MW00636474

A HISTORY OF THE CRUSADES

Kenneth M. Setton, GENERAL EDITOR

A HISTORY OF THE CRUSADES

Kenneth M. Setton, GENERAL EDITOR

I The First Hundred Years

II The Later Crusades, 1189–1311

III The Fourteenth and Fifteenth Centuries

IV Civilization and Institutions

V Influence and Consequences, with Genealogies and Bibliography

VI An Atlas and Gazetteer of the Crusades

Volume I

THE FIRST HUNDRED YEARS

Krak des Chevaliers

A HISTORY OF
THE CRUSADES

KENNETH M. SETTON
GENERAL EDITOR

Volume I

THE FIRST HUNDRED YEARS

EDITED BY
MARSHALL W. BALDWIN

THE UNIVERSITY OF WISCONSIN PRESS
Madison, Milwaukee, and London, 1969

Published by
The University of Wisconsin Press
Box 1379, Madison, Wisconsin 53701

The University of Wisconsin Press, Ltd.
27–29 Whitfield Street, London, W.1

First Edition, 1955, University of Pennsylvania Press

Printed in the United States of America
Library of Congress Catalog Card Number 68–9837

DIS MANIBVS

JOHANNIS L. LAMONTE

ET

DANAE C. MVNRO

ATQVE

GENIIS ADHVC FLORENTIBVS

FREDERICI DVNCALF

ET

AVGVSTI C. KREY

HOC OPVS

DEDICAMVS

EDITORES

Deus vult, Deus vult

CONTENTS

ILLUSTRATIONS

MAPS

FOREWORD

For some four or five years I have been waiting for the opportunity to write this foreword. Since there are so many footnotes in the pages which follow, I am moved to employ them even here. This book is the first of five volumes. Its appearance has been long delayed. During the years of waiting, however, there has often gone through my mind the wise maxim attributed to Augustus, of which Petrarch once reminded Boccaccio: Whatever is being done well enough is being done soon enough.[1] If, then, both contributors and editors have done their jobs well enough, our readers will forgive us the long wait. I hope so, for I foresee now some further delay before we can bring out the remaining volumes. Since we have had very familiar terrain to traverse in the first volume, we have gone far; we have covered the first hundred years of the crusades, and the second volume will reach the beginning of the fourteenth century.

The third volume will be devoted chiefly to the crusades of the fourteenth and fifteenth centuries. The fourth will cover the political and ecclesiastical organization of the crusader states, propaganda, financing, legal and political theories relating to the crusades, and the like. If chief emphasis is given in the early volumes to the history of the states established in Syria, Palestine, and Cyprus, no less attention will be given, as we proceed, to the history of the Latin Empire of Constantinople, to the more durable states in continental Greece and the Morea, and to those in the islands of the Aegean. Some fine chapters have already been written on agricultural conditions in the crusader states in Syria and Palestine; on commerce and industry, as well as on the Genoese and Venetian empires; and others are now being prepared on numismatics, sigillography, and heraldry. Five excellent chapters on art and architecture were written five years ago, and last year their authors patiently revised them; I think that we shall be able to include four of them in the third volume. Volume V will

[1] *Epp. rerum senilium*, XVI [XVII], 2, in *Opera*, Basel, 1581, II, 965: "...et saepe mihi per animum recursat sententia Caesaris illi[us] sapientissimi principis Augusti: Sat celeriter fieri quicquid fiat satis bene."

deal with the influence of the crusades upon European thought and literature, the arts and architecture, and economic and social life. It will also contain an extended bibliography.

The source from which this work ultimately derives is the ambition which the late Professor Dana C. Munro long nurtured to write a comprehensive history of the crusades. An inspiring teacher, Munro aroused a vast interest in the crusades among students in his seminars at the Universities of Pennsylvania and Wisconsin and at Princeton. At one time or another Munro's students included — and this list could be expanded — August C. Krey and Frederic Duncalf, William E. Lingelbach and Louis J. Paetow, Eugene H. Byrne and Einar Joranson, Charles W. David, Thomas C. Van Cleve, and Marshall W. Baldwin, the last of whom has been my fellow editor of this volume. It was the hope and expectation of all Munro's students that the results of his years of research would finally be embodied in a two- or three-volume history of the crusades. He had intended to write such a work and had accumulated and organized much material for this purpose. Munro's desire for perfection was an obstacle to literary production throughout his life. One of his closest friends, the late Professor Edward P. Cheyney, has described how the years were to make of his high standard of scholarship almost a disability: "From the beginning Munro insisted on the most rigorous scientific method.... No statement... [is to] be made in historical writing for which a satisfactory reference to a contemporary source cannot be given. His influence has thus been marked on a long series of younger scholars. This practice also was probably responsible, at least in part, for the slow progress of what was to be his *magnum opus*, a detailed and scholarly history of the Crusades, based on an exhaustive and critical use of the contemporary sources and vivified by a careful study on the ground of the regions traversed and occupied by the Crusaders. For the latter purpose he made two visits to the Near East. The work was still incomplete at his death."[2] In a sense the work was unbegun at his death; and in another sense this is the first volume of that work.

Munro was prevented from writing much not only by his perfectionism but also by the demands made upon his time by uni-

[2] "Dana Carleton Munro (1866–1933)," *Dictionary of American Biography*, XIII (1934), 330; cf. Cheyney's memoir of Munro, in the *American Historical Review*, XXXVIII (1933), 618–620; and A. C. Krey, in Munro's lectures on *The Kingdom of the Crusaders* (New York, 1936), pp. vff., 205ff. Munro's former students presented to him in December 1926, as retiring president of the American Historical Association, the valuable volume on *The Crusades and Other Historical Essays* (New York, 1928).

versity, state, and federal authorities, who often had recourse to his wide knowledge and abundant wisdom. He was devoted to his former students, and they took much of his time. When L. J. Paetow's untimely death in 1928 left unfinished the revision of his *Guide to the Study of Medieval History*, Munro undertook its completion, assisted by Professor Gray C. Boyce, who now prepares the third edition of Paetow, and whose wide bibliographical knowledge has been placed at the disposal of this *History of the Crusades*, for he will be the editor of Volume V. After Munro's death in 1933, on the eve of his retirement from Princeton, it soon became clear that all the writing he had been able to do for some time before his death was *The Kingdom of the Crusaders*, which Professor August C. Krey prepared for the press in 1935. But Munro had often discussed his plans for a detailed history of the crusades with his friends and former students, especially with Krey and with Professor Frederic Duncalf. The latter's summer home at Waquoit, Massachusetts, was the scene of several such sessions, which still remain most treasured memories to Duncalf and to Krey. It is to these two that we owe the inception of this *History*, although the project gained a vast momentum when the twain was made a trio by the addition of the late Professor John L. LaMonte.

The friendship of Krey and LaMonte began about 1930 when LaMonte taught Krey's courses while Krey was on a year's leave of absence from the University of Minnesota. Duncalf and LaMonte met for the first time in December 1935 at the annual meeting of the American Historical Association, held that year in Chattanooga, Tennessee. It was Duncalf who first proposed that a coöperative history of the crusades be undertaken by Munro's former students together with others who might be interested in joining them in such a venture. Krey was, of course, a firm supporter of the idea. Nothing was done, however, until three years later. At the meeting of the Historical Association held in Chicago in 1938, with Duncalf in the chair, LaMonte read a paper on "The Crusades Reappraised,"[3] which was later published as "Some Problems in Crusading Historiography."[4] After discussion, a committee of medievalists was formed to make plans for a coöperative history of the crusades; LaMonte proved to be a very popular preacher, and recruits were gathered for this crusade of scholarship from the chief universities in the United States. Duncalf was

[3] *Annual Report of the American Historical Association for the Year 1938* (Washington, D. C., 1939), p. 22; *American Historical Review*, XLIV (1939), 486.
[4] In *Speculum*, XV (1940), 57–75.

chosen editor and LaMonte secretary of the project. Always Krey was on hand, ready to give stout assistance. In the following year (1939), when the Association met in Washington, plans were made which envisaged four volumes (later expanded to six, and now contracted to five). At the next meeting of the Association, in New York in 1940, conferences were continued among those participating in the projected history, and various editorial details were discussed. But the war was already more than a year old in Europe, and another year was to see the United States involved in the conflict. LaMonte went into the navy, serving in the Pacific, with lasting detriment to his health, and other scholars associated with the history were quickly caught up in wartime activities.

In the spring of 1941, however, the plan of the work had been submitted to the Mediaeval Academy of America, which was glad to sponsor the project but unable to make any financial commitment thereto. Although nothing could be done for the duration of the war, in 1945–1946 the proposal for a coöperative history of the crusades was revived, and now expanded to include British and European scholars. Duncalf, Krey, and LaMonte assumed official editorship of the work, and in the spring of 1946 the administration of the University of Pennsylvania generously agreed to underwrite the full costs of publication. LaMonte was enabled to make a contract to this effect with the University Press, providing also for the publication of other monographs on the crusades. Since neither editors nor contributors were able to abide by the provisions of the first contract, the present writer renegotiated various details of this agreement in January 1954, in pretty much the same terms as the first contract, but no longer providing for the publication of any additional monographs. At the annual meeting of the American Historical Association in New York in 1946, since Duncalf and Krey were obliged by physicians' advice to reduce their activities, those contributors to the work who were present, acting as a committee for the whole, elected LaMonte, the youngest of the trio, as managing editor of the work.[5]

LaMonte threw himself into the task with his customary energy. In April 1947 he sent out to all contributors, and to other interested persons, a report on "The Project for an International Coöperative History of the Crusades." After two years of arduous endeavor, on the very day before he was to sail to the Levant for a year of historical study and observation relating to this *History*,

[5] On December 28, 1946, both Krey and LaMonte read papers, the latter giving a "Progress Report on 'The History of the Crusades.'"

LaMonte died of a heart attack at the age of forty-seven (on October 2, 1949). It is now five years since anyone has heard his booming voice and felt the hearty warmth of his handshake. John LaMonte was not only widely respected for his scholarly achievement, he was deeply beloved by those who knew him best for his kindness and generosity, for a largeness of heart and spirit which always placed his time and strength at the disposal of the friends and students, historians old and young, who turned to him for help. A lover of witty stories, an amiable companion, a thoughtful host, LaMonte had a buoyant nature which had held off death, with courage and without complaint, through three hard years of ill health, *anima qualem non candidiorem terra tulit*! This *History of the Crusades* is thus curiously bound up with the academic lives of four men, and to these four this volume and those to come are dedicated. If Munro and LaMonte are gone, Duncalf and Krey are very much with us, and to them in Byzantine fashion we wish "many years".

In March 1950 the present writer was appointed LaMonte's successor in the University of Pennsylvania and soon thereafter became editor-in-chief of the *History*. Since that time two brief reports of our slow progress have been published.[6] At last we have produced the first volume, and we have incurred many obligations in its production and in the accumulation of the many chapters on hand for subsequent volumes. The editors owe much to the board of advisors whose names appear on a preceding page; I give especial thanks to Professors Austin P. Evans of Columbia and Joseph R. Strayer of Princeton, to whom I have often turned for help most readily given. Mention must be made of the consistent interest taken in this work by Dr. Charles R. D. Miller, executive secretary of the Mediaeval Academy of America, under whose auspices and sponsorship the work appears. We are most grateful to President Gaylord P. Harnwell of the University of Pennsylvania and to former President George Wm. McClelland for the financial undertakings which have made this volume possible and assured the publication of its successors. Dr. Edwin B. Williams, Provost of the University of Pennsylvania, a distinguished philologist and good friend of sound learning, has supported the *History of the Crusades* with unceasing encouragement from its inception.

[6] Kenneth M. Setton, "The Pennsylvania *History of the Crusades*," *Speculum*, XXVI (1951), 578–581, and "History of the Crusades," *Year Book of the American Philosophical Society*, 1952, pp. 222–226.

Dr. William H. DuBarry, Vice-President of the University, has done likewise. It is a pleasure to express our thanks to Dean Roy F. Nichols and Professor Albert C. Baugh; I hope this volume may not fall short of their own exacting standards of scholarship. To my good friends, Mr. Phelps Soule, former director of the University of Pennsylvania Press, and Dr. Morse Peckham, present director, both editors and contributors are under deep obligation. Dr. Peckham has especially been called upon to assist us in the solution of our problems. Finally and very importantly, the editors give renewed expression of their thanks to the officers of the American Philosophical Society, especially to Dr. Luther P. Eisenhart, for the grant of one thousand dollars which the Society gave us for general administrative expenses.

The initial editing of this volume was done by Professor Baldwin; he has cut here and added there, to avoid duplication and to effect literary sutures; with discernment and patience he has combined footnotes, and so on, and himself retyped a good deal of manuscript. He has put much work into this book. Dr. Hazard has prepared the maps and the gazetteer, standardized the oriental names throughout the volume, translated Professor Cahen's chapter from the French original, and rendered a dozen other services with great readiness. Quick in perception and in execution, Hazard possesses stupendous energy, no little of which he has most generously poured into this volume, and Professor Baldwin joins me in extending to him our sincerest thanks. Miss Sarah S. Landers helped us by typing. Mrs. Setton read most of the manuscript and retyped parts of it; she also assisted in the proof-reading. The illustrations were chosen by President T. S. R. Boase, Magdalen College, Oxford. The conclusion to this foreword can only be a restatement of our debt to the University of Pennsylvania and of our hope that this volume may merit some of the support which the University has given it.

KENNETH M. SETTON

[*University of Pennsylvania, 1955*]

FOREWORD TO THE SECOND EDITION

There is a universal assumption that an historical work should have a foreword as well as an index. The need for the latter is abundantly clear, and I yield again to the categorical imperative in supplying a foreword to the second edition of Volumes I and II. In fact I am very glad of the opportunity to express my gratitude to President Fred Harvey Harrington of the University of Wisconsin for his willingness to take over the *History of the Crusades* from the University of Pennsylvania, which published the first edition of these volumes. The University of Wisconsin Press will publish the remainder of the work.

Republication of the present two volumes has made possible the complete redoing of the maps by the University of Wisconsin Cartographic Laboratory under the direction of Professor Randall D. Sale, whose labors have been lightened by the continued cooperation of Dr. Harry W. Hazard, my fellow crusader for many years. Moreover we now plan to add as a sixth volume to this work *An Atlas and Gazetteer of the Crusades*, to be done by Dr. Hazard and Professor Sale.

The conscientious efforts of Mr. Thompson Webb, Jr., director of the University of Wisconsin Press, and his vigilant staff have made the production of the second edition a painless process, painless at least for me if not for them. I want them to know how grateful I am. Special acknowledgment must be made of the help of Professor C. Julian Bishko of the University of Virginia, who revised the first part of Volume I, Chapter II, on the Spanish *reconquista* before 1095.

We have been able to correct a few slips in these volumes, typographical and otherwise, as well as to augment the gazetteers which accompany the maps. The Wisconsin Press has also effected other improvements of style and format.

KENNETH M. SETTON

The Institute for Advanced Study
Princeton, New Jersey
July 2, 1968

PREFACE

Some years ago, our late colleague John L. LaMonte remarked that modern crusading historiography has expanded notably in two directions.[1] First, the chronological scope has been extended to include not only the background of the eleventh century and even earlier, but also what have sometimes been called the "later crusades" of the fourteenth and fifteenth centuries. Second, there has been in recent years a more extensive consideration of those aspects of civilization in the eastern Mediterranean and its hinterland which affected both the launching of the crusades and the development of the Latin states. The present volume, the first in the series, illustrates both these tendencies. It is appropriate, for example, that it include a discussion of the manifold problems which confronted the government of Constantinople, the origins and consequences of the schism of 1054, and the stake of Byzantine diplomacy in the Near East. Equally significant are such matters as the history of the Selchükid Turks, the vicissitudes and divisions of the caliphate, and the major movements within Islam.

Within European Christendom two lines of development were to converge in the First Crusade: pilgrimage and the holy war. The first is the older of the two, indeed, nearly as old as Christianity. As the practice developed it received direction and ultimately became associated with the penitential system of the church. Deeply ingrained in western thinking, the idea of pilgrimage inspired even the most worldly of the crusaders. The Norman adventurer, Bohemond, did not assist his fellow warriors in the capture of Jerusalem because he was busy securing valuable territory elsewhere for himself. But he did fulfil his vow to visit the Holy Sepulcher later. In papal exhortations and in medieval narratives the crusade is a pilgrimage, the "way to Jerusalem". The notion that war against the infidel could be a holy thing is in Christian history a distinctively western development. The Byzantine emperor Heraclius, it is true, restored the Holy Cross to Jerusalem. And something resembling the crusade idea seems to

[1] John L. LaMonte, "Some Problems in Crusading Historiography," *Speculum*, XV (1940), p. 60.

have animated the great military emperors of Byzantium in the tenth century. Notwithstanding, Constantinople generally regarded the Moslem states much as it had formerly regarded Persia. They were established powers with whom it was necessary to deal. War was often mandatory as an instrument of policy. But so also was diplomacy; and the latter was preferable. Significantly it was a western historian, William of Tyre, who commenced his narrative of the crusade with Heraclius and the restoration of the Holy Cross, and a continuation of William's story came to be known as *L'Estoire de Eracles Empereur*.

Perhaps western Europe with its inferior military and political organization during the feudal age felt itself more endangered than did Byzantium. For a long time it was vulnerable in Spain, in Sicily, even occasionally on the southern Mediterranean littoral. But clearly there was something more to the concept of holy war which developed in the west than a heightened sense of urgency. European feudalism was an expansive thing. And it was belligerent. Peace of God and Truce of God were of little avail. Equally futile were ecclesiastical prohibitions of tournaments. As subsequent pages will demonstrate, Italian merchants were not pacifists. Thus, it would appear that war gradually came to be accepted as an honorable occupation. By the eleventh century war against the infidel was already regarded as in some way religious. Pope and Italians launched a "crusade" against North African ports. Norman expansion in Sicily received ecclesiastical approbation as, of course, also did the Spanish reconquest.[2] Therefore, when toward the end of the eleventh century a great pope spoke to western knights urging them to a new war against Islam, the astonishing response represented everything that western feudal civilization had come to be, all its energy, its religious zeal, its belligerence.

When the goal had been achieved some warriors elected to remain in the east, and they and their successors faced the manifold tasks of a "colonial" administration. Vastly inferior in numbers to the heterogeneous native population, they created in an eastern environment a civilization which was fundamentally western. Ties with Europe were close. Pilgrims, fighting men, and churchmen travelled back and forth. Italian merchants were pro-

[2] A significant discussion of the development of the holy war idea in western Christendom is C. Erdmann, *Die Entstehung des Kreuzzugsgedankens* (Stuttgart, 1935). For a review of the equally significant subsequent discussion of "Erdmann's thesis" see M. W. Baldwin, "Some Recent Interpretations of Pope Urban's Eastern Policy," *Catholic Historical Review*, XXV (1940), 459–466, and A. C. Krey, "Urban's Crusade, Success or Failure?" *American Historical Review*, LIII (1948), 235–250. The subject is also considered in chapter VII, below.

fitably established in all the major ports. Notwithstanding, these Europeans of the east, these "creoles", to use the expression of Rubió y Lluch, Grousset, and others, inevitably acquired something of the viewpoint of the eastern Mediterranean. Basically western and no less brave than their forbears, they nevertheless lost much of the crusading ardor of the men of 1095 or of those who came from Europe in later expeditions. A cleavage between "natives" and "newcomers" was evident in the middle of the twelfth century and was especially prominent during and after the Second Crusade.

Despite their more oriental attitude, western colonials were never able for long to act in concert with Byzantium. During the period covered in this volume there were, it is true, many apparently fruitful diplomatic exchanges, marriage alliances, and the like. But more than one favorable opportunity for increasing the military security of the Latin states or even of extending their frontiers was lost because Latin and Greek could not agree. By the end of the first century of the crusades little hope remained of healing the breach. It is difficult to overemphasize the significance of this failure. As much as any other single factor the break-down of the military alliance between Jerusalem and Byzantium underlies the ultimate loss of the crusaders' states. And the failure goes deeper. Western Europe's brilliant achievement in the middle ages, of which the crusades were a part, was not accomplished without the loss of its former eastern half. Although blame may be attached to both sides, certainly the crusades were an element in a schism whose consequences are felt to this day.

The present volume describes what might be called the classical period of the crusades. It carries the reader from the great surge of the eleventh century and the establishment of colonies to the Moslem counter-offensives of Zengi, Nūr-ad-Dīn, and Saladin. The cultural and institutional history of the Latin states will be found in later volumes, as indicated by Professor Setton in the Foreword. Here, rather, is a narrative of war, diplomacy, and politics. It was precisely these matters which most interested contemporaries and which fill the pages of the chroniclers. Accordingly, the contributors to this volume are following in the footsteps of illustrious predecessors in presenting one more "continuation" of the crusade story. Moreover, like the crusaders themselves they are men of different national backgrounds who have joined together in a common enterprise.

MARSHALL W. BALDWIN

[*New York University, 1955*]

A NOTE ON TRANSLITERATION AND NOMENCLATURE

One of the obvious problems to be solved by the editors of such a work as this, intended both for general readers and for scholars in many different disciplines, is how to render the names of persons and places, and a few other terms, originating in languages and scripts unfamiliar to the English-speaking reader and, indeed, to most readers whose native languages are European. In the present volume, and presumably in the entire work, these comprise principally Arabic, Turkish, Persian, and Armenian, none of which was normally written in our Latin alphabet until its adoption by Turkey in 1928. The analogous problem of Byzantine Greek names and terms has been handled by using the familiar Latin equivalents, Anglicized Greek, or, occasionally, Greek type, as has seemed appropriate in each instance, but a broader approach is desirable for the other languages under consideration.

The somewhat contradictory criteria applied are ease of recognition and readability on the one hand, and scientific accuracy and consistency on the other. It has proved possible to reconcile these, and to standardize the great variety of forms in which identical names have been submitted to us by different contributors, through constant consultation with specialists in each language, research in the sources, and adherence to systems conforming to the requirements of each language. I wish to record here our debt to my ever-helpful and admirably patient colleagues at Princeton: Professors Philip K. Hitti and R. Bayly Winder for Arabic, Lewis V. Thomas for Turkish, and T. Cuyler Young and Dr. N. S. Fatemi for Persian.

The most common of these languages in the first volume is Arabic, and fortunately it presents the fewest difficulties, since the script in which it is written is admirably suited to the classical language. The basic system used, with minor variants, by all

English-speaking scholars was restudied and found entirely satisfactory, with the slight modifications noted. The chief alternative system, in which every Arabic consonant is represented by a single Latin character (ṯ for th, ẖ for kh, ḏ for dh, š for sh, ġ for gh) was rejected for several reasons: needless proliferation of diacritical marks to bother the eye and multiply occasions for error, absence of strong countervailing arguments, and, most decisively, the natural tendency of non-specialists to adopt these spellings but omit the diacritical marks. The use of single letters in this manner leads to undesirable results, but the spellings adopted for the present work may be thus treated with confidence by any writer not requiring the discriminations which the remaining diacritical marks indicate.

The letters used for Arabic consonants, in the order of the Arabic alphabet, are these: ', b, t, th, j, ḥ, kh, d, dh, r, z, s, sh, ṣ, ḍ, ṭ, ẓ, ', gh, f, q, k, l, m, n, h, w, y. The vowels are a, i, u, lengthened as ā, ī, ū, with the *alif bi-ṣūrati-l-yā'* distinguished as â; initial ' is omitted, but terminal macrons are retained. Diphthongs are *au* and *ai*, not *aw* and *ay*, as being both philologically preferable and visually less misleading. The same considerations lead to the omission of *l* of *al-* before a duplicated consonant (Nūr-ad-Dīn rather than Nūr-al-Dīn). As in this example, hyphens are used to link words composing a single name (as also 'Abd-Allāh), with weak initial vowels elided (as abū-l-Ḥasan). Normally *al-* (meaning "the") is not capitalized; *abū-* is not capitalized when it means "father of", but is in the name Abū-Bakr and the place Abū-Qubais; *ibn-* is not when it means literally "son of", but is otherwise (as Ibn-Khaldūn, Usāmah Ibn-Munqidh).

Some readers may be disconcerted to find the prophet called "Mohammed" and his followers "Moslems", but this can readily be justified. These spellings are valid English proper names, derived from Arabic originals which would be correctly transliterated "Muḥammad" and "Muslimūn" or "Muslimīn". The best criterion for deciding whether to use the Anglicized spellings or the accurate transliterations is the treatment accorded the third of this cluster of names, that of the religion "Islam". Where this is transliterated "Islām", with a macron over the *a*, it should be accompanied by "Muslim" and "Muḥammad", but where the macron is omitted consistency and common sense require "Moslem" and "Mohammed", and it is the latter triad which have been considered appropriate in this work. All namesakes of the prophet, however, have had their names duly transliterated

"Muḥammad", to correspond with names of other Arabs who are not individually so familiar to westerners as to be better recognized in Anglicized forms.

All names of other Arabs, and of non-Arabs with Arabic names, have been systematically transliterated, with the single exception of Ṣalāḥ-ad-Dīn, whom it would have been pedantic to call that rather than Saladin. For places held, in the crusading era or now, by Arabs the Arabic names appear either in the text or in the gazetteer, where some additional ones are also included to broaden the usefulness of this feature.

Large numbers of names of persons and groups, however, customarily found in Arabicized spellings because they were written in Arabic script, have been restored to their underlying identity whenever this is ascertainable. For example, Arabic "Saljūq" misrepresents four of the six component phonemes: *s* is correct, *a* replaces Turkish *e*, for which Arabic script provides no equivalent, *l* is correct, *j* replaces the non-Arabic *ch*, *ū* substitutes a non-Turkish long *u* for the original *ü*, and *q* as distinguished from *k* is non-existent in Turkish; this quadruple rectification yields "Selchük" as the name of the eponymous leader, and "Selchükid" — on the model of 'Abbāsid and Timurid — for the dynasty and the people. Arabic forms of Turkish names, as well as hybrids like "Ortoq" and "Zangī", are cross-referenced in the index.

It might be thought that as Turkish is now written in a well conceived modified Latin alphabet, there would be no reason to alter this, and this presumption is substantially valid. For the same reasons as apply to Arabic, *ch* has been preferred above *ç*, *sh* above *ş*, and *gh* above *ğ*, with *kh* in a few instances given as a preferred alternate of *h*, from which it is not distinguished in modern Turkish. No long vowels have been indicated, as being functionless survivals. Two other changes have been made in the interest of the English-speaking reader, and should be remembered by those using map sheets and standard reference works: *c* (pronounced dj) has been changed to *j*, so that one is not visually led to imagine that the Turkish name for the Tigris — Dijle/Dicle — rhymes with "tickle", and what the eminent lexicographer H. C. Hony terms "that abomination the undotted ı" has, after the model of *The Encyclopaedia of Islām*, been written ĭ.

Spellings, modified as above indicated, have usually been founded on those of the Turkish edition, *İslâm Ansiklopedisi*, hampered by occasional inconsistencies within that work and especially by the fact that it has appeared in fascicule form only as far as "K" to date, which has necessitated pursuit of elusive individuals through relevant articles in the available volumes, usually but not invariably successful. All names of Turks appear thus emended, and Turkish equivalents of almost all places within or near modern Turkey appear in the text or the gazetteer.

In addition to *kh*, Middle Turkish utilized a few other phonemes not common in modern Turkish: *zh* (modern *j*), *dh*, *ng*, and *ä* (modern *e*); the first three of these will be used as needed, while the last-mentioned may be assumed to underlie every medieval Turkish name now spelled with *e*. Plaintive eyebrows may be raised at our exclusion of *q*, but this was in Middle Turkish only the alternate spelling used when the sound *k* was combined with back instead of front vowels, and its elimination by the Turks is commendable.

Persian names have been transliterated like Arabic with certain modifications, chiefly use of the additional vowels *e* and *o* and replacing *ḍ* and *dh* with *ẓ* and *ẕ*, so that Arabic "Ādharbaijān" becomes Persian "Āẕerbaijān", more accurate as well as more recognizable. Omission of the definite article from personal names was considered but eventually disapproved.

Armenian presented great difficulties: the absence of an authoritative reference source for spelling names, the lack of agreement on transliteration, and the sound-shift by which classical and eastern Armenian *b*, *d*, *g* became western Armenian *p*, *t*, *k* and — incredible as it may seem to the unwary — *vice versa*; similar reciprocal interchanges involved *ts* and *dz*, and *ch* and *j*. The following alphabet represents western Armenian letters, with eastern variants in parentheses: a, p (b), k (g), t (d), e, z, ē, ĭ, ṭ, zh, i, l, kh, dz (ts), g (k), h, ts (dz), gh, j (ch), m, y, n, sh, o, c͜h, b (p), ch (j), ṛ, s, ṿ, d (t), r, t͜s, u or v, ṗ, ḳ, ō, f. When the original sources used consecutive consonants, this has been retained without introducing unwritten vowels (Smpad and Shnchrig, for example). Most spellings are based on the Armenian texts in the *Recueil des historiens des croisades*.

In standardizing names of groups, the correct root forms in the respective languages have been hopefully identified, with the ending "-id" for dynasties and their peoples but "-ite" for sects, and with plural either identical with singular (as Kirghiz) or plus "-s" (Khazars) or "-es" (Uzes). In cases where this sounded hopelessly awkward, it was abandoned (Nuṣairīs, not Nuṣairites; Qarmaṭians, not Qarmaṭites; Muwaḥḥids, not Muwaḥḥidids or Muwaḥḥidites and certainly not Almohads; Murābiṭs, not Murābiṭids or Murābiṭites and definitely not Almoravids, which is, however, like Almohads, cross-referenced).

Technical terms and other common nouns appear for the first time in any chapter italicized, with diacritical marks and notation of language and meaning; thereafter, they are used as English words with plural in "-s" instead of trying to reproduce native plurals; thus "magistrates (Arabic singular, *qāḍī*)", but thereafter "qadis".

The use of place names is explained in the note preceding the gazetteer, but may be summarized by saying that in general the most familiar correct form is used in the text and maps, normally an English version of the name by which the place was known to Europeans during the crusades. Variant forms are given and identified in the gazetteer, and are cross-referenced in the index.

Despite conscientious efforts to perfect the nomenclature, errors will probably be detected by specialists; they are to be blamed on me and not on individual contributors or editorial colleagues, for I have been accorded a free hand. Justifiable suggestions for improvements will be welcomed, and used to bring succeeding volumes nearer that elusive goal, impeccability in nomenclature.

HARRY W. HAZARD

[*Princeton, New Jersey, 1955*]

ABBREVIATIONS

AHR *American Historical Review*, I (1895) and ff.

AOL *Archives de l'Orient latin*, Société de l'Orient latin, 2 vols., Paris 1881–1884.

Byz. Zeitschr. *Byzantinische Zeitschrift*, I (1892) and ff.

CSEL *Corpus scriptorum ecclesiasticorum latinorum*, editum consilio et impensis Academiae litterarum caesareae Vindobonensis, 1866 and ff.

CSHB *Corpus scriptorum historiae byzantinae*, eds. B. G. Niebuhr, Imm. Bekker, and others, 50 vols., Bonn, 1828–1897.

Hagenmeyer, "Chronologie" Heinrich Hagenmeyer, "Chronologie de la première croisade, 1094–1100," *ROL*, VI–VIII (1898–1901); and "Chronologie de l'histoire du royaume de Jérusalem, 1101–1118 [actually to 1105]," *ROL*, IX–XII (1902–1911).

Hagenmeyer, *Epistulae* Heinrich Hagenmeyer, *Epistulae et chartae ad historiam primi belli sacri spectantes: Die Kreuzzugsbriefe aus den Jahren 1088–1100*, Innsbruck, 1901.

Hist. Zeitschr. *Historische Zeitschrift*, I (1859) and ff.

MGH *Monumenta Germaniae historica*, ed. G. H. Pertz, T. Mommsen, and others (Hanover, 1826ff.). Reichsinstitut für ältere deutsche Geschichtskunde, Hanover, 1826 and ff. [*SS* = *Scriptores*, etc.].

MPG, PG *Patrologiae graecae cursus completus* ..., ed. J.-P. Migne, 161 vols., Paris, 1857 and ff.

MPL, PL *Patrologiae latinae cursus completus* ..., ed. J.-P. Migne, 221 vols., Paris, 1844 and ff.

Munro Essays *The Crusades and other Historical Essays Presented to D. C. Munro*, ed. L. J. Paetow, New York, 1928.

Neues Archiv *Neues Archiv der Gesellschaft für ältere deutsche Geschichtskunde*, Reichsinstitut für ältere deutsche Geschichtskunde, I (1876) and ff.

PPTS *Palestine Pilgrims' Text Society*, 13 vols. and Index, London, 1896–1897.

RH *Revue historique*, I (1876), and ff.

RHC *Recueil des historiens des croisades*, Académie des inscriptions et belles-lettres, Paris, 16 vols. in fol., 1841–1906:
- *Arm.* *Documents arméniens*, 2 vols., 1869–1906.
- *Grecs* *Historiens grecs*, 2 vols., 1875–1881.
- *Lois.* *Assises de Jérusalem*, 2 vols. 1841–1843.
- *Occ.* *Historiens occidentaux*, 5 vols., 1841–1895.
- *Or.* *Historiens orientaux: Arabes*, 5 vols., 1872–1906.

RHGF *Recueil des historiens des Gaules et de la France*, ed. Martin Bouquet [1685 to 1754] and others, 24 vols. in fol., Paris, 1738–1904.

RISS *Rerum italicarum scriptores* ..., ed. L. A. Muratori [1672–1750], 25 vols. in 28, Milan, 1723–1751; new edition by G. Carducci and V. Fiorini, Città di Castello, 1900 and ff.

ROL *Revue de l'Orient latin*, 12 vols., Paris, 1893–1911.

Volume I

THE FIRST HUNDRED YEARS

1. Western Europe and the Mediterranean (*Map by the University of Wisconsin Cartographic Laboratory*)

I

WESTERN EUROPE ON THE EVE OF THE CRUSADES

The crusades had their origin in eleventh-century western Europe and to understand them one must know something of the environment in which they emerged. No mere static description of the land and its people can serve this purpose. The picture must be a moving one that shows the basic forces that were slowly molding medieval civilization, for the crusades were a natural product of these forces. The eleventh was the first of the three great creative centuries of the Middle Ages — an era of pioneers, soldiers, and statesmen. During its span the political and economic institutions that had been gradually taking shape since the sixth century were firmly cemented together to form the foundations of medieval civilization. While many of those who were to make the twelfth century an age of saints, scholars, artists, and creative literary men were born before the first crusaders set out for Palestine, their day lay in the future. The great lay figures of the eleventh century, William the Conqueror, the emperors Henry III and Henry IV, Roger I of Sicily, and Alfonso VI of Castile, were soldier-statesmen, and their ecclesiastical counterparts, pope Gregory VII, the early abbots of Cluny, and archbishop Lanfranc, were priestly statesmen. They sought essentially power, order, and efficiency. Even the chief monastic order of the period, that of Cluny, represented administrative rather more than spiritual reform. The hardy peasants who cleared forests and drained marshes to bring new land under cultivation and the Genoese and Pisan seamen who swept the Moslems from the coasts of Europe must have been moved by the same vigorous spirit as their conquering lords. In short, both expansion and organization marked the eleventh century. The crusades were a part of the former and were made possible by the latter.

Medieval western Europe had two basic patterns of settlement — the hamlet and the village. In general the hamlet was found in the least productive regions such as Scotland, Wales, Ireland, Brittany, and the mountainous districts of France. While it is possible that the hamlet was essentially a Celtic institution, it seems just as likely that it was simply the natural form of settlement in the barren lands into which the Celts had been driven by their Germanic foes. The rest of western Europe was a land of villages. There would be a cluster of houses, or rather huts, each with a small fenced garden and perhaps a fruit tree, a church, and usually a manor house or castle. Around the village lay its arable land and meadow — beyond lay the pasture, waste, and woodland. The men who lived in these villages and hamlets used three fundamentally different ways of cultivating their arable land. The crudest of these is commonly called the infield and outfield system. Although it was not completely confined to the regions of hamlets, it was most common there. Under this system the farmer had a small garden or infield near his house that he kept in continuous cultivation by using the manure from his animals. Then he would go out and plow a piece of land some distance away, grow crops on it until it lost its fertility, and then abandon it and plow another piece. This method of exploitation was suited to a region with a large amount of available land, none of which was very fertile.

Another system was to divide the arable land of a village into rectangular plots assigned to the various houses. This was the standard practice in southern France and in Italy. But over the major portion of western Europe the dominant method of cultivation was what we call the two- or three-field system. The arable land of the village was divided into two or three large fields. When there were two fields, one was cultivated and one allowed to lie fallow each year. When there were three fields, two were cultivated and one lay fallow. It seems likely that originally all villages used the two-field system and that the third field was adopted as an improvement in the more fertile regions. These large fields were divided into long, narrow strips and each house in the village had an equal number of strips in each field. The region of the two- and three-field systems comprised the richest and most populous part of western Europe, extending from the border of Wales through England, northern France, and the major part of Germany.

The agricultural methods of the eleventh century were not very efficient. As the plows were heavy and clumsy and the harness poorly designed, from four to eight oxen were required for a plow team. Moreover, the slowness of the oxen made the area that a team could care for rather small. The sole crop in the arable fields was grain. It was sown broadcast to the delight of the birds. The seed was simply a part of the previous year's crop. The land as a rule received no fertilizer beyond the manure deposited by the cattle that grazed upon it while it lay fallow. Hence the production per acre, per bushel of seed, and per man was extremely low. This meant that if the people of the village were to have enough to eat, all land that could be plowed had to be utilized. As good meadow should be as fertile as arable land, there was nearly always an acute shortage of meadow and therefore of hay. Most villages could only hope to gather enough hay to keep their plow teams and a few breeding cattle alive through the winter. The pasture land was usually poor and often simply waste. In summer the cattle found a meager living in the pastures and in the fall most of them were slaughtered.

In some regions such as England and parts of Germany the grain grown on the arable supplied both food and drink. It is estimated that in England about half the grain was used for bread and the other half for ale. The wine-growing districts were more fortunate, as land too steep to plow would grow vines. From the gardens behind their houses the villagers obtained a few common vegetables. The cattle were valued for their hides, milk, and meat. The milk was made into cheese. Every village had a few sheep to supply wool for clothing and chickens for meat and eggs. But the chief source of meat was the pig. Pigs could find their own food in the woods in both summer and winter. In Domesday Book the size of a village's woodland is commonly measured by the number of pigs it could feed.

Each house or tenement in the village had its strips in the fields and a share of the meadow. The other resources of the village territory were used in common. The villager pastured his cattle in the common pasture and waste, fed his pigs and gathered his firewood in the common woodlands, and fished in the village stream. All the agricultural activities of the village were conducted by the community as a whole. The villagers decided when to plow, when to plant, and when to harvest, and all worked together. Certain men were assigned special tasks such as herding.

The villager lived in a rude hut with a thatched roof. A hole in the roof let out some part of the smoke from the fire. His clothes were crudely fashioned from the hides of his cattle and the wool from his sheep. He was never far removed from the threat of starvation. In general, throughout the village region thirty acres of arable land seems to have been considered a normal tenement and experts have calculated that this would support a family in ordinary years. But many tenements were smaller than thirty acres and there were bound to be bad years. And the high cost of transportation by ox-cart over bad roads meant that even a local crop failure would result in a famine.

For the mass of the population of western Europe the village was the political, economic, social, and religious unit. The villager found his amusement in the village fetes. The village priest performed the sacraments and gave his flock what little knowledge they had of the world of ideas. As he was likely to be barely literate, this knowledge was bound to be slight. The villagers were both devout and superstitious. The countryside abounded in miracle-working springs and trees and its people venerated a multitude of local saints never officially recognized by the church.

The legal status of the villagers and the proportion of their produce that they could keep for their own use differed sharply from region to region and even from village to village. By the end of the third quarter of the eleventh century the seignorial system was firmly established in England, France, and western Germany. In these broad regions almost every man who worked the land owed some form of rent or service to a lord. In Saxony and parts of eastern Germany the villagers still depended directly on the king, but the seignorial system was spreading rapidly, aided by the political anarchy of the last quarter of the century. But even where the seignorial system reigned there were striking differences in conditions. In southern England, most of France, and Alsace and Lorraine, the vast majority of the villagers were unfree, bound to the soil and with no property rights against their lords. In eastern and northeastern England, the ancient Danelaw and East Anglia, a fair proportion, probably over half, of the villagers were freemen who paid rents and certain carefully defined services to their lords. Some parts of France such as the region about Bordeaux contained many freemen. In eastern Germany the free villagers were gradually being reduced to serfdom but the process was by no means complete.

The seignorial system was a set of institutions through which the feudal class, soldiers and prelates, drew their support from those who tilled the land. In most of the vast region occupied by villages using the two- and three-field systems it was based on what we call manorial organization. The lord of the village had his demesne, strips in the fields that his tenants cultivated for him. The villagers plowed the demesne, sowed it, harvested the crops, and stored them in the lord's barns. The demesne might occupy as much as a third of the arable land, but was usually rather less. Then the villagers paid the lord a percentage of the crops grown on their own strips. The lord considered that he owned the common resources of the village and charged his tenants for their use. Thus the villager paid a rent in pigs for feeding his swine in the woodlands and in cheese for having his cattle in the common pasture. When the villager fished, the lord got a share of the catch. In short, the tenants owed a rent in kind for the use of every resource of the village. In addition, they worked for the lord at cultivating his demesne, harvesting his hay, or any other task he might set. Sometimes these labor services occupied as much as three days a week. The lord and his household obtained their food from the rents and the produce of the demesne. The lord's clothes were made from the wool of his sheep spun and woven by the village women under his wife's direction. His dwelling was built by his tenants' labor services.

The rents and services mentioned in the last paragraph were due to the lord as the owner of the land. In addition, the lord usually had extensive and profitable rights that were essentially political. As the feudal system developed, the functions and powers of government had been parceled out among the members of the feudal hierarchy. Although in strict theory they exercised these rights as representatives of the king, the fact that the powers were hereditary made them regard them as their own property. The extent of these seignorial powers differed according to the custom of the land and the status of the lord. In England the king kept a firm grip on the higher criminal jurisdiction and the lords of villages could have little more than what we would call police-court justice. In Normandy the duke was equally jealous of his rights. But in most of France and western Germany a man of importance in the feudal hierarchy would have complete jurisdiction over the people of his villages. A lesser lord would have more limited rights. These rights of jurisdiction were important to a lord from several points of view. For one thing they contributed to his prestige — lords with powers of life and death considered their gallows one of their prized possessions. Then they gave a firm control over tenants and complete freedom to discipline them at will. Finally they were extremely profitable. When a man was hanged, the lord could seize all his possessions, and the penalty for many offenses was a fine. The possession of seignorial authority gave a lord many opportunities for profit. He could hold a market in his village and collect a toll or sales tax on all goods sold. He could establish fees for crossing a bridge or sailing down a stream. He could also establish monopolies. Thus many a lord compelled his tenants to have their grain ground at his mill and to bake their bread in his ovens, paying generous fees in grain and flour. He forbade his tenants to keep doves while his waxed fat on their crops.

The unfree villager was almost completely subject to his lord, especially when the latter had rights of jurisdiction. In theory criminal justice was a function of the state and the unfree as well as the free were subject to it. In England this theory was a reality. Except in minor offenses the lord had no criminal jurisdiction over his unfree tenants and if he committed a crime against one, he could be haled into a royal court. But in France and western Germany the governmental powers were so distributed that if the lord of a village could not hang his serfs, the lord next above him could, and would be delighted to do so at his request. Nowhere did unfree tenants have any civil rights against their lord. He could demand any rents and services he desired and take any of their property that struck his fancy. The arbitrary authority of the lord was, however, restrained by several circumstances. The men of the Middle Ages were basically conservative — their tendency was to do what their ancestors had done and distrust innovations. Hence a lord hesitated to increase the customary dues of his villagers. Then it was obviously to his interest to keep his labor supply alive and this in itself limited the rents and services he could demand. Finally the church insisted that serfs had souls and urged the lords to treat them as fellow Christians. Rather grudgingly the lords admitted that serfs could marry, but they insisted on calling their families *sequelae* or broods.

Throughout history progress in agricultural methods has been slow and gradual. As our information concerning the eleventh century is extremely scanty, it is almost impossible to say to what extent and in what ways agricultural techniques were improved. There is some evidence that villages were changing from the two- to the three-field system and thus increasing their utilization of their arable land. It seems likely that improvement in the design of plows and the harnessing of oxen was allowing a reduction in the size of the plow teams and by this means lessening the demands on the meadows. Perhaps the chief problem connected with eleventh-century agriculture is the extent to which the available arable land was increased by reclamation. We have clear evidence that in the early twelfth century there was extensive clearing of wood and brush land and that some inroads were made on the edges of the great forests. There was also some draining of marshes, especially when it could be done by a system of dikes. In the twelfth and early thirteenth centuries colonists from all over Europe settled the lands to the east of the Elbe in Germany. There is evidence that this great reclamation movement started early in the eleventh century, at least to the extent of returning to cultivation the lands that had been deserted during the Viking invasions, but it is impossible to estimate how much was accomplished. It seems clear that the initiative in this movement was taken by lords who wanted to utilize as much of their lands as possible. They made attractive offers to peasants who would reclaim land and settle it — greater personal freedom and lower rents and services. The result was an increase in the lord's resources both material and human. His total rents were larger and more people lived on his lands. In short, during the eleventh and twelfth centuries the productive capacity of western Europe and its population were greatly increased by colonization and reclamation, but it is impossible to say how far this process had gone when the crusades began.

Although western Europe in the eleventh century was overwhelmingly rural and agricultural, the revival of industry, commerce, and urban life was well under way. This development was particularly marked in Italy. There urban life had never disappeared to the extent that it had in the north. Even though they might have little industry and trade, the Italian towns had remained populated. And a number of Italian towns had maintained a flourishing trade with Constantinople. Under the protection of the Byzantine fleet, ships plied steadily between the capital of the empire and such Italian ports as Amalfi and Venice. By the second half of the eleventh century Venice had a powerful fleet of her own. At about this same time Genoa and Pisa began to trade along the Mediterranean coast to Marseilles, Narbonne, and Barcelona. These two cities also took the offensive against the Moslem fleets that had been raiding their harbors and seizing their vessels. Naval expeditions were made against Corsica, Sardinia, and even Tunis. In the inland towns of Tuscany and Lombardy, industry, particularly the manufacture of textiles, began to flourish. The last years of the century saw the beginnings of the communal movement that was to break the power of the bishops and transform the towns of north Italy into independent if rather turbulent republics. In short, the towns were an important element in the civilization of eleventh-century Italy. Two of them at least, Genoa and Pisa, were to play a vital part in the First Crusade.

Outside the Mediterranean region the revival of urban life had made far less progress. Unfortunately, lack of evidence makes it extremely difficult to be very specific. It seems clear that great lay and ecclesiastical lords were encouraging their tenants who lived in their chief seats to acquire specialized skills. Thus there were craftsmen living around castles, cathedrals, and monasteries who made articles for the use of their lords. In Flanders the spinners and weavers were already manufacturing more woolen cloth than they could use and were selling it to others. There were also merchants engaged in inter-regional commerce. Men of Rouen carried wine to England to satisfy the thirst of the Norman favorites of king Edward the Confessor. When William of Normandy conquered England, Norman merchants swarmed over to settle in the English boroughs. By the end of the century, certainly, London was a great town with several rich and powerful merchant families. But all these phenomena were merely the beginnings of the movement of urban revival that was to mark the twelfth century. Although western Europe had industry, commerce, and urban life, these were still insignificant elements in its civilization.

One of the most important features of the eleventh century was the crystallization and extension of the feudal system. Feudal institutions had been developing since the eighth century. Charles Martel had given benefices to men who swore loyalty to him and were ready to serve him as soldiers. By the time of Charles the Bald benefices were becoming hereditary in practice if not in theory and the same tendency was affecting the countships and other royal offices. In eleventh-century France the benefice had become the hereditary fief. Although the office of count was not absolutely hereditary, a competent heir was practically certain of the inheritance. When an office changed hands, this was less likely to be the result of royal action than of the successful aggression of a powerful rival. Moreover, during the ninth and tenth centuries when civil war combined with Viking raids to keep France in a state of anarchy, the landholders had but two practical alternatives. One could obtain military support and protection by becoming the vassal of a powerful neighbor or one could sink into the category of an unfree villager. Almost every landholder whose resources permitted him to equip himself as a soldier chose the former course. Only the most powerful and most stubborn could stay outside the feudal system. Although eleventh-century France contained *allods*, that is, lands held from no lord, they were quite rare and most of them disappeared in the twelfth century. In short, eleventh-century France, especially in the north, was almost completely feudalized and the principle so dear to feudal lawyers of "no land without a lord" was nearly true of it.

As the feudal system spread over France its members became arranged in a hierarchy. At the head stood the Capetian king, who was suzerain of the great lords of the land. Below him came a group of feudal potentates who may best be described as feudal princes — the men whom a later age called the "peers of France". According to the theory developed in the twelfth century, there were six lay peers — the count of Flanders, the duke of Normandy, the count of Champagne, the duke of Aquitaine, the count of Toulouse, and the duke of Burgundy. The powerful counts of Anjou were not called peers because they were considered vassals of the Capetian king in his capacity of duke of France, the title held by the family before its elevation to the throne, but they were far more important than the vassals of the royal demesne in the Île de France such as the lords of Coucy and Montmorency. Each of these great lords who held directly of the king had his own vassals many of whom were counts or had usurped that title. It was by no means uncommon for a vigorous lord to wake up some bright morning and decide he was a count, and usually no one bothered to dispute the claim. These secondary vassals in turn had their own vassals and rear-vassals, and the hierarchy continued down to the simple knight who had just enough land and peasant labor to support him. This minimum unit of the feudal system, the resources that would enable a man to be a knight, was called the knight's fief or fee. To make this hierarchy clear let us cite a concrete example. In the lands along the Bay of Biscay known as Bas-Poitou the simple knights held their fiefs of two barons, the lords of La Garnache and Montaigu. They in turn were vassals of the viscount of Thouars, who held his fief from the count of Poitou, who was in turn a vassal of the duke of Aquitaine, a peer of France. Actually the same man was count of Poitou and duke of Aquitaine, but the offices were distinct.

Each member of the feudal hierarchy had obligations to his lord and his vassals. These obligations were defined by feudal custom. Whenever a dispute arose between lord and vassal, it was settled in the lord's *curia* or court. There the lord acted as presiding officer and the vassals rendered the decision. In every fief the feudal custom for that fief was created by these decisions in the lord's court. Thus feudal custom varied from fief to fief. Moreover, in the eleventh century the formation of this custom was far from complete, for questions were decided only when they arose and many came up but rarely. Take for instance the customs governing inheritance. It was generally accepted that if a man had sons, one of them was his heir, but in the eleventh century the idea of primogeniture was by no means absolutely accepted. If the eldest son looked unpromising as a warrior, the vassals felt free to choose one of his younger brothers. If the two eldest sons were twins, the fief might be evenly divided between them. When a man died leaving a son under age, who cared for the fief and performed the service due from it? Sometimes it was the nearest male relative on the mother's side, sometimes on the father's side. In other fiefs the custody of minors belonged to the lord. But despite the variations from fief to fief it is possible to make certain general statements about feudal obligations that are reasonably valid.

The fundamental purpose of the feudal system was coöperation in war. Every lord was bound to protect his vassal from enemies outside the fief and every vassal owed military service to his lord. In some cases the vassal owed only his own personal service; in others he was bound to lead a certain number of knights to his lord's army. By the thirteenth century the military service owed by vassals was carefully defined and limited, but this process was not complete in the eleventh century. In most fiefs a distinction was made between offensive and defensive campaigns and the length of time a vassal had to serve in the former was limited — forty days was usual in the thirteenth century. When the fief was in danger, obviously the vassals were bound to stay in service as long as they were needed. Then the feudal system was political as well as military. When there was a question of feudal custom to be decided, the vassals were bound to obey the lord's summons to his court. Moreover, as the vassals had a strong interest in the welfare of their lord and his fief, they expected him to consult them before making an important decision. When their lord was about to marry, he was expected to summon his vassals to aid him in deciding what lady had the most useful marriage portion and the most potent relatives. If a lord wanted his vassals to serve him with enthusiasm in a war against a neighbor, he sought their counsel before embarking on it. In short, the important business of the lord's fief was conducted in his court. Finally a man's prestige in the feudal world depended very largely on the number and importance of his vassals. When he wanted to display his power and dignity, he summoned his vassals to "do him honor". Thus attendance at the lord's court was second in importance only to military service as a feudal obligation.

In addition to service in his lord's court and army the vassal had certain obligations that were essentially economic. One of these was known as relief. By the twelfth century, relief was a money payment due to the lord when an heir succeeded to a fief, but there is evidence to indicate that in some fiefs at least in the eleventh century it was also demanded when a new lord came into his inheritance. Moreover, in the eleventh century it was often, perhaps usually, paid in horses and armor rather than in money. When a lord had a need for additional resources for some purpose that he considered important for his fief as a whole, he asked his vassals for an aid. By the twelfth century feudal custom defined very strictly the occasions on which a lord could demand an aid — for other purposes he could simply request one. The accepted occasions were the knighting of the lord's eldest son, the wedding of his eldest daughter for the first time, and the paying of ransom for the lord if he were captured. In all probability this clear definition had not been achieved by the eleventh century. When a lord wanted an aid, he asked his vassals for it and unless the request seemed too unreasonable, he received it. This form of income probably played a large part in financing the crusades. Vassals could hardly refuse to assist their lord in so worthy an enterprise. Finally, in some fiefs in the twelfth and thirteenth centuries, the vassals were obliged to entertain the lord and his household when he visited them, and there is reason for believing that this obligation had been more general and more important in the eleventh century.

Beyond the actual services owed by the vassal the lord had certain rights over the vassal and his fief. As the marriage of a vassal's daughter gave a male from outside the family an interest in her father's fief, the bridegroom had to be approved by the lord. If a vassal died leaving an unmarried daughter as an heir, it was the lord's right and duty to choose a husband for her. This was a valuable prerogative as it allowed the lord to reward a faithful knight at no cost to himself. When a vassal died leaving children under age, the lord could insist that someone be found to perform the service due from the fief unless custom gave him the custody of the heirs and their lands. If a vassal died without heirs that were recognized by the custom of the fief — second cousins were rarely accepted and more distant relatives practically never — the fief escheated, that is, returned to the lord. In case a vassal violated the feudal bond by some offense against his lord and was condemned by his fellow vassals in the lord's court, he could forfeit his fief. Forfeiture was rather rare. The assembled vassals hesitated to declare a fief forfeited because each of them felt that he might be in the same position some day.

When a man became a vassal, he did homage and swore fidelity to his lord. There has been a great deal of essentially fruitless discussion about the distinction between homage and fidelity. The fact that prelates often were willing to swear fidelity but refused to do homage would seem to indicate that fidelity was personal loyalty while homage represented a promise to perform the services due from a fief. But household knights who held no fief often swore fidelity and did homage. Actually it seems doubtful that there was any clear, generally accepted distinction. Ordinarily the two were part of a single ceremony. The vassal knelt before his lord, put his hands between his lord's hands, and swore to be faithful to him "against all men living or dead". Often the lord then gave the vassal a clod of earth to symbolize the granting of the fief. The personal relationship between lord and vassal was an important element in feudalism — each was expected to be loyal to the other. It was a horrible crime for a vassal to slay or wound his lord or seduce his wife or daughter, but a lord was also bound not to injure his vassal in person or honor. The vassal was expected to aid his lord in every way possible.

As a form of government feudalism had both advantages and disadvantages. It supplied a military force of heavy cavalry at every stage in the hierarchy. Thus each barony, each county, and each kingdom had its army. It also furnished vigorous and interested local government. The extensive reclamation of land and the founding of towns were largely the result of the desire of feudal lords to increase their resources. It is highly doubtful that mere agents working for the benefit of a central government could have accomplished so much. But as a means of keeping peace and order the feudal system was no great success, for it was based on the assumption that there would be continual warfare. In theory, quarrels between lords and vassals and between vassals of the same lord were settled in the feudal courts. Actually when two vassals of a lord quarreled, they went to war and the lord did not intervene unless he thought one might be so seriously weakened that he could not perform his service. And no spirited vassal accepted an unfavorable decision by his lord's court until he was coerced with armed force. Between vassals of different lords there was no hindrance to war. In short, in eleventh-century France, feudal warfare was endemic and it was a fortunate region that saw peace throughout an entire summer. The church tried to limit this warfare by declaring the Peace and Truce of God. The Peace of God forbade attacks on noncombatants, merchants, women, and peasants while the Truce prohibited fighting on weekends and on religious days. Unfortunately, neither Peace nor Truce was taken very seriously by the feudal lords.

Fighting was the chief function of the feudal male. From early youth he was conditioned to bear the weight of knightly armor and drilled rigorously in the use of arms. He had to learn the extremely difficult feat of hitting a target with his spear while riding at full gallop with his shield on his left arm. When he was considered adequately mature and trained he was made a knight. This was a simple ceremony in the eleventh century. An experienced knight gave him his arms and then struck him a terrific blow with his hand or the flat of his sword. Throughout his life the knight spent most of his time in practising with his arms or actually fighting. Dull periods of peace were largely devoted to hunting on horseback such savage animals as the wild boar. The knight ate enormous meals of pastry and game washed down with vast quantities of wine or ale. He kept his wife continuously pregnant and saw that his house was well supplied with concubines to while away his leisure hours. In short, the ordinary knight was savage, brutal, and lustful. At the same time he was, in his own way, devout. He accepted without question the teachings of the church and was deeply interested in the welfare of his soul. He had a private chaplain, commonly chosen for the speed with which he could say mass, who performed the sacraments in his chapel and heard his confessions. Most knights scrupulously observed the rites of religion. They were, however, little troubled by Christian ethics. The giving of generous gifts to a family monastic establishment or even the founding of a new one was the usual way of atoning for one's sins. The crusades with their plenary indulgences were particularly useful for this purpose.

The women of the feudal class held a rather ambiguous position. A woman was never her own mistress. Before marriage she was in the care of her father; then she passed into the custody of her husband; if he died, she was the ward of her lord or her eldest son. A woman could not do homage or hold a fief in her own hands though she could carry one to her husband. Her testimony was unacceptable in court except in respect to a rape committed on her or the murder of her husband in her presence. She had no rights against her husband. He could dispose of her property and beat her whenever she annoyed him. The *chansons de geste* show clearly that feudal husbands beat their wives savagely with no qualms of conscience. Moreover, the marriage bond was far from firm. Although the church consistently preached the permanence of marriage, by the eleventh century it had still failed to convince the feudal class that unwanted wives could not be calmly laid aside. Yet there is a brighter side to the picture. Although a wife had no rights against her husband, she enjoyed his status as against all others. When her lord was away, the lady was the mistress of the fief. She also ruled her side of the household — the women and girls who spun and wove. Here it seems she was little gentler than her husband. Church councils continually decreed that it was mortal sin for a lady to beat her maids to death. Moreover there is evidence that the feudal lady used the bottle as gaily as her spouse. The *chansons* abound in tales of drunken ladies and their misadventures.

A simple knight and his lady usually lived in a crude wooden house surrounded by a moat and palisade. A baron would possess at least one castle. In the eleventh century most castles were of what is termed the motte-and-bailey type. The lord's peasants would dig a circular ditch some nine or ten feet deep and perhaps thirty feet wide, piling the excavated earth into a mound encircled by the ditch. On the inner edge of the ditch or moat and around the top of the mound they would erect palisades. Then on the summit of the mound inside the palisade would be built a wooden tower of two or three stories. The lowest floor would be used for storing supplies and prisoners. On the second floor would be the hall where the lord transacted business, entertained guests, and feasted with his retainers. In it the retainers and servants slept at night. On the third floor the lord and lady would have their chamber where they reposed in a great bed, while their personal servants slept on the floor. A few great lords had some stone work in their castles — perhaps a stone gate with towers. Others built great stone *tours* or towers like the White Tower in the Tower of London built by William the Conqueror. These had massive walls ten to twenty feet thick. The door was on the second floor and was reached by a wooden stairway easily cut away in time of danger. If an enemy appeared, the door would be closed and the inhabitants of the tower would sit quietly inside. The enemy could not get at them, but neither could they get at him unless he came so close to the walls that stones or boiling oil could be dropped on him from the roof.

The castle was an extremely vital factor in feudal politics. If adequately supplied and garrisoned a castle could hold out almost indefinitely against the siege methods of the day. Rarely could a feudal army be held together long enough to take a resolutely defended castle. Hence its lord was practically independent. If a baron was so unfortunate as to be condemned by his lord's court, he could simply retire to his castle until his discouraged suzerain was ready to make peace. Not until the advent of mercenary troops who would stay in service as long as they were paid and the invention of improved siege engines was it possible for a lord to exert any effective authority over a vassal who possessed a strong castle. And the castle was an integral part of feudalism. When feudal institutions spread to a new land, castles soon appeared. Within a century of the Norman conquest there were some twelve hundred castles in England.

At the beginning of the eleventh century France was the only feudal state in Europe. The Capetian king was essentially a feudal suzerain supporting his court on the produce of his demesne manors and raising his army from his vassals in the duchy of France and the tiny contingents that the great lords were willing to send him. The peers of France readily acknowledged that they were the king's vassals, but rarely bothered to render him any services. Actually France was not a single state but an alliance of feudal principalities bound together by the feeble suzerainty of the king. In real power the king was weaker than most of his great vassals. His demesne was small and he could not control the barons of the Île de France. The monarchy survived largely because of the support of the church, which was inclined to prefer one master to many, and the resources that could be drawn from church fiefs. While some of the great lords such as the count of Flanders and the dukes of Normandy and Aquitaine had obtained control of the bishops within their lands, the prelates of Burgundy and Champagne depended on the king. The bishops had large, rich fiefs with many knightly vassals. Hence the man who appointed the bishops had the use of extensive resources. Nevertheless, the Capetian monarchy of the early eleventh century could do little more than survive. In the Île de France it had little authority and outside none whatever.

Along the borders of France feudal institutions had spread into other regions. The county of Barcelona, once Charlemagne's Spanish March, was a thoroughly feudal state and there were strong feudal elements in the kingdoms of Aragon and Navarre. In Germany, Lorraine and Franconia were essentially feudal. The kingdom of Germany and the Holy Roman Empire ruled by the emperors of the Saxon dynasty did not constitute a feudal state. The base of the royal power lay in the duchy of Saxony, which was almost untouched by feudalism. It was a land of free farmers, noble and non-noble, who were always ready to follow their duke to war. Outside Saxony the imperial authority depended almost entirely on the prelates. The bishops and abbots of Germany, Lombardy, and Tuscany were imperial appointees with wide, delegated authority. Their great fiefs and their resources were at the emperor's disposal. Although the counts of Germany were non-hereditary royal agents, they were essentially judicial officers, and the military control rested in the hands of the dukes. The emperors, dukes, counts, and other landholders occasionally granted fiefs, but the offices of duke and count were not fiefs. The power of a duke depended on the extent of his estates and his ability to inspire the loyalty of the people of his duchy. Thus the dukes of Franconia, Swabia, and Bavaria were usually powerful figures while the duke of Lorraine was likely to be a mere figurehead. In this same period England was still a Teutonic monarchy. Small men commended themselves to great men, swore oaths of fidelity to them, and occasionally held land in return for military service, but there were neither vassals nor fiefs in the continental sense.

During the course of the eleventh century feudalism expanded rapidly. The conquest of England by duke William of Normandy created a new feudal state. King William retained the powers that had been enjoyed by his Anglo-Saxon predecessors. In every shire there was a sheriff appointed by the king and removable at his pleasure who presided over the popular courts, supervised the king's demesne manors, and collected his dues. William also collected the land tax called Danegeld and was the only monarch of western Europe to have a source of revenue of this type. Moreover, when king William established a complete and formal feudal hierarchy in England, he made certain innovations in feudal custom. In France a vassal's primary obligation was to his lord, and if the lord waged war against the king, it was the vassal's duty to follow him. William insisted that every freeman owed basic allegiance to the crown. In the famous Salisbury Oath the freemen of England swore fidelity to him as against all others. If an English baron rose in revolt, his vassals were expected to desert him. Then William absolutely forbade private warfare. The vassals of an English baron owed him military service only when the baron himself was engaged in the king's service. Finally the Conqueror was extremely niggardly in granting rights of jurisdiction. All lords of any importance were given "sac and soc" or police court authority over their own tenants. A few great lords had the right to have their agents preside over local popular courts. But the higher ranges of justice were kept firmly in the hands of the crown. In short, William created a feudal state, but it was one in which the monarch had extensive non-feudal powers and resources and in which feudal custom was modified to favor royal authority.

At about the same time that William of Normandy established a feudal state in England a group of Norman adventurers were doing the same thing in southern Italy and Sicily. In the third decade of the eleventh century William, Drogo, and Humphrey, sons of a petty Norman lord named Tancred of Hauteville, entered the continuous quarrels between rival factions in southern Italy. First they served as mercenary captains, but soon they established themselves in lands and fortresses. They then sent for their younger brothers, Robert Guiscard and Roger. When Humphrey, the last of the elder brothers, died in 1057 the Hautevilles were masters of Apulia. Robert Guiscard took the title duke of Apulia and set his brother Roger to work conquering Calabria. In 1061 both brothers joined forces to attack Sicily, which was held by the Moslems.[1] After some thirty years of continuous war the conquest was completed and Roger became count of Sicily as his brother's vassal. Robert, duke of Apulia and overlord of Sicily, did homage to the pope for his lands and was a firm ally of the papacy against the German emperors. But the possession of southern Italy failed to satisfy his ambition. He and his turbulent son Bohemond viewed with greedy eyes the Byzantine lands across the

1 See below, chapter II, section C.

Adriatic and contemplated the conquest of Greece if not that of the whole Byzantine empire. Robert and Bohemond invaded Greece and might well have conquered it if their communications had not been cut by the Venetian fleet, which aided the emperor in return for extensive commercial rights in the empire. Robert Guiscard and Roger of Sicily built a strong feudal state on much the same lines followed by William of Normandy. There was a feudal hierarchy strictly controlled by a strong and effective central government.

In Germany the two great emperors of the Salian house, Henry III and Henry IV, attempted to build a strong, centralized monarchy on the foundations laid by the Saxon emperors. Already master of Franconia and with extensive estates in Swabia, Henry III planned to add Thuringia and south Saxony to the family domains and thus gain a firm basis of power in the heart of Germany. He built a strong castle at Goslar, the chief town of south Saxony and the site of valuable silver mines, and strewed the neighborhood with fortresses garrisoned by troops from his Swabian lands. His son Henry IV continued his policy. But the nobles and freemen of Saxony fiercely resented the king's intrusion into the duchy and, led by the Billung family, which claimed the ducal dignity, they rose in revolt against Henry IV. At the same time the great pope Gregory VII chose to attack the very cornerstone of the imperial government — the emperor's control over the prelates. The German lords, who had no desire to see a strong monarchy, combined with the pope and the Saxon rebels against Henry. The emperor held his own and died victor over his foes in the year 1106. But the long struggle had ruined the hopes of the Salian kings for establishing a strong monarchy. The first half of the twelfth century was to be a period of anarchy in Germany in which feudal institutions were to spread rapidly until the Hohenstaufen emperors created a feudal state. On the eve of the crusades the so-called Roman empire of the Saxon and Salian emperors was crumbling.

What had earlier been border lands of western Europe also evinced marked activity in the eleventh century. In Spain, for example, the Christian kingdoms of the north were taking the offensive against the Moslem masters of the rest of the peninsula. This will be treated at length in a later chapter.[2] It will suffice here to observe that, as all the energies and resources of the Spanish states were needed for their internecine wars and the

[2] See below, chapter II, section A.

struggle against the Moslems, they took part neither in the affairs of Europe as a whole nor in the early crusades to the Holy Land.

The eleventh century was a high point in the history of the Scandinavian states, but, except for the conquest of England by king Swein of Denmark and Canute his son, they had little to do with the rest of western Europe. During the century Norway, Sweden, and Denmark were evangelized and their kings built reasonably firm national governments. Under the vague overlordship of these kings the Viking chieftains ruled their vast island domain — the Orkneys, the Shetlands, the Faroes, Iceland, Greenland, and the Isle of Man. It was also the age of the Viking settlements on the North American coast, while princes of Kiev, descendants of Swedish adventurers, ruled a large state on the Russian plains. A great proportion of the vigor of the eleventh century was centered in the Scandinavian blood. The Normans, who were only a century removed from their Viking ancestors, ruled the strongest feudal principality in France, the kingdom of England, and southern Italy and Sicily. It is interesting in this connection to notice that of the eight chief lay leaders of the First Crusade four were Normans and a fifth had a Norman wife who supplied most of his ardor. Robert, duke of Normandy, and Bohemond, son of Robert Guiscard, are easily recognizable as Normans, but in addition Godfrey of Bouillon, duke of Lower Lorraine, and his brother Baldwin were sons of the Norman count of Boulogne.

To the east of the German empire lay the vast Slavic lands cleft in twain by a wedge of Magyars who occupied the Hungarian plain and Pechenegs in the steppes north of the Black Sea. To the north of this wedge were three important Slavic states — Bohemia, Poland, and Russia. The Přemyslid dukes of Bohemia and Moravia had a status that is hard to define. They were masters of their own lands and dealt as they pleased with their eastern neighbors, but they acknowledged themselves vassals of the kings of Germany and supported their policy in the west. Duke Vratislav II (1061–1092) was a loyal follower of the emperor Henry IV. Poland was an independent state ruled by its own kings. To the east of Poland lay the Russian principalities. Yaroslav the Wise, the last powerful prince of Kiev, died in 1054. Under his descendants the state was divided into a number of principalities under the vague suzerainty of the prince of Kiev.

In religion and culture Bohemia and Poland were part of the Latin west. Their bishops acknowledged the pope at Rome and their political organizations were essentially borrowed from the German state. Russia on the other hand was thoroughly Byzantine. The princely descendants of the Viking Rurik had been converted to Christianity by Byzantine missionaries and their commercial and diplomatic relations were largely with Constantinople. Kiev was a Byzantine city. Its churches were Byzantine in style and its scholars pursued Byzantine learning. By the latter part of the eleventh century the conquest of the steppes north of the Black Sea by the Pechenegs made actual communication with Constantinople difficult, but this did not affect the basic tone of Russian culture.

The Asiatic wedge that divided the Slavic peoples consisted of two distinct elements. The Pecheneg masters of the Black Sea steppes held the northern bank of the Danube as far as the Carpathian mountains. The Hungarian plain was occupied by the Magyars. After their crushing defeat by the emperor Otto I the Magyars had gradually settled down in Hungary. Toward the end of the tenth century prince Géza united the Magyar clans and brought in missionaries — chiefly from Bohemia. His son Stephen organized Hungary as a Latin Christian state. The land was divided into counties and dioceses, and in the year 1000 Stephen was crowned king with the approval of the pope. On the eve of the crusades Hungary enjoyed a period of prosperity and comparative peace under the strong hand of king Ladislas I (1077–1095). His successor, Coloman, was to face the problem of handling the crusading armies marching down the Danube.

interesting

This period saw the southern Slavs largely dependent on other peoples. In 1018 the Byzantine emperor Basil II, called "the Bulgar-slayer", finally crushed the Bulgarian state and incorporated it into his empire. Despite fierce revolts in 1040 and 1073 the Bulgars remained Byzantine subjects for over a century. The Serbs were divided into many tribes under local princes. Sometimes one of these princes would be recognized as a paramount chief, but such authority was usually short-lived. All the Serbian princes acknowledged the overlordship of the Byzantine emperor, but only under extremely strong rulers did this relationship have any meaning. As a rule the Serbs were independent and divided. To the north of Serbia lay Croatia. In the last years of the eleventh century Croatia was a separate state ruled by the Hungarian kings. In culture and religion the Bulgars and Serbs were Byzantine while the Croats were Latin.

While the peasants were improving their agricultural methods and reclaiming forest, marsh, and waste, and the knights were developing and extending feudal institutions, the churchmen were making similar progress. The local administration of the church was clarified and strengthened and an effective central government was created. At the same time missionaries converted the Scandinavian lands and labored among the Slavs. Christian Europe was both strengthened and extended. One of the most interesting developments in local church organization was the development of cathedral chapters. The bishops had always had officers and clergy who aided them in serving their cathedrals. In the eleventh century the more important members of the cathedral clergy began to form corporations. Of great assistance to this movement was the inclination of lay lords to endow seats or canonries in the cathedral that could be used as refuges for unwarlike sons. The chapter was composed of the episcopal officials such as the chancellor, treasurer, sacristan, and archdeacon and a number of priests or canons. The chapter had an elected head called a dean. The chapter soon became the body that formally elected the nominee of the lord when an episcopal vacancy was to be filled. In the eleventh century also the itinerant agents of the bishop called archpriests settled down as parish priests with supervisory powers over their fellows.

During the ninth and tenth centuries the church had become deeply involved in secular affairs. The extensive lands of the bishops and abbots were held of lay lords by feudal services, and the prelates had to perform the functions of vassals either personally or by deputy. Some doughty bishops led their troops in battle wielding a mace, which they insisted did not violate canon law as it drew no blood, but most had secular agents called advocates to head their levies. But the prelates were appointed by the secular lords and invested by them with the insignia of their holy office. They served the lords as counselors and administrators. As we have seen, the Capetian monarchy owed what little power it had to the prelates it controlled and the German empire was based on an episcopacy devoted to the emperor. This situation was harmful to the spiritual functions of the church. A bishop should be primarily devoted to his episcopal duties rather than to the service of a lay prince, and an abbot who was essentially a baron was unlikely to be an effective father to his monks.

As early as the tenth century this situation had alarmed many devout men. In the hope of improving the monastic system duke William of Aquitaine had in 911 founded the abbey of Cluny. Cluny was forbidden to hold lands by feudal service. A donor to this foundation had to make his gift in free alms — that is, the only service owed was prayers for his soul. Cluny adopted a modified form of the Benedictine rule. St. Benedict had directed his monks to spend long hours at manual labor, but once a monastery grew rich in land and peasant labor, it was impossible to get the monks to work in the fields. The Cluniac rule greatly extended the hours to be devoted to performing the services of the church in the hope of keeping the monks occupied in that way. By the eleventh century Cluny had many daughter houses. Some were new foundations while others were old monasteries that were more or less willingly reformed by Cluniac monks. The order also developed a highly centralized administration. There was only one abbot — the abbot of Cluny. Each daughter house was headed by a prior who was subject to the abbot of Cluny, who was supposed to visit regularly and inspect every house of the order. In the eleventh century Cluny had enormous influence. With the support of the emperor Henry III Cluniac monks reformed many German monasteries and men inspired by Cluny revived English monasticism. All enthusiastic and devout churchmen tended to gravitate toward Cluny.

These enthusiasts were not willing to limit their reforms to the monasteries. They were anxious to remedy the abuses that were common among the secular clergy. The most serious of these was lay appointment of ecclesiastics. The great lords appointed bishops and abbots, and the lords of villages appointed the parish priests. Closely related to this was the sin of simony, the payment of money to obtain church offices. The lay lords were extremely inclined to bestow offices on the highest bidder. Another abuse that seriously troubled conscientious churchmen was the marriage of priests. To some extent this was a moral question — canon law required priests to be celibate. But it also vitally concerned the material interests of the church. A married priest was inclined to think of his family before his priestly duty and was most likely to use church property to endow his children even if he did not succeed in making his office hereditary. There were, of course, other abuses that interested the reformers, but these were the ones on which they concentrated their attention.

The reformers realized that there was but one way to achieve their ends. Even if the bishops of Europe could be made enthusiastic supporters of reform, they were as individuals helpless before the power of the lay princes. Only a strongly organized church with an effective central government could hope to make much progress. Hence their eyes turned toward the papacy. The pope was elected by the clergy and people of Rome, which meant in practice by the dominant faction of the Roman nobility. But when a strong monarch occupied the imperial throne, his influence could be decisive. Neither of these methods of choice pleased the reformers. If the papacy was to lead in the reform of the church, it had to be removed from lay control. The emperor Henry III was a pious as well as an efficient ruler, and he gladly supported the reformers by appointing popes favorable to their aims. The first important step was the creation of the college of cardinals. The six bishops who were suffragans of the pope as bishop of Rome, the pastors of the more important Roman churches, and some of the deacons of the Roman church were formed into a corporation. When a pope died, these men were to meet and elect his successor. If outside pressure was put upon them, the election was to be void.

The next problem was to increase the pope's authority over the church as a whole. Several devices were used for this purpose. It had long been customary for the pope to summon peculiarly worthy archbishops to Rome to receive the *pallium* from his hands. If the prelate to be honored was unwilling to go to Rome, the pope sent him the *pallium*. The reformers advanced the theory that as soon as an archbishop was elected, he must go to Rome to seek the *pallium* and could not perform the functions of his office until he did so. This gave the pope an effective veto on archiepiscopal elections and a chance to instruct the new prelate. In theory it had always been possible to appeal a decision rendered by an archbishop's court to the papacy, but the journey to Rome was long and costly and only the rich could make such an appeal. The reformers established a system by which cases could be heard by local prelates appointed by the pope. If anyone wanted to appeal a case to the papal court, he wrote to the pope asking him to appoint delegates to hear the appeal. The pope then directed a group of ecclesiastics in the region where the appellant lived to hear and determine the case. This device greatly increased the business of the papal courts, and enormously expanded the pope's influence. But the most important official was the papal legate. The legate was an agent of the pope sent to carry out his master's will in some part of Christendom. Sometimes a legate was sent to deal with a particular problem, but more often he was given a broad commission to carry out papal policy in a region. Armed with the full spiritual authority of the papacy he was an effective agent. Through his legates the pope could take an active part in the affairs of the church as a whole.

One of the ablest and most energetic members of the papal *curia* under the first reforming popes was an ecclesiastic named Hildebrand. Deeply imbued with the ideas of the Cluniac group, he was convinced that the church must be independent of all secular control and that the pope must be the absolute master of the church. In 1073 he was elected pope and took office under the name of Gregory VII. During the pontificates of Gregory's five predecessors much progress had been made. The college of cardinals had been established, papal legates and judges-delegate introduced, and stern decrees issued against simony and married clerks. The emperor Henry III was in favor of these reforms and supported them. But when reformers remarked that bishops should be chosen without lay interference, Henry turned a deaf ear. Control of the prelates was the very foundation of his power and he had no intention of abandoning it. Gregory found the imperial throne occupied by Henry IV, who had but recently come of age. The pope informed the emperor that bishops should be elected according to canon law — that is, by the clergy and people of the diocese. Henry ignored the warning and went on his way. Gregory wrote a stern letter of rebuke. The emperor replied by calling the German prelates together at Worms and having them declare Gregory a false pope improperly elected. Gregory then excommunicated Henry. This gave the emperor's enemies in Germany, the Saxons and the great lords who feared he would become too strong, a perfect excuse for revolt. They rose in rebellion and informed the emperor that unless he obtained absolution from the pope, they would choose a new ruler. To make his search for absolution impossible of success, they carefully guarded the Alpine passes. But Henry slipped through his kingdom of Burgundy into Lombardy where the bishops and their levies promptly rallied around him. The emperor met the pope at the castle of Canossa in northern Tuscany, went through a humiliating form of penance, and was absolved. All this was dramatic and picturesque but it accomplished little. Henry would not abandon his claim to the right to appoint and invest bishops and Gregory was determined to win his point. The pope continued to support the German rebels against the emperor and used his Norman vassals to check the imperial power in Italy. Gregory died in 1085 in exile with his Norman allies while imperial troops occupied Rome. After the short pontificate of Victor III, pope Urban II continued with enthusiasm the quarrel with the emperor. This quarrel was the chief reason for the meagerness of the German participation in the First Crusade preached by Urban in 1095.

Although the investiture question was the chief cause of the bitter controversy between Gregory VII and Henry IV, it was not the only point at issue. Gregory was advancing a novel concept of the proper relation between secular and ecclesiastical authority. During the ninth and tenth centuries the church had bent every effort to support the authority of the kings against their powerful subjects. It had preached that the royal office was a sacred one instituted by God and that an anointed king had priestly characteristics. Gregory maintained that the pope was God's viceroy on earth and all men were subject to him. Kings were merely high grade police chiefs to protect the church and suppress criminals. If an emperor or king refused to obey the pope, the pope could depose him.

The fact that Gregory was kept well occupied by his struggle with the emperor was a great boon to the other princes of Europe. Philip I of France was a cheerful sinner who was in continual difficulties with the church. Gregory's legates attempted to stop lay investiture in France, but they made little progress. Philip did not openly defy the pope; he simply ignored his commands. On the very eve of the First Crusade, pope Urban II excommunicated Philip for stealing the wife of the count of Anjou and making her his queen, but this did not trouble the king very gravely. Most interesting of all were Gregory's relations with William the Conqueror. As duke of Normandy William had appointed bishops as he saw fit and he continued the practice in England. Moreover, he forbade any papal legate to enter his realm without his express permission. But William, as a rule, made respectable episcopal appointments, and Gregory felt that he could not afford to be at odds with all the monarchs of Europe. When the English king complained that a papal legate was making a nuisance of himself in Normandy, Gregory hastily ordered his agent to stay out of the duchy. Incidentally, the Norman conquest of England had been a major victory for the papacy. The Anglo-Saxon church had been firmly under the control of the kings and largely independent of Rome. The conquest brought it into the orbit of the centralized government being developed by the papacy.

Although the eleventh century cannot be called a great era in the history of European culture, it was by no means unimportant even in this respect. Perhaps its most significant contribution was in a field closely related to the work of the reforming popes — canon law. The fundamental bases of ecclesiastical law were the Bible and the patristic writings — especially those of Ambrose, Jerome, and Augustine. To this mass of material were added the decrees of popes and councils. From the sixth century to the eleventh the churches of the various European states had been developing their own canon law in their own local councils. Obviously if the church was to have an effective centralized administration, it needed a common, generally accepted canon law that might be applied throughout Christendom. Fortunately, the eleventh century was marked by great interest in legal studies. Roman law as expounded in the works of Justinian's jurists and practical handbooks based on them had been continuously studied and applied in Italy, but one of the most valuable parts of Justinian's monument, the *Digest*, had apparently been forgotten. It was rediscovered in the eleventh century and spurred what was probably already an active interest in law. Bologna became particularly noted as a center of legal studies. Lanfranc, abbot of Bec and later archbishop of Canterbury, had studied Roman law in Italy. Equipped with their legal training many ecclesiastics set to work to produce codes of canon law for the church. Gregory VII had a group of canonists at work on codes that would emphasize the papal authority. The complete reconciliation of the divergent versions of ecclesiastical law had to await Gratian in the twelfth century, but the process was well begun in the eleventh.

In theology and philosophy the eleventh century was completely overshadowed by the twelfth. Anselm, abbot of Bec and archbishop of Canterbury, was a powerful and rather original thinker whose proof of the existence of God was greatly admired throughout the later Middle Ages. Lanfranc and Anselm made the monastic school at Bec the chief center of scholarship in northern Europe. The great cathedral schools of Laon, Chartres, and Paris had their beginnings in the eleventh century. This period also saw the first literature in French. The *Chanson de Roland* clearly existed in some form before the end of the century, and the first troubadours were at work in the south of France at the same time. The best known of the early troubadours, duke William IX of Aquitaine, took part in the abortive crusade of 1101. In the north the eleventh century was the great age of the Norse sagas. In architecture this era saw the rapid development of the Romanesque style with its massive barrel vaults, ingeniously carved capitals, and extensive exterior sculpture. Appropriately enough the queen of all Romanesque churches graced the abbey of Cluny.

In all the varied phases of civilization the eleventh century was a period of vital growth and energetic development. The twelfth and thirteenth centuries were to see the flowering of medieval civilization, but the plant matured and the buds were formed in the eleventh. The men of western Europe had faith in God and in their own strong arms. They also had a willingness to adventure, to innovate, and to organize. The two great complexes of institutions, the church and the feudal system, had achieved the strength of maturity without losing their capacity for further development and expansion. And it was the church and the feudal system that made the crusades possible.

2. Central Europe and the Mediterranean (*Map by the University of Wisconsin Cartographic Laboratory*)

II
CONFLICT IN THE MEDITERRANEAN BEFORE THE FIRST CRUSADE

A. *The Reconquest of Spain before 1095*

Before the northward advance of the Moslem forces had run its full course at least one center of Christian resistance had made its appearance at the northern edge of the Hispanic peninsula. By the middle of the ninth century the princes of Asturias-Leon had extended their holdings southward across the Cantabrian mountains for a distance of some sixty miles from the coast of the Bay of Biscay. On the eastern coast of the peninsula, to the immediate south of the eastern Pyrenees, lay the Catalan counties of the Spanish March, Barcelona chief among them. In the western Pyrenees Navarre and immediately to her east Aragon were in a rudimentary stage of development. Within a century after the completion of the Moslem conquest, the centers of resistance from which the Christian reconquest of the peninsula was to emanate had all made their beginnings, but it was to be another two centuries before any semblance of concerted and continuing Christian aggression against the Moslem conquerors would be discernible.

Excellent guides to source materials and the modern literature are: P. Aguado Bleye, *Manual de historia de España* (9th ed., 3 vols., Madrid, 1963——), I, chapters 25–35, and L. G. de Valdeavellano, *Historia de España* (3rd ed., Madrid, 1963——), I, i (pp. 359–509) and ii (pp. 9–386). A. Ballesteros y Beretta, *Historia de España* (2nd ed., rev., 11 vols., Barcelona, 1943–1956), I–II, is helpful but dated. The long standard work of A. Herculano, *História de Portugal* (9th ed., Lisbon, n. d.), I, should be supplemented by L. Gonzaga de Azevedo, *História de Portugal* (6 vols., Lisbon, 1935–1944), II–III. Cf. also D. Peres, *Como nasceu Portugal* (5th ed., Porto, 1959); E. Lévi-Provençal, *Histoire de l'Espagne musulmane* (3 vols., Paris, 1950–1953); J. Pérez de Urbel, *Sancho el Mayor de Navarra* (Madrid, 1950); R. Menéndez Pidal, *La España del Cid* (4th ed., 2 vols., Madrid, 1947), and English translation by H. Sunderland from 1st ed., *The Cid and His Spain* (London, 1934). H. Livermore's *History of Spain* (London and New York, 1958) and *History of Portugal* (Cambridge, England, 1947) provide introductory surveys.

The earliest firm tradition of a victory by Christian remnants and refugees after the final defeat of the Visigothic monarchy is localized in the Asturias, a region lying in the rugged terrain between the Cantabrian mountains and the north coast of the peninsula. It is adjacent to Galicia on its west and is separated from Cantabria to its east by the Picos de Europa. To the south of the Asturias, across the Cantabrian mountains lies Leon, early an object of Asturian conquest.

According to the tradition, after the defeat and death of king Roderic a certain Pelayo was acclaimed as king, and thereafter led his followers to victory over a Moslem force in the valley of Covadonga near his capital at Cangas de Onís. Although the earliest written account of the battle of Covadonga which has reached our time dates from some two centuries after the event, it is recorded by several Arabic historians unlikely to have made use of the Latin chronicle, and is so firmly established in tradition that there seems no reason for denying its foundation in fact. After allowance is made for exaggeration in numbers and embellishment with the miraculous or with supernatural interpretation of natural phenomena—arrows turning back from the mountain wall against the enemy, a mountain moving to engulf the retreating foe—the account may be accepted as the record of a successful skirmish fought by local inhabitants, Visigothic and other Christian refugees, following a long series of defeats. It is generally believed that Pelayo, whether or not that was his true name, was a member of the Gothic aristocracy, if not of royal blood. There is a tradition that he was in Cordova, presumably to attempt a negotiated settlement with the Moslem rulers, a year before the traditional date of the battle (718). At least this establishes at an early date the pattern of the frontier *caudillos*, often ready to treat with the Moslem in terms of alliance or feudal submission if such were the surest means for securing possessions and authority.

Pelayo was succeeded by his son, and subsequent successors are traced to relationship with him by blood or by marriage. The third prince in the succession, Alfonso I (737–756), son of the duke of Cantabria and son-in-law of Pelayo, broadened the base of operations by bringing the adjacent provinces into personal union with the Asturias and by moving westward into Galicia. In the latter move, he was able to take advantage of a Berber revolt which drew southward the scant Berber garrisons with which the Moslems had sought to hold the northwest of the peninsula. Although Alfonso I was able to strengthen the internal organization of his dominions to some degree, the counts of Galicia were by no means fully subjected and this northwest corner of Spain remained for generations a center for recurring revolt against hereditary succession and monarchical control. With the relaxation of their hold on the northwest, the Moslems established a frontier of firmly held places which may be traced from Coimbra through Coria, Talavera, Toledo, and Guadalajara to Pamplona. The last, however, was soon lost. This line left a rough square in the northwest corner of the peninsula, bounded by the northern wall of the Tagus valley below Talavera and following up the course of the river eastward and northward from that point to rest on the Pyrenees or, in the ninth century, on the boundaries of the Spanish March or its succession states.

The boundaries of Christian and Moslem tenure were not contiguous. Until the tenth century the line of the Douro was the outermost objective of durable Christian reconquest. Prior to the eleventh century, it was only temporarily and under the most favorable conditions that the Christian princes of the northwest were able to penetrate southeastern Castile to the Guadarrama mountains. Between the two cultures lay a no-man's-land, a desert, subject to repeated and destructive raids from both sides.

At the death of Alfonso I almost all Spain except the rectangle in the northwest corner was held in Moslem hands. Little progress was made toward the expansion of this territory during the next century and a half. Nevertheless, the Asturian monarchy showed its ability to survive internal dissension and attack from without. On the slopes of the Pyrenees and in Catalonia, Carolingian intervention forced back the Moslem frontier to some extent, and laid the foundations for Navarre, Aragon, and Catalonia.

In the Asturias, Alfonso II, "the Chaste" (791–842), had to sustain three devastating Moslem attacks which carried deep into his own territory. He was, however, able to take advantage of the internal disorders under al-Ḥakam I to raid Moslem territory as far as Lisbon. He undertook the restoration of Braga in northern Portugal, and carried back from his raids numerous Christian subjects of the emir. These were used in repopulating the devastated areas of the frontier. He established his capital at Oviedo and undertook to improve the internal organization of the state by reactivating Gothic law, which had fallen into disuse. The first raids of the Northmen struck the shores of Galicia during this reign, and Alfonso had to overcome a revolt by the Galician nobility. Discovery of what were believed to be the remains of St. James, and the founding of the shrine at Compostela, had even greater significance for the future than for Alfonso's own day. Not only was the possession of the relics a great inspiration to the Christian cause, but the shrine of Santiago de Compostela became a pilgrimage center of major importance for the Christian world, and the numerous pilgrims insured a substantial flow of wealth into Galicia. Alfonso turned to Charlemagne for alliance against the Moslems, and styled himself a client of the Frankish king. Although the reign of Alfonso II added little or no territory, its length and vigor and boldness proved the durability of the Asturian monarchy.

During the first decade of the ninth century, the foundation of the Frankish March of Spain was completed. The forces of Charlemagne had captured Gerona in 785 and Barcelona in 801, and subsequent campaigns carried the conquest to the Ebro. Peace was concluded with the Moslems in 810. Among the several counties established by the Franks Barcelona soon became preëminent. With the relaxation of monarchical controls in the course of the century, its counts became in effect independent.

The Basques of the western Pyrenees had traditionally opposed both Moslem and Frankish control. The reconquest of Navarre was therefore in the first instance a conquest from the Frankish counts. The chieftains at Pamplona found allies in the Banū-Qasī, the semi-independent Moslem princes of Saragossa. Liberated from the Franks, they were able to find allies in the counts of Cerdagne and Aragon for protection against the Moslems.

Ordoño I (850–866) was a vigorous campaigner. He overran and pillaged the territory between Salamanca and Saragossa—southern Leon, Castile, and the southern portion of what was later to become the kingdom of Aragon. He is particularly significant for rebuilding and repopulating devastated and deserted places and areas within his borders, among them Tuy on the northern bank of the lower Minho, Astorga in Leon, and the city of Leon itself. Orense on the Minho in Galicia was lost and won again. The rebuilding of Leon, which was to become the new capital of the dynasty, may have symbolized the emergence of the monarchy from the narrow limits of Asturias and Cantabria.

The son and successor of Ordoño, Alfonso III (866–909), continued the military and repopulation policies of his father. He attempted to establish himself south of the Douro. In Portugal between the Douro and the Mondego, the towns Lamego, Viseu, and Coimbra, and in Leon, Salamanca were successfully taken. On the upper course of the Douro he established strong points at Zamora, Toro, Simancas, and Dueñas. His raids carried him deep into Moslem territory. After repulsing a Moslem attack from Zamora he followed the retreat to Toledo but accepted a ransom to leave the city unharmed. At the end of his reign the populated southern frontier of the kingdom had been materially advanced from its location in the middle of the eighth century. The Mondego-Douro line was now firmly held in Portugal, Leon, and Castile. It is in the time of Alfonso III, about 884, that Burgos, seat of the early county of Castile, was founded by count Diego Rodríguez.

This reign of Alfonso III fell in a period of opportunity for the Christians, when the emirate was weakened by internal dissension. His reign ended in a disastrous division of territory forced on him by the revolt of his wife and his sons. During the tenth century, rivalries within the dynasty and struggles with an unruly aristocracy absorbed the energies of the Oviedo kings at a time when they were confronted with a comparatively strong Moslem state under ʿAbd-ar-Raḥmān III and then the chamberlain al-Manṣūr. It was to be more than a hundred years before the Christian states could recover from their weakness and division in the face of strength.

The three sons of Alfonso III were assigned respectively Leon, Galicia and Lusitania (Portugal), and the Asturias. The disastrous effect of this division of inheritance was not immediately apparent. The oldest son reigned only three years, after which Ordoño II (914–924) reunited Leon and Galicia. In alliance with the king of Navarre he fought ʿAbd-ar-Raḥmān, winning one battle but losing a second. Following the death of Ordoño, his sons disputed the succession. During this period a separatist movement led by the counts of Castile began to make its appearance. This movement was comparable to the particularist movements in Galicia. Control over the counts on the frontier was seldom adequate. Negotiation with the enemy and disobedience to the sovereign were not uncommon. Under Ramiro II (931–950), the revolt of count Fernán González of Castile virtually nullified the advantage gained by a victory over ʿAbd-ar-Raḥmān III (939). The fame of the caliph—a title assumed by the emir in 929—was by this time so great that the victory was one of the few events of the peninsula to be noted by chroniclers north of the Alps. Although Fernán González was defeated and imprisoned, his following was so considerable that Ramiro was forced to release him, subject to an oath of allegiance and an arranged marriage between the count's daughter and the king's son, all to little effect.

The foundation of Ramiro's policy was a firm alliance with Navarre, which was governed by the dowager queen Tota, on behalf of her infant son. This vigorous lady was in the habit of leading her troops in battle. She had married her two daughters to the count of Castile and the king of Leon respectively. It was this complex of family alliances which was ultimately to accomplish a temporary unification which would save the Christian states from complete subservience to the caliphate.

In the period following the death of Ramiro, the Christian states became almost completely dependent. Directly and indirectly the Moslem power was able to interfere in internal affairs of the states by treaty, intervention, and negotiations with disloyal vassals. The case of Ramiro's second son Sancho "the Fat" is illustrative: His mother was a princess of Navarre. Tota, his grandmother, was still regent in Navarre. When the nobles of Leon deposed Sancho, ostensibly because he was too fat to cut a proper royal figure, he took refuge at his grandmother's court at Pamplona. Tota got in touch with 'Abd-ar-Raḥmān III who was delighted, first to supply a physician and then to welcome king Sancho and his grandmother Tota to the court at Cordova as honored suppliants. Sancho returned to Leon without his surplus weight but with a Moslem army and with treaty obligations involving delivery of certain towns to the caliphate. Having regained his throne he showed no interest in fulfilling his promises until forced to do so. After Sancho had been conveniently poisoned, his successor, Bermudo II (984–999), was plundered and exploited by his nobility until he appealed to the Moslem commander, the chamberlain al-Manṣūr. The Moslem demanded submission, in return for which al-Manṣūr placed Moslem garrisons in most of the Leonese fortresses. The king's efforts to escape from this burden led ultimately to the punitive sack and plundering of the shrine of Santiago at Compostela (997). The wealth of plunder reported to have been carried away is revealing. Large numbers of the turbulent Leonese and Galician nobility participated in the raid. In the west the Christian frontier retreated to the Douro.

Neither Bermudo II nor al-Manṣūr long outlived the sack of Compostela. Bermudo's son and successor, Alfonso V (999–1027), was barely five years of age when he came to the throne. The caliphate in 1008 began to totter toward its fall. Alfonso succeeded in effecting a substantial reorganization of the kingdom and attended to the rebuilding and repopulation of devastated places. He held a council in his capital of Leon (1020) and granted a charter to the city. He pressed the campaign against the Moslems beyond the Douro in Portugal and died at the siege of Viseu. The ability of the count of Castile at this time to stand off and bargain with opposing Moslem factions who sought his services is a signal of the approaching disintegration of the caliphate. Bermudo III (1027–1037) succeeded his father on the throne. He was married to the sister of García, count of Castile. Another sister of García was the wife of the king of Navarre, Sancho "the Great" (1000–1035). Count García was murdered in 1028 as the result of a feud with another comital family. Immediately Sancho of Navarre advanced the claims of his wife to the county of Castile. War followed between Navarre and Leon. Difficulties were, at least temporarily, settled by mediators. Bermudo III was relegated to Galicia, and Sancho's second son Ferdinand was married to Bermudo's sister.

Sancho of Navarre now ruled over an impressive territory including in addition to Navarre, now extended beyond the Ebro, Leon with the Asturias, and Cantabria, the Basque provinces, the counties of Aragon, and suzerainty over the Catalan counties. Even though his authority over the Basque provinces east of Navarre and over Barcelona rested on a somewhat variable allegiance, his dominions included some third of the peninsula and extended from the Atlantic to the Mediterranean. With the end of the caliphate of Cordova (1031) and the division of Moslem Spain into a score of rival petty emirates, no power in the peninsula could compare to his. But Sancho could not avoid a return to the practice of dividing his vast possessions among his heirs. His political testament recognized García as his successor in Navarre but established the second son, Ferdinand (1035–1065), in Castile with the title of king. Sobrarbe and Ribagorza were given to Gonzalo but soon passed to the illegitimate son Ramiro, whom Sancho had named king in Aragon. Thus two new royal titles were created, and a new political history of Aragon had its beginning.

After the death of Sancho the Great, warfare between Ferdinand I and his brother-in-law Bermudo III of Leon again broke out. In 1037 Bermudo died in battle. Leon, Galicia, and Castile were united under the hand of Ferdinand.

In the meantime, after the death of al-Manṣūr the counts of Barcelona had regained their capital and other Catalan possessions which had been lost to the great Moslem commander and his son. In 1025 Berenguer I inherited the county.

Ferdinand I, to win the support of his new subjects, held a council in 1050 at which he confirmed all public charters granted by Alfonso V. He was drawn into conflict with his brother, García of Navarre, who sought to restore the unity of their father's dominions. García was defeated and killed in 1054. It was now possible for the king to address himself to the reconquest. He seized Lamego and Viseu in Portugal south of the Douro (1057/1058); and in 1064, with his conquest of the important city of Coimbra, carried his western border to the banks of the Mondego. He next attacked the Moslem territories to the south of Aragon and then seized additional fortresses south of the Douro, and raided the territory of the kingdom of Toledo as far as Alcalá de Henares. The petty kings (Arabic, *muluk aṭ-ṭawā'if*; Spanish, *reyes de taifas*) of Toledo, Badajoz, and Saragossa became his tributaries. Toward the end of his life he raided the lands of Seville, destroying villages and crops until her 'Abbādid king agreed to payment of an annual tribute. Ferdinand again divided his holdings, but his second son, Alfonso VI (1065–1109) of Galicia, succeeded in uniting the entire inheritance after long civil war.

Hitherto concerted action toward reconquest had been sporadic and dependent upon the fortunate accident of strong leadership combined with weakness in the enemy. Unity of action among the Christian princes was still far in the future. But in 1064 an international army, composed of Catalan, Aragonese, Norman, Aquitanian, and Burgundian (but not, as often alleged, papal and Italo-Norman) contingents, launched a successful attack against the Moslem stronghold of Barbastro, only to lose the thoroughly plundered town the following year.[1] Whether pope Alexander II's fragmentary letters relating to French warriors en route to Spain to fight *contra Sarracenos*, and issuance of a plenary indulgence on their behalf, relate to

[1] Cf. P. David, *Études historiques sur la Galice et le Portugal* (Lisbon and Paris, 1947), pp. 341–439; and chapter VII, below.

this expedition or to a second, abortive one being organized in 1073 by Ebles II, count of Roucy, remains unclear. In any case, the crossing of the Pyrenees by French knights (a movement the chroniclers Raoul Glaber and Adhémar of Chabannes carry back to the time of Sancho the Great) and the intervention in the reconquest of the reform papacy (leading Gregory VII in 1073 and 1077 to claim suzerainty over all territories recovered from the infidel, and indeed all Spain) demonstrate how these extra-Iberian forces now viewed the peninsular struggle against Islam as a Christian holy war. At the same time Ferdinand I and Alfonso VI, in alliance with Cluny, and as self-proclaimed emperors of Hispania (i. e., all Iberia, Christian and Moslem), moved vigorously to reduce the Taifa kingdoms to vassalage or outright annexation through imposition of economically ruinous annual tributary exactions *(parias)*.

After the reunion of Castile, Leon, and Galicia, Alfonso intensified the raids against the weak emirs. The tribute collected supplied his war chest, and on May 25, 1085, he occupied Toledo, bringing the frontier of Castile well to the south of the Tagus. By raids and seizures his forces made themselves felt against the Moslem borders in all directions, penetrating southward to the vicinity of Granada. Threatened with subjection or destruction, the Moslems reluctantly sought outside help. Al-Muʿtamid, the ʿAbbādid ruler of Seville and chief survivor of the internecine warfare among the petty kingdoms, sought help from Morocco. The Murābiṭ (hispanized Almoravid) sect of veiled Touaregs from the Sahara[2] had unified Morocco under Yūsuf ibn-Tāshfīn, who now acceded to al-Muʿtamid's request for aid, crossed to Andalusia in 1086, and annihilated Alfonso's army near Badajoz on October 23. His mission accomplished, he withdrew to Africa but returned with his Murābiṭs in 1090 and quickly conquered all Moslem-held Spain except Ṣaragossa, an exposed outpost ruled by the Banū-Hūd. He also reconquered many of the border towns taken by the Christians.

Alfonso was able to retain Toledo while Rodrigo Diaz of Vivar, called the Cid, established himself in Valencia and was able for a time to oppose the advance of the Moslems into northeastern Spain. In 1095 the territory of the peninsula was fairly evenly divided between the Spanish Christians in the north and the African and Andalusian Moslems in the south. Military power was in precarious and sensitive balance.

[2] For detailed consideration of the Murābiṭs of Morocco and Andalusia and their rise to power, see the chapter on Moslem North Africa in volume III (in preparation).

B. The Italian Cities and the Arabs before 1095

Long before pope Urban II made his impassioned plea at Clermont, the Italian cities were fighting the Saracens on land and sea. During the four centuries preceding 1095 they suffered from seemingly endless raids and plunderings; sometimes they allied themselves with the enemy to attack other cities; on occasion they met him with force, and these occasions increased in number and gained in success. Eventually, in 915 the southern cities, in alliance with Byzantine and papal forces, drove the Saracens from their last stronghold on the peninsula, and a century later the northern cities attacked the various Arab maritime bases nearby. Finally, in the eleventh century the Pisans and Genoese raided the African coast itself, and forced terms of peace upon the Saracen leader, among them the promise to refrain from further piracy. With this victory and peace, made in 1087, control

accounts of this use crusade rhetoric [handwritten marginal note]

The principal primary sources are: M. Amari, *Biblioteca arabo-sicula* (3 vols., Turin and Rome, 1880–1889); *Annales Barenses* (*MGH, SS.,* V); *Annales Bertiniani* (*MGH, SS.,* I); *Annales Laurissenses* (*MGH, SS.,* I); *Annales Laurissenses maiores et Einhardi* (*MGH, SS.,* I); *Annales Pisani di Bernardo Maragone* (*RISS,* VI, part 2); *Chronica Sancti Benedicti Casinensis* (*MGH, Scriptores rerum Langobardicarum*); L. de Mas-Latrie, *Traités de paix et de commerce et documents divers contenant les relations des chrétiens avec les arabes d'Afrique septentrionale au moyen-âge* (Paris, 1866); *La Cronaca Veneziana del Diacono Giovanni* (*Fonti per la storia d'Italia,* IX, Rome, 1890); Lupus Protospatarius, *Annales* (*MGH, SS.,* V).

Among the secondary sources which should be consulted are the following: M. Amari, *Storia dei musulmani di Sicilia,* (3 vols., Catania, 1933–1939); J. B. Bury, "The Naval Policy of the Roman Empire in Relation to the Western Provinces from the Seventh to the Ninth Century," *Centenario della nascità di Michele Amari,* vol. II (Palermo, 1910), 21–34; R. Caddeo (et al.), *Storia marittima dell'Italia dall'evo antico ai nostri giorni* (Milan, 1942); *Cambridge Medieval History,* vol. II, chapters x–xii; vol. III, chapters ii, iii, vii; vol. IV, chapters v, xiii; vol. V, chapter v; Daniel C. Dennett, "Pirenne and Muhammed," *Speculum,* XXIII (1948), 165–190; F. E. Engreen, "Pope John the Eighth and the Arabs," *Speculum,* XX (1945), 318–330; U. Formentini, *Genova nel basso impero e nell'alto medioevo* (Milan, 1941); J. Gay, *L'Italie méridionale et l'empire byzantin depuis l'avènement de Basile Ier jusqu'à la prise de Bari par les Normands* (Paris, 1904); L. M. Hartmann, *Geschichte Italiens im Mittelalter* (4 vols., Leipzig, 1900–1915), and *Wirtschaftsgeschichte Italiens im frühen Mittelalter* (Gotha, 1904); W. Heywood, *A History of Pisa* (Cambridge, 1921); P. K. Hitti, *History of the Arabs* (5th ed., London, 1951); R. J. H. Jenkins, "The 'Flight' of Samonas," *Speculum,* XXIII (1948), 217–235; H. Kretschmayr, *Geschichte von Venedig* (2 vols., Gotha, 1905–1934); Abbé J. Lestoquoy, "The Tenth Century," *Economic History Review,* XVII (1947), 1–14; A. R. Lewis, *Naval Power and Trade in the Mediterranean, A. D. 500–1100* (Princeton, 1951); R. S. Lopez, "Mohammed and Charlemagne: a Revision," *Speculum,* XVIII (1943), 14–38; A. Schaube, *Handelsgeschichte der romanischen Völker des Mittelmeergebiets bis zum Ende der Kreuzzüge* (Munich and Berlin, 1906); and A. A. Vasiliev, *A History of the Byzantine Empire* (Madison, 1952).

over the western Mediterranean passed from the Arabs to the Italian cities.

The first period in the Italo-Arab relations ran from 652 to 827. During these years the Arabs attacked and plundered the south Italian cities and especially the nearby islands almost at will, because the Byzantines and Italians were unable to maintain garrisons everywhere. The attackers shifted their raids in accordance with the Italian defense and preparedness. But they remained mere pirates, since their mainland and maritime forces were occupied elsewhere. The Arabs, by force and diplomacy, had to subdue the Berbers of North Africa; temporarily united with them, the Arabs reached Gibraltar and easily crossed into Spain and advanced to the Pyrenees. Not until the Arabs were stopped in 732 and driven from Gaul in 769, that is, not until they had been stopped in western Europe, did they direct their main attacks upon mid-Europe, upon Italy and its neighboring islands.

The earliest recorded Arab raid upon Sicily took place in 652. A general of Mu'āwiyah, 'Abd-Allāh ibn-Qais, directed it, very likely from Syria, seemingly as part of a determined campaign against Byzantine sea power. Syracuse felt the impact most and lost much of its wealth and treasures and many of its citizens to the plunderers. In 669 an Alexandrian fleet of two hundred ships pillaged Sicily again. These two expeditions, originating in the eastern Mediterranean, were possible because the Arabs had shattered Byzantine eastern naval power in a series of battles between 649 and 655. Western Byzantine naval strength suffered a disastrous defeat in 698, when the Arab land and sea forces of Hassān ibn-an-Nu'mān captured Carthage. With its capture the Arabs acquired another maritime base of operations and began their control over the western Mediterranean. Both were of ominous significance for Italy and the Italian cities.

Mūsâ ibn-Nuṣair, who became governor of North Africa shortly after the capture of Carthage, recognized the possibilities and need of maritime power. At Tunis he ordered the construction of harbor facilities and shipyards, and eventually of a fleet of one hundred ships. Nearby Italy soon felt the results of his activities. In 700 the Arabs took over Pantelleria, in 704 they successfully plundered western Sicily, and in 705 they attacked Syracuse, but lost ships and men in a storm. Elsewhere, the first Arab raid upon Sardinia took place in 711 and upon Corsica in 713, and both islands were soon controlled by Arab forces. Again in 720 Arab raiders touched upon Sicily and in almost every year between 727 and 734; negotiations were undertaken and a truce was signed in 728, but the truce did not prevent the raids of 180 ships in the next year. In 740 the Syracusans preferred to pay tribute to the attackers to avoid a greater loss of property and life. Not till 733 and 734 did the Arabs meet with resistance from Byzantine naval forces, and in 752 and 753 Byzantine ships and defenses again held off the Arabs, this time seemingly intent upon conquest rather than upon plunder. Thereafter, for about fifty years the Italians enjoyed a respite from Arab attacks. When the military successes and advances in Gaul stopped, and as the control of the eastern caliphs lessened, civil wars in North Africa broke out; through them strong-armed Berber and Arab leaders set up independent states in Spain and North Africa. Among these the Aghlabid state around Kairawan, the Idrīsid state centered in Morocco, and Umaiyad Spain initiated and carried out raids and campaigns against Italy. When the Aghlabids began in earnest their conquest of Sicily in 827, the Italians realized that a new period in their relations with the Arabs had arisen.

The second period in the Italo-Arab relations, roughly covering the ninth century, was a disastrous period for the south Italian cities. The dukes of these cities fought one another instead of offering a united defense against the Saracens, and quite often in their inter-municipal rivalries they called in the common enemy. In their ambition for power and hope of independence they limited and curtailed the power and forces of old Byzantium in the east, of the new Carolingian empire in the west, and of the Roman papacy, none of which was capable of defeating the Saracens single-handedly.[1] On the other hand, the various Arab groups, even though disunited, were strong enough individually to establish settlements because of the inadequate Christian forces. As a result, all south Italy, cities and country alike, suffered from Arab plunder and occupation. Not until the end of the period, when the two empires had already obtained partial successes and when the papacy offered vigorous leadership, did the south Italian cities make common cause with them, to defeat the Arabs at the Garigliano river.

The century began auspiciously. In 805 Ibrāhīm ibn-al-Aghlab, the emir at Kairawan, signed a ten-year truce and trade agreement

[1] However, it must also be noted that Byzantine naval policy toward the west deserved little loyalty and gratitude from the Italian dukes and cities. That it was a policy of short-sighted neglect has been pointed out by John B. Bury, "The Naval Policy of the Roman Empire in Relation to the Western Provinces from the Seventh to the Ninth Century," *Centenario della nascità di Michele Amari* (2 vols., Palermo, 1910), II, 21–34, esp. pp. 25 f.

with Constantine, the patrician of Sicily; the emir needed his forces and strength to consolidate his holdings in Africa, and he hoped that this arrangement might serve to curb the ambitions of the Spanish Umaiyads and the western Idrīsids. In Europe Charlemagne fitted out an Aquitanian and an Italian fleet, partially built and manned by Italians, to patrol the western Mediterranean. But as before, the truce proved ineffective. On his side, the emir at Kairawan was in no position to speak for the other Saracens beyond his state, and Constantine could hardly control the actions and plans of the Byzantine emperor, of Charlemagne, and of the pope. Charlemagne's son, king Pepin of Italy, and his constable Burchard had minor successes, but failed to wrest Corsica from the Arabs in campaigns between 806 and 810. In one of these, in 806, Hadumarus, the first Frankish count of Genoa, lost his life. Both Corsica and Sardinia remained under Arab control. The Aghlabids directed other assaults upon Lampedusa, off the African coast, and upon Ponza and Ischia, off the Italian shore near Naples, all in 812. A Byzantine fleet under the patrician Gregory, refused aid by Naples, but helped by Gaeta and Amalfi, eventually defeated the attackers, and another truce was arranged in the next year. But while the Aghlabids were curbed, Umaiyads from Spain swept over the Tyrrhenian Sea and plundered Nice, Civita Vecchia, Corsica, and Sardinia, despite the defensive measures of Charlemagne and pope Leo III.

In 827 the Aghlabid conquest of Sicily began in earnest; it was not complete till 902. Ziyādat-Allāh I, the third emir of Kairawan, felt himself strong enough to undertake an expedition of expansion, similar to the one into Spain a century before. Like that one, too, the Sicilian expedition was prompted by civil war and by a traitorous appeal for help by Euphemius, the Byzantine leader, who had set himself up as emperor. For Arab help and recognition of his imperial position in Sicily Euphemius agreed to accept the emir as his titular overlord and to pay a tribute consonant with that relationship. After considerable debate the Arab leader agreed to help, but the size of the Arab force indicated that the Arabs had plans quite different from those of Euphemius. A fleet of seventy or one hundred ships carried 10,000 foot-soldiers and seven hundred horsemen from Susa in Tunisia to Mazara in western Sicily, not merely to plunder and return, nor to help a usurper, but to conquer and remain. The Saracens defeated the outnumbered but heroic Byzantine garrisons, disregarded Euphemius and his troops, and moved inward and eastward, toward Syracuse.

That all-important city the Arabs besieged by land and sea for over a year; not until famine and pestilence had decimated some of their forces, and a Byzantine-Venetian fleet threatened the rest, did they raise the siege. They burned their own ships and fled into the interior; driven from Mineo and Enna and abandoning Agrigento, they returned to Mazara, their starting point two years before. Spanish Arabs, who unexpectedly appeared for purposes of plunder, supported the retreating Aghlabids, renewed the attack, and plundered as far as Mineo, but then retreated to Mazara, whence they sailed to Spain. At the same time, in 828, a Frankish fleet under count Boniface of Tuscany cleared the waters around Corsica and Sardinia and successfully plundered the African coast between Utica and Carthage. Byzantine land and sea forces, aided by the Venetians, had frustrated for the moment the Arab conquest of the island.

The second effort at conquest, however, succeeded and eventually led to the occupation of the entire island. In 830 an African fleet of three hundred ships and some Spanish squadrons attacked and besieged Palermo, the second city on the island. After a year the strategic port fell to the besiegers, for whom it became the base of operations against the rest of the island and, more significantly, against the mainland. In spite of active Byzantine resistance and occasional successes the Arabs consolidated and increased their holdings. They took a decade to drive out stubborn garrisons and to capture strongholds; by 840 they controlled western Sicily and could turn to other parts of the island. In 843 they captured Messina after a long siege and a surprise land attack; with its capture they controlled the Strait of Messina and so could prevent the entrance of Byzantine naval forces into western waters. Actually, they were assisted by the Neapolitans, on whose behalf they had intervened against duke Sikard of Benevento, when the latter had laid siege to their city in 837. Not only political, but economic considerations, too, prompted the Christians of Naples to aid the enemy, for only in friendly alliance with the Arabs were they able to carry on their commerce since the eastern Mediterranean was already closed to them, by other Arabs and by the Venetians.[2]

With Palermo and Messina in hand, the Arabs turned to the southeastern part of the island, especially toward Syracuse. They

[2] Both Pirenne and Gay emphasize the commercial reasons for these alliances with the Arabs. Henri Pirenne, *Mohammed and Charlemagne* (New York, 1939), pp. 182 f. Pirenne quotes J. Gay, *L'Italie méridionale et l'empire byzantin* (Paris, 1904), p. 129. A very recent and concise review of Moslem trade has been made by Robert S. Lopez in *Cambridge Economic History*, II (Cambridge, 1952), 281–289.

easily overran the countryside, and from its plunder and enslaved inhabitants they lived, but much more slowly did they conquer the fortified cities. But by constant attack, through devastation of the countryside, aided by starvation and plague, and on occasion by treachery, they took the cities that guarded the approaches to the all-important port. Modica fell in 845, Lentini in 847, and Ragusa in 848. Stubborn Enna in central Sicily was given to them by treachery in 859. The sea outpost Malta was captured in 870. Syracuse itself fell in 878 after a heroic nine-month defense against Saracen land and sea forces. One Byzantine fleet was defeated and partially captured during the period, and another was awaiting favorable winds in Greece when the siege ended. In 902 Taormina, the last Byzantine stronghold on the island, fell to the Saracens. Here no heroic defense could be made, because the Byzantine admiral Eustace was in conspiracy with the enemy. The Arab conquest of Sicily was complete.

Even before the Arabs had acquired that island base, they had attacked the Italian cities on the mainland. Neither the measures of the Byzantine and Carolingian empires nor the appeals and plans of the Roman popes were sufficient to forestall Saracen plunder and settlement, while the inter-municipal rivalries and the constant strife between the coastal cities and the dukes of Benevento often were opportune for just such activities of the enemy.

The Arabs first appeared on the Italian mainland in 837, when the Neapolitans begged them for help against the ambitious duke Sikard of Benevento, who was besieging their city. For the Neapolitans it was an act of desperation, since their earlier appeals to Louis the Pious and other Christians remained unanswered. But the Arabs came, lifted the siege of the angry duke, plundered his own lands, and signed a treaty of friendship and trade with Naples. The latter reciprocated by aiding the Saracens at Messina in 842–843. But the friendship did not restrain the Arabs from occupying the islands of Ponza and Ischia and Cape Miseno on the mainland. Arab ships threatened the coastal shipping, and their land forces plundered the countryside. The new duke at Naples, Sergius I, repudiated the earlier policy and initiated an alliance with Gaeta, Amalfi, and Sorrento in 845; these cities fitted out ships to protect the Campanian shores and already in 846 duke Sergius broke up an Arab siege of his own city and led this fleet to victory over the Arabs off Point Licosa. In 846, too, Rome was visited by an Arab force of 73 ships and 11,000 men. In spite of the walls rebuilt at the request of pope Gregory IV and the repeated warnings of the imminent attack, Ostia and Porto were overrun, and at Rome the basilica of St. Peter and the cathedral of St. Paul, on the right bank of the Tiber and outside the city-walls, were plundered. The Romans themselves and the small Frankish garrison were unable to stop the enemy, while the land forces of Louis II and the naval forces from the cities arrived too late to prevent the incursion. However, when the Saracens, already laden with Roman treasures, laid siege to Gaeta, they were stopped by allied fleets from Gaeta, Naples, and Amalfi. They were allowed to depart peaceably, only to be destroyed by storm; they lost their ships and their stolen treasures, but they retained their bases for further attack.

At Rome pope Leo IV wisely began the refortification of the city. The old walls and towers, partially destroyed in 846, were rebuilt and others were added, and the Porta Portuensis was constructed to guard and close the Tiber in case of another sea attack. All the Vatican area in which St. Peter's stood was walled in, to become the *Civitas Leonina*. The costs of construction were borne by the church and individual monasteries, by the nobles and citizens of Rome, and by the people of the Frankish empire, in which the emperor Lothair ordered a general subscription for the purpose. Leo IV also provided fortified places of refuge for Corsicans and others at Lorto and Leopoli, and at Orte and Ameria in interior Tuscany. Before the defenses were finished, however, the Saracens appeared. In 849 a large Saracen fleet assembled off the Sardinian coast and then sailed toward Ostia. The south Italian cities recognized the common threat and Caesarius, son of duke Sergius I of Naples, led a fleet from Naples, Gaeta, and Amalfi northward. Received with caution by the Romans, then hailed with joy, the fleet was blessed by pope Leo IV before giving battle to the enemy. During the battle a storm destroyed most of the enemy ships; many survivors were hanged, and others were put to work on the walls and towers. Of the Italian fleet little is known, but at least it had waylaid the Saracens until the storm approached. In the same year the Saracens also raided the Italian coast from Luni to Provence.

The Saracens were also active in the Adriatic and in southeast Italy, and here as on the other side of the peninsula they were aided by the differences among the Italians. In 838 they occupied Brindisi and ravaged the area about, but were driven out of the burnt-out city by duke Sikard of Benevento. In 840 his successor,

Radelgis, hired Saracen mercenaries to fight the duke of Salerno, and provided them with a landing and camping place just outside Bari. It was foolhardy. The Saracens made a surprise night-attack upon the city, murdered many of the inhabitants, enslaved others, and took command of the city. They used it as their Adriatic base of operations for the next thirty years. In the same year they also occupied Taranto and to the west plundered throughout Calabria and southern Apulia. In the Adriatic their naval squadrons harassed Christian shipping. Venice, in alarm over these events, gladly answered the plea of the emperor Theophilus and sent out sixty ships to wrest Taranto from the marauders, but the entire force was lost. The Adriatic cities themselves suffered intermittently from attacks. Ancona was plundered and burned in 840; Adria, in the delta of the Po, was unsuccessfully attacked in the same year; across the sea Ossero on the island of Cherso was pillaged and burnt. On the sea two Venetian fleets were defeated, one near Ancona in 840, another at Sansego, just south of Cherso, in 842, and everywhere Venetian merchantmen were robbed and captured. Venetian control over the Adriatic was disappearing, and Venetian trade with Sicily and Byzantium was becoming hazardous.[3]

Many Saracens settled down in these southern bases, while others, some in compliance with the orders of Radelgis of Benevento, some in defiance of him, moved into the interior. Saracen bands plundered from Cannae to Capua and moved northward. Duke Siconolf of Salerno also called upon the Saracens of Taranto to join him against Radelgis and the Saracens at Bari. The rivalry of the two men brought the Saracen peril to all south-central Italy. Under the circumstances king Louis II, pope Leo IV at Rome, the doge Peter of Venice, and duke Sergius of Naples in 847 took a hand against the two dukes and the Saracen danger which the ducal rivalry had encouraged. The two dukes were forced to agree to a truce and to join the drive against the Saracens. An imperial force defeated and drove one Saracen group back to Bari, but it could not take the city; another force defeated the Saracens who were in the employ of Radelgis at Benevento. Unfortunately, the Arabs still maintained their control over Bari and Taranto, in which they strengthened the walls and towers, and over the southern provinces of the peninsula. In these areas other Arabs settled

[3] References to early Venetian trade with the Saracens are found in A. Schaube, *Handelsgeschichte der romanischen Völker des Mittelmeergebiets bis zum Ende der Kreuzzüge* (Munich and Berlin, 1906), pp. 21–24, but the references are generally for a later period. In 971 the Byzantine emperor forbade the Venetians to send iron, arms, and timber to Moslem countries.

to give protection to the coastal bases. From them the Saracens repeatedly raided the interior and threatened Monte Cassino and San Vincenzo. King Louis, called in by the monasteries in 852, again failed before the walled cities. Within the same decade the threatened monasteries bought off other Saracen bands, and cities like Naples and Capua were plundered, all the duchy of Benevento was overrun, and most of Campania also. As long as the Saracens held their naval bases, they remained a threat, since neither the imperial nor the ducal forces were willing or able to drive them out.

Finally, in 866 Louis II, now emperor, heeded the persistent pleas of Benevento and Capua. He recruited large forces in north and central Italy and compelled the south Italian dukes and cities to abandon their local rivalries and to join him in a full-scale campaign against the Saracens at Bari. He carried out a methodical, but often interrupted, plan of attrition against the enemy by destroying or occupying the fortress towns in the approaches to the naval base. Canosa, Venosa, and Matera were occupied, but again he could not take Bari because of the lack of sea power. In 868 a large Byzantine fleet did appear before the city, but then the imperial land forces were inadequate and the four hundred Byzantine ships sailed back to Corinth when negotiations for the marriage between Louis's daughter and Basil I's son failed to reach a satisfactory conclusion. A Venetian force, however, crippled a Saracen fleet off the port of Taranto in 867. The emperor also had to protect his land forces against attack from the rear by those Saracens who were coming into Italy through Naples, since there duke Sergius II, in order to maintain his independence of the emperor, had aligned himself with the enemy. However, the emperor was fortunate in having the active support of Venice and the Dalmatian towns. While their naval forces blockaded the port, he attacked the city on the land side. After four years of intermittent warfare the emperor successfully concluded the campaign by taking Bari in 871. It was a decisive blow to the Arabs and initiated the gradual lessening of their power on the mainland. But the leadership and success of the emperor Louis were repaid with treachery. Sergius of Naples, Waifar of Salerno, Lambert of Spoleto, and Adelchis of Benevento conspired against him, their henchmen ambushed him, and they held him prisoner till he swore never to return to southern Italy. In that way they hoped to maintain their independence of imperial sovereignty. But when a force of 30,000 African Saracens threatened Salerno it was another story. In 872 the traitors again welcomed the imperial forces, which drove out the Saracens and raised the siege of Salerno.[4]

But the Saracen threat continued, and the Christian defense deteriorated in the last decades of the century, before the final decisive battle. The death of the emperor Louis II introduced civil war among the claimants to the imperial throne, and the eventual winner, Charles the Bald, could have little interest in southern Italy when his authority was questioned and his own Gallic domains were threatened. In southern Italy itself the cities and their dukes fought one another as before, made commercial and military agreements with the Saracens instead of presenting a united front, and so permitted the enemy to regain the initiative. In the Adriatic Saracens, possibly from Crete, in 872 ravaged the Dalmatian coast, especially the island of Brazza, and appeared before Grado and burned out Comacchio in 875, but Venetian squadrons maintained their supremacy there, even though limited by the Saracen occupation of Sicily and Crete. On land, only the revived Byzantine authority at Bari stopped the ravages in southeast Italy and in 880 a Byzantine force regained Taranto.

But these successes were neutralized by setbacks on the west coast. There, fear of the revived Byzantine power, hope of avoiding Saracen plunder, and expectation of commerce with Sicily prompted the Italian cities again to align themselves with the Moslems. Naples, Gaeta, Salerno, Capua, even Amalfi, joined with the Saracens to raid the Roman littoral in 876 and 877; Naples served as the base of Saracen operations. Pope John VIII was unable to prevent the spoliation of monastic lands and the capture of monks and nuns. Since he could not obtain aid from Charles the Bald, he was dependent upon the south Italian cities, who already had made common cause with the enemy, and upon Byzantium with which he was in conflict over the status of the patriarch Photius. Eventually, by threat and cajolery, by promise and gift, by negotiation to have the hated Byzantines patrol the Tyrrhenian Sea, he momentarily detached the cities from their Saracen alliance, but they returned to it when it served their interests. Amalfi agreed to protect the Roman coast against attack, but withdrew when the promised papal subsidy was not completely paid. Thus in 878 pope John VIII had to buy off the Saracens. To his dismay,

[4] Evidence for trade between Amalfi and the African Saracens appears in this episode. Merchants of Amalfi trading in Mahdia were told by an Arab of the impending attack upon Salerno, and he urged them to warn count Waifar. Michele Amari, *Storia dei Musulmani di Sicilia* (3 vols., Catania, 1933–1939), I, 524–526. The episode appears in the *Chronicon Salernitanum* (*MGH. SS.*, III), p. 528.

the Amalfitans not only refused to return the 10,000 *mancusi* already paid to them, but they formed an alliance with the Saracens. A proposal for combined action by Salerno, Benevento, and the Byzantine forces, which had already gained control over Calabria, also was nullified by the petty rivalry between the two cities over Capua after the death of its duke in 879. The cities and duchies of southern Italy refused to form a common anti-Saracen front under papal auspices;[5] they coöperated with the Byzantines and aligned themselves with the Saracens in accordance with their individual ambitions and needs. As a result of this policy, the abbeys of San Vincenzo on the Volturno and the more famous Monte Cassino were burned and destroyed around 883, the abbey of Farfa was besieged in 890, and Subiaco was also destroyed. The Arabs entrenched themselves firmly and comfortably along the Garigliano river at Trajetto and, more closely to Rome, at Ciciliano and Saracinesco; from these bases they plundered at will. Finally, pope John X succeeded in organizing a successful campaign against them. He won over the Byzantines, some of the south Italian princes, and even cities like Naples, Gaeta, Capua, and Salerno. At the Garigliano river, in 915, this alliance — and pope John was on the field — defeated the last remaining Arab force on the Italian mainland; even in this battle the princely leaders of Naples and Gaeta connived to help the enemy escape. It was of no use; the Saracens were hunted down; and the period of Arab occupation in Italy was over.[6]

In the final period of these relations, the chief, although not the exclusive, activity came from the northern cities of the peninsula. Like those of the south, they at first suffered from Arab attacks, but unlike those of the south they never formed alliances with them and very quickly took the offensive against them. To Genoa and Pisa falls the honor of having done most to clear the western Mediterranean of the Arab menace.

From Sicily and from Africa the Arabs harassed the southern cities after the events of 915. Taking Reggio in 918, the Arabs overran Calabria and sold many inhabitants into slavery in Sicily

[5] On the policy of pope John VIII (872–882) against the Arabs, cf. Fred E. Engreen, "Pope John the Eighth and the Arabs," *Speculum*, XX (1945), 318–330.

[6] In this survey there is no place for an analysis of the revisionist attacks upon Pirenne's views on the lack of western Mediterranean commerce during this period. His latest statements are found in *Mohammed and Charlemagne*, pp. 166, 172f., 179, 181–185. The arguments of the revisionists are best presented by Robert S. Lopez, "Mohammed and Charlemagne: a Revision," *Speculum*, XVIII (1943), 14–38, and Daniel C. Dennett, "Pirenne and Muhammed," *ibid.*, XXIII (1948), 165–190. Both refer to the arguments of Sabbe and Ganshof. Cf. also Abbé J. Lestoquoy, "The Tenth Century," *Economic History Review*, XVII (1947), 1–14.

and Africa. They easily overcame the Byzantine resistance and laid siege to Naples.[7] By continued threats and assaults upon Christian shipping they extorted tribute from the coastal cities, and when the latter refused to pay, they attacked them as well. Such was the case in 1016–1017 when Salerno was besieged and occupied, only to free itself with the aid of pilgrims returning from Jerusalem. In the southeast both Taranto and Bari suffered from similar assaults; in 1002 Bari was saved by the timely aid of a Venetian fleet which came to the aid of the Byzantine forces. In a three-day battle the Venetians won a brilliant victory to enhance their own prestige and the standing of the doge Orseolo II. But smaller raids always took place and shipping was never secure.

In the tenth century the northern littoral also felt the fury of the Arab bands. Here around 888 Spanish Arabs established themselves at La Garde-Freinet (Fraxinetum) in Provence, in an almost impregnable position. On land they very soon controlled the Alpine passes and so endangered, and at times stopped altogether, the course of pilgrims and merchants between the west and Italy. They destroyed the abbey of Novalesa in 906 and plundered Aix-en-Provence around 935. In 931 a Byzantine fleet and Provençal land forces attacked, but did not eliminate, the base; and a more successful attack in 942 was partially nullified by king Hugh of Italy, who made a separate peace with the Arabs on their promise to hold the Swabian passes against Berengar of Ivrea. In 972 the Arabs finally overreached themselves by capturing the revered abbot of Cluny, St. Maiolus, and fellow pilgrims in the Great St. Bernard Pass. The Cluniacs raised the enormous ransom demanded by the Arabs, but the count of Provence and Ardoin of Turin united to clear the enemy out of the passes and La Garde-Freinet.

Genoa and Pisa also suffered from various Arab fleets. In 934 and 935 the whole area between Genoa and Pisa suffered from Fāṭimid attacks originating in Africa. Genoa especially was subjected to massacre, many women and children were enslaved, and many of the treasures of the city and churches were robbed. But Pisa suffered on several other occasions, in 1004, 1011, and 1012. In 1015 Spanish Arabs from Denia and the Baleares occupied Sardinia and raided the coast between Genoa and Pisa. From their many bases the Arabs easily controlled the western waters and so limited

[7] In 965 a Byzantine fleet was disastrously defeated in the Strait of Messina; so the Arabs found no great opposition except from the northern cities. Cf. Archibald R. Lewis, *Naval Power and Trade in the Mediterranean, A. D. 500–1100* (Princeton, 1951), p. 187.

the economic life of the north Italian cities. In the previous period the coastal cities had suffered, to be sure, but the Saracens, once in control of or in alliance with these cities, were more active in the country and against the monastic centers. In this period, the country was relatively safe, but the coastal cities suffered most because their all-important commerce was being ruined, for they were the special targets of the Arab raiders, and their ships were the special goal of the Arab pirates.

That threat convinced the two northern communes that more than mere defensive measures were necessary. In the eleventh century Pisa and Genoa took the offensive, at times in joint enterprises, at times singly, to make the Tyrrhenian Sea and, if possible, the western Mediterranean safe for Christian merchants and ships. Pisa carried out a small raid of vengeance against Reggio in 1004 and united with the Genoese in the larger expedition against the new Arab settlements on Sardinia. In 1015 and 1016 the fleets of the two cities, encouraged by pope Benedict VIII, finally drove the Arabs from the island and the Pisans occupied it; al-Mujāhid barely escaped, leaving wife and sons in the hands of the Italians. Several years later, in 1034, the Pisans, and possibly also the Genoese and Provençals, carried the offensive to Bona, the Saracen base in North Africa; the captured booty they gave to the monastery of Cluny. In 1062 or 1063 the Pisans forced their way into the harbor of Palermo and destroyed the Saracen arsenal, burned five merchantmen, and used the booty from a sixth to start construction of their duomo, Santa Maria Maggiore. In 1087 a combined force of Italian cities again carried the attack to an African base, this time against Mahdia. From this base, the capital of Tamīm, prince of the Zīrid dynasty, Saracen pirates had plundered and captured Italian ships and merchants. Therefore pope Victor III found it easy to persuade the victims, Pisans, Genoese, Romans, and Amalfitans, to send a force of three to four hundred ships and 30,000 men against such an enemy; the expedition served under the papal legate, bishop Benedict of Modena. The assault was tremendously successful, even though Tamīm had warning of the threat. The Italians captured all of Zawīlah, a merchant suburb, and almost all of Mahdia itself before Tamīm asked for terms of surrender. He paid out, according to various Arab sources, 30,000 to 100,000 dinars of gold and granted to the Pisan and Genoese merchants free access to Mahdia and the area under his jurisdiction. In addition he freed his Christian prisoners and promised to stop piratical raids. The incidental plunder in gold, silver, silks, and vessels was extraordinary, and with it the Pisans and the Genoese began the construction of their churches dedicated to St. Sixtus, on whose feast day (August 6) the victory was gained.[8]

In the Pisan annals of Bernardo Maragone the next reference is to the call of pope Urban II and to the Pisan participation in the First Crusade. It is not surprising. The Italian cities had fought and defeated the Arabs in the western Mediterranean, often upon the request of the Roman popes and under the leadership of papal legates. They had carried the battle to the Arab bases in Africa, Spain, and the Mediterranean islands, and in the last great campaign of 1087 they had won commercial rights and privileges. For them participation in the First Crusade was natural.

[8] Ubaldo Formentini, *Genova nel basso impero e nell'alto medioevo* (Milan, 1941), p. 265.

C. The Norman Conquest of Sicily

Although the Norman conquest of Sicily was probably the greatest triumph of Christians over Moslems in the eleventh century, it is hardly exact to describe it as a duel between Cross and Crescent. Count Roger invaded the island for the same reasons which had spurred the Hauteville brothers to many wars against Christians, including the pope and both the eastern and the western emperor. "He was always eager to acquire," as his official historian and apologist, friar Geoffrey Malaterra, candidly states.[1] He began the war as the ally of one of the rival emirs of Sicily, employed Moslem as well as Christian Calabrese auxiliaries as early as the

M. Amari, *Storia dei Musulmani di Sicilia* (2nd ed. revised by the author and edited by C. A. Nallino, 3 vols., Catania, 1933–1939), and F. Chalandon, *Histoire de la domination normande en Italie et en Sicile* (2 vols., Paris, 1907) are still fundamental, although the latter is almost half a century old, and the former originally appeared almost a hundred years ago. This is largely owing to the admirable quality of both works — Amari was a great master, Chalandon was far less inspired but industrious and careful — but it also shows that the problem has not been adequately reconsidered in recent times. G. Fasoli, "Problemi di storia medievale siciliana," *Siculorum Gymnasium*, n. ser., IV (1951), intelligently presents a list of open questions; the symposium *Il Regno Normanno* (Messina and Milan, 1932) includes some good articles but does not aim at originality; the summary of G. Libertini and G. Paladino, *Storia della Sicilia* (Catania, 1933), chaps. XIII and XIV, is mediocre and often inaccurate; the sketch of P. K. Hitti, *History of the Arabs* (5th ed., London, 1951), chap. XLII, is an uncritical panegyric; charity forbids mention of some other brief surveys. On the other hand, there are some valuable monographs on certain special problems. On legal history see E. Besta, *Il diritto pubblico nell'Italia meridionale* (Padua, 1939), and its bibliography. On intellectual history, besides the short but brilliant essay of F. Gabrieli, "Arabi di Sicilia e Arabi di Spagna," *Al-Andalus*, XV (1950), 27–45, see A. De Stefano, *La cultura in Sicilia nel periodo normanno* (Palermo, 1938), and its bibliography. On monastic history, see L. T. White, *Latin Monasticism in Norman Sicily* (Cambridge, Mass., 1938), and the remarks of G. A. Garufi, "Per la storia dei monasteri di Sicilia del tempo normanno," *Archivio storico per la Sicilia*, VI (1940). On naval history see C. Manfroni, *Storia della marina italiana dalle invasioni barbariche al trattato di Ninfeo* (Livorno, 1899), and W. Cohn, *Die Geschichte der normannisch-sicilischen Flotte unter der Regierung Rogers I und Rogers II* (Breslau, 1910). On population problems, G. Pardi, "Storia demografica della città di Palermo," *Nuova Rivista Storica*, III (1919), 180–208, 601–631, is fair, but not fully reliable; see also the remarks of J. Beloch, *Bevölkerungsgeschichte Italiens*, I (Berlin and Leipzig, 1937). Some aspects of Sicilian economic and social life have been recently discussed in F. Gabrieli, *Storia e civiltà musulmana* (Naples, 1947). Further bibliography is found in R. Morghen, "L'unità monarchica nell'Italia meridionale," *Questioni di storia medioevale* (E. Rota editor, Como and Milan, 1946), and in the invaluable *Archivio storico Siciliano*.

[1] G. Malaterra, *De rebus gestis Rogerii Calabriae et Siciliae comitis et Roberti Guiscardi ducis*, II, 1; the best edition is that of E. Pontieri in *Rerum Italicarum Scriptores*, V (1927). See also the well-balanced judgment of C. H. Haskins, *The Normans in European History* (Boston, 1915), chap. VII.

first year of the war, and throughout the war displayed toward Moslem, Greek, and Latin adversaries alike that peculiar admixture of cruelty and moderation, cunning and straightforwardness, avarice and generosity which was the secret of the stunning Norman successes. His conduct and that of his followers definitely disproves the rationalizations of ecclesiastical chroniclers who extolled the Normans as ardent champions of the faith. Obviously it was good politics to make capital of the difference of religion and to favor Latin Catholicism whenever it brought dividends. Inasmuch as the Normans were Catholic, closer identification of their interests with those of the Roman church in the long run became unavoidable, but we must not confuse a by-product with an original cause. The process was opposite to that of the crusades: the religious motivation was not a prime incentive gradually pushed into the background by material incentives, but a thin cloak for material appetites which very slowly grew into a sincere sentiment.

Regardless of religious considerations, Sicily was a better prize than any of the other lands which the Normans had previously attacked. The island had not suffered as terribly as the Italian mainland from the wars among Goths, Byzantines, and Lombards, and it had never been severed from the cultural and economic community of the eastern world, which throughout the early Middle Ages was vastly superior to the barbarian west. Therefore it was easy for the Moslems to build a better structure upon solid Byzantine foundations. They lightened somewhat the heavy burden of Byzantine taxation, and they split many *latifundia* into small estates intensively cultivated by tenants and peasant proprietors. Agriculture remained by far the largest source of wealth, and grain continued to be the main crop, but commerce received a new impulse from the inclusion of Sicily in the immense economic commonwealth of Islam, and agricultural production was enhanced by the introduction of new methods and new plants. Industry does not seem to have progressed to the same extent. There were thriving craftsmen who supplied fine wares for the leisure class in the towns and catered to the humbler needs of the peasants, but one type of cloth is the only manufactured product mentioned as a Sicilian export in the sources before the Norman period. Moslem writers, on the other hand, stress the wealth of metals and other minerals, one of which, salammoniac, was a valuable export. More important was the bilateral staple trade with nearby North Africa, which sent oil in exchange for Sicilian grain. Of the new plants which the Moslems introduced, cotton, sugar cane, and date palms were probably unsuited to the climate and gave small rewards for great efforts. Their culture has now disappeared. Hard wheat, sorghum, and bitter oranges (from which the sweet orange later developed) were durable acquisitions. Still more significant was the progress of market gardening. A supercilious visitor from the east deplored the heavy production and consumption of onions, which, in his opinion, depressed the intelligence and paralyzed the imagination of the inhabitants. We are not afraid of onions and we delight in spinach, melons, and other vegetables which Sicily transmitted from the Moslem to our world. It is worth noting that Arabic treatises on agriculture cite as a model the Sicilian horticultural methods and praise the skill of the Sicilians in growing cotton in inferior soils.[2]

It is impossible to decide what share of the credit for this economic progress should be given the native Christian population and what was owing to the newcomers, nor is it possible to determine the proportions of Christians and Moslems in the agricultural population. We know that the Roman equalizing varnish already covered various layers of Greek colonists, North African Semites, and other immigrants besides the older Sicilian peoples. The Germans left small traces in the ethnic structure of the country, but the Byzantine period brought greater changes. The Slavic invasion of Greece toward the end of the sixth century, the Moslem conquest of North Africa during the seventh, and probably many of the other military, political, and religious commotions of the Byzantine empire drove to Sicily large numbers of refugees, who founded new villages and restored to cultivation stretches of deserted land. This, and the influence of the Byzantine government, partly offset centuries of Romanization and caused Greek rites and culture to reëmerge.[3] Then came several waves of Moslem invaders, chiefly Arabs and Berbers from North Africa, but also adventurers from Spain and the east, with a sprinkling of negroes and

[2] See in addition to Amari and other works quoted above, Ch. Parrain, "The Evolution of Agricultural Technique," and R. S. Lopez, "Mediaeval Trade in Southern Europe," *Cambridge Economic History*, I, chap. III, and II, chap. V.

[3] See P. Charanis, "On the Question of the Hellenization of Sicily and Southern Italy during the Middle Ages," *American Historical Review*, LII (1946), 74–86, and the remarks of K. M. Setton, "The Bulgars in the Balkans in the Seventh Century," *Speculum*, XXV (1950), 516ff. While I agree with Charanis on his main thesis as to the Hellenization of Sicily and southern Italy, I think that he overstates his case when he says (*op. cit.*, p. 84) that documentation is lacking with regard to immigration of refugees during the Arabic invasions. To quote only one instance, see the account of the "Riyāḍ an-nufūs" on the emigration of the people of Carthage — which included many Greeks — to Sicily after the Arab conquest, in M. Amari, *Biblioteca arabo-sicula* (translation, 2 vols., and an appendix, Turin and Rome, 1880–1889), I, 297–298.

Slavs. The flow of immigration continued throughout the tenth century. As late as 1005 a famine in Africa drove hungry crowds off to Sicily; in 1018 and 1019 many Shī'ite heretics found shelter in the island. Conversions also swelled the Moslem element, especially in the western and southern provinces; in eastern Sicily, which was conquered last, the overwhelming superiority of Greek Christians was never shaken and there was a strong Latin minority. Judging from very meager sources, differences between Moslems and "infidels" were sharp only at the extremes. The aristocracy of fighters (Arabic, *jund*) who lived on stipends was exclusively Moslem; the slaves were unconverted descendants of Byzantine slaves, unransomed Christian war prisoners, and strangers imported by slave merchants. The rustic masses consisted of hard-working tenants, often bound to the land, and of small proprietors who paid heavy taxes and were too busy making a living to be ardent supporters of any faith or party. The infrequency of peasants' revolts even in times of civil war and invasion shows that their lot was not unbearable, and that they were resigned to it. We catch glimpses of their feelings in the account of a chronicler which shows the Christians of Val Demone as bringing "gifts" to count Roger while assuring the Moslem authorities that they had been forced to do so.[4] During World War II there were Sicilian farmers who, caught between two armies, endeavored to escape punishment by similar acrobatics.

Leadership rested with the military, civil, and commercial upper class in the towns. Palermo, long the capital of the provincial governors sent from Africa and then that of the virtually independent Kalbid emirs, was now ruled by its own assembly of notables (Arabic, *jamā'ah*) where Arabs of old noble stock held first place. It was the religious metropolis of both the Moslems and the Christians, one of the largest cities in the Moslem world, and larger than any Christian town except Constantinople. Hundreds of school teachers, lawyers, scholars, and poets made it one of the greatest intellectual centers in the world. It was a port of the first rank, an active center of ship-building and other crafts, and the residence of wealthy Jewish, Moslem, and Christian businessmen. Its stately buildings of stone, marble, and bricks sprawled from the old fortified center to many new suburbs brightened by gardens and fountains. Along the sea shore were the quarters of voluntary

[4] Malaterra, *De rebus gestis*, II, 14. Unfortunately most of the information on the rural classes comes from documents of the Norman period, which to some extent reflect the earlier conditions. See now E. Besta, "Le classi sociali," in *Il Regno Normanno*.

warriors for the faith — those fierce ghazis (Arabic singular, *ghāzī*) who caused al-Maqdisī, the great Palestinian geographer, to extol "Sicily, the fertile island whose people never tire of fighting the holy war."[5] Farther south the inland town of Agrigento was a capital of peasants and the moral center of the Berbers, who often rose against the more refined and cosmopolitan but more relaxed Arab aristocracy of the north. Not far from it Enna, in a dominant position on a mountain top, was now the residence of Ibn-al-Ḥauwās, the strongest of the petty emirs who had gained control of the country after the collapse of the Kalbid monarchy. His brother-in-law and rival, Ibn-aṭ-Ṭumnah, from Catania endeavored to extend his rule all along the eastern coast. Here Syracuse, the former Byzantine capital, and Messina were slowly recovering after their last-ditch fight against the invaders; the Christian population had lost its autonomy, but it shared with the Moslem minority the benefits of a fairly enlightened and progressive economic and administrative regime. There were many other thriving towns.

Yet this proud, brilliant civilization bore the germs of a disease which delivered it into the hands of an adventurer of genius. If we are to believe the poisoned pen of Ibn-Ḥauqal, in the late tenth century, already the ghazis of Sicily were nothing but "evildoers, rebels, rabble of many nations, panderers, contemptible men;" the teachers in Palermo were incompetent hypocrites who had embraced their profession to dodge military service; as for the other classes, here is how he summed up the state of Islam in the Mediterranean: "The Romans are attacking the Moslems, who find nobody to help them .... Our proud, greedy princes cowardly bow before the enemy; men of learning forget God and future life to do their pleasure...; the wicked merchants neglect no opportunity of illicit profit...; the bigots sail with every wind that blows."[6] This indictment is of course exaggerated. It was not the lukewarmness of Islam but the recovery of Christian peoples that gradually turned the tide in the Mediterranean. The bands of holy warriors, like those of the crusaders, included many desperadoes,

[5] Amari, *Bibliot. arabo-sicula*, app., p. 86. The population figures suggested for Palermo by Amari (300–350,000) and Pardi (250,000 at most) are too high, and nearly all figures of contemporary Arab writers are unreliable. More significant is the comparative statement of al-Maqdisī (*Bibliot. arabo-sicula*, II, 670), who makes Palermo larger than Old Cairo; even if he was too optimistic in regard to Palermo, the town must have had well over 100,000 inhabitants.

[6] *Bibliot. arabo-sicula*, I, 18–19, 24, 27. In regard to the ghazis in other Moslem frontier regions, see G. Salinger, "Was the *futūwa* an Oriental form of Chivalry?" *Proceedings of the American Philosophical Society*, XCIV (1950), 481–493, with bibliography.

but they fought bravely; as late as 1035 many were killed while raiding Italy and Greece, and others were to show their gallantry in the fight against the Normans. What especially undermined Sicily was the chronic anarchy of Moslem society, which could be overcome for the sake of gaining a specific objective, but which reëmerged soon after victory, as Ibn-Khaldūn, the greatest historian of the Middle Ages, has so incisively stated. Neither the African Aghlabids who wrested Sicily from the Byzantines nor the Sicilian Kalbids who ruled it afterwards exceeded the one hundred and twenty years which Ibn-Khaldūn regarded as the normal life span of a dynasty. In the early eleventh century rival Moslem factions called to their help respectively the Byzantines from southern Italy and the Zīrids from North Africa. The former, led by George Maniaces, conquered the eastern part of the island; the latter swept through the rest of the country. The Sicilians had already repented of their rash appeals when fortune rid them of both invading armies. Court intrigues and more pressing wars led to the recall of Maniaces and his troops; the disastrous invasion of nomad tribes from the desert crippled the Zīrids in North Africa and precipitated the departure of their armies.[7] Sicily, left to itself, relapsed into anarchy. Its weakness whetted the appetite of the Normans, who were in the process of conquering the Byzantine and Lombard possessions of the Italian mainland. As early as 1059 Robert Guiscard styled himself "by the grace of God and St. Peter duke of Apulia and Calabria and, with their help, hereafter of Sicily." In 1061 Ibn-aṭ-Ṭumnah invited Robert's brother and vassal, count Roger of Calabria, to help him fight Ibn-al-Ḥauwās. He did not talk to deaf ears.

Inasmuch as the Zīrids soon afterwards sent new contingents to Sicily, the struggle superficially recalled that of 1038–1042, when a duel between Christian and African "allies" overshadowed the strife of local factions but for a short time. Further progress of the nomads, however, had now cut so deeply into the Zīrid state that this was no longer capable of a sustained effort. Both the assets and the liabilities of the Normans also were different from those of Maniaces. Count Roger was at the same time a ruler and a general, perhaps a greater general than the able Maniaces and certainly a better statesman than any Byzantine emperor after Basil II. Though operations on the Italian mainland sometimes distracted

[7] On the struggle between Zīrids and nomads, see G. Marçais, *La Berbérie musulmane et l'orient au moyen âge* (Paris, 1946); earlier bibliography in E. Gautier, *Les Siècles obscurs du Maghreb* (Paris, 1927). A study of Maniaces and his times is still a desideratum.

him from the Sicilian campaign, he did not have to worry about distant wars in Asia. His financial resources, however, were far slimmer than those of the Byzantine treasury, his land army was small, and for a long time he had no fleet of his own. At the beginning of his career he had not been above stealing horses and robbing peaceful merchants. He soon learned how to make war by plundering enemy territory and levying high taxes on his own, so that his solvency steadily increased, but the Norman avarice in Sicily as in Italy bred much hatred and alienated populations whose friendliness would have been valuable. So did the atrocities which sullied the Norman campaigns especially during the first years. Their only moral justification, if there was any, was that which a beaten enemy, Ibn-Ḥamdīs, invoked for earlier Moslem atrocities: "It was not cruelty, but [the self-defense] of the few who were surrounded by the many."[8]

As a matter of fact, count Roger had at his disposal only a few hundred or, at the most, a few thousand Norman knights with perhaps three times as many armed valets — some of the knights, not including Roger's own son, proved trustworthy for the whole duration of the war — besides auxiliary forces from his county of Calabria, some intermittent and interested help from his brother, duke Robert Guiscard, and any other Christian or Moslem reinforcements which he might be able and willing to obtain through alliance. The number of non-Norman fighters and the part which they played is not easily assessed, because the only detailed accounts come from two Norman friars, Geoffrey Malaterra and Aimé of Monte Cassino, who did not like to squander credit outside their own nation. It is evident that what naval activity was displayed must be ascribed to Italian auxiliaries since the Normans in Sicily were land troops. There are indications that auxiliaries and perhaps a Sicilian fifth column were at times useful in the battlefield and in the rear, but the Normans undoubtedly bore the brunt of the fight. They were splendid soldiers, probably the best in their time. Their exploits in France, in England, in Spain, in Italy, in the Byzantine empire filled the Norman chronicles, deeply impressed the conquered peoples, and were magnified in heroic literature.[9] Actually the Normans were much like the ideal of the sagas and

[8] Amari, *Bibliot. arabo-sicula*, II, 396. Needless to say, the Moslems during the conquest of Sicily and in their raids from Sicily against the Italian mainland did not show any greater consideration for the civilians than did the Normans. War is seldom considerate.

[9] Besides the works quoted above see H. Grégoire and R. de Keyser, "La Chanson de Roland et Byzance," *Byzantion*, XIV (1939), 265–316; H. Grégoire, "La Chanson de Roland de l'an 1085," *Bulletin de l'académie royale de Belgique, Classe des lettres*, ser. 5, XXV (1939), 211–273.

Check?

chansons de geste — they were adventurous, fearless, unruly, insatiable, exceedingly gallant to willing and unwilling ladies of any social class, indiscriminately hard on unwarlike peasants and bourgeois of any nation, and frequently very devoted to Christ if not to his commandments. A handful of Normans, including two of Roger's elder brothers, already had assisted Maniaces in smiting Saracens and scorching the country, but their part had been far less important than certain sagas and chronicles represented it. Now a larger, if still fairly small, number were poised under the command of a ruthless and extremely gifted man of their own race. They outmatched their Moslem counterparts, the ghazis, and overpowered large militias of less martial men fighting for home and liberty. Though the numbers of their adversaries have been multiplied by the same chroniclers who passed by their allies, the very duration of the struggle — thirty years — shows that victory went not to the larger but to the braver army.

The background of the Sicilian campaign is more interesting than the campaign itself.[10] The war was important for its results, not for its methods; there were innumerable skirmishes, raids, and counter-raids, but few battles, only one memorable siege, and no new weapons or tactics that had not been widely used elsewhere. Even before receiving the invitation of Ibn-aṭ-Ṭumnah, Roger had carried out an exploratory raid across the Strait of Messina, which was unsuccessful but may have been instrumental in gaining the invitation (1060).[11] A second raid with the armed support of Ibn-aṭ-Ṭumnah was equally unsuccessful; the Normans were driven back to the coast and feared total destruction as a storm prevented them from recrossing the Strait. Happily Roger, as the chroniclers tell us, calmed the waters by dedicating what booty he had taken to the reconstruction of a church in Calabria. Finally, in 1061, more careful preparation, shrewder strategy, and the personal intervention of Robert Guiscard enabled a larger number of Normans to dodge the fleet which Ibn-al-Ḥauwās had sent to blockade the Strait, capture Messina, obtain the submission of Rametta, and reconquer for Ibn-aṭ-Ṭumnah a large part of the northeastern region. The count and the emir did not succeed in capturing Enna, the fortress capital of Ibn-al-Ḥauwās, but Palermo made overtures

[10] Detailed accounts of the Sicilian campaign are found in Amari (with a pro-Moslem bias), in Chalandon (with a pro-Norman bias) and, for naval history, in Manfroni (with a pro-Italian bias). These authors discuss at length the sources and their reliability; the writer does not always agree with their judgments.

[11] On the legendary character of the *Brevis historia liberationis Messanae*, which mentions an imaginary invitation of Roger by the Christian population of the town, see N. Rodolico, "Il municipalismo nella storiografia siciliana," *Nuova Rivista Storica*, VII (1923), 57–72.

to embrace the party of the winners. So far the Normans had acted as allies of a Moslem emir, but this had not prevented them from killing or enslaving the Moslem inhabitants of Messina, nor had the friendly attitude of the Christian farmers restrained the undisciplined heroes from looting and raping. As a reward for their intervention they retained Messina and a few other places — probably by agreement with Ibn-aṭ-Ṭumnah — and thus they secured a bridgehead across the narrow Strait, which even their small naval force could easily control. Meanwhile some Sicilian refugees easily persuaded the Zīrid emir — the same al-Muʿizz who twenty years earlier had intervened against Maniaces — to send a powerful fleet to the relief of their party. But a storm scattered the ships; those who were not drowned went back to Africa, where the nomads and other rebels intensified their attacks against the old and discredited emir.

Then, in 1062 and 1063, the tide seemed to turn against the Normans, who were saved only by their desperate bravery. Ibn-aṭ-Ṭumnah was killed while fighting without their help and his successors withdrew from the struggle; the Christian population was so exasperated by their coreligionists that it made common cause with their enemies; Roger and Robert, back in Calabria, had a bitter fight which nearly wrecked their uneasy coöperation; Tamīm, the new Zīrid ruler, sent to Sicily two of his sons with a fairly large army which crossed over safely, gained control of the larger part of the island including Palermo, and joined forces with Ibn-al-Ḥauwās. Robert had remained on the mainland. Roger, alone in a hostile country, was almost besieged with a few hundred knights in the small town of Troina. But he broke out, made some successful raids, and defeated near Cerami a Zīrid-Sicilian force which greatly outnumbered his troops. A chronicler, repeating and embellishing what he may have heard from some imaginative veteran, states that St. George took part in the battle, that one hundred and thirty-six Norman knights crushed 50,000 enemies, killing 15,000 of them, and that Roger sent four camels loaded with booty to pope Alexander II, who reciprocated with a blessing and a standard. Subsequent events show that the combat removed for the Normans the danger of being thrown back to the sea, but apart from this it was of no great consequence.[12] When,

[12] It is strange that serious historians have placed so much reliance upon the obviously fictional story of Malaterra, who is almost our only source for the battle of Cerami since Aimé of Monte Cassino, perhaps on account of gaps in the extant manuscript, does not mention it and the so-called Anonymus Vaticanus is strongly suspected of being but an abridgment of Malaterra: see Chalandon, I, xxxvii–xxxviii, and bibliography. The silence of all Arabic

a few weeks later, a Pisan fleet arrived at an eastern Sicilian port and invited Roger to take part in a combined attack on Palermo — possibly in execution of plans which had been made in agreement with Robert — Roger was unable to leave his corner around Troina. The Pisans alone broke into the port of Palermo and captured some ships, but they did not dare to storm the city without some help from land forces, and withdrew with the booty.[13] The following year (1064) Robert Guiscard brought fresh troops and together with Roger tried to take Palermo by a land siege, but the attempt failed. Robert returned to the mainland — according to Aimé of Monte Cassino, he realized that without "a multitude of ships" he could not stop the flow of supplies and reinforcements[14] — and Roger alone during the four years that followed could do little to check the progress of the Zīrid princes in western and central Sicily.

Once again, as twenty years earlier, the African allies became the masters of the Sicilian Moslems. Aiyūb, the elder of the Zīrid princes, became virtually the ruler of Agrigento, whose Berber inhabitants had a leaning towards African men and customs. Ibn-al-Ḥauwās was killed as he endeavored to recover the town. His former followers and Palermo itself proclaimed Aiyūb their sovereign. Had Aiyūb been able to obtain reinforcements from Africa and to inflict a serious defeat upon the Normans, the fate of Sicily would have anticipated that of Spain, where the African Murābiṭs (Almoravids) came as allies, defeated the Christians, and remained as conquerors. Tamīm, however, had no reserves to spare, and Roger in 1068 beat the army of Aiyūb at Misilmeri. Then the population of Palermo, which had forgotten how to obey, came to blows with the negro guard of the Zīrids. Civil war broke out in the town and spread to other regions. Before the end of 1069 the disheartened Zīrid princes returned to Africa with their troops and with a large number of Sicilians who read the writing on the wall and chose to follow them. One Ibn-Ḥammūd, probably of a family which had given rulers to Cordova and Malaga, became the lord of Enna and Agrigento; Palermo recovered its liberty but for a short time. As a matter of fact, while Sicily was returning to independence and particularism, Robert

sources also is significant; it is natural that they deëmphasize a defeat, but they could hardly have ignored it if it had been a great disaster.

[13] On the possible connection with an earlier agreement, see Amari, III, 104, and n. 2; and see the preceding section in this chapter.

[14] Aimé of Monte Cassino, *Storia de' Normanni*, V, 26; the most recent edition is that of V. de Bartholomaeis in *Fonti per la Storia d'Italia, Scrittori* (Rome, 1935).

Guiscard with Roger's assistance built up the sea power which he had lacked in 1064. He captured Bari, next to Venice the greatest Adriatic seaport and trading center, and he completed the conquest of the other maritime towns of Apulia.

Bari surrendered in April 1071 after a siege which lasted more than three years. In July 1071 Robert and Roger, accompanied by a brother of the Lombard prince of Salerno and by other barons, sailed to Sicily in an armada of fifty-eight vessels manned by Apulian, Calabrese, and Greek sailors. Their army included not only a substantial number of Norman knights but also conscripts and volunteers from southern Italy and perhaps other regions. The Normans inaugurated their campaign by entering the port of Catania as allies — the heirs of Ibn-aṭ-Ṭumnah while desisting from active operations had remained friendly — and treacherously occupying the town as conquerors. Then they laid siege to Palermo by land and sea. The town resisted for several months, and it received some naval help from Africa, but famine and discord slowly undermined the morale. The final assault began January 7, 1072; the old section of the town, attacked by Roger, held out, but Robert broke into a lightly defended suburb. While some of the citizens wanted to fight to the last, others opened negotiations which on January 10 led to surrender. Palermo preserved a large measure of autonomy and full freedom of worship, but the main mosque on the site of the former cathedral again became a cathedral, and the Normans built or restored two fortresses to teach discretion to Christians and Moslems alike. Mazara, the oldest Moslem possession on the island, after learning the fate of Palermo surrendered on similar conditions. Remarkably enough the chroniclers, who describe in glowing terms the happiness of the victorious Christian army, say nothing of the feelings of the local Christians.[15] The Moslems on the whole seem to have accepted the foreign rule of the Norman "infidels" more easily than that of their African brothers, but many of the poets and scholars who had been the glory of Palermo became honored refugees in the several Moslem states from Spain to the Near East. Some of them wrote nostalgic poems and prophecies of revenge; one, abū-l-ʿArab, showed himself a spiritual neighbor of Dante, another poet and exile born in Italy of another faith. "O my fatherland," he wrote, "you have abandoned me; I shall make my fatherland the

[15] The silence of the chroniclers in this respect contrasts with their detailed accounts of the behavior of the Christians in northeastern Sicily and with the description of the welcome which the Christians of Malta extended to the Normans in 1091.

saddles of generous steeds. On the earth I was born, any earth is my fatherland, any man is my brother!"[16]

After the fall of Palermo victory was so well assured that Robert and Roger partitioned the island between themselves. Robert, the suzerain, retained Palermo with some other places and struck coins with the Arabic inscription "King of Sicily".[17] Roger, however, claimed the larger part of the island, which after the death of Robert was to become all his, to be bequeathed to Roger II, the first crowned king. Still it took nineteen years to subdue southern Sicily — and during these years two savage Moslem raids on the Calabrese coast recalled to the unfortunate population terrible memories of the ninth and tenth centuries. The first raid, which was followed by a landing in Mazara one year later, was a result of a short resumption of activity by the Zīrids (1074–1075); but Roger I averted further interference by concluding a treaty with Tamīm. The emir had lost nearly all the African hinterland; he depended on Sicilian grain and free trade for his maritime cities.[18] The second and wilder raid (1085) was one of many enterprises of the last Moslem leader in eastern Sicily, the emir of Syracuse, who fought bravely and ferociously to the last. But the struggle between the cornered, disunited defenders and the Normans whose land and sea forces continuously grew could not last forever; it would have lasted less long if Roger had not frequently diverted his activity to the Italian mainland. Some towns capitulated after a long resistance; others came to terms without direct pressure when their doom seemed imminent; the emir of Enna, whose wife had been captured by Roger, accepted baptism and was granted an estate in Calabria. The conquest was

division of Sicily after Norman Conquest - check this further —

[16] We are quoting from the translation of Gabrieli, "Arabi di Sicilia," p. 39, which differs from that of Amari and its revision by De Stefano, "La cultura in Sicilia," in *Il Regno Normanno*, p. 135; compare the letter of Dante to his Florentine friends. Hitti's statement that the case of the poet Ibn-Ḥamdīs who went into exile "was exceptional" (p. 607) is not borne out by the sources, which list a good number of intellectuals and other leaders who left Sicily. The number would probably have been still larger but for the fear of crossing "the sea, which belongs to the Romans," a fear which caused abū-l-ʿArab to hesitate before accepting the invitation of his fellow-poet, the ruler of Seville; cf. H. Pérès, *La Poésie andalouse en arabe classique au XIe siècle* (Paris, 1937), p. 216. Aristocrats of true or pretended Sicilian origin are still enjoying special prestige in Morocco; see C. A. Nallino, "Sicilia," in *Enciclopedia Italiana.*

[17] On the royal coinage of Robert, see B. Lagumina, *Catalogo delle monete arabe esistenti nella Biblioteca Comunale di Palermo* (Palermo, 1892), pp. 226–234; in general on Sicilian numismatics of the period, see G. C. Miles, *Fāṭimid Coins* (New York, 1951), and R. S. Lopez, "Il ritorno all'oro nell'Occidente duecentesco, I," *Rivista Storica Italiana*, LXV (1953), 19–55. The terms of the partition between Robert and Roger are given in detail by many sources, but the sources do not fully agree with one another.

[18] The alliance stood the test of disaster when, in 1087, Tamīm's capital was captured by northern Italian sailors in what has been called "the dress rehearsal of the crusades".

completed in 1091 with the bloodless, negotiated surrender of Noto and of the island of Malta.

Reconstruction and reorganization of the island began long before the end of the war. In this trying task the statesmanship of count Roger and of his son and successor, king Roger II, proved equal to their military achievements. During thirty years of warfare the population had been diminished by starvation, death in battle, deportation into slavery, and voluntary exile. Many of the splendid Arab buildings in the towns had been ruined and some villages had been wiped out.[19] The uneasy equilibrium which long association had established among Moslems, Greeks, and Latins had been upset. The Norman knights and the "Lombards" (continental Italians) who immigrated in the early period of the Norman rule added other sharply discordant pieces to the tessellated pavement of Sicily. The feelings of the average Norman toward other nations can be surmised when we read in Fra Malaterra's chronicle that both the Sicilian Greeks and the Calabresi are "ever wicked races"; the equally wicked Apulian Lombards are "never tired of betraying"; the Romans are shamelessly venal and disloyal; the Pisans are cowards interested only in commercial gain; and the Moslems, of course, are the scum of the earth. Granted that bigoted expressions of this kind are not uncommon in medieval writings and may still be heard too often in our own day, they were not a good omen for the moral unification of the Norman state.[20] It took much wisdom and firmness for the new sovereigns to bring out of confusion and hatred one of the most brilliant and harmonious civilizations of the Middle Ages.

Roger I and Roger II owed their outstanding success as sovereigns of Sicily to the fact that they used indiscriminately the talents and labor of all their subjects, and that they chose from every culture the elements which seemed to function best. The local autonomies and religious or national differences they re-

[19] To quote only one instance, here is how Malaterra, *De rebus gestis*, II, 36, describes the passing of Robert Guiscard through a village near Agrigento in 1064: "Bugamum oppugnare vadunt, civibusque eiusdem castri enerviter reluctantibus, funditus diruunt, incolas omnes cum mulieribus et liberis omnique supellectili sua captivos adducunt . . . . Dux itaque digressus, in Calabriam veniens . . . Bugamenses, quos captivos adduxerat, Scriblam, quam desertaverat, restaurans, ibi hospitari fecit." Bugamo was not restored and no longer appears on the map. Of the Arab monuments which were described in glowing terms in pre-conquest sources none survives in the island, although some of them were incorporated into Norman monuments, a few of which are extant.

[20] Malaterra, *De rebus gestis*, II, 29; I, 28, 6, and 14; III, 38; II, 34, and *passim*. Aimé is equally biased. William of Apulia, of course, is more favorable to his fellow nationals, the Lombards of southern Italy. As a matter of fact the Lombards were closer to the Normans in customs and civilization and usually were treated with greater consideration.

spected and indeed protected enough to rule a divided country, yet not so much that the country might be split asunder. These policies have been justly praised by many medieval and modern historians of different nations, but they should be called opportunism rather than tolerance. True tolerance appeared only in the later years of the Norman state, under William II, who was a devoted Christian ruling a majority of old or new Christians, but who ignored the Moslem religious practices of baptized pages in his own palace. Mere opportunism guided Roger I, who created a new Latin hierarchy to by-pass the pope, protected the Greek monasteries to counterbalance the Latin church, and forbade Christian propaganda among Moslem soldiers whose undivided devotion he needed against Christian enemies; it also guided Roger II, who subsidized the useful research of al-Idrīsī and accepted his fulsome praise, but closed his reign with the *auto-da-fé* of his admiral, charged with apostasy but guilty only of military bungling. Still it was a blessing to all concerned that the Machiavellianism of the princes spared Sicily much of the suffering which men of all faiths were about to encounter in Palestine and Syria during the crusades.

Check all this.

Lastly, it should be remembered that the main lines of the Norman policies largely followed examples which had been set by the earlier rulers of the Sicilian mosaic of peoples — the Romans, the Byzantines, and the Moslems. The Normans may have excelled all of them in many respects, but they did not escape the fate which Ibn-Khaldūn predicts for conquerors. Their dynasty did not outlast one hundred and twenty years.

D. The Pilgrimages to Palestine before 1095

It is a common trait among men and women to wish to visit the sites connected with the lives of those whom they admire; and the idea of pilgrimage has played a large part in most of the great religions of the world. Before ever the Christian era began pious Buddhists were traveling to pay their respects at the shrines where the Buddha and his chief disciples had lived and taught. Later on Islam was to teach that the journey to Mecca should be the aim of every pious Moslem.

From the earliest times Christians felt a desire to see for themselves the places hallowed by the incarnate God, where Christ was born and preached and suffered. They inherited from the Jews a particular respect for the city of Jerusalem, and as the scene of the crucifixion it became doubly holy to them. Moreover, there soon arose a feeling that the martyrs when suffering for the faith were able to grant a special remission of sins, a *libellus* or warrant of reconciliation with God; and gradually it was believed that the spot where a martyrdom had occurred acquired something of the remissory power.[1] Calvary, sanctified by the greatest martyrdom of all, was inevitably held to be peculiarly potent. At the same time relics, either the bodily remains of the saints or objects that had played a part in the life of Christ or of a saint, were popularly supposed to possess the same power; and in time, through stages that we cannot now trace, the church gave recognition to what had become an almost universal belief.

During the first two centuries of the Christian era it was not easy to make the pilgrimage to Palestine. Jerusalem itself had been destroyed by Titus, and the Roman authorities did not approve of journeys thither. The fall of Jerusalem had resulted in the triumph of St. Paul's conception of Christianity over that of St. James, and the church sought to stress its universality at the expense of its Jewish origins. But the holy places were not forgotten. It is significant that Hadrian, when he rebuilt Jerusalem, deliberately erected a temple to Venus Capitolina on the site of

[1] See P. H. Battifol, *Études d'histoire et de théologie positive* (Paris, 1906), I, 112–120.

Calvary. When, after the triumph of the Cross, the empress Helena came to Palestine, the tradition that she found there was strong enough for her to be able to identify all the sacred sites. Even before her time pilgrims had travelled to Palestine. We hear of a bishop, Firmilian of Caesarea-Mazaca (Kayseri), who visited Jerusalem early in the third century, and of another Cappadocian bishop, Alexander, who followed a few years later.[2] Origen about the same time talks of the "desire of Christians to search after the footsteps of Christ."[3]

The official recognition of Christianity, combined with Helena's voyage and her pious labors, which her son Constantine endorsed by building the great churches of the Holy Sepulcher at Jerusalem and the Nativity at Bethlehem, let loose a stream of pilgrims bound for Palestine. The first to leave an account of his travels was a man from Bordeaux, who wrote out his itinerary in the year 333, when the emperor had barely completed his buildings.[4] Some fifty years later an indefatigable lady called Aetheria, who probably came from France or Spain, wrote in detail of her experiences, which included a visit to Egypt and to Mount Sinai.[5] About the end of the century St. Jerome moved to Palestine and settled at Bethlehem, and in his train came a number of fashionable but godly ladies from Rome.[6] By the beginning of the next century the number of monasteries and hostels in Jerusalem where pilgrims could be housed was said to be over three hundred.[7]

The fathers of the church were not altogether happy about this new fashion. Even Jerome, though he recommended a visit to Palestine to his friend Desiderius as an act of faith and declared that his sojourn there enabled him to understand the Scriptures more clearly, confessed that nothing really was missed by a failure to make the pilgrimage.[8] St. Augustine openly denounced pilgrimages as being irrelevant and even dangerous.[9] Of the Greek fathers, St. John Chrysostom, while wishing that his episcopal duties did not prevent him from traveling, mocked at the sight of

[2] Jerome, *De viris illustribus*, 54 (*PL* XXIII, 700B); Eusebius, *Historia ecclesiastica* (tr. J. E. L. Oulton and H. J. Lawlor, Loeb Classical Library, Cambridge, Mass., 1953), II, 37.

[3] Origen, *In Joannem*, VI, 29 (*PG* XIV, 269).

[4] Published in *PPTS*, vol. I, with a translation by A. Stewart.

[5] Published in *PPTS*, I, under the name of *The Pilgrimage of Saint Silvia of Aquitaine*, translated by J. H. Bernard. For her identity see Dom Cabrol, *Étude sur la Peregrinatio Silviae* (Paris and Poitiers, 1895), and M. Ferotin, "Le Véritable auteur de la Peregrinatio Silviae: la vierge espagnole Ethéria," *Revue des questions historiques*, LXXVI (1903), 367–397.

[6] Jerome, *Ep.* XLVI (*PL* XXII, 483ff.), letter from Paula and Eustochium to Marcella.

[7] See A. Couret, *La Palestine sous les empereurs grecs* (Grenoble, 1869), p. 212.

[8] Jerome, *Liber paralipomenon*, praefatio (*PL* XXVIII, 1325–1326).

[9] Augustine, *Ep.* LXXVIII (*PL* XXXIII, 268–269); *Contra Faustum Manichaeum*, 21 (*PL* XLII, 384–385).

a whole world in motion merely to look at Job's dung-hill.[10] St. Gregory of Nyssa remarked that pilgrimages were nowhere enjoined by Holy Writ, and he saw no merit in visiting Jerusalem, which was a rather ordinary town, indeed fuller than most towns of wicked persons, merchants, actors, and prostitutes.[11] But the general public ignored such strictures, preferring to believe that the interesting journey brought spiritual merit as well.

In the middle of the fifth century the empress Eudocia, wife of Theodosius II, settled in Jerusalem. It was then highly fashionable to reside there; and the empress showed her support of another fashion when she sent to her sister-in-law at Constantinople one of the most precious relics that she could find there, a portrait of the Mother of God said to have been painted by St. Luke.[12] To many of the pilgrims crowding to Palestine half the point of the journey was the possibility of buying some important relic with which to sanctify their churches at home. The greater number of the early saints and martyrs had lived in the east, and it was in the east that their relics could be found. It was now generally held that divine aid could be obtained at the graves of the saints, as the Spaniard Prudentius and the Italian Ennodius taught, while St. Ambrose himself believed in the efficacy of relics and sought to discover some.[13] St. Basil of Caesarea was a little more cautious. He was prepared to believe that relics might have some divine power, but he wished to be absolutely certain of their authenticity.[14] Here again popular enthusiasm was undeterred by the caution of the fathers. The major Christian relics remained in the east, those of Christ being gradually moved from Jerusalem to Constantinople and those of the saints being preserved at their native homes. But it was often possible for a lucky pilgrim to acquire some lesser relic, while others were brought to the west by enterprising merchants. Not only did the hope of successful relic-hunting send more and more pilgrims to the east, but also the arrival and possession of the relic of some eastern saint in their home town would inspire western citizens to visit the lands where their new patron saint had lived. Whole embassies would be despatched with orders to bring home relics. Avitus, bishop of Vienne, sent special envoys to find him a piece of the True Cross

[10] John Chrysostom, *Ad populum Antiochenum*, V, 1 (*PG* XLIX, 69); *Hom. VIII in Ep. ad Ephesios*, 2 (*PG* LXII, 57).

[11] Gregory of Nyssa, *Ep.* II (*PG* XLVI, 1009).

[12] Nicephorus Callistus, *Historia ecclesiastica*, XIV, 2 (*PG* CXLVI, 1061 A).

[13] Prudentius, *Carmina* (*CSEL*, LXI [1926]), pp. 132–135; Ennodius, *Libellus pro synodo* (*ibid.* VI [1882]), p. 315; Ambrose, *Ep.* XXII (*PL* XLI, 1019ff.).

[14] Basil of Caesarea, *Ep.* 197 (*PG* XXXII, 709–713).

at Jerusalem. St. Rhadegund, ex-queen of Clothar the Frank, employed agents who brought her a rich haul, including a fragment of the Cross, acquired at Constantinople, and the finger of St. Mamas of Cappadocia, several of whose other bones were obtained by pilgrims from Langres. Women were particularly zealous in this pursuit. It was a lady from Guienne who returned home with a phial containing the blood of St. John the Baptist, and a lady from Maurienne who brought back his thumb.[15]

Throughout the sixth century pilgrims continued to visit the east in great numbers, and several *Itineraries* were written to help them on their way, such as those of the travelers Theodosius and Antoninus Martyr. There were still constant trade connections with the east; and it was not difficult for a pilgrim to obtain a passage in a merchant-ship, probably Syrian-owned, traveling between Provence or Visigothic Spain and the ports of Syria and Egypt.[16]

With the Arab conquest of Syria and Egypt, the pilgrim-traffic was necessarily interrupted. For some centuries there was no sea-borne trade between the Moslem east and the Christian west. Pirates infested Mediterranean waters. The new rulers of Palestine were suspicious of strangers; and in any case the journey was increasingly expensive, and wealth in the west was declining. But intercourse was not entirely broken off; and the western church still thought with sympathy and longing of the holy places. Many of the popes were still of oriental origin and had oriental connections. In 652 pope Martin I was accused of friendly dealings with the Moslems and acquitted himself by showing that his motive was to be able to send alms to Palestine.[17] While most pilgrims now contented themselves with journeys to nearer shrines, such as Rome, there were still some hardy enough to brave the perils of the east. In 670 the Frankish bishop, Arculf, set out on travels that brought him to Egypt, Syria, and Palestine and home by Constantinople, but he was away for many years and suffered many hardships.[18] We hear of other pilgrims of the time, such as the Picard, Vulphy of Rue, and the Burgundians, Bercaire and Waimer of Montier-en-Der.[19]

[15] For the question of relics see H. Delehaye, *Les Origines de culte des martyres* (2nd ed., Brussels, 1938), pp. 73–91; Jean Ebersolt, *Orient et occident* (Paris and Brussels, 1928), I, 32–39.

[16] The itineraries of Theodosius and Antoninus are given in *Itinera Hierosolymitana* (ed. Tobler and Molinier, Société de l'orient latin, I, Geneva, 1880), p. 2.

[17] Pope Martin I, *Ep.* XV, in *PL* LXXXVII, 199–200, letter to Theodore.

[18] Arculf's journey was described by his disciple, Adamnan, *De locis sanctis*, tr. J. R. Macpherson (*PPTS*, III).

[19] *Vita S. Wlphagii* (*Acta sanctorum*, Iun. tom. II, June 7), pp. 30–31; *Miracula S. Bercharii* (*Acta sanctorum ordinis S. Benedicti*, saec. II), p. 849.

In the eighth century the numbers increased. Pilgrimage was now fashionable amongst the English and the Irish, and seems to have been encouraged by the appearance of numerous *Poenitentialia*, little books written by some hierarch recommending types of private penance. They were used first by the Celtic church; and the Anglo-Saxon expansion, combined with the missionary activities of such Celts as St. Columban, introduced them into general usage in the western church. They recommended pilgrimage as a means of penance, though they did not mention specific destinations.[20] The most eminent of the English pilgrims was Willibald, who was to die as bishop of Eichstädt in Bavaria. In his youth, from 722 to 729, he made a long and uncomfortable journey from Rome to Jerusalem and back.[21] Relations between the west and the Moslems soon improved. When Charlemagne entered into some sort of alliance with the caliph Hārūn ar-Rashīd, there was a sufficient number of pilgrims coming to Jerusalem for the emperor to find it worth while to obtain permission to have a hostel set up for them in the holy city. There were women again amongst the pilgrims, and there were Spanish nuns living attached to the Holy Sepulcher.[22] There was another slight interruption in the course of the ninth century, owing to the growth of Moslem power in the Mediterranean and the establishment of Arabs in Crete and Sicily and southern Italy. When the Breton Bernard the Wise set out in 870, he had to obtain a passport from the Moslem emir of Bari, which, however, did not permit him to land at Alexandria. When he eventually reached Jerusalem he found Charlemagne's establishments still in working order, but they were shabby and the number of visitors had sadly declined.[23] At the same time the beginning of the Norse invasions of the west added to the perils of travel and brought poverty in their train. Pilgrimages were for a while too expensive for the average man and woman.

By the beginning of the tenth century conditions in the Mediterranean had improved. The Moslems had lost their foothold in southeast Italy and were soon to lose their last pirate-nests in southern France. Crete was recovered for Christendom half way through the century; and the Byzantine fleet was already able to provide an effective police force. The Italian maritime cities were beginning to open up direct commerce with the Moslem

[20] For the *Poenitentialia*, see J. Tixeront, *Histoire des dogmes*, III, 400–402.
[21] Willibald's *Hodoeporicon*, tr. W. R. Brownlow (*PPTS*, III).
[22] *Commemoratorium de casis vel monasteriis* (*Itinera Hierosolymitana*), I, 2, pp. 303–305.
[23] *Itinerary of Bernard the Wise*, tr. J. H. Bernard (*PPTS*, III [1893]), from A. D. 870.

ports. In the east the ʿAbbāsid caliphate was declining. Its viceroys in Palestine were ready to welcome visitors who brought money into the country and who could be taxed; and when the Ikhshīdids, and after them the Fāṭimids, succeeded to the possession of Palestine, the appearance of good-will increased. It was now not difficult for a pilgrim to take a boat at Venice or Bari or Amalfi which would take him direct to Alexandria or some Syrian port. Most pilgrims, however, preferred to sail in an Italian ship to Constantinople and visit the renowned collection of relics there, and then go on by land to Palestine. Land travel was always cheaper than sea travel, and the Byzantine roads through Anatolia down into Syria were excellent. Most of the pilgrims had no other motive than a pious desire to see the holy places; but that certain holy places endowed the visitor with peculiar spiritual merit was now generally accepted. Shrines such as those of St. James at Compostela in Spain or of the archangel Michael at Monte Gargano in Italy, and all the shrines at Rome itself were held to have this quality, but those connected with the actual life of Christ in Palestine naturally outshone the others. The penitential value of a pilgrimage was also widely recognized. The first pilgrim whose name has survived as having made his journey for definitely expiatory reasons was a nobleman called Fromond who went from France to Jerusalem in the mid-ninth century.[24] In the tenth century we hear of many distinguished criminals who followed his example. The crime of murder in particular needed such an expiation. The system had a practical value, for it removed criminals from the community for several months; and if they survived the arduous journey they returned spiritually refreshed.

The names of the pilgrims that are known to us are all of eminent personages, such as Hilda, countess of Swabia, who died on her journey in 969, or Judith, duchess of Bavaria, sister-in-law to Otto I, who was in Palestine in 970. Amongst the pilgrim-noblemen of the tenth century were the counts of Ardèche, Arcy, and Anhalt, Vienne, Verdun, and Gorizia. Amongst the churchmen were the bishop of Olivola, who made his journey in 920, and the abbots of Aurillac, Saint-Cybar, Saint-Aubin, and Flavigny. St. Conrad, bishop of Constance, made the pilgrimage on three separate occasions, and St. John, bishop of Parma, no less than six. Most of these important travelers were accompanied by a number of

[24] *Peregrinatio Frotmundi* (*Acta sanctorum*, Oct. tom. X, Oct. 24), pp. 847 ff. See E. van Cauwenbergh, *Les Pèlerinages expiatoires et judicaires dans le droit communal de la Belgique au moyen-âge* (Louvain, 1922), *passim*; and M. Villey, *La Croisade: Essai sur la formation d'une théorie juridique* (Paris, 1942), pp. 141 ff.

humbler followers who took advantage of the security that a large and distinguished company offered.[25] It is doubtful if during the early years of the century many poor folk ventured to set out without the protection of some magnate. But in 910 count William I of Aquitaine founded the abbey of Cluny, and in a few decades Cluny became the center of a vast ecclesiastical nexus, closely controlled by the mother-house, which itself owed obedience to the papacy alone. The Cluniacs took an interest in pilgrimage, and soon organized the journey to the Spanish shrines. By the end of the century they were popularizing the journey to Jerusalem and were building hostels along the route for the benefit of poorer pilgrims. They particularly encouraged pilgrims from the neighborhood of their great houses. It was due to their persuasion that the abbot of Stavelot visited Palestine in 990 and the count of Verdun in 997. The great abbot Odilon, though he never succeeded in making the journey himself, induced many of his friends to go. The dukes of Normandy and the counts of Anjou both were devoted patrons of the Cluniac movement; and we find Fulk Nerra of Anjou making three journeys to Palestine, all well merited by his sins, and Richard III of Normandy collecting alms for the Palestinian shrines, which his brother duke Robert visited at the head of a large company in 1035. But it was the poorer folk that the Cluniacs particularly helped and enabled to go east in smaller independent groups.[26]

Political events aided the Cluniacs in their work. About the beginning of the eleventh century the mad Fāṭimid caliph al-Ḥākim began to persecute the Christians throughout his dominions and to destroy their churches, including the church of the Holy Sepulcher itself; and during his reign pilgrimage was dangerous. Later, he persecuted the Moslems as well; and after his death there was a reaction in favor of religious toleration. The Byzantine emperor Romanus III made a treaty with al-Ḥākim's successors allowing him to rebuild the Sepulcher, and the treaty was confirmed in the time of Constantine IX, who sent his own workmen to set about the work.[27] The frontier between Byzantium and the Fāṭimid caliphate now ran to the Mediterranean near the town

[25] L. Bréhier, *L'Église et l'orient au moyen-âge: les croisades* (Paris, 1928), pp. 32–33; J. Ebersolt, *Orient et occident*, I, 72–73.

[26] For the influence of Cluny see J. H. Pignot, *Histoire de Cluny* (Paris, 1868), II, 108ff. and J. Longnon, *Les Français d'outremer* (Paris, 1929), pp. 2–5. Its importance has been challenged by A. Fliche, *L'Europe occidentale de 888 à 1125* (Paris, 1930), p. 551, but reasserted by A. Hatem, *Les Poèmes épiques des croisades* (Paris, 1932), pp. 43ff.

[27] See G. Schlumberger, *L'Épopée byzantine*, III (Paris, 1905), 23, 131, 203–204. On the caliph al-Ḥākim see below, chapter III.

of Tortosa; and the frontier-officials were used to pilgrims. In Europe the Hungarians were converted to Christianity in 975; and in 1019 the emperor Basil II, the "Bulgar-slayer", annexed the whole Balkan peninsula to the empire. A pilgrim from central Europe or Flanders could therefore travel through the lands of the western emperor till he reached the Hungarian frontier near Vienna. He then crossed Hungary to the Byzantine frontier-town of Belgrade, and on through the Byzantine empire past Constantinople till he reached the Fāṭimid frontier between Latakia and Tortosa. It was a simple journey and, for a pilgrim that went by foot, not at all expensive. Pilgrims from France or Italy preferred to go by road to Apulia and cross the narrows of the Adriatic, a short and cheap sea-journey, to Dyrrachium and so on to Constantinople by the Via Egnatia, now cleared of all dangers from Bulgarian marauders. There were several hospices in Italy at which a pilgrim could stay, and a great hospice at Melk in Austria. At Constantinople the hospice of Samson was reserved for western pilgrims and the Cluniacs had a hospice nearby, at Rodosto (Tekirdagh); and at Jerusalem, when many of the older hospices fell into decay the merchants of Amalfi built about 1070 a great hospital dedicated to St. John the Almsgiver.[28]

Sea routes were not abandoned, but were used now mainly by pilgrims from the Scandinavian sphere. From the early years of the tenth century the emperor at Constantinople recruited Norsemen for his palace guard, and by the end of the century they were numerous enough to form a separate regiment, the Varangian Guard. Many Scandinavians would come, either by the old route up and down the Russian rivers and across the Black Sea, or still more, now, past Britain and the Strait of Gibraltar, to Constantinople, and after serving for some years in the emperor's armies and amassing a comfortable fortune there, they would visit Palestine before returning home. Others came merely to visit the holy places. A Varangian officer called Kolskeggr went to Palestine in 992. Harald Hardråde, most illustrious of the Varangians, was there in 1034. The missionary to Iceland, Thorvald Kódransson Vidtförli, made a pilgrimage to Jerusalem about the year 990. After Olaf Tryggvesson, first Christian king of Norway, mysteriously vanished in 1000, many Norse pilgrims claimed to have seen him at the holy places. The Norse princes were particularly given

[28] Ordericus Vitalis, *Historia ecclesiastica* (ed. Le Prevost), II, 64; William of Tyre (*RHC*, I), pp. 872–876; Aimé of Monte Cassino, *Chronicon* (ed. Delarge), p. 320. See Paul Riant, *Expéditions et pèlerinages des scandinaves en terre sainte* (Paris, 1865), p. 60.

to the crime of murder, and expiatory pilgrimages were therefore common amongst them. The half-Dane, Svein Godwinsson, set out barefoot with a party of Englishmen in 1051 to seek pardon for a murder, and died of exposure while crossing the mountains of Anatolia. Lagman Gudrödsson, king of the Isle of Man, who killed his brother, found peace for his conscience at Jerusalem. Most of the Scandinavian visitors made a round trip, coming by way of Gibraltar and returning by the Russian route.[29]

By the middle of the eleventh century pilgrimages were undertaken on an enormous scale. An endless flow left western Europe in the early spring, uncertain when they would return, traveling sometimes in tiny groups and sometimes in parties of a thousand or more.[30] The great pilgrimage led by German bishops in 1064 to 1065 was said to number over ten thousand men and women and probably in fact numbered seven thousand. It seems that great lords were allowed to bring an armed escort, so long as it was well under control. But most pilgrims traveled unarmed. The pilgrimage was seldom risky to life, apart from the hazards of the weather in the Anatolian mountains. The roads were usually well policed, and food and water were usually available. The pilgrims were usually given a cordial reception by the local Orthodox at Jerusalem.[31] But there were difficulties at times. When the Normans began to attack the Byzantine possessions in southern Italy, Norman pilgrims were treated very coldly by the emperor's officials.[32] There were occasional troubles in Syria when some local emir rebelled against Fāṭimid rule. In 1055 the Byzantine governor of Latakia refused an exit-visa to bishop Lietbert of Cambrai, on the grounds that it was not safe for Christians to cross the frontier. The bishop, furious at this solicitude, was forced to go instead to Cyprus. He met several hundred Christians who had been turned out of Palestine.[33] The great German pilgrimage, which crossed into Moslem territory against the advice of the Byzantines, found conditions there very unsatisfactory. It must, indeed,

[29] The Scandinavian pilgrimages are fully described by Riant, *op. cit.*, pp. 97–129.

[30] The names of many of the pilgrims are given in Bréhier, *op. cit.*, pp. 42–45, and Ebersolt, *op. cit.*, I, 75–81.

[31] The pilgrim, Ingulf (Fell, *Rerum anglicarum scriptores*, I, 74), says that in 1065 the patriarch Sophronius received him and his company with music and illuminations.

[32] Bréhier, *L'Église et l'orient*, p. 42, assumes that the "schism" of 1054 created ill-will between Byzantium and the western pilgrims. It is far more likely that the Norman invasions of southern Italy made the Byzantines suspicious of pilgrims. The Normans had first come to southern Italy as pilgrims to Monte Gargano.

[33] *Vita Lietberti*, in d'Achery, *Spicilegium sive collectio veterum aliquot scriptorum* (1st ed., Paris, 1655–77), IX, 706–712. *Miracula S. Wulframni Senonensis* (*Acta sanctorum ordinis S. Benedicti*, saec. III), I, 381–382, tells of Christians being ejected from Jerusalem in 1056.

have been difficult for the Moslem authorities to find food for so large and sudden an invasion, and the numbers roused resentment amongst the local Moslem population. There was trouble near Tripoli and a serious skirmish at Ramla.[34] There were perpetual complaints of taxes and tolls levied by local authorities on travelers. The emperor Basil II told his customs-officials to levy a tax on pilgrims and their horses. Pope Victor II asked the empress Theodora to rescind the order in 1056. At the same time he complained that her officials levied taxes at the Holy Sepulcher itself. Presumably the Byzantines claimed the right to collect money there to pay for the work of restoration.[35]

Such inconveniences were not frequent. Throughout the middle years of the eleventh century the travelers grew in numbers, encouraged by the ecclesiastical authorities. Eleventh-century literature bears frequent testimony to the desirability of the pilgrimage. The pilgrim was the exile of Christ, *peregrinus Christi*, or the poor man of Christ, *pauper Christi*.[36] It seemed to the German pilgrims of 1064 that their coming to Jerusalem was the fulfilment of a prophecy.[37] Pope Gregory VII condemned Cencius, who led a revolt against him in 1075, to the pilgrimage to Jerusalem.[38] There seems to have been some doubt how effective one pilgrimage alone was in remitting the sins of great sinners. In 1049 the citizens of Narni saw a multitude of men dressed in glowing raiment passing through their town, and one of these radiant beings declared that they were all souls who had earned everlasting felicity, but were still obliged to continue without ceasing on an endless penitential journey to the holy places. So essential was it considered now to make the pilgrimage that the heroes of the past were provided by popular legend with a journey to the Holy Land. King Arthur was said to have visited Jerusalem, while the pilgrimage of Charlemagne came to be given universal credence.[39] The

[34] For this pilgrimage, which is described in *Annales Altahenses majores*, see E. Joranson, "The Great German Pilgrimage of 1064–1065," *The Crusades and Other Historical Essays Presented to D. C. Munro* (New York, 1928), pp. 3–43. On the question of armed pilgrimage and the relation of pilgrimage to the First Crusade see below, chapter VII, p. 243–244.

[35] *Letter of Victor II* (wrongly attributed to Victor III, *PL*, CXLIX), cols. 961–962; P. Riant, *Inventaire critique des lettres historiques des croisades* (Paris, 1881), pp. 50–53.

[36] For these terms, see Villey, *La Croisade*, p. 86, and P. Rousset, *Les Origines et les caractères de la première croisade* (Neuchatel, 1945), pp. 40–41.

[37] See note 34 above.

[38] Hefele-Leclercq, *Histoire des conciles*, V, 1, p. 150. Cencius did not go to Jerusalem, but instead fled to the protection of Henry IV.

[39] G. Paris, *Histoire poétique de Charlemagne* (Paris, 1905), pp. 337ff., and L. Bréhier, "Les Origines des rapports entre la France et la Syrie," *Congrès français de Syrie* (Marseilles, 1919), II, 36–38. The anonymous Norman author of the *Gesta francorum* describes the route that Charlemagne took as far as Constantinople. The Arthur legend was probably copied from that of Charlemagne. See G. Paris, "La Chanson du pèlerinage de Charlemagne," *Romania*, IX (1880), 1ff.

effect of it all was to create and sustain in the west an undying interest in the Holy Land and the road to Jerusalem, and to rouse indignant interest when the road seemed likely to be blocked.

The Turkish invasions of Palestine from 1071 onwards did not at first interfere much with the pilgrims. The first Turkish governors, Atsïz and Artuk, were cultured princes who had no wish to suppress a harmless source of revenue. But the collapse of Fāṭimid power meant the emergence of a number of petty emirates along the road from the north, and every petty emir wished to extract his share of tolls. Every few miles there was a new greedy and officious tax-collector; and when Artuk died in 1091, his sons were less complaisant, fearing that the Christians were working for a Fāṭimid restoration; and a large number of priests were exiled from the city. The Turkish invasions of Anatolia increased the difficulties of pilgrims. In the course of wars and raids and migrations of whole districts, roads went out of use, villages decayed, bridges fell down, and wells dried up or were deliberately blocked.[40] A few well armed and equipped expeditions like that of count Robert I of Flanders in 1089 succeeded in penetrating through to the Holy Land; but most pilgrims suffered the fate of Peter the Hermit who was turned back with insults by the Turks while he was still on his way.[41]

That such difficulties should arise at a moment when the pilgrimage to Jerusalem played so large a part in the minds of western Europeans gave a great impetus to any movement that advocated direct action. Pope Urban's phenomenal success when he preached the crusade at Clermont was due to his combination of the idea of pilgrimage with that of the holy war.

[40] See articles "Tutush" by Houtsma and "Ortoḳids" by E. Honigmann in the *Encyclopaedia of Islām*, III, 1001 ff.; also C. Cahen, "La Ṭuğrā Seljuḳide," *Journal asiatique*, CCXXXIV (1943–1945), 167–172. On the Fāṭimid collapse see below, chapter III, pp. 92–94. For the effects of the Selchükid invasions, see below, chapter V, p. 160.

[41] Anna Comnena, *Alexiad*, VII, 6 (ed. Leib, II, 105). The exact date of his pilgrimage is uncertain. H. Hagenmeyer, *Le Vrai et le faux sur Pierre l'hermite* (tr. Furcy Raynaud, Paris, 1883), pp. 64–74.

Jerusalem: The Dome of the Rock

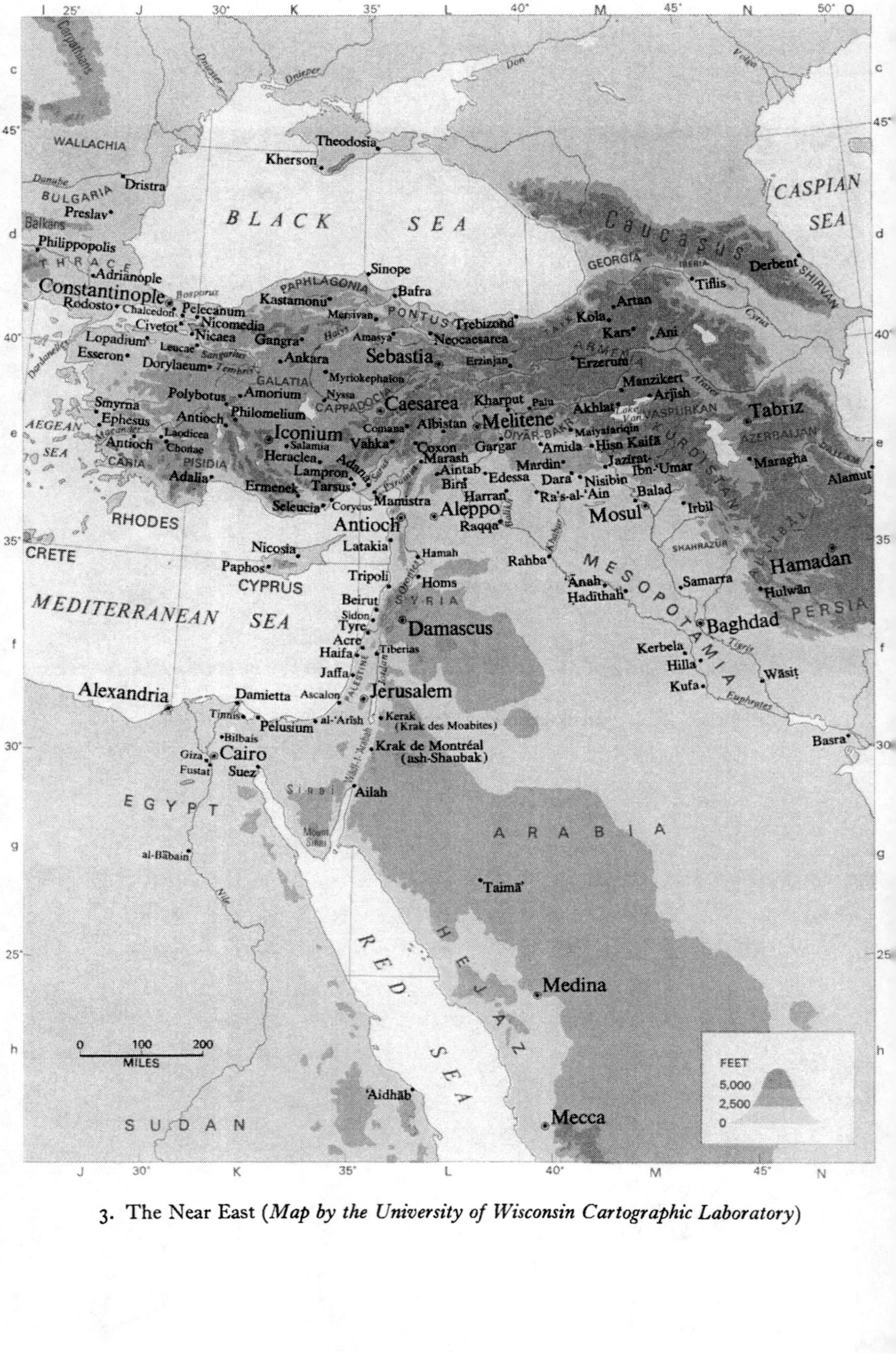

3. The Near East (*Map by the University of Wisconsin Cartographic Laboratory*)

III

THE CALIPHATE AND THE ARAB STATES

Under the rule of the first caliphs, or "successors" of the prophet Mohammed, at Medina, the tribesmen of Arabia, organized into the armies of Islam, had rapidly overrun Syria, Iraq, western Persia, and Egypt, and established themselves in garrison cities in the conquered provinces. Dissensions between the tribesmen and their governors led to the murder of the third caliph, 'Uthmān, in 656, and a civil war, which ended with the constitution of a new caliphate at Damascus (661), hereditary in the house of the Meccan clan of Umaiyah, and dependent for its power largely upon the Arab tribesmen of Syria. Under the Umaiyad caliphs the Arab empire continued its expansion into eastern Persia, Turkestan, northwestern Africa, and Spain, in spite of repeated insurrections among the tribesmen in Iraq and growing discontent in many sections of the general population. The burden of defending so vast an empire ultimately exhausted the Syrian Arabs, whose unity was, in addition, disrupted, like that of the Arab settlements in every province from Spain to Khurasan, by violent feuds between the rival factions of Muḍar and Yaman, or "northern" and "southern" Arabs. The Umaiyad caliphate succumbed in 750 to a general revolt of the Yaman faction combined with other

For the general history of the Arabs, see Sir William Muir, *The Caliphate, its Rise, Decline, and Fall* (Edinburgh, 1915; reprinted 1924), and P. K. Hitti, *History of the Arabs* (5th ed., New York, 1951). For Egypt and the Fāṭimids: G. Wiet, *L'Égypte arabe, de la conquête arabe à la conquête ottomane* (Paris, 1937; vol. IV of *Histoire de la nation égyptienne*, ed. G. Hanotaux), and the appropriate titles listed in the bibliographical note to chapter IV. The *Encyclopaedia of Islām* (Leyden-London, 1908-1938, 4 vols. and *Supplement*; revision in progress) has useful articles on dynasties, sovereigns, and religious sects. For Syria in the tenth century: M. Canard, *Histoire de la dynastie des H'amdanides de Jazira et de la Syrie*, vol. I (Algiers, 1951). For the eleventh century the principal sources are: Ibn-al-Qalānisī, *Dhail ta'rīkh Dimashq* [*Continuation of History of Damascus*] (ed. H. F. Amedroz, Leyden, 1908); Kamāl-ad-Dīn ibn-al- 'Adīm, *Zubdat al-ḥalab fī ta'rīkh Ḥalab* [*History of Aleppo*], vol. I (ed. Sāmī ad-Dahhān, Damascus, 1951); Yaḥyâ al-Anṭākī, *Continuation of the History of Eutychius* (ed. and tr. I. Kratchkowsky and A. A. Vasiliev, *Patrologia Orientalis*, vols. XVIII and XXIII, Paris, 1924, 1932). The data from the latter sources, together with contemporary Greek and Armenian materials relating to northern Syria, are summarized by E. Honigmann, *Die Ostgrenze des byzantinischen Reiches* (vol. III of A. A. Vasiliev, *Byzance et les Arabes*, Brussels, 1935).

discontented elements, both Arab and non-Arab, and was replaced by a third line of caliphs, descended from the prophet's uncle al-'Abbās, who built themselves a new capital at Baghdad.

The strength of the 'Abbāsid caliphate rested, politically, upon the Arab and Islamized population of Iraq (with an important exception, to be noted later) and the Arab colonists and Iranian aristocracy of Khurasan. Militarily, it depended on a standing army drawn from Khurasan, of mixed but mainly Arab composition, stationed in Iraq and capable of reinforcement from its home province in case of need. Such elements of opposition as existed in Syria and Egypt were disabled by the persistence of the Muḍar-Yaman feud, and suppressed in northwestern Africa by the settlement of a Khurasanian garrison in Kairawan. With the growth of urban civilization and the development of trade, the Arab settlers in the former garrison cities of Iraq were transformed into townsmen and ceased to constitute effective military units. Those of Syria and upper Mesopotamia continued, under 'Abbāsid command, their established routine of frontier warfare against the Greeks in Anatolia. On the other hand, the tribesmen in central and northern Arabia and in the Syrian desert, no longer held in check by imperial armies of their own kin, or able to find an outlet for their martial spirit by enrolment in the paid forces of the empire, were reverting to their former rebelliousness towards the civil authorities in Iraq and to their traditional occupation of raiding.

The latent conflict between Iraq and Khurasan, on the one hand, and between the settled population of Iraq and the bedouins (Arabic, *badawī,* desert-dweller), on the other, flared into action on the occasion of yet another civil war in 812–813, resulting from Hārūn ar-Rashīd's ill-advised attempt to give his son al-Ma'mūn an independent position in Khurasan, outside the control of his elder brother, the caliph al-Amīn. Al-Ma'mūn owed his victory to a new Khurasanian army, more pronouncedly Iranian in composition and leadership, with which he reconquered Iraq, Mesopotamia, Syria, and Egypt, and restored some semblance of control over the tribesmen. The price he paid for it was the virtual abandonment of the direct rule of the caliphate over Persia and the eastern provinces. The government of Khurasan was made over to the commander-in-chief Ṭāhir, and it, together with the chief military command in Baghdad, became hereditary in his family.

Partly in order to offset the power of the Tāhirids, the caliphs now formed a private guard in which Turkish slaves, captured in frontier warfare on the steppes, soon predominated. A new cantonment for these troops was built in 835 sixty miles north of Baghdad, at Samarra, which for some sixty years replaced Baghdad as the seat of administration. Isolated among the Turkish guards, the caliph fell increasingly under their control, and between 861 and 870 no fewer than four caliphs perished by assassination or in armed conflict with the Turks. The prestige and authority of the ʿAbbāsids, already shaken by the civil war of 812 and the murder of the caliph al-Amīn by the Khurasanians, could scarcely survive these calamities. The lesson that power was to be had for the taking by the strong and the skillful unleashed in every part of their former empire ambitions which found support among the victims of the misgovernment and financial oppression resulting from anarchy at the center. In Persia the Ṭāhirids were swept away by local risings; in the Arab provinces the beneficiaries were the Turkish governors and the bedouins.

In the struggle that followed, rivalry between the Turks and the bedouins was, after the manner of political forces in the Near East, coupled with or colored by differences of religious allegiance. During the Umaiyad caliphate the bedouin revolts in northern Arabia and Mesopotamia had as a rule been organized under the banner of the Khārijite "heresy", which maintained an extreme puritan and equalitarian doctrine and found a sympathetic echo in tribal democracy and resistance to external control. At the other pole, the tribesmen of Kufa in lower Iraq constituted themselves the defenders of the hereditary right to the caliphate of the house of ʿAlī, son-in-law of the prophet and father of his only surviving descendants, and fourth caliph, who had transferred the capital from Medina to Kufa at the time of the first civil war.

For a century or so the cause of the *Shīʿah* or "Party" of ʿAlī gained little acceptance outside Kufa and its dependencies, except in the Yemen and as a cloak for revolutionary coteries. Under the early ʿAbbāsid caliphs it began to supplant Khārijism as the religious substrate or symbol of revolt; and after the civil war between al-Amīn and al-Maʾmūn a Shīʿite rebellion in Kufa in 815 found general support among the bedouins of northern Arabia and the desert fringes of Iraq. From then onwards bedouin movements became increasingly associated with the profession of Shīʿism in one or other of its sectarian varieties, and more especially of the activist — and, from the point of view of the moderate Shīʿites, heterodox — wing, known as the Ismāʿīlites.[1] Among the negro slaves also, Shīʿism gained a following, and many bedouins joined the negroes in the great slave revolt which from 869 to 883 convulsed lower Iraq. Scarcely was this put down than the Ismāʿīlite tribesmen of northeastern Arabia and the Syrian desert, under the name of Qarmaṭians or "Carmathians" (Arabic, *qarāmiṭah* or *qarmaṭī*), carried fire and slaughter from Basra to Antioch and only in 907 were reduced temporarily to quiescence.

The Turkish principalities in the Arab provinces, on the other hand, were founded by generals who combined a supple independence with rigorous Sunnite orthodoxy. Since the reign of al-Ma'mūn's successor, al-Muʿtaṣim, the practice had grown up of assigning whole provinces as fiefs to Turkish generals at the capital. The fiefholder drew the revenue from the crown estates in the province, and was represented in its actual government by a deputy. It was in this way that the Turkish *mamlūk* (trooper of slave origin) Aḥmad ibn-Ṭūlūn, appointed deputy-governor of Egypt in 868, obtained the leverage by which he not only built up a factually independent power there, though officially he remained deputy-governor to the end of his life, but added Syria to his dominions and founded a dynasty which lasted until 905. Such an independent power was, however, maintained, not by enrolling the support of the local population, but by creating a private army of Turkish mamluks strong enough to hold the imperial forces at bay.

Even when Turkish generals seized provinces for themselves, however, as they did also in Mesopotamia, Armenia, and elsewhere, they did not thereby renounce their allegiance to the caliph; on the contrary, they formally petitioned for a diploma of investiture and duly received it, sometimes with the grant of hereditary rights in addition. Fictitious in a sense though such diplomas may have been, they served two genuine purposes. One was of internal order: to legitimize the proceedings of the law courts and the decisions of the qadis (Arabic singular, *qāḍī*, magistrate) and other religious officials appointed by the local rulers, as well as marriages, inheritances, and bequests. The other was political: to check the spread of Shīʿism and the resurgence of the bedouins in those areas where the caliph's forces were themselves unable to intervene.

[1] The Ismāʿīlites were so called from their belief in the imamate of Ismāʿīl, the eldest son of the sixth imam, Jaʿfar aṣ-Ṣādiq. The term covered at this time a medley of local groups, of which the "Carmathians" were one, and is not to be equated completely with the systematic Ismāʿīlism of the Fāṭimids. See below and chapter IV, *passim*.

But such a system of uneasy and suspicious alliances against a common enemy could not stop up all the cracks in the decaying fabric. Before the end of the ninth century, Shīʿism had gained a strong and permanent base in Persia, in the highlands southwest of the Caspian Sea, known as Dailam, and another permanent base in the highlands of the Yemen. It was not only in such relatively remote regions, however, nor only amongst the bedouins that Shīʿism continued to make headway. The discontent with the prevailing misrule and disorder, and the millennial aspirations which had broken out in the Qarmaṭian risings, found an echo among educated and pious citizens, philosophers, and men of letters, even while they abhorred the crude violence and excesses of the peasantry and tribesmen. The opportunity offered by this widespread dissatisfaction with the prevailing state of affairs was seized by the leaders of a reorganized and systematized Ismāʿīlite propaganda on behalf of a "Hidden Imam", whose headquarters at Salamyah, east of Homs, were on the fringes of Ṭūlūnid territory. Here there was planned the audacious scheme which, repeating the method by which the ʿAbbāsids had seized the caliphate, but in the reverse direction, was aimed at their overthrow. An enterprising Ismāʿīlite missionary from the Yemen had already gained a footing among the Berber hillmen of Tunisia; and from this base, utilizing the reserves of Berber manpower and Egypt as a stepping-stone, with the active or passive aid of partisans in all provinces, a Shīʿite universal empire was to inaugurate the reign of justice under the house of the prophet.

The first steps were successfully accomplished. Fleeing from Salamyah before the Qarmaṭian ravagers, and eluding the agents of the restored ʿAbbāsid government of Egypt, the "Hidden Imam" made his way to northwestern Africa; there, in 909, after the victory of his missionary's Berber army, he inaugurated the Fāṭimid caliphate in Tunisia, taking for himself the millennial title of *al-Mahdī*. But the next step miscarried; twice, in 915 and 921, the ʿAbbāsid armies, in a last flicker of imperial power, drove the Fāṭimid invaders out of Egypt, and before the attempt could be renewed the Fāṭimids were involved in a long and dangerous Berber rising at home. It was only in 969 that at last Egypt was occupied, almost without opposition, by a Fāṭimid general, to become, for the next two hundred years, the seat of their rival caliphate.

Much, of course, had happened in the meantime, and the distribution of forces which now confronted the Fāṭimids in Asia bore no resemblance to the situation in 909. The ʿAbbāsid caliphate, as a political power, no longer existed. Exhausted by the military effort involved in checking the Qarmaṭians and in recovering and holding Egypt, and weakened by financial disorders and factional rivalries in the imperial forces, it had been unable to prevent the reëmergence of local dynasties and the revival of military ambitions. Egypt had again become the seat of a factually independent Turkish dynasty, founded by an officer of the former Ṭūlūnid forces, Muḥammad ibn-Ṭughj, surnamed al-Ikhshīd, whose government embraced also Damascus and the Hejaz. The Arab tribes of northern Syria and Mesopotamia were organized under the chiefs of the house of Ḥamdān, whose two principalities, based on Mosul and Aleppo, remained linked by fraternal ties. In northeastern Arabia the Qarmaṭian state of Bahrain (the Hasa coast) still maintained relations with the tribes of the Syrian desert. In western Persia the Dailamites, having broken out of their mountains and ravaged the settled provinces, had at length been brought under the organized control of three brothers of the house of Buwaih. The Buwaihids, whose relations with each other in the first and second generations were marked by a rare spirit of concord, established themselves in a bloc of principalities extending along the eastern frontiers of Iraq from the Caspian Sea to the Persian Gulf, and thus cut the caliphate off from the only major Sunnite power in Asia, the Sāmānids of Khurasan and Transoxiana.[2]

Two features distinguished this second disintegration of the ʿAbbāsid empire in the tenth century from its earlier disruption in the second half of the ninth. One was the relatively greater strength and more organized character of the new states. This fact, together with the divisions in the caliphs' armies, had its effect on their attitude towards the caliphate itself, and led to a struggle between the rival principalities to establish their control over the caliphs. The competition was won by the Dailamites, when the Buwaihid prince of Khuzistan, Muʿizz-ad-Daulah, entered Baghdad and annexed Iraq to his principality in 946. In the second place, all the new dynasties — with the exception of the Ikhshīdids in Egypt and the Kurds in Diyār-Bakr and northwestern Persia — were Shīʿites. That, in such circumstances, the Buwaihids did not dethrone the ʿAbbāsid caliphs was probably due to political calculation; the possible cost in Sunnite rebellion and administrative disorder, since the official classes were over-

[2] On the Buwaihids and Sāmānids, see below, chapter V.

whelmingly Sunnite, was too high a price to pay, and being themselves uninhibited by any respect for ʿAbbāsid authority they had no wish to set up a new spiritual authority with which they would have to share their power.

The Fāṭimids, therefore, after their conquest of Egypt, found themselves confronted in Asia, not by a discredited government of Sunnite caliphs against whom they could rally the forces of Shīʿism, but by successive layers of Shīʿite principalities, extending without interruption to the frontiers of Khurasan. And although the Ḥamdānids of Aleppo and the Qarmaṭians of Bahrain were not opposed in principle to recognizing the spiritual suzerainty of the Fāṭimid caliphs, they were far from ready to submit to their temporal control; while the Buwaihids, belonging to a rival Shīʿite sect which denied the spiritual and doubted even the genealogical claims of the Fāṭimids, now found their tolerant patronage of the ʿAbbāsid caliphate paying a political dividend in support against the expected advance of the Fāṭimid armies.

In fact, however, the Fāṭimids were never to challenge Buwaihid dominion in Iraq. During the whole of the century following their conquest of Egypt they were engaged in a never-ending and finally unsuccessful effort to establish their control over Syria. Since it was this struggle — with the added complications of Turkoman immigrations and Selchükid principalities, to be described in a later chapter[3] —which determined the general features of the internal political life of Syria in the century preceding and into the period of the crusades, it is necessary to describe here in some detail its course and consequences.

The main factor underlying the confused political history of Syria during this period was the recovery of the Arab tribes from the severe control maintained by the ʿAbbāsid governors and their agents after the fall of the Umaiyad caliphate. The major tribal confederations had, however, remained intact; these were now the Yamanī or "southern" Arab groups of Ṭaiy (or Ṭaiyiʾ) in Palestine and Kalb in central Syria, and the Qaisī or "northern" groups of Kilāb in northern Syria and Numair and ʿUqail in Mesopotamia. All these groups had relations with the Qarmaṭians, and both Ṭaiy and Kalb took part in the Qarmaṭian risings at the beginning of the tenth century. In 944 the Ḥamdānid chief Saif-ad-Daulah, himself descended from the old-established Mesopotamian tribe of Taghlib, seized Aleppo from the Ikhshīd and established an independent Syro-Mesopotamian principality. After

[3] See below, chapter V.

long struggles with the Qaisī tribes he gained the support of Kilāb and ʿUqail, and could also rely on the other tribesmen to take his part against the Turkish government of Egypt, which in turn maintained its hold on Damascus only by coming to terms with the local tribes.

Saif-ad-Daulah, however, devoted most of his energies to warfare with the Greeks, and gained for a time a measure of success which not only enhanced his own reputation but also went far to strengthen the self-assurance and sense of independence of the Arabs. On the other hand, it eventually provoked a Byzantine counterattack which, beginning in 962, penetrated the Islamic defenses more and more deeply and in 968 swept over all northern Syria. For the Fāṭimids, fresh from their triumph over the Greeks in Sicily and at that moment preparing for their descent on Egypt, the Greek invasions were highly opportune; they not only weakened the Ḥamdānids of Aleppo but furnished Fāṭimid propaganda with the theme, which seemed all too evidently justified, that the Fāṭimids were the only Moslem power capable of stopping and throwing back the Greeks. The Fāṭimid caliph al-Muʿizz had also negotiated with the Qarmaṭians of Bahrain, in order to forestall a possible intervention by hostile forces from the east, and in the same year 968 a Qarmaṭian army entered Syria and, with its local Arab allies, exacted tribute from the Ikhshīdid governor of Damascus.

Everything thus seemed to be in train for a rapid Fāṭimid occupation of Syria as soon as Egypt had been conquered. Suddenly, on the advance of the Fāṭimid expeditionary force into Syria, the Qarmaṭian commander, for reasons which have never been fully explained, came to terms with the Ikhshīdid commander. Nevertheless, the Fāṭimid troops entered Damascus at the end of 969 and for five months besieged the Greeks in their newly-recaptured stronghold of Antioch, only to be faced by a coalition of Qarmaṭians, Ikhshīdid troops, and tribesmen, who drove them out of Syria and pursued them into Egypt (971). Not until a second Qarmaṭian attack on Cairo had been beaten off in 974 were the Fāṭimids able to renew the Syrian campaign. In the meantime the Greek raids had been renewed and Aleppo reduced to vassalage; but the final campaign of John Tzimisces into central Syria in 975 was countered by Fāṭimid forces at Tripoli. It was only after three more years of fighting that the independent Turkish commander at Damascus, Aftigin, and his Qarmaṭian allies were defeated by the Fāṭimid caliph al-ʿAzīz, Damascus was annexed, and the Qarmaṭians finally withdrew from the contest.

The effect of this conquest was not so much to establish Fāṭimid rule in southern Syria as to divide Syria into two protectorates: a Byzantine protectorate in the north over Aleppo and its dependencies, with a strongly-held base at Antioch, and an Egyptian protectorate over Damascus and the south, with its principal base at Tripoli. Berber troops of the Fāṭimid army were posted in Damascus, to the detestation of its citizens, and garrisoned the coastal cities, but the countryside was largely out of control. This weakness was no doubt due in some degree to the qualities of the Berber forces, who were no match for disciplined Turkish cavalry and could just hold their own against the Arab tribesmen. But it seems probable that the Fāṭimid caliphs in general placed an excessive confidence in the influence of propaganda. The elaborate organization of the "mission" was the feature by which their administrative system was especially distinguished, the chief missioner (*dā'ī* of dā'īs) being one of the highest officers at the court; and it was for missionary training that the most enduring monument of their rule, the college mosque of al-Azhar, was founded. The assumption that conquest would be facilitated by a thorough preliminary campaign of propaganda had served them well in Tunisia and again in Egypt, but in Syria it was never more than a broken reed. The reason was not that the Syrians rejected their religious claims; on the contrary, with the exception of Damascus, whose stiffly orthodox population was never reconciled to Fāṭimid rule, the citizens and tribesmen, both "northern" and "southern", were in principle more attached to the Fāṭimid than to the 'Abbāsid caliphate and some, especially in the north, were its fervent partisans. For anything on a larger scale than local operations the Fāṭimid government relied to a great extent on the coöperation of the Ṭaiy and Kalb tribes, as the Ḥamdānids relied on the Kilāb. But the division of the country, and the absence of effective control over the tribesmen, fostered the natural appetite for independence amongst the latter, and encouraged others also to aim at independence, or at least autonomy.

From this time, therefore, the history of Syria begins to take on the baffling complexity which characterized it down to the middle of the twelfth century. Not only were the Fāṭimid governors, the Ḥamdānids, and the Greeks of Antioch engaged in a shifting sequence of hostilities and alliances, but lesser chiefs in various parts of the country insinuated themselves into these rivalries and sought to play them off against one another in their own interest. The prefects of Damascus were constantly tempted to exploit for their own profit the hostility of the citizens towards the Berbers and the Fāṭimids; on the other hand, the Ḥamdānids at Aleppo reinsured themselves against their Byzantine suzerains by overtures to the Fāṭimids. But whenever Fāṭimid armies marched on Aleppo, they appealed to Antioch for assistance; and in their hour of most extreme danger, after the forces of Aleppo and Antioch had been routed in two successive campaigns (992, 994) and the city itself was besieged by the governor of Damascus, it was delivered in 995 by the emperor Basil II in person. Basil's subsequent campaigns in Syria, however, failed to weaken the Fāṭimid defenses, and in 1001 the first of a series of ten-year truces between the two empires was arranged. In 1009 a Fāṭimid army from Tripoli supported the succession of a new governor at Aleppo against Basil's protegé. A few years later the Kilābī Arabs, who had grown increasingly restive as the power of the Ḥamdānids weakened, broke out in open rebellion under their chief Ṣāliḥ ibn-Mirdās. He, to gain his ends, made common cause with the supporters of the Fāṭimids, and in 1016 Aleppo submitted for the first time to the rule of a Fāṭimid governor.

It is remarkable that these successes in Syria coincided with the reign of the eccentric Fāṭimid caliph al-Ḥākim (996–1021). In addition to many measures vexatious to his Moslem subjects, al-Ḥākim opened in 1008 a seven-year persecution of Jews and Christians, confiscated the possessions of the churches, and ordered their demolition. Among those destroyed was the Holy Sepulcher at Jerusalem, which was torn down in 1009. In Syria, at least, where the population had suffered from Greek invasions for fifty years, this was the most popular act of al-Ḥākim's administration, although it was followed by an order from Basil prohibiting commercial intercourse between Egyptian and Byzantine territories.

The fragility of the new conquests was soon to be demonstrated. From the first the Fāṭimid government had had to deal with persistent tribal revolts. The most turbulent of its Arab subjects was the very tribe which supplied the bulk of its auxiliary forces, the Ṭaiy of Palestine and the Transjordan. These former allies of the Qarmaṭians revolted in 980, and again in 998 and 1011; their shaikhs, of the house of Jarrāḥ, set up on each occasion as independent princes of Palestine, and on the third renounced the Fāṭimids in favor of the caliphate of the sharīf of Mecca. At the same time or later they also opened negotiations with the Greeks at Antioch, and in 1011 Ibn-Jarrāḥ even began to rebuild the church of the Holy Sepulcher.

The Kilāb, for their part, resented the Fāṭimid occupation of Aleppo, which they regarded as their rightful prize. In 1024, after the death of al-Ḥākim, the Kilābī chief Ṣāliḥ ibn-Mirdās formed a league of Arab tribes on the basis of an agreement to partition Syria among Kilāb in the north, Kalb in the center, and Ṭaiy in the south, and himself occupied Aleppo. The general revolt shook the Fāṭimid government out of its indolence. A strong force sent from Egypt under a Turkish officer, Anushtigin ad-Dizbirī, routed Ṣāliḥ and his Arab allies at al-Uqḥuwānah, on the Lake of Tiberias (1029), and set about reorganizing a stable administration in the south. In the meantime the Byzantine emperor reimposed the Greek tribute on Ṣāliḥ's son and successor at Aleppo (1030), and Greek forces from Antioch, accompanied by the fugitive Ṭaiyī, Ibn-Jarrāḥ, engaged the tribesmen in the north. In 1032 George Maniaces, commanding the Euphrates frontier, seized Edessa (Urfa) from the Kurds of upper Mesopotamia, and subdued the tribesmen of Numair who had seized Harran and Sarūj. In the same year Anushtigin reopened negotiations with Antioch and Constantinople. Hostilities were suspended, but it was not until 1038 that a peace was signed by which, in return for the release of his Moslem prisoners, the emperor obtained permission to rebuild the church of the Holy Sepulcher. Anushtigin, for his part, having agreed to continue payment of the Greek tribute, drove the Kilāb out of Aleppo and reoccupied the rest of the former Ḥamdānid principality.

This was the high-water mark of Fāṭimid power, and it roused extravagant hopes in Cairo. The Buwaihids in Iraq were by now weakened and disorganized by internal conflicts; the "mission" was reorganized and spurred on to fresh efforts; Persia was honeycombed with Fāṭimid agents, who were making converts among all classes in the eastern kingdoms; alliances and ententes were established not only with the Byzantine emperor, but also with the princes of Georgia, the Turks in Central Asia, and even the Hindu rajah of Delhi. But again the Syrian Arabs intervened. On the death of Anushtigin, Aleppo was recovered by the Mirdāsids with Greek support (1042), and the Ṭaiy rebelled once more in Palestine and were not reduced to order until their most turbulent sections were transported a few years later to the Delta. The disproportion between the propagandist aims and the real resources of the Fāṭimids was displayed at this moment by the fantastic episode of al-Basāsīrī at Baghdad. Al-Basāsīrī, a Turkish officer of the last Buwaihid prince, driven out of Baghdad by the Selchükids in 1055, appealed to Cairo for support. After receiving a substantial gift of money and arms, he reëntered Baghdad in December 1058, and forced the ʻAbbāsid caliph to recognize his Fāṭimid rival. But in the circumstances no military support could be sent to him from Egypt or Syria, and a year later the ʻAbbāsid caliph was restored by the Selchükids. The only result of the incident was to encourage the Selchükids in their hostility to the Fāṭimids to take advantage of the violent outbreak of anarchy in Egypt in this same year (1060), which practically put an end to Fāṭimid rule in Syria and left it open to the Turkoman and Selchükid invasions.[4]

Apart from the coastal cities between Ascalon and Tripoli, one relic of Fāṭimid dominion remained in Syria. This was the heretical Ismāʻīlite sect called the Druze (Arabic, Durūz), after the name of the Persian missionary (ad-Darazī), who had brought about their conversion to the new belief in the divinity of the Fāṭimid caliph al-Ḥākim.[5] The origins of the cult and the reasons for its spread are still obscure, but it took root among the mixed population of the highlands south of Lebanon and spread from there into the hill country between the Orontes and Aleppo (called Jabal as-Summāq), in spite of the attempts of both the Byzantine governors and the adherents of "orthodox" Fāṭimid Shīʻism to eradicate it. Extremist Shīʻism had already established itself in various forms in northern Syria during the previous century. The chief of these sects was that of the Nuṣairīs, whose missionaries, favored by the Ḥamdānids, had gained a strong establishment among the sedentary "Yamanī" clans in the Jabal Bahrā' (now called, after the sectaries, Jabal Anṣārīyah), south of Antioch. The Druze sect may perhaps have been intended to serve a political end by linking up with these extremist Shīʻite groups in the north; but apart from theological controversy little or nothing is known of the relations between them at this period. In the event, however, Druzism ebbed back into its original home in Lebanon, and except for adding yet another to the varieties of religious belief represented in Syria, and yet another independent fraction to its political structure, played little part in the history of the next centuries.

The principal cause of the severe, but short-lived, internal crisis in Egypt was the outbreak of armed rivalry among the three divisions of the Fāṭimid army: the Berbers, the Sudanese infantry, and the regiments of Turkish cavalry whom the caliphs had grad-

[4] On the Selchükids, see below, chapter V.
[5] On the Ismāʻīlites, see below, chapter IV.

ually enrolled in their service, and who now numbered some 10,000. Since the caliphs of Baghdad had initiated in the ninth century the practice of constituting regiments of guards of Central Asian Turks, acquired by purchase or as prisoners of war, the superior military qualities of these Turkish "slaves" (mamluks) had made it necessary for all who held or aspired to independent rule in western Asia to do the same, in spite of the political dangers which all too often followed from the practice. Every prince must have his *'askar*, or standing regiment of Turkish guards, varying in number with his resources from some thousands to a few hundreds. But their highly developed *esprit de corps* which made them such a valuable military instrument became also, under weak rulers, a source of danger, leading to conflicts with regiments of other nationalities, mutinies, and open revolts under ambitious generals. One after another, the dynasties and principalities of western Asia during the tenth and eleventh centuries suffered from and eventually succumbed to the violence of their Turkish troops.

It was a conflict of this kind in which the Fāṭimid caliphate now became involved. After seven years of fighting, the Turks, commanded by the Ḥamdānid Nāṣir-ad-Daulah, and allied with the Berber regiments, drove the Sudanese into upper Egypt. Six more years followed during which the countryside was ravaged by the Turks, the Sudanese in the south, and Berber tribesmen from Libya in the north, and Cairo was besieged and looted. After the assassination of Nāṣir-ad-Daulah by his Turkish officers (1073), the caliph al-Mustanṣir, in desperation, called in the aid of his Armenian general Badr al-Jamālī, the governor of Acre. His arrival by sea with his Armenian guard took the Turks by surprise, and he was able to enter Cairo in January 1074 and to put down the turbulent officers and their troops by massacre and other vigorous measures. In three further years of constant campaigning the Sudanese, bedouins, and Libyan Berbers were brought under control, and by 1077 Badr had accomplished his task of restoring peace and stability in Egypt.[6]

During these seventeen years Syria had perforce been left to its own devices. At Damascus the Turkish and Berber troops fought with one another, or against the local militia or the Kalbī Arabs, and no governor could maintain himself between the rival factions. Badr twice attempted the task, in 1064 and 1068, and was twice driven out, and withdrawing to Acre he there set about building up the Armenian guard with which he was afterwards to occupy

[6] On the subsequent rulers of Egypt, see below, chapter IV, pp. 105 ff.

Cairo. The governors of Tripoli and Tyre both broke with the Fāṭimid government in 1070 and made themselves independent — probably for commercial as much as for political reasons. These local events were overshadowed by graver portents. In 1064 the first band of Turkomans entered northern Syria, to take a hand in the conflict between rival Mirdāsid princes for the possession of Aleppo. Other bands followed under different chiefs. When Badr besieged Tyre in 1070 the new ruler called in the aid of one such Turkoman chief, who forced the attackers to retire. Badr himself, shortly afterwards, followed his example; when Nāṣir-ad-Daulah attempted to stir up the Ṭaiyī Arabs against him, he called in a band led by a certain Atsïz to counter their activities. The consequence was that Atsïz occupied Palestine and looted Jerusalem, and after Badr's removal to Egypt besieged and captured Damascus (1075). In the next year he attempted to follow up this success by invading Egypt, but was met and defeated by Badr in February 1077. Badr in turn marched on Damascus but failed to recapture the city in two successive campaigns; after the second, Atsïz surrendered it to the Selchükid prince Tutush, to become the capital of the new Selchükid principality of Syria (1078).

Henceforward Badr, avoiding any conflict with the Selchükid power, devoted himself to the reorganization of Egypt and the restoration of its prosperity. Thanks to his firm and orderly government and that of his son al-Afḍal Shāhānshāh after him, the Fāṭimid caliphate endured for another century. His achievement was even more remarkable, indeed; for the general principles on which he reorganized the administration were so soundly conceived that they remained operative for centuries, notwithstanding wars, revolutions, and dynastic changes. The most striking feature of his system was the combination of military government with civil administration. From this time forward, the Fāṭimid caliphs no longer, or only for rare and brief intervals, were the effective rulers of the country. The ruling power lay in the hands of the military dictator, called the vizir (Arabic, *wazīr*) or, in later times, the sultan (Arabic, *sulṭān*), supported by an army whose officers were paid from military fiefs. Yet, although the government remained a military government at its head, a powerful civil administration was built up, which controlled the entire financial organization, including the payment of the troops, and regulated the distribution of the fiefs.

Scarcely less remarkable is the revolution which Badr and his son introduced into the external policy of Egypt. Whether or not they accepted it as a fact that the Selchükid power put all dreams of territorial expansion out of court, the only military action which they took outside Egypt was to recover its naval bases at Acre, Tyre, and other ports (1089), and to maintain a defensive bridgehead in Palestine. On the approach of the crusaders, Tyre and Sidon were refortified, and Jerusalem was recaptured in 1098 from the Artukid Turkoman chiefs who held it as a Selchükid fief. The assumption that al-Afḍal attempted to negotiate a division of Syria with the crusaders seems to be belied by the fact that the Frankish envoys who went to Cairo in that year were imprisoned. It is more probable that he saw in their establishment in northern Syria a useful counterpoise to the ambitions of the Selchükids.[7]

In effect, Egypt, from being the intended springboard for a universal Shī'ite empire, was re-formed as a closely knit and self-contained kingdom. Although the parties in opposition to the Selchükids in Syria continued to recognize the Fāṭimid caliphate, no serious attempt was made to capitalize on their religious allegiance for political ends. So far from this, indeed, were Badr and al-Afḍal that they would almost seem to have deliberately undermined the whole Fāṭimid mission organization, except in the Yemen. It was an essential article of Ismā'īlite doctrine that the spiritual office inherited by the descendants of 'Alī passed in a direct line from father to son by explicit nomination; and it had hitherto passed always to the eldest, or eldest surviving, son. Thus Nizār, the eldest son of the caliph al-Mustanṣir, was regarded in the mission as his destined successor, and may even have been so proclaimed; and a vigorous militant propaganda on this understanding had already achieved its first successes in Persia by the foundation of the new "Assassin" movement. Yet, on the death of al-Mustanṣir in 1094, al-Afḍal recognized his youngest son as his successor, with the title of al-Musta'lī, and Nizār's revolt in Alexandria was crushed.

It can hardly be supposed that so intelligent a governor as al-Afḍal was not aware that the consequence of this act would be to split the Fāṭimid mission into two rival sections, and that the militant eastern section would support the claim of Nizār. We can only surmise, therefore, that among the reasons for his action was a desire to dissociate the Fāṭimid caliphate in Egypt from the terrorist activities already initiated by the Assassins, and thus to avoid a conflict with the Selchükid sultanate, whose imminent

[7] But on this see below, chapter X, pp. 315–316.

decline he could not, of course, have foreseen.[8] Whether or not he himself was an orthodox Sunnite, as the contemporary Damascus chronicler asserts, it is evident that he was regarded with bitter hostility by the more activist elements among the Ismā'īlites, who eventually compassed his death. But on the other hand he seems to have been concerned to build up the Musta'līan section and mission in the Yemen.

This apparent inconsistency may serve to throw further light on the policy of Badr al-Jamālī and al-Afḍal. Relations between the Fāṭimids and the Yemen go back, as has already been noted, to before the establishment of the Fāṭimid caliphate. But from the middle of the eleventh century they took on a new importance. About this time the maritime trade in the Indian Ocean, which had hitherto generally taken the Persian Gulf route, began, owing to the unsettled state of Persia and Iraq, and the relative stability of Egypt, to adopt increasingly the route via Aden and the Red Sea, where merchandise was disembarked at the port of 'Aidhāb, on the African coast, and transported to the Nile.[9] It is at the same period, in the second half of the eleventh century, that trading relations between Alexandria and Amalfi and Genoa begin to be documented. The connection between these facts is obvious, and certainly did not escape the notice of the rulers of Egypt. That they actively encouraged trade with the commercial cities of Italy by the grant of charters of protection to their merchants is certain, not only from the fragmentary evidences that survive from the years between 1070 and 1120, but from the indisputable documents of the following decades. The existence and fostering of these commercial relations thus contributed on the one hand to the economic prosperity and self-sufficiency of Egypt, and on the other discouraged its rulers from warlike activities which might disturb them. It was only at a later period, when the Egyptian trade had become a firmly established institution, that Saladin, as will be seen, was able to exploit them as an instrument in his struggle with the Syrian Franks.

It should be clear from this survey that there is little justification for the view which represents the conflict between the Sunnite Moslems, or supporters of the 'Abbāsid caliphate, and the Shī'ites, who supported the Fāṭimid caliphate, as the principal or primary cause of the weakness or disunity in the Islamic

[8] Note that even under the Fāṭimid caliphate Sunnism still had a strong following in Egypt, especially, it would seem, in Alexandria.

[9] It is significant in this connection that the Fāṭimids commanded a following on the coasts of Kerman and Baluchistan, as well as in Sind and Gujerat.

world at the time of the First Crusade. It is true that the division existed, and that the Selchükids, as will be shown in a later chapter, made it their professed aim to reunite all Islam in allegiance to the ʿAbbāsids.[10] But the sectarian divergence was not, even after the establishment of the Selchükids, at the bottom of the political and military conflicts which continued to split up western Asia into a network of independent principalities, and least of all in Syria. The fundamental cause was the spirit of particularism and personal and local jealousies, which offered opportunity of personal aggrandizement to ambitious princes, governors, and generals, and because of which every political structure lacked stability and was destined, after the disappearance of the temporary factors that had brought it into being, to end in disruption.

Furthermore, not only did the question of Sunnite or Shīʿite allegiance count, in this atmosphere of *Realpolitik*, for little more than diplomatic form, but — in northern Syria, at least — even the distinction between Moslem and Christian faith had lost much of its former sharpness. After the passing outburst of feeling in the time of al-Hākim, relations between Moslems and Christians seem to have become remarkably easy, and, under the protection of the Byzantine treaties, trade and intercourse between the Greeks and the Syrians were actively pursued. With the establishment of Byzantine governments in Antioch and Edessa, Christian principalities took their place in the normal political framework of Syria and Mesopotamia, and Christian protectorates over Aleppo and parts of inner Syria were not only tolerated, but actually demanded on occasion against Moslem rivals. Moslems and Christians were mingled with one another, especially after the large Armenian immigration into northern Syria; Christians ruled over Moslems, and Moslems over Christians, without serious friction on either side. Greeks and Armenians served in Moslem armies, and Moslems fought against Moslems under Greek generals. It was these facts which determined the comparative indifference of the Moslem princes towards the Latin crusaders when they first arrived in Syria. Their occupation of Antioch and Edessa did no more than restore the *status quo ante*, and even the conquest of Jerusalem and the organization of the kingdom roused few apprehensions, providing, as it did, a buffer between Egypt and inner Syria.

Thus the Egyptian counter-offensive was intended primarily to defend the coastal cities, although on the first occasion al-Afḍal

[10] See below, chapter V.

may have hoped to prevent Jerusalem from falling into the hands of the Franks. It is noteworthy that Jaffa was captured by the Genoese even before the siege of Jerusalem and that the principal object of Baldwin's policy during the first five years of his reign was to gain possession of the seaports, and more especially of the harbor of Acre. That this determined the military objective of the Egyptians seems to be clear from the strategy, such as it was, of their campaigns in 1101, 1102, 1103, and 1105. Again, however, we have most probably to see in this aim not so much the desire to defend their territorial possessions as to preserve their commercial advantages, and above all to prevent the Franks from gaining direct access to the profitable Red Sea trade.[11]

Al-Afḍal had not reckoned with the intervention of the Genoese and Venetian fleets, and the fall of one seaport after another compelled him before long to take a more serious view of the situation. Ascalon, at least, had to be held, both for strategic and for commercial reasons. Its importance as a commercial base to the Franks had been underlined by the fact that, if Ekkehard is to be believed, Godfrey had already made a commercial treaty with it, as well as with Damascus. Consequently, after the failure of the earlier campaigns, al-Afḍal opened negotiations with Tughtigin of Damascus for combined operations in 1105. The failure of this attempt also seems to have convinced him that there was nothing to be gained from an offensive policy toward the Franks, and from this time onwards he contented himself with securing the defense of Ascalon by land and sea, save for occasional sorties by the garrison troops. Even for this purpose, however, an alliance with Damascus had more than merely diplomatic value. After the narrow escape of Ascalon in 1111, when a rebel governor negotiated its surrender to Baldwin, therefore, al-Afḍal acquiesced in the occupation of Tyre by Tughtigin in 1112, and again, after the raid on Egypt during which Baldwin I died (April 1118), the Egyptian and Damascene armies joined in a military demonstration outside Ascalon. But neither these sporadic operations nor the more energetic attempt made by the Egyptian government after al-Afḍal's assassination in 1121 to organize a joint campaign against the Franks implied any real breaking down of the barriers to coöperation. The counter-crusade had to wait on the growth of a psychological or spiritual unity strong enough to overcome the obstacles of regionalism and private interest, and to heal the lingering effects of religious schism.

[11] On Frankish policy at this time, see below, chapters X and XII.

IV

THE ISMĀ'ĪLITES AND THE ASSASSINS

The death of the prophet Mohammed created something in the nature of a constitutional crisis in the infant Moslem community. It was solved by the appointment of Abū-Bakr, one of the leading converts, as "deputy" (Arabic, *khalīfah*) of the prophet, and the creation, almost incidentally, of the great historic institution of the caliphate. There was at the very beginning of the caliphate a group of people who felt that 'Alī, the son-in-law and cousin of the prophet, had a better title to the succession, some of them perhaps from legitimist scruples, most of them for the reason, far more congenial to the Arabian mind, that 'Alī was the best man for the job. This group came to be known as the *shī'atu 'Alī*, the party of 'Alī, and then simply as the *Shī'ah*. In the course of time it gave rise to the major religious schism of Islam. In its origins,

Detailed studies on the Assassins in Syria will be found in E. Quatremère, "Notice historique sur les Ismaëliens," *Fundgruben des Orients*, IV (Vienna, 1814), 339–376; C. Defrémery, "Nouvelles recherches sur les Ismaéliens ou Bathiniens de Syrie," *Journal asiatique*, 5th series, III (1854), 373–421, and V (1855), 5–76; S. Guyard, "Un Grand Maître des Assassins au temps de Saladin," *Journal asiatique*, 7th series, IX (1877), 324–489; B. Lewis, "The Sources for the History of the Syrian Assassins," *Speculum*, XXVII (1952), 475–489. On the parent sect in Persia see J. von Hammer, *Geschichte der Assassinen aus morgenländischen Quellen* (Stuttgart, 1818; English translation by O. C. Wood, *The History of the Assassins*, London, 1835); C. Defrémery, "Documents sur l'histoire des Ismaéliens ou Bathiniens de la Perse," *Journal asiatique*, 5th series, XV (1860), 130–210. For an annotated bibliography of works on the Ismā'īlite and Fāṭimid movements in general see J. Sauvaget, *Introduction à l'histoire de l'orient musulman* (Paris, 1943), pp. 136–139. Among the numerous writings of W. Ivanow on Ismā'īlite doctrine and history mention may be made of his article "Ismā'īlīya," *Encyclopaedia of Islām*, supplement, and his book *A Brief Survey of the Evolution of Ismailism* (Leyden, 1952). While many Ismā'īlite works have come to light and been published in recent years, there is very little of Syrian provenance. Some religious texts were published and translated by S. Guyard in "Fragments relatifs à la doctrine des Ismaélis," *Notices et Extraits*, XXII (1874), 177–428. A legendary and anecdotal Syrian Ismā'īlite biography of Sinān was published, translated, and examined in S. Guyard, "Un Grand Maître. . . ." The Arabic inscriptions of the Syrian Ismā'īlites were edited and discussed by M. van Berchem, "Épigraphie des Assassins de Syrie," *Journal asiatique*, 9th series, IX (1897), 453–501. The main sources for events in Syria are the general Arabic historical works which are examined in B. Lewis's article, cited above, in *Speculum*. Further bibliographical information, including editions, etc., will be found in C. Cahen, *La Syrie du nord à l'époque des croisades* (Paris, 1940), pp. 33–93. The whole problem of the Assassins will be treated at greater length in a book which is now being written by the author of this chapter (Bernard Lewis).

however, the Shī'ah was purely political, consisting only of the adherents of a political pretender, with no distinctive religious doctrine and no greater religious content than was inherent in the very nature of Islamic political authority.[1]

The vast expansion of the Arabs under the early caliphs brought into the Islamic fold great numbers of imperfectly Islamized converts who carried with them from their Christian, Jewish, and Iranian backgrounds many religious and mystical ideas unknown to primitive Islam. These new converts, though Moslems, were not Arabs, and the inferior social and economic status imposed on them by the ruling Arab aristocracy created a sense of grievance which made them a rich recruiting ground for messianic and revolutionary sects. The great increase in numbers among the Arabs during the first century of Islam brought important social differentiations among the conquerors, and many of the Arabs themselves, especially among the sedentarized or semi-sedentarized southern tribes, began to share the resentments of the non-Arab converts. Most of these had traditions of political and religious legitimism, the latter exemplified in the Judaeo-Christian Messiah of the house of David and the Zoroastrian *Saoshyant* of a God-begotten line through which the divine light is transmitted from generation to generation. Once converted to Islam, they were readily attracted by the claims of the house of the prophet as against the ruling caliphs, who were associated for them with the existing regime of Arab aristocratic hegemony. All new faiths need their martyrs, and the emergent Shī'ite heresy was watered with blood by the murder of 'Alī in 661 and the dramatic slaying of his son Ḥusain and his family at Kerbela in 680.

The fusion between the pro-'Alid party and the nascent heresies did not take long. In 685 one Mukhtār, a Persian Moslem of the Arab garrison city of Kufa, led a revolt in favor of an 'Alid pretender, and after the disappearance and reputed death of the latter, preached that he was not really dead but was in concealment, and would in course of time return and establish the rule of justice on earth. Here for the first time we find a clear statement of the characteristic Shī'ite doctrine of the *Mahdī*, the divinely guided one, a messianic personage who, after a period of concealment, will manifest himself and initiate a new era of righteousness and divine law. With Mukhtār and his followers Shī'ism develops from a party to a sect.

During the early years of its development the Shī'ite heresy

[1] See above, chapter III, pp. 83ff.

was extremely fluid, both in doctrine and in organization. Innumerable pretenders appeared, claiming with varying plausibility descent from the prophet or authority from one of his descendants, and, after enriching the description of the awaited Mahdī with some new detail, followed one another into eschatological concealment. Their doctrines varied from moderate, semi-political opposition resembling that of the original pro-'Alids to the most extreme forms of religious heterodoxy, often reflecting gnostic, Manichaean, and even Indian ideas. In different parts of the empire vigorous local variants appeared, crystallized out of Shī'ism by the action of earlier local beliefs. The nominal leadership of the Shī'ah was transmitted from father to son through a series of 'Alid pretenders known to their adherents as imams (Arabic singular, *imām*). These were descended from 'Alī in several different lines. The most active in the Umaiyad period was the line of Muḥammad ibn-al-Ḥanafīyah (d. 700/701), a son of 'Alī by a wife other than Fāṭimah. It was this group that gave rise to the 'Abbāsid revolution and perished in the hour of its victory. More important in the long run were the imams of the line of 'Alī and Fāṭimah, the daughter of the prophet, through their son Ḥusain (d. 680). How far the Fāṭimid pretenders of this time were themselves associated with their more extreme followers is not known. Their relative freedom from molestation by the caliphs and the frequent denunciation of the extremist leaders in the traditions of the imams suggest that the connection was not close.

The first half of the eighth century was a period of intensive activity among the extremists. Countless sects and subsects appeared, especially among the mixed population of southern Iraq and the coasts of the Persian Gulf. Their doctrines varied widely, often recalling the wilder speculations of earlier Near Eastern mysticism, and in the fluid state of the sects transition was easy and frequent from one doctrine and leader to another. The Moslem sources name many heretical leaders of the time who led revolts and were put to death, and attribute to some of them doctrines which were later characteristic of the Ismā'īlites. One group practised the strangling of opponents with cords as a religious duty — an obvious reflection of Indian Thuggee, and a foreshadowing of the "assassinations" of later centuries.[2]

The decisive split between extremists and moderates occurred after the death in 765 of Ja'far aṣ-Ṣādiq, the sixth Fāṭimid imam

[2] See G. van Vloten, "Worgers in Iraq," *Feestbundel . . . aan Dr. P. J. Veth* (Leyden, 1894).

of the line of Ḥusain. Ja'far's successor by primogeniture would have been Ismā'īl. For reasons which are not quite clear, and probably because of his association with the more extreme elements, Ismā'īl was disinherited, and a large part of the Shī'ah recognized his brother Mūsâ as seventh imam. The line of Mūsâ continued until the twelfth imam, who disappeared about 873, and is still the "awaited imam" or Mahdī of the great majority of the Shī'ah at the present day. The followers of the twelve Imams, usually known as *Ithnā'asharī* or Twelver Shī'ah, represent the moderate branch of the sect. Their difference from the main body of Sunnite Islam is limited to a certain number of points of doctrine, which in recent years have become ever less significant.

Around Ismā'īl and his descendants a sect was formed which by its cohesion, organization, and intellectual maturity far outstripped its competitors. In place of the chaotic speculations of the early heresiarchs, a series of distinguished theologians elaborated a system of religious doctrine on a high philosophic level, and produced a literature that is only now beginning to achieve recognition at its true worth. Ismā'īlite doctrine is eclectic, drawing especially on Neoplatonism. Extraneous ideas were introduced into their Islam by means of the so-called *ta'wīl al-bāṭin*, esoteric interpretation, which was one of the characteristic features of the sect and gave rise to the term Bāṭinite, by which it was often known. The Koran (Arabic, *Qur'ān*) and all religious precepts were believed to bear two meanings, one literal and exoteric, the other allegoric or esoteric, and known only to the initiate. After the creation of the world by the action of the universal mind on the universal soul, human history falls into a series of cycles, each begun by a "speaking" imam, or prophet, followed by a succession of "silent" imams. There were cycles of hidden and of manifest imams, corresponding to the periods of persecution and success of the faith. The imams — in the current cycle the heirs of 'Alī through Ismā'īl — were divinely inspired and infallible, and commanded the unquestioning obedience of their followers.

The intellectual influence of Ismā'īlism on Islam was very great indeed. During the heyday of its expansion poets, philosophers, theologians, and scholars flocked to the Ismā'īlite centers and produced works of a high order. Owing to the anti-Ismā'īlite reaction that followed the fall of the Fāṭimids, most of them are preserved only among the Ismā'īlites themselves, and have only recently begun to come to light. A few works of Ismā'īlite inspiration have, however, for long been widely known, and many of the great Arabic and Persian classical authors show at least traces of Ismā'īlite influence. The famous "Epistles of the Sincere Brethren", an encyclopedia of religious, philosophic, and scientific knowledge compiled in the tenth century, is saturated with Ismā'īlite thought, and exercised a profound influence on the intellectual life of Islam from Persia to Spain.

Extremist Shī'ism in its origins was, as we have seen, closely connected with the revolt of those elements which, for one reason or another, were opposed to the established order. Serious and sustained opposition to the theocratic state tended to take the form of heresy against the dominant faith. This was not because scheming men used religion as a cloak or mask for material purposes, but because, in an age when the problems of faith and worship took first place in men's minds, and when the state itself was conceived to be an instrument of the divine law, religion provided the necessary and inevitable expression, in terms of both doctrine and action, of all major differences and discontents. With its strong stress on social justice and reform, its belief in a Mahdī — no vague, eschatological figure, but a rebel leader waiting to strike and to "fill the earth with justice and equity as it is now filled with oppression and tyranny" — Ismā'īlism appealed especially to the growing and discontented urban population. Orthodox polemicists against Ismā'īlism made it quite clear that they regarded the menace of the sect as social no less than religious. Several orthodox sources assert that the Ismā'īlites preached and practised communism of property and women. There is no record of this whatever in Ismā'īlite sources, and, while perhaps true of some of the earlier extremist heresies, it is quite out of keeping with the general tenor of Ismā'īlite thought in the developed stage. There is on the other hand strong reason for believing that the Ismā'īlites were closely associated with the early development of the Islamic craft-guilds, which they attempted to use as an instrument of organization and propaganda.[3]

Another element ready to welcome the new preaching was the nomadic Arab tribes of Arabia and more especially of the Syrian and Mesopotamian border-lands. By the ninth century these had lost the position of power and privilege they had once held in the Islamic state, and were suffering more and more from the consequences of the establishment of Turkish military rule in the cen-

[3] See L. Massignon, articles "Ṣinf," "Shadd," in the *Encyclopaedia of Islām,* and "Guilds (Islamic)," *Encyclopaedia of Social Sciences;* B. Lewis, "The Islamic Guilds," *Economic History Review,* VIII (1937), 20–37.

ters of civilization. A doctrine which impugned the legitimacy and justice of the regime that had ousted them and which gave them a rallying cry for an attack upon it, could count on their willing acceptance.

For the first century and a half of the existence of the sect the imams of the line of Ismāʿīl remained hidden, and were protected from the attention of the authorities by a series of devices. The organization of the sect was run by a hierarchy of missionaries (Arabic singular, *dāʿī*), who preached allegiance to the hidden imams and the newly elaborated doctrine and built up centers of Ismāʿīlite strength in widely separated parts of the Islamic empire. As might be expected, they achieved special success in those places, like southern Iraq, the Persian Gulf provinces, and parts of Persia, where the earlier forms of Shīʿite extremism had already won a following. At the end of the ninth century a branch of the sect known as the Qarmaṭians, or "Carmathians" — their precise relationship with the main Ismāʿīlite body is uncertain — was able to seize power in Bahrain (the Hasa coast of Arabia), establish a republic, and conduct a series of raids on the communications of the ʿAbbāsid empire. A Qarmaṭian attempt to seize power in Syria at the beginning of the tenth century failed, but the episode is significant and reveals some local support for Ismāʿīlism even at that early date.

The final success of the sect came in another quarter. An Ismāʿīlite mission in the Yemen had achieved considerable success by the end of the ninth century, and was able to send missionaries to a number of other countries, including North Africa, where they succeeded so well that in 909 the hidden imam was able to emerge from hiding and establish a Fāṭimid caliphate, challenging the ʿAbbāsids of Baghdad for supremacy in the Islamic world.[4] After a period of incubation in Tunisia, the new empire swept eastward, and in 973 al-Muʿizz, the fourth Fāṭimid caliph, established his new capital of Cairo. The Fāṭimid caliphate at its height included Egypt, Syria, the Hejaz, the Yemen, North Africa, and Sicily, and commanded the allegiance of countless followers in the eastern lands still subject to the ʿAbbāsids of Baghdad. The great college mosque of al-Azhar, founded by the Fāṭimids as the intellectual center of their faith, turned out innumerable missionaries and agents who, under the aegis of the chief daʿi, the head of the religious hierarchy in Cairo, went out to preach and to organize in Iraq, Persia, Central Asia, and India.

[4] On the Fāṭimid caliphate, see above, chapter III, pp. 85 ff.

The Fāṭimid threat to Baghdad was economic as well as religious. The European commercial connections formed by the North African caliphs were retained and extended by the rulers of Cairo. Fāṭimid control of both shores of the Red Sea and of the ports of the Yemen opened the way for Fāṭimid trade and propaganda in India, and deflected a large part of the vital Near Eastern transit trade from Persian Gulf to Red Sea ports.

The very successes of the Fāṭimids brought Ismā'īlism its first serious internal conflicts. The needs and responsibilities of an empire and a dynasty necessarily involved some modifications in the earlier doctrine, and in the elaboration and reorganization of the Ismā'īlite religious system that followed the establishment of the Fāṭimid caliphate, the last links with the old extremist heresies were cut. From the beginning purists were not wanting to complain against the alleged corruption of the faith. The spearhead of resistance was formed by the Qarmaṭians of Bahrain, who, after first supporting the Fāṭimids, turned against them and fought unsuccessfully against the armies of al-Mu'izz in Syria and Egypt. At a later date the Qarmaṭians seem to have returned to the Fāṭimid allegiance and the sect sank into oblivion as a separate entity.[5]

Another schism occurred after the disappearance, in obscure circumstances, of the caliph al-Ḥākim in 1021. A group of Ismā'īlites preached the divinity and "concealment" of al-Ḥākim and, refusing to recognize his successors, seceded from the main body of the sect. The Druzes (Arabic, Durūz), as they are known, after their leader ad-Darazī, made a determined effort to win over the Ismā'īlite sectaries in Syria, and they are still to be found in Lebanon, Syria, and Israel at the present day.[6]

It was during the long reign of the caliph al-Mustanṣir (1036 to 1094) that Ismā'īlism suffered its greatest internal schism. The Fāṭimid empire in its heyday was administered by a civilian bureaucracy, presided over by a civilian vizir (Arabic, *wazīr*),and under the supreme control of the religious and spiritual imam. Since the death of al-Ḥākim, however, the military had been steadily increasing its power at the expense of the caliph and the civil administration. This process of transfer of the center of power was completed in 1074, when the Armenian general Badr al-Jamālī

[5] See M. J. de Goeje, *Mémoire sur les Carmathes du Bahrain et les Fatimides* (Leyden, 1886); B. Lewis, *The Origins of Ismā'īlism* (Cambridge, 1940); W. Ivanow, *Ismaili Tradition concerning the Rise of the Fatimids* (Oxford and Bombay, 1942).

[6] On the Druzes see Silvestre de Sacy, *Exposé de la religion des Druzes*, 2 vols. (Paris, 1838), and above, chapter III, p. 92.

came with his army from Syria to take control of affairs in Egypt. Henceforth the real ruler of Egypt was the *amīr al-juyūsh*, commander-in-chief, a military autocrat ruling through his troops, and the army was the final repository of authority in the state. Just as the ʿAbbāsid caliphs of Baghdad had become the helpless puppets of their own praetorians, so now the Fāṭimids became mere figureheads for a series of military dictators. The military domination of the emirs, some of them not even Ismāʿīlite, and the shrunken stature of the Fāṭimid caliphs were clearly incompatible with the ecumenical ambitions of the Ismāʿīlite sect and organization. Soon the world-wide ambitions of the Ismāʿīlite mission were abandoned, and the descendants of al-Muʿizz became a local Egyptian dynasty — secularized, militarized, and in decay.

Such a change inevitably awoke widespread discontent and opposition among the more active and consistent of the sectaries, the more so since it coincided with a period of extraordinary activity among the Ismāʿīlites in the newly created Selchükid empire in Asia, where, under the leadership of al-Ḥasan ibn-aṣ-Ṣabbāḥ (Persian, Ḥasan-i-Ṣabbāḥ), a veritable Ismāʿīlite renaissance was taking place. Al-Ḥasan was a Persian and, according to an old legend, a fellow student of Omar Khayyám (ʿUmar al-Khaiyām) in the academy of Nishapur. In 1078, already a prominent figure among the eastern Ismāʿīlites, he visited Cairo, where he made contact with the leaders of the sect. Between the future leader of the Assassins and the military autocrat there can have been little in common. The two men soon came into conflict, and, according to some sources, al-Ḥasan was deported from Egypt.

The replacement of Badr al-Jamālī by his son al-Afḍal made little change in the state of affairs, and when, by the death of al-Mustanṣir, al-Afḍal was confronted with the need to choose a successor, his choice was not difficult. On the one hand was Nizār, an adult, already appointed heir by al-Mustanṣir, known and accepted by the Ismāʿīlite leaders; on the other, his brother al-Mustaʿlī, a youth without allies or supporters, who would consequently be entirely dependent on al-Afḍal. It was certainly with this object in mind that al-Afḍal arranged a marriage between his own daughter and al-Mustaʿlī. In choosing al-Mustaʿlī, al-Afḍal split the sect from top to bottom, and alienated, perhaps intentionally, almost the whole of its following in the eastern lands of Islam. Even within the Fāṭimid boundaries there were movements of opposition; the eastern Ismāʿīlites, under the leadership of al-Ḥasan ibn-aṣ-Ṣabbāḥ, refused to recognize the accession of al-Mustaʿlī, and, proclaiming their allegiance to the deposed Nizār and his line, broke off all relations with the attenuated Fāṭimid organization in Cairo. Thus the divergence between the state and the revolutionaries, the first open expression of which was the conflict between al-Muʿizz and the Qarmaṭians at the time of the conquest of Egypt, was complete. It is significant that even those Ismāʿīlites who had remained faithful to al-Mustaʿlī broke away a little later. In 1130, on the death of the caliph al-Āmir at the hands of the Assassins, the remaining Ismāʿīlites refused to recognize the new caliph in Cairo, and regarded al-Āmir's infant son Ṭaiyib as the hidden and awaited imam. The last four Fāṭimid caliphs in Cairo were not recognised as imams, and did not even themselves claim this title. The final extinction of the dynasty at the hands of Saladin can have made little difference to the Ismāʿīlites in the east.[7]

While the Mustaʿlīan branch stagnated in the remoter outposts of Islam, the Nizārites on the other hand began a period of most intensive development, both in doctrine and in political action, and for a while played a vital role in the history of the Near East.

In the eleventh century the growing internal weakness of the Islamic world was revealed by a series of invasions, the most important of which, that of the Selchükid Turks, created a new military empire from Central Asia to the Mediterranean.[8] Social upheaval in such a period of change was inevitable. The new ruling caste of Turkish soldiers replaced or subjugated the Arab and Persian landowners, traders, and bureaucrats who had been the dominating element in earlier times. The military power of the Turks was unchallengeable. But there were other methods of attack, and to the many malcontents of Selchükid Persia Ismāʿīlism, in its new form, once again brought a seductive doctrine of revolution, now associated with a new and effective strategy of attack.

[7] See C. Cahen, "Quelques chroniques anciennes rélatives aux derniers Fatimides," *Bulletin de l'institut français d'arch. or.*, XXXVII (1937), 1–27; S. M. Stern, "The Succession to the Fatimid imam al-Āmir, the Claims of the Later Fatimids to the Imamate, and the Rise of Ṭayyibī Ismailism," *Oriens*, IV (1951), 193–255. After the break with Egypt the main center of the Mustaʿlīan branch was in the Yemen, where many of its followers still live. Many of the Indian Ismāʿīlites refused to accept the "reformed" Ismāʿīlism of al-Ḥasan ibn-aṣ-Ṣabbāḥ, and, reinforced from the centers in the Yemen, developed into an important community. They are known at the present day as Bohras. Mustaʿlīan Ismāʿīlism, often known as the "old preaching", to distinguish it from the "new preaching" of the Assassins, continued in the main doctrinal traditions of the Fāṭimid period, and it is among the Mustaʿlīans of the Yemen and India that most of the Fāṭimid classics have been preserved. With the disappearance of the Mustaʿlīan imams after the break with Egypt on the death of al-Āmir, the leadership of the sect passed to the hereditary chief daʿis, resident in the Yemen and later in India.

[8] On the Selchükids, see below, chapter V.

According to Ismā'īlite tradition Nizār and his son were murdered in prison in Egypt, but an infant grandson was smuggled out to Persia and there brought up by al-Ḥasan ibn-aṣ-Ṣabbāḥ to found a new line of Nizārite imams. Al-Ḥasan and his two successors in the grand-mastership of the Ismā'īlites in Persia, Kiyā Buzurg-Umīd (1124–1138) and Muḥammad (1138–1162), claimed only to be emissaries of the imam, but the fourth grand master, known as al-Ḥasan 'alâ-Dhikrihi-s-Salām (1162–1166), proclaimed himself to be the son of the infant brought from Egypt, and the first of a new cycle of open imams. Nizārite doctrine differs in some particulars from the unreformed Fāṭimid system. The esoteric element is given greater stress at the expense of the exoteric, while the imamate increased in status, under the influence of old oriental "light" beliefs. The imam is a hypostasis of the divine will, which is transferred, from father to son, through the line of imams.

Of greater significance to the outside world was the adoption by the Persian Nizārites of the procedure that has come to be known, after them, as "assassination". Murder as a religious duty was not new to extremist Shī'ism, and was practised as early as the eighth century by the strangler sects of southern Iraq. After the suppression of the stranglers by the Umaiyad authorities nothing is heard of religious as distinct from private or political murder in the Near East until the appearance of the Assassins. Here too, murder clearly has a religious, even a sacramental value. It is significant that the Assassins always used a dagger; never poison, never missiles. Some sources even speak of the grand master's consecrating the daggers of Assassins setting out on a mission. The Ismā'īlites themselves use the term *fidā'ī*, or *fidāwī*, devotee, of the actual murderer, and an interesting Ismā'īlite poem has been preserved praising their courage, loyalty, and pious devotion.[9] The use of this term for the sectaries as a whole, it may be noted in passing, is an error. The name Assassin, by which the sectaries are known in both Moslem and western sources, is now known to be a corruption of *ḥashīshī*, taker of hashish, or Indian hemp, which the sectaries were believed to use in order to induce ecstatic visions of paradise and thereby fortify themselves to face martyrdom. The stories told by Marco Polo and other eastern and western sources of the "gardens of paradise" into which the drugged devotees were introduced to receive a foretaste of the eternal bliss that awaited them after

[9] W. Ivanow, "An Ismaili Ode in Praise of Fidawis," *Journal of the Bombay Branch of the Royal Asiatic Society*, n. s., XIV (1938), 63–72.

the successful completion of their missions are not confirmed by any known Ismā'īlite source.

The open history of the sect begins in 1090, when al-Ḥasan ibn-aṣ-Ṣabbāḥ, by a combination of force and guile, seized the castle of Alamut, in an impregnable fastness south of the Caspian, some two days' march northwest of Kazvin. The adjoining provinces of Dailam and Azerbaijan had long been centers of extremist heresy, and offered a ready recruiting ground from which al-Ḥasan formed his corps of fida'is, the fanatical and utterly devoted instruments of his war of terror against the Selchükids. The numerous Ismā'īlite followers and sympathizers scattered through the Selchükid realms facilitated their task, and before long the Assassins were able to seize other castles in Iraq, in the neighborhood of Isfahan, and in other parts of Persia. By the end of the eleventh century al-Ḥasan commanded a network of strongholds all over Persia and Iraq, a tried and tested corps of devoted murderers, and a "fifth column" of unknown size in all the camps and cities of the enemy. In Alamut, which remained the headquarters of the sect until its capture by the Mongols in the thirteenth century, the grand master presided over a hierarchy of Assassins, propagandists, and lay brothers, and directed the policies and activities of the sect in all areas. Selchükid attempts to capture it and stamp out the menace at its source were unavailing, and soon the daggers of the faithful were claiming many victims among the generals, governors, and princes of the Selchükid states. The comprehensive nature of the Assassin threat to Islamic society was well realized by the Selchükid authorities, who took steps to protect the minds of their subjects from Ismā'īlite sedition. In this they were in the long run more successful than in protecting the persons of their servants against the Ismā'īlite reign of terror. In Baghdad and later in other cities great theological colleges (Arabic singular, *madrasah*) were founded, to formulate and disseminate orthodox doctrine and to counter the Ismā'īlite propaganda that came, first from the colleges and missions of Fāṭimid Egypt, later in a more radical form from the emissaries of the Nizārites.

It was at the beginning of the twelfth century that the Persian Assassins seem to have begun to extend their activities to Syria. The terrain was favorable. Between 1070 and 1079 the Selchükids had conquered Syria, carrying with them many of the problems that had made Persia so excellent a field for Assassin propaganda. The irruption of the crusaders at the end of the century completed the political fragmentation of the country begun by the dissensions of the Selchükid princes. Among the native population of the country extremist Shīʿism already had a hold. Since the fall of the Umaiyads and the transfer of the capital to Iraq, Syria had been a discontented province, unreconciled to its loss of metropolitan status, severed by mutual distrust from the government in the east. The first Shīʿite pretender appeared in Syria only a few years after the fall of the Umaiyads, and by the end of the ninth century and the beginning of the tenth the hidden imams of the Ismāʿīlites could count on sufficient local support to make Syria the seat of their secret headquarters and the scene of their first bid for power. The spread of the Fāṭimid empire eastwards from North Africa brought Syria under intermittent Ismāʿīlite rule in the late tenth and eleventh centuries, and opened the country to the free dissemination of Ismāʿīlite propaganda. Here and there were sects which, though not actually Ismāʿīlite, were near enough to Ismāʿīlism in outlook to encourage the emissaries of Alamut. The Druzes in Mount Lebanon had only recently broken away from the main body, and had not yet developed that ossified exclusiveness that distinguished them in later times. The Nuṣairīs, an offshoot of the Twelver Shīʿah, much influenced by extremist doctrine, were powerful in the hill-country east and northeast of Latakia, and perhaps also in Tiberias and the Jordan district. The ignominious weakness of the Fāṭimid state under the successors of al-Mustanṣir would incline many Ismāʿīlites in Syria, threatened by both Turks and crusaders, to transfer their allegiance to the more active branch. Even among the Turkoman tribes migrating into Syria there were many who had been affected by extremist Shīʿite propaganda in the east. Some of the Shīʿites in Syria remained faithful to their old several allegiances. Many, if not the majority, rallied to the Assassin emissaries, who seemed to offer the only effective challenge to the invaders and rulers of the country.[10]

The first Assassin leader in Syria of whom we hear is the personage known as al-Ḥakīm al-Munajjim, "the physician-astrologer," who appeared in Aleppo at the beginning of the twelfth century. Aleppo was a city with an important Shīʿite population, and was conveniently near to the Shīʿite strongholds in the Jabal as-Summāq and Jabal Bahrā'. Its ruler, the Selchükid prince Riḍvan, was disposed to favor the sectaries, possibly in the hope of win-

[10] Ivanow, *Ismaili Tradition concerning the Rise of the Fatimids*, pp. 158ff.; Keuprulu [Köprülü] Zadé Mehmed Fuad, *Les Origines du Bektachisme* (Paris, 1926), *passim*.

ning support among the Shī'ites, more probably in the hope of compensating for his military weakness as against his rivals in Syria. A few years earlier Riḍvan had not scrupled to proclaim Fāṭimid allegiance for a short time when it suited him, and then to return as easily to political orthodoxy. In the lax religious atmosphere of the time, he had no hesitation in supporting even the Assassins when it seemed politically expedient. Riḍvan allowed the Assassins full freedom in the practice and propagation of their religion. Of special importance was the opportunity to establish a *dār ad-da'wah*, "house of propaganda," and to use the city as a base for further activities. That Riḍvan, as some sources suggest, himself inclined to Ismā'īlism is uncertain and on the whole unlikely.

Riḍvan's policy paid quick dividends. On May 1, 1103, Janāḥ-ad-Daulah, the ruler of Homs and a rival of Riḍvan, was stabbed to death by three Persians in the great mosque. The assassins, who were dressed as sufis (Arabic singular, *ṣūfī*), acted on a signal from a shaikh who accompanied them. A number of Janāḥ's officers were killed with him and, significantly, most of the Turks in Homs fled to Damascus. The assassins themselves were killed. Most sources agree that the murder was instigated by Riḍvan.[11]

Two or three weeks after the murder of Janāḥ-ad-Daulah, the physician-astrologer himself died, and was succeeded in the leadership of the Syrian Assassins by another Persian, abū-Ṭāhir aṣ-Ṣā'igh, the goldsmith. From that time until the accession of the famous Rāshid-ad-Dīn Sinān in, or shortly after, 1162,[12] the main efforts of the Syrian mission were directed to the seizure and consolidation of castles in country inhabited by sympathetic populations, to be used after the Persian model. The leaders as far as they are known to us were all Persians, sent from Alamut and operating under the orders of al-Ḥasan ibn-aṣ-Ṣabbāḥ and his successors. The endeavor to win strongholds falls into three main campaigns. The first, conducted from Aleppo and directed by abū-Ṭāhir, was concentrated on the Jabal as-Summāq and ended with the death of abū-Ṭāhir in 1113 and the reaction against the Ismā'īlites in Aleppo after the death of Riḍvan. The second, conducted from Damascus by the chief da'is Bahrām and Ismā'īl al-'Ajamī, was aimed at Banyas and the Wādī-t-Taim, and ended in

[11] Lewis, "The Sources for the History of the Syrian Assassins," pp. 485–486, and "Three Biographies from Kamal ad-Din," *Mélanges Köprülü* (Ankara, 1953), pp. 325–326, 329–332. Cf. Defrémery, "Ismaéliens de Syrie," *Journal asiatique*, III, 377.

[12] Guyard, "Un Grand Maître," p. 35 (cited from a reprint); Lewis, "Three Biographies," p. 328.

failure and death by 1130. The third, conducted from unknown bases by a number of chiefs of whom only a few are known by name, succeeded between 1132 and 1151 in winning and consolidating a group of strongholds in the Jabal Bahrā' (now called the Jabal Anṣārīyah after its Nuṣairī population).

The population of the Jabal as-Summāq had long been affected by Ismā'īlism and related doctrines. The hidden imam had stayed there for a while in the late ninth century, and in 1036/1037 al-Muqtanâ, the Druze missionary, addressed a special epistle to the Ismā'īlites of that area exhorting them to join the Druzes. He asked them to draw up lists of reliable men and to meet secretly in various places in groups of from seven to nine men.[13] From the beginning the emissaries of Alamut seem to have been able to call on local support in Sarmīn and other places, and may even have controlled a few localities. At an unknown date they seized Kafarlāthā, which however they lost to Tancred, prince of Antioch, by 1110.[14] The first documented attempt came in 1106, in Apamea. Its ruler, Khalaf ibn-Mulā'ib, had been expelled from Homs by the Turks in 1092, and had sought refuge in Egypt. When a request for a ruler came to Cairo from the Ismā'īlite inhabitants of Apamea, Khalaf was sent to take over as Fāṭimid representative. In 1096 he seized the town from Riḍvan and embarked on a career of brigandage. Though a Shī'ite and presumably an Ismā'īlite, Khalaf was apparently unwilling to throw in his lot with the Assassins, and on February 3, 1106, he was killed by emissaries acting under the orders of abū-Ṭāhir in Aleppo. These were assisted by an Assassin from Sarmīn residing in Apamea, called abū-l-Fatḥ.[15] After the murder and the seizure of the citadel and town abū-Ṭāhir himself arrived to take charge, nominally on behalf of his patron Riḍvan. But this attempt, despite its promising start, did not succeed. Tancred, who had already occupied much of the surrounding country, now attacked Apamea, possibly at the request of the Christian population, who feared Assassin rule. After a first inconclusive siege, he returned and in September received the capitulation of the town. Abū-l-Fatḥ was put to death by torture, while abū-Ṭāhir ransomed himself from captivity and returned to Aleppo.[16]

[13] De Sacy, *Exposé de la religion des Druzes*, I, dviii. The text is in MS. Marsh, 221 (Bodl.), folios 179–180.

[14] Defrémery, "Ismaéliens de Syrie," *Journal asiatique*, III, 387; Quatremère, "Notice historique sur les Ismaëliens," *Fundgruben des Orients*, IV, 342.

[15] This is a more probable reading than the form abū-l-Qinj given by some sources.

[16] Lewis, "Three Biographies," pp. 326, 329, 332–336; Defrémery, "Ismaéliens de Syrie," *Journal asiatique*, III, 380–384; Quatremère, "Notice historique sur les Ismaëliens," *op. cit.*, p. 342. On Tancred, see below, chapter XII, p. 392.

Another attempt was made in 1113/1114, to seize Shaizar from its holders, the Banū-Munqidh, by a group of Assassins from Apamea, Sarmīn, Maʿarrat-an-Nuʿmān, and Maʿarrat-Miṣrīn. After an initially successful surprise attack the men of Shaizar recovered, and were able to defeat and exterminate the attackers.[17]

In the same year, 1113, the Syrian Assassins achieved their most ambitious coup to date — the murder in Damascus of Maudūd, the Selchükid emir of Mosul and commander of the eastern expeditionary force to Syria. Most sources are agreed that the Assassins performed the deed. Contemporary gossip, as recorded by Ibn-al-Athīr and William of Tyre, suggests that Tughtigin, the regent (Turkish, *atabeg*) of Damascus, had a hand in it. Along with the other independent Moslem rulers of Syria, Tughtigin might well have feared an increase in Selchükid power and influence among them, and his later dealings with the daʿi Bahrām show that he did not disdain such allies. But Maudūd's position as commander of an eastern Selchükid army would alone have sufficed to mark him down as a dangerous enemy of the Assassins, and in this respect it is significant that the Assassins of Aleppo rallied to the support of Riḍvan when, in 1111, he closed the gates of Aleppo against Maudūd and his army.[18]

The danger to the Assassins of eastern Selchükid influence became clear after the death of their patron Riḍvan on December 10, 1113. Assassin activities in Aleppo had made them increasingly unpopular with both the Sunnite and the moderate Shīʿite townsmen, and in 1111 an unsuccessful attempt on the life of one abū-Ḥarb ʿĪsâ ibn-Zaid, a rich Persian from Transoxiana and a declared anti-Ismāʿīlite, was followed by a popular outburst against the sectaries. After Riḍvan's death the storm burst. His son Alp Arslan at first followed his father's policy, even ceding them a

[17] Ibn-al-Qalānisī, *Dhail ta'rīkh Dimashq* [*Continuation of History of Damascus*] (ed. H. F. Amedroz, Leyden, 1908), pp. 190–191 (extracts tr. H. A. R. Gibb, *The Damascus Chronicle of the Crusades*, London, 1932, pp. 147–148); Defrémery, "Ismaéliens de Syrie," *Journal asiatique*, III, 395–397 (based on Ibn-al-Athīr). Quatremère, "Notice historique sur les Ismaëliens," p. 348, following Ibn-al-Furāt, puts this ten years later.

[18] Defrémery, "Ismaéliens de Syrie," *op. cit.*, III, 389–391; C. Cahen, *La Syrie du nord*, p. 267; Ibn-al-Qalānisī, p. 187 (tr. Gibb, pp. 140–141); al-ʿAẓīmī, *Ta'rīkh*, (ed. C. Cahen, "La Chronique abrégée d'al-ʿAẓīmī," *Journal asiatique*, CCXXX [1938]), p. 382; anonymous, *Bustān al-jāmiʿ* (ed. C. Cahen, "Une Chronique syrienne du VIe–XIIe siècle: le Bustān al-Jāmiʿ," *Bulletin d'études orientales de l'institut français de Damas*, VII–VIII [1937–1938]), p. 117; Ibn-al-Athīr, *Al-kāmil fī-t-ta'rīkh* (ed. C. J. Tornberg, *Chronicon*, 14 vols., Leyden-Upsala, 1851–1876), X, 347–348; *Ta'rīkh ad-daulah al-atābakīyah mulūk al-Mauṣil* (*RHC, Or.*, II, part. 2; cited as *Atābeks*), p. 36; Sibṭ Ibn-al-Jauzī, *Mir'āt az-zamān* (ed. J. R. Jewett, Chicago, 1907), p. 31 (*RHC, Or.*, III, 551); Bar Hebraeus, *Chronography* (ed. and tr. E. A. W. Budge, 2 vols., Oxford, 1932), p. 246; Michael the Syrian, *Chronique* (ed. and tr. J. B. Chabot, 4 vols., Paris, 1899–1910), III, 216; William of Tyre, XI, 20. On the episode at Aleppo see Ibn-al-Qalānisī, pp. 159–160.

castle outside Bālis on the Aleppo-Baghdad road. But the reaction soon came. Kamāl-ad-Dīn, the historian of Aleppo, tells of a letter from the Selchükid sultan Muḥammad to Alp Arslan warning him of the Assassin danger and urging him to make a clean sweep. The main initiative in Aleppo came from Ṣā'id ibn-Badī', the prefect (Arabic, *ra'īs*) of the city and commander of the militia, who adopted a series of vigorous measures. Abū-Ṭāhir and other leaders were put to death, and about two hundred of their followers killed or imprisoned. A number escaped and fled to various parts, including, according to Ibn-al-Qalānisī, the lands of the Franks. Ḥusām-ad-Dīn ibn-Dumlāj, who commanded the Ismā'īlite levies in Aleppo, fled to Raqqa and died there, while his henchman Ibrāhīm al-'Ajamī (the Persian), who had held the castle of Bālis in the Ismā'īlite interest, fled to Shaizar.[19]

Despite this setback, and their failure to secure a permanent castle-stronghold so far, the Persian Ismā'īlite mission had not done too badly during the tenure of office of abū-Ṭāhir. They had made contacts with local sympathizers, winning to the Assassin allegiance Ismā'īlites of other branches and extremist Shī'ites of the various local Syrian sects. They could count on important local support in the Jabal as-Summāq, the Jazr, and the Banū-'Ulaim country — that is, in the strategically significant territory between Shaizar and Sarmīn. They had formed nuclei of support in other places in Syria, and especially along their line of communication eastwards to Alamut. The Euphrates districts east of Aleppo are known as centers of extremist Shī'ism in both earlier and later periods, and although there is no direct evidence for these years, one may be certain that abū-Ṭāhir did not neglect his opportunities.

Even in Aleppo itself the Assassins, albeit weakened, held on for a while. In 1119 their arch-enemy Ṣā'id ibn-Badī' was expelled from the city by the shiftless Alp Arslan, and fled to Īl-Ghāzī in Mardin, to beg him to return to Aleppo. On his way he was attacked by two Assassins at Qal'at Ja'bar (Dausar), on the Euphrates, and killed, together with his two sons.[20] In the following year they were again strong enough in Aleppo to demand the small

[19] Ibn-al-Qalānisī, pp. 189–190 (tr. Gibb, pp. 145–146); Ibn-al-Athīr, *Kāmil*, X, 349 (*RHC, Or.*, I, 291); Ibn-ash-Shiḥnah, *Ad-durr al-muntakhab fī ta'rīkh mamlakat Ḥalab* (ed. J. Sauvaget, *Les Perles choisies*, Beirut, 1933), p. 27; Defrémery, "Ismaéliens de Syrie," *Journal asiatique*, III, 387–395; Quatremère, "Notice historique sur les Ismaëliens," *op. cit.*, pp. 342–343; Cahen, *La Syrie du nord*, p. 268.

[20] Kamāl-ad-Dīn, *Zubdat al-ḥalab fī ta'rīkh Ḥalab* (*RHC, Or.*, III), p. 616; al-'Aẓīmī, p. 386; Defrémery, "Ismaéliens de Syrie," *op. cit.*, III, 398–399; Quatremère, *op. cit.*, pp. 345–346.

citadel (Qalʿat ash-Sharīf) from Īl-Ghāzī. He, unwilling to cede it to them and afraid to refuse, resorted to the subterfuge of having it hastily demolished and then pretending to have ordered this just previously. Ibn-al-Khashshāb, who conducted the demolition, was "assassinated" in 1125.[21] The end of Ismāʿīlite power in Aleppo seems to have come in 1124, when Belek, having seized the city, arrested the agent of Bahrām, the chief daʿi, and ordered the expulsion of the sectaries, who sold up their property and departed. In the following year the Ismāʿīlites of Amida (Diyarbakir) were set upon by the local population and several hundred of them killed.[22]

In 1124 it was the agent of the chief daʿi, and not the chief daʿi himself, who was arrested as leader of the Assassins in Aleppo. After the death of abū-Ṭāhir the chief daʿis no longer resided in that city. His successor, Bahrām, transferred the main activities of the sect to the south, and was soon playing an active part in the affairs of Damascus. Like his predecessors, Bahrām was a Persian, the nephew of an Assassin leader executed in Baghdad in 1101 by order of the Selchükid sultan Berkyaruk. He fled to Syria, and appears to have succeeded to the headship of the sectaries after the debacle in Aleppo in 1113. For a while, in the words of Ibn-al-Qalānisī, "he lived in extreme concealment and secrecy, and continually disguised himself, so that he moved from city to city and castle to castle without anyone being aware of his identity."[23] He almost certainly had a hand in the assassination of Aksungur al-Bursukī in Mosul on November 26, 1126. Al-Bundārī, the chronicler of the Selchükids, suggests that the assassination was arranged by Qiwām-ad-Dīn Nāṣir ibn-ʿAlī ad-Dargazīnī, the vizir of the Selchükid sultan and a secret Ismāʿīlite. Some at least of the murderers came from Syria. Ibn-al-Athīr mentions Sarmīn as their place of origin, while Kamāl-ad-Dīn tells an interesting story of a youth from Kafr Nāṣiḥ, in the neighborhood of ʿAzāz, who was the sole survivor of the expedition. On his return home in safety his aged mother, who had previously rejoiced on hearing of his mission, was unhappy and ashamed at his survival. The death of al-Bursukī freed the Assassins from a redoubtable enemy.[24]

[21] Defrémery, "Ismaéliens de Syrie," *op. cit.*, III, 399–401; Quatremère, *op. cit.*, p. 346; Cahen, *La Syrie du nord*, pp. 347–348.

[22] Kamāl-ad-Dīn (*RHC, Or.*, III), p. 640; Defrémery, "Ismaéliens de Syrie," *op. cit.*, III, 408; Quatremère, *op. cit.*, pp. 348–349. On the massacre in Amida, see Sibṭ Ibn-al-Jauzī (ed. Jewett), p. 69. See also Ibn-al-Athīr, *Kāmil*, X, 441; Defrémery, "Ismaéliens de Syrie," *op. cit.*, III, 405; Cahen, *La Syrie du nord*, p. 348, note 2.

[23] Ibn-al-Qalānisī, p. 215 (tr. Gibb, pp. 179–180).

[24] Ibn-al-Qalānisī, p. 214 (tr. Gibb, p. 177): al-ʿAẓīmī, p. 397; Kamāl-ad-Dīn (*RHC, Or.*, III), pp. 654–656; Sibṭ Ibn-al-Jauzī (ed. Jewett), p. 71, with the date A. H. 519; Ibn-al-

As early as 1126 Assassin militia from Homs and other places joined the troops of Tughtigin in an unsuccessful attack on the Franks. Towards the end of 1126 Bahrām appeared openly in Damascus with a letter of recommendation from Īl-Ghāzī. He was received with honor and given protection, and soon acquired a position of power in the city. In pursuance of the usual Assassin policy he sought to obtain a castle which he could fortify as a stronghold, and the atabeg Tughtigin ceded him the frontier-fortress of Banyas. Even in the city itself the Ismā'īlites received a building as headquarters, variously described as a "palace" and a "house of propaganda". Ibn-al-Qalānisī, the chronicler of Damascus, places the main blame for these events on the vizir abū-'Alī Ṭāhir ibn-Sa'd al-Mazdaganī who, though not himself an Ismā'īlite, was the willing agent of their plans and the evil influence behind Tughtigin's compliance. Tughtigin, though strongly disapproving of these proceedings, tolerated them for tactical reasons and bided his time until an opportunity offered to strike against the Assassins. Ibn-al-Athīr on the other hand, while recognizing the role of the vizir, places the blame squarely on Tughtigin, and attributes his action in large measure to the influence of Īl-Ghāzī, with whom Bahrām had established relations while still in Aleppo.

In Banyas Bahrām rebuilt and fortified the castle, and embarked on a course of military and propagandist action in the surrounding country. "In all directions," says Ibn-al-Qalānisī, "he dispatched his missionaries, who enticed a great multitude of the ignorant folk of the provinces and foolish peasantry from the villages and the rabble and scum. . . ." From Banyas, Bahrām and his followers raided extensively, and may have captured some other places. But they soon came to grief. The Wādī-t-Taim, in the region of Ḥāṣbaiyā, was inhabited by a mixed population of Druzes, Nuṣairīs, and other heretics, who seemed to offer a favorable terrain for Assassin expansion. Baraq ibn-Jandal, one of the chiefs of the area, was captured and put to death by treachery, and shortly afterwards Bahrām and his forces set out to occupy the Wādī. There they encountered vigorous resistance from Ḍaḥḥāk ibn-Jandal, the dead man's brother and sworn avenger.

Athīr, *Kāmil*, X, 446–447 (*RHC, Or.*, I, 364); *Atābeks*, p. 58; *Bustān* (ed. Cahen), p. 120; *Anonymous Syriac Chronicle*, in *Corpus scriptorum christianorum orientalium, Scriptores Syri*, series III, vol. XV; tr. A. S. Tritton with notes by H. A. R. Gibb, "The First and Second Crusade from an Anonymous Syriac Chronicle," *Journal of the Royal Asiatic Society*, 1933, pp. 69–101, 273–305; Defrémery, "Ismaéliens de Syrie," *Journal asiatique*, III, 408–411; Quatremère, "Notice historique sur les Ismaëliens," p. 351; Cahen, *La Syrie du nord*, p. 304.

In a sharp engagement the Assassins were defeated and Bahrām himself was killed.[25]

Bahrām was succeeded in the command of Banyas by another Persian, Ismāʿīl, who carried on his policies and activities. The vizir al-Mazdagānī continued his support. But soon the end came. The death of Tughtigin in 1128 was followed by an anti-Ismāʿīlite reaction similar to that which followed the death of Ridvan in Aleppo. Here too the initiative came from the prefect of the city, Mufarrij ibn-al-Ḥasan ibn-aṣ-Ṣūfī, a zealous opponent of the sectaries and an enemy of the vizir. Spurred on by the prefect, as well as by the military governor Yūsuf ibn-Fīrūz, Böri, the son and heir of Tughtigin, prepared the blow. On Wednesday, September 4, 1129, he struck. The vizir was murdered by his orders at the levée, and his head cut off and publicly exposed. As the news spread, the town militia and the mob turned on the Assassins, killing and pillaging. "By the next morning the quarters and streets of the city were cleared of the Bāṭinites and the dogs were yelping and quarrelling over their limbs and corpses." Among the victims was a freedman called Shādhī, a disciple of abū-Ṭāhir and, according to Ibn-al-Qalānisī, the root of all the trouble. The number of Assassins killed in this outbreak is put at 6,000 by Ibn-al-Athīr, 10,000 by Sibṭ Ibn-al-Jauzī, and 20,000 by the author of the *Bustān*. In Banyas Ismāʿīl, realizing that his position was untenable, surrendered the fortress to the Franks and fled to the Frankish territories. He died at the beginning of 1130. Ibn-al-Athīr's story of a plot by the vizir and the Assassins to surrender Damascus to the Franks is not confirmed by other sources, and is probably an invention of hostile gossip.[26]

Böri and his coadjutors took elaborate precautions to protect themselves against the vengeance of the Assassins, wearing armor and surrounding themselves with heavily armed guards; but without avail. The Syrian mission seems to have been temporarily disorganized, and it was from the center of the sect in Alamut that

[25] Ibn-al-Qalānisī, pp. 215, 221–222 (tr. Gibb, pp. 179–180, 187–191); Ibn-al-Athīr, *Kāmil*, X, 445–446, 461–462 (*RHC, Or.*, I, 366–368, 383–384); al-ʿAẓīmī, pp. 397, 400–401; *Bustān*, pp. 120–121; Sibṭ Ibn-al-Jauzī, p. 72; Michael the Syrian, *Chronique* (ed. J. B. Chabot, 4 vols., Paris, 1899–1910), III, 239–240; *Anonymous Syriac Chronicle*, tr. A. S. Tritton, pp. 98–99; Defrémery, "Ismaéliens de Syrie," *op. cit.*, p. 411; Quatremère, *op. cit.*, pp. 348 to 351; Cahen, *op. cit.*, p. 347.

[26] Ibn-al-Qalānisī, pp. 223–224 (tr. Gibb, pp. 192–194); Sibṭ Ibn-al-Jauzī, p. 80 (abridged in *RHC, Or.*, III, 567); Ibn-al-Athīr, *Kāmil*, X, 461–463 (*RHC, Or.*, I, 384–385); *Bustān*, p. 121; William of Tyre, XIV, 19; Bar Hebraeus, p. 254; Defrémery, "Ismaéliens de Syrie," *Journal asiatique*, III, 413–414; Quatremère, "Notice historique sur les Ismaëliens," pp. 350–351; Cahen, *La Syrie du nord*, p. 348. On the surrender of Banyas and the plot concerning Damascus, see below, chapter XIII, p. 430.

the blow was struck. On May 7, 1131, two Persians, who, disguised as Turkish soldiers, had entered the service of Böri, struck him down. The assassins were at once hacked to pieces by the guards, but Böri himself died of his wounds in the following year. Despite this successful coup the Assassins never recovered their position in Damascus, and indeed, in so rigidly orthodox a city, can have had but little hope of doing so.[27]

During this period the Assassins were fighting another enemy besides the Turks. The supporters of the Nizārite line of imams had not yet given up hope of installing their own candidate in place of the, to them, usurping Fāṭimid caliph in Cairo. During the first half of the twelfth century more than one pro-Nizārite revolt broke out and was suppressed in Egypt, and the government in Cairo devoted much attention to countering Nizārite propaganda among their subjects. The caliph al-Āmir issued a special rescript defending the claims of his own line to the succession and refuting the Nizārite case. In an interesting appendix to this document the story is told how, when the Fāṭimid emissary read it to the Assassins of Damascus, it caused an uproar and so impressed one of them that he forwarded it to his chief, who added a refutation in the blank space at the end. The Nizārite read this refutation to a Fāṭimid meeting in Damascus. The Fāṭimid emissary asked the caliph's aid in answering it, and received a further statement of the Musta'līan arguments. These events may be connected with the murder by an Assassin in Damascus in 1120 of a man alleged to have been spying on the Assassins for the Fāṭimid government.[28]

The Assassins also used stronger and more characteristic arguments against their Fāṭimid rivals. In 1121 al-Afḍal, the commander-in-chief in Egypt and the man primarily responsible for the dispossession of Nizār, was murdered. Though Ibn-al-Qalānisī dismisses the attribution of this crime to the Assassins as "empty pretense and insubstantial calumny", and lays the blame on al-Āmir's resentment of al-Afḍal's tutelage, it is not impossible that the Assassins were involved in a murder so much to their advantage. There is no doubt at all about the murder of al-Āmir himself in 1130, by ten Assassins in Cairo. His hatred of the

[27] Ibn-al-Qalānisī, p. 230 (tr. Gibb, pp. 202–204); Ibn-al-Athīr, *Kāmil*, X, 471–472; Sibṭ Ibn-al-Jauzī, p. 83; al-'Aẓīmī, p. 404; *Bustān*, p. 122; *Anonymous Syriac Chronicle*, p. 273; Michael the Syrian, *Chronique*, III, 240; Defrémery, "Ismaéliens de Syrie," *op. cit.*, III, 416; Quatremère, *op. cit.*, p. 352.

[28] S. M. Stern, "The Epistle of the Fatimid Caliph al-Āmir," *Journal of the Royal Asiatic Society*, 1950, pp. 20–31. Cf. Defrémery, "Ismaéliens de Syrie," *op. cit.*, III, 402–403; Quatremère, *op. cit.*, p. 347.

Nizārites was natural and well-known, and it is related that after the death of Bahrām, his head, hands, and ring were taken by a native of the Wādī-t-Taim to Cairo, where the bearer received rewards and a robe of honor.[29]

Little is known of Assassin relations with the Franks in this period. Stories in later Moslem sources of Ismā'īlite collaboration with the enemy are probably a reflection of the mentality of a later age, when the holy war for Islam filled the minds of most Near Eastern Moslems. At this time, the most that can be said is that the Assassins shared the general indifference of Moslem Syria to religious divisions. No Frankish victims to the daggers of the fida'is are known, but on at least two occasions Assassin forces came into conflict with the crusading armies. On the other hand, Assassin refugees from both Aleppo and Banyas sought refuge in Frankish lands. The surrender of Banyas to Frankish rather than Moslem rulers, when it had to be abandoned, was in all probability merely a matter of geography.

The next twenty years are taken up with the third, and successful, attempt of the Assassins to secure fortress-bases in Syria, this time in the Jabal Bahrā', just to the northwest of the scene of their first endeavor, in the Jabal as-Summāq. Their establishment followed an unsuccessful attempt by the Franks to win control of the area. In 1132/1133 Saif-al-Mulk ibn-'Amrūn, lord of al-Kahf, sold the mountain fortress of al-Qadmūs, recovered from the Franks in the previous year, to the Assassins. A few years later his son Mūsâ ceded them al-Kahf itself in the course of a struggle with his cousins for the succession. In 1136/1137 the Frankish garrison in Kharībah was dislodged by a group of Assassins, who succeeded in regaining control after being temporarily dislodged by Ibn-Ṣalāḥ, the governor of Hamah. Maṣyāf, the most important of the Assassins' strongholds, was captured in 1140/1141 from Sungur, a governor appointed by the Banū-Munqidh, who had purchased the castle in 1127/1128. The other Assassin castles of al-Khawābī, ar-Ruṣāfah, al-Qulai'ah, and al-Manīqah were all probably acquired about the same period, though little is known of the date or manner of their acquisition.[30]

[29] On the murder of al-Afḍal, see Ibn-al-Qalānisī, p. 203 (tr. Gibb, p. 163); Sibṭ Ibn-al-Jauzī, p. 64; Ibn-al-Athīr, *Kāmil*, X, 416; Ibn-Muyassar, *Akhbār Miṣr* (ed. H. Massé, *Annales d'Égypte*, Cairo, 1919), p. 63; Defrémery, "Ismaéliens de Syrie," *op. cit.*, III, 403–405. On that of al-Āmir, see al-Maqrīzī, *Al-khiṭaṭ* (2 vols., Būlāq, 1853/1854), II, 182; *Itti'āẓ al-ḥunafā'*, MS. Saray 3013, Istanbul (ed. Jamāl-ad-Dīn ash-Shaiyāl, Cairo, 1948), folio 132a of MS; Ibn-Ḥammād, *Akhbār mulūk Banī-'Ubaid* (ed. and tr. M. Vonderheyden, Algiers and Paris, 1927), pp. 60, 92; Ibn-Muyassar, p. 72; Defrémery, "Ismaéliens de Syrie," *op. cit.*, III, 415–416.

[30] Cahen, *La Syrie du nord*, pp. 353–354, where the main sources are reviewed.

During this period of quiet consolidation, the Assassins made little impression on the outside world, and in consequence little is heard of them in the historians. Very few of their names are known. The purchaser of al-Qadmūs is named as abū-l-Fatḥ, the last chief da'i before Sinān as abū-Muḥammad. A Kurdish Assassin leader called 'Alī ibn-Wafā' coöperated with Raymond of Antioch in his campaign against Nūr-ad-Dīn, and perished with him on the battlefield of Inab in 1149. Only two assassinations are recorded in these years. In 1149 Ḍaḥḥāk ibn-Jandal, the chief of the Wādī-t-Taim, suffered the vengeance of the Assassins for his successful resistance to Bahrām in 1128.[31] A year or two later they murdered count Raymond II of Tripoli, at the gates of that city — their first Frankish victim.[32]

Of the general policy of the Assassins in these years only the broadest outlines can be seen. To Zengi and his house they could feel only hostility. The Turkish rulers of Mosul had always been the most powerful of the atabegs. Lying across the Assassin line of communication with the Persian centers and in friendly relations with the Selchükid rulers of the east, they offered a constant threat to the position of the Assassins, aggravated by their recurrent tendency to spread into Syria. Maudūd and al-Bursukī had already been assassinated. The Zengids were more than once threatened. After the Zengid occupation of Aleppo in 1128 the danger to the Ismā'īlites became more direct. In 1148 we find Nūr-ad-Dīn abolishing the Shī'ite formulae used hitherto in the call to prayer in Aleppo.[33] This step, which aroused intense but ineffectual resentment among the Ismā'īlites and other Shī'ites in the city, amounted to an open declaration of war against the heretics. In the circumstances it is not surprising to find an Assassin contingent fighting beside Raymond of Antioch, the only leader in Syria at the time who could offer effective resistance to the Zengids.

Meanwhile the greatest of all the Assassin chiefs of Syria had taken command. Sinān ibn-Salmān ibn-Muḥammad, surnamed Rāshid-ad-Dīn, was a native of 'Aqr as-Sudan, a village near Basra, on the road to Wāsiṭ. He is variously described as an alchemist, a schoolmaster, and, on his own authority, as the son of one

[31] Ibn-al-Qalānisī, p. 303. On Raymond of Antioch, see below, chapter XVII, p. 533.

[32] Ibn-al-Furāt, *Ta'rīkh ad-duwal wa-l-mulūk* (vols. VII–IX ed. C. K. Zurayk, 4 vols., Beirut, 1936–1942), VIII, 79; William of Tyre, XVII, 19; Defrémery, "Ismaéliens de Syrie," *Journal asiatique,* III, 421; Quatremère, "Notice historique sur les Ismaëliens," pp. 352 ff. On Raymond II, see below, chapter XVII, p. 535, where the assassination is dated 1152.

[33] Ibn-al-Qalānisī, p. 301. On Zengi and Nūr-ad-Dīn, see below, chapters XIV and XVI.

of the leading citizens of Basra. An early interest in extremist Shīʿism led to his abrupt departure from home, and a sojourn in Alamut, where he was well received by the grand master Kiyā Muḥammad, and well indoctrinated with Ismāʿīlite theology and philosophy. After Kiyā Muḥammad's death in 1162, his successor sent Sinān to Syria as delegate of Alamut. A historian quoted by Kamāl-ad-Dīn reports a contemporary's description of a visit to Sinān, and a conversation with him, in the course of which Sinān is quoted as giving this account of his journey to Syria: "He [the grand master] delegated me to Syria. . . . He had given me orders and provided me with letters. I arrived in Mosul and stayed at the mosque of the date-sellers. Thence I went to Raqqa. I had a letter to one of our comrades there, and when I delivered it to him he furnished me with provisions and lent me a mount to carry me to Aleppo. There I met another to whom I gave a letter, and he lent me a mount and sent me on to al-Kahf, where I was ordered to stay. I stayed there until Shaikh abū-Muḥammad, who was in command, died in the mountains." Sinān then describes a dispute as to the succession, and his own eventual accession by order of Alamut. The main points of this narrative are confirmed by other sources, and amplified by the Ismāʿīlite biography of Sinān, which gives his period of waiting at al-Kahf as seven years.[34]

Once established, Sinān's first task was to consolidate his new realm. He rebuilt the fortresses of ar-Ruṣāfah and al-Khawābī, and rounded off his territory by capturing al-ʿUllaiqah by means of a stratagem and refortifying it. According to a narrative reproduced by Kamāl-ad-Dīn, the grand master of Alamut feared his power and independence, and sent a number of emissaries to kill him, all of whom were foiled by the watchfulness of Sinān. This has been taken to mean that Sinān, alone among the Syrian Assassin leaders, threw off the authority of Alamut and pursued an entirely independent policy. For this view there is some support in the doctrinal fragments bearing his name, preserved into modern times among the Syrian Ismāʿīlites. These make no reference to Alamut, its grand masters, or its Nizārite imams, but acclaim Sinān himself as supreme leader and incarnation of divinity. This claim is also mentioned by Syrian Moslem sources and by the Spanish Arab traveller Ibn-Jubair, who visited the area in 1184/1185. Some of his followers went too far even for

[34] On Sinān see Defrémery, "Ismaéliens de Syrie," *Journal asiatique*, V, 5 ff.; Guyard, "Un Grand Maître;" Ivanow, "Rāshid ad-Dīn Sinān," *Encyclopaedia of Islām*; Lewis "Three Biographies," pp. 327–328, 336–344.

Sinān. In 1176/1177, says Kamāl-ad-Dīn, the people of the Jabal as-Summāq, declaring that Sinān was their God, "abandoned themselves to all kinds of debauchery and iniquity. Calling themselves 'the Pure', men and women mixed in drinking sessions, no man abstained from his sister or daughter, and the women wore men's clothes. One of them stated that Sinān was his God." Al-Malik aṣ-Ṣāliḥ sent the army of Aleppo against them, and they took to the mountains, where they fortified themselves. Sinān, after making an inquiry, disclaimed responsibility, and, persuading the Aleppans to withdraw, himself attacked and destroyed them. Other sources speak of similar groups of ecstatics in these years.[35]

Our information about the policies of the Assassins under Sinān deals principally with a series of specific events in which they were involved: the two attempts on the life of Saladin (Ṣalāḥ-ad-Dīn), followed by his inconclusive attack on Maṣyāf; the murder of Ibn-al-'Ajamī in Aleppo; the fire in Aleppo; and the murder of Conrad of Montferrat. Apart from this there are only vague accounts of threatening letters to Nūr-ad-Dīn and Saladin, and a reference by Benjamin of Tudela, in 1167, to a state of war between the Assassins and the county of Tripoli. The rise of Saladin as the architect of Moslem unity and orthodoxy and the champion of the holy war (Arabic, *jihād*) won him at first the position of chief enemy of the Assassins, and inevitably inclined them to look more favorably on the Zengids of Mosul and Aleppo, now his chief opponents. In letters written to the caliph in Baghdad in 1181/1182, Saladin accuses the rulers of Mosul of being in league with the heretical Assassins and using their mediation with the infidel Franks. He speaks of their promising the Assassins castles, lands, and a house of propaganda in Aleppo, and of sending emissaries both to Sinān and to the count, and stresses his own role as defender of Islam against the threefold threat of Frankish infidelity, Assassin heresy, and Zengid treason.[36] The author of the Ismā'īlite biography of Sinān, himself affected by the jihad mentality of later times, depicts his hero as a collaborator of Saladin in the

[35] Ibn-Jubair, *Riḥlah* (ed. William Wright, rev. by M. J. de Goeje; Leyden and London, 1907), p. 255; tr. by R. J. C. Broadhurst, *The Travels of Ibn Jubayr* (London, 1952), p. 264. *Bustān*, p. 136, alone puts these events in A. H. 561. See also Kamāl-ad-Dīn, MS 193b (Blochet, *ROL*, IV [1896], 147–148); Lewis, "Three Biographies," p. 338; Defrémery, "Ismaéliens de Syrie," *op. cit.*, V, 8–9; Quatremère, "Notice historique sur les Ismaëliens," pp. 354–355; Cahen, *La Syrie du nord*, p. 377.

[36] Abū-Shāmah, *Kitāb ar-rauḍatain* (2 vols., Cairo 1871, 1872), II, 23–24; Defrémery, "Ismaéliens de Syrie," *op. cit.*, V, 29–30; B. Lewis, "Saladin and the Assassins," *Bulletin of the School of Oriental and African Studies*, XV (1953), 239–245. See also below, chapter XVIII, p. 576.

holy war against the crusaders. As we shall see, both statements may be true for different dates. Though Saladin's account of the degree of collaboration among his opponents is probably exaggerated in order to discredit the Zengids, it was natural enough to begin with that his various enemies should concentrate their attacks on him rather than on one another. The curious story told by William of Tyre of an Assassin proposal to embrace Christianity may reflect a genuine rapprochement between Sinān and the kingdom of Jerusalem.[37]

The first Assassin attempt on Saladin's life occurred in December 1174 or January 1175, while he was besieging Aleppo. According to the biographers of Saladin, Gümüshtigin, who governed the city on behalf of the Zengid child who was its nominal ruler, sent messengers to Sinān, offering him lands and money in return for the assassination of Saladin. The appointed emissaries penetrated the camp on a cold winter day, but were recognized by the emir of Abū-Qubais, a neighbor of theirs. He questioned them, and was at once killed. In the ensuing fracas many people were killed, but Saladin himself was unscathed. In the following year Sinān decided to make another attempt, and on May 22, 1176, Assassins, disguised as soldiers in his army, attacked him with knives while he was besieging ʿAzāz. Thanks to his armor Saladin received only superficial wounds, and the assailants were dealt with by his emirs, several of whom perished in the struggle. Some sources attribute this second attempt also to the instigation of Gümüshtigin. After these events Saladin adopted elaborate precautions, sleeping in a specially constructed wooden tower and allowing no one whom he did not know personally to approach him.

While it is by no means impossible that, in organizing these two attempts on Saladin's life, Sinān was acting in concert with Gümüshtigin, it is unlikely that Gümüshtigin's inducements were his primary motive. What is far more probable is that Sinān, acting for reasons of his own, accepted the help of Gümüshtigin, thus gaining both material and tactical advantages. The same may be said of the statement contained in a letter sent by Saladin to the caliph from Cairo in 1174, that the leaders of the abortive pro-Fāṭimid conspiracy in Egypt in that year had written to Sinān, stressing their common faith and urging him to take action against Saladin. The Nizārite Ismāʿīlites of Syria and Persia owed no allegiance to the last Fāṭimids in Cairo, whom they regarded as

[37] William of Tyre, XX, 29–30; Quatremère, "Notice historique sur les Ismaëliens," pp. 353–354. See below, chapter XVII, note 23.

usurpers. That Fāṭimid elements sought the aid of the Syrian Assassins is likely enough — some half century previously the Fāṭimid caliph al-Āmir had attempted to persuade them to accept his leadership. But the Nizārites had refused, and al-Āmir himself had fallen to their daggers. It is not impossible that Sinān, again for tactical reasons, may have been willing to collaborate with the Egyptian conspirators, though it is unlikely that he would continue to act in their interests after the definitive crushing of the plot in Egypt. A more likely immediate cause for Sinān's action against Saladin is to be found in a story told by Sibṭ Ibn-al-Jauzī, though not, oddly enough, by the contemporary chroniclers. In 1174/1175, according to Sibṭ, ten thousand horsemen of the Nubuwīyah, an anti-Shī'ite religious order in Iraq, raided the Ismā'īlite centers in al-Bāb and Buzā'ah, where they slaughtered 13,000 Ismā'īlites and carried off much booty and many captives. Profiting from the confusion of the Ismā'īlites, Saladin sent his army against them, raiding Sarmīn, Ma'arrat-Miṣrīn, and Jabal as-Summāq, and killing most of the inhabitants. Sibṭ unfortunately does not say in what month these events took place, but if, as seems likely, Saladin's raid was carried out while his army was on its way northward to Aleppo, it may serve to explain the hostility of the Assassins towards him. Even without this explanation, however, it is clear that the emergence of Saladin as the major power in Moslem Syria, with a policy of Moslem unification, would mark him down as a dangerous adversary.

In August 1176 Saladin advanced on the Assassin territories, in search of vengeance, and laid siege to Maṣyāf. There are different versions of the circumstances of his withdrawal. 'Imād-ad-Dīn, followed by most of the other Arabic sources, attributes it to the mediation of Saladin's uncle Shihāb-ad-Dīn Maḥmūd ibn-Takash, prince of Hamah, to whom his Assassin neighbors appealed for intercession. Ibn-abī-Ṭaiyī adds the more convincing reason of the Frankish attack on the Biqā' valley, which urgently required Saladin's presence elsewhere. In Kamāl-ad-Din's version it is Saladin who invokes the mediation of the prince of Hamah, and asks for peace, apparently as a result of the terror inspired by Assassin tactics. In the Ismā'īlite version, Saladin is terrified by the supernatural antics of Sinān, and the prince of Hamah intercedes on his behalf with the Assassins, to allow him to depart in safety. Saladin agrees to withdraw, Sinān gives him a safe-conduct, and the two become the best of friends. The Ismā'īlite account is obviously heavily overlaid with legend, but seems to contain this element of truth, that some sort of agreement was reached. Certainly we hear of no overt acts by the Assassins against Saladin after the withdrawal from Maṣyāf and there are even some hints of collusion.[38]

The next murder, on August 31, 1177, was of Shihāb-ad-Dīn abū-Ṣāliḥ ibn-al-'Ajamī, the vizir of the Zengid al-Malik aṣ-Ṣāliḥ in Aleppo, and former vizir of Nūr-ad-Dīn. This assassination, which was accompanied by unsuccessful attempts on two of the vizir's henchmen, is attributed by the Syrian historians to the machinations of Gümüshtigin, who had forged the signature of al-Malik aṣ-Ṣāliḥ on a letter to Sinān requesting this action. The authority for this story is the confession of the Assassins, who claimed, when questioned, that they were only carrying out the the orders of al-Malik aṣ-Ṣāliḥ himself. The truth came out in subsequent correspondence between al-Malik aṣ-Ṣāliḥ and Sinān, and Gümüshṭigin's enemies seized the opportunity to bring about his downfall. Whatever the truth of this story, the death of the vizir and the ensuing discord and mistrust cannot have been unwelcome to Saladin. The breach between Aleppo and Sinān continued. In 1179/1180 al-Malik aṣ-Ṣāliḥ seized al-Hajīrah from the Assassins. Sinān's protests producing no result, he sent agents to Aleppo who set fire to the marketplaces and wrought great damage. Not one of the incendiaries was apprehended — a fact which suggests that they could still command local support in the city.[39]

Although it will carry us beyond the terminal date of the present volume, which closes on the eve of the so-called Third Crusade, it seems best to continue with, and in this chapter to conclude, the history of the Assassins. On April 28, 1192, they brought off their greatest coup — the murder of the marquis Conrad of Montferrat in Tyre. Most sources agree that the murderers disguised themselves as Christian monks and wormed their way into the confidence of the bishop and the marquis. Then, when an opportunity arose, they stabbed him to death. Bahā'-ad-Dīn, whose account is based on the exactly contemporary report of Saladin's envoy in Tyre, says that when the two Assassins were put to the question they confessed that the king of England had instigated the murder. In view of the testimony of most of the oriental and some of the occidental sources, there seems little doubt that some such confession was indeed made. Richard's obvious interest in the disappearance

[38] On the two attempts on Saladin and the attack on Maṣyāf, see Lewis, "Saladin and the Assassins." Cf. also below, chapter XVIII, pp. 567, 570.

[39] Defrémery, "Ismaéliens de Syrie," *Journal asiatique*, V, 20–25; Quatremère, "Notice historique sur les Ismaëliens," pp. 355–357; Lewis, "Saladin and the Assassins," n. 21.

of the marquis, and the suspicious speed with which his protégé count Henry of Champagne married the widow and succeeded to the throne of the Latin kingdom, lent some color to the story — and one can readily understand that it found widespread credence at the time. But whether or not the Assassins were telling the truth when they confessed is another question. Ibn-al-Athīr, for whose dislike of Saladin due allowance must be made, mentions the attribution to Richard simply as a belief current among the Franks. He himself names Saladin as the instigator, and even knows the sum of money paid to Sinān for the work. The plan was to kill both Richard himself and the marquis, but the murder of Richard proved impossible. The Ismā'īlite biography attributes the initiative to Sinān, with the prior approval and coöperation of Saladin; but here too allowance must be made for the author's obvious desire to present his hero as a loyal collaborator of Saladin in his holy war. He adds the unlikely information that, in reward for this deed, Saladin granted the Assassins many privileges, including the right to set up houses of propaganda in Cairo, Damascus, Homs, Hamah, Aleppo, and other cities. In this story we may perhaps discern an exaggerated recollection of some definite recognition accorded to the Assassins by Saladin in the period after the agreement at Maṣyāf. 'Imād-ad-Dīn, on the other hand, tells us that the murder was not opportune for Saladin, since Conrad, though himself one of the leaders of the crusaders, was an enemy of the more redoubtable Richard, and was in communication with Saladin at the time of his death. Richard, aware of this, himself inclined to negotiation and peace. But the murder of Conrad freed him from anxiety and encouraged him to resume hostilities.[40]

This and the preceding murder raise an important general issue in the history of the Assassins. Of a score of murders recorded in Syria between 1103 and 1273, almost half are attributed by one or another source to the instigation of third parties. Sometimes the story is based on an alleged confession by the actual murderers. Yet it must be remembered that the Assassins were no mere band of hired cut-throats, but the fanatically devoted adherents of a religious sect, dedicated ultimately to the achievement of nothing less than the establishment of a new Fāṭimid empire over all

[40] Bahā'-ad-Dīn, *An-nawādir as-sulṭānīyah*, p. 165; abū-Shāmah, II, 196; 'Imād-ad-Dīn, *Al-fatḥ al-qussī* (ed. C. de Landberg, *Conquête de la Syrie...*, Leyden, 1888), pp. 420 to 422; Ibn-al-Athīr, *Kāmil*, XII, 51 (*RHC, Or.*, II, 58–59); Bar Hebraeus, p. 339; Nicetas Choniates, *Historia* (*RHC, Grecs*, I), p. 318; Defrémery, "Ismaéliens de Syrie," *op. cit.*, V. 25–30; Quatremère, *op. cit.*, p. 357; Lewis, "Saladin and the Assassins," n. 23.

Islam, under the rule of the imams of the house of Nizār. Though Sinān may have permitted himself some deviations from this ideal, and though some of the murders may have been arranged with the temporary allies of the sect, it is in the highest degree unlikely that in this period of their prime the daggers of the fida'is were for hire. Even when murders were politically or otherwise arranged, it is still more unlikely that the actual murderers would know the identity of the instigator or ally concerned. But the Assassin setting forth on a mission might well have been given what in modern parlance would be called a "cover story", implicating the likeliest character on the scene. This would have the additional advantage of sowing mistrust and suspicion in the opposing camp. The murders of Ibn-al-ʿAjamī and of Conrad of Montferrat are good examples of this. The suspicion thrown on Gümüshtigin in Aleppo and on Richard among the Franks must have served a useful purpose in confusing the issues and creating discord.

The murder of Conrad was Sinān's last achievement. In 1192/1193 or 1193/1194 the redoubtable Old Man of the Mountain himself died, and was succeeded by a Persian called Naṣr.[41] With the new chief the authority of Alamut seems to have been restored, and remained unshaken until after the Mongol conquest. The names of several of the chief daʿis at different dates are known to us from literary sources and from inscriptions in the Ismāʿīlite centers in Syria; most of them are specifically referred to as delegates of Alamut. They are, with the dates of mention: Kamāl-ad-Dīn al-Ḥasan ibn-Masʿūd (after 1221/1222); Majd-ad-Dīn (1226/1227); Sirāj-ad-Dīn Muẓaffar ibn-al-Ḥusain (1227 and 1238); Tāj-ad-Dīn abū-l-Futūḥ ibn-Muḥammad (1239/1240 and 1249); Raḍī-ad-Dīn abū-l-Maʿālī (1256 ff.).[42]

About 1211 the sources record a curious episode that is worth considering. In that year, the Persian sources tell us, the grand master of Alamut, Jalāl-ad-Dīn al-Ḥasan III, decreed a return to orthodoxy. He renounced the heretical teachings of his predecessors, burnt their books, restored orthodox religious practices, and, most significant of all, recognized the ʿAbbāsid caliph an-Nāṣir, from whom he received a diploma of investiture. Because of these changes he received the Persian sobriquet *Nau-Musulmān*, New Moslem. The Syrian historians also report these events, and add that he sent messengers to Syria, ordering his Syrian

[41] *Bustān*, p. 151; Sibṭ Ibn-al-Jauzī, p. 269; Bar Hebraeus, p. 343; Lewis, "Three Biographies," pp. 338–339; Defrémery, "Ismaéliens de Syrie," *op. cit.*, V, 31.
[42] Van Berchem, "Épigraphie des Assassins," *passim*.

followers to follow his example. The circumstances of this episode are obscure, but it is certainly connected with the policies of the caliph an-Nāṣir, the last ʿAbbāsid to pursue an independent line. He was himself known as a Shīʿite sympathizer, and sought whatever allies he could find in his struggle against the Mongols and other enemies.[43]

The "reform" seems to have had little permanent effect on the religious beliefs of the Ismāʿīlites in either Persia or Alamut, though it may have affected their practice. It is striking that in Syria, in the presence of the enemies of Islam, no further assassinations of Moslems are recorded, though several Christians were still to fall. The first of these was Raymond, son of Bohemond IV of Antioch, who was killed in the church in Tortosa in 1213. His father, thirsting for vengeance, led an expedition against the Ismāʿīlite fortress of al-Khawābī. The Ismāʿīlites, who were now clearly on good terms with the Aiyūbids, appealed for help to Aleppo, the ruler of which, al-Malik az̧-Z̧āhir, sent a force to relieve them. Az̧-Z̧āhir's forces suffered a set-back at the hands of the Franks, and he appealed to al-Malik al-ʿĀdil in Damascus, who sent an army which compelled the Franks to raise the siege and withdraw in 1215/1216.[44]

About this time the Assassins became tributary to the Knights of the Hospital. In the year 1226/1227, according to the author of the *Ta'rīkh al-Manṣūrī*, the chief da'i Majd-ad-Dīn received envoys from the emperor Frederick II, bringing gifts worth almost 80,000 dinars. On the pretext that the road to Alamut was too dangerous because of the rampages of the Khorezmians, Majd-ad-Dīn kept the gifts in Syria and himself gave the emperor the safe-conduct he required. In the same year the Hospitallers demanded tribute from the Assassins, who refused, saying: "Your king the emperor gives to us; will you then take from us?" The Hospitallers then attacked them and carried off much booty. The

[43] Sibṭ Ibn-al-Jauzī, p. 363; abū-Shāmah, *Tarājim rijāl al-qarnain* (ed. Muḥammad Zāhid, Cairo, 1947), pp. 78, 81; al-Juvainī, *Ta'rīkh-i-Jahān-Gushā*, vol. III (ed. Mīrzā Muḥammad Qazvīnī, Leyden and London, 1937), 243–248; Bar Hebraeus, p. 366; Defrémery, "Ismaéliens de Syrie," *op. cit.*, V, 38–40; J. von Hammer, *History of the Assassins*, pp. 141 ff.; van Berchem, "Épigraphie des Assassins," p. 27, note 1, 28 (cited from a reprint).

[44] Defrémery, "Ismaéliens de Syrie," *op. cit.*, V, 40–45; Cahen, *La Syrie du nord*, pp. 620 to 621. This version of the Frankish withdrawal from al-Khawābī is based on Kamāl-ad-Dīn, MS. 235v–236r (Blochet, *ROL*, V [1897], 48–49). A somewhat different version is given by Ibn-al-Furāt (Quatremère, "Notice historique sur les Ismaëliens," p. 358), according to which al-Malik az̧-Z̧āhir himself led his army to relieve the Ismāʿīlites. The Franks raised the siege on hearing of his approach. Az̧-Z̧āhir then reinforced al-Khawābī, and warned the Franks against attacking the Ismāʿīlites. This version is also to be found in the manuscript of Ibn-Wāṣil, *Mufarrij al-kurūb fī akhbār Banī-Aiyūb* (Cambridge, *Or.* 1079, pp. 538–539), with whom it probably originates.

text does not make it clear whether the tribute to the Hospitallers dates from this event or was already in existence.[45]

An interesting indication of how far the Assassins had become a recognized and even an accepted part of the Syrian political scene is given by Ibn-Wāṣil, under the year 1239/1240. In that year, says Ibn-Wāṣil, who was himself a native of central Syria, the qāḍī of Sinjar, Badr-ad-Dīn, sought and obtained refuge among the Assassins from the anger of al-Malik aṣ-Ṣāliḥ 'Imād-ad-Dīn. The chief of the Assassins was then a Persian called Tāj-ad-Dīn, who had come from Alamut. Ibn-Wāṣil does not hesitate to add that he knew him personally and was on terms of friendship with him. The same Tāj-ad-Dīn is named in a Maṣyāf inscription dated Dhū-l-Qa'dah 646 (February or March 1249).[46]

Only one group of events remains to be recorded before the political extinction of the Assassins — their dealings with St. Louis. The story of an Assassin plot against St. Louis while he was still a youth in France can, like all the other stories of Assassin activities in Europe, be dismissed as a product of over-vivid imaginations. But the account in Joinville of St. Louis's dealings with the Assassins after his arrival in Syria is of a different order, and bears every mark of authenticity. Emissaries of the Assassins came to the king in Acre, and asked him to pay tribute to their chief, "as the emperor of Germany, the king of Hungary, the sultan of Babylon [Egypt], and the others do every year, because they know well that they can only live as long as it may please him." Alternatively, if the king did not wish to pay tribute, they would be satisfied with the remission of the tribute which they themselves paid to the Hospitallers and the Templars. This tribute was paid, explains Joinville, because these two orders feared nothing from the Assassins, since, if one master was killed, he would at once be replaced by another as good, and the Assassin chief did not wish to waste his men where nothing could be gained. In the event, the tribute to the orders continued, and the king and the chief da'i exchanged gifts. An interesting addendum is the story of the Arabic-speaking friar Yves le Breton, who accompanied the king's messengers to the Assassins and discussed religion with their chief. Through the mists of ignorance and prejudice one can faintly discern some of the known doctrines of Ismā'īlite religion.[47]

[45] Amari, *Biblioteca arabo-sicula*, Appendix II, 30–31.
[46] Van Berchem, "Épigraphie des Assassins," p. 19 (cited from a reprint).
[47] Joinville (ed. Wailly), pp. 88, 162, 246ff.; Defrémery, "Ismaéliens de Syrie," *Journal*

The end of the power of the Assassins came under the double assault of the Mongols and of their deadliest enemy, the Mamlūk sultan Baybars. In Persia the Mongol general Hulagu succeeded where all Moslem rulers had failed, and captured the Assassin castles one by one, with surprisingly little difficulty. In 1256 Alamut itself fell, and the last grand master Rukn-ad-Dīn Khūr-Shāh was compelled to surrender himself. He was hanged shortly thereafter. The remaining Assassin strongholds in Persia were soon subjugated, and their treasures dispersed.

In Syria, as one would expect, the Assassins joined with the other Moslems in repelling the Mongol threat, and sought to win the good graces of Baybars by sending him embassies and gifts. Baybars at first showed no open hostility to them, and, in granting a truce to the Hospitallers in 1266, stipulated that they renounce the tribute they were receiving from various Moslem cities and districts, including the Ismā'īlite castles, whose tribute is given by al-Maqrīzī as "1,200 dinars and a hundred *mudd* of wheat and barley." The Ismā'īlites prudently sent emissaries to Baybars offering him the tribute which they had formerly paid to the Franks, to be used in the holy war.

But Baybars, whose life-work was the liberation of the Moslem Near East from the double threat of the Christian Franks and the heathen Mongols, could not be expected to tolerate the continued independence of a dangerous pocket of heretics and murderers in the very heart of Syria. As early as 1260 his biographer Ibn-'Abd-aẓ-Ẓāhir reports him as assigning the Ismā'īlite lands in fief to one of his generals. In 1265 he ordered the collection of taxes and tolls from the "gifts" brought for the Ismā'īlites from the various princes who paid them tribute. Among them the sources name "the emperor, Alfonso, the kings of the Franks and the Yemen". The Assassins, weakened in Syria and disheartened by the fate of their Persian brothers, were in no position to resist. Meekly accepting this measure, they themselves paid tribute to Baybars, and soon it was he, in place of the departed grand master in Alamut, who appointed and dismissed them at will.

In 1270 Baybars, dissatisfied with the attitude of the aged chief Najm-ad-Dīn, deposed him and appointed in his place his more compliant son-in-law Ṣārim-ad-Dīn Mubārak, Assassin governor of al-'Ullaiqah. The new chief, who held his office as representative of Baybars, was excluded from Maṣyāf, which came under the

asiatique, V, 45–46; Quatremère, "Notice historique sur les Ismaëliens," p. 262; van Berchem, *op. cit.*, pp. 30–32 (reprint).

direct rule of Baybars. But Ṣārim-ad-Dīn, by a trick, won possession of Maṣyāf. Baybars dislodged him and sent him as a prisoner to Cairo where he died, probably poisoned, and the now chastened Najm-ad-Dīn was reappointed, conjointly with his son Shams-ad-Dīn, in return for an annual tribute. They are both named in an inscription in the mosque of al-Qadmūs, of about this date.

In February or March 1271 Baybars arrested two Ismā'īlites sent from al-'Ullaiqah to Bohemond VI of Tripoli and, according to Ibn-al-Furāt, suborned to assassinate Baybars. Shams-ad-Dīn was arrested and charged with intelligence with the Franks, but released after his father Najm-ad-Dīn had come to plead his innocence. The two Ismā'īlite leaders, under pressure, agreed to surrender their castles and live at Baybars' court. Najm-ad-Dīn accompanied Baybars. He died in Cairo early in 1274. Shams-ad-Dīn was allowed to go to al-Kahf "to settle its affairs". Once there, he began to organize resistance to Baybars, but in vain. In May and June 1271 Baybars' lieutenants seized al-'Ullaiqah and ar-Ruṣāfah and in October, Shams-ad-Dīn, realizing his cause was hopeless, surrendered to Baybars and was at first well received. Later, learning of an Ismā'īlite plot to assassinate some of his emirs, Baybars deported Shams-ad-Dīn and his party to Egypt. The blockade of the castles continued. Al-Khawābī fell in the same year, and the remaining castles were all occupied by 1273.[48]

With the fall of al-Kahf on July 9, 1273, the last independent outpost of the Assassins had fallen. Henceforth the sect stagnated as a minor heresy in Persia and Syria, with little or no political importance. In the fourteenth century a split occured in the line of Nizārite imams. The Syrian and Persian Ismā'īlites followed different claimants, and from that date onward ceased to maintain contact with one another.[49]

The Mamlūk sultans in Egypt were quick to realize the possible uses of their once redoubtable subjects. As early as April 1271 Baybars is reported as threatening the count of Tripoli with assassination. The attempt on prince Edward of England in 1272 and perhaps also the murder of Philip of Montfort in Tyre in 1270 were instigated by him. Later chroniclers report several instances of the use of Assassins by Mamlūk sultans against their enemies,

[48] Defrémery, "Ismaéliens de Syrie," *op. cit.*, V, 48–65; Quatremère, *op. cit.*, pp. 363–365; van Berchem, *op. cit.*, p. 47 (reprint); Cahen, *La Syrie du nord*, p. 719.

[49] W. Ivanow, "A Forgotten Branch of the Ismailis," *Journal of the Royal Asiatic Society*, 1938, pp. 57–79.

and Ibn-Baṭṭūṭah, in the early fourteenth century, gives a detailed description of the arrangements adopted.[50]

In Persia the sect survived in rather greater numbers. A son of the last grand master Rukn-ad-Dīn was hidden while still a child, and lived to sire a whole series of imams, about whom unfortunately little is known. In the nineteenth century the imam migrated from Persia to India, where the majority of his followers were by then to be found. His grandson is well known as the Aga Khan.

[50] Defrémery, "Ismaéliens de Syrie," *Journal asiatique*, V, 65–74.

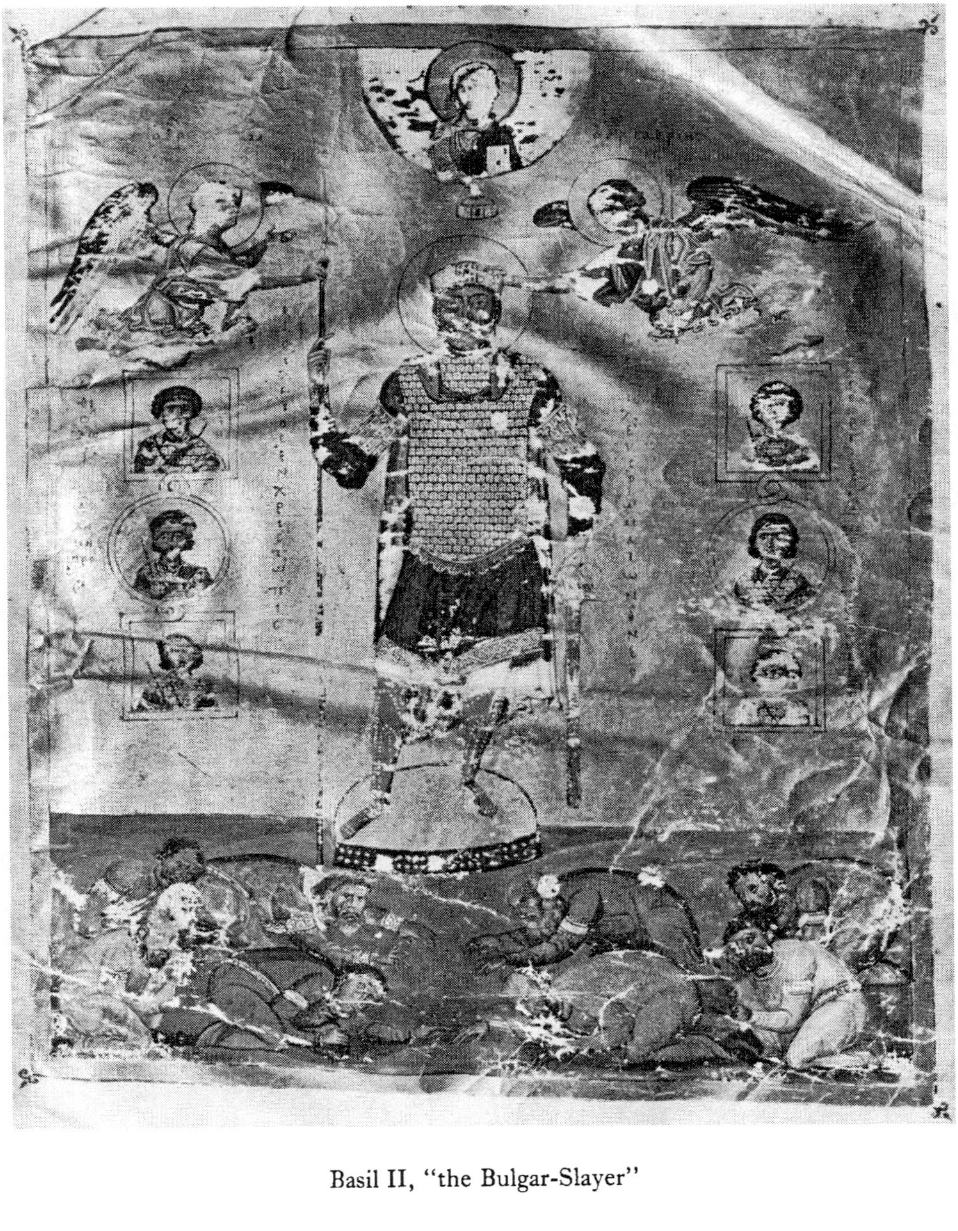

Basil II, "the Bulgar-Slayer"

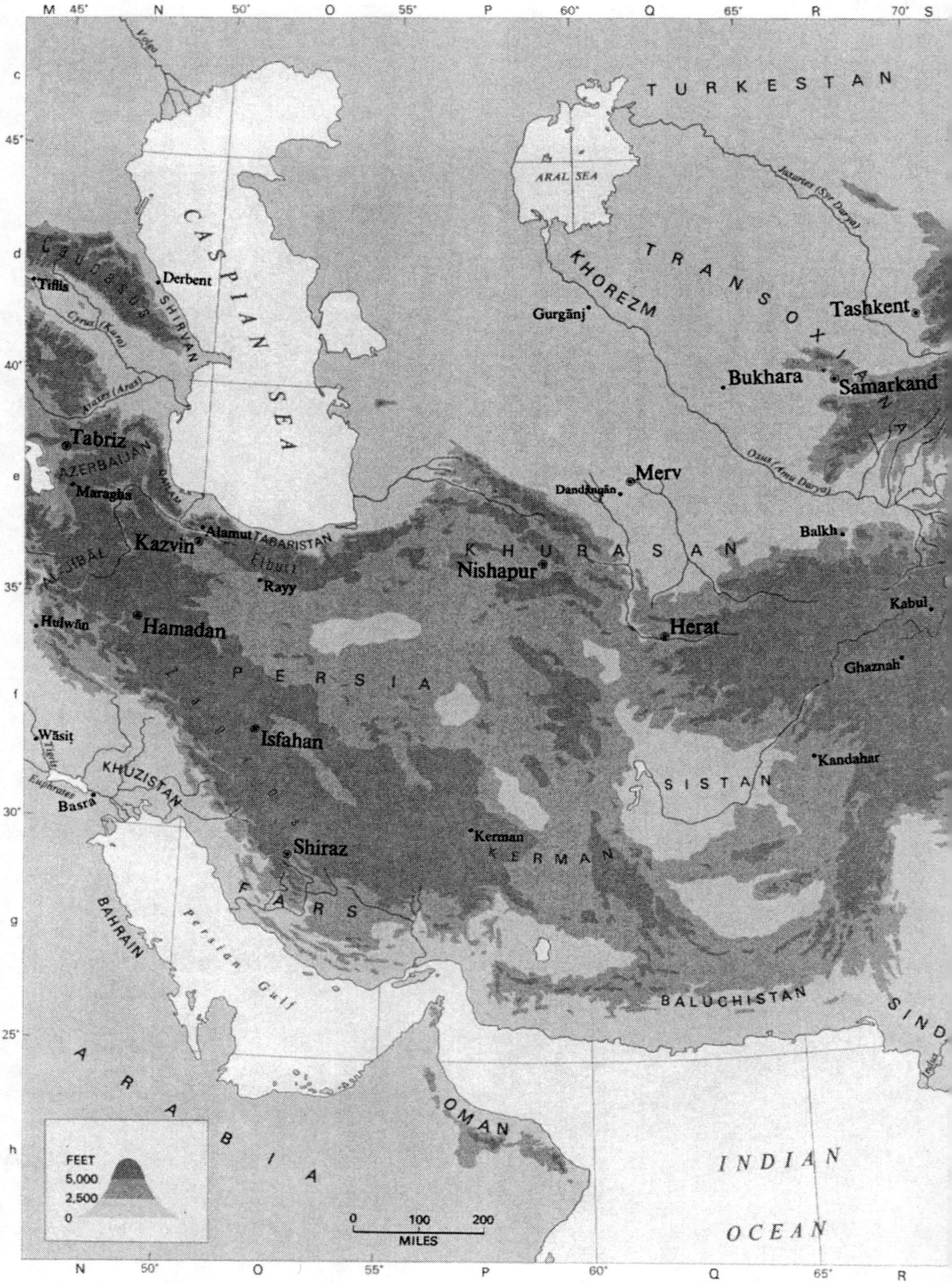

4. Persia and Adjacent Regions (*Map by the University of Wisconsin Cartographic Laboratory*)

V

THE TURKISH INVASION: THE SELCHÜKIDS

The appearance of the Turks, starting with the eleventh century, in most of the Moslem world and then of the Byzantine empire, inaugurated a profoundly new phase in the history not only of eastern Christianity, but also of Islam. It is true that the transformations which it brought about were in some respects the culmination of a previous internal evolution, but it precipitated and, in certain respects, disrupted this. There is thus the problem, to which insufficient attention has been directed, of identifying with precision the circumstances, the characteristics, and the scope of this intervention. But to attempt to offer here an inclusive analysis of its history would force us both to remain on too elementary a level and to depart from the general plan of the present work. We shall, therefore, lay particular stress on those of its aspects which affected the international relations of the occident and the orient.

No comprehensive scholarly history of the Selchükids exists; the pages devoted to them in the general histories of Islam or of the Turks are inadequate. It must be understood that the views expressed in this chapter, being based on personal studies in preparation, cannot always be documented. In general, the best course is to refer to the *Encyclopaedia of Islām*, especially the articles "Turks" and "Seldjuks", or still better, if possible, to the portion thus far published of the Turkish revision, *Islâm ansiklopedisi* (Istanbul, 1941 ff.). Views of a breadth extending far beyond their geographic base are to be found in the two works of W. Barthold: "Zwölf Vorlesungen über die Geschichte der Türken Mittelasiens," *Die Welt des Islams*, XIV–XVII (1932–1935), French translation, *Histoire des Turcs d'Asie centrale*, Paris, 1945, and *Turkestan down to the Mongol Invasion*, Gibb Memorial Series, new series, V (Oxford, 1928), a slightly revised translation from the Russian original of 1902. See also C. Cahen, "La Première pénétration turque en Asie Mineure," *Byzantion*, XVIII (1948), 5–67; and A. Z. V. Togan, *Umumi türk tarihine giris* [General Survey of Turkish History] (Istanbul, 1948).

A study of all the sources for Syrian history in the time of the crusades can be found in C. Cahen, *La Syrie du nord à l'époque des croisades* (Paris, 1940). For the beginning of the twelfth century the principal sources are: the Damascus Chronicle of Ibn-al-Qalānisī, *Dhail ta'rīkh Dimashq* (ed. H. F. Amedroz, Leyden, 1908; parts translated by H. A. R. Gibb, *The Damascus Chronicle of the Crusades*, London, 1932); the Aleppan sources were transmitted in the following century by Ibn-abī-Ṭaiyī (preserved in Ibn-al-Furāt, *Ta'rīkh ad-duwal wa-l-mulūk*, on which note C. Cahen, *Chronique chiite*, Académie des inscriptions et belles-lettres, Comptes-rendus des séances, 1935); and Kamāl-ad-Dīn ibn-al-'Adīm, *Zubdat al-ḥalab fī ta'rīkh Ḥalab* (ed. Sāmī ad-Dahhān, Damascus, 1951 ff.; extracts in *RHC, Or.*, III.)

[This chapter has been translated from the French original by Dr. Harry W. Hazard.]

There had long been Turks within the Moslem world. Some tribal groups had established themselves, well before the eleventh century, on the eastern confines of the Islamic domain, cut off from the main body of their relatives.[1] From the ninth century on, especially heavy recruiting of Turkish slaves had been undertaken in order to enlarge or replace the former unreliable indigenous armies, and from their ranks had emerged numerous governors of provinces, some of whom had become autonomous, as had the Ṭūlūnids of Egypt and the Ghaznavids of eastern Iran. It is unlikely that these men had retained no Turkish elements in their memories or, especially, in their characters. Since, however, they had been removed at an early age from their original environments and integrated into the structure of Moslem society, they cannot be considered as representing a real penetration by the Turkish world into that of Islam. When the true Turkish conquest occurred, these elements were no less opposed to it than were the natives, just as "barbarian"-born chieftains had defended the Roman empire against the "barbarians". And even though they may unconsciously have facilitated certain transitions, nothing would have been more foreign to them than any concept of Turkish solidarity. It was the same with the many Turkish mercenaries introduced into the Byzantine army during the eleventh century. During the First Crusade, for example, the troops of the basileus were led by a commander of Turkish origin in their effort to reconquer Anatolia from the Turks.

In order to avoid misunderstanding, however, it should be stated immediately that, in our judgment, the Turkish conquest was achieved as much from within as from without. This was done, as we shall try to make clear, in another fashion.

On their side the Turks were not, in the eleventh century, novices in politics. Almost certainly Turkish in all save name were the Huns who, having been forced towards Europe at the time of Attila, were the indirect forerunners of the Bulgar states on the Volga and the Danube and of the Khazars between the Black Sea and the Aral Sea. In the sixth century, Turks — by this time even in name — founded around the Altai range an empire which formed a link between Byzantium and China and left splendid memories in Central Asia, of which we have an eighth-century record in the first of the famous Orkhon inscriptions. Likewise Turkish, in the same region, were the eighth-century Uyghur

[1] R. N. Frye and Aydîn Sayîlî, "Turks in the Middle East before the Saljuqs," *Journal of the American Oriental Society,* LXIII (1943), 194–207.

realm and the ninth-century Kirghiz (or Kirgiz, Kïrghïz) kingdom. From the time of the first Turkish empire the eastern Turks, in contact with Chinese civilization, are to be distinguished from those of the west, leading nomadic lives to the north of Transoxiana. The pressure of new peoples, largely Mongol, caused a progressive withdrawal of the Turks from the east towards the west and the consequent transformation of the western steppes, until then half-Iranian, into that "Turkestan" which has retained their name ever since. Some groups, such as the Pechenegs, even reached Europe. The majority stayed in Asia, among them most of the Oghuz group who, having already been among the chief actors in the events just related, were to dominate later history.[2]

The Turks, generally shamanistic and hence originally alien to any exclusive or circumscribed religion, had been exposed to Nestorian, Manichaean, and Buddhist influences brought in by pilgrims and by merchants from Soghdia and elsewhere as they crossed Central Asia. The Khazars had similarly been open to Jewish influences. The Arab conquests of the seventh century placed them in contact with Islam, and, once the newly-conquered territory was Islamized, Moslem traders in their turn brought into the Turkish zone the influence of their new faith. In the tenth century large groups of Turks were won to Islam, from the Bulgars of the middle Volga to those whom the Kara-Khanids were about to unite on both sides of the mountains separating Russian from Chinese Turkestan. As had formerly been the case among the Arabs of Arabia, Islam was able to constitute for the Turks a common political bond, so that under this dynasty the first great Turkish Moslem realm came into being.

Most of the Moslems who had ventured among the Turks had come from Transoxiana, from Khurasan, and from Khorezm. Thus it was in the special forms which had been developed in the north-eastern Iranian region that the Turks came to know both Islam as a religion and the general civilization from which they were unable to distinguish it. It should be stressed that its spread had been accomplished not by orthodox theologians but by merchants

[2] F. Altheim, "Die Wanderung der Hunnen," *Nouvelle Clio*, I (1949), 71–86; R. Grousset, *L'Empire des steppes* (Paris, 1948); anonymous, *History of the Turkmens* (Tashkent, 1940, in Russian); A. Yakubovsky, "Seldjukskoe dvijenie i Turkmenui b XI beke" [The Selchükid Invasion and the Turkomans in the Eleventh Century], *Akademiia Nauk S. S. S. R., Isvestiia* [*Proceedings of the Academy of Science of the U.S.S.R.*] (Moscow, 1936); W. Barthold, article "Turks", in the *Encyclopaedia of Islām*; and his two works cited above in the bibliographical note; Osman Turan, "Türkler ve Islâmiyet" [The Turks and Islam], Ankara Üniversitesi: *Dil ve tarih-coğrafaya Fakültesi dergisi*, V (1945–1946), 457–485; P. Wittek, "Türkentum und Islam, I," *Archiv für Sozialwissenschaft*, LIX (1928), 489–525.

and plebeian mystics. Although the princes, on adopting Islam, associated themselves with orthodox groups, the mass of Turks remained no less Moslem, but professed a folk-Islam very different from orthodoxy. And naturally the Turks, on adopting the new faith, did not entirely forget all the customs, beliefs, and practices of their non-Moslem ancestors.

Even though the Turks lived, like all nomads, in symbiosis with the sedentary oasis-dwellers, and though some of them had themselves become sedentary, the overwhelming majority remained pastoral migrants from steppe to steppe. It has often been emphasized that nomad societies usually ignore or challenge the property limits which administrative states establish, as well as the frontiers which these states erect in an attempt to reserve for themselves the right to use certain territories. The Oghuz were not different. Like their "Scythian" precursors, they constantly launched against their neighbors and the sedentary inhabitants rapid raids which were hardly more than adventurous episodes in their perpetual wandering, although in times of drought the booty they secured was almost essential to life. The sedentary population referred to the Oghuz nomads and analogous neighboring groups as Turkomans (Turkish, Türkmenler; Arabic, Turkumān).

Along the northern border of Transoxiana, therefore, the Moslems continued against the nomads the old Iranian tradition of frontier defense. A special military organization provided this, and since their original opponents were unbelievers, it attracted all those whose enthusiasm was aroused by the Moslem ideal of holy war (Arabic, *jihād*), namely the ghazis (Arabic singular, *ghāzī*). Their tactics, matching those of their adversaries, stressed flexibility and speed, and were adapted to a strategy of incursions. Organized into martial brotherhoods in which the spiritual and military leaders simultaneously encouraged religious fanaticism and developed combat skills, the ghazis often represented, for the rulers of eastern Iran, a source of internal unrest and at the same time a bulwark against external enemies; the Ṣaffārid dynasty in Sistan originated among them.

The conversion to Islam of a growing proportion of the Turkomans adjacent to Transoxiana upset this whole system. Against the others, still non-Moslem, the Moslem Turks became ghazis in their turn. Obviously this entailed an extension of the Islamic domain, but it also meant the disappearance of the former fortified frontier. From place to place along that line the former ghazis and the new Turkish ghazis mingled, all the more readily because in many respects their ways of life and of war were alike. Against such an infiltration, if it should appear menacing, it would be impossible to mobilize the ghazis of the interior, as they would not fight against Moslems. The idleness to which they found themselves reduced aggravated social discontent. The Sāmānid sovereigns of Transoxiana and Khurasan found themselves compelled, in imitation of the rest of the Moslem world, to increase the slave element in their armies. It was their misfortune that at the same time the Turkish invasions of Russia had ruined commerce on the Volga, from which they and their subjects had derived great profit. Forced on this account to increase tax burdens, the Sāmānids alienated the mass of the people, and by making an effort to reduce this unpopularity by concessions to heretics, they also alienated the leaders of orthodox Islam. No one but the slaves had any apparent interest in defending the Sāmānid realm against the Moslem Turkish chieftains.[3] By this combination of reasons is to be explained the conquest of Transoxiana by the Turkish Kara-Khanid princes, while the balance of the Sāmānid domains fell into the hands of the Ghaznavids, the offspring of Turkish slaves, who kept their warlike elements occupied by inaugurating at the end of the tenth century a new aggressive policy against the Hindu plain. Moreover, the advance of the new Turkish population modified the ethnic character of these hitherto Iranian regions, such as Khorezm, which within two centuries was to become wholly Turkish.

The reciprocal interpenetration of the ghazis and the Turkomans meant for the latter the assimilation of Moslem civilization in the special ghazi form, which was so well suited to their habits. The frontier zones, where they set up a quasi-autonomous government, they called marches (Turkish singular, *uj*). Their moral cohesion, in default of any administration, was assured by the preachers (Turkish singular, *baba*) and the learned (Persian singular, *dānishmend*), heirs of the shamans, who continued to live among them, teaching and judging, and who sometimes succeeded in acquiring the prestige of chieftains.

One of the principal Turkish groups on the Moslem borders who were converted to Islam in the second half of the tenth century

[3] B.Zakhodar, "Khorasan i Obrazovanie Gosudarstva Sel'dzhukov" [Khurasan at the Beginning of the Selchükid Regime], *Voprosy istorii*, V–VI (1945), 118–142; M. S. Günaltay, "Selçuklular'în Horasan'a indikleri zaman İslâm dünyasînîn sîyasal, sosyal, ekonomik ve dini durumu" [The Moslem World at the Time of the Selchükid Conquest of Khurasan], Türk tarih kurumu [Society for Turkish History], *Belleten*, VII, (1943), 59–99; Barthold, *Turkestan down to the Mongol Invasion.*

had as chief one Selchük (also written Selchuk, Seljuk, Seljük; Arabic, Saljūq), of the Kinik tribe of the Oghuz.[4] He had established himself on the lower Jaxartes (Syr Darya). At the end of the tenth century this group was hired by the Sāmānids to resist the Kara-Khanids, and at the start of the eleventh century by the prince of this latter family who held Bukhara and Samarkand to support his revolt against the others. The Selchükids, with their men, therefore settled in Transoxiana, in the old Iranian Moslem land, where they received grazing grounds for their flocks. Closely associated with the princes in their activities, as leaders of one of the principal elements of their military forces, they could begin to familiarize themselves with the traditional Moslem ways of life and administration and to form ties with the orthodox Moslem leaders.

In 1025 a portion of the Selchükid Oghuz were settled in Khurasan itself by Maḥmūd the Ghaznavid who, victorious over their Kara-Khanid protector, was probably desirous of depriving him of their strength.[5] But very soon these nomads, by the necessary conditions of their life, set themselves up as a troublesome element, destroying harvests around the towns and thus causing misery and unrest, as well as a decrease in tax revenues. Military operations against them, conducted by troops less mobile than they, succeeded in driving them back but not in destroying them; the result was the diversion of their disorderly activity towards central and western Iran. The revolt of Mas'ūd, son of Maḥmūd, against the immediate successor of his father stripped Khurasan of its army; while the tendency of Mas'ūd to minimize the danger, which seemed to him merely to call for police action, and to use his army for profitable raids on India left the Turkomans practically uncontrolled.

In 1035 the rest of the Selchükid Oghuz, who had embroiled themselves with the new princes of Samarkand and Bukhara, moved to Khorezm with a rebellious vassal of Mas'ūd; then, threatened by a neighboring prince, they crossed the Oxus (Amu Darya) without difficulty, since the principality of Khorezm straddled the river, and in their turn made an unauthorized entry into Khurasan, in the territories left vacant by the departure of their predecessors, where they naturally behaved as had the others.

[4] C. Cahen, "Le Malik-nâmeh et l'histoire des origines seljukides," *Oriens* (*Journal of the International Society for Oriental Research*), II (1949), 31–65.
[5] M. Nāzim, *The Life and Times of Sulṭān Maḥmūd of Ghazna* (Cambridge, 1931).

The population of the commercial cities of Khurasan had no reason to be faithful to the Ghaznavids — whose government, entirely devoted to the military, was fiscally oppressive — except when this dynasty guaranteed their security. When it appeared unable or unwilling to do this, the leaders decided that the most practical way of avoiding disaster would be to recognize Selchükid suzerainty, which could be done without religious qualms since they affected a severe orthodoxy. At least, concerned for the prosperity of these cities, they would deflect elsewhere the disorders of their people. This was done by Merv and then, in 1037, by Nishapur, the capital of Khurasan.

It is scarcely to be doubted that the chiefs of this second Selchükid group, two brothers, grandsons of Selchük, Tughrul-Beg and Chagrî-Beg, were willing to form a state, making use of their Turkomans, but in accordance with concepts strange to them. From the start they had their authority recognized by the caliph under the title "clients of the commander of the faithful", which legitimized in Islamic eyes their actual power over their men, and established a claim to enlarge it. For although the groups which, lured by booty, followed Tughrul and Chagrî recognized them as warrior chiefs, they did not consider that this recognition conferred on them any rights in regard to the internal affairs of the tribes, nor that it prevented any Turkoman tribe from leaving the confederation whenever it wished. Tughrul and Chagrî were merely first among equals. But, charged by the commander of the faithful with the responsibility for imposing on their men the word of Allāh, Tughrul and Chagrî found their justification for claiming an authority which they could not otherwise have exercised. After their subsequent accession to the rank of territorial princes, they found themselves automatically integrated into the old Moslem organization. This brought the brothers a new power foreign to their functions as chieftains of nomads, but it led them to desire in their turn to preserve their territories from the depredations of the same men to whom they owed their acquisition.

The capitulation of the great cities opened the eyes of Mas'ūd to the political danger threatening him and he led his forces back into Khurasan. This was followed by several years of exhausting struggle in which the enemy always fled into the desert, to reappear unexpectedly and attack in a different quarter. In a country which the nomads had impoverished it was difficult to maintain a large army, poorly prepared for this style of warfare. The soldiers complained and the hard-pressed inhabitants did not assist

Mas'ūd. At last the Selchükids dared to attack. In 1040 at the battle of Dandānqān in the province of Merv the Ghaznavid army was annihilated.[6] Mas'ūd fled to India. Khurasan was lost, and the Iranian plateau was wide open. The evolution of the Iranian and Turkish worlds had led the former to admit the Turks into its own bosom. Like that of the Germans in the Roman empire, the conquest by the Turks, from then on, was accomplished from inside.

Among the simple yet powerful ideas which the Selchükid chieftains found in Iran was that of the scandal involved in the oppression of the caliph by the heretical Buwaihids. Already Maḥmūd and Mas'ūd had spoken of going to his relief, had begun the subjection of the Buwaihids of Iran, and had persecuted heretics. A "crusade" was in the air, and it can scarcely be doubted, from the course of ensuing events, that Tughrul-Beg promptly decided to profit from it. He immediately received the support of the orthodox notables of Khurasan, both for ideological reasons and for the sake of the profits they expected from exercising administrative control over the new conquests. For naturally it was through them that the Selchükids, whose Turkomans had had no administrative experience, would have to govern their territories. In certain respects the entry of the Turks into Baghdad would reproduce the earlier Khurasanian conquests of the 'Abbāsids over the Umaiyads and of al-Ma'mūn over al-Amīn.

At the same time, the occupation of Khurasan allowed the Selchükids to add to their Turkoman bands an army of the traditional Moslem type, supplied with weapons suitable for taking cities, which the men of the desert had lacked. Moreover, this army diminished their dependence on their Turkomans. The latter remained, nevertheless, their basic force, which required almost no pay and alone assured their superiority over their adversaries. The main problem of the Turkomans was the locating of new pastures. In religion their attitude was that of the ghazi, which was not that of the orthodox against the heretic but rather that of the Moslem of every description against the unbeliever; and they remained opposed to any Selchükid domination over them except the purely military.

In some respects the two attitudes might in practice coincide. This may be seen in the division of tasks which Tughrul and Chagrï agreed upon following Dandānqān. Chagrï retained, in addition to most of Khurasan, the Selchükid homelands, to be defended against the Kara-Khanids and the Ghaznavids. He accomplished

[6] B. Zakhodar, "Dendanekan," *Istoricheskii Zhurnal*, III–IV (1943), 74–78.

this by annexing Khorezm and the upper Oxus and, at first through the intermediary of some cousins, the provinces of Herat and Sistan. But in this direction expansion halted there, not only because it was made difficult by the presence of other Turks in the northeast and by mountains to the southeast, but also because in fact the majority of the Turkomans were not oriented thither. Even though, towards the south, a son of Chagrï named Kavurd occupied Kerman and went beyond to seize the entrance to the Persian Gulf and impose his power on Oman, these excessively hot deserts could not greatly attract the Turkomans.

On the other hand Tughrul, to whom had been allotted whatever he could conquer towards the west, was able to take advantage of the more normal area of expansion which the steppes of the northern and western portions of the Iranian plateau presented to the Turkomans, as they had to many others before them. The Buwaihids and other Iranian princes, torn apart by dissensions, poorly supported by troops who, more than elsewhere, were attached to the soil by land-grants (Arabic singular, *iqṭāʿ*), were no longer in a position to organize any real resistance. Tughrul had no trouble in taking Rayy or in leaping forthwith to the opposite edge of the plateau to capture Hamadan, at the same time that, on his flanks, he had his "suzerainty" recognized in Tabaristan and, in 1043, Isfahan. This advance was considered menacing by the first wave of Turkomans to have entered western Iran. Fleeing the Selchükids, they spread over upper Mesopotamia where, cut off from their bases, they were annihilated by the Arabs and Kurds, who had formed a coalition against their ravaging pastoral competitors.

The situation of Tughrul with his own Turkomans was complex. It was chiefly in the direction of Azerbaijan that the convergence of the Iranian routes caused them to reassemble, and in addition they were drawn by the proximity of frontiers — Georgian, Armeno-Byzantine, and Caucasian — which suggested the possibility of resuming the ghazi activity which they had had to abandon in the east. In itself this did no harm to Tughrul, who thus assured at slight expense the covering of his northern flank and might look forward to further conquests. In any event, it was preferable for their flocks to browse on pastures other than his. But there were disadvantages; Tughrul needed the Turkomans at hand for his own operations, which had become much less attractive to them now that, as we shall see, he often forbade pillage and did not let them take their families for permanent settlement. On the other hand, the Turkomans could give asylum and assistance beyond Tughrul's reach to ambitious rebels or, even without any preconceived plan, might end by founding a separate state. For all these reasons it was essential that Tughrul participate in the activities of the Turkomans in order to direct and channel them. And since, as Saif-ad-Daulah had just shown, the ideal of holy war still inspired the Moslems, he could derive increased prestige, redounding to the benefit of his other undertakings, from engaging in it beside his Turkomans.

Thus can be discerned, amidst the jumble of episodes monotonously narrated in the chronicles, the permanent balancing of two great trends: the expansion northwestward and the consolidation of power within Iran. The former began with intervention in northwestern Iran to enforce recognition of Selchükid authority, and in addition, following the traditional invasion routes, isolated Turkoman raids against the Georgians, the Armenians, and the Byzantines. In 1048 came the campaign of Ibrāhīm Înal (or Yînal), half-brother of Tughrul, into Armenia and the sack of Erzerum, and in 1054 that of Tughrul himself further south, capturing Arjish and besieging Manzikert. There he was also motivated by the desire to reconquer and strengthen the old Moslem frontier against the expansionism of Byzantium, whose response to the first Turkoman pressure from Azerbaijan had been the direct annexation of the hitherto autonomous Armenian kingdoms. The Byzantine government, renouncing a militarist policy, negotiated and purchased a peace which it expected the Selchükid to guarantee, and, by initiating closer ties with the 'Abbāsid caliphate for this purpose, succeeded only in cooling the friendship of the Fāṭimids, whose support would prove to be lacking at the decisive moment.

Meanwhile a ten-year period was devoted to establishing solid Selchükid dominance over the entire region between Khurasan and Baghdad through the direct annexation of vassal principalities, through the penetration of the Kurdish hill province (Arabic, al-Jibāl), where Ibrāhīm Înal combined military operations with diplomatic play on the rivalries of the indigenous tribal chieftains, and through utilization of similar rivalries and fear of the Turkomans to set up in Mesopotamia itself a faithful circle of petty princelings. In the province of Baghdad itself all pillaging was forbidden; Tughrul knew what he wanted.

At Baghdad, with the decline in the authority of the last Buwaihid of Iraq, the rule had fallen to his Turkish general and fellow-

Shī'ite, al-Basāsīrī, the oppressor of both people and caliph.[7] The latter, however, took advantage of the Buwaihid collapse to reconstitute a sketchy caliphal government for which he needed orthodox support against al-Basāsīrī. He had long enjoyed pleasant relations with Tughrul. In 1051 the famous jurist, al-Māwardī, at the same time that he had urged him to restrain the pillagers, had conferred on the Selchükid prince titles superior to those borne by anyone else. Tughrul had spoken of his desire to liberate the caliph, to assure the security of the pilgrimage, to subdue domestic heretics, and to deprive those abroad of Syria and Egypt, while disowning any intention of effecting direct seizure of Iraq. Pushed by al-Basāsīrī to extreme measures, the caliph thought of summoning the conqueror of Iran as a protector. Even the Buwaihid thought he might deal better with him than with al-Basāsīrī. The latter, uneasy and too weak, left Baghdad. In 1055, after everything had been solemnly prepared, Tughrul-Beg made his entry into Baghdad at the head of his troops without striking a blow. There he was welcomed by the vizir (Arabic, *wazīr*) of the caliph.

This moral triumph, it is true, was soon followed by a very grave crisis. Most of the Arabs, who were worried about their pastures and who were Shī'ite, gathered around al-Basāsīrī in his refuge on the Syrian border. From there he appealed to the Fāṭimids, who sent ambassadors and money, and led him to hope for reinforcements. Difficult operations ensued in upper Mesopotamia. The Turkomans grew discontented. For them, long accustomed to contact with Iranians and to a similar climate, northwestern Iran was not a strange land. But because of its heat and because of the language and customs of its inhabitants, Mesopotamia was. Further, they were prevented from establishing themselves there comfortably by the presence of nomadic Arabs and Kurds and by the policy of Tughrul; they had to leave their women in Iran; they suffered from a lengthy separation uncompensated by adequate booty. Moreover, Tughrul, to gain acceptance from his new subjects, surrounded himself with Arabs and overwhelmed them with favors. He adopted the manner of a sovereign. All these things offended the Turkomans and the Selchükid princes. In the midst of the Mesopotamian war Ibrāhīm İnal deserted to instigate a revolt among the Turkomans in Iran. Tughrul had to leave Mesopotamia; al-Basāsīrī returned to Baghdad, proclaimed Fāṭimid sovereignty, and expelled the caliph, who was sheltered by an Arab chief.

[7] H. Bowen, "The Last Buwayhids," *Journal of the Royal Asiatic Society*, 1929, pp. 225 to 245. Cf. also above, chapter III, pp. 91–92.

The assistance which Tughrul as a last resort obtained from the sons of Chagri-Beg saved him. The Turkoman revolt was stifled, Ibrāhīm Inal strangled, Iraq retaken, al-Basāsīrī hunted down and killed, and the caliph restored. All the Mesopotamian chieftains, especially the ʿUqailid of Mosul, now hurried to make their peace with the omnipotent victor. By 1059, and this time definitively, Tughrul-Beg was master of Mesopotamia as far as the Byzantine and Syrian frontiers.

Obviously thereafter, in Iraq as elsewhere, it was Tughrul who exercised the real power, but not in exactly the way the Buwaihid had; and the caliph was the beneficiary of the change. He was indeed sometimes made to feel that his domains had been left to him as a favor and that his government was subject to the agreement of Tughrul, as when in 1060 he tried to refuse his daughter's hand to the sultan. It was nevertheless noteworthy that he did have a civil government which, with the Turkish garrison, ruled Baghdad, and that he did hold domains commensurate with his rank. Above all, Tughrul, whether sincere or merely aware of the moral authority he derived from him, showed a real respect for the caliph. It was he who, as master, tried to avoid offense by not leaving too many Turks in Baghdad; he who, ill at ease amid the welter of Arab intrigues, preferred not to visit Baghdad often; and he who, above all, fought for the faith and for orthodoxy, and to whom for that reason the caliph gave his sincere support.

The title of sultan (Arabic, *sulṭān*) which the caliph conferred on him — long since a part of the current vocabulary, though Tughrul seems to have been the first to bear it officially — meant that he exercised all material power, on behalf of Islam in the service of the caliph, who was the supreme religious leader. It was a somewhat novel situation. The ninth-century caliphs had actually ruled; those of the tenth century were not even recognized as their religious superiors by the Buwaihids; and the principalities where they were so recognized, like the Sāmānids', were so distant that they were forgotten there. Now there was a true symbiosis which might suggest that which had existed in western Christendom between Charlemagne and the papacy.[8]

The two long reigns which followed that of Tughrul-Beg, those of Alp Arslan (1063–1072) and Malik-Shāh (1072–1092), witnessed

[8] W. Barthold, "Khalif' i sultan," *Mir Islama*, I (1912), 345–400, in Russian (analyzed by C. H. Becker in *Der Islam*, VI [1916], 350–412); J. H. Kramers, "Les Noms musulmans composés avec Dīn," *Acta Orientalia*, V (1927), 53–67; A. H. Siddiqi, "Caliphate and Kingship in Medieval Persia," *Islamic Culture*, IX (1935), 560–579; X (1936), 97–126, 260–279, 390–408; XI (1937), 37–59.

the development of both the Selchükid empire and the Turkoman power.[9] It is impossible to describe here in detail events the characteristics of which were not new.

The deaths of Chagrî-Beg and the childless Tughrul-Beg led to the unification of all the Selchükid domains except Kerman under the rule of a son of Chagrî named Alp Arslan. It could have been a source of weakness for the sultan to have to keep watch simultaneously over the whole of so extensive a frontier. In fact, even though Alp Arslan happened to die in Transoxiana, neither the Kara-Khanids, who were disunited, nor the Ghaznavids, whose ambitions were deflected toward India, were to cause him or his successor serious trouble. The bulk of their external affairs concerned the west. Tughrul had received from the caliph the title "king of the east and the west", investing him in advance with all he might conquer from the heretical Fāṭimid. Alp Arslan, as will be evident, remained aware of this mission. It was not, however, from this quarter that he was to acquire his glory in the eyes of posterity, but from that where he became involved in the expansion of the Turkomans themselves.

Since the later years of Tughrul-Beg's reign, these nomads had been making deep raids into Byzantine Armenia. The weakening of the Byzantine army, the internal revolts, the indiscipline and rivalries of the Armenian frontier chieftains, and especially perhaps the unsuitability of a system of large garrisons in widely-spaced fortresses for intercepting light troops crossing the countryside — for, once across the frontier, these no longer feared any army — these are the explanations of how such raids could have been accomplished with so little risk. Each year they had penetrated a little further. After 1057, when they sacked Melitene (Malatya), those who were perhaps most closely in touch with Selchükid policy had ranged southward along the Byzantine-Moslem border, descending the Euphrates as far as Syria; but the boldest were those who, for whatever reason, had fled Selchükid authority and who wanted to carve out by main strength a refuge inside Byzantine territory. In 1067–1068 they were to be found in Anatolia proper, at Amorium, at Iconium (Konya), and in Cilicia, and in 1070 at Chonae. Sometimes they were hired by Byzantines, as was a brother-in-law of Tughrul-Beg in 1070. Another leader, who had served the Marwānid Kurds on the upper Tigris and

[9] For this whole topic see C. Cahen, "La Première pénétration turque en Asie Mineure," *Byzantion*, XVIII (1948), 5–67; P. Wittek, "Deux chapitres de l'histoire des Turcs de Roum," *Byzantion*, XI (1936), 285–319; J. Laurent, *Byzance et les Turcs seldjoucides jusqu'en 1081* (Paris, 1914).

then the Byzantines, ended by serving the Mirdāsid Arabs of Aleppo against the Byzantines. A third, Atsïz, having escaped from Anatolia, landed in Palestine in 1071 and was engaged by the Fāṭimids to pacify insurgent bedouins (Arabic singular, *badawī*). It had long been the practice of "civilized" governments to hire for use against each other whatever "barbarian" bands offered their services.

It can be seen how indispensable it was for Alp Arslan, for the same reasons as for Tughrul-Beg but even more urgently, to intervene on the Byzantine frontiers. In 1065 he took Ani and about 1068 annexed some Georgian territory, thus making sure not only of the fidelity of his native vassals in Azerbaijan, but also of firm bases for activities in connection with the Turkomans. At length Byzantium reacted. The soldierly emperor Romanus Diogenes in 1068–1069 conducted a campaign into Syria and then along the upper Euphrates, by which he acquired or strengthened the frontier fortifications. The appearance of bands of Turks far to his rear demonstrated the futility of this method, and his army suffered from the devastation inflicted by the Turkomans on the regions through which it passed. In 1070 Alp Arslan could consider his realm safe.

It was then that he revived the old project of war with Egypt, to which he was the more receptive because of the welcome found by the Turkoman Atsïz in the Fāṭimid possessions. Though on his way he occupied several Christian places in consolidating his Euphrates frontier, his real goal was Aleppo. This strategically placed junction, autonomous but under Egyptian influence, he subdued and officially restored to ʿAbbāsid control. From there he was prepared to continue southward, but he received word that Romanus Diogenes, profiting from his extended advance, was preparing an offensive in his rear. He reversed his movements in the Turkoman way, leading unprepared observers to assume a rout, but he reunited his troops at the assembly point.

A battle which has been embellished by legend, but which has always been fascinating because it was the first meeting in centuries between a Byzantine emperor in person and a comparable Moslem sovereign, took place near Manzikert in Armenia in the summer of 1071. The Byzantine army, heterogeneous, suffering from the mute hostility of the native population and of the mercenaries composing it, frightened by a poorly known adversary, and fearing treason because of the presence in its ranks of a Turkish contingent, fell victim to the classical nomad maneuver, a simulated flight permitting a return-offensive envelopment. The Byzantine army was annihilated and, for the first time in history, the Byzantine emperor himself was brought captive to the feet of his vanquisher.[10]

The battle of Manzikert marked the beginning of a new period. Not that Alp Arslan had any idea of dismembering the Byzantine empire; he was satisfied to demand a tribute and the cession of the formerly Moslem border towns, provisions which the overthrow of Romanus Diogenes at Constantinople rendered meaningless. What the sultan wanted was a guarantee of neutrality or alliance in his enterprise of unifying the Moslem world, and the eventual aid of the basileus against rebels who fled into Byzantine territory. But Manzikert completed the ruin of the Byzantine military strength; the Turkomans, instead of retiring after each raid, no longer had any reason not to stay in the territory of the empire. The populations of Armenia and Cappadocia, hostile to Byzantium for fiscal and religious reasons, no longer able to rely on the Byzantines for defense, treated with the invader just as had the inhabitants of Khurasan. Certain of their component elements — military colonists planted on the frontier and others — had less in common with the Byzantines than with the border Moslems with whom for centuries they had alternately had minor battles and courteous exchanges, and who sometimes mingled with the Turkomans. At times these groups joined the newcomers. The Byzantine system had, moreover, become disorganized by the action of the Constantinopolitan government itself in annexing Armenia and Edessa (Urfa) and thereby advancing its frontier beyond the prepared zone. Distrusting its new subjects, it had replaced them as soldiers with mercenaries hateful to the inhabitants, who under the pretext of protecting them from the Turks were deported to Cappadocia and Cilicia. Thus the area where anti-Byzantine quarrels and bitterness prevailed was permanently enlarged.

A few years sufficed to eliminate the last traces of Byzantine administration from the main routes of Armenia and Cappadocia. It was not that they had been formally expelled, but in a flat land held by nomads and deserted by whatever peasants survived, how could taxes be collected? The cities remained as foreign bodies which surrendered in order to escape famine. And even though the Turkomans necessarily allowed them to govern themselves,

[10] C. Cahen, "La Campagne de Mantzikert d'après les sources musulmanes," *Byzantion*, IX (1934), 613–642. On Manzikert and its consequences to the Byzantine empire, see below chapter VI, pp. 192–193.

they lost all contact with the Byzantine government. No deliberate seizure of Byzantine territory by the Turkomans had occurred; they were in a land which they knew belonged to "Rome" (Arabic, Rūm), but that sovereignty had been emptied of any reality.

By themselves the Turkomans could perhaps not have progressed as rapidly as they did. It was the Byzantines who had brought them into the heart of the empire. Since Byzantium had commenced the habitual enrollment of "barbarians" as mercenaries, the Turks who had for a century or two regularly offered their services were strangers no longer. Even if they had been, what difference would it have made to all the generals competing for the throne? Had Romanus Diogenes himself not called upon his late enemy, the sultan, for aid in regaining power? From Manzikert on, and especially from 1078 to 1081, others successively brought them in, opening to them the Greek villages of Asia Minor, even establishing them on the shore of the Sea of Marmara and near the Bosporus at Nicaea or along the coasts of the Aegean Sea.

Assuredly these Turkomans, though theoretically responsible to the Byzantines through the leaders who imported them, were none the less autonomous Turks whose perpetual pillaging by land and soon by sea was an obvious danger to Byzantium, and not only to Byzantium but also to the sultan, from whose control they had completely escaped. In the last years of Tughrul-Beg's life one of his cousins, Kutulmish (or Kutlumush), whose father had formerly been the eldest and foremost member of the family, had withdrawn with some Turkomans into the mountains south of the Caspian Sea. Proceeding into open revolt against Alp Arslan, the sons of Kutulmish sought safety in Anatolia amidst some free Turkomans. It was with them in particular that the Byzantines had dealings and doubtless it was they or their Turkomans who wished to set themselves up as a state in Anatolia, or at least as a force capable of resuming the contest with their Iranian cousins. From 1075 on they were involved in Syria as allies of the Fāṭimids against a Selchükid adherent. In the Taurus mountains a former general of Romanus Diogenes, an Armenian named Philaretus (Filardos), had gathered under his authority the people of Cilicia and of the region from Antioch to Edessa and Melitene. The Byzantine emperor Alexius Comnenus allowed — if nothing more — Sulaimān, the last survivor of the sons of Kutulmish, who was installed at Nicaea, to take from Philaretus, in the capacity of a Byzantine lieutenant, Cilicia, Antioch, and Melitene. At Iconium, he was in complete possession of one of the two great east-west

Anatolian routes and hence at the border of Selchükid Mesopotamia and Syria, a grave danger to Malik-Shāh in 1084–1085.

On a smaller scale, the same problem was posed by Atsïz further south. Though summoned by Egypt, he had promptly embroiled himself with her and, together with Jerusalem and Damascus, had formed an autonomous principality which he now sought to consolidate by recognizing Malik-Shāh, thus provoking the Egyptian appeal to the sons of Kutulmïsh. Atsïz defeated the coalition and, in his new power, could hardly have inspired much confidence in Malik-Shāh.

Indeed, this sultan's policies seemed much more concerned with the avoidance of such dangers than with the further extension of his empire. It is true that he had cleared the Persian Gulf region of the Qarmaṭians who had infested it, and had disputed with the Fāṭimids the allegiance of Mecca, but those were minor undertakings. Young, born to the "purple" and not to the steppe like his father, he was less a soldier than a proponent of the diplomacy counselled by his vizir Niẓām-al-Mulk. The latter knew that the unity of the empire needed careful safeguarding, and that every prolonged absence of the sovereign in one quarter could be utilized by fomenters of trouble elsewhere.

He also knew that within the Selchükid family itself, where the tradition still lingered of rule by the family rather than by a single sovereign, there could arise new discontents like those of Ibrāhīm Ïnal and Kutulmïsh, recently quelled. Though Malik-Shāh had removed, by executing him, the embarrassment of his uncle, Kavurd of Kerman, who had claimed as eldest of the family to supplant him, it appeared that it might be useful to create appanages for the young princes. Such a course would please them, propitiate local sentiment, and avoid unnecessary travel by the sultan. This was the solution Malik-Shāh adopted for Syria, among other places, in response to an appeal by Atsïz concerning an Egyptian attack. Tutush, brother of Malik-Shāh, received central Syria and Palestine, and in 1079 rid himself of Atsïz. As for Aleppo, distracted by the ravages of the Turkomans, which Tutush was unable to prevent, and deceived by princes incapable of giving protection, it yielded to the 'Uqailid of Mosul, an Arab allied by marriage to the Selchükids and vassal to them. Malik-Shāh left Aleppo alone for the time being, but he sent an army to Anatolia to combat the sons of Kutulmïsh.

Meanwhile the Selchükid government also gradually limited the autonomy of the indigenous population, and that policy of perpetual small-scale local encroachment would continue long after the Selchükid empire had been broken into fragments. It was thus that the Shabānkārah Kurds of Fars were subdued, and that the vassal states of extreme northwestern Iran were, except for Shirvan, annexed little by little. Those situated on frontiers or on main strategic routes were in particular danger. Some remained more or less openly Shī'ite, like the 'Uqailid, who clashed with Tutush and intrigued with Philaretus and even with Egypt. On the other hand there was the more vulgar greed of the lieutenants of sultan and caliph, when they knew a treasury was rich. This was one of the reasons for the suppression of the Kurdish principality of the Marwānids, innocuous though it was otherwise. Against the 'Uqailid an assault was prepared, for he had feared the consequences of the disappearance of the Marwānids, and had come to their aid. But it happened that Sulaimān, the son of Kutulmïsh, having just taken Antioch, got into a dispute with him and killed him. Sulaimān thought it wise to be reconciled with Malik-Shāh, but was attacked and killed by Tutush.

Chance favored Malik-Shāh. The bedouin victims of the Turkomans, the victims of Sulaimān, of the 'Uqailid, and of Tutush, all those who were exasperated by the continued devastations appealed to him, asking only to submit to him. He arrived without striking a blow, annexing Mosul, Aleppo, Antioch, and the rest of Philaretus's holdings. He had been seen at Samarkand; he now appeared on the shore of the Mediterranean. This time Mesopotamia and Syria were wholly incorporated into the Selchükid empire. Tutush remained, but in 1086–1087 the other captured cities received as governors freedmen from the Selchükid army — Buzan at Edessa, Yaghï-Sïyan at Antioch, and Aksungur al-Ḥājib at Aleppo.

There remained only one dark spot, Anatolia. For the death of Sulaimān, though it had enabled Malik-Shāh to occupy Antioch, had not contributed to the subjugation of the Turkomans of Anatolia. Against them Malik-Shāh, at the same time that he sent troops, tried to obtain as an ally Alexius Comnenus, whom he recognized as legitimate possessor of all the former Byzantine territories. This was a necessary procedure, for how could one organize a Moslem administration in territories where there were no Moslems except the Turkomans ? But Alexius hesitated, not knowing whether to prefer the troops of the powerful Selchükid or the bands which he hoped in the long run to neutralize by playing them against one another. Malik-Shāh was to die without having concluded this agreement or having accomplished anything important against the Turkomans. Subsequent events, it is true, were to demonstrate that once they had left the empire, the Turkomans could not make much headway against it.

It is impossible here to consider exhaustively the internal administration and the civilization of the Selchükid empire, subjects about which very little is known.[11] It will suffice to describe certain general characteristics necessary to the understanding of events which will be mentioned in this work.

The Selchükid regime can be defined as an orthodox dictatorship accepted by the majority of the population, administered by Khurasanians, and relying upon a dual military basis of Turkish slaves and Turkomans. In the domain of culture it was the period of Omar Khayyám ('Umar al-Khaiyām), when the revival of the Persian language, which began at the end of the tenth century, culminated in the progressive elimination of Arabic from the land of Iran, even as the language of learning. In Selchükid art Khurasanian influences are evident. The administrative personnel, even in the Arab areas on at least the upper levels, was basically Iranian.

The great organizers of the regime, the vizir of Tughrul-Beg, 'Amīd-al-Mulk al-Kundurī, and the vizir of Alp Arslan and Malik-Shāh, the illustrious Niẓām-al-Mulk, who left us a *Treatise on Government*, started as functionaries of the Ghaznavids, and belonged to the petty aristocracy of Khurasan. They were in complete charge of internal administration, for the Turks had had no experience along that line, and the sultan left it in their care. Especially under Malik-Shāh, who had become sultan while young and who owed to Niẓām-al-Mulk's ability his ascendancy over the other princes of his family, the vizir was the actual master. He had an enormous following, mostly Khurasanian, an army of slaves, and numerous sons on whom the most lucrative posts were bestowed, to such an extent that for nearly twenty years after his death it would be almost impossible for the Selchükids to

[11] While awaiting a complete study, which would require knowledge of the earlier Turkish and Moslem institutions, see A. K. S. Lambton, *Contribution to the Study of Seljuk Institutions* (manuscript thesis, University of London); M. F. Köprülü, "Bizans müesseselerinin Osmanlî müesseselerine te'siri hakkînda bâzî mülâhazalar" [Remarks on the Influence of Byzantine Institutions on Ottoman Institutions], *Türk hukuk ve iktisat tarihi mecmuasî*, I (1931), 165–298, and "Les Institutions juridiques turques au moyen âge," *IIe Congrès turc d'histoire* (1937), pp. 383–418; I. H. Uzunçarsîlî, *Osmanlî devleti, teskilâtîna medhal* [*Introduction to the Organization of the Ottoman Empire*] (Istanbul, 1941); C. Cahen, "Contribution à l'histoire de l'iqtâ'," *Annales: économies, sociétés, civilisations*, VIII (1953), 25–52.

secure vizirs not of his family. This power, it is true, aroused envy among those who, perhaps even with the complicity of Malik-Shāh, procured his assassination early in 1092.

The power which the regime derived from its conquests, from the elimination of its foes, and from the unification of a territory almost as vast as that of the ʿAbbāsid caliphate at its start — except for the far west nothing important was lacking but Egypt — equipped it for action on a huge scale. Its military strength was its foundation, permitting it, paradoxical though it seems, by holding the military power in leash to restore the primacy of the civil administration, which had fallen into neglect under the Buwaihids. In this administration, as in the whole social structure, it was necessary to construct a solid orthodox framework. While up to this time Jews, Christians, and Shīʿites could be found on all levels of the bureaucracy, now the Jews were eliminated as much as possible except in wholly subordinate positions, and the Shīʿites were rooted out. The training of officials was no longer left to chance.

Education had long been left mainly to private initiative, and had been directed toward the development of learning rather than the inculcation of orthodoxy. This had been altered somewhat, to the benefit of Ismāʿīlism, under the Fāṭimid caliphate. Among the Sunnites, perhaps as a reaction, an analogous movement had been spreading through eastern Iran since the time of the later Sāmānids, and was doubtless further encouraged by the Ghaznavids, resulting in the establishment of schools (Arabic singular, *madrasah*) distinct from the public mosques (Arabic singular, *masjid*) where until then instruction had usually been dispensed. The Selchükids extended this movement throughout their realm, especially in the former Buwaihid domain, where it was a complete innovation. Even if the idea was not wholly novel, in practice they created a new situation by the vigorous interest they took in the widespread diffusion of the madrasahs and the material help they afforded to the schools, their students, their teachers, and their libraries. The most distinguished of these madrasahs was the Niẓāmīyah, founded at Baghdad by Niẓām-al-Mulk for the great philosopher abū-Isḥāq ash-Shīrāzī. Soon, with the notables competing out of ardor, conviction, or a desire to flatter their master, the Moslem world was covered with madrasahs, Iran from the late eleventh century, the Arab world during the twelfth. Of the four rites two in particular were encouraged, the Shāfiʿite, which was that of most Arabic-speaking easterners and of Niẓām-al-Mulk, and the Ḥanafite, which predominated in Khurasan and had thus become that of the Turks and of their sultans.

Among the mass of the people the dominant influence was that of the sufis (Arabic singular, *ṣūfī*) who, because of their indifference to rites and laws, had often been unfavorably regarded by those in power, and who were riddled with heretical tendencies. But a new form of sufism was beginning to appear in the east, organized into congregations. Their rule was indeed outside the classical practices of Islam, but their influence might, according to circumstances, be exercised either in the direction of official orthodoxy or against it. The westward thrust of the Turks and Khurasanians promoted and accelerated the diffusion of these congregations. The Selchükids, their Persian vizirs, and their Turkish officers, sincerely devoted to saintly individuals and aware of their usefulness in the spiritual control of the urban masses, favored certain of these orders. At the same time as the madrasahs appeared the orders dotted the empire with their headquarters (Persian singular, *khānaqāh*).

Finally, it is from this functional point of view, among others, that it is fitting to note the construction of numerous splendid new mosques and richly endowed hospitals, which served indeed to proclaim the glory of the dynasty, but a glory which it attached to all pious institutions susceptible of strengthening the Islamic social structure and binding it to the regime.

Paradoxical though it may sound, however, the Selchükid regime might in certain respects be considered rather non-clerical in comparison with other Moslem states. Power, although exercised in behalf of the Islamic faith, was in the hands of the sultan, whose role, in contrast to that of the caliph, was not primarily religious. It had been the same under the Buwaihids, but the very real priority accorded by the Selchükids to military and political matters, coupled with their intervention in spiritual affairs, meant for the "clerics", as well as material wealth and an enhancement of their social function, a decrease in their independence in that role.

Even in the structure of the Selchükid administration itself this secular characteristic was emphasized by an organic development. In the ʿAbbāsid and Buwaihid state, in addition to the daily justice of the magistrates (Arabic singular, *qāḍī*) the sovereign exercised a sort of supreme jurisdiction on appeal, the *maẓālim* sessions. In spite of edifying anecdotes told about the great caliphs this justice does not seem to have been very effective. In the Sāmānid and Ghaznavid states, one has the impression that it acquired more actual importance, being directed by a special functionary named on the same level as the other great heads of state departments, the *amīr-dād*. The Turks conceived of it as continuing their tribal tribunal, the *yavlak*. The Selchükids adopted and extended to the rest of their empire this institution which seemed so novel and so admirable to officials trained in the Buwaihid state, like the historian ar-Rūẕrāvarī. And even though in theory this justice was of course based on the principles of the religious law alone, it was in practice far more flexible than that of the qadis and more responsive to considerations of common sense and political utility.

It is difficult to say, in the present state of our knowledge, whether differences more fundamental than mere nomenclature and the exact division of responsibilities existed between the other great state services of the Sāmānids and the Ghaznavids – which the Selchükids adopted for their empire with their heads – and their counterparts in the ʿAbbāsid and Buwaihid domains. These were the vizir, the director of finances (Persian, *mustaufī*), the controller general (Arabic, *mushrif*), the steward of the palace and the royal domain (Arabic, *wakīl*), the supervisor of the army (Arabic, *ʿāriḍ*), and the director of the postal system. The provinces were similarly organized, and their civil governors were recruited, like the heads of the central departments, from an upper category of civil servants entitled amids (Arabic singular, *ʿamīd*). The garrison commanders (Arabic singular, *shiḥnah*) did not, under the great Selchükids, encroach on the civil authority of the amids. In certain instances the administration of a district was farmed out. It could happen that the compensation of the tax-farmers, in place of or in addition to payment of cash, might include a land-grant (*iqṭāʿ*), but these were never confused, nor was an administrative district ever treated by the official as a land-grant; the state was strong enough to assure respect for its rights. The information and espionage services, which were said to be repugnant to Tughrul-Beg, were nevertheless set up without delay.

It is not easy to disentangle and identify whatever portion of all this might stem from Turkish traditions, that vague heritage of administrative experience derived either from certain Turkish groups in the past or from transfer of nomadic Oghuz usages. The sultans remained Turkish in their personal and family lives, the emancipation of their women for example, and in their language. The seal (Turkish, *tughra*) with which they affirmed their sovereign authority on their decrees was in the form of that bow which had signified such authority among the Oghuz. Their safe-conducts were in the form of arrows for the same reason. More fundamentally, we have seen and shall again see persist among them the tribal idea of the preëminence of a family ruled by the eldest member, beside the contrasting Moslem idea of a monarch who would be succeeded by his sons. Finally, whoever glances over the whole of Turkish history, however cursorily, can hardly avoid receiving the impression that the temperament or the experience of the Turks, as compared to other peoples, had induced a sense of political and military command like that which the first Buwaihids had displayed in a lesser degree.

In the immigrant Turkish population there naturally persisted the traditions and some of the literature, mainly oral, of the Oghuz of Central Asia. It is difficult to determine whether some of this passed into certain aspects of the life and culture of the Iranians and Arabs in the Selchükid period. On the whole, while the Turkish aristocracy tended to adopt Iranian culture and to become diluted in the issue of mixed matings, the bulk of the Turkomans were, because of their nomadic way of life, a body foreign to the society in the midst of which they had come to live, though it seems likely that in certain regions they mingled with the native peasantry. The narrative of events has shown how these nomads were both an indispensable source of strength and a permanent danger to the regime.

It is difficult to compute the number (twenty or thirty thousand ?) of these Turkomans or to be sure which among the twenty-four Oghuz tribes of Central Asia, most of whose names reappear among the population of the modern Near East, had already played, before the new ethnic dislocations of the twelfth and thirteenth centuries, a major role in the migration associated with the Selchükid conquest. The Avshar, the Döger, the Salgur (or Salghur, Salur), and the İva (Yİva) seem to have predominated. The Turkomans were generally able to stay in tribal groups, but fractions swarmed or were transferred to all corners of the vast new domains, and as a result of these movements, of the chances of war, and of discord, new groupings arose under chieftains who were not always members of the former ruling tribal families. They were numerous in eastern Iran, where many had stayed, in Fars and Khuzistan, on the great arteries of central al-Jibāl province, and in Diyār-Bakr province. Above all they were massed in Azerbaijan, which has remained Turkish until today. There were also those who had ranged as far as Palestine or, in ever-growing numbers, had crossed Byzantine Armenia and reached the shores of the Aegean Sea.

In every case, as pastoral nomads, the newcomers had to try to procure grazing lands with a minimum of damage to the rest of the inhabitants. They were aided by their dispersion, by the loose pattern of agricultural utilization of the western Asian countryside, and by their concentration in frontier regions accustomed to receiving military settlers and to relying for food on their enemies. It was necessary to concede to them, or to their chiefs, vast fiefs suitable for grazing, inside which they would live in semi-autonomy.

An attempt to insure their fidelity was made by attracting to the court, through the promise of an education qualifying them for great futures, the sons of their notables, and by using them on occasion on productive military undertakings. Such was the case, for example, with Artuk, chief of a group of the Döger, who as a feudatory of Ḥulwān on the Mesopotamian edge of al-Jibāl was employed by Malik-Shāh in Anatolia, in Bahrain (the Hasa coast of Arabia), and in upper Mesopotamia. There he was circumvented by the ʿUqailid and thence, at the death of the latter, he fled in fear of Malik-Shāh to the service of Tutush, who bestowed Jerusalem on him.

What permitted the Turkoman force to be held in check was the regular army recruited from slaves. It was of the classical type of the armies of almost every nation of Islam at this period, and composed in large part of Turks, but, thanks to the conquests whose further extension it made possible, much larger, with 46,000 or even 70,000 horsemen, according to unreliable medieval estimates. The economy of the Selchükid domain, which was for many reasons less mercantile than at the start of the tenth century, thereby rendered correspondingly even less practicable the creation of such an army by the sheer expenditure of money, or of property. The Buwaihids had installed and developed a system of supporting troops by the practice of distributing grants of land and its revenues. It is probable that Niẓām-al-Mulk, in particular, perfected this system, applying it in a way which ended by interesting the concessionaires in improving their lands and by regularizing the responsibility of certain chieftains holding huge concessions for the maintenance of specified contingents. Thus there was what might be termed a feudal system functioning in the service of the state, which was able to maintain control by reason of the superiority of the resources which remained to it throughout its immense empire.

Although of course the regime functioned on behalf of the military and religious aristocracy, the reappearance of a regular administration and political unity after periods of fragmentation, and in places anarchy, seems to have given a feeling of relief to the people in general. After Alp Arslan, with his aura of military glory, Malik-Shāh and Niẓām-al-Mulk appeared in the eyes of posterity as the ideal sovereign and vizir.

The remarkable fact is that this was true not only of Moslems but of Christians of all sects. Of course the ecclesiastics deplored the territorial losses sustained by Byzantium, and they all lamented the ravages of the Turkomans, but they generally held the Byzantines responsible for the former and were the more grateful to the great peacemaker Malik-Shāh for his praiseworthy suppression of the latter. Whether one listens to the testimony of the Armenians, Matthew (Madṭēos) of Edessa and Sarkavag, or the opinions of the Syrian Monophysites transmitted later by Michael the Syrian, or those of the Nestorians recorded in the chronicle of ʻAmr, or even those of Copts outside the Selchükid domain as given in the *History of the Patriarchs of Alexandria*, Christian sentiment is unanimous, even in writings subsequent to the death of Malik-Shāh and therefore free of any imputation of venality.

This favorable opinion was even extended, as soon as the Turkoman ravages ceased, to chiefs like Sulaimān at Antioch or Artuk at Jerusalem. This was so because even though the ghazi spirit entailed the subjugation of unbelievers, it did not allow their persecution after submission, thus resembling the spirit of classical Islam. Moreover, in the frontier regions, where Selchükid control was less effective, the struggle between the Turkomans and the old Arab or Byzantine aristocracy worked, insofar as any administration continued, to the advantage of the natives, including numerous Christians of churches happy to be free of the trickery of the Greek clergy. And even the Greek patriarchs of Antioch and Jerusalem could stay in their metropolitan sees; the former was to be imprisoned and the latter expelled by the Egyptians only in reprisal, upon the approach of the army of the crusaders and the Greeks. The sole persecution of Christians inside Islam was that of al-Ḥākim, the half-insane Fāṭimid caliph, fifty years before the appearance of the Turks in the region of Iran.

Also it would be absolutely incorrect to imagine, merely because the crusades did occur, that the native Christians had hoped for liberation from outside. Of course some Hellenized elements might have hoped for a Byzantine resurgence in Anatolia or Armenia, but naturally, although they had heard of Frankish mercenaries, they could have conceived of no reconquest other than Byzantine. But the immense majority either were reasonably satisfied or else, if they had anything to complain of, placed their hopes on Malik-Shāh. The most that can be said is that in the disorders which were to follow his death, those hopes would no longer have a focus. It has been established that no oriental appeal, except Byzantine, was ever sent westward either to the pope or to anyone else. It may be added that such an appeal would in no respect have corresponded to the mentality of the Christians of the orient. When these latter, after the event, wished to explain the crusade, they borrowed from the occident their explanation, the mistreatment of the pilgrims.

Certainly pilgrims, who often took the land route by Constantinople, suffered from the loss of Anatolia and the anarchy prevalent there. Some of the pilgrims might even have suffered at Jerusalem itself, because of the disorders at the time of Atsiz. But it should not be forgotten that we know of robberies of pilgrims by bedouins before the Turkomans arrived, and we know of none committed by the Turks. In any event, these grievances applied only to certain places at certain times of disorder.[12] By sea Mediterranean commerce and pilgrimages continued. Of course the Turkoman holy war had been a catastrophe for Byzantium, but for it alone. Perhaps it was the very vigor of commerce and pilgrimage which made what had previously been endured without difficulty suddenly seem intolerable, especially since Byzantium was no longer able to extend to Christians in its jurisdiction the protection which it had provided for three generations. On the contrary, the Latin influence among them was increasing. The schism between Constantinople and Rome dating from the middle of the century caused only slight echoes in Antioch and Jerusalem, even among the Melkites, natives Greek in faith and Arab in speech. The idea of taking over in the orient from a weakened Byzantium might have arisen in Rome. It is not extraordinary that in poorly informed western Europe the remote and the recent past should be confused, and that such a confusion, perhaps skillfully induced, should envisage a Byzantine disaster as a great hardship for the eastern Christians.[13]

[12] For a somewhat different interpretation of the difficulties encountered, see above, chapter II, section D, p. 78.

[13] C. Cahen, "En Quoi la conquête turque appelait-elle la croisade ?" *Bulletin de la faculté des lettres de Strasbourg* (1950); G. Every, *The Byzantine Patriarchate* (London, 1947); S. Runciman, *A History of the Crusades*, I (Cambridge, 1951); E. Cerulli, *Etiopi in Palestina*, 2 vols. (Rome, 1943–1947), who discusses all the Jacobites. Cf. below, chapter VII, p. 238.

Not all, however, was strength with the Selchükid empire. The moral cohesion was not complete. It was not that there had been grave moral friction between Turks and natives. But there remained heretical Moslems. The Ismā'īlite propaganda, directed from Cairo, had not disappeared. Hunted down, it had become more secret. The dissensions which, in Egypt in the final quarter of the eleventh century, had ranged those who remained faithful to the ruling Fāṭimids against the partisans of the ousted prince Nizār had weakened the control of the Fāṭimids over the propagation of Ismā'īlism.

The dissident faction was reorganized into new autonomous forms and, as was normal in view of the terror hanging over them, its adepts themselves became terrorists. Their history is to be found treated in detail in another chapter.[14] Here it will suffice merely to recall that the new sect, founded by al-Ḥasan ibn-aṣ-Ṣabbāḥ (Persian, Ḥasan-i-Ṣabbāḥ) — whose followers, lured by the joys of hashish (Arabic, *ḥashīsh*), were termed *ḥashīshīyah* — succeeded in creating, late in the reign of Malik-Shāh, a formidably defended camp around the fortress of Alamut, in the Elburz mountains south of the Caspian Sea. From there action was initiated in the form of those political murders which gave its present meaning to the word "assassin", derived from *ḥashīshī*. These exploits spread far and wide the dread of the Assassins, whose first victim of note — if indeed they were the perpetrators of the crime, which was incited by his other foes — was the vizir, Niẓām-al-Mulk.

A second danger lay in the nature of the dynasty itself. As has been seen, the Selchükids never entirely abandoned the tribal concept of power. Among the Oghuz, as among the Buwaihids, there prevailed the idea of tribal government less by a prince who was to be succeeded by his sons than by a family whose eldest members were chiefs in turn. Niẓām-al-Mulk had been able to make the monarchist principle triumph on behalf of Alp Arslan's son, Malik-Shāh, by ousting Kavurd, the eldest of the family, but the familial idea was nevertheless to persist visibly until the end of the dynasty. Even during the lifetime of Malik-Shāh it was strong enough to force the minister and his sovereign to consent to share the power by distributing appanages to the princes "of the blood" such as Tutush. Even among the sons of the ruler no Moslem dynasty was ever able to fix the order of succession by primogeniture or otherwise, and polygamy aggravated this difficulty by adding the rivalries of the women to those of their sons. Finally, the semi-

[14] See chapter IV, above.

feudal system gave power to a small number of great chiefs, the danger of which is illustrated by too many examples to need particularization.

These perils were not so great when there was in power a capable prince, wise enough to keep in his possession all the necessary resources. Already the minority of Malik-Shāh could have given rise to serious dangers if it had not been for the strong personality of Niẓām-al-Mulk and the resources in his control dating from the reign of Alp Arslan. When Malik-Shāh died young in 1092, closely following his great minister, he left only small children with ambitious mothers and no vizir in control of the situation. The caliph, in spite of his desire to do so, could not impose his moral authority to arbitrate. Hence there developed quarrels among the sons of Malik-Shāh and between them and his brothers, their uncles, each supported by his adherents and the adherents of vizirial rivals, these uncles being enemies of the family of Niẓām-al-Mulk.

This situation resulted in a partition of the empire, devastation, administrative disorder, and universal usurpation. For what had begun in 1092 got worse with every later change of ruler. Each prince in an effort to secure allies disposed of resources and territories and thus weakened himself by that much. They died young and left their infants in the care of military chiefs (Turkish singular, *atabeg*) whom they judged, or rendered, strong enough to be able to defend their rights; inevitably these atabegs worked above all to secure for themselves the real power and expected some day to liquidate a nominal dynasty which had become useless.

To these struggles the Turkomans, especially in Fars and Azerbaijan, were always ready to lend their weight, for they no longer had other outlets. The road to Asia Minor was blocked by their kinsmen; a stable Christian kingdom had been established in the mountains of Georgia to resist the invader; and a certain attachment to the soil kept them from planning great new migrations. It was doubtless in order to keep these Turkomans under tighter control that the sultans constantly bestowed Azerbaijan as an appanage or an autonomous march, but the scheme invariably boomeranged because the grantee found there an army ready for any revolt. The Kurds, including the Shanbānkārah of Fars and others, the Lurs, the bedouins, the Khafājids of Khuzistan, all profited from the disorder, as did especially the Mazyadids of Hilla, who ranged from the outskirts of Baghdad itself as far as Basra and who, under Ṣadaqah and his son Dubais, made life miserable for the caliphs and sultans for the first quarter of the twelfth century.

Asia Minor permanently escaped any effort to incorporate it into the Selchükid empire. The Byzantine administration had disappeared there, but no Moslem administration had yet established itself, for lack of native Moslems. In places the inhabitants had fled. The Turkomans were the rulers and sometimes in the rural districts were the only residents. There, truly, one was outside the classical world to such an extent that for generations the Moslem chroniclers ignored almost everything that happened in that area. But it was this void itself which was to make Asia Minor more important in Turkish history than the Selchükid empire; the Turks flowed thither, and it was there, and not in the empire they had won for their first chiefs, that they created a new "Turkey", which alone bears that name today. From the start, on the Arab side, the limits of Turkish habitation were almost where they are today. Perhaps, if there had been no crusade, the most important of these Turks would have been then, as they were to be later in the time of the Ottomans, those on the shores of the Straits and those who, farther south along the Aegean, joined the traditionally maritime natives to become corsairs. The crusade and the accompanying Byzantine reconquest pushed them back onto the plateau, and Iconium succeeded Nicaea as the residence of their sovereign; the disaster inflicted on the Crusade of 1101 proved that their control of the plateau was effective.[15]

After the death of Malik-Shāh the theoretical sovereign of Asia Minor was a son of Sulaimān named Kilij (or Kilich) Arslan, who, being called Ibn-Sulaimān, was known as Solomon to the crusaders. He had escaped from his Selchükid relatives in Iran. But though he directly dominated the road from Nicaea to Iconium and the passes of the northern Taurus range farther east, he was not master of all Asia Minor. In Armenia, facing the Greeks of Trebizond and the Georgians, Turkoman chiefs who were to attract attention were established at Erzerum — the Saltukids — and at Erzinjan — the Mengüchekids (or Mengüjükids). Farther west, on the northern roads, Sebastia (Sivas), Amasya, Caesarea (Kayseri), and Ankara belonged to a man whose descendants would be very important, but whose connections with the Selchükids are obscure. This was a Turkoman chief whose Persian title of *dānishmend* suggests that his power had the spiritual origin which was mentioned earlier in this chapter as attaching to that title. Thus there arose in Anatolia an opposition

[15] On the First Crusade in Asia Minor see below, chapter IX; for the Crusade of 1101, see below, chapter XI.

— which the captivity of Bohemond would illustrate — between the Turkomans, interested primarily in raiding the Greeks, and the Selchükid princes, whose strength rested on the Turkomans, but who sought to organize, with the help of some Iranians in their entourage and of an alliance with the Byzantines, the rudiments of a government, and to return, if opportunity offered, to play their part in the quarrels of their cousins to the east. To do this they had to make sure of their liaison with the Turkish hinterland, but this was also the concern of Malik-Ghāzī ibn-Dānishmend, who was eager to keep open the path of Turkoman reinforcement; hence their rivalry for the possession of Melitene, which after Bohemond's capture in 1100 Malik-Ghāzī took in 1103 from its Armenian chief, Gabriel (Armenian, Khōril), and which Kilij Arslan occupied in 1106 after the death of his rival.[16]

But the appeal which, as will be seen, the upper Mesopotamian chieftains in revolt against their sultan sent him on that occasion was to culminate for Kilij Arslan in his defeat and death during 1107. Thereafter, the Turks of Anatolia, cut off from their kinsmen to the east, would have to govern themselves in isolation. When non-Turkish Moslems gradually resumed relations with them, these Moslems would be Iranians and not Arabs, because the establishment of crusaders from Cilicia to Edessa impeded communications between Anatolia and Arab Islam, at least in Syria, which was nearest.[17]

Within the Selchükid empire proper, Syria and upper Mesopotamia, regions which the crusaders were to reach, were the first to break up. At the death of Malik-Shāh his brother, Tutush, had desired to claim his heritage. He was recognized in Syria and upper Mesopotamia, but, after he had conquered and killed Buzan and Aksungur al-Ḥājib, who had deserted him, he died in battle in Iran in 1095. His sons, Ridvan and Dukak, fell out, with each taking part of his realm, the former at Aleppo and the latter at Damascus and in the province of Diyār-Bakr. New tensions embroiled the former with his atabeg, Janāḥ-ad-Daulah, who entrenched himself at Homs, and with Yaghi-Siyan, still master of Antioch. None of these chiefs, in these circumstances, had any real power at his disposal. Moreover, the Turkomans had abandoned Syria and Palestine, bringing ruin to the Turkish populations of these lands. Led by Tutush to the conquest of upper

[16] For Bohemond's capture, see below, chapter XII, p. 380; for the title *dānishmend*, see above, p. 139.

[17] F. Chalandon, *Essai sur le règne d'Alexis I Comnène* (Paris, 1900); C. Cahen, "La Première pénétration turque..." (cited above).

Mesopotamia, they had stayed there, mingling with their kinsmen who had never left.

Thus the princelings of Syria, when the crusaders arrived, had for making war only the handful of slaves which the revenues from their meager provinces enabled them to buy. The local pride of the Damascenes, their Sunnism, the protection afforded by their geographical situation, and the skill of Dukak's atabeg, Tughtigin, unified them around these two leaders. But Ridvan, surrounded by Arabs who were largely Shī'ite, held in check by the armed townsmen, and knowing no other source of help, relied, after a Fāṭimid interval, on the Assassins, who thus acquired a foothold in Syria. Obviously the crusade, by stripping these princelings of their richest districts, along the coast, and by posing a constant threat to their security, further intensified their impotence. In the cities the real leaders were the notables, Sunnite or Shī'ite, qadis or headmen (Arabic singular, *ra'īs*), together with their adherents and militia (Arabic collective, *aḥdāth*) — Shī'ite qadis of the Banū-l-Khashshāb and Sunnite headmen of the Banū-Badī' of Iranian origin at Aleppo, to a lesser degree headmen of the Banū-ṣ-Ṣūfī at Damascus, and qadis at several coastal ports, of whom the most illustrious were the Banū-'Ammār, whom we shall meet again.

On the other hand, Syria and upper Mesopotamia have always been lands of intense geographic, social, religious, and ethnic fragmentation; there had been no opportunity there for the religious unification which elsewhere mitigated the political disunity, but on the contrary the opposition between the new orthodox princes and the frequently Shī'ite people introduced an extra element of moral division. Dynastic fragmentation often found support in local particularism, and the resulting weakness left a free field for others. Arab lords sprang up, like the Banū-Munqidh at Shaizar on the Orontes, whose life mingled literary diversions with hunting and the petty wars which the Franks were to find so familiar. The Nuṣairīs were fairly independent in their mountains; the Ismā'īlite pro-Fāṭimid Khalaf ibn-Mulā'ib set himself up at Apamea; at Tripoli the family of the Banū-'Ammār, sheltered between mountain and sea, for a third of a century constituted an autonomous non-Ismā'īlite Shī'ite principality, spiritually and materially prosperous and untroubled by the Turkomans. The Arab tribes, such as the Numairids around Harran, freed themselves, while the Armenians further north found themselves free by default; at Edessa, at Melitene, at Marash, and elsewhere the crusaders found them under the command of their own leaders, Ṭoros, Gabriel, and Kogh Vasil. And the decline of the Turkish power in the south allowed Egypt, which had been reorganized by the vizirs Badr al-Jamālī and al-Afḍal, to regain the ports, though the intervention of the crusaders was required to induce them to retake Jerusalem itself from the sons of Artuk, who had died in 1091.[18]

The Syria to which the crusaders were to come was thus, of all Islamic regions, the least capable of resistance. The loss of the coastal strip would add to its impotence. It was in upper Mesopotamia, to which it was bound geographically and which had already so often absorbed it politically, that it must find help. As in proportion to the increase of Frankish power such help became more urgent, and as Diyār-Bakr and Mosul had meanwhile become stable local states, it became more and more inevitable that Aleppo at least would rely on their aid and hence come under their sway. The history of the first three decades after the First Crusade was to confirm this conclusion. But it was an irregular process, for these helpers themselves were sometimes paralyzed by the internecine wars of Iraq and Iran, or when this was not the case were arrayed against each other. In any event the Syrians could not view without distrust these "orientals" whom they suspected of aspiring to replace them. This fear was so strong that, as will be seen, it was to lead the Moslems of Syria to ally themselves on occasion with the new Syrians, which in a sense the Franks were to become, against those very foes whom they had on previous occasions summoned for help against them.[19]

Unexpected as it may appear to the westerner, it must be clearly realized that the crusades did not produce much of an impression on the Islamic world in general. In the traditions of the Turkomans of Anatolia almost no trace was left by the crossing of the Frankish army. Of what importance was it, in fact, to the nomads that they had been roughly handled in regions of which they had promptly regained control, or that they had lost some towns outside their grazing area? Moreover, at first the crusade was considered as related to those earlier Byzantine expeditions, ephemeral and limited to territories traditionally accustomed to frequent changes of masters, incompletely converted to Islam, distant from Baghdad and Cairo, and negligible since

[18] On the Egyptian capture of Jerusalem see also above, chapter III, p. 95; on the Armenians see below, chapter IX, p. 299.

[19] C. Cahen, *La Syrie du nord*, and P. K. Hitti, *History of Syria* (London, 1951), *passim*; H. A. R. Gibb, *The Damascus Chronicle of the Crusades*, introduction.

commerce never suffered from the changes. They had supplied the opportunity for worthy exploits and for romantic encounters sung on both sides of the frontiers by the poets in the circle of Saif-ad-Daulah or in the Byzantine Digenis. At most it was deemed necessary to try to reduce the ravages of the unbeliever; his expulsion was hardly imagined. Among the eastern Christians is to be found, in their description of the crusades, a certain amount of oratorical exaggeration, but even there difficult to appraise, as stylistic emphasis was usual with them. Among the Moslems, even in those of their narratives which have survived — all were compiled considerably later than the crusade and had already undergone fundamental revision — the wars with the Franks were invariably treated like any other wars. In the literatures of Iraq and Egypt these wars were scarcely mentioned, in that of Iran not at all. It was to be the length and nature of the Frankish occupation which would gradually provoke a reaction. At the start the crusaders were merely one more pawn on an already overcrowded political chessboard, a pawn indistinguishable from its fellows. The trend of history in the surrounding region was not at all affected by it.

Of the history of the later Selchükids in Iran and Mesopotamia only the broad outlines are appropriate to this work. Before the crusade, Berkyaruk, the eldest son of Malik-Shāh, had triumphed successively over an infant brother, who soon died, and, in 1095, over his uncle Tutush. Between 1097 and 1099, while the crusaders were conquering Syria, he was subduing another uncle and various relatives in Khurasan, and taking the grave step of constituting it the appanage of his brother, Sanjar. Scarcely had this situation been thus regulated when he was faced with the revolt of another brother, Muḥammad, with whom, in 1103 after four years of war, he decided to share the sultanate. His death in January of 1105 permitted the energetic Muḥammad to reunite the remains of the power of western Iran and of most of Mesopotamia in the capacity partly of a sovereign and partly of a leader of a confederation. At least he could now divert the ambitions of certain great chieftains toward the pursuit of a policy of counter-offensive, in the line of Selchükid tradition, against the enemies of Islam whether external — the Franks — or internal — the Assassins, the former perhaps as a pretext and certainly as an occasion to attempt to restore his preponderance in Syria.

Khurasan, however, owed to the longevity of Sanjar, who lived until 1156, a calmer internal history. The reign of this prince, whose last years were so difficult, and whose death was so tragic, had opened with three decades of effective rule; he made laws at Samarkand for the Kara-Khanids and, what Malik-Shāh had never done, at Ghaznah for the Ghaznavids. Muḥammad's death in 1118 made him the eldest of the Selchükid family. Without aspiring to reunite the whole empire under his sway, he insisted that his nephews accord him a certain primacy. His intervention at the succession of Maḥmūd safeguarded the unity of the whole; Maḥmūd could neutralize his brothers Tughrul and Mas'ūd and the Mazyadid chief Dubais sufficiently to assist in the war against the Franks with whom Dubais was now allied, and to participate personally in organizing a campaign against the Georgians.

Under Maḥmūd's successor, his brother Mas'ūd (1131–1150), the disintegration was accelerated. Six years of fairly savage warfare against Sanjar, Tughrul, his nephew Dā'ūd, the caliphs al-Mustarshid and ar-Rāshid, and Dubais ended, it is true, by assuring him of victory and a monopoly of the sultan's title. But of what did this sultanate consist? Fars, Azerbaijan, and soon Iraq, not to mention more distant or smaller territories, constituted autonomous principalities. Even the sultan, at the end of his reign, was the prisoner of chieftains who shared the spoils of the empire and from whom he could only rarely gain an illusory liberty by intriguing to shatter their fragile coalitions. His successors would be mere powerless wards of the atabeg of Azerbaijan whom we should hardly mention except that the last of them, Tughrul, at the end of the century won a final pale reflection of the glory of his ancestors by dying in battle against the troops of Khorezm.

The emancipation of Iraq deserves special mention, because it also involved the emancipation of the caliph. The diminution of the revenues of the sultans had led them to consider Iraq as their last financial reserve, and thus rendered their authority harsher to the caliphs at the same time that it became less justified by services rendered to the Moslem community. But elsewhere, in the rivalries of pretenders, the caliph was sought as arbitrator, and he sold his awards high. Gradually he recovered a real measure of autonomy, at the head of a principality in Iraq analogous to the others. Even the Turkish soldiers, fearing the vengeance of a conqueror, entered his service. But the winning sultan was not always the one he favored, and even when he was, this independence of the caliph at the time that the sultan had greatest need of the resources of Iraq necessarily led to conflict. The gravest of these occurred (1134–1138) during the reign of Mas'ūd. It ended with a fierce siege of Baghdad, the successive execution of the two caliphs al-Mustarshid and ar-Rāshid, and the forced installation of the candidate of Mas'ūd, al-Muqtafī. But the decline of the sultanate nonetheless produced under this same al-Muqtafī the result which Mas'ūd had sought to avoid. By the middle of the century the caliph was an autonomous territorial sovereign, perhaps more than he was a real caliph, to judge from his remarkable indifference to the holy war.

Up-river from Iraq, the province of Mosul was, in the first quarter of the twelfth century, a kind of autonomous march whose governor was usually designated by the sultan and charged both with the holy war against the Franks and the reduction to obedience of the Turkomans of the upper Tigris and the Syrian princes. After the occupation of Mosul by Tutush and his subsequent death, the city fell into the hands of a former freedman of Aksungur al-Ḥājib, Kerbogha, who had had himself recognized by Berkyaruk and was to gain fame among the crusaders through the disastrous campaign he undertook against them in 1098.[20] At his death in 1102 he was replaced, thanks to the wars between Berkyaruk and Muḥammad, by the governor of Jazīrat-Ibn-'Umar, Chökürmish, whom Berkyaruk approved. But the reconciliation of the two princes, with Mosul falling to the lot of Muḥammad, and the subsequent death of Berkyaruk complicated the situation of Chökürmish, who was attacked in 1106 by the successor whom the sultan had designated, Chavlï Saqaveh. Chökürmish died in the fighting. It was then that his son appealed to Kïlïj Arslan, whom almost all the local chiefs at first supported against the return of Muḥammad to power but then deserted when they realized that they had merely exchanged one master for another, causing the disaster of Kïlïj Arslan at the Khabur in 1107. Chavlï Saqaveh, however, in his turn quickly became suspect to the sultan by too independent behavior. We shall see how, when the sultan sent Maudūd against him, he went so far as to ally himself in 1108 with the Franks of Edessa, but then received his pardon and the governorship of Fars. Maudūd conducted four campaigns against the Franks, with uneven results; during the final one he was "assassinated" in 1113 at Damascus.

Aksungur al-Bursukī, who replaced him, remained for only one year, because of the failure of the campaign he undertook in 1114 against the Franks. He stayed at Rahba, however, and later, after having been governor of Iraq, regained the governorship of Mosul

[20] For the campaign of 1098 see below, chapter X, pp. 316ff.

in 1124, while in 1126 his son was to be the last lieutenant of the sultan there before Zengi.[21] Meanwhile, in 1114, Muḥammad named to Mosul Juyūsh-Beg, as atabeg of his second son Mas'ūd, but this time the command of the holy war was entrusted not to the atabeg but to a great emir (Arabic, *amīr*) from Hamadan, Bursuk ibn-Bursuk, who, with the Kurd Aḥmad-Il of Maragha and Sokman of Akhlat (or Khilat) on Lake Van, had already participated in the preceding campaigns. The campaign of 1115 culminated in disaster, as will be seen, and thereafter for ten years no expedition into Syria would be organized at Mosul or elsewhere. Juyūsh-Beg spent ten years at Mosul until 1124, when he was compromised by the attempts at insubordination of his pupil Mas'ūd against sultan Maḥmūd, who replaced him with his predecessor Aksungur al-Bursukī. The latter and his son were the last governors of Mosul who can be termed dependents of the sultan. Under Zengi, still in theory atabeg of a Selchükid, the civil war between Mas'ūd and the caliph, in which Zengi was to participate, would end in fact in the complete independence of the latter. His successors would retain power without being even in theory atabegs of any Selchükid.

None of the governors of Mosul had succeeded, on his own behalf or on the sultan's, in subjugating the Turkomans of Diyār-Bakr province. On the contrary, the earlier fragmentation of the region had gradually given way to a territorial concentration for the benefit of a Turkoman family, that of the Artukids, whom Zengi would later partially reduce but not evict, and who would survive until the fifteenth century as vassals of all the subsequent empires. The principal city north of the Tigris, Maiyafariqin, successively center of the governments of Dukak, who had inherited it from Tutush, of Kilij Arslan, and finally of Sokman of Akhlat, the vassal of Muḥammad, was not destined to fall into the hands of the Artukids until 1118. On the Tigris, Amida (Diyarbakir) would be until the time of Saladin (Ṣalāḥ-ad-Dīn) the capital of a small autonomous principality. Various Turkoman chiefs, between the Tigris and Lake Van, subsisted as vassals either of the Artukids or of the "Shah-i-Armīn", like Kizil Arslan, probably the "Red Lion" of the crusade poems. But the most important and most renowned family was always that of the descendants of that Artuk whom we have met in the service of Malik-Shāh and Tutush.

Ousted from Jerusalem by the Egyptian and Frankish con-

[21] On Maudūd see below, chapter XII, pp. 399–403; for Aksungur al-Bursukī see below, chapter XIII, pp. 420–427.

quests, and from Sarūj, between Syria and upper Mesopotamia, by the Frankish conquest, the Artukids thereafter made a career both in the service of the sultans — as did Īl-Ghāzī in the time of Berkyaruk — and as chiefs of the Turkomans in the land of the upper Tigris where their father had once brought them. To the flat country, which they doubtless dominated very quickly, were added Mardin in 1097, Ḥiṣn Kaifā in 1102, Kharput in 1115, and Maiyafariqin in 1118, not to mention Aleppo, which they held six years but did not keep. At the start the best known of them, as much in Diyār-Bakr as in Syria and the Frankish county of Edessa, was Sokman ibn-Artuk. After his death in 1104 his brother Īl-Ghāzī, whose sojourn in Iraq was terminated by the accession of Muḥammad, came to Diyār-Bakr to assume the leadership of the family. By the end of his life the family had become a real power, was allied with Dubais in Iraq, and was importuned for aid against the Georgians, and against the Franks to such a degree that, under conditions which we shall detail, the Aleppans were to offer to surrender to them. Īl-Ghāzī's nephew Belek, who had carved out his own domain around Kharput in spite of a coalition of Dānishmendids and Greeks from Trebizond, succeeded him briefly (1122–1124) at Aleppo and in the holy war.

In the struggles of the sultans against each other or of agents against foes of the sultans, as well as in the holy war, the Artukid policy was a perpetual double game with a single goal, the acquisition and retention of autonomous territories. Sokman had participated in the expeditions of Kerbogha in 1098 and of Chökürmish in 1104 against the Franks. Īl-Ghāzī, embroiled simultaneously with Chökürmish and with sultan Muḥammad, but avoiding direct conflict with the latter, fought both Kilij Arslan, an ally of the son of Chökürmish, and partisans of Muḥammad like Sokman of Akhlat, who, opportunely for him, died in 1110, and Aksungur al-Bursukī, whom he opposed in 1114. When, however, a large army of the sultan needed his support for the holy war, he joined in 1110, 1113, and 1114 only to desert, contributing by his equivocal attitude to its divisions and setbacks, when Sokman of Akhlat was with it in 1110, for example, or Aksungur al-Bursukī in 1114. Threatened with vengeance by the sultan in 1115, as we shall see, he joined the other adversaries of the sultan in Syria, including the Franks, and, after a grave accident, was one of the architects of their triumph over the sultan's army in that year. Once the danger from the sultan had been cancelled, he deserted the friends of the Franks — now uneasy at the power of the latter — to resume on his own account, at the call of the Aleppans, the holy war which was to redound to his benefit.

After the deaths of Īl-Ghāzī and Belek, the family remained permanently divided into two branches, one descended from Īl-Ghāzī at Maiyafariqin and Mardin whose representative at the time of Zengi was to be Timurtash, the other descended from Sokman at Ḥiṣn Kaifā and Kharput whose representative was to be Dā'ūd. The coins of the first Artukids are famous for bearing the Christian creed of the native artisans on whom they had to rely to coin them. Later Artukids were to become ordinary territorial princes and participate in the general movement of orthodox reorganization which the Zengids were to initiate.[22]

In Syria the eviction of Yaghī-Siyan from Antioch by the crusaders and the assassination of Janāḥ-ad-Daulah of Homs in 1103 left Rīdvan at Aleppo and Dukak at Damascus practically alone in the field. The death of the latter in 1104 marked the end of the dynasty in that city, for his son and relatives were set aside by his erstwhile close collaborator and atabeg, Tughtigin. Actually this collaboration meant that no change of policy resulted from the change of family. Though Damascus, better governed perhaps, better protected from the Franks, less directly in the path of oriental ambitions, had on the whole a firmer and better balanced policy than Aleppo, and though Dukak and Tughtigin stood for orthodoxy while Rīdvan was the accomplice of the heterodox, their policies were similar in the distrust they felt for each other, for the Franks, and for the easterners. Thus there arose all the combinations and shifting alliances, to try to save their little holdings by offsetting and neutralizing one another. This mediocre policy exasperated their subjects, particularly at Aleppo, conscious of the over-riding necessity of forming a common Moslem front to meet the Frankish menace. It is essential, however, for the understanding of the vicissitudes of the Frankish conquest, to summarize also the zigzag politics of Aleppo and Damascus.

Rīdvan tried in general to banish the Frankish danger with cash, and not to wage war except with minimal risk. He had scarcely defended Antioch and had not participated in the expedition of Kerbogha, in which, on the other hand, Dukak and Janāḥ-ad-Daulah had figured. Although he had in 1104 risked profiting from the Frankish defeat on the Balikh, he was to lose in the following year the districts he had acquired. Although an "assassination"

[22] C. Cahen, "Le Diyār Bakr au temps des premiers Urtukides," *Journal asiatique*, CCXXVII (1935), 219–276; "Artuk Oğullarī", in *İslâm ansiklopedisi*.

had rid him of the pro-Fāṭimid Khalaf of Apamea, he allowed the place to fall into Frankish hands in 1106. In 1106 and 1107 he helped his former subordinate Il-Ghāzī against Chökürmish of Mosul, and then against Kilij Arslan of Anatolia, in the hope of getting equivalent reinforcements against the Franks, but in 1108 he was allied with Tancred against Chavli Saqaveh, the new lord of Mosul and ally of Baldwin of Edessa, an alliance which on both sides crossed religious lines to satisfy personal quarrels. Among the Shī'ites as among the Sunnites, Ridvan had the reputation of being a rapacious miser, but he bought a precarious peace from the Franks at a very high price.

Meanwhile Dukak and Tughtigin were consolidating their power over central and southern Moslem Syria, even installing vassals at Homs — Karaja — and at Hamah —'Alī Kurd. They directed their policy of defense against the Franks toward an alliance with Egypt, disregarding former sectarian differences, and helped with the land defense of the Syrian ports which it defended by sea. They did not neglect opportunities for territorial aggrandizement which appeals for help from local rulers offered them; and, having no desire for the expulsion of the Franks, which would leave them in dangerously direct contact with Egypt, readily agreed to arrange truces with the Franks or to abstain from serious hostilities. They had embroiled themselves with Ibn-'Ammār of Tripoli by supporting Jabala's revolt against him in 1101. Ibn-'Ammār could no longer count on Egypt, which aspired to reconquer his city. At the start he had, like the others, willingly treated with the Franks. When he had nevertheless to defend himself against them, he was one of the first to send an appeal to Baghdad, where he went in 1108 and would later end his career after the fall of Tripoli. Three years later the Aleppans made a noisy demonstration in the open mosque at Baghdad, to shame the Moslem world for its disunity in the face of the Frankish peril. Like Ibn-'Ammār most of these men, who pinned their hopes on the capital of Sunnite Islam, were Shī'ites, proof that for the people and some at least of their chiefs, sectarian differences were disregarded in times of danger, and that Moslem solidarity was beginning to develop in reaction to past divisions.

After 1110, as we have seen, the sultan, whose policy this newly born movement complemented, was organizing expeditions against the Franks, the first directed only at Edessa, the others into Syria. Ridvan tried to profit from them by participating as little as possible, and by hastily quitting them to buy his pardon from the

Franks, dreading a coalition of his subjects and the eastern emirs against him. In 1111 he asked these latter to raise the siege of Tell Bashir and hurry to succor Aleppo, and, when they arrived, refused to let them enter the city or to join them in the countryside. When Tughtigin came to meet them in order to try to lead them, by-passing Damascus, to retake Sidon or Tripoli from the Franks, Riḍvan tried in vain to have him "assassinated", but then made friends by sending tardy help to save Tyre in return for formal recognition of his sovereignty over Damascus.

In 1113 a double "accident" occurred. At Damascus the commander of the eastern army, Maudūd, was "assassinated". Although it was almost certainly an act of vengeance by the Assassins against Maudūd, who had been their fierce enemy in the east, public rumor aimed at Tughtigin an accusation symptomatic of the atmosphere of universal distrust.[23] Tughtigin, until then much more favorable to the sultan's expeditions than was Riḍvan, since they menaced him less, at once became suspect in connection with the holy war, and was rebuffed into alliance with the Franks. Then Riḍvan died. The population, weary of reprisals against the Assassins, forced the young Alp Arslan, his son, to have them massacred; but by doing so, he deprived himself of his only possible support. He tried to put himself under the protection of Tughtigin, but thus aroused the distrust of the Shī'ite majority; finally he was in his turn slain.

That was practically the end of the Syrian Selchükid dynasty. The slaves of Riḍvan and the civic notables who one after the other, in the midst of universal anarchy, tried to take the reins of government had insufficient strength either to impose their authority on all the residents of Aleppo or to raise effective armies for the defense of their territory. Fearing the army of the easterners, in which they well knew the people had put their hopes, they too were thrown into alliance with the Franks. Il-Ghāzī, as we have seen, had also broken with the sultan's party. In 1115 Tughtigin, the Aleppans, and Il-Ghāzī made common cause with the Franks against the army of the sultan under Bursuk ibn-Bursuk, who had come intending to fight them as much as he had to fight the Franks.[24] It is true that the sultan had found a new partisan in Syria, which he had promised to concede to him, in the person of Ḳir-Khan, son of Ḳaraja, who, at Homs, hoped to liberate himself from the control of Tughtigin, and who once captured Il-Ghāzī, though Tughtigin forced his release. It will be seen how this situ-

[23] Cf. above, chapter IV, p. 113.
[24] Cf. below, chapter XII, p. 404.

ation culminated — partly because of the jealousy of the easterners for Kîr-Khan — in a Frankish victory more complete than Tughtigin had wished. The latter then felt it necessary to visit Baghdad to make his peace with the sultan, bringing back in 1116 an official investiture.

The disaster of 1115 meant for the sultan a permanent check to all his Syrian dreams, and the recognition of Tughtigin was the only way for him to save even appearances. For Tughtigin, now that all the Selchükids of Syria had vanished, it conferred the legitimate succession on him as opposed to his adversaries. Two years later Muḥammad died, and under Maḥmūd there was even less likely to be any resumption of activity in Syria by the easterners, at least before an internal reorganization which the sultan could not accomplish. This does not mean that there was to be no more collaboration between Syria and Iraq; on the contrary; but henceforth it would be with the autonomous princelings of Iraq, whom the policy of the sultan no longer restrained, and who concluded treaties of mutual advantage with the Syrian states, or who at least, being less foreign, were more readily accepted by the Syrians. Before the time of Zengi, Aksungur al-Bursukī, recently repulsed by some as oriental, but having become semi-Syrian at Rahba in the interval, would be summoned by the same ones in 1124.[25]

The pattern of the Asiatic Moslem world was thus about to be reconstructed on a new framework. Iran, and to a lesser degree Mesopotamia, were to survive almost entirely apart from the western provinces, so much so that in connection with the crusades their further history would be irrelevant were it not for the grave events then being prepared in Central Asia which would, in the following century, brutally reintroduce them into Syrian history. A new alignment of regions, from Mosul to Aleppo, then to Damascus and on to Cairo, would arise and take over the lead, not only in the battle against the Franks, which is self-evident, but also, and perhaps partially because of that, in the whole of Moslem, especially Arab, life.

This is not to say that there did not remain from the Selchükids, in default of political unity, an important heritage, even in the old Moslem countries. In some places a Turkish population, and almost everywhere an aristocracy under Turkish command, had

[25] C. Cahen, *La Syrie du nord*; H. A. R. Gibb, "Notes on the Arabic Materials for the History of the Early Crusades," *Bulletin of the School of Oriental Studies*, VII (1933–1935), 739–754; W. B. Stevenson, *The Crusaders in the East* (Cambridge, 1907); H. Derenbourg, *Vie d'Ousama ibn Munqidh* (Paris, 1889).

superimposed themselves on the former inhabitants. A policy of orthodoxy had been initiated, and all the subsequent regimes until the Mongol invasion would follow it. The reaction which the Frankish invasion provoked little by little among its Moslem neighbors did not result from it, but the organizational forms it would adopt followed exactly the lines of Khurasanian initiative which the Selchükid conquest had strongly developed in extent and in depth. Nūr-ad-Dīn and Saladin are inconceivable without Tughrul-Beg and Niẓām-al-Mulk.

VI
THE BYZANTINE EMPIRE IN THE ELEVENTH CENTURY

With the death of Basil II in 1025 there came to an end the most brilliant period in the history of Byzantium. During this period of roughly one and a half centuries, beginning with 867 when Basil I ascended the throne and ending with 1025 when Basil II died, the Byzantine empire had reëstablished itself as the great power of the Christian and Moslem worlds. Its armies had humbled the Saracens, subjugated the Bulgars, virtually cleared

The following are the principal Greek narrative sources: Michael Psellus, *Chronographie* (ed. and tr. E. Renauld, 2 vols., Paris, 1926, 1928); English translation by E. R. A. Sewter, *The Chronographia of Michael Psellus* (London, 1953); Michael Attaliates, *Historia* (Bonn, 1853); Cedrenus-Skylitzes, *Historiarum compendium*, vol. II (Bonn, 1839); John Zonaras, *Epitomae historiarum*, vol. III (Bonn, 1897); Nicephorus Bryennius, *Commentarii* (Bonn, 1836); Anna Comnena, *Alexiad*, 2 vols. (Bonn, 1839, 1872); a new edition with a French translation by B. Leib, 3 vols. (Paris, 1937, 1943, 1945); also an English translation by E. Dawes (London, 1928); *The Strategikon of Cecaumenus* (ed. V. G. Vasilievsky and V. Jernstedt, *Cecaumeni strategicon et incerti scriptoris de officiis regiis libellus*: Zapiski istoriko-filologicheskago Fakulteta Imp. S. Peterburgskago Universiteta, XXXVIII, St. Petersburg, 1896). A new edition with an English translation prepared by the late Georgina Buckler is expected to come out soon. Significant also are the discourses and letters of Psellus, on which see C. N. Sathas, *Bibliotheca graeca medii aevi*, vol. IV (Paris, 1874), 303 ff., and vol. V (Paris, 1876); L. Bréhier, "Un Discours inédit de Psellus," *Revue des études grecques*, XVI (1903), 375–416, and XVII (1904), 35–75; E. Kurtz and F. Drexl, *Michaelis Pselli scripta minora*, vol. I (Milan, 1936). Less important than the chronicles already cited are the following: Michael Glycas, *Chronicon* (Bonn, 1836); Constantine Manasses, *Synopsis chroniké* (Bonn, 1836); Joel, *Chronographia* (Bonn, 1836); and a chronicle in verse with no definite title by Ephraem (Bonn, 1840).

Among the oriental sources mention should be made of Michael the Syrian, *Chronique* (ed. and tr. J. B. Chabot, 4 vols., Paris, 1899–1910); Bar Hebraeus, *Chronography* (tr. E. A. W. Budge, London, 1932). More important is the work of Matthew of Edessa, for which see E. Dulaurier, *Chronique de Matthieu d'Édesse* (Bibliothèque historique arménienne, Paris, 1858). See also Arisdaguès de Lasdiverd, *Histoire d'Arménie* (tr. M. S. Prud'homme, Paris, 1864).

Documents, which for this period are fairly numerous, will be cited elsewhere in the course of this chapter. Important guides to these are: F. Dölger, *Regesten der Kaiserurkunden des oströmischen Reiches*; part I, *Regesten von 565–1025* (Munich, 1924), and part II, *Regesten von 1025–1204* (Munich, 1925); G. Moravcsik, *Byzantinoturcica*, vols. I and II (Budapest, 1942–1943); and V. Grumel, *Les Actes des patriarches*, I, fascs. 1–3 (1932–1947).

The most detailed secondary account for the period from 1025 to 1057 is still G. Schlumberger, *L'Épopée byzantine à la fin du dixième siècle*: part 3, *Les Porphyrogénètes Zoé et* the Mediterranean of corsairs, and strengthened its hold in southern Italy. Its missionaries, aided by diplomats and sometimes by armies, spread the gospel among the southeastern Slavs, a development of the greatest significance. Byzantium was the center of Mediterranean civilization.

In less than sixty years after the death of Basil II this great political and military structure was no more. The armies of the empire had been decimated; internal order had broken down; hordes of barbarians, the Selchükids in Asia Minor, the Pechenegs and Uzes in the Balkans, were ravaging its territories; and in southern Italy a new power, the Normans, had arisen which not only had engulfed what possessions the empire still had in that peninsula, but threatened its very existence. It is this disintegration of the Byzantine empire which created the conditions without which the crusading movement would not have taken place, at least not in the form which it assumed.

One living at the time of the death of Basil II might very well have felt that no external power could disturb the internal security and peace of the empire. For the first time in its long ex-

Théodora, 1025–1057 (Paris, 1895). For Theodora and her immediate successors see H. Mädler, *Theodora, Michael Stratiotikos, Isaak Komnenos* (Plauen, 1894). The best general accounts covering the eleventh century are: C. Neumann, *Die Weltstellung des byzantinischen Reiches vor den Kreuzzügen* (Leipzig, 1894; French translation by E. Renauld, *ROL*, X [1905], 57–171); N. Skabalanovich, *Byzantine State and Church in the Eleventh Century* (St. Petersburg, 1884). (The writer's knowledge of the Russian language is limited, but he has been able to consult this book and the others cited in this chapter with the aid of Miss Nathalie Scheffer.) See also W. Fischer, *Studien zur byzantinischen Geschichte des XI Jahrhunderts* (Plauen, 1883). For portraits of the emperors the best account in English is that by J. B. Bury, "The Roman Emperors from Basil II to Isaac Komnenos," *EHR*, IV (1889), 41–64, 251–285, reprinted in *Essays*, ed. H. Temperley (Cambridge, 1930), pp. 126–215. For the intellectual life of the empire, see J. M. Hussey, *Church and Learning in the Byzantine Empire, 867–1185* (Oxford, 1937); L. Bréhier, *La Civilization byzantine* (Paris, 1950); B. Tatakis, *La Philosophie byzantine* (Paris 1949); on institutions, L. Bréhier, *Les Institutions de l'empire byzantin* (Paris, 1949). Among the general histories of Byzantium the following should be cited: A. A. Vasiliev, *Histoire de l'empire byzantin*, 2 vols. (Paris, 1932); new English edition (Madison, Wisconsin, 1952); G. Ostrogorsky, *Geschichte des byzantinischen Staates* (Munich, 1952); L. Bréhier, *Vie et mort de Byzance* (Paris, 1947). In connection with what Ostrogorsky has to say about the eleventh century one should also consult J. M. Hussey, "The Byzantine Empire in the Eleventh Century: Some Different Interpretations," *Transactions of the Royal Historical Society*, 4th series, vol. XXXII (1950), 71–85. See further R. J. H. Jenkins, *The Byzantine Empire on the Eve of the Crusades* (London, 1953: a pamphlet — General Series: G. 24 — of the Historical Association); S. Runciman, *A History of the Crusades*, I (Cambridge, 1950); and B. Leib, "Jean Doukas, César et moine, son jeu politique à Byzance de 1067 à 1081," *Mélanges P. Peeters*, II (= *Analecta Bollandiana*, LXVIII, 1950), 163–180.

On Byzantine Italy the fundamental book still is J. Gay, *L'Italie méridionale et l'empire byzantin depuis l'avènement de Basile I, jusqu'à la prise de Bari par les Normands, 867–1071* (Paris, 1904). For Alexius Comnenus the principal work is still that by F. Chalandon, *Essai sur le règne d'Alexis I Comnène, 1081–1118* (Paris, 1900). The most important geographical treatise on the frontiers of the empire in Asia Minor is E. Honigmann, *Die Ostgrenze des byzantinischen Reiches von 363 bis 1071* (A. A. Vasiliev, *Byzance et les Arabes*, vol. III, Brussels, 1935). The writer wishes to thank the American Philosophical Society and the Rutgers University Research Fund for the financial assistance which they gave him to work on this chapter.

istence Byzantium had no well organized and powerful states on its borders. The eastern caliphate still existed to be sure, but it had been greatly weakened by internal divisions, while the more powerful emirs had been defeated and humiliated by the Byzantine armies. The Saracens might still make incursions into Byzantine territories, but they had been so deeply impressed by the might of the Byzantine armies that they were ready to accept humiliating terms the moment they heard that an army was marching against them.

Farther north, in the regions south of the Caucasus, the frontiers of the empire had been rounded off by the annexations which Basil II had made. These annexations included the domain of David (East Armenian, Daviṭ) of Taik, acquired by Basil in 1000, which extended from Manzikert, north of Lake Van, to Erzerum, near the upper Euphrates, and northward to the district of Kola and Artanr (Ardahan), northwest of Kars, and the realm of Vaspurkan, ceded to Basil in 1021 by its king, who had found himself unable to protect it against the incursions of the Turks. The acquisition of Vaspurkan extended the frontiers of the empire from Lake Van eastward to the chain of mountains which today separates Turkey from Iran. About the same time (1022) Sempad (East Armenian, Smbat) of Ani, king of Greater Armenia, yielded his kingdom to the Byzantine emperor on condition that he remain its ruler until his death. These regions were inhabited predominantly by Armenians and some Georgians. The dispossessed Armenian princes were given lands elsewhere in the empire whither they were followed by other Armenians. It is said, for instance, that the prince of Vaspurkan, who was given important domains in Cappadocia, was followed there by 14,000 of his compatriots, in addition to their women and children. Other Armenians were forcibly evacuated and settled in other provinces.[1]

If in the east the Saracens no longer offered a serious threat, the situation in the Balkan peninsula was still more favorable, for the state which had so often challenged the empire was no more. Ever since its foundation in the second half of the seventh century, the Bulgarian kingdom had been a thorn in the side of Byzantium and at times a serious menace to its very existence. But Basil II put an end to this kingdom and annexed its territories. These territories were inhabited by masses of Slavs who would not always be happy with their new status and would at times rebel, but

[1] René Grousset, *Histoire de l'Arménie des origines à 1071* (Paris, 1947), p. 554; Honigmann, *Die Ostgrenze des byzantinischen Reiches*, p. 162.

whatever disturbances these Slavs might thus cause could not be as dangerous as the devastating attacks for which the Bulgarian kingdom had so often been responsible. The destruction of the Bulgarian kingdom extended the frontiers of the empire to the Danube and the Drava. On the Dalmatian coast its control, direct or indirect, extended as far as Istria and, as Venice was still a semi-dependency of the empire, this made the Adriatic a Byzantine lake.

The prestige of the empire was also high in southern Italy. Calabria and Apulia were firmly under its control, and its influence in the Lombard principalities of Benevento, Capua, and Salerno was not insignificant. The rebellion which had broken out in Apulia in 1017 under the leadership of Melo, a wealthy citizen of Bari, and in which Norman mercenaries participated — the first known appearance of Norman mercenaries in southern Italy — was decisively put down. Basil Bojoannes, the Byzantine governor who had defeated Melo, gave to the country a wise administration and assured its defenses by the foundation of a number of fortified towns, of which the most famous was Troia, in the plains between the Ofanto and the Fortore rivers. The effectiveness of these fortifications was demonstrated in 1021 when Henry II, the German emperor, failed to occupy Troia and had to give up his invasion of Apulia. So impressed were the Byzantines by the work of Bojoannes that they attributed to him the subjugation of "all Italy as far as Rome".[2]

Basil II transmitted to his successors an empire whose prestige, power, and territorial extent had never been greater since the days when Heraclius triumphantly entered the Persian capital. The men who succeeded Basil were neither statesmen nor military leaders; nevertheless, the empire was able to keep its prestige and position substantially unimpaired for some time after his death.

In the east the Saracens still made incursions and in 1030 the emir of Aleppo defeated the emperor Romanus III Argyrus. His victory, however, was not decisive and he was soon forced to put himself again under the suzerainty of the empire as did the other emirs along the frontiers. The city of Edessa (Urfa) was ceded to Byzantium and this put its frontiers beyond the Euphrates. Farther north, the attempt made in 1038 to annex Ani and Greater Armenia did not succeed, but the annexation was achieved a few years later during the reign of Constantine IX. On the sea, several piratical expeditions, one in 1027, another in 1032,

[2] Cedrenus [after Skylitzes], *Historiarum compendium*, II, 546.

and still another in 1035, launched by the Saracens of Sicily and North Africa, were successfully dealt with. In the Balkan peninsula, the Slavs, discontented over the transformation of the taxes from levies in kind to levies in money, rallied around Peter Deljan, apparently a descendant of Samuel, the last great Bulgarian king, and a formidable revolt broke out in 1040. The rebels besieged Thessalonica and sent an army which devastated Greece, but the dissensions which soon broke out among the leaders enabled the Byzantines to suppress the rebellion. In 1043 the Russians, aroused apparently by some misunderstanding concerning their trade privileges in the Byzantine capital, a misunderstanding which had already resulted in the death of a high-ranking Russian, attacked Constantinople, but their expedition, headed by the prince of Novgorod, Vladimir, was broken up and their fleet virtually destroyed. In Italy the situation had somewhat deteriorated as a result of the recall of Bojoannes in 1028, but the position of the empire was not yet definitely compromised. In 1038 an expedition, commanded by the redoubtable George Maniaces, was launched for the conquest of Sicily in order to bring to an end the piratical depredations of the Saracens of this island as well as of North Africa. The Byzantine forces occupied a considerable part of the island, but the recall of Maniaces as a result of a quarrel with the brother-in-law of the emperor, who commanded the sea forces, and the incompetence of his successor, enabled the Saracens to reëstablish themselves.

This record of the Byzantine armies during the two decades which followed the death of Basil II, if not brilliant, is by no means wanting in success. Byzantine forces suffered reverses here and there and incursions by the enemy at times disturbed the internal security of the empire, but on the whole the frontiers were well protected and even expanded. But while the old enemies were kept at bay new and more vigorous enemies appeared along the frontiers. Their apparently insignificant raids in the period immediately following the death of Basil II became increasingly more frequent and devastating until finally they shattered the political and military power of the empire. Among these enemies the most important were the Pechenegs, the Normans, and the Selchükid Turks.

The Pechenegs, called Patzinaks by the Byzantines, a nomadic people of Turkish origin, were not unknown to the Byzantines before the eleventh century.[3] They had made their appearance

[3] The fundamental work on the Pechenegs (Patzinaks) is V. G. Vasilievsky, "Byzantium

sometime in the ninth century and occupied the territory roughly between the lower Danube and the Dnieper, which today is Rumania and southwestern Russia. The emperors of the tenth century pursued a friendly policy toward them and sought to use them to keep Russians, Magyars, and Bulgars at bay. "So long as the emperor of the Romans is at peace with the Pechenegs," writes Constantine Porphyrogenitus, "neither Russians nor Turks [Magyars] can come upon the Roman dominions by force of arms, nor can they exact from the Romans large and inflated sums in money and goods as the price of peace, for they fear the strength of this nation which the emperor can turn against them while they are campaigning against the Romans .... To the Bulgars also the emperor of the Romans will appear more formidable, and can impose on them the need for tranquillity, if he is at peace with the Pechenegs."[4] But with the annexation of Bulgaria the situation changed. The Pechenegs now became the immediate neighbors of the empire along the Danube and, as they were pressed from behind by other Turkish tribes, the Kumans (elsewhere called Kîpchaks or Polovtsy), they turned their eyes toward the empire and began a series of raids which lasted almost throughout the eleventh century.

There was virtually no reign from the accession of Constantine VIII in 1025 to the end of the eleventh century which did not witness some Pecheneg invasion of the territories of the empire in the Balkan peninsula. Pechenegs crossed the Danube during the reign of Constantine VIII and were driven back only after they had caused considerable damage, killed many people, including high-ranking officers, and carried with them numerous prisoners who were ransomed only during the reign of Romanus III Argyrus. In July 1032 there was another destructive raid upon Bulgaria and during the reign of Michael IV there were no less than four different invasions which spread desolation and death and resulted in the taking of many captives, including five generals. It was, however, with the reign of Constantine IX

and the Patzinaks," *Journal of the Ministry of Public Instruction*, CLXIV (1872); also in Vasilievsky, *Works*, vol. I (St. Petersburg, 1908, in Russian), 1–175. For their early history see J. Marquart, *Osteuropäische und ostasiatische Streifzüge* (Leipzig, 1903), pp. 63ff.; V. Minorsky (ed. and tr.), *Ḥudūd al-ʿĀlam*: "*The Regions of the World*," *a Persian Geography* (London, 1937), pp. 312–315. On the Pechenegs in the eleventh century one may consult C. A. Macartney, "The Pechenegs," *The Slavonic Review*, VIII (1929–1930), 342–355; G. Schlumberger, *L'Épopée byzantine*, pp. 565–595; Chalandon, *Alexis I Comnène*, pp. 2–5; H. F. Gfoerer, *Byzantinische Geschichten*, vol. III (Gruz, 1877), 474–507; and G. Moravcsik, *Byzantinoturcica*, I (Budapest, 1942), 46ff., where the reader will find a detailed bibliography.

[4] Constantine Porphyrogenitus, *De administrando imperio* (edited by G. Moravcsik and translated into English by R. J. H. Jenkins, Budapest, 1949), pp. 51f.

Monomachus, which witnessed one of the most devastating Pecheneg invasions, that the Pecheneg menace became very serious, as we are told by the Byzantine historians themselves.

A quarrel between two Pecheneg chieftains was the first in a series of events which led to the devastation of the Balkan peninsula by the Pechenegs during the reign of Constantine IX. Tirakh (or Tirek, called Τυράχ by the Byzantines), a man of noble birth, was the khan of the Pechenegs, while Kegen (Byzantine, Κεγένης), a man of humble origin, was their military leader. Kegen had risen to this position through his own merits, but the reputation which he enjoyed among his fellow tribesmen alarmed Tirakh, who plotted to put him out of the way. Kegen, however, learning of the plot escaped, and after many adventures found refuge on a small island near the mouth of the Danube with 20,000 of his followers. He then appealed to the Byzantine emperor for permission to settle on imperial territory. Kegen was granted this permission, was honorably received in Constantinople, and was given the title of patrician. In return he accepted Christianity and promised to have his followers do likewise. The latter were settled along the Danube where they were given lands and assumed the obligation of defending the frontier against the incursions of their fellow tribesmen who had remained on the other bank of the river. But Kegen and his followers were not content to remain on the defensive; they took the offensive and began a series of raids across the river. These raids aroused Tirakh. He protested to the emperor, but as his protests remained unheeded, he countered by launching a terrible invasion of the empire. He crossed the Danube, which had frozen thickly, in December 1048 with a force estimated by a Byzantine historian, no doubt with gross exaggeration, at 800,000,[5] and spread terror and death everywhere. The barbarians, however, were not accustomed to the rich food of civilization and overindulgence proved fatal. Dysentery soon broke out among them and this together with the extreme cold carried thousands away. At the same time the armies of the European provinces concentrated against the Pechenegs. Tirakh, with what remained of his forces, finally capitulated. The khan and the other chieftains were taken to Constantinople where they were well received and accepted Christianity. Their followers were settled in the deserted regions of Sofia (Sardica) and Nish (Naissus) to cultivate the land, pay taxes, and furnish recruits to the army.

[5] Cedrenus, *Historiarum compendium*, II, 585.

In the meantime the frontier regions of the empire in Asia Minor were threatened with another invasion by the Selchükid Turks. To help meet this invasion an army of 15,000 men was raised among these Pechenegs and was sent to Asia Minor under the command of four of their own chieftains. Their destination was the province of Iberia, but before they had gone very far in Bithynia they revolted and, forcing their way back, they continued on to cross the Bosporus, whence they marched to the region of Sofia and induced their fellow tribesmen to rebel also. They were soon joined by those who had been settled around Nish and they all retired toward the Danube, where they established themselves in well protected places and then began to raid the Thracian regions of the empire. To meet this new danger the emperor turned to Kegen and summoned him to Constantinople together with his followers. But while the forces of Kegen were encamped before the capital waiting for orders, an unsuccessful attempt was made to take the life of their leader. The conspirators were themselves Pechenegs, however, and when they were brought before the emperor, they declared that Kegen planned to join the rebels. Kegen was arrested, and when the news of his arrest reached his followers, they immediately joined the rebels. The emperor now released Tirakh, who promised upon oath that he would reduce the rebels to obedience. But once Tirakh regained his freedom, he ignored his oath, and put himself at the head of the rebellion. In the meantime the army of the western provinces was defeated near Adrianople. The whole Pecheneg world was in an upheaval, and all the country from the Danube to Adrianople was at their mercy.

The emperor combined the armies of the Asiatic and European provinces under one command and sent them against the Pechenegs beyond the Balkan mountains. The combined armies, however, were routed and their camp was taken by the nomads. This took place in 1049. In the following year, as the Pechenegs continued to plunder the country at will, another army, again drawn from the eastern and western provinces, was sent against them. The encounter with the barbarians took place in June 1050, near Adrianople, but the barbarians were again victorious and, although the timely arrival of reinforcements forced them to flee northward, they continued to ravage the country without fear. The emperor now tried diplomacy and sent Kegen to the Pechenegs. But Kegen, whose object was to create dissension among them and thus bring about their submission, was killed by them.

In the meantime, however, an army under the command of Nicephorus Bryennius defeated three detachments of Pechenegs in three different engagements, two near Adrianople and the other near Chariopolis. These defeats made them more cautious, but did not stop their incursions, which continued throughout 1051 and 1052. In 1053 the emperor made another all-out effort against the Pechenegs, but his army, which attempted to dislodge them from the Bulgarian city of Preslav near the Danube, was again defeated. Despite their victory, however, the Pechenegs now asked for peace, and an agreement to that effect which was supposed to last for thirty years was concluded. The Pechenegs, showered with gifts and titles, remained south of the Danube.

The peace was not kept. To be sure, Constantine IX had no further trouble with the Pechenegs, and there is no evidence that they made any incursions during the short reigns of Theodora and Michael VI, but in 1059 they "crawled out of the caves in which they were hidden," and joined the Hungarians in an attack upon the empire. Isaac I Comnenus immediately took the field. While he was at Sofia the Hungarians, who had sent an embassy to him, concluded peace and he was free to direct his attention against the Pechenegs. But before any encounter took place, the Pecheneg chieftains, with the exception of one named Selte (Σελτέ), asked for, and obtained, peace. Isaac now turned against Selte, defeated him, and destroyed his stronghold. Selte fled into the marshes of the Danube. While campaigning against Selte, the emperor Isaac barely escaped a stroke of lightning and, upon returning to Constantinople shortly afterwards, he fell ill and abdicated.

During the reign of Constantine X Ducas, Isaac's successor, the Pechenegs resumed their incursions, extending their activities as far as Sofia where they were defeated by Romanus Diogenes, the future emperor. But more destructive than the ravages of the Pechenegs during this reign were those of the Uzes, another nomadic people of Turkish origin, a "race," according to a Byzantine historian, "more noble and numerous than the Pechenegs",[6] but distantly related to them. The Uzes crossed the Danube in 1065, defeated the Byzantine garrisons that were opposed to them and took their generals, Basil Apokapes and Nicephorus Botaniates, prisoners. It was a mass migration, the fighting strength alone of

[6] Cedrenus, *Historiarum compendium*, II, 654. The Uzes are merely the Oghuz in Byzantine form, but the distinction is useful in separating those who crossed the Russian steppe from those who crossed the Persian plateau.

the barbarians being said to have numbered six hundred thousand. As the Uzes entered the empire, they divided into groups, one group going as far as Thessalonica, and even beyond into Greece. They destroyed and killed, and took whatever booty they could carry. Their ravages were so terrible, and their numbers so overwhelming, that the native inhabitants of the European provinces of the empire despaired of safety and began to think of emigrating.[7] Meanwhile the emperor, although much distressed, was slow in taking any measures either, as some thought, because he was too parsimonious to raise an army, or, in the opinion of others, because he felt that the barbarians were too strong to be met successfully in the field. He tried at first to win the barbarian chieftains by means of gifts and other inducements, but finally left the capital, presumably in order to take the field. By that time, however, the backbone of the Uzes' invasion had been broken. Famine, disease, and cold had decimated their ranks, and as they moved northward, Bulgars and Pechenegs fell upon them and further reduced their numbers. Some of them surrendered to the imperial authorities and were settled in Macedonia to cultivate the land and furnish recruits to the army. Leading members among these settlers were honored with the rank of senator and other dignities. The disaster suffered by the barbarians was attributed by the Byzantines to divine intervention.

Pechenegs and Uzes again invaded the empire in 1073, during the reign of Michael VII. On the advice of his minister, the clever but unprincipled Nicephoritzes, Michael VII had failed to make the payments which were due to the garrisons of the fortified towns of the Danube. This put the soldiers in a state of rebellion and they all flocked to the standard of the Byzantine governor of the region, a former slave of Constantine X, Nestor by name, who took advantage of the situation to rebel against the emperor. But besides the garrisons of the towns, which were doubtless composed of barbarians, Nestor obtained also the assistance of Pechenegs and Uzes from across the river. Nestor directed his forces straight to the capital and demanded the dismissal of Nicephoritzes; his rebellion finally collapsed and the Pechenegs returned beyond the Danube, but before they did so they plundered the country all the way from the capital.

During the struggle for the possession of the throne following the overthrow of Michael VII, the Pechenegs and Uzes were busily engaged in ravaging the country. Pechenegs were in the army of

[7] Attaliates, p. 84.

the rebel Basilacius, and Pechenegs and Kumans, another Turkish people, plundered the regions of Adrianople while the armies of the rivals for the throne were engaged with each other. Nicephorus Botaniates made peace with the Pechenegs and the Uzes, but the Pecheneg menace remained undiminished. It was one of the most serious problems that Alexius Comnenus would have to face.

The conquest of southern Italy by the Normans, which was to have such an important effect on the relations between Byzantium and the west, has been treated in more detail in an earlier chapter.[8] It may, however, be noted here that the Norman campaign was brought to a successful end in 1071 when, under the leadership of Robert Guiscard, the Normans captured Bari. The capture of Bari made Guiscard the unquestioned master of southern Italy, but already before this event the Byzantines had reconciled themselves to the loss of their Italian possessions and adopted a policy designed to win the friendship of the Norman leader. This policy was initiated by the emperor Romanus IV Diogenes, who proposed the marriage of one of his sons to one of Guiscard's daughters. The proposal, which must have been made either immediately before or during the siege of Bari, was rejected by Guiscard.

Diogenes' policy was revived by his successor, Michael VII. In the hope that he might use the Normans to check the Selchükid Turks in Asia Minor, and at the same time protect the empire from further attacks by Guiscard, Michael VII definitely abandoned his claims to the former possessions of the empire in southern Italy and sought the friendship of the Norman leader. This we are told by Cedrenus, and the two letters in which Michael VII asked for the alliance of Guiscard and the chrysobull to Guiscard, by which he confirmed the conditions of the alliance which he succeeded in concluding with him, have survived. The first letter was most probably written late in 1071 or early in 1072; the second letter was written either in 1072 or 1073; and the chrysobull bears the date August 1074.

The subject of the two letters is a proposal for the marriage of the emperor's brother, Constantine, to one of Guiscard's daughters in return for Guiscard's friendship and alliance. Of the two letters the first is rather general. It puts the emphasis on the common religion of the two leaders; praises the greatness and

[8] See above, chapter II, section C; and cf., in general, Einar Joranson, "The Inception of the Career of the Normans in Italy: Legend and History," *Speculum*, XXIII (1948), 353–397. On the documentation of what follows concerning the Normans and Byzantium, see P. Charanis, "Byzantium, the West, and the Origin of the First Crusade," *Byzantion*, XIX (1949), 17–24.

intelligence of Guiscard; recognizes by implication Guiscard's conquest of southern Italy; and declares that the two rulers should in the future identify their interests. The second letter is more specific. In return for the marriage of one of his daughters to the emperor's brother, Guiscard was to become the rampart of the Byzantine frontiers, spare the princes who were vassals of the empire, furnish aid to Byzantium in all things, and fight with the Byzantines against all the enemies of the empire. Guiscard rejected both proposals.

In 1074 the Byzantine court tried again. This time the emperor proposed, as the basis of the alliance which he sought, the marriage of his own son with one of Guiscard's daughters. Guiscard accepted this proposal, and in August 1074 Michael VII issued a chrysobull which he addressed to the Norman leader and by which he confirmed the conditions of the alliance the two leaders had reached. The agreement provided for the marriage of the emperor's son Constantine to Guiscard's daughter, who subsequently took the name Helen; it gave imperial titles to the young couple; granted to Guiscard the title of *nobilissimus*; allowed him to name one of his sons *curopalates*; and put at his disposal eight other titles of varying rank which he was free to grant to anyone among his followers. Some of these titles carried with them an annual payment. Guiscard, in return, agreed not to violate the territories of the empire, but to defend them against its enemies. The agreement was, as far as the Byzantine empire was concerned, a defensive and offensive alliance. The Turks are nowhere mentioned, but we are told by Cedrenus (or rather Skylitzes) that Michael's motive was the hope that with the assistance of the Normans he might be able to drive the Turks out of Asia Minor.

Guiscard concluded the alliance with the Byzantine emperor at a time when his relations with the papacy were bad, and it is indeed extremely probable that he decided on this course in order to prevent any agreement being reached between Byzantium and the papacy. For while they approached Guiscard the Byzantine authorities carried on negotiations also with the papacy, and it is significant that these negotiations stopped as soon as the alliance with the Norman leader was concluded. But Byzantium derived no benefit from its treaty of alliance with Guiscard. Guiscard was restlessly ambitious, and it was not long before he began to focus his eyes upon the imperial title itself. In the overthrow of Michael in 1078 he thought he saw an opportunity to realize his ambition and used the treaty which he had concluded with Michael as an excuse to justify his action. Meanwhile Guiscard had settled his differences with the papacy, and pope Gregory VII, who had been bitterly disappointed over the failure of his negotiations with Byzantium, sanctioned his aggressive plans against the Byzantine empire. On July 25, 1080, Gregory wrote to the bishops of Apulia and Calabria, asking them to lend all possible help to Guiscard in the expedition which he was about to undertake against Byzantium. Guiscard, with the pope's blessing, was on the point of invading the empire as Alexius Comnenus ascended the throne. The issue at stake was no less than the very existence of the empire.

While Pechenegs and Uzes roamed within and devastated the Balkan provinces of the empire, and the Normans in Italy threatened the very existence of the state, the situation in Asia Minor had so deteriorated that one did not know precisely what regions still belonged to the empire. This situation was created by the advance of the Turks known as Selchükids, a name born by the family which furnished them their leaders. Like the Uzes, to whom they were related, the Selchükid Turks were nomads, but they could easily adapt themselves to the ways of civilization. Already converted to Islam and accustomed to the life of the frontier regions, they were motivated both by the desire for booty and by religious fanaticism. The men who led them showed remarkable qualities of statesmanship. The aim of these men was to conquer the more advanced regions of Islam — Mesopotamia, Syria, Egypt — but they allowed the nomads, whose movements they could not really effectively control, to penetrate the Byzantine provinces of eastern Asia Minor. It was this penetration, which the Byzantines utterly failed to stop, that undermined the position of the empire in Asia Minor and created conditions which were to determine the history of the Near East for centuries.[9]

The Armenians of Vaspurkan were the first to feel the pressure of the movement of the Selchükid Turks toward Asia Minor. It is said that it was because the king of Vaspurkan felt himself unable to check this pressure against his realm that he ceded it to the Byzantines (1021), receiving in return important domains in Cappadocia as well as the governorship of that province. Against the Byzantine empire itself no serious Selchükid incursions are recorded

[9] On the Selchükids see above, chapter V, and J. Laurent, *Byzance et les Turcs seldjoucides dans l'Asie occidentale jusqu'en 1081* (Nancy, 1913); H. M. Loewe, "The Seljuqs," *Cambridge Medieval History*, IV, 299–317; and especially C. Cahen, "La Première pénétration turque en Asie-Mineure (seconde moitié du XIe siècle)," *Byzantion*, XVIII (1948), 5–67. On the social conditions in Asia Minor which enabled the Turks to consolidate themselves see P. Wittek, "Deux chapitres de l'histoire des Turcs de Roum," *Byzantion*, XI (1936), 285–319, and *The Rise of the Ottoman Empire* (London, 1938), pp. 16–33; and also G. Moravcsik, *Byzantinoturcica*, I, 66ff., with bibliography.

until the reign of Constantine IX Monomachus. It is indeed with that reign that Byzantine historians date the beginning of the Selchükid menace and the eventual loss of the major part of Asia Minor.

Two major Selchükid raids in Byzantine territory took place during the reign of Constantine IX, one in 1048 under Ibrāhīm İnal (or Yinal) and the other in 1054 under the sultan, Tughrul-Beg himself. Both times the situation was favorable to the invaders, for they found the eastern provinces stripped of the major part of their troops: in 1048, because these troops had been recalled in order to suppress the revolt of Leo Tornicius, which had broken out in Adrianople in 1047; and in 1054, because they were being used in an effort to stop the Pechenegs.

Ibrāhīm İnal ravaged the province of Iberia and the back country of Trebizond, but it was on Erzerum, a city of commerce, wealth, and population, that he inflicted the greatest disaster. The city was burned to the ground; the major part of its population — one hundred and forty thousand, according to one Byzantine historian — was destroyed;[10] and its wealth was plundered and carried away. The Byzantine governors of Vaspurkan and Iberia at first hesitated as to what action to take, but when they were joined by the Iberian prince Liparites (East Armenian, Liparit), a vassal of the empire, they came to grips with Ibrāhīm İnal only to be defeated. Liparites himself was taken prisoner. An exchange of ambassadors between the Byzantine emperor, who was in no position to send reinforcements to the east, and the Turkish sultan followed, and Liparites was liberated; but there was no stop to the Turkish raids, and in 1054 it was the sultan himself who led the expedition into Byzantine territory. His forces plundered the regions between Lake Van, Erzerum, and the mountains of the back country of Trebizond; they also laid siege to Manzikert, but failed to take it. The sultan withdrew, but not all of the marauders left the territory of the empire. Three thousand under a certain Samuk (called Σαμούχης in Byzantine sources) remained to continue their pillaging; they were active during the reign of Michael VI (1056–1057).

These incursions under Ibrāhīm İnal and Tughrul-Beg were the beginning of a series of raids which became increasingly more frequent. On this fact all the Byzantine historians agree.[11] In 1057, when the troops of the Armenian provinces were withdrawn in

[10] Cedrenus, *Historiarum compendium*, II, 578.

[11] See, for instance, Bryennius, *Commentarii*, pp. 31–32; Zonaras, *Epitomae historiarum*, III, 640–641; Glycas, *Chronicon*, p. 597.

order to support Isaac Comnenus in his rebellion against Michael VI, the Turks under Samuk ravaged the regions where the two branches of the Euphrates join. But it was especially during the reign of Constantine X Ducas that the Turkish raiders roamed far and wide. In 1059 Sebastia (Sivas) was pillaged; in 1064 or 1065 Alp Arslan, the successor of Tughrul-Beg, took Ani; from 1065 onward both Edessa and Antioch were continuously on the defensive; in 1067 Caesarea (Kayseri) in Cappadocia was ruined. About the same time we find Samuk active as far as Galatia and Phrygia. The Byzantine emperor meanwhile made no serious effort to counteract these raids.

The death of Constantine X Ducas, however, brought to the Byzantine throne Romanus IV Diogenes, a soldier by profession. The desires of the widow of Constantine X no doubt had something to do with the choice of Diogenes, but the Selchükid menace was the primary consideration. Romanus was a brave, if somewhat rash, soldier who had already distinguished himself against the Pechenegs near Sofia. He ascended the throne in January 1068; a few months later he was in the field against the Selchükids, but his army, which was hastily brought together, was neither well armed nor well organized. He achieved some success, but nothing decisive. He succeeded indeed in intercepting a Turkish band which had sacked Pontic Neocaesarea (Niksar), and forced it to abandon its booty, and in the southeast he was able to take Artāḥ near Antioch and Manbij northeast of Aleppo, thus assuring communications between Edessa and Antioch. But while he was active in Syria a fresh band of Selchükids penetrated into the heart of Asia Minor and pillaged Amorium. Diogenes returned to Constantinople, but in 1069 he again took the field. He first defeated the Norman chieftain Crispin, who had rebelled with his troops, and then proceeded to clear the regions around Caesarea in Cappadocia which were inundated with Turkish bands. Near Melitene (Malatya) he left a part of his army with Philaretus (West Armenian, Filardos), a general of Armenian descent, with instructions to bar the passage of the Turks, while he himself proceeded toward the Armenian provinces in order to assure their defenses. But Philaretus was defeated and Turkish bands broke into Asia Minor to pillage Iconium (Konya). When Romanus heard of the sack of Iconium he turned back in order to intercept the raiders, but neither he nor his lieutenants were able to destroy them, although they forced them to give up their booty. Romanus then returned to the capital where he remained throughout 1070, entrusting the campaign against the marauders of the east to his youthful general Manuel Comnenus. But, after a minor success, Manuel was defeated near Sebastia and taken prisoner, while another Turkish band penetrated deep into Asia Minor and sacked Chonae. Meanwhile Alp Arslan, who was preparing an expedition against the Fāṭimids of Egypt, was willing to come to some agreement with the Byzantines, and a truce seems to have been concluded. But Alp Arslan was in no position to stop the Turkish raids into the territory of the empire, for they were often made without his knowledge and sometimes even against his will. Under such conditions the truce, if indeed there was a truce, could have no lasting effects. But Alp Arslan seems to have been taken by surprise when in the spring of 1071 Romanus Diogenes launched his third and last campaign against the Selchükids.

The campaign of 1071 was the greatest effort made by Byzantium to stop the incursions of the Selchükids. Oriental sources put the strength of the army which Romanus led deep into Armenia at 300,000 and say further that it was well equipped with various weapons and siege engines.[12] This is, of course, an exaggeration. This army, no doubt, was numerically superior to the previous armies that Romanus had led into Asia Minor. In morale, cohesiveness, and equipment, however, it was no better than they. It was a motley force composed of Greeks, Slavs, Alans, Uzes, Varangians, Normans, Pechenegs, Armenians, and Georgians. Some of these groups, as, for instance, the Greeks and the Armenians, did not trust each other; others, the Uzes, for example, were Turks related to the Selchükids to whom they might, as in the event they did, desert. But even the numerical strength of the army had been considerably reduced by the time of the decisive engagement; for the Normans under Roussel of Bailleul and a contingent under the Georgian Joseph Tarchaniotes had been dispatched to take Akhlat (or Khilat) on Lake Van, while others had been sent elsewhere to seek provisions. These troops were recalled, to be sure, but they failed to arrive. Then too at a critical moment of the campaign a contingent of the Uzes deserted to the enemy, and this defection introduced doubts and distrust into the camp of the Byzantines. It is said that at the time of the engagement Romanus had no more than one third of the army which he had brought with him. Still the Byzantine forces made a powerful impression and Alp

[12] For this campaign see above, chapter V, pp. 148–149, and C. Cahen, "La Campagne de Mantzikert d'après les sources musulmanes," *Byzantion*, IX (1934), 629ff., and cf. M. Mathieu, "Une Source négligée de la bataille de Mantzikert: les 'Gesta Roberti Wiscardi' de Guillaume d'Apulie," *Byzantion*, XX (1950), 89ff.

Arslan, who commanded the Turkish troops, made an effort to avoid a battle, but his overtures for peace were rejected by the Byzantine emperor. He had made too great an effort to return without meeting the enemy. The decisive battle took place on August 26, 1071, near Manzikert. Romanus fought bravely, but his forces were completely routed and he himself was taken prisoner, the first Byzantine sovereign to be captured by a Moslem opponent. After Manzikert there was no effective force to stop the penetration of the Turks, who now came not only to raid, but to stay.

Alp Arslan treated Romanus Diogenes generously and liberated him at the end of eight days. The Byzantine emperor, however, agreed to pay a huge ransom and an annual tribute. It is said also that he promised to cede the cities of Manzikert, Edessa, Manbij, and Antioch, but this is extremely doubtful. For the moment at least, Alp Arslan did not envisage the annexation of Byzantine territory, while the Byzantine emperor would have preferred to die rather than agree to anything that was not worthy of his dignity.[13] The two men agreed to keep the peace and to exchange prisoners. Diogenes was then given a Turkish guard and was allowed to return to his country. But in the meantime the authorities in Constantinople had declared him deposed and had replaced him by the eldest son of Constantine X Ducas, Michael VII. The result was civil war during which Diogenes called the Selchükids to his assistance. He was finally defeated and captured; he died shortly afterwards as a result of having been blinded. Alp Arslan vowed to avenge his death and gave his bands freedom of action. They soon inundated Asia Minor, where they were destined to remain. They were helped in this, as will be seen later in this chapter, by the military anarchy which broke out in the empire during the reign of Michael VII.

In less than twenty-five years after they had begun their activities in earnest, the nomads from the east and the adventurers from the west had reduced the empire to impotence and had threatened its very existence. How this came about is a question that cannot be easily answered, but an examination of the internal conditions of the empire during this period may yield at least a partial explanation.

Between 1025 and 1081, when Alexius Comnenus ascended the throne, thirteen sovereigns, two of them women, occupied the throne. This gives an average of little more than four years for

[13] Bryennius, *Commentarii*, p. 44.

each reign, but this figure is less revealing than the actual duration of each reign. Eight emperors occupied the throne for not more than three years, and only one ruled for more than ten years, a fact which contemporaries did not fail to notice. Of the remaining four reigns two lasted for seven years, one for six, and the other for nine.[14] Five emperors were overthrown by force, one died under questionable circumstances, and another abdicated, probably under pressure. Moreover, virtually every reign was troubled by some uprising aimed at the overthrow of the emperor. Among the emperors who ruled during this period, four owed the throne to Zoë, daughter of Constantine VIII; Romanus III Argyrus, Michael IV, and Constantine IX Monomachus married Zoë, and Michael V was adopted by her.

The emperors, with one or two possible exceptions, were persons of no ability, of a caliber greatly inferior to what the situation required. Constantine VIII was an old man when he became sole emperor, but at no time in his life had he shown any interest in government. The pursuits which attracted him the most were horse-racing, hunting, dice-playing, and eating luxurious dishes. In his scant three years on the throne he managed to dissipate the vast surpluses which his frugal brother, Basil II, had accumulated. Romanus III Argyrus had many pretensions, but nothing in his record shows that they were founded in fact. He was neither a good general nor a good administrator. Nor did he have strength of character, as his indifference to the infidelities of

[14] The narrative sources for the internal history are the same as those listed in the bibliographical note. But these should be supplemented by the documentary evidence, the principal collections of which are the following: F. Miklosich and J. Müller, *Acta et diplomata graeca medii aevi sacra et profana*, 6 vols. (Vienna, 1860–1890); *Actes de l'Athos*, vols. I–VI (edited by Petit, Regel, Kurtz, and Korablev and published as appendices to *Vizantiiskii Vremennik*, vols. X (1903), XII (1906), XIII (1907), XVII (1911), XIX (1912), XX (1913); T. Florinsky, *Athonskie Akte* (St. Petersburg, 1880); G. Rouillard and P. Collomp, *Actes de Laura* (Paris, 1937). On this see F. Dölger, "Zur Textgestaltung der Lavra-Urkunden und zu ihrer geschichtlichen Auswertung," *Byz. Zeitschr.*, XXXIX (1939), 23–66. See also P. Lemerle, *Actes de Kutlumus* (Paris, 1945). Most of these documents belong to the period later than the eleventh century. See also Zachariae von Lingenthal, *Jus Graeco-Romanum*, vol. III (Leipzig, 1857); F. Dölger, *Aus den Schatzkammern des Heiligen Berges*; *Textband* (Munich, 1948); P. Charanis, "The Monastic Properties and the State in the Byzantine Empire," *Dumbarton Oaks Papers*, IV (1948), 98, note 135. The best modern treatments are those of Neumann and Skabalanovich cited in the bibliographical note. The standard study on the financial administration of the empire is that by F. Dölger, *Beiträge zur byzantinischen Finanzverwaltung, besonders des 10. u. 11. Jahrhunderts* (Leipzig, 1927). Important also is the work of G. Ostrogorsky, "Die ländliche Steuergemeinde des byzantinischen Reiches im X. Jahrhundert," *Vierteljahrschrift für Sozial- und Wirtschaftsgeschichte*, XX (1927), 1–108. Reference should also be made to the book of D. A. Xanalatos, *Beiträge zur Wirtschafts- und Sozialgeschichte Makedoniens im Mittelalter, hauptsächlich auf Grund der Briefe des Erzbischofs Theophylaktos von Achrida* (Munich, 1937). For a general account of the rural life of the empire, see G. Rouillard, *La Vie rurale dans l'empire byzantin* (Paris, 1953). This book, published posthumously, consists of a series of lectures which the author delivered at the Collège de France in 1944.

his wife, which were to cost him his life, shows. His reign is noted for the favors he bestowed upon the aristocracy to which he belonged. Michael IV, a Paphlagonian upstart, had a sense of duty and was not incapable of action, but he was subject to epilepsy, which sapped his strength and in the end deprived him of his life. Michael V was certainly mentally unbalanced, and Zoë and Theodora could not rise above the foibles and petty interests of their sex. Constantine IX Monomachus was a sick man, coarse and uncouth in his tastes and pleasures, more disposed to seek the embraces of his mistresses than the hardships of the camp or the cares of government. Michael VI was an old man, simple and inoffensive, a tool of his ministers. Isaac I Comnenus and Romanus IV Diogenes were soldiers of the old school, active and ready to take the field, men who saw clearly what the empire needed, but neither the one nor the other was able to withstand the pressure of intrigue. Constantine X Ducas was educated and not intemperate in his habits, but he failed utterly to grasp the gravity of the situation. Michael VII was considered by his contemporaries as insignificant and there is not much that can be said in favor of Nicephorus Botaniates.

These men, while enjoying the privileges of power, generally shied away from its responsibilities, which they entrusted to their ministers. Some of these ministers, as, for instance, Leichudes, who served under Constantine IX Monomachus and again under Isaac I Comnenus, or Leo Paraspondyles, who guided Theodora and Michael VI, were honest and conscientious, but they were not always sound — this is especially true of Paraspondyles — in their judgment as to the policy that would best serve the interests of the state. Others, men like John the Orphanotrophus under the Paphlagonians, the eunuch John who served Constantine IX during the last years of his reign, or Nicephoritzes under Constantine X and Michael VII, sought their own aggrandizement or that of their families; still others, as, for instance, Michael Psellus, who served virtually every one of these emperors, intrigued and maneuvered in order to stay in power. Byzantium, at one of the gravest moments of its existence, lacked what it most needed — the guiding hand of a soldier-statesman.

The factor which lay at the bottom of the political instability in Byzantium in the eleventh century was the conflict between the landed aristocracy as a military class and the imperial court. The antecedents of this conflict go back to the tenth century. Basil II had met and defeated the aristocracy in the field and had then proceeded, by a series of measures, to undermine the sources of their power. Among these measures the severest was that of 1002, the law concerning the *allelengyon*, which required the landed aristocracy to pay the tax arrears of peasants too poor to meet their own obligations. After the death of Basil his measures were not enforced and the law concerning the *allelengyon* was actually repealed, but a certain distrust of the military magnates persisted. This is strikingly illustrated by the fact that under the patriarch Alexius of Studium in 1026 a synodal decision was obtained pronouncing an anathema against all rebels and excommunicating priests who might admit them to communion.[15] It was, however, during the reign of Constantine IX that opposition to the military magnates took a systematic form. A political faction, composed principally of members of the civil bureaucracy, emerged during the reign of this emperor. It had as its aim the elimination of the military from the administration of the empire. But the effort to achieve this aim plunged the empire into a series of civil wars which squandered its resources and manpower at a time when they were needed to cope with the new enemies.

Constantine IX was no soldier emperor; he preferred, as we have noted, the comforts and pleasures of the palace to the hardships of the military camp. This, no doubt, was a factor in his anti-military bias, but it was not the principal factor. If he made peace the keynote of his foreign policy, as he did, it was not primarily because of his aversion to the military life; it was because of the general feeling that there was no longer any need to follow a policy of expansion. The great military triumphs of the tenth and eleventh centuries, the crushing of the Saracens and the Bulgars and the pushing of the frontiers to the Euphrates and the Tigris in the east, and to the Danube in the Balkans, seemed to have assured the external security of the empire. Here and there, as in the case of Greater Armenia, it might be necessary to make further annexations in order to round off the frontiers, but these were not major operations. The protection of the frontiers might be assured by the maintenance of a mercenary force under the direct control of the capital. Continued expansion was not only unnecessary, but too expensive for the empire to support. The maintenance of peace on the other hand would reduce the financial burdens of the state; it would also reduce the influence of the army in the administration and eliminate the danger of

[15] Zachariae von Lingenthal, *Jus Graeco-Romanum*, III, 320–321; *Jus Graeco-Romanum*, cura J. Zepi et P. Zepi (Athens, 1930), I, 273.

revolts. Constantine took into his service a number of intellectuals, men like Constantine Leichudes, John Xiphilinus, Michael Psellus, and John Mauropus, and with their help refounded the University of Constantinople, one of whose objectives must have been, no doubt, the training of civil functionaries for the state. Constantine did not retain the services of these men, however, although to the end of his reign he relied principally on his civil servants and ignored the generals, many of whom he retired from service. Moreover, he deprived the soldiers of the frontier regions of the payments which they were accustomed to receive, diverting these funds to other purposes. These acts of the emperor created wide discontent among the military leaders. Two serious rebellions broke out during his reign. One, headed by the redoubtable George Maniaces, had as its cause the private grievances of that general, but the other, under the leadership of Leo Tornicius, was the work of generals who had been deprived of their posts. The failure of both rebellions strengthened the party of civil officials. This party kept its hold upon the government to the end of the reign of Constantine, and when Theodora, who had succeeded him, died in 1056, it was instrumental in putting on the throne Michael VI (1056–1057), "a simple and inoffensive man," who was already advanced in years. Neither Constantine nor his advisers seem to have realized the significance of the incursions of the new enemies of the empire. The Byzantine historians who wrote after the battle of Manzikert, however, attributed the beginnings of the misfortunes of the empire to the reign of this emperor, mentioning especially his extravagance and his neglect of the army.[16]

The struggle between the civil and the military factions came to a head during the reign of Michael VI. The influential generals, men such as Michael Bourtzes, Constantine and John Ducas, Isaac Comnenus, Catacalon Cecaumenus — all of them great magnates of Asia Minor — openly resented the favoritism shown by this emperor to his civil servants. The generals demanded that some consideration be given to them also. But, as the emperor paid no attention to them, and continued to treat their remonstrances with derision, they countered by conspiring to bring about his overthrow. The revolution which put Isaac Comnenus on the throne in 1057 had the support of important elements in Constantinople, including the patriarch Cerularius, but it was primarily the work of the generals who had become exasperated

[16] For instance, Cedrenus, *Historiarum compendium*, II, 608–609. See also C. Diehl, *Figures byzantines* (Paris, 1909), vol. I, 273 ff.

by the anti-military policy of Michael VI. It may be recalled that it was at the time of this revolt, when the troops of the Armenian provinces were withdrawn in order to support Isaac Comnenus, that the Turk Samuk made a devastating incursion into the territory of the empire.

Isaac Comnenus was a soldier-emperor, the first soldier-emperor since Basil II had passed away. That there should be no mistake as to where he stood on the issues of the day, he had himself represented on coins with sword in hand. But the task which he faced was overwhelming. The army was disorganized, the treasury empty, and the enemies of the empire many and active. He put himself to work with diligence and took the field in person, something which no emperor had done since Michael IV. The reorganization of the army he considered his most pressing problem, but this reorganization could not be done without money. In order to find this money he practised the strictest economy, collected all taxes with care, annulled land grants that his predecessors had made to various persons, and confiscated properties of the monasteries. These measures were applauded by some as most desirable, but they aroused the opposition of powerful elements.[17] Isaac might have successfully resisted the intrigues of these elements, but when in addition to these intrigues he had to cope with a serious illness, he decided to abdicate. He designated Constantine Ducas as his successor. This was perhaps his most serious mistake.

Constantine X Ducas belonged to an illustrious family of military chieftains, but he himself disliked the life of the soldier. He had come under the influence of the civil party, and this combined with his own inclinations to bring about a reaction against the military policy of his predecessor. During his reign the disorganization of the army became complete. Its expenditures were cut, and its leaders removed from the rolls. Constantine freely distributed dignities and honors, but these dignities and honors did not go to the soldiers; they went to the civil functionaries. The profession of the soldier which in the great days of Byzantium carried with it prestige, honor, and position had no longer any value and so, as Skylitzes says, "the soldiers put aside their arms and became lawyers or jurists."[18] But the empire did not need lawyers and jurists; it needed soldiers. The Selchükid Turks in Asia Minor and the Pechenegs and Uzes in the Balkans roamed

[17] Attaliates, *Historia*, pp. 60–62.
[18] Cedrenus [i. e., Skylitzes], *Historiarum compendium*, II, 652.

freely, and there was no one to stop them. That Constantine X had gone too far in his neglect of the army even some of the most intimate among his civil advisers realized. Psellus declares that the most serious fault he committed was to ignore the disorganized state of the army at a time when the empire was hard pressed by enemies from every side.[19]

Romanus Diogenes, who succeeded Constantine X in 1068, tried to rebuild the army. The task was overwhelming and the new emperor had neither the means nor the time required to bring it to a successful completion. His failure at Manzikert enabled the civil party to get control of the government and to replace him with Michael VII, the eldest son of Constantine X Ducas. Educated according to the best literary standards of the period, a pupil of Psellus, Michael VII was more interested in rhetoric, philosophy, and poetry than in governing the empire. His reign marked the complete disintegration of the state. Rebellions broke out everywhere. In the European provinces Nicephorus Bryennius, the governor of Dyrrachium (Durazzo), threatened with disgrace, proclaimed himself emperor; the magnates of Asia Minor declared for Nicephorus Botaniates, himself a magnate of Asia Minor; Botaniates overthrew Michael VII, and then his soldiers under the command of Alexius Comnenus defeated Bryennius. But Botaniates himself was shortly overthrown by Alexius; in the meantime Nicephorus Melissenus had rebelled in Asia Minor. Order was reëstablished with the triumph of Alexius in 1081. But these civil wars enabled the Selchükids to establish themselves in western Asia Minor.

Thus between 1042, when Constantine Monomachus became emperor, and 1081, when Alexius Comnenus became emperor, a period which saw the appearance of new and formidable enemies, the imperial government, with the exception of the two short reigns of Isaac Comnenus and Romanus IV Diogenes, had made it a point of policy to curtail the power of the army (and had weakened its efficiency). The ultimate objective of this policy was to lessen the power and influence of the great military magnates. In the end this objective was not achieved, but the effort to achieve it had plunged the empire into a series of civil wars. But more serious still was the increasingly depressed condition of the enrolled soldiers, men who held small estates granted to them by the state in return for their services, and who had played such an important role in the great military triumphs of the tenth century. Writing

[19] Psellus, *Chronogr.*, II, 146f.

of the army that took the field in one of the expeditions which Romanus IV Diogenes commanded against the Selchükids, Skylitzes states: "The army was composed of Macedonians and Bulgars and Cappadocians, Uzes, Franks, and Varangians and other barbarians who happened to be about. There were gathered also those who were in Phrygia [the theme Anatolikon]. And what one saw in them [i.e., in the enrolled soldiers of the theme Anatolikon] was something incredible. The renowned champions of the Romans who had reduced to subjection all the east and the west now numbered only a few, and these were bowed down by poverty and ill treatment. They lacked weapons, swords, and other arms such as javelins and scythes. . . . They lacked also cavalry and other equipment, for the emperor had not taken the field for a long time. For this reason they were regarded as useless and unnecessary, and their wages and maintenance were reduced."[20] The enrolled soldiers, depressed and forgotten, became more and more a minor element in the Byzantine army. The bulk of this army in the eleventh century came to be composed almost entirely of foreign mercenaries: Russians, Turks, Alans, English, Normans, Germans, Pechenegs, Bulgars, and others.[21] These mercenaries were swayed more by their own private interests than by those of the empire. The harm which they did was much greater than the services they rendered.

Among these mercenaries the most turbulent and intractable were the Normans. Their chiefs were given important positions in the army and were even given land, but the slightest provocation was enough to make them rebel. The Byzantine historians single out three of these chiefs for their turbulent, warlike, and sanguinary spirit: Hervé, Robert Crispin, and Roussel of Bailleul.[22] Hervé deserted to the Turks in 1057 and Crispin openly rebelled in 1068. But more ambitious and more terrible in his devastations was Roussel of Bailleul, who seems to have passed into the service of the Byzantines about 1070 with a large group of his com-

[20] Cedrenus, *Historiarum compendium*, II, 668.

[21] Zachariae von Lingenthal, *Jus Graeco-Romanum*, III, 373. Cf. *Byzantion*, XIV (1939), 280ff. On the Anglo-Saxons in the Byzantine army, see A. A. Vasiliev, "The Opening Stages of the Anglo-Saxon Immigration to Byzantium in the Eleventh Century," *Annales de l'Institut Kondakov*, IX (1937), 39ff.; S. Blöndal, "Nabites the Varangian, with some Notes on the Varangians under Nicephorus III Botaniates and the Comneni," *Classica et Mediaevalia*, II (1939), 145ff.; and "The Last Exploits of Harold Sigurdsson in Greek Service," *ibid.*, 1ff.; R. M. Dawkins, "The Later History of the Varangian Guard: Some Notes," *Journal of Roman Studies*, XXXVII (1947), 39ff.

[22] On these Normans see G. Schlumberger, "Deux chefs normands des armées byzantines au XIe siècle," *RH*, XVI (1881), 289–303; L. Bréhier, "Les Aventures d'un chef normand en Orient," *Revue des cours et conférences de la faculté des lettres de Paris*, XX (1911), 172–188.

patriots. At Manzikert he played a doubtful role; two years later he openly rebelled against the government and sought to play the role of emperor-maker. Defeated in this, he retired into the interior of Asia Minor where he tried to carve out a principality for himself, to do what his compatriots had done in Italy. It was only by treachery that he was finally delivered into the hands of the Byzantines. His captor was the youthful Alexius Comnenus, who was then in the service of Michael VII.

Besides the Normans, there were in the service of the empire other foreign troops whose loyalty was doubtful. The Uzes, for instance, deserted to the enemy at Manzikert, a desertion which greatly contributed to the final defeat of the Byzantine forces. But the foreign troops in the Byzantine forces which profited most from the disturbed conditions in which the empire found itself after Manzikert were the Selchükid Turks, who had entered the service of the various Byzantine generals. It was with Turkish auxiliaries that Romanus IV Diogenes tried to regain his throne after he had been liberated by Alp Arslan, his captor at Manzikert. His example was followed by almost all his successors. When Roussel of Bailleul openly rebelled, Michael VII called upon Turkish auxiliaries to track him down. The same emperor tried to suppress the rebellion of Nicephorus Botaniates with the help of the bands of Manṣūr and Sulaimān, two brothers related to the Selchükid sultan Alp Arslan. It was indeed this use of Turkish auxiliaries that enabled the Selchükids to establish themselves in western Asia Minor. Manṣūr and Sulaimān had agreed to come to the assistance of Michael VII, but they were ready at the same time to listen to the highest bidder, and they soon transferred their services to Botaniates. Botaniates installed them in Nicaea, and there they established themselves as masters. It was in this way that Nicaea was lost to the empire. In this way also were lost the cities of Galatia and Phrygia. Nicephorus Melissenus, who rebelled against Botaniates, was supported almost entirely by Turkish mercenaries. The cities of Galatia and Phrygia opened their gates to him; he installed Turkish garrisons in them, but while he never became emperor, the Turkish garrisons took over the cities in which he had installed them. The Byzantines, in using the Turks as mercenaries, thus made them masters of western Asia Minor between 1078 and 1081.

Besides its serious effects upon the military position of the state, the decline of the enrolled soldiers also had serious consequences for the social structure of the empire. The establishment of the military estates in the seventh and eighth centuries had contributed greatly to the growth of the class of the small peasant proprietors. For, while the eldest son of an enrolled soldier inherited his father's plot, together with the obligation of military service, the rest of the family were free to reclaim and cultivate land that was vacant, thus adding to the number of the free peasant proprietors. But now the depression of the enrolled soldiers reduced the free element in the agrarian structure of the empire and helped to bring about the decline of the small peasant proprietors.[23] The fundamental cause, however, for the decline of the free peasantry in Byzantium was the greed and love of power of the aristocracy, which used its wealth and official position to absorb the holdings of the peasantry. The decline of the free peasantry and the growth of the large estates constitute the characteristic features of the social history of Byzantium in the tenth and eleventh centuries.

The great emperors of the tenth century had realized the dangerous social and political implications of this development and tried to check it.[24] Every major emperor from Romanus Lecapenus up to and including Basil II, with the exception of John Tzimisces, issued more than one novel for this purpose. These emperors sought to preserve the free peasantry because they considered it an essential element in the health of the state. As Romanus Lecapenus put it in one of his novels (in 934): "It is not through hatred and envy of the rich that we take these measures, but for the protection of the small and the safety of the empire as a whole. . . . The extension of the power of the strong . . . will bring about the irreparable loss of the public good, if the present law does not bring a check to it. For it is the many settled on the land, who provide for the general needs, who pay the taxes and furnish the army with its recruits. Everything falls when the many are wanting."[25] The strictest among the measures taken for the protection of the free peasantry was that taken by Basil II concerning

[23] Cf. G. Ostrogorsky, "Agrarian Conditions in the Byzantine Empire in the Middle Ages," *The Cambridge Economic History*, I (Cambridge, 1941), 196.

[24] For the bibliography on this, see P. Charanis, "On the Social Structure of the Later Roman Empire," *Byzantion*, XVII (1944–1945), 52, note 51. To this bibliography there should now be added: E. Bach, "Les Lois agraires byzantines du Xe siècle," *Classica et Mediaevalia*, V (1942), 70–91; John Danstrup, "The State and Landed Property in Byzantium to c. 1250," *ibid.*, VIII (1946), 221–262; and Kenneth M. Setton, "On the Importance of Land Tenure and Agrarian Taxation in the Byzantine Empire, from the Fourth Century to the Fourth Crusade," *American Journal of Philology*, LXXIV (1953), 225–259, with references. Additional references are in P. Charanis, "Economic Factors in the Decline of the Byzantine Empire," *Journal of Economic History*, XIII (1953), 412ff.

[25] Zachariae von Lingenthal, *Jus Graeco-Romanum*, III, 246–247.

the *allelengyon*, to which reference has already been made. But with the death of Basil the effort to stop the growth of the large estates came to an end. His law concerning the *allelengyon* was repealed, and the other measures, although kept on the books, were not enforced. The fate of the free peasantry was thus definitely decided. The struggle which in the eleventh century the central government waged against the military magnates was not fought for the protection of the free peasantry. Indeed, the government, by the grants which it made to its partisans, promoted the further growth of the large estates. Henceforth the large estates were to constitute the dominant feature of the economic landscape of Byzantium. These estates were worked by tenant farmers, the *paroikoi* of the Byzantine texts, people who were personally free, but who were tied to certain obligations and *corvées* which curtailed their movement. Some free peasant proprietors continued to exist, but they had become hardly distinguishable from the *paroikoi*. Besides working for the lord, the *paroikoi* had allotments of their own for which they paid rent and performed various obligations and from which, after the passage of a number of years, they could not be evicted. These allotments were transmissible from father to son.

The free peasantry, as Romanus Lecapenus declared, had constituted the principal element of the strength of the empire. This class cultivated the land, provided for the general needs, paid the taxes, and furnished the army with recruits. But, as the holdings of the free peasantry decreased and the large estates increased, this element of strength was undermined. All land in Byzantium was in theory subject to taxation, but it was not always easy to collect from the great magnates, whose influence in the administration enabled them to obtain important exemptions. Throughout the eleventh century there was a continuous cry for money, prompted in part no doubt by the extravagances of some of the emperors, but in part by the reduction in the revenues resulting from the granting of various exemptions and from the failure to collect all the taxes. The things with which Isaac Comnenus was reproached and which rendered him unpopular were his cancellation of privileges and grants made by his predecessors and his careful collection of the taxes. But if large magnates could escape the payment of taxes, it was otherwise with the peasants, the vast majority of whom were now tenants. They had to bear the ever-increasing burden of taxation and, in addition, numerous *corvées*. The welfare of the state no longer had any meaning for them. The peasantry of the interior of Asia Minor offered no resistance to the Turks. The military class which might have offered the necessary resistance had also been undermined both by the expansion of the large estates and the struggle between the military and civil parties in the eleventh century. The enrolled soldiers, neglected and reduced to poverty, had neither the will nor the equipment to fight. The mercenaries who replaced them helped to complete the disintegration of the state.

The growth of the large estates and the consequent depression of the peasantry resulted also from the development of what has been called, by some scholars, Byzantine feudalism. This feudalism was based on institutions which had their origin or became fully developed in the eleventh century. These institutions were the *pronoia*, the *charistikion*, and the *exkousseia*.[26]

The *pronoia*, which consisted in the assignment by the government of a revenue-yielding property to a person in return for certain services, usually but not always military, rendered or to be rendered, made its appearance about the middle of the eleventh century. The grant consisted usually of land, but it could be a river or a fishery; its holder was known as a *pronoiarios*. The size of the grant varied from a territory of considerable extent to a single village or estate sufficient to take care of one family. The grant was made for a specific period, usually but not always for the lifetime of the holder. It could be neither alienated nor transmitted to one's heirs, and it was subject to recall by the imperial treasury. The *pronoiarios* served in the army as an officer and was expected, upon call, to furnish some troops, the number of them depending upon the size of his *pronoia*. But at the beginning the *pronoia* was not granted primarily for military service; it became primarily military under Alexius Comnenus and his successors. Its extensive use contributed greatly not only to the growth of the large estates but to the development of the appanage system, and thus weakened the central administration.

The *charistikion* was a development associated with the manage-

[26] For the discussion which follows see P. Charanis, "The Monastic Properties and the State in the Byzantine Empire," *Dumbarton Oaks Papers*, IV (1948), 65–91, where the sources, including translations of important passages, and essential bibliography, are cited. See also Ostrogorsky, *Geschichte des byzantinischen Staates*, Munich, 1952, pp. 230–232, 295–296. The fundamental work on the Byzantine *pronoia* now is that by Ostrogorsky, *Pronoia: A Contribution to the History of Feudalism in Byzantium and in South-Slavic Lands* (Belgrade, 1951) (in Serbian). The first seven chapters of this work have appeared in a French translation: H. Grégoire, tr., "La Pronoia," *Byzantion*, XXII (1952), 437–518. There is also a lengthy summary in English: I. Ševčenko, "An Important Contribution to the Social History of late Byzantium," *The Annals of the Ukrainian Academy of Arts and Sciences in the United States*, II (1952), 448–459. (Grégoire's translation has just been completed, and now appears under the title *Pour l'histoire de la féodalité byzantine*, Brussels, 1954.)

ment of monastic properties. In Byzantium the monastic and ecclesiastical properties were very extensive. It has been estimated by a competent authority on the internal history of Byzantium that at the end of the seventh century about one third of the usable land of the empire was in the possession of the church and the monasteries. Much of this property had been confiscated by the iconoclastic emperors in the eighth century, but with the defeat of iconoclasm it began to accumulate again. The attempt made by the emperors of the tenth century, Nicephorus Phocas in particular, to check this growth met with no success. About the middle of the eleventh century the monastic properties "were in no way inferior to those of the crown."[27]

The financial difficulties into which the empire had fallen in the eleventh century led Isaac Comnenus to envisage the confiscation of monastic properties. Isaac was primarily interested in finding the funds which he needed for the military rehabilitation of the empire, but it was hoped that this measure would also help to ameliorate the condition of the peasantry. The historian Attaliates, who reports this measure, writes that "it appeared to be profitable in two ways: [1] it freed the ... peasants from a heavy burden, for the monks, relying upon their extensive and wealthy estates, were wont to force them to abandon their lots ...; and [2] the public treasury which was forced in diverse ways to spend its resources obtained an addition and relief which were not inconsiderable without doing any harm at all to others."[28] But the measure rendered Isaac unpopular and was no doubt one of the factors involved in the intrigues which brought about his abdication. His immediate successors abandoned the policy of direct confiscation, but at the same time they did not refrain from the use of monastic properties. They used these properties, however, not for the financial rehabilitation of the empire, but in order to reward friends and favorites. They did this by exploiting an old Byzantine institution, the *charistikion*, an institution not unlike the western *beneficium*.

The *charistikion* was a grant which consisted of one or more monasteries and their properties. Monasteries thus granted remained monasteries and did not lose title to their properties, but their management was put under the direction of the persons to whom they were granted, who, while undertaking to support the monks and maintain the buildings, appropriated for themselves

[27] Attaliates, *Historia*, p. 61.

[28] *Ibid.*, pp. 60–62. For a complete translation of this passage see Charanis, "The Monastic Properties and the State ...," p. 68.

what remained of the revenue. The *charistikion* seems to have developed as early as the fifth century and may have been invented by the ecclesiastical hierarchy itself in order to get around the canons of the church, which did not permit the alienation of monastic properties. It was greatly exploited by the iconoclastic emperors in their efforts to weaken monasticism, but with the defeat of iconoclasm it fell into disuse. It appeared again in the tenth century and reached its widest prevalence in the eleventh. Originally only monasteries which had fallen into decay were involved in such a grant, the aim being to have them restored. Gradually, however, prosperous monasteries came to be included, and they were granted not for their benefit and upkeep, but for the profit of those who obtained them. This was so in the eleventh century. Many of the *charistikia* granted in this century were granted by the ecclesiastical hierarchy, but there were not a few which were granted by the emperors. The emperors made their grants to friends and favorites. In this way they assured themselves of the momentary support of those persons, but they added to the landed aristocracy whose growth in wealth and power threatened to undermine the central government. The holder of a *charistikion* was known as a *charistikarios*, and the grant was usually made to him for life.

Monastic and other large properties, although theoretically subject to taxation and other obligations, were in actual fact the beneficiaries of numerous exemptions. These exemptions were made by a specific grant; they constitute the *exkousseia* of the Byzantine documents.

The date of the origin of the *exkousseia* is still a matter of dispute, but the institution already existed in the tenth century and it was widely used in the eleventh.[29] The term itself is no doubt the hellenized form of the Latin *excusatio* (*excusare*); as an institution it comprised the exemptions from taxes and *corvées* and meant independence from the judicial administration (this independence being limited); such grants were made by the government to monasteries and large estates. Most of the documentation concerning the *exkousseia* dates from the second half of the eleventh century, and this may mean that it was during this period that this institution became crystallized. Thus, by the second half of the eleventh century it became a regular practice to grant immunities, especially from taxation, and this at a time when the treasury needed all the resources that it could command.

[29] Dölger, *Aus den Schatzkammern des Heiligen Berges*: *Textband*, n. 56, p. 155; Charanis, "The Monastic Properties and the State ...," pp. 65–67.

The battle of Manzikert decided the fate of Asia Minor and determined much of the subsequent history of the Byzantine empire. But Manzikert was only a battle, and what was lost there might have been retrieved had the society of the empire been healthier and more vigorous. Despite its wide territorial extent, however, and its seemingly great power the empire, such as it was in the eleventh century after the death of Basil II, was not a healthy organism. The depression of the peasantry deprived it of a strong pillar of support; the struggle between the military and the civil parties dissipated its energies and consummated the decay of that group of soldiers which had been its stoutest defenders. The mercenaries who replaced them pursued their own interests and did infinitely more harm than good. At the same time the extensive use of the institutions of the *pronoia*, the *charistikion*, and the *exkousseia* planted the seeds of further disintegration.

The most significant fact affecting the Byzantine church in the eleventh century was the quarrel with Rome.[30] The ecclesiastical events of 1054 have come down in history as marking the definite separation of the Greek and Roman churches. In actual fact, however, these events only accentuated and made worse a situation which already existed. Rome and Constantinople had not been in communion with each other for at least thirty years when the quarrel between cardinal Humbert and the Byzantine patriarch took place. In 1054 no one knew when and under what circumstances the break had come about, and modern research has not been able to throw much light on this problem. One thing is

[30] The sources, which are almost entirely documentary, have been brought together by C. Will, *Acta et scripta quae de controversiis ecclesiae graecae et latinae saeculi XI composita exstant* (Leipzig, 1861), and by Migne, *PG*, CXX (Paris, 1880), 735–820, 835–844; and *PL*, CXLIII (Paris, 1853), 744–781, 930–1003. Important guides are V. Grumel, *Les Regestes des actes du patriarcat de Constantinople*, vol. I: *Les Actes des patriarches*, fasc. II, *Regestes de 717 à 1043* (Istanbul, 1936); fasc. III, *Regestes de 1043 à 1206* (Paris, 1947); P. Jaffé and G. Wattenbach, *Regesta pontificum romanorum*, vol. I (Berlin, 1885). For Psellus on Cerularius, see C. N. Sathas, *Bibliotheca graeca medii aevi*, IV, 303–387; L. Bréhier, "Un Discours inédit de Psellos," *Revue des études grecques*, XVI (1903), 375–416; XVII (1904), 35–75.

Secondary literature includes: J. Hergenröther, *Photius von Constantinopel*, vol. III (Regensburg, 1869), 703–789; L. Bréhier, *Le Schisme oriental du XIe siècle* (Paris, 1899); J. Gay, *L'Italie méridionale et l'empire byzantin depuis l'avènement de Basile I jusqu'à la prise de Bari par les Normands* (Paris, 1904), pp. 469–501; A. Michel, *Humbert und Kerullarios*, vol. I (Paderborn, 1925), 1–44; vol. II (Paderborn, 1930), 1–40. But see the reviews of the first volume by V. Laurent, *Échos d'Orient*, XXXI (1932), 97–111, and M. Jugie, *Byzantion*, VIII (1933), 321–326. See also L. Bréhier, "The Greek Church: Its Relations with the West up to 1054," *Cambridge Medieval History*, IV, 246–274; M. Jugie, *Le Schisme byzantin: Aperçu historique et doctrinal* (Paris, 1941), pp. 187–246; George Every, *The Byzantine Patriarchate* (London, 1947); Adhémar d'Alès, "Psellos et Cérulaire," *Études publiées par la Compagnie de Jésus*, CLXVII (1921), 178–204; V. Laurent, "Le Titre de patriarche oecuménique et Michel Cérulaire," *Studi e testi*, CXXII (*Miscellanea Giovanni Mercati*, vol. III, Vatican City, 1946), 373–386.

certain, however; the break took place before 1024, for in that year the patriarch of Constantinople offered to resume relations with Rome, provided Rome recognized Constantinople as the head of the churches in the east. Rome apparently refused, but her refusal did not affect in any practical way the actual position of the Byzantine church in the east. The church of Constantinople was in fact the head of the orthodox churches in the east and what Rome thought made little difference.

This state of affairs might have continued indefinitely if the situation in southern Italy had not provoked a new crisis. For some time past the Normans had been conquering the country and threatened to occupy all the territories which Byzantium still held there. To check their advance the Byzantine emperor, Constantine IX Monomachus, resolved to enter into an alliance with the papacy and appointed a new governor for his Italian possessions with instructions to form such an alliance. The new governor was Argyrus, the son of that Melo who in 1017 had hired the Normans to help him in his rebellion against the Byzantines.

Argyrus was Italian by birth, of Lombard origin, and Latin in religion and tradition. He had not always been a loyal subject, but the ruthlessness of the Normans had led him definitely to embrace the Byzantine cause. He came to Constantinople and there exerted his influence in favor of the alliance with the papacy as the means of checking the Normans. Argyrus was the first native Italian to become Byzantine governor in Italy. But if he won the confidence of the emperor, there were important elements in the Byzantine capital, especially among the clergy, who were hostile to him and looked upon his appointment with suspicion. The patriarch himself had on several occasions exchanged bitter words with Argyrus when the latter was in Constantinople and had more than once refused him the communion of his church.[31] Argyrus arrived in Apulia in 1051 and soon entered into negotations with the papacy.

The pope with whom Argyrus sought alliance was Leo IX. Leo, who, as is well known, belonged to the party of reform, had no sooner been elected pope than he began a vigorous campaign in southern Italy for the elimination of simony and the enforcement of clerical celibacy. His activities, to be sure, were directed against the offenders among the Latin clergy under his jurisdiction, but the campaign for reform, especially the drive for the celibacy of the clergy, was bound eventually to affect the Greek clergy as

[31] Will, *Acta et scripta*, p. 177.

well. For with the Greek clergy in southern Italy continuing to marry, it would have been difficult, if not impossible, to impose celibacy on their Latin colleagues.[32] But this was a matter which affected seriously the interests of the Byzantine patriarchate since the Greek clergy in southern Italy were under its jurisdiction.

The man who then occupied the see of Constantinople was Michael Cerularius. Cerularius was a powerful personality and a clever and ambitious politician. He had come near, at one time, to occupying the imperial throne, and when he became patriarch (1043), his ambition was to render his church independent of the state. Already disturbed by the appointment of Argyrus, Cerularius saw in the alliance with the papacy and the activities of the pope in southern Italy a definite threat to the interests of the patriarchate, and this threat he determined to eliminate. His plan was to provoke a crisis calculated to render ineffective, at least in so far as it might involve his church, the alliance with the papacy. He began by closing the Latin churches in Constantinople (1052 or 1053), and then issued, through Leo, archbishop of Ochrida, a manifesto against certain usages of the Latin church, particularly the use of unleavened bread in the celebration of the Eucharist.[33] This manifesto was addressed to John, bishop of Trani, who, although Latin, was friendly to the Byzantines, and through him to all the bishops of the west, including the pope. Subsequent developments in Italy, the failure of the Byzantines and of Leo IX to stop the Normans, together with the captivity of Leo IX, made it more imperative for pope and emperor to coöperate, and Cerularius wrote the pope a more conciliatory letter in which he said nothing of the Latin usages which he had previously criticized, but in which he implied that he was the pope's equal.[34] The pope now set aside the sharp rejoinder which he had prepared against the manifesto of Leo of Ochrida and drew up a reply to the letter of Cerularius. But if in this reply he toned down the sharpness of his rejoinder to the manifesto of Leo of Ochrida, he made it clear that on the fundamental issue, the subordination of Constantinople to Rome, he was offering no compromise.[35]

The papal delegation which carried the letter of the pope to the Byzantine patriarch was headed by cardinal Humbert. No less

[32] Cf. Gay, *L'Italie méridionale*, pp. 479f.

[33] The Greek text of the letter is in Will, *Acta et scripta*, pp. 56–60; and the Latin translation, *ibid.* pp. 61–64.

[34] Will, *Acta et scripta*, p. 91.

[35] *Ibid.*, pp. 89–92; *MPL*, CXLIII, 773–777; Jaffé-Wattenbach, *Regesta*, vol. I, 548, no. 4332. Cf. Jugie, *Le Schisme byzantin*, p. 195.

suitable a man could have been found to head this delegation. Humbert was a man of limited learning, obstinate, arrogant, and tactless, and easily given to polemics. No sooner had he arrived in Constantinople than his behavior completely alienated the Byzantine patriarch. Humbert made matters worse by raising the question of the *filioque*, a question to which the Byzantine patriarch had not referred, and charged that the Byzantines had tampered with the Nicene creed by suppressing that phrase, when in truth it was the western church that had done the tampering by inserting the controversial phrase. In the meantime Leo IX died (April 13, 1054), and his successor, Victor II, a creature of the German emperor Henry III, did not take office until April 3, 1055. It is questionable whether Humbert still had the authority to keep up his activities in Constantinople.[36] But he continued to make charges against the Byzantine patriarch, and, as the latter refused to listen or enter into any negotiations, he resolved to hurl against him and his followers the sentence of excommunication. On Saturday, July 16, 1054, at the moment when the clergy of Hagia Sophia were about to celebrate the holy liturgy, the Roman delegation, with Humbert at the head, marched toward the principal altar and there deposited the sentence of excommunication while the Byzantine clergy and people looked on. The sentence of excommunication was couched in language which could hardly have been more arrogant and libelous.[37]

It was now the turn of the Byzantine patriarch to act. He had been shocked and angered by the contents of the sentence of excommunication and determined to obtain satisfaction. He straightway transmitted the document to the emperor and declared that he could not endure to have such audacity and effrontery go unpunished. Meanwhile the papal legates had left the capital to return to Rome. They had reached Selymbria (Silivri) when a message reached them from the emperor, urging them to return, and indicating that Cerularius was ready to have an interview with them. The legates returned, but no interview with the Byzantine patriarch ever took place. What actually happened is difficult to determine since only the accounts of Humbert and Cerularius have survived, and they are contra-

[36] But on this see A. Michel, "Die Rechtsgültigkeit des römischen Bannes gegen Michael Keroullarios," *Byz. Zeitschr.* XLII (1942), 193–205; E. Herman, "I legati inviati da Leone IX nel 1054 a Constantinopoli erano autorizzati a scommunicare il patriarca Michele Cerulario?" *Orientalia Christiana Periodica*, VIII (1942), 209–218.

[37] Latin text in Will, *Acta et scripta*, pp. 151–154; *MPL*, CXLIII, 1002–1004; Greek text in Will, *op. cit.*, pp. 161–165; *MPG*, CXX, 741–746; French translation, Jugie, *Le Schisme byzantin*, pp. 206–208.

dictory. This much seems certain, however. When Cerularius turned to the emperor, he did not intend to make amends to the papal legates; he demanded amends instead. But when the papal legates were asked to return, they were not informed of the true temper of the Byzantine patriarch. It was only after they had returned to the capital that they learned that what he wanted from them was a retraction and an apology for the sentence of excommunication. This they would not give, and, as the populace was in an uproar in support of its patriarch, they decided to leave. The emperor himself, who seems finally to have realized the seriousness of the situation, urged them to go.

The situation in the capital had indeed become very serious. The populace, angered by the sentence of excommunication against Cerularius, was in a riotous mood, and the refusal of the papal legates to make amends accentuated its temper. A tumult broke out, which forced the emperor to yield to the demands of the patriarch. Cerularius now proceeded to take formal action against Humbert and his associates. On July 20, 1054, in the presence of twenty-one bishops and an embassy from the emperor, he cast the anathema upon the impious document of excommunication, its authors, and all those who had participated in any way in its composition and circulation. He decreed further that all copies of the document were to be burned. The original, however, was to be kept in the archives of the patriarchate "to the everlasting dishonor and permanent condemnation of those who had cast such blasphemies against God." Four days later, on Sunday, July 24, the same bishops sitting in synod renewed the condemnation in an atmosphere of greater solemnity.[38] It was then read to the public.

Scholars have tended to attribute the schism of 1054 to the Byzantine patriarch. This is because Cerularius was responsible, by his sponsorship of the manifesto of Leo of Ochrida, for provoking the controversy. That the manifesto of Leo of Ochrida was provocative there can be no doubt, but Cerularius, as his letter to Leo IX shows, was not indisposed to compromise. Any compromise, however, had to take into account the actual position of the Byzantine patriarchate. Cerularius presided over the Byzantine church at a time when the see of Constantinople had achieved the widest territorial extent in its history, and its prestige and power had reached their highest point. The failure of the papal legates to realize this was what made all negotiations im-

[38] For the text of this synodal edict see Will, *Acta et scripta*, pp. 155–168.

possible. As Jugie writes, "the Roman legates were under illusions concerning the sentiments of the Byzantines on the whole toward the Latins. They had wished to separate the cause of the patriarch and his clergy from that of the emperor and the people, to treat Cerularius like a black sheep of St. Peter's flock, to act in Constantinople as they would have acted in a city of the west. And they did not notice that in Constantinople they cut the figures of arrogant strangers with insupportable airs. It was enough for their sentence to be known to provoke a popular tumult." The same scholar writes with reference to the sentence of excommunication against the Byzantine patriarch: "From every point of view this theatrical act was deplorable; deplorable, because it could be asked whether the legates were duly authorized to take a measure so serious at a time when the Holy See was vacant; deplorable, because useless and ineffectual, for Humbert and his companions had no means of having the sentence executed; deplorable especially by the contents of the sentence itself and the tone in which it was drawn up. Besides the well founded grievances, it reproached Cerularius and his partisans, and indirectly all the Byzantines, with a series of imaginary crimes and heresies."[39]

The Greek chroniclers of the period make no mention of the schism of 1054. This is somewhat puzzling, although there are other events in the history of Byzantium which contemporary historians do not record. Quite possibly this schism was not considered significant enough to be recorded. Unlike previous schisms, that of 1054 did not involve any division in the Greek church itself. The exchange of anathemas between Humbert and Cerularius no doubt left some bitterness in its wake, but it did not greatly affect the actual state of the relations between the two sees. The names of the popes, which for some years before 1054 had not been in the diptychs of the Constantinopolitan church, simply remained off, and the Byzantine church continued in its own independent way. There is some evidence that Leichudes, who succeeded Cerularius, communicated with the pope, Alexander II, in 1062, but it is not known what prompted him to do so. The point of the communication was to ask the pope to furnish irrefragable proof of the doctrine of the *filioque*.[40] Ten years later pope Alexander II made an effort to end the schism, but the Greeks showed no desire to enter into negotiations.[41]

[39] Jugie, *Le Schisme byzantin*, pp. 218, 205–206.
[40] *Byz. Zeitschr.*, XLIII (1950), 174.
[41] *De S. Petro Episcopo Anagniae in Italia*, in *Acta Sanctorum*, Aug. tom. I (1867), p. 236.

The deterioration in the external situation of the empire finally induced the Greeks to try to establish better relations with the papacy. In 1073 Michael VII addressed a letter to Gregory VII which was supplemented by an oral message imparted to the pope by those who brought the letter. Neither the letter nor a record of the oral message has survived, but a careful study of Gregory's reply and his various letters relating to the east indicate that the problem of the union of the churches and the need of the empire for military assistance in order to check the Turks constituted the subject matter of the imperial messages.[42] Gregory was very much impressed by the emperor's messages and sent his representative to Constantinople for further investigation, but nothing came out of the negotiations. A few years later the relations between Rome and Constantinople actually became worse as a result of Gregory's open support of Guiscard's invasion of the Byzantine empire. On July 25, 1080, Gregory wrote to the bishops of Apulia and Calabria asking them to lend all possible help to the expedition which Guiscard was about to undertake against Byzantium. Guiscard attacked the Greeks as schismatics. Thus, as Alexius Comnenus ascended the throne, the empire faced, in addition to its other enemies, the active enmity of the papacy. The reason for this was the refusal of the Greeks to agree to the union of the churches on conditions dictated to them by the papacy.

The civil wars which followed Manzikert ended in 1081 when Alexius Comnenus ascended the throne. The empire which the youthful Alexius now undertook to rule was on the brink of dissolution. Its treasury was empty; its armies were still disorganized; its enemies were many and active. In the Balkan peninsula, Guiscard, with the blessings of Gregory VII, was on the point of invading the territories of the empire; the Serbs were restless and hostile; and the Pechenegs and Kumans were ready to launch new attacks. In Asia Minor the effective control of the empire was restricted to localities on the coast of the Sea of Marmara, including Nicomedia, but even these were threatened by the new Turkish state which was arising in Nicaea. At the same time the Turkish adventurer Chaka (called Τζαχᾶς in Byzantine sources) established himself in Smyrna (İzmir), built a fleet, seized some of the islands of the Aegean, and threatened Constantinople itself.

[42] P. Charanis, "Byzantium, the West, and the Origin of the First Crusade," pp. 20ff. For a different view, W. Holtzmann, "Studien zur Orientpolitik des Reformspapsttums und zur Entstehung des ersten Kreuzzuges," *Historische Vierteljahrschrift*, XXII (1924–1925), 173, 190. See also below, chapter VII, p. 223.

That the empire was able to survive was due primarily to the remarkable ability and almost inexhaustible energy of Alexius.[43] He found the funds which he needed immediately by the confiscation of the valuables of the church; he improvised an army by enrolling numerous mercenaries; he neutralized, by overtures and concessions, some of his enemies in order that he might deal with them singly. Alexius was well versed in the technique of Byzantine diplomacy and used very expertly the principle of divide and rule.

When Guiscard invaded the empire in the spring of 1081, Alexius was engaged with the Selchükids of Nicaea, but he quickly came to terms with them. About the same time he entered into negotiations with Henry IV of Germany and tried to sow dissension among the Normans in southern Italy. He also concluded a treaty with the Venetians whereby he obtained their naval support in return for commercial privileges (1082). The essential element of these privileges consisted in the right to buy and sell in certain stipulated localities of the empire free from all duties. The granting of these privileges was destined to undermine the economic prosperity of the empire, but for the time at least it obtained for Alexius an important source of support in his struggle against the Norman leader. Alexius's first encounter with Guiscard near Dyrrachium ended in disaster; Dyrrachium soon fell to the enemy and the way was opened to Thessalonica and thence to Constantinople. But the negotiations of Alexius with Henry IV and his intrigues among the Normans in southern Italy now bore fruit. While Henry IV marched upon Rome to resolve his differences with Gregory VII, a revolt broke out in southern Italy against the authority of Guiscard. These events forced Guiscard to return to Italy, leaving his son, Bohemond, to carry on the war against the emperor. Bohemond met with initial successes, but Alexius kept after him with remarkable tenacity and succeeded in breaking the backbone of the invasion. In 1083 Bohemond returned to Italy. In the following year Guiscard organized another expedition; it won some successes at first, but, when Guiscard suddenly died in 1085, it was abandoned. The Norman danger, for the present at least, was over.

But not so the tribulations of Alexius. For it was now the turn of the nomads from the north, the Pechenegs and Kumans, to try their fortunes against the forces of the empire. This time they

[43] The fundamental work on Alexius is still that by Chalandon, *Essai sur le règne d'Alexis I Comnène, 1081–1118* (Paris, 1900).

had the coöperation of the Bogomiles,[44] adherents of a heretical sect, who dwelt in the region of Philippopolis and whose hostility to the Greeks was no secret. Urged by the Bogomiles, the Pechenegs and Kumans broke into Thrace in 1086, defeated one Byzantine general, but were stopped by another. They returned in 1087 only to be driven beyond the Balkans. But in the autumn of the following year they inflicted, near Dristra (Silistra) on the lower Danube, a terrible defeat on the Byzantine emperor, who had taken the offensive against them. Alexius barely escaped with his life. The situation was momentarily saved by the quarrel over the spoils which broke out between the Pechenegs and the Kumans. This momentary relief was further extended by a treaty of peace which Alexius concluded with the Pechenegs but the respite thus gained was only of short duration. The crisis came in the winter of 1090–1091, provoked this time by the adventurer Chaka, who conceived the grandiose plan of making himself emperor of Constantinople. He induced the Pechenegs to attack the empire by land while he himself besieged the capital by sea and abū-l-Qāsim, the sultan of Nicaea, attacked Nicomedia in Asia Minor. Chaka had forged a ring around the Byzantine capital.

The Pechenegs broke into Thrace, defeated the emperor, and fought their way to the environs of the capital. The diplomacy of Alexius saved the situation. Alexius entered into negotiations with the Kumans and induced them to take up arms against their former confederates. The decisive encounter took place on April 29, 1091. The Pechenegs were literally cut to pieces and, as a people, almost disappeared from history.

Chaka still remained active, but the diplomacy of Alexius eliminated him also. The peaceful relations which Alexius had established with the Selchükids of Nicaea at the time of the invasion of the empire by Guiscard were disturbed following the death of Sulaimān, the sulṭan of Nicaea, who had been killed in 1085 while trying to extend his rule over Syria. His successor at Nicaea was abū-l-Qāsim, the man who coöperated with Chaka by attacking Nicomedia. Abū-l-Qāsim, following the annihilation of the Pechenegs, planned to attack Constantinople itself, but he was beaten by the Byzantine forces and decided to accept a treaty of alliance which Alexius offered to him. Meanwhile his

[44] On the Bogomiles one may consult H. C. Puech and A. Vaillant, *Le Traité contre les Bogomiles de Cosmas le Prêtre* (Paris, 1945); S. Runciman, *The Medieval Manichee: A Study of the Christian Dualistic Heresy* (Cambridge, 1947); D. Obolensky, *The Bogomiles: A Study in Balkan Neo-Manichaeism* (Cambridge, 1948); also A. Soloviev, "Autour des Bogomiles," *Byzantion*, XXII (1952), 81–104.

relations with the great sultan Malik-Shāh, ruler, in theory at least, of all the Selchükids, were not cordial, and this led to his death in 1092. Shortly after this event Nicaea fell into the hands of Kilij (or Kilich) Arslan, the son of Sulaimān. Alexius, whose sea and land forces were making some progress against Chaka, pointed out to Kilij Arslan that the growth of the power of Chaka would endanger his own lands and induced him to accept the alliance which he offered him. Chaka went to see Kilij Arslan, but the latter murdered him after a banquet. Constantinople was now free from any immediate danger.

Meanwhile Alexius consolidated his position inside the empire.[45] He did this by the creation of a coterie of friends, with the members of his family as the nucleus, upon whom he could rely and to whom he could entrust the administration and defense of the empire. To keep their loyalty he compensated these men by land grants and other favors. "To his relatives and favorites," writes Zonaras, "Alexius distributed the public goods by wagon loads; he granted to them sumptuous annual revenues. The great wealth with which they were surrounded and the retinue which was assigned to them were more becoming to kings than to private individuals. The homes which they acquired appeared like cities in size and were no less magnificent than the imperial palace itself." More detailed and precise information about this is given in documents which Alexius himself issued. These documents deal with the land grants that Alexius made to his partisans. For instance, in 1084 Alexius granted the entire peninsula of Cassandria to his brother Adrian. But in this Alexius made no radical innovations. He exploited more extensively institutions which were already in existence. This was particularly true of the *pronoia* and the *charistikion*.

Alexius also established better relations with the papacy. The initial step in this was taken by Urban II, but the matter was really pushed by Alexius.[46] In 1089 Alexius received a letter from Urban II in which the pope urged the establishment of peace and harmony in the church, complained that the papal name had been

[45] On this see Charanis, "The Monastic Properties and the State in the Byzantine Empire," *Dumbarton Oaks Papers*, IV (1948), 69 ff.

[46] For this and what follows, see W. Holtzmann, "Die Unionsverhandlungen zwischen Kaiser Alexios I und Papst Urban II," *Byz. Zeitschr.*, XXVIII (1928), 38–67; P. Charanis, in *AHR*, LIII (1948), 941–944. See also August C. Krey, "Urban's Crusade, Success or Failure?" *AHR*, LIII (1948), 235–250; B. Leib, *Rome, Kiev, et Byzance à la fin du XIe siècle* (Paris, 1924), pp. 25–26, and "Les Patriarches de Byzance et la politique religieuse d'Alexis Ier Comnène [1081–1118]," in *Mélanges Jules Lebreton*, II (= *Recherches de science religieuse*, XL [1952]), 201 ff.

removed from the diptychs of the Constantinopolitan church, without canonical justification, and made the request that it be restored. In order that the papal request might be considered, a synod was held in Constantinople in September 1089. It was attended by the patriarch of Constantinople, the patriarch of Antioch, eighteen metropolitans, and two archbishops, and was presided over by Alexius.

When the synod met, Alexius submitted to it the papal proposal, asked for the documents attesting the separation of Rome from Constantinople, and inquired whether it was because of these documents that the name of the pope was not in the diptychs of the church of Constantinople. The ecclesiastics present replied that no such documents existed, but that there were between the two churches important differences of a canonical nature which it was necessary to regulate. Alexius then expressed the view that, since there was no official record of the separation of Rome from Constantinople, the papal name had been uncanonically removed from the diptychs and it should be put back. To this the ecclesiastics replied that too much time had elapsed since the removal of the papal name from the diptychs to put it back before the elimination of the objections which they had against the Latins. The synod, with Alexius agreeing, finally reached the following compromise.

Urban II should first of all send to Constantinople his profession of faith. If the pope's profession of faith were found to be sound, if he accepted the seven ecumenical councils and the local synods which the latter had approved, if he condemned the heretics and the errors which the church condemned, and if he respected and accepted the holy canons which the fathers of the church had adopted at the sixth ecumenical council, then his name would be put back in the diptychs of the church of Constantinople. This arrangement was to be temporary, pending the holding of a council in Constantinople which was to regulate and eliminate the differences between the two churches. This council was to be held within eighteen months after the receipt of the papal profession of faith and was to be attended either by a papal delegate or by the pope himself. The synod urged the patriarchs of Alexandria and Jerusalem to accept this compromise.

At the same time a message from the patriarch of Constantinople, Nicholas III, was sent to Urban II. In this message the patriarch expressed his joy over the receipt of the papal letter, apparently the letter which Urban had sent to Alexius requesting that his name be reëntered in the diptychs. He was pained to hear, however, that he had been represented to the pope as ill-disposed towards the Latins and as excluding them from the churches. The Latins, he declared, were free to enter the churches and to celebrate their religious services, and he was aware that the same freedom was enjoyed by the Greeks of southern Italy. But the pope would have acted well if he had sent him, as was the custom of old, the announcement of his elevation to the papal see together with his profession of faith. He could still do it, however. The patriarch himself desired, with all his heart, the unity of the church. But if the patriarch desired the unity of the church, on the fundamental questions which separated Rome from Constantinople he was far from willing to yield. This is quite clear from a letter which he addressed to the patriarch of Jerusalem. The letter in question is without title, signature, date, or address, but Grumel has produced sufficient evidence in support of his view that it was written in 1089 by the patriarch of Constantinople, Nicholas III, to Symeon II, patriarch of Jerusalem. In this letter the patriarch of Constantinople defended the position of the Greek church on the question of the *filioque*, the azyme, and the primacy of the papacy. He wrote to the patriarch of Jerusalem in order to counteract the effects of a letter which the pope had sent to the patriarch of Jerusalem in which he expressed his desire for the unity of the churches, urging that there should be one head for the church, and that the pope of Rome, as the successor of St. Peter, should be that head.[47]

It is not definitely known what the reaction of Urban II was to the compromise offered to him by Alexius and the Byzantine clergy. There is some evidence that he accepted it and that as a consequence the communion between the two churches was provisionally reëstablished. But the step which was to make this communion permanent was never taken. The realization of the union on a permanent basis was indeed a most difficult task. For the crucial point, the fundamental difference between the two churches, was the primacy of Rome, and on that the Byzantine clergy, as is shown by the attitude of the patriarch of Constantinople, were in no mood to compromise. Yet Alexius did succeed in removing some of the differences which separated him from the papacy and in establishing good personal relations with the pope.

Thus by 1095 Alexius had removed the dangers which had threatened Constantinople, had consolidated his own position in

[47] Grumel, *Échos d' Orient*, XXXVIII (1939), 104–117.

the empire, and had established better personal relations with the papacy. He was now ready to undertake the offensive which he hoped would enable him to recover Asia Minor from the Turks. This task was difficult indeed, but he hoped to accomplish it with the aid of the west. It was for this reason that in 1095 he appealed to Urban II for help. And to succeed in obtaining this help he used the argument that it was necessary to liberate the Holy Land from the Turks.[48] The result was the First Crusade.

[48] On this see Charanis, "Byzantium, the West, and the Origin of the First Crusade," *Byzantion*, XIX (1949), 24–36.

VII
THE COUNCILS OF PIACENZA AND CLERMONT

The crusade was first proclaimed by Urban II at the Council of Clermont on November 27, 1095. So we must believe, unless evidence of earlier publicity is found. Some have thought that the pope preached the crusade earlier in the same year at the council which he held at Piacenza, but if this was the case, what he said failed to produce any widespread popular response. To be sure, contemporary writers were not immediately impressed by the historical significance of his November speech, and, as Chalandon

The crusade inspired considerable contemporary historical literature, but is not mentioned in any existing document written before the Council of Clermont, and seldom in sources that appeared before the undertaking had come to a successful end. For letters which give information about the beginning of the movement, consult P. Riant, *Inventaire critique des lettres historiques des croisades* (*AOL*, I, 1881), pp. 1–224. The letters of Gregory VII are found in *MGH*, *Epistolae selectae* (ed. E. Caspar), II, and any others that contain references to immediate antecedents are in H. Hagenmeyer, *Epistulae et chartae ad historiam primi belli sacri spectantes*: *Die Kreuzzugsbriefe aus den Jahren 1088–1100* (Innsbruck, 1901). For the Council of Piacenza the chief source is Bernold of St. Blaise, *Chronicon* (*MGH*, *SS.*, V): Bernold died in 1100. See D. C. Munro, "Did the Emperor Alexius I Ask for Aid at the Council of Piacenza?" *AHR*, XXVII (1922), 731–733.

The earliest account of the Council of Clermont and its antecedents is that of Fulcher of Chartres, *Gesta Francorum Iherusalem peregrinantium* (ed. H. Hagenmeyer, Heidelberg, 1913). Fulcher was an intelligent, observant man who had read the classics at Chartres. He went on the crusade and spent the rest of his life in the east, and although he wrote the first part of his history about 1101, he may have revised it later. See on this D. C. Munro, "A Crusader," *Speculum*, VII (1932), 321–335.

Another contemporary historian who had first-hand knowledge of the east, having accompanied the crusaders in 1101, was the German, Ekkehard, author of a universal chronicle. About 1115, he wrote his *Hierosolymita*, an account of the crusade, which was intended to be a part of his *Chronicle* (ed. H. Hagenmeyer, Tübingen, 1877), and which contains some observations about conditions just before the crusade.

Three other historians of the crusade, who did not accompany the expedition, but were at the Council of Clermont, wrote their accounts in the early twelfth century: Guibert of Nogent (*Historia quae dicitur Gesta Dei per Francos*, in *RHC*, *Occ.*, IV) was a well-educated and critical person for his time — "the theologian" of the crusade, Villey calls him. Most of Guibert's history is based on the anonymous *Gesta* (see the following chapter), but the reflections and observations in the first part of his work are very interesting and useful. Another historian who, like Guibert, undertook to put the material in the *Gesta* in what was then regarded as good literary form, was Baldric of Dol (*Historia Jerosolimitana*, *RHC*, *Occ.*, IV), who wrote about 1107–1110. Robert the Monk (*Historia Hierosolymitana*, *RHC*, *Occ.*, III) also used the *Gesta* as the source of his history, but added other information, including an account of the council at Clermont. His work was very popular, and was not written before 1122, according to C. Cahen (*La Syrie du nord à l'époque des croisades*, Paris, 1940, p. 10, note 1). Another contemporary, William of Malmesbury (*Gesta regum*, ed. W. Stubbs, Rolls has indicated, neither Raymond of Aguilers nor the anonymous author of the *Gesta Francorum* mentions Clermont. But, although these early chroniclers were eager to get on with the story of the expedition in which they participated, others, who attended the council, were careful not to neglect it. Thus Robert the Monk, when he undertook to rewrite the *Gesta* soon after the turn of the century, complained that his source did not have its proper beginning at Clermont. The glorious success of the crusade brought fame to the council where it originated.

At first Urban was regarded as the author of the movement that began at Clermont. Bernold, writing while the crusade was in progress, said "the lord pope was the chief author of this expedition." Writing from Antioch in 1098, the leaders asked the pope to come over and finish the war "which is your very own".[1] But Urban had said that it was "God's work", that "Christ was the leader" — and so plausible did such propaganda seem that the success of the movement was regarded as divinely assured. If

Series, 2 vols. London, 1887–1889), wrote about the council some thirty years after. As he was not there, he depends chiefly on Fulcher, but adds information gained from others who attended.

The beginnings of the crusade have interested recent historians. C. Erdmann, *Die Entstehung des Kreuzzugsgedanken* (Stuttgart, 1935), traces the ideas which contributed to crusading from patristic times, and is a rich source of information for all antecedents. He has been criticized for not distinguishing between holy war and crusade. M. Villey, *La Croisade: Essai sur la formation d'une théorie juridique* (Paris, 1942), indicates that Urban was the originator of the crusade as an institution. P. Rousset, *Les Origines et les caractères de la première croisade* (Neuchatel, 1945), reveals ideas and attitudes in contemporary literature. B. Leib, *Rome, Kiev, et Byzance à la fin du XIme siècle* (Paris, 1924), emphasizes church union. Two articles by W. Holtzmann, "Studien zur Orientpolitik des Reformspapsttums und zur Entstehung des ersten Kreuzzuges," *Historische Vierteljahrschrift*, XXII (1924), 167–199, and "Die Unionsverhandlungen zwischen Kaiser Alexios I und Papst Urban II im Jahre 1089," *Byzantinische Zeitschrift*, XXVIII (1928), 39–67, give other views of the significance of church union. F. Chalandon, *Histoire de la première croisade* (Paris, 1925), suggests that the importance of the Council of Clermont has been overemphasized. M. W. Baldwin, "Some Recent Interpretations of Pope Urban's Eastern Policy," *The Catholic Historical Review*, XXV (1940), 459–466, and A. C. Krey, "Urban's Crusade, Success or Failure?" *AHR*, LIII (1948), 235–250, hold union of the churches to have been Urban's guiding motive. D. C. Munro, "The Speech of Pope Urban II at Clermont," *AHR*, XI (1906), 231–242, analyzes the versions of the pope's speech as reported by chroniclers who were present. R. Crozet, "Le Voyage d'Urbain II et ses négotiations avec le clergé de France," *RH*, CLXXIX (1937), 271–310, and "Le Voyage d'Urbain II en France," *Annales du Midi*, XLIX (1937), 42–69, has traced the pope's itinerary, and A. Fliche, "Urbain II et la croisade," *Revue de l'histoire de l'église de France*, XIII (1927), 289–306, suggests the possible effect of the journey in France on Urban's decision to preach the crusade.

Among other recent discussions of origins may be noted: E. Joranson, "The Spurious Letter of Emperor Alexius to the Count of Flanders," *AHR*, LV (1950), 3–43; S. Runciman, *A History of the Crusades*, vol. I, *The First Crusade* (Cambridge, 1951); F. Duncalf, "The Pope's Plan for the First Crusade," *The Crusades and Other Historical Essays Presented to D. C. Munro* (New York, 1928), pp. 44–56; U. Schwerin, *Die Aufrufe der Päpste zur Befreiung des Heiligen Landes von den Anfängen bis zum Ausgang Innocenz VI* (Ebering, Historische Studien, 301, Berlin, 1937).

[1] Bernold, *Chronicon* (*MGH, SS.*, V), p. 464; H. Hagenmeyer, *Epistulae*, p. 164: "... bellum, quod tuum proprium est."

it was "not human but divine", as Ekkehard said, whoever started it was merely an agent of the Lord. A legend, which was given a long life by the popular historian of the crusades, William of Tyre, indicated that Peter the Hermit was the divine agent who was sent to persuade the pope to initiate the crusade, and it was believed that he carried a letter from heaven as his credential. Not until the last of the nineteenth century did history finally discredit this legend and restore credit to the great pope who was the author of the plan which he proposed at Clermont.[2]

But how much of the proposal was originated by Urban II? Although it seems to have taken contemporaries by surprise, the crusade was so quickly accepted that it is clear the public was ready for it. Quite simply the author of the *Gesta* says that the crusade came when "the time was at hand" for all to take up crosses and follow Christ. The modern way of putting it is that the crusade was preceded by a long trend of thought which conditioned minds to the idea of holy war.[3] Urban had only to propose carrying the holy war to the eastern Mediterranean to show that such a proposal had an immediate appeal to the popular imagination. Nevertheless, it must be recognized that the scheme which the pope devised to put this proposal into effect was original, not so much in the elements of which it was composed as in the synthesis of parts which were known and understood. The "time" for such attention to the practical problems of organization did not come until a human mind capable of such planning was ready to apply itself to the problem of how to raise large armies to serve the church. Unfortunately, the antecedents of this papal plan are not evident. There is no mention of the crusade in any source written before Clermont that is now in existence.

The idea of carrying the holy war against the Moslems to the eastern end of the Mediterranean (but not any way of implementing the idea) seems to have come to Urban from his famous predecessor, Gregory VII, who had proposed an expeditionary force to aid the Byzantine Christians in their struggle with the Selchükid Turks. Inasmuch as Urban undertook to carry out Gregory's ideas, to be his *pedisequus*, as he put it, it may be assumed that he felt it to be his duty to put Gregory's proposal into effect. He did so with the same remarkable success that he had in advancing the Gregorian reform program; waging a winning

[2] H. Hagenmeyer, *Peter der Eremite* (Leipzig, 1879).
[3] C. Erdmann, *Die Entstehung des Kreuzzugsgedankens* (Stuttgart, 1935).

struggle with Henry IV; and, in general, restoring to the papacy the prestige which Gregory had lost.

Just two years before Gregory became pope in 1073, the disastrous defeat of the Byzantine army at Manzikert had opened up all Anatolia to the raids of nomad Turks. In the meantime, Byzantine rule in southern Italy had been overthrown by the Normans, and the imperial forces were unable to deal with the Pechenegs in the Balkans. In this desperate situation, the young basileus, Michael VII, disregarded the controversial separation of Greek and Latin churches which followed the so-called schism of 1054 and made an appeal to the newly chosen pope for aid. When an imperial embassy with a friendly letter to Gregory had been well received, Dominic, patriarch of Grado (who, as a Venetian, may have had contacts at Constantinople), was chosen to carry a favorable reply back to Michael. Gregory, of course, hoped to bring about a reunion of the churches under the recognized dominance of Rome.[4]

Although it is not known that anything was said about military aid from the west in this diplomatic exchange of good will, Gregory soon after proposed that some of the *fideles* of St. Peter should go to the help of the Greeks. On February 2, 1074, the pope wrote to William, count of Burgundy, asking him to fulfil the vow that he had taken to defend the possessions of St. Peter, and to notify Raymond, count of St. Gilles, Amadeo, count of Savoy, and other *fideles* of St. Peter to join the countess Beatrice and her husband, Godfrey of Lorraine, in an expedition to pacify the Normans in southern Italy by a show of force, and then cross over to Constantinople, where the Christians "are urging us eagerly to reach out our hands to them in succor."[5] On March 1, the pope called for recruits because he had learned that the pagans "have been pressing hard upon the Christian empire, have cruelly laid waste the country almost to the walls of Constantinople and slaughtered like sheep many thousand Christians." But by September 10, Gregory seemed to think that the urgency had passed, for he wrote William VII, duke of Aquitaine and count of Poitou, "the report is that the Christians beyond seas have, by God's help, driven back the fierce assault of the pagans, and we are waiting for the counsel of divine providence as to our future course."

[4] Riant, *Inventaire* (*AOL*, I), pp. 59–60.

[5] For the six letters that Gregory wrote concerning this plan, see his *Registrum* (*MGH*, *Epistolae selectae*, II), pp. 69–71, 75–76; 126–128, 165–168, 173. Quotations are from Emerton's translations in *The Correspondence of Pope Gregory VII* (Columbia University, Records of Civilization, New York, 1932).

Three months later, the pope was no longer in doubt when he wrote to young Henry IV, king of Germany: "I call to your attention that the Christians beyond the sea, a great part of whom are being destroyed by the heathen with unheard-of slaughter and are daily being slain like so many sheep, have humbly sent to beg me to succor these our brethren in whatever ways I can, that the religion of Christ may not utterly perish in our time — which God forbid."

With exaggerated optimism, Gregory told the young king that 50,000 men were prepared to go "if they can have me for their leader," and suggested that they might "push forward even to the sepulcher of the Lord." Naively, he even asked Henry to protect the Roman church during his absence. December 16, the pope followed with a general call to *fideles* beyond the Alps, and at the same time wrote to the countess Matilda that he hoped she would accompany the empress Agnes, who was expected to go. But January 22, 1075, when he wrote to his former abbot, Hugh of Cluny, he made no mention of any expedition to aid Greek Christians, although he complained that they were "falling away from the Catholic faith".

When Gregory became involved in the desperate conflict with the western emperor, he had to give up his hopes of winning friends at Constantinople, and instead of helping the Greeks to repel Turkish invaders, the pope gave his blessing to an invasion of the empire by Normans. Although he had tried to check Norman aggression in southern Italy during the early years of his pontificate, as the letter to the count of Burgundy indicates, he had to reverse his policy when hard pressed by Henry IV. In 1080, by concessions, he induced Robert Guiscard to become his ally, and when the Normans prepared to invade the Balkan peninsula, Gregory gave his support to this buccaneering enterprise. He had excommunicated Nicephorus III Botaniates, who had deposed Michael in 1078, and Guiscard asserted that he intended to restore Michael, whose son had been betrothed to the Norman's daughter, to the throne. Although it was known that the real Michael was living in a monastery, Guiscard exhibited a Greek monk who pretended to be the deposed emperor. Gregory seems to have accepted this fraud, and on July 24, 1080, he wrote to the bishops in Apulia and Calabria that all *fideles* of St. Peter should aid Michael, "unjustly overthrown," and that all fighting men who went overseas with the emperor and Robert should be faithful to them, which obviously referred to the pretender.[6] When Guiscard's undertaking

[6] *Registrum* (*MGH, Epp. selectae*), II, 523–524.

seemed successful, the pope congratulated him, while trying to impress him with the danger that threatened the Roman church, for Henry IV, subsidized by Byzantine gold, was closing in on the city of St. Peter. Alexius Comnenus, who became emperor in 1081 by deposing Nicephorus III, at first had asked the pope to restrain the Normans, but when it became clear that Gregory was a "Norman pope", he gave his support to Henry IV. Thus, at Constantinople, the pope, who had once wished to send military aid to the empire, came to be regarded as a hated enemy.[7]

Thus, all Gregory's hopes of ending the schism between east and west were destroyed when political necessity drove him into the Norman alliance. However, in 1085 the death of both Guiscard and his papal ally relieved the tension, and better understanding between east and west seemed possible. But, although the abbot of Monte Cassino, who became Victor III, had been in friendly correspondence with Alexius, he was too dependent on Norman support to do much to restore papal prestige. Not until the Frenchman, Odo of Lagery, became pope on March 12, 1088, did the church have a leader capable of saving the papacy from the crisis into which Gregory VII had precipitated it.

Odo, who took the name of Urban II, had been a pupil of Bruno, the founder of Chartreuse, at Rheims, where he became canon and archdeacon. Later he became a monk and prior of Cluny, and it was on abbot Hugh's recommendation that he entered the service of Gregory VII, who made him cardinal-bishop of Ostia, and sent him on the difficult mission of being papal legate in Germany, where he was when Gregory died. Odo supported Victor III, whom other reformers opposed because he was not a strong supporter of Gregory's reform program, and it is said that Victor nominated Odo as his successor. Certainly no one was better qualified to restore the prestige of the papacy, which had sunk so low that Bernold relates that only five German bishops recognized the new pope. Although the countess Matilda of Tuscany loyally supported the rightful pope, much of northern and central Italy was dominated by the partisans of Clement III, the anti-pope, while the Romans, who had seen their city looted by the followers of Gregory's Norman ally, favored the schismatics. "Guibert [Clement III], however, urged on by the support of the aforesaid emperor and by the instigation of the Roman citizens, for some time kept Urban a stranger to the church of

[7] See the violent condemnation of Gregory by Anna Comnena. *Alexiad*, I, xiii, 2–7 (ed. Leib, I, pp. 47–49).

St. Peter." But, according to Bernold, Urban would not use force to obtain possession of the city and, except for a few months when Clement had to leave, his visits to Rome were clandestine and brief. During most of the first five years that he was pope, he found it necessary to wander about in Apulia and Calabria, where he was assured of Norman protection. It is not surprising, therefore, that a few days after being consecrated, he set out to find count Roger, Guiscard's brother, most influential of the Norman chiefs, who was then completing the conquest of Sicily. There the pope held a conference with him at Troina.

One topic that the pope brought up for consideration was the advisability of reopening diplomatic relations with Constantinople. Geoffrey Malaterra, historian of the Italian Normans, says that the pope asked the count's advice about accepting an invitation to a church council at Constantinople for consideration of the differences between the two churches. Roger urged acceptance, but, as Malaterra tells the story, Urban was prevented from participating in such a meeting by the hostility of the antipope and his partisans at Rome.[8] It seems clear, however, from evidence given by Walter Holtzmann that what Urban wanted to know was whether the count had any intention of renewing the war on Alexius, which had undone the efforts of Gregory VII to maintain close relations with the eastern church. When the pope was able to assure the basileus that there would be no further Norman aggression, he, not the basileus as Malaterra thought, made a move to open negotiations. He asked that his name be put on the diptychs at Constantinople inasmuch as it was not excluded by any synodal acts. Alexius, finding that this was true, induced a synod to grant the request, but on condition that Urban send his profession of faith in the customary systatic letter, and participate in person, or through representatives, in a council to be held at Constantinople eighteen months later for the purpose of settling the controversial issues that divided the churches. The patriarch also assured the pope, who had complained that Latins were not allowed to worship in their own fashion in the empire, that they had the same freedom as Greeks in the territories under Norman rule. Urban also made another friendly move at this time, September 1089, by removing from Alexius the excommunication which Gregory had imposed on Nicephorus III.[9]

[8] Malaterra, *Chronicon*, iv, 13 (*MPL* CXLIX, 1191, 1192).

[9] W. Holtzmann, "Unionverhandlungen zwischen Kaiser Alexios I und Papst Urban II im Jahre 1089," *Byz. Zeitschr.*, XXVI (1920), 38–67. See P. Charanis, *AHR*, LIII (1948), 941–944, for an analysis of the documents published by Holtzmann, and above, chapter VI, pp. 216ff.

There is no evidence to show that Urban ever sent a profession of faith, and he did not accept the invitation to discuss the union of the churches. No doubt he knew that the Greeks would not accept the supremacy of Rome, which the reform movement in the west was striving to establish. On other points of difference, the Greeks may have been more conciliatory, but here also the Gregorian program offered little hope of compromise. Urban, usually the tactful diplomat, seems to have been much the partisan at Bari in 1098. When the discussion held there with Greek churchmen of southern Italy did not go to his liking, he called upon Anselm of Canterbury to defend the Latin cause, and when this champion seemed to overwhelm the Greeks by his dialectic, Urban exulted. Such is the report of Eadmer, the biographer of Anselm.[10]

There is reason to assume that Urban did not wish to enter into negotiations about ecclesiastical matters in 1089, because controversy might have marred the friendly relations that he had established with the Byzantine emperor. He could be well satisfied with the significant diplomatic victory that he had won, for he had brought about a reversal of Greek policy in the west. As long as the Normans were a serious menace to the empire, it had been imperial policy to cause trouble for them in Italy by subsidizing Henry IV. Furthermore, as long as this alliance lasted, the anti-pope, Clement III, had hoped to obtain recognition at Constantinople. Urban had changed all this by being able to assure Alexius that the Normans were no longer to be feared. By obtaining the favor of the eastern emperor, the pope had gained an important advantage over his enemies in Italy.

It has been asserted that Alexius was glad to have cordial relations with the pope because he hoped to get military help from the west. Later, of course, the pope did recruit large armies, but what military aid did the emperor hope to obtain from a pope who was virtually an exile in Norman Italy? It was not until later, when papal prestige had risen, that there was much possibility of obtaining such help. "The fact that Alexius had frequently asked for aid before the Council of Piacenza is universally admitted."[11] But mercenaries, not armies going forth to holy war, was the kind of military aid the basileus wanted. Anna Comnena says that her father did all that he could to collect a mercenary army by letters,

[10] Eadmer, *Historia novorum in Anglia* (ed. M. Rule, Rolls Series, no. 81 [1884]), pp. 104 to 106.

[11] D. C. Munro, *AHR*, XXVII (1922), 733, note 11.

and even indicates that he awaited a mercenary army from Rome about 1091.[12] It is more plausible to assume that Anna's statement refers to the military contingent promised to Alexius by the count of Flanders.

Robert the Frisian, count of Flanders, went on a pilgrimage to Jerusalem about 1087 to 1090 or 1091. On his return trip he was received with great honor by Alexius, who apparently asked him to send mercenaries. Robert, binding himself by the sort of oath that Anna thought was customary among the Latins, pledged himself to send five hundred mounted warriors when he returned to Flanders. The count kept his word, and the contingent reached Alexius with a gift of one hundred and fifty excellent horses, and the emperor was able to purchase all other horses which were not needed by these western horsemen.[13] It may be that the emperor wrote to the count of Flanders at this time, and that his letter became the basis for the famous *epistula spuria*, which was used later for propaganda.[14] Ekkehard, without saying when, tells us that the emperor wrote "not a few" letters to the pope asking aid for the defense of the eastern churches.[15] Returning pilgrims, who may have been indoctrinated by Byzantine propaganda as well as disturbed by their own experiences, added their testimony to the requests made at higher levels. The pope, we may feel sure, was well informed about the situation in the east. Nevertheless, there is no evidence to show that he made any effort to send help to the emperor before the Council of Piacenza in 1095.

In the meantime, as contemporary sources do make clear, Urban was very busy trying to combat the "schismatics", and to build up papal prestige in the west. At one stage, his position seemed so desperate that his staunchest supporter, the countess Matilda, actually tried to negotiate a compromise peace with the triumphant German emperor, and, although more than forty years old, she married seventeen-year-old Welf (V) of Bavaria in order to win him over to the papal cause. Urban endeavored to secure the support of prominent prelates by relaxing the severity of the reform program in special instances, and in 1093 his diplomacy was successful in inducing Conrad, Henry's heir, to rebel against

[12] *Alexiad*, VIII, v, 1 (ed. Leib, II, 139). Urban, who did not have any authority in Rome, could not have sent troops from the city at this time.

[13] *Alexiad*, VII, vi, 1; VII, 4; VIII, iii, 4 (ed. Leib, II, 105, 109, 135).

[14] For the best and most recent discussion of this letter, see E. Joranson, "The Spurious Letter of Emperor Alexius to the Count of Flanders," *AHR*, LV (1950), 811–832. The conclusion is that the letter in the form in which it has come down to us was used in 1105 by Bohemond in his campaign to recruit an army with which to attack the emperor.

[15] Ekkehard, *Hierosolymita*, V, 2, 3 (ed. Hagenmeyer, pp. 81–82).

his father. By this time, as the emperor was losing support in Italy, Urban was able to enter Rome, where early in 1094 he secured possession of the Lateran, which the abbot of Vendôme obtained by bribing a partisan of the anti-pope to surrender it. Later in 1094, Urban moved north, visiting Pisa, Pistoia, and Florence. "Now that he had prevailed nearly everywhere," says Bernold, he issued a call for a council to meet at Piacenza early the next year, "among the schismatics themselves and against them, to which he summoned bishops from Italy, Burgundy, France, Allemania, Bavaria, and other countries."[16] The council was in session the first week in March 1095, and its agenda consisted of ecclesiastical matters, chiefly of measures for the furtherance of the Gregorian reform program, and condemnation of the "schismatics". The presence at Piacenza of important lay personages shows how greatly the prestige of the pope had increased. Praxeda, the discarded wife of Henry IV, was there to make scandalous accusations against her royal husband. King Philip of France sent representatives to argue against his excommunication for adultery which had been imposed at the Council of Autun the preceding year, while king Peter of Aragon became the vassal of the papacy and agreed to pay an annual tribute. Lastly, and most impressive of all, no doubt, was the embassy from Constantinople with a request from the emperor that the pope urge western fighting men to aid in the defense of the eastern church, which the pagans had almost destroyed in the regions which they had occupied, extending almost to the walls of Constantinople. When he preached outside the city in the open fields to a crowd too large for any church, the pope incited many to give such help, and urged those who intended to go to take oath that they would give faithful aid to the emperor to the best of their ability.[17] It has often been suggested that this means that the pope preached the crusade at Piacenza, but all that Bernold says is that Urban urged warriors to go to aid Alexius, which was what Gregory had proposed earlier. It is possible, of course, that the pope had in mind much of what he proposed a few months later at Clermont, for it

[16] Bernold, *Chronicon* (*MGH*, *SS.*, V), p. 461.

[17] Formerly Bernold (*MGH*, *SS.*, V), p. 462, was the only source for this Byzantine appeal and the papal response to it. Confirmation by another contemporary source was found by D. C. Munro (*AHR*, XXVII [1922], 731–733). Bernold's reference to the oath is interesting in view of the vow to complete the pilgrimage to the Holy Sepulcher that crusaders were required to take (see below, p. 247) and the insistence of Alexius that the leaders of the crusade bind themselves to him by oath (see below, p. 284). Bernold says, "Ad hoc ergo auxilium domnus papa multos incitavit, ut etiam jurejurando promitterent, se illuc Deo annuente ituros et eidem imperatori contra paganos pro posse suo fidelissimum adjutorium collaturos. . . ."

does not seem probable that he thought out all the ideas in his plan for the crusade in the short time between Piacenza and Clermont, but what Bernold reports has little or no resemblance to the later proposal.[18]

Urban stayed at Piacenza for a month before moving on to Cremona, where Conrad, son of Henry IV, became a vassal of the papacy. After visiting other Lombard cities, Vercelli, Milan, Como, he arrived at Asti about June 27. A month later the papal party was at Valence, and, although the usually reliable Bernold says that the trip was made by sea, it seems more likely that Fulcher of Chartres, who went from France to Italy with the crusaders the next year, was right in reporting that the pope crossed the mountains.[19] Urban was glad to revisit Cluny, where he had been a monk. When he dedicated the altar of the abbatial church in the famous monastery, he announced that his main reason for coming to France was to do honor to Cluny,[20] and the charters and confirmations to Cluniac houses that mark his trail throughout southern France indicate that his desire to favor Cluny was not mere rhetoric.

There was, in fact, much ecclesiastical business to justify the journey to France, where the condition of the church and papal influence had greatly deteriorated during the preceding centuries of disorder, and the Gregorian reform program and the struggle over investiture had added to ecclesiastical confusion. Consequently, there were many jurisdictional disputes that papal legates had not been able to settle but which might be adjusted by the personal diplomacy of Urban himself. Furthermore, the pope, as he became more influential, became more and more firm in urging the clergy to conform to the ecclesiastical reform. Urban desired to have the churchmen of France discuss and legislate in councils such as the one held at Piacenza. The business transacted is indicated by the acts of the papal chancery and local charters by which the itinerary has been traced. There is no reason to

[18] See A. Fliche, "Urbain II et la croisade," *Revue de l'histoire de l'église de France*, XIII (1927), 289–293. B. Leib (*Rome, Kiev, et Byzance*, pp. 180ff.) holds that the union of churches must have come up for discussion. Bernold's only mention of the church is that the emperor asked help for its defense (*ut aliquod auxilium sibi contra paganos pro defensione sanctae ecclesiae conferrent*), which cannot be used to imply anything more than it says. Inasmuch as Alexius had formerly proposed a council to consider the obstacles to union, and had found the pope not interested, it seems improbable that he would raise the question again. There is no evidence to indicate that Urban had become any more willing than before to become involved in arguments with the Greeks.

[19] Fliche, who decided that Urban visited St. Gilles twice before going to Clermont, accepts Bernold's statement. Crozet, who has made a careful study of Urban's itinerary in France, thinks that Fulcher, who is supported by Albert of Aix, is correct.

[20] *MGH, SS.*, XIV, 100; Bouquet, *RHGF*, XIV, 101.

doubt Urban's statement that he came to Gaul on ecclesiastical business.[21]

But Urban also said that he came to France with the intention of appealing for aid to the eastern Christians. The pope gave this explanation for his journey in his letter to the Flemings, which was written soon after the Council of Clermont.[22] Fulcher, writing after the crusade, having recalled all the troubles of both clergy and laity that the pope wished to correct, goes on to say: "When he heard, too, that interior parts of Romania were held oppressed by the Turks, and that Christians were subjected to destructive and savage attacks, he was moved by compassionate pity; and prompted by the love of God, he descended the Alps and came into Gaul; in Auvergne he summoned a council to come together from all sides in a city called Clermont."[23] But there is no way for us to know how much the desire to send aid to eastern Christians may have influenced Urban to cross the mountains. Neither can it be determined when he prepared a plan for a crusade, so different from what he had preached at Piacenza. It can only be suggested that he probably found encouragement to mature his plans in southern France, where holy war was well understood.

Feudal France, at this time, had a considerable surplus of fighting material. Young men, trained to the profession of arms and knowing no other, who were without prospect of inheriting feudal holdings, turned to robbery at home or adventure abroad. The church, especially in southern France, had endeavored to control feudal anarchy by creating the institutions known as the Peace of God and the Truce of God. But the mass meetings, oaths, and other means used in this eleventh-century peace movement were not enough to check private warfare and brigandage, and it was fortunate for French society that many young warriors went abroad to fight for booty or lands in England, Spain, and southern Italy and Sicily. That France, then, was an excellent recruiting ground for a crusade, we may assume Urban understood. But, if we can believe the writers who reported his speech later, he was also interested in bringing peace within Christendom by siphoning off many of the troublemakers in a foreign war.[24]

Many French warriors had participated in the reconquest in

[21] Crozet, *RH*, CLXXIX, 272, quotes from the Cartulary of St. Sernin of Toulouse, "Factum est cum in partes Gallie pro negotiis ecclesiasticis venissemus."

[22] Hagenmeyer, *Epistulae*, p. 136.

[23] Fulcher, *Gesta Francorum* (ed. Hagenmeyer), I, 3, p. 121.

[24] See L. C. MacKinney, "The People and Public Opinion in the Eleventh-Century Peace Movement," *Speculum*, V (1930), 181–206.

Spain, and Cluny had done much to give this struggle the character of a holy war. As the black monks had established their colonies in the territories recovered from the Moslems, they were much interested in extending their holdings, and by the close of the eleventh century, Cluny was so well established in the Christian part of the peninsula that almost every prelate of importance there had been taken from one of her houses. In her monasteries along the "French road" that went to Compostela, the pilgrims heard the legends, containing much propaganda for holy war, which provided the material for the epic poems. The monks prayed for those who went forth to do battle for the faith, and, in gratitude, the warriors gave a share of their plunder to the monasteries. At Cluny, and the Cluniac priories where he stopped, Urban, who was planning to send aid to Christians who were being attacked by Moslems in the east, found sympathetic listeners who were interested in the holy war in Spain.

The small Christian kingdoms in northern Spain had received much aid from France in the reconquest, and Spanish kings had become closely connected with the noble families of southern France. Thus Raymond of St. Gilles, count of Toulouse, was the half-brother of two counts of Barcelona, and his third wife was the daughter of the king of Castile, Alfonso VI. This Spanish ruler had first married a daughter of the duke of Aquitaine, and later a daughter of the duke of Burgundy. Peter I, king of Aragon, whose mother was a sister of the French lord, Ebles of Roucy, married another daughter of William VIII, duke of Aquitaine and count of Poitou, who headed the French expedition that captured Barbastro in 1064, a deed which was celebrated in a *chanson de geste*. In 1073, Ebles of Roucy went to Spain with an army that Suger said was fit for a king.[25]

The disastrous defeat of Alfonso at Zallaca, in 1086, permitted the victorious Murābiṭs (Almoravids) to advance northward again, and caused the Spanish Christians to send urgent appeals for help to friends and kinsmen beyond the Pyrenees. According to one report, Alfonso threatened to permit the enemy to pass through his territories into France if he did not receive aid.[26] French lords, among them the duke of Burgundy, crossed into

[25] M. Defourneaux, *Les Français en Espagne*, pp. 136–137; *La Siège de Barbastre* (ed. J. L. Perrier, Les Classiques français du moyen-âge, Paris, 1926); Suger, *Vita Ludovici* (ed. Waquet, *ibid.*, Paris, 1929), p. 26. On the Spanish reconquest, see above, chapter II, section A.

[26] Defourneaux, *Les Français en Espagne*, p. 143, note 3, and chapter III; Erdmann, *Entstehung*, pp. 88, 89, 124; P. Boissonade, *Du nouveau sur la chanson de Roland* (1929), calls all these expeditions to Spain crusades. Rousset, *Première croisade*, p. 35, holds that they were not crusades.

Spain about this time, but seem to have accomplished little in arresting the Moslem advance. As this had happened a few years before Urban came to France, it is evident that he found many who had recent first-hand knowledge of the holy war in Spain.

Popes before Urban had been interested in the reconquest.[27] Gregory VII had insisted that Spain "was from ancient times subject to St. Peter in full sovereignty," and "it belongs to no mortal, but solely to the Apostolic See." In 1073, he announced that Ebles of Roucy had agreed that all conquered territory in Spain was to be held in fief of St. Peter, and he forbade anyone to take part in his undertaking unless this was understood.[28]

In his younger days, before he left France to serve Gregory VII, Urban, we may be sure, had learned much about the reconquest, especially when he was a Cluniac monk and prior. No doubt he had observed French interest in this peninsular war, and could have known about the expedition of Ebles of Roucy at first hand. Soon after becoming pope, while the papacy was in rather desperate straits, Urban revealed his interest in the holy war in Spain. In 1089, he assured all who would participate in the rebuilding of the frontier post of Tarragona that by so doing they would secure the same help toward salvation as from a pilgrimage to Jerusalem or other holy places.[29]

The pope left Italy accompanied by an entourage of distinguished prelates. In addition to four cardinals, there were two archbishops (one of whom, Daimbert of Pisa, was to become patriarch of Jerusalem), several bishops, and John of Gaeta, the famous papal chancellor. Other ecclesiastical dignitaries joined along the way, to assist in affairs that concerned their own jurisdiction as well as to enjoy the opportunity of being with the pope and his influential associates. The party found lodging and entertainment in wealthy monasteries, where Urban had conferences with influential persons, ecclesiastical and lay, from the regions about. One is naturally inclined to assume that the pope was eager to sound out public opinion in regard to interest in the sufferings of the eastern Christians before he undertook to recruit

[27] M. Villey, *La Croisade*, p. 69, questions Erdmann's belief that Alexander II initiated or directed the expedition that captured Barbastro, or that he granted an indulgence to those who participated. There is no proof that Raymond, count of St. Gilles, participated in this expedition. The fact that his third wife was the natural daughter of Alfonso VI creates a probability that he was in Spain at some time.

[28] M. Villey, *La Croisade*, pp. 70–73, says that there is no indication that the papacy gained any such temporal advantage.

[29] Villey, *La Croisade*, p. 72; Riant, *Inventaire*, *AOL*, I, 68–71; Erdmann, *Entstehung*, p. 292.

important lay leaders for the expedition that he was planning to organize. But the sources tell only of ecclesiastical business, and only one bit of evidence gives a clue to any such effort to interest anyone in the crusade. Baldric of Dol says that after the pope had delivered his famous oration at Clermont, envoys from Raymond, count of Toulouse, appeared and announced that their lord had taken the cross.[30] If this is a fact, it is clear that Raymond knew what the pope intended to do at Clermont, and, no doubt, had been solicited by Urban. If the count had been enlisted, it is very probable that others had been approached, and possibly recruited. Such a shrewd politician as Urban would not have ventured to launch his undertaking without having assurances of adequate human support, even though he believed it all to be "God's work".

The pope was at Le Puy when he issued his call for the council at Clermont. Here he had opportunity to confer with the bishop, Adhémar of Monteil, who came from a noble Valentinois family. A good horseman, trained in the use of arms, he had defended his church from neighboring lords with vigor, and, according to one rumor, he had been on a pilgrimage to Jerusalem.[31] Inasmuch as Urban was to make Adhémar his papal legate for the crusade some three months later, it may be assumed that the matter had been under discussion at Le Puy. Fliche, without any evidence, surmises that Adhémar proposed that the pope go to consult with the count of St. Gilles.[32] At any rate, after a stop at the monastery of Chaise-Dieu, August 18, which seems to have been frequently visited by Raymond, the papal party moved rather rapidly southward and arrived at St. Gilles about the end of August.

Fliche thinks it is probable that Raymond was in the vicinity of St. Gilles at the time of Urban's weeklong stay at this famous monastery. In June he had attended the marriage of his son, Bertram, to a daughter of Odo, duke of Burgundy. Having recently inherited the county of Toulouse and other family holdings on the death of his brother, Raymond had become the greatest lord in southern France, as he was count of Rodez, Nîmes, Narbonne, and Toulouse, as well as marquis of Provence. Although he had been excommunicated for a consanguineous marriage, and had supported simoniacal prelates, he had been suggested for an expedition overseas as one of the *fideles* of St. Peter by Gregory

[30] Baldric of Dol, *Historia* (*RHC, Occ.*, IV), p. 16; Fliche, "Urbain II et la croisade," *Revue de l'histoire de l'église de France*, XIII (1927), 296–299.

[31] Devic and Vaissete, *Histoire générale de Languedoc*, IV, 147.

[32] Fliche, "Urbain II et la Croisade," pp. 290–297.

VII in his letter to the count of Burgundy, and probably the reforming papacy had found him as coöperative as any of the great lords of the time. He had formed matrimonial alliances with two rulers who were at war with the Moslems; his second wife was a daughter of count Roger of Sicily, and his third, who accompanied him on the crusade, was a daughter of king Alfonso VI of Castile. It has been suggested that Raymond had the very natural ambition to be chosen leader of the crusade, but there is no proof to indicate that the pope ever entertained this idea. Certainly, if the pope had desired a lay leader, he would have considered the count, who, as far as we know, may be regarded as the first crusader.

It has also been intimated, again by Fliche, that Urban may have hoped to enlist the support of Odo, duke of Burgundy, who had fought in Spain, although the prospect that Philip I, king of France, might be induced to join the expedition could not have been seriously entertained as Philip seemed to be so enamored of Bertrada of Montfort, wife of Fulk Rechin, count of Anjou, that he was prepared to defy all ecclesiastical discipline. At the Council of Autun, in 1094, where Hugh of Die, archbishop of Lyons and papal legate, presided, the sentence of excommunication had been imposed on the king, who had appealed his case to the pope at Piacenza. Urban had reserved decision until he should be in France, hoping to induce the king to mend his ways. No doubt this was the matter discussed at a meeting between Philip and Hugh at Mozac, which is near Clermont, not long before the council met.[33] The duke of Burgundy was present at this conference, and it is the guess of Fliche that the crusade was discussed and that Odo was so loyal to his suzerain that he would not support the pope's plans unless the king's adultery was condoned. If so, it is a most unusual example of loyalty to a king when the great lords of France had so little respect for Capetian weakness.

After a leisurely journey up the Rhone valley, with stops for dedications, consecrations, and ecclesiastical affairs, the party reached Cluny about October 18, and remained at the famous monastery, where Urban had once been a monk, until the end of the month. It has been said that Cluny, which had promoted pilgrimages to Jerusalem as well as to Compostela, and had en-

[33] A. Fliche, *Le Règne de Philippe Ier, roi de France* (Paris, 1912), pp. 58–59, and "Urbain II et la croisade," p. 300.

[34] A. Hatem, *Les Poèmes épiques des croisades* (Paris, 1932), pp. 63–78; Erdmann, *Entstehung*, pp. 60 ff., 285, note 4, 304; Fliche, "Urbain II et la croisade," p. 300. On the role of Cluny in promoting pilgrimage, see above, chapter II, section D.

couraged holy war in Spain, contributed much to the initiation of the crusade.[34] But surely the pope had the very mature plan, which he presented at Clermont a month later, well prepared by this time. No doubt he asked his former abbot, Hugh, for advice, because he certainly wished to have the support of Cluny, but there is no evidence to show that Hugh had anything to do with initiating the plan that Urban was to propose. But the abbot did accompany the pope on his long journey through southern France, and may have done much to arrange the itinerary so that the papal party would be entertained at Cluniac houses, and the pope rewarded such hospitality by favors in the form of grants of privileges which often included exemption from secular control.

By November 14, the party had reached Clermont, and the pope opened the council on the 18th. The responsibility of arranging for the entertainment of the delegates in his city seems to have been too much of a strain on bishop Durand, who died that night. The estimates of how many churchmen were there vary from one hundred and ninety to four hundred and three. Fulcher of Chartres and Guibert of Nogent put the figures at three hundred and ten and four hundred bishops and abbots, but the bull dealing with the primacy of Lyons, a controversial affair on which some may not have cared to be counted, was signed by twelve archbishops, eighty bishops, and ninety abbots. This, Chalandon thinks, may be regarded as a sort of official roll call of the members. In his letter to the faithful of Bologna, Urban made a much more extravagant claim, when he said that the plenary indulgence decreed at Clermont had been endorsed by nearly all the archbishops and bishops of Gaul.

It was southern France, as Crozet has shown, that was best represented in the council; the Burgundies, Anjou, Poitou, Aquitaine, and Languedoc sent large delegations. On the other hand, there were only two bishops from the Capetian sphere of influence, although we have Urban's statement that king Philip did not prevent others from going. William II of England did forbid his clergy to go, and only three bishops and one abbot represented Normandy, although it is not reported that duke Robert interfered in the matter. A few came from regions farther north, including the bishops of Toul and Metz, while an archbishop, two bishops, and an abbot came from Spain. The hardships and dangers of travel and infirmity may have prevented some prelates from attending, and a few sent excuses. Lambert, bishop of Arras, was kidnapped near Provins by a robber lord named Guarnier

Trainel, and the pope had to threaten to excommunicate the offender in order to get Lambert released.[35]

Although the Council of Clermont became famous for initiating the crusade, it devoted so much of its time and energy to ecclesiastical business that, at first, contemporaries seem to have regarded it as not very different from Piacenza, or the synods at Tours and Nîmes which came after. There were various controversial issues, some of long standing, that came up for decision. Thus, the archbishop of Sens, who took the side of the king in his efforts to keep his mistress without being excommunicated, would not recognize the primacy of Hugh of Die, archbishop of Lyons, and was suspended. But as the count of Anjou had made formal complaint about his wife's being, as everyone knew, the royal mistress, and as Philip would not promise to give her up, Urban could no longer find pretext to postpone action, and excommunicated the guilty pair. Nevertheless, Hugh, the king's brother, did take the cross and lead a contingent on the crusade.

The legislation passed by the council consisted chiefly of reform measures passed by earlier councils, with further definition and provision for better regulation. Only two canons can be regarded as having any bearing on the crusade. The first canon, which proclaimed the Truce of God, might be regarded as papal confirmation of the peace movement, which up to this time had been a matter of regional action, but, although he believed that the crusade would promote peace in the west, the pope must have realized that peace at home might make men more willing to enlist in an expedition which would take them far away for a long period. The second canon was obviously intended to stimulate recruiting, inasmuch as it promised plenary indulgence to all who would go to liberate the church of God in Jerusalem. If they were animated by devotion, and not by the desire for fame or money, the journey (*iter*) would take the place of all penance.[36]

On November 27, when the ecclesiastical business of the council had been completed, Urban went outside the city to address an

[35] F. Chalandon, *Histoire de la première croisade*, pp. 24–28; Hagenmeyer, *Epistulae*, p. 137; R. Crozet, "Le Voyage d'Urbain II," *RH*, CLXXIX (1937), pp. 282–287; *Letter from Urban to Guarnier Trainel* (*PL* CLI), cols. 429–430.

[36] As the canons of the council have not survived in any official copy, they have been taken from a list which apparently belonged to bishop Lambert of Arras (Mansi, *Sacrorum conciliorum amplissima collectio*, XX, 815–820) and from the summaries given by Ordericus Vitalis and William of Malmesbury. See Chalandon, *Première croisade*, pp. 33–35; Riant, *Inventaire* (*AOL*, I), p. 109, note 3. Urban had previously endorsed the Truce at Melfi in 1089, and at Troia in 1093 (A. Fliche, *La Réforme grégorienne*, Paris, 1926, p. 283). In his letters from Antioch to the archbishop of Rheims, Anselm of Ribemont hopes that there is peace at home (Hagenmeyer, *Epistulae*, pp. 144, 160). See also Hagenmeyer, *Epistulae*, pp. 136–137.

audience which was too large for any church.[37] It is understandable that the prospect of listening to a pope and seeing so many high prelates had drawn many people from the neighboring region. In a letter from the archbishop of Rheims to Lambert, bishop of Arras, in which the papal summons to the council was transmitted, it was suggested that the bishop bring Baldwin, count of Mons, with him, and Urban wrote to the Flemings shortly after the council that he had urged (*sollicitavimus*) the princes of Gaul and their followers to liberate the eastern Christians. From these slender bits of evidence it might seem that Urban made some effort to have lay lords in his audience, but later writers have given greatly exaggerated estimates of such attendance. Passing over Ekkehard's one hundred thousand (for which a loudspeaker would seem necessary), we have Baldric reporting "innumerable powerful and distinguished laymen, proud of their knighthood . . . from many regions." Robert mentions bishops and lords from France and Germany, but qualifies his statement by adding that no lay lord, qualified to be chosen leader, was there. Chalandon thinks that the failure of both Raymond of Aguilers and the author of the *Gesta* to mention Clermont indicates that this council did not seem very different from any of the others that Urban was holding to promote church reforms.[38] Such vague references do not tell us how many of the "great multitude" that departed in 1096 may have been the first fruits of the papal oratory. But, after all, the number of immediate recruits was not significant if many could be enlisted later, and the assembly at Clermont provided a favorable opportunity for the pope to give publicity to his plan. It was not to laymen but to ecclesiastics that Urban entrusted the task of promoting the enterprise, and immediately after the main address, or possibly the next day, we are told that he urged the bishops to proclaim the crusade in their churches, "with their whole souls and vigorously to preach the way to Jerusalem." The crusade had such popular appeal that Urban would have conferred fame on any place where he decided to announce it.

The idea caught popular imagination and the undertaking soon inspired an outburst of writing. The deeds done overseas seemed

[37] J. Gay, *Les Papes du XIe siècle et la chrétienté* (Paris, 1926), p. 375, says that just as the council was about to dissolve, the pope decided to preach the crusade. I find no evidence to support this. It is more reasonable to assume that the whole affair was carefully planned.

[38] The failure of Bernold, in his notes for 1095, to mention that the crusade was preached at Clermont may add something to this argument from silence, but in his notes for 1096 he tells of a great multitude starting for Jerusalem and says that the pope had earnestly preached the crusade at all previous synods (Bernold, *Chronicon*, *MGH*, *SS.*, V, pp. 463–464).

to provide the only contemporary material heroic enough for the *chansons de geste*, and the chronicles written about it have much of the epic spirit.[39] Writing the history of the expedition was started by participants — the anonymous author of the *Gesta Francorum* (completed by 1101), Raymond of Aguilers, and Fulcher of Chartres. Of these, Fulcher is the only one who tells of what happened at Clermont, where it is generally assumed he was present.[40] Three other writers, who were there, wrote accounts of the assembly soon after the turn of the century when the undertaking was known to be a glorious success, and all three, Baldric of Dol, Robert the Monk, and Guibert of Nogent, used the *Gesta* as their main source, endeavoring to rewrite the simple story of an eyewitness in the stilted Latin then regarded as the mark of good style. Nevertheless, all three added, what the *Gesta* had omitted, an account of the beginning at Clermont. Robert says that an abbot Bernard showed him a history (the *Gesta*) which displeased him because of its literary crudity, and because it did not have the beginning of the story at Clermont. He suggested that Robert, who had been there, should do it over, and put "a head on such acephalous material." The story of Clermont, as first told by these four writers, was to be used again and again by later chroniclers and modern historians.

Although it is probable that all four were present, they relate what happened after the oration somewhat differently. Robert says that the emotional enthusiasm awakened by the pope culminated in a great shout of *Deus lo volt* (God wills it), and Baldric recalled how many applauded by stamping on the ground, while others were moved to tears, and that discussion soon became animated. Then Adhémar came forward, knelt before the pope, took the vow to go to Jerusalem, and received the papal blessing, all of which seems so dramatic that it may have been prearranged. Urban then commanded all who were going, to obey Adhémar as their leader (*dux*). He also directed all who took the vow to go to sew cloth crosses on their shoulders as a symbol or badge of their profession to follow Christ, who had said, "If anyone wishes to come after Me, let him deny himself, take up his cross, and follow Me." Fulcher says, "O how fitting it was, how pleasing to us all to see these crosses, beautiful, whether of silk, or woven

[39] Marc Bloch, *La Société féodale*, I (Paris, 1939), 157; Ordericus Vitalis, *Historia ecclesiastica*, IX, 1 (ed. A. Le Prevost, Société de l'histoire de France, 5 vols., Paris, 1838–1855), III, 458, says, "Nulla, ut reor, unquam sophistis in bellicis rebus gloriosior materia prodiit. . . ."

[40] Munro, "The Speech of Urban II at Clermont, 1095," *AHR*, XI (1906), 232, note 10, says that he finds no evidence that Fulcher was there.

gold, or of any kind of cloth, which these pilgrims, by order of pope Urban, sewed on the shoulders of their mantles or cassocks or tunics once they had made the vow to go." To Baldric it seemed to be the mark of an honorable profession like the belt of knighthood. Thus Urban initiated a most effective advertising device, for everywhere people would want to know about these *cruce signati*.[41] Finally, after the cardinal Gregory had led the crowd in the *Confiteor*, Urban dismissed his audience with his blessing. He had launched the crusade. What had he said to do that?

All four chroniclers, Fulcher, Baldric, Robert, and Guibert, tell what they claim they had heard the pope say at Clermont, but, as they were trying to recall it all several years later, it is not surprising that their speeches differ. Chalandon suggests that what they wrote must be regarded as just rhetorical exercises; and medieval chroniclers, in the manner of classical historians before them, often made up imaginary speeches. Naturally Urban's oration, which had initiated the glorious crusade, seemed famous enough to deserve the very best rhetorical treatment, and these writers were not inhibited by any appreciation of the importance of accurate reporting. In fairness to them, however, it must be noted that they frankly say that they are not giving the exact words of the pope.[42] Furthermore, whenever they agree, as they frequently do, there is a fair probability that they are recalling ideas that Urban used in his speech.[43]

According to Munro, the pope seems to have made at least three speeches about the crusade. Fulcher first reports what must have been the pope's inaugural address with which he opened the council. "When these and many other things were well disposed of, all those present, clergy and people alike, gave thanks to God and welcomed the advice of the lord pope Urban, assuring him, with a promise of fidelity, that these decrees of his would be kept." He spoke of the evils in society, denounced simony, and urged the clergy to stay free from secular control. In short, this was an ap-

[41] Erdmann, *Entstehung*, pp. 318–319, suggests that this was the first army badge and the first step in the direction of a uniform. According to the *Gesta*, when Bohemond first learned of crusaders coming to Italy, he asked what emblem they wore, and was told that they wore the cross of Christ on the right shoulder or between their shoulders. *Gesta*, I, 4 (ed. Bréhier), p. 18.

[42] "His ergo etsi non verbis, tamen intentionibus usus est." — Guibert. "Haec et id genus plurima peroravit." — Robert. "His vel hujus modi aliis." — Baldric.

[43] For a study of the ideas given in the reports of the speech, see D. C. Munro, "The Speech of Urban II at Clermont, 1095," *AHR*, XI (1906), 231–242. Paul Rousset, *Les Origines et les caractères de la première croisade*, p. 58, does not approve of the method used by Munro. He prefers to follow Hagenmeyer, and accepts ideas from Baldric, Fulcher, and Robert, but not from Guibert.

peal for conciliar action on church reform, and it ended with insistence on the Truce of God. "Let him who has seized a bishop be considered excommunicate" must have sounded timely to prelates who probably knew that the bishop of Arras had just been kidnapped by a robber baron. Fulcher next goes on to the main speech, and under the heading, "the pope's exhortation concerning the expedition to Jerusalem," he says: "Since, O sons of God, you have promised the Lord to maintain peace more earnestly than heretofore in your midst, and faithfully to sustain the rights of Holy Church, there still remains for you, who are newly aroused by this divine correction, a very necessary work, in which you can show the strength of your good will by a further duty, God's concern and your own. For you must hasten to carry aid to your brethren dwelling in the east, who need your help, which they have often asked."[44]

The purpose of the address was to persuade fighting men to enlist in this holy war, and to induce the bishops and abbots of the council to promote the undertaking. Consequently, it seems clear, the pope used what he believed were convincing arguments, the sort of propaganda that came to be called *excitatoria*, and the ideas attributed to Urban were to be used over and over by popes and crusading preachers. But it must not be forgotten that the reports of the speech that we have were written several years later and were most certainly colored by what the chroniclers knew about the ideas and emotions which had actually inspired the great popular movement. It is possible to make some check on the speeches written by the chroniclers by comparing them with Urban's letters to the people of Flanders and Bologna. But in the letters, as in the speech, there were the arguments, the propaganda by which the pope was trying to persuade people to take the cross. He was not trying to give historical causes.[45]

No doubt Urban began by appealing to the Franks, as Robert puts it, a "race chosen and loved by God," whose epic hero, Charlemagne, had overthrown the kingdoms of the pagans.[46] According to Fulcher, the pope asked these valorous Franks to go

[44] Quotations are from translations in A. C. Krey, *The First Crusade* (Princeton, 1921).

[45] Rousset, *Les Origines*, pp. 59–62, confuses causes, purposes, and arguments.

[46] Guibert revealed some such racial pride when he said to an archdeacon of Mainz, "If you think the French are such weaklings and cowards that you can injure by ridicule a name whose fame extends to the Indian Ocean, tell me to whom pope Urban called for aid against the Turks. If the Franks had not with strength and courage interposed a barrier to the Turks, not all you Germans, whose name is not even known in the east, would have been of use." Guibert, *Gesta Dei per Francos* (*RHC, Occ.*, IV), p. 136. The title of his history, he says, was intended to honor his people.

to the aid of the eastern Christians in the Byzantine empire because the Turks had "advanced as far into Roman territory as that part of the Mediterranean which is called the Arm of St. George. . . ." Fulcher, of course, had verified this when he went on the crusade, but Robert, who stayed at home, also refers to the losses of the eastern empire. "The kingdom of the Greeks is now dismembered by them [Turks] and deprived of territory so vast in extent that it cannot be traversed in a march of two months." Although Guibert recalled only that the pope lamented the sufferings of the pilgrims, Baldric, who does not mention the Greeks, has the pope emphasize the religious unity that should exist among all Christians, who were all blood-brothers, "sons of the same Christ and the same church: . . . It is charity to risk your lives for your brothers." That Urban did plead for aid to eastern Christians, as reported by the chroniclers after the crusade, is made certain by the pope himself in his letter to the Flemings written soon after he spoke at Clermont.[47]

But much as Urban wished to aid fellow Christians in the east, he likewise intended that the crusade should benefit the people of the west by substituting foreign war for private warfare at home. As reported by the chroniclers, he was brutally frank in condemning internecine war and brigandage. "You, girt about with the belt of knighthood, are arrogant with great pride; you rage against your brothers and cut each other to pieces. . . . You the oppressors of children, plunderers of widows; you, guilty of homicide, of sacrilege, robbers of another's rights; you who await the pay of thieves for the shedding of Christian blood — as vultures smell fetid corpses." So Baldric reports. Robert's version indicates a plea for peace: "Let, therefore, hatred depart from among you, let your quarrels end, let wars cease, and let all dissensions and controversies slumber." The crusade, then, was intended to supplement the Truce of God which the council had already endorsed, and Fulcher says: "Let those who have been accustomed to make private warfare against the faithful, carry on to a successful conclusion a war against infidels, which ought to have been begun ere now. Let those who for a long time have been robbers now become soldiers of Christ. Let those who once fought brothers and relatives now fight against barbarians as they ought."

[47] It is interesting to note that Baldric and Robert put the pope's plea for the eastern Christians so emphatically although they were in sympathy with Bohemond's drive to raise an army to make war on the emperor Alexius. See A. C. Krey, "A Neglected Passage in the *Gesta*," *Munro Essays*, pp. 57–78.

Was it possible to interest men who committed such crimes against their Christian neighbors in the sufferings of far-away eastern Christians? Did Urban expect to arouse western warriors and robbers by such appeals to altruistic sentiments? Gregory VII, it would seem, had tried to arouse interest in the troubles of the Greeks by a similar appeal without results. But Urban went on to tell of the desecration of churches and holy places, perhaps knowing that injuries to sacred places or things seemed greater atrocities to his contemporaries than the sufferings of human beings. Many feudal lords had made the pilgrimage to Compostela; others had made the long, hard journey to Jerusalem; the count of Anjou, Fulk Nerra, had atoned for his many crimes by making the trip three times. Such men, who had slight regard for human life or human suffering, seem to have felt that it was a shame that the most sacred of all Christian shrines, the Holy Sepulcher, should be in the "defiling" hands of "infidels". Guibert's report of Urban's speech consists largely of a learned disquisition on the religious significance of Jerusalem, and Robert has the pope declaim that it "is the navel of the world; the land is fruitful above all other lands, like another paradise of delights." In Baldric's summary, we read that it was intolerable that the place sanctified by the presence of Christ should be subjected to the abominations of the unbelievers. Gregory VII had made a casual suggestion about going on to Jerusalem, but Urban preached holy war for the recovery of the holy city, which became the goal toward which the crusaders directed their march. Contemporary writers called them the "Jerusalemites" (*Hierosolymitani*), who followed the way (*iter*) to the Holy Sepulcher, or the "Jerusalem route".

Bohemond was told that the crusaders appearing in Italy were going to the Lord's Sepulcher.[48] Urban told the people of Flanders that he had urged war to liberate the eastern churches and "the holy city of Christ, made illustrious by his passion and resurrection." He wrote another letter because he was pleased to know that citizens of Bologna had decided to go to Jerusalem.[49]

To go to pray at the Holy Sepulcher was the best of all Christian pilgrimages. The crusaders were fighting pilgrims who set out to open up the route to Jerusalem, which had been obstructed by

[48] *Gesta*, I, 4 (ed. Bréhier, p. 18). Bernold says that a large multitude began to go to Jerusalem in 1096. The histories of both Robert and Baldric are entitled *Historia Hierosolymitana*; that of Fulcher, *Gesta Francorum Hierusalem peregrinantium*.

[49] "Nonnullos vestros in Hierusalem eundi desiderium concepisse audivimus, quod nobis plurimum complacere noveritis" (Hagenmeyer, *Epistulae*, p. 137).

the Selchükids, and to liberate the holy city. Previously pilgrims had not even been armed for defense; the *milites Christi* were pilgrims undertaking a war of offense.[50] To liberate Jerusalem, the crusaders did much fighting and endured extreme hardships, and when they finally got inside the holy city, they all went weeping to pray in the church of the Holy Sepulcher. Soon after, the purpose of their journey fulfilled, most of them turned their faces homeward. It would seem that Urban found the pilgrimage to be the most effective means of sending armies to the east. But Villey thinks that we must not fall into the error of believing that Jerusalem was the fundamental end of the expedition for Urban; the chroniclers, he suggests, made it into what it was not originally — a war for the Holy Sepulcher.[51] If the pope did send crusaders to Jerusalem, as he did, in order to get them to aid the Greeks, it seems obvious that either he was guilty of deliberately deceiving all those who went, or he was misunderstood. There is no reason, however, to assume that he did not have as strong a desire to recover Jerusalem as the men who actually did liberate it, and, after all, it is only conjecture that he was more interested in sending aid to Byzantium than in recovering the holy city.[52]

The pope did not neglect to hold out the promise of material gains which would be derived from holy war against the Moslems, stronger incentives to his feudal contemporaries than any altruistic suggestions of fighting and dying for the eastern "brethren". In Baldric's version, Urban held out the prospects of loot, which had made the reconquest in Spain so attractive to French warriors. "The possessions of the enemy will be yours, too, since you will make spoil of his treasures...."[53] To plunder, according to Robert, was added the hope of conquest: "wrest that land (*terra sancta*) from the wicked race, and subject it to yourselves, that land which, as the scripture says, 'floweth with milk and honey' ...." Urban seemed to believe that the French needed *Lebens-*

[50] "Decisive evidence has never been adduced to prove that pilgrims, prior to the crusades, had begun to arm for defense." E. Joranson, "The Great German Pilgrimage," *Munro Essays*, p. 40. But see above, chapter II, section D, p. 76.

[51] Villey, *Croisade*, pp. 83, 95. Erdmann, *Entstehung*, pp. 374, 363, note 2, holds that modern research has shown that Urban intended the crusade to help Byzantium. Jerusalem, he says, was the *Marschziel*, not the *Kampfziel*. P. Charanis (*Speculum*, XXIV, 93, 94) gives a statement from a thirteenth-century Greek writer, who says that Alexius "exploited the feeling, widely prevalent in the west, that the domination of the Holy Land by the Turks was intolerable."

[52] "Le but véritable de la croisade, c'est le Saint-Sépulchre qu'il faut délivrer, la route de Jérusalem qu'il faut rendre libre. Tous les chartes parlent du voyage de Jérusalem, de cette ville, terme du pèlerinage guerrier" (Rousset, *Les Origines*, p. 73).

[53] The propagandistic *epistula spuria* to the count of Flanders told of the material gains to be obtained in the Byzantine empire.

raum for colonization. Their land, Robert quotes him as saying, "is too narrow for your large population; nor does it abound in wealth; and it furnishes scarcely enough food for its cultivators. Hence it is that you murder and devour one another." And, of course, migration, especially of landless troublemakers, would relieve pressure and promote peace in the west.

Plunder, conquest, and adventure were strong incentives to unemployed fighting men, but the pope emphasized the religious gains to be obtained in the undertaking. Unlike other wars, recruiting for the crusade was carried on by preaching. Urban strove to awaken enthusiasm for the liberation of eastern Christians and the holy places by urging enlistment in the holy war, which was God's work, in which He was the omnipotent leader, and, according to the chroniclers, the crusaders believed that God was always with them, aiding them in battle, withholding such support when their sins demanded. Their feudal wars were sinful, but robbers could become soldiers of Christ by taking the cross. Guibert argues that wars for the protection of the church are legitimate, and because men had become so filled with greed that both knights and common folk were engaged in mutual slaughter, God instituted this new way of salvation "in our time". By becoming crusaders it was possible to obtain God's favor without leaving the world as was necessary in taking the vows of a religious order, and giving up liberties or lay garments.[54] Thus the pope offered the opportunity for a new kind of religious service, in which, without giving up their customary pursuits of fighting and brigandage, knights could obtain moral and spiritual rewards. The privileges that Urban offered were definite and precise.

It later became customary for popes to grant such privileges in a bull of the crusade. But, although Eugenius III, in his bull for the Second Crusade, said that he was reissuing what Urban II had enacted for his expedition, there is no record that such regulations were incorporated in any bull for the First Crusade.[55] As already indicated, one very important privilege is to be found in the list of canons adopted by the Council of Clermont, namely, that an indulgence was to be granted to all who should go to liberate Jerusalem,[56] provided they were motivated not by desire for honor or money, but by devotion only. This was not "remission of sins", although Urban used the phrase in his letter to the Flemings. It

[54] Guibert, *Gesta Dei per Francos* (*RHC, Occ.*, IV), p. 124.

[55] Villey, *Croisade*, p. 106. On the bull issued by pope Eugenius III see below, chapter XV, p. 466.

[56] "Iter illud pro omni poenitentia reputetur" (Mansi, XX, 816).

was remission of the penance which the church imposed for sins, as the pope makes clear in his letter to the faithful of Bologna, in saying that the pilgrimage would take the place of penance for all sins for which they would make "true and perfect confession". Just what the religious value of pilgrimages had been before is not clear, although when Urban offered those who would rebuild Tarragona the same advantages that were attached to the pilgrimage to Jerusalem, it would seem he assumed that whatever religious gain this might be was generally understood. At any rate, what was granted in precise terms by the canon at Clermont was something more. Pope Eugenius III, in his crusading bull of 1145, says this form of indulgence was originated by Urban. Villey says it is the first instance of plenary indulgence to be found in canon law.[57]

Inasmuch as the canon specified that the indulgence should be granted to those who went to liberate the church at Jerusalem, it may be asked whether unarmed pilgrims, of whom there were many on the crusade, obtained full remission of all penance. According to Robert, the pope had said: "We do not command or advise that the old, or the feeble, or those unfit for bearing arms, undertake this journey. . . . For such are more of a hindrance than an aid. . . ." In his letter to the pilgrims of Bologna he said that neither clerks nor monks should go without the permission of their bishops or abbots, and he further directed that bishops should see to it that priests and clerks did not go without their knowledge and approval. "For this journey would profit them nothing if they went without such permission," writes Robert. Evidently the pope intended that the clergy should screen out unarmed pilgrims who were not qualified to be *milites Christi*.

Urban intended that the clergy should have control of enlistment by requiring all recruits to take a solemn vow to pray at the Holy Sepulcher, and the cross was put on as the sign that they had taken such a vow. According to Robert, Urban proclaimed that whoever decided to go on the pilgrimage, after making this promise, and offering himself "as a living sacrifice", should "wear the sign of the Lord's cross".[58] For Guibert, putting on the cross was somewhat similar to joining a religious order. "He [Urban] instituted a sign well suited to so honorable a profession [vow] by making the figure of the cross, the stigma of the Lord's passion, the emblem of chivalry, or rather what was to be the chivalry of

[57] Villey, *Croisade*, pp. 142–145
[58] Robert, *Historia* (*RHC, Occ.*, III), pp. 729, 730.

God." Fulcher says that the cross was put on after taking "the vow to go". In 1099, Manasses, the archbishop of Rheims, said, "those who have taken the vow of pilgrimage have put on the sign of the cross."[59] Urban, therefore, intended that the act of joining the army of the Lord should be a sort of solemn initiation, which the clergy could use to eliminate those who were unfit to go. That crowds of unarmed pilgrims followed the armies is proof that the papal injunctions were not carried out.[60]

As the way was long and beset with peril and hardship, and the pope knew that the initial enthusiasm, aroused by preaching, would not last, the vow to pray at the Holy Sepulcher was intended to hold the "wearers of the cross" to their task. Furthermore, the "sword of anathema" threatened all who became fainthearted and turned back. Guibert says: "He commanded that if anyone, after receiving this emblem, or after openly taking this vow, should shrink from his good intent through base change of heart, or any affection for his parents, he should be regarded as an outlaw forever, unless he repented and again undertook whatever of his pledge he had omitted." Writing from Antioch, in 1097, Adhémar said that all wearers of the cross who had stayed home were apostates and should be excommunicated. In 1099, Manasses, archbishop of Rheims, urged Lambert, bishop of Arras, to round up all who had failed to fulfil their vows unless sickness or lack of means had prevented them from making the journey. In December of the same year, pope Paschal II wrote to the clergy of Gaul to raise more recruits for the aid of the crusaders in the east. Those who had put on the cross, he said, should be compelled to go, and all who had deserted the army at Antioch were to remain excommunicate until they went back to finish their pilgrimage.[61] This was no idle threat as Stephen, count of Blois, discovered. Since he had run away from Antioch and returned home, either public opinion, or his wife, or both, forced him to join the crusading armies of 1101 and complete the journey to Jerusalem. Thus, to the attractive offer of plenary indulgence, Urban added the vow to complete the pilgrimage, and it seems that violation of this vow was regarded as desertion from the *militia Christi*, to be punished with severe ecclesiastical penalty.

For the many who died before reaching the Holy Sepulcher to obtain the "remission of sins", it was generally believed that their

[59] Hagenmeyer, *Epistulae*, p. 176.
[60] W. Porges, "The Clergy, the Poor, and the Non-Combatants on the First Crusade," *Speculum*, XXI (1946), 2.
[61] Hagenmeyer, *Epistulae*, pp. 142, 175, 176.

souls would go to heaven. Guibert reports that Urban said, "We now hold out to you wars which contain the glorious reward of martyrdom." Baldric quotes Urban's exhortation thus: "... and may you deem it a beautiful thing to die for Christ in that city in which He died for us. But if it befall you to die on this side of it, be sure that to have died on the way is of equal value, if Christ shall find you in his army." Fulcher's version of Urban's words is: "And if those who set out thither should lose their lives on the way by land, or in crossing the sea, or in fighting the pagans, their sins shall be remitted. This I grant to those who go, through the power vested in me by God.... Let those who have been hirelings at low wages now labor for an eternal reward." The chroniclers are sure that this promise was fulfilled. The author of the *Gesta* said that those who died at Nicaea obtained martyrdom, and even the poor folk who died of famine in Christ's name triumphantly assumed the mantle of the martyrs in heaven.[62] Stephen of Blois wrote his wife that the souls of Christians who had been killed had entered the joys of paradise. From Antioch in 1098, the leaders reported that three thousand of their followers were dead in peace, "who without any doubt glory in eternal life."[63] Spiritual rewards seemed certain to all who persevered.

The pope offered temporal as well as religious privileges in his drive to win recruits to his enterprise. Inasmuch as the crusaders were soldiers of Christ engaged in a war sponsored by the church, not only were they taken under ecclesiastical protection, but the church also undertook to protect both their families and property so that they would not leave wives, children, or holdings to the uncertainties of feudal society. In a sense this was the Truce of God which had been approved by the Council of Clermont, but the pope seems to have made it especially applicable to crusaders for three years, or as long as they were absent.[64] Fulcher says that Urban urged the clergy to enforce the Truce, and Guibert reports that Urban "condemned with a fearful anathema all those who dared to molest the wives, children, and possessions of these who were going on this journey for God...." In December 1099, pope Paschal II ordered that their property should be restored to the returning crusaders just as Urban himself had established "by synodal definition". In 1122, pope Calixtus II granted such pro-

[62] *Gesta* II, 8 (ed., Bréhier), p. 42.

[63] Hagenmeyer, *Epistulae*, pp. 150, 154; Rousset, *Les Origines*, pp. 81–83.

[64] Whether the council acted on this protection of families and property is not certain. See E. Bridrey, *La Condition juridique des croisés et le privilège de la croix* (Paris, 1900), pp. 8, 113, note 2.

tection to crusaders, "just as had been done by pope Urban."[65] It seems clear enough that Urban initiated the "Privileges of the Cross", and that it was an innovation is indicated by the request made by Ivo of Chartres, a famous canon lawyer, for an interpretation of this "new institution", inasmuch as he was not sure that he had jurisdiction in a case which involved the loss of his holding by a crusader.[66]

What the pope was asserting was that the possessions of crusaders, *milites Christi*, were to be temporarily as exempt from secular control as the property of the church. Obviously this was a very considerable extension of ecclesiastical jurisdiction. Temporal rulers were to be deprived of the services and payments of vassals who enlisted in the papal armies for an indefinite period of service overseas. Once William the Conqueror had punished a vassal, than whom he knew of no better warrior, by taking away his fief because he went off to fight Moslems in Spain without permission.[67] But so popular was this holy war that neither kings nor feudal lords seem to have made protest against the invasion of their feudal rights.

Pope Urban II, then, had come to Clermont with a well-prepared scheme for raising an army with which to make holy war on the enemies of Christianity. It was a method of recruiting that worked so well that popes were to continue to use the same method of launching crusades at home as well as abroad. It does not seem reasonable to assume that so effective a plan had been conceived quickly, say in the period between Piacenza and Clermont, and it may be noted that there is no trace of it in anything that Gregory VII had proposed. Urban assumed responsibility for this new form of holy war which he was initiating. Unable to go himself, he said that he had appointed a churchman "in our place". Bishop Adhémar, he said, was to be the leader (*dux*), and all who went should obey his legate's commands as they would his own. There is no evidence that the pope had any intention of selecting a layman to head the forces he intended to recruit by offering religious inducements for military service. To be sure, the legate was a fighting bishop who marched at the head of his own contingent and led his men into battle. But the legate associated himself with the much larger army of the count of Toulouse, and it was the news that Raymond, the greatest lord in France, had

[65] Hagenmeyer, *Epistulae*, p. 175.

[66] Bridrey, *op. cit.*, pp. 132–135; Villey, *Croisade*, pp. 151, 152.

[67] Ordericus Vitalis, *Historia ecclesiastica* (ed. Le Prevost, III), p. 248.

taken the cross that gave Urban assurance that there would be a crusade. Perhaps Urban did not realize that his preaching and the religious incentives which he had proclaimed would result in a widespread popular movement, and it may be, as Fliche suggests, that he did not anticipate that Adhémar would have the difficult task of controlling several lay leaders. At any rate, he suggested that Flemings who wished to go should join Adhémar's forces before the date of departure.[68] That the bishop of Le Puy was regarded as their head was so stated by the leaders, when after Adhémar died, they wrote from Antioch asking the pope to come and finish his war.[69] There can be no doubt about its being Urban's war.

Urban stayed in France for more than eight months after the Council of Clermont. The records of the dedications, confirmations of grants, and privileges with which he rewarded the monasteries where he was entertained, and the records of other matters of ecclesiastical business, naturally do not refer to the crusade. Other sources tell little more. There is, of course, the letter that the pope himself wrote to the Flemings not long after Clermont, and there is evidence that the pope preached the crusade at Limoges, where he celebrated Christmas, and at Angers in February.[70] He held two more councils, and we are told that at Tours, as at Piacenza and Clermont, he preached in the open air. We may assume without authority for doing so that he urged his hearers to take the cross. As for the synod held at Nîmes in July, the only suggestion that the crusade was considered is the probability that Raymond, count of Toulouse, was there. Nevertheless, it must be assumed that Urban used such gatherings to arouse enthusiasm and spread knowledge of his undertaking. Surely, as a later chronicler said, wherever he went he endeavored to induce men to go and free Jerusalem from the Turks.[71]

The papal party moved on into the Limousin after leaving Clermont on December 2, instead of going northward into Capetian territory. Possibly, as has been suggested, the pope assumed that he would not be able to promote either crusade or ecclesiastical business successfully where the king was excommunicate and was

68 "... eiusque comitatui tunc se adhaerere posse" (Hagenmeyer, *Epistulae*, p. 137); Fliche, "Urbain II et la croisade," p. 303.

69 The leaders referred to Adhémar as "ille Podiensis episcopus, quem tuum vicarium nobis commiseras," and "qui ab Urbano suscepit curam Christiani exercitus" (Hagenmeyer, *Epistulae*, pp. 164, 141).

70 Hagenmeyer, *Chronologie* (*ROL*, VI), nos. 14, 18.

71 "Ubicumque fuit praecepit cruces facere hominibus et pergere Jerusalem et liberare eam a Turcis et aliis gentibus" (quoted by Crozet, *op. cit.*, p. 272).

supported by high churchmen. After successful preaching at Limoges, the pope moved on to the pleasant city of Poitiers, where he may have found that obdurate young man, William IX, the troubadour, count of Poitou and duke of Aquitaine, son of the old Spanish campaigner, Guy-Geoffrey. But, although the pope visited Poitiers twice and spent some time traveling through Aquitaine, there is no evidence to show that this early troubadour, who had little respect for the clergy, ever met the pope. Certainly he did not decide to atone for his sins by becoming a crusader till later. In fact, he seems to have deliberately waited until Raymond was safely on his way to the Holy Sepulcher to move in and take over Toulouse, to which his wife had a claim, being the daughter of the former count, Raymond's elder brother.[72] Neither do we know whether Urban conferred with Fulk, count of Anjou, whose wife had deserted him for the king of France. However, it was at Angers, where he preached the crusade, that the pope commissioned Robert of Arbrissel, who later founded the Order of Fontevrault, to preach the crusade in the Loire valley.[73] No doubt it was at the pope's urging that Hélie, count of Maine, took the cross, and at Le Mans, Urban commissioned Gerento, abbot of St. Bénigne of Dijon, to promote the crusade in Normandy and England. Then, without entering Normandy, the pope turned southward for the council at Tours, and another visit in Poitiers before moving on through Aquitaine.

During the month of April 1096 the party visited monasteries in Aquitaine, where the pope consecrated the cathedral at Bordeaux on May 1. Moving on through Gascony into the lands of count Raymond, after a brief stop at Toulouse, where he arrived on May 7, Urban went northward to visit the famous Cluniac monastery of Moissac, where he found much interest in Jerusalem as well as the holy war in Spain.[74] Returning to Toulouse he had opportunity to discuss plans for the crusade with count Raymond, who was present when Urban consecrated the church of St. Sernin, and it is possible that Raymond accompanied the pope as he traveled through Languedoc, with stops at Carcassonne and various monasteries. It may be that when Urban preached at Maguelonne, on June 28, he persuaded William of Montpellier, who

[72] J. L. Cate, "A Gay Crusader," *Byzantion*, XVI (1944), 503–526, and below, chapter XI, p. 348.

[73] *Vita B Roberti de Arbrissello, Acta Sanctorum*, Febr. tom. III, Febr. 25, p. 611.

[74] A. Gieysztor, "The Genesis of the Crusades; the Encyclical of Sergius IV," *Medievalia et Humanistica*, V, 1–25; VI, 2–33. According to this study, the encyclical was propaganda written at Moissac.

was present, to take the cross. At Nîmes, where he opened the council on July 5, he dedicated the cathedral with count Raymond and important prelates of the region present. In a grant made at this time Raymond specified that he was going to Jerusalem.[75] Before the council ended on July 14, the pope was informed that the brother of the king of France would lead a contingent of crusaders, and that Philip had repented and agreed to give up his mistress. Although the king's repentance turned out to be short-lived, it seems certain that Urban could be satisfied that his plan for an expeditionary force to invade the Moslem east would be carried through. As he prepared to return to Italy, he sent two bishops to Genoa, where they preached so successfully that many prominent citizens took the cross, and the city prepared a fleet of thirteen vessels which eventually set sail in July 1097.[76]

After a second visit to the monastery of St. Gilles, the pope prepared to leave France, and he was crossing the Alps by August 15, the date that he had set for the departure of the crusaders. A month later, while at Pavia, he wrote his letter of explanation to citizens of Bologna who were interested in the pilgrimage to Jerusalem. By November 1096 crusaders from France, the duke of Normandy and the counts of Flanders and Blois, stopped long enough to obtain his blessing at Lucca as they marched toward the ports on the Adriatic. The sight of their armies on the way to rescue the Holy Sepulcher assured Urban that his carefully prepared plan for the crusade was going to be carried out.

[75] Devic and Vaissete, *Histoire générale de Languedoc*, V, 472–473.
[76] Caffaro, *De liberatione civitatum orientis* (*RHC, Occ.*, V), pp. 49, 50.

VIII
THE FIRST CRUSADE: CLERMONT TO CONSTANTINOPLE

When the pope announced his plan for a holy war against the Moslems in the east for the recovery of the Holy Sepulcher, he directed his appeal to fighting men. Plenary indulgence and other inducements seem to have been intended for those who would fight their way through to Jerusalem or die in the attempt. To men who regarded fighting as an honorable profession, what could

Information concerning the march of the crusaders to Constantinople must be obtained chiefly from Latin chroniclers, as only one Greek source has much on this subject; this is Anna Comnena, *Alexiad* (ed. B. Leib, Collection byzantine de l'association Guillaume Budé, 3 vols. Paris, 1937–1945; also parts relating to the crusade in *RHC*, *Grecs*, I). There is also an English translation by E.A. S. Dawes (London, 1928). Anna was well informed, but as she wrote forty years after, her work suffers from the defects which so often characterize memoirs, and she does not hesitate to eulogize her father, Alexius. But the impression left on her as a young girl by the crusaders remained vivid, and she makes clear the Greek attitude toward the crusade.

For those who followed, or attempted to follow, the route from Germany through Hungary and Bulgaria, with the exception of a few references in Ekkehard, the main source is Albert of Aix, *Liber Christianae expeditionis pro ereptione, emundatione, restitutione sanctae Hierosolymitanae ecclesiae* (*RHC*, *Occ.*, IV). The author, who did not go on the crusade, wrote his chronicle sometime between 1119 and the middle of the century. He collected much information from returning pilgrims and crusaders, which is often so precise that it gives the assurance of accuracy even when it cannot be checked. Albert also incorporated material more suited to romance and epic poetry than history, but he is indispensable. Although it is necessary to use his history with care, it is not too difficult to decide what the author obtained, as he says, from those "qui praesentes adfuissent."

Although the author is unknown, the [*Anonymi*] *Gesta Francorum et aliorum Hierosolimitanorum* (ed. H. Hagenmeyer, Heidelberg, 1890; ed. L. Bréhier, Les Classiques de l'histoire de France au moyen âge, Paris, 1924), was much used by contemporary historians and has acquired great respectability in recent times. It was read in Jerusalem in 1101 by Ekkehard, copied by Tudebod, a Poitevin crusader, and done over into what was regarded as more popular form by Guibert of Nogent, Baldric of Dol, and Robert the Monk. It is a factual account of the expedition by a follower of Bohemond, presumably a knight of no particular prominence (cf. A. C. Krey, "A Neglected Passage in the *Gesta*," *The Crusades and Other Historical Essays Presented to Dana C. Munro* [New York. 1928], pp. 57–76).

Raymond of Aguilers, chaplain of count Raymond of St. Gilles, began writing in 1098, and probably finished in 1099 his *Historia Francorum qui ceperunt Iherusalem* (*RHC*, *Occ.*, III). The author early became prejudiced against the Greeks, and was credulous and naïve, but more interested than other writers in the poor pilgrims.

The principal secondary works include, for the early bands known as the Peasants' Crusade: H. Hagenmeyer, *Peter der Eremite* (Leipzig, 1879), the work which first revealed the falsity of the Peter legend; T. Wolff, *Die Bauernkreuzzüge des Jahres 1096: ein Beitrag zur Geschichte des ersten Kreuzzuges* (Tübingen, 1891); and F. Duncalf, "The Peasants' be better, as a troubadour saw it, than to escape hell by doing deeds of honor?[1] But crowds of lesser folk, noncombatant pilgrims, became enthusiastic about making the trip to the holy places in the wake of armed forces; and Urban, when he realized that such folk would be a hindrance to the expedition, made some effort to prevent them from going. Thus, in his letter to the people of Bologna, he definitely excluded old people, those unfit to fight, women without husbands or guardians, clerics without consent of their superiors, or laymen without clerical blessing. Robert reports that Urban had said that the benefits of the journey were not for the members of the clergy who went without the consent of their bishops. But the urge to go became too strong to be restrained by such regulations. Much more effective, as the story of the march to Constantinople reveals, was the necessity of having the means to meet the expenses of the journey.

The chroniclers tell how the news of this new way to salvation, "constituted by God," literally flew about the world.[2] Robert the Monk, for whom modern wireless would have been no surprise, says that it was known everywhere on the very day that it was announced at Clermont. But Urban instructed the churchmen to

Crusade," *AHR*, XXVI (1921), 440–453. For Godfrey the most useful study is the recent monograph by J. C. Andressohn, *The Ancestry and Life of Godfrey of Bouillon* (Bloomington, 1947).

For Bohemond, the excellent study of R. B. Yewdale, *Bohemond I, Prince of Antioch* (Princeton, 1917), may be supplemented by R. L. Nicholson, *Tancred, A Study of His Career and Work in Their Relation to the First Crusade and the Establishment of the Latin States in Syria and Palestine* (Chicago, 1940). Other studies of crusading leaders are J. H. Hill, "Raymond of Saint Gilles in Urban's Plan of Greek and Latin Friendship," *Speculum*, XXVI (1951), 265–276; M. M. Knappen, "Robert II of Flanders in the First Crusade," *Munro Essays*, pp. 79–100; and C. W. David, *Robert Curthose, Duke of Normandy* (Cambridge, 1920).

The march to Constantinople is also treated in the histories of the crusade, of which the most detailed is that of R. Röhricht, *Geschichte des ersten Kreuzzuges* (Innsbruck, 1901), but now superseded by more recent works as, of course, is the first really modern history of the First Crusade, that of H. von Sybel, *Geschichte des ersten Kreuzzuges* (2nd ed., Leipzig, 1881). More recent and very instructive, although a posthumous publication, is F. Chalandon, *Histoire de la première croisade* (Paris, 1925), whose earlier *Essai sur le règne d'Alexis Ier Comnène* (Paris, 1900), had suggested that the emperor wanted mercenaries, not crusaders. L. Bréhier, *L'Église et l'orient au moyen âge: les croisades* (Paris, 1928), gives a brief summary but is not trustworthy in details. Satisfactory as a general history is S. Runciman, *A History of the Crusades*, I, *The First Crusade* (Cambridge, 1951); and especially helpful for the march to Constantinople, his article, "The First Crusaders' Journey across the Balkan Peninsula," *Byzantion*, XIX (1949), 201–221.

H. Hagenmeyer, "Chronologie de la première croisade," *ROL*, VI–VIII (1898–1901), is an indispensable guide, especially for dates. The hopeless problem of the size of the armies has been considered by F. Lot, *L'Art militaire et les armées du moyen âge* (2 vols., Paris, 1946), and by Runciman in Appendix II of his *History of the Crusades*, vol. I. Const. Jiriček, *Die Heerstrasse von Belgrad nach Constantinopel und die Balkanpässe* (Prague, 1877), is still very useful.

[1] M. Bloch, *La Société féodale*, II (Paris, 1940), 20.

[2] "Solutum est concilium, et nos unusquisque properantes redivivimus ad propria. Praedicant episcopi, et voce liberiori iam illud idem vociferabantur laici" (Guibert, *Gesta Dei per Francos*, *RHC*, *Occ.*, IV, i, 6, p. 16).

go home from the council and preach the crusade. As Baldric relates, "And turning to the bishops, he said, 'You, brothers and fellow bishops; you, fellow priests and sharers with us in Christ, make the same announcement through the churches committed to you and with your whole soul vigorously preach the journey to Jerusalem.'" The importance of the clergy as publicists of the pope's undertaking is made clearer by Ekkehard, who believed that the "eastern Franks" had remained in ignorance of the movement until crusaders came trooping through their country because the schism had prevented any of their clergy from going to Clermont and bringing back the news. Southern Italy also seems to have learned about the crusade late, if we can believe the author of the *Gesta*, who says that Bohemond did not know about this "new way of penance" until crusaders came into Italy from France.[3] It seems likely that Norman Italy thus did not have members of the clergy returning from Clermont. Also, we know a little about the pope's use of churchmen. Gerento, abbot of St. Bénigne, was delegated to promote the crusade in Normandy and England, and two bishops were sent to rouse the citizens of the maritime republic of Genoa. Robert of Arbrissel, and possibly Peter the Hermit, received papal encouragement to preach the crusade. It was, of course, an exciting idea, and once made public by the clergy, it spread rapidly among the people.

The chroniclers give ridiculously exaggerated estimates of the numbers of those who responded to the call. Fulcher mentions a "countless multitude, speaking many languages;" while Guibert says that the movement took in "the whole of Christendom capable of bearing arms." If it was God's work, as contemporaries believed, the numbers given had to be sufficient to justify such inspiration, and there was no need to ask about contributory mundane conditions or causes. Ekkehard was exceptional in noting that the eastern Franks were more easily persuaded to leave their homes because they had been afflicted for some time by civil strife, famine, and pestilence. Guibert also took note of economic conditions in saying that the French had suffered much from famines. Some modern historians have been intrigued by this eleventh-century suggestion, and have labored the notion that recruiting for the crusade was facilitated by unfavorable economic conditions, especially famines, in the west.[4]

Such statistical evidence as may be obtained by counting up

[3] *Gesta* (ed. Bréhier), p. 18.
[4] Röhricht, *Gesch. d. ersten Kreuzzuges*, p. 24; T. Wolff, *Bauernkreuzzüge*, pp. 108–119.

references to famines does not prove that conditions were more unfavorable at this time, and many of the famines reported were local. But it is now quite generally believed that the last half of the eleventh century was a period of rising prosperity, marked by reviving trade, industry, town life, and expansion of agriculture. Money was beginning to circulate more widely, and there is evidence to indicate that pilgrims and crusaders obtained money by mortgaging or selling their property. Ready cash was necessary for the journey, as large numbers of people could not get very far on the way toward the Holy Sepulcher by depending upon foraging or charity. Guibert says that when the "cry of crusade" came, "the famine disappeared and was followed by abundance ... each one hastened to convert into money everything that he did not need for the journey.... What cost most were goods needed for the journey, others sold for nothing."[5] As cartularies indicate, the church did a good business in mortgaging and buying the property of crusaders who needed money for the long journey.

Alexius, it may be assumed, hoped to have fighting men to serve in his armies — mercenaries, according to Chalandon — and as reported by Bernold, when Urban called for volunteers at Piacenza, he told those who might go to take an oath to obey the emperor. But the basileus became alarmed when he learned the extent of the movement of people who were coming to help; "all the barbarians between the Adriatic and the Pillars of Hercules," his daughter Anna rhetorized. He knew from experience how dangerous these westerners were when aroused, that they were greedy and fickle fellows who could not be bound by any agreements. The first problem that confronted the emperor, however, was how to get them through the Balkan provinces without trouble, and arrangements to do this were made much more difficult because the armies were accompanied by an unarmed multitude of pilgrims.[6] Practically the only information about Byzantine plans to handle this sudden influx from the west is found in the *Alexiad* of Anna Comnena, who was an impressionable girl of thirteen when it happened, but did not write about it until forty years later. She describes the plans of the imperial government so clearly that it may well be that she obtained her information from an official document.[7]

[5] Guibert, *Gesta Dei* (*RHC, Occ.*, IV), p. 141. Baldric of Dol (*RHC, Occ.*, IV), p. 17, says that an inner desire was aroused in Christians "ut pene omnes iter arriperent, si stipendiorum facultas eis suppeteret."

[6] Runciman has estimated that from 70,000 to 100,000 made the journey to Constantinople during 1096 and 1097 (*Byzantion*, XIX, 220–221, and *History of the Crusades*, I, Appendix II, pp. 336–341).

[7] *Alexiad*, X, v, 9 (ed. Leib, II, 209).

There were two main routes through the Balkans that led to Constantinople. Earlier in the eleventh century many pilgrims from Germany had gone through Hungary to enter the empire at Belgrade, and had then followed the road that went through Nish (Naissus), Sofia (Sardica), Philippopolis, and Adrianople to the Byzantine capital.[8] But as the result of disorders in Bulgaria, this route had become less popular than the old Via Egnatia, which began at Dyrrachium (Durazzo), and ran through Ochrida, Monastir, Vodena, and Thessalonica, and on to Constantinople. The northern road, of course, was an all-land route. It was, naturally, necessary for travelers to cross the Adriatic to get to Dyrrachium, unless they went around the northern end of this sea through wild and desolate regions. It was Anna's recollection that all the crusaders came over the southern road, probably because her cousin, John Comnenus, was stationed in the western part of the empire, and a large military force was sent there to guard against a Norman effort to capture Dyrrachium again.[9]

To handle the crowds expected from the west, the imperial government planned to send officials who would be provided with interpreters familiar with Latin. Commanders of Byzantine ships, who watched for pirates in the Adriatic, were instructed to bring word of approaching pilgrim transports, so that the officials could greet them and take them in hand. Military forces were to serve as escorts, and "discreetly" put them back on the road by light skirmishing if they strayed out of bounds. Finally, and what was very necessary if foraging was to be prevented, the government planned to have stores of provisions at the larger towns on the routes so that pilgrims and crusaders could provide themselves with food — provided they could pay for it, of course. That these plans were carried out is evident from the accounts of western chroniclers.

Unfortunately, bands of pilgrims and crusaders began to arrive in Bulgaria before Byzantine officials were ready to take care of them. Possibly the imperial government had assumed that the date set by the pope, August 15, 1096, would be observed, or, as may be inferred from Anna, it had been assumed that the northern route would not be much used. And it is entirely probable that Urban himself was surprised that crusading bands went off ahead of the time set and did not wait for his legate, Adhémar, as he

[8] Jireček, *Heerstrasse von Belgrad nach Constantinopel*; R. Röhricht, "Pilgerfahrten nach dem Heiligen Lande vor den Kreuzzügen," *Historisches Taschenbuch*, V (1875–1876), 275 ff.

[9] *Alexiad* (ed. Leib), II, 220, note 1.

had proposed to the Flemings. But early in February, while the pope was north of the Loire in western France, a group of lords met at Paris, and, in the presence of their excommunicated king, chose his brother, Hugh, count of Vermandois, to lead them on the crusade. At the same time, lesser folk, aroused by the preaching of Peter the Hermit, were marching north through Capetian territories, and it was this popular movement, which is known as the Peasants' or People's Crusade, that was responsible for the premature appearance of bands of crusaders and pilgrims on the northern road into the Byzantine empire.[10]

Peter had high credentials. He carried a letter which was said to have fallen from heaven, and it contained a prophecy that the Christians would drive the "infidels" from the holy places if they tried. According to another story, the Hermit had seen Christ in a vision as he prayed at the Holy Sepulcher, for it was long believed that he had gone on a pilgrimage to Jerusalem, and that on his return he had persuaded pope Urban to launch the crusade This legend, related by Albert of Aix, was given wider currency by William of Tyre. Thus it came to be believed that Peter, not Urban, initiated the crusade, and this explanation was accepted until late in the nineteenth century, when it finally became clear that there was no evidence to show that Peter had any influence on the pope.[11]

Peter, who seems to have been born in Picardy, was a small man, "short in stature, but great in heart and eloquence." At a time when popular preaching was unusual, he had great influence, and many followed him as he moved northward from Berry through Capetian territory. At Étampes he enlisted Geoffrey Burel, known as Master of the Footmen, and at Poissy he was joined by a knight named Walter, with his nephews, Walter Sans-Avoir ("the Penniless"), William, Matthew, and Simon. Reginald of Bray came from the vicinity of Liége. It was with a considerable following that Peter arrived at Trier in April, and a few days later he was preaching at Cologne. But the "proud Franks" became impatient, and under the leadership of Walter Sans-Avoir started off toward Constantinople. Albert says there were only eight knights in this band, which clearly consisted largely of pilgrims. Walter, an outstanding knight, according to Fulcher of Chartres,

[10] F. Duncalf, "The Peasants' Crusade," *AHR*, XXVI (1921), 440–453; T. Wolff, *Die Bauernkreuzzüge* (Tübingen. 1891).

[11] H. Hagenmeyer, *Peter der Eremite* (Leipzig, 1879). According to Anna, Peter started on such a pilgrimage but was unable to get through Anatolia because of the Turks. Cf. *Alexiad*, X, v, 5 (ed. Leib, II, 207).

proved to be a capable leader, and his followers seem to have been well prepared, and they were orderly and peaceful on their journey.[12]

The Germans ridiculed these pilgrims for having sold their property in order to go on what they thought was a foolish journey, saying that they had exchanged the certain for the uncertain, and had abandoned the land of their birth for a doubtful land of promise. But the Germans, who knew little about the movement at first, changed their attitude as they saw the crowds, who seem to have been very orderly, cross through their country. Certainly, king Coloman did not hesitate to grant Walter's request for permission to cross Hungary with the privilege of buying food along the way. This concession was made, the chronicler says, because Walter seemed a worthy man, who had undertaken his journey with the best of intentions. Hungarians, of course, were accustomed to pilgrim travel through their country.[13]

After marching through Hungary, Walter's band crossed the Sava river into Bulgaria. Nicetas, the Byzantine governor of Bulgaria, who was stationed at Nish, either was without instructions about how to handle crusading bands, or had not informed whoever was in command at Belgrade, and Walter's request for market privileges was denied. To complicate matters at this time, sixteen stragglers, who had remained behind at Semlin, in Hungary, came in with complaints of being robbed. Walter wisely refused to consider retaliation. In the meantime, further trouble had arisen at Belgrade, where, unable to buy food, his people had spread out in the countryside to forage. Some sixty pilgrims were surrounded in a church, where they were burned to death. Walter, to avoid further trouble, hurried his band off along the road to Nish through the Bulgarian forests. When they arrived at this town on June 18, Nicetas granted market privileges and even made good the losses, at the same time assuring Walter that his people would be able to buy provisions on the rest of the way to Constantinople.[14] Conducted by an escort, this band reached Constantinople without further

[12] Albert of Aix is our chief source for the Peasants' Crusade. Although his sources of information are not definitely known, he gives so many precise details that it is reasonable to assume that he obtained them from eye-witnesses, as he says, "ab his qui praesentes adfuissent."

[13] Ekkehard of Aura, *Hierosolymita*, IX, 1, 2 (ed. Hagenmeyer, pp. 100–113). Albert of Aix says that Walter reached Hungary on March 8, which William of Tyre gives as the date of departure. Hagenmeyer substitutes May for March. Hagenmeyer puts the date of arrival on the Hungarian border at May 21. Cf. "Chronologie," *ROL*, VI (1898), nos. 21, 22, 35.

[14] Runciman (*Byzantion*, XIX, 212) suggests that Nicetas held Walter at Nish until he received instructions from Constantinople.

difficulty, and the only incident recorded on this last stage of the journey is the death of the older Walter, whose body was found to be marked with a cross. At the capital city, where they arrived about mid-July, Walter and his people made camp outside the walls to await the coming of Peter. They had behaved very well, and had asked only for the right to buy their food, which was precisely what the Byzantine government had planned to provide.

Peter, the preacher who could arouse emotions, was not as capable a leader as the knight, Walter. Nevertheless, it seems certain that he intended to have a peaceful journey, as his followers were prepared to pay their way and do not seem to have been guilty of the persecution of the Jews which became so prevalent in the Rhine valley after their departure. Peter, to be sure, had a letter from French Jews advising their brethren elsewhere to aid Peter for the good of Israel, which may mean that he threatened them to obtain money; and later on we learn that he had a treasure chest.[15] Peter's following, after the departure of the French, probably consisted mainly of Germans who were recruited in the Rhineland. Ordericus Vitalis says that he added many by his preaching at Cologne, and it seems that he was accompanied by two German counts and a bishop. Albert mentions French, Lorrainers, Swabians, and Bavarians, the last being added on the march through southern Germany.[16] At Ödenburg (Sopron) on the Hungarian boundary, Peter waited until he received permission to march through Hungary, which was granted by king Coloman with the stipulation that there should be no pillaging nor disputes about markets. Peter agreed to the terms, and his band was orderly until Semlin was reached, where some of the crusaders became so indignant at seeing the clothing and arms of the sixteen stragglers from Walter's band, hanging defiantly from the walls, that they captured the town by assault.[17] They were also disturbed by a rumor that one of Coloman's officials, named Guz — Runciman suggests that he may have been a Ghuzz (the Arabic form of Oghuz) Turk — was plotting with Nicetas against them. Peter seems to have lost control of the

[15] Hagenmeyer, "Chronologie," no. 27.

[16] A list of south German nobles is given in the *Chronicle of Zimmern* which Hagenmeyer believes was taken from a contemporary source. See Hagenmeyer, "Étude sur *la Chronique de Zimmern*," *AOL*, II (1884), 72.

[17] Such is Albert's account here, but later (*RHC, Occ.*, IV, 300) he inserts a letter from Coloman to Godfrey, in which the king complains that Peter's people had violated the *emendi licentia* by pillaging and killing some 4000 Hungarians. This contradiction may be the result of confusing his information about Peter with that about later bands.

hotheads in his band, and, fearing retaliation, he made haste to get his people out of Hungary.

As few boats were available, his people had to take time to construct rafts, watched by Pechenegs, Byzantine mercenaries, gathered on the Bulgarian side of the Sava, possibly to act as an escort.[18] After a brush with these mercenaries, in which a few were captured, the crossing was made, and the band moved on to Belgrade, which they found deserted. By July 2 they reached Nish, where the chronicler says Nicetas had collected Bulgars, Kumans, Pechenegs, and Hungarians for the defense of the town. But he granted markets on condition that hostages, Walter of Breteuil and Geoffrey Burel, should be given as a pledge for good behavior, who, as all went well, were released the next morning.

According to Albert's information, some Germans who had become quarrelsome while trading with citizens set fire to some mills outside the walls, and imperial troops then attacked the baggage train which was in the rear of the departing crusaders and pilgrims, and captured women and children. Albert thought these unfortunates were still in captivity when he was writing his history more than a quarter of a century later. Peter hurried back and ordered his people to do nothing until he could negotiate with Nicetas for the return of the prisoners, but, disregarding orders, headstrong young men attempted to storm the walls of the town, only to be repulsed with heavy losses. In the meantime, Peter had sent Bulgars, who had joined his pilgrimage, to ask Nicetas for a cessation of fighting until the troubles could be discussed. The Byzantine governor accepted the proposal, but "the footmen", unwilling to wait any longer, began to load up their wagons again and march away; although Peter, Fulcher, and Reginald tried to persuade them to stay. To the imperials, it seemed that Peter and his leaders were trying to hurry their people away to avoid negotiating, and they again attacked; in the rout that followed, many were killed, and the rest sought refuge in the surrounding forests.[19]

When Peter finally united his band, Albert's informant thought that a fourth of them had been lost. Stopping at a deserted town, which has been identified as Palanka, they spent three days in

[18] Runciman, *History of the Crusades*, I, 124–125, suggests that they were there to conduct a holding operation to permit Nicetas to retire from Belgrade to Nish, because he had insufficient forces to deal with "such a horde".

[19] Albert may be presenting a favorable case for Peter's people, but it should be noted that all crusading armies had similar trouble. Note, for example, the Second Crusade, below, chapter XV, pp. 484–485, where the Germans who preceded the French foraged and committed atrocities.

gathering and parching grain, on which they fed themselves till they reached the next town, Sofia, on July 12. Here Byzantine officials from Constantinople took charge, promising free markets for the rest of the way, with the stipulation that the band should not stay more than three days at any market town. At Philippopolis, the eloquent Peter told his story of misfortunes with such fervor that the citizens gave his people gold bezants, silver coins, horses, and mules. At Adrianople, imperial messengers urged Peter to hurry on, saying that the emperor had heard much about him and was eager to see him. On August 1, the band arrived at Constantinople, having been on the way from Cologne three months and eleven days.[20]

Other bands that were formed soon after Peter's departure failed to get through Hungary because they expected to live off the country. The followers of a certain Folkmar passed through Saxony and Bohemia into Hungary. As Albert does not mention him, and Ekkehard is very brief, little is known about him. It may be assumed that the persecutions of Jews at Magdeburg and Prague were the work of this band. Ekkehard merely says that Folkmar traversed Bohemia to Nitra where his band was broken up, some being killed and others captured, because "sedition was incited" (*seditione concitata*). It is not very enlightening to learn further that survivors attributed their escape to a cross which they saw in the heavens.[21]

Gottschalk, a German priest from the Rhineland, was inspired by Peter to preach the pilgrimage to Jerusalem. With followers from eastern France, Lorraine, and southern Germany, he followed Peter's route into Hungary. Although Albert, who twice says that his information was derived from eye-witnesses, specifies that these people, both horsemen and footmen, had collected money and equipment for the journey, and were peaceful on their march through Germany, Ekkehard calls Gottschalk "a false servant of God" (*mercenarius, non pastor*). Nevertheless, king Coloman had a favorable enough impression of this band to grant them the privilege of markets in his country on condition that they were not disorderly. But, while negotiating for permission to enter Hungary, Bavarians, Swabians, and "other fools", who became drunk on stolen wine, took grain, cattle, and sheep from

[20] For this estimate and other dates, see Hagenmeyer, "Chronologie," in *ROL*, VI ff.

[21] The Annalist of Magdeburg, copying Ekkehard, corrects him when he calls Folkmar "a certain priest" (*MGH, SS.*, XVI, 179). Chalandon rightly discounts Hagenmeyer's suggestion that Folkmar and the Fulcher of Orléans in Albert are the same person. See also Cosmas, *Chronicon* (*MGH, SS.*, IX), p. 103.

the Hungarians, who were soon roused to retaliate. The pilgrims were forced to seek refuge in the monastery of St. Martin, and in the negotiations that followed, Gottschalk and his followers were persuaded to surrender both arms and money, "the means of supporting life on the way to Jerusalem." Then the Hungarians killed or captured most of the band, "just as they affirm who were there and barely escaped." Such is the improbable account given by Albert. Ekkehard merely says that the band established a fortified camp and engaged in foraging. The "massacre" probably took place in July.

Folkmar's band and possibly Gottschalk's followers were involved in the wave of anti-semitism that swept through the Rhineland at this time. Jews, who had been encouraged to settle in the growing cities along the Rhine, were protected by the ecclesiastical princes and the emperor. Money-lending at usurious rates of interest made them prosper, and riches gained by such unchristian practices, as well as their ostentation and exclusiveness, made these strangers (*exsules*) unpopular and even hated, and crusaders, going forth to fight the enemies of their faith, were easily persuaded to persecute and rob Jewish "unbelievers". Especially ready to sack the Jewries were poor crusaders who needed money to finance their journey. Was not the purpose of their expedition to oppose the enemies of Christianity ? The chronicler Ekkehard praised the persecution of "these execrable people", who were "enemies within the church". But Cosmas of Prague, it is interesting to note, held it uncanonical to force baptism on them, for, as Albert put it, "God is a just judge who has not ordained that anyone should be brought into the Christian obedience unwillingly by force." Actuated by more selfish reasons, no doubt, Henry IV later declared that Jews who had been forced to become Christians could return to their own faith, and the ecclesiastical princes made efforts to protect their Jewish wards from mob violence. According to a late Jewish source, Godfrey of Bouillon threatened to avenge the blood of Christ on the Jews, but denied that he had ever intended to harm them when Henry IV advised both lay and ecclesiastical lords to protect them. Nevertheless, he did collect a thousand marks of silver from the Jewries of Mainz and Cologne to help defray the expenses of his crusade, and it may be assumed that Godfrey had Jew-baiters in his army, although the worst of the persecutions were over before he departed for the east.

The most fanatical pogroms may be attributed to the various bands that came together under the leadership of count Emicho of Leiningen, who had feudal holdings between Mainz and Worms, and was said to be "most powerful in that region". This robber baron had an evil reputation for oppression, and Ekkehard asserts that he "usurped leadership" over pilgrims by deluding them with reports of divine revelations which he had received "like another Saul". He was joined by another adventurer, who had acquired his bad reputation in Spain, William the Carpenter, viscount of Melun and Gâtinais, and kinsman of Hugh of Vermandois. Other French lords, Clarebold of Vendeuil, Thomas of La Fère, and Drogo of Nesle, also joined Emicho, whose band consisted of "pilgrims and crusaders" (*cruce signati*) from France, England, Flanders, Lorraine, and southern Germany in addition to his original followers from the Rhine region. To Albert it was a sinful collection of men, women, and children, who regarded the pilgrimage as a pleasure trip, but he notes that they provided themselves with whatever was needed by people taking the road to Jerusalem.[22]

Early persecutions in the Moselle valley may be attributed to bands moving toward the Rhine. (It does not seem possible to distinguish various bands as Wolff has attempted to do.[23]) Early in May, a few Jews who refused to be baptised were killed at Metz, and, at Speyer, a massacre was prevented because bishop John gave asylum to Jews in his palace. At Worms, similar action by the bishop was not effective, and on May 18, crusaders and a mob from the surrounding countryside forced their way into the episcopal palace and killed all within. This pogrom may have been the work of Emicho's band, as was that which took place soon after at Mainz, where this "enemy of all the Jews" arrived on May 25, to find the gates closed against him. But the Jews who paid the archbishop Ruthard to protect them seem to have been betrayed. Their enemies were admitted to the city two days later and a massacre followed. Later, when the archbishop was accused of having taken money from the Jews, he fled without defending himself.[24]

When Emicho arrived at Cologne, on May 29, Jewish sources say that most of their brethren were saved either by finding protection in the houses of Christian friends or by escaping from the city. When Albert says that two hundred attempted to escape to

[22] See also Ekkehard, *Chronicon universale* (*MGH, SS.*, VI), pp. 208 ff.; *Gesta* (ed. Bréhier), p. 78; *Bibliothèque de l'école des chartes*, 2nd ser., I, 239; Hagenmeyer, "Chronologie," no. 24.

[23] T. Wolff, *Bauernkreuzzüge*, pp. 159–169.

[24] Hagenmeyer, "Chronologie," nos. 25, 26, 30, 31, 32, 35, 36, 37.

Neuss, he may have in mind the massacre that occurred in that place later. He also believed that many were killed at Cologne, where he says the mob found "much money" to divide. After the departure of Emicho, other bands carried out a series of persecutions farther down the Rhine valley.[25] This outbreak of anti-Semitism probably came after the departure of Emicho from Cologne, where he had waited for the various bands to gather.

Emicho, Clarebold, and Thomas led that "intolerable crowd of men and women" (twelve thousand is Ekkehard's figure), laden with loot from the ghettos, as far as Hungary on the way to Jerusalem. Their route led from the Rhine, up the Main and down the Danube, and on the way they were joined by count Hartmann of Dillingen-Kyburg with a contingent of Swabian nobles. At the town of Wieselburg, which was fortified and flanked by swamps, at the juncture of the Leitha river with the Danube, they were halted, and Coloman refused to permit them to enter his kingdom, possibly because, as Ekkehard says, he had heard that the Germans were as willing to kill Hungarians as pagans. Finding advance effectively blocked, Emicho and his colleagues undertook to construct a bridge, an operation which took six weeks. During this time, the crusaders resorted to foraging, and engaged in many skirmishes with the Hungarians, while the leaders quarreled about who should have Hungary when they had conquered this land.

When the bridge was completed, the crusaders crossed to attack the town, and by means of machines soon breached the walls. Just as victory seemed certain, for some reason that the chronicler was unable to explain, the crusaders were seized by sudden panic, and, in their haste to return to the other bank of the river, many were drowned. The Hungarians rallied to pursue and succeeded in completely destroying this band of marauders. The leaders, having good horses, escaped. Thomas, Clarebold, and William the Carpenter made their way southward into Italy, where they may have joined William's kinsman, Hugh of Vermandois.[26] The only explanation for this sudden defeat offered by Ekkehard is that it was the will of God. "Men of our race, having zeal for, but not knowledge of, God," he says, "in the very militia which Christ provided for liberating Christians, began to attack other Christians ...," thus bringing the crusade into bad repute.

[25] Neuss, June 24; Wevelinghofen, June 25; Altenahr, June 26–27; Xanten, June 27; Mörs, June 29–July 1 (Hagenmeyer, "Chronologie," nos. 43, 44, 45, 46, 48).

[26] Albert, *Historia*, pp. 299, 304, 305, 427. Hagenmeyer, "Chronologie," no. 64, suggests that this defeat occurred about the middle of August.

Too many eager pilgrims, inspired by religious enthusiasm, and too few fighting men, had marched away in these early bands. Forty years after, Anna Comnena still believed that the preaching of Peter had aroused the religious fervor of the crusading movement, but, she explains, shrewd, perverse men, such as Bohemond, made use of these simple folk to promote their own selfish ends. Her father understood all this quite well, she says, because he knew how naive the westerners were, and she makes the vanity of Hugh of Vermandois seem ridiculous. Nevertheless, most of our information about Hugh's journey comes from her account.[27]

Hugh, whom she calls Ubos, announced his departure from France in a bombastic letter to Alexius, making the preposterous claim that he was the "basileus of basileis, the greatest on earth," and being of royal blood, he demanded that he be honored with an appropriate reception when he arrived at Constantinople. The second son of king Henry I and his second wife, Anna, the princess of Kiev, Hugh had obtained his feudal possessions by marrying the daughter of the count of Vermandois. He departed about the middle of August 1096, with a respectable following. When he reached Rome, the pope gave him the standard of St. Peter, an honor of which he proudly informed the emperor when he sent a second announcement of his coming.[28]

Alexius, his daughter recalled, instructed his nephew, John Comnenus, then stationed at Dyrrachium, to welcome Hugh when he arrived. Before setting sail from Bari, Hugh sent a delegation of twenty-four resplendent knights to warn the governor that he was coming. Fulcher briefly states that Hugh, "the first of the heroes who crossed the sea, landed at the city of Dyrrachium in Bulgaria, with his personal following, but having imprudently departed with a scant army, he was detained by the citizens there and taken to Constantinople, where he was detained for a time, not altogether free." There are other references to his not being free, but according to Anna, he arrived with "a scant army" because most of his followers had been lost in a storm. Only good fortune had permitted Hugh to land on the shore somewhere between Cape Pali and Dyrrachium, where he was picked up bedraggled and forlorn and taken before John Comnenus, who fed and refitted him, and sent him on to Constantinople under the escort of a high official.

[27] *Alexiad*, X, vii, 1–5 (ed. Leib) II, 213–215.

[28] For his surname "the Great" or "Magnus" which the chroniclers use, see Bréhier, *Gesta*, p. 14, n. 3, who explains that "magnus" was a corruption of "mainsné," the younger, i. e. *moins né* or the "cadet".

Godfrey of Bouillon departed from the west about the same time as Hugh, but, as he followed the northern route, he was longer on the way.[29] If Godfrey, like all "Celts" [Κελτοί], was proud of his race, as Anna says, it was not without good reason, as he was descended from Charlemagne. A second son, like Hugh, he did not inherit the county of Boulogne and the extensive English holdings of his father. A promising future seemed to open in his fifteenth year, when his maternal uncle, Godfrey the Hunchback, duke of Lower Lorraine, was assassinated, and on his deathbed designated his nephew as his heir. But the emperor, Henry IV, gave the duchy to his own infant son, Conrad, conferring the margraviate of Antwerp on Godfrey by way of consolation. This and the county of Bouillon, with other family possessions in the neighborhood, made Godfrey a feudal lord of some importance. He aided the emperor in his wars, and may have participated in the siege of Rome.[30] Finally, in 1089, Henry made him duke of Lower Lorraine; but, either because ducal authority had deteriorated, or because Godfrey was a poor administrator, he seems to have derived neither power nor wealth from the duchy. Certainly he had to finance his crusade chiefly from his hereditary holdings and was able to sell or mortgage Verdun for a sum said to have been substantial, while the bishop of Liége gave either 1,300 or 1,500 marks of silver for Bouillon. As there is no evidence that he realized anything from his duchy, Anna's statement that "the man was very rich" is not justified.

No trustworthy evidence explains why Godfrey took the cross. The *Chronicle of Zimmern* relates that he decided to go on this pilgrimage while he was ill during the siege of Rome. Caffaro says that he went on some such pilgrimage, then visited Raymond of St. Gilles and Adhémar, and with them initiated the crusade. All this is as legendary as his later reputation for piety, to which William of Tyre contributed by saying that he took monks with him on the crusade, "notable for their holy lives," to celebrate the divine offices. In reality, he had ruined monasteries in the neighborhood of Bouillon by his exactions, and it was his mother, the pious Ida, who induced him to make a few donations to churches to save his reputation before he departed. When crusading excitement spread throughout the Walloon region, and neighboring lords made

[29] See J. C. Andressohn, *The Ancestry and Life of Godfrey of Bouillon*. Albert is the chief source for his march.

[30] At least Albert, p. 440, has Godfrey recall, while pestilence raged at Antioch in 1098, that five hundred knights perished similarly before Rome.

ready for the pilgrimage, Godfrey decided to go along. Being the duke, he was made leader of the army.

The more important of Godfrey's companions, *fortissimi milites et principes clarissimi*, seem to have come chiefly from the region about Godfrey's holdings. Baldwin, the duke's younger brother, who cautiously took time to make up his mind, was accompanied by his wife. Another Baldwin, of Le Bourg, was a kinsman of Godfrey, possibly a cousin. The oldest brother, Eustace, count of Boulogne, who inherited his father's extensive lands in England, also went on the crusade, but whether with Godfrey or with Robert of Normandy is uncertain.[31] A third Baldwin, count of Hainault, Reginald, count of Toul, and a bishop, the schismatic Otto of Strassburg, are mentioned. Godfrey's followers seem to have been adequately prepared, and he may have maintained a personal following from his own resources. The size of this army cannot be estimated from the dubious figures in the chronicles.[32]

Albert says that Godfrey was on the march by the middle of August, and was at the Hungarian border for three weeks in September. The delay was due to the suspicions that king Coloman had of the intentions of any armed forces after the troubles he had had with Folkmar, Gottschalk, and Emicho. So, while his people were encamped at Tollenburg (either Bruck an der Leitha or possibly Tulln), Godfrey sent forward a delegation of twelve, headed by Geoffrey of Esch, who had been engaged in previous negotiations with the Hungarian king. According to Albert, they rather tactlessly asked Coloman why he had been killing Christian pilgrims, and he replied that he had found it necessary to exterminate them because they were unholy robbers. He demanded a personal conference with Godfrey, and the two met on a bridge; but, still unconvinced, the king invited the duke to visit at his court. Godfrey accepted, and after eight days finally obtained permission to march through Hungary, on condition that his brother Baldwin and his family be given as hostages to guarantee that there would be no pillage. When Godfrey returned to camp with this proposal, Baldwin angrily refused, but yielded when the duke offered to be hostage himself. Godfrey then ordered heralds to proclaim that anyone guilty of foraging would be put to death,

[31] C. W. David, *Robert Curthose*, Appendix D. He seems to have returned home with Robert.

[32] Baldwin of Stavelot and others were "ex familia ipsius ducis" (Albert, p. 300). When the final march on Jerusalem began, Godfrey's army was rated as equal to that of Robert of Normandy and larger than those of Tancred and Robert of Flanders (Raymond of Aguilers, *Historia*, in *RHC, Occ.*, IV, 271).

while Coloman warned his people that all who failed to provide necessities at fair prices would be punished, and he undertook to escort the crusaders with a strong force of horsemen.

The march through Hungary was without incident, and the army reached Semlin late in November. As soon as the army had crossed the Sava into Bulgaria, king Coloman appeared on the other bank and surrendered the hostages. As Belgrade was deserted, the crusaders marched on toward Nish. Byzantine officials met them on the way with assurances that free markets would be available at towns along the route, and Godfrey promised that his people would take nothing except fodder for their horses. At Nish, Godfrey received a generous supply of food as a gift, and his people found abundant supplies for sale. As equally satisfactory markets were provided at Sofia and Philippopolis, the army halted to rest and replenish supplies at both places. Before leaving the latter city, however, Godfrey was greatly disturbed by a rumor that Hugh, William the Carpenter, Drogo, and Clarebold were prisoners of the emperor, and he immediately sent a demand to Alexius that the captives be released. But Baldwin, count of Hainault, and Henry of Esch, excited by the report of handsome imperial gifts to Hugh, departed at dawn in order to reach Constantinople before the generosity of the basileus might be dried up by Godfrey's ultimatum.[33]

At Selymbria (Silivri) on the Sea of Marmara, Godfrey permitted eight days of pillage in the surrounding region because the emperor was holding Hugh and his companions, Albert says. But, when Alexius sent two Franks with the assurance that the count of Vermandois either was, or would be, released, Godfrey called in the foragers, and moved on to the outskirts of Constantinople just in time to celebrate Christmas there. Tension was relieved when Hugh came out to the camp, and imperial officials invited Godfrey to an audience with the emperor. But Godfrey, still suspicious of Alexius, declined. Albert explains that certain men, "from Frankish lands," secretly advised Godfrey not to enter the city because the Greeks were not to be trusted. Also unconfirmed, and still less plausible, is a tale about Bohemond proposing that Godfrey join him in an attack on Constantinople.[34]

[33] Albert, pp. 304–305.

[34] Anna says that a "count Raoul" arrived soon after with some 15,000 followers, both horse and foot. Leib says that he has not been identified, but Runciman suggests that he may have been Reginald, count of Toul, and that instead of following Godfrey, he may have gone down into Italy and taken the southern route. He ingeniously suggests that Anna telescoped "Rainald de Toul" into "Raoul": *Alexiad* (ed. Leib), II, p. 227, n. 1; Runciman, *History of the Crusades*, I, 152–153.

Bohemond crossed the sea fifteen days after Hugh. It was a familiar crossing to this eldest son of Robert Guiscard, who had been his father's second in command during the war in Albania from 1081 to 1085. So confident had Guiscard been at that time that he had made Bohemond heir to all future conquests on the eastern side of the Adriatic; Roger Borsa, second son by a second marriage, was to inherit his Italian possessions.[35] When Guiscard died and the bold adventure overseas failed, Bohemond returned to wrest what land he could from his less capable half-brother, and although Borsa had the powerful support of his uncle, count Roger of Sicily, Bohemond became one of the strongest lords in southern Italy. Nevertheless, what he could hope for there was not enough to satisfy his ambition, and he welcomed the greater opportunity that the crusade offered.

The historian of his expedition, the author of the *Gesta*, would have his readers believe that Bohemond did not know about the armies that were forming beyond the mountains until French crusaders came down into Italy. When certain that they were fighting men, and on their way to rescue the Holy Sepulcher, he quickly made up his mind to take the cross. This was seven or eight months after Clermont while he was coöperating with his brother and uncle in besieging Amalfi. Dramatically he cut an expensive cloak into crosses, and won so many followers for his crusade that the siege had to be raised. There were many young men in Italy, says Malaterra, "who were eager for something new, as is natural at that age."

The dominating personality of this large, powerful man, whose eyes flashed fire, fascinated young Anna Comnena. At the age of forty, probably because of his military experience in Albania, he raised an army more quickly than any of the other leaders. How he financed his expedition is very obscure, although it is not likely that he undertook to provide for any followers, except those in his personal following, and this *famulatus*, mentioned in the *Gesta*, may have been composed of his kinsmen. Tancred, his twenty-year-old nephew, it is said, had to be persuaded by gifts, flattery, and the position of second in command, whereas his brother William, without waiting for Bohemond, joined Hugh and was escorted with him to Constantinople. Also mentioned are two cousins, Richard of the Principate and Rainulf with his son Richard. Bohemond's army was small, Anna says, "because he

[35] R. B. Yewdale, *Bohemond*, pp. 23–24. The first marriage seems to have been dissolved on grounds of consanguinity. Anna jeers that he was not of noble birth.

lacked money." As he did not transport all his people at one time, it may be inferred that shipping facilities were not available to many of the pilgrims always so eager to follow crusading armies.[36]

The Normans landed between Dyrrachium and Avlona. Byzantine officials were ready for them, and provisions seem to have been plentiful at a place called "Dropuli", in the valley of the Viyosa river, where the different contingents became united into one army. Then marching from village to village, the anonymous author of the *Gesta* says, they came to Castoria, where Christmas was celebrated. This was familiar territory to Bohemond, but his previous occupation of this region had not been forgotten by the natives, who, from either hatred or fear of the Normans, refused to sell them provisions. Bohemond, although he was anxious to allay Greek suspicions of his intentions, and had ordered that his men do no foraging, had to permit them to get food. They took cattle, horses, asses — "everything that we found," says the chronicler. Somewhere on the way between Castoria and the Vardar, they felt justified in destroying a town because it was inhabited by heretics, Paulicians. At the Vardar, the imperial escort caught up with them, and attacked those in the rear who had not crossed the river. Tancred and others recrossed and drove the imperials away.

After passing Thessalonica, they were met by the delegation which Bohemond had sent to Constantinople after his landing, and with them was an important Byzantine official. Although he gave assurance that provisions would be available the rest of the way, Norman propensities to pillage were not easily restrained. When young Tancred proposed to storm and loot a town which was full of supplies, Bohemond became very angry. The citizens, when they realized that he had saved them, were so grateful that they came forth in a procession, bearing crosses to bless him as their protector. It seems, however, that Bohemond was not able to prevent all foraging, and after hearing the complaints of imperial officials, he ordered his men to return all the animals that they had stolen. At Roussa (Keshan), Bohemond decided to accept the invitation of Alexius to leave his army and hurry on to Constantinople. But no sooner was he gone than young Tancred, who as second in command was left in charge of the army, gave

[36] Lupus Protospatarius, *Annales* (*MGH, SS.*, V), p. 62, says that more than 500 knights took the cross at Amalfi. For Tancred see R. H. Nicholson, *Tancred*; Radulf of Caen, *Gesta Tancredi*, iii (*RHC, Occ.*, III), p. 607. Anna's remarks about her father's suspicions were justified by later events, and may be hindsight on her part. The same may be true of William of Malmesbury's statement that Bohemond actually originated the crusade to provide an excuse for conquest in the empire: William of Malmesbury, *Gesta regum* (Rolls Series), II, 390. (The "Principate" was Salerno.)

them their long-desired chance to live off the country. "Seeing the pilgrims buying food," as the anonymous author of the *Gesta* puts it, he "at once led them off the main road into a pleasant valley, where they could live happily because they found all good things there." In the meantime, Bohemond arrived at the capital city on April 10, eager to make a favorable impression on his former enemy, Alexius. He was assigned quarters outside the city. According to a rumor, he made his servants eat the food provided in order to see whether it contained poison.

The largest army on the crusade was that of Raymond, count of Toulouse, who was accompanied by Adhémar, bishop of Le Puy, the papal legate.[37] Raymond, the great lord of southern France, the wealthiest of all the crusading leaders according to the chroniclers, aided many poor soldiers to equip themselves for the journey. The pope, in his letter to the Flemings, had suggested that Raymond would provide for the needy. But this army also had the largest following of noncombatants, and Raymond seems to have felt that it was his duty to help all pilgrims. Raymond of Aguilers says that this army was composed of those who came from Burgundy, Auvergne, Gascony, and Gothia, who were called Provençals, while all others were French (*Francigenae*), but to the enemy all were known as Franks.[38] These provinces, situated along the Mediterranean, were developing a brilliant civilization, and, because of interest in the holy war in Spain, this was the region upon which Urban probably counted most for support of the crusade.

Raymond, aged about fifty-five years, was decidedly old for that period when the life expectancy of the military class was low, and it is not surprising that he was ill oftener than others, once almost to death. However, he survived Adhémar, a younger man, the papal legate, who was a fighting prelate, a good horseman who knew how to wear the armor of a knight.[39] The reports that Raymond took a vow never to return home, and sold all his possessions, may have arisen because he was old, but it is more likely that they arose because he stayed in the east until he died. Also,

[37] The account of the march of this army is given by Raymond's chaplain, Raymond of Aguilers, who wrote a history of the crusade, *Historia Francorum qui ceperunt Iherusalem*, i–ii (*RHC, Occ.*, III), pp. 235–238.

[38] Raymond of Aguilers, *Historia*, p. 244; Baldric of Dol (*RHC, Occ.*, IV), p. 16; W.Porges, "The Clergy, the Poor, and the Non-Combatants on the First Crusade," *Speculum*, XXI (1946), 10–11.

[39] "Gracilis ad equitandum" and "lorica vestitus et casside" (Robert the Monk, *Historia* [*RHC, Occ.*, III], p. 834). There were rumors that both men had been on pilgrimages to Jerusalem, and that Raymond had lost one eye in a fight with the doorkeeper of the Holy Sepulcher.

he took his wife and youngest son with him and left Bertram, his son by his first wife, in charge of his possessions in Languedoc. About all that can be learned about how he financed his expedition comes from a few charters; grants to such abbeys as St. Gilles, Chaise-Dieu, and the church of Le Puy, together with a suggestion that he sold Forez. Inasmuch as Raymond of Aguilers noted that none died of starvation during the march through Dalmatia where little or no food could be obtained along the way, Raymond and the nobles who went with him seem to have made adequate preparation. Among the lords of southern France known to have been in his army, several were his own vassals. Perhaps because of Adhémar, the clergy were well represented and seem to have exerted considerable influence on the conduct of the crusade. The chaplain of Adhémar, Bernard of Valence, became patriarch of Antioch.[40]

Either the march through northern Italy and around the northern end of the Adriatic was not recorded by Raymond of Aguilers, or the first section of his account has been lost, and so his story begins with the entrance into Dalmatia (which he calls *Sclavonia*), in which wilderness they wandered for forty days, at least. They saw neither wild animal nor bird, partly because of the fog and mist, which the good chaplain says was often so thick that it had to be pushed away. As it was winter, the roads through this mountainous region were difficult, and the natives would neither sell provisions nor offer guidance. Moreover, some of them followed the rear of the army to rob and kill stragglers, "the poor, aged, and infirm." The count tried to protect them, and was always the last to seek rest, sometimes not till the cock crew; and once when he was caught in an ambush he nearly lost his life. Savagely he retaliated by mutilating prisoners and leaving them behind to terrify others. When they reached Scutari (now in Albania), the count induced the local chieftain to agree to grant markets, but the only outcome seems to have been quarrels in which some of his men were killed. They hurried on, anxious to reach Byzantine territory, where they believed that the people were their Christian brothers and allies.

But the good chaplain and the hungry pilgrims also were disappointed when imperial troops attacked "peaceful folk" in groves and villages far from the camp, and although "the duke", John Comnenus, promised peace, two noble lords were killed. But Raymond, it seems clear, was willing to coöperate with Byzantine

[40] J. H. Hill, in an unpublished doctoral dissertation, gives a very useful list. See also Porges for the clergy (*Speculum*, XXI, 21–23).

policy, for his chronicler complains that although there were opportunities to retaliate, it seemed wiser to continue the march. But the military escort, he bitterly complains, was always in front and behind, on the right and on the left, carrying out the imperial instructions, as indicated by Anna. Unfortunately, in the valley of Pelagonia, when Pecheneg mercenaries found the papal legate away from camp, they threw him from his mule, and injured him severely with a blow on the head. Fortunately for Adhémar, his captors made so much commotion that crusaders rushed forth to rescue him. Not long after, because of an ambush, Raymond says, the crusaders attacked the imperial troops, killing some and putting the rest to flight. And so suspicious of the Greeks was Raymond of Aguilers that he was not impressed by a friendly letter which arrived from the emperor about this time when they were still hemmed in by Byzantine troops. Following the Egnatian way, the army reached Thessalonica about the beginning of April, where Adhémar, who had not recovered from his injury, decided to wait for his brother, Hugh of Monteil, who had been delayed at Dyrrachium by illness.

At Roussa, where the author of the *Gesta* notes that the Normans had been welcomed some two weeks earlier, the Provençals met a reception so little to their liking that they stormed over the walls, shouting "Toulouse, Toulouse", and joyfully looted the town. As Runciman suggests, it is probable that the Normans and also the Flemings had exhausted the stock of supplies intended for the crusaders and pilgrims.[41] At Rodosto (Tekirdagh) another brush with imperials took place, but it was not serious enough to prevent Raymond from accepting the invitation of Alexius to come to Constantinople ahead of his army. Chaplain Raymond was bitter about this when he wrote his history, and it was his belief that Raymond had been misled by his own envoys whom he had sent to Constantinople earlier. They had been corrupted because they had accepted money from the emperor, who had promised them much for the future. But he adds that Raymond was told that Bohemond, Robert of Flanders, and Godfrey were eager to see him. The count reached Constantinople April 21, where he was well received.

Friendly negotiations with Alexius were interrupted by news that the Provençals had been disastrously defeated by imperial troops. Raymond of Aguilers was so mortified by what happened that his lamentations merely reveal that the crusaders fled before

[41] Runciman, *History of the Crusades*, I, 161–162.

their attackers and abandoned arms and baggage. No doubt they had given provocation by excessive pillage, and like the armies of Godfrey and Bohemond, the Provençals had exhausted their resources sufficiently to resort to foraging on the last stage of the march. But the reaction of the Byzantine troops on this occasion seems to have been unusually vigorous, and count Raymond became so angry that he flew into a rage and had to be calmed by the other leaders. His army arrived at Constantinople on April 27.

The account of the march to Constantinople given by Raymond of Aguilers indicates that the imperial military escort had much trouble with this army. As it was a large army, Byzantine officials may have had difficulty in providing enough food along the way, and the poor pilgrims — of whom there were many — were always ready to forage. *Provinciales ad victualia* was their reputation according to Radulf (Ralph) of Caen.[42] The good chaplain undoubtedly reflects the general resentment of his people, who were opposed to any police restrictions, but it must be noted that he is quite definitely anti-Greek in his history.

Robert of Flanders had arrived at Constantinople before Raymond, but we have no account of his march across the Balkan peninsula. When he crossed the Adriatic in the winter, and left his companions Robert of Normandy and Stephen of Blois behind in southern Italy, the chronicler, Fulcher of Chartres, stayed with them. Robert II, count of Flanders, dubbed the "Jerusalemite", was the son of Robert I, "the Frisian", who had made a pilgrimage to Jerusalem sometime between 1087 and 1091, possibly to atone for complicity in the assassination of Godfrey the Hunchback, the maternal uncle of Godfrey of Bouillon. After his return he sent five hundred horsemen to Alexius, and probably he was the recipient of the original of the "spurious" letter from Alexius to a count of Flanders. His son, therefore, had every opportunity to learn about the east, and Urban may have had this in mind when he wrote his letter to the Flemings soon after Clermont. The pope had every reason to be satisfied with the response made to his appeal by Robert, who seems to have been much influenced by the religious appeal of the crusade. "The Holy Ghost fired his heart to check the wickedness of the pagans," the motive attributed to him in a document subscribed to by his wife, seems to be a fairly accurate statement. He gave evidence of pious inclinations while on the expedition.[43]

[42] Radulf of Caen, *Gesta Tancredi*, lxi (*RHC, Occ.*, III), p. 651.
[43] M. M. Knappen, "Robert II of Flanders in the First Crusade," *Munro Essays*, pp. 79–100.

Robert had inherited a prosperous feudal state which his father had reduced to reasonably good order, and he seems to have been able to raise funds adequate for the demands of the journey. At least he preferred a gift in relics to gold, silver, and jewels when he was in southern Italy. He was able to raise an effective army, and by his decision to make the rough winter crossing of the Adriatic he probably discouraged most of the Flemish pilgrims who may have followed him to Italy. The military strength of his possessions may have been as great as 1,000 horsemen, but how many of these volunteered for the crusade cannot be ascertained. In 1099, when count Raymond sought to subsidize other leaders for the march on Jerusalem, he estimated that Robert's strength was six-tenths of that of Godfrey or Robert of Normandy. His wife thought that he departed with a very large following.[44]

With Robert went his first cousin, Robert of Normandy, and his cousin by marriage, Stephen of Blois, husband of Adèle, sister of Robert of Normandy. As noted above, it is not clear whether his neighbor, Eustace III of Boulogne, elder brother of Godfrey, marched with his brother or with Robert of Normandy.[45] Robert, duke of Normandy, oldest son of William the Conqueror, was rapidly losing control over his duchy, partly because of inefficient government on his own part and partly because his brother, William II, king of England, was endeavoring to take it away from him. The crusade offered an opportunity to escape from this unpleasant situation, and he was quite ready to mortgage Normandy for money for his expenses. This was made possible by the negotiations of Gerento, abbot of St. Bénigne of Dijon, whom Urban had commissioned to make peace between the brothers and, when he was in England in April, the abbot seems to have persuaded William to make a loan of 10,000 marks of silver to the duke, with Normandy pledged as security. To obtain such a large sum, king William levied taxes on the English people, including the clergy, who protested vigorously, but in September when he crossed over to Normandy he paid Robert the whole amount. With finances arranged, Robert, as the chroniclers say, took the cross "at the admonition of pope Urban" and "by the counsel of certain men of religion." A crusading army was recruited, a "great army" in the eyes of the chronicler, and in addition to a goodly following of adventurous Norman lords, it contained con-

[44] "Copiosa manu armata" (Hagenmeyer, *Epistulae*, p. 142); F. Lot, *L'Art militaire et les armées du moyen âge*, I, 130; Runciman, *History of the Crusades*, I, 339, estimates that Robert could have had 600 cavalrymen.

[45] See above, p. 268. In the east, however, Eustace served under his brother.

tingents from the neighboring feudal states of Brittany, Perche, and Maine. But the Norman lords in England were still too busy establishing themselves in that conquered land to be lured away, and only two are known to have followed the duke. Representing the Norman church were two bishops who were at Clermont, Odo of Bayeux and Gilbert of Évreux. Robert also took along as chaplain his sister's tutor, Arnulf of Chocques, who was destined to have an important career overseas.[46]

In the meantime, another lord in western France was preparing to go crusading. Stephen, count of Chartres and Blois, was a person of importance in the feudal world, ruler of as many castles as the days in the year, says Guibert. He has revealed himself in the letters which he wrote to impress "his sweetest and most amiable wife", Adèle, daughter of William the Conqueror.[47] His colleagues thought well enough of him to elect him quartermaster general for a time and, even after he had disgraced himself by deserting the expedition, Fulcher of Chartres, the historian who accompanied him, could say "all of us grieved since he was a very noble man and valiant in arms."[48] He was ready to depart with his brother-in-law, Robert of Normandy, and his wife's cousin, Robert of Flanders, in October. The abbot Gerento and his secretary, Hugh of Flavigny, went as far as Pontarlier to say farewell as they began the crossing of the Alps.

As the pope was at Lucca, the leaders "and others of us who wished, spoke with him and received his blessing," says Fulcher. At Rome, in the church of St. Peter, they were annoyed by partisans of the anti-pope, but they did not stop to retaliate. Marching "down the old Roman road," they stopped at Monte Cassino to commend themselves to St. Benedict, before going on to the seaport of Bari, where more prayers were said in the church of St. Nicholas. "We thought to cross the sea at that time," but the winter weather was so unfavorable in the opinion of the sailors that Robert of Normandy and Stephen were glad to accept the hospitality of the south Italian Normans. Robert of Flanders was urged to do likewise by his sister and her husband, Roger Borsa, who gave him relics, said to be some hair of the Virgin

[46] C. W. David, *Robert Curthose*, pp. 90–96, and the list of Robert's followers in Appendix D, pp. 221–226. For England, see David, *De expugnatione Lyxbonensi* (Records of Civilization, XXIV), pp. 4–12.

[47] Hagenmeyer, *Epistulae*, nos. IV, X, pp. 138–140, 149–152. Unfortunately, the first letter from Stephen of Blois to his wife, Adèle, has been lost. It gave a description of his experiences on the way to Constantinople.

[48] For Robert of Normandy and Stephen of Blois see Fulcher of Chartres, *Historia Hierosolymitana* (ed. Hagenmeyer), pp. 154–170.

Mary and bones of Saints Matthew and Nicholas, which he sent home to his wife. Then, no doubt with the help of his brother-in-law, he was able to obtain passage and crossed the Adriatic, to hurry on to Constantinople.[49]

If the mysterious *komes prebentzas* who followed Bohemond, according to Anna, was Baldwin II of Alost, count of Ghent, a follower of Robert of Flanders, his crossing probably took place during the winter or early spring.[50] The count, whoever he was, leased, for 6,000 gold staters, a large pirate ship that had three masts and two hundred rowers. Unfortunately, the Byzantine fleet was on the lookout for pirates and attacked and boarded the ship. The hero, in the long story told by Anna, was Marianus Mavrocatacalon, who commanded the attacking squadron. The count and his party were eventually landed, and it may be assumed that they went on to Constantinople to join the other crusading armies.[51]

When spring came, Robert and Stephen collected their followers at Brindisi, where ships were ready to transport them to Epirus. On April 5, as the embarkation was beginning, a large ship broke in two, and four hundred persons, as well as horses and mules, were drowned; also, "much money" was lost. This catastrophe discouraged many who were waiting from risking their lives on the deceptive water, and they gave up their pilgrimage forthwith and turned homeward. The others "thrust themselves upon the sea," to find it very peaceful as the wind died down, and they were virtually becalmed for three days. Not until the fourth day were they able to land at two places near Dyrrachium. Then, as Fulcher says, "joyfully we resumed our dry-land journey."

The march along the Via Egnatia did not provide many incidents that seemed worthy of note to the chronicler, although he listed the towns to which they came along the way. A swollen mountain stream swept a few pilgrims to their death; others were saved by knights who rode their horses into the torrent. The Vardar was successfully forded, and soon after they found Thessalonica to be a "city abounding in all goods". The arrival at Constantinople was about May 14, 1097. No brushes with a Byzantine escort are reported, and there seems to have been no difficulty about obtaining food, which indicates that the crusaders

[49] Fulcher of Chartres, *Historia*, pp. 167–168.

[50] Runciman, *History of the Crusades*, I, 167, n. 1, accepts this identification from A. Maricq, "Un 'comte de Brabant' et des 'Brabançons' dans deux textes byzantins," *Bulletin de la classe des lettres*, Royal Academy of Belgium, ser. 5, XXXIV (1948), 463–480.

[51] *Alexiad* (ed. Leib), II, 215–220.

were able to buy what they needed. No doubt the long wait in Apulia, and the fear and cost of transportation by sea, had eliminated many of the impecunious pilgrims. While encamped without the walls, small parties were permitted to enter the city to visit the churches. Among these visitors was the chronicler Fulcher, who was greatly impressed by the sights of this "excellent and beautiful city".

With the arrival of Robert of Normandy and Stephen, the first stage of the crusade, the march of the armies to Constantinople, was ended. That the Byzantine officials had handled the large numbers of crusaders and pilgrims very successfully is indicated by the rarity, as a whole, of the complaints made by the western chroniclers who accompanied the armies. But it must also be noted that the crusading leaders had managed their undisciplined crowds very well, especially in restraining the propensity of their men to forage. For, although most of the crusaders, and also the noncombatant pilgrims, seem to have understood that they had to have the means to buy food, they were all ready enough to forage when the opportunity came. Certainly, this was true of the Lorrainers, the Normans from southern Italy, and the Provençals. That they were difficult folk to manage, Alexius knew very well, and as they arrived at Constantinople, he undertook to come to terms with the leaders, one by one.

IX
THE FIRST CRUSADE: CONSTANTINOPLE TO ANTIOCH

The journeys of the crusaders through the Balkan peninsula gave the emperor Alexius time to plan his policy toward their leaders when the armies should arrive at Constantinople. However little he might have wanted an expedition of the type that was coming, he could see that, if they were carefully directed, the crusaders could be of great advantage to his empire, which he not unreasonably regarded as the main bulwark of Christendom. But they must be handled delicately. In 1096 the empire was enjoying a lull in the Turkish wars. Alexius had not yet been able to win back much territory, except along the coasts of the Sea of Marmara and the Aegean. But the emir Chaka of Smyrna (İzmir), the most menacing of the empire's enemies, had been murdered in 1092 by his son-in-law, the Selchükid Kilij (or Kilich) Arslan, at the emperor's instigation. Kilij Arslan himself, established at Nicaea and calling himself sultan (Arabic, *sulṭān*), was alarmed by the growing power of the Dānishmendid dynasty farther to the

The story of the crusaders' march across Anatolia is covered by the same Latin sources as for the previous chapter and by Anna Comnena. As the crusade moved eastward, Armenian sources are more important, in particular, Matthew of Edessa (extracts in Armenian, with a not always accurate French translation, in *RHC*, *Arm.*, I, and a full translation of the *Chronique* by E. Dulaurier, Paris, 1858). Matthew wrote before 1140. He hated the Byzantines, about whom his information is copious but inaccurate. He is more objective about the Franks, and seems to have obtained information from some Frankish soldiers. About his own city and compatriots he is reliable. Of Jacobite sources, Michael the Syrian, patriarch of Antioch, who wrote at the end of the twelfth century, provides a little information (*Chronique de Michel le Syrien*, ed. and tr. J. B. Chabot, 4 vols., Paris, 1899–1910). Bar-Hebraeus copies from him, and he is supplemented by an anonymous chronicle of which only the first portions have been properly edited (A. S. Tritton and H. A. R. Gibb, "The First and Second Crusades from an Anonymous Syriac Chronicle," *Journal of the Royal Asiatic Society*, 1933, pp. 69–101, 273–305). Arabic sources are of negligible importance until the crusade reaches Antioch.

The same secondary sources are valuable as in the preceding chapter, with the addition of articles by J. Laurent on the Armenians, notably, "Des Grecs aux croisés: étude sur l'histoire d'Édesse," *Byzantion*, I (1924), 367–449, and "Les Arméniens de Cilicie," *Mélanges Schlumberger*, I (Paris, 1924), 159–168. The military history of the march across Anatolia is covered in C. W. C. Oman, *History of the Art of War in the Middle Ages* (2nd ed., 2 vols., London, 1924), and F. Lot, *L'Art militaire et les armées du moyen âge*, 2 vols. (Paris, 1946).

east and of the emir Ḥasan of Cappadocia. It was the emperor's aim to follow the traditions of Byzantine diplomacy and play off the Turkish princes against each other until the Christians could collect a force strong enough to deal them a deadly blow. In the meantime it was essential to avoid any premature and precipitate attack that might frighten the Turks into union.[1]

The first crusaders to reach Constantinople presented a problem to the emperor's police rather than to his politicians. In the middle of July 1096, Walter Sans-Avoir ("the Penniless") arrived before the capital at the head of two or three thousand French peasants. This was the vanguard of the huge disorganized rabble that the preaching of Peter the Hermit and his fellows had urged eastward. As the preceding chapter has indicated, the Peasants' or People's Crusade had not been willing to wait while the princes organized their expeditions; and Walter and his Frenchmen had been more impatient even than Peter the Hermit, whom they had left at Cologne. Walter had had trouble with the Byzantine authorities when he entered the empire at Belgrade, but by the time that he approached Constantinople his company was satisfactorily controlled by the imperial police. The visitors were established in a camp in the suburbs. There they were joined by a stream of pilgrims from Italy, who had crossed the Adriatic from Apulia and had tramped along the Via Egnatia to Constantinople.

Peter the Hermit and the main body of the People's Crusade, which now included thousands of Germans, arrived at Constantinople about a fortnight after Walter, on August 1. Their passage across the Balkans had been turbulent and unfortunate; but the emperor considered that they had been sufficiently punished for their misdeeds and had sent Peter while he was still at Adrianople a gracious message of forgiveness. There seems to have been amongst the Byzantines a sympathetic interest in these humble, enthusiastic pilgrims who had left their homes to fight for Christendom. In spite of their lawlessness they were well received. The emperor himself was eager to see Peter, who had already acquired an almost legendary renown. Peter was summoned to the palace, where he was given handsome presents and good advice. Peter's expedition was not at all impressive from a military point of view. Alexius therefore urged him strongly to wait till the organized armies of the crusading princes arrived.

Peter was impressed by the emperor's counsel, but his followers were more impatient; and in the meantime they alienated sym-

[1] On the Turkish and Byzantine situations see chapters V and VI.

pathy by endless acts of violence. Hardly were they settled in a camp in the suburbs before they began to raid the neighboring villages, breaking into farms and villas and even stealing the lead off the roofs of churches. They were too numerous to be easily controlled by the police. The authorities decided that the sooner they were conveyed across the Bosporus and settled in some camp farther away from the great city, the better. On August 6 the whole expedition, Peter's and Walter's men as well as the Italians, was conveyed across the straits and began to march down the road that ran eastward along the shore of the Sea of Marmara, to Nicomedia. It was an unruly journey. Houses and churches along the way were pillaged. At Nicomedia, which had lain deserted since it had been raided by the Turks a few years before, a quarrel broke out between the Germans and Italians on the one hand and the Frenchmen on the other. The former broke away from Peter's leadership and elected their own chief, a petty Italian noble called Reginald. But they continued to march in conjunction. Probably on the emperor's instructions, they rounded the head of the Gulf of Nicomedia and went westward along its southern shore toward Helenopolis, at the mouth of the Dracon, to a fortified camp by the coast, called by the Byzantines Cibotus and by the Franks Civetot or Civitot. It had been constructed by Alexius a few years previously to house his English mercenaries and seemed a suitable resting place for the expedition till the other crusaders arrived. The district was fertile, and it was easy to keep in touch with the camp by sea from Constantinople.

Unfortunately Civetot was close to the Turkish frontier; and the proximity of the "infidel" proved too great a temptation to the impatient crusaders. They began to raid the villages in the immediate neighborhood, which were inhabited by Christian Greeks. Then they ventured into Turkish territory. Peter, remembering the emperor's advice, tried vainly to restrain them. He no longer had any authority over the Germans and Italians, and even his own Frenchmen turned from him to follow the more dashing leadership of Geoffrey Burel. In the middle of September a large party of Frenchmen penetrated as far as the gates of Nicaea, sacking the villages on the outskirts, rounding up the flocks and herds that they found, and torturing and massacring the villagers, who were Christians, with appalling savagery. They were even said to have roasted babies on spits. The Turkish troops sent out from the city to oppose them were driven back. They returned to Civetot laden with booty.

Their success roused the jealousy of the Germans, who set out in force a few days later under Reginald, and marched past Nicaea, pillaging as they went but sparing Christian lives, till they came to a castle called Xerigordon.[2] They surprised it and finding it well stocked with provisions decided to hold it as a center from which to raid the countryside. On hearing the news Kilij Arslan sent out a strong expedition from Nicaea which arrived before the castle on September 29 and invested it. After the summer the castle cisterns were dry, and the only well was outside the walls. The besieged Germans were soon desperate from thirst. After eight days of misery Reginald surrendered on receiving a promise that his and his friends' lives would be spared if they renounced their faith. All those that remained true to Christianity were slaughtered. Reginald and his fellow apostates were sent into captivity in the east.

The first news to reach Civetot from Xerigordon told of its capture by the Germans; and it was followed by a rumor, sedulously put around by two Turkish spies, that Nicaea too had been taken. The Turks hoped thus to lure the eager crusaders out into ambushes that they had prepared. The trick would have succeeded had not a messenger arrived to tell the true story of Reginald's fate and to warn that the Turks were massing. The excitement in the camp turned into panic. Peter the Hermit set sail at once for Constantinople to beg for additional help from the emperor. Without his restraining influence the crusaders decided to attack the Turks at once. Walter Sans-Avoir persuaded them to await Peter's return; but when Peter delayed at Constantinople, Walter and his friends were overruled by Geoffrey Burel, who shared the general impatience. It was arranged that the whole armed force of the expedition should march out at dawn on October 21.

Some three miles out of Civetot the road to Nicaea passed through a narrow wooded valley, by a village called Dracon. There the Turks lay in ambush. As the horsemen in the van entered the valley they fell on them and drove them back on to the infantry behind. In a few minutes the whole Christian army was fleeing in disorder back to the camp, with the Turks on their heels. There followed a general massacre. Hardly a Christian, soldier or civilian, survived, except for a few boys and girls whose appearance pleased the Turks, and a few soldiers who with Geof-

[2] Xerigordon has not been identified. Albert of Aix, I, 17 (*RHC, Occ.*, IV, 285), places it at three miles from Nicaea; the *Gesta*, I, 2 (ed. Bréhier, p. 6), at four days' journey beyond Nicaea. Anna Comnena, X, vi, 2 (ed. Leib, II, 210), gives no geographical particulars.

frey Burel managed to reach an old castle by the shore, where they improvised defenses. After sundown a Greek with the survivors managed to find a boat and sailed to Constantinople with the news of the disaster. The emperor at once sent a squadron of naval vessels to Civetot. On its approach the Turks retired. The survivors, nearly all severely wounded, were taken off and were settled, deprived of their arms, in a suburb of the capital.[3]

A few days after the collapse of the People's Crusade in the autumn of 1096 the first of the crusading princes arrived at Constantinople. As we have seen in the preceding chapter, this was Hugh of Vermandois, brother to the king of France. Alexius had by now decided on his policy towards the princes. Hugh was received honorifically and given sumptuous presents. In return Alexius demanded of him a promise to restore to the empire lands that it had owned up till the time of the Turkish invasions and an oath of allegiance for any further lands that he might conquer in the east. It was a reasonable demand. The crusaders might well be expected to help the empire to recover its recent frontiers; and if they wished, as Alexius rightly suspected, to carve themselves principalities farther to the east, it was natural that Alexius, as emperor in the east, should be accepted as overlord. That small states should be sovereign and independent was unthought of at that time; and though some of the crusaders may have envisaged the pope rather than any lay potentate as their suzerain, the claims of the eastern emperor could not be disregarded.

Hugh of Vermandois made no objection to taking the oath. He had only a small following with him; and Alexius saw to it, tactfully but firmly, that he was not allowed liberty of movement. But Hugh bore him no resentment for it and was ready to further his policy.[4]

The next prince to arrive was less amenable. Godfrey of Bouillon, duke of Lower Lorraine, arrived at Constantinople on December 23, with his brothers Eustace of Boulogne and Baldwin, and a large and well-equipped army. Some of his followers had

[3] The fullest account of Peter's expedition in Asia is given by Albert of Aix, I, 16–22 (*RHC, Occ.*, IV, 284–289). It seems to have been provided by some responsible friend of Peter's and is not markedly anti-Byzantine. The shorter account in the *Gesta*, I, 2 (ed. Bréhier, pp. 6–12), presumably given to the author by some survivor, is strongly hostile to Byzantium. Anna's account, X, vi, 1–6 (ed. Leib, II, 210–212), on the whole corroborates Albert's, although she believes Peter to have been with the army at the time of the disaster. The Zimmern chronicle (*Chronique de Zimmern*, ed. H. Hagenmeyer, *AOL*, II, 29), lists the Germans killed at Civetot.

[4] Anna Comnena, X, vii, 2–5 (ed. Leib, II, 213–215), admitting that Hugh was not allowed complete liberty; *Gesta*, I, 3 (ed. Bréhier, p. 14); Albert of Aix, II, 7 (*RHC, Occ.*, IV, 304); Fulcher of Chartres (ed. Hagenmeyer), p. 165.

arrived before him; but Godfrey had delayed in Thrace, where his troops had ravaged the countryside, on the news, Godfrey said, that the emperor was keeping Hugh of Vermandois in prison. Two Frenchmen in the emperor's service, Ralph Peeldelau and Roger, son of Dagobert, were able to pacify Godfrey and persuaded him to come on to the capital. He encamped near the head of the Golden Horn.

Alexius at once sent Hugh to Godfrey to ask him to visit the palace and to take the oath of allegiance. Godfrey hesitated. He was suspicious of Hugh's role. He had probably met some of the survivors of the People's Crusade, who chose to blame the emperor for their disaster. It may be that, having taken a personal oath of allegiance to the western emperor when he was appointed to Lorraine, he felt that he could not also pay allegiance to a rival emperor. In any case he wished to wait for the other princes, to see what they intended. He would not fall in with Hugh's suggestions.

Alexius was annoyed, and cut off the supplies that he had promised for Godfrey's troops, whereupon Godfrey's brother Baldwin raided the suburbs till the blockade was lifted. Godfrey at the same time agreed to move his camp to Pera, across the Golden Horn, where it would be better protected from the winter winds and more easily watched by the imperial police. For the next three months Godfrey's army remained there. Discipline was maintained; and Alexius supplied sufficient food. At the end of January 1097, Godfrey was again invited to the palace, but only sent some vassals who would make no promises on his behalf. At the end of March, on the news that other crusader armies were approaching, Alexius brought matters to a head by cutting off supplies once more. Again Baldwin riposted by raiding the suburbs and had a slight success in a skirmish against the emperor's Pecheneg police. Emboldened by this, Godfrey moved his camp from Pera, which he pillaged, and established himself outside the city walls, by the palace of Blachernae, which he began to attack. It was the Thursday in Holy Week, April 2. The city was unprepared for an onslaught; and Alexius was deeply shocked at having to fight on such a day. He calmed the growing panic of the citizens and drew up his troops. His cavalry made a demonstration outside the walls, and his archers on the walls fired over the Franks' heads. Godfrey soon retired, having slain only seven Byzantines. Next morning Hugh of Vermandois went out to make another attempt to induce Godfrey to meet Alexius, but in vain;

and when later in the day an imperial embassy went out towards the camp, Godfrey's men at once attacked them. Alexius then sent out seasoned troops to attack the Franks, who turned and fled. Godfrey realized at last that he was no match for the emperor. He agreed to take the oath and to have his men transported across the Bosporus.

On Easter Sunday Godfrey, Baldwin, and their leading vassals all solemnly promised to restore to the empire its recently lost lands and to regard the emperor as overlord for their further conquests. They were then entertained at a rich banquet and rewarded with gifts of money. Immediately afterwards Godfrey's army was shipped across the straits, and marched from Chalcedon to a camp at Pelecanum, on the road to Nicomedia.[5]

During the next few days a miscellaneous host of crusaders, mainly vassals of Godfrey who had preferred to travel through Italy and along the Via Egnatia, arrived at Constantinople. Their leaders agreed, grudgingly, to take the required oath; and Godfrey and Baldwin were invited to attend the ceremony. It was on this occasion that a boorish knight sat himself down on the emperor's throne, and was severely reproved by Baldwin.

Next week, on April 9, Bohemond of Taranto reached the capital, leaving his nephew Tancred in command of his army, a day's journey from the walls. Bohemond, who had a high reputation as a warrior, was an old enemy of the empire; and Alexius was anxious how he would behave. He arranged at once for a private audience with him. But Bohemond showed himself correct and even friendly and helpful. He took the oath of allegiance without hesitation. Then he asked for appointment as grand domestic of the east, that is, commander-in-chief of all the imperial forces in Asia. It was an ingenious request. As imperial commander he would be in a position to control the whole allied expedition. He would have authority over all the other potential vassals of the empire, and all the recovered territory would be handed over to him. He could later decide what use to make of his power.

It was also an embarrassing request. Alexius distrusted Bohemond but wished to retain his goodwill. He temporized noncommittally, saying neither yes nor no. Meanwhile he discussed with Bohemond the help that the empire could most usefully give to the whole crusading expedition. Bohemond's army was sum-

[5] Anna Comnena, X, ix, 1–X, x, 7 (ed. Leib, II, 220–230), and Albert of Aix, II, 9–16 (*RHC, Occ.*, IV, 305–311), are the two fullest accounts. See F. Chalandon, *Histoire de la première croisade*, pp. 119–129.

moned to Constantinople and taken at once across the Bosporus, to join Godfrey's at Pelecanum. Tancred and his cousin, Richard of Salerno, who did not comprehend Bohemond's game and were unwilling to take the oath to Alexius, slipped through the capital by night.[6] That same day Raymond of St. Gilles, count of Toulouse, arrived and was at once admitted to an interview with the emperor. His army waited behind at Rodosto (Tekirdagh).

Raymond's journey had been uncomfortable, and his temper was frayed. When he came to the palace and found Bohemond apparently on excellent terms with Alexius, he was suspicious. His aim had been to be considered the lay leader of the expedition, and he felt that Bohemond was his chief rival. There were rumors that Bohemond was to become the imperial commander. If this were true, Raymond by accepting the emperor's suzerainty might find himself under Bohemond's orders. He told the emperor that he had come east to do God's work, and God was now his only suzerain. But he added that if the emperor himself were to lead the imperial forces he would serve under him. The other western princes in vain tried to make Raymond change his mind; and Bohemond even said openly that he would support the emperor should Raymond have recourse to arms. Alexius made no attempt to put pressure on Raymond, but withheld gifts from him. Eventually on April 26, Raymond swore a modified oath promising to respect the life and honor of the emperor and to see that nothing was done, by himself or his men, to the emperor's hurt. Such an oath of non-injury was often taken by vassals to their overlord in southern France; and Alexius was satisfied with it. As soon as the oath was taken, Bohemond left to rejoin his army in Asia, and Raymond's army was brought to Constantinople. Raymond took it across the Bosporus two days later, and then returned to Constantinople, to spend a fortnight at the imperial court.

At the end of this visit Raymond and Alexius were on excellent terms. It is possible that Adhémar of Le Puy, armed as legate with the pope's instructions, made it his business to placate the emper-

[6] Anna Comnena, X, xi, 1–7 (ed. Leib, II, 230–234); Albert of Aix, II, 18 (*RHC, Occ.*, IV, 312); *Gesta*, II, 6–7 (ed. Bréhier, pp. 28–34). The last named contains a passage (p. 30, lines 14–20) describing a secret treaty between Alexius and Bohemond, giving the latter Antioch. A. C. Krey, "A Neglected Passage in the *Gesta*," *The Crusades and Other Historical Essays Presented to D. C. Munro* (New York, 1928), pp. 57–78, shows this to be an interpolation made later on Bohemond's orders, before he brought the text of the chronicle to Europe in 1105. Miss Evelyn Jamison, "The Sicilian Norman Kingdom in the Mind of Anglo-Norman Contemporaries," *Proceedings of the British Academy*, XXIV (1938), 245, 279–280, believes that the *Gesta* came to France with Robert of Normandy in 1099–1100, in which case it is hard to see when Bohemond could have inserted the interpolation. The story as the *Gesta* tells it is, however, so unconvincing that Krey's solution can safely be accepted.

or. But a surer bond was the distrust that both count and emperor felt for Bohemond. Henceforward, though he never took a more definite oath, Raymond was a loyal friend to Alexius, who came to like and respect him.[7]

The fourth great crusading army arrived at Constantinople in May. It was led by Robert, duke of Normandy, and his brother-in-law Stephen, count of Blois. Their cousin, Robert of Flanders, who had started out with them, had hurried ahead and had arrived soon after Bohemond. None of these leaders made any difficulty about taking the oath required by Alexius. Stephen of Blois was particularly pleased and impressed by his reception and the gifts that were made to him, and wrote to his wife a warm eulogy of Alexius.[8] When this last army was across the Bosporus Alexius could breathe again. The huge crusading host had been safely escorted through his European provinces and past his wealthy capital, with no serious incident apart from the skirmishes with Godfrey's men. The crusaders were now safely in Asia, ready to fight against the Turks for the recovery of imperial territory; and if they chose later to create buffer states beyond the imperial frontier, they might well add to the security of the frontier, as the emperor's overlordship was apparently assured. But the success of the whole scheme depended on the crusaders' keeping their oath, and a clear decision on what was admittedly former imperial territory. It also required that the emperor's troops should take an active part in the campaign.

The first objective of the crusaders and their imperial ally was Nicaea. Not only was it a city hallowed in Christian history, but it was the capital of the Selchükid potentate, Kilij Arslan ibn-Sulaimān, and it lay on the main military road across Anatolia. Its capture was a necessary preliminary to any advance into Turkish territory. Nicaea, which lay at the eastern end of Lake Ascanius, had been powerfully fortified by the Byzantines, and its fortifications were in good repair. It formed a rough pentagon, its western wall rising straight out of the shallow lake. The inhabitants were still mainly Christian, but it contained a large garrison of Turks as well as the officials of the Selchükid court. The moment for the siege was well chosen. After his easy victory

[7] Anna Comnena, X, xi, 9 (ed. Leib, II, 234–235); Raymond of Aguilers (*RHC, Occ.*, III), p. 238; *Gesta*, II, 6 (ed. Bréhier, p. 52). For Raymond's motives, see S. Runciman, *History of the Crusades*, I (London, 1951), 164 and note.

[8] Fulcher of Chartres, I, viii (ed. Hagenmeyer), pp. 168–176; *Letter of Stephen of Blois* (H. Hagenmeyer, *Epistulae et chartae ad historiam primi belli sacri spectantes: Die Kreuzzugsbriefe aus den Jahren 1088–1100* [Innsbruck, 1902], pp. 138–140).

over Peter the Hermit's rabble, Kĭlĭj Arslan was inclined to despise the whole crusading movement and had gone with his main army eastward, to dispute the suzerainty of Melitene (Malatya) with the Dānishmendid emir. When he heard that a formidable Christian army was advancing against Nicaea, it was too late for him to bring back his full fighting force to defend it.[9]

Godfrey of Bouillon's army left Pelecanum on about April 26 and marched to Nicomedia, where it waited for three days, while Bohemond's army came up, under the command of Tancred, as Bohemond was still at Constantinople, negotiating with the emperor about supplies. They were joined also by Peter the Hermit and the survivors of his party and by a small detachment of Byzantine engineers, with siege machines, under the command of Manuel Butumites. The whole force moved cautiously to Civetot and up through the valley of the Dracon, where the People's Crusade had perished. Scouts and engineers went ahead to open up the track, which was then marked with wooden crosses. On May 6 the army reached Nicaea. Godfrey encamped outside the northern wall and Tancred outside the eastern, leaving the southern for Raymond's army, which arrived ten days later, on May 16. Bohemond had joined his army two or three days before. Robert of Normandy and Stephen of Blois followed with their troops a fortnight later, on June 3. The arrangements that Bohemond had made with the emperor insured a steady supply of provisions to the crusader camp. Alexius himself moved to Pelecanum, where he was in touch with both Nicaea and his capital.

Messengers, one of whom was intercepted by the crusaders, had been sent by the Turkish garrison to urge Kĭlĭj Arslan to rush troops into the city before its investment was complete. But the first Turkish relieving force came too late, a day or two after Raymond's arrival had blocked the southern gate. After a brief skirmish with Raymond's troops it withdrew, to await the main Turkish army. When the commanders of the garrison saw its withdrawal, they established contact with the Byzantine general Butumites to discuss terms of surrender. But almost at once news came that Kĭlĭj Arslan was not far off; and negotiations were abandoned.

Kĭlĭj Arslan was now seriously alarmed. He had not foreseen that the crusading army would be so strong; and he had left his wife and family and much of his treasure in Nicaea. He patched

[9] Matthew of Edessa, *Chronique* (tr. Dulaurier), II, cxlix-cl, pp. 211–212, 215.

up a truce with the Dānishmendids and brought his whole army by forced marches across Anatolia. On May 21 he appeared in the plain before the city and at once attacked Raymond's army. Raymond was for a time hard pressed, as neither Godfrey nor Bohemond dared leave his section of the walls unguarded. But the Flemish contingent came to his aid. The battle raged all day long; but the Turks could make no headway. In the open ground before the walls the crusaders with their better physiques and better arms outmatched their enemies. Their losses were heavy. Many leading knights, including the count of Ghent, were killed, many others severely wounded. But the Turkish losses were heavier. At nightfall Kilij Arslan led off his troops to retreat into the hills and leave Nicaea to its fate.

The crusaders were elated with their victory. They took delight in catapulting the heads of the Turkish dead into the city; and they discovered with glee the ropes that the Turks had brought for binding the prisoners that they had thought to take. But the fortifications were still formidable, and the besieged garrison fought well. Attempts by Raymond to mine the walls failed. Moreover it was found that supplies and messages were reaching the city by way of the lake. It was necessary to ask Alexius to provide a flotilla to blockade the lake. It seems that Alexius deliberately waited for the westerners to make this request in order that they should realize how essential was his coöperation. He sent a few ships, which he put under the command of Butumites, and at the same time added to his military contingent.

Kilij Arslan had told the garrison that it must do as it thought best; he could give no more help. When it saw the emperor's ships and reinforcements, it reëstablished contact with Butumites and opened negotiations. But it still played for time, hoping perhaps that the sultan would make another attempt at its relief. Only when it was told, probably by Butumites, that the crusaders were planning a general assault, did it yield.

The assault was ordered for June 19. But when dawn broke the imperial standards were already waving over the city. The Turks had surrendered during the night to Butumites, who had rushed his troops in through the gates that opened on to the lake. The crusader leaders had probably known that negotiations were in progress; but they certainly had not been told of the final stages. They could not, however, disapprove. Nicaea would have had to be restored to the emperor, and it was satisfactory that it should be taken without further loss of life. But they were hurt that they had not been consulted; while their rank and file, who had hoped to pillage the city and hold the Turkish notables for ransom, found themselves robbed of their prey. Alexius had no intention that his future subjects should undergo a sack, nor did he wish unnecessarily to worsen his relations with the Turks. The crusaders were only allowed in small groups into the city, closely watched by the police, while the sultan's family and nobles were conveyed with all their movable possessions to Constantinople. There the nobles were permitted to ransom themselves. The sultana, the emir Chaka's daughter, and her children were sent back to Kilij Arslan without a ransom, after some months' delay.[10]

Such generosity to the "infidel" enemy struck the average crusader, who already felt himself cheated, as treason to Christendom. Alexius was, however, generous to the crusaders themselves. Every soldier was presented with a special gift of food, and their leaders were summoned to Pelecanum and there were given gold and jewels from the sultan's treasury. Stephen of Blois, who traveled there with Raymond of Toulouse, wrote home to boast of the riches that he had received, and to say that, unlike his comrades, he quite understood that the emperor should not have been able to come in person to Nicaea. In return for the gifts that he made, Alexius insisted that the chief knights who had not yet taken the oath to him should now do so. Tancred demurred and made a truculent scene in the emperor's presence; but in the end Bohemond persuaded him to comply.[11]

However disappointed they might be over the emperor's behavior, the crusaders were cheered by the liberation of Nicaea and looked forward to an easy progress to Palestine. Stephen of Blois wrote hopefully to his wife that in five weeks they would be at Jerusalem, unless, he added, they were held up at Antioch. News of the victory was sent to the west and induced many hesitant crusaders there, notably in the Italian cities, to decide to join the movement.[12]

[10] Anna Comnena, XI, i–ii, 10 (ed. Leib, III, 7–16); *Gesta*, II, 7–8 (ed. Bréhier, pp. 34–40); Fulcher of Chartres, I, x (ed. Hagenmeyer, pp. 182–189); Albert of Aix, II, 20–37 (*RHC, Occ.*, IV, 313–328); Raymond of Aguilers (*RHC, Occ.*, III, 239).

[11] Anna Comnena, XI, iii, 1–2 (ed. Leib, III, 16–17); *Gesta*, II, 9 (ed. Bréhier, p. 42); Raymond of Aguilers (*RHC, Occ.*, III, 239–240); Fulcher of Chartres, I, x (ed. Hagenmeyer, pp. 188–189); *Letters of Stephen of Blois and Anselm of Ribemont* (Hagenmeyer, *Epistulae*, pp. 140, 145). Raymond says that the emperor promised the crusaders all the booty from Nicaea but broke his word. The other western sources comment on his generosity. Anna's account of Tancred's oath-taking is too circumstantial to be doubted, though Radulf of Caen, xviii–xix (*RHC, Occ.*, III, 619–620), later gave the version that Tancred wished to be believed.

[12] Stephen of Blois, *loc. cit.* Most western European chronicles briefly mention the capture of Nicaea.

The next problem was to choose the route across Anatolia. The great military road of the Byzantines ran eastward from Nicaea to the Sangarius (Sakarya) valley, which it left at a village called Leucae to go southeast across the hills to Dorylaeum, near the modern Eskishehir. Thence it continued just south of east, bypassing Ankara, to Caesarea-Mazaca (Kayseri), then across the Anti-Taurus range to Marash and down the valley to the east of the Amanus range to Antioch. But it was not at the moment practicable; the whole section from Dorylaeum to Caesarea was occupied by the Turks. There was a post-road that led from Dorylaeum to Amorium and thence across the salt desert straight to the Cilician Gates. It was the shortest route, but it led across long waterless tracts of country and was suitable only for swiftly moving cavalry. The third road after passing Dorylaeum skirted the salt desert to the south, past Philomelium (Akshehir) and Iconium (Konya) to Tyana, where it forked, one branch crossing the Cilician Gates and the other turning northeast to join the military road at Caesarea-Mazaca. It was this third road which the crusaders decided to take, probably on the emperor's advice. It went through territory into which the Turks had not yet penetrated in full force, and in the past it had been supplied with wells and cisterns at regular intervals.

Whichever road was taken, the next objective must be Dorylaeum. On June 26 the crusader vanguard began to move from Nicaea, and during the next two days the various divisions of the army followed, accompanied by a Byzantine detachment under the general Taticius, who was to supply the guides. A few crusaders, probably those who were still recovering from wounds, stayed behind at Nicaea, in the emperor's service, and were employed to repair and garrison the fortress.

At Leucae the princes met together to plan the order of the march. It was decided to keep the army in two sections, the one to precede the other at a day's interval. The first consisted of the Normans of southern Italy and northern France, the troops of the counts of Flanders and Blois, and the Byzantines, the second of the southern French and the Lorrainers and the troops of Hugh of Vermandois. Bohemond was to be military commander of the former and Raymond of the latter force. As soon as the council was over, Bohemond set out with his army, while Raymond and his comrades, who had ridden ahead of their troops, waited for them to come up.

Kilij Arslan was waiting in the hills; and the common danger had induced the Dānishmendid emir and Ḥasan of Cappadocia to bring detachments to join him. On June 30 the Turkish army was encamped in the valley of the river Tembris (Porsuk) when scouts reported that Bohemond's troops were coming down into the valley of the Bathys a few miles away beyond a low range of hills. The crusaders encamped that evening in the plain. During the night the Turks crept over the hills, and at sunrise they swooped down on to the camp.

Bohemond was ready for an attack. The noncombatants were in the center of the camp, where there were springs; and the women were allotted the task of carrying water up to the front line. Tents were quickly dressed, and knights told to dismount and remain on the defensive. Meanwhile a messenger was sent to the second army, urging it to hurry. One knight, the rude Frenchman who had seated himself on the emperor's throne, disobeyed Bohemond's orders and with his followers charged into the enemy, to be routed with ignominy. The rest of the army patiently awaited the onslaught.

The Turks, whose numbers seemed to be infinite, attacked from all sides, with archers running to the front to discharge their arrows, then making room at once for others. As the hot July morning advanced the Christians wondered how long they could hold out against such a rain of missiles. But Bohemond rode ceaselessly round the lines encouraging them and telling them that flight was impossible and surrender would mean life-long captivity. About midday the vanguard of Raymond's army appeared, with Godfrey and Hugh in front, and Raymond himself close behind. The Turks, who had thought that they had entrapped the whole Christian army, faltered. Godfrey was able to break through into the camp. Then, when Raymond came up, the united army formed a long front, with Bohemond, Robert of Normandy, and Stephen of Blois on the left, Raymond and Robert of Flanders in the center, and Godfrey and Hugh on the right, and moved forward against the enemy. The Turks were not prepared to meet an offensive, and their ammunition was running out. As they hesitated, suddenly they saw another army coming over the hills behind them. It was Adhémar of Le Puy, at the head of a detachment of southern Frenchmen. He had himself planned this diversion and procured a guide to take him over the mountain paths. Taken by surprise the Turks turned and fled eastward, leaving in their panic their encampment intact. When the victors moved over the hill, they found the tents of the sultan and the emirs undefended and full of treasure.[13]

It was a tremendous and heartening victory, won by the generous coöperation of all the crusaders. They lost some of their best soldiers, including Tancred's brother, William; and the battle had taught them to respect the Turks as fighters. Indeed, they could not withhold their admiration for the Turks. The anonymous author of the *Gesta* declared that, if only they were Christians, they would be the finest of races; and he recalled a legend that made Franks and Turks alike the descendants of the Trojans, a legend that justified them both in hostility towards the Greeks. Such praise made the victory seem the greater. But it was hardly needed; for the battle of Dorylaeum permitted the crusade to cross Anatolia. After two days' repose to recover from the struggle the army set out again, on July 3, taking the road to Philomelium and Iconium. It marched now as one unit, to avoid a recurrence of the risk run at Dorylaeum.

Kilij Arslan had now lost his capital, his tent, and the greater part of his treasure. When he met in his flight some Syrian Turks who had come too late for the battle, he told them that the Franks were stronger and more numerous than he had expected and he could not oppose them. He sent orders out to evacuate the cities along the crusaders' route, and he and his people took to the hills after ravaging the countryside and blocking the wells.[14]

Taticius and his Byzantines provided the crusade with guides. But their task was not easy. After twenty years of raids and warfare much of the Christian population had moved away. Villages were deserted and fields uncultivated. Bridges and cisterns had fallen into disrepair, and the deliberate "scorched earth" policy of the Turks completed the devastation. The guides themselves could not know the road as it now was, and information was not always available from the sparse population. But whenever things went wrong the guides were suspected by the Franks of treachery. Resentment in the army grew against the Greeks.

After starting out along the road to Iconium, the army soon made a detour, from Polybotus (Bolvadin) to Pisidian Antioch,

[13] *Gesta*, III, 9 (ed. Bréhier, pp. 44–52); Fulcher of Chartres, I, xi (ed. Hagenmeyer, pp. 189–197); Raymond of Aguilers, iii–iv (*RHC, Occ.*, III, 240–241); Albert of Aix, II, 38–42 (*RHC, Occ.*, IV, 328–332); *Letter of the Princes to Urban II* (Hagenmeyer, *Epistulae*, p. 161); Anna Comnena, XI, iii, 4 (ed. Leib, III, 18), a brief account which mentions the French knight. For the site of the battle see S. Runciman, *Crusades*, I, 186, note 1.

[14] *Gesta*, IV, 10 (ed. Bréhier, pp. 52–54).

and thence back to the main road at Philomelium by a track over the bare range of the Sultan Daghi. This was probably because Pisidian Antioch had not been destroyed by the Turks and supplies could be obtained there. From Philomelium the road ran along desolate country between the mountains and the desert. In the heat of high summer there was no vegetation nor any shade. Water was very scarce, with the wells blocked or dry, and the cisterns that they saw all ruined. The horses died in great numbers. Many knights were forced to go on foot, despite their heavy armor. Others rode on oxen. Sheep, goats, and dogs were captured and harnessed to the baggage carts. The men themselves, continually thirsty and unprepared for such heat, vainly chewed thornbushes. The older pilgrims and the women suffered terribly. Even the leaders' health began to fail. Godfrey of Bouillon was wounded by a bear when hunting close to the road, and his wounds took long to heal. Raymond fell desperately ill and was even given extreme unction by the bishop of Orange. But the general morale remained high. To Fulcher of Chartres the fellowship of the soldiers and pilgrims, coming from so many different lands and speaking so many different tongues, seemed to be inspired by God.

About the middle of August the army reached Iconium. The town itself was deserted; but the green valley of Meram, in the foothills close to the city, was full of running water and orchards laden with fruit. There the weary crusaders rested and recovered their strength. Both Godfrey and Raymond were restored to health. After about a week the army was able to move on again much refreshed. Taking the advice of some friendly Armenians settled there, the soldiers carried with them sufficient water to last them till their next halting place in the fertile valley of Heraclea (Ereghli).[15]

Near Heraclea a Turkish army was waiting, composed of the troops of the Dānishmendids and of Ḥasan of Cappadocia. The emirs probably hoped by their presence in force to induce the crusade to turn southward over the Taurus mountains and so leave their own possessions untouched. But at the sight of the enemy the Franks at once attacked, led by Bohemond, who personally sought out the Dānishmendid emir. The Turks had not wished for a pitched battle and rapidly retired. A comet

[15] *Gesta*, IV, 10 (ed. Bréhier, p. 55); Fulcher of Chartres, I, xiii (ed. Hagenmeyer, pp. 199–203); Albert of Aix, III, 104 (*RHC, Occ.*, IV, 339–342).

passed across the sky that night as though in celebration of the victory.[16]

A few miles beyond Heraclea the road branched. The shortest route to Antioch led over the Taurus through the great pass of the Cilician Gates, into Cilicia, and then over the Amanus range, through the Syrian Gates, to the Orontes valley. The road was hardly suitable for a large army. As it winds up through the Cilician Gates it is at times so steep and narrow that quite a small hostile force can easily cause havoc to a slow-moving expedition. Cilicia was in Turkish hands; and the climate there in September is at its worst. The Syrian Gates, though less sensational than the Cilician, were almost as difficult to cross. On the other hand, the defeat of the Turks at Heraclea opened the alternative road, which led to Caesarea-Mazaca. The Byzantine military road could be joined at Caesarea. From Caesarea it ran over the Anti-Taurus to Marash, through mountainous country, but country held for the most part by Christians, Armenian princelings who were, nominally at least, vassals of the emperor. From Marash to Antioch the road was easy, running over the low, broad pass known as the Amanus Gates. It seems that Taticius and the Byzantines advised the route through Caesarea and Marash, which would have the additional value of reëstablishing contact between the emperor and his distant isolated vassals. Tancred and the crusader princes hostile to Byzantium therefore opposed this route; and when they were outvoted, Tancred decided to separate from the main army and lead his own expedition of southern Italians into Cilicia. About September 10 he left the camp by Heraclea with a company of a hundred knights and two hundred infantrymen, and made straight for the Cilician Gates. His example was followed by Godfrey's brother Baldwin, who, like Tancred, was the landless cadet of a great family and was determined to found a principality in the east. His company was considerably larger than Tancred's. His cousin, Baldwin of Le Bourg, together with Reginald of Toul and Peter of Stenay and five hundred knights and two thousand infantrymen drawn from the Low Countries and Lorraine, set out with him a few days later. They were too numerous to take the rough track followed by Tancred to the head of the pass, but kept to the main road, through Tyana and Podandus. Neither party was encum-

[16] *Gesta, loc. cit.*, Fulcher of Chartres, I, xiv (ed. Hagenmeyer, pp. 203–205); Anna Comnena, XI, iii, 5 (ed. Leib, III, 18–19). She especially mentions Bohemond's part in the battle. Her informant must have been Taticius.

bered by noncombatants. Baldwin's wife, Godvere of Tosni, and her young children remained with the main army.[17]

While Tancred and Baldwin crossed into Cilicia the other crusading princes moved northeastward. At a village called Augustopolis they caught up with Ḥasan of Cappadocia's army and defeated it again, but did not pause to capture a castle of Ḥasan's that stood not far from the road. The villages through which they passed were handed over to a local Armenian lord, at his request, to hold under the emperor. They found Caesarea, which they reached at the end of September, quite deserted, but they hurried on at once southeastward to Comana, or Placentia, a prosperous town inhabited by Armenians. The Dānishmendid Turks had been laying siege to it, but retired when the crusade approached. Bohemond with some of his knights set out at once in pursuit of them, but, though he followed them for several days, he never established contact. Meanwhile the Armenians of Comana enthusiastically welcomed their rescuers, who asked Taticius to nominate a governor to rule the town for the emperor. Taticius chose Peter of Aulps, a Provençal knight who had in the past served under Guiscard before he entered the emperor's service. It was a tactful appointment and showed that the Franks and Byzantines could still coöperate.

From Comana the road led on to Coxon (Göksun), whose Armenian inhabitants were equally friendly. The crusaders remained there for three days, collecting supplies for the passage over the last portion of the Anti-Taurus, which lay just ahead. While they were there, a rumor came that the Turks had abandoned Antioch. Bohemond had not returned from his pursuit of the Dānishmendids; so Raymond, without consulting any of his colleagues, sent Peter of Castillon with five hundred knights to ride there at full speed and occupy the city. They reached a castle held by Paulician heretics not far from the Orontes, and there they learnt that the rumor was false. On the contrary, the Turks were pouring in reinforcements. Peter of Castillon returned, to report to Raymond; but one of his knights, Peter of Roaix, with a few comrades went off to the east and, with the help of local Armenians, occupied some forts and villages in the valley of Rugia, towards Aleppo. When Bohemond later returned to the camp and heard of Raymond's maneuver he was furious. Relations between them grew strained, and most of the princes sympathized with Bohemond.[18]

[17] See note 21 below.

[18] *Gesta*, IV, 11 (ed. Bréhier, pp. 60–62); *Letter of Stephen of Blois* (Hagenmeyer, *Epistulae*, p. 150); Baldric of Dol (*RHC, Occ.*, IV, 38–39); Anna Comnena, XI, iii, 6 (ed. Leib, III, 19).

For some reason unknown to us the crusaders did not take the usual road from Coxon to Marash. Perhaps they learnt that it was ambushed by the Turks. Instead, they took a track to the south, which was at the best of times a difficult path, very narrow and steep as it climbed up and down the gorges that they had to cross. It was now early October, and the rains had begun. For miles the army had to pass along a muddy ledge overhanging precipices. Horses slipped and fell over the edge. Baggage-animals, roped together, dragged each other into the abyss. Riding was impossible. The knights, struggling on foot through the mud, tried to sell their heavy armor to lightly equipped infantrymen or else threw it away in despair. Many more lives were lost on the pass than at the hands of the Turks. It was with great relief that at last the army emerged into the plain before Marash.[19]

In Marash too the population was Armenian, and was commanded by a former imperial official called Ṭaṭoul. He was confirmed in his authority by Taticius, and gave the crusade all the help that he could. The army paused three or four days there. Bohemond rejoined it, after his fruitless pursuit of the Dānishmendids; and Baldwin came hurrying up from Cilicia, presumably to see his wife, who was dying; nor did her children survive her. On her death, as will presently be discussed, he went off again, towards the east. The main army left Marash on about October 15, along the easy road to Antioch. On October 20 it reached the Iron Bridge across the Orontes, at three hours' distance from the city.[20]

It was four months since the crusade had left Nicaea. For so large an army, heavily encumbered by noncombatants, traveling in the full heat of the Anatolian summer through barren country that lay open to a mobile and formidable enemy, the achievement was remarkable. Without zeal and a burning faith it could never have been achieved; and it had required the sincere coöperation of the various component parts of the crusade. Except for a growing tension between certain of the leaders, in particular between Bohemond and Raymond, the army had been singularly free from quarrels. In a lyrical passage Fulcher of Chartres lauds the divinely inspired comradeship of the soldiers, coming as they did from so many diverse lands and speaking so many diverse

[19] *Gesta*, IV, 11 (ed. Bréhier, p. 63); Albert of Aix, III, 27–29 (*RHC, Occ.*, IV, 358–359). The description of the road as given by Robert the Monk (*RHC, Occ.*, III, 770–771), who merely rewrote the account in the *Gesta*, is almost identical with that given by Hogarth in Murray, *Guide to Asia Minor* (1895 ed.).

[20] *Gesta, loc. cit.*; Albert of Aix, *loc. cit.*; Matthew of Edessa, *Chronique*, II, clxvi (tr. Dulaurier, pp. 223–230).

languages. It had required, too, the coöperation of Byzantium. Though many of the soldiers and a few of the leaders were deeply suspicious of the Byzantines and were inclined to blame them for anything that went wrong, as yet relations between the emperor's representative, Taticius, and the Frankish command were correct if not cordial. Towns captured on the journey had been duly handed back to the emperor's nominees. Taticius on his side seems to have sent favorable reports back to Constantinople; for when Anna Comnena came later to write her history she must have used such reports, and it is noteworthy that, though she came to loathe Bohemond, she pays tribute to his prowess and the courage of his comrades when she describes the march across Anatolia.

It was as well for the harmony of the crusade that its two most turbulent princes had left the main army to seek their fortunes in Cilicia. Cilicia had formed part of the Byzantine empire up till the Turkish invasions. Now the Turks occupied the plain, while the Taurus mountains behind were in the hands of Armenians, refugees who had retreated there from Greater Armenia in the course of the past few decades to escape the Turkish invaders. There were two Armenian principalities in the mountains. To the west of the Cilician Gates was the territory of Ōshin, son of Heṭoum, with his headquarters at the castle of Lampron, on a spur of the range overlooking Tarsus. Ōshin professed loyalty to the emperor, who had given him the title of *strategopedarch* of Cilicia. He made occasional incursions into the plain and in 1097 took advantage of the Turks' preoccupation with the crusade to attack Adana and occupy half the town. East of the great pass Constantine, son of Reuben (West Armenian, Ṛoupen), was established. He claimed to be heir of the Bagratid dynasty, and as such was a passionate adherent of the Separated Armenian Church and hostile to Byzantium. His seat was the castle of Partzapert, behind Sis (Kozan). To the east of the Ṛoupenids, along the Anti-Taurus range and into the Euphrates valley, there were other Armenian princelings, of whom the chief were Ṭaṭoul, whom the crusade found at Marash, Kogh Ṿasil (Basil the Robber) to the east of him at Raban and Kesoun, Gabriel (Armenian, Khōril) farther north at Melitene, and Ṭoros of Edessa (Urfa) across the Euphrates. Ṭaṭoul, Gabriel, and Ṭoros were former officials of the empire and Orthodox in religion. Kogh Ṿasil belonged to the Separated Church. The position of them all was precarious. It was only by paying tribute to the neighboring Turkish lords, whom they tried to play off against each other, that they managed to maintain themselves. They were eager to make use of the crusaders as allies.

Tancred's motive in invading Cilicia was probably pure ambition, a desire to found quickly his own principality away from the dominating personality of his uncle Bohemond. But Baldwin of Boulogne was definitely interested in the Armenian question. He had taken onto his staff an Armenian called Pakrad, the brother of Kogh Vasil and a former imperial officer, on whom he relied for advice. Pakrad was concerned with the welfare of the Armenians nearer the Euphrates, where his family was settled; but when Tancred decided to set out for Cilicia, Baldwin and Pakrad felt that it would be unwise to allow any other crusader chieftain to be the first to embark on an adventure that would involve Armenian interests.

When Tancred moved down from the Cilician Gates, he marched straight on Tarsus, which was still the chief city of the plain. It was held by a small Turkish garrison, which came out to meet the invaders but was repulsed. The Greek and Armenian inhabitants of Tarsus made contact with Tancred and promised him help; but the garrison held firm, until, three days later, Baldwin and his far greater army were seen approaching. That night the Turks fled under cover of the darkness, and at dawn the Christians opened the gates to Tancred. When Baldwin came up later in the morning, Tancred's banners were flying from the towers. Tarsus should have been restored to the emperor, but, even had Tancred been minded to abide by the treaty, there was no imperial official at hand to take over the city. In Baldwin, however, he had a far more dangerous rival. Baldwin insisted that Tarsus should be transferred to his rule. Tancred, whose army was hopelessly outnumbered by Baldwin's, was furious but had to agree. He withdrew his men and moved eastward to Adana.

Hardly had he gone before another three hundred Normans, who had decided to follow him, came down over the pass to Tarsus. Baldwin would not allow them into the city. They were obliged to camp outside the walls; and during the night the former Turkish garrison crept up and massacred them to a man. The disaster was rightly blamed on Baldwin, even by his own followers, and his position might have been difficult had not news come of the arrival of a Christian fleet off Longiniada, the now-vanished port of Tarsus at the mouth of the Cydnus, under the command of Guynemer of Boulogne.

Guynemer was a professional pirate who realized that the crusade would need naval help. He had collected an armada of Danes, Frisians, and Flemings, and had sailed from the Low Countries early in the spring and was now trying to make contact with the crusade. He was delighted to find himself close to an army under a prince from his native town. He sailed up to Tarsus and did homage to Baldwin, who borrowed three hundred men from him to act as a garrison for Tarsus, apparently under Guynemer as governor. Baldwin then followed Tancred eastward.

Adana was in a state of confusion. Ōshin of Lampron held half of the town. Other parts were still occupied by the Turks, who fled when the Normans approached; and a Burgundian knight called Welf, who had probably broken away from Baldwin's party, had managed to force his way into the citadel. Ōshin and Welf both welcomed Tancred. The former was probably glad to extricate himself from a risky adventure. With his approval Welf was confirmed by Tancred in the possession of all the town, while, on Ōshin's advice, Tancred continued eastward to Mamistra (Misis), where there was an Armenian population eager for deliverance from the Turks. He reached Mamistra early in October. The Turks fled before him, and the Armenians opened the gates to him.

Meanwhile Baldwin, having wrecked Tancred's chance of founding a Cilician principality, had decided to rejoin the main crusading army. He may have had news that his wife was dying; he may have wished to consult his brothers; or he may, on Pakrad's advice, have considered that his true destiny lay farther east on the Euphrates. While Tancred was at Mamistra, Baldwin came up with his army. His intent was now peaceable, but Tancred was naturally suspicious, and would not let him into the town. Baldwin and his men had to camp on the far side of the river Pyramus (Jeyhan). Tancred's brother-in-law, Richard of the Principate, could not bear to let Baldwin's crime at Tarsus go unavenged. He and his friends persuaded Tancred to join them in a surprise attack on the camp. Their army was far smaller than Baldwin's, which easily repulsed them. After this unedifying conflict both leaders felt ashamed. There was a formal reconciliation where it was agreed that neither party would remain in Cilicia. Baldwin moved hastily on to catch the main crusading army at Marash, while Tancred, after leaving a small garrison at Mamistra, turned southward round the head of the Gulf of Alexandretta to the town of Alexandretta (İskenderun). He had sent a message to Guynemer at Tarsus to ask for his help, which, now that Baldwin had left the province, was willingly given. With Guynemer's help Alexandretta was captured. Tancred garrisoned it, then marched over the Amanus mountains to join the crusading army just as it arrived before Antioch.

The Cilician diversion had not been entirely valueless. The presence of Frankish garrisons in the principal towns of eastern Cilicia prevented the district from being used by the Moslems as a base for relieving Antioch, and helped to put a wedge between the Syrian and the Anatolian Turks. But it had revealed how precarious was the friendship between the more ambitious princes of the crusade. The natives, Christian and Moslem alike, learned that they could be played off one against another.[21]

Unlike Tancred, Baldwin did not again join the main crusade. He spent only a few days at Marash with his brothers. After his wife had died he set out again eastward, with the Armenian Pakrad to advise him. A smaller company than before traveled with him. Perhaps his brothers would not spare so many men, with the siege of Antioch in view, or perhaps his own popularity had suffered as a result of the affair at Tarsus. He now had only a hundred horsemen. As chaplain he took with him the historian, Fulcher of Chartres. While the main army moved southwest toward Antioch he turned southeastward to Aintab (Gaziantep). As he journeyed he managed, with Pakrad's help, to get into touch with the Armenians of the neighborhood and their princes. Everywhere the Armenians welcomed him as a liberator. The Syrian Jacobites, who formed the rest of the population, were more doubtful but did not oppose him. The only important Moslem lord of the district, the Turk Balduk, emir of Samosata, made only half-hearted efforts to oppose him. Two local Armenian lords, whom the Latins called Fer and Nicusus, joined their small levies to the Franks. With their help Baldwin captured the two main fortresses between Aintab and the Euphrates, Ravendan and Tell Bashir, known to the Latins as Ravendel and Turbessel. Ravendan was given to Pakrad to hold under Baldwin's suzerainty and Tell Bashir to Fer.

While Baldwin was at Tell Bashir an embassy reached him from

[21] The story of the Cilician expeditions is given by Albert of Aix, III, 5–17 (*RHC, Occ.*, IV, 342–350), by Radulf of Caen, xxxii–xlvii (*RHC, Occ.*, III, 629–641), and, briefly, in the *Gesta*, IV, 10. All these accounts are hostile to Baldwin. For Ṭoros, Gabriel, and Ōshin, see Laurent, "Des Grecs aux croisés," pp. 405–410, and "Les Arméniens de Cilicie," pp. 159–168. Pakrad's connection with Baldwin is mentioned by Albert of Aix, III, 17 (*RHC, Occ.*, IV, 350–351). William of Tyre, VII, 5 (*RHC, Occ.*, I), identifies him as Kogh Ṿasil's brother.

Ṭoros, prince of Edessa. Ṭoros had started his career as an imperial official and had later been one of the chief lieutenants of the Armenian, Philaretus (Filardos), who between 1078 and 1085 had ruled from Cilicia to Edessa. On Philaretus's death Edessa had been taken by the Turks; but Ṭoros had recaptured it in 1094, and held it as a fief from the Selchükid sultan, whose garrison, however, he had managed to eject. But his position was insecure. As an Orthodox Christian he was disliked both by his Armenian subjects, who were of the Separated Church, and by the Jacobite Syrians. The Turks resented him; and he feared that the great army which Kerbogha, regent (Turkish, *atabeg*) of Mosul, was planning to bring to the defense of Antioch would suppress him as it passed by. He had, it seems, already invited Baldwin to come to Edessa to serve under him; but Baldwin had no wish to be a mere mercenary. The embassy that Ṭoros now sent was empowered to offer Baldwin the whole heritage of Edessa. Ṭoros would adopt him as his son and at once coöpt him as partner in the government. It was not what Ṭoros had envisaged; but he was old and childless and desperate. It seemed the best solution. Others of the Armenians were less pleased. Before Baldwin left Tell Bashir, Fer reported to him that Pakrad at Ravendan was plotting against him. Fer was doubtless jealous of Pakrad, who may have done no more than get privately into touch with his brother, Kogh Vasil. But Baldwin was taking no risks. He rushed men to Ravendan to arrest Pakrad, who was tortured to make him confess. He revealed very little and soon escaped, to take refuge with his brother. But it was now clear to the wiser Armenians that Baldwin had come not to liberate them but to build up a dominion for himself.

Early in February 1098, Baldwin left Tell Bashir for Edessa, with only eighty horsemen. Balduk of Samosata, informed of his movements, rushed troops to ambush him where he was expected to cross the Euphrates, probably at Bira (Birejik); but he slipped round them and forded the river a few miles to the north. He arrived at Edessa on February 6, and was welcomed enthusiastically by the whole population. Ṭoros at once formally adopted him as his son at a ceremony whose ritual fascinated the Frankish chroniclers. Baldwin was stripped to the waist, while Ṭoros put on a wide shirt which was passed over Baldwin's head, and the two of them rubbed their bare chests against each other. The ceremony was then repeated with the princess, Ṭoros's wife.

Baldwin's first action as co-regent of Edessa was to attack Balduk of Samosata, whose raids endangered life in the Edessan countryside. He secured the help of a vassal of Ṭoros, Constantine, the Armenian lord of Gargar. But the expedition was not a success. The Edessan soldiers were surprised and routed by the Turks. Baldwin, however, with his Franks, captured a village called St. John near Samosata and installed a Frankish garrison there, which served as a check on Balduk's raids. The achievement enhanced his reputation.

A few days later the Armenians of Edessa, helped by Constantine of Gargar, hatched a conspiracy against Ṭoros. Baldwin officially had nothing to do with it, but the plotters informed him that they intended to dethrone Ṭoros in his favor, and they clearly knew that they could count on his support. On Sunday, March 7, a riotous mob marched on the palace. Ṭoros was deserted by his troops, and Baldwin would not come to his rescue. He agreed to abdicate, merely asking that he and his wife might retire to Melitene, whose prince, Gabriel, was her father. Baldwin guaranteed him his life, but he was not allowed to leave the palace. On the Tuesday he tried to escape through a palace window, but was taken and torn to pieces by the mob. The fate of the princess is unknown. On Wednesday, March 10, at the invitation of the people of Edessa, Baldwin formally took over the government. Thus, some months before the crusade entered Antioch, a Frankish state was formed in the east, to the envy of all the crusading princes. The news undoubtedly incited Bohemond to follow suit as soon as he could and determined him to make a bid for Antioch.[22]

Edessa had formed part of the Byzantine empire before the Turkish invasions and so should have been restored to the emperor. But it was far away. The only imperial representative there had been Ṭoros, who himself had invited Baldwin; and Baldwin could further claim that he had taken over the government not by conquest from the "infidel" but by the wish of the local Christian population. The emperor Alexius could do nothing about it and did not even make a formal protest. But the rights of Byzantium were remembered at the imperial court, to be revived when a better occasion should recur. For the moment the problem of Edessa was dwarfed by the far more serious problem of Antioch.

[22] Fulcher of Chartres, I, xiv–xix (ed. Hagenmeyer, pp. 209–243), who accompanied Baldwin to Edessa; Albert of Aix, III, 17–25 (*RHC, Occ.*, IV, 350–357); Matthew of Edessa, *Chronique*, II, cliv–clv (tr. Dulaurier, pp. 219–221). See also Laurent, "Des Grecs aux croisés," pp. 418–438.

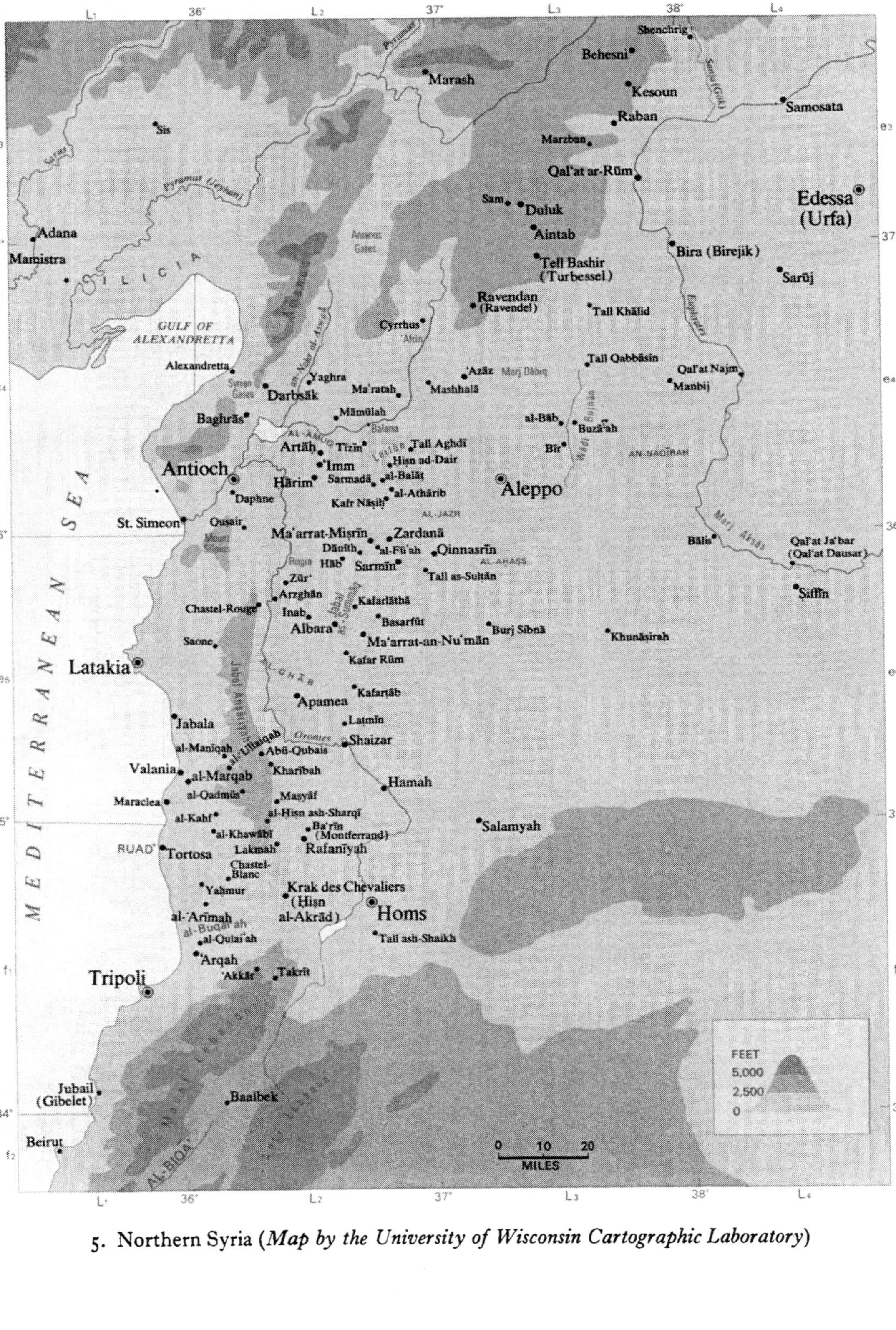

5. Northern Syria (*Map by the University of Wisconsin Cartographic Laboratory*)

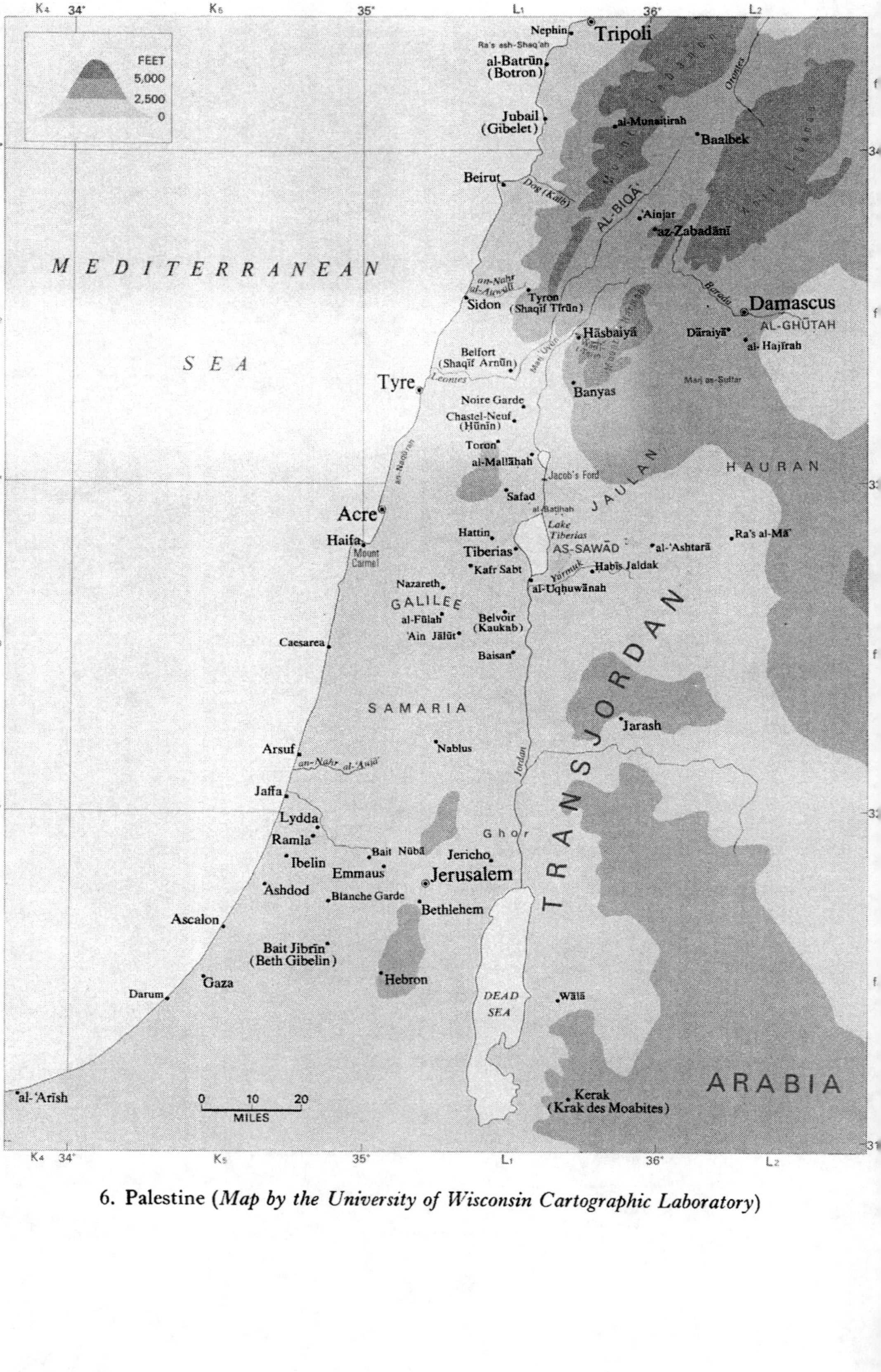

6. Palestine (*Map by the University of Wisconsin Cartographic Laboratory*)

The Land Walls of Constantinople

X
THE FIRST CRUSADE: ANTIOCH TO ASCALON

The city of Antioch lies on the southeastern bank of the river Orontes, some twelve miles from the sea, in a plain three miles long and a mile and a half deep, between the river and Mount Silpius. It was surrounded by great fortifications built by Justinian and repaired by the Byzantines when they reconquered the city a century before the crusaders arrived. To the northwest the walls rose out of a marshy ground by the river, but at either end they climbed steeply up the slopes of Mount Silpius, and to the southeast they ran along the summit of the ridge to a citadel a thousand feet above the town. Four hundred towers were built along the walls, each within bowshot of its neighbors. The Gate of St. Paul, at the northeastern corner, admitted the high road from the Iron Bridge and Aleppo. At the opposite end of the city the Gate of St. George admitted the road from the suburb of Daphne and from Latakia. The third great gate opened straight on to a fortified bridge across the river, carrying the road to St. Simeon, the port at the mouth of the river, and to Alexandretta (İskenderun). Smaller gates, those of the Duke and of the Dog, between the fortified bridge and the Gate of St. Paul, led to the gardens by the river; and there was a postern, called the Iron Gate, on the edge of the gorge where a torrent broke through the ram-

To the sources mentioned for the preceding two chapters Arabic accounts must be added. Of these the most important are: Ibn-al-Qalānisī, *Dhail ta'rīkh Dimashq* [*Continuation of History of Damascus*] (Arabic text ed. H. F. Amedroz, London, 1908; relevant passages tr. H. A. R. Gibb, *The Damascus Chronicle of the Crusades*, London, 1932); Kamāl-ad-Dīn, *Zubdat al-ḥalab fī ta'rīkh Ḥalab* [*Chronicle of Aleppo*] (extracts in *RHC, Or.*, III, 577–690); Ibn-al-Athīr, *Al-kāmil fī-t-ta'rīkh*, (extracts in *RHC, Or.*, I, 187–744; full Arabic text ed. C. J. Tornberg, 14 vols., Leyden-Upsala, 1851–1876), and *Ta'rīkh ad-daulah al-atābakīyah mulūk al-Mauṣil* [*History of the Atabegs of Mosul*] (extracts with French translation, *RHC, Or.*, II, part 2). Ibn-al-Qalānisī was almost contemporary with the First Crusade (he wrote his history about 1140), and as an official in Damascus was well informed, but was not much interested in events that did not concern his native city. Kamāl-ad-Dīn and Ibn-al-Athīr wrote rather more than a century later, but both made careful use of earlier sources now mainly lost. Of modern works, C. Cahen, *La Syrie du nord à l'époque des croisades* (Paris, 1940), is especially valuable, owing to the author's wide knowledge and citations from Arabic sources.

part of Mount Silpius. Inside the fortifications there were gardens as well as houses and some pasture ground for flocks, and water was abundant.

Antioch had been captured by the Selchükids in 1085. In 1087 Malik-Shāh installed as its governor a Turkoman called Yaghi-Siyan. Late in February 1095 Ridvan of Aleppo became overlord of Antioch; but Yaghi-Siyan had been a disloyal vassal, openly intriguing with Dukak of Damascus and with Kerbogha of Mosul against Ridvan. Consequently, when Yaghi-Siyan heard of the Franks' approach and sought eagerly for allies, Ridvan would do nothing to help him. Ridvan's rivals were more amenable. Yaghi-Siyan's son, Shams-ad-Daulah, went to Damascus and secured a promise from Dukak that he would send an army to rescue the city; and Dukak's regent (Turkish, *atabeg*), the Turkoman Tughtigin, and the emir of Homs, Janāḥ-ad-Daulah, both promised to join the expedition. Help was also offered by Kerbogha, who had long wanted to establish himself as overlord of Antioch in order ultimately to control Aleppo.[1]

In the meantime, as the crusade was marching across Anatolia, Yaghi-Siyan sought to clear Antioch itself of disloyal elements. The population was mainly Christian. Hitherto he had treated the Christians with tolerance. Now he felt that only the Syrian Jacobites, who hated the Greeks and the Armenians, could be trusted. The Greek patriarch, John the Oxite, who had till now been allowed to officiate in the city, was thrown into prison, and the cathedral of St. Peter was desecrated, to become a stable for the emir's horses. Many leading Greeks and Armenians were forcibly exiled. Others fled. There was some persecution in the villages in the suburbs, which provoked massacres of the Turkish garrisons as soon as the Franks drew near.

On October 20, 1097, the crusading army entered Yaghi-Siyan's territory at the village of Ma'ratah, whose Turkish garrison fled as they approached. Robert of Flanders led a detachment off to Artāḥ, to the southeast, where the Christian population had massacred the garrison, while the main army attacked the Iron Bridge across the Orontes. The bridge was fortified by two towers flanking its entrance, but the Frankish onslaught, which was directed by Adhémar of Le Puy, was immediately successful. Their swift victory enabled the Franks to capture on the other side of the river a large convoy of cattle, sheep, and corn that was on its way to revictual Antioch. Next day Bohemond led the

[1] For the Turkish situation see above, chapter V.

vanguard up to the walls of the city, and the whole army followed close behind.[2]

It was through treachery that the Turks had captured Antioch in 1085; and treachery was what Yaghi-Siyan most feared. His garrison was not very large. If he was to man the walls and police the city adequately he could not afford engagements that might reduce his strength in men. He allowed the invaders to install themselves around the walls and left them for a fortnight unmolested. When they arrived, Bohemond took up his position opposite the Gate of St. Paul, with Raymond on his right, opposite the Gate of the Dog, and Godfrey beyond him, opposite the Gate of the Duke. Work was at once begun on a bridge of boats to cross the river from Godfrey's camp. It was completed quickly, and detachments of the army moved across to camp opposite the fortified bridge and to open the road to the sea.

Yaghi-Siyan had expected an immediate assault on the city; but among the crusaders only Raymond wished to storm the walls at once. God would carry them to victory, he said. The other leaders were less hopeful. They could not afford to lose men, and they expected reinforcements. Tancred was due to arrive from Alexandretta, and there were rumors of help coming by sea. Bohemond, whose opinion carried most weight in the army, counseled delay. He had his own reasons for so doing. Almost certainly he already planned to secure Antioch for himself and intended therefore that it should be surrendered to him personally. Raymond pleaded in vain; and the one chance of capturing the city quickly was lost. Yaghi-Siyan had been thoroughly frightened and might not have been able to put up a vigorous resistance; but with the delay his confidence was restored.

It was easy for Bohemond to make friends within the city. There were local Christians in the camp who had relatives in Antioch; and as yet it was possible to pass to and fro through the Gate of St. George on the west. But, while the Franks found agents within the walls, Yaghi-Siyan equally well found agents

[2] The story of the siege of Antioch is told in detail in the *Gesta Francorum*, V, 12 — VIII, 20 (ed. Bréhier, pp. 66–110), and by Albert of Aix, III, 2 — IV, 2 (*RHC, Occ.*, IV, 358–432), and by Raymond of Aguilers, v–ix (*RHC, Occ.*, III, 241–259). Fulcher of Chartres, I, xv–xviii (ed. Hagenmeyer, pp. 216–233), who was not present, gives a shorter account. William of Tyre and the chronicles based on the *Gesta* add a few details. There are accounts in Anna Comnena, XI, iv, 1–7 (ed. Leib, III, 19–23), and Matthew of Edessa, II, cli–cliv (tr. Dulaurier, pp. 217–222). The Arabic chroniclers pass over the siege briefly (Kamāl-ad-Dīn, pp. 579–582, and Ibn-al-Athīr, *Kāmil*, pp. 192–193). An account by a contemporary Armenian monk is published by P. Peeters, "Un Témoignage autographe sur le siège d'Antioche par les croisées en 1098," *Miscellanea historica Alberti de Meyer* (2 vols., Louvain, 1946), I, 373–390. A critical summary of the sources is given in C. Cahen, *La Syrie du nord*, pp. 211–218.

in the camp. From them he learned of the Franks' reluctance to attack; and he began to organize sorties. He kept in touch with his garrison at Ḥārim, east of the Iron Bridge, and in conjunction with them he would cut off the foraging parties that were sent out from the camp. He was further cheered by the news that an army from Damascus was approaching.

The crusaders too were cheered by reinforcements. Tancred's arrival had enabled them to control the road to the fortified bridge. In the middle of November a Genoese squadron of thirteen vessels put into the port of St. Simeon, with a useful consignment of armaments. About the same time Bohemond managed to lure out and destroy the Turkish garrison of Ḥārim, which he occupied. Meanwhile, to protect the camp from sorties through the Iron Gate, the crusaders built a tower on the slopes of Mount Silpius, close outside the walls. It was known as Malregard; and the princes took turns to provide it with a garrison. Raymond's troops had already moved from the low ground between the walls and the river to encamp opposite the fortified bridge.

As autumn turned to winter, a new problem arose in the Christian camp. When the Franks had arrived in the plain of Antioch they had found it well stocked with foodstuffs. They had eaten well and had made no provision for the winter. Now the stocks were falling low, and something must be done to replenish them. Just after Christmas it was arranged that Bohemond and Robert of Flanders should go on a raiding expedition up the Orontes, to gather what food they could find in the villages there. The camp was to be left in the charge of Raymond and of Adhémar. Godfrey at the time was seriously ill. Bohemond and Robert set out on December 28 with almost half the fighting force of the crusade. Yaghī-Sīyan was delighted to see them go. He had recently learned that his son Shams-ad-Daulah had at last left Damascus with Dukak and Tughtigin and a considerable army. He hoped that the Damascene army would be able to surprise Bohemond, while he himself attacked the depleted besiegers.

On the night of December 29 Yaghī-Sīyan made a sudden sortie across the fortified bridge. Raymond's troops were unprepared, but Raymond was able to muster his knights and charge at the attackers. So fierce was his onslaught that the Moslems were driven back across the bridge, and many of the Christian knights followed them into the city before the great gates could be swung shut. For a moment it seemed that Raymond was to take the city by storm, when a horse of one of the foremost knights threw its rider and bolted back onto the knights on the bridge. It was very dark; and in the confusion the Christians panicked. They fled back across the bridge, pursued by the Turks, but soon rallied by their camp; and the Turks retreated again. Losses had been heavy on both sides, particularly amongst the Frankish horsemen. Adhémar's own standard bearer was among the dead.

Bohemond and Robert were meanwhile moving southward, in ignorance of the battle by the bridge, and in ignorance, too, that the Damascene army was coming up. On December 30 the Moslems reached Shaizar, where they learned that the crusaders were near Albara. They marched on at once, and next morning they came on Robert's army, which was a little ahead of Bohemond's. Robert was taken by surprise and was all but surrounded; Bohemond arrived in time to see what was happening. He kept his troops back till the Moslems thought that victory was theirs, then flung them into the battle. His attack discomfited the enemy, who retired with heavy losses to Hamah. But the crusaders, though they had been victorious, had lost too many men to follow up the victory. They sacked one or two villages, then returned to the camp before Antioch, with far less food than they had hoped to obtain.

The next weeks were gloomy for the crusaders. There had been an earthquake on December 30, and a frightening display of the aurora borealis next evening. During the following weeks rain fell incessantly, and it was bitterly cold. Stephen of Blois wrote home to say that he could not understand why people complained of too much sunshine in Syria. The weather did indeed oblige Dukak of Damascus, already depressed by his heavy losses, to retire home, leaving Antioch to its fate. But, while Yaghi-Siyan could keep his men dry and warm within the city and still had supplies of food, the chilled crusaders in their damp tents were near starvation. Adhémar ordered a three days' fast, to avert the wrath of God; but in fact everyone was fasting all the time, and soon one man in seven was dying of hunger. Missions were sent as far as the Taurus mountains to collect food; and the local Christians brought what they could spare to the camp. But they were not philanthropists; they charged high prices. A donkey-load of provisions cost eight bezants, and few could afford to pay such sums. The horses fared even worse than the men, till only seven hundred were left in the camp.

Some help came from the island of Cyprus, where the Orthodox patriarch of Jerusalem, Symeon, was living in exile. Adhémar, no doubt on pope Urban's instructions, had hastened to enter into relations with him, and treated him with a respect which belies the theory that Urban intended to bring the eastern church under his direct control. Symeon had in the past written a treatise against Latin usages; but he was ready to coöperate with the Latins. When Adhémar in October had sent a report to the west on the progress of the crusade, he had written it in Symeon's name as well as his own; and his next appeal to the west for reinforcements was drafted as an appeal from Symeon alone; and in it Symeon was given the titles and authority of an independent pontiff. In return for this friendliness Symeon sent from Cyprus across to Antioch all the fruit, bacon, and wine that he could collect. But, generous though his gifts were, they could do little to alleviate the general hunger.[3]

In their despair soldiers began to desert the army and seek transport back to Europe. The first deserters were humble folk; but one January morning it was found that Peter the Hermit had fled from the camp, together with an old comrade, William, viscount of Melun. William was an adventurer who had already deserted from a crusade in Spain. Presumably he persuaded Peter that it was useless to waste time on a hopeless expedition. Tancred went at once to pursue the fugitives. When they were brought back, Peter was pardoned in silence, but William was made to stand all night in Bohemond's tent. In the morning he was sternly lectured and obliged to swear to stay with the army till it reached Jerusalem. Later he broke his oath.

Early in February of 1098 the emperor's representative, Taticius, suddenly left the army. He had recommended a closer blockade and the occupation of castles commanding the approaches to the city, but his advice was unheeded. His story, when he reached Alexius, was that Bohemond sent for him one day and warned him that the army believed the emperor to be secretly encouraging the Turks, and that there was a plot against his life. Such was the temper of the army that Taticius was convinced by the story. Besides, he may well have despaired of the crusaders' ever taking the fortress. He announced that he must go to arrange for a better system of revictualment, and took a ship from St. Simeon to Cyprus. To show that he meant to return he left most of his staff with the army. But as soon as he was gone, Bohemond's friends put it about that he had fled from cowardice

[3] The letters sent in Symeon's name are given in Hagenmeyer, *Epistulae*, pp. 141–142, 146–149. Albert of Aix, VI, 39 (*RHC, Occ.*, IV, 489), reports Symeon's gift to the army.

in face of the coming Turkish attack, if not from actual treachery. When the emperor's representative acted so dishonorably, surely there was no obligation to regard the emperor's claims to Antioch.[4]

It was now known that another Turkish relieving force was on the march; so Bohemond next declared that it was time for him to return to his home. He had been away a long time, he said, and his estates needed his presence. As he expected, the army was horrified. He had proved himself its ablest commander; to lose him now would be disastrous. So he let it be understood that, if he were promised the lordship of Antioch, he would think it worth his while to remain. The other princes were not taken in; but there was much sympathy for him in the rank and file.

The Turkish army coming to relieve Antioch was led by Rîdvan of Aleppo, with whom Yaghî-Sîyan had made his peace when Dukak failed him. Rîdvan now regretted his earlier inaction, and had brought with him his cousin, Sokman the Artukid, emir of Amida (Diyarbakîr), and his father-in-law, the emir of Hamah. Early in February he reoccupied Ḥārim. As he approached Antioch the Franks on Bohemond's advice sent out all their cavalry to lure him to the narrow terrain where the lake of Antioch comes nearest to the Orontes. When he moved toward the Iron Bridge, the Franks attacked. They made no impression on the mass of the Turks, but succeeded in drawing them away from the bridge to the chosen battlefield. There Rîdvan had no opportunity to make use of his numbers to outflank the Franks; and when the heavily armed knights charged again and again into the tightly packed Turks, the latter fell back in confusion and soon were in full flight. As they passed through Ḥārim the garrison joined them in panic, and the town was reoccupied by the Christians.

Yaghî-Sîyan had meanwhile come out in full force against the infantry defending the camp and was gaining ground when the triumphant knights returned. When he thus learned that Rîdvan had been defeated, he retired into the city.

The victory raised the Franks' morale, though it did not ease their food situation. They determined to tighten the blockade on Antioch by building towers to command the gates. Raymond had

[4] Raymond of Aguilers, vi (*RHC, Occ.*, III, 245–246), says that Taticius left the army when his suggestion of a tighter blockade was rejected, but that he allotted Cilician towns to Bohemond first (an extremely unlikely transaction; presumably Bohemond put the story about). The *Gesta*, VI, 16 (ed. Bréhier, pp. 78–80), says that he fled from cowardice, pretending to arrange for better provisioning for the army; Albert of Aix, III, 38, IV, 40 (*RHC, Occ.*, IV, 366, 417), that he had always meant to flee. Anna Comnena's story, based presumably on Taticius's own reports, is that Bohemond frightened him into leaving. See the *Alexiad*, XI, iv, 3 (ed. Leib, III, 20).

long desired to have a tower built opposite the fortified bridge; but materials were lacking. On March 4 a fleet put in at St. Simeon manned by Englishmen and carrying a number of Italian pilgrims. It had called at Constantinople, where it had taken on board a number of siege materials and mechanics and had found the exiled English prince, Edgar Atheling, who took command.[5] On the news of its arrival both Raymond and Bohemond, neither trusting the other, went down to meet it and to escort the men and material to the camp. Two days later, as they returned heavily laden, they were ambushed by some of Yaghi-Siyan's troops. The Franks fled in panic, leaving their loads in the enemy's hands. A few stragglers reached the camp, and said that Raymond and Bohemond were killed. Godfrey at once planned to go to the rescue, but was attacked by Turks of the garrison, who hoped to clear the way for the raiders to return into the city. He held the attack; and suddenly Raymond and Bohemond came up, with the remnant of their forces. Their arrival enabled Godfrey to drive the Turks back into the city. The Franks then fell on the raiders and routed them, recovering all the lost material. The Turkish losses were very heavy. That night the Turks crept out to bury their dead in the Moslem cemetery across the river. They were unmolested; but next morning the Franks dug up the corpses for the sake of the ornaments that they had on them.

With their new material the princes first constructed a fortress at the mosque by the Moslem cemetery, opposite the fortified bridge. They called it "the Mosque" or *La Mahomerie*. It was put under Raymond's control. Next, a tower was built close outside the Gate of St. George, and given to Tancred to garrison. Thenceforward the only access to and from the city was over the steep slopes of Mount Silpius or through the narrow Iron Gate. Food convoys could no longer easily reach the garrison.

As spring advanced the besiegers found it easier to obtain provisions, while starvation began to be felt inside the city. But Yaghi-Siyan did not despair, for he learned that Kerbogha, atabeg of Mosul and the Moslem soldier with the greatest reputation, was gathering his forces. Other Moslem powers were prepared to let the Franks have Antioch. In March an embassy reached the camp from the Fāṭimid caliph of Egypt. Alexius had advised the Franks to make friends with the Egyptians, who hated the Turks and

[5] Ordericus Vitalis, *Historia ecclesiastica* (ed. A. Le Prevost, 5 vols., Paris, 1838–1855), IV, 70–72, says that Edgar was with the fleet. C. W. David, *Robert Curthose* (Cambridge, Mass., 1920), pp. 236–237, denies his presence as he was still in Scotland in 1097. But he may well have joined the fleet at Constantinople.

would willingly work against them. But the caliph's suggestion that Turkish Syria should be partitioned, the Franks taking the north and the Egyptians Palestine, did not meet with the crusaders' approval. The Egyptian ambassadors were hospitably entertained and returned to Cairo accompanied by a Frankish mission; but no agreement was reached.[6] The Egyptian vizir al-Afḍal therefore sent troops to reconquer Palestine without waiting for an alliance. In August 1098 the Egyptians captured Jerusalem and by autumn they had reoccupied the country as far north as the Dog river, beyond Beirut.

Kerbogha left Mosul in the first days of May. The sultans of Iraq and Persia sent him detachments; many of the Artukid princes of northern and central Mesopotamia joined him, and Riḍvan had reinforcements waiting for him at Aleppo. The crusader princes were anxious. Yaghi-Siyan was hard-pressed, but if he could hold out till Kerbogha arrived, there would be small chance of taking Antioch. The city must be captured at once. Fortunately for them Kerbogha delayed on the way to attack Edessa (Urfa). He feared the existence of a Frankish state that might cut his communications; but he overrated Baldwin's offensive strength and underrated the defensive strength of Edessa itself. He paused for three weeks in front of Edessa but could make no impression against its walls. It was not till the last days of May that he continued his march.

During these precious three weeks Bohemond had been busy. At some time he established a connection with one of Yaghi-Siyan's captains, a certain Fīrūz, who was probably a renegade Armenian. Fīrūz agreed to betray the city to him. Bohemond told none of his fellow princes of the negotiations. He now openly demanded Antioch for himself; and as the emperor was far away and his representative had left the army, most of the princes were prepared to promise it to him, with the exception of Raymond. Raymond was bitterly jealous of Bohemond, who was his chief rival as lay leader of the crusade. He had moreover made friends with Alexius at Constantinople and genuinely wished to be loyal to his friendship. It is probable that Adhémar agreed with him. After some discussion the princes decided that, if Bohemond's troops were the first to enter the city and if the emperor never came in person to receive it, then it should be Bohemond's. Even so, Raymond demurred. Meanwhile Bohemond publicly

[6] For a different interpretation of Egyptian policy, see above, chapter III, p. 95. On Kerbogha, see above, chapter V, p. 169.

emphasized the dangers ahead, in order the better to conceal his plots.

His propaganda was highly successful. When it was known that Kerbogha had raised the siege of Edessa and was continuing his march, there was some panic in the camp. Deserters slipped away in such numbers that they could not be stopped. On June 2 a large body of northern French took the road to Alexandretta, led by Stephen of Blois. Stephen, though he had recently written an optimistic letter home to announce that he had been elected to a high administrative post in the army, had now lost his nerve. His departure was to have consequences that were unexpectedly useful for Bohemond[7].

Had Stephen waited only a few hours he might have changed his mind. That same day Fīrūz sent to Bohemond to say that he was ready to betray the city. It was later said that he had hesitated till the previous night, when he discovered that his wife had been seduced by a Turkish colleague. He now commanded the tower of the Two Sisters, opposite the tower of Tancred, with the two adjacent towers and the wall between them. He now urged Bohemond to assemble the whole crusading army and march eastward as though to intercept Kerbogha, then bring the army back after dark to his section of the wall, with scaling-ladders. The garrison's watch would be relaxed, and he himself would be there to admit them. He would send his son that night as a hostage and a sign that he was prepared.

Now at last Bohemond revealed his plot to his colleagues. Antioch would be theirs that night, he said. Whatever Raymond may have thought, he and the other princes gave their support to the scheme. Just before sunset the Christian army set out ostentatiously towards the Iron Bridge. In the middle of the night it wheeled back. Bohemond's party reached the Gate of St. George and the tower of the Two Sisters just before dawn, while the bulk of the force remained outside the fortified bridge. A ladder was set against the tower, and sixty knights climbed up. Fīrūz asked anxiously in Greek for Bohemond himself, but he need not have worried. The knights took over the other towers under Fīrūz's command, then summoned Bohemond. His ladder broke behind him, but already some of the knights had opened the Gate of

[7] Stephen of Blois had been elected "ductor" (*Gesta*, IX, 27; ed. Bréhier, p. 140) or "dictator" (Raymond of Aguilers, xi; *RHC*, *Occ.*, III, 258) or "dominus atque omnium actuum provisor et gubernator" (his own letter in Hagenmeyer, *Epistulae*, p. 149). As he certainly was not commander-in-chief, he was presumably quartermaster general in charge of the administration and commissariat.

St. George, while others were running through the streets arousing the Christian citizens, with whose help they flung open the gates at the bridge. Soon the whole Frankish army was pouring into the city. Greeks and Armenians joined them in massacring every Turk that they met; and many Christians died in the confusion. Yaghi-Siyan was awakened by the tumult. He thought that all was lost, and fled with his bodyguard on horseback up the gorge that led to the Iron Gate, and out to the hills. His son, Shams-ad-Daulah, kept his head. Gathering all the men that he could find, he made for the citadel. When Bohemond reached the citadel gate, he could not force an entrance; but he placed his purple banner on the highest point that he could reach, to cheer the crusaders as they rushed through the streets far below. He made a second and stronger attack on the citadel which also failed, and he himself was wounded. So, leaving men to contain it, he returned into the city. Soon he was consoled by the gift of Yaghi-Siyan's severed head. Yaghi-Siyan had been thrown from his horse as he hurried over a mountain path. His escort left him as he lay there, and he was found, half-stunned, by some Armenian peasants who killed him and came to Bohemond, who gave them a rich reward.[8]

By nightfall on June 3, 1098, Antioch was once more in Christian hands, and not a Turk was left alive there. The streets were full of corpses; the houses, Christian as well as Moslem, had been looted, and their treasures scattered or destroyed. Only the citadel remained unconquered.

The capture of Antioch was a great achievement; but the crusaders were not very much better off in consequence. They could now protect themselves behind the great fortifications, which had received no damage during the siege. Their noncombatant followers were now safely sheltered. The Turkish army defending the city had been almost annihilated. But the long line of walls now needed defense. The citadel had to be picketed, and its garrison could watch everything that took place within the city. The crusade was still short of fighting men. Moreover, they found no

[8] *Gesta*, VII, 20 (ed. Bréhier, pp. 100–110), is the most vivid account, although it omits mention of Bohemond's own failure at the citadel; Raymond of Aguilers, ix (*RHC, Occ.*, III, 251–253), supplying information about the citadel. William of Tyre's account contains probably legendary details such as the story of Fīrūz's wife (V, 18–23; *RHC, Occ.*, I, 222–223). Fīrūz is called an Armenian by Anna Comnena (IX, iv, 2; ed. Leib, III, 19) and by Radulf of Caen (lxii; *RHC, Occ.*, III, 651), and a "Turcatus", i.e. a renegade Christian, by Raymond. The *Gesta* calls him "Pirrus"; Ibn-al-Athīr, *Kāmil*, p. 192, "Fīrūz"; Kamāl-ad-Dīn (*RHC, Or.*, III, 581–582), calls him "Zarrād", the maker of cuirasses. William of Tyre says that he belonged to the "Beni Zarra", which he says means "filii loricatoris". Ibn-al-Athīr, *Kāmil*, p. 193, describes Yaghi-Siyan's death.

huge stores of food within the city, and they had wantonly destroyed most of its wealth. The Christian population, especially the Syrians, were not reliable. And two great problems lay ahead. First, the vast army of Kerbogha had to be beaten; and secondly, agreement must be reached about the future of Antioch.

The first task was to cleanse the city. Soldiers and civilians had to clear the streets and bury the corpses before an epidemic should be started. Then the defense of the walls had to be allotted among the princes. Meanwhile Adhémar of Le Puy released the patriarch John from the prison where Yaghi-Siyan had kept him and restored him to his throne, and the cathedral of St. Peter was purified and reconsecrated.[9]

Hardly were the crusaders installed in Antioch before Kerbogha arrived. His army reached the Iron Bridge on June 5 and encamped outside the walls on June 7. His first action was to take over the citadel from Shams-ad-Daulah and to place it under his trusted lieutenant Aḥmad ibn-Marwān. His first plan was to attack the city from the citadel; but the crusaders had built a rough wall isolating the fortress, and they were able to hold it against a heavy assault launched by Aḥmad on June 9. Kerbogha then decided to encircle the city and starve it into surrender. A crusader sortie on June 10 was driven back with heavy losses.[10]

That night a group of deserters led by Bohemond's brother-in-law, William of Grant-Mesnil, broke through the enemy lines and reached St. Simeon. They told the Genoese ships in the harbor that the crusade was doomed and persuaded them to carry them to Tarsus. There they joined Stephen of Blois, who had thought of returning to Antioch when he heard of its capture, but had been deterred by a distant view of Kerbogha's army. With Stephen they sailed from Tarsus to Adalia (Antalya) and began to march back across Anatolia. Their desertion and Kerbogha's close blockade cast gloom over the besieged city. Food soon was short. A small loaf cost a bezant, an egg two, and a chicken fifteen. It seemed that the only chance of salvation would be the arrival of the emperor and the army of Byzantium.

It was known that Alexius had started out from Constantinople. His cousin, John Ducas, had already cleared western Anatolia of the enemy and opened the road to Adalia. With his rear thus secure, Alexius marched early in June as far as Philomelium

[9] Albert of Aix, IV, 3 (*RHC, Occ.*, IV, 433), mentions John's reënthronement, calling him "virum Christianissimum".

[10] For Kerbogha's expedition, see Cahen, *La Syrie du nord*, pp. 213–218, with a good summary of the sources.

(Akshehir). There he met the fugitives from Antioch, who told him, to justify their own flight, that it was too late to save the crusade. At the same time Peter of Aulps came hurrying from his post at Comana to say that a huge Turkish army was planning to fall on Alexius before he could reach Antioch. Alexius had no reason to doubt these stories. If Antioch had already fallen to the Turks, and there was another Turkish army besides Kerbogha's in the field, then it would be madness to advance farther into hostile and difficult country. He had the welfare of his empire to consider; he could not involve his army in such a risky and unpromising adventure. Only one of his staff, Bohemond's half-brother Guy, begged him to continue his march, to rescue the survivors of the crusade. His other advisers counseled retreat; and the great imperial army turned back northward, leaving a cordon of waste land to protect the recovered territory.[11]

The emperor's retreat was strategically justified; but it was a grave political mistake. The crusaders could not know what information he had received; they could not appreciate his wider responsibilities. It seemed to them that he had refused to help them when help was most needed; he was apparently indifferent to their fate and the fate of Christian Antioch. By his own action he had, they alleged, forfeited his rights over the city. Bohemond's claim to be given Antioch was immeasurably strengthened. But it was realized that Stephen also was to blame. He returned home universally labeled as a coward, to a wife who would not rest till she had sent him out again to redeem his name.

Kerbogha meanwhile continued to press the siege. On June 12 he nearly captured one of the southwestern towers; and Bohemond was obliged to demolish many houses near the walls to allow his troops greater freedom of movement. The morale of the defenders was very low, when suddenly their faith in the supernatural came to their aid. On the morning of June 10 a poorly dressed peasant in count Raymond's army came to the count demanding to see him and the bishop of Le Puy. He was called Peter Bartholomew and he was the servant of a Provençal pilgrim called William-Peter. The story that he had to tell was of visions in which St. Andrew had appeared to him, on no less than five occasions during the last six months. The saint had bidden him to chide the bishop for neglecting his duties as a preacher and to reveal to the count

[11] The account in the *Gesta* (IX, 27; ed. Bréhier, pp. 140–146) of Stephen's interview with Alexius seems to have been interpolated after Bohemond's break with the emperor. See Bréhier's preface, p. vii. Anna Comnena's account is more convincing (XI, vi, 1–2; ed. Leib, III, 27–28).

the hiding-place of one of the holiest relics of Christendom, the lance that had pierced the side of Christ. This was in the southern chapel of the cathedral of St. Peter. Bishop Adhémar was not impressed. He had doubtless remarked a better authenticated lance in the relic collections of Constantinople; and he learned that Peter Bartholomew was considered to be unreliable and disreputable. But Raymond, whose piety was simpler, was at once convinced. He arranged to attend a solemn search for the lance in five days' time; and meanwhile he confided Peter Bartholomew to the care of his chaplain.

News of the vision spread, and bred other visions. The crusader army was half-starved and desperately anxious, ripe for supernatural experiences. That evening, as the princes were meeting in council, a Provençal priest, Stephen of Valence, was shown in to them and told them of a vision that he had had of Christ and the Virgin, in which Christ told him that if the army repented of its sinful ways, it would receive a token of his favor in five days' time. Stephen was a reputable cleric and swore on the gospel that his story was true. Adhémar therefore accepted it, and, finding the princes deeply moved, he at once made them swear not to leave the army without the consent of all the others. On June 14 a meteor was seen to fall into the Turkish lines. Next morning a party of twelve, including count Raymond, the bishop of Orange, and the historian Raymond of Aguilers, accompanied Peter Bartholomew to the cathedral and began to dig there in the promised spot. They dug in vain all day, and the count left disappointed. Then Peter Bartholomew himself leapt into the hole and soon produced a piece of iron. Raymond of Aguilers tells us that he himself embraced it while it was still half-embedded. The story of its discovery was delightedly heard by the army, and the "relic" was taken in triumph to count Raymond's quarters.

It is possible that Peter Bartholomew had buried the piece of iron himself, or that he had the diviner's ability to detect the presence of metal. It is remarkable that, in an age when no one thought miracles to be impossible, Adhémar continued to believe him to be a charlatan, and there were others who shared that view. But the bulk of the army accepted the authenticity of the relic with enthusiasm, and no one wished openly to spoil its effect. Peter himself somewhat shook his supporters by another vision in which instructions were given for the services to be held in celebration of the discovery. The bishop of Orange was suspicious of so much liturgical detail, particularly when Peter untruthfully declared that he was illiterate. Moreover St. Andrew soon reappeared, to recommend five fast-days, after which the crusaders were to go out and attack Kerbogha. This advice conveniently coincided with Bohemond's known wishes.[12]

Bohemond, who was now in sole command, as Raymond had fallen ill, had learned of difficulties in Kerbogha's camp. His great army was not homogeneous. The bedouins from the desert disliked the Turks from Mesopotamia. The emir of Homs had a feud with the emir of Manbij; and none of the emirs relished being under the command of a mere atabeg. Kerbogha decided that Riḍvan's help was needed, but to court Riḍvan meant to offend Dukak. There were quarrels in the Moslem camp, and desertions became more frequent.

The Christian princes were aware of this and hoped that perhaps Kerbogha could be persuaded to raise the siege on terms. On June 27 they sent an embassy to him, composed of Peter the Hermit and a Frank called Herluin, who spoke both Arabic and Persian. Peter was chosen partly as the most eminent non-military figure in the army and partly that he might redeem his reputation, damaged by his attempted flight. He fulfilled the task bravely; but Kerbogha made it clear that he would consider only unconditional surrender. The ambassadors returned empty-handed, but Herluin may have learnt something of the enemy's difficulties.

On the failure of the embassy Bohemond easily persuaded the princes to risk a battle. Early on Monday, June 28, he drew the army up for action, in six divisions. The first, the French and Flemish, was led by Hugh of Vermandois and Robert of Flanders; the second, the Lorrainers, led by Godfrey; the third, the Normans of Normandy, under duke Robert; the fourth, Raymond's army, under bishop Adhémar, as Raymond was still ill; and the fifth and sixth of Italians and Normans of Italy, under Bohemond and Tancred. Raymond, from his sickbed, was to command the two hundred men left to contain the citadel. After a service of intercession, the troops marched out across the fortified bridge and wheeled right up the river bank. Though many of the knights had to fight on foot for lack of horses, the general morale was high.

[12] The fullest contemporary account of Peter Bartholomew's visions is given by Raymond of Aguilers, who believed completely in them (x; *RHC, Occ.*, III, 253–255). The author of the *Gesta* (IX, 35; ed. Bréhier, pp. 132–134) seems also to have believed, and omits the story of his later fiasco. The princes in their letter to Urban II were also convinced at the time (Hagenmeyer, *Epistulae*, p. 163). For the story of the lance, see S. Runciman, "The Holy Lance Found at Antioch," *Analecta Bollandiana*, LXVIII (1950), 197–205.

Each division bore its princes' standards; and the historian Raymond of Aguilers had the honor of carrying the holy lance.

As the Christian divisions emerged, Kerbogha's Arab commander, Waṣṣāb ibn-Maḥmūd, wished to attack them at once one by one. But Kerbogha preferred to wait till he could destroy them at one stroke. When he saw their full array he hesitated; they were more formidable than he had thought, and he was unsure of his own men. He sent a herald to offer to discuss a truce. But the Franks ignored his messenger and continued to advance. Kerbogha tried to lure them on, in the usual Turkish way, then poured arrows into their ranks. He also sent a detachment to take them on their left flank, where they were unprotected by the river. But Bohemond was ready for it, and had formed a seventh division, under Reginald of Toul, to hold the attack. Despite the rain of arrows the crusaders pressed on against the Turkish center, encouraged by visions of the saints fighting for them. The Turks began to waver. And many of the emirs began to desert Kerbogha's cause, not sorry that his arrogance should be humiliated. Dukak of Damascus, who had heard disquieting news of an Egyptian advance into Palestine, was the first to draw off his men. His retirement caused a panic. Kerbogha set fire to the dry grass in front of his line, in an attempt to keep the crusaders off while he restored order. But the solid mass of their cavalry trampled out the flames. There was fierce hand-to-hand fighting with heavy losses on both sides. Again bishop Adhémar's standard bearer was amongst those slain. Soon the whole Moslem army was in flight. Sokman the Artukid and the emir of Homs remained with Kerbogha till at last he saw that he could no longer hope to rally his men, and abandoned the battle. The crusaders, resisting the temptation to plunder Kerbogha's camp, followed closely after the fugitives as far as the Iron Bridge. They slew great numbers of them, while the Christian peasants of the countryside finished off most of the stragglers. Kerbogha reached Mosul with a remnant of his army, with his prestige and his power ruined.

Aḥmad ibn-Marwān, watching from the citadel, saw that the battle was lost and sent a herald into the town to offer his surrender. Raymond at once dispatched men with his banners to take over the fortress, but Aḥmad would not admit them. It seems that he had made a secret pact to surrender to Bohemond alone, in the event of a Christian victory; and it was only when Bohemond appeared in person that he opened the gates. The garrison was allowed to march out unharmed; and Aḥmad, with many of his men, became converts to Christianity and joined Bohemond's army.

The spectacular victory ensured the Christians' possession of Antioch, but did not decide which Christian was to hold it. By the treaty of Constantinople it should have gone to the emperor. But the emperor had no representative now with the army and had not appeared in person. Bohemond openly claimed the city. As he had organized its capture and had directed the recent battle, and the citadel had surrendered to him, most of the princes supported his claim. Only Raymond, partly from jealousy of Bohemond and partly because he thought the goodwill of Byzantium important, remembered the emperor's rights. Adhémar of Le Puy agreed with him. Probably at Adhémar's suggestion, Hugh of Vermandois, who wished to return to France, was deputed to go and secure the emperor's leadership. Hugh left Antioch early in July. After an arduous journey, in the course of which his comrade Baldwin of Hainault disappeared during a skirmish with the Turks, he found Alexius already back at Constantinople. There could be no question of a Byzantine expedition to Syria that year and thus the empire's only real opportunity to regain this province was lost.[13]

Meanwhile the crusaders decided to wait at Antioch till November 1, to rest the soldiers and wait till the summer heat was over before advancing farther. The waiting did not improve their nerves. While lesser princes rode off to visit Baldwin at Edessa or raid villages and capture forts, Bohemond established himself in the citadel and most of the city, even giving a charter to the Genoese as its ruler; and Raymond countered by occupying the palace and the fortified bridge. Soon a serious epidemic broke out, probably of typhoid; and on August 1 it claimed its first distinguished victim, Adhémar of Le Puy.

Adhémar, as the pope's legate and friend, was the one crusader whose authority was unquestioningly respected; and his personal qualities, his courage, his charity, and his tact, had made him universally beloved, even by the obstreperous Normans. His death was a disaster. He had been determined to work with the eastern Christians, and to prevent any open breaches within the crusade. Only one man was delighted by his disappearance. The visionary Peter Bartholomew had not forgiven him for his skepticism, and

[13] *Gesta*, X, 28–29 (ed. Bréhier, pp. 146–158); Albert of Aix, IV, 47–56 (*RHC, Occ.*, IV, 421–429); Raymond of Aguilers, xii (*RHC, Occ.*, III, 259–261); *Letter of Anselm of Ribemont* (Hagenmeyer, *Epistulae*, p. 160); Ibn-al-Athīr, *Kāmil*, pp. 195–196; Kāmil-ad-Dīn (*RHC, Or.*, III, 583).

promptly had a vision in which he was given a sentence in hell for his unbelief. At the same time St. Andrew told Peter that Antioch should be given to Bohemond, that the crusade should march off at once to Jerusalem, and that a Latin patriarch should be installed in Antioch. These revelations irritated Adhémar's many admirers and threw discredit on Peter Bartholomew, though Bohemond's friends approved of the political suggestions; and they embarrassed Raymond, who was proud of his possession of the lance.

As the epidemic spread, the princes took refuge in the countryside. Bohemond went to Cilicia, to reinforce the garrisons left there by Tancred. Godfrey established himself in Tell Bashir (Turbessel) and Ravendan, handed over to him by his brother Baldwin. The movements of Raymond and Robert of Flanders are unknown. Robert of Normandy went to Latakia, which had been temporarily occupied by Guynemer of Boulogne, then by Edgar Atheling in the emperor's name. Edgar had insufficient men to garrison it, and so appealed to the crusade. Robert governed there for a few weeks, but his rule was so exorbitant and unpopular that the citizens forced him to leave, and accepted instead a Byzantine garrison from Cyprus.[14]

In September, when the epidemic abated, the princes returned to Antioch, and on September 11 they met to draft a letter to the pope, reporting the death of his legate. They probably knew by now that Alexius was not coming to Antioch; so they suggested that Urban himself should take over this see of St. Peter. They would await his coming. It was a compromise, evolved to postpone a decision and excuse further delay; but it was ominous in its implied rejection of the claims of the Greek patriarch and in its note of hostility towards all the eastern Christians.

While they waited for an answer, the princes raided the countryside in order to secure food for the winter. They began to interfere in Moslem politics, supporting the emir of ʿAzāz against his overlord, Riḍvan of Aleppo. Godfrey even accepted the emir as a vassal, though the vassalage did not last for long. In October Raymond occupied Chastel-Rouge on the Orontes, and Albara, some miles across the river. Albara was a Moslem town, but Raymond turned its mosque into a cathedral and set up a Latin bishopric, the first in the east, under one of his priests, Peter of Narbonne. Peter went to Antioch to be consecrated by the Greek

[14] For the complicated question of the history of Latakia during the First Crusade, see F. Chalandon, *Essai sur le règne d'Alexis Comnène* (Paris, 1900), pp. 205–212; David, *Robert Curthose*, pp. 230ff.; Runciman, *Crusades*, I, 255, and note 2.

patriarch, John; but his appointment encouraged those crusaders who wished to see a Latin church in the east replacing the Orthodox Greek.

Early in November the princes rode again to Antioch to discuss plans. On November 5 they met together in the cathedral. Bohemond's friends opened by claiming Antioch for him. Raymond retorted by reminding them of the oath sworn to the emperor. Godfrey and Robert of Flanders, who supported Bohemond, were afraid to speak up for fear of being accused of perjury. The spokesmen of the army, waiting impatiently outside, broke in to say that, unless the princes settled the Antioch question and prepared to continue the crusade, they themselves would raze the city's walls. The princes then met in a more intimate gathering, and at last Raymond agreed to abide by their common decision on the future of Antioch so long as Bohemond swore to march with the army to Jerusalem; and Bohemond solemnly swore not to delay or harm the crusade. Bohemond was meanwhile left in possession of the citadel and three quarters of the city; but Raymond retained the bridge and the palace of Yaghī-Sīyan. The date of departure for Jerusalem was still unfixed. But to occupy the troops meanwhile it was decided to attack the fortress of Maʻarrat-an-Nuʻmān.

The siege of Maʻarrat-an-Nuʻmān lasted from November 27 to December 11, when Raymond's mining operations opened a breach in the walls. Bohemond thereupon offered the citizens their lives if they would meet in a certain hall and surrender to him. Many accepted his offer, but they were no more spared than were the citizens who resisted. Bohemond's action intensified his quarrel with Raymond, which grew still worse when he refused to remove his troops from the town unless Raymond retired from his portion of Antioch. He began also openly to question the authenticity of the lance.

About Christmas representatives of the army told Raymond that they would accept him as leader of the crusade if he would lead them on now to Jerusalem. He felt he must accept, and moved from Maʻarrat-an-Nuʻmān to Chastel-Rouge, to organize the journey. Bohemond thereupon agreed to leave Maʻarrat-an-Nuʻmān also, and it was placed under the bishop of Albara. Raymond then asked all the princes to meet him at Chastel-Rouge and attempted to bribe them to admit his leadership. He offered 10,000 *solidi* to Godfrey and to Robert of Normandy, 6,000 to Robert of Flanders, 5,000 to Tancred, lesser sums to the lesser lords, and nothing to Bohemond. But his offers were rejected.

While the princes conferred at Chastel-Rouge, the army at Ma'arrat-an-Nu'mān took action. Disregarding the protests of the bishop of Albara the soldiers destroyed the fortifications. Raymond saw now that he could delay no longer. He went to Ma'arrat-an-Nu'mān and collected his troops and any other men that would join him. On January 13, 1099, he marched out of Ma'arrat-an-Nu'mān at the head of his men, going barefoot as befitted the leader of a pilgrimage. All his vassals came with him, including the garrison that he had left at Antioch. Robert of Normandy at once set out to join him, accompanied by Tancred, who doubtless came to represent Bohemond's interests. Godfrey and Robert of Flanders held back, disliking to admit Raymond's leadership; and Bohemond, in spite of his oaths, remained firmly at Antioch, of which he was now the unquestioned master.[15]

Kerbogha's defeat had discouraged and disorganized the Turks. The two Selchükid princes of Syria, Ridvan of Aleppo and Dukak of Damascus, were too jealous of each other for either to be able to take the lead against the Franks, and the latter was further worried by the Egyptians' recent reconquest of Palestine from the Artukids. The lesser emirs thought only of their own interests, while the two chief Arab dynasties, the Banū-Munqidh of Shaizar and the Banū-'Ammār of Tripoli, were ready to help any enemy of the Turks. Raymond therefore met with little opposition as he moved southward. At Kafarṭāb he was joined by Robert of Normandy and Tancred. The emir of Shaizar sent guides to take the army through his territory and across the Orontes. By mistake one of them introduced the Franks into the valley where the local peasants were hiding their herds. The Franks rounded them up, in such quantities that the knights were able to sell the surplus and buy pack-horses in Shaizar and in Hamah, whose rulers freely admitted them. Raymond's plan was now to march straight over the Nuṣairī mountains (Jabal Anṣārīyah) to the coast, where he would be in touch with Antioch and Cyprus. But Tancred pointed out that it would be unsafe to march down the coast without capturing all the cities there, and the army was too small and ill-equipped for that. He suggested a direct route up the Orontes and down the Biqā' valley to the head of the Jordan. But that would undoubtedly rouse Dukak to action, and supplies might be difficult. A compromise was reached. The army

[15] *Gesta*, X, 31–34 (ed. Bréhier, pp. 166–178), giving Bohemond's point of view over the negotiations between the princes; Raymond of Aguilers, xiii–xiv (*RHC, Occ.*, III, 262–272), giving that of the southern French, sometimes critical of Raymond of Toulouse. On Bohemond's establishment in Antioch see below, chapter XII.

decided to march down the Buqai'ah and strike the sea near Tripoli.

After leaving the Munqidh lands, the crusade passed through Maṣyāf, whose emir made a treaty with them, to Rafanīyah, which was deserted but full of supplies. The army stayed there for three days, then entered the Buqai'ah valley, pausing to attack the fortress of Ḥiṣn al-Akrād, because of the herds that were known to be sheltering there. The garrison, after one successful skirmish, lost heart and fled, leaving the castle full of supplies. While Raymond stayed there, to celebrate the feast of the Purification, an embassy reached him from the emir of Hamah offering gifts, which was followed by one from the emir of Tripoli, who asked for a Frankish embassy to come to his capital to discuss the safe passage of the crusade through his lands. Raymond sent envoys, who returned much impressed by the riches and the unwarlikeness of the Tripolitans and their emir. They suggested that, if the crusaders attacked one of the emir's towns, he would undoubtedly pay them a large indemnity to buy immunity for his other towns. Raymond, who was short of money, took this advice, and marched down to lay siege to 'Arqah, some fifteen miles from Tripoli, where the Buqai'ah opened to the sea. He arrived there on February 14. Meanwhile he encouraged two of his vassals, Raymond Pilet and Raymond of Turenne, to lead an expedition to the towns on the north Syrian coast. They hurried to Tortosa, where by a ruse they induced the governor, a vassal of the Banū-'Ammār, to believe that they commanded considerable forces and to evacuate the town, which opened its gates to them. The governor of Maraclea, ten miles further north, thereupon recognized Raymond's suzerainty.

News of these successes reached Antioch; and the princes remaining there were jealous and decided to join Raymond. At the end of February Bohemond, Godfrey, and Robert of Flanders set out together down the coast; but Bohemond turned back at Latakia, reflecting that it would be dangerous to leave Antioch exposed to a possible attack from the emperor. Godfrey and Robert went on to besiege the small town of Jabala. When they were there, messengers from Raymond arrived, to beg them to join him at 'Arqah.

The siege of 'Arqah had not been going well. The town was defended with unexpected vigor, and the Franks lacked siege engines. It is possible that the soldiers made no great effort, for life was comfortable in the camp, amid the rich fields of the plain.

But Raymond could not abandon the siege lest the Moslems should recognize his weakness too clearly. In March there was a rumor that the caliph of Baghdad himself was coming with a great army to relieve 'Arqah. The news was false, but it alarmed Raymond into summoning Godfrey and Robert of Flanders. They made a truce with the emir of Jabala, who accepted their overlordship, and with great reluctance joined Raymond before the end of March.

Raymond had been for two months the accepted leader of the crusade. Even Tancred had admitted his authority in return for 5000 *solidi*. But neither Godfrey nor the two Roberts were ready to regard him as their superior; and now Tancred moved over to Godfrey's camp, saying that Raymond had not paid him enough. The men of the various armies, seeing their leaders quarreling, followed suit and would not work together. The quarrels were embittered by the arrival of a letter from the emperor early in April. Alexius announced that he was about to start out for Syria, and if they would wait till the end of June, he would be with them by St. John's Day, and would lead them on to Palestine. Raymond wished to accept the offer; and many of his men, such as Raymond of Aguilers, who disliked the Byzantines, felt that at least they would have in the emperor an undisputed leader for the expedition. But none of the other princes desired the presence of an imperial overlord; and the bulk of the army was impatient to move on. The emperor's offer was rejected. It is probable that Alexius was not surprised. He was in touch with the Fāṭimid court; and it seems that before waiting for the crusaders' reply he had written to Cairo to repudiate any connection with their advance into Fāṭimid territory. His obligations in Palestine were to the Orthodox community there; and he may well have thought that the Orthodox would be better off under the Fāṭimids, who had usually shown them great tolerance, than under the Franks, whose behavior at Antioch indicated growing hostility. But the subtleties of Byzantine diplomacy were unintelligible to the Franks, and when later they captured copies of his correspondence with Egypt they were horrified at his "treachery".

They blamed him because the embassy that they had sent from Antioch to Cairo had been so long detained. In fact the ambassadors returned a few days after the emperor's letter arrived. They bore the final offer of the Fāṭimids, who would ally with the crusaders so long as they did not advance into Palestine, and who offered every facility for Christian pilgrims bound for Jerusalem. The offer was at once rejected.

In spite of the general desire to resume the march, Raymond would not leave ʿArqah untaken. To speed matters up Peter Bartholomew announced on April 5 that he had just had another vision in which St. Peter and St. Andrew told him that ʿArqah must be stormed at once. The opposition to Raymond challenged the vision. Led by Robert of Normandy's chaplain, Arnulf of Chocques (called "Malecorne"), the Normans and northern French openly declared that Peter Bartholomew was an impostor and the holy lance a fraud, and they recalled Adhémar's disbelief. The Provençals rallied to Peter's support, many of them citing visions that confirmed his. Arnulf professed to be convinced, but others still doubted, till Peter in a fury demanded to be tested by the ordeal of fire. He was clearly convinced now of his own divine inspiration.

On Good Friday, April 8, two piles of logs, blessed by the bishops, were erected in a narrow passage and set alight. Peter, clad in a tunic and with the lance in his hand, leapt across the flames. He emerged horribly burned and, had he not been held by a friend, would have fallen back into the flames. He died in agony twelve days later. The Provençals loyally declared that he had been pushed back into the flames, and count Raymond still kept the lance in his chapel. But with the bulk of the army the lance was now utterly discredited; and Raymond's prestige suffered.

Nevertheless, Raymond succeeded in keeping the whole army before ʿArqah for another month. There was heavy fighting and many crusaders lost their lives, including Anselm of Ribemont, whose letters to the archbishop of Rheims, his liege lord, provide some of the most vivid descriptions of the crusade. At last on May 13 Raymond yielded and with tears in his eyes ordered the camp to be struck. There was some discussion about the route to be followed. The local Christians told Raymond that the easiest road ran inland, through Damascus, but though food was plentiful, water would be short. The road over Mount Lebanon and through the Biqāʿ was well-watered but difficult for baggage-animals. But local prophecies declared that the deliverers of Jerusalem would come down the coast; and the coast road was chosen, less because of the prophets than because it might provide contact with the Genoese and English fleets cruising in Levantine waters. On the other hand it exposed the crusade to attacks from the Fāṭimid navy, whose presence would make it impossible for the westerners, already handicapped by a lack of siege materials, to take the cities along the coast.

When the crusade approached Tripoli, the emir hastened to release some three hundred Christian captives that were in the town and to send them with 15,000 bezants and fifteen fine horses to the Frankish camp; and he provided pack-animals and provender for the whole army. He was also believed to have undertaken to embrace Christianity, should the Christians defeat the Fāṭimids. His prompt action saved the rich suburbs of Tripoli from spoliation. The crusaders left Tripoli on Monday, May 14; and guides lent by the emir took them safely round the cape of Ra's ash-Shaq'ah and past his towns of al-Batrūn and Jubail. On May 19 they crossed the Dog river, just north of Beirut, and entered Fāṭimid territory.

The Fāṭimids kept no troops, apart from garrisons in the towns, in their northern province; but the Egyptian fleet was in the offing. As the crusaders were afraid of running short of food, they were anxious to pass around every city as quickly and peaceably as possible. When the citizens of Beirut offered food and an unmolested passage on condition that their orchards and gardens were unharmed, the princes accepted the offer and abided by it. The army moved on to Sidon, whose garrison was less accomodating and attacked the Christians as they were encamped by the river, an-Nahr al-Auwalī. The sortie was repulsed and, in reprisal, the suburban gardens were ravaged; but the army thought it wise to hurry on to Tyre. There the garrison stayed behind its walls, and the crusaders were able to spend two days in peace in its pleasant orchards, waiting for Baldwin of Le Bourg and a party of knights who had ridden from Edessa to join the expedition. The army left Tyre on May 23, and passed unchallenged up the Ladder of Tyre and the heights of an-Naqūrah, arriving next day outside Acre. Its governor, like his colleague of Beirut, bought immunity for the suburbs by an ample gift of provisions. After pausing for the night the crusaders moved on past Haifa and around Mount Carmel, and reached the outskirts of Caesarea on May 26. The garrison of Caesarea ignored them; and, as it was the Whitsun weekend, they spent four days there. During their stay a pigeon killed by a hawk fell into the camp. It was found to be a carrier with a message from the governor of Acre urging the Moslems of Palestine to resist the invaders.

From Caesarea the army moved down the coast to Arsuf, then above Jaffa turned inland on the road to Jerusalem through Ramla, which it reached on June 3, without meeting any opposition. Ramla was a Moslem town and had been till recently the capital of the province of Palestine. Since the Turkish invasions it had fallen into a decline and its fortifications were in disrepair. As they were too far inland to be helped by the Egyptian navy, the inhabitants abandoned the town, after first burning down the great church of St. George at Lydda, a mile away. When Robert of Flanders rode up at the head of the crusading army, the place was deserted. The crusaders were delighted at their occupation of a Moslem city in the heart of Palestine. They vowed at once to rebuild the church and to erect Ramla and Lydda into a lordship as patrimony for the saint. A Norman priest, Robert of Rouen, was appointed bishop and administrator of the fief. Public opinion amongst the crusaders still considered that territory acquired in Palestine should be given to the church.

At Ramla the princes discussed their next move. There were rumors that the Egyptians were sending an army to Palestine; and some of the princes wished to advance towards Egypt to meet it, for Egypt was the real enemy, and it would be madness to attempt to attack the fortress of Jerusalem in the height of summer when they lacked the proper machines. But the army was impatient to reach the holy city; and others of the princes, trusting in the help of God, believed that if they could install themselves in the great fortress before the Egyptians arrived, they could hold it. After some debate it was decided to continue into the hills, up the road past Emmaus. The march was resumed on June 6.

At Emmaus envoys from Bethlehem came to the camp, asking that their town, which was entirely Christian, should be liberated from the Moslems. Tancred, with Baldwin of Le Bourg and a few knights, rode off at once over the hills and reached the town after dark. The inhabitants first thought them to be the vanguard of an Egyptian army, but when dawn broke and the knights' Christian insignia were recognized, the whole population came out in procession, with all the relics of the church of the Nativity, to welcome their rescuers and to kiss their hands. Tancred entered the town at the head of the knights, and the citizens set his banner up over the church of the Nativity.

All through the night of June 6 and the next day, while Tancred was at Bethlehem, the main army toiled up the road towards Jerusalem. During the night an eclipse of the moon presaged the defeat of the crescent. In the course of the morning a hundred knights rode back to say that Bethlehem was freed; and about noon, when the army reached the summit of the road, at the mosque of the prophet Samuel, on a hill-top that the pilgrims called Montjoie, Jerusalem itself came into sight. By nightfall on Tuesday, June 7, the Christian force was encamped before the holy city.[16]

Strategists less certain of divine aid would have hesitated long before attempting to attack Jerusalem at that moment. The city was a renowned fortress, and its great walls were in good condition. On the east, the south, and the west they were protected by ravines, except where they cut across Mount Sion, at the southwest corner. Only there and from the north could they be approached without insuperable difficulty. The Fāṭimid governor, Iftikhār-ad-Daulah, had an adequate garrison of Arab and Sudanese troops. The city cisterns, built by the Romans, were amply filled with water; and Iftikhār had rounded up flocks and herds from the neighboring countryside and driven them inside the walls. He had taken the further precaution of expelling all Christians, Orthodox and heretic alike, from the city, thus decreasing by more than one half the number of mouths to be fed and at the same time removing possible traitors. The Jews were allowed to remain. He also poisoned all the wells in the neighborhood, except for the Pool of Siloam, which he could command from the south walls. His armaments were better than the Franks'; and he had time to strengthen his towers with sacks of cotton and hay. He knew that an army was on its way from Egypt to relieve him. He could confidently hope to hold out till it came.

His optimism was reasonable. The Franks were operating in a country that they did not know. Their communications were tenuous, and they were short of arms. Even had the terrain allowed it, they were not numerous enough to invest the whole city, nor to prevent sorties from the garrison. According to Raymond of Aguilers, they numbered 1200 or 1500 knights and 12,000 infantrymen capable of bearing arms. The summer sun burned down on them, and there was little shade to be found. Water was soon a problem. Parties had to journey six miles or more to find springs that were safe, and raiders from the garrison would fall on them as they came back heavily laden. Food began to run short; and though the Christian villages in the neighborhood were friendly

[16] *Gesta*, X, 34–37 (ed. Bréhier, 180–194). Apparently the author accompanied Tancred. Raymond of Aguilers (another eye-witness), xiv–xx (*RHC*, *Occ.*, III, 272–292), describes Peter Bartholomew's ordeal with sympathy (see p. 330 above). Albert of Aix, V, 13 (*RHC*, *Occ.*, IV, 452), and Fulcher of Chartres, I, xviii (ed. Hagenmeyer, pp. 238–241), neither of whom was present, are skeptical, and Radulf of Caen, Tancred's apologist, was openly hostile (cviii; *RHC*, *Occ.*, III, 682). The *Gesta* is silent about it.

they had little to spare after Iftikhār's requisitioning. The only hope for the crusade was somehow to take the city by assault as quickly as possible.

They concentrated their strength on the sectors where they could approach the walls. Robert of Normandy took up his position at the east end of the north wall, opposite the Gate of Flowers. On his right was Robert of Flanders, opposite the Gate of the Column, the modern Damascus Gate. Godfrey of Bouillon took over the west end of the north wall and the north end of the west wall, aided by Tancred, who came up from Bethlehem a day later. Raymond was to the south of him, but, finding that the terrain did not let him approach the walls, he moved up after two days on to Mount Sion. But, owing to the shortage of siege machines, no general assault was attempted.

On June 12 the princes went in pilgrimage to the Mount of Olives. There they met an aged hermit, who ordered them to attack the walls on the morrow. When they protested that they lacked the necessary machines he reproved them, saying that if they had faith, God would give them the victory. They followed his advice, and next morning a general assault was ordered. So fervent was the attack that the outer defenses to the north wall were stormed; but not all their faith could provide them with enough scaling-ladders for the wall itself. After some hours of fighting they withdrew with heavy losses.

The princes had learned their lesson. At a council on June 15 they decided that many more mangonels and ladders must be constructed before another attack could be attempted. But they did not know where to find the material, when, almost as an answer to their prayers, on June 17 a squadron of six Christian ships put into the harbor of Jaffa, which they found deserted by the Moslems. There were two Genoese galleys, under the Embriaco brothers, and four ships that probably came from the English fleet. They carried ample foodstuffs, and ropes, nails, and bolts for making siege machines and ladders. A messenger hurried up to the camp before Jerusalem, and troops were sent down to establish contact. They were ambushed on the way and were only saved by a rescuing force led by Raymond Pilet. Meanwhile, the Egyptian fleet came up and blockaded Jaffa. One of the English ships broke through and sailed back to Latakia. The other ships were abandoned by their crews as soon as the goods were landed, and the sailors marched up with Raymond Pilet and his party to Jerusalem. Their provisions and the armaments that they brought were very welcome, but it was still necessary to find wood for the ladders and other machines. The hills around Jerusalem were treeless, and expeditions had to be sent long distances to collect the quantities that were needed. At last Robert of Flanders and Tancred penetrated to the forests of Samaria. It was a Moslem district, and they made many captives there, whom they used to transport logs and planks back to the camp; and work could be started on the ladders, while both Godfrey and Raymond set about the construction of great wooden castles on wheels.

It was slow work; and meanwhile conditions worsened in the camp. Water was a perpetual problem. The local Christians pointed out the springs, but they were far away; and detachments would often travel right to the Jordan in search of sufficient supplies. The men all went short, and many of the pack-animals and the beasts collected for food died of thirst. The heat was intense, and for several days a sirocco blew, fraying everyone's temper. The princes quarreled again. Tancred had offended them all by raising his banner over the church of the Nativity, a place too holy to be given to one secular lord. They began to bicker over the future of Jerusalem itself, many knights desiring to see a king for Palestine, while others and all the clergy declared that no man should call himself king in the city where Christ was crowned. Some of the host despaired. A company went down to the Jordan, to be rebaptized in the holy water, and then, after gathering palm leaves from its banks, made their way to Jaffa, hoping to find some transport back to Europe.

Early in July news came that the Egyptian army was really on the move. In a month at most it would be at Jerusalem. The princes saw that they could no longer delay their attack, and laid aside their quarrels. The morale of the army was low, but, as at Antioch, a vision came to its support. On the morning of July 6 a Provençal priest, Peter Desiderius, who had already reported visions in support of Peter Bartholomew, announced that he had seen bishop Adhémar during the night, and the bishop, after deploring the selfish feuds of the princes, ordered the whole army to hold a fast and then walk barefooted around the city walls. If they did so with true repentance in their hearts, then within nine days the city would fall to them. Peter Desiderius's previous vision had not carried conviction, but now the whole crusade was hungry for a sign from God and from the beloved bishop whom they had lost. The instructions were carefully obeyed. A fast was immediately ordained and strictly kept. On the evening of the third day, Friday, July 8, the Moslems, watching in derision from the walls, saw a solemn procession winding round the path at their feet. First came the bishops and all the clergy, carrying crosses and relics, then the princes and knights, then the foot-soldiers and the pilgrims. No one who could walk was absent. After finishing the circuit the whole host ascended the Mount of Olives. There Peter the Hermit preached to them with all his old eloquence. He was followed by Raymond's chaplain, Raymond of Aguilers, then by Arnulf Malecorne, Robert of Normandy's chaplain, who was considered the finest preacher in the army. Everyone was deeply moved, and even Raymond and Tancred forgot their enmity and swore to work together for the faith.

For the next two days, despite their sufferings, the men worked hard to complete the siege towers. Even old men and women helped, sewing ox-hides and camel-hides to nail onto the exposed parts. On July 10 the two great structures were ready. One was wheeled up to face the north wall and the other to face the wall across Mount Sion. A third, slightly smaller, was brought up opposite the northwest corner. The garrison had not seen the construction of the towers and was surprised and alarmed. Iftikhār hastily strengthened the weaker sections of the defenses, and began a steady bombardment of the towers with stones and with Greek fire.

The attack was timed to begin on the night of July 13–14. A feint would be made on the northwest wall, but the main forces would attack simultaneously on the eastern sector of the north wall and on Mount Sion. The first task was to bring the wooden towers right up to the walls, which involved filling up the ditch outside the walls. The whole day of July 14 was spent on this work, while stones and liquid fire were poured down from the walls. By evening Raymond's tower had closed in against the wall. But Iftikhār himself was in command of the defense on the Mount Sion sector; and Raymond's men could not establish themselves on the wall itself. Early next morning Godfrey's tower was in place, close to the Gate of Flowers, with Godfrey and his brother Eustace commanding from the upper story. About midday their men succeeded at last in making a bridge from the tower to the top of the wall; and two Flemish knights, Letold and Gilbert of Tournai, led a party across, followed soon by Godfrey himself. Once a section of the wall was taken, it was possible to use scaling-ladders, and more and more of the Lorrainers climbed up, followed by Tancred and his men. While the Lorrainers fought their way to open the Gate of the Column to the main army, Tancred penetrated through the streets towards the Temple area, al-Ḥaram ash-Sharīf. The Moslems fled before him, hoping to use the mosque called al-Aqṣâ as their last defense. Tancred barely stopped to desecrate and pillage the Dome of the Rock, before he was on them. Seeing that all was lost, they surrendered to Tancred, who promised them their lives, and set his banner to wave over the mosque. Others of the crusaders rushed through the main streets, pushing the defenders in confusion to the southwest corner, where Iftikhār was with difficulty holding out against Raymond. Early in the afternoon Iftikhār gave up the struggle. He had retired to the fortress of the Tower of David, by the Jaffa Gate, and he offered to hand it over to Raymond, with all the treasure that it contained, if he and his bodyguard were allowed to leave the city. Raymond accepted his terms and occupied the Tower, and provided Iftikhār with an escort to take him through the lines and leave him free to join the Egyptian garrison at Ascalon.

Iftikhār and his bodyguard were the only Moslems to save their lives. The crusaders rushed through the streets and into the houses slaying everyone that they saw, man, woman, and child. The refugees in the Aqṣâ mosque found Tancred's banner no protection. Early next morning a party of crusaders broke into the mosque and killed them all. The Jews fled in a body to their chief synagogue. But the building was set on fire and they all perished within. When the carnage stopped, the streets were running with blood, and round the Temple area one stepped over corpses all the way. The horror of the massacre in the holy city was never forgotten nor forgiven by Islam.[17]

The crusade had attained its goal. The capture of the great fortress of Jerusalem had been an achievement remarkable for even so fanatically brave and confident an army. But in itself it did not assure the success of the crusade. There was still a large Egyptian army in the field; and there was the future government of the conquered land to be arranged. The first task was to establish some order in Jerusalem itself. On Sunday, July 17, the princes met to discuss their plans. First, they dealt with adminis-

[17] The siege and capture of Jerusalem are described by the *Gesta* (X, 37–38; ed. Bréhier, pp. 194–206) and Raymond of Aguilers (xx; *RHC, Occ.*, III, 293–300). Albert of Aix's long account (V, 46–VI, 28; *RHC, Occ.*, IV, 463–483) is not entirely reliable. Fulcher of Chartres gives a brief account (I, xxvii; ed. Hagenmeyer, 295–301). The Moslem sources, Ibn-al-Qalānisī, *Damascus Chronicle* (tr. Gibb), p. 48; Ibn-al-Athīr, *Kāmil*, pp. 198–199; abū-l-Fidā', *Al-Mukhtaṣar* ... (extracts in *RHC, Or.*, I), p. 4, give brief accounts, with special emphasis on the massacres. Ibn-al-Athīr specifically exonerates Raymond. The capture of Jerusalem is noted in every contemporary chronicle, eastern, Greek, and western.

trative matters on which they could all agree. The streets and buildings had to be cleared of the corpses. Quarters had to be allotted to the troops. The orderly return of the local Christians had to be arranged. Preparations must be made to meet the coming attack of the Egyptian army. Then there were delicate personal problems to be faced. Was, for instance, Tancred to be allowed to keep the eight huge silver lamps and the other loot that he had taken from the Dome of the Rock? In the midst of the discussion someone raised the question of the election of a king. The clergy at once protested. Spiritual needs came first. A patriarch must be appointed who could preside over the election. Had the Orthodox patriarch, Symeon, been in Jerusalem, his rights would probably have been respected. But he was in exile in Cyprus with all his higher clergy; and he was known to be old and very ill. In fact he had died a few days before the capture of the city. Adhémar, whom everyone would have gladly accepted and whose guidance was sorely needed, was dead. After Adhémar, William of Orange had been the most revered of the bishops; but he too had died. There was no outstanding ecclesiastic. When Arnulf, bishop of Marturana, proposed his friend Arnulf Malecorne, the Lorrainers were unenthusiastic and the southern French regarded it as a Norman plot. No other candidate came forward. The patriarchal election was postponed.

But a secular governor was essential. There were four princes from whom the choice could be made, Raymond of Toulouse, Godfrey of Bouillon, Robert of Flanders, and Robert of Normandy. Tancred did not carry enough prestige, and Eustace of Boulogne was overshadowed by his brother Godfrey. Of the four, Robert of Flanders was the ablest; but he was known to wish to return to Flanders. Robert of Normandy was popular and was respected as the head of the Norman people; but he lacked a strong personality, and he too was unwilling to remain in the east. The only serious candidates were Raymond and Godfrey. Raymond was a man of mature age and experience and great wealth. He had been the close associate of bishop Adhémar and the only prince whom pope Urban had consulted. But his colleagues resented his pretensions. His policy of coöperation with Byzantium was unpopular, even with his own men. The siege of ‘Arqah had not added to his reputation as a skilled commander-in-chief; and he had lost prestige over the holy lance. His piety and courage were acknowledged, but neither his politics nor his generalship inspired confidence. Godfrey, on the other hand, was popular and respected. He was descended from Charlemagne, and had held the high post of duke of Lower Lorraine. He too was renowned for piety and courage, and he had been the first prince to enter Jerusalem. He had not been a very efficient duke in Lorraine, and he had shown a weak obstinacy at Constantinople. But his failings were unknown to the ordinary crusader, who respected him as a gallant and godly man.

The electoral body consisted probably of the higher clergy and the knights who were tenants-in-chief to a prince at home. The crown was first offered to Raymond, who refused it, probably because he felt that the offer did not command general support. He declared that he would not be king in Christ's earthly kingdom, hoping no doubt thus to prevent anyone else from accepting the kingship. The electors then turned to Godfrey, whom the two Roberts were known to support. He accepted the post of prince for the purpose of fighting the "infidel", and, while likewise refusing a royal title, he decided to be called *Advocatus Sancti Sepulchri*, the dedicated defender of the Holy Sepulcher, a title which gave him secular authority but did not prejudice the rights of the church. His piety was sincere. He seems to have shared the view of the average crusader that the Holy Land should be an ecclesiastical patrimony. It was only after the greater part of the crusade had gone home and left a handful of adventurers to colonize and rule the country that public opinion demanded a king.[18]

Raymond thought that he had been tricked and took Godfrey's election badly. He possessed the Tower of David, surrendered to him by Iftikhār, and he refused to give it up. Only after the two Roberts remonstrated with him did he agree to leave it in the hands of the bishop of Albara, till a council of the church decided on the whole case. As soon as he had moved out, the bishop handed it to Godfrey, telling Raymond, untruthfully, that he could not have defended it for lack of arms. Raymond angrily declared that he would return home, and meanwhile moved with all his troops down to Jericho, where he led them in a solemn pilgrimage to the Jordan, following a ritual that Peter Bartholomew had ordained in one of his visions. He refused to return to Jerusalem.

[18] For Godfrey's position see below, chapter XII, p. 375. Raymond of Aguilers (xx; *RHC, Occ.*, III, 301), and Albert of Aix (VI, 33; *RHC, Occ.*, IV, 485–486) mention Raymond's refusal of the crown. William of Tyre (IX, 1–4; *RHC, Occ.*, I, 364–369) supplies information about the patriarchate from ecclesiastical sources at his disposal. Fulcher of Chartres (I, xxx; ed. Hagenmeyer, p. 308) says that no patriarch was elected until the pope's advice was received.

With the southern French away, the Normans were able to control the council that now met to elect a patriarch. Arnulf Malecorne's supporters were successful in securing his appointment. The southern French vainly pointed out that Arnulf was not even a sub-deacon and that his lack of morals was notorious. Arnulf's elevation was generally welcomed, though his enemies remembered that it was not strictly canonical. He set about reorganizing the church of the Holy Sepulcher and starting exclusively Latin services there, to the disgust of the local Christians of every rite, whose clergy were banished from the shrine.[19]

Godfrey's relations with his colleagues worsened after his elevation. Somehow he offended Robert of Normandy; and Robert of Flanders seems to have grown less friendly to him. But before there was any open breach, the expected Egyptian attack had to be met. The vizir al-Afḍal was himself in command of the forces which had now crossed into Palestine and were approaching Ascalon. He sent an embassy to Jerusalem to reproach the Franks for having invaded Fāṭimid territory unprovoked and to order them to evacuate the province. The ambassadors were dismissed at once, and Godfrey prepared to lead the crusading army down to the plain to meet the enemy. His brother Eustace had gone with Tancred a few days previously to occupy the country round Nablus. A messenger from Godfrey summoned them to descend towards Ascalon and discover the strength and the movements of the Egyptians. Meanwhile Godfrey mustered his own troops and called on his colleagues to join him. Robert of Flanders answered the call at once; but Robert of Normandy and Raymond, who was still at Jericho, hung back. They would wait, they said, till the seriousness of the invasion was confirmed.

On August 9 Godfrey and Robert set out from Jerusalem with all their men, accompanied by the patriarch Arnulf. At Ramla they met Eustace and Tancred, who reported that the enemy was in full force at Ascalon. The bishop of Marturana was sent back to impress on Robert of Normandy and on Raymond that their help was needed at once. They were convinced now, and followed with their armies, catching up with Godfrey on August 11 at Ibelin, a few miles beyond Ramla. Only a handful of soldiers were left in Jerusalem, where Peter the Hermit was instructed to hold daily services of intercession, attended by Latins and native Christians alike.

By the evening of August 11 the whole Christian army reached

[19] William of Tyre, IX, 4 (*RHC, Occ.*, I, 367).

Ashdod, where the herds that the Egyptians had brought to feed their troops were grazing. The herdsmen were surprised and killed and the beasts rounded up. After a brief night's rest the Christians hurried on to arrive at sunrise in the fertile plain of al-Majdal, just to the north of the fortress of Ascalon. The whole Egyptian army was encamped in the plain, completely ignorant that the enemy was so near. The Christian lines were formed with Raymond on the right, next to the sea, the two Roberts and Tancred in the center, and Godfrey on the left. Finding the Moslems unprepared, they charged at once in a curved line onto the camp. The Egyptians were barely awake before the Frankish knights were upon them. They hardly attempted to resist. Raymond on the right drove numbers of them to perish in the sea. In the center Robert of Normandy and Tancred drove right into the heart of their camp, and Robert's bodyguard captured the vizir's tent with his banner and many of his possessions. Farther inland other Egyptians took refuge in a tangled sycamore grove, which was set alight, and they were burned to death. Al-Afḍal himself fled with his bodyguard behind the walls of Ascalon, whence a few days later he took ship for Egypt. Within a few hours the whole Egyptian host had been slaughtered or put to flight, and the Christians were masters of the field.

The booty captured at the battle was immense. Few of the soldiers did not return the richer. Robert of Normandy bought the vizir's standard from the soldier that had taken it for twenty silver marks and presented it to the patriarch. The vizir's sword was sold by another Norman to one of the princes for sixty bezants. A vast amount of bullion and jewelry was discovered in the camp, together with stores of armaments and numbers of horses. On Saturday, August 13, the army returned in a triumphal procession to Jerusalem, bearing the captured treasures with them. What they could not carry was burnt on the spot.[20]

The victory at Ascalon was the complement to the capture of Jerusalem. It ensured the crusaders' possession of Palestine. It crowned the great adventure of the First Crusade. The Holy Land had been rescued for Christendom. The problem now was how to maintain and govern it.

[20] *Gesta*, X, 39 (ed. Bréhier, pp. 208–216); Raymond of Aguilers, xxi (*RHC, Occ.*, III, 304–305). Both end their histories with the first battle of Ascalon. See also Albert of Aix, VI, 44–50 (*RHC, Occ.*, IV, 493–497). Brief accounts are given in Ibn-al-Qalānisī, *Damascus Chronicle* (tr. Gibb), p. 49, and Ibn-al-Athīr, *Kāmil*, p. 202.

Alexius I Comnenus

XI

THE CRUSADE OF 1101

With the capture of Jerusalem on July 15, 1099, the crusaders had gained their principal objective, and their victory over the Egyptians at Ascalon four weeks later removed for the moment the most immediate threat against the Christian holdings. The official report of the campaign, written by Daimbert and others from Latakia in September, was triumphant in tone and justly so. The

The sources for the Crusade of 1101 are about as plentiful as those for the First Crusade, but in general were written at second hand. Some of the chroniclers of the First Crusade included also an account of the later movement. The best of these are: Bartolf of Nangis, *Gesta Francorum expugnantium Iherusalem* (*RHC, Occ.*, III); Fulcher of Chartres, *Gesta Francorum Hierusalem peregrinantium* (ed. H. Hagenmeyer, *Fulcheri Carnotensis Historia Hierosolymitana* [1095–1127], Heidelberg, 1913); Guibert of Nogent, *Gesta Dei per Francos* (*RHC, Occ.*, IV); Ordericus Vitalis, *Historia ecclesiastica* (ed. A. Le Prevost and L. Delisle, vol. IV, Paris, 1852); Radulf [Ralph] of Caen, *Gesta Tancredi* (*RHC, Occ.*, III); William of Malmesbury, *Gesta regum Anglorum* (ed. W. Stubbs, Rolls Series, 2 vols., London, 1887–1889); William of Tyre, *Historia rerum in partibus transmarinis gestarum* (*RHC, Occ.*, I, and tr. E. A. Babcock and A. C. Krey, *A History of Deeds Done Beyond the Sea: by William, Archbishop of Tyre*, Columbia University, Records of Civilization, 2 vols., New York, 1943). Ekkehard of Aura was a participant during part of the crusade; his *Hierosolymita* (ed. H. Hagenmeyer, Tübingen, 1877) is valuable in spots but is less useful than the author's reputation would suggest. Albert of Aix, *Historia Hierosolymitana* (*RHC, Occ.*, IV), is by far the fullest and most interesting account. His version of this story was attacked as erroneous and inconsistent by H. von Sybel, *Geschichte des ersten Kreuzzuges* (2nd ed., Leipzig, 1881), but defended effectively, it would seem, by B. Kugler, *Albert von Aachen* (Stuttgart, 1885). The continuators and minor crusading historians add nothing of value.

Detailed information about the participants may be found in a number of local sources — cartularies and annals. Of the latter, the following are the most useful. For the Lombards: Landulf of San Paulo, *Historia Mediolanensis* (*MGH, SS.*, XX); Caffaro de Caschifelone, *De liberatione civitatum orientis liber* (*RHC, Occ.*, V). For the French: *Chronica prioratus de casa Vicecomitis* and *Chronicon S. Maxentii Pictavensis* (both ed. P. Marchegay and E. Mabille, *Chroniques des églises d'Anjou*, Paris, 1869); *Gesta Ambaziensium dominorum* (ed. L. Halphen and R. Poupardin, *Chroniques des comtes d'Anjou*, Paris, 1913). For the German: *Annales Augustani* (*MGH, SS.*, III); *Annales Mellicences* (*MGH, SS.*, IX); Otto of Freising, *Chronica* (ed. A. Hofmeister, Hanover, 1912); *Historia Welforum Weingartensis* (*MGH, SS.*, XVI).

Of the non-Latin sources, the most useful is Anna Comnena, *Alexiad* (*RHC, Grecs*, I, and ed. Bernard Leib, 3 vols., 1937–1945). Some information, never very full or accurate, may be had from the following histories: Matthew of Edessa, *Chronique* (*RHC, Arm.*, I); Ibn-al-Athīr, *Al-kāmil fī-t-ta'rīkh* (extracts in *RHC, Or.*, I, 187–744); Ibn-al-Qalānisī, *Dhail ta'rīkh Dimashq* (extracts tr. H. A. R. Gibb, *The Damascus Chronicle of the Crusades*, London, 1932); *Anonymous Syriac Chronicle* (ed. and tr. A. S. Tritton and H. A. R. Gibb, "The First and Second Crusades from an Anonymous Syriac Chronicle," *Journal of the Royal Asiatic Society*, 1933, pp. 69–101, 273–305).

We know of no monograph on the Crusade of 1101. It is treated in most standard histories of the crusades, perhaps most satisfyingly in René Grousset, *Histoire des croisades et du royaume franc de Jérusalem*, vol. I (Paris, 1934), and S. Runciman, *A History of the Crusades*, vol. II (Cambridge, 1952). The present writer has tried elsewhere to give an interpretation of the crusade: see J. L. Cate, "A Gay Crusader," *Byzantion*, XVI (1942–1943), 503–526.

Christian position was far from secure, however, and this the magnates recognized as they set about organizing the new state. Most of the important seaports, upon which their control of Syria and Palestine ultimately depended, had yet to be taken, and recent acquisitions inland needed to be consolidated. For the tasks at hand there was not enough manpower: some westerners had elected to stay on in the Levant but most of them, homesick and pilgrims at heart rather than colonizers, turned homeward as soon as their vows were fulfilled and as transportation became available. Within a few months Godfrey's army had shrunk until he could count on no more than a few hundred knights and one or two thousand footmen. In 1100, when Baldwin became king, Fulcher of Chartres believed, not unreasonably, that there were not enough Christians left to defend Jerusalem from the Saracens "if only they dared attack us".

Long before this rapid demobilization the leaders of the crusade had felt the need for reinforcements. Their letters home as they moved into enemy territory had punctuated stirring accounts of victories with pleas for prayers, subsidies, and recruits. These requests they continued to send westward by letter and word of mouth as pilgrims returned after the taking of Jerusalem. Even earlier than the princes, Urban II had understood that the hot flame of enthusiasm he had kindled on the plain outside Clermont would not insure the permanent conquest of the Holy Land. After the departure of the hosts in 1096 he had continued to urge, by letter and by voice, the Jerusalem way. He had thus enlisted the aid of the maritime cities of Italy, without whose ships Jerusalem could not have been taken or held, and he had tried as well to raise additional armies. In his last councils, at Bari (October 1098) and Rome (April 1099), Urban introduced crusading business, and it is possible that he considered seriously the invitation to come out with fresh recruits and assume command of the crusade he had launched.[1]

It was Urban's tragedy that he died on July 29 without learning of the victory at Jerusalem a fortnight earlier. His work went on without a break, however. New armies were recruited in Europe and marched out bravely toward the Holy Land. Fulcher of Chartres referred to the movement as a second crusade and so it was, though modern usage has preferred the less accurate desig-

[1] H. Hagenmeyer, *Epistulae et chartae ad historiam primi belli sacri spectantes*; *Die Kreuzzugsbriefe aus den Jahren 1088–1100* (Innsbruck, 1901), epp. VI, VIII, IX, XII, XV, XVI, XVII, pp. 59ff.; C. J. Hefele, *Histoire des conciles*, tr. H. Leclercq, V (Paris, 1912), 460–461.

nation of Crusade of 1101. Whatever it be called, the expedition was an utter failure which drew sharp criticism from historians of the time and scant attention from those of later centuries. But there is some value in describing that failure in order to make clear the difficulties inherent in the overland approach to Jerusalem.

Urban's successor was Rainerius of Blera, who was enthroned as Paschal II on August 14, 1099. As a young monk — whether of Cluny or Vallombrosa is uncertain — Rainerius had favorably impressed Gregory VII. Called to Rome, Rainerius had advanced rapidly in the papal curia, being named cardinal-priest of St. Clement's. He had enjoyed Urban's favor too, serving as his legate in Spain, and it was reported that Urban had suggested Rainerius as his successor. With his background, it was inevitable that Paschal should continue the crusading policy of Urban and should use the techniques that had already proved successful.[2]

Paschal must have heard of the crusaders' crowning success soon after his elevation, but it was late in 1099 before Daimbert's report was brought to him by Robert of Flanders. Paschal's reply, dated April 28, 1100, accredited to the crusaders a new legate, cardinal-bishop Maurice of Porto, and urged that the Christian forces stay on in the east to complete their task. Several months earlier, as he learned from returning pilgrims something of the precarious situation in the Holy Land, the pope had addressed a letter to the clergy of Gaul, directing them to preach a new crusade. All soldiers should be asked to enlist, with a promise of the privileges instituted by Urban, but special pressure was to be used on all who had failed to make good crusading vows taken earlier. In spite of the threat of excommunication, this latter group seems to have been quite large. It included laggards who had never left home, faint-hearted pilgrims who had deserted in Italy or elsewhere along the road and, most odious of all, the "rope-dancers" who had fled the siege of Antioch. Letters from the east had been particularly insistent that the slackers be returned to combat; for the sake of discipline and morale Paschal was forced to stress their case, though he hoped also to attract a large number of new volunteers.[3]

In retrospect his task appears less difficult than Urban's had been in 1095. True, Paschal could count on little help from the

[2] *Liber pontificalis* (ed. J. M. March, Barcelona, 1925), pp. 132–135; B. Monod, *Essai sur les rapports de Pascal II avec Philippe Ier* (Paris, 1907), pp. 1–4; H. K. Mann, *Lives of the Popes in the Middle Ages*, VIII (2nd ed., London, 1925), 5–11.

[3] Hagenmeyer, *Epistulae*, XVIII, XIX, XXII, pp. 103ff.

monarchs of western Europe. His attitude toward Henry IV was as stern as had been that of his predecessors. Philip I of France was sunk in sloth and at odds with the papacy because of his matrimonial ventures. In England William Rufus was as cynically realistic as he had been in 1095; when Henry I succeeded him in August 1100, it was without regard for the claims of Robert of Normandy and in apparent contradiction of the latter's crusading privileges. The Spanish monarchs had Saracens enough along their own frontier. Paschal, who knew something of the unending demands of the *reconquista*, released from their crusading vows knights from Castile and Leon, sent home others who had already started for Jerusalem, and made plain to Alfonso VI that his task was in Spain.[4] But these handicaps were not prohibitive. The First Crusade had succeeded, as Guibert of Nogent observed, without benefit of kings; what was needed now was not so much ambitious monarchs, with their interests rooted in Europe, as a supply of soldiers and colonists willing to serve under experienced leaders in the Levant. And to attract such recruits Paschal had a signal advantage in the manifest success of Urban's expedition. References in contemporary sources — chronicles and charters, sermons and songs — show how widely the news of the capture of Jerusalem spread; that news moved many to follow the heroes whose names were soon to be legendary in Europe. Some of the recruits were repeaters, largely from northern France, but for the most part they came from regions moved only lightly by the excitement of 1095–1096: from Aquitaine and Burgundy, from Germany and Lombardy.

In that last region there was little left for the new pope to do. A center of opposition to the reform papacy, Lombardy had contributed few troops to the First Crusade, but sentiment had changed as the movement had prospered. A few months before his death Urban II wrote to Anselm of Buis, a staunch supporter who had recently been installed as archbishop at Milan, asking him to lead his people on crusade. This plea was seconded by letters from the Holy Land circulated in Lombardy by the Genoese late in 1099. Anselm accepted the invitation, named a suffragan to act in his stead, and levied on the income of his clergy to help defray expenses. The archbishop's preaching won over men of all ranks, who took the cross singing "Ultreja, ultreja!" At least two bishops went, William of Pavia and Guido of Tortona, and many clergy. There were women too, and children, and the chroniclers — not

[4] Migne, *PL* CLXIII, col. 45 (letters XXV and XXVI) and col. 63 (letter XLIV).

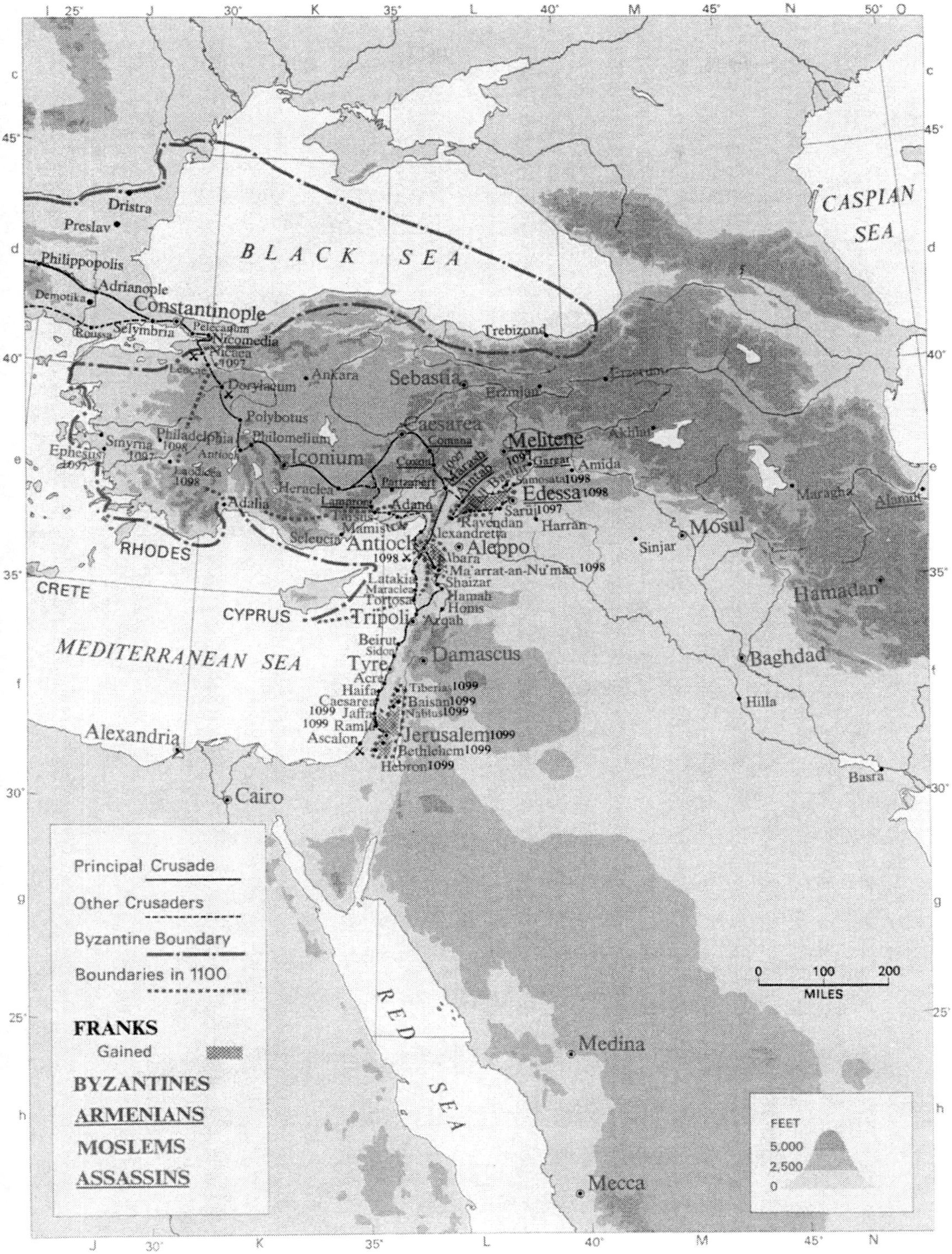

7. The Near East during the First Crusade, 1097–1100 (*Map by the University of Wisconsin Cartographic Laboratory*)

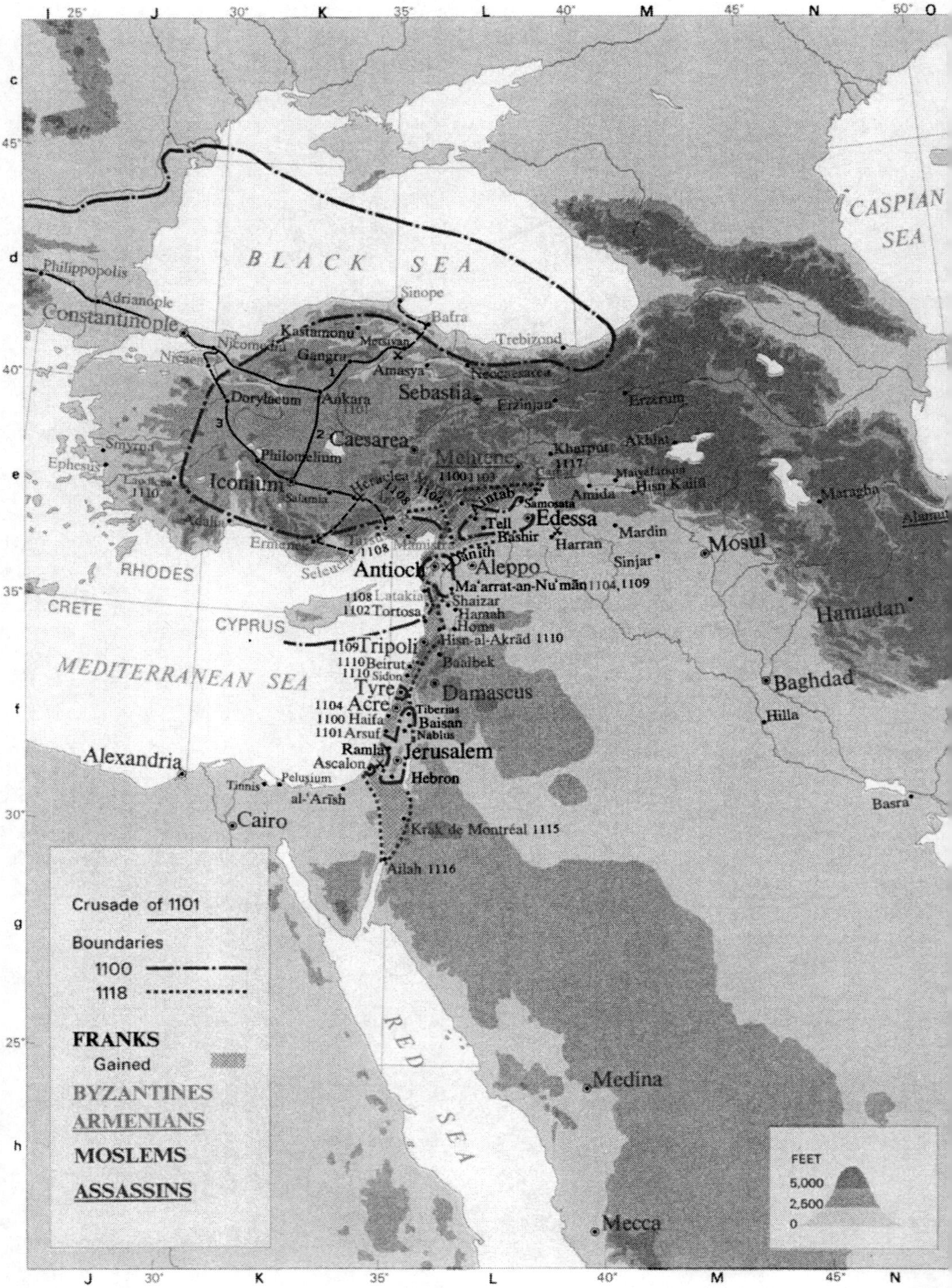

8. The Near East during the Reign of Baldwin I, 1100–1118 (*Map by the University of Wisconsin Cartographic Laboratory*)

Italian — were to accuse the Lombard host of poor discipline and lack of stamina in battle. The lay leaders were of respectable rather than exalted rank: count Albert of Biandrate, with his brother Guido and his nephew Otto Altaspata; Hugh of Montebello; and count Albert of Parma. This last Albert has been identified as a brother of the anti-pope Guibert, who died just as the crusaders marched off in September of 1100, and Albert's enlistment has been cited as a posthumous token of Urban's victory.[5]

It was in France that Paschal II made his chief effort and had his chief success, though it is impossible of course to say how much that owed to the formal campaign of the church, how much to an aroused public opinion. In response to Paschal's encyclical letter archbishop Manasses II of Rheims wrote to bishop Lambert of Arras, repeating the pope's call for soldiers and adding the pleas of Godfrey and Arnulf from Jerusalem. Presumably Manasses wrote also to his other bishops. Perhaps other Gallic metropolitans did likewise: our information in the case of Rheims results from a chance survival of a bishop's correspondence. At any rate when Hugh of Die, archbishop of Lyons, convoked a synod at Anse in the spring or summer of 1100 four archbishops and nine bishops joined him in promulgating Paschal's crusading decree. Hugh had served both Gregory VII and Urban II as legate in France, but Paschal had decided to use Italians rather than natives in that office so Hugh took the cross, later obtaining the pope's permission to make the pilgrimage and an appointment as legate in Asia.[6]

Soon after the meeting at Anse, Paschal's new legates, the cardinals John of St. Anastasia and Benedict of St. Eudoxia, arrived in France. They held a council at Valence toward the end of September and, passing through Limoges, came to Poitiers where they convoked another council on November 18, fifth anniversary of the opening of Clermont. At Poitiers certainly, and apparently at the other cities, the legates preached the crusade, "violently exciting the people that they should quickly aid the faithful in God's war." As at Clermont, the response was im-

[5] Landulf of San Paulo, *Historia Mediolanensis* (*MGH, SS.*, XX), p. 22; Caffaro, *De liberatione*, xii (p. 58); Ekkehard, xxii (p. 221); Albert of Aix, VIII, i (p. 559); Riant, "Un Dernier triomphe d'Urbain II," *Revue des questions historiques*, XXXIV (1883), 247–254. Bishop Aldo of Piacenza was probably in the army too: G. Tononi, "Actes constatant la participation des plaisançais à la première croisade," *AOL*, I (1881), pp. 395–401.

[6] Hagenmeyer, *Epistulae*, XX, p. 175; Hugh of Flavigny, *Chronicon* (*MGH, SS.*, VIII), p. 487; *Gallia Christiana*, IV, 97–98; *Cartulaire de l'abbaye de Savigny* (ed. A. Bernard, Paris, 1853), no. 819, p. 433; A. Fliche, *Le Règne de Philippe Ier* (Paris, 1912), p. 363.

mediate and enthusiastic: nobles, clergy, and simple folk "assumed the sign of Christ's cross."[7]

The most powerful layman to enlist at Poitiers was William IX, duke of Aquitaine and count of Poitou. He had resisted Urban's call in 1095, staying in France to prey on the lands of his crusading neighbor, Raymond of Toulouse. William, a light-hearted young man who has since become famous as the first of the troubadours, had been in trouble with the church, and now incurred further displeasure by his belligerent defense of his suzerain Philip I before the legates at Poitiers, so that some have thought that his vow was in expiation of his violence at the council. But there is evidence to show that he had tried to raise funds for a crusade by mortgaging his duchy to William Rufus before the latter's death on August 2, and it seems probable that the duke was moved more by reports of glorious deeds done in the east than by ecclesiastical strictures.[8]

William was able to muster a large army from his own and neighboring territories. Among the leaders were count Geoffrey of Vendôme, Herbert, viscount of Thouars, and his brother Geoffrey, Hugh of Lusignan (a half-brother of Raymond of Toulouse who apparently bore no bitter grudge against William), and many clergy including bishops Reginald of Périgueux and William of Auvergne. The clergy added a not unneeded touch of respectability, for while some crusaders set out with their wives, William IX left his spouse to manage his estates and took with him a bevy of damsels.[9]

Save in the case of a few princes there is no information concerning the circumstances under which men vowed to go to Jerusalem. One would suppose that French preachers, local or itinerant, repeated the pope's message as others had done in 1096. For example, two of the most celebrated pulpit orators of the day — Robert of Arbrissel and Raoul Ardent — were at Poitiers and the latter is supposed to have gone to the east with his patron William IX; it would have been strange if such men had not helped speed the new call. Enthusiasm was aroused in many

[7] *Vita B. Hilarii* (*RHGF*, XIV), p. 108; *Vita B. Bernardi abbatis de Tironio* (*ibid.*), p. 166; *Chronicon S. Maxentii Pictavensis*, ad ann. 1100, p. 420; Geoffrey of Chalard, *Dictamen de primordiis ecclesiae Castaliensis* (*RHC, Occ.*, V), p. 348.

[8] On William IX's enlistment, Cate, "A Gay Crusader," *Byzantion*, XVI (1942–1943), 503–512. The negotiations with William Rufus are mentioned in Ordericus Vitalis, X, xii (IV, 80), and William of Malmesbury, IV, 333 (II, 379).

[9] *Chronica prioratus de casa Vicecomitis*, ad ann. 1101, p. 340; *Gesta Ambaziensium dominorum*, p. 86; Geoffrey of Vigeois, *Chronicon*, ad ann. 1101 (*RHGF*, XII), p. 391; Abbé Cousseau, "Mémoire historique sur l'église de Notre-Dame de Lusignan," *Mémoires de la Société des antiquaires de l'ouest*, XI (1844); Guibert of Nogent, VII, xxiii (p. 243).

places by the display of relics brought back from Outremer, and everywhere by the tales of the returning veterans.[10]

In northern France, whence many volunteers had gone out in 1096, there were quite a few deserters who now reënlisted, though the inordinate attention they received from the chroniclers stemmed from their rank and notoriety rather than from their great number. Best known of the group were Stephen of Blois and Hugh of Vermandois. Clerical threats were strongly reinforced by popular indignation over their supposed cowardice and, in the case of Stephen — if we may believe the report of a gossipy monk who certainly was no eyewitness — by complaints uttered by his spirited wife during their most intimate marital relations. Another defaulter from Antioch, Guy Trousseau of Montlhéry, was represented by two kinsmen: Guy II ("the Red"), count of Rochefort and seneschal to Philip I; and Miles of Bray, viscount of Troyes, probably second of that name and grandson of Guy I. Other nobles from the region, with no stigma of desertion, included Odo Arpin, viscount of Bourges, Hugh Bardulf II of Broyes, Baldwin of Grandpré, Dodo of Clermont, and Walbert, seneschal of Laon. There were three bishops in the host: William of Paris, Ingelrand of Laon, and Hugh of Soissons; William had attended the synod at Anse, the other two that at Poitiers.[11]

The response in eastern France was equally enthusiastic. William II, count of Nevers, Auxerre, and Tonnerre, enlisted; the contingent he raised from his territories, while not so numerous as that from Aquitaine, was to act as a separate army. Volunteers from neighboring Burgundy, on the other hand, joined with Stephen of Blois's forces. The two most important leaders were Odo, duke of Burgundy, and Stephen, count of Burgundy and Mâcon. Unfortunately the chroniclers have confused these two persons so that it is usually impossible to determine which is referred to, but charters of the time show that both were among the crusaders who left in 1101. Duke Odo was a veteran of the Spanish wars against the Moslems and a sometime benefactor of Molesme and Cîteaux, but he had recently incurred papal dis-

[10] J. de Petigny, "Robert d'Arbrissel et Geoffroi de Vendôme," *Bibliothèque de l'école des chartes*, 3rd ser., XV (1854), 1–30; Fliche, *Philippe Ier*, p. 69; *Histoire littéraire de la France*, IX, 254–265. Examples of relics brought back by crusaders are widely spread; see, for example, Sigebert of Gembloux, *Chronica* (*MGH, SS.*, VI), p. 395; *Chronicon S. Maxentii*, ad ann. 1100, p. 419; Ortlieb, *Chronicon Zwifaltense* (*MGH, SS.*, X), pp. 88–89; *Narratio Acquicinensis* (*RHC, Occ.*, V), pp. 248–251; C. W. David, *Robert Curthose* (Cambridge, 1920), p. 227.

[11] Ordericus Vitalis, X, xix (IV, 118); Guibert of Nogent, VII, xxiv (p. 243); Albert of Aix, VIII, vi (p. 563); Suger, *Vita Ludovici* (ed. H. Waquet, Paris, 1929), pp. 37–39; *Gallia Christiana*, VII, 52–55; IX, 353–354, 525–526.

pleasure by infringing on the lands of Cluny in spite of the complaints of his sainted uncle, abbot Hugh. Excommunicated by the legates at Valence, Odo had made retribution and had taken the cross. Count Stephen had been ruling for his elder brother Reginald, who had gone out to Jerusalem; another brother, archbishop Hugh of Besançon, accompanied Stephen in 1101.[12]

In Germany, as in Italy, the favorable reaction to crusading propaganda was in some degree a measure of the increased prestige of the papacy. As Ekkehard of Aura noted, it was the strife between emperor and pope that had kept the Germans aloof during the First Crusade. Germany was now enjoying a respite from civil war, and at the death of Guibert in 1100 there was for a time some hope that the papal schism might be healed. At any rate, Henry IV interposed no objections to enlistments in Germany (he was to propose a pilgrimage himself two years later), and some of his adherents were among those who now took the cross. One small band was led by Conrad, called Henry's constable but otherwise unidentified. There was a second and much larger army. Chroniclers speak of recruits from all the duchies, but most of the persons actually named were from Bavaria and its marches. The ranking layman was Welf IV of Bavaria. The old duke had fought first for Henry IV, then on the papal side, but had latterly made his peace with the emperor and now had determined to go to Jerusalem in expiation of his sins. He was accompanied by Ida of Austria, widow of Leopold II and mother of the ruling margrave, Leopold III; by count Frederick of Bogen and the burgrave Henry of Regensburg; and by one Bernhard, sometimes identified as count of Scheyern. Among the many clergy attached to the army were archbishop Thiemo of Salzburg, bishop Ulrich of Passau, abbot Giselbert of Admont, and, fortunately for us, the historian Ekkehard of Aura.[13]

Welf's army was accounted large by contemporaries. So for that matter were the forces raised at the same time in other lands.

[12] Albert speaks only of "Stephen" of Burgundy, but uses both titles, duke and count; Guibert speaks of the duke of Burgundy without naming him. Ordericus names both duke Stephen and count Stephen. Many of the other sources identify count Stephen. The documentary evidence can be found in *Cartulaire de l'abbaye de Molesme* (ed. J. Laurent, 2 vols., Paris, 1907–1911), II, 13, 18, 143; and *Recueil des chartes de l'abbaye de Cluny* (6 vols., Paris, 1876–1903), V, no. 3809. Other evidence is given in E. Petit, *Ducs de Bourgogne* (9 vols., Paris, 1885–1905), I, 234–264.

[13] Albert of Aix, VIII, vi (p. 562), and VIII, xxxiv (p. 579); Ekkehard, ix (pp. 109–113), and xxii (p. 227); *Historia Welforum Weingartensis*, xiii (*MGH, SS.*, III), p. 13; G. M. Knonau, *Jahrbücher ... Heinrich IV und Heinrich V* (7 vols., Leipzig, 1890–1909), V, 134–136; S. Riezler, *Geschichte Bayerns* (Gotha, 1878), I, 560–562.

The medieval man had many virtues, but accuracy in statistics was not one of them. No scholar today accepts the huge figures cited by the chroniclers. Some have made ingenious attempts to scale such numbers down to a more reasonable estimate, but this author is skeptical of the utility of such an exercise, at least in the case of the armies of 1101. Not only are the grand totals fantastically large; even in dealing with small groups where one might expect some semblance of accuracy the chroniclers too often use symbolic numbers such as 700. Albert of Aix says that Conrad's band numbered 2,000 and that of William of Nevers 15,000. The absence of other important magnates in either force would suggest, as Albert is saying, that these groups were smaller than the other armies, but there is no reason to suppose that the sizes varied in proportion to his figures. Indirect evidence in the sources — rather than the numbers cited — and the population of the several areas drawn from seem to indicate that the Lombard and Aquitanian armies were the two largest to set out. Ekkehard thought that the total forces were almost as great as those of 1096, Guibert of Nogent that they were quite as large.[14] A rough comparison of the status of the leaders in each case makes either estimate sound reasonable; unfortunately we do not know how many went out in 1096. On one point the sources were in complete agreement — that in each of the bands in 1101 there were too many noncombatants. In spite of the advice of experienced crusaders and contrary to papal decree, the fighting men were accompanied by many women of varying degrees of honesty and by children. The clergy who went along may have served a more useful military purpose, but they were too numerous.

On the whole the crusaders seem to have been adequately provided with funds; at least they were able to purchase supplies wherever a normal market existed and they still had rich treasures when defeated in Asia Minor. Financing was done partly by the individual pilgrim, partly by aid from the wealthy leaders. Other prelates probably followed the practice of Anselm of Milan and Hugh of Lyons in exacting a subsidy from their clergy. For most

[14] Ekkehard, xxii (p. 221); Guibert of Nogent, VII, xxiii (p. 243). The figures cited for the Crusade of 1101 are as follows. Albert of Aix: Lombards, 30,000; Lombards and northern Franks, 260,000, of whom 60,000 were slain in the battle that almost annihilated the army; Aquitanians and Bavarians, 160,000; Nivernais, 15,000; Conrad's Germans, 2000. Ekkehard: Lombards, 50,000; Aquitanians and Bavarians, 160,000; total forces, 300,000. Anna Comnena: Lombards and northern Franks, 50,000 cavalry, 100,000 infantry. William of Malmesbury: Aquitanians and northern Franks, 60,000 cavalry, more than that number of infantry. Ordericus Vitalis: Aquitanians, 300,000 departed, but when joined by other Franks and Lombards, only 50,000. Fulcher of Chartres: 100,000 killed in Asia Minor. Ibn-al-Athīr, 300,000 in Christian army.

laymen it was a matter of raising money from their estates. William IX, balked in his plan to borrow from William Rufus, was said to have given up his questionable title to Toulouse in return for a lump sum. Odo Arpin sold his *vicomté* of Bourges to Philip I for an alleged sum of 60,000 *solidi* in one of the first permanent accretions to the royal domain.[15] The cartularies, which are the richest mine for this sort of information, show how large a part the monasteries played in financing this crusade, as men sold or hypothecated, under terms that seem not disadvantageous to the abbey, a field or vineyard here, an allod or meadow there. The charters tell too of pious donations made on the eve of departure and they sometimes add a bit of precise detail to enliven the dry narrative of the chronicles.[16]

There is no record to show that Paschal had a general plan for the crusade. There was some effort to coördinate the movements of the several armies, and for that he may have been responsible. As in 1096 there was no single layman to command the hosts; there was not even the unity furnished by Adhémar of Le Puy, for Hugh of Lyons, Paschal's legate to Asia, seems to have reached Jerusalem without traveling with any of the large bands. But the various leaders operated according to a plan based on that of the First Crusade, whether by papal direction or by common knowledge of what had happened before. They knew something of the intentions of each other and in some instances planned a rendezvous along the route through eastern Europe; all expected to gather in Constantinople before beginning the trek across Asia Minor.

The Lombards, first to muster, were first to leave, departing from Milan on September 13, 1100. They marched northeastward, crossing Carinthia with permission of the duke, Henry of Eppenstein, and passed peacefully through Hungary, probably down the Sava to join Godfrey's earlier path at Belgrade. On entering Bulgaria, the Lombards sent messengers to Alexius, requesting market privileges as they traversed his realm, and this, subject to good behavior, the emperor granted. He specified as open markets the

[15] Robert of Torigny, *Chronica* (*Chronicles of the Reigns of Stephen, Henry II and Richard*, Rolls Series, 4 vols., London, 1884–1889), IV, 202; William of Newburgh, *Historia rerum Anglicanorum*, II, x (*ibid.*, I, 121–122); Ordericus Vitalis, X, xix (IV, 119); M. Prou, *Recueil des actes de Philippe Ier* (Paris, 1908), p. 368.

[16] These are too numerous to cite in full, but for interesting examples see the following: *Das Saalbuch des Benedictiner-Stiftes Gottweig* (*Fontes rerum Austriacarum*, II, Abt. VIII), pp. 14–15; T. Mayer, "Einige Bemerkungen über die Familie der Stifter von Seitenstetten," *Archiv für österreichische Geschichte*, XXI (1859), 372; *Codices traditionum ecclesiae Pataviensis*, no. XLVI; *Monumenta Boica*, XXIX, iii; *Recueil des chartres de l'abbaye de Cluny*, V, no 3737.

following towns: Roussa (Keshan), Panidos, Demotika (Didymoteikhon), Philippopolis (Plovdiv), Adrianople (Edirne), Rodosto (Tekirdagh), Selymbria (Silivri), and a place called "Natura". The crusaders wintered in Bulgaria; in spite of their agreement with Alexius they began to pillage. They seized cattle and fowl without paying for them — a not unusual practice for soldiers whether in friendly or enemy territory — and they compounded their felony by eating the meat in Lent and on fast days. They turned then to graver crimes, violating Greek shrines and committing sordid atrocities. These disorders were at least in part the work of camp-followers and without the sanction of the Lombard leaders; when Alexius learned of the misdeeds, he ordered the Lombards to proceed to Constantinople directly, and the leaders obeyed.[17]

The army arrived at the capital late in February or early in March and by imperial command pitched camp outside the city on the Arm of St. George. There they remained for two months, awaiting reinforcements from Germany and France. Again the Lombards began to pillage and Alexius attempted, as he had in 1096–1097, to move his guests across the strait where they might stay in safety at Civetot (Cibotus) or "Rufinel" until joined by the other bands. When the Italians refused to move, Alexius cut off their market privileges and after three days of hunger they armed themselves and attacked the imperial palace of Blachernae, where they killed a young kinsman of the emperor and a pet lion — an act that was responsible for Ordericus Vitalis's quaint belief that Alexius had a bodyguard of lions. Embarrassed by this violence, Anselm, Albert of Biandrate, and other leaders rounded up the rioters — who included knights as well as common folk — and got them back to camp. The leaders then went to Alexius and, having cleared themselves of guilt by an oath, attempted to assuage his wrath. The emperor still insisted on ferrying the crusaders across the strait and resorted to his usual practice of reinforcing his requests with rich gifts, which only Anselm refused. Eventually concord was reached, partly through the good offices of Raymond of St. Gilles, count of Toulouse.

Count Raymond had left the Holy Land in August 1099 after the capture of Jerusalem and the subsequent victory at Ascalon. His Provençal troops were anxious to return to their homes, and Raymond himself was far from happy over the installation of

[17] Albert of Aix, VIII, i–iii (pp. 559–560); Ekkehard, xxiii, p. 227; *Notae S. Mariae Mediolanensis* (*MGH, SS*,. XVIII), p. 386 (giving the date of departure).

Godfrey as Advocate of the Holy Sepulcher. He had come to Constantinople from Latakia in the summer of 1100 and was now a firm ally of the emperor. Indeed, as preceding chapters have indicated, Raymond had always favored a close association with Alexius.[18] A more recent bond between them was their dislike of Bohemond, who had thwarted them both.

Thus it was that amid mutual promises of peace, Alexius restored to the crusaders the right of buying supplies and a few days after Easter (April 21) the army crossed the Bosporus and camped at Nicomedia. There they were joined by the German band led by Conrad, who had brought his troops through Greek lands without serious trouble and, after a favorable reception by Alexius, had crossed into Asia Minor. Much larger reinforcements arrived from France, the forces led by Stephen of Blois and those from Burgundy. Apparently they had left home early in the spring, but of their march to Constantinople we know nothing. At the request of the crusaders, Alexius gave them Raymond of Toulouse and the Greek general Tsitas as advisers and a force of mounted native auxiliaries known as Turcopoles — estimated at five hundred — to serve as guides. The European reinforcements came in May, and early in June the host moved out.[19]

Stephen of Blois and other men of experience proposed to follow the familiar route along which they had marched in 1097. The Lombards had other ideas. At Constantinople they had learned of the capture of Bohemond the previous summer by Malik-Ghāzī ibn-Dānishmend, the Turkish emir of Sebastia (Sivas), who now held him at Pontic Neocaesarea (Niksar). They were determined to invade Pontus or, as they called it, "Khorassan," to release Bohemond and perhaps conquer that land. Stephen, Raymond, and Alexius tried to dissuade the Lombards from this foolish diversion, but in vain; rather than split the host, in which the Italians constituted the most numerous force, the French magnates finally acquiesced.

The crusaders left Nicomedia early in June with Raymond and the Turcopoles in the van. Provisions were plentiful, discipline lax. On June 23 they came through the mountains to attack Ankara. After almost wiping out the Turkish garrison they re-

[18] See above, chapters VIII, IX, and X.

[19] Albert of Aix, VIII, ii–vi (pp. 560–563); Ekkehard, xxiii, (p. 227); Anna Comnena, (*RHC, Grecs*, I) pp. 70–71; Ordericus Vitalis, X, xix (IV, 120–124); Ordericus Vitalis, who shows throughout a curious and garbled affinity with Albert, puts the Aquitanian army with the Lombards in these incidents. H. Hagenmeyer, "Chronologie de l'histoire du royaume de Jérusalem," *ROL*, IX (1902), no. 573, p. 437, dates the crossing at "about" June 3.

stored the town to the Greeks in accordance with the oath which Alexius usually exacted from western princes. Turning northeastward, the crusaders came to Gangra (Chankîrî); they found the fortifications too strong to storm and had to content themselves with burning the crops in the neighborhood. From this point on, the westerners were constantly harassed by the soldiers of Kîlîj (or Kîlîch) Arslan, the Selchükid sultan of Rūm.[20]

When the Turks began to cut off stragglers, the Christian leaders set a vanguard of Franks and a rear guard of Lombards. The latter broke under a sudden attack and permitted the mounted Turkish archers to slaughter many of the road-weary pilgrims. The rear guard then became the post of honor with the several leaders rotating in command there. First the Burgundians, then Raymond's Provençals and Turcopoles, performed more creditably in that assignment than had the Italians, and by tightening up their line of march the crusaders were able to go forward without excessive losses.

It is impossible to reconstruct from the sources the exact route followed. From Gangra the direct way to Neocaesarea went eastward across the Halys (Kîzîl) river and through Amasya. But Albert reports that after the crusaders had passed several towns and castles which he could not identify, Raymond was bribed by the Turks to lead them astray and that thereafter the way led through wilderness and desert. The Christians now began to suffer from shortages of food. There was no lack of money but they found no markets, and only those wealthy persons who had brought provisions by cart from Nicomedia or Civetot had plenty. Lesser folk had to forage, a difficult way of life, what with the rough country and the even rougher Turks. By Albert's account the army had gone far north of the road to Neocaesarea — at least he shows one large body of footmen searching for food in the vicinity of Kastamonu. Intent on gathering young barley (in the grain but not yet ripe in July) and crabapples, the Christians were trapped in a valley and burned to death in a great brush fire.

[20] The account that follows in the next few paragraphs derives chiefly from Albert of Aix, VIII, vii–xxi (pp. 563–573), and Anna Comnena (*RHC, Grecs*, I), pp. 70–72. Most of the other sources tend to confuse this battle with the defeat of the other Christian armies. See, for example: Fulcher of Chartres, II, xvi (pp. 430–432); Ordericus Vitalis, X, xix (IV, 125–128); Guibert of Nogent, VII, xxiv (pp. 243–245); Ibn-al-Athīr, p. 203; Matthew of Edessa, xxii (pp. 56–57). Hagenmeyer's date of August 5 is logically derived but by no means certain ("Chronologie ... du royaume de Jérusalem," no. 589). On the geography of this campaign, see W. Tomaschek, "Zur historischen Topographie von Kleinasien im Mittelalter," *Sitzungsberichte der kaiserlichen Akademie der Wissenschaften, philos.-hist. Classe*, CXXIV (1891), 87–88, and Kugler, *Albert von Aachen*, pp. 313–314.

The news of this slaughter frightened the crusaders; having been a fortnight on the march from Gangra they turned back to the road toward Neocaesarea. After crossing the Halys they came to a town inhabited by Greek Christians. These the westerners allegedly slew in a senseless massacre. Six days after the ambush below Kastamonu the army debouched from the mountains of Paphlagonia and camped on a plain below. Here for the first time they met the main Turkish army, comprising troops of Malik-Ghāzī of Sebastia, Rîdvan of Aleppo, and Karaja of Harran. It had been the internal dissension among the Selchükid sultans and the local emirs that had made possible the success of the First Crusade; now the coöperation between the Moslem princes of Anatolia was the undoing of the Christians.

Albert of Aix's detailed account of the fighting thereafter has an epic quality that may derive from a source more literary than the tales of survivors that he cites; his details are suspect, but the general picture receives some corroboration from Anna Comnena. The battle lasted several days during the early part of August. On the first day the Turkish horsemen surrounded the camp, yelling horribly after their fashion and shooting at the Christians with their bows of horn and bone. By holding together compactly the crusaders repulsed this assault. Next day a very large foraging party under the German Conrad and his nephew Bruno attacked and seized a Turkish stronghold in the neighborhood of Mersivan (Merzifon), taking what victuals and plunder they found, but they were trapped during their return to camp and lost all their spoils and many men. On the morrow both armies rested; Albert says it was Sunday and one may marvel at this curious observance of the Truce of God.

On Monday the archbishop of Milan preached to the whole crusading host, exhibiting a relic of St. Ambrose and the "Holy Lance" which Raymond had brought along, and exhorting the multitude to confess. The army was then ordered in five "battles": the Burgundians, Raymond and his troops, the Germans, the western Franks, and the Lombards. The Lombards, placed in the van, were driven back after heavy fighting and so in sequence were the Germans, Burgundians, and French. Toward dusk Raymond took refuge on a crag whence he in turn was rescued by Stephen and Conrad.

The Christians had sustained heavy losses and the day had certainly gone to the Turks, but the latter had suffered too and the issue was still in balance as each force settled in camp for the night. Then panic struck among the crusaders. According to Albert it was Raymond who began the flight; Anna Comnena says the other leaders first sought from Raymond and Tsitas the location of some imperial stronghold whither they could flee. Regardless of who ran first, the flight became general as the horsemen rode off leaving behind their women and children and the infantry. The nonchalance with which the knights deserted their ladies in this and subsequent battles (without serious chiding from the chroniclers) is a sad commentary on the practices, as opposed to the theories, of chivalry.

The Turks, learning during the night of the stampede, swarmed into the crusaders' camp at dawn. There was a wild scene of rape and carnage. Some of the handsomer women and youths were saved for the slave market and the rest were killed. Then the tents were looted. After these important preliminaries the Turks went in pursuit of the broken army. The footmen they cut down like ripe grain. One small band held together and fought its way to Byzantine territory, but most of the Christians perished in the battle or the rout. Albert lists a number of knights killed: Baldwin of Grandpré, Dodo of Clermont, Walbert of Laon, Eraldus and Enguerrand of Châlons-sur-Marne, Arnulf, and Walter of Châtillon. These were all from northern France; presumably the other contingents suffered equally.

Many of the magnates escaped, however. Raymond fled northward to the Black Sea port of Bafra and thence to Sinope where he embarked for Constantinople. Stephen of Burgundy, Stephen of Blois, Guy of Rochefort, Hugh Bardulf, Anselm, the bishops of Laon and Soissons, and others made their way to Sinope. With such followers as they could round up, they then returned overland to Constantinople. There they were received in kindly fashion by Alexius, who tried to make good their losses by his gifts and an offer to support them until they could continue their pilgrimage. The archbishop of Milan, worn out by the campaign, died on September 30 and was buried at Constantinople.[21]

Most of the western sources, written in an atmosphere unfriendly toward the Greeks, accuse Alexius of complicity in the defeat near Mersivan. This charge will be examined later in the context of similar disasters to the other armies of 1101. Here it is appropriate to note that Albert, like other authors, links Ray-

[21] Albert of Aix, VIII, xxii–xxiv (pp. 573–574); Anna Comnena (*RHC, Grecs*, I), p. 73. The date for Anselm's death is given in *Catalogus archiepiscoporum Mediolanensium* (*MGH, SS.*, VIII), p. 105.

mond with the basileus in his alleged act of perfidy. But Albert is not consistent. He shows the emperor and Raymond opposing the Lombards in their mad diversion toward Pontus, and Raymond fighting valiantly against the Turks even after his alleged agreement with them. His flight was no more disgraceful than that of the other magnates, yet Albert shows the emperor upbraiding Raymond for having deserted his companions. There is no real evidence of a plot on the part of the emperor or his Provençal ally. The crusaders were defeated because of their own willful stupidity.

Meanwhile other crusading forces had passed through Constantinople. That led by William of Nevers poses a peculiar problem. Among the chroniclers it is only Albert of Aix who treats the Nivernais as a separate army, and for want of substantiating evidence some scholars have supposed that they went out with either the Burgundians or the Poitevins. But most of the chroniclers tend to confuse the various contingents, sometimes to the extent of joining them all into one huge force; even Ekkehard knew little about the armies after they entered Asia Minor. Albert's account on the contrary is circumstantial and consistent enough to warrant some credence.

A charter to Molesme indicates that William of Nevers was preparing to set out for Jerusalem on January 30, 1101, and he probably left soon after. He led his troops down through Italy to Brindisi and crossed to Avlona. The way then was by Thessalonica, the same that Bohemond had followed in 1096. William's army maintained excellent discipline and received decent treatment from the natives. The emperor received the crusaders with kindness, giving them a camp site on the Arm of St. George, but after three days insisted that they cross the strait. On the Asiatic shore they camped for a fortnight while William was in daily attendance upon Alexius.[22]

By Albert's chronology, the Nivernais had arrived toward the middle of June — about the 14th by Hagenmeyer's reckoning. At that time the German and Poitevin bands had already begun to assemble at Constantinople, and it would have been natural for William to have joined forces with them. Instead, shortly after June 24, he led his troops to Civetot and then hurried on in an attempt to overtake the Lombard-Frankish army. By the time he reached Ankara William had found that effort hopeless and after

[22] *Cartulaire de l'abbaye de Molesme,* II, 40–43; Albert of Aix, VIII, xxv–xxvi (pp. 574–575); Le Blanc, *Recherches historiques et statistiques sur Auxerre* (Auxerre, 1830), I, 147–153; Hagenmeyer, "Chronologie ... du royaume de Jérusalem," no. 574.

a day's stop turned south toward Iconium (Konya), where he might await reinforcements. While on this leg of the journey his army was attacked by Turks, perhaps local troops rather than (as Albert says) the victors from Mersivan. After a running fight of three days the Nivernais arrived in mid-August at Iconium, where they found the citadel so strongly garrisoned by Turks that attempts to storm the wall failed. The army moved on to Heraclea (Ereghli, east of Iconium) which the enemy had deserted after destroying all sources of water supply. When the Christians had been weakened by several days of thirst, the Turks surrounded them and attacked in force. After a vain defense the Frankish cavalry broke and fled, leaving the infantry and noncombatants to be slain or captured. As at Mersivan, many women were carried off as slaves. William, with his brother and a standard-bearer, William of Modena, led a small group of knights in flight southwestward to Ermenek. There he hired some imperial Turcopoles to guide the party to Antioch, but the guides proved faithless, robbing the pilgrims and leaving them naked and afoot in the wilderness.[23]

Eventually the unhappy pilgrims found their way to Antioch, where Tancred was ruling in Bohemond's stead. Tancred made good part of their losses and entertained William at his court for a while. The count stayed on at Antioch through the winter, gathering other fugitives who like himself wished to go on to Jerusalem in the spring. By that time their number had been swelled by the remnants of a third defeated army.

The Aquitanians under William IX had left home in the second week in Lent, March 12–19, and marched overland, apparently through northern Italy and Carinthia. Somewhere along the route they joined the main Bavarian army led by Welf IV, which had set out about April 1, and the combined forces went together peacefully through Hungary. In Bulgaria, which they entered early in May, the westerners were greeted by friendly messengers from Alexius, but they were also dogged by his mounted mercenaries, Pechenegs and Kumans. Ekkehard of Aura, travelling with a German group in the wake of Welf's army, complained of attacks by these soldiers; this was no more than retribution for the misdeeds of those crusaders who had preceded him. The Poitevins, an "unrestrained and incorrigible people," got into a fight with some Bulgarians and injured their leader, Guzh. Ac-

[23] Albert of Aix, VIII, xxvii–xxxiii (pp. 575–578).

cordingly, when the crusaders reached Adrianople and wished to enter, they found the long bridge leading into the city blocked by Guzh and his troops. The Poitevins attacked, firing the suburbs and attempting to push across the bridge. Ralph of Saintonge, a relative of William's, was killed, Ardouin of St. Médard and others were captured. But Guzh was taken by the Poitevins and after some parley peace was restored and prisoners were exchanged.[24]

Relations between the crusaders and the Byzantines seem to have been improved by the blood-letting. Guzh allowed the westerners to enter Adrianople and buy supplies, and he furnished an escort which led them to Constantinople without further difficulty.

The main army reached the capital about the beginning of June and was augmented during the next fortnight by the daily arrival of new troops. Alexius received the princes as "sons" and showered them with gifts, but he also exacted from them an oath of fealty similar to that sworn by the crusaders in 1097. Several of the chroniclers picture William IX as a haughty young duke who refused to take the oath and offered gratuitous insults to the emperor, but there is no evidence of any disorders. Alexius distributed money among the lesser folk and made markets available to all, but he also hurried the pilgrims across the straits. The stay in the environs of Constantinople dragged on for five weeks while the pilgrims purchased supplies for the journey and the leaders met in daily council with Alexius. It was probably during this long halt that William of Nevers passed through the capital and his failure to unite with the Poitevins and Bavarians can perhaps be explained by their inordinate delay.[25]

Nor was William's the only band to go on alone. During their long halt the Germans — probably the rank and file rather than the princes — became suspicious of Alexius. They had heard no news of the Lombards, but they suspected — wrongly — that the Greek had forced the crusaders into enemy territory before the arrival of reinforcements; now the Germans began to fear that Alexius was preparing to betray them to the Turks. The pilgrims were seized with panic. Some sold their horses and bought passage

[24] Albert of Aix, VIII, xxxiv–xxxvi (pp. 579–580); Ekkehard, xxii–xxiii (pp. 226–232); *Historia Welforum Weingartensis*, p. 462. The date of William IX's departure is accepted from *Chronica prioratus de casa Vicecomitis*, ad ann. 1101, p. 341, in preference to William of Malmesbury's erroneous estimate of September. Cf. *Gesta regum*, IV, 383 (II, 447). On the German departure, see Hagenmeyer, "Chronologie ... du royaume de Jérusalem," no. 548.

[25] Matthew of Edessa, xxii (pp. 58–59); Ordericus Vitalis, X, xix (IV, 123); Guibert of Nogent, VII, xxiii (p. 243); William of Malmesbury, IV, 383 (II, 447–448); *Narratio Floriacensis de captis Antiocha et Hierosolyma* (*RHC, Occ.*, V), p. 360.

on ships bound for the Holy Land. When warned that Alexius could destroy them at sea as well as on land, many who had already boarded ship debarked and refitted themselves, at great loss, for the overland trip. Ekkehard describes, with evident emotion, the terrible confusion as the German army, already less numerous than the Aquitanian, split into two groups. He himself, after much wavering, elected to go by sea with a sizeable party and arrived safely at Jaffa after a voyage of six weeks.[26]

The more important German leaders and a majority of their followers chose to march on with the French. The combined forces left about the middle of July, having accepted from Alexius a band of Turcopole guides. According to Ekkehard, who now is dependent like Albert on reports from survivors, the army then turned away from the southeasterly road through Rūm and marched east toward Pontus. This was what William of Nevers had done shortly before and like him William IX and Welf were perhaps hoping to join the Lombards. Albert mentions no such deviation from the main military road to Syria. He shows the crusaders marching by way of Nicomedia and Nicaea, and thence to Philomelium (Akshehir), which they destroyed. The early part of the journey was pleasant enough, but after entering enemy territory the Christians began to suffer. The provisions they brought from the coast ran short; the Turks burned the ripe grain and ruined cisterns, wells, and springs. Squadrons of Turkish cavalry punished them in harassing attacks without risking a pitched battle. Passing Iconium, the crusaders destroyed Salamia (Ismil), then headed for Heraclea, early in September.

Near that city they came to a river where they hoped to slake their thirst. But Kilij Arslan and his allies lay in ambush among the growth along the other bank and just as the Christians drew near the water the Turks loosed a volley of arrows and charged. Caught by surprise and weakened by hunger and thirst, the crusaders could not stand up to the fierce assault. After a desperate stand in the marshy land along the river (where their heavy equipment must have been a hindrance) the army dissolved. Some crusaders tried vainly to hide in the marsh grass, some escaped by following the stream up to its source, and others fled into the mountains. Most of the Christians were either killed or enslaved.[27]

[26] Ekkehard, xxiv (pp. 235–239).

[27] *Ibid.*, xxv–xxvi (pp. 239–252); Albert of Aix, VIII, xxxvii–xxxviii (pp. 580–581); *Narratio Floriacensis* (*RHC, Occ.*, V), p. 361; Matthew of Edessa, xxii–xxiii (pp. 59–61); *Anonymous Syriac Chronicle*, pp. 74–75; Bartolf of Nangis, lvi–lvii (pp. 532–533). Kugler, *Albert von Aachen*, pp. 312–313, 332, explains satisfactorily Albert's apparent mistake in the

Among the many women reported to have been carried off into captivity were Corba, wife of Geoffrey Burel, and Ida of Austria. Albert was not certain whether Ida had been captured or killed, but others came to believe that she had lived on in the harem of a Moslem prince to whom she bore a famous son, Zengi. This is an early instance of what was to become a conventional literary theme; it is matched in interest — and lack of credibility — by the legend of Thiemo of Salzburg. The archbishop was carried off by a Turkish emir and being a metal worker of sorts, he was commanded to repair a certain "Mohammedan idol". When the idol began to speak blasphemously, Thiemo broke it and for this he was martyred.[28]

As in the previous defeats, an undue proportion of those who escaped were leaders, perhaps because of their superior horses. The bishop of Auvergne, however, walked out. Welf got away by shedding arms and armor and riding through the mountains. Two of his counts, Bernhard and Henry of Regensburg, made their way to the coast. William IX fled with a single squire and reached Longiniada, the port for Tarsus, then ruled by Bernard the Stranger. Bernard treated them well. After a few days Tancred, learning of William's misfortunes, sent an escort of knights to conduct him to Antioch, where the duke was lavishly entertained. Less certain is the case of Hugh of Vermandois. He was wounded in the knee by an arrow, but escaped to Tarsus, where he died on October 18 and was buried in the church of St. Paul. The chroniclers tell of his reënlistment in France and of his death, but nothing of his activities on crusade. The context suggests that he was with William IX at Heraclea, but the record is none too clear.[29]

With the disaster at Heraclea the military significance of the Crusade of 1101 vanishes. Remnants of the several bands continued their way to Jerusalem but in effect the crusade had become a pilgrimage. Ekkehard saw some of the survivors at Rhodes, Paphos, Jaffa and other ports. But for the magnates, with such fol-

location of the cities in question. Cf. Tomaschek, *op. cit.*, p. 89. In the *Chronica prioratus de casa Vicecomitis*, p. 342, the battle site is identified as "valles Lampadarum". Matthew calls it the plain of Aulos.

[28] For Corba, see *Gesta Ambaziensium dominorum*, p. 103. For Ida, see Albert of Aix, VIII, xxxix (p. 581), and *Historia Welforum Weingartensis*, p. 462. For Thiemo, see *Passio Thiemonis archiepiscopi* (*MGH, SS.*, XXI), p. 462. There are a number of versions of this story. See Riant, "Le Martyre de Thiemo de Salzburg," *Revue des questions historiques*, XXXIX (1906), 218–237. Otto of Freising, who accepted the tradition in a general way, had the good sense to point out that the Moslems did not have idols. Cf. *Chronica*, VII, vii (ed. Hofmeister, pp. 316–317).

[29] Albert of Aix, VIII, xxxix–xl (pp. 581–582); Ekkehard, xxvi (p. 247); Matthew of Edessa, xxiii (p. 61); Fulcher of Chartres, II, xvi (pp. 431–433); William of Tyre, X, xiii (p. 418); Radulf of Caen, *Gesta Tancredi*, cv (p. 680); Guibert of Nogent, VII, xxiii (p. 243).

lowers as they could muster, Antioch served as a new rendezvous. During the autumn and winter, stragglers who had fled overland from the defeats in southern Asia Minor were joined by those fugitives from the first army who had returned to Constantinople and had come on from there by ship to St. Simeon. By the end of February 1102 the newly formed band, which included Albert of Biandrate, Conrad, Stephen of Blois, Stephen of Burgundy, William of Aquitaine, Welf, Raymond of Toulouse, and a number of prelates, was ready to depart.[30]

Raymond's welcome had been less than cordial. Landing at Longiniada, he had been seized by Bernard the Stranger and delivered to Tancred at Antioch. The charge was that Raymond had betrayed his comrades to the Turks; the real reason lay in the feud between Raymond and Bohemond, and the anxiety with which Tancred viewed Raymond's arrival with a band of warriors and the backing of Alexius. The crusading princes interceded for Raymond as they had earlier at Constantinople, and the Latin patriarch, Bernard, added his pleas. Tancred then released his prisoner, first exacting from Raymond a solemn oath that he would not attack any territories between Antioch and Acre.

The crusaders, thanking Tancred for his kindness, marched southward with Raymond in their band. With the aid of a Genoese fleet they attacked Tortosa and after a short siege captured the city. Anxious to get on to Jerusalem, the pilgrims gave the city into the custody of Raymond, who remained there. If Albert's description of the oath is accurate, this constituted an early breach of the agreement; perhaps the chronicler was wrong in believing that Tancred's interest extended so far south as Acre. At any rate, Tortosa was to be the base for further operations on count Raymond's part, leading ultimately to the foundation of the county of Tripoli.[31]

Duke Welf of Bavaria had avoided the siege, going to Jerusalem in the company of Reginald of Burgundy, the brother of count Stephen who had come out earlier. Reginald died on the journey, but Welf performed his devotions at the Holy Sepulcher. He then

[30] Fulcher of Chartres, II, xvi (p. 433); Albert of Aix, VIII, xli (p. 582); Bartolf of Nangis, lvii (p. 532); Radulf of Caen, cxlvii (p. 709). Albert puts the date "mense Martio inchoante". Hagenmeyer, "Chronologie ... du royaume de Jérusalem," no. 629, puts it at "about February 10".

[31] Albert of Aix, VIII, xlii (p. 582); Matthew of Edessa, xxii (pp. 57, 58); Fulcher of Chartres, II, xvii (pp. 433–435); William of Tyre, X, xiii (p. 418); Caffaro, xxiii (p. 69). Albert says Bernard captured Raymond at St. Simeon, but this is evidently an error for Longiniada. See Cahen, *La Syrie du nord à l'époque des croisades* (Paris, 1940), pp. 232, note 10, and 233, note 12. On count Raymond and the establishment of the county of Tripoli, see below, chapter XII.

began the voyage home but died on the island of Cyprus and was buried at Paphos.[32]

The other crusaders, leaving Tortosa, went by way of ʿArqah, Tripoli, and Jubail. Near Beirut they were met by king Baldwin, who had waited there for eighteen days to escort them through a dangerous pass at the Dog river. This service was at the request of the pilgrims themselves; it was a measure of their failure that instead of bringing substantial aid to Baldwin they should now be dependent on his small army. After a joyous meeting the combined forces went on to Jaffa. They reached that port on March 23 to find that some crusaders had already arrived by ship. They stayed a week at Jaffa, celebrating Palm Sunday there on the 30th.

Next day they went on to Jerusalem, where they spent Holy Week in prayer and fasting. They were joined by two belated comrades, Conrad and bishop Ingelrand of Laon, and on Easter all united in celebrating the resurrection of the Lord. While offering thanks for their own safe arrival, the pilgrims persuaded Baldwin to negotiate with Alexius for better treatment of those who might follow in their steps.[33]

Thus the pilgrims had released themselves from their vows and few felt any obligation to stay on. Soon after Easter the group began to break up, as individuals sought some way to return home. A number of them secured passage at Jaffa. William IX sailed from that port either for Europe, as seems more likely, or for Antioch where Albert says he was with Tancred in September. In either event he had arrived at Poitiers by October 29, 1102.[34] Some were less fortunate, being held back by adverse winds. These rejoined Baldwin and during an Egyptian counter-attack in May they were drawn willy-nilly into the defense of the realm.

Baldwin, relying on faulty intelligence, underestimated the strength of the Egyptians as they marched from Ascalon toward Ramla. Without waiting for the considerable force available at Jaffa, he decided to attack with the small body of knights who were with him at Jerusalem. Among them were some survivors of

[32] Albert of Aix, VIII, xliii (p.583); Ekkehard, xxvi (pp. 249–250); *Historia Welforum Weingartensis*, p. 462; *Annales Augustani* (*MGH, SS.*, III), p. 135. Three brothers from the comital family of Burgundy died in the Holy Land during this year: Reginald, Stephen, and Hugh of Besançon. See the letter of pope Calixtus II, who was a fourth brother, cited in Mann, *Lives of the Popes*, VIII, 144.

[33] Fulcher of Chartres, II, xvii (p. 435); Albert of Aix, VIII, xliv–xlv (pp. 583–584); Bartolf of Nangis, lvii (p. 533); William of Tyre, X, xix (p. 428).

[34] William of Tyre, X, xix (p. 429). The date of his presence in France is taken from J. Besly, *Histoire des comtes de Poitou* (Paris, 1647), *Preuves*, p. 416. For William's reputation thereafter, see Cate, "A Gay Crusader," *Byzantion*, XVI, 523–526.

the recent crusading armies: Stephen of Blois, Stephen of Burgundy, Hugh of Lusignan, Geoffrey of Vendôme, Conrad, and others. Stephen of Blois advised caution but his sound advice was flouted now as it had been earlier by the Lombards; his flight from Antioch had stamped him as a coward whose counsel was overly timid.

When Baldwin discovered the size of the Egyptian army it was too late to retreat. He and his knights charged impetuously and with some momentary success. But against tremendous odds they could do little more. Those who survived the first onslaught fled, some to Jaffa, Baldwin and others to Ramla. This was on May 17. That night Baldwin escaped and two days later reached Arsuf. The remnants of his band sought refuge in a tower in Ramla. The Egyptians broke into the city and attempted to fire the tower. After enduring heat and smoke for two days the Christians sallied forth to sell their lives as dearly as possible. After a desperate melée they were overwhelmed. Most of the knights were killed — Hugh of Lusignan, Miles of Bray, Geoffrey of Vendôme, and Stephen of Blois, whose death did something to brighten a tarnished reputation.[35]

A few were carried off into Egypt as captives. Among these were Conrad, whose prowess had impressed the enemy, and Odo Arpin. They were kept at Cairo for three years and then released through the intercession of Alexius. Both returned to Europe, Conrad to serve his emperor again and Odo Arpin to enter Cluny in gratitude for his deliverance.[36] From various bits of evidence we learn of the eventual return to Europe of other pilgrims: William of Nevers, who later refused to go on the Second Crusade in 1147; Hugh Bardulf; and a number of prelates — Hugh of Lyons and the bishops of Soissons and Laon. The only person of importance whom we know to have remained in the east was Joscelin of Courtenay, later to become count of Edessa.

Judged by any standards, the Crusade of 1101 had been a failure. Of the thousands who had marched eastward only a few hundreds reached Jerusalem; still fewer stayed on to give Baldwin the help he had hoped for. Their one achievement was the capture of Tortosa; their one battle for Baldwin, that at Ramla,

[35] Fulcher of Chartres, II, xvii–xx (pp. 436–446); Albert of Aix, IX, i–vi (pp. 591–594); William of Tyre, X, xx–xxii (pp. 429–435); Bartolf of Nangis, lviii (pp. 533–535), who gives judgment on Stephen; Ibn-al-Athīr, A. H. 495, pp. 213–214; William of Malmesbury IV, 384 (II, 448–450); Ordericus Vitalis, X, xxi (pp. 132–136).

[36] Albert of Aix, IX, viii (p. 595), and X, xxxix (p. 649); Guibert of Nogent, VII, xxiv (p. 245); Ordericus Vitalis, X, xxii (pp. 137–139); Ibn-al-Athīr, p. 214.

was a defeat. Chroniclers found this failure an unpleasant contrast to the marvelous success of the First Crusade, and they believed that the destruction of the armies of 1101 was God's punishment for their manifest sins: their pride, their atrocities against fellow Christians, their wantonness. God's agent, though an evil one, was the emperor Alexius.

Friction between the Latins and Greeks, rooted in ethnic and cultural differences, had been in evidence during the First Crusade. The antagonism had been sharpened in 1101, largely through the undisciplined actions of the crusaders and Alexius's precautionary moves. Most of the western writers who describe the Crusade of 1101 accuse the basileus, either directly or indirectly, of betraying the armies of that year to the Turks. Those authors, writing at some remove from the events, were infected by the growing hostility to Alexius, the result partly of Bohemond's propaganda in the west in 1106, partly of an earlier incident described by Albert of Aix. When the pilgrims at Jerusalem in April 1102 had asked Baldwin to negotiate with the emperor, the king had complied. He sent an embassy to Constantinople and in the conversations which followed Alexius cleared himself by oath of all charges and promised to deal kindly with future pilgrims. Among Baldwin's ambassadors was a bishop whom Albert calls Manasses of "Barzenona"; his name first appears as one of the Italian prelates who survived the battle at Mersivan and reached Antioch early in 1102. Manasses was commissioned to exonerate Alexius before Paschal II on his return to Europe, but he became piqued over an imagined affront and at the Council of Benevento later in the year impeached rather than defended the emperor. The charges, Albert reports, were spread throughout Gaul.[37]

Some of the sources that repeat those charges contain details so fanciful that they deserve no credence. Ekkehard, the only western author who was an eye-witness, knew of rumors of treachery but had no evidence. Albert of Aix repeats the charges in several places but tends to disprove them by other statements. He and other authors show that Alexius and Raymond, far from sending the first army off on a wild goose chase into Pontus, had pleaded with the leaders to go directly to Syria. These statements are corroborated by the emperor's evident interests. His negotia-

[37] Albert of Aix, VIII, xli (p. 582), and VIII, xlv–xlviii (pp. 584–585). Albert speaks in the first citation of "Manases de Barzenona, alii quoque episcopi Italiae." I cannot identify him. Certainly Albert does not mean Barcelona in Spain, whose bishop, Berengar, was then in his own see. Cf. D. S. Puig y Puig, *Episcopologio de la sede Barcinonense* (Barcelona, 1925), pp. 135–137; Runciman, *Crusades*, II, 35, note 1.

tions with the princes and the oaths he secured from them at considerable expense show clearly that he expected to profit by their fighting as he had by the victories of the earlier crusaders. He was not the man to destroy potential allies out of spite because of their disorders and insults, and certainly he was not the man to send them out to rescue his archenemy Bohemond.[38]

The failure of the crusade can be explained without making a traitor of Alexius. The crusaders had planned to meet at Constantinople, but the several armies missed the rendezvous by a very narrow margin of time; this was partly the result of their own behavior, partly a matter of chance. Separately they fell before a temporary alliance of Moslem princes; together they might have fought their way through to Syria. Perhaps they would not have been able to do so. Their leadership was poor, their knowledge of the enemy's territory and tactics slight. For any army so long a march through a rugged and skillfully defended area is a prodigious task that requires good organization, a sound system of logistics, and a bit of luck. The crusaders of 1101 had no organization, no system, no luck, and so they set a pattern of failure that was to be followed by those of 1147 and 1190. Of more immediate importance was their failure to reinforce the Latin kingdom. The newly established states of the crusaders were forced, therefore, to rely largely on their own resources for both defense and administration. These resources were very limited, and herein lies the major problem of the ensuing years.

[38] For Alexius' character I have relied heavily on F. Chalandon, *Essai sur le règne d'Alexis Ier Comnène* (Paris, 1900), especially chapter VII, which deals with the Crusade of 1101, and on his briefer treatment in the *Cambridge Medieval History*, IV, chapter XI.

XII

THE FOUNDATION OF THE LATIN STATES, 1099–1118

After the capture of the city of Jerusalem on July 15, 1099, most of the crusaders felt that their work was done. They remained long enough to establish a government to protect the Holy Sepulcher and to repel a Moslem attack from Ascalon on August 12. Then the majority set out for their homes in Europe, marching back to northern Syria in order to embark in Byzantine ships. As we have seen in the preceding chapter, the crusaders of 1101–1102 did the same thing in their turn, and so we must now consider the situation which these crusaders were leaving behind in Palestine and Syria.

The following are the more important primary sources used in this chapter. The principal Arabic sources are Ibn-al-Qalānisī, *Dhail ta'rīkh Dimashq* (extracts tr. and ed. H. A. R. Gibb, *The Damascus Chronicle of the Crusades*, London, 1932); Ibn-al-Athīr, *Al-kāmil fī-t-ta'rīkh* (extracts in *RHC, Or.*, I, 187–744); Kamāl-ad-Dīn, *Zubdat al-ḥalab fī ta'rīkh Ḥalab* (extracts in *RHC, Or.*, III, 577–690); and Sibṭ Ibn-al-Jauzī, *Mir'at az-zamān* (extracts in *RHC, Or.*, III, 517–570). The most valuable is Ibn-al-Qalānisī, a Damascene chancery official who wrote between 1140 and 1160, and who has many details and is excellent in his chronology. The other Arabic writers listed are of the thirteenth century and though they rely upon Ibn-al-Qalānisī to some extent they each supply a great deal of information not found elsewhere.

The chief Armenian source is Matthew of Edessa, *Extraits de la chronique de Matthieu d'Édesse* (*RHC, Arm., I*). Matthew, a monk, intensely patriotic, wrote before 1140 and was very well informed regarding Armenian affairs.

The principal Byzantine source is Anna Comnena, *Alexiad* (ed. B. Leib, 3 vols., Paris, 1937–1945). Anna, the daughter of the emperor Alexius I Comnenus, wrote forty years after the events she describes. She is unreliable in her chronology and reflects the anti-western prejudices of the Byzantines of her day, but presents much of value from her point of vantage.

The most important Latin chronicles are Fulcher of Chartres, *Historia Hierosolymitana* (ed. H. Hagenmeyer, Heidelberg, 1913); Albert of Aix, *Liber christianae expeditionis* (*RHC, Occ.*, IV); and William of Tyre, *Historia rerum in partibus transmarinis gestarum* (*RHC, Occ.*, I). William's chronicle has been translated and supplied with valuable notes by E. A. Babcock and A. C. Krey, *History of Deeds Done Beyond the Sea: by William, Archbishop of Tyre* (Columbia University, Records of Civilization, 2 vols., New York, 1943), and will be cited by book and chapter. Fulcher, chaplain of king Baldwin I, is well informed but often brief. Albert, writing after 1120, though he never visited the Latin states, has the fullest account, partly legendary but mostly very useful. William, chancellor of the kingdom of Jerusalem and a distinguished historian (d. probably 1185), relying upon Fulcher, Albert, and on private sources, is remarkable for his discriminating judgment. Letters of the crusaders may be found in H. Hagenmeyer, *Epistulae et chartae ad historiam primi belli sacri spectantes: Die Kreuzzugsbriefe aus den Jahren 1088–1100* (Innsbruck, 1901), H. Hagenmeyer, "Chronologie de la première croisade," *ROL*, VI–VIII (1898–1901), and "Chronologie de l'histoire du royaume de Jérusalem" (incomplete), *ROL*, IX–XII (1902–1911), are extremely useful for chronology, but should be checked with Ibn-al-Qalānisī, to whom Hagenmeyer did not have access.

About three thousand Frankish fighting men, in addition to the clergy and other noncombatants, remained in and about Jerusalem, a larger number in and about Antioch, and a small band at Edessa (Urfa). Antioch was three hundred and ten miles to the north of Jerusalem, across hostile territory; Edessa was one hundred and sixty miles northeast of Antioch, and forty-five east of the Euphrates. There were thus three isolated groups of western European invaders left in a foreign land. It was an ancient land whose Semitic inhabitants had seen many changes of fortune in the past, and whose upper classes were superior to the Franks in manners, breeding, and education.

The region in which these newcomers had chosen to find their homes is essentially a narrow strip between the Mediterranean Sea and the Syrian desert. First there is a coastal plain of sandy wastes interspersed with cultivable areas. At places this narrows to nothing as at Dog river pass near Beirut where a road is cut into the face of the cliffs fronting the sea. This coastal area contains a number of seaports such as Latakia, Tripoli, Beirut, Sidon, Tyre, and Acre which since time immemorial have exported both caravan goods and local manufactures to the west. Back of the coastal plain is a series of mountain ranges running north and south. They vary in elevation up to five thousand feet in northern Syria, to eleven thousand feet in the Lebanon, and to nearly four thousand feet in Palestine. There is a valley running north and south between these ranges with its high point at Baalbek. Northward flows the Orontes until it breaks through the mountains at Antioch to reach the sea. Southward runs the Jordan until it reaches the depression of the Dead Sea 1,292 feet below sea level, about twenty miles east of Jerusalem.

From November to March moisture-laden winds from the Mediterranean bring rains to the western slopes of the mountains. This causes the land to bloom in the spring. Although much water runs off, more so now than in medieval times owing to deforestation and overgrazing by sheep and goats, some of it soaks into the underlying limestone strata. This water accounts for the springs and streams, some of which continue to flow in the dry season when the winds blow in from the desert. Consequently irrigation has ever been important in Syria and Palestine, and the land has always had a significant agricultural as well as commercial population. This is true even on the eastern side of the mountains where the occasional streams eventually lose themselves in the desert. Here nourished in fertile areas are located cities famous since ancient times for manufactures and the caravan trade. Such are Aleppo, Hamah, Homs, and Damascus. These cities were never conquered by the crusaders.[1]

With the exception of the county of Edessa the Frankish conquests were to hug the coast, dependent upon sea communications with Europe and reaching back into the highlands only for an average distance of fifty miles. Under these circumstances the enemy was seldom more than a day's ride away. Therefore the Frankish states had to be garrison states, and their history is in large part military. Let us first examine the Moslem lands surrounding the Franks in 1099, and then the Latin Christian states themselves.

Southwest of Jerusalem, across the Sinai peninsula, lies Egypt. At the end of the eleventh century it was one of the wealthiest countries of the world with a dense though not warlike population. Its ships dominated the coasts of Palestine and Syria northward to the Byzantine sphere of control around Cyprus. In Ascalon, Palestine, it had an advanced base only forty miles from Jerusalem. As preceding chapters have made clear, Egypt was technically ruled by the Fāṭimid caliph of Cairo, al-Musta'lī, but was actually governed by a capable vizir, al-Malik al-Afḍal. This caliphate championed the Shī'ite school of Moslem belief, and represented a challenge to the older Sunnite caliphate of the 'Abbāsid dynasty in Baghdad. In the latter part of the eleventh century the caliphs of Cairo had lost control of Syria and most of Palestine to the warlike Selchükid (Arabic, Saljūq) sultans who had begun to dominate the 'Abbāsid caliphate of Baghdad in 1055.[2] Consequently the Moslems were badly divided by the religious and political rivalries of the two caliphates when the crusaders arrived.

Between Jerusalem and Antioch Syrian affairs were in great confusion. The two most powerful centers of authority were Damascus and Aleppo, east of the mountain ranges and facing the Syrian desert. In 1099 they were governed by two Selchükid princes, brothers and rivals, Riḍvan of Aleppo and Dukak of Damascus. Their father, Tutush, governor of Syria, had aspired to succeed his own brother, the Selchükid sultan Malik-Shāh,

[1] See P. K. Hitti, *History of Syria* (New York, 1951), pp. 30–53; and D. C. Munro, *The Kingdom of the Crusaders* (New York and London, 1935), pp. 3–29.

[2] For the politics of the Moslem states and the conditions in Syria and Palestine see H. A. R. Gibb, *The Damascus Chronicle*, intro.; R. Grousset, *Histoire des croisades*, I (Paris, 1934), i–lxii; Hitti, *op. cit.*, pp. 573–592; S. Runciman, *A History of the Crusades*, II (Cambridge, 1952), 3–17; and above, chapters III and V.

who died in 1092. Tutush was killed in battle with his nephew, the sultan Berkyaruk, son of Malik-Shāh, in 1095. Berkyaruk was thereafter much more concerned with the rivalry of his brother Muḥammad in Iraq and Iran than with affairs in Syria and Palestine. Riḍvan seized Aleppo and aspired to rule all of Syria, but Dukak seized Damascus. Selchükid affairs in Syria were therefore, aside from Fāṭimid hostility, hopelessly muddled when the crusaders arrived in 1097, a fact of great importance to the invaders. After the Franks had come, Riḍvan and Dukak continued to be primarily jealous of each other, and of any real authority to be exerted by the sultan in Baghdad. They were not disposed to attack the crusaders unless the latter threatened them.

The rest of Syria, the region of the coast and the mountains, went its own way after the death of Tutush. The wealthy seaport towns were generally ruled by ex-Fāṭimid governors who had repudiated Fāṭimid political but not religious authority, and who would call upon Egypt for naval aid when necessary. In the mountains were the Nuṣairī Shī'ite sect in the north; the neo-Ismā'īlite Shī'ite Bāṭinites (the so-called "Assassins") in the direction of Aleppo; the Maronites, Syriac-speaking Monothelite Christians, in Mount Lebanon, and the Druzes, a Shī'ite sect, around Mount Hermon.[3] All three Shī'ite groups hated one another and also the Sunnite Moslems, but hated Christians more. Shaizar, between Damascus and Aleppo, defended by an immensely strong fortress, contained a considerable Christian population, but was ruled by an Arab family, the Banū-Munqidh. Other than the Shī'ite sects and the Maronites the rural peoples were generally Syrians who had gone over to Sunnite Islam and to the Arabic language. They hated the Turks who had recently conquered them. The towns of Syria contained important Christian elements, Jacobite, Nestorian, Greek Orthodox, and Armenian, which grew larger the farther north one went. These native Christians were disposed to coöperate with the Franks against the Turks.

North of Antioch in the Taurus mountains and their southern foothills lay a series of Armenian principalities. The Armenians had moved into this region from their ancient homeland in Greater Armenia around Lake Van in the late eleventh century as a result of both Byzantine and Turkish pressure. Consequently their

[3] On the Ismā'īlites and the Assassins see above, chapter IV; C. E. Nowell, "The Old Man of the Mountain," *Speculum*, XXII (1947), 497–519 and Bernard Lewis, "The Sources for the History of the Syrian Assassins," *ibid.*, XXVII (1952), 475–489.

princes were disposed to welcome the Franks as allies. One of them, however, Ṭoros of Edessa, had been displaced in 1098 in favor of Baldwin of Boulogne. This was described in an earlier chapter.[4] Baldwin thus became count of Edessa, and his was the first of the Latin states in the east. Moreover, he had subsequently strengthened his position by marrying Arda, the daughter of an Armenian noble; and he had conquered Samosata on the Euphrates, about thirty miles northwest of Edessa, and Sarūj, about the same distance southwest of his capital. Having consolidated his position Baldwin remained in his principality and did not rejoin the army of crusaders marching south.

North of the Taurus range was the Anatolian plateau. In the western part the Byzantine emperor, Alexius Comnenus, was expanding his territories at the expense of the Selchükid sultan, Kilij (or Kilich) Arslan of Iconium (Konya), who had been greatly weakened by the progress of the crusaders through his realm in 1097. Eastern Anatolia was held by a powerful Turkish prince, Malik-Ghāzī ibn-Dānishmend, the emir of Sebastia (Sivas). South of the Armenian principalities lay the crusader states of Antioch and Edessa. East and southeast of Edessa lay Iraq, the main center of Selchükid power. In its capital, Baghdad, resided the impotent 'Abbāsid caliph, al-Mustaẓhir, and his real master, the Selchükid sultan. In 1099 the latter was Berkyaruk, more concerned with the rivalry of his brother and eventual successor, Muḥammad, than with Syria and Palestine, as we have seen.

Antioch was at first clearly the strongest of the Frankish states. It extended northward into Cilicia, eastward to the frontiers of Edessa and Aleppo, and southward a vague distance into the no man's land of central Syria. The population was largely Christian — Jacobite, Nestorian, Armenian, and Greek Orthodox. In fact this area had been nominally Byzantine territory as late as 1085. The city of Antioch still retained some of its ancient commercial importance. It was also powerfully fortified. A major source of the new state's strength lay in its ruler, Bohemond, one of the ablest of the crusader princes. Many of the Franks had remained there with him. But Bohemond was also a source of weakness. He was the son of the Norman adventurer Robert Guiscard, who had wrested much of south Italy from the Byzantines. Robert and his son had been bold enough to make, in Albania, a major attack upon the Byzantine empire itself in 1081–1085. Bohemond was like his father ambitious and crafty. Like most of the Latin princes

[4] See chapter IX.

he had sworn an oath at Constantinople in 1097 to return Antioch, when captured, to the emperor Alexius Comnenus. But, as we already know, he had seized possession of Antioch for himself in 1098–1099 after it had been captured.[5] Very plainly Bohemond had embarked upon the crusade in order to secure a dominion for himself rather than to recover the Holy Sepulcher for the church.

Bohemond's usurpation naturally made Alexius an enemy of the Franks in Antioch. It also prevented Alexius from aiding in the capture of Jerusalem and ruined whatever chance there may have been for a rapprochement of the Latin and Greek churches based upon a common crusade to the Holy Sepulcher, as seems to have been a part of pope Urban's plan in starting the First Crusade. Bohemond's ambition had also offended Raymond of St. Gilles, count of Toulouse, whom Urban had consulted before preaching the crusade in 1095, and who had hoped to be regarded as its secular leader under the papal legate, bishop Adhémar of Le Puy.[6]

Let us now examine Bohemond's problem after he had seized possession of Antioch. He was faced by a hostile Byzantium. Three of his logical maritime outlets, Latakia, Valania, and Maraclea, had been turned over to Byzantine officers by count Raymond of Toulouse when the latter continued with the crusade to Jerusalem in 1099. Byzantium now controlled Bohemond's coastal waters, as well as the island of Cyprus to the west. The emperor Alexius, learning of Bohemond's usurpation of Antioch and violation of the oath made at Constantinople, protested at once, and was rebuffed. Alexius dispatched an army to seize Cilicia and from there to operate against Antioch. It took only Marash, the Cilician Armenians preferring the Franks to the Greeks. But in 1099 a Byzantine fleet occupied the ports of Corycus (Korgos) and Seleucia (Silifke) on the Cilician coast, basing a squadron at Seleucia to harry Bohemond's sea communications.[7] Possession of

[5] Chapter X, pp. 324, 326–327. It is even held by B. Kugler, *Boemund und Tankred* (Tübingen, 1862), p. 2, and E. Kühne, *Zur Geschichte des Fürstentums Antiochia* (Berlin, 1897), pp. 2, 11, that Bohemond's seizure of Antioch was evidence of an ambition to found a great military power in the east.

[6] Raymond, the most powerful of the crusader princes, apparently felt a special obligation to Urban II, since he had been involved in the initial plans for the crusade. He had also been close to Urban's legate, Adhémar of Le Puy, whose death made it easier for Bohemond to mature his plans for the seizure of Antioch. Raymond undoubtedly felt that if Antioch fell to Bohemond, Alexius' good will would be permanently forfeited and Urban's great plan for a Greek-Latin concord would be ruined beyond repair. Hence Raymond must have been a prime mover in the resolution of the princes (July 5, 1098) to invite the emperor to come to Antioch and join them. For Urban's plan for the First Crusade see above, chapters VII and VIII.

[7] Anna Comnena, *Alexiad* (ed. Leib, II), pp. 34, 39–41, 45–46.

Cyprus and these ports gave the Byzantines several strategically located naval bases.

During this time Bohemond had begun the siege of the important port of Latakia. Suddenly, late in the summer of 1099, a great Pisan fleet of one hundred and twenty ships arrived. Though sent to take part in the crusade against the Moslems and very probably to get commercial concessions in captured Syrian and Palestinian ports, this fleet, on the way out, had engaged in hostilities against the Byzantines. It had seized Corfu and wintered there, and had fought a punitive Byzantine naval squadron near Rhodes in the spring of 1099.[8] The dominating personality in this fleet, archbishop Daimbert of Pisa, was accordingly in a receptive frame of mind when Bohemond accused the Greeks in Latakia of being enemies of the crusaders, although Bohemond was more properly an enemy of the Greeks. The upshot was that Daimbert joined Bohemond in the siege of Latakia. At this juncture, in September, there arrived three of the principal chieftains of the First Crusade, Raymond of St. Gilles, Robert, duke of Normandy, and Robert, count of Flanders, leading their troops home from the conquest of Jerusalem. The three princes vigorously protested against this attack upon fellow Christians. This is excellent evidence that they were still strongly motivated by pope Urban's original plans for reconciliation with the Greek church, as well as by their oaths to Alexius. They won over Daimbert and forced Bohemond to desist. Raymond must have had another motive; he must have also desired to embarrass his old rival Bohemond. Robert of Normandy, Robert of Flanders, and most of Raymond's Provençal army now returned home, by way of Constantinople, in ships furnished by the Byzantines. Raymond himself wintered at Latakia among the Greeks, and went on to visit Alexius at Constantinople the next year.

Bohemond meanwhile was in an uneasy position. He realized that he did not have the support of the other Latins in his war with the Byzantines. He had violated his oath to Alexius and the intent of Urban's crusade, and had not even fulfilled his vow to go to Jerusalem. But Bohemond was resourceful. He invited Baldwin of Edessa, who likewise had not fulfilled his vow, and archbishop

[8] The fact that the Pisan fleet wintered in Corfu is among the reasons why A. C. Krey, "Urban's Crusade, Success or Failure?" *AHR*, LIII (1948), 241, note 21, and his student J. Bohnstedt, to both of whom I am indebted, believe that Daimbert and the Pisan fleet left Italy before the news of the death, August 1, 1098, of the papal legate, bishop Adhémar of Le Puy, could have been brought back to Italy from Syria. Hence Daimbert could not have been sent out from Italy as legate in succession to Adhémar, as has been widely assumed.

Daimbert to accompany him to Jerusalem to celebrate Christmas at the Holy Sepulcher. As a result the three leaders arrived with a large force, principally Bohemond's, at Jerusalem, December 21, 1099.

Now let us examine the situation at Jerusalem when Bohemond, Baldwin, and Daimbert arrived. The dominating influence there was Godfrey of Bouillon, duke of Lower Lorraine, who now held the title of Advocate of the Holy Sepulcher. Godfrey's greatest immediate problem was the safety of the city and the surrounding area. After the battle of Ascalon, disagreements between Godfrey and the other leaders and his unwillingness to permit any advantage to Raymond of St. Gilles prevented further coöperation. There were two unfortunate consequences. First, Ascalon did not surrender and, indeed, was only captured with great labor a half century later. Second, there followed an almost wholesale exodus of crusaders led, as we have seen, by count Raymond and the two Roberts. The chronicler Albert of Aix writes that about twenty thousand left with them. Of the leaders only Godfrey and Tancred, a nephew of Bohemond, remained. Godfrey begged the departing princes to send him aid when they returned home. Albert reports that Godfrey had about three thousand men that fall (1099). Next spring it was estimated that Godfrey had only two hundred knights and a thousand footmen. William of Tyre writes that men who had originally decided to stay deserted their holdings and went back to Europe.[9]

The little state of Jerusalem was thus left an island in the sea of Islam. It consisted of Godfrey's own domain in southern Palestine and of a semi-independent barony begun by Tancred around Tiberias. Godfrey's domain chiefly comprised the port of Jaffa and the inland towns of Lydda, Ramla, Bethlehem, and Jerusalem. At first it consisted of little more than these towns. The peasants of the countryside, largely Arabs, were hostile and given to ambushing the unwary on the highways. The towns were depopulated, short of food, and subject to plundering by the Arabs at night. The nearest possible source of help was Tancred, seventy-five miles to the north, and Tancred's resources were even more insignificant than those of Godfrey. Godfrey had no sea power. Saracen squadrons from Sidon, Tyre, Acre, Caesarea, Ascalon, and Egypt scoured his coast and threatened traffic into Jaffa.

[9] Albert of Aix (*RHC, Occ.*, IV), pp. 503, 507, 517; William of Tyre, IX, 19. For discussion of conditions in Jerusalem see J. Prawer, "The Settlement of the Latins in Jerusalem," *Speculum*, XXVII (1952), 491–495.

What saved the tiny state was al-Afḍal's failure to renew a prompt and vigorous offensive.

Godfrey's first step in providing for the defense of the country was to attempt to gain control of the Palestinian seaports. Thus he could make safe the entry of pilgrims and supplies from Europe, could deprive the Saracens of bases for raids by sea and land, and could gain control of the commerce of the hinterland. An attempt to gain the surrender of Ascalon after the battle near there, August 12, was foiled by the rivalry of Raymond, who disliked the selection of Godfrey as Advocate of the Holy Sepulcher at Jerusalem and who wanted the surrender of Ascalon for himself. Albert of Aix relates that a few days later an attempt to gain Arsuf, forty miles to the north, was spoiled by the obstinacy of Raymond.[10] Godfrey was so infuriated that he wanted to attack St. Gilles, and was only dissuaded by Robert of Flanders. Godfrey tried again to take Arsuf that fall, but failed because of approaching winter and the lack of men and ships. The next spring he succeeded, with the aid of Daimbert's Pisan fleet, in compelling Arsuf to pay tribute. Meanwhile in January he strongly fortified Jaffa with the help of Daimbert's men. This, and the presence of the Pisan fleet, so alarmed the Saracen governors of Ascalon, Caesarea, and Acre that they also agreed to pay tribute. Soon after, the shaikhs of the Transjordan, seeing that the new state might prove to be more than transitory, made treaties with Godfrey. Their merchants gained the right to come to Jerusalem and Jaffa. Likewise the merchants of Ascalon could come to Jerusalem, and those of Jerusalem to Ascalon. This is interesting evidence of how soon commercial activity brought the two sides together. But Godfrey ordered the death penalty for any Moslem who came in by sea. He wanted the Saracens of Palestine and the Transjordan to be economically and politically dependent upon him, and not upon Egypt.

Godfrey set up a feudal system on the western European model to defend Palestine. Albert of Aix writes that on the fourth day after the arrival of Godfrey's brother and successor, Baldwin I, every knight and important man was called in to account for his arms, revenues, and fiefs (*beneficia*), including his fief in money revenues from the cities. Then the oath of fealty was exacted. The principal fiefs were in land. The greatest territorial vassal was Tancred. This prince, immediately after the fall of Jerusalem, had

[10] Albert of Aix, p. 498. For the rivalry of Godfrey and Raymond see J. C. Andressohn, *The Ancestry and Life of Godfrey of Bouillon* (Bloomington, 1947), pp. 109–111.

taken about eighty knights and had begun to carve out a domain in northern Palestine, the future principality of Tiberias. Within a year Tancred controlled Nablus, Tiberias, Baisan, and Haifa. His domain served as a march over against Damascus. In the west Godfrey promised Arsuf as a fief to Robert of Apulia. In the south, according to Albert of Aix, he gave a large fief called St. Abraham, centering around Hebron, to Gerard of Avesnes. This all agrees with the statement in one manuscript of the chronicle of Baldric of Dol that Godfrey's own domain extended north to Nablus, south to St. Abraham, and eastward to the Jordan and Dead Sea. It included the city of Jerusalem and the port of Jaffa. Stevenson has remarked that the countryside lent itself to the establishment of manorial holdings, that the natives, accustomed to foreign masters, lived in small villages whose headmen were easy to coerce.[11]

Godfrey's position in the realm was therefore seriously challenged when Bohemond of Antioch, Baldwin of Edessa, and archbishop Daimbert of Pisa came to Jerusalem. Bohemond had a considerable army and Daimbert a badly needed fleet at his disposal. Godfrey was very weak by land and sea, and had just given up a heartbreaking siege of Arsuf when these guests arrived.

Daimbert and Bohemond immediately reopened the question of the patriarchate of Jerusalem. Arnulf of Chocques, chaplain of duke Robert of Normandy, had been chosen patriarch on August 1 by the influence of the princes favorable to Godfrey. This was over the objections of those of the clergy who felt that the patriarch should be the ranking official in a state dedicated to the Holy Sepulcher, and that there should be a lay advocate or defender as his assistant. Arnulf was instead willing to be the assistant of the lay advocate, Godfrey. Daimbert and Bohemond now insisted that Arnulf, as yet unconfirmed by the pope, step down and that Daimbert be chosen in his place. Daimbert apparently acted on his own responsibility, for Krey has shown that he does not seem to have been sent out by the pope either as a legate or as a prospective patriarch. Behind Daimbert were two compelling arguments, the Pisan fleet and the military forces of Bohemond. As a result Arnulf was ousted and Daimbert installed. Bohemond and

[11] Albert of Aix, pp. 532, 516; Baldric of Dol (*RHC, Occ.*, IV), p. 111, MS. G.; W. B. Stevenson, *The Crusaders in the East* (Cambridge, 1907), p. 37. The best study of the manorial organization of the kingdom is H. G. Preston, *Rural Conditions in the Kingdom of Jerusalem* (Philadelphia, 1903), pp. 5–17. A subsequent volume in this work will contain a chapter on agricultural conditions in the kingdom by Jean Richard. See now also Richard, *Le Royaume latin de Jérusalem* (Paris, 1953), pp. 80ff., 113ff.

Godfrey became vassals of the new patriarch. As Yewdale has pointed out, Bohemond in doing homage to the patriarch of Jerusalem hoped that he had secured a title to Antioch which would be acceptable to the Latin world.[12] Up to this time he had felt his position compromised by his violation of his oath to restore Antioch to the emperor Alexius. Having secured a title at the price of acquiring an absentee sovereign who would trouble him not at all, Bohemond departed for Antioch after Christmas. Baldwin of Edessa left at the same time. There is no record that he defended Godfrey's position against Bohemond and Daimbert. Probably he was not strong enough to oppose Bohemond. Nor is there any record that he did homage to Daimbert. He had nothing to gain by doing so. Arnulf was given what consolation he could find in the important position of archdeacon of the Holy Sepulcher.

Godfrey was left to deal with his new suzerain. Daimbert was an able and ambitious man. He had dominated the affairs of Pisa as if it were, in the words of Moeller, "a sort of episcopal republic,"[13] and at a time when Pisa was extending its influence in Corsica, Sardinia, Sicily, and even Valencia. He stood high in the counsels of pope Urban, who had elevated him to the rank of archbishop in 1092, and had used him as a legate in Castile and Sardinia. Daimbert had accompanied Urban to the Council of Clermont in 1095 and on the great speaking tour that followed the next winter and spring. They were both supporters of the Cluniac reform movement in the church, which sought to free the latter from domination by the feudal princes. Such a man, though he seems, as we have noticed, to have been neither papal legate nor patriarch-designate, would play no modest role in Jerusalem. He at once demanded possession of the city of Jerusalem with its citadel, of the Tower of David, and of the port of Jaffa, the essential link with Europe. Godfrey, weak in resources and probably conscious of the need of church support from the west, reluctantly made formal cession of a fourth part of the port of Jaffa, February 2, 1100, and of the city of Jerusalem itself on Easter Sunday, April 1. Title was vested in the church of the Holy Sepulcher, to which as well as to the patriarch the Advocate of the Holy Sepulcher swore homage. But on the latter occasion Godfrey inserted the provision that he would retain physical possession of

[12] Krey, "Urban's Crusade," *AHR*, LIII (1948), 245, n. 32; R. B. Yewdale, *Bohemond I, Prince of Antioch* (Princeton, 1924), p. 91.

[13] C. Moeller, "Godefroy de Bouillon et l'avouerie du saint-sépulchre," *Mélanges Godefroid Kurth* (Liége and Paris, 1908), p. 79. See also W. Heywood, *History of Pisa* (Cambridge, 1921), pp. 12–13.

Jaffa and Jerusalem until such time as he could conquer one or two other cities, Babylon (the Frankish term for Cairo or, more precisely, its suburb Fustat) being suggested according to William of Tyre.[14]

We may conclude that Daimbert, confident that he represented official church views but lacking direct papal authority, on his own initiative took the position that the crusade had been an ecclesiastical enterprise, that its conquests were church conquests, and that the patriarch of Jerusalem was the trustee and ruler for the church of the Holy Sepulcher, in which title to Jerusalem was vested. He considered that Bohemond and Godfrey were merely lay vassals and defenders. Bohemond was out of the way in the outer province of Antioch, and Godfrey might be got out of the way elsewhere, in Cairo, for example. Such were the ambitious views of Daimbert. In his letter to the Christians of Germany in April 1100, the patriarch spoke of his difficulties in defending the Holy Land, and did not even mention Godfrey.[15] But Daimbert's whole position, at first so favorable, changed rapidly with the homeward departure of the Pisan fleet after Easter, the death of Godfrey, and the arrival of Godfrey's brother Baldwin of Edessa in the fall of 1100.

Godfrey died July 18, 1100, after falling ill while helping Tancred in the region east of Tiberias. What this famous but little understood man would have accomplished, had he lived, no one can say. He faced appalling difficulties in his one year as advocate, and he faced them with singular courage and pertinacity. His followers, huddling in the ruins of Jerusalem, were few, their communications with the outside world precarious, and their morale at the breaking point. The imperious Daimbert presented a special problem. He had to be humored because he represented both naval strength and prevailing ecclesiastical opinion. But Godfrey had enough of both personal ambition and practical military common sense not to yield actual control of Jerusalem. Tenacious, shrewd, and tactful, rather than the pious zealot of later legend, he managed to avoid a break with the patriarch. He

[14] William of Tyre, IX, 16; letter of Daimbert to Bohemond, quoted by William (X, 4). E. Hampel, *Untersuchungen über das lateinische Patriarchat von Jerusalem* (Breslau, 1899), p. 25, accepts the naming of Babylon (Cairo). Babcock and Krey, *William of Tyre*, I, 418, n. 11, are doubtful.

[15] Hagenmeyer, *Epistulae et chartae*, no. XXI, pp. 176–177. Daimbert seems to have desired, without evidence of papal authority, to make Jerusalem an ecclesiastical state ruled by the patriarch. Jerusalem does not seem to have been claimed as a papal fief until 1128, and not afterwards. Cf. M. W. Baldwin, "The Papacy and the Levant during the Twelfth Century," *Bulletin of the Polish Institute of Arts and Sciences in America*, III (1945), 281–283.

held together the tiny state. His reputation rests upon a solid foundation of achievement.

When Godfrey died the patriarch Daimbert had his great opportunity to make Jerusalem a church-state. He should have gone to Jerusalem at once. But suspecting no danger he remained with Tancred, who was undertaking the siege of Haifa, until about July 25.[16] Meanwhile a group of Lotharingian knights, hitherto obscure, seized the Tower of David, the citadel of Jerusalem, and summoned Godfrey's brother, count Baldwin I of Edessa. Their leader was Warner of Gray, a cousin of Baldwin. High in their counsels was archdeacon Arnulf, bitter against Daimbert and from this time on the firm ally of Baldwin. Daimbert, when he realized his peril, sent an appeal to Bohemond of Antioch, his nominal vassal, to stop Baldwin, by force if necessary. The message never reached Bohemond. That redoubtable prince was captured in the middle of August by the Turkish chieftain, Malik-Ghāzī ibn-Dānishmend of Sebastia, in an ambush on the road to Melitene (Malatya).[17] Meanwhile Daimbert remained with Tancred. He promised the latter the fief of Haifa when Tancred became suspicious that Godfrey had promised it to another, Galdemar Carpinel. Daimbert and Tancred, both ambitious men, must each have had hopes of becoming the dominant figure in Jerusalem. Certainly victory would have made them rivals. But for the time they coöperated. Meanwhile Tancred was tied down by the siege of Haifa, where he had the indispensable but temporary help of a Venetian blockading squadron. At the same time the little group of Lorrainers remained in control in Jerusalem.

When Haifa was taken in August Tancred delayed a little, establishing himself there. During the next month he was suddenly called to Latakia by cardinal Maurice of Porto, newly arrived as papal legate. Maurice, and the commanders of the Genoese fleet that had brought him, invited Tancred, about September 25, to assume the regency of Antioch in the emergency created by the capture of Bohemond.[18] But Tancred, rather than trying to seize Antioch, whose authorities after all had not invited him, hurried back to Palestine where he had more pressing business. This time he went to the gates of Jerusalem and demanded entrance. He was refused because he would not swear allegiance to Baldwin.

[16] For an excellent discussion of Daimbert's position upon arrival see J. Hansen, *Das Problem eines Kirchenstaates in Jerusalem* (Luxemburg, 1928), pp. 29–77.

[17] See above, chapter V, p. 164.

[18] Caffaro, *Liberatio civitatum orientis* (*RHC, Occ.*, V), p. 59, and *Annales Ianuenses* (*MGH, SS.*, XVIII), pp. 11–12.

Tancred considered Baldwin a dangerous enemy, for Baldwin had once quarreled with Tancred over possession of Tarsus, in Cilicia, in 1097, and had compelled the latter to yield. Enraged, Tancred now withdrew to Jaffa where he besieged the small Lotharingian garrison. He was so engaged when Baldwin appeared in Palestine.

Count Baldwin of Edessa, upon being informed of his brother's death, "grieved a little, but rejoiced more over the prospect of his inheritance," according to Fulcher of Chartres, his chaplain and biographer. He named as his successor in Edessa his kinsman, Baldwin of Le Bourg. He then levied heavily upon Edessa for his expenses, and departed on October 2 with nearly two hundred knights and seven hundred footmen. He went by way of Antioch. Here, according to Albert of Aix, he was offered the regency, but declined.[19] No doubt he felt that Jerusalem would offer him more possibilities of prestige and of material support from Europe than would either Antioch or Edessa. He turned south, and after fighting his way through a dangerous ambush at Dog river near Beirut, reached his new dominion, in the vicinity of Haifa, about October 30.

Baldwin, who had the qualities of statesmanship, arrived determined to conciliate Tancred if possible. He did not try to enter Haifa, wishing to avoid trouble with Tancred, whose garrison held the place. Tancred, hearing of Baldwin's approach, dropped the siege of Jaffa, fifty-four miles to the south, and hastened by a circuitous route to the security of his own domains around Tiberias. Baldwin reached Jerusalem about November 9, and was welcomed by his Lotharingian friends. Patriarch Daimbert, who had come back to the city late in August, too late to take advantage of Godfrey's death, remained in seclusion. Baldwin did not bother him. Instead, as we have seen, he called in Godfrey's vassals to an accounting on the fourth day, and received from them an oath of loyalty. Then on November 15, before the week was out, feeling it necessary to overawe the Arabs of the south and east who might be tempted to harass the tiny state, he took one hundred and fifty knights and five hundred footmen and departed on a campaign to the south. He first made a demonstration before Ascalon and then, boldly marching east into the region of the Dead Sea, terrorized the natives of that area. He returned to Jerusalem on December 21. Baldwin then constrained patriarch Daimbert, who had had time

[19] Fulcher of Chartres (ed. Hagenmeyer), pp. 352–354; Albert of Aix, p. 527. Albert states that Edessa was granted as a *beneficium* (fief) to Le Bourg. Cf. R. Röhricht, *Geschichte des Königreichs Jerusalem*, p. 10, and J. L. LaMonte, *Feudal Monarchy in the Latin Kingdom of Jerusalem*, p. 190.

for reflection, to crown him king four days later, December 25, 1100. But Daimbert succeeded in salvaging some of his prestige. He crowned Baldwin in Bethlehem, not in the capital, Jerusalem. This was because Baldwin was to be regarded not as king of Jerusalem but of something else, as king of Asia, or king of Babylon (Cairo) and Asia, for example. Daimbert clung to his technical position as suzerain-lord of Jerusalem. As Kühn says, Daimbert regarded Baldwin as a resident of the patriarch's domain, and expected him like Godfrey to go out and conquer one of his own.[20]

All during the winter of 1100–1101 Tancred remained sullenly aloof in his fief around Tiberias. He did not intend to recognize Baldwin. The latter gently but persistently sought to bring Tancred to terms. Twice Baldwin sent Tancred a formal summons to his court, but was ignored. The third time Tancred, who had sworn no oath to Baldwin, agreed to meet the latter on opposite banks of an-Nahr al-'Aujā', a little stream between Jaffa and Arsuf. At this meeting, February 22, nothing was decided except that Baldwin and Tancred were to meet again in fifteen days. By then, early in March, Tancred had been offered the regency of Antioch by a delegation from that city. Antioch needed a strong leader during the captivity of Bohemond in the hands of Malik-Ghāzī. The Franks of Antioch were unable to get any help from Bohemond's *princeps militiae*, Baldwin of Le Bourg. The latter, now count of Edessa, was himself then obtaining help from Antioch following a defeat by Sokman ibn-Artuk of Mardin at Sarūj early in 1101. Tancred decided to accept the offer. He agreed with king Baldwin on March 8 to give up his fiefs in northern Palestine, with the right of resuming them in fifteen months. This was obviously based upon the calculation that Bohemond might be ransomed within that time. The next day Tancred left for Antioch with all his knights and about five hundred footmen. He never came back to recover these lands.

Baldwin, having settled with Tancred, now turned upon his other rival, the patriarch Daimbert. By this time, in the spring of 1101, Baldwin had captured two cities, Arsuf and Caesarea, putting Daimbert in a logical position to demand that Baldwin vacate the patriarch's domain, the area of Jerusalem and Jaffa. Baldwin forestalled this by a vicious attack upon Daimbert, accusing the latter of attempting a conspiracy with Bohemond against his life,

[20] F. Kühn, *Geschichte der ersten lateinischen Patriarchen von Jerusalem* (Leipzig, 1886), pp. 33–34. See also Hampel, *Untersuchungen über das lateinische Patriarchat*, p. 33, n. 3, and Munro, *Kingdom of the Crusaders*, pp. 74–75.

and of high living while the state needed money for defense. Baldwin, aided by archdeacon Arnulf, made Daimbert's life so miserable that the latter retired to Jaffa in the fall of that year, and to the protection of Tancred at Antioch the next spring.

But Daimbert clung tenaciously to the plan of making Jerusalem a church-state. He returned in the fall of 1102 with Tancred and Baldwin II of Edessa who brought military support to Baldwin of Jerusalem following a defeat of the latter by the Egyptians earlier in that year. As a result Daimbert was briefly restored to his office. Possibly, as Hansen says, they felt that the quarrel at Jerusalem would impair the necessary good relations with the church in the west. Tancred, as far as he was concerned, had private reasons for resentment against king Baldwin. But Daimbert's restoration was subject, at Baldwin's insistence, to an immediate inquiry by a local synod. This court, presided over by cardinal Robert of Paris, a new papal legate, and packed by the king's friends, promptly decreed Daimbert's removal, October 8, 1102. It thereupon elected Evremar of Chocques, a fellow townsman of Arnulf, and Tancred had to accept this situation.[21]

Daimbert returned to Antioch with Tancred, and in 1104 to Italy with Bohemond. In 1107 he was declared the official holder of the patriarchal office by pope Paschal II, but he died that year at Messina on the way back. There is no evidence that Paschal restored or indeed had ever recognized Daimbert as feudal suzerain of the Holy Land. Hansen, indicating that Paschal was heavily involved with the emperor Henry V in the celebrated contest over the lay investiture of bishops, believes that the pope told Daimbert to return and arrange a *modus vivendi* with Baldwin. La Monte, speaking of subsequent papal policy, goes so far as to suggest that the papacy accepted the situation at Jerusalem, not wishing to exalt a potential rival in the strategic patriarchate of Jerusalem. Certainly after Daimbert's death the papacy allowed king Baldwin a free hand with the patriarchate. It permitted Evremar to be locally deposed in 1108, a victim of Arnulf's intrigues. It thereafter recognized the patriarchs of Jerusalem who were Baldwin's nominees — Gibelin of Arles (1108–1112) and Arnulf himself (1112–1118). With Daimbert's eviction in 1102 died

[21] See Hansen, *Das Problem eines Kirchenstaates*, pp. 102–108. Albert of Aix, pp. 538–541, 545–548, 598–600, gives a long account of Baldwin's persecution of Daimbert. The sources do not indicate what attitude Robert took regarding Daimbert. Hansen suggests that Robert was won over to Baldwin's view of the need for a strong secular government, but says that opinion must be reserved for lack of evidence (p. 106, note 1). For the role of Tancred see R. L. Nicholson, *Tancred* (Chicago, 1940), pp. 132–134.

any chance to make Jerusalem a church-state ruled by the patriarch as suzerain-lord and defended by a lay advocate. Feudal monarchy had won. Yet there was deference for ecclesiastical feeling for a long time. Baldwin usually used some oblique formula such as "Ego Balduinus, regnum Ierosolimitanorum dispositione Dei optinens" in his official documents, as in 1114, rather than the "Dei gratia Latinorum rex" of his successors.[22]

While Baldwin was contending with Tancred and Daimbert for the domination of the Holy Land, he was facing a precarious military situation. This was especially true during his first winter, 1100–1101, until the arrival of a Genoese squadron at Jaffa in April relieved the situation. Baldwin's chaplain, Fulcher of Chartres, says that in the beginning the king had scarcely three hundred knights and as many footmen to garrison Jerusalem, Ramla, Jaffa, and Haifa. There were so few men that they dared not lay ambushes for enemy marauders. The contemporary writer of the *Gesta Francorum Iherusalem expugnantium* reports that Baldwin's power extended scarcely twelve miles from the capital city. Land communication with Antioch was through hostile territory. Sea communication was also precarious. Fulcher also states that the Saracen corsairs were so numerous that pilgrim ships could only slip into Jaffa, the port of Jerusalem, by ones, twos, threes, or fours. He adds that while a few of the new arrivals would stay in the Holy Land the others would return home, and that for that reason the kingdom was always weak in manpower. A typical instance of this occurred in the spring of 1102, and was described in the preceding chapter. A number of the knights of the Crusade of 1101 joined the king against an Egyptian attack at Ramla. Many were killed in the ensuing disaster and almost all the survivors returned to Europe. Thus the hope of permanent reinforcements offered by the Crusade of 1101 proved vain.[23]

One of Baldwin's most pressing problems, therefore, was the organization of a military system. His first step was to swear in Godfrey's vassals, holders of fiefs in money and in land. An indication of the nature of the first is given by Albert of Aix who states that Gerard, a knight of the king's household, held a part of the revenues of Jaffa for his services. The great land fiefs were:

[22] Hansen, *op. cit.*, pp. 108–111; La Monte, *Feudal Monarchy*, p. 205. For Baldwin's royal formula see E. de Rozière, *Cartulaire de l'église du saint-sépulchre* (Paris, 1849), nos. 10–12, 25, 29, 36, 42, 122; R. Röhricht, *Regesta regni Hierosolymitani* (Innsbruck, 1893), pp. 5 ff.; Kühn, *Geschichte des ersten lateinischen Patriarchen*, pp. 33–34.

[23] Fulcher of Chartres, pp. 387–394; *Gesta Francorum Iherusalem expugnantium* (*RHC, Occ.*, III), p. 523. The latter chronicle, probably anonymous, has been ascribed to Bartolf of Nangis, otherwise unknown. On the Crusade of 1101 see above, chapter XI.

Tiberias, given to Hugh of Falkenberg when Tancred left for Antioch in 1101; Haifa, given to Galdemar Carpinel at the same time; St. Abraham, given to Hugh of Robecque; and Caesarea and Sidon, given after capture to Eustace Garnier. There is no record that Baldwin granted out Montréal (ash-Shaubak) as a fief when it was established in 1115. In general he held more of the land in his own domain than did the later kings of Jerusalem.

King Baldwin had other resources. He had paid garrisons in Jerusalem and Jaffa, his capital and chief port. To pay these men he demanded a share of the patriarch's Easter pilgrim receipts in 1101. Albert of Aix relates that in 1108 two hundred knights and five hundred footmen of the garrison of Jerusalem captured a large caravan beyond the Jordan to provide money for their pay. The annual influx of pilgrims provided a welcome though temporary source of manpower. La Monte sees in Baldwin's appeal to patriarch Evremar in 1102 a request for sergeanty service. He adds that on unusual occasions, such as the determined attack upon Acre in 1104, Baldwin called for a levy en masse (*arrière-ban*) from the kingdom. There is no record that Baldwin used Moslem troops in his own service although Albert of Aix writes that queen Adelaide brought some over from Sicily in 1113. Baldwin never had a navy. He had to depend upon naval agreements with squadrons from Europe, usually Genoese, Pisan, or Venetian, in return for commercial concessions.[24] The famed military orders of the Knights Hospitaller and Knights Templar came after his time. On occasion, we shall find, Baldwin campaigned in alliance with Moslems.

The king's greatest problem, after consolidating his power at home, was to conquer the seaports along his coast. He started with two, Jaffa and Haifa. Ascalon, Arsuf, Caesarea, Acre, Tyre, Sidon, and Beirut were all in the hands of Saracen emirs dependent upon al-Afḍal, vizir of Egypt, for support. In Saracen hands these cities could serve as bases for hostile operations on sea or land, and choke both communications with Europe and the export trade of the hinterland. Therefore it was vital for Baldwin to capture these ports. Godfrey had tried to make a start, as we have seen, but failed, partly owing to the rivalry with count Raymond and partly owing to lack of sea power.

[24] Albert of Aix, pp. 636, 653, 697; LaMonte, *Feudal Monarchy*, pp. 138–165, especially p. 159. For commercial concessions to Italian cities consult W. Heyd, *Histoire du commerce au moyen âge* (tr. F. Raynaud, 2 vols., Leipzig, 1885–1886), E. H. Byrne, "The Genoese Colonies in Syria," *Munro Essays* (New York, 1928), pp. 139–148; and LaMonte, *op. cit.*, pp. 261–275. Baldwin tended to favor the Genoese over the Pisans, compatriots of Daimbert.

Arsuf and Caesarea were the first to fall to Baldwin. He took them in the spring of 1101 with the help of a Genoese fleet. By agreement he gave the Genoese a third of the spoils, and perpetual rights to a street (as a market place) in each town. Acre was besieged in 1103, but not taken until 1104 when Baldwin had the aid of another Genoese fleet.

The offensive against the coast towns was halted during the years 1105–1108. In 1104 Shams-al-Mulūk Dukak, ruler of Damascus, died. Ẓahīr-ad-Dīn Tughtigin, a very able man who as *atabeg* (regent or tutor) for Dukak had been the power behind the scenes, now assumed full control as atabeg for Dukak's infant son Tutush. King Baldwin interfered by sheltering a disappointed heir, Ertash (Bektash). As a result the government of Damascus, hitherto unfriendly to the Fāṭimid regime in Cairo, now became a partner in opposition to Baldwin. The effect of this new alignment was soon apparent. Al-Afḍal, vizir in Cairo, made a last serious effort to overthrow the Latin state of Jerusalem in 1105. He gathered a large army, to which Tughtigin contributed thirteen hundred cavalry, and sent it to the plain of Ramla. Here Baldwin met and defeated it, August 27, but otherwise only held his own in that year. During the next three years pressure by Tughtigin in the north and al-Afḍal in the south prevented Baldwin from making any conquests, although he attacked Sidon in 1106 and 1108 when he had the necessary help of fleets from the west. Soon after the latter event Baldwin and Tughtigin made a truce that lasted four years. Apparently it applied strictly to their own territories, for they fought elsewhere, around Tripoli in 1109 and Edessa in 1110.[25]

King Baldwin played a leading role in the capture of Tripoli in 1109. But since Tripoli became the capital of one of the four Latin states in the east, this event will be discussed later. Baldwin continued his offensive. He took Beirut in May 1110, with the help of a Genoese squadron. He secured Sidon at last, in December of that year, with the aid of a fleet of Norwegian crusaders and adventurers under the youthful king Sigurd (1103–1130), "Jorsalfar" or Jerusalem-farer, son of Magnus Barefoot.[26] This force had been four years in preparation and three years en route, wintering in England, Spain, and Sicily, fighting Moors and being

[25] For Turkish and Egyptian policies at this time see above chapter III, p. 98, and chapter V, pp. 172–173.

[26] See Snorre Sturlason, *Heimskringla*: *Norges Kongesagaer* (eds. J. V. Jensen and H. Kyrre, 3 vols., Copenhagen, 1948), III, 184–185; English tr. Erling Monsen and A. H. Smith (New York, 1932), p. 612.

entertained by friends as it went along. King Baldwin made an attempt to obtain Ascalon by conspiracy in 1111. He plotted with Shams-al-Khilāfah, a governor traitorous to al-Afḍal of Cairo, and even succeded in introducing three hundred men into the city as guards for Shams-al-Khilāfah. But at that juncture Baldwin was called north to help Tancred against the Selchükids of Iraq, and when he returned found that his confederate had been overthrown and his men killed. It would have been a very great advantage to the state of Jerusalem if this intrigue had succeded for Ascalon remained an Egyptian advanced base until it fell in 1153. King Baldwin I made a most determined effort to take Tyre by siege in the winter of 1111–1112. But a skillful and bitter defense, aided by operations by Tughtigin of Damascus in the rear, forced Baldwin to desist in April 1112. Tyre was not to be taken until 1124, by Baldwin II.

By 1112 the efforts of Baldwin I to reduce the coast towns were over. He had all but Ascalon and Tyre, and although they were important he could get along without them. In the remaining years of his life he was busy in the larger cause of the defense and unity of all the Frankish states, and later in extending his own domains in the south.

Let us now examine the history of the Latin states in the north, starting with Antioch. We have observed that this principality was founded by Bohemond early in 1099, and that it came into the hands of Tancred as regent in March 1101, after Bohemond's capture by Malik-Ghāzī of Sebastia the summer before. Tancred's first act was to expel the partisans of Baldwin of Le Bourg, Bohemond's *princeps militiae*. Le Bourg, kinsman of Baldwin of Jerusalem, had been the latter's successor as count of Edessa since October 1100. Tancred thus made himself more secure in Antioch but he embittered relations with a powerful neighbor whom he should have had as a friend and ally. Nevertheless, he did have a friend and ally in the new Latin patriarch, Bernard of Valence, whom Bohemond had appointed to replace the Greek, John the Oxite.

Tancred immediately began to extend his power. First, by the end of 1101 he recovered the Cilician cities of Mamistra (Misis), Adana, and Tarsus which he had helped to conquer for Bohemond in 1097 and which the latter had let slip to the Byzantines. Second, he took Latakia from the Greeks in the spring of 1103, after a siege of a year and a half. Third, he intervened in the affairs of

Baldwin of Jerusalem. As a result of a disastrous defeat administered to king Baldwin near Ramla by the Egyptians in the spring of 1102 Tancred and Baldwin of Le Bourg appeared in the southern realm with large supporting forces in September. Tancred used this occasion to insist upon the restoration of patriarch Daimbert, but with only momentary success, as we have seen.

One project which the regent Tancred did not push was the ransoming of his uncle, Bohemond. Albert of Aix relates that Bohemond was released from Turkish captivity in the following way. Tancred's pressure upon the Byzantines led the emperor Alexius to desire Bohemond as a hostage and to make a bid for his possession. This led to jealousies between Bohemond's captor, Malik-Ghāzī, and Ḳiliĵ Arslan, sultan of Iconium. The wily Bohemond offered Malik-Ghāzī favorable terms, including an alliance against Ḳiliĵ Arslan and Alexius in return for freedom. Bohemond's friends then raised the necessary funds for his ransom. They included the Latin patriarch, Bernard of Antioch, the Armenian lord, Kogh Vasil of Kesoun, and Baldwin of Le Bourg of Edessa, Tancred's rival. Tancred contributed nothing although he did not hinder collections. Bohemond, freed, promptly went to Antioch and assumed complete authority, in May 1103. Radulf of Caen says that Bohemond left Tancred with scarcely two small towns (*oppidula*).[27] It was a bitter humiliation for the proud and ambitious young Norman.

Bohemond was in an excellent position after his release. His territory had been strengthened by Tancred's conquests of the valuable port of Latakia and of the Cilician cities. Baldwin of Edessa and the Armenian Kogh Vasil were his friends. Bohemond had embroiled his enemies, the emperor Alexius and Ḳiliĵ Arslan, with Malik-Ghāzī. In Iraq the Selchükid Turks were weak at the center of their power. Berkyaruk and Muḥammad, sons of the late great sultan Malik-Shāh (d. 1092), were still quarreling over their vast inheritance. Bohemond's immediate neighbor Riḍvan, lord of Aleppo, was jealous of his independence and suspicious of the Selchükids of Iraq. Riḍvan cared nothing for Moslem solidarity, but instead had a leaning toward the Assassins.[28]

Riḍvan's peculiar attitude did not prevent the Franks from seriously threatening him. Successes by Bohemond and Baldwin

[27] Albert of Aix, pp. 611–613; Radulf of Caen (*RHC, Occ.*, III), p. 709.

[28] On Selchükid politics at this period see above chapter V, pp. 167, 172–173; for the Assassins, see chapter IV, pp. 110–111.

of Le Bourg in 1103 apparently alarmed Ridvan's nominal overlord, the Selchükid sultan Muḥammad. In January 1104, the latter had been allotted Syria and northern Iraq as a share in a division of his paternal inheritance. Certainly two powerful Mesopotamian emirs, Shams-ad-Daulah Chökürmish of Mosul and Sokman ibn-Artuk of Mardin, were moved to act. They composed their differences, gathered a large force, and advanced upon Edessa in the spring of 1104. Baldwin of Le Bourg called for help. Bohemond, accompanied by Tancred, united with Le Bourg's chief vassal, Joscelin of Tell Bashir, and marched to the aid of Baldwin. The four leaders then moved to attack Harran, a strategic stronghold twenty-three miles south of Edessa. This move created a diversion in favor of Edessa, for it brought down the Turkish army.

Chökürmish and Sokman employed the old ruse of pretended flight which the Parthians had used against Crassus and the Romans at the same place in 53 B.C., and with the same decisive result. The Turks retreated south for three days, causing the Franks to separate into two bodies, which were successively annihilated May 7, 1104. Baldwin of Le Bourg and Joscelin were captured. Bohemond and Tancred escaped with difficulty to Edessa with a handful of followers.

The Frankish defeat at Harran had far-reaching results. As in the time of Crassus it put a limit to Latin conquests eastward. It ended forever any chance the Franks might have had to penetrate Iraq. It ruined Bohemond's hope of building up a major power around Antioch. It saved Aleppo and the Moslem position in north Syria by preventing Antioch and Edessa from using the strategic location of Harran to cut off contact with the east.

The immediate results of the battle of Harran were several. Tancred became regent of Edessa. Bohemond, his uncle and patron, though shaken was now without question the dominant Latin prince in the north. Thus out of general disaster the two Normans snatched some personal gain. The return of Baldwin of Le Bourg would have disturbed this situation. Consequently Bohemond and Tancred seem to have neglected the matter of Baldwin's ransom, although the subject was broached both by the Turks and by king Baldwin in Jerusalem. As a result Le Bourg endured a captivity of four years. On the other hand Chökürmish and Sokman profited little from their victory. They conquered nothing although the former tried to take Edessa. Their chief gain was two valuable prisoners, Joscelin who was held by Sokman and Le Bourg who was kidnapped from Sokman's tent by Chökürmish. Rīdvan of Aleppo, who had done nothing, profited greatly. With almost no fighting he won back from Antioch the barrier fortresses of al-Fū'ah, Sarmīn, Ma'arrat-Miṣrīn, and Artāḥ, whose people admitted his men, and Laṭmīn, Kafarṭāb, Ma'arrat-an-Nu'mān, and Albara, whose garrisons fled. Of these Artāḥ, the gateway to Antioch, was particularly valuable. Likewise, according to Anna Comnena, the Byzantine admiral Cantacuzenus seized Latakia, though not the citadel, and al-'Ullaiqah, al-Marqab, and Jabala to the south. The Greek general Monastras occupied Tarsus, the adjacent port of Longiniada (not now extant), and Adana and Mamistra, being welcomed by the Armenian population.[29] The Byzantines already held the island of Cyprus with its naval bases off the Syrian coast, and from them were helping Bohemond's enemy, Raymond of St. Gilles, establish himself around Tripoli to the south of Antioch, as we shall see.

Bohemond's position was therefore rendered desperate by pressure on all sides from the Byzantines and Aleppo. With many of his troops lost at Harran, his home garrisons demoralized, Edessa weak, and now himself in debt for his ransom of 1103 and unable to secure more men, Bohemond was at the end of his resources. He might remain and face defeat or decay, or he might return to Europe and embark upon a bold new venture. He chose the latter course. He appointed Tancred his regent in the east, and sailed for Italy, arriving in January 1105.

Bohemond's plan was nothing less than to make a frontal attack on the Byzantine empire through Albania, as his father, Robert Guiscard, with Bohemond as second-in-command, had done in 1081–1085. Bohemond's experience convinced him that he might succeed, particularly if he could channel the mounting anti-Byzantine prejudices of the west into support of his venture. These prejudices were born of the friction and misunderstanding engendered by the passage of the hungry and ill-disciplined forces of the First Crusade through the Byzantine empire, and by the disaster of the Crusade of 1101, which Alexius was widely suspected of sabotaging. The wily Norman, therefore, decided to promote a new "crusade", directed not against the Moslems but against the Byzantines. Its real purpose was not to protect the Holy Sepulcher, but to increase the power of Bohemond. To start a crusade he

[29] For the gains of Rīdvan see Kamāl-ad-Dīn (*RHC, Or.*, III), p. 592, and for those of the Byzantines, Anna Comnena, *Alexiad*, III, 47–49; Radulf of Caen, p. 712.

would have to have the sanction of pope Paschal II. He saw the pope in 1105. As a result Paschal appointed bishop Bruno of Segni as legate to preach a new crusade.

Although the reports of the Council of Poitiers where the crusade was formally launched in 1106 mention the "way to Jerusalem" rather than Byzantium, it seems likely that Paschal succumbed to the anti-Byzantinism of the day and fell in with Bohemond's plans. At any rate there is no record that the pope denounced Bohemond's purpose when it became publicly apparent. Indeed, in his relations with the Norman, Paschal does not emerge as a strong character.

The prince of Antioch made a triumphal tour of Italy and France in 1105–1106, everywhere greeted as a hero of the First Crusade, and everywhere calling for volunteers for his new venture. As bases for propaganda against Alexius he carried in his train a pretender to the Byzantine throne, and circulated copies of the anonymous *Gesta Francorum et aliorum Hierosolimitanorum*, a pro-Norman chronicle of the First Crusade, which Bohemond had brought over from Antioch and into which he seems to have had inserted a passage saying that Alexius had promised Antioch to him.

By the fall of 1107 Bohemond was able to sail from Apulia to Albania with 34,000 men. He took Avlona and laid siege to Dyrrachium (Durazzo). Alexius however was ready for Bohemond. He blockaded him by land and sea and forced the proud Norman to ask for terms in September 1108. The treaty required Bohemond to take an oath of vassalage for Antioch in western style, and to return to Italy. Bohemond, a broken and discredited man, never went back to Antioch. He spent the few remaining years of his life in Apulia, dying there in 1111.[30]

Bohemond's death ended the career of one of the boldest and most ambitious men of the time. He saw in the First Crusade an opportunity to establish himself as a powerful prince. He did succeed in founding a principality at Antioch, but it was much less than he had expected. His seizure of this city in 1098, his denuncia-

[30] For Bohemond's war with Alexius, see F. Chalandon, *Essai sur le règne d'Alexis I Comnène (1081–1118)* (Paris, 1900), pp. 242–250; R. B. Yewdale, *Bohemond I, Prince of Antioch* (Princeton, 1924), pp. 106–133; S. Runciman, *Crusades*, II, 47–51. For Bohemond's use of the *Gesta Francorum*, see A. C. Krey, "A Neglected Passage in the *Gesta* and its Bearing on the Literature of the First Crusade," *Munro Essays*, pp. 57–78. For the view that Bohemond deceived Paschal II as to his real intentions, see M. W. Baldwin, in *Bulletin of the Polish Institute of Arts and Sciences*, III (1945), 283–284. See also J. L. LaMonte, "To What Extent was the Byzantine Empire the Suzerain of the Latin Crusading States?" *Byzantion*, VII (1932), 253–264.

tions of the Byzantines, and his wars against them wrecked whatever chance the crusading movement may have had to realize the apparent hope of pope Urban, a new understanding between Latin and Greek Christendom.

Let us now return to Tancred when Bohemond left him as regent of Antioch in 1104. He had now to rebuild his power. He appointed as his governor at Edessa his kinsman, Richard of Salerno (also known as Richard of the Principate). Thus Edessa became for a time a dependency of Antioch although king Baldwin in Jerusalem had originally given it to Baldwin of Le Bourg. Tancred attacked Ridvan of Aleppo in the spring of 1105. He took the key fortress of Artāḥ, completely shattering an army Ridvan led to its relief, and then scoured the country, capturing Tall Aghdī and Sarmīn, and threatening Aleppo itself. Ridvan was dismayed. He seems to have made a submission to Tancred for he gave no more trouble for five years. In 1106 Tancred took the powerful fortress of Apamea. He could now threaten the important emirate of Hamah, to the south of Aleppo. He also gained prestige by marrying Cecilia, a natural daughter of king Philip I of France, a bride sent him by Bohemond.

The young regent of Antioch set out to regain what had been lost to the Byzantines in 1104. He attacked Mamistra, the key to Cilicia, in the year 1107, when Bohemond was attacking Dyrrachium. Apparently he took it late in 1107 or early in 1108, and then moved south to recapture Latakia, the chief port of his principality. By the spring of 1108 Tancred had regained nearly all that Bohemond had lost, and he was overlord of Edessa in addition. It is true that Bohemond in the treaty of Deabolis in 1108 had recognized Alexius as suzerain lord of Antioch, but Tancred treated the emperor's claims with contempt. Bohemond was partly responsible for Tancred's success, as his attack in Albania drew off Byzantine troops toward the west.

If Tancred, regent of Antioch and overlord of Edessa, felt in 1108 that he was at the height of good fortune after his Cilician victories, he was due to be rudely disillusioned by the loss of Edessa. It is at this point necessary to review the history of Edessa up to 1108. We have seen that Baldwin of Boulogne became its ruler in 1098. When he took over Jerusalem in 1100 he gave Edessa to his kinsman, Baldwin of Le Bourg. The latter immediately strengthened his position in Edessa in several ways. He married an Armenian princess, Morfia, daughter of the wealthy Gabriel (Armenian, Khōril) of Melitene. He received Basil, patriarch of the Armenian Church, with great honor, probably in 1103. Thus he sought the favor of his Armenian subjects. He chose as his chief vassal his kinsman Joscelin of Courtenay, recently arrived from France. He gave Joscelin the great fief of Tell Bashir, lying between the Euphrates and the borders of Antioch. Finally, in 1103 he helped procure the ransom of Bohemond of Antioch, with whom he could coöperate, in place of Tancred, with whom he could not. We have seen that the immediate results were the attacks upon Ridvan of Aleppo in 1103, and the Harran campaign of 1104, which led to the capture of Baldwin and Joscelin by the Turks. Then followed the short regency of Tancred in Edessa, the departure of Bohemond for Europe, the second regency of Tancred in Antioch, and Tancred's bestowal of Edessa upon his cousin, Richard of Salerno, all in the year 1104.

Richard lacked ability. He did not hold in check the tyranny and greed of his Frankish followers. He rapidly lost the loyalty of his Armenian subjects. Stevenson is doubtless correct in saying that the authority of the Franks was confined to the garrison towns. As a result the territory of Edessa was open to invasion. Chökürmish of Mosul raided the countryside in 1105 and Kilij Arslan of Iconium did the same in 1106 and 1107. Therefore Richard's rule of Edessa (1104–1108) was a period of great weakness for this exposed northern state.

While Richard governed Edessa, Baldwin of Le Bourg experienced changing fortunes in captivity. Shortly after his capture in 1104 by Sokman of Mardin he was kidnapped by Chökürmish of Mosul. He fell into the hands of Chavli Saqaveh when the latter conquered Mosul, probably late in 1107. The growth of Chavli's power soon aroused the jealousy of the Selchükid sultan Muḥammad, son of the great conqueror Malik-Shāh. Muḥammad commissioned Sharaf-ad-Dīn Maudūd, of whom we shall hear later, to take Mosul from Chavli. Chavli now did an astonishing thing. He offered Le Bourg liberty in return for an alliance against Maudūd, in addition to a ransom. Baldwin accepted, and was released, probably in the summer of 1108. He went to Antioch and demanded of Tancred the return of Edessa. According to Matthew of Edessa, Baldwin was refused because he would not accept it as a fief from Tancred. Tancred's selfishness blinded him to the fact that he and Baldwin of Le Bourg, by taking the side of the rebel Chavli, could deal the Selchükid power a dangerous blow. Le Bourg at once turned for support to the Armenian prince Kogh Vasil of Kesoun, who feared Tancred, and to Chavli. Border fighting developed,

with Tancred holding his own. Shortly afterwards Tancred and
Le Bourg were reconciled, largely through ecclesiastical intervention according to Ibn-al-Athīr. Edessa was then restored to count
Baldwin, September 18, 1108.[31] Thus Tancred, earlier in the year
at the pinnacle of power, not only lost the suzerainty of Edessa but
embittered its rightful lord, Baldwin of Le Bourg.

Then began a strange double civil war between Tancred and
Rĭdvan of Aleppo on one side and Le Bourg and Chavlĭ on the
other. Chavlĭ, who had left the defense of Mosul in the hands of his
wife, appeared in the district of Rahba, east of Aleppo, in order
to recruit allies. His capture of the stronghold of Bālis alarmed
Rĭdvan, lord of Aleppo. Rĭdvan called upon Tancred, with whom
he apparently had had a truce since 1105, for aid. He pictured the
plight of the Franks in Syria if Chavlĭ should seize Aleppo. Tancred
came, perhaps moved in part by resentment against Chavlĭ for
freeing Baldwin of Le Bourg. Chavlĭ now became alarmed. He
called upon Le Bourg and Joscelin for help. They responded, bitter
against Tancred. In the battle which ensued Tancred scattered his
enemies near Tell Bashir in the early fall of 1108. He besieged
Le Bourg in Duluk for a short while, but was driven off by
threatening moves made by Chavlĭ.

Thus ended the civil war of 1108. The Franks might have destroyed the power of the Turks in the region around Edessa while
the latter were fighting among themselves. They could even have
had the help of one of the Turkish factions. Such an opportunity
was not to come again soon, for Maudūd, a very able man, established himself in Mosul in September and the renegade Chavlĭ
succeeded in making his peace with the sultan Muḥammad. On the
other hand the Turks had lost an opportunity. If they had been
united, they could have attacked the Franks when the latter were
divided. The whole episode is illuminating because it shows how
quickly the Frankish and Moslem princes could forget rivalries
and become allies when private diplomatic and military considerations so warranted.

The capture of the city of Tripoli by the Franks, one of the key
events of the period, occurred during the next year, 1109. This became the capital of the Latin county of the same name. The origin
of this state is intimately connected with the name of Raymond of
St. Gilles, count of Toulouse. Raymond, it will be recalled, had,
come out on the First Crusade having sworn to devote his life to

---

[31] Matthew of Edessa, pp. 85–86; Ibn-al-Athīr, pp. 257–263; Michael the Syrian, *Chronique*
(ed. J. B. Chabot, 4 vols., Paris, 1899–1910), III, ii, 195.

the cause. But the establishment of his rival Godfrey as ruler of Jerusalem and the homesickness of his Provençal troops had forced Raymond to leave Jerusalem in August 1099. He marched his men to Latakia where most of them embarked for Europe, as we have seen. Raymond, now a leader without an army, went on to Constantinople the next year to seek whatever aid he could get from the emperor Alexius. The bond between them was dislike of Bohemond of Antioch, who had thwarted them both.

About the beginning of 1102 Raymond returned by sea to Syria. In the year 1101 he had assumed the leadership, with the approval of the emperor Alexius, of a host of crusaders, principally Lombards, who had reached Constantinople fired by enthusiasm generated by the success of the First Crusade. It was now Raymond's hope that he might appear in Syria and Palestine with this new army at his back and dictate a settlement more in accord with his conception of the original purposes of the crusade. It was Alexius's hope that Raymond would reopen Anatolia to Byzantine occupation, and would reduce Antioch to a dependency of Byzantium.

As we saw in the preceding chapter, however, the crusaders of 1101 were virtually exterminated by Kilij Arslan of Iconium and Malik-Ghāzī of Sebastia (Sivas). If Raymond of St. Gilles had arrived in Syria in 1101 with a large and victorious army, it is presumable that the Byzantines would have recovered the Anatolian provinces in his wake, that he might have been able to restore Antioch to them, and that the Greeks would thereafter have played a much more important and friendly role in the history of the Latin states. It is also presumable that Raymond, who had been consulted by pope Urban in 1095 in planning the First Crusade, and who thought that he more truly represented its original purposes than did the other princes, would have had a large influence upon the disposition of affairs in general in Syria and Palestine. Grousset goes further and suggests that Raymond and his large army might have conquered Aleppo and Damascus and made possible the establishment of a Latin power much stronger and more stable than Edessa and the three coastal states that did result from the efforts of the Franks.[32] However in the Crusade of 1101 not only were the hopes of Alexius and Raymond defeated, but when Raymond returned to Syria in 1102 he was virtually without a following. The old count endured the humiliation of

[32] *Histoire des croisades*, I, 332–333. For details of the Crusade of 1101 see above, chapter XI.

arrest and delivery into the hands of the youthful Tancred, regent of Antioch for Bohemond, then a prisoner of Malik-Ghāzī. Tancred compelled Raymond to swear to make no conquests between Antioch and Acre, and released him. Observance of this oath would have virtually excluded St. Gilles from any acquisitions on the coast of Syria and Palestine.

The count of Toulouse now proceeded to do just what Tancred had feared. He started the conquest of an area south of Antioch in Tancred's natural sphere of expansion. By now his hopes had to be reduced to the immediate business of getting a foothold in Syria. Raymond had passed through this area twice in 1099, and had become familiar with it. Grousset suggests that it reminded him of his native Midi.[33] Raymond began by capturing the port of Tortosa in 1102, and used it as a base for further operations. Then he laid siege to Ḥiṣn al-Akrād (Castle of the Kurds, later Krak des Chevaliers), which he had taken and abandoned in 1099. He gave up this siege when the assassination of Janāḥ-ad-Daulah of Homs in May 1103 seemed to offer an excellent opportunity to seize that rich and powerful emirate. However, Homs delivered itself to Dukak of Damascus and Raymond retired. Then in 1103 the count of Toulouse found his objective at last. He established a permanent camp on a hill outside the important port of Tripoli, living off the hinterland with a few hundred followers and blockading the city by land. Gradually he transformed this camp into a fortress, *Mons Peregrinus* (Pilgrim Mountain), with the help of workmen and materials sent by Alexius's officials in Cyprus. In 1104 Raymond with Genoese naval aid captured the port of Jubail, twenty miles to the south. The Genoese admiral, Hugh Embriaco, received Jubail and established a hereditary fief around it. But on February 28, 1105, count Raymond died, his ambition to conquer Tripoli still unrealized. Disappointed in his hopes to carry through the plans of pope Urban, Raymond had remained to play out the role of a petty conqueror. His monument was to be the county of Tripoli, the smallest of the four Latin states.

Raymond's successor in Syria was his cousin, William Jordan, count of Cerdagne. For four more years William, with slender resources, kept up the land blockade of Tripoli from Pilgrim Mountain. Then in the beginning of March 1109, there arrived from France Raymond's son, Bertram of St. Gilles, to claim his paternal inheritance. Bertram had left France with an army of four thousand men convoyed in a fleet largely Genoese. On the way out he

[33] Grousset, *Histoire des croisades*, I, 335.

had come to an understanding with the emperor Alexius, a step consistent with the policy of his father. On the other hand he incurred the enmity of Tancred by stopping at St. Simeon and laying claim to that part of Antioch originally held by his father in 1098. Tancred stiffly ordered Bertram to leave the principality of Antioch.

Bertram then sailed with his forces to Tortosa, a port controlled by William Jordan. He immediately claimed a part of his father's estate. William, the defender and possessor for four years, rebuffed him. But William, fearing his cousin's large forces, appealed to Bertram's enemy, Tancred, offering to become a vassal in return for protection. Tancred, eager for power and desirous of checking St. Gilles, accepted the proposal and prepared to join William Jordan.

Count Bertram, fearing Tancred's intervention, hastened to Tripoli and laid siege to it by land and sea. He hoped to settle the matter by seizing the great prize before William and Tancred could act. William's small garrison in the stronghold of Pilgrim Mountain looked on helplessly.

The young count of St. Gilles had another resource. He sent word to king Baldwin of Jerusalem, Tancred's rival of other days, offering to become a vassal in return for help. Baldwin accepted. He welcomed the opportunity to extend his power northwards and to forestall Tancred. He was glad to help reduce another Saracen port and he could hope for an alliance with the Genoese fleet for further attacks upon coastal towns. But to Baldwin, who had the qualities of statesmanship, there was still a greater opportunity. He saw then the possibility of ironing out differences among all the Franks and of uniting their energies as crusaders under the leadership of the regime at Jerusalem.

For these reasons king Baldwin formally summoned Tancred to meet him at Tripoli to give satisfaction to the complaints of Bertram, and also to those of Baldwin of Edessa and Joscelin of Tell Bashir. But Tancred owed no allegiance to king Baldwin. Therefore Baldwin summoned him in the high name of the church of Jerusalem,[34] a formula which reminds us of the stand originally taken by the ecclesiastics and others regarding the proper regime to be established in the holy city. Soon two coalitions faced each other outside Tripoli. On one side were king Baldwin, Bertram, Baldwin of Le Bourg, and Joscelin. On the other were Tancred and William Jordan with a smaller following. Under the circum-

[34] Albert of Aix, p. 667, "universae ecclesiae Iherusalem."

stances Tancred proved conciliatory. King Baldwin achieved the great personal triumph of sitting in judgment and hearing the complaints of Le Bourg versus Tancred and of Bertram versus William Jordan.

A number of compromises were worked out. First, Tancred gave up his claims in Edessa and recognized the restoration of Baldwin of Le Bourg, kinsman of king Baldwin. In return king Baldwin granted Tancred the fiefs of Tiberias, Nazareth, Haifa, and the *Templum Domini* (now the shrine Qubbat aṣ-Ṣakhrah) in Jerusalem. Tancred formally became Baldwin's vassal for these fiefs. This meant that, if Bohemond returned to Antioch, Tancred could expect to resume the place in the state of Jerusalem that he had left in 1101. It was provided that meanwhile he could enjoy the revenues from these fiefs. Tancred did not become Baldwin's vassal for Antioch. Second, it was agreed that William Jordan should keep 'Arqah and apparently Tortosa. William became a vassal of Tancred. Thus the northern part of the territory of Tripoli was to be under Tancred's influence. Third, Bertram was to get the remainder of his father's inheritance, that is, the area around Tripoli and Tripoli itself when it should fall. He became a vassal of king Baldwin. It was a great day for Baldwin I. Edessa and Tripoli were thereafter dependent upon him, while Tancred of Antioch could expect to control only the northern part of Tripoli. The prestige of king Baldwin had never been so high. Tancred, thwarted and disappointed, marched off, and besieged and captured the ports of Valania and Jabala in May and July, 1109. He thus forestalled Baldwin I and Bertram by extending his rule about a third of the way south from Latakia toward Tripoli.

The city of Tripoli surrendered July 12, 1109. It was divided between Bertram, who received two-thirds, and the Genoese, who received one-third in return for their naval help. In addition Bertram inherited the holdings of William Jordan, who was killed a little before the fall of Tripoli. Thus Bertram extended his possessions as far north as Tancred's territory. This deprived Tancred of the influence he had expected to have as the suzerain of William Jordan. A year or two later Tancred seized Tortosa from Bertram. Beyond this, king Baldwin was the beneficiary of the Tripolitan campaign, for the county of Tripoli remained a fief of the southern kingdom.[35] Its history may be treated with that of the latter.

[35] J. Richard, *Le Comté de Tripoli sous la dynastie Toulousaine, 1102–1187* (Paris, 1945), pp. 26–43, presents some evidence that, while the counts of Tripoli owed liege homage to Alexius for Maraclea and Tortosa, they also owed liege homage for these cities to Tancred of Antioch. After Pons of Tripoli became friendly with Antioch in 1112 (see below) this con-

For a number of years after the Franks took Tripoli the history of all four Latin states tended to run in the same channel. This was because the Turks of Iraq, aroused by the fall of Tripoli, were now disposed to unite and take the offensive. Therefore, the Latin states had to stand together. The *jihād* of the Turks was authorized by the Selchükid sultan Muḥammad. There soon emerged as its moving spirit a devoted Moslem, Sharaf-ad-Dīn Maudūd, lord of Mosul since 1108, and a worthy forerunner of ʿImād-ad-Dīn Zengi, Nūr-ad-Dīn, and Saladin (Ṣalāḥ-ad-Dīn). Maudūd acted as Muḥammad's commander-in-chief. It was his mission to lead the Selchükids of Iraq in a series of dangerous attacks upon the Franks.[36]

Maudūd's first campaign was in 1110. He ravaged the lands of Edessa in the spring. Baldwin of Le Bourg called for help. Baldwin of Jerusalem, after finishing the siege of Beirut, May 13, appeared in the north in the early summer. Bertram of Tripoli and two Armenian princes, Kogh Vasil of Kesoun and abū-l-Gharīb (West Armenian, Ablgharib) of Bira (Birejik), also came. Tancred did not respond. He resented Le Bourg's possession of Edessa. King Baldwin, wishing to preserve the unity attained the year before at Tripoli, summoned Tancred to join the rest of the Franks, and if he had grievances, to present them. It was apparently a direct appeal, not a feudal summons, for Antioch was not a fief of Jerusalem. Its sanction was both crusader sentiment and the power of the coalition, which Albert of Aix says disposed of twenty-five thousand men. Tancred came, reluctantly, went through the forms of reconciliation with Le Bourg, and soon withdrew. The other allies, not daring to remain long absent from their lands, prepared to go home also. They provisioned and garrisoned the city of Edessa, evacuated the agrarian population, and crossed the Euphrates. Maudūd, now joined by Tughtigin of Damascus, appeared and killed five thousand Armenians before they could cross. He then devastated the whole countryside of Edessa on his way back to Iraq. The county of Edessa, especially the part east of the Euphrates, never recovered from this blow. Nor was this all. The Franks of Edessa now in their weakness became suspicious,

nection with Byzantium became increasingly nominal. Tripoli thereafter depended more heavily upon her feudal relationship to Jerusalem for protection, however, although retaining a very real independence.

Regarding the relation between Jerusalem and Antioch, Cahen, *La Syrie du nord*, p. 246, and Nicholson, *Tancred*, p. 186, respectively write that Baldwin had only a moral not a feudal ascendancy over Antioch.

[36] For Maudūd's career see H. S. Fink, "Mawdūd of Mosul, Precursor of Saladin," *The Muslim World*, XLIII (1953), 18–27.

vengeful, and cruelly extortionate, and were hated by the people they had originally been welcomed to defend.

The Turks made a second effort in 1111. An offensive by Tancred caused individuals from Aleppo, rather than the weak and suspicious Rîdvan, to clamor for aid from both the sultan and the caliph in Baghdad. As a result Maudūd assembled a new coalition of Iraqian princes, invaded the county of Edessa, and then in August marched south to join Rîdvan in a war against Tancred. But Rîdvan shut the gates of Aleppo. He feared the greed of the Mesopotamian emirs more than that of Tancred. He cared nothing for the holy war or Moslem unity, for as we have said he sympathized with the esoteric and heretical sect of Assassins. Accordingly Rîdvan's would-be deliverers ravaged his lands for seventeen days, doubtless confirming him in his suspicions of them.

Maudūd and his Iraqian allies marched farther south, early in September, to join Tughtigin of Damascus, who desired an attack upon Tripoli. Tripoli was the natural maritime outlet for Damascus. But Maudūd's Mesopotamian allies, tired of the long campaign, balked at this and went home. Only the zealous Maudūd remained with Tughtigin.

Meantime Tancred had taken alarm. He called for help, although he had been unwilling to help others the year before. Baldwin of Jerusalem came, abandoning the promising intrigue to gain Ascalon. Count Baldwin of Edessa and his vassal Joscelin of Tell Bashir, Bertram of Tripoli, and a number of Armenian princes also gathered at the meeting place, Chastel-Rouge, thirty miles south of Antioch up the Orontes valley. There was a little skirmishing near Shaizar, and then both sides warily withdrew and went home.

One may conclude in regard to the whole campaign of 1111 that the splendid prospects of the Turks were ruined by internal dissensions, and that the policy of unity and coöperation sponsored by king Baldwin in 1109 and 1110 was brilliantly justified. However it is a matter of irony that the selfish Tancred was the principal beneficiary of this solidarity, and that king Baldwin, who was responsible for it, lost a promising opportunity to gain Ascalon.

In the years 1111–1112 Bertram and especially king Baldwin made another contribution to the cause of Latin unity. The emperor Alexius, following the death of Bohemond in Italy in 1111, again demanded Antioch of Tancred, in accordance with Bohemond's treaty of 1108. Tancred rebuffed him. Alexius then sent an envoy, Butumites, to bribe Bertram and king Baldwin into an alliance against Tancred. Bertram dallied with the idea but Baldwin's refusal was decisive for them both. Such a scheme was hardly consistent with Baldwin's policy of Frankish unity and coöperation. For Bertram it meant dropping his father's historic quarrel with the Normans of Antioch and ceasing the intrigues with Alexius.

As a result the courts of Antioch and Tripoli became friendly. Ibn-al-Qalānisī writes that when Bertram died, probably a little before February 3, 1112, the guardians of his young son Pons sent the latter to Antioch for training as a knight. He also states that Pons was given four fiefs by Tancred — Tortosa, Ṣāfīthā (later Chastel-Blanc), Ḥiṣn al-Akrād, and Maraclea. After Tancred died (probably December 12, 1112), Pons was also given Tancred's young wife, Cecilia of France. This was by wish of Tancred, according to William of Tyre.[37] Thus ended the old quarrel begun at Antioch in 1098 by Raymond of St. Gilles and Bohemond. This policy of friendship was continued by Tancred's successor in the regency of Antioch, Roger of Salerno, son of Richard of the Principate, former regent of Edessa.

Tancred's death ended the career of the youngest of the leaders of the original crusading expedition. He was certainly one of the ablest, ranking immediately below Bohemond and Baldwin I. The young Norman was perhaps more than Bohemond the real founder of the principality of Antioch. He rather than his uncle, who was usually an absentee, established the state upon a permanent foundation. A restless fighter, Tancred extended his conquests as long as he lived. Usually he fought Moslems but he was unscrupulous enough to fight fellow Christians, whether Byzantines, Armenians, or even the Franks of Edessa, if he saw a chance to gain an advantage. He was more concerned with the immediate expansion of his own power than with the larger interests of the Latin states. Yet on the whole the career of Tancred belongs on the credit side of the Latin ledger. He built up the principality of Antioch into a powerful military state that considerably outlasted the southern kingdom of Jerusalem.

Maudūd's third campaign against the Franks was in 1112. This time he came alone. He harassed the city of Edessa from April to June, and nearly captured it by corrupting some of the Armenian guards. When this failed he returned home. The pro-Turkish plots of some Armenians inside Edessa, notably in 1108 and 1112,

[37] Ibn-al-Qalānisī, p. 127; William of Tyre, XI, 18. For Tancred's death see Nicholson, *Tancred*, p. 224, note 3. Grousset believes that Bertram died at the beginning of the year 1113, shortly after the death of Tancred (*Hist. des crois.*, II, 889).

led Baldwin to take vigorous counter-measures, including a mass deportation to Samosata in 1113, rescinded in 1114. Baldwin's poverty after the constant Turkish devastations east of the Euphrates, contrasted with the prosperity of Joscelin at Tell Bashir, led him in 1113 to imprison his chief vassal briefly, strip him of his fief, and expel him. Joscelin was welcomed at Jerusalem by Baldwin I and given the fief of Galilee.

The Selchükids attacked the Franks again in 1113. This time Maudūd passed by Edessa and straightway joined Tughtigin of Damascus, who had been suffering from raids from the Franks of Jerusalem. The combined Turkish army boldly took position south of Lake Tiberias, east of the Jordan, across from the village of aṣ-Ṣinnabrah. King Baldwin summoned what was probably his maximum strength, seven hundred knights and four thousand footmen according to Albert of Aix, and marched north. At the same time he called upon Roger of Antioch and Pons of Tripoli for help. Baldwin, always aggressive and usually shrewd, this time blundered into the enemy at aṣ-Ṣinnabrah, June 28. He lost twelve hundred infantry and thirty knights, and himself barely escaped. The next day Roger and Pons arrived at Tiberias, and reproached their senior colleague for his rashness.

But the end was not yet. The Frankish force, inferior in numbers, took refuge on a hill west of Tiberias where though safe they suffered from lack of sufficient water. Ibn-al-Athīr writes that the Franks were immobilized here for twenty-six days. For two months Turkish raiding parties roamed the kingdom to the environs of Jaffa and Jerusalem itself. The Arab peasantry assisted the Turks in the plundering and devastation. However the towns, except Nablus and Baisan, held out behind their walls. As the summer wore on the Frankish army, which stayed around Tiberias, grew by accretion of pilgrims from Europe until it numbered about sixteen thousand men according to Albert of Aix. At the same time Maudūd's Iraqian allies became more and more insistent upon returning home, and eventually did so. Maudūd dismissed his own men, and himself went to Damascus with Tughtigin, September 5.[38] He intended to prepare for a campaign the next year.

Maudūd's invasion of the kingdom in 1113 was strikingly like that of Saladin in 1187. In each case the Moslems entered via the

[38] The best sources for the history of this remarkable invasion are Ibn-al-Qālanisī, pp. 133–139; Albert of Aix, pp. 694–696; Fulcher of Chartres, pp. 565–572; and William of Tyre, XI, 19. See also Ibn-al-Athīr (*RHC, Or.*, I), p. 289.

Tiberias gateway, and caused the kingdom to muster its full strength which the invaders then disastrously defeated. Both times the Franks were marooned on a hill short of water. But there were three differences. King Baldwin's troops were not entirely without water, he received reinforcements, and he was astute and had the respect of his colleagues in spite of his error. King Guy in 1187 would enjoy none of these advantages.

The danger to the Franks implicit in the existence of the able and energetic Maudūd ended with the murder of that prince, October 2, 1113. He was struck down in the presence of Tughtigin, probably by a member of the fanatical sect of Assassins. It is hard to escape the conclusion that Tughtigin, jealous of his autonomy and annoyed at the continued presence in his capital of the sultan's generalissimo, was involved. For the Franks the results were wholly fortunate. First, the murder removed a most powerful, persistent, and capable adversary. Second, Tughtigin, though he posed as innocent, became suspect in the court of sultan Muḥammad at Baghdad. As a result Tughtigin was driven to making a permanent truce with king Baldwin in 1114, and even to an alliance with the Frankish princes in 1115. Thus the circumstances of Maudūd's death bred suspicions among the Turks and destroyed much of the unity it had been his life work to create.[39]

Maudūd's death did not, however, cause sultan Muḥammad to abandon the holy war. He named Aksungur al-Bursukī to be Maudūd's successor as governor of Mosul and leader in the war. Aksungur made a futile attack upon Edessa, in May of 1114. A more positive achievement was the acceptance of an offer of loyalty from the widow of the Armenian prince Kogh Vasil (d. 1112). Her husband had suffered from aggression by Tancred in 1112. By her action Marash, Kesoun, and Raban, all northwest of Edessa, were included in the Turkish sphere of influence.

However, Aksungur permitted himself to be badly defeated by a Mesopotamian rival, Īl-Ghāzī ibn-Artuk of Mardin, probably late in 1114. As a result Īl-Ghāzī, fearing the vengeance of the sultan, made an alliance with Tughtigin of Damascus. According to Ibn-al-Athīr the two princes even made an agreement with Roger of Antioch.[40] A wide breach was opened in the ranks of the Turks. A second result of Aksungur's defeat was his replacement as Muḥammad's generalissimo by Bursuk ibn-Bursuk of Hamadan.

[39] On Maudūd's assassination see above, chapter IV, p. 113. For a discussion of Moslem politics at this period see above, chapter V, pp. 169–170.

[40] Ibn-al-Athīr, p.294.

Bursuk was ordered to punish Īl-Ghāzī and Tughtigin as well as carry on the holy war against the Franks.

In the spring of 1115 Bursuk gathered a large army of Iraqian contingents, threatened Edessa briefly, and then moved on, intending to make Aleppo his base of operations. But the eunuch Lu'lu', atabeg in that city for the child Alp Arslan, son of Ridvan (d. 1113), was as unwilling to open his gates to the army of the sultan as had been Ridvan in 1113. Lu'lu' called upon Īl-Ghāzī and Tughtigin for aid, and they in turn called upon Roger of Antioch. As a result the troops of these strange allies took position in two camps, one Turkish and one Frankish, near Apamea, to watch Bursuk. Roger in turn called upon the other Frankish princes for support. King Baldwin, Pons of Tripoli, and Baldwin II of Edessa all gathered at Apamea by August. The stage was now set for a great battle between the sultan's army under the command of Bursuk, and the coalition of Latin princes and Turkish rebels. But there was no battle, the Latin-Turkish allies being very cautious. After eight days Bursuk slyly retreated into the desert and his enemies scattered to their homes. The whole affair is excellent evidence that the Franks and Syrian Turks though given to fighting each other could close ranks against others from outside Syria.

Bursuk's withdrawal was a ruse, however. He slipped back to capture Kafarṭāb, a mountain fortress of Roger's, and to menace the lands of Antioch and Aleppo. Roger took the field and succeeded in ambushing Bursuk at Dānīth half way between Apamea and Aleppo, September 14. The rout was complete and appalling. Bursuk himself escaped but the Franks slaughtered three thousand male camp followers, enslaved the women, and committed the children and old men to the flames. The prisoners who remained, other than those held for ransom, were sent to Tughtigin, Īl-Ghāzī, and Lu'lu'. It took the Franks two or three days to divide the spoils, which were worth three hundred thousand bezants according to Fulcher of Chartres.

The battle of Dānīth made a deep impression upon the Moslems. According to Grousset, Roger, as "Sirojal" (Sire Roger), became a legendary figure among them something like Richard the Lionhearted after the Third Crusade.[41] Tughtigin of Damascus broke with his dangerous ally at once and made his peace with sultan

[41] Fulcher of Chartres, p. 589; Grousset, *Histoire des croisades*, I, 510. In addition to the usual chronicle sources see Walter the Chancellor, *Bella Antiochena* (ed. Hagenmeyer, Innsbruck, 1896), pp. 65–76. For a discussion of the importance of this battle see Cahen, *La Syrie du nord*, p. 274.

Muḥammad the next spring. Nor do we hear more of Īl-Ghāzī as an ally of Roger. This catastrophe broke the offensive spirit of the Selchükids for some time. Maudūd was dead and there was none to take his place. The Frankish states now, until Roger's defeat by Īl-Ghāzī at Darb Sarmadā in 1119, enjoyed more security than they had ever known before.

The safety enjoyed by the Latin states permitted them to go their separate ways. They could unite in danger but not in victory. Pons of Tripoli, possibly in the summer of 1116, began to plunder the Biqā' valley, the country around Baalbek. As a result he was badly defeated by Tughtigin of Damascus and Aksungur al-Bursukī of Rahba. The latter, probably to regain the laurels lost in 1114, had come down to coöperate with Tughtigin in a holy war of their own. The two years following Dānīth were spent by Baldwin II of Edessa in a war upon the neighboring Armenian principalities. It will be remembered that one at least, Kesoun, antagonized by Tancred's brutality, had sympathized with Aksungur in 1114. Baldwin acquired the territory of Dgha Ṿasil, son of Kogh Ṿasil, by torturing Dgha Ṿasil; that of abū-l-Gharīb of Bira after a year-long siege of the latter's capital; and that of Pakrad of Cyrrhus and Constantine of Gargar also by violence. Baldwin of Le Bourg thus rounded out his territories in the Euphrates valley to the west and north, and in a measure recovered the strength he had lost in 1110. His county was secure when he left it in 1118 to become king of Jerusalem.

Roger of Antioch, strange as it may seem, apparently was not actively aggressive for two years after his great victory. Probably his chief concern was Aleppo. As long as the weak and incompetent Lu'lu' was alive Roger seems to have been satisfied. But when Lu'lu was murdered in 1117 there began a confused struggle for the control of the city. It was Roger's role to combine with each successive faction dominant in Aleppo to keep out powerful candidates such as Īl-Ghāzī of Mardin, active probably in 1118 or early 1119. This able prince purchased an expensive truce from Roger, made plans with Tughtigin, went home, proclaimed a holy war, and raised a large army. He then returned to defeat and kill Roger at Darb Sarmadā near al-Athārib, west of Aleppo, June 28, 1119. This disaster, called the "field of blood" (*ager sanguinis*), will be discussed more fully in the following chapter. But the Franks of the north lost in 1119 much of the security that they had gained in 1115. They now faced a powerful and active prince in Aleppo, where there had always been a weak ruler. But this is beyond the limits of our story. In 1118 the results of Dānīth still stood. Roger's brief rule of Antioch was, states Cahen, "the moment of greatest prestige in its history."[42]

Let us now turn and see what king Baldwin of Jerusalem was able to do with his own dominions after the lapse of the Turkish peril in 1115. In the fall of that year he built in the Transjordan the castle of ash-Shaubak, or Krak de Montréal, as it was called in his honor. This was on a commanding height south of the Dead Sea eighty-five miles from Jerusalem and eighty miles north of the Red Sea. Its fine strategic position enabled the Franks not only to protect the kingdom in that quarter, but to levy tribute upon the Moslem caravans passing between Damascus and Egypt and also between Damascus and the holy cities of Medina and Mecca.

The next year Baldwin extended his influence still farther south by leading a military force to Ailah at the head of the gulf now called Aqaba, on the Red Sea. This town, one hundred and fifty miles south of Jerusalem, became the southernmost point in his kingdom. According to Albert of Aix, Baldwin now visited the Greek monastery of Mount Sinai, which is ninety miles to the southwest, but made no claim upon the territory in this area.[43]

Late in 1116 Baldwin put away his queen, Adelaide of Sicily. He had put aside Arda, his Armenian queen, in 1113, in order to marry Adelaide. He wanted to secure a rich dowry and the friendship of Adelaide's son, count Roger II of Sicily. It was agreed that Roger should inherit the kingdom if the royal pair should be childless. It is presumable that this political marriage had the approval of Baldwin's close friend and adviser, patriarch Arnulf. Arnulf, a royal partisan during the patriarchates of Daimbert (1099–1102), Evremar (1102–1108), and Gibelin (1108–1112), and privy to the removal of the first two, became patriarch in 1112. But there was enough of clerical opposition to his policy of subordinating the church to the interests of a strong monarchy, and of personal opposition to Arnulf himself, to secure his deposition in a papal legatine court in 1115. Arnulf promptly went to Rome and was reinstated in 1116. At this time he agreed to urge Baldwin to give up his bigamous union with Adelaide. King Baldwin, becoming very sick late in 1116, and still childless, fell in with this idea. It is probable, as Kühn suggests, that both Baldwin and

[42] Cahen, *op. cit.*, p. 266. For the events around Aleppo see especially Kamāl-ad-Dīn (*RHC, Or.*, III), pp. 611–618. For Roger's death and the *ager sanguinis* see below, chapter XIII, p. 413.

[43] Albert of Aix, p. 703.

Arnulf felt that the little kingdom could not be safely left to an absentee king, for Roger's most important interests would be in Sicily. Therefore with Arnulf's connivance the marriage with Adelaide was annulled. Although Baldwin, when he died two years later, left the kingdom to a resident sovereign, he had forfeited permanently the friendship of the wealthy Sicilian court.[44] The affair of Adelaide is also significant because it shows the close support given the throne, even the strong influence upon royal policy, by the patriarchate under Arnulf. But it was an influence exerted for a strong monarchy, not an independent church.

In the spring of 1118 Baldwin led a small reconnoitering expedition into Egypt for the first time. He plundered Pelusium (al-Faramā'), southeast of modern Port Said, late in March. He then pushed on to Tinnis on one of the mouths of the Nile. Here he became fatally ill. He attempted to return to Jerusalem but died at al-ʿArīsh, sixty miles southwest of Ascalon, April 2, 1118. He was succeeded by Baldwin of Le Bourg, whose formal consecration as king of Jerusalem took place on April 14 of that year. As a result another Latin state, the county of Edessa, also changed hands, for Baldwin of Le Bourg gave it to Joscelin of Courtenay in 1119. In the year 1118 there died several others identified with the early history of the Latin states, namely pope Paschal II, Adelaide of Sicily, patriarch Arnulf, and emperor Alexius Comnenus.

The reign of Alexius Comnenus, whose death occurred in August, four months after that of Baldwin I, had been advantageous to his empire and not inimical to the Franks.[45] He had reorganized and strengthened the administration and had restored the security and prosperity of his people, while protecting his frontiers against the usual attacks in the Balkans, the pseudo-crusade of the avaricious and vindictive Norman, Bohemond, and the menacing raids of the Turks in Anatolia. He had preserved his realm against the threat implicit in the presence of large western armies, too often composed of ambitious and unprincipled leaders with bigoted and undisciplined followers, only too willing to blame all their hardships and misfortunes on the Greeks, whom they regarded as wily profiteers, as schismatics, and eventually as treacherous renegades. However accurate these accusations might be against certain of

[44] William of Tyre, XI, 21, 26, 29; letter of Paschal II in de Rozière, *Cartulaire*, no 11; Kühn, *Geschichte der ersten lateinischen Patriarchen*, pp. 55–57.

[45] The whole period of the Comneni and the Angeli of Byzantium (1081–1204) will be examined in a chapter of volume II, where another chapter will consider the complex history of the Selchükids of Rūm and their Moslem neighbors, chief among whom in the twelfth century were the Dānishmendids.

Alexius' successors, they had no basis in his own conduct, but originated chiefly in the shrewd propaganda attempt of his enemy Bohemond to cast a cloak of justification over his own marauding.

Alexius had profited from the First Crusade and from his maritime strength by recovering the Anatolian littoral, but this territorial gain was partially offset by the loss of Cilicia — acquired only in 1099, lost in 1101, and retaken in 1104 — definitively in 1108 to Tancred, and by the suppression of his nominal Armenian vassals by the counts of Edessa between 1097 (Tell Bashir) and 1117 (Gargar and Cyrrhus), with Gabriel of Melitene overwhelmed by the Turks in 1103. By 1118 no portion of the crusading arena was under Greek control, and none under that of Armenians except in the Taurus mountains north of Cilicia, where Ṭoros (1100–1129) — son of Constantine, son of Ṛoupen — still held Partzapert and Vahka, and Heṭoum, son of Ōshin, ruled at Lampron. The population of Cilicia, and of that part of the county of Edessa which lay west of the Euphrates, remained largely Armenian, with a mutually antagonistic admixture of Orthodox Greeks and Syrian Jacobites, all of whom had quickly learned to detest their Frankish overlords.

The year 1118 therefore marks the end of an era. This is particularly true because of the death of Baldwin I of Jerusalem. He was the last of the original leaders of the First Crusade, with the exception of Robert of Normandy, who died in 1134, after many years as a prisoner of king Henry I of England. Godfrey, Raymond, Bohemond, and Tancred, all of whom had elected to stay in the east as builders of states, had passed. Of these Baldwin was probably the ablest. He was certainly the most successful as a prince. He founded the first Latin state in the east, the county of Edessa. He was virtually the founder and was for eighteen years the ruler of another, Jerusalem, which he transformed from an ecclesiastical state into a monarchy. He even had a hand in the capture of the city of Tripoli and in the establishment of the fourth and last state, the county of Tripoli.

With small means Baldwin accomplished much. He founded the county of Edessa with a mere handful of knights. As Godfrey's successor at Jerusalem he took over a weak state torn by factionalism and surrounded by enemies. He left it united and powerful. He found it in economic ruin. He revived and maintained commerce with the people he had come to fight, the Moslems. When he arrived he controlled but one port, Jaffa. When he died he ruled all but two along his coast, Tyre and Ascalon. He never had a fleet, yet he found Italian naval help for coastal conquests and for the protection of the vital sea routes to the west. Baldwin rarely had more troops than a modern battalion or regiment. Yet he was able to protect his small state, leave it secure and aggressive, aid the Latin states in the north, and extend his own dominions. He was a conqueror to the day of his death. His powerful enemies al-Afḍal of Egypt and Tughtigin of Damascus early gave up any notion of conquering him. As a king he had very scanty revenues. He relied upon customs duties, upon contributions from pilgrims, upon raids and tribute, and upon the economic prosperity he revived in his kingdom. He fostered this prosperity by conciliating and protecting the natives, both Christian and Moslem, who formed the bulk of the wealth-producing population of his "Latin" kingdom. He induced the Christian peasants of the Transjordan and adjacent districts to migrate to his kingdom and replace the hostile Arabs, in lieu of the potential colonists lost in the disastrous crusade of 1101.

King Baldwin had become the leader of the Franks in the Levant although he had no real means with which to coerce the three other Latin princes. It is true that he was suzerain of Tripoli, and had granted Edessa to its lord, yet their feudal rulers could have defied him if they had wished. Baldwin was statesman enough to know that the Franks would stand or fall together. He had sufficient moral authority to unite and lead them, even the reluctant Tancred, against the Turkish peril in the north. When Baldwin died his kingdom was first in dignity, power, and leadership among the Latin states in the east. All, even the exposed county of Edessa, were secure. King Baldwin's passing marks the end of the formative period of these states. It was now the turn of others to maintain what had been won.

XIII
THE GROWTH OF THE LATIN STATES, 1118–1144

The death of the childless king Baldwin I of Jerusalem on April 2, 1118, while returning from a campaign in Egypt brought to an end the rule of the direct line of the house of Boulogne. Their vigorous policies, both in the domestic and foreign fields, had greatly benefited the infant kingdom of Jerusalem. On his death the leading men of the kingdom assembled to select a successor. Among them were patriarch Arnulf, the archbishops, bishops, and other prelates of the church together with various lay leaders in-

The principal western sources are: Albert of Aix, *Christiana expeditio pro ereptione, emundatione, restitutione sanctae Hierosolymitanae ecclesiae* (*RHC, Occ.*, III); Fulcher of Chartres, *Historia Hierosolymitana, 1095–1127* (ed. H. Hagenmeyer, Heidelberg, 1913); Walter the Chancellor, *Bella Antiochena* (ed. H. Hagenmeyer, Innsbruck, 1896); William of Tyre, *Historia rerum in partibus transmarinis gestarum* (*RHC, Occ.*, I), and translated into English by A. C. Krey and E. A. Babcock, *A History of Deeds Done Beyond the Sea: by William, Archbishop of Tyre* (2 vols., Columbia University, Records of Civilization, New York, 1943).

The chief Moslem chronicles are: abū-l-Mahāṣin Yūsuf, *An-nujūm az-zāhirah* (extracts in *RHC, Or.*, III, 481–509); Ibn-al-Athīr, *Al-kāmil fī-t-ta'rīkh* (extracts in *RHC, Or.*, I, 187–744); Ibn-al-Qalānisī, *Dhail ta'rīkh Dimashq* (extracts tr. and ed. Ḥ. A. R. Gibb, *The Damascus Chronicle*, London, 1932); Kamāl-ad-Dīn, *Zubdat al-ḥalab fī ta'rīkh Ḥalab* (extracts in *RHC, Or.*, III, 577–690); Sibṭ Ibn-al-Jauzī, *Mir'āt az-Zamān* (extracts in *RHC, Or.*, III, 517–570). See also Usāmah Ibn-Munqidh, *Kitāb al-i'tibār* (tr. H. Derenbourg, Paris, 1896; also tr. G. R. Potter, London, 1929; and tr. P. K. Hitti, *An Arab-Syrian Gentlemen ... of the Time of the Crusades*, Columbia University, Records of Civilization, New York, 1929).

Byzantine and oriental Christian writers include: "The First and Second Crusade from an Anonymous Syriac Chronicle," ed. A. S. Tritton and H. A. R. Gibb, *Journal of the Royal Asiatic Society*, 1933, pp. 69–101, 273–305; John Cinnamus, *Epitome rerum ab Ioanne et Alexio Comnenis gestarum* (*RHC, Grecs*, I); Gregory abū-l-Faraj (Bar Hebraeus), *Chronography* (tr. E. A. Wallis Budge, London, 1932); Gregory the Presbyter, *Chronique* (*RHC, Doc. arm.*, I); Matthew of Edessa, *Chronique* (*RHC, Doc. arm.*, I); Michael the Syrian, *Chronique* (ed. J. B. Chabot, Paris, 1899); Nicetas Choniates, *Historia* (*RHC, Grecs*, I).

Among secondary works the following are especially useful: C. Cahen, *La Syrie du nord à l'époque des croisades et la principauté d'Antioche* (Paris, 1940); F. Chalandon, *Les Comnène: Jean II Comnène (1118–1143) et Manuel I Comnène (1143–1180)* (Paris, 1912); René Grousset, *Histoire des croisades et du royaume franc de Jérusalem*: vol. I, *L'Anarchie musulmane et la monarchie franque*; vol. II, *Monarchie franque et monarchie musulmane: l'équilibre* (Paris, 1934–1935); B. Kugler, *Geschichte der Kreuzzüge* (Berlin, 1880); J. L. LaMonte, *Feudal Monarchy in the Latin Kingdom of Jerusalem, 1100–1291* (Cambridge, 1932); E. Rey, "Histoire des princes d'Antioche," *ROL*, IV (1896), 321–407, and *Les Colonies franques de Syrie aux XIIme et XIIIme siècles* (Paris, 1883); R. Röhricht, *Geschichte des Königreichs Jerusalem 1100–1291* (Innsbruck, 1898); S. Runciman, *History of the Crusades*, vol. II, *The Kingdom of Jerusalem* (Cambridge, 1952); W. B. Stevenson, *The Crusaders in the East* (Cambridge, 1907); and Jean Richard, *Le Royaume latin de Jérusalem*, Paris, 1953.

cluding Joscelin, lord of Tiberias, to choose his successor. Some, apparently swayed by the late king's request that they select his brother Eustace if he should come to Jerusalem, urged that they wait for his arrival and not interfere with the ancient law of hereditary succession. But others, fearful that an interregnum would imperil the safety of the kingdom, opposed this view and urged the immediate selection of a king. Joscelin, already apprised of the patriarch's support, sided with the latter group and argued that Baldwin's kinsman, Baldwin of Le Bourg, who had recently repaired from his state, the county of Edessa, to visit the holy places and to confer with the king, be made the new ruler. The assembly, unaware that Joscelin hoped by this move to succeed later to the county of Edessa and recalling the harsh treatment accorded to him by Baldwin of Le Bourg, believed in his sincerity and accordingly elected Baldwin of Le Bourg to the kingship. Perhaps the alternate suggestion of the late ruler to the effect that Baldwin of Le Bourg be made his successor if Eustace were unavailable also recommended Joscelin's pleas to them. The claim of the new sovereign to his throne was uncontested, since Eustace, who had reluctantly accepted the offer of a group of nobles to assume the kingship and had, indeed, proceeded as far as Apulia in quest of it, now abandoned it rather than provoke civil strife. Accordingly, Baldwin II was consecrated king of Jerusalem on April 14, 1118.[1]

The new ruler, despite his advanced years, was well suited for his new role, because of his abundant experience in war and government and pronounced sense of duty. Events were soon to prove the need of all these political and military assets, for the Moslems, after long years of disunity, were now slowly beginning to unite once more.[2] Desiring to come to terms with one of his chief antagonists, Baldwin dispatched envoys to Tughtigin, the emir of Damascus, with terms of truce. Tughtigin replied that he would accept them on condition that Baldwin relinquish his share of the revenues of a number of territories east of the Jordan. Upon the king's refusal and threat to wage war on him, the emir advanced upon Tiberias and its environs and pillaged them in May 1118. Meanwhile, al-Afḍal, the ruler of Egypt, invaded the

[1] William of Tyre, XII, 3; Matthew of Edessa, *Chronique* (*RHC, Arm.*, I), p. 119. A. C. Krey, *William of Tyre*, I, 521, note 11, and J. L. LaMonte, *Feudal Monarchy*, p. 8, differ in their views concerning the time of the sending of the embassy to Eustace, the former believing that it occurred after, the latter that it occurred before the selection of Baldwin of Le Bourg. Cf. Röhricht, *Königreich Jerusalem*, p. 126, note 3.

[2] For further details on Moslem politics at this time, especially the significance of Aleppo, see below, chapter XIV.

kingdom in the summer of 1118 and encamped before Ascalon. Tughtigin thereupon repaired to Ascalon, assumed command of the Egyptian forces, and received from the garrison's commander a promise of complete coöperation, in accordance with the instructions of his government. The kingdom, now threatened by Damascus and Ascalon on the northeast and southwest respectively, presently had to meet a new danger on the northwest, for a number of the enemy's warfleet had sailed from Ascalon to the important naval base at Tyre, apparently with the consent and approval of the Moslem commanders there.

Baldwin, foreseeing these moves, had summoned troops from the principality of Antioch and the county of Tripoli and had assembled his own warriors in the plain of the Philistines. He now camped very close to the Egyptian lines. A military stalemate of two or three months ensued with neither side daring to attack, whereupon Tughtigin elected to withdraw and return to Damascus, and the remainder of his forces retired to Egypt. Similarly the Frankish forces departed and returned to their respective lands.

Apparently in retaliation for Tughtigin's invasion of the kingdom, the Franks now invaded and pillaged the Damascus country. Tughtigin dispatched his son Tāj-al-Mulūk Böri against them, whereupon the invaders retired to a neighboring mountain. In defiance of his father's order, Tāj-al-Mulūk Böri met them in battle and suffered a crushing defeat. Pursuing the policy of the offensive, the Franks then struck at Aleppo and ravaged the surrounding country. Tughtigin promised aid to the Aleppans, but was defeated by Joscelin.

Despite the Frankish counter-attack, Tughtigin pursued his plans, and, having joined forces with Īl-Ghāzī, the sultan of Aleppo, successfully sought the latter's help against the southern Franks, who continued to ravage the Hauran. But these plans were soon shelved in favor of agreements that Īl-Ghāzī should marshal his troops at Mardin and join Tughtigin in a campaign against Antioch in the summer of 1119. The change of plans resulted from the threat to Aleppo arising from the capture of ʻAzāz, an important stronghold belonging to Īl-Ghāzī, in late 1118 by the united efforts of Roger, the ruler of Antioch, and Leon, an Armenian chieftain in Cilicia, and also from the seizure of Buzāʻah by the Franks.

In accordance with these agreements, Īl-Ghāzī, after a pause before Edessa (Urfa), crossed the Euphrates at the beginning of June 1119 and invaded the Tell Bashir (Turbessel) country. Apprised of his impending danger, Roger appealed to Joscelin, Pons, the count of Tripoli, and Baldwin for help. Baldwin hastily mustered an army and joined forces with Pons. Meanwhile, Roger, chafing under the delay, left Antioch and encamped before the stronghold of Artāḥ. Then, after waiting several days for the arrival of the king and the count, he spurned the views of the patriarch, followed the advice of some of the local nobles, who were anxious to have his army protect their lands, and ordered his army to advance. At length on June 20 he took up an untenable position at al-Balāṭ between two mountains located near Darb Sarmadā north of al-Athārib in the mistaken belief that the difficulty of the terrain would thwart the enemy. Īl-Ghāzī, meantime, was awaiting the arrival of Tughtigin at Buzā'ah, a town situated northeast of Aleppo, to draw up a plan of campaign, but his emirs, weary of delays, demanded immediate action. Īl-Ghāzī consented. The Moslem forces broke camp on June 27 and took up a position under cover of darkness near the unsuspecting Franks, who believed that the attack would be launched by way of al-Athārib or Zardanā. When dawn broke, the Moslems closed in on the Latins from three sides. A rout and butchery of the Franks ensued, which came to be known as the "field of blood" (*ager sanguinis*). Roger himself was slain, seventy of his knights were captured, and their leaders were taken to Aleppo for ransom. This annihilation of the Norman chivalry effected a permanent decrease of Norman influence in Syria as against Provençal and east-central French.

Fortunately for the Franks, Īl-Ghāzī did not clinch his triumph over them, but contented himself with plundering operations in the principality of Antioch. Instead of striking at the now well-nigh defenseless city of Antioch, manned by the Frankish clergy and citizens under the direction of the patriarch Bernard of Valence, Īl-Ghāzī advanced on the far lesser prizes of al-Athārib and Zardanā and captured them. Then, after reorganizing the administration of Aleppo, he returned to Mardin. Meanwhile, Baldwin had hastened on to Antioch, and, establishing his domination over it, had repaired its shattered defenses with the help of Roger's widow. The cavalry and infantry forces were reconstituted, and the widows of the fallen were married to the survivors. Baldwin also called upon the Edessan Franks for aid in the coming battles with the foe.

Īl-Ghāzī's capture of Zardanā aroused Baldwin and Pons. Accordingly, they immediately departed from Antioch to search out the enemy. Directing their march toward the Rugia valley, they presently encamped on a hill near Dānīth (Tall Dānīth) where Roger had won a victory in 1115.[3] Meanwhile, Īl-Ghāzī, informed of the Frankish plans, summoned his chiefs and prepared for a predawn attack on the Franks, but the latter passed a sleepless night in preparation for the contest. An inconclusive battle was fought on the following day, August 14. Īl-Ghāzī together with Tughtigin fled from the field; the former repaired to Mardin to gather fresh forces. The Franks retired as well, Baldwin returning to Antioch.

The indecisive character of the second battle of Dānīth is indicated by the fact, illustrative of Moslem weakness, that Baldwin was able to reconquer during the autumn of 1119 the Moslem strongholds of Zūr', Kafar Rūm, Kafarṭāb, Sarmīn, and Ma'arrat-Miṣrīn. But al-Athārib and Zardanā did not fall into Frankish control, and the continued Moslem mastery of these bastions meant the end, at least for the time being, of the threat to Aleppo's security. The death of Roger and the decimation of the north Frankish soldiery were advantages of the first importance to the Moslems.[4]

The political vacuum created in the principality of Antioch endangered the very existence of the north Frankish political establishment. Accordingly, the lay and clerical leaders of Antioch gave Baldwin *carte blanche* to govern the principality. Continuing with the policies he inaugurated between the death of Roger and the second battle of Dānīth, Baldwin bestowed the goods of the fallen warriors on their children, provided the widows with new spouses of equal rank, and reëquipped the several fortresses. More important still, he became the ruler of Antioch, for the Antiochenes now entrusted their state to his care with the understanding that he would grant it to Bohemond II, Bohemond I's son, when he attained his majority. The king's ensuing rule, which continued until the arrival of Bohemond II in 1126, indicated that he was as careful of the principality as if it had been his own country. Baldwin shortly thereafter completed his stabilization of the north Frankish possessions and that of the county of Edessa, in particular, by calling Joscelin from Tiberias, and, following his swearing of an oath of fealty, investing him with the county of Edessa in late August or early September 1119 and charging him with the the task of opposing the Moslem incursions. Baldwin's decision was a wise one, as Matthew of Edessa observes, for Jos-

[3] Cf. above, chapter XII, p. 404.
[4] See also S. Runciman, *History of the Crusades*, II, 155.

celin was a chief renowned among the Franks for his shining valor, recent examples of which he had displayed in vigorous although unsuccessful attacks on the Hauran and Ascalon districts in the late winter, spring, and summer of 1119.

The new ruler of Edessa, continuing his policy of the offensive, twice successfully invaded the Wādī Buṭnān and the Syrian bank of the Euphrates. He then advanced on Manbij, Naqīrah, and the eastern part of the province of Aleppo. But, upon his arrival at Ravendan in pursuit of a body of Turks who had crossed the Euphrates, a battle ensued in which he suffered defeat and sustained the loss of many of his warriors.

Apparently encouraged by the reverse administered to Joscelin, Īl-Ghāzī and his nephew Belek now launched twin blows at the Franks. The former invaded the principality of Antioch but suffered defeat. The latter assembled a large army, advanced on and encamped before Edessa for four days, and ravaged the entire countryside. Departing in May 1120, he passed by Sarūj and stealthily crossed the Euphrates on May 26 and proceeded from Tell Bashir to Kesoun. Joscelin hastened from Raban, a stronghold in the northern part of the county of Edessa, to Kesoun and Behesni, where he raised an army. Setting out in pursuit of the Turks, he fell on them and killed a thousand warriors. Īl-Ghāzī thereupon fell back and, turning towards the principality of Antioch, encamped near ʿAzāz. Then, following a single day's pause before Antioch and a few days' halt in the territory of Rugia, he retired toward Qinnasrīn. The lack of booty, together with persistent Frankish attacks, led to growing discontent in his army and increasing desertions. Fortunately for Īl-Ghāzī, Tughtigin arrived with reinforcements in the nick of time. Meanwhile the Franks, in response to an appeal from Antioch for aid, marched out in June from Jerusalem to do battle under Baldwin's banner and effected a juncture with Joscelin's forces in Antioch. Despite the lack of food and water and constant harassing attacks by the Moslems, they maintained their ranks and reached Maʿarrat-Miṣrīn safely. Aware of the superiority of the Frankish cavalry horses and the inferiority of their own and, in consequence, fearful of a sudden and victorious Frankish attack, the Moslem commanders withdrew their troops to Aleppo; thereupon the Franks returned to Antioch. An armistice providing for the undisturbed possession of Maʿarrat-Miṣrīn, Kafarṭāb, and Albara by the Franks until March 1121 was arranged shortly thereafter. But this considerable gain by the Franks was partly offset by Īl-Ghāzī's destruction of Zardanā in June 1120 to prevent its capture by the Franks.

Apparently believing that he was not obligated to observe Baldwin's truce with Īl-Ghāzī, Joscelin ravaged Naqīrah and al-Aḥaṣṣ in January 1121 on the pretext that the governor of Manbij had seized one of his prisoners and had ignored his protests.[5] Proceeding thence, he devastated the Wādī and then repaired to Tell Bashir to obtain new troops for further raids. The Edessan chieftain's harsh treatment of his captives evoked indignant protests from the governor of Aleppo to Baldwin, but the latter replied that he had no authority over him. Joscelin then led a successful expedition against the Moslems located in the territory of Ṣiffīn to the south of the Euphrates, attacked the town of Buzā'ah, located northeast of Aleppo near the Wādī Buṭnān, and succeeded in burning a part of its walls. In return for a money payment on the part of the besieged, Joscelin raised the siege and returned to his own county.

Shortly thereafter with the expiration of the truce between Baldwin and the Moslems, the Franks resumed the offensive (April-June 1121). After a successful raid upon the Shaizar country, which terminated in a short truce, the Antiochene Franks, with Joscelin presumably one of their number, unleashed two such unremitting attacks on the Moslem stronghold of al-Athārib at the beginning of May and so gravely threatened Aleppo that Īl-Ghāzī ordered his son Sulaimān, the governor of al-Athārib, to make peace with the Franks. Joscelin, one of the chief negotiators, required the Turks to relinquish their claims to Sarmīn, al-Jazr, Lailūn, and the northern part of the province. In addition, all the environs of Aleppo were divided equally between the Franks and the Moslems. Īl-Ghāzī accepted the Frankish demand that he surrender al-Athārib, but the garrison stoutly refused to carry out his promise and hence it remained in Moslem hands. Baldwin presently left Jerusalem and ratified the new treaty.[6]

Meanwhile, Tughtigin, believing that Baldwin's dual role as king of Jerusalem and *bailli* of Antioch prevented him from ruling both states effectively, invaded the kingdom of Jerusalem and devastated the lands about Tiberias. When Baldwin quickly

[5] Kamāl-ad-Dīn (*RHC, Or.*, III), pp. 625–626. Grousset, *Croisades*, I, 578, concludes that the "comte d' Édesse ... ne s'était peut-être pas fait inclure dans la trêve."

[6] Kamāl-ad-Dīn (*RHC, Or.*, III), pp. 626–628; Usāmah Ibn-Munqidh (ed. and tr. Derenbourg), I, 122–123. E. Rey, "Histoire des princes d'Antioche," *ROL*, IV (1896), 351, believes that the refusal of the Moslem garrison of al-Athārib to surrender caused the treaty to remain a dead letter until the end of Baldwin's campaign in October 1121.

mobilized his forces and advanced to meet him, Tughtigin retired to his own country. Thereupon, Baldwin advanced southward and invested and captured Jarash, a fortress constructed by Tughtigin the preceding year. Following its capture, the Franks razed it (July 1121) because of the prohibitive cost and difficulty of maintenance.

The signal victories gained by the Franks over Il-Ghāzī and Tughtigin continued throughout the summer of 1121 and were augmented by the revolt of Sulaimān against his father. Taking advantage of the opportunity thus presented to them, the Franks invested, captured, and fortified Zardanā (August–September) and, advancing on Aleppo, inflicted a serious defeat on the defenders. Baldwin then besieged and captured the citadels of Khunāṣirah (Khānaṣir), Burj Sibnā, Naqīrah, and al-Aḥaṣṣ. Sulaimān in alarm sent an envoy to Baldwin and proposed peace, but the parleys broke down over Baldwin's insistence that al-Athārib be surrendered to him. The king then besieged al-Athārib but returned to Antioch after only three days. Il-Ghāzī and Sulaimān presently composed their differences (November 1121), and the former effected a temporary peace with the Franks, whereby he once more surrendered the territories which they had held when they were the masters of al-Athārib and Zardanā.

Despite the signal defeats inflicted upon him by the Franks, Il-Ghāzī resumed the offensive. Taking advantage of Baldwin's absence — Pons' reluctance to recognize Baldwin as his overlord required the king's presence in Tripoli to exact his submission — he returned to Syria at the end of June 1122 accompanied by Belek.[7] Il-Ghāzī besieged some of the Frankish fortresses, among them Zardanā, on July 27. Upon receipt of the news from Zardanā's lord, Baldwin summoned Joscelin to his aid. The two chieftains, in company with the Antiochene leaders, marched against Il-Ghāzī. The Moslems withdrew, whereupon Baldwin returned to Antioch. The Moslems then resumed the siege, but again withdrew in simulated flight on the approach of Baldwin. When the king refused to be tricked by their maneuver, Il-Ghāzī, who had in the meantime been struck down by apoplexy, retired from Zardanā with the other Moslem leaders in September. Before they

[7] Kamāl-ad-Dīn (*RHC, Or.*, III), p. 632; William of Tyre, XII, 17. A. C. Krey, *William of Tyre*, I, 539, note 55, comments as follows, "Perhaps the campaign represented an effort by Baldwin II to extend his authority over Tripoli and to make himself real ruler of all the Latin states of Syria. His regency of Antioch together with the personal dependence of Joscelin of Edessa upon him created a favorable opportunity for such a move. The basis of his demand upon Pons was the homage which Bertram had shown to Baldwin I in 1109...."

reached Aleppo, however, the stricken leader died, November 3, 1122. Meanwhile Baldwin had returned to Antioch.

The military advantages and opportunities presented to the Franks by the illness of their redoubtable adversary, Īl-Ghāzī, were presently negatived by the capture of the Frankish hammer, Joscelin. Upon his return from Zardanā, Belek laid siege to Edessa, but, finding the resistance too stout, retired. The Franks, apparently fearing that Belek would return, sent some of their number to Bira (Birejik) to report Belek's activities to Joscelin. That leader, who had taken as his second wife Maria of Salerno, the sister of Roger of Antioch, and had received ʻAzāz as a dowry, was spending the night at Bira with its lord Galeran of le Puiset, who had been granted it by Baldwin in 1117. Urged on by Galeran, who was alarmed by Belek's presence in his territory, Joscelin with a hundred knights sought to surprise the Artukid. Belek, however, learned of their plan and, preferring an ambush to a pitched battle, stationed his forces at a marshy spot near Sarūj. The Frankish cavalry traversing this area were soon hopelessly mired, whereupon the Moslems, launching a merciless hail of arrows, captured Joscelin, Galeran, and twenty-five to sixty knights on September 13, 1122. After vainly demanding the surrender of Edessa, Belek imprisoned his two noble captives together with the other Frankish prisoners in the fortress of Kharput northeast of Edessa. Belek's good fortune was soon increased, for Īl-Ghāzī bequeathed his estates as well as the care of his sons Sulaimān and Timurtash to his nephew.

In the face of the several disasters which had overtaken the north Syrian Franks, Baldwin undertook a vigorous counter-offensive against the Moslems in the autumn of 1122 and launched an attack on the Aleppan territories near Tall Qabbāsīn north of the town of al-Bāb (Bāb Buzāʻah) in October. The Moslems garrisoned at Buzāʻah hastened forth, but suffered a total defeat at the hands of the Franks. Then, apprised of Īl-Ghāzī's death, Baldwin ravaged the valley of Buzāʻah, reduced to submission and collected tribute from the citizenry of al-Bāb, and laid siege to Bālis. Upon the approach of Belek's forces, Baldwin returned to the valley of Buzāʻah and invested Bīr. That town capitulated and Baldwin took its garrison to Antioch.

The precarious condition of the leaderless county of Edessa also occupied Baldwin's attention. Assuming the rule of the county, he repaired at once to Edessa and placed the city under the command of a garrison commanded by Geoffrey the Monk, lord of Marash, until the fate of Joscelin should be ascertained. The fortresses of Tell Bashir and Edessa placed themselves under the king's supervision and through his efforts were kept in a good state of defense. These effective administrative and military measures were complemented by Baldwin's peace treaty with Sulaimān ibn-al-Jabbār of Aleppo on April 9, 1123, which provided for the surrender of the stronghold of al-Athārib to the Franks. Yet Baldwin's task of administration of both Edessa and Antioch was now a crushing burden, as Grousset points out.[8]

But an even more signal Moslem triumph and Frankish defeat followed Joscelin's capture, for Baldwin himself became a Saracen prisoner in April 1123. Having assembled an army to attack Belek, who was then besieging the castle of Gargar, and to effect the release of Joscelin and Galeran, Baldwin advanced toward Raban on April 8. Belek was already engaged in plundering operations in this very area. The rival forces were unaware of each other's presence. The king encamped at Shenchrig, whereupon Belek, informed of the enemy's nearness, arranged an ambush and then hurled his forces at the surprised Franks and effected the capture of Baldwin and his nephew on April 18. After obtaining the surrender of Gargar from Baldwin, Belek imprisoned his captives in Kharput, where Joscelin and Galeran were already imprisoned.

The royal prisoners presently began to plot escape and succeeded in enlisting the support of a number of Armenians living around the prison. These, in turn, communicated with their compatriots in Edessa. Soon fifty soldiers disguised as merchants departed from Edessa and, proceeding to Kharput, gained admission to the inner gates of the castle (May 1123). Using as a pretext an insult which they claimed had been imposed upon them, the conspirators approached the leader of the guardians of the castle gates. Then, having drawn knives from their garments and killed him, the rescuers seized spears and made short work of the Turkish garrison which now sallied forth. Baldwin as well as the other captives were liberated. But before the rescuers and rescued could effect an escape, a large Turkish force approached Kharput and invested it on all sides. The besieged Franks decided that Joscelin should seek help, and the Edessan leader agreed. Accompanied by three

[8] Grousset, *Croisades*, I, 584; William of Tyre, XII, 17; Ibn-al-Qalānisī, p. 166; Kamāl-ad-Dīn (*RHC, Or.*, III), p. 635; Sibṭ Ibn-al-Jauzī (*RHC, Or.*, III), p. 564; Ibn-al-Athīr (*RHC, Or.*, I), p. 349. See also Stevenson, *Crusaders in the East*, p. 109. LaMonte, *Feudal Monarchy*, p. 192, observes that "the kings of Jerusalem were often baillies for one or another of the great counties [Tripoli and Edessa] during the captivity of the lord of the county or during a minority. But the bailliage seems to have been held as a result of invitation by the barons and people of the county rather than by any right derived from their legal relationship."

servants, he left Kharput, successfully crossed the enemy lines and the Euphrates, and then with a friendly Armenian peasant acting as a guide at length reached Tell Bashir.

Joscelin now undertook the task of rescuing his overlord. After dispatching messengers to the Byzantine emperor and the several Armenian chieftains, he departed in August 1123 and proceeded, by way of Kesoun and Antioch, to Jerusalem to rally help for the release of Baldwin. His fervent appeal for help had an instantaneous response, for the feudality rose as one man to meet the dreadful challenge hurled at them by the exultant Belek. Joscelin then proceeded to Tripoli. Soon a combined force of warriors from Jerusalem, Tripoli, and Antioch advanced toward Tell Bashir. There they learned the disquieting news that Baldwin and the fortress of Kharput had again fallen into Belek's hands on September 16. Informed of the release of his prisoners and Joscelin's escape on August 6, Belek abandoned the siege of Kafarṭāb which he had recently begun and returned to Kharput. After fruitless dickering with Baldwin to secure a peaceful surrender, Belek stormed and captured the fortress and then reimprisoned Baldwin, his nephew, and Galeran at Harran.

The Frankish rescuing force accordingly decided to abandon the project of rescuing Baldwin and his fellows, but determined to harm the enemy at the time of the passage of the Frankish contingents by Aleppo. Meanwhile, Joscelin, following his appeal for help in Jerusalem, began his return trip to Tell Bashir, but learned en route of Belek's recovery of Kharput. He then attacked Buzā'ah, al-Bāb, and Aleppo. The main body of the Franks, upon their arrival at Aleppo, scored some successes over the defenders, but a dearth of food supplies forced them to depart. In consequence, they, together with Joscelin, returned to their respective bailiwicks in October.

Equally indecisive results attended the ensuing Franco-Moslem warfare in north Syria during the autumn of 1123 and the early months of 1124. Apparently believing that the best defense of his own territories and those of the now leaderless principality of Antioch lay in offense, Joscelin attacked Belek's dominions. Belek retaliated shortly thereafter when, with the forces of Tughtigin and Aksungur al-Bursukī, the regent (Turkish, *atabeg*) of Mosul, as his allies, he advanced upon and invested 'Azāz in the early winter of 1124, but was defeated by a relieving force of Franks. Better luck attended his next sally in April when he defeated a Frankish force at Mashḥalā. Yet Frankish pressure seemingly was not without effect, for, perhaps as a precautionary measure, he transferred Baldwin and the other captives from Harran to Aleppo during late February or early March 1124.

Meanwhile, important events had occured in the kingdom of Jerusalem during Baldwin's captivity. Upon learning of the king's imprisonment, the feudality together with the patriarch Gormond of Picquigny, who had succeeded Arnulf of Chocques in 1118, and the prelates agreed unanimously that the constable of the kingdom, Eustace Garnier, should act as regent until Baldwin's release. Foreign affairs soon came to occupy the constable's attention, for the Ascalon Moslems, having heard of Baldwin's captivity, attacked the kingdom by land and sea in mid-May 1123. The Franks effectively repulsed the Moslem land forces near Jaffa on May 29, whereupon the Moslem naval squadron which was closely investing Jaffa returned to Ascalon. This victory, together with the selection of the able William of Bures, the lord of Tiberias, to replace Eustace Garnier after his death on June 15, augured well for the kingdom, but still the danger of new and perhaps more menacing attacks had not been averted. Fortunately for William of Bures, help was near at hand. A strong Venetian naval force under the command of the doge of Venice, which had set out for the Holy Land in the late autumn of 1122 in response to an appeal from Baldwin and which was now at Corfu, learned of the threat to the kingdom through messengers and now proceeded post-haste towards Ascalon. The ensuing naval battle between the Venetians and the Moslems ended in a smashing Moslem rout.

The fresh accretions of strength from Europe inspired hope in the ranks of the leaders of the kingdom that additional prizes might be wrested from the Moslems. Accordingly, William of Bures and the other chieftains initiated conferences with the Venetians in late December 1123. The bitter quarrel which followed between the advocates of an attack upon Tyre and the proponents of an assault upon Ascalon was at length resolved by a resort to lots. Tyre was chosen. Thereupon, a treaty was drawn up providing for grants to the Venetians of one third of the city of Tyre, if it were captured, a quarter in Jerusalem, various judicial privileges in Tyre, and freedom of trade without tolls in all parts of the kingdom. Preparations for the siege were now undertaken, and the allies began their investment by land and sea on February 16, 1124.

Utilizing to the utmost their strategic location, massive fortifications, and abundant food supplies, the Tyrians for a time successfully repulsed the fierce attacks of the besiegers, but the arrival of fresh Frankish forces coupled with the steady dwindling of their provisions at length compelled the defenders to appeal to their lords, Tughtigin of Damascus and the caliph of Egypt, for assistance. Tughtigin's ready compliance with an assisting force proved unavailing, however, for the Franks devised a counter-strategy so effective that Tughtigin decided to withdraw. Meanwhile, the Venetian doge, having investigated and proved false rumors that an Egyptian fleet was about to succor Tyre, redoubled his attacks upon the city. At last relieved of fears that Tughtigin would intervene decisively, the Frankish armies pressed forward with unrelenting assaults against the now frenzied defenders. At length Tughtigin, having vainly appealed to the Egyptian Moslems for aid, made peace overtures to the allies. An agreement for surrender was finally reached, with the proviso that the Tyrians be allowed to remain or depart as they desired with no molestation of their homes and possessions. The victors took possession on July 7, 1124, the terms of surrender were executed, and, in accordance with the treaty, two parts were assigned to the king and one to the Venetians.[9]

With Baldwin and Galeran once more firmly in his grasp, Belek ceased to fear effective Frankish attack, and hence turned his attention again to the perennial internecine Moslem warfare. Resolving to settle accounts with Ḥassān, the governor of Manbij, he entrusted the command of an army corps to his cousin Timurtash in April 1124 with orders to proceed to Manbij and to invite Ḥassān to participate in an attack on Tell Bashir. If Ḥassān agreed, then Timurtash was to seize him. Timurtash accepted the command and entered Manbij, but was met with a formal refusal by 'Īsâ, Ḥassān's brother. Timurtash accordingly arrested Ḥassān and imprisoned him in the fortress of Palu. 'Īsâ, in retaliation, wrote to Joscelin and offered to surrender Manbij to him if he would drive away Belek's troops. Fearful that Belek would be a more dangerous neighbor than Ḥassān, Joscelin traveled to Jerusalem, Tripoli, and all the other Frankish areas, raised an army, and advanced on Manbij. Shortly thereafter a battle followed with Belek. A complete Frankish defeat ensued and Joscelin himself fled to Tell Bashir on the following day, May 6. Belek thereupon executed all the prisoners taken in the battle and then advanced on

[9] As might be expected William of Tyre (XIII, 1–14) gives considerable space to the siege of Tyre and includes a detailed description of the city. The inaction of the Fāṭimids stemmed from the murder of the capable vizir al-Afḍal in December 1121.

Manbij to resume the siege, planning to leave the conduct of the investment in the hands of Timurtash and to proceed himself to the rescue of Tyre which was then being besieged by the Franks. But all his designs came to naught when he was killed immediately thereafter on May 6 by an arrow discharged by the besieged. Timurtash now succeeded Belek in the rule of Aleppo — the dead chieftain had been so enraged by his cousin Sulaimān's surrender of al-Athārib in 1123 that he had come to regard him as incapable of effective leadership and had, accordingly, invested and captured Aleppo in June 1123 — and presently transferred Belek's several noble captives, including Baldwin and Galeran, to Shaizar.

The signal good fortune for the several crusading states and Edessa, in particular, stemming from Belek's death was soon heralded by fresh attacks upon the Moslems. Joscelin's lieutenant ravaged the canton of Shabakhtan in May 1124. 'Umar al-Khāṣṣ, Timurtash's subordinate, met the Franks in battle near Marj Aksās and succeeded in killing most of them including their leader. In compensation for his services, Timurtash rewarded him with the civil and military rule of Aleppo.

The reverse suffered by the Moslem cause by the death of Belek in May was now intensified by Timurtash's rash decision to release Baldwin, who agreed on June 24 to surrender 'Azāz and to pay a very large ransom in return for his freedom. In addition, he promised to make war on Dubais, the Arab chieftain of Hilla and Iraq and the mortal enemy of Timurtash. Joscelin and the queen of Jerusalem negotiated with Timurtash concerning Baldwin's release and surrendered to him as hostages Joscelin [II], Joscelin's son, and Baldwin's young daughter Yvette together with fifteen other persons. Baldwin was released shortly thereafter on August 29. Count Galeran and the king's nephew, however, remained in Timurtash's hands and were presently executed.

Immediately thereafter, on September 6, Baldwin broke his agreement to surrender 'Azāz, alleging that the patriarch had forbidden him to do so. Then, to make matters worse for Timurtash, Joscelin and Baldwin entered into negotiations with Dubais, and, informed by him of the sympathy of the Aleppan population, agreed not only to attack Aleppo but also, following its capture, to cede it to him with the proviso that the authority over the property and population of Aleppo be reserved to the Franks. Dubais thereupon advanced upon Marj Dābiq and routed the forces of Timurtash. Despite Baldwin's treaty-breaking, Timurtash continued his negotiations with him concerning the Frankish and

Moslem hostages. He prepared, however, for any eventuality by a visit to Mardin, where he requested the assistance of his brother Sulaimān and recruited troops.

The Franco-Aleppan agreements were definitely sundered in late September when Baldwin marched to Artāḥ and threatened Aleppo, arriving before the latter city on October 6. Meanwhile, Joscelin and Dubais, proceeding from Tell Bashir, invaded the valley of Buzā'ah and conducted widespread devastations of the crops. They soon effected a junction with Baldwin before Aleppo. The Frankish chieftains and their followers, together with their Moslem allies, namely Dubais and his son Ṣadaqah and lesser leaders with their forces, numbering no less than two hundred Frankish and one hundred Moslem tents, now established a close investment of Aleppo. The ensuing siege was marked by a bitter struggle. The besieged leaders, failing in their negotiations to end hostilities, sorely pressed because of the paucity of their forces, and suffering together with the citizens from famine, decided at length to send envoys to Timurtash, who was at Mardin, to obtain his assistance. Intent on the occupation of Maiyafariqin, the bequest of his recently deceased brother, Sulaimān, who was the former ruler of that city, and preoccupied with negotiations with Aksungur al-Bursukī of Mosul for an anti-Frankish coalition, Timurtash ignored the envoys' pleas for assistance and continually temporized with them. At length, angered by their complaints and by the receipt of a letter from Aleppo which seemed to him to disguise the seriousness of the situation to the end of causing him to succor Aleppo with too small a rescuing force, he ordered them to be imprisoned. But they escaped and presently sought Aksungur's aid. He complied with the appeal, and having urged the rulers of Damascus and Homs to aid him, raised an army and advanced on Aleppo, arriving after nightfall on January 29, 1125. Dubais urged his Frankish allies to give him an army to prevent Aksungur from crossing the Euphrates until the Franks had captured Aleppo. This sensible advice went unheeded, and, as a result, Aksungur succeeded in raising the siege when the inhabitants were on the point of surrender. On his approach Baldwin and his several allies retired from Aleppo, deeming it wiser to retreat than to risk battle with the numerically superior enemy.[10] Aksungur pursued the retreating Franks as far as al-Athārib and cut off stragglers and plundered their baggage. The Franks, however, succeeded in withdrawing without great loss. Loath to risk a defeat at the hands of

[10] For a discussion of Aksungur al-Bursukī and Aleppo, see chapter XIV, p. 453.

the enemy by a determined pursuit, Aksungur retired to Aleppo. As the new ruler of that city, he retained the hostages surrendered by Baldwin at the time of his release. Meanwhile, the Frankish forces reached Antioch, where they separated. Baldwin returned to Jerusalem, reaching it on April 3, 1125, following an absence of nearly three years. Dubais contented himself with ravaging Mosul and Aksungur's other territories.

Pursuing his recent victory over the Franks, Aksungur, having formed an alliance with Tughtigin, advanced into Syria and besieged and captured the Frankish stronghold of Kafarṭāb. His next intended prize, Zardanā, succeeded in repelling his attacks. Then, together with Tughtigin, he advanced on Joscelin's fortress of ʿAzāz with a picked force and invested it fiercely. Capitulation seemed certain. Help was soon forthcoming, however, for Baldwin, having learned that Aksungur had returned to Aleppo, repaired at once to Antioch and assembled a large force with the active assistance of Joscelin, Pons, and Mahuis, the count of Duluk. The united force then proceeded by way of Cyrrhus to ʿAzāz. Learning of the Frankish advance, Aksungur returned to ʿAzāz and reëstablished the investment.

The ensuing battle of June 11, 1125, ended with a signal Frankish victory, despite initial setbacks. Baldwin shrewdly resorted to the strategy of withdrawal toward al-Athārib in order to cause the investing Moslem forces to abandon their siege and to pursue the retreating Franks into an ambush. Aksungur fell into the trap. The Franks halted their retreat, and, falling on their pursuers, annihilated them, harrying the survivors as far as the gates of Aleppo.

Baldwin, who now apparently sought a *modus vivendi* with the Saracens, paid his ransom to Aksungur and the latter, in turn, released Yvette and Joscelin [II]. A truce agreement providing for the division of the revenues of Jabal as-Summāq and other contested areas between the Franks and the Moslems was also made. Aksungur then departed for Aleppo and, having left his son there, repaired to Mosul to assemble a new army and renew the war.

This favorable turn in Frankish fortunes was further marked in the autumn of 1125 by new and successful assaults on the economic resources and military bastions of the Moslems. In October Baldwin constructed a castle on a mountain six miles distant from Beirut as a means of extracting tribute from the local Saracens. Then, following the expiration of his recent truce with

Tughtigin, Baldwin made a successful raid into the Damascus area. Thereafter, he turned his forces southward and advanced on the city of Ascalon, the garrison of which had recently been strengthened by the Egyptian Moslems. The king administered a sharp rebuff to the defenders.

Continuing his unceasing attacks on the foe, Baldwin prepared an expedition against Tughtigin and led his army out from Tiberias across the Jordan on January 13, 1126. The Franks at length joined battle in the Marj aṣ-Ṣuffar on January 25 with the troops of Tughtigin and his son, who had advanced out of Damascus on the preceding day after calling on their fellow emirs for assistance. The contest ended in a Moslem defeat. Tughtigin retired to Damascus and Baldwin then returned to Jerusalem, capturing two towers on his homeward journey.

The county of Tripoli and the county of Edessa also made their contributions to Frankish expansion in 1126. At the request of Pons, Baldwin hastened to Rafanīyah, a dependent town in the hills west of Homs, and aided him in its investment for eighteen days in March. Shams-al-Khawāṣṣ, its governor, sought the assistance of Aksungur, but the former's son, who was now entrusted with the active defense of the city, was of another mind and surrendered the stronghold to the Franks on March 31. The Franks then invaded and ravaged the territory of Homs in May. Aksungur immediately assembled a new army and advanced to Raqqa at the end of May and continued his march without pause to Naqīrah. Apparently desiring a buffer state for the more distant Frankish domains, Joscelin proposed a division of the territories included in the area between ʿAzāz and Aleppo, but the continuation of the existing state of war in all the other territories. Aksungur concurred and an agreement was drawn up on this basis.

Aksungur now sent his son ʿIzz-ad-Dīn Masʿūd to the rescue of Homs and the latter succeeded in dislodging the Franks. Upon his son's return from Homs, Aksungur left him in Aleppo and, after relieving Babek, the governor of Aleppo, of his duties, replaced him with the eunuch Kāfūr and then departed for al-Athārib on July 1. Babek, acting on Aksungur's orders, meanwhile repaired to Ḥiṣn ad-Dair with an army corps and miners and presently became master of it by capitulation. Babek's victorious forces then proceeded to ravage crops and pillage the peasantry and at length launched an attack on the Frankish stronghold of al-Athārib. Although two of the outer bastions fell to them, the Moslems were unable to capture the town.

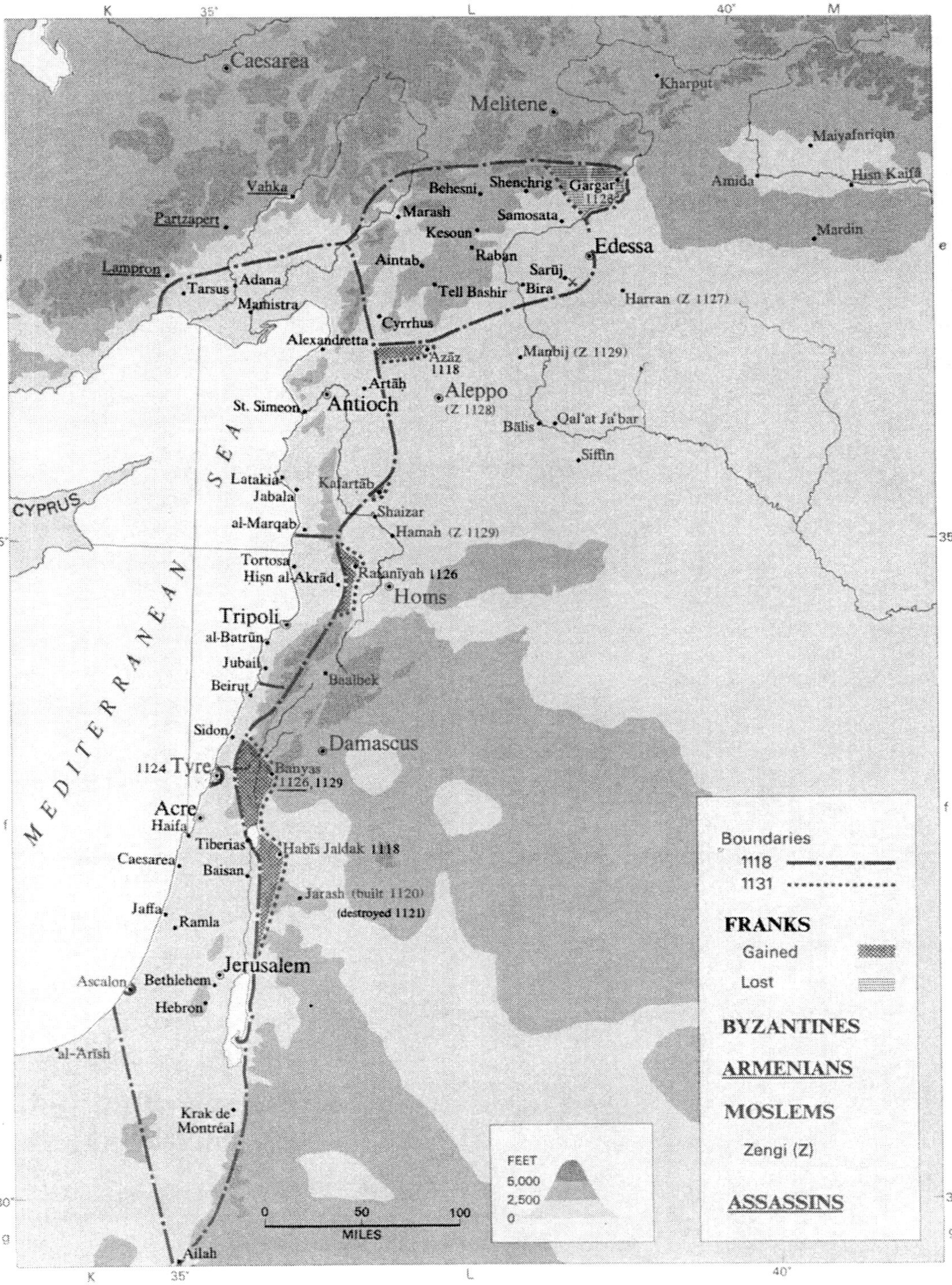

9. The Latin States during the Reign of Baldwin II, 1118–1131 (*Map by the University of Wisconsin Cartographic Laboratory*)

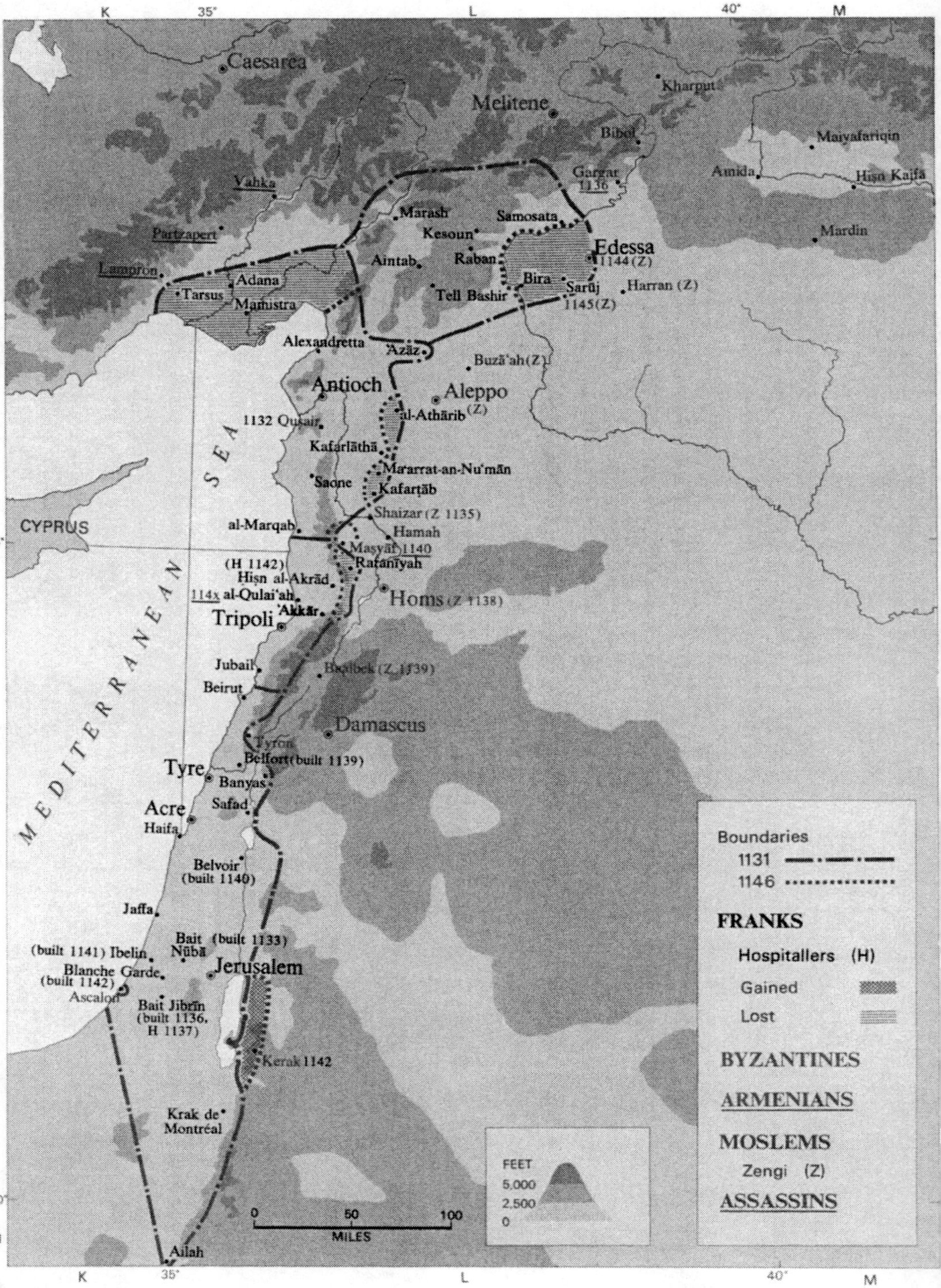

10. The Latin States during the Time of Zengi, 1131–1146 (*Map by the University of Wisconsin Cartographic Laboratory*)

Apprehensive of this threatening surge of Moslem power, Baldwin advanced from Jerusalem with his entire army, united his forces with those of Joscelin, and, having encamped before Artāḥ and ʿImm, a town thirty-three miles west of Aleppo, sent a messenger to Aksungur with an offer to surrender Rafanīyah if he would withdraw from the country. Recalling his defeat at ʿAzāz and fearing a similar disaster, Aksungur decided not to fight and concluded a truce, the terms of which were that the siege of al-Athārib should be raised and that its commander should depart with its troops and possessions. But the Franks broke their agreement, stating that they would abide by it only if the territories granted to Aksungur in the agreement of the preceding year were abandoned completely by the Moslems. He refused and remained for some time at Aleppo exchanging messages with the Franks without reaching an agreement. Then he departed early in August for Qinnasrīn and Sarmīn, while his army proceeded toward al-Fūʿah and Dānīth. Meanwhile, the Franks encamped near the reservoir of Maʿarrat-Miṣrīn until August 6. Then, being short of provisions, they returned to their own territories.

Resuming the attack, Aksungur, together with the atabeg Tughtigin, who had joined him at Qinnasrīn, proceeded to Aleppo. There Tughtigin became ill, and, after leaving instructions with Aksungur, had himself carried on a litter to Damascus. Aksungur now entrusted the government to his son ʿIzz-ad-Dīn Masʿūd and then returned to Mosul in November 1126. There, on Friday, November 26, he met death at the hands of assassins of the Bāṭinite sect.[11]

This signal good fortune for the Franks was soon followed by others, for ʿIzz-ad-Dīn Masʿūd soon fell to quarreling with Tughtigin and the anti-Frankish coöperation of Damascus and Aleppo ended. ʿIzz-ad-Dīn Masʿūd presently died of poison and the ensuing contest in Aleppo among the several claimants for the purple revived the chronic disunity among the Moslems. At length Badr-ad-Daulah Sulaimān ibn-al-Jabbār, the Artukid nephew of Īl-Ghāzī who had inherited Aleppo but had been ousted by Belek some years before, gained control of the city and proceeded to arrest the followers of his ejected rival Kutlug Abeh, whose excesses had led the Aleppans to recall the Artukid line. Informed of the hap-

[11] Ibn-al-Qalānisī, p. 177; Kamāl-ad-Dīn (*RHC, Or.*, III), p. 654; Matthew of Edessa, *Chronique* (*RHC, Arm.*, I), pp. 145–146; Ibn-al-Athīr (*RHC, Or.*, I), pp. 364–365, 378; William of Tyre, XIII, 20. Stevenson, *Crusaders*, p. 118, has rightly remarked that "once more Islam had lost its champion . . . . It is El Burski's [Aksungur al-Bursukī's] fame to have saved Aleppo from its greatest peril." On the Assassins, see above, chapter IV, p. 115.

penings in Aleppo, Joscelin advanced upon that city in October 1127, presumably in the hope of taking advantage of the anarchy and thereby becoming the master of Aleppo, but soon departed in return for a cash payment.

Meanwhile a serious quarrel had temporarily broken the unity of the Franks which had stood them in such good stead in their struggle against Aksungur. Bohemond II, the son of Bohemond I, sailed from Apulia, in September 1126, for the Holy Land and arrived at the port of St. Simeon in October or November. He had come in response to the invitation extended to him by the citizenry of Antioch during Baldwin's captivity as well as that offered later by Baldwin himself. Baldwin, who had been Antioch's regent ever since Roger's death in 1119, now, in accordance with the promise which Roger had made to Tancred on his deathbed that he would surrender the government of the principality to Bohemond or his heirs, turned over to him Antioch and all Cilicia. Having obtained recognition of his supremacy from Joscelin and Pons, Bohemond II then proceeded to Antioch with a body of troops and presently married Baldwin's second daughter, Alice, in the closing days of September 1127.[12]

Soon enmity developed between Joscelin and Bohemond and at length led to open hostilities. Joscelin summoned Turkish forces to his banner and with their aid ravaged the principality of Antioch during the summer of 1127 and compelled the Antiochenes to recognize his rule. Bohemond was absent at the time, engaged in war with the Turks in another theater. When rumors of this quarrel reached Baldwin, he was greatly disturbed. Realizing that this new division in the ranks of the Franks might afford the Moslems an excellent opportunity to harass them, and desiring peaceful relations between his cousin and his son-in-law, he speedily journeyed to Antioch to effect a reconciliation. Joscelin was ready to accept mediation. He was now so dangerously ill that he vowed he would become reconciled with Bohemond II, render him satisfaction, and pay him rightful homage, if his life should be spared and his health should be restored. The patriarch of Antioch now offered his good offices, and Baldwin soon ended the altercation between his vassals. Perhaps making doubly certain of

[12] Matthew of Edessa, p. 147; Bar Hebraeus, *Chronography* (tr. E. A. Wallis Budge), p. 253; Fulcher of Chartres (ed. Hagenmeyer), pp. 805–809, 819–822; William of Tyre, XII, 10; XIII, 21; Usāmah (tr. Potter), pp. 160–161; ed. and tr. Derenbourg, p. 136; Michael the Syrian, *Chronique* (ed. and tr. Chabot), p. 224. Stevenson, *Crusaders*, p. 119 and note 2, observes that "Baldwin laid aside with equal gladness the burden of administering the northern princedom." Cf. A. C. Krey, *William of Tyre*, II, 32, note 45.

Joscelin's sincerity, the patriarch ordered that all the churches be closed, church bells be silenced, and prayers be discontinued until Joscelin surrendered all his booty to Bohemond II. Joscelin swore fealty to his erstwhile foe and remained true to his pledge thereafter. The king then returned to Jerusalem.[13]

The tide of Moslem reaction, which Īl-Ghāzī, Belek, and Aksungur had led with only partial success because of the continued internecine quarrels prevailing among the various Moslem factions, now surged ahead under the able leadership of a new chieftain, Zengi. His rise to power began in April 1127 when the sultan conferred on him the function of commissioner in Iraq and the principalities of Mosul and Aleppo in recognition of his manifest military abilities.[14] Zengi's significance lay not only in the fact that he determined from the first to become the master of all Moslem Syria, but; more significantly, in his policy of deliberately refraining from serious attack on the Latin states and concentrating his assaults on his Moslem rivals. His program of the *status quo* in respect to the Franks was of course designed to give him a free hand in his endeavors to best his Moslem foes and did give a badly needed breathing spell to the Christians. But when his consolidation was completed, the respite proved to be illusory, for the effect of the consolidation was to create an effective dam to the spreading Frankish tide and to cause the loss of the county of Edessa.

Having quickly established his rule over Mosul in September 1127, Zengi soon obtained control of Nisibin, Sinjar, and Harran from his Moslem rivals. Shortly thereafter he dispatched an envoy to Joscelin with a request for a short truce. Joscelin agreed. The remainder of Moslem Syria and the important prize of Aleppo soon fell under Zengi's sway, for his troops occupied Aleppo in January 1128, and he himself seized Manbij and Buzā'ah in June 1129. The Sultan recognized his *de facto* control of Syria and whetted his ambitions for still further conquests when he con-

[13] Grousset, *Croisades*, I, 652, remarks rightly about "une opportune maladie de Joscelin ayant ramené celui-ci à la peur salutaire de l'enfer." LaMonte, *Feudal Monarchy*, p. 200, observes, in regard to Baldwin's arbitrament of this dispute and Baldwin I's settlement of the quarrel between Tancred and Baldwin of Le Bourg in 1109, that "it was in the court of the king that disputes between the great counts were occasionally settled, but here it was a case of the king arbitrating between his peers rather than a lord summoning his unruly vassal into his court. . . . There was no matter here of a legal right to try the suits and quarrels of vassals; it was merely that the king could sometimes get himself accepted as mediator." See also Runciman, *Crusades*, II, 180–181, for illuminating comments on the rivalry of Bohemond II and Joscelin, and cf. in general R. L. Nicholson, *Joscelyn I, Prince of Edessa*, Urbana, Ill., 1954.

[14] On the career of Zengi, see below, chapter XIV.

ferred on him, shortly after the death of Tughtigin, in February 1128 a royal diploma granting to him all Syria and adjacent countries. Flushed with his military and diplomatic triumphs, Zengi, having successfully summoned Tāj-al-Mulūk Böri, Tughtigin's son and the new ruler of Damascus, to a *jihād* against the Franks, treacherously betrayed his new ally and imprisoned his son Sevinj in Aleppo. Then, with the connivance of his fellow conspirator, Kîr-Khan, the ruler of Homs, he captured Hamah in September 1129 and conferred the rule of that city on Kîr-Khan. But Kîr-Khan soon suffered deposition from his new post at Zengi's hands. Not until the autumn of 1129 when Moslem Homs successfully resisted Zengi's investment did the expanding power of the new leader of the Moslem world receive a check.[15]

Meanwhile the Franks, unaware of the import of Zengi's maneuvers, were concentrating their attention upon Damascus. Baldwin and the other leaders sent Hugh of Payens, the first master of the Knights of the Temple, to Europe in 1128 to obtain help. Considerable success attended his efforts, for he returned to Palestine in 1129 with many companies of noblemen and Fulk, the count of Anjou.

Virtually simultaneous developments in Damascus itself perhaps quickened the tempo of the Frankish planning operations and hastened the attack. The vizir of Damascus, with the approval and connivance of a local sect of Assassins and their leader Ismā'īl, wrote the Franks and offered to surrender Damascus to them in exchange for Tyre. They agreed. However, the plot was discovered and the vizir, many of his henchmen, and the Assassins were executed on September 4, 1129. Ismā'īl, fearing that he, too, would fall victim to Damascus' reprisals, wrote to the Latins and offered to surrender Banyas to them in exchange for asylum. They concurred and the long-planned expedition began.[16]

The attacking forces advanced on Banyas, and, having received its surrender from Ismā'īl, proceeded to Damascus and encamped nearby at the end of November 1129. Battle was joined in the Marj aṣ-Ṣuffar, some miles southwest of Damascus, and the Mos-

[15] See Stevenson, *Crusaders*, p. 125, n. 9, for arguments against the dating given in Kamāl-ad-Dīn (*RHC, Or.*, III), pp. 656ff. (A. H. 524, practically 1130), and the date, 1130, for Zengi's alliance with Tāj-al-Mulūk Böri and the ensuing betrayals of Sevinj and Kîr-Khan. These observations may be equally well applied to the identical dating given by Sibṭ Ibn-al-Jauzī, pp. 568–569, abū-l-Mahāsin Yūsuf (*RHC, Or.*, III), pp. 499–500, and Ibn-al-Qalānisī, pp. 183–184, 290–292. See also Kugler, *Geschichte der Kreuzzüge*, p. 115, and Röhricht, *Königreich Jerusalem*, p. 188. See also below, chapter XIV, p. 456, for the traditional chronology.

[16] But on the plot to surrender Damascus see above, chapter IV, p. 117.

lems scored a great triumph over the Franks. This disaster was soon followed by another, for winter rains and fog now set in and made military operations impossible. Accordingly, the Franks abandoned their project and returned home on December 5 with their rearguard closely pressed by the enemy. Although failure had attended the expedition proper, yet the not unimportant town of Banyas was now a Frankish possession.

The favorable military trends for the Moslems in the closing weeks of 1129 were soon complemented by political ones as well, for the fortunes of the principality of Antioch were imperilled by the death of its valiant ruler, Bohemond II, at the hands of Dānishmendid troops in February 1130 during the course of a campaign in Cilicia, and by the machinations of his widow Alice, daughter of Baldwin. Bereft of their young leader, the Antiochenes held a council and then called on Baldwin for assistance. The king, fearful for the safety of Antioch in this crisis, complied. Meanwhile, Alice was scheming, despite the solid opposition of her chief men and the entire population, to obtain the rule of Antioch for herself and to disinherit her daughter, Constance, the legal heir. In order to effect her plan, she called upon Zengi for assistance. Unluckily for her, the messenger was captured by the Franks, and, upon being interrogated by Baldwin, confessed the plot. Baldwin hastened to Antioch, but Alice forbade him entrance to the city. However, a number of lay and clerical leaders disobeyed her commands and by a prearranged plan permitted Fulk and Joscelin to enter. Thereupon Baldwin entered Antioch and at length secured Alice's reluctant capitulation. He decreed that she be forcibly expelled from Antioch and that the rule of Antioch and its dependencies be entrusted to Joscelin and the principal men of the city, who should administer them for Constance until her marriage. Her husband would then become lord of Antioch. Then, tempering his wrath, he granted to Alice the coast cities of Latakia and Jabala, which her late husband had deeded as a dowry to her at the time of her marriage. The king then returned to Jerusalem.

Encouraged by the manifest disaffection in the ranks of the Latins, Zengi invaded the principality of Antioch in the spring of 1130 and laid siege to al-Athārib. When the Franks, including Baldwin, advanced to the relief of the beleaguered city, Zengi's officers advised him to retreat, but he scorned their advice. A battle followed, and the Moslems were victorious. Zengi then advanced on the fortress of Ḥārim on the outskirts of Antioch but was persuaded by the inhabitants to abandon his siege in return for half of the revenues of the district. A truce was concluded, and he returned to his own territories. The ending of Zengi's campaign of 1130 marked the beginning of a considerable respite from major warfare with him for the Franks, for his energies were consumed in war with a league of rivals in the latter part of 1130, in struggles with the revived caliphate in the period 1131–1133, and in a war with the Kurds in 1134.

Fortunate it was for the Franks that the early 1130's marked a lull in the Moslem offensive, for 1131 marked the passing of those veritable shields and bucklers of the crusading states, Baldwin and Joscelin. Baldwin died on August 21 in Jerusalem after committing the rule of the kingdom to his eldest daughter Melisend, his son-in-law Fulk, and his two-year-old grandson Baldwin.[17] Fulk, who became the fourth ruler of the kingdom on the following September 14, had come out to the Holy Land in the spring of 1129 in response to an invitation from Baldwin to marry Melisend. A mature man of thirty-eight with a background and training befitting him for his new duties, he had had much experience as a military and political chieftain in France in his role of count of Touraine, Maine, and Anjou, as Baldwin's lieutenant from 1129 to 1131, and as the ruler of the cities of Tyre and Acre which he received at the time of his marriage to Melisend.

Less lucky was the county of Edessa. Joscelin continued his vigorous yet politic rule in the north during 1130 and 1131, invading the northern Aleppan country and battling successfully with Sevar, Zengi's representative in Aleppo, and suffering, in retaliation, Sevar's attacks on al-Athārib's suburbs. Perhaps seeking the sultan's support against Zengi, Joscelin refused asylum to his erstwhile ally, Dubais, when that worthy fell afoul of the sultan's displeasure. But injuries incurred in 1130 during the course of a siege of a Moslem castle at length had their cumulative effect and he died shortly after Baldwin. Joscelin II, markedly inferior to his illustrious sire, suceeded to the rule of the county of Edessa.[18]

[17] For the grudging praise of an unfriendly but fair-minded contemporary, see Ibn-al-Qalānisī, pp. 207–208, and note 1, p. 208: "On many occasions he [Baldwin] fell into the hands of the Muslims as a prisoner, in times both of war and of peace, but he always escaped from them through stratagems. After him there was none left amongst them possessed of sound judgment and capacity to govern." This is balanced by the reluctant admission of Ibn-al-Athīr concerning the Frankish dominance in the later 1120's, for which Baldwin was assuredly responsible to a large degree. His last years were complicated by a dispute with the patriarch, Stephen of La Ferté (1128–1130), over ecclesiastical privileges; this dispute was resolved in favor of the monarchy by Stephen's death and the elevation of the more pliable William of Messines (1130–1147).

[18] Although William of Tyre, XIV, 3, declares that Joscelin II was distinguished for military prowess, he is obliged to admit that his lack of energy was responsible for the loss of the entire county of Edessa.

This was a disaster, indeed, for a state facing the steadily waxing ambition of Zengi.

Fresh troubles in Antioch occupied much of Fulk's attention during the first years of his rule. Alice revived her claim to Antioch and enlisted as her supporters Pons and Joscelin II. But other nobles, resentful of Alice's aspirations, appealed to Fulk. Much perturbed, the king hastened north by land as far as Beirut, but was obliged to continue his journey by sea because of Pons' refusal to allow him to pass through the county of Tripoli. At length he reached St. Simeon and was met by influential leaders of Antioch who now gave him the command of the principality and city of Antioch. Pons, however, refused to capitulate and strengthened his fortresses, Chastel-Rouge and Arzghān. Fulk thereupon raised an army and, meeting Pons in a bitterly contested battle at Chastel-Rouge in the summer of 1132, gained the victory and put him and his followers to flight. King and count were at length reconciled, but Fulk, aware of the general fear that sedition might appear once more, agreed to tarry in Antioch and assumed the role of *bailli*. He busied himself with affairs of state, with the advice and consent of the chief nobles, and then placed Reginald Masoier in charge of the principality as constable.

The new *entente* between the kingdom of Jerusalem and the county of Tripoli was soon tested, for the long dormant Damascus and Tripolitan frontiers awoke to activity in the closing weeks of 1132. Shams-al-Mulūk Ismā'īl, the son and successor of Tāj-al-Mulūk Böri in the rule of Damascus, upon learning that the Franks of Beirut had seized the goods of various Damascene merchants in violation of their treaty with Damascus, tried vainly to obtain satisfaction for them. Then, seeking revenge, he secretly made military preparations, and, leading out his troops against Banyas, captured the town on December 21 before Fulk was able to succor it.[19]

Although the fall of Banyas spread much fear among the Franks, still more alarming news came from Tripoli at the same time to the effect that a Turkoman force had invaded Tripoli and had defeated Pons in battle. Pons and his companions retired to Ba'rīn which

[19] Stevenson, *Crusaders*, p. 131, and Röhricht, *Königreich Jerusalem*, p. 200, believe that a quarrel between Fulk and one of his vassals, Hugh of Jaffa, which resulted in a ruling in 1132 that the latter should go into exile permitted Shams-al-Mulūk to recover Banyas. A full account is provided by William of Tyre, XIV, 18. See also Grousset, *Croisades*, II, 20, 26–29. LaMonte, *Feudal Monarchy*, p. 13, and Cahen, *La Syrie du nord*, p. 351, note 12, also date the quarrel in 1132. A. C. Krey, *William of Tyre*, II, 71, note 2, dissents with the dating of 1132 on the ground that Hugh's name appeared on a grant by Alice of Antioch as late as 1134.

the Turkomans promptly invested. Then, fleeing to Tripoli, he summoned help from the other Frankish chiefs; a gratifying response followed. Perhaps his most valuable ally was Fulk, who at the moment was marching north to assist Antioch against new Moslem incursions. Learning at Sidon of Pons' plight from his wife Cecilia, he abandoned his northern campaign and went to his vassal's rescue. When Pons believed that he was strong enough to take the field, he advanced upon Baʿrīn again and raised the siege. The ensuing battle was indecisive, for the Franks retired to Rafanīyah in good order after considerable battle losses, and the Turkomans likewise withdrew.[20]

Fulk now resumed his advance, reached Antioch, and presently captured the nearby fortress of Quṣair from the Moslems. Informed that Moslem troops commanded by Sevar had concentrated at Qinnasrīn and were planning to use it as a base of operations, he led out his forces from Antioch and encamped near the fortress of Ḥārim. After waiting vainly several days for the enemy to move, Fulk suddenly attacked and soundly whipped the surprised Saracens. Then, having imposed a truce upon them (January 1133), he returned to Antioch with much booty.[21]

Fulk's favor with both the masses and classes of Antioch was now greater than ever before. Shortly before his return to Jerusalem, the Antiochene nobility, seeking a more stable government for their principality, requested him to obtain a husband for Constance, who was still a minor. With their approval he selected Raymond, son of the count of Poitou, and a mission was accordingly sent to him, with the greatest possible secrecy.

Although the victory of Qinnasrīn relieved pressure on the

[20] William of Tyre's statement (XIV, 6) that Zengi was the leader of this Turkoman force is erroneous, as Zengi was fully occupied at this time with his quarrels with the caliphate. See also Cahen, *La Syrie du nord*, p. 352, note 18, and below, chapter XIV, pp. 456–457.

[21] There is considerable disagreement concerning the date of the battle of Qinnasrīn; Kamāl-ad-Dīn (*RHC, Or.*, III), p. 665, places it in January 1134; Michael the Syrian (ed. Chabot), pp. 233–234, dates it the closing days of 1134 or the beginning of 1135, while Bar Hebraeus, *Chronography*, p. 257, refers in a rather unclear passage to a defeat administered by Baldwin (should not Fulk be read ?) to the Turks and dates this engagement in 1134. See also William of Tyre, XIV, 7; Ibn-al-Qalānisī, pp. 222–223; Ibn-al-Athīr (*RHC, Or.*, I), p. 792. Similar disagreement prevails among modern writers, Stevenson, *Crusaders*, p. 132, dating the battle in January 1133, whereas Röhricht, *Königreich Jerusalem*, p. 197, fixes it in December 1132. A. C. Krey, *William of Tyre*, II, 57, note 19, and Grousset, *Croisades*, II, 17, note 2, differ in their interpretation of Ibn-al-Qalānisī's dating of the battle, the former believing that he dates it in January 1134, the latter arguing that he places it in the period between December 11, 1132, and January 10, 1133. In favor of Grousset's view is the fact that Ibn-al-Qalānisī includes the account of the battle under the heading of the Moslem year, A. H. 527 (November 12, 1132, to October 31, 1133). Secondly, the acceptance of Krey's dating requires the lapse of more than a year between Fulk's assistance in raising the siege of Baʿrīn and his appearance in the Antiochene area, which he originally planned to succor at the time of the receipt of news of Pons' plight in December 1132. This seems quite improbable.

Aleppan front, the Damascus front once more became very menacing for the Franks. Encouraged by his capture of Banyas and learning that the caliph of Baghdad was planning to besiege Zengi in Mosul, Shams-al-Mulūk Ismā'īl now turned his attention to his Moslem rivals and obtained Hamah by surrender from Zengi's commander on August 6, 1133. Presently he obliged Moslem Shaizar to become tributary to him. Then, having returned to Damascus in September 1133, he advanced on Tyron (Shaqīf Tīrūn), a Moslem stronghold near Sidon, and captured it in November from its commander Ḍaḥḥāk, who had pursued anti-Moslem as well as anti-Frankish tactics. Disturbed by Shams-al-Mulūk Ismā'īl's waxing power, the Franks invaded the Hauran in 1134, whereupon Shams-al-Mulūk Ismā'īl, having ascertained the enemy's superior power, invaded the country around Acre, Tiberias, and Tyre in a counter-stroke designed to make them withdraw. Success rewarded his efforts, and the Franks retired from the Hauran in October 1134 after securing a temporary peace from him in September. But before he could effect his program in Moslem as well as in Latin Syria, he was murdered on January 30, 1135. He was succeeded by his brother, Shihāb-ad-Dīn Maḥmūd, in the rule of Damascus.

Meanwhile, Zengi, at long last free from major involvements with his Moslem enemies, now returned to his goal of the mastery of Moslem and Frankish Syria.[22] Quickly taking advantage of the political embarrassments of Damascus resulting from the assassination of its ruler, he advanced upon that city and began its investment in the late winter of 1135. But the Damascenes, commanded by their *mamlūk* Mu'īn-ad-Dīn Unur (or Önör), so stoutly resisted him and so coldly rebuffed his demand for their surrender that he made peace with the mamluk and withdrew on March 16. Although Zengi's dream of mastery over Damascus had not been realized, his other program of gaining the mastery of the Frankish and Moslem fortresses which still threatened Aleppo went ahead unchecked. Inflicting major defeats on the principality of Antioch, he easily captured al-Athārib in the course of a whirlwind campaign on April 17, 1135, and Zardanā, Tall Aghdī, Ma'arrat-an-Nu'mān, Ma'arrat-Miṣrīn, and Kafarṭāb shortly thereafter. The Moslem stronghold of Shaizar presently capitulated to him, and then, after a brief feint against the Frankish citadel of Ba'rīn, he advanced on unwary Moslem Homs and devastated its environs. Hearing that Frankish forces under the command of Pons were

[22] For Zengi's movements see below, chapter XIV.

now engaged in Qinnasrīn, Zengi advanced upon that city and by skillful maneuvering forced them to withdraw. Thereupon he returned to Homs, and after unsuccessful attacks upon it in the opening days of August, repaired immediately thereafter to Mosul and thence to Baghdad.

Zengi was absent from the Syrian scene during the next year, his energies being consumed in squabbles between the caliph and the sultan, with a consequent personal postponement of his long-run program. But the program itself did not suffer, for his able lieutenant Sevar continued to defend his master's interests. He assailed Homs so vigorously in the autumn of 1135 that the sons of its ruler, Kīr-Khan, recognizing their own weakness and Sevar's might, surrendered Homs to Shihāb-ad-Dīn Maḥmūd. Thereupon, Sevar, nothing daunted, invaded the Damascus country and obtained a peace treaty from Shihāb-ad-Dīn Maḥmūd. The troublesome Damascus front was at long last pacified. Even more important triumphs soon followed, for Sevar, thoroughly cognizant of Frankish weaknesses, invaded the principality of Antioch in April 1136, and, after pillaging a hundred villages, reached the coast and, surprising the unwary defenders of Latakia, devastated the city and obtained many prisoners and much booty. So badly shaken was the Frankish power that no reprisal could be made. In the words of a Moslem contemporary, "Such a calamity as this has never befallen the northern Franks."

Why had Moslem arms under Zengi and Sevar gained such signal triumphs, comparable only to the Saracen victory at Harran in 1104, and why had their Frankish enemies failed to capitalize on the victory of Qinnasrīn? The answer may be found in the dissensions rampant in the ruling circles of Antioch, in the failure of Antioch's two major neighbors to do much more than mark time and remain on the defensive during the rise of Zengi, and in the flaccid policies pursued by Fulk in respect to the north Syrian areas. Despite the exile imposed upon her by her father, Alice returned to Antioch in 1135 and, ignoring her daughter Constance, assumed the active rule of the principality with the approval of her sister Melisend, Fulk's wife, who persuaded her spouse not to interfere. No longer inhibited by the restraining influence of her kinsfolk, Alice sought the support of the Byzantine emperor John by offering Constance's hand to his son Manuel. John assented. Then, to make matters worse, Ralph, the crafty patriarch of Antioch, in order to obtain Alice's support against his clerical enemies, convinced her that the mission which had recently requested Raymond of Poitiers to repair to Antioch desired to have him marry her. Great was her wrath when Raymond married Constance, in accordance with his oath of fealty to Ralph and an agreement made with him upon his arrival in the latter half of 1136. Alice, sadly disillusioned, withdrew from Antioch and opposed Raymond with relentless fury. Ralph, believing that his position was now secure, behaved presumptuously and arrogantly toward Raymond, who now retaliated by aligning himself with Ralph's foes.[23] The political and religious schisms wracking Antioch made it an easy prey for Sevar.

Almost equally conducive to Sevar's strategy of the offensive was the time-serving, defensive policy pursued by the county of Edessa and the kingdom of Jerusalem. Neither state sought to capitalize on the victory over Sevar which they had scored at Qinnasrīn. Sevar attacked Zardanā and Ḥārim in 1134 and boldly invaded the districts of Ma'arrat-an-Nu'mān and Ma'arrat-Miṣrīn and then returned to Aleppo laden with booty. There was no organized reprisal on the part of Edessa. The kingdom of Jerusalem, under Fulk's leadership, pursued its new southern policy of guarding its immediate interests and, following the unsuccessful Damascus campaign of 1134, contented itself with the construction in 1136 of a fortress at Bait Jibrīn on the southern frontier as a means of checking the constant forays of the nearby garrison of Ascalon. This was a development of the policy inaugurated in 1133 of building Chastel-Arnoul near Bait Nūbā to guard the Jaffa-Jerusalem road for the pilgrims against recurrent attacks from Ascalon.[24]

The full storm of the Moslem *revanche* broke in the opening months of 1137. Doubtless spurred on by Sevar's triumphant march to the sea, Beza-Uch, the commander of the Damascus forces, invaded the county of Tripoli in March 1137 and routed the forces of the Tripolitan Franks in a bitterly fought battle. Pons, presently betrayed by the Syrians living on Mount Lebanon, fell into enemy hands, and was put to death on March 25. Then, after capturing the castle of Ibn-al-Aḥmar and a rich booty,

[23] Röhricht, *Königreich Jerusalem*, p. 203, sees in Raymond's oath of allegiance to Ralph a factor aggravating the differences between the two men. See also Stevenson, *Crusaders*, p. 138. Kugler, *Geschichte der Kreuzzüge*, p. 119, dates these events in the beginning of 1136. Ralph (Radulf) of Domfront succeeded Bernard of Valence in 1135 and was himself succeeded in 1139 by Aimery of Limoges, who was patriarch until his death, probably in 1196.

[24] Stevenson, *Crusaders*, pp. 135–136, believes that Fulk's abstention from Antiochene affairs was also the result of his acceptance of the position of those who believed the king should concentrate his efforts in the kingdom of Jerusalem itself. This mistaken northern policy of "separatism" replaced the united-front policy of Baldwin I with fatal results for Antioch and Edessa.

Beza-Uch returned to Damascus. Meanwhile, Raymond II, Pons' son and heir to the county, having rallied his forces, struck savagely in retaliation at the Syrians on Mount Lebanon, capturing, torturing, and executing many of their leaders.

Thereupon, Zengi, having obtained an armistice from and having established a friendly agreement with Shihāb-ad-Dīn Maḥmūd, once more repaired to Syria, arriving in June 1137. He at once dispatched his chief negotiator, Ṣalāḥ-ad-Dīn, to the Damascene fortress of Homs with instructions to obtain its surrender by negotiation from its commander, Mu'īn-ad-Dīn Unur. When negotiations failed, Zengi himself began the investment of the city. Failing after several weeks of fruitless alternate military action and threats to achieve his aim and learning that the defenders were about to be aided by the Franks — this latter consideration indicates that the Latins were at long last understanding balance-of-power politics — he departed on July 11 and began the siege of the nearby Frankish stronghold of Ba'rīn in the county of Tripoli. Raymond II besought and obtained Fulk's support. But when Fulk arrived in Tripoli, he learned the disheartening news that the principality of Antioch was now being invaded by the emperor John Comnenus and that the Antiochenes were seeking his aid. Fulk immediately held a council; the decision was that Ba'rīn should be helped first and then Antioch. Accordingly, the Franks advanced upon Zengi, whereupon the latter abandoned the siege of Ba'rīn, fell upon the Franks, and decimated their infantry. Raymond II and some of his knights were captured. Fulk recognized the futility of further resistance and retired into the fortress with the loss of all the baggage intended for the succoring of Ba'rīn. The Moslems again resumed the siege of Ba'rīn, whereupon the imprisoned Franks appealed to Antioch, Jerusalem, and Edessa for aid. A *levée en masse* followed. Jerusalem, Antioch, and Edessa answered the appeal. Grave indeed as was the plight of the kingdom of Jerusalem, it now became still more serious, for Beza-Uch took advantage of its defenseless state and attacked and plundered the unfortified city of Nablus with impunity. Meanwhile Zengi pressed his attack unremittingly. But, learning of the approach of the armies of Edessa and Jerusalem and fearing the loss of his prize, he offered peace terms providing for the surrender of Ba'rīn and a safe-conduct for the besieged. The Franks, unaware of the approach of the relief forces, accepted the offer and marched out safely only to meet the Frankish columns which presently arrived, too late.

Meanwhile, the sadly harried principality of Antioch had to meet new menaces from the north. Emperor John, continuing the policies of his father Alexius, had laid claim to Antioch with all the adjacent provinces. The immediate cause of the revival of these claims was the receipt of the news that the Antiochenes had betrothed Constance to Raymond of Poitiers instead of John's son Manuel. Another motive for this action was his desire to recover the Cilician towns taken by Leon the Ṛoupenid. John, therefore, assembled an army and conquered Leon's states. At length he reached Antioch and began investing it on August 29. Apprised of the developments at Antioch, Raymond of Poitiers hastened home from Ba'rīn and took personal charge of the defense. John pressed his attack so fiercely that at length Raymond sought peace and sent emissaries to the emperor. An agreement was drawn up with Fulk's approval in September 1137 providing that Raymond would become John's vassal with Antioch as his fief, and would surrender Antioch to him if John should recover Aleppo, Shaizar, Hamah, and Homs, and would grant them as fiefs to Raymond. Raymond, together with Raymond II of Tripoli and Joscelin, tendered their oaths of fealty to the emperor, and the latter, having promised to campaign against the Moslems in 1138 to recover the designated towns, returned to Cilicia to spend the winter.

The markedly anti-Moslem hue of the newly established Graeco-Antiochene *entente* became clearly visible in the latter part of February 1138 when Raymond of Antioch arrested several Moslem merchants and Aleppan travelers in Antioch.[25] Then, in alliance with John, the Antiochene Franks began military operations on March 31 and advanced due east on Buzā'ah, capturing it on April 9. Allied expeditions were now dispatched from Buzā'ah in all directions and scoured even the trans-Euphratean countryside in early April. Zengi, apprised at Homs, which he was then besieging, of the recent events, sent reinforcements under Sevar's command to Aleppo, whereupon the allies advanced west on Aleppo and reached it on April 14, five days after Sevar's reinforcements arrived. The brief siege ended on April 20 with the allies withdrawing to the west and south. Several easy triumphs were now gained by the allies with the capture of al-Athārib following its abandonment by its garrison on April 21 and the capture of Kafarṭāb following a short struggle. Believing that the indepen-

[25] Grousset, *Croisades*, II, 100, and F. Chalandon, *Jean II Comnène et Manuel I Comnène*, pp. 134–135. See also, below, chapter XIV for Zengi's movements.

dent emir of Shaizar would be less resolute in its defense than Zengi himself, the allies advanced on Shaizar and reached it on April 28.

The ensuing siege of twenty-four days was futile because of the formidable character of the defense, the slothfulness and lackadaisical attitudes of Joscelin II and Raymond of Antioch, and the menacing activities of Zengi. Disgusted with his vassals' noncoöperation, disturbed by Zengi's preparations to march on Shaizar in force with large contingents and by his divisive propaganda in the ranks of the besiegers, and fearful, in the face of a Moslem invasion of Cilicia, for the safety of that important Byzantine province, the emperor recognized the uselessness of further effort. Accordingly, he accepted a bribe from the emir of Shaizar and some of its citizens and announced his intention of withdrawal to Antioch. Unaware of John's plans, Raymond and Joscelin belatedly protested his decision but to no avail. The allies withdrew from Shaizar on May 21.

Upon his arrival in Antioch the emperor demanded the cession of the citadel of Antioch, free access to the city proper, and the use of its military equipment on the part of his troops, alleging that these grants were essential for the conquest of Aleppo. The Franks feared that the acceptance of these demands would involve the loss of Antioch to the Greeks and accordingly requested a delay, ostensibly to consider the matter with the nobles. John assented. Thereupon Joscelin sent *agents provocateurs* into the streets to inform the populace of the emperor's demands and to rouse them to arms. Presently Antioch was convulsed by angry crowds. Joscelin then rushed into the emperor's presence, stating that he had been pursued by a mob of angry citizens seeking his life as a base traitor. The ruse succeeded. When the fury of the populace mounted and members of the emperor's own retinue fell victim to their wrath, John, apprehensive for his own safety, withdrew his demands and agreed to withdraw from Antioch. The leaders silenced the mobs, and the Greeks left the city on the following day. Shortly thereafter, envoys dispatched from Antioch appeased the emperor with honeyed words designed to establish Raymond's innocence and the mob's responsibility for the recent disturbances. Although he was not deceived by these maneuvers, John did not want to break with the Franks, and, in consequence, accepted the explanation. He then returned to Cilicia and eventually to Constantinople.[26]

[26] William of Tyre, XV, 5. Krey, *William of Tyre*, II, 101, note 5, disagrees with Chalandon, *Jean II Comnène et Manuel I Comnène*, pp. 149–150, in his acceptance of the reason

Meanwhile, Zengi, despite the blight placed upon his hopes of becoming the master of Frankish Syria, prudently continued to pursue his first goal, dominion over Moslem Syria, the *sine qua non* for the ousting of the Franks.[27] He contented himself with the recovery of Kafarṭāb, which the Graeco-Frankish allies abandoned on May 21 during their retreat from Shaizar, and harassed the retiring Greeks with cavalry forces upon their refusal to cede Apamea to him. Seeking the more immediately important Moslem prizes, he returned once more to Homs and demanded its surrender from Shihāb-ad-Dīn Maḥmūd. An exchange of correspondence followed, and soon Shihāb-ad-Dīn Maḥmūd agreed and received Ba'rīn, Lakmah, and al-Ḥiṣn ash-Sharqī in exchange. The political arrangements were now cemented by marriage alliances between the families of the erstwhile rivals in June. Zengi, recognizing her influence at Damascus and hoping thereby to become its master, espoused Shihāb-ad-Dīn Maḥmūd's mother and betrothed his daughter to Shihāb-ad-Dīn Maḥmūd.

With the consolidation of his Moslem rear now secured, Zengi once more turned his attention to the Franks. He captured and destroyed 'Arqah in the summer of 1138, seized Buzā'ah on September 27, and mastered al-Athārib on October 10. Despite the economic and population losses attendant upon the severe earthquakes which visited Aleppo and al-Athārib and their environs from October 20 until the following summer, despite the questionable success of his lieutenant Sevar against the Franks in the first half of 1139, and despite his own renewed time- and resource-consuming conflict with his Artukid rivals, the year which followed Zengi's 'Arqah-Buzā'ah-al-Athārib campaign may nevertheless be regarded as one of continued ascendancy on Zengi's part, for Frankish power had been sapped by the loss of the Cilician towns to the Greeks, and Latin initiative had been dulled by the realization of the difficulties attendant upon the capture of Aleppo.

An even greater opportunity for aggrandizement seemingly presented itself to Zengi in the assassination of Shihāb-ad-Dīn Maḥmūd on June 22, 1139. Mu'īn-ad-Dīn Unur now took command of the situation and invited the slain man's brother, Jamāl-

advanced by William of Tyre for John's departure from Antioch and observes, "there were deeper reasons than this ruse of Joscelin for the resentment of the Latin populace against the Greeks. The overlordship of Antioch by John carried with it, expressed or implied, the reëstablishment of a Greek patriarch. Innocent II, alarmed by John's conduct in Cilicia, issued a bull forbidding Latin Christians to serve in the army of the Greeks."

[27] Cf. below, chapter XIV, p. 459.

ad-Dīn Muḥammad, the ruler of Baalbek, to assume the rule of the city. The latter accepted the invitation. Meanwhile, Mu'īn-ad-Dīn Unur expelled another brother and claimant, Bahrām-Shāh, who thereupon repaired to Aleppo to enlist Zengi's aid. He was assisted in his quest by his mother, Zengi's wife, who urged her spouse to avenge her dead son. Determined to find in this incident an occasion whereby he could dominate the country, Zengi quickly responded by marching on Damascus. Finding the Damascenes on guard and determined to repel him, he changed his plans and began an investment of Baalbek, which Mu'īn-ad-Dīn Unur had recently received as a fief from Jamāl-ad-Dīn Muḥammad on August 20. The *entente* of the preceding summer was no more and Zengi's ambitions were apparent to all.

Undaunted by this crisis, Mu'īn-ad-Dīn Unur resumed the negotiations with the Franks for an alliance which he had unsuccessfully carried on in 1133 and 1138. Appealing for their assistance against a common foe, he dispatched envoys to Fulk with a promise of the cession of Banyas as soon as Zengi had been driven from Damascus. Recognizing the cogency of Mu'īn-ad-Dīn Unur's arguments and attracted by his promise of Banyas, which was now controlled by an emir friendly to Zengi, the Frankish leaders agreed to his proposal.

Meanwhile, Zengi's military progress continued for a time unabated with the capture of Baalbek in October and with the routing of Mu'īn-ad-Dīn Unur's contingents on the outskirts of Damascus in December. Yet final victory eluded his grasp. Jamāl-ad-Dīn Muḥammad at first entertained favorably his offer of Baalbek and Homs in exchange for Damascus, but changed his mind when his advisers pointed out Zengi's untrustworthiness. Even Jamāl-ad-Dīn Muḥammad's death on March 29, 1140, with all its potentialities for governmental paralysis in Damascus, proved to be only a temporary gain for him, for Mu'īn-ad-Dīn Unur and other Damascene leaders kept tight control of affairs and appointed the dead man's son Mujīr-ad-Dīn Abak to fill the vacant post. Hoping to capitalize on the supposed discords between the Damascene leaders, Zengi now attacked Damascus, but was met by stubborn and united resistance. Even the Franks eluded him. Learning of the recently contracted Franco-Damascene alliance and seeking to battle the Franks before they united with the Damascenes, he abandoned his siege of Damascus on May 4 and advanced into the Hauran to attack the Franks. When they failed to appear he returned to the Damascus country on

May 25 and laid waste the countryside. Apprised of the Frankish advance on Tiberias to join the Damascene forces and loath to meet two hostile armies, Zengi retired to the north to Baalbek and remained there during the Franco-Damascene siege of Banyas.[28]

Meanwhile, the Franks and Damascenes, having united their forces, proceeded to invest Banyas closely in May. The besieged, despairing of Zengi's aid and unable to stem the allies' determined assault, at length accepted the offer of surrender tendered by Mu'īn-ad-Dīn Unur and the Franks and capitulated on June 12, 1140. Mu'īn-ad-Dīn Unur received the captured city and turned it over to the Franks. After choosing Adam, the archdeacon of Acre, and Rainier of Brus as the new bishop and ruler respectively of Banyas, the Franks repaired to Jerusalem.

The formidable Franco-Damascene alliance had done its work well. It had saved Damascus from possible capture, had effected the reduction of an important stronghold of Zengi's, had sharply checked the growing unification of the Moslems under Zengi's leadership, and now served, together with Zengi's fear of a new Byzantine invasion, to expel him from the Syrian area. After one more plundering operation in the Hauran and a sally against Damascus on June 22, 1140, he retired from Syria and spent the next few years in war against his several Moslem rivals.

The withdrawal of Zengi from Syria, the pacific and pro-Frankish policies pursued by Mu'īn-ad-Dīn Unur of Damascus, the continuance of the isolationist, southern policy of Fulk, the quiescence of the Ascalon Moslems, and the arrival in the seat of political power of a new generation content to rest on the laurels gained for it by the hard-fighting leaders of the First Crusade and their immediate successors in the Holy Land and to seek a *modus vivendi* with its Moslem neighbors gave to the history of the Frankish crusading states from 1140 to 1144 a character quite different from that of the preceding two decades, permitting the historian to narrate their fortunes largely independently of each other. With the passing of the offense, preserving the *status quo* became more and more the rule.

Perhaps the best example of the new viewpoint is to be found in the kingdom of Jerusalem. With its northern and eastern frontiers at long last quiet, with little likelihood of Byzantine intervention following Raymond's successful defiance of John's claims

[28] Kugler, *Geschichte der Kreuzzüge*, p. 121, observes that as long as Fulk, Raymond of Antioch, and Mu'īn-ad-Dīn Unur lived, Zengi was effectively checkmated and only Fulk's death broke the solidarity of the strong anti-Zengi triumvirate.

on Antioch in the autumn of 1142, and with his own successful avoidance of John's expressed desire to proceed to Jerusalem to visit the holy places and be permitted to lend aid against the Moslems, Fulk turned his attention to the potentially troublesome southern frontier, and resuming his policies of the middle 1130's, built a number of castles, including that of Blanche Garde eight miles from Ascalon.[29] Fulk died on November 10, 1143, and was succeeded by his son Baldwin III, a boy of thirteen years. Because of his youth his mother, Melisend, assumed the royal power as regent. The early years of her regency were marked by mature wisdom, skillful rule, and a conscious following of Fulk's policies, in which she was aided by the capable patriarch William of Messines (1130–1147). She was, however, unable to impose the royal authority on Raymond and Joscelin, so disunity in the north was to be in sharp contrast to tranquillity in the south.

The county of Tripoli received an important accretion of strength with the arrival of the Knights Hospitaller. Raymond II bade them welcome and, having granted them the important stronghold of Ḥiṣn al-Akrād, as well as Rafanīyah if they could recapture it, stated that any peace he might make with the Saracens would be subject to the approval of the Hospitallers. Fulk, too, had welcomed them and had allotted them Bait Jibrīn as a stronghold protecting the pilgrim road from Jaffa to Jerusalem.

Not nearly as peaceful and uneventful was the experience of the principality of Antioch. Although Zengi's withdrawal from Syria terminated major clashes between Franks and Moslems, still petty warfare continued. Turkoman invasions of the principality were avenged by Latin incursions into the Aleppan country in 1140. Frankish pillaging of Sarmīn and Kafarṭāb in 1141 provoked retaliations about January 1142 by Sevar and Lajah, a Damascene emir who had taken service with Sevar. Sevar continued the offensive with an invasion of Antioch in April 1142; Raymond replied with an unsuccessful assault on Buzāʿah in April 1143. But a truce quickly followed, for the more pressing and menacing problem of the Byzantines was now at hand.

[29] William of Tyre, XV, 21. Krey, *William of Tyre*, II, 126, note 27, is of the opinion that "this polite refusal of any but a pious visit from John indicated the resistance of Jerusalem to John's plans for a general overlordship of Christian Syria." See also Chalandon, *Jean II Comnène et Manuel I Comnène*, p. 191, and Cahen, *La Syrie du nord*, p. 367. For a study of the reign of John Comnenus and of his Turkish contemporaries, see the chapters, in the forthcoming second volume of the present work, on the Comneni and Angeli (1081–1204) and on the Selchükids of Rūm. According to Deschamps, *La Défense du royaume de Jérusalem*, p. 11, and Grousset, *Croisades*, II, 156–157, the fortress of Blanche Garde was built by king Fulk in 1142, although it has also been attributed to the regency of Melisend in 1144.

Four years after his departure from Antioch in 1138 John revived his claims on the north Syrian Franks and laid plans to establish a principality comprising Adalia (Antalya), Cyprus, and Antioch for his son Manuel. Accordingly, he returned with a large army, invaded the county of Edessa, and encamped before Tell Bashir. Joscelin, wholly unprepared, speedily capitulated and, accepting John's demand for hostages, surrendered his daughter Isabella. Thereupon the emperor advanced on Antioch and encamped in its environs on September 25, 1142. Raymond flatly refused his peremptory demand that Antioch together with its citadel and fortifications be surrendered to him, alleging in extenuation of his repudiation of his agreement of September 1137 that his promises were invalid because the Frankish nobles contended that he had no legal power to make such covenants. Aware that the temper of the Antiochenes and the approach of winter made impossible the capture of the city, John withdrew and after a brief foray against Tripoli repaired to Cilicia, planning to return in the spring of 1143.

Although John's accidental death during the course of a hunt in Cilicia in April 1143 led to a change of rulers in Byzantium — his son Manuel succeeded him — the mutual hostility of Frank and Greek continued. Raymond's invasion of Cilicia in 1143 was met by a Byzantine invasion of Antioch in 1144, and Raymond was at length beaten and forced to visit Constantinople in person and become Manuel's vassal. The reign of John Comnenus (1118–1143) had almost exactly coincided with those of Baldwin II and Fulk, and we may pause in our narrative long enough to assess some of its results. The son of Alexius I had, as we have seen, made good his father's failure to intervene in person in Frankish affairs, had restored Byzantine control of Cilicia by his victorious campaign of 1137–1138, and had retrieved the northern Anatolian territory lost in the 1120's to the Dānishmendids. His internal administration and European policies had been notably successful. Nevertheless, his apparent accomplishments in Asia were hollow and valueless. What use to the real purposes of the Byzantine empire were the nominal suzerainty over Antioch, the possession of devastated countrysides and isolated towns in northern and west central Anatolia, the military promenade in Syria? No effective occupation could resist the steady Turkoman encroachment on the agricultural areas; no military sweep could restore the commercial prosperity of the towns or assure the security of the roads between them; no form of allegiance could reconcile the conflicting interests of Norman and Byzantine and Armenian, or the passionate mutual hatred of Latin and Greek and Syrian Christians. The cost of John's eastern expeditions was disproportionately high when matched against the small ephemeral results, while for the Franks he was both a moderate restraint on Zengi and a difficult political problem. But he had dealt with them firmly and fairly, and had given no legitimate ground for accusations on the part of Frankish Christians; his death, though welcomed by them, was to prove a disaster to their cause.

The fourth and most exposed of the Latin states, the county of Edessa, just as the other three, pursued an isolationist policy in the early 1140's. But here the dangers of this policy were accentuated by the slothfulness and indifference of the ruler in vital matters of security. Joscelin abandoned his father's policy of maintaining permanent residence in the city of Edessa and established his residence in the castle of Tell Bashir, which provided greater opportunities for leisure and pleasure. Since Edessa's inhabitants were for the most part traders unfamiliar with arms, the defense of the city depended on mercenaries. But even these follies do not complete the dismal tale, for Joscelin and Raymond were openly hostile to each other and felt no responsibility for the welfare of each other's dominions.[30]

Meanwhile, Zengi concluded his quarrels with his Moslem rivals and made a peace treaty with the chief of them, the sultan, in 1143. Then, with his attention at long last undivided, he resumed his war with the Franks and invaded the county of Edessa. Having attacked and captured several castles, he then secured them by garrisoning with his own troops. A number of Frankish merchants and their soldier escorts presently became his captives in October 1144. Joscelin led most of his army towards the Euphrates to cut Zengi off from Aleppo, whereupon the residents of Harran informed Zengi of Edessa's plight. Indeed, Harran's governor urged him to seize it. This information, together with a report of the dissensions rampant between prince and count, crystallized his plans. After mustering a large cavalry and infantry force, Zengi advanced on Edessa in a circuitous fashion in order to allay the suspicions of the Franks and with the support of numerous Moslem chieftains laid close siege to the city on November 28, 1144.

[30] William of Tyre, XVI, 4. Krey, *William of Tyre*, II, 141, note 9, explains the defensive system of Edessa as follows: "the use of paid troops, including even knights, was probably more extensive in Edessa than elsewhere, owing to the fact that the large Armenian and other native Christian population had not been dispossessed by western nobles. Doubtless the mercenaries at times included Moslems."

Joscelin dispatched messengers to Raymond of Antioch and queen Melisend and besought their aid. Raymond, who was preoccupied with his quarrels with the new Byzantine emperor, Manuel, refused, but Melisend at once dispatched a relief force, which arrived, however, too late to assist the defenders. Meanwhile, the outnumbered defenders put up a stout resistance and boldly spurned Zengi's peace proposals and demands for their surrender. But it was to no avail. The Moslem chieftain pressed on unceasingly and at length captured Edessa in late December 1144. Zengi presently followed up his triumph over Edessa by a victorious sweep through the trans-Euphratean part of the county of Edessa.[31]

The price of political disunity had been heavy. The generation of the 1140's, no more prescient of future disaster than that of the 1930's, had played the isolationist game and had lost. The Moslem *revanche*, now in its crescendo, had scored its first signal triumph. It is important to understand the course of this development and the nature of Zengi's success in its Moslem setting, to which we turn in the next chapter.

[31] On Zengi's Edessan campaign, see below, chapter XIV, p. 461.

Cilicia: Armenian Fortress at Anamur

XIV
ZENGI AND THE FALL OF EDESSA

With the establishment of the county of Tripoli, a rough balance of power was struck in Syria between crusaders and Moslems. Jerusalem faced Damascus, Antioch faced Aleppo, and Tripoli faced the group of lesser cities in the upper Orontes valley. Although Aleppo lay between Antioch and Edessa, they, too, lay between Aleppo and the Moslem principalities to east and north, as Jerusalem lay between Damascus and Egypt. The dynasties in the crusading states were, unconsciously but effectively, absorbed into the system of Syrian politics, with its shifting play of alliances and counter-alliances, temporary treaties, sudden realignments, and petty gains and losses.

The point of balance of the whole system was Aleppo. Its effective absorption by Damascus, or Mosul, or the northern crusaders, would involve a major regrouping of the forces on either side. But the local strength of Aleppo lay in its alliance with the Assassins, and when, after the death of Riḍvan in 1113, the zeal of a new governor, Lu'lu', regent for Riḍvan's son, led to a breach with the Assassins, it became too weak to stand by itself and was forced to seek external support. But support was one thing, in the eyes both of its governors and of its Shī'ite population, and absorption quite another. The main thread in the history of Moslem Syria during the next decade was the conflict which

The principal contemporary sources for the history of Moslem Syria to the death of Nūr-ad-Dīn are the history of Damascus of Ibn-al-Qalānisī (ed. H. F. Amedroz, Leyden, 1908; partial translation by H. A. R. Gibb, *The Damascus Chronicle of the Crusades*, London, 1932); the "memoirs" of Usāmah Ibn-Munqidh (ed. P. K. Hitti, Princeton, 1930; tr. Hitti, *An Arab-Syrian Gentleman in the Period of the Crusades*, Columbia University, Records of Civilization, New York, 1929); the citations from 'Imād-ad-Dīn and other lost Syrian sources in abū-Shāmah, *Ar-rauḍatain* (Cairo, 1870–1871; partial translation in *RHC, Or.*, IV–V); the Syriac chronicle of Michael (vol. III, ed. and tr. J. B. Chabot, Paris, 1910); and for Mesopotamia, the history of Maiyafariqin by Ibn-al-Azraq al-Fāriqī (partially published in notes to Ibn-al-Qalānisī). For northern Syria the data from these and other fragmentary sources are coördinated by C. Cahen, *La Syrie du nord à l'époque des croisades* (Paris, 1940), and for Mesopotamia by C. Cahen, "Le Diyâr Bakr au temps des premiers Urtuqides," *Journal Asiatique*, CCXXVII (1935), 219–276. For the history of Egypt, see G. Wiet, *L'Égypte arabe* (Paris, 1938).

raged round Aleppo, as it oscillated between its more powerful neighbors, now appealing for their help and now playing them off against one another.

The first to be approached was Tughtigin at Damascus. But he, realizing after a personal inspection that the defense of Aleppo in its disorganized and unstable condition would be a liability so serious as to overstrain his forces, returned to Damascus. By renewing his treaty with Baldwin, however, he kept his hands free for eventualities. Lu'lu' then murdered his sovereign, broke with Tughtigin, and appealed to the Selchükid sultan of Iraq, who dispatched the governor of Hamadan, Bursuk ibn-Bursuk, to "restore order in Syria and engage the Franks." Scarcely had Bursuk set out in June 1115 than Lu'lu' formed an alliance with Tughtigin and the Artukid chief Īl-Ghāzī, at the time a refugee in Syria; Roger of Antioch also, fearing the surrender of Aleppo, joined in the coalition and brought both Baldwin and Pons of Tripoli into it as well. The unexpected junction of the Moslem and Christian princes against Selchükid intervention, and the subsequent destruction of Bursuk's army at Dānīth by Roger, left uneasy feelings on the Moslem side. Tughtigin, after a brush with Pons, found it advisable to repair in person to Baghdad to reinsure himself with the sultan, and returned to Damascus laden with honors and the grant of full legal powers over his principality.[1]

The isolation of Aleppo and the confusion which followed the assassination of Lu'lu' in 1117 led Tughtigin to support an attempt by Aksungur al-Bursukī, a former governor of Mosul now established at Rahba, to occupy the city. Its commander appealed both to Roger and to Īl-Ghāzī, once more established at Mardin; the former, on payment of tribute, forced the withdrawal of Aksungur, so that Īl-Ghāzī, on his arrival, was coldly received and withdrew to await events.

During Tughtigin's engagements in the north Baldwin had consolidated his hold on the Transjordan, but avoided direct hostilities with Damascus. After Baldwin I's death in 1118, however, Tughtigin entered into an alliance with the Egyptians, which detained him in the south. As Aksungur was simultaneously engaged in the conflicts in Iraq which followed the death of sultan Muḥammad in the same month, Roger seized the opportunity to open an attack on Aleppo on his own account. The citizens urgently recalled Īl-Ghāzī, who bought a truce with Roger and made arrangements with Tughtigin for a combined campaign in the

[1] For further details on Frankish policy, see above chapter XII, pp. 404–405.

following year. In June 1119 the two allies prepared to take the field. Īl-Ghāzī, arriving first with a motley host of Turkomans and volunteers, began to raid the valley of Rugia, and Roger, apparently unaware of the alliance and imagining that he had to deal only with the usual haphazard incursions, marched out in haste, to anticipate an attack on al-Athārib. Īl-Ghāzī wished to await the disciplined forces of Damascus, but was overborne by the impatient Turkomans, whose mobility enabled them to take Roger unawares in the rock-strewn region of Darb Sarmadā (June 28, 1119).[2]

The *ager sanguinis*, as the Franks called Roger's defeat, relieved the Frankish threat to Aleppo only for the time being, but committed Īl-Ghāzī to the onerous responsibility of defending the city. The Artukids, as has been shown in an earlier chapter, were the chiefs of an important group of Turkomans, who were associated with the Selchükids in their conquest of Syria, but had moved up into the highlands of Mesopotamia after the opening of the First Crusade.[3] There the two brothers Īl-Ghāzī and Sokman had constituted around their main castles of Mardin and Ḥiṣn Kaifā respectively principalities which they maintained by means of continual raids upon their neighbors. With the governors of Mosul, whose principal task it was to keep them under some sort of control, they were, of course, at perpetual feud; during Zengi's governorship, as will be seen, he devoted far more time and energy to warfare with them than with the Franks of Syria, and at later moments in the careers of both Nūr-ad-Dīn and Saladin (Ṣalāḥ-ad-Dīn) they played a decisive part against Mosul. As the chiefs of the largest Turkoman groups in the region, they were a valuable source of auxiliary troops. On the other hand, they were frequently divided by military and political rivalries, not only between but also within the two branches, and their Turkomans and Kurdish irregulars, though highly mobile, lacked the discipline and the stability of the organized Turkish regiments. Though hardy fighters, the main object of the Turkomans in warfare was booty, and they were quickly discouraged by a long and unsuccessful campaign. It was difficult, therefore, for their chiefs to keep them in the field, and this fact, together with their divisions, made it impossible for the Artukids to build up stable political organizations.

The Artukid connection thus gave a very imperfect shelter to Aleppo from the steady pressure and encroachments of Baldwin

[2] On Roger see above, chapter XII, p. 404, and chapter XIII, p. 413.

[3] See above, chapter V, pp. 170–171.

from Antioch and Joscelin from Edessa (Urfa). Īl-Ghāzī gained few additional resources from his new possession, and was compelled in any case to devote most of his attention to his Mesopotamian holdings, where he was shortly afterwards engaged in a disastrous conflict with the Georgians. But when his son Sulaimān, whom he had left as his representative at Aleppo, revolted in the summer of 1121, he returned to Aleppo, cemented the alliance with the Selchükids by marrying Rīdvan's daughter, and prepared to resume the offensive against the Franks.

Īl-Ghāzī's death in November 1122 left Aleppo still more isolated, until his nephew Nūr-ad-Daulah Belek, after capturing Baldwin, occupied it in June 1123 and began energetically to reëstablish its security. His death while besieging Manbij on May 6, 1124, was the climax of the city's misfortunes, since it was now reduced to dependence on Īl-Ghāzī's indolent son and successor at Mardin, Timurtash. At this juncture a fresh claimant appeared in the person of the Arab chief Dubais ibn-Ṣadaqah, formerly prince of Hilla in Iraq, who had been driven out by the combined forces of the caliph and Aksungur al-Bursukī, now governor of Mosul again, and had fled to his fellow-countryman, the ʿUqailid prince of Qalʿat Jaʿbar. With his assistance, Dubais opened negotiations with the Franks and the Shīʿite citizens of Aleppo, on whose support he, as a Shīʿite, counted against the Sunnite Turks and Turkomans. In June 1124, accordingly, Timurtash released Baldwin, on his undertaking to surrender ʿAzāz and other fortresses, to pay a ransom of 80,000 gold pieces, and to have no dealings with Dubais. So far from honoring his word, Baldwin, once free, refused to surrender the fortresses and formed a league with Dubais. Timurtash, giving up all hope of holding Aleppo, retired to Mesopotamia, leaving the city to be defended by five hundred horsemen and the citizens.

The long struggle for Aleppo had, however, brought into play a new factor in the conflict. Ever since the *ager sanguinis* the feeling between Moslem and Christian had grown more hostile, and the ferocity displayed by Joscelin in his raids in 1123, after his escape from Kharput, had roused the bitterness of the population of Aleppo to an intense degree. When, therefore, Baldwin and Joscelin commenced the siege of the city on October 6, 1124, with their Moslem allies, including not only Dubais and the Arab chief of Qalʿat Jaʿbar, but also a son of Rīdvan and a minor Artukid, they were met by a vigorous and unflinching resistance. After vain appeals to Timurtash, the citizens, in desperation, were forced to beg for what they had so long and so tenaciously resisted, the protection of Mosul. Aksungur al-Bursukī acted at once, and advanced with such speed and secrecy that the besiegers, taken by surprise on the night of January 29, 1125, withdrew without a combat.[4]

Although Aleppo had thus by a chain of accidents become a dependency of Mosul it was not thereby reabsorbed into the Selchükid state. Whatever its formal status may have been, Aksungur, like Zengi after him, saw it rather as a means by which to establish an independent and hereditary principality. For this purpose Mosul alone, owing to its proximity to the centers of Selchükid power, was insufficient. The possession of Aleppo gave depth to his holding, and might, once he regained control of its territories, provide additional material and financial support. In a tactical sense it was even more valuable, for by its position as an outpost of Islam against the Franks its possession invested the governor of Mosul with the character of a champion of the faith against the "infidel", and the strength of Moslem feeling would make it difficult for the sultan to take vigorous action against him.

Although the union with Mosul removed from Aleppo the immediate menace of a Frankish conquest, there was an active party among the citizens to whom it came as a severe blow. These were the Assassins, who had by favor of the Artukids recovered their strength during the troubled decade. The occupation of Aleppo by an "easterner" boded them no good, and the all-but-inevitable consequence followed when Aksungur, after some minor operations in conjunction with Tughtigin during 1125 and 1126, was struck down in the great mosque of Mosul in November 1126.[5]

His son Masʿūd received at once the allegiance of Aleppo and the sultan's confirmation of his governorship of the two cities. But a growing party of the citizens, among them it may be suspected the Assassins, showed some resistance; and Masʿūd, on his way to seize Hamah from Tughtigin, died suddenly while besieging Rahba in May 1127. Although his nominee Kutlug Abeh succeeded in occupying Aleppo, the citizens rebelled, proclaimed allegiance to an Artukid prince, and besieged the garrison in the citadel. Joscelin seized the opportunity to make a fresh attack, but was bought off, and was afterwards prevented from further aggression by hostilities with Bohemond II of Antioch.

[4] Cf., above, chapter XIII, pp. 424–425, for a discussion of Aksungur's policies in relation to the Latin states.

[5] See above, chapter IV, p. 115.

Meanwhile a deputation of notables from Mosul to Baghdad had been persuaded to ask sultan Maḥmūd to appoint as their governor ʿImād-ad-Dīn Zengi, the son of an earlier Aksungur, al-Ḥājib, who had been appointed governor of Aleppo by sultan Malik-Shāh in 1086 and executed by Tutush in 1094. He had succeeded Aksungur al-Bursukī of Mosul as military governor of Iraq in 1126. In consideration of "a handsome contribution" to the treasury, the sultan granted the diploma for Mosul to Zengi, in the capacity of atabeg or regent for his son, the *malik* Alp Arslan. Zengi took over Mosul in September 1127 without opposition, set about reducing its outlying dependencies, and in January 1128 sent a detachment to occupy Aleppo. The general Ṣalāḥ-ad-Dīn al-Yaghisiyanī (or al-Ghisyanī) was nominated as its governor, and shortly afterwards Zengi himself marched into Syria and entered the city on June 18. In thus restoring the union between Mosul and Aleppo, however, Zengi had gone beyond the terms of his appointment. When he presented himself at the court some months later he found the sultan unwilling, not without reason, to endow so ambitious an officer with such extensive domains, and only on the intercession of the caliph did he consent to grant him the diploma for Aleppo also.

The first effects of the altered balance of Moslem power in the north were felt by Damascus. Baldwin I had directed the brunt of his attacks on Egypt and the Egyptian possessions in Asia, and endeavored to maintain the neutrality of Damascus. Baldwin II, on the other hand, on all occasions when he was free to take the initiative, directed his attacks towards Damascus.[6] The disaster at the *ager sanguinis*, however, by involving Baldwin in the north, freed Tughtigin not only to join in the campaigns in the north but also to negotiate with Egypt. There in December 1121, the powerful vizir al-Afḍal had been assassinated and replaced by al-Ma'mūn, who gave immediate evidence of his intention to adopt a more active policy in Palestine and Syria, and took measures to build up the Egyptian fleet. Hoping for support from Tughtigin after Belek's capture of Baldwin, he dispatched a force by sea to Jaffa in May 1123, but the expected assistance from Damascus failed to arrive. The Egyptians were defeated on land near Ibelin (Yabnâ) by the constable Eustace Garnier, and on sea by the Venetians under the doge Domenico Michiel. The double defeat made it impossible to send relief to Tyre when it was besieged in the following year, and Tughtigin could do no more than negotiate

[6] For a discussion of Baldwin II's policies see above, chapter XIII, pp. 411 ff., 426.

the terms of surrender of the city, no doubt ensuring that satisfactory arrangements were made for commercial relations with Damascus.

In his negotiations with Egypt, Tughtigin had associated Aksungur with himself, and these continued even after Aksungur's occupation of Aleppo. In all probability, it was this tentative movement towards closer relations among Egypt, Damascus, and Aleppo which explains Baldwin's attack on Ascalon in November 1125, followed by an invasion of Damascus territory in January 1126. The defeat inflicted on the army of Damascus by this reconnaissance in force accomplished the object, if such it was, of forestalling any concerted action, and prepared the way for the invasion three years later.

It is in connection with this battle that the coöperation of the Assassins with the army of Damascus is mentioned for the first time. That the Assassins, discouraged by the union of Aleppo with Mosul, had decided to try their fortunes at Damascus seems clear, and it is equally clear that this was done with the consent of Tughtigin. In this policy is to be seen his reaction to the new situation in the north. The union of Aleppo with Mosul had the effect of placing Damascus in the precariously isolated position from which Aleppo had just escaped, at the price of its independence. Alliance with the Franks was out of the question, in view of the hostile attitude of Baldwin II, and equally so any effective alliance with Egypt. The only course open to Tughtigin was to mobilize in its support all the strength which could be gained from local Syrian forces, and even their enemies did not deny the courage and gallantry of the Assassins. It is certainly the fact that, after his defeat by Baldwin, Tughtigin openly acknowledged the alliance by assigning the frontier castle of Banyas to the leader of the Assassins in November 1126.[7]

A month after Zengi's occupation of Aleppo, Tughtigin died (February 1128) after a prolonged illness. He was succeeded by his son Böri, who proved himself to be equal to the successive dangers to which Damascus was exposed. On Tughtigin's death the Assassins at Banyas resumed their terrorist activities, under the shelter of the vizir at Damascus. Fortunately for Böri, they were severely worsted in a conflict with the Druzes of Wādī-t-Taim, and he seized the opportunity to root them out of the city (September 1129), but at the cost of Banyas, which they surrendered

[7] Cf. above, chapter IV, p. 116. For Baldwin's expeditions into the areas of Ascalon and Damascus, see chapter XIII, p. 426.

to the Franks. Two months later Baldwin, reinforced by the arrival of Fulk of Anjou and the troops of the northern principalities, marched on Damascus. Böri, forewarned, had enlisted in its defense some thousands of Turkomans and Arabs, who threw a cordon round the crusading army, and dispatched a strong force to waylay a foraging expedition to the Hauran under William of Bures. The defeat suffered by the latter and the consequent retreat of the crusaders was recognized on both sides as an event that put an end, for many years, to Baldwin's policy of attack on Damascus, and shortly afterwards a treaty was negotiated to regulate their political and commercial relations.[8]

The third, and still greater, threat to Böri's principality followed in the spring or early summer of 1130, when Zengi returned to Syria and called for the coöperation of Damascus "to prosecute the holy war". With natural suspicion, Böri swore him to good faith before dispatching a strong contingent and instructing his son Sevinj, at Hamah, to join it with his own forces. He had already suffered a serious loss in the defection of Sevar, one of the ablest Turkish generals of his age, who joined Zengi at Aleppo and was rewarded with its governorship. On their arrival at Zengi's camp Sevinj and the Damascene officers were seized and placed in confinement at Aleppo; at the same time Zengi occupied the now undefended stronghold of Hamah and marched on Homs, notwithstanding his engagements towards its prince, Kîr-Khan, who, with his forces, was actually serving in his army. But the garrison and citizens of Homs refused to surrender and after a fruitless siege Zengi returned to Mosul, taking his prisoners with him. The capture of Dubais ibn-Ṣadaqah by Böri's Arab auxiliaries in the following year enabled him to negotiate the release of Sevinj and his officers in return for the surrender of Dubais to Zengi; but the whole episode had given clear warning that the first objective of Zengi's "holy war" in Syria was none other than Damascus.

It was some years, however, before the attempt was renewed. The death of sultan Maḥmūd in September 1131 was followed by a struggle between his brothers for the succession to the sultanate of Iraq, into which Zengi was inevitably drawn as a partisan of sultan Masʿūd. At the height of the struggle he, in association with Dubais, attempted even to seize Baghdad, but was defeated by the forces of the caliph al-Mustarshid, who retaliated a few months later by besieging Mosul (August–October 1133). Warned by this experience to abstain from further adventures in Iraq for

[8] On Frankish policy, see above, chapter XIII, pp. 430–431.

the time being, Zengi turned his attention to the Artukid principalities in Mesopotamia. Profiting by the rivalry between Timurtash, the son of Īl-Ghāzī, and his cousin Dā'ūd ibn-Sokman of Ḥiṣn Kaifā, he made an alliance with the former and in 1134 seized and transferred to him many of Dā'ūd's northern fortresses, but failed in an attempt to subdue the independent fortress of Amida (Diyarbakir). In the midst of these operations, an unexpected invitation to take possession of Damascus brought him back in haste to Syria in February 1135.

In June 1132 Böri had died as the result of wounds inflicted by Assassins, and was succeeded by his son, Shams-al-Mulūk Ismā'īl.[9] After a successful start with the recapture of Banyas (December 1132) and of Hamah (August 1133), followed by a devastating raid on the county of Galilee in retaliation for a Frankish raid on the Hauran (September 1134), he alienated by his tyrannical conduct both his troops and his subjects. Realizing, apparently, their growing exasperation, he wrote secretly to Zengi urging him to come with all speed to receive the surrender of Damascus, and threatening to deliver it up to the Franks if he should delay.

Whatever their grievances against Shams-al-Mulūk Ismā'īl, the army and the citizens were equally resolute in their hostility to Zengi, "knowing as they did," in the words of the Damascus chronicler, "what the conduct of Zengi would be if he should capture the city."[10] Ismā'īl having been disposed of by the palace guards and his brother Maḥmūd proclaimed in his place, the population under the command of the general Mu'īn-ad-Dīn Unur (or Önör) effectually prevented Zengi from pressing his siege. An opportune command from the caliph to withdraw from Damascus and to take over the government of Iraq gave him an opening for negotiations, and he marched north on March 15. But not at once to Iraq, for after regaining Hamah on the way he opened a lightning campaign against the unsuspecting Franks.

During the intervening years Sevar had engaged in minor hostilities with Antioch and Tell Bashir, but little change had been made in the general situation of Aleppo, which was still under close surveillance from the castles held by the Franks to north and west. Within a few weeks Zengi cleared the whole of its western

[9] For the assassination of Böri see above, chapter IV, pp. 117–118.

[10] All contemporary sources bear witness to Zengi's ferocity. His namesake, the secretary 'Imād-ad-Dīn, describes him as a "tyrant, striking at random, and a raging blast of calamities, tigerish in nature, lionlike in malevolence, ignorant of no severity and acquainted with no gentleness, feared for his violence, shunned for his roughness, inordinate in conduct and pride, the death of his enemies and of his subjects." Cf. the abridgement by al-Bundārī (Houtsma, *Textes relatifs à l'histoire des Seldjoucides*, II, Leyden, 1888), p. 205.

and southwestern approaches, by the capture of al-Athārib, Zardanā, Ma'arrat-an-Nu'mān, and other fortresses, while Sevar moved against 'Azāz and Aintab (Gaziantep). Then, after vainly besieging Homs again, Zengi returned to Mosul, leaving Sevar to follow up his offensive with the aid of the Turkoman irregulars, who were at this time moving into Syria in increasing numbers. As soon as he had gone, the sons of Kīr-Khan negotiated the surrender of Homs to Damascus; it was given in fief to Unur, and had immediately to sustain incursions by Sevar, until an armistice was signed. The Turkomans were compensated by an extensive and profitable raid on the district of Latakia in April 1136.

Zengi's second intervention in Iraq was little more successful than the first. In the autumn of 1135 the caliph al-Mustarshid had attempted to organize a coalition against sultan Mas'ūd, and Zengi, accompanying the Selchükid *malik* Dā'ūd ibn-Maḥmūd, moved up to Baghdad to join in the alliance. Al-Mustarshid had in the meantime marched out against the sultan, but was deserted by his Turkish troops, defeated, captured, and killed by Assassins. Dā'ūd and Zengi then proclaimed his son ar-Rāshid caliph and swore to support his cause, but no sooner did sultan Mas'ūd move on Baghdad than they both fled. Ar-Rāshid followed Zengi to Mosul, but Zengi, having sent an envoy to the sultan and obtained from him additional fiefs and honors, refused to receive the fugitive caliph, who was forced to take refuge with Dā'ūd in Azerbaijan, and was subsequently killed by Assassins while besieging Isfahan.

In the spring of 1137 Zengi returned to Syria and renewed his attack on Homs, but again failed to overcome Unur's resistance. Concluding an armistice with Damascus, he turned northwards on July 11 to attack Ba'rīn, and had the good fortune to surprise Fulk, who threw himself into the castle. The advance of a relieving army from Antioch and Edessa, together with the news of the approach of John Comnenus to Antioch, forced him to allow the garrison to evacuate the castle on payment of ransom. He withdrew to Aleppo and set the population to work on its fortifications against a Greek attack, until he was relieved by the temporary withdrawal of the emperor and an exchange of embassies with him, when he led his forces back into Damascus territories, and captured 'Ainjar and Banyas. He then returned to his attack on Homs, and was still besieging it when the Greek offensive took him by surprise at the beginning of April 1138.[11]

[11] On Frankish policy and the Greek intervention, see above chapter XIII, pp. 438–439.

The short delay of the Greek army at Buzā'ah (April 3–9) was just long enough to give warning to the garrison of Aleppo and to allow of their reinforcement by detachments from Zengi's squadrons. The emperor halted outside Aleppo for two days only (April 18–20), and marched on Ma'arrat-an-Nu'mān and Kafarṭāb, while a detachment occupied al-Athārib. Zengi hastily withdrew the rest of his forces to Salamyah, sent his baggage-train to Raqqa, and himself with his light-armed cavalry remained on guard. At the end of April the emperor laid siege to Shaizar. Zengi's cavalry could only harass his flanks until a force of Turkomans, sent by Dā'ūd of Ḥiṣn Kaifā, and a detachment from Damascus came up to reinforce him; at the same time news of the attacks upon his lines of communications by the Dānishmendids and Selchükids decided John Comnenus to raise the siege after twenty-three days, and he withdrew to Antioch.

The effect of this futile Greek campaign was only to enhance Zengi's reputation. Scarcely were the Greeks gone before he negotiated an agreement with Damascus, and received Homs (in exchange for Ba'rīn) as dowry on his marriage with the queen-mother (June 1138). Kafarṭāb, al-Athārib, and Buzā'ah were rapidly reoccupied and the territories of Edessa were overrun by the Turkomans of Timurtash and Dā'ūd. Leaving Sevar once more in command of his Syrian possessions, Zengi returned to Mosul, and in the following year took Dara and Ra's al-'Ain from Timurtash as dowry for another marriage, with the daughter of Timurtash.

Again Zengi was recalled to Damascus, this time at the invitation of his wife, the queen-mother, who was indignant at the murder of the prince Maḥmūd and his replacement by his brother Muḥammad, formerly governor of Baalbek (June 23, 1139). Baalbek was besieged and captured, and its garrison crucified notwithstanding his oath of security. After refortifying it Zengi withdrew to the Biqā' valley and tried to negotiate the surrender of Damascus. On the rejection of his demands, he blockaded the city from December until the following May, without result. During the siege the prince Muḥammad fell ill and died, and Unur set up his young son Abak in his place without opposition. Despite the determination of both troops and population to resist Zengi, however, Unur realized that in its isolated situation the city could not hold out indefinitely, and fell back on the only remaining source of external support. A formal alliance was negotiated with the kingdom of Jerusalem against the common enemy, and in return for the assistance of the crusaders Unur undertook to pay 20,000 pieces of gold per month for their expenses, to give hostages, and to restore Banyas to them after Zengi's withdrawal.[12]

When the crusaders began to assemble at Tiberias, Zengi retired to the Hauran (May 4), before the Franks and Damascenes could join forces. In his absence the allies besieged Banyas; Zengi remained strangely inactive, and the governor, at the end of a month, surrendered to Unur on terms. Unur delivered the castle up to Fulk, but before he could return to Damascus Zengi reappeared in the Ghūṭah and devastated it for three days. He retired northwards, but a week later attempted a sudden *coup de main* at dawn, and when it failed finally withdrew with an immense booty.

Five years passed before he returned to Syria, if ever, and during this time little but border raids are recorded between the Moslems and the Franks. The treaty between Damascus and Jerusalem was apparently maintained in force, and the Greek expedition of 1142 involved no Moslem troops in action. One small but influential new political force had, however, established itself between the Moslem and Latin principalities during the preceding years. This was the Assassins who, beginning with the purchase of al-Qadmūs in 1132–1133, after their expulsion from Banyas, had gradually acquired other strongholds in the Nuṣairī mountains (Jabal Anṣārīyah), and in 1140–1141 seized Maṣyāf as their headquarters.

From his base at Mosul Zengi was actively engaged for the next three years in operations directed mainly against the Artukid Dā'ūd and the small Kurdish baronies to the north. He began also to feel his way cautiously back into Iraq, and in 1143 captured Ḥadīthah and ʿĀnah on the Euphrates. Sultan Masʿūd was at the time occupied in dealing with rebellions in various quarters, which he ascribed, with some justice, to Zengi's intrigues in order to prevent him from intervening. Having at length restored order, the sultan assembled his forces at Baghdad and prepared to settle his account with Zengi, at the same time investing his own brother Dā'ūd with the command of the holy war in Syria. Zengi, in extreme alarm, made his submission, and the sultan, for reasons not specified, found it advisable to reach a reconciliation with him.

The chronology of these and the following events, and the relation between them, is still uncertain in detail. In August 1144 Dā'ūd ibn-Sokman died and was succeeded by a younger son, Kara Arslan. Zengi immediately overran most of his territories and then, since Kara Arslan had, apparently, begun to negotiate with Joscelin, occupied the eastern fortresses of the county in

[12] Cf., above, chapter XIII, p. 442.

Shabakhtan, on the headwaters of the Khabur river, in order to cut communication between them. On Zengi's return to renew his assault on Amida, Kara Arslan offered to surrender to Joscelin the fortress of Bibol, north of Gargar, in return for his assistance. Joscelin at once set out towards the west, taking with him a strong contingent of his forces, whereupon Zengi, informed of the temporary weakness of the garrison at Edessa, advanced by forced marches and encircled it (November 24). Before Joscelin and his outnumbered army could intervene, Zengi, calling up all his available vassals and auxiliaries, smothered the defense and broke into the city on December 24. The citadel fell two days later, and Zengi, first killing all the Franks and destroying their churches, but sparing the native Christians and their churches to the best of his ability, gave the city in fief to the commander of his guard, Zain-ad-Dīn 'Alī Küchük.[13]

The reactions to this event were almost as widespread in the east as in the west. By his fortunate conquest Zengi acquired the reputation of a "defender of the faith", which went far to atone for his defects of character and grasping policies. The caliph showered on him presents and titles, including that of *al-malik al-manṣūr*, "the victorious king," and the contemporary chronicles bear witness to the resounding fame of his exploit throughout the Moslem world. For himself, he energetically prosecuted the advantage he had gained, cleared Sarūj and other strongholds, and besieged Bira (Birejik), which guarded the Euphrates crossing to Tell Bashir (March 1145).

At this juncture one of the Selchükid princes in his care, Farrukh-Shāh ibn-Maḥmūd, seized the occasion of his absence to murder the governor of Mosul (May 1145) and to proclaim himself ruler. Though the revolt was put down with ease by the garrison troops, the incident reawakened all his fears. Hastily ordering 'Alī Küchük to proceed to Mosul, he himself made first for Aleppo in order to forestall possible repercussions there.[14] On his return to Mosul, he brought the other Selchükid prince, Alp Arslan, out

[13] Cf., above, chapter XIII, pp. 446–447.

[14] See *Anonymous Syriac Chronicle* (in the *Corpus scriptorum Christianorum orientalium, Scriptores Syri*, ser. III, vol. XV, ed. J.-B. Chabot, Paris, 1916), tr. A. S. Tritton and H. A. R. Gibb, "The First and Second Crusades from an Anonymous Syriac Chronicle," *Journal of the Royal Asiatic Society*, 1933, p. 287. Zengi had stored two-thirds of his treasure at Aleppo and Sinjar against the eventuality of a Selchükid coup at Mosul. Cf. Ibn-al-Athīr, *Atābeks* (*RHC, Or.*, II), p. 143. Apparently after Zengi lifted the siege of Bira, its citizens voluntarily submitted to Artukid suzerainty to forestall any resumption, but as this was one of the towns ceded by Beatrice to Manuel in 1150 (cf. below, chapter XVII, p. 534), this suzerainty must have been merely nominal.

of confinement and thereafter carried him with him on his expeditions.

Late in the same year he began to make preparations for a decisive attack on Damascus and had actually set out when, early in 1146, an Armenian plot to restore Edessa to Joscelin changed his plans. Probably moved by suspicions of an understanding between Joscelin and his former ally, the Artukid Timurtash, he turned against the latter, seized Tall ash-Shaikh, and after further operations moved southwards to reduce another ally of the Franks, the ʿUqailid Arab prince of Dausar, or Qalʿat Jaʿbar, at the eastward bend of the Euphrates. Here, on the night of September 14, 1146, he was assassinated by one of his slaves.

The first reactions of the troops on the report of Zengi's death showed that his fears of a Selchükid revolution in Mosul had not been without foundation. An eye-witness account describes their demonstrations against Zengi's officers and vizir in favor of the Selchükid *malik* Alp Arslan. But before he could seize the opportunity, ʿAlī Küchük, who had been left in command at Mosul, in agreement with the vizir Jamāl-ad-Dīn, summoned Zengi's eldest son, Saif-ad-Dīn Ghāzī, from his fief at Shahrazūr and installed him. On his advance towards the city Alp Arslan was seized, imprisoned, and never seen again. While the issue at Mosul was still in doubt the governors of Hamah and Aleppo, al-Yaghisiyanī and Sevar, led back the Syrian contingents accompanied by Zengi's second son Nūr-ad-Dīn Maḥmūd, and set him up in his father's place at Aleppo. The era of Moslem expansion which had begun under Zengi was to continue with almost unabated success under Nūr-ad-Dīn.

XV
THE SECOND CRUSADE

In histories of the crusading movement the Second Crusade generally figures briefly as a fiasco, modeled slavishly on the First Crusade, but without its mystic power, and lacking the vigorous secular quality of the Third and Fourth Crusades. This estimate is partly deserved; but existing records show that the Second Crusade had a complicated character of its own and formed a turning point in the development of the crusades. Without doubt its leaders followed the example of Urban and Godfrey of Bouillon in that they tried to adapt and regularize the phenomena of the

The chief contemporary Latin source for the Second Crusade is Odo of Deuil, *De profectione Ludovici VII in orientem*. There are several editions including: Migne, *PL*, CLXXXV; that of H. Waquet (Paris, 1949); and the Latin text with English translation and notes by V. G. Berry (Columbia University, Records of Civilization, New York, 1948). References to the Berry edition are given in the notes to this chapter. There is also important material in William of Tyre, *Historia rerum in partibus transmarinis gestarum* (*RHC*, *Occ.*, I, and tr. E. A. Babcock and A. C. Krey, *A History of Deeds Done Beyond the Sea*, 2 vols., Records of Civilization, New York, 1943); Otto of Freising, *Chronicon* (*MGH*, *SS*., XX, and the English translation by C. C. Mierow, *The Two Cities: A Chronicle of Universal History to the Year 1146, by Otto, Bishop of Freising*, Records of Civilization, New York, 1928); the same author's *Gesta Friderici I imperatoris* (ed. G. Waitz, 3rd ed., Hanover, 1912, also tr. C. C. Mierow, Records of Civilization, New York, 1953); John of Salisbury, *Historia pontificalis* (ed. R. L. Poole, Oxford, 1927); *De expugnatione Lyxbonensi* (ed. and tr. C. W. David, Records of Civilization, New York, 1936); Helmold, *Cronica Slavorum* (ed. B. Schmeidler, 2nd ed., Berlin, 1909, and tr. F. J. Tschan, *The Chronicle of the Slavs by Helmold, Priest of Bosau* Records of Civilization, New York, 1935); Caffaro, *Annales Ianuenses* and *Historia captionis Almarie et Turtuose* (ed. L. T. Belgrano, *Fonti per la Storia d'Italia*, XI, Rome and Genoa, 1890); *Liber iurium reipublicae Genuensis*, I (*Historiae patriae monumenta*, Turin, 1854); *Prefatio de Almeria* (ed. L. T. Belgrano, *Atti della Società Ligure di Storia Patria*, XIX, Genoa, 1887); *Cronica Adephonsi imperatoris* (ed. H. Florez, in *España sagrada*, XXI, Madrid, 1766); Gerhoh of Reichersberg, *De investigatione Antichristi* (ed. F. Scheibelberger, Linz, 1875); *Annales Palidenses*, *Annales Magdeburgenses*, and *Annales Herbipolenses* (all in *MGH*, *SS*., XVI); *Chronicon Mauriniacense* (*RHGF*, XII); *Sancti Bernardi opera omnia* (*MPL*, CLXXXII–CLXXXV); and tr., in part, by S. J. Eales, *The Life and Works of St. Bernard* (3 vols., London, 1889–1896) and by B. Scott James, *The Letters of St. Bernard of Clairvaux* (London, 1953); *Wibaldi epistolae* (ed., P. Jaffé, *Monumenta Corbeiensia*, Berlin, 1864); *Epistolae Eugenii III papae* (*MPL*, CLXXX); *Epistolae Conradi, Ludovici, Sugerii* (all in *RHGF*, XV); Suger, *De glorioso rege Ludovico Ludovici filio*, in *Vie de Louis le Gros* (ed. Molinier, Paris, 1877).

Greek sources include: John Cinnamus, *Epitome rerum ab Ioanne et Alexio Comnenis gestarum* (*CSHB*); Nicetas Choniates, *Historia* (*ibid.*); *Epistolae Manuelis* (*RHGF*, XV); and Franz Dölger, *Regesten d. Kaiserurkunden d. oströmischen Reiches*, pt. 2: *Regesten von 1025–1204*, Munich and Berlin, 1925. See also W. Ohnsorge, "Ein Beitrag zur Geschichte Manuels I von Byzanz," *Festschrift für Albert Brackmann* (ed. L. Santifaller, Weimar, 1931), pp. 371–393; C. Neumann, *Griechische Geschichtschreiber und Geschichtsquellen im 12. Jahrhundert* (Leipzig, 1888).

First Crusade without changing its essential character. Eugenius's bull with its careful attention to the status and privileges of the crusaders; the insistence on authorized preachers; the reliance on experienced military leaders; the desire for the orderly departure of the crusade through territories whose rulers had been consulted

Chief among the Arabic sources generally accessible are: Ibn-al-Qalānisī, *Dhail ta'rīkh Dimashq* (extracts tr. H. A. R. Gibb, *The Damascus Chronicle of the Crusades*, London, 1932; also ed. H. F. Amedroz [Leyden, 1908]); Ibn-al-Athīr, *Al-kāmil fī-t-ta'rīkh* (extracts in *RHC, Or.*, I, 187–744), and *Ta'rīkh ad-daulah al-atābakīyah mulūk al-Mauṣil* (*RHC, Or.*, II, part 2); Usāmah Ibn-Munqidh, *Kitāb al-i'tibār* (tr. P. K. Hitti, *An Arab-Syrian Gentleman ... in the Period of the Crusades*, Records of Civilization, New York, 1929); other editions by H. Derenbourg (Paris, 1889), and G. R. Potter (London, 1929); Kamāl-ad-Dīn, *Zubdat al-ḥalab fī ta'rīkh Ḥalab* (extracts in *RHC, Or.*, III, 577–690, and tr. E. Blochet, *ROL*, III–VI, 1895 to 1898); abū-Shāmah, *Kitāb ar-rauḍatain* (*RHC, Or.*, IV–V).

Syrian and Armenian chronicles include that of Matthew of Edessa, continued by Gregory the Presbyter (*RHC, Doc. Arm.* I); Michael the Syrian, *Chronique* (ed. J.-B. Chabot, 4 vols., Paris, 1899–1910); Bar-Hebraeus, Gregory abū-l-Faraj, *Chronography* (tr. E. A. Wallis Budge, London, 1932); St. Nerses Schnorhali, *Elègy on the Taking of Edessa* (*RHC, Doc. Arm.* I). See also W. R. Taylor, "A New Syriac Fragment dealing with Incidents in the Second Crusade," *Annual of the American School of Oriental Research*, XI (1929–1930), 120–131; A. S. Tritton and H. A. R. Gibb, "The First and Second Crusades from an Anonymous Syriac Chronicle," *Journal of the Royal Asiatic Society*, 1933, pp. 69–101, 273–305; J.-B. Chabot, "Une Episode de l'histoire des croisades," *Mélanges Schlumberger* (2 vols., Paris, 1924), I, 169–179. Important recent comment on oriental literature of the period can be found in C. Cahen, *La Syrie du nord* (cited below), pp. 33–100, and M. Bertsch, *The Attitude of Twelfth Century Arabic Historians towards the Crusades* (University of Michigan, dissertation, Ann Arbor, 1950).

The classic studies on the Second Crusade remain those of B. Kugler, *Studien zur Geschichte des zweiten Kreuzzuges* (Stuttgart, 1866), and the modifications and additions found in his *Analekten zur Geschichte des zweiten Kreuzzuges* (Tübingen, 1878), and *Neue Analekten* (Tübingen, 1883). These supersede earlier treatments. While no entire volume since Kugler's has been devoted to the Second Crusade, important later contributions to various aspects of the subject have been made by W. Giesebrecht, *Geschichte der deutschen Kaiserzeit*, IV (2nd ed., Leipzig, 1877); H. von Kap-Herr, *Die abendländische Politik Kaiser Manuels* (Strassburg, 1881); C. Neumann, *Bernhard von Clairvaux und die Anfänge des zweiten Kreuzzuges* (Heidelberg, 1882); W. Bernhardi, *Konrad III* (Leipzig, 1883), a very full study; G. Hüffner, "Die Anfänge des zweiten Kreuzzuges," *Historisches Jahrbuch* VIII (1887), 391–429, a satisfactory summary and resolution of many problems; E. Vacandard, "Saint Bernard et la seconde croisade," *Revue des questions historiques*, XXXVIII (1885), 398–457, and *Vie de Saint Bernard*, vol. II (Paris, 1895); F. Chalandon, *Histoire de la domination normande en Italie et en Sicile*, vol. II (Paris, 1907); and *Jean II Comnène (1118–1143) et Manuel Comnène (1143–1180)* (Paris, 1912); P. Rassow, "Die Kanzlei Bernhards von Clairvaux," *Studien und Mitteilungen zur Geschichte des Benediktinerordens und seiner Zweige*, new series, III (1913); H. Cosack, "Konrads III Entschluss zum Kreuzzug," *MIOG*, XXXV (1914), 278–296; E. Caspar, "Die Kreuzzugsbullen Eugens III," *Neues Archiv*, XLV (1924), 285–300; P. Pfeiffer, "Die Cistercienser und der zweite Kreuzzug," *Cistercienser Chronik*, XLVII (1935); H. Gleber, *Papst Eugen III* (Jena, 1936); V. Cramer, "Kreuzpredigt und Kreuzzugsgedanke von Bernhard von Clairvaux," *Palästina-Hefte des deutschen Vereins vom Heiligen Land*, XVII–XX (1939); C. Cahen, *La Syrie du nord à l'époque des croisades* (Paris, 1940); A. Cartellieri, *Der Vorrang des Papsttums zur Zeit der ersten Kreuzzüge* (Munich, 1941); H. Conrad, "Gottesfrieden und Heeresverfassung in der Zeit der Kreuzzüge," *Zeitschrift der Savigny-Stiftung für Rechtsgeschichte, Germanistische Abteilung*, LXI (1941), 71–126; J. Richard, *Le Comté de Tripoli sous la dynastie toulousaine (1102–1187)* (Paris, 1945); S. Runciman, *History of the Crusades*, vol. II (Cambridge, 1952); G. Constable, "The Second Crusade as Seen by Contemporaries," *Traditio*, IX (1953), which reëxamines the western sources with particular reference to the scope of the crusade, the role of the papacy, and the explanations advanced for the failure of the expedition; and E. Willems, "Cîteaux et la seconde croisade," in *Revue d'histoire ecclésiastique*, XLIX (1954), 116–151, where the activities of St. Bernard are explored in some detail.

beforehand — all are facts which show an extension and clarification of concepts present in the First Crusade. This interest in organization and regularization is a sign of the times which had given rise to the orders of the Templars and the Hospitallers in the interval between the two crusades.

For direction the Second Crusade looked to the papacy in the main, although it was not as peculiarly the work of Eugenius as the First Crusade had been of Urban. The pope, of course, formulated the crusade. St. Bernard, with all his personal prestige and eloquence, was his deputy. Louis and the other rulers implemented his plan, while the papal legates exerted considerable weight in the crusading armies. Far more than in the First Crusade, however, lay rulers like Louis of France and Conrad of Germany coöperated in planning and negotiations, and Louis's determination to aid the east did much to make the first stages of the crusade possible.

In scope the Second Crusade was never duplicated in medieval times. Besides the great allied armies that went east for the Palestinian crusade, there were expeditions against the Moors in Portugal and Spain and against the Wends in Pomerania, all in all a grandiose conception far surpassing the aims of the First Crusade and pointing to later adaptations of the crusading idea.

As in the First Crusade, however, the combination of pilgrimage and military expedition proved troublesome. The armies, made unwieldy by many noncombatants, were slow, difficult to provision, and sometimes unruly; while religious goals and military objectives were not always identical. Then, too, the Palestinian expeditions proved to be too predominantly land-based. Fleets from Scandinavia, Genoa, Pisa, southern France, and the Iberian peninsula were engaged in the Wendish and Spanish crusades; while the Sicilians, Venetians, and part of the Byzantine fleet were occupied by a war outside the crusade and extremely detrimental to it. In both the Wendish and Palestinian armies the crusaders displayed little realistic knowledge of the conditions they were to meet. Preparations against the Wends were particularly hasty; but the Jerusalem crusaders, in spite of more thorough and efficient planning, did not understand the situation in the east, which was far more complicated than in 1096–1097. Fifty years after the First Crusade, the Turks were stronger and more unified. The Greeks looked for harm rather than aid from the westerners; and Palestine had changed from a land of opportunity which could be wrested from the Moslems to a loosely knit feudal kingdom as various in interests and alliances as its European prototypes and without the black-and-white view of Moslem-Christian relations entertained in the west. Thus the ill-informed crusaders were often disappointed and embittered by the confusing and contradictory conditions which they encountered; and they failed to unite under strong leadership or to bring their great coalitions to a successful outcome in the east or Pomerania. The conquests of the Second Crusade were Lisbon, Almeria, Tortosa, Lerida, and Fraga, far removed from the Palestinian theater and the central plans for the crusade. In the east the crusaders actually harmed the Latin states when the Moslems learned how easily their armies could be vanquished; and the friction between French and Germans, French and Greeks, Germans and Syrians, and newly-arrived crusaders and inhabitants of Outremer made coöperation on a grand scale impossible for a long time to come.

Like the First Crusade, the Second received its impetus from the east. As early as the summer of 1145 pilgrims and travelers coming home from Jerusalem had spread the sad news of the fall of Edessa in the preceding December, and the Armenian bishops who came shortly afterward to consult pope Eugenius about the possible union of the Roman and Armenian churches must have enlarged the pope's information about affairs in the east. In addition, messengers were sent west to appeal for help. We have no record of any from count Joscelin of Edessa; but Raymond of Antioch, the suzerain of Edessa and the Latin prince whose lands lay next in the path of the Moslems, apparently recognized that his troops and Joscelin's were not sufficient for the reconquest and asked for aid from the Franks or other parts of Europe. The *Chronicle of Morigny* speaks of emissaries from both Antioch and Jerusalem, "begging with supplication that the unconquerable force of the Franks should dispel the danger that had come and drive away future harm;" and Otto of Freising heard bishop Hugh of Jabala, a city in the principality of Antioch, at the papal curia in November 1145, "bewailing in tearful fashion the peril of the church beyond the sea after the capture of Edessa and on account of this wishing to cross the Alps to the king of the Romans and the Franks to stir up aid."

We do not know whether Hugh of Jabala made his journey to France and Germany, but his pleas and those of the Armenian bishops apparently helped to influence Eugenius III to call for a new crusade by issuing the bull *Quantum praedecessores* from Vetralla on December 1, 1145. The pope had been moved by the plight of Edessa. Like Urban, he also hoped that the crusade would further the union of the Christian churches. Although leaning heavily on the example of Urban and other popes, Eugenius's *Quantum praedecessores*, the first crusading bull ever issued, is a virtual charter of the crusade rather than a letter or appeal and as such is of great importance not only to the Second Crusade but to those which followed. Addressing "his dear son Louis, the illustrious and glorious king of the Franks, and his cherished sons the princes and all the faithful living throughout Gaul," Eugenius recalled Urban's summons to the First Crusade, which resulted in the conquest of Jerusalem and other sites in the Holy Land and the retention of those places and additions to their number until the sins of the faithful had brought about the recent capture of Edessa; and he exhorted the Franks and Italians, and especially the powerful nobles among them, to emulate their forefathers and "gird themselves courageously to oppose the multitude of unbelievers which is rejoicing that it has obtained a victory over us, ... to defend the eastern church... to snatch from their hands the many thousands of captives who are our kinsmen." To those vowing to go on the crusade he promised remission of penance, protection of wives, children, and possessions, freedom from legal action from the time of taking the cross until their return or death, cancellation of the obligation to pay interest on debts, and permission to mortgage property in order to gain funds for the journey.[1]

A strange silence concerning *Quantum praedecessores* follows. The next plan for succor of Edessa comes from another quarter — the Christmas court Louis VII of France held at Bourges a few weeks later. There the king "revealed for the first time to the bishops and magnates of the realm, whom he had purposely summoned in greater numbers than usual for his coronation, the secret in his heart" (i. e., his desire to go to the aid of the east) and Godfrey, bishop of Langres, gave an address "concerning the devastation of Edessa, the oppression of the Christians, and the arrogance of the heathen and ... admonished all that together with their king they should fight for the King of all in order to succor the Christians." There is no allusion to the pope nor to a crusade,

[1] On the bull, see Jaffé-Wattenbach, *Regesta pontificum Romanorum*, II, no. 8796. For the text, cf. Otto of Freising, *Gesta*, I, 36; *RHGF*, XV, 429; *MPL*, CLXXX, 1065. Hüffer, "Die Anfänge," and Hefele-Leclerq, *Histoire des conciles*, V, 804–807, summarize the arguments about the date of this much-discussed bull. See also E. Caspar, "Die Kreuzzugsbullen," *passim*; M. Villey, *La Croisade: Essai sur la formation d'une théorie juridique* (Paris, 1942), pp. 106–205; U. Schwerin, *Die Aufrufe der Päpste zur Befreiung des Heiligen Landes* (Ebering, Historische Studien, Berlin, 1937), pp. 74 *ff.*; A. Gottlob, *Kreuzablass und Almosenablass* (Stuttgart, 1906), pp. 91–115; E. Bridrey, *La Condition juridique des croisés et le privilège de la croix* (Paris, 1900), pp. 9–10.

with its inducements of pardon and other privileges for those taking the crusading vow. Instead Odo of Deuil and Otto of Freising seem to describe a desire for a military expedition to aid Edessa as an answer to the pleas from the east, similar in character to the forces raised by Hugh of Payens in 1129 for an attack on Damascus. To this plan the assembly did not respond favorably; and abbot Suger of St. Denis, the senior statesman of the court, openly opposed the king's participation. Finally Louis and his nobles agreed to meet again at Easter and meanwhile to ask the opinion of St. Bernard, "as if he were a divine oracle." This decision, too, suggests that the papal bull had not reached Louis; for if it had, a direct appeal to Eugenius would have been in order.[2]

When consulted St. Bernard refused to make a decision, saying that such an important matter should be referred to the pope; and so an embassy went to Eugenius, and the early months of 1146 were given over to negotiations which can be considered the starting point of the actual organization of the Second Crusade. The pope granted Louis's wish to go to the east by enlisting the young king in the papal crusade. Since he was busy coping with the political situation in Rome, where Arnold of Brescia was fomenting discord against him, Eugenius authorized St. Bernard to preach the crusade in his place. On March 1, 1146, he reissued *Quantum praedecessores* to emphasize his guidance of the movement from its inception.[3]

Despite this marked papal guidance, however, it is well to notice that without the support of Louis VII *Quantum praedecessores*

[2] Odo of Deuil, *De profectione* (tr. Berry), p. 7; Otto of Freising, *Gesta*, I, 34–35. Many motives for going to the Holy Land have been ascribed to Louis: his natural piety, stirred into action by the news about Edessa; the desire to carry out his dead brother Philip's vow to go to Jerusalem; remorse about the burning of Vitry in 1144; expiation for breaking an oath that Peter of La Châtre should not enter the city of Bourges as archbishop; or a combination of all these. See also A. Luchaire in Lavisse, *Histoire de France*, III (Paris, 1901), 12; Cartellieri, *Der Vorrang des Papsttums*, pp. 339–340; Bernhardi, *Konrad III*, pp. 517–518; R. Hirsch, *Studien zur Geschichte Königs Ludwigs VII von Frankreich (1119–1160)* (Leipzig, 1892), pp. 40ff. Otto of Freising, who was a Cistercian, is particularly enthusiastic about St. Bernard. On the bishop of Langres, see H. Wurm, *Gottfried, Bischof von Langres* (Würzburg, 1886). On Suger's attitude, see *Guilelmi vita Sugerii* (ed. A. Lecoy de la Marche, Paris, 1867), p. 394.

[3] Source material concerning the original bull is too scanty to furnish a definitive answer to the problem of dating. See Hefele-Leclerq, *Conciles*, V, pp. 804–807; Hirsch, *Ludwig VII*, pp. 104–105; Vacandard, "Saint Bernard et la seconde croisade," pp. 404ff.; Gleber, *Papst Eugen III*, pp. 39ff. For a criticism of Odo of Deuil and Otto of Freising as sources, and a reconstruction of events, see Hüffer, "Die Anfänge," pp. 399–411, and Bernhardi, *Konrad III*, pp. 515ff. At first St. Bernard struggled against Eugenius's suggestion that he preach the crusade. See *Vita Bernardi*, III (*RHGF*, XIV), 378; Bernard, *De consideratione*, II (*PL* CLXXXII), 741; Otto of Freising, *Gesta*, I, 37. The March version of the bull has been edited by P. Rassow (*Neues Archiv*, XLV [1924]), pp. 302–305. E. Caspar (*ibid.*, pp. 287–296) points out that the only real variations between the versions serve to heighten the prohibitions against luxury in the March version, and he considers Bernard responsible for the change. Conrad ("Gottesfrieden und Heeresverfassung") links the Templar rule with these clauses.

might have come to nothing. No popular response to the bull has been recorded. As we have seen, the French nobles at Bourges, who were most likely to offer aid to the east, were apathetic or opposed to such an expedition when first approached and apparently ignorant of the pope's wishes. Unlike the First Crusade this movement, then, was not entirely the work of the pope. Although Eugenius alone could establish it as a crusade, Louis's initial persistence in desiring to aid the east and Bernard's inspired preaching made the crusade an actuality.

At Vézelay on March 31 Louis met again with his court, fortified by the pope's approval and three months of preparation, which were far more effective than the sudden revelation of his project at Bourges. Since there was no building large enough to contain the crowd, the assembly met in the fields. Wearing the cross sent him by the pope, Louis accompanied St. Bernard onto the platform. The abbot of Clairvaux read the papal bull and delivered an eloquent address. Immediately the audience responded with fervor and cried out for crosses until Bernard had exhausted his supply and had to rip pieces of cloth from his own garments in order to satisfy the demands. Among those who enrolled were Louis's queen, Eleanor of Aquitaine, a niece of Raymond of Antioch; the bishops of Noyon, Langres, and Lisieux; Thierry of Alsace, count of Flanders, a kinsman of the king of Jerusalem; Henry, son of count-palatine Theobald of Blois; Robert count of Perche and Dreux, Louis's brother; count Alfonso Jordan of Toulouse, son of Raymond, who had led an army on the First Crusade; the counts of Nevers, Tonnerre, Bourbon, Soissons, and Ponthieu; William of Warenne, earl of Surrey; barons like Enguerrand of Coucy, Geoffrey of Rancon, Hugh of Lusignan, and William of Courtenay; Everard of Barres, later grand master of the Temple, with a group of Templars; many other nobles and knights and throngs of lesser folk. Recruiting had begun most successfully.[4]

Before leaving Vézelay the leaders decided that they must have a year for preparation before the crusade could depart. Since it was necessary to enter into diplomatic negotiations with the rulers of the countries through which the crusaders might pass on their way to Anatolia, Louis VII wrote to Roger of Sicily, the Byzantine emperor Manuel, Conrad of Germany, and Géza of Hungary describing the plans for the large army of crusaders being recruited and

[4] Odo of Deuil, *De profectione*, p. 8; *Chronicon Mauriniacense* (*RHGF*, XII), p. 88; *Historia Vizeliacensis monasterii* (*ibid.*), p. 319; *Historia gloriosi regis Ludovici VII* (ed. Molinier), pp. 157–159; Otto of Freising, *Gesta*, I, 37.

asking for the privilege of securing food supplies and free passage through their lands. The pope also wrote to Manuel (and most likely to the other rulers involved) announcing the expedition and its purpose. Favorable replies were not slow in coming. Conrad and Géza assented. Roger sent Louis an embassy "which pledged his realm as to food supplies and transportation by water and every other need and promised that he or his son would go along on the journey." These promises were very attractive because they held out the possibility of avoiding the difficult overland route. Furthermore, Roger had been successful in expeditions against the Arabs in North Africa and knew the ways of the Moslems. Yet Roger's great political ambitions made an alliance with him a delicate matter. As pretender to the throne of Antioch he was the enemy of Raymond, queen Eleanor's uncle, who had solicited aid for Edessa, while the expansion of his power in the so-called kingdom of Sicily had alienated his interests from those of Conrad, the pope, and Manuel.

Manuel's reply was a partial answer, more cautious in essence than Roger's. While he indicated willingness to assist the crusaders in preparation of the route, crossing over to Asia Minor, and market privileges, he had detained two Templars from the embassy while he prepared a more detailed answer, "since the matter is great and demands consideration." Recalling the throng of soldiers who came to Constantinople during the First Crusade and the agreements which Alexius had exacted then, Manuel wanted time to draw up the conditions on which he would fulfil Louis's requests. He also held out some hope that he would join in the fight against the Turks, since they had been the aggressors at Edessa. Manuel wrote to Eugenius, too, saying that he would consent to receive the crusaders well, but wanted them to agree to honor him "just as the Franks who formerly came honored my famous grandfather," that is, by taking an oath of homage to him; and he asked Eugenius to strive for this and to write to him again.[5]

In other words, the Greeks, too, wanted to profit from their experiences in the First Crusade and in 1101 and to control the movements of the crusaders while they were in the Byzantine empire. The situation of the Greeks had altered greatly, to the disadvantage of the crusaders. At the time of the First Crusade Alexius had asked for help from the west to start an offensive

[5] Manuel's letter to Louis (*RHGF*, XVI), p. 9; his letter to Eugenius (*ibid.*, XV), pp. 440 to 441; Odo of Deuil, *De profectione*, p. 16.

against the Turks, who had been turned back from Constantinople only recently and still occupied land formerly held by the Byzantine empire. Manuel had made no such appeal. In 1146 the Greeks did not dread the Moslems nor see such a pressing need to regain lost territory, since the First Crusade had helped to reëstablish them in some of their territories in Asia Minor and had created the Latin states which served as buffers between the Greeks and Moslems. Talk of a new crusade revived memories of previous armies from the west and made the Greeks fear that the crusaders would turn their attack against Constantinople as Bohemond had done in 1107. Furthermore, the appeal for the crusade had stemmed in part from Raymond of Antioch and was suspect to Manuel as a device to strengthen Raymond until he would not need Byzantine help and could put the Greek protectorate over northern Syria into question once more. Louis and his advisors apparently did not sense these ramifications. They saw only that Manuel had expressed willingness to help them.

In addition to the negotiations with foreign rulers, undertaken together with the pope, Louis had many domestic matters to look after. He needed to raise money to maintain himself and his followers during the crusade. The pope had authorized the crusaders to cease paying interest on debts and to mortgage their property to gain funds for the journey. The king needed additional resources and apparently employed something like a forced loan or an extension of the feudal aids to collect considerable sums of money before he left. The details and nature of the levy are not clear from the evidence at hand, but it may have foreshadowed the famous Saladin Tithe of the Third Crusade.[6]

While the pope and the king of France were looking after the ways and means of the crusade, Bernard plunged at once into additional recruiting by letter and by word of mouth. Eloquently he pictured the Turkish conquest of Edessa as the prelude to an attack on Jerusalem and the very shrine of the Christian religion unless his hearers worked to prevent it. "What are you brave men doing? What are you servants of the cross doing? Will you thus give a holy place to dogs and pearls to swine?" he demanded. Declaring that God was making a trial of the Christians and giving them an opportunity for salvation in his service, Bernard exhorted his audience to receive the blessed arms of the Christian

[6] Hirsch, *Ludwig VII.*, p. 45; Bridrey, *La Condition juridique des croisés*, pp. 67–69; *De tributo Floriacensibus imposito* (*RHGF*, XII), 94–95; *Epistola Johannis abbatis Ferrariensis* (*RHGF*, XV), 497; *Letter of Peter the Venerable to Louis* (*ibid.*), p. 641.

zealously. Wherever St. Bernard went he excited great reverence because of his impassioned preaching and the many miracles of healing which he performed. Everywhere, too, his preaching and letters were accompanied by the papal bull, with its official appeals and promises. The combination of the pontifical appeal and the inspired preacher was extremely successful. Bernard was soon able to write to Eugenius: "You have commanded and I have obeyed, and the authority of him who gives the command has made my obedience fruitful; whenever I have announced and spoken of the crusade, the crusaders have been multiplied beyond number. Cities and castles are emptied...."[7]

Unfortunately news soon came of uprisings stirred against the Jews by the unauthorized preaching of the crusade in northern France around Sully and Carentan by a Cistercian monk named Radulf.[8] As in the First Crusade it had proved all too easy to heighten the propaganda for fighting the enemies of the Holy Land in Palestine to include the Jews and then to encourage persecution of the Jews close at hand. Anti-Semitic feeling in France was widespread, but St. Bernard set himself against this sentiment and sent a message to northern France asking the inhabitants to follow the teachings of Christ and abstain from persecution. When his letter went unheeded, Bernard set out for northern France and Flanders, intent on preaching the crusade there and utilizing the excitement aroused by Radulf for more orderly preparations. But at the same time he continued to widen the scope of the entire movement by letter, sending one to Manfred of Brescia in midsummer and another soon after to England, where the Flemish enthusiasm for the crusade had spread.[9]

St. Bernard's journey to the north was highly successful. Radulf

[7] *MPL*, CLXXXII, 257. Bernard dictated letters for places he would not be able to visit. For a penetrating discussion of Bernard's crusading letters see Rassow, "Die Kanzlei St. Bernhards," and H. Cosack, "Konrads III Entschluss zum Kreuzzug." Propaganda against the Moslems is not one of Bernard's main themes. He puts more stress on the sinfulness of man and the present opportunity for salvation. For a full discussion of these themes, see Cramer, "Kreuzpredigt und Kreuzzugsgedanke," pp. 49–55, and Constable, "Second Crusade," pp. 247–254.

[8] The chief contemporary account of the persecution from the Jewish point of view is that of Ephraim bar Jakob of Bonn (ed. and tr. M. Stern, *Hebräische Berichte über die Judenverfolgungen während der Kreuzzüge*, Berlin, 1892). Dom Pitra traced St. Bernard's journey (*MPL*, CLXXXV, cols. 1792–1822). Also of interest is G. Hüffer, *Vorstudien zu einer Darstellung des Lebens und Werkens des heiligen Bernard von Clairvaux*, vol. I (Münster, 1886).

[9] Rassow, "Die Kanzlei St. Bernhards," pp. 269–272, includes some interesting sidelights on the relation of the British part of the crusade to St. Bernard. Other material on the British participation is in W. Morris, *Britain and the Holy Land prior to the Third Crusade* (University of Minnesota, 1940, unpublished thesis), and Constable, "Second Crusade," *Traditio*, IX (1953), 261.

fled before him, and countless numbers were enrolled in the crusade. On his return, however, Bernard again received complaints about Radulf, this time from the archbishop of Mainz. Escaping Bernard's orbit, the monk had gone into Germany in August to continue his inflammatory preaching and to arouse the people of Cologne, Mainz, Worms, and Speyer against the Jews. Once more Bernard attempted to quell Radulf by a letter of condemnation to be read in public. When this made little impression the abbot of Clairvaux widened the scope of his enlistment by writing directly to the affected groups in Speyer and Cologne in an effort to incorporate them into an orderly and useful army. Complimenting them on their zeal for the work of God, he called on them to abjure their private wars and the persecutions of the Jews in order to take the cross and participate in the spiritual rewards of the army of Christ. With his customary desire for an orderly expedition, he recalled Peter the Hermit and his ill-fated army as a horrible example and told the Germans not to listen to unauthorized preachers, not to set out before the main army was ready to go, and not to choose leaders unless they were experienced military men who could keep the army strong and well-disciplined.

Letters, however, continued to be less effective than Radulf's fiery harangues. In late October St. Bernard went to Germany to preach the crusade in person and to stop Radulf's activities once and for all. As enrollment in the crusade had spread, St. Bernard's ideas of its scope had widened, too, and while following and encouraging the popular demand he apparently began to hope to unite all Christendom against the Moslems. Hence, after encountering Radulf in Mainz and sending him back to the cloister, Bernard went on to Worms and other cities, arriving at the end of November in Frankfurt, where Conrad III of Germany was holding court. Ostensibly he came to discuss a truce between Albero of Trier and Henry of Namur with a view to their participation in the crusade; but he was also eager to enlist Conrad, since in Bernard's expanding plans the emperor was the logical strong leader for the Germans then being recruited. Conrad refused. Momentarily discouraged, Bernard thought of returning to Clairvaux and the French phase of the crusade, but the bishop of Constance prevailed upon him to preach the crusade to the Swiss, a course approved by the other bishops and by Conrad, who was not hostile to the idea of raising recruits in German territory.[10]

[10] Otto of Freising, *Gesta*, I, 38; *Annales Rodenses* (*MGH, SS.*, XVI), p. 8; Ephraim bar Jakob; *Epistolae Bernardi* (*PL* CLXXXII), 363, 365, 570; J. Greven, "Die Kölnfahrt

Accordingly, St. Bernard set out on still another journey for the crusade. Although he had to speak through an interpreter, people flocked to hear him wherever he went, eager to witness the miracles which he performed and to join the crusade he advocated. While in Constance he was near the south German seat of the Welfs and apparently made his influence felt in the Welf circle through the medium of count Conrad of Zähringen. Fresh from these new achievements Bernard returned to Speyer on December 24 and after several days succeeded in gaining Conrad's promise that he would consult his nobles about the advisability of his going on crusade. Bernard saw that Conrad showed signs of weakening. At the daily mass held for the court the abbot unexpectedly insisted on preaching a sermon and directed his closing remarks to Conrad, not as a king but as a man. Dramatically he pictured Conrad standing before Christ to be judged and Christ saying, "O man, what is there that I should have done for you and did not do?" During the enumeration of kingship, wealth, wisdom, active courage, and bodily strength which Conrad possessed, the emperor cried out in acknowledgment of the divine gifts which he had received and in revulsion from his own ingratitude, "I am ready to serve Him." Those present also called out in witness of the glory of God, and Bernard received Conrad as a crusader and gave him the banner from the altar for his use in the army of God. Frederick of Swabia, Conrad's nephew, and countless others of all ranks enrolled in the army.[11]

Bernhards von Clairvaux," *Annalen des historischen Vereins für den Niederrhein*, CXX (1952), 44–46. Bernhardi, *Konrad III*, pp. 532–533, indicates Conrad's valid reasons for not wanting to go on the crusade. Affairs in Poland needed attention. In Italy the emperor's coronation, the conflict between the pope and the Romans, and relations with Roger of Sicily were especially pressing. Even in Germany Conrad's place was not secure since Welf of Bavaria and Henry of Saxony were hostile.

Cosack, "Konrads III Entschluss zum Kreuzzug," pp. 283–288, believes that Conrad and Bernard agreed to meet again at the Christmas court at Speyer, and that Conrad may have made his participation in the crusade conditional on Welf's joining. It seems more likely, however, as Vacandard, "Saint Bernard et la seconde croisade," p. 425, suggests, that Bernard went to Speyer to see whether his appeal had borne fruit and whether these additional crusaders might help him to enlist the emperor.

[11] J. Greven, "Die Kölnfahrt Bernhards von Clairvaux," p. 3, gives the itinerary in Switzerland and literature on this subject. See also *Vita Bernardi*, vi (*RHGF*, XIV), p. 378; Otto of Freising, *Gesta*, I, 40. Cosack, *op. cit.*, pp. 285–289, explains Conrad's act as hinging upon Welf's becoming a crusader on December 24 at Peiting, following Bernard's journey in that neighborhood, with news of this act coming to St. Bernard on the morning of the 27th and communicated to Conrad by Bernard during their private meeting. This has not been accepted by A. L. Poole, "Germany, 1125–1152," *Cambridge Medieval History*, V, 353, or by A. Cartellieri, *Der Vorrang des Papsttums*, p. 347. (Cosack has succeeded, however, in showing the steps which led to Conrad's joining and has demonstrated that the turning point was not as abrupt as first appears in the *Vita*, but was probably caused by a mixture of motives, including religious ones, and the desire not to harm royal prestige by staying outside the great and strong current which the Second Crusade had now become.)

When Conrad took the cross Bernard felt that his dearest wish concerning the preaching of the crusade had been accomplished. He called it "the miracle of miracles". Certainly it was a turning point; the crusade was no longer a French expedition under Louis, with auxiliary forces from Italy, Britain, and other parts of the west, but a joint movement on the part of the two mightiest sovereigns of Europe. In magnitude it had far surpassed the original request for aid and the plans which Eugenius and Louis had formed. St. Bernard had inspired such enthusiasm as had not been felt since the First Crusade and had raised it to such a pitch that it seemed as if most of Europe would be affected; but he had also enlisted two princes whose royal rank and conflicting diplomatic interests were to weaken the papal dream of strong leadership.

Eugenius did not share St. Bernard's extreme enthusiasm for Conrad's decision. He apparently had not thought that the emperor would go to the east and had hoped that Conrad would soon help to establish him in Rome. The news overtook him in northern Italy, where he was preaching the crusade before going to France to participate in the final plans before the crusaders departed. For nearly two months he delayed answering Conrad and concentrated on the Italian aspects of the crusade, which also had expanded and taken a different turn. Recruiting for the Palestinian crusade had been relatively slow there, even though Eugenius had sent a special bull in the previous October exhorting the clergy to recruit their parishioners. The colonies in Syria and Palestine seemed to have lost some of their importance to commercial cities like Genoa and Pisa, partly because the second generation of crusaders showed much less friendliness to them than the first generation had done and partly because of similar opportunities closer home. Hence interest had shifted to another sector of the battle against the Moslems: Spain and North Africa.

Sometime after the launching of the crusade at Vézelay, however, Eugenius had received and granted a request from Alfonso VII, king of Castile, for an extension of the crusaders' indulgence to Spaniards undertaking a campaign against the Moslems in their part of the world. In so doing the pope had followed the example of his predecessors. When the First Crusade began to draw knights from the "holy war" in Spain, Urban had pressed them not to abandon their enterprise at home, since it was as meritorious as the Palestinian crusade, by promising them indulgences and participation in life eternal; and Paschal II, a former legate in Spain, wrote in 1101 a letter to Castile, saying, "Do not abandon the war against the Moors to go to the east; go back home, and in combat there you will accomplish your penance." Thus Spain became the first country in Europe to keep knights at home to combat the Moslem instead of joining the great crusades to the east.

In 1146–1147 the Spaniards were not the only ones involved in this new development of the Second Crusade. The pope permitted the Genoese to join the campaign in Spain, and forces from the sea-faring towns of southern France were also to make up part of the expedition. During the early part of 1147 the pope worked to establish peace in Tuscany, so that the crusaders could rely on the support of the Pisan fleet. By no means all his efforts, however, were directed towards the Spanish phase of the crusade. Most outstanding of those whom Eugenius enrolled in the Palestinian crusade at this time was count Amadeo III of Savoy and Maurienne, who was to be the leader of the Lombard pilgrims.[12]

At last the pope wrote to Conrad reproaching him for undertaking such a great project as the crusade without papal advice and warned and exhorted him to make careful plans for the regulation of his realm during the crusade. He must have pointed out Conrad's unstable position in Germany and Italy and expressed the fear that a long absence during his son's minority would weaken that position still further; but Cosack's theory that

[12] For convenience in this section the armies are called "German," "French," and "Spanish," although they were composed of forces from various countries. Information about the Spanish phase of the crusade is particularly scanty. Eugenius's bull against the Wends and his letter to Alfonso of Castile in April 1148 mention it (Jaffé-Wattenbach, *Regesta*, nos. 9017, 1255). A letter from St. Bernard to the Spanish on the subject of the crusade, *Ad peregrinantes Jerusalem*, is said to exist in the Archives of the Crown of Aragon in Barcelona and should be informative when made available. Other sources are Caffaro, *Annales Ianuenses*, *Historia captionis Almarie et Turtuose*, *Liber iurium*, I, and *Cronica Adephonsi imperatoris*. G. Constable, "The Second Crusade," pp. 227 ff., has treated the topic more thoroughly than has been done before and has collected a bibliography. See also Villey, *La Croisade*, pp. 196–198; M. Defourneaux, *Les Français en Espagne aux XIe et XIIe siècles* (Paris, 1949); H. Krueger, "Post-war Collapse and Rehabilitation in Genoa (1149–1152)," *Studi in Honore di Gino Luzzatto*, vol. I (Milan, 1949), 117–128; O. Langer, *Politische Geschichte Genuas und Pisas im XII. Jahrhundert* (Leipzig, 1882).

It seems unlikely that a grant of indulgence was extended to Portugal. As C. Erdmann points out, "Der Kreuzzugsgedanke in Portugal," *Hist. Zeitschr.*, CXLI (1930), pp. 23–53, the known crusading action of the popes in the first third of the twelfth century concerned only the eastern part of the Iberian peninsula, and the Portuguese, unlike the Spanish, do not seem to have thought in terms of an official crusade. There is only one unconfirmed mention of Eugenius's giving indulgences to Portugal. On the contrary, the bishop of Oporto in speaking to the Lisbon crusaders did not offer such an inducement, but spoke of the importance of living rightly on the way to Jerusalem as a motive for besieging the Moors at Lisbon.

On the Savoy pilgrims, see C. W. Previté-Orton, *The House of Savoy* (Cambridge, 1912), p. 309. Carutti, *Regesta comitum Sabaudiae* (Bibliotheca Storica Italiana, V, Turin, 1889), p. 107, gives a list of knights thought to have accompanied Amadeo on the crusade although its accuracy has sometimes been questioned. See also Constable, *op. cit.*, p. 216.

the pope urged Conrad to set aside his crusading oath does not seem tenable.[13]

In the same period St. Bernard was spurred on to even greater activity as the time for the departure of the crusading armies drew near. Instead of going directly from Speyer to France he went via Cologne, preaching the crusade along the lower Rhine. On February 2 he arrived at Châlons-sur-Marne, where Louis VII was conducting interviews with French and German nobles and messengers from Conrad and Welf. For two days they discussed the conduct of the crusade. It was a time for pooling information, drafting final arrangements, and altering the general plan of the crusade to accommodate the participation of Conrad and others recruited during Bernard's absence in Germany and Switzerland. One of the main problems discussed must have been the route or routes which the armies would follow. Since Conrad and Roger of Sicily were enemies, the German army never considered going to the east via Sicily, and so had already decided on the land route through Hungary and the Balkan peninsula. Now the French and their allies had to decide whether to follow the same plan or to strike out independently. It was necessary also to consider the business to be introduced at the general meeting to be held at Étampes in two weeks, the choice of regents for the realm, and a change in the date of departure so that the French and German armies would not overlap during the journey and overtax the provisions and other facilities available. Conrad's messengers must have received information as to the present state of affairs and an indication of what remained to be done in the next few months.

The large general meeting of the French crusaders and magnates took place at Étampes on February 16, 1147. They heard St. Bernard's report on the splendid progress of enrollment in the crusade and then turned their attention to the letters and envoys from different countries involved in the expedition or from those guaranteeing passage and markets for the crusaders. Next they chose the route which Louis's army would follow. There can be no doubt that the debate was long and heated. Among the French there was a party, including Godfrey of Langres, with strong sympathy for Roger of Sicily and a distrust of the Greeks which had been fostered either by experience in the east or by reading prejudicial accounts of the First Crusade and the period since then. To them the sea route seemed far preferable; but Conrad's example and the tradition of Godfrey of Bouillon's army carried the day. At

[13] Cosack, "Konrads III Entschluss zum Kreuzzug," pp. 290 ff.

this the disappointed Sicilian envoys departed with dire predictions about the future, and there was no further talk of Roger or his son participating in the crusade. Finally the assembly chose Suger and count William of Nevers as regents during the king's absence and decided to postpone their departure from Easter to June 15.[14]

After Étampes St. Bernard had to attend another important meeting, the great assembly at Frankfurt on March 13. Busy with affairs at Châlons and Étampes, he had not been able to attend the court Conrad had held at Regensburg a month earlier and hence had entrusted the preaching of the crusade there to the Cistercian abbot, Adam of Ebrach. After reading the papal bull and Bernard's letter to the East Franks and Bavarians, Adam had signed a multitude of crusaders ranging in rank from Conrad's half-brother, bishop Otto of Freising, to a vast crowd of robbers who had repented of their sins. Despite the huge numbers already enlisted further efforts were still being made. To bishop Henry of Olmütz, who took the cross at that time, were probably entrusted a copy of the papal bull and Bernard's recruiting letter addressed to Vladislav of Poland, couched in the usual terms and pointing out that a large army of the Lord which was going to set out at Easter planned to pass through Hungary.

As at Étampes the assembly at Frankfurt had much business to settle. The pope's exhortations for the security of the realm and whatever advice he offered may have had some influence on Conrad when he received them during the diet. Certainly he, too, wanted to leave the empire in as strong a position as possible. Peace was ordained and confirmed mutually through all the empire, and Conrad's ten-year-old son was elected and acclaimed king and successor to his father, with the archbishop of Mainz as his guardian and regent and Wibald of Stavelot (later of Corvey) as another guardian. Messengers from Louis were present to preserve the rapport between the two kings. The route through Hungary was announced. Also the German crusaders set mid-May as the date of their departure, so that they could precede the

[14] Suger did not wish to accept the regency "because he considered it a burden rather than an honor," and did so only in obedience to the pope. Cf. *Vita Sugerii*, pp. 393–394; *Breve chronicon sancti Dionysii* (*RHGF*, XII), pp. 215–216. The count of Nevers had already vowed to become a Carthusian and could not be dissuaded from entering the monastery (*Origo et historia brevis Nivernensium comitum*, in *RHGF*, XII, p. 316; *Historia Vizeliacensis monasterii*, *ibid.*, pp. 318–319). Samson, archbishop of Rheims, and Raoul I, count of Vermandois and Valois, were later associated with Suger in the regency. See Odo, *De profectione*, pp. 14, 20; A. Luchaire, *Études sur les actes de Louis VII* (Paris, 1885), especially pp. 170–176. O. Cartellieri, *Abt Suger von St. Denis* (Berlin, 1898), examines the regency very thoroughly.

French army by several weeks on the overland march and join forces only at Constantinople.

Once again events took an entirely new turn. A portion of the crusaders, composed mainly of Saxons, declared that they wanted to go on crusade against their pagan Slavic neighbors east of the Elbe rather than against the Moslems in Palestine. The circumstances of the movement are not at all clear, but it appears to have been of popular origin (though not from the actual border country) and to have been countenanced by St. Bernard as analogous to the Spanish part of the crusade which had already been authorized by the pope.[15] A special sign, the cross on the orb, was selected for this Wendish crusade and the feast of Saints Peter and Paul indicated as the date for the participants to set out from Magdeburg. Many joined at once.

Conrad's envoys to Eugenius, the bishops of Worms and Havelberg and abbot Wibald, left the diet to meet the pope at Dijon on March 30 and probably acquainted the pontiff with the situation. Those conversations and a meeting with St. Bernard at Clairvaux a week later apparently satisfied the pope in regard to the Wendish crusade. His bull *Divini dispensatione*, issued on April 13, established the expedition as a crusade coexisting with the Palestinian and Spanish ones. He granted the crusaders' indulgence to participants if they had not enrolled in the Jerusalem crusade previously, if they retained their devout purpose throughout, and if they did not allow the Wends to buy their freedom from conversion. Conversion or destruction was to be the watchword. As papal legate he designated Anselm of Havelberg, one of the messengers whom Conrad had sent from Frankfurt.

Although friendly relations now existed between him and Conrad, Eugenius did not go to Strassburg to confer on German matters. Instead he went to Paris with Louis and helped to convince Suger that he should overcome his reluctance to act as regent of the kingdom, then celebrated Easter at St. Denis, and took part in much of the business relating to the final arrangements for the crusade. At this time the pope received a second

[15] St. Bernard's role in regard to the Wendish crusade is puzzling. His letter, no. 457 (*PL* CLXXXII, 651) and Otto, *Gesta*, I, 42, seem to show him authorizing the movement as part of the papal crusade at once and without recourse to Eugenius. Such an action is unlike Bernard's constant assertion that he acted at the command of the pope, and is unorthodox because the pope alone could create a crusade with its special privileges. Perhaps Bernard yielded to pressure in the belief that Eugenius's willingness to modify his plans to include the Spanish crusade augured well for the authorization of the Wendish crusade, which would similarly utilize popular enthusiam and enlarge the Christian orbit. Cf., however, Constable, "The Second Crusade," pp. 256–257.

letter and embassy from Manuel, embodying the emperor's considered conclusions concerning the passage of the French army through his realm. He indicated that the routes and supplies requested had been readied for the French, but that Louis and his magnates for their part would have to guarantee not to harm the Byzantine empire in any way during their passage and would have to promise to return to the Byzantines any cities captured from the Turks which had originally belonged to the empire. This latter provision was further defined by a list of cities involved, which had been sent along with the messengers. Manuel asked the pope for coöperation in inducing Louis to agree to these provisions. To show his assent Eugenius was to send a cardinal with the French army and some other sign which would be unmistakable to the French, and by these means to restrain irresponsible members of the army from harming Byzantine territory. Finally Manuel asked for more news from the pope and touched on the attractive possibility of union between the papacy and the eastern church.[16]

Eugenius did appoint cardinals as legates to accompany the two main armies to Palestine. They were probably chosen before Manuel's letter arrived; Eugenius had already designated a legate for the Wendish crusade in April and would not have neglected the opportunity of doing likewise for the longer established Palestinian expeditions. He chose two of the most illustrious members of his curia as his representatives: Theodwin, cardinal-bishop of Porto, to accompany the Germans, and Guido of Florence, the cardinal-priest of San Chrysogono, to go with the French. Eugenius envisaged their powers on a grand scale; they were to keep the sovereigns in peace and amity and to provide for their well-being in both spiritual and temporal matters. Without doubt the cardinal Guido was told of the pope's correspondence with Manuel and urged to preserve the peace between the Greeks and the westerners. In addition the pope later named bishop Henry of Olmütz as a special legate to aid and advise the cardinals and to work particularly for the union of the churches. This proved impossible, however, because the bishop had decided to join the Wendish crusade instead. Even so the crusading army was rich in ecclesiastics of official position, since Arnulf of Lisieux and Godfrey of Langres claimed legatine authority over the Anglo-Norman and French contingents respectively. Although their position was nominally subordinate to that of the cardinal legates, the two bishops,

[16] Text in W. Ohnsorge, "Ein Beitrag zur Geschichte Manuels I von Byzanz," *Festschrift für Albert Brackmann* (ed. L. Santifaller, Weimar, 1931), pp. 391–393.

who were very unlike in temperament and sympathies, were more suited to dissipate the unity of the legatine authority than to augment it.[17]

Almost all Europe was now engaged in last-minute preparations for the crusade. In France and Germany crusaders from all parts of the west had been gathering since February and March. The Castilian king and his allies were preparing to attack the Moslem town of Almeria. Recruiting for the expedition against the Wends continued; both Bernard's letter and the papal bull were sent to Moravia, and the papal legate Hubald carried the bull to Denmark, with the result that the Danes who might have taken an active part in the eastern crusade found this an easy and accessible way to accomplish their vows and expiate their crimes.[18]

On April 27 the first party of crusaders had begun their journey. Men from Flanders, Frisia, Normandy, and Cologne set out for England, where they were joined by Scottish and English crusaders. In general these were sea-faring men, accustomed to dealing with other lands in their voyages. No princely leader directed the expedition; but before they left Dartmouth on May 19, they had set up a very strict code of behavior, which has been recorded by the author of *De expugnatione Lyxbonensi* as follows: "Among these people of so many different tongues the firmest guarantees of peace and friendship were taken; and furthermore, they sanctioned very strict laws, as, for example, a life for a life and a tooth for a tooth. They forbade all display of costly garments. Also they ordained that women should not go out in public; that the peace must be kept by all, unless they should suffer injuries recognized by the proclamation; that weekly chapters should be held by the laity and the clergy separately unless some great emergency should require their meeting together; that each ship should have its own priest and keep the same observances as are prescribed for parishes; that no one retain the seaman or the servant of another in his employ; that everyone make weekly confession and communicate on Sunday; and so on through the rest of the obligatory articles with separate sanctions for each. Furthermore they constituted for every thousand of the forces two elected members who were to be called judges or *coniurati*, through whom the cases of the constables were to be settled in accordance with

[17] Eugenius's letters to bishop Henry of Moravia in A. Boczek, *Codex dipl. et epist. Moraviae* (Olmütz, 1836), p. 257, no. CCLXXVI, and p. 258, no. CCLXXVII; *Letters of Arnulf of Lisieux* (ed. F. Barlow, London, 1939), pp. xxv–xxvi; *Historia pontificalis*, p. 24.

[18] P. Riant, *Expéditions et pèlerinages des Scandinaves en terre sainte au temps des croisades* (Paris, 1865), p. 225.

the proclamation and by whom the distribution of moneys was to be carried out."[19]

After suffering stormy weather in the first part of the voyage they proceeded along the north coasts of Spain and Portugal and arrived at Oporto on June 16. There they were met by the bishop of the city, who explained that his sovereign, Alfonso I of Portugal, was warring against the Moors and had succeeded in capturing the city of Santarem three months before; and that when he had heard that the crusaders were coming by sea he went further south to besiege Lisbon, leaving the bishop of Oporto to welcome the crusaders and to induce them to help in the siege. Reaction to this proposal was mixed. Since the struggle against the Saracens in Portugal was not part of the crusade on which they were bound, some thought that they should not interrupt their journey to the Holy Land for this enterprise; but since they would be combating the Moors at Lisbon, too, and would also replenish their coffers with booty and ransom, they finally decided to go to Lisbon and negotiate with the king. There they agreed to take part in Alfonso's plans, with the understanding that they would have the right of plundering and that the plundered city would then belong to the king. Operations began July 1; and shortly afterwards the attacking army gained control of the suburbs outside the city and set up the siege. The crusaders suffered several setbacks when the Moslems destroyed their siege machinery, but the city had great difficulty in gaining supplies and was not able to secure aid from neighboring Moorish chiefs. At last the walls were breached, and on October 24, 1147, the city capitulated. The crusaders realized their hope of rich booty; then Alfonso occupied Lisbon and the neighboring castles of Cintra and Palmela. An Englishman, Gilbert of Hastings, was made bishop and some others of the men decided to remain as settlers. Most of those on the expedition, however, were to spend the winter only and to leave for the east on February 1. With the conquest of Lisbon they had already at-

[19] *De expugnatione Lyxbonensi* (ed. C. W. David), p. 57. The other armies also adopted codes which have not been recorded in such detail, but were probably similar in many respects and may have been influenced by canon law and the ideas of the pope and of St. Bernard. The *De expugnatione* is the chief source of information for this part of the crusade. The editor gives full information about other editions. Other sources are: *Annales Magdeburgenses* (*MGH, SS.*, XVI), p. 189; Duodechin's letter in *Annales Sancti Disibodi*, 1147 (*MGH, SS.*, XVII), pp. 27ff.; Arnulf (*RHGF*, XIV), p. 325. See also U. Cosack, *Die Eroberung von Lissabon* (Halle, 1875); F. Kurth, "Der Anteil niederdeutscher Kreuzfahrer an den Kämpfen der Portugiesen gegen die Mauren," *Mittheilungen des Instituts für österreichische Geschichtskunde*, Ergänzungsband, VIII (1911), 131–159; G. Constable, "The Second Crusade," pp. 221–222, and "The Route of the Anglo-Flemish Crusaders," *Speculum*, XXVIII (1953), 525–526.

tained the high point of their expedition and had made one of the few territorial acquisitions of the Second Crusade.

By a coincidence the Spanish crusaders, who were entirely separate from the Portuguese in their efforts against the Moslems, succeeded in capturing Almeria on October 17, just a week before Lisbon fell. In this enterprise the Genoese took the main initiative. Alfonso of Castile and Raymond Berengar of Aragon-Catalonia directed soldiers from Christian Spain, and boats and troops from the ports of Languedoc fought under the leadership of count William of Montpellier. At the end of the following year Raymond Berengar, William of Montpellier, the Genoese, Narbonnese, and Béarnaise went on to capture Tortosa; and in 1149 they consolidated this victory by gaining possession of Fraga and Lerida, the last remnants of Moslem domination in Catalonia.[20]

In the middle of May, while the Lisbon crusaders were getting under way, Conrad of Germany began his journey to the east as the commander of a far more heterogeneous army, composed mainly of Franconians, Bavarians, and Swabians in such great numbers that the rivers and surrounding countryside could hardly accomodate them. The German crusaders ranged from bishops, princes, and magnates advancing with fully equipped troops to include at the other extreme not only those with no equipment or money and no realization of the implication of the long, hard journey, but also the robbers and other criminals whose enlistment had been hailed as a special sign of divine grace. Problems of discipline, maintenance, and provisioning must have been inherent in such a huge and loosely-knit group from the beginning; but they were not yet critical.[21]

The German crusaders went from Nuremberg to Regensburg. There the emperor paused to negotiate a truce with king Géza of Hungary, who had defeated the Germans at the battle of Leitha the year before and who now feared that Conrad and his army might retaliate and succeed in placing the pretender Boris on the Hungarian throne. During the last week in May the crusaders went to Ardagger and thence to Vienna where more crusaders, including Ottokar of Styria, joined the army, and negotiations with Géza were continued. The Hungarian king finally agreed to allow

[20] See *Ex gestis comitum Barcinonensium* (*RHGF*, XII), pp. 376–377; Caffaro, *Annales*, pp. 33–36, and *Historia captionis Almarie*, pp. 409–423; *Cronica Adephonsi imperatoris*, pp. 399–409; *Liber iurium*, I, cols. 118–132; Defourneaux, *Les Français*, pp. 175–178; Constable, "The Second Crusade," pp. 226–234.

[21] Otto, *Gesta*, I, 46; Gerhoh, ch. 67; *Annales Rodenses* (*MGH, SS.*, XVI), 44; Bernhardi, *Konrad III*, pp. 596ff.

the huge army to pass through his realm and to pay Conrad a large sum of money levied from the Hungarian church in order to guarantee that the passage of the army would be peaceful. Soon after the middle of June the crusaders crossed the border and entered Hungary in martial array, as if it were an enemy land; they managed to observe the terms of the truce, however, and without untoward incident arrived around July 20 at Branits on the Bulgarian border, where the ancient road to Constantinople begins. Apparently a few Hungarian crusaders had joined the army during its transit.[22]

The emperor Manuel had been alarmed by the news of Conrad's participation in the crusade and had apparently thought that it might indicate a shift away from the German-Byzantine alliance against Roger to a concentration of the forces of western Europe against Constantinople. He had therefore taken the precaution of strengthening the fortifications of Constantinople and equipping and readying his home troops, some of whom were detailed to remain in the city and others to follow the Germans in order to insure that they should pass through the Byzantine realm peacefully. In addition he sought to maintain diplomatic relations with the leaders of the crusading armies. Here at the entrance to Byzantine territory two Greek messengers came to Conrad bringing greetings from Manuel and seeking to ascertain the German emperor's intentions. They said that the Germans could not traverse the Byzantine empire unless they swore not to injure the emperor's interests in any way; whereupon the chief nobles in the army swore that they had not entered Byzantine territory to injure the Greeks, but were going to fight the Turks in Anatolia. Satisfied with this assurance, the ambassadors promised to furnish provisions during the passage of the army. The crusaders then took the highway along the Morava to Nish and Sofia, which led through difficult mountainous terrain. At both cities they were treated well and received ample provisions; and the Greeks had no serious complaint to make against the Germans. When they reached the richer land around Philippopolis, however, relations became more strained. There were instances of plundering, of rough treatment of the people bringing provisions to the camp, and even of armed conflict between the rear guard and the natives. Conrad

[22] *Marci Chronicon* (ed. Fr. Toldy, Budapest, 1867), xcvi–xcvii; J. Hannenheim, *Ungarn unter Bela II und Geisa II in seinen Beziehungen zu Deutschland* (Hermannstadt, 1884); F. Ludwig, *Untersuchungen über die Reise und Marschgeschwindigkeit im 12. und 13. Jahrhundert* (Berlin, 1897); C. Jireček, *Die Heerstrasse von Belgrad nach Constantinopel* (Prague, 1877).

appeared neither willing nor able to enforce discipline in these matters, a circumstance not entirely surprising when one remembers the miscellaneous character of his army and the long march which it had already accomplished without any major incidents like the fighting around Belgrade in the First Crusade. A Byzantine force under general Prosouch, however, followed the Germans at a little distance, quashing the inroads of stragglers and, when the raiders were unusually fierce, coming into more open conflict for a short time near Philippopolis.

Sometimes, as at Adrianople, Greek elements were guilty of breaking the peace. Perhaps because of his experience of disorders around Philippopolis, Conrad did not stop at Adrianople, but led his army on beyond. Unfortunately, a relative who remained in the city because of illness was killed by Greek marauders and the inn where he was lodging burned and looted. The emperor's nephew, Frederick (later Frederick I), returned to avenge the incident by burning a monastery in which the sick man had lodged, capturing and killing some men, and searching for the lost money. Open warfare seemed sure to result, but Prosouch and others managed to make peace.

Aware of the tension between the crusaders and his people and still fearful for the safety of his capital, Manuel asked Conrad to cross the Dardanelles at Sestus rather than the Bosporus at Constantinople. To this route, which was actually more direct and favorable than the one he chose, Conrad would not agree, perhaps because he did not care to have Manuel dictate his route or because he had agreed to meet Louis at Constantinople or because the armies of the First Crusade had not gone that way. It remained for Frederick I to make use of the route through Sestus during the Third Crusade. Conrad and his army continued according to their original plan, and Manuel went on strengthening his capital and sent additional forces to police the Germans on their journey.

Nature administered the next rebuff to the crusaders. On September 8 the German army encamped in a pleasant meadow called the plain of the Choerobacchi, which was watered by the Melas river. During the night the river became swollen with torrential rains and swept away many men and animals and much equipment in a flash flood. The crusaders were stricken by the thought that this was a sign of divine disapprobation and were full of sorrow when they viewed the wreckage. Again Manuel sent messages, of comfort this time and inviting the German sovereign to a conference. Conrad seems to have refused unless the emperor would come to meet him as he approached the city, and so the negotiations were abandoned.[23]

By September 10 the Germans were before Constantinople. During the rest of the month they remained outside the city, first at the inclosure known as the Philopatium, which is on the land side, and then in the suburb of Pera, from which they crossed the Bosporus. Although the rulers did not meet, and the crusaders were not allowed inside the city, the army took the opportunity to rest from the long march. Some looting and reprisals took place, and there is a tradition that Conrad observed the defenses of the city with interest and threatened to return and invest the city in the following year. Actually negotiations were never broken off entirely, partly perhaps because of the good offices of Manuel's empress, Bertha of Sulzbach, who was Conrad's sister-in-law. The army was furnished with supplies, and Manuel pressed Conrad to cross over into Asia Minor. He also seems to have suggested some interchange of forces, with the idea of giving Conrad the support of some Greek troops in Asia Minor if the German commander would leave part of his army in Constantinople for Manuel's use.

At that time Roger of Sicily, who had been their common enemy for a long time, was attacking the Byzantine empire. After Roger withdrew from the crusade at Étampes, he decided that the time was propitious for him to attack the Byzantine empire and establish himself more firmly in southern Italy, since Conrad and Manuel were both occupied. He alleged that Manuel had insulted him by refusing to allow his son to marry Manuel's daughter. Corfu and Cephalonia fell to Roger; and he plundered Corinth, Thebes, Euboea, and possibly Athens. Manuel had to call in the Venetians as allies and probably would have used the German reinforcements, too, against Roger or a possible coalition between Roger and the French. Conrad would not agree with this plan, but finally decided to go on to Asia Minor without waiting for Louis. When he crossed at the end of September, he and his army received gifts from Manuel. At the same time the Lorrainers, who had preceded the main part of the French army, were forced to cross, too, and they waited for their comrades on the shore of Asia Minor. But Conrad had had enough of waiting. He and his army pressed on, eager to arrive before Edessa and begin the conflict.[24]

[23] Cinnamus, *Epitome*, II, 12–14; Nicetas, *Historia*, I, 4–5; Otto, *Gesta*, I, 47; Odo, *De profectione*, pp. 43–47.

[24] Otto, *Gesta*, I, 34. Bernhardi, *Konrad III*, pp. 616ff., discusses the relations of the two sovereigns at Constantinople very thoroughly. See also Kugler, *Studien zur Geschichte des zweiten Kreuzzuges*, pp. 124ff.; Chalandon, *Les Comnène*, pp. 278–279; W. Cohn, *Das Zeit-*

Metz had been chosen as the assembly point for the French army. The large army gathering there in June included Lotharingian crusaders under Stephen of Metz and Henry of Toul, Thierry of Alsace, count of Flanders, Reginald of Bar, and Hugh of Vaudémont. From northern Italy came the rulers of Savoy and Montferrat. There were contingents from Brittany, Burgundy, central France, and Lorraine, and, of course, Eleanor's men from Poitou and Aquitaine. The large band from Provence, however, did not go at this time. They could afford to wait until August, since they had chosen the sea route which would be less time-consuming. They sailed from the mouth of the Rhone under the aegis of Alfonso Jordan, the count of Toulouse, bearer of the proud crusading name of St. Gilles.[25]

At this time Louis enacted laws necessary for securing peace and maintaining discipline in the army, probably similar to those agreed upon by the Lisbon crusaders; and the leaders of the various parts of the army confirmed these by solemn oath. Also he dispatched the bishop of Arras and the abbot of St. Bertin to Worms to prepare a fleet to take the crusaders across the Rhine at that point. On June 29 Louis and his army arrived in Worms, were honorably received, and crossed the river safely. They encamped on the other side to await the arrival of bishop Arnulf of Lisieux and his Norman and English troops and sent men on to Regensburg to meet the Greek messengers who had been expecting the king for a long time. While here some friction and altercations arose between the crusaders and the citizens of Worms who were looking after the provisions. Prices soared. Because of this and the congestion in the army, the counts of Auvergne and Savoy and the marquis of Montferrat decided to leave the main group and take their troops through the Alps to Apulia and thence across to Constantinople.

At Regensburg the army crossed the Danube on a new bridge and found a fleet prepared to carry their baggage and many of the people as far as Bulgaria. Louis gave audience to the Byzantine ambassadors, who delivered letters from Manuel. Conciliatory in the main and seeking to secure the good will of the crusaders, the letters contained two important stipulations which Manuel had already revealed to the pope but does not seem to have in-

alter der Normannen in Sizilien (Bonn, 1920); E. Caspar, *Roger II* (Innsbruck, 1904); Tafel and Thomas, *Urkunden zur älteren Handels- und Staatsgeschichte der Republik Venedig* (*Fontes rerum Austriacarum*, Venice, 1856–1857).

[25] C. Devic and J. Vaissete, *Histoire générale de Languedoc*, III (Toulouse, 1872), p. 754; *Chronicon Turonense* (*RHGF*, XII), p. 473.

cluded in the German negotiations: namely, that the king should not seize any city or stronghold in Manuel's realm and that if he drove the Turks from any place in Anatolia which had belonged to Byzantium, that place should be restored to Manuel. These stipulations the nobles were to confirm by oath. At once a great discussion arose. The nobles were willing to endorse the first clause but could not agree about the second, even though the messengers resorted to threats, saying that the emperor would destroy the supplies gathered for them if they delayed much longer, since he would consider their hesitation a sign of hostility. Even so the crusaders refused to comply. The presence of an anti-Greek party, including Godfrey of Langres and Louis's brother, Robert of Perche, made itself felt, but at last a compromise was reached. Some of the leaders swore on behalf of the king to guarantee the security of the Greek realm, and the ambassadors confirmed the promise of a sufficient market, suitable exchange, and other necessary privileges. Consideration of the much-debated provision about restoration of conquered lands to the emperor was postponed until Louis and Manuel could meet together. One of the messengers took the news to Constantinople at once; the other accompanied the French army until legates had been selected to go with him to the Byzantine capital ahead of the main army and prepare for the negotiations with Manuel.

The French followed the route of the German army along the Danube to Passau and then to Vienna and the Hungarian border without outstanding incident. They continued to use the bridges which Conrad had built and were well received at the principal cities. In the more mountainous, wooded, and often swampy country of Hungary the going was harder; but as the result of early negotiations between Louis and king Géza the army received ample supplies. The relationship between the two sovereigns was far more amicable than the armed neutrality which Conrad and Géza had observed. They met together, established a common peace, and provided that French pilgrims could pass through Hungary in safety in the future; and Géza presented Louis with horses, vessels, and garments. Relations were impaired, however, when Géza discovered that the pretender Boris had secretly joined the French army, and Louis refused to hand him over because Boris had sought asylum with him. The Hungarian king therefore withdrew to a part of his kingdom which did not lie along the crusaders' route, and the army continued peaceably as far as the Bulgarian border, and there stocked up on provisions, supplied in great part by the Hungarians, before undertaking the passage of the difficult western part of that country.[26]

From the first the French crusaders were not satisfied with the rate of exchange the Greeks offered them, and they had to suffer from the antagonism which the passage of the German army had kindled in the inhabitants. Louis, however, worked to disperse misunderstandings. He was aided by Michael Branas, the duke of Sofia, who had been appointed to accompany him through the Balkan peninsula and who established peace with the inhabitants along the route and helped to procure markets. Louis shared the provisions thus obtained with rich and poor alike in his army, and so it was possible for him to maintain peace more easily than for the commanders of troops who had less prestige and less money to insure the provisioning of their followers and had to resort to plundering when the markets were not sufficient. The drain even on the royal treasury was great; from the edge of Hungary and at many later points Louis had to write urgently to Suger for additional funds to cover his heavy daily expenses.[27]

In addition to the problems of Greek-French relations, there were also some altercations between the advance part of the French army and the rear of the German army as to who should secure supplies at the Greek markets. The French army had traveled at a faster rate than the Germans, who had set out a month earlier, and so the advance party of Lorrainers was in Constantinople by mid-September while Louis, going more slowly, was still in Philippopolis. During the journey across Bulgaria Louis received no news from the ambassadors whom he had sent to Constantinople, but he had many reassuring messages from Manuel and his empress. Again the Greeks urged the crusaders to by-pass Constantinople by taking the road from Adrianople to Sestus, and like Conrad, Louis refused to fall in with this plan.

When a day away from Constantinople, Louis at last met his messengers. They brought the disquieting news that, contrary to their original plan, Conrad had crossed the Bosporus without waiting for the French and that the Lorrainers had been forced to accompany him. In addition some members of the French army who had reached Constantinople in September and refused to cross over had been attacked by Byzantine mercenaries; and they had been rescued from this dilemma only by the intercession of the

[26] Odo, *De profectione*, II, 21–39, is the fullest account. See also *Marci Chronicon*, xcvi to xcvii; Cinnamus, *Epitome*, II, 17.
[27] *RHGF*, XV, 487.

French envoys. To these indications of haste and lack of coöperation on the part of the Germans and coercion on the part of the Greeks was added the news that Manuel had concluded a treaty with the Selchükid sultan of Iconium (Konya). Such an action was not comprehensible to the French. They remembered Manuel's writing to Louis that although the Greeks had been more or less at peace with the Turks, the capture of Edessa broke the peace, and so influenced Manuel to collect an army to go against them. Since then, however, Manuel's attitude had changed. He had been frightened by the great increase in the crusading forces and by the participation of the German emperor; he had become aware of the strong preparations embarked upon by the sultan of Iconium; and he had experienced western hostility in the form of Roger's attacks.

On hearing of the Turkish alliance the anti-Greek party in the army advised the king along the very lines which Manuel feared: to retreat and capture a foothold in the rich and populous countryside through which they had just passed, and then with the aid of Roger and his fleet to attack Constantinople. This advice did not prevail, however; the king and his army followed their original plan and arrived at Constantinople on October 4. Unlike their reception of Conrad the Greeks gave Louis a splendid welcome and conducted him to an audience with Manuel in the imperial palace. There the two sovereigns discussed the crusaders' plans in a friendly fashion, and the emperor promised to give whatever aid he could. Louis and his retinue were housed in the Philopatium, as the Germans had been; but in contrast to his cool treatment of Conrad, Manuel spared no pains in entertaining Louis and conducted him on a tour of the famous shrines of the city, invited him to a fabulous banquet, and sent a group of special clergy to celebrate the feast of St. Denis in Louis's presence. Meanwhile the army camped outside the city, whose gates were closed to all except the king and his retinue. As before, the Greeks furnished an ample market and suitable rates of exchange, but the crusaders did a certain amount of plundering and destruction of property, some of which was held in check by punishments meted out by the king. The fiery bishop of Langres kept urging the French to capture the city before which they stood, pointing out its weaknesses and stirring up hostility by citing the wrongs which John Comnenus, Manuel's father, had done to Antioch and the enmity between Greek and Roman bishops in Asia Minor. This effort to sidetrack the crusade was fruitless as far as an actual change in goal was concerned, but it must have damaged the morale of the army by adding to the already present distrust and hostility towards the Greeks. Unlike the members of the Fourth Crusade who were convinced by similar arguments, the majority of crusaders in 1147, according to Odo, agreed with those who cited the pope's call to the crusade as controlling their plan of action. The papal legate, cardinal Guido of Florence, must have been the one who pointed out that Eugenius had called not for an attack on Constantinople, but for a pilgrimage to the Holy Sepulcher and the destruction or conversion of the Moslems. Thus Manuel's request for help from Eugenius in restraining hotheads in the French army had been granted. Certainly papal policies exerted a greater influence over the course of the crusade after it left western Europe than critics like John of Salisbury have acknowledged. Unfortunately neither cardinal legate was able to dominate the army under his spiritual guidance as Adhémar of Le Puy had, or as St. Bernard could have done, and to carry it forward with a positive plan. Despite their good qualities Theodwin was considered barbarous and crude by the French, and Guido exhibited more interest in books and dialectics than in battles. Their leadership lacked vigor and was further reduced to a monitory position by contrast with more aggressive ecclesiastics like the bishops of Langres and Lisieux and by strong lay interests.

During this critical time Louis was waiting for the lords of Savoy, Auvergne, and Montferrat who had left the main army at Worms and were now coming to Constantinople via Brindisi and Dyrrachium (Durazzo). Manuel was suspicious of the long delay and probably distrusted the new forces, since they were coming by way of the Norman kingdom of Sicily. Therefore he had part of the market removed. Especially effective was the circulation of rumors about the Germans' progress in Asia Minor. They were credited with slaughtering 14,000 Turks, capturing Iconium, and asking Manuel to come and hold the city while they sped ahead to further conquests. These stories caused such discontent in the French army that Louis finally agreed to cross the Bosporus before his allies arrived. Using Greek boats and accompanied by Greek provisioners and money-changers, the army entered Asia Minor.

As yet, after nearly two weeks of proximity, the Byzantine and French sovereigns had not come to any agreement about their relations in Asia Minor. Once he had succeeded in removing the French from their potentially dangerous position before Constantinople, Manuel detained them on the opposite shore with a series of diplomatic exchanges. At last his terms were clear: an alliance between one of Louis's kinswomen and Manuel's nephew and the homage of the barons in return for guides, fair exchange, markets where possible, the right of plunder where markets were not available, and suitable gifts for the king and his barons. At once Robert of Perche and some comrades abducted the French noblewoman who had figured in Manuel's plans and went to Nicomedia without paying homage to the emperor. Again the rest of the anti-Greek party urged bold action, advising Louis to seize Constantinople; but the milder and more expedient counsel which stressed the crusaders' need for guides, supplies, and the friendship of the Byzantines won out once more. In the meantime the long-awaited contingent which had traveled through Italy managed to cross over without the help of the Greeks, who had wished to split the army by detaining them; and the reunited army determined to set out on its march through Asia Minor. Only then did Manuel hold the long-deferred meeting, and he and Louis came to the following agreement: that the king would not take from the emperor any town or stronghold which was under his jurisdiction; that the emperor should send along two or three of his chief barons as guides and should furnish market facilities; that the crusaders should have the rights of plunder where supplies were not offered.

The barons then paid homage to Manuel and received gifts from him. Manuel had also hoped to induce Louis to enter into an alliance against Roger, but he was unsuccessful. This may account in part for his detached attitude towards the French crusaders thereafter. In addition, of course, he was opposed to the establishment of independent Latin principalities in Anatolia and was bound by a treaty of peace with the Moslems. Thus the participants in the Second Crusade did not receive active assistance from the Greeks in any way comparable to that rendered by Alexius during the First Crusade, and this proved a grave handicap during their penetration of Anatolia.[28]

While the Lisbon expedition, the Spanish crusade, and the various armies of the Palestinian crusade were embarking upon their various journeys and campaigns, the Wendish crusade, the latest comer to the scene, was still in a state of preparation.[29]

[28] Odo, *De profectione*, II–IV, 40–82: Cinnamus, *Epitome*, II, 17; *Historia pontificalis*, XXIV, 54–56; Chalandon, *Les Comnène*, pp. 317–323; Kugler, *Studien*, pp. 143–147.

[29] On the Wendish crusade: *Helmoldi presbyteri Bozoviensis cronica Slavorum* (ed. B. Schmeidler, Berlin, 1909); idem (tr. F. J. Tschan, *The Chronicle of the Slavs*), I, 62–66; *Annales Magdeburgenses* (*MGH, SS.*, XVI), p. 188; Vincent of Prague (*MGH, SS.*, XVII),

Apparently the agitation for a crusade against the Slavs had not come as the result of any recent invasion or at the instance of the people living nearest them. By 1147 count Adolf of Holstein had managed to build up his position in connection with the Wends quite successfully. He had brought in German colonists and reëstablished Lübeck, had restored churches like Neumünster, and had won the friendship of Niklot, the Obotrite prince who was the chief leader of the Wends. News of the crusade disrupted these arrangements; although Niklot asked Adolf to remain his ally, it was impossible for the count to oppose the holy war. The pact had to be broken off. Niklot retired to the northeast, establishing a strong fortress, and mustering an army, and on June 26 took the offensive before the crusaders arrived. He sailed into the harbor of Lübeck, burned parts of the city, killed many of the citizens or took them prisoners, and captured much booty. Then he proceeded to lay waste the surrounding country, so that all the recently won advantages were lost.

June 29 had been set as the time for the crusade to leave Magdeburg, but as usual recruits were slow in coming. Finally approximately 40,000 men set off from Artlenburg in the middle of July under the leadership of the duke of Saxony, Conrad of Zähringen, archbishop Adalbero of Bremen, and others. Anxious to punish Niklot, they crossed the lower Elbe and arrived at the Wends' stronghold, Dobin. There the Saxons were joined by a large army and fleet of Danes who had come to retaliate for sea-raids which Niklot had perpetrated. The Wends, however, made a successful foray against the Danes and took many prisoners; and their allies the Rani attacked the fleet and partially destroyed it. In reply the Danes harassed the inhabitants along the coast and rescued much of their fleet. Despite this lively beginning, it early became apparent that the siege was being conducted with mixed feelings. The Saxons apparently thought that it was not to their advantage to devastate a land belonging to them and to harass a people which was becoming more and more dependent on them. Those who had come to seek fiefs found little encouragement; and those who had come in order to fulfil the crusading vow and return home as quickly as possible grew restive. Furthermore the Danes were anxious to regain their men who had been captured. And so a truce and then a peace were concluded on the following terms: Idolatry was to be discontinued; the Danish prisoners were to be

p. 663; *Wibaldi epistolae* (ed. Jaffé), no. 150; Giesebrecht, *Kaiserzeit*, IV, 296–302; Bernhardi, *Konrad III*, pp. 563–578.

released; and Niklot was to become an ally of count Adolf of Holstein again and to pay tribute. The first two conditions were never really carried out. In practice the fanatic vow "to convert or to destroy" had dwindled to a clause which was not enforced; and the prisoners returned were for the most part infirm. The alliance between count Adolf and Niklot was resumed, however, and continued along the lines which had been established before the crusade was announced.

Early in August the papal legate, Anselm of Havelberg, led the main body of crusaders from Magdeburg. Their numbers included bishop Henry of Olmütz, the palgrave Hermann of the Rhine, Frederick of Saxony, Albert the Bear and his two sons, Wibald of Corvey, and many others, totalling perhaps 80,000 men. They planned to attack the tribe of the Liutizi. Crossing the Elbe, they rested at Havelberg and then stormed into enemy country, bringing devastation. The natives fled before them, however; and the crusaders were not able to meet them in hand to hand fighting until part of the army set up a siege before Demmin. Here again the crusaders proved less ruthless in carrying out their vow against the Slavs than one might expect. Discontent broke out in the besieging army; and in early September the crusaders returned home after doing little more than devastate some of the open countryside.

While part of their number had encamped before Demmin the rest had gone to Stettin. This was a singular choice, since Christianity had already been established there; and it was possibly dictated by Albert the Bear's desire to gain more land. Many of the crusaders were amazed when crosses were displayed on the walls and a group of citizens led by bishop Adalbert of Stettin came to treat with the army and to point out that this was not a heathen city and would profit more from preaching than from being put to the sword. On hearing this the bishops in the army entered into negotiations with Ratibor, the Christian prince of the Pomeranians, and with bishop Adalbert; and peace was concluded. From there the crusaders, unsatisfied with the turn of events, went home.

Thus the expedition against the Wends had accomplished little or nothing beyond interrupting for a time the more peaceful relations which were being established between the Saxons and the Slavs. The desire to split off from the Palestinian crusade apparently rose mainly from the application of two familiar crusading motives to local conditions: that of the clerics who wished to extend the influence of the church to the north and that of the lay princes who were eager to augment their domains and eliminate inroads from the Slavs. At the outset each group had endorsed a policy of extermination or conversion of the heathen; but when faced with the sieges of pagan Dobin and Demmin the lay nobles whose interests were involved hesitated to destroy valuable property and potential allies and so carried out their crusading vows as expediently as possible, while at Stettin the crusade was diverted against a Christian city in order to satisfy a desire for territorial expansion and then was brought to a halt when this became clear. The disparity between the ambitions of the crusaders and the actual conditions obtaining among the Slavs and their neighbors was very great. The Wendish crusade thus stands in marked contrast to the more realistic campaigns carried out in Portugal and Spain.

In Europe the crusade, despite the meager accomplishments against the Wends, had made a satisfactory beginning. Crusaders like the conquerors of Lisbon and Almeria had finished their immediate battles successfully and could wait for the spring before setting out again. The armies for the Palestinian crusade, however, were still traveling towards their goal.[30] The French army hastened past Nicomedia and Nicaea, eager to join the Germans and participate in and emulate their conquests. At this sanguine moment when the long journey and wearisome negotiations promised to give way to the accomplishment of their hopes, they learned that the German army had not captured Iconium as the Greeks had reported but had been defeated by the Turks and forced to retreat in disorder towards Nicaea. Conrad had planned to combat the Turks as soon as possible and without waiting for the French. Apparently he had hoped to accomplish this scheme with the support of the military forces in his army while sending the pilgrims to Jerusalem by another route, but this sensible idea caused great dissatisfaction among the crusaders and could not be carried out. A group did leave Conrad's forces and travel south along the coast under the leadership of the emperor's half-brother, the bishop of Freising, but the army was not pared down to a purely military expedition. At Nicaea Conrad gathered provisions for the march

[30] Odo, *De profectione*, V, 88–98; Cinnamus, *Epitome*, II, 16; *Annales Palidenses* (*MGH, SS.*, XVI), p. 82; Nicetas, *Historia*, I, 6; Conrad's letter to Wibald (*Wibaldi epistolae*, no. 78); *Annales Herbipolenses*, ad ann. 1147 (*MGH, SS.*, XVI), pp. 4ff.; William of Tyre, *History*, XVI, 22–23; Gerhoh, *De investigatione*, ch. 58, 69. On the relations between the French and the Germans, see Cinnamus, *Epitome*, II, 18. See also Kugler, *Studien*, p. 164.

on the sultan's capital of Iconium and prepared to follow a short-cut through the mountains which the Greek guides showed them.

The unwieldy army found the mountains very difficult to traverse and went so slowly that they exhausted their supplies before they emerged from the confusing mountainous terrain. Somewhere near Dorylaeum (near modern Eskishehir) they suffered an ambush from the Turks, who had been building up their strength against the crusaders for some time. The German cavalry charged the enemy in vain, because the Moslems feigned flight until they had tired the crusaders and drawn them away from the main army, which sustained terrible losses. After this catastrophe Conrad yielded to the request of the princes and nobles and led the expedition back towards the sea in the hope of renewing its strength and keeping it relatively intact for an engagement when conditions should be more favorable. The retreat was dreadful. Although begun in an orderly fashion, it degenerated into a rout. The hungry crusaders withdrew slowly because of their weariness and their attempts to secure food, and the Turks became more daring day by day in harassing them and finally succeeded in killing count Bernard of Plötzkau and his men who had been protecting the rear of the army. Then they molested all parts of the column at will. Fatalities and injuries were numerous, and Conrad was wounded. When the army finally reached Nicaea at the beginning of November it broke up. Most of its members tried to return home via Constantinople, a terrible undertaking for them with their reduced or vanished strength and equipment. Conrad and a nucleus of his barons sent messengers to tell Louis of the disaster and to ask him to meet the emperor and be ready to aid and counsel him in his time of need.

The French army was grieved and stupefied by this turn of events. Cries against the treachery of the Greeks broke forth, but it is worth noting that Conrad in his letters to Wibald of Corvey did not mention this factor in his account of the disaster, even though he could have shifted responsibility from himself in this way. Instead, the Germans tended to blame themselves for an over-bold reliance on their own strength and for the offense which their sins had given God. Odo records what must have been the comment of the military party of both armies: "When the holy father forbade dogs and falcons and restricted the nature of knights' clothing and arms, men who did not concur with this command acted with a lack of wisdom and utility which equaled the presence of wisdom and utility in his command. But would that he had instructed the infantry in the same way and, keeping the weak at home, had equipped all the strong with the sword instead of the wallet and the bow instead of the staff; for the weak and helpless are always a burden to their comrades and a source of prey to their enemies." The vast number of pilgrims on the crusade was proving a hazard to the military aims.

Louis and his nobles offered Conrad money and equipment and agreed to wait at Lopadium until Conrad could collect more supplies before continuing the journey. Markets became scarcer in the interim, and the French resorted to plundering the countryside, as their agreement with Manuel permitted. To this the enraged inhabitants responded by molesting and sometimes killing members of the weakened German forces who followed after and finally had to be conducted to the rendezvous at Lopadium by a French escort.

In the council held at this time Conrad expressed a desire to continue the crusade in Louis's company and asked to be stationed in the middle of the army, since he and his forces were not strong enough to guard the front or rear. At his request for additional troops Louis designated Amadeo of Savoy, the marquis of Montferrat, the bishop of Metz, the count of Bar, and others as additions to the emperor's forces. In this order they arrived at Esseron (near Balîkesir) sometime after November 11. Louis had originally planned to travel to Antioch through Philadelphia (Alashehir) on a good road which was less direct than the one Conrad had taken in the direction of Iconium but shorter than the coastal route which Otto and his men had chosen. Reports that the way through Philadelphia afforded meager supplies, however, caused Conrad, in reaction from his former desire for speed, to persuade Louis and his advisers to change their minds and follow the longer but better supplied road near the sea.

The army found that this road, too, crossed mountainous country and rivers which were swollen with the winter rains, while food was expensive and difficult to obtain from the fortified cities located at intervals. Some crusaders managed to take passage in ships; some remained behind in the service of the Greeks; but the majority arrived at Ephesus around mid-December. Here they were greeted by Greek messengers who warned Louis that the Turks had gathered a large force to combat the crusaders and urged him to take refuge in the imperial strongholds. It seems likely that this message was bona fide and that the Turks, encouraged by their success in dispersing the German army, had pushed into Byzantine territory to repeat their tactics against the French, while the Greek inhabitants who had been alienated by the disorders during the passage of the western army were not going to oppose the Turks and may have been willing to coöperate with them in some instances. This time, however, Louis did not put credence in the emperor's news, and he refused to give in to fear of the Turks. Thereupon the imperial messengers produced other letters listing injuries which the king and his army had been responsible for in Byzantine territory and serving notice that Manuel could not restrain his men from vengeance in the future. The Franco-Greek alliance, on which so much time and effort had been spent, had become extremely shaky, particularly since the German defeat in Asia Minor had removed one source of anxiety from the Greeks.

At Ephesus Conrad became ill and failed to recuperate quickly enough to continue with the army. When Manuel and his wife heard this they invited Conrad to come to Constantinople to convalesce. There is no doubt that Manuel was very glad to separate the two western sovereigns and to have an opportunity to strengthen the old agreement with Conrad against Sicily and Hungary, now that the German emperor was powerless to threaten Constantinople, and Conrad on his part must have been happy to exchange the lesser place which he had to accept in Louis's army for the attentions lavished upon him at the Greek court. Byzantine diplomacy had reversed itself. Now it was the German sovereign who was wooed by the court while the French king marched at the head of his army through Asia Minor. Manuel himself acted as Conrad's physician until the illness had been cured; and the difficult winter season, passed among the amenities of life in Constantinople, was fruitful in strengthening pre-crusade ties between the Byzantines and the Germans, but not in promoting unity among the crusading armies.

Meanwhile the French army had continued on its stubborn way. The first contact with the Turks came in a successful skirmish on Christmas eve near Ephesus. After this heartening incident winter weather, with torrents of cold rains, began in earnest. On the way to Laodicea ad Lycum the crusaders found Turkish forces blocking the ford of the swollen Maeander river and using their usual tactics of harassing the army as it advanced; but after two days the Turks were finally routed and the crusaders came to Laodicea on January 3 or 4, 1148. The French rightly felt themselves in a kind of no man's land where Turkish forces could appear suddenly and, when defeated, as at the Maeander, seek refuge in Greek towns like Carian Antioch. It was impossible to secure enough food at Laodicea for the journey to Adalia (Antalya), but the army had to go on rather than exhaust its strength in vain waiting. Turks and some of the inhabitants lurked threateningly around them; worst of all, the crusaders saw gruesome evidence of the destruction of part of Otto of Freising's army just a week or so before. Therefore Louis drew his troops into battle array and stationed himself with his body-guard at the rear while Geoffrey of Rancon, one of the chief Poitevin barons, and Amadeo of Savoy took command of the van. Unfortunately for the crusaders, not all the army had taken the warning signs seriously. Perhaps overconfident because of their success thus far, the vanguard disregarded the royal order to spend an entire day in crossing a mountain near Cadmus. When the passage was not too difficult, they outdistanced the rest and climbed a second mountain, pitching camp on the other side. This confused the center part, which stopped and piled up while trying to discover where the vanguard had gone. In the midst of this turmoil the watchful enemy closed in, attacking the unprotected middle of the army before the rear guard came up. Louis heard the noise of the struggle and arrived on the scene as quickly as possible, sending his chaplain to the vanguard to tell them of the situation. They were prevented from returning, however, by the onrush of men fleeing the battle. Louis and his nobles, unaccompanied by the foot soldiers or sergeants which he would have provided for a pitched conflict, managed to charge against the Turks and distract their attention from the noncombatants, who fled to safety; but in the ensuing engagement the Turks destroyed almost all of the royal guard. Fortunately for the crusaders, Louis was not recognized and fought his way to safety. The approach of night and fear of a surprise attack finally halted the Turks, who collected their rich spoils and departed without pressing their advantage further. Thus the king was able to join the baggage train which was still crossing the mountain; and then he encountered the reinforcements coming from the van. They decided, however, that it would be unwise to launch a counterattack during the night. Louis alleviated the needs of those in his army as generously as he could from his own supplies; and the next day he led the army on, with the enemy continuing its policy of harassing the troops.

The French still had twelve days of hard marching before they could reach Adalia, and there were not enough provisions for the journey. Louis and his magnates must have feared that the army would break up in disorder as the Germans had on the road between Dorylaeum and Nicaea. Apparently there was no serious talk of retreat, since they had found little protection and few supplies at Laodicea. The French continued doggedly towards Adalia as best they could. At this time the Templars, who had had more experience of this sort of warfare in west and east than the other knights, stood out because of their ability to look after their own equipment and protect the people around them; and so by common consent it was agreed that the army should form a sort of fraternity with the Templars during the emergency, all taking an oath that they would not flee the field and that they would obey in every respect the officers assigned them. The knights were divided into groups of fifty and each group put under the command of Gilbert the Templar or one of his associates. They had to learn to endure Turkish attacks without being drawn away in fruitless pursuit, to attack only when ordered, and to return from pursuit at once when the signal was given. Also they were taught to maintain an order of march in which each man kept the position given him. The archers on foot were drawn up at the rear of the army to combat the Turkish bowmen; and nobles who had lost or sold their equipment on the journey were included in this group.

The new system worked well. The crusaders managed to rout enemy attacks four times or so in the days that followed and to go ahead in an orderly fashion with forces intact. Since the Turks and Greeks had burned the stores of food and destroyed the pasturage and crops in the fields by allowing flocks and cattle to graze ahead of the advancing army, many of the horses succumbed and many packs, tents, clothing, arms, etc. had to be abandoned and destroyed. The army subsisted on horse-meat and bread baked in the ashes of the campfires. At last they arrived at Adalia on January 20.[31]

As William of Tyre has pointed out, Adalia belonged to the Byzantine empire but was so close to Moslem territory that it had had to establish a working agreement with the Turks and so maintained a trade in necessary articles with them.[32] To this town Manuel had sent a messenger who forced the French nobles to reconfirm

[31] Odo, *De profectione*, VI, 108–128; Nicetas, *Historia*, I, 6; letter of Louis to Suger (*RHGF*, XV), p. 496; William of Tyre, *History*, XVI, 24–26; Kugler, *Studien*, pp. 170ff.; C. H. Walker, "Eleanor and the Disaster at Cadmos Mountain," *AHR*, LV (1949–1950), 857–861. Chalandon, *Les Comnène*, pp. 310–311, thinks the country may have been stripped by the survivors from Otto of Freising's army. For a description of similar methods of fighting on other occasions, see William of Tyre, *History*, XVI, 12.

[32] William of Tyre, *History*, XVI, 27.

their pact with the emperor in return for market privileges. Food was obtainable, though at high prices; but it was impossible to obtain grain for the starving horses, and the Turks lingering outside the city prevented access to the surrounding pastures. Furthermore, the crusaders could not obtain animals in the city to replace the ones lost on the journey. In this new emergency the king was eager to march on to Antioch, but his barons recommended going by sea in order to avoid the forty days' journey which would traverse the same type of barren countryside infiltrated with enemy forces which they had experienced since leaving Ephesus and to which their depleted strength was not equal. The Greeks had promised to collect a large fleet from the neighboring villages and islands and had told the crusaders that the trip to Antioch would take only three days by sea. Still reluctant to endorse this plan, Louis offered to equip the knights from his own resources and to go with them along the route which the soldiers of the First Crusade had taken to Antioch via Tarsus, while he suggested sending the pilgrims by ship. Once again the hope of separating the military forces from the noncombatants was not realized. The barons opposed the king's proposal as unsuitable since they were "sluggish with idleness and ailing with weariness and annoyances" and in many cases without weapons and horses.

When it proved impossible to reëquip the knights the French approached the commandant of the city and Manuel's messenger to secure passage by water; and they were promised enough ships to transport the entire army. Then winter storms set in and continued for almost a month, delaying the fleet. Prices in the town sky-rocketed, and the crowded conditions were unpleasant. When the ships did come, accomodation on them proved to be expensive and inadequate for the numbers in the army. Louis apportioned the first ships among his bishops and barons. Next came a long wait for more vessels. At last it became evident that no more ships were coming. Then the greater part of the army, which had no place on shipboard, took the only alternative open to them: the decision to march to Antioch. With his usual generosity Louis tried to provide for their needs. He gave the commandant and the emperor's messenger five hundred marks to insure that they and a large troop of men would accompany the crusaders across two nearby rivers, which the enemy was guarding, and then give the French an escort to lead them safely to Tarsus; those unfit for the journey were to be sheltered in the city until they recovered and could get an opportunity to follow their comrades. Accordingly, the invalids were admitted to the city and the troops for the overland journey made preparations for their departure. All the horses which the king could collect were furnished to knights of proven valor.

After appointing the counts of Flanders and Bourbon to see that the agreement was carried out, Louis embarked for Antioch. He left behind him the larger part of the army which he had led for more than eight months across Europe and down the wintry and unfriendly coast of Asia Minor and for whose requirements he had provided as well as he could throughout. This large, slow-moving expedition of mixed character had been far different from that envisioned in his first plan for a military force which would go to succor Edessa and the east. Louis, like Conrad, had hoped eventually to separate the pilgrims from the soldiers in order to accomplish his military aims efficiently, but not in the manner in which the severance came about at Adalia. Here and elsewhere between Constantinople and Jerusalem the lack of a friendly supporting fleet was particularly disastrous. If the army could have been provisioned and rearmed by ships, or if the noncombatants could have been transported easily, the fate of the large western armies in 1147–1148 might have been far different. The sea-faring peoples were engaged, however, in the Spanish, Wendish, and Lisbon expeditions or the Sicilian-Byzantine struggle.

As it was, Louis had clung somewhat timidly, and perhaps in reaction from Conrad's unfortunate dash toward Iconium, to nominally friendly territory with the apparent idea of reaching Jerusalem before launching his offensive. Thus his barons had not had ready opportunities for practicing their warlike arts and replenishing their resources by attacking enemy strongholds. Instead, the initiative had been taken by the enemy, whose large concentrations of troops and knowledge of the country and the necessary movements of the crusaders enabled them to pick the time and place for conflicts. Also unsatisfactory relations with the Greek inhabitants and their emperor had embittered and confused the French still further. The most lurid tales of Manuel and his treachery are admittedly not true; but his desire to separate the western armies and their commanders, his truce with the Turks, and his lack of any substantial support of the crusaders in Anatolia, while they may be justified as dictated by self-interest (and suggested by the Norman attack upon Greece), cannot be ignored as factors in the dispersal of the large pilgrim armies.

The morning after Louis departed the Turks descended on the crusaders, but were beaten off. Then the Greeks said that the winter season and the presence of the Turks made it impossible to take the army to Tarsus; and after several days of argument forced the king's representatives to leave Adalia on the ships which returned for them. The end of the army left behind came swiftly. Many were killed in combat with the Turks outside Adalia; some were led into slavery by the Moslems or were admitted to Greek service; others died of the plague which raged in the city. Only a small percentage of the original number could have managed to get through to Tarsus and Antioch.

Louis did not arrive at St. Simeon, the port for Antioch, in three days as promised. Although some of the ships did so, he was driven off course by unfavorable winds and may even have touched Cyprus before reaching the port more than two weeks later, on March 19.[33] There he received a warm and splendid welcome from prince Raymond of Antioch and his people. Raymond was Eleanor's uncle, and he had been one of the first to send messages to the west asking for aid. Consequently his pleasure at the arrival of Louis and his barons after three years of anticipation was very great. He escorted the king and his followers to Antioch with pomp and ceremony unlike anything which they had experienced since Constantinople and showered them with attentions and gifts. In return Raymond counted on their support in a campaign against the cities of Aleppo and Shaizar in order to alleviate Turkish pressure on the hard pressed northern section of the Latin states. To his surprise and growing disgust Louis was inclined to do no such thing. Even though the neighboring Turks feared the recently arrived French, and Raymond thought the situation promising for conquest, Louis was not sympathetic. The powerful preaching of the crusade had wrought a great change in the early, simple plan of a military expedition for the aid of the east; the concepts of holy war and pilgrimage had been impressed on those who enlisted, and Louis was of the temperament to respond to such ideas. Privately and in council he announced that he planned to go on to Jerusalem in order to fulfil his crusading vow.[34] After

[33] Amadeo of Savoy, who died at the beginning of April, is buried at Nicosia and may have been left behind there as an invalid during the journey to Antioch. Cf. C. W. Previté-Orton, *The House of Savoy* (Cambridge, 1912), p. 312, n. 2.

[34] William of Tyre, *History*, XVI, 27; Cahen, *La Syrie du nord*, p. 381. I cannot agree with Runciman, *Crusades*, II, 279, that Louis's desire to go to Jerusalem was a mere excuse. At Constantinople the pope's advice to Louis and the crusaders was cited as "to visit the Holy Sepulcher and to wipe out their sins by the blood or conversion of the infidels." Edessa, Antioch, and northern Syria were not mentioned as primary goals. Jerusalem and its holy

visiting the holy places, Louis apparently hoped to plan a joint campaign with Conrad, other western crusaders, and the knights of the Latin principalities. Then, too, the French crusaders had been reduced to a tenth or less of their original numbers during their journey to Antioch and now consisted mostly of knights without substantial numbers of sergeants and archers to reinforce their strength. A more vigorous general than Louis or a less travel-worn army might have overcome their scruples and welcomed the opportunities which Raymond offered for extending and protecting the northern section of the Latin states, just as the maritime crusaders had agreed to turn aside to help the king of Portugal defeat the Moslems at Lisbon, but for this group the attractions of Jerusalem were too many and too close at hand. Furthermore, Raymond's device of interesting Eleanor in his schemes in order to sway Louis was not a happy one. The queen entered into her uncle's plans wholeheartedly and enjoyed the diversions offered her in Antioch as well; but Louis distrusted this enthusiasm, and gossiping courtiers apparently misconstrued and magnified her lively enjoyment of the visit. The final step in a worsening situation came when Raymond lost his patience with Louis and tried to injure the French king by advising Eleanor to remain in Antioch if her husband left and to divorce him on the ground of consanguinity. Louis countered these moves by taking his queen and his people away from Antioch sooner than he had planned and setting out quietly for Tripoli.[35]

Raymond had not been the only prince looking forward to the arrival of the crusaders and hoping to make use of their resources, manpower, and prestige. Joscelin of Edessa, Raymond of Tripoli, and Baldwin and Melisend of Jerusalem hoped to attract Louis to their domains, too. Since the rulers of Jerusalem feared that the French might be detained in Antioch or Tripoli, they sent Fulcher of Angoulême, the patriarch of Jerusalem (1147–1157), to invite Louis to visit their kingdom. We can be sure that the patriarch pointed out that Otto of Freising and survivors from his army had reached Jerusalem on April 4 and that Conrad had arrived a

places had become the first objective, with no specific campaign planned against the "infidel". The same attitude appears among the Lisbon crusaders, whose goal was Jerusalem too, and who required some persuasion by the bishop of Oporto before they interrupted their journey to besiege Lisbon. In contrast, Conrad wished to go directly to Edessa, though he hoped to send the pilgrims in his army to the holy city.

[35] William of Tyre, *History*, XVI, 28; *Historia pontificalis*, xxiii. For a reasonable account of Eleanor's role, see A. Richard, *Histoire des comtes de Poitou* (Paris, 1903), II, 93–94. More recent and accessible are C. H. Walker, *Eleanor of Aquitaine* (Chapel Hill, 1950), and A. Kelly, *Eleanor of Aquitaine and the Four Kings* (Cambridge, 1950).

week or so later. The German ruler had parted from Manuel on the best of terms, laden with many splendid gifts, and had travelled with a Greek fleet. On landing at Acre he went to Jerusalem, where Fulcher had helped to welcome him outside the city and to conduct him within to the sound of hymns and chants. There the emperor had established himself in the house of the Templars and had visited the shrines of the holy city. He had intended to accomplish his vows and then to gather an army and set out for Edessa, which he had been unsuccessful in rescuing the autumn before; but in Jerusalem he was influenced to consider an expedition against Damascus to redress the failure of a campaign of the summer before.[36] Conrad needed to build up his army again and so set out for Acre to secure the services of the men arriving at the seaport. Probably among them were the Lisbon crusaders.

The emergence of Damascus as a goal for the crusading armies was abrupt. From the time of the first appeal for aid in 1145, Edessa and northern Syria had been to the fore. Jerusalem, however, had been mentioned as needing protection from further inroads by the Moslems and it was always the goal of the crusaders' religious aspirations. At the court of Jerusalem Conrad had encountered local and feudal ambition as marked as, and even less far-seeing than, that which Louis had found in Antioch, but harder to recognize. The glamor of the holy city, the authoritative position which Baldwin held for westerners as the king of the Latin state, and the reputation which the Templars had for military sagacity made the arguments for a Damascene campaign weighty. No one seems to have objected seriously that the young king and his barons should have been more mindful of the precarious welfare of the northern principalities than of the aggrandizement of their comparatively secure domain. Damascus, like Aleppo, was a desirable city whose capture had long been wished for. Also, Conrad was probably told that the devastation of Edessa in 1146 had been so complete that its repossession would be of doubtful value. Thus the problem of the city whose fall had stirred the west to the monumental crusade was pushed aside.

Louis was eager to lead his army to Jerusalem; and the news that Conrad was preparing for a joint expedition with the eastern Franks and recruiting his ranks from newly-arrived crusaders

[36] William of Tyre, *History*, XVI, 28–29; Otto, *Gesta*, I, 57, 62; *Wibaldi epistolae*, no. 78; Cinnamus, *Epitome*, II, 19; Gerhoh, *De investigatione*, p. 143. The wide dispersal of the German forces after their defeat is shown by the fact that some landed at Acre and some at Tyre, while others appeared between Tyre and Sidon. On the campaign of the previous year, see Grousset, *Histoire des croisades*, II, 211–225.

must have raised new hopes of military conquest in Palestine, with an army in full strength and shorn of its non-military elements. Louis could count on gaining added strength from the contingents from Provence and Languedoc who had come to Acre in late April with count Alfonso Jordan of Toulouse and his son Bertram. Unfortunately the count of Toulouse himself furnished an incident for dissension between the crusaders and the eastern Franks. As the son of Raymond of Toulouse, who had founded the county of Tripoli, he was rumored to aspire to that principality, which was being governed by Raymond II, the grandson of the French count's elder brother. On the road south to Jerusalem, Alfonso Jordan died at Caesarea, the victim, it was said, of poison administered at the command of the count of Tripoli and his sister-in-law, queen Melisend of Jerusalem. Bertram continued his journey and later took part in the siege of Damascus; but Tripoli appears to have been in a state of unrest after the death of Alfonso Jordan, and rumors over this latest incident between the Franks of the east and west were as rampant as they had been in Antioch.

On reaching Jerusalem, Louis was given the same ceremonious welcome which Conrad had experienced, and he and his nobles were conducted to the holy places. After he had accomplished the devotions customary for a Jerusalem pilgrim, a general court was announced for June 24 at Acre, "to consider the results of this great pilgrimage, the completion of such great labors, and also the enlargement of the realm." The roster of rulers and lay and ecclesiastical lords who attended was brilliant. Conrad was accompanied by Otto of Freising, the bishops of Metz and Toul, the papal legate Theodwin of Porto, the dukes of Bavaria and Swabia, duke Welf, margrave Hermann of Verona, Berthold of Andechs, William of Montferrat, and count Guy of "Blandras" (Biandrate) as his principal advisors. Louis's train included the bishops of Langres and Lisieux, the papal legate Guido of Florence, the counts of Perche, Troyes, Flanders, and Soissons, and Bertram of Toulouse; while king Baldwin and his mother were supported by patriarch Fulcher, the archbishops of Caesarea and Nazareth, the bishops of Acre, Sidon, Beirut, Banyas, and Bethlehem, Robert of Craon, called the Burgundian, master of the Temple, and Raymond of Le Puy, master of the Knights of St. John, the royal constable, the lords of Nablus, Tiberias, Sidon, Caesarea, the Transjordan, Toron, and Beirut. No representatives from the principalities of Antioch, Edessa, or Tripoli are known to have been present, however. The rulers of Edessa and Antioch were

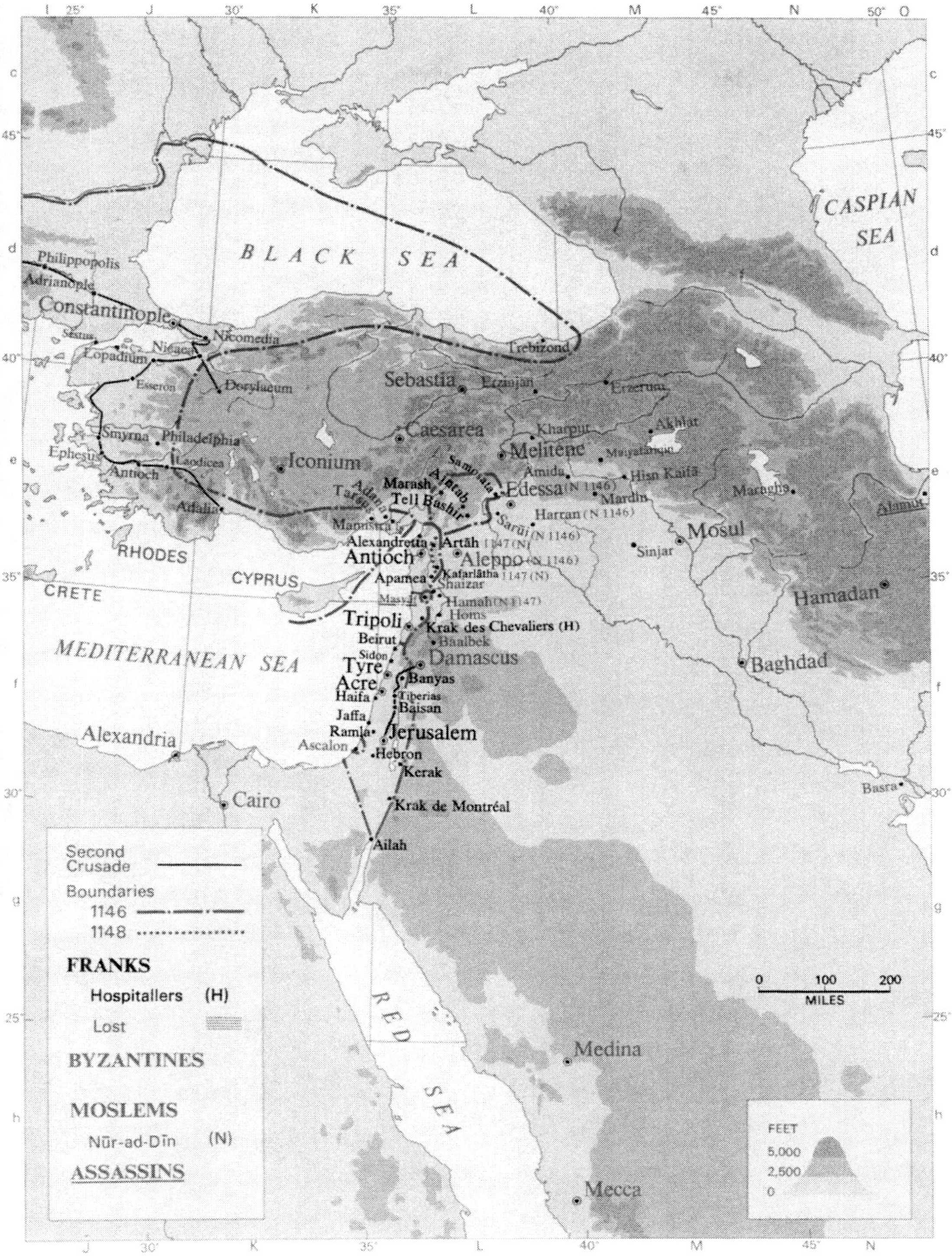

11. The Near East during the Second Crusade, 1146–1148 (*Map by the University of Wisconsin Cartographic Laboratory*)

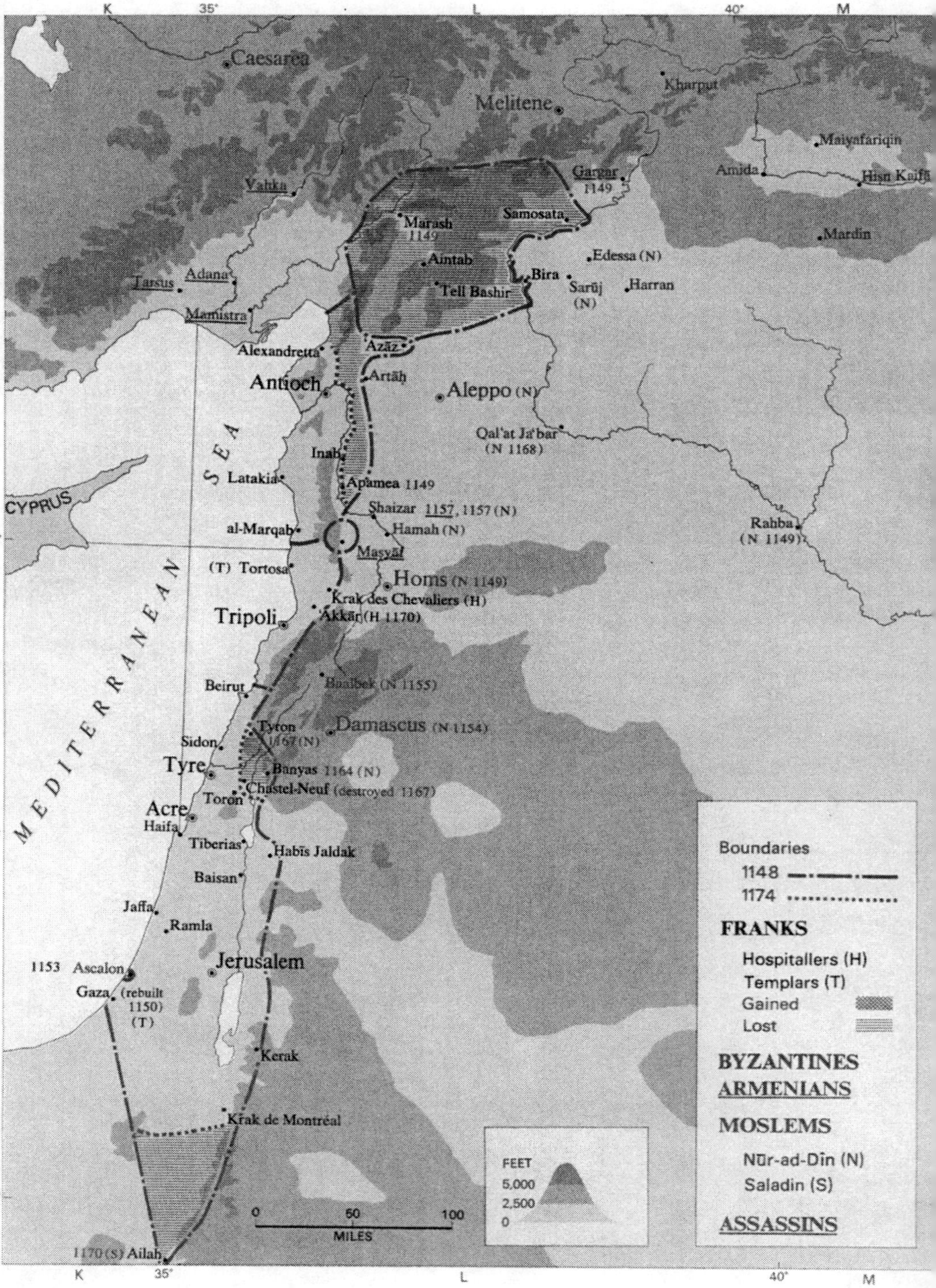

12. The Latin States during the Time of Nūr-ad-Dīn, 1148–1174 (*Map by University of Wisconsin Cartographic Laboratory*)

engaged in defending their lands against Nūr-ad-Dīn, and the count of Tripoli had serious internal problems to settle.

In his description of the court William of Tyre characterizes the nobles of the realm of Jerusalem as possessing an accurate knowledge of affairs and places, attributes which were normal enough for the inhabitants of the country, but in sharp contrast to the elementary and romantic notions that the European crusaders entertained concerning the Holy Land. On foreign soil, among situations which had repeatedly proved far more complex than they had suspected, the western princes felt and were made to feel that they needed the advice of men who knew the place intimately. The day was past when they could afford to dash ahead into practically unknown territory or plod ahead without a vigorous plan for a campaign. With the nobles of Jerusalem they entered into careful consideration as to what action would be most expedient. Various plans were presented before the council and discussed. Some crusaders like the count of Flanders and Arnulf of Lisieux were eager to leave the Holy Land behind and to go home without attempting the campaign, and Conrad seemed to be turning to that point of view. Louis and his warlike supporters like the bishop of Langres wanted to stay and perform some deed worthy of their country and their ancestors. Surely there must have been advocates for the northern campaign planned by Raymond of Antioch or for the relief of Edessa. In the end, however, the recommendation of the more belligerent Syrian barons won out, even though there was a native faction which considered an expedition against a city as consistently friendly as Damascus unwise. At this decision some of the crusaders like Welf did go home; but the greatest part of the troops, numbering at least 50,000 and commanded by Baldwin, Louis, and Conrad, assembled at Tiberias in mid-July.[37]

Fired by the sight of the True Cross, the Christian army marched to Banyas for a further conference about strategy. Here the leaders received the advice of men well acquainted with the situation of Damascus and its surroundings, and in council with the barons and prelates decided to attack from the west, where the city's strongest fortifications were protected by orchards that

[37] William of Tyre, *History*, XVI, 28–29; XVII, 1–2; Otto, *Gesta*, I, 62; *Historia pontificalis*, xxiv; *Historia Welforum Weingartensis* (*MGH, SS.*, XXI), p. 27. The *Syriac Fragment* (ed. Taylor), pp. 123–124, after speaking of the second fall of Edessa, mentions the many refugees from Edessa among the great crowds in Jerusalem in 1148. See also Giesebrecht, *Kaiserzeit*, IV, 288–289; Devic et Vaissete, *Histoire générale de Languedoc*, III, 754; IV, 223–224; Jean Richard, *Le Comté de Tripoli*, p. 6ff.; Grousset, *Histoire des croisades*, II, 270; Bernhardi, *Konrad III*, pp. 663–665.

would assure the attacking army a supply of food and water. Going by Mount Lebanon, they arrived at Dāraiyā, a few miles southwest of Damascus, on July 23.[38] There they arranged the armies in battle formation and decided upon the order of march, to eliminate disorder and rivalry as much as possible during the siege. First went the forces of the eastern Franks, whose superior knowledge of the country fitted them for finding the best route and opening the attack. Louis and his men followed close behind to strengthen and aid the Jerusalemite army, while Conrad commanded the rear in anticipation of a possible surprise attack from that direction. In this way they advanced on the following day through the plain before the city, which was irrigated by canals and thickly set with mud-walled orchards whose density and narrow paths made the approach extremely difficult. The Damascenes harassed the army from hiding places among the trees, openly blocked the paths, shot arrows from towers in the orchards, and hid behind perforated walls in order to stab the attackers with lances. Despite this vigorous defense the crusaders killed or captured many of the Moslems and drove the rest back into the city. As they emerged from the gardens, however, they found the cavalry and archers of Damascus and its allies massed on the bank of the Barada river, which flowed beside the city. After some hesitation the crusaders rallied and began to attack, but were not able to break through until Conrad and his knights rushed from the rear in a powerful charge and then began hand to hand fighting. With great courage and ferocity they drove the Moslems back from the river and inside the city. Thus the army was established in a good position, with access to food and water. They had gained some booty in the gardens and had timber at hand to use for defenses; at the same time they were able to destroy bridges which were necessary to the enemy.

Inside the walls the Damascenes were terrified. Their vizir, Mu'īn-ad-Dīn Unur (or Önör), had sent urgent messages for help to Saif-ad-Dīn of Mosul and his brother Nūr-ad-Dīn. Both had raised large forces to come to the aid of Damascus, but the citizens were afraid that they could not hold out until help came. Unur, however, was indomitable. He stirred his people by displaying

[38] William of Tyre, *History*, XVII, 3–5; *Historia pontificalis*, xxiv; *Wibaldi epistolae*, no. 144; Ibn-al-Qalānisī (tr. H. A. R. Gibb), pp. 283–286; Ibn-al-Athīr, *Kāmil* (*RHC, Or.*, I), p. 460; *Atābeks* (*RHC, Or.*, II, part 2), p. 161; Bar Hebraeus, *Chronography* (tr. E. A. Wallis Budge), p. 274; Usāmah, *I'tibar* (tr. P. K. Hitti), p. 124; Grousset, *Histoire des croisades*, II, 255–268; Runciman, *History of the Crusades*, II, 281–284. On Nūr-ad-Dīn, see below, chapter XVI.

the Koran of the caliph 'Uthmān while they tried desperately to fortify the city from within. The next day he led a counter-attack which was not successful in forcing the crusaders from their position but did kill and wound many of their number. This example of courage heartened the Damascenes; and the situation remained the same during that night and the next day, with no serious attack made by either side. By this time Saif-ad-Dīn and Nūr-ad-Dīn had reached Homs, and Saif-ad-Dīn had notified Unur that he would fight the crusaders if a man of his choice could command Damascus during the conflict. Although he said that he would return the city to Unur if the Moslems won, the vizir of Damascus was in a dilemma. Because of his former friendly relations with Jerusalem he had incurred the hostility of the Moslems and felt that Saif-ad-Dīn would not really return the city.

Unur had apparently written to the Syrian Franks in an attempt to induce them to raise the siege. According to Ibn-al-Athīr he pointed out that if Damascus fell, the foreign Franks would expect it for themselves and would claim additional land which belonged to the kingdom of Jerusalem, and that, if he gave the city to Saif-ad-Dīn, Jerusalem would be readily accessible for the next Moslem campaign. The effect of this message was heightened by the fact that Saif-ad-Dīn had written to the crusaders saying that he would seize them if they did not leave Damascus alone. All this news appalled the Syrian Franks, and Unur has been credited with increasing his advantage by sending money to encourage them to withdraw. Furthermore the Palestinian barons had been annoyed when the three kings had agreed to grant Damascus to the count of Flanders when it fell, since they felt that it should go to Guy of Beirut. They decided to raise the siege and draw Louis and Conrad away.

The crusaders knew that the western part of the city, which they faced, had been well fortified during their delay and the eastern part held open for flight if that became necessary. Since the proximity of the great Moslem armies now made it necessary to capture the city quickly, the council advocated a shift in position. During the night of July 26 the new view of the situation and the proposed change in tactics were discussed. Finally the crusaders, whose belief in the experts must have been somewhat shaken by this time, agreed to the plan, and on July 27 they advanced to the east. Here they found themselves in a worse position than before, lacking water and with very little food at hand, since they had counted on entering the city quickly. The walls were too thick to storm at once, and the large armies of Nūr-ad-Dīn and his brother still threatened from the rear. The folly of the move was apparent to all; and it was impossible to return to the western approach, which the Moslems had reoccupied and where the army would have been obliged to repeat their first arduous offensive in order to gain a foothold. Retreat from the city seemed the only solution, but the bishop of Langres and the most belligerent part of the French army advocated remaining and fighting it out. At last Conrad, the count of Flanders, and the native barons induced Louis to agree with them. This he did for the common good and as a token of his respect for Conrad. Thus the armies withdrew, suffering Moslem attacks as they went.

The failure at Damascus gave rise to much bitterness and many accusations of treachery against various persons and groups. The Templars, the Palestinian barons, and Raymond of Antioch were named most often. Even Conrad, who was too cautious to name names, wrote to Wibald that betrayal had been encountered where least expected when the city was declared unassailable in the west and the armies were moved intentionally to another place where there was not a suitable approach or water supply for the army. Thus the great alliance was destroyed in one short campaign. Although the troops besieging Damascus had agreed on their return to attack Ascalon and had fixed a day and place for the assembly of the expedition, the atmosphere was full of accusations and charges which discouraged coöperation. When Conrad arrived at the rendezvous he found few others there, and after eight days' waiting for a muster that never occurred he decided that he had been deceived a second time and made plans to leave Palestine as soon as possible and to winter in Constantinople on the way home. The crusade had been a series of shattering defeats for him, but he consoled himself with the reflection that he and his army had accomplished everything which God had wished or the people of the land had permitted. He felt the kind of antagonism for the inhabitants of the Latin principalities which the French vented on the Greeks; and so he turned his attention to the one advantage which his eastern journey seemed to offer: a closer alliance with the Byzantine emperor Manuel. This was built partly on the marriages of Manuel and Bertha and Manuel's niece Theodora and Henry of Bavaria, the second of which was celebrated at this time. Bertha's dowry had been southern Italy; Theodora's seems to have been part or all of Austria. To ensure the possession of these portions a coalition was established among Manuel, Conrad, the duke of

Bohemia, the margrave of Istria, Henry of Carinthia, Henry of Bavaria-Austria, William of Montferrat, Venice, Genoa, Pisa, Poland, Galicia, and the Kumans against Hungary, Sicily, and their allies, among whom duke Welf was numbered once more, now that he had returned from the crusade.[39]

Louis was less eager to depart from Palestine. He still dreamed of achieving something helpful to the Holy Land. To Suger's urgent pleas that he come home, he replied that in view of the oppression of the church and the emergency existing in the east he had been moved by piety and by the prayers of the eastern church to remain until after the following Easter. In the meantime he did what he could financially to aid the inhabitants who were suffering from frequent Moslem inroads. The defeat of the crusade had reduced the prestige of the Christians to a very low level and had emboldened the Turks to attempt things which they had not dared to do before, particularly in northern Syria. When Louis did leave Palestine in 1149 his mind was still full of the necessity to aid Outremer, but now Byzantium figured as an enemy rather than an ally in future plans. This conviction was strengthened by the journey home. Louis had chosen to sail on a Sicilian vessel and so narrowly escaped being captured by part of the Byzantine navy, which was still at war with Roger. The king did lose a ship on which some of his retinue were traveling, and Eleanor was detained for a while. This misadventure added fuel to the French hatred and distrust of the Byzantines, which had grown tremendously in the past year and a half. When Louis landed in Calabria, he was glad to claim Roger as an ally, and together they spoke of launching a new crusade to bring effective aid to the east and to avenge themselves on the Greeks. Louis crowned Roger king; then he journeyed home, stopping at the papal curia to tell of his experiences and to sound out the pope on the idea of a new expedition. Eugenius assented to this plan, and St. Bernard and Suger supported it, too; but there was no real response to the new crusade among the nobles and the people. They were exhausted by the grueling experiences of the Second Crusade and its tremendous expenditure of resources and strength in the east without any positive achievement. Conrad, of course, was not willing to be drawn into such a scheme. His antipathy for the Latin east

[39] *Wibaldi epistolae*, no. 144; K. Heilig, "Ostrom und das deutsche Reich um die Mitte des 12. Jahrhunderts," *Kaisertum und Herzogsgewalt im Zeitalter Friedrichs I* (Leipzig, 1944), pp. 148–167. G. Constable, "The Second Crusade," pp. 266–276, gives a more detailed discussion of the various accusations made regarding responsibility for the failure.

and his entente with Manuel were more than enough to alienate him.[40]

There was to be no epilogue to recover the fortunes of the Second Crusade in Palestine. The vision of all the forces of Christendom on the march against the pagan Slavs and the Moslem world had been dissipated by the mixture of military and non-military elements in the armies, divided leadership, conflicting interests within Christendom, lack of knowledge and understanding of the countries invaded, and the growing strength of the Moslems in the east. The smaller, more concentrated, essentially military expeditions in Portugal and Spain had achieved the successes of the crusade; and they foreshadowed the shift from the vast miscellaneous outpourings of the First and Second Crusades to the more limited personnel and more definite objectives of the Third and Fourth Crusades.

[40] Louis's letters to Suger (*RHGF*, XV), pp. 502, 509. R. Röhricht, *Beiträge zur Geschichte der Kreuzzüge*, II (Berlin, 1878), p. 79, thinks that the crusade cost the Germans about a million men.

XVI
THE CAREER OF NŪR-AD-DĪN

When Nūr-ad-Dīn Maḥmūd succeeded his father Zengi at Aleppo in mid-September of 1146, he was a young and hitherto, apparently, inexperienced man, who was now faced with the task of establishing himself. He was surrounded by actual or potential enemies and rivals, and there were jealousies between his emirs. The division of Zengi's principality seemed to dissipate at one stroke all the gains made in the past twenty years, except for the capture of Edessa. Unur at Damascus had lost no time in compelling Zengi's governor, Najm-ad-Dīn Aiyūb, to surrender Baalbek, in detaching Homs from Aleppo, and even in gaining over al-Yaghīsiyanī at Hamah. After the repulse by Shīrkūh, who had also accompanied Nūr-ad-Dīn to Aleppo, of a raid by Raymond, a more serious threat presented itself in Joscelin's attempt to recapture Edessa. In this crisis, Nūr-ad-Dīn showed for the first time what he was made of; he raced to its defense, not only to counter the crusaders, but also to forestall his brother Saif-ad-Dīn of Mosul, and prevented any future attempts of the kind by destroying its Armenian and Jacobite population.[1]

This striking success over the Franks had in all probability a considerable effect in consolidating Nūr-ad-Dīn's position. For he had still to reach a direct settlement with his brother at Mosul, whose liberty of action was hampered for the time being by the rising of the Artukid princes Timurtash and Alp Arslan, and their recovery of their former possessions in the north. That there were some tensions between Aleppo and Mosul seems to be indicated by a number of small details, such as Nūr-ad-Dīn's refortification of Qalʿat Najm, guarding the bridge over the Euphrates on the Harran-Aleppo road; and it would appear that one of the main stabilizing factors in the situation was the friendship between the Mosul vizir Jamāl-ad-Dīn and the Kurdish emir Shīrkūh, who made it their aim to maintain the two principalities separate but in close alliance. Whether, as Ibn-al-Athīr asserts, the two brothers,

[1] For the second siege of Edessa and Frankish policies at this time, see below, chapter XVII, p. 531.

with many precautions, met outside Aleppo and came to a friendly agreement, or not, it is clear that Saif-ad-Dīn accepted the situation.[2] Nūr-ad-Dīn had, in fact, gained the support not only of the regular regiments of Aleppo but also of the Yürük Turkoman tribes who had recently migrated into northern Syria, and was already able at the time of the attack on Edessa to put an army of 10,000 horsemen in the field. So powerful a force not only guaranteed his independence against his brother, though it would appear that Saif-ad-Dīn was regarded formally as Nūr-ad-Dīn's suzerain during his lifetime, but also convinced Unur of the advantages of a reconciliation with him. In the following March the two Syrian princes were united by Nūr-ad-Dīn's marriage with Unur's daughter; al-Yaghīsīyanī at Hamah returned to his former allegiance; and the alliance was signalized by joint operations in May against the Franks in the Hauran, where a rebel governor, Altīntash, had sought assistance from Jerusalem.

Back in the north, Nūr-ad-Dīn prepared to defend himself against a more powerful rival. The Selchükid sultan of Rūm ("Rome", central Anatolia), Mas'ūd (1116–1155), now at peace with Manuel, was turning his arms southwards and engaging the northern garrisons of Antioch. Nūr-ad-Dīn joined in, to occupy the fortresses in the 'Afrīn valley south of 'Azāz and on the eastern fringe of the 'Amuq depression, followed, in spite of Raymond's attempted counter-attack, by the capture of Hāb and Kafarlāthā, which guarded the passage from the Rugia valley to the plain of Aleppo. But before the end of 1147 the news of the approaching Second Crusade brought operations to an end, as all parties in Syria awaited, in hope or fear, what it might bring.[3]

How far, even yet, the Moslem princes were from the conviction of a common cause against the "infidel" is shown by the absence of any consultations or arrangements for mutual defense. It was not until the decision to attack Damascus became known that Unur sent out appeals for assistance. The panic caused at Aleppo and Damascus by the early reports of the vast host on the way had already been alleviated by the disasters in Asia Minor, and was even giving place to some degree of confidence when the forces actually engaged in the campaign were found to be so much smaller than had been expected. In the interval Saif-ad-Dīn had joined forces with Nūr-ad-Dīn and begun to move southwards, but had advanced no farther than Homs when the siege of Damas-

[2] Ibn-al-Athīr, *Atābeks* (*RHC, Or.*, II, part 2), p. 158.
[3] On the Second Crusade, see above, chapter XV.

cus was abandoned July 28. There can be little doubt that their prospective intervention was a factor in the decision to do so, yet the ultimate consequence was to drive a still deeper wedge of suspicion between Aleppo and Damascus.

The failure of the Second Crusade, coupled with the curious incident that followed in September, when Raymond II of Tripoli called in the united forces of the Zengids and Damascus to dislodge the son of Alfonso Jordan from the castle of al-ʿArīmah, was utilized by Nūr-ad-Dīn to attack the Frankish castles in central Syria. He then turned north to raid the lower reaches of an-Nahr al-Aswad, in order to counter a raid by Raymond of Antioch into Selchükid territory. In spite of a reverse at Yaghra, due to the jealousy of Shīrkūh at the favor shown by Nūr-ad-Dīn to his minister Ibn-ad-Dāyah, he continued his operations towards Apamea in the following spring, while Unur, calling in the Turkomans, harassed the kingdom until an armistice was signed in May 1149.

Relieved from further anxiety in the south, Unur was able to answer Nūr-ad-Dīn's appeal for reinforcements in the north, and the combined armies, some 6,000 strong, set out to besiege Inab, on the borders of the Rugia valley. Raymond of Antioch, hastening to its defense and forced by his barons to engage the superior Moslem forces, was disastrously defeated June 29 and himself killed in the battle.[4]

This, the most spectacular of Nūr-ad-Dīn's victories over the Franks, and coming at this early stage in his career, seems to have been the turning-point in his own conception of his mission and in the history of Moslem Syria. In the eyes of all Islam he had become the champion of the faith, and he now consciously set himself to fulfil the duties of that role. His first task was to deal with the heretics within his gates. On first occupying Aleppo he had shown some indulgence towards the Shīʿites, but in the last months of 1148, he had perhaps already begun to take measures against them and to break up their leadership. The Assassins of Maṣyāf were making common cause with the Franks; their chief, ʿAlī ibn-Wafā', had contributed to the reverse at Yaghra and was killed on the Frankish side at Inab. But negative measures were not enough; the new counter-crusade was henceforth to be placed under the banner of orthodoxy, and Nūr-ad-Dīn gave active encouragement to all the elements that could contribute to the revival of the faith, by the foundation of schools, mosques, and sufi (Arabic, *ṣūfī*) convents, and to the unity of popular feeling,

[4] Cf. below, chapter XVII, pp. 532–533.

by the service of preachers, poets, and romancers. It entered into his political ambitions also. The campaigns soon to be opened against Damascus were preceded and accompanied by poetic denunciations and pointed demonstrations of the injury done to the cause of Islam by the alliance of its political chiefs with the Franks. Later on, it was to range him against the Fāṭimids of Egypt. Whatever part private ambition may have had in his policy, it cannot be questioned that in the twenty-five years that lay ahead of him he was to go far towards creating the general unity and even exaltation of spirit amongst the Moslems of Syria of which Saladin was to reap the benefit after him.

For the moment he set himself to make the most of his victory at Inab, and even hoped to seize Antioch in its temporary state of defenselessness. Foiled in these hopes by the patriarch Aimery and the speed of Baldwin's advance to its support, he rejoined al-Yaghisiyani, whom he had previously detached to invest Apamea. After its surrender, he returned to the north and seized Ḥārim and all the remaining castles east of the Orontes before concluding an armistice with Antioch. Mas'ūd, the sultan of Rūm, also joined in the scramble for spoils, and having captured Marash, Sam, and Duluk, laid siege to Tell Bashir and appealed to Nūr-ad-Dīn for assistance.

But Nūr-ad-Dīn's interest at this moment lay in a different direction. On August 28 Unur of Damascus had died, and a violent struggle broke out between the prince Abak and rival parties among his officers. Before Nūr-ad-Dīn could seize the opportunity to intervene, however, his brother Saif-ad-Dīn Ghāzī of Mosul died also (September 6). On receipt of this news Nūr-ad-Dīn rode hell-for-leather toward Mosul with a small party of followers, and reached and occupied Sinjar. A faction in the army of Mosul was favorable to his interest, but 'Alī Küchük and the vizir set up a younger brother, Quṭb-ad-Dīn Maudūd, as their prince, and when Nūr-ad-Dīn was joined by the Artukid Kara Arslan, the Mosul forces marched out to give battle. The fratricidal strife was finally averted by the vizir, who persuaded Nūr-ad-Dīn to surrender Sinjar in return for the surrender to him of Homs and Rahba.

On his return to Syria Nūr-ad-Dīn, after sending Shīrkūh to join the sultan Mas'ūd at Tell Bashir, negotiated the raising of the siege on payment of tribute by Joscelin. His ally, the Artukid Kara Arslan, was engaged during the autumn and winter months in conquering the fortresses of Joscelin's Armenian vassals on the upper Euphrates, including Gargar. But Nūr-ad-Dīn himself was mainly preoccupied with the affairs of Damascus. On the pretext of punishing the Franks for their raids on the Hauran he demanded reinforcements from its prince. The prefect, Mu'aiyid-ad-Dīn Ibn-aṣ-Ṣūfī, who had by now established his control of the city, pleaded the treaty with Jerusalem. In the spring of 1150 Nūr-ad-Dīn marched south, encamped outside the city, and repeated his demand for a thousand men to join him in an expedition to relieve Ascalon and Gaza. Although it is evident from the language of the Damascus chronicler that the popular sympathies lay with Nūr-ad-Dīn, the prefect, no doubt remembering the former occasion when Damascus troops were sent under Sevinj to coöperate in the "holy war" with Nūr-ad-Dīn's father, refused the request in peremptory terms; but in the face of Nūr-ad-Dīn's threats he agreed to recognize Nūr-ad-Dīn's suzerainty, though without admitting him into the city.

During his absence in the south, his Turkoman troops remained actively engaged against the territories of Tell Bashir and succeeded in capturing Joscelin. Instantly, the county was invaded from three sides. The Artukid Timurtash of Mardin seized Samosata and Bira, with other fortresses; the Selchükid sultan Mas'ūd reappeared before Tell Bashir and was joined by Nūr-ad-Dīn, who had already captured 'Azāz. On the transfer of Tell Bashir to the Greek emperor Manuel, the siege was raised, but the two Moslem forces vigorously harassed the Franco-Armenian garrison and population on their evacuation to Antioch. During his withdrawal Mas'ūd seized Kesoun, Behesni, Raban, and Marzban, while Nūr-ad-Dīn occupied in the course of the same autumn and winter Tall Khālid, Cyrrhus, and Ravendan. Early in the next year (1151) his general Ḥassān of Manbij renewed the siege of Tell Bashir, and with its surrender on July 12 the former county of Edessa was extinguished.[5]

Nūr-ad-Dīn's absence in the north brought little relief to Damascus, where, in addition, the internal conflict was still unappeased. During the autumn of 1150 his Turkomans were sent to detach the province of Hauran and fought a pitched battle with a detachment of Damascene troops. In the spring of 1151 he again encamped outside the city and though he deprecated the shedding of Moslem blood, his forces engaged in skirmishes with the local

[5] For a slightly different chronology on the liquidation of the remnants of the county of Edessa and the intervention of the emperor Manuel, see below, chapter XVII, pp. 533–534, and above, map 12.

forces and the villages of the Ghūṭah were plundered by the undisciplined followers of both sides. This attack on Damascus was the more pointed in that the Egyptian vizir Ibn-as-Sallār, perhaps taking Nūr-ad-Dīn's protestations of a desire to relieve the growing pressure on Ascalon at their face value, had in May 1150 sent an embassy to him to arrange for a joint attack on the Franks and had received his promise to participate. But when, in the following spring, the Egyptian fleet attacked the Syrian coastal towns from Jaffa to Tripoli, Nūr-ad-Dīn remained inactive.

On the approach of the Franks in June, he withdrew to az-Zabadānī and sent a squadron to the Hauran, which subsequently engaged the Franks there and forced them to retire. He then resumed the siege of Damascus early in July and cut off its supplies, but held firmly to his decision not to engage in regular hostilities with its troops and citizens. Before the end of the month a fresh agreement was reached between the parties, the negotiators including Shīrkūh on the one side and his brother Najm-ad-Dīn Aiyūb on the other. The agreement was duly ratified in October by a ceremonial visit of the prince Abak to Aleppo, when he was formally recognized as Nūr-ad-Dīn's lieutenant in Damascus.

Even yet, however, Nūr-ad-Dīn was not satisfied. The Damascenes still regarded themselves as bound by their treaty with Jerusalem, and the Yürük Turkoman irregulars, with or without the knowledge or consent of Nūr-ad-Dīn, continued to operate in the districts of Damascus. In December 1151 they inflicted heavy losses on the Frankish garrison of Banyas and were engaged in consequence by the forces of Damascus; but Aiyūb at Baalbek had almost immediately to take measures against a reprisal raid by the Franks in the Biqā' valley. While Nūr-ad-Dīn, in the following spring, was engaged in the north, where he seized Tortosa and Yaḥmur, Abak strengthened himself by restoring his control over the Hauran, which had been shaken by the Turkomans.

Early in 1153 Nūr-ad-Dīn determined to exert his authority once more at Damascus and ordered Abak to join him with the whole of his regular forces in order to relieve the pressure on Ascalon. The combined armies, after capturing Aflis, marched to Banyas, where they split up in disorder and retired (May–June). This was the last straw, and while the disorders broke out afresh in Damascus, and Ascalon fell to the crusading armies, Nūr-ad-Dīn, encamped at Homs, blockaded Damascus by preventing the passage of grain convoys. At the end of March 1154 Shīrkūh appeared before the city, but was met with hostility. In April Nūr-ad-Dīn himself arrived, and after brushing aside a show of resistance forced an entrance on April 25 "to the joy of the people, troops, and militiamen" (Arabic singular, *'askarī*). Abak surrendered and was recompensed with fiefs at Homs, and Shīrkūh was invested with the governorship of the city. Baalbek still resisted, Aiyūb having been replaced as governor of the citadel before the fall of Damascus by another officer, Ḍaḥḥāk; but in June 1155, after concluding an armistice with the kingdom of Jerusalem for one year, Nūr-ad-Dīn forced its surrender.[6] Aiyūb rejoined Nūr-ad-Dīn's service either before or after this event, and was appointed governor of Damascus with Shīrkūh as military commandant.

Immediately after the occupation of Damascus Nūr-ad-Dīn, in addition to reorganizing its defenses, began to apply there also his program of religious revival by the foundation of colleges and convents. Two other institutions of his deserve special note. One was the hospital (*Māristān*), which long remained one of the most famous of medieval infirmaries. The other was the *dār al-'adl* or palace of justice, whose counterpart he had already instituted in Aleppo, where he himself, during his periods of residence in the city, sat in audience twice a week to deal with complaints, especially against the officers of the army and the administration. The stress which he laid on this part of a ruler's duties is recognized in the title conferred on him by the caliph, apparently in this same year 1154, of *al-malik al-'ādil* "the just king".

With the unification of all Moslem Syria, as well as the former county of Edessa, under his rule, Nūr-ad-Dīn's military power was now consolidated. Although little direct or detailed information on his military organization is preserved in the sources, it certainly followed the Selchükid feudal system, in which the officers and a number of the regular troops were assigned estates in lieu of pay, on condition of presenting themselves with adequate equipment and provisions for active service when called upon. The officers received estates graduated in size according to their rank, and were required to maintain a corresponding number of troops from their revenues; in the case of general officers placed in command of districts or provinces, these numbered several hundreds.[7] The feudal army thus consisted of the ruler's own regiments of guards, numbering perhaps some 2,000 under Nūr-ad-

[6] Cf. below, chapter XVII, pp. 538–539.

[7] For example, Shīrkūh as governor of Homs maintained a regiment of 500 regular troopers.

Dīn, plus the regiments of his district commanders and vassals. The combined forces of Aleppo and Damascus at Inab amounted, as already noted, to 6,000 horse; and it is probable that the regular armies under Nūr-ad-Dīn's direct command never much exceeded this figure. When reinforced by the Artukid princes or from Mosul, or by auxiliary bodies of Turkomans or Arab tribesmen, his armies may well have reached 10,000 or even 15,000, exclusive of foot-soldiers and volunteers.

In one feature Nūr-ad-Dīn's regular forces differed from most of the Selchükid armies, namely in the enrolment of large numbers of Kurds alongside the Turkish *mamlūks*. The brothers Aiyūb and Shīrkūh were, though the most prominent, by no means the only Kurdish officers who attained high rank under him; and these in turn naturally attracted large numbers of their fellow-countrymen, both as regulars and as auxiliary troops. The local Arab sedentaries and militia, on the other hand, who had played so large a part in Syria during the preceding century, seem to have been suppressed or discouraged, no doubt as potential elements of insubordination. They are scarcely mentioned in the annals of Nūr-ad-Dīn's campaigns, and reappear under Saladin only as auxiliary infantry and siege troops.

Shortly after the capture of Baalbek, Nūr-ad-Dīn returned to the north to intervene in the complicated struggle between the Selchükid and Dānishmendid princes in Anatolia that followed the death of sultan Masʿūd I in 1155. While his successor Kilij Arslan II engaged and defeated the Dānishmendid Yaghi-Basan of Sebastia (Sivas) at Aqserai in September, Nūr-ad-Dīn seized the opportunity to annex Aintab, Duluk, and Marzban. The indignant sultan retaliated by attempting to organize a coalition against him with Ṭoros of Cilicia and Reginald of Antioch, but the only immediate action taken was a raid toward Aleppo by Reginald, who was overtaken and defeated near Ḥārim by Ibn-ad-Dāyah in the following spring. In the autumn amicable relations were restored between the two Moslem princes.

The next five years were filled with anxieties, external and internal, for the preservation of the newly unified kingdom of Syria. In September 1156 began a series of severe earthquakes which repeatedly destroyed cities and fortifications in the northern half of his territories. In spite of the renewal of the truce with Jerusalem on the payment of a tribute of 8,000 Tyrian dinars, it was broken again and again by attempts on the part of the Latins to take advantage of the disordered conditions in the country. Nūr-ad-Dīn, preoccupied with measures for the defense of the ruined cities, established himself near Baalbek and sent out squadrons to deal with these attacks, at the same time sending an envoy to Egypt to organize coöperation with the Egyptian forces against the Franks.

Encouraged by two successful engagements in April 1157, in which his brother Nuṣrat-ad-Dīn severely handled a force of Hospitallers and Templars on their way to Banyas with supplies, and Shīrkūh with a body of Turkomans repulsed the raiders in the north, Nūr-ad-Dīn concentrated his armies at the beginning of May for an assault on Banyas. Retiring before Baldwin's advance, he counterattacked the Frankish troops in camp at al-Mallāḥah on June 19 and destroyed the greater part, Baldwin himself barely escaping by flight.[8] William of Tyre relates that Nūr-ad-Dīn then returned to the attack on Banyas, but was forced to retire by the conjunction of the troops of Antioch and Tripoli with those of the kingdom. It seems more probable, however, that the reason for his withdrawal was a renewed series of earthquake shocks which began on July 4 and continued into November, with particularly serious results in Homs, Hamah, Apamea, and Shaizar, where the whole household of its Arab princes, the Banū-Munqidh, perished. Having attempted without success to renew the armistice with Baldwin, he left a force in the field to protect the territories of Damascus and himself moved north in August to occupy Shaizar and protect the other cities. By this move he forestalled the advance of the combined Latin forces, following on the arrival of Thierry of Alsace, count of Flanders, on the third of his four personal crusades, and on their concentration at Antioch Nūr-ad-Dīn took up his position at Inab in readiness to meet the expected attack.

Here he was attacked by a severe illness early in October, and after giving instructions that in the event of his death his brother Nuṣrat-ad-Dīn should be his successor at Aleppo, with Shīrkūh as his lieutenant at Damascus, he withdrew to the citadel of Aleppo. Amidst the confusion which followed, Shīrkūh moved south to protect Damascus. The rest of the army was temporarily disorganized, and the crusaders, reinforced by Ṭoros and his Armenians, advanced on Shaizar without opposition. But the Assassins of Maṣyāf had long coveted its possession and seized the opportunity first; their stubborn defense of the citadel gave time

[8] Cf. below, chapter XVII, p. 539, where the Christian defeat is described as an ambush at Jacob's Ford.

for disputes to break out between the Frankish leaders, and the enterprise was abandoned.[9]

Meanwhile, in Aleppo itself the Shī'ites, thirsting to escape from the severe control of Nūr-ad-Dīn, had, after extracting from Nuṣrat-ad-Dīn promises in their favor, forced the city gates, and organized a violent demonstration against the governor of the citadel, Ibn-ad-Dāyah. But ocular proof that Nūr-ad-Dīn was still alive was enough to quell the disturbance, and Nuṣrat-ad-Dīn was dispatched as governor to Harran. The army was still disorganized, however, and during Nūr-ad-Dīn's long convalescence failed to intervene when Baldwin, with the forces of Antioch and Tripoli, besieged and recaptured Ḥārim in January or February 1158.[10] Shīrkūh had lately rejoined Nūr-ad-Dīn at Aleppo, apparently with the object of reorganizing the Zengid forces, but his absence gave an opening to raiders from the kingdom of Jerusalem, who ravaged the country south of Damascus with impunity. In early spring, however, while contingents from Egypt began an extensive series of raids in the south of Palestine, Nūr-ad-Dīn and Shīrkūh returned from Aleppo and, after a raid on Sidon by the latter, joined forces in an attack on the stronghold called Ḥabīs Jaldak, on the south bank of the Yarmuk river (in May). On Baldwin's advance to the northeast of Lake Tiberias, where he threatened the Moslem lines of communication, Nūr-ad-Dīn joined battle but suffered a defeat, retrieved only by his personal courage (July 15). His proposals for an armistice having been rejected, Nūr-ad-Dīn remained at Damascus, continuing the negotiations with the Egyptian vizir, but again fell seriously ill at the close of the year.

In face of the imminent danger to Aleppo implied in the emperor Manuel's sudden invasion of Cilicia, Nūr-ad-Dīn had the oath of allegiance taken by his officers to his brother Quṭb-ad-Dīn and sent envoys to Mosul to acquaint him with the decision, but before Quṭb-ad-Dīn could arrive with his troops Nūr-ad-Dīn recovered and himself set out towards Aleppo in March 1159. Although Manuel had already opened communications with Nūr-ad-Dīn, his entry into Antioch at the end of March and the subsequent advance of the combined Greek and Latin forces to 'Imm made it necessary to neglect no precautions. On Nūr-ad-Dīn's urgent summons the forces of Mosul and contingents from all the vassal and allied principalities in Mesopotamia joined him east of Aleppo, and the city was further strengthened by an outer wall. But

[9] On the capture of Maṣyāf by the Assassins see above, chapter IV, p. 119.
[10] Cf. below, chapter XVII, p. 542.

Manuel had little reason to desire the destruction of Nūr-ad-Dīn's power, wishing rather to utilize him, negatively, to hold the Latins in check in Syria, and, positively, as an ally against Kilij Arslan in Anatolia. Negotiations were accordingly set in train at the end of May, and in return for Nūr-ad-Dīn's surrender of Bertram of Toulouse, Bertrand of Blancfort, the master of the Temple, and other Frankish prisoners, the alliance was formed and Manuel withdrew to Anatolia, "having earned thanks and praise, and without injuring a single Moslem."[11]

The immediate advantages which accrued to Nūr-ad-Dīn from this situation were limited to the occupation of Raban, Kesoun, Behesni, and Marash while Kilij Arslan was engaged against the emperor and the Dānishmendid Yaghi-Basan, in the course of 1160. During the same year Reginald of Châtillon fell into his hands, captured by Ibn-ad-Dāyah on his return from a raid against Aintab in November. But in spite of the confusion which resulted from this in Antioch, Nūr-ad-Dīn seems to have been unable to turn it to profit, and indeed after some raiding, he concluded an armistice with Baldwin. Either before or after this, however, he made an attack on Ḥārim, which was repulsed by a combined force of Latins, Greeks, and Armenians, but succeeded in recovering Arzghān, which had been retaken earlier by Reginald.

The two-year armistice with Baldwin relieved Nūr-ad-Dīn's anxieties over Damascus and the south, which had been exposed, almost unprotected, to some raiding during his northern campaign in 1160. But the course of events in Egypt set him a new, and even embarrassing, problem. When Shavar, driven out by Dirgam in August 1163, appealed for military assistance to reinstate him, Nūr-ad-Dīn, already burdened with the task of maintaining his extensive territories with relatively small forces, hesitated. Finally, however, he was persuaded to accept the proposal by Shīrkūh, "a man of great bravery and strength of character, and impervious to fear," on the understanding that Nūr-ad-Dīn should receive one-third of the revenues of Egypt, less the pay of his troops. Shīrkūh set out late in April 1164, accompanied by his nephew Saladin, and defeated and killed Dirgam under the walls of Cairo in August. Shavar's failure to observe his engagement led Shīrkūh to occupy the province of Sharqiya; the vizir then called on Amalric for assistance on the former terms, and the joint forces of the Latins and Egyptians besieged Shīrkūh in Bilbais for three months.[12] At length Amalric agreed to treat;

[11] On the Byzantine intervention see below, chapter XVII, pp. 543–545.

[12] For further discussion of Amalric's Egyptian policy, see below, chapter XVII, pp. 549–550.

Shīrkūh, already hard-pressed, consented to evacuate the town and return to Syria, and his withdrawal in October was followed by that of the Franks.

Amalric's eagerness to leave Egypt was occasioned by the disasters which Nūr-ad-Dīn, profiting by the engagement of large Latin forces in Egypt, had inflicted on the Franks during his absence. Although his first diversionary raid towards Tripoli had ended in the all-but-total destruction of his force at Krak des Chevaliers (Ḥiṣn al-Akrād) in May, he had immediately called for and received substantial reinforcements from Mosul and the Artukid princes of Ḥiṣn Kaifā and Mardin, and with these he renewed the attack on Ḥārim. All the available forces from Tripoli and Antioch, together with the Armenians and Greeks from Cilicia, rallied to its defense, but were drawn into battle and totally defeated in the plain of Artāḥ at the beginning of August 1164. Bohemond III, Raymond III of Tripoli, the Greek duke Coloman, and Hugh of Lusignan were among the prisoners.

The surrender of Ḥārim followed in a few days. Nūr-ad-Dīn, anxious to avoid drawing the Greeks into the defense of Antioch, and hoping to utilize the opportunity of Humphrey's absence in Egypt, with Amalric, dismissed the Mesopotamians and made a surprise march on Banyas. The garrison, deprived of all hope of relief, surrendered the castle on October 18, and the victory was signalized by an agreement to divide the revenues of Tiberias.[13] In spite of the failure of Shīrkūh's expedition to Egypt, therefore, the net result had been to consolidate Nūr-ad-Dīn's possessions in Syria and to raise his prestige to new heights in the Moslem world.

But the continued evidences of Byzantine interest in Antioch deterred him from further military activities in the north, and led to a rapprochement with sultan Kilij Arslan, to whom he restored Behesni, Kesoun, and Marash in 1166 or 1167. Minor raids were probably undertaken in central Syria, and the Damascus troops under Shīrkūh captured two cave strongholds, one near Sidon and the other east of the Jordan. But on the whole it seems clear that Nūr-ad-Dīn was biding his time, and watching with caution and possibly with anxiety the course of events both as between Latins and Greeks and in Mosul. Here his young and feckless brother Quṭb-ad-Dīn had dismissed and imprisoned the vizir Jamāl-ad-Dīn in the summer of 1163. The removal of his strong and experienced hand had created new tensions at Mosul, which the commandant, 'Alī Küchük, was unable to control. In 1167/1168,

[13] Cf. below, chapter XVII, p. 551.

now half blind and deaf, he surrendered all his fiefs and governorships, except Irbil, to which he retired and which, on his death shortly afterwards, he left to his son Gökböri as his successor, under the control of his mamluk Mujāhid-ad-Dīn Qaimāz. His place at Mosul was taken by a white mamluk of Zengi's, Fakhr-ad-Dīn 'Abd-al-Massīḥ, under whom matters continued to deteriorate.

In January 1167 Shīrkūh again invaded Egypt, at the head of a detachment of Nūr-ad-Dīn's troops, with Turkoman reinforcements. No reason is assigned for this expedition except Shīrkūh's own desire to avenge himself on Shavar.[14] As on the previous occasion, Nūr-ad-Dīn, on Shīrkūh's departure, summoned the aid of Quṭb-ad-Dīn's forces from Mosul and engaged in widespread raiding and destruction in the territories of Tripoli, capturing al-Munaiṭirah (Le Moinestre) and destroying Chastel-Neuf (Ḥūnīn). Shīrkūh's and Amalric's return, and dissensions between the troops of Aleppo and Mosul, brought the campaign to an end, and Nūr-ad-Dīn made over Raqqa to Quṭb-ad-Dīn, who occupied it on the way back. In the following spring the rebellion of a governor — a rare event in Nūr-ad-Dīn's career — involved an expedition to Manbij to displace him and a personal intervention at Edessa. Barely had he returned to Aleppo in April 1168 when the 'Uqailid prince of Qal'at Ja'bar, Mālik ibn-'Alī, was captured by the Kalb Arabs and brought to him as a prisoner. For many months, in spite of promises and threats, the 'Uqailid refused to surrender his fortress, which withstood all the assaults of the Aleppo armies, but finally consented to exchange it for Sarūj and other fiefs, and it was made over in October to Majd-ad-Dīn Ibn-ad-Dāyah.

With this conquest Nūr-ad-Dīn put an end to the last of the independent principalities in northern Syria and became fully master of the territories to the west of the principality of Mosul. Only a few weeks later he received the urgent appeal from the Fāṭimid caliph and the vizir Shavar which led to Shīrkūh's third and final expedition to Egypt. Its addition, in January 1169, to the list of provinces which acknowledged him as sultan or as suzerain seemed to be the apogee of Nūr-ad-Dīn's career.[15] But his ambitions were growing with the extension of his power. Many years before, he had been foiled in the attempt to assert his authority over Mosul itself, and he had since watched for an opportunity to

[14] Cf. below, chapter XVII, p. 552.

[15] For the effect of this on the Latin states, see below, chapter XVII, p. 556; for further details regarding Saladin's role in Egypt see below, chapter XVIII, pp. 564–566.

achieve this purpose. In 1166 or 1167, the Artukid prince Kara Arslan of Ḥiṣn Kaifā on his death had left his son and heir Nūr-ad-Dīn Muḥammad under the guardianship of Nūr-ad-Dīn, who sharply intervened to restrain his brother Quṭb-ad-Dīn at Mosul from asserting his suzerain rights over the principality. This protectorate served Nūr-ad-Dīn's purpose when Quṭb-ad-Dīn died, at the age of forty, in August 1170, and the succession was disputed by his elder son 'Imād-ad-Dīn and younger son Saif-ad-Dīn Ghāzī. Hastily assembling a light troop, Nūr-ad-Dīn crossed the Euphrates, invested and reoccupied Raqqa, halted at Nisibin where he was joined by his Artukid namesake and other troops, took Sinjar by force and bestowed it on his nephew 'Imād-ad-Dīn, and advanced to Balad on the Tigris. A few days later Mosul surrendered, and Nūr-ad-Dīn, having received the caliph's diploma for the city and its dependencies, reinstated Saif-ad-Dīn as his vassal, and placed his own mamluk Sa'd-ad-Dīn Gümüshtigin in command of the citadel. After receiving homage from Gökböri and Qaimāz of Irbil, he installed his own governors in the cities of upper Mesopotamia, and returned to Aleppo in March 1171.

This expedition to Mosul could be made with the greater impunity since in the summer of 1170, beginning towards the end of June, a further series of earthquakes had laid in ruins a number of cities and their fortifications in northern Syria, including Antioch, Tripoli, Jabala, and Latakia, as well as Aleppo, Hamah, and Homs. Both sides, faced with the necessity of rebuilding their fortresses, agreed to a truce. In the autumn of 1171 this was broken by the seizure of two Egyptian merchant ships at Latakia. Nūr-ad-Dīn in retaliation called up the troops of Mosul and upper Mesopotamia and engaged in a violent raiding campaign in the territories of Tripoli, during which he captured 'Arqah. Immediately afterwards he arranged with Saladin, now his lieutenant in Egypt, to join him in an attack on Kerak (Krak des Moabites), and in October moved south to meet him there. Saladin set out from Cairo at the end of September, but returned without meeting Nūr-ad-Dīn, who abandoned the siege before the Latins under Humphrey could intervene. In the autumn of the next year he was again engaged against Frankish raiding parties in the Hauran, and sent a counter-raid against Tiberias. Although he was still actively seeking to stimulate public feeling in his territories in favor of the *jihād*,[16] this was apparently his last contest with the Franks of Syria.

[16] One remarkable initiative in this direction was his order in 1169 to construct a *minbar*

For already, although he had built up a powerful war machine to be used against the crusaders, his ambitions had implicated him in a series of operations in the north which were to lead him into conflict with the Moslems of Anatolia instead. On the death of Ṭoros of Cilicia in 1168, his brother Mleh, who held Cyrrhus as a fief from Nūr-ad-Dīn, invaded Cilicia with the support of a contingent from Aleppo, which remained in his service and assisted him to drive out the Templars and Greeks from the fortresses and, in 1173, the cities which they held in Cilicia. An expedition organized by Amalric after his return from Constantinople in 1171 was interrupted by Nūr-ad-Dīn's attack on Kerak, and Mleh remained master of Cilicia until Nūr-ad-Dīn's death.

During these events in Cilicia the Selchükid Kïlïj Arslan had been actively breaking up the Dānishmendid principalities and annexing their territories, Albistan, Caesarea (Kayseri), and Ankara. In 1170 or 1171 he attacked Melitene (Malatya), but was repulsed, owing to the intervention of the Artukid Nūr-ad-Dīn of Ḥiṣn Kaifā. He then attacked the last Dānishmendid stronghold, Sebastia, whose prince appealed to Nūr-ad-Dīn. In the spring of 1173 he set out from Damascus, and after capturing Marash and Behesni, joined forces in August or September with Mleh and the troops of Melitene, and marched on Qalʿat ar-Rūm, on the Euphrates north of Bira. At this point Kïlïj Arslan sent overtures for peace. The precise terms of the agreement are uncertain; according to some sources Kïlïj Arslan consented to restore Ankara and Sebastia to their princes, and Nūr-ad-Dīn sent the former vizir of Mosul, ʿAbd-al-Massīh, with a contingent of his own troops to garrison Sebastia, but these returned to Aleppo on the news of his death.

On his return, Nūr-ad-Dīn made a leisurely journey to Damascus, where shortly afterwards he fell seriously ill, and died on May 15, 1174, leaving only a minor son as his heir. Almost instantaneously the territorial and military organization which he had built up with so much labor fell to pieces. But, in contrast to his father Zengi, he had by his life and conduct laid the foundations for that moral unification of Moslem forces on which alone a real political and military unity could be reared. It is ironical that the great name and reputation which he left was to prove one of the major obstacles to the efforts of his true successor, Saladin, to resume his task and bring it to fruition.

or pulpit destined for the Aqṣâ mosque in Jerusalem after its recovery. The work was finished only after his death, but was duly installed in Jerusalem by Saladin.

XVII
THE LATIN STATES UNDER BALDWIN III AND AMALRIC I
1143–1174

The period of forty years or so which followed the death of king Fulk began and ended in defeat. In 1144 Edessa (Urfa) fell. Jerusalem was taken by Saladin in 1187. Yet for the three states, Antioch, Tripoli, and Jerusalem, the intervening years were prosperous and brought to fruition their development as western European "colonies". Western usages, political, religious, economic, and military, modified to suit eastern conditions, were successfully implanted in Palestine and Syria, and the European conquerors reached a *modus vivendi* with the native population, both Moslem and Christian.

Since this chapter is concerned with the political history of the kingdom of Jerusalem and the other Latin states, the following select bibliography does not include works on strictly economic, religious, or institutional developments.

The standard Latin source for the period from 1143 to 1174 is William of Tyre, *Historia rerum in partibus transmarinis gestarum* (on which cf. the bibliographical notes to earlier chapters): the Latin text with an Old French version is given in *RHC, Occ.*, I. A. C. Krey has discussed William's life and work thoroughly in his introduction to the English translation and in "The Making of an Historian in the Middle Ages," *Speculum*, XVI (1941), 149–166. In 1167 William was commissioned by king Amalric to record his Egyptian campaigns and in 1170 a more ambitious history of the kings of Jerusalem was undertaken. He was also tutor to the king's son, the future Baldwin IV, and was as a rule well informed regarding important developments. The period covered in this chapter was probably written after 1180.

The principal Moslem sources are Ibn-al-Athīr, *Al-kāmil fī-t-ta'rīkh* (extracts in *RHC, Or.*, I, 187–744) and *Ta'rīkh ad-daulah al-atābakīyah mulūk al-Mauṣil* (*RHC, Or.*, II, part 2); Ibn-al-Qalānisī, *Dhail ta'rīkh Dimashq* (extracts translated by H. A. R. Gibb, *The Damascus Chronicle of the Crusades*, London, 1932); abū-Shāmah, *Kitāb ar-rauḍatain* (*RHC, Or.*, IV–V); Kamāl-ad-Dīn, *Zubdat al-ḥalab fī ta'rikh Ḥalab* (tr. E. Blochet, "Histoire d'Alep," *ROL*, II–VI, 1894–1898): Usāmah Ibn-Munqidh, *Kitāb al-i'tibār*, tr. P. K. Hitti, *An Arab-Syrian Gentleman in the Period of the Crusades* (Columbia University, Records of Civilization, New York, 1929); al-Maqrīzī, *Akhbār Miṣr* (tr. E. Blochet, "Histoire d'Égypte," *ROL*, VI–IX, 1898–1902).

The Byzantine historians John Cinnamus and Nicetas Choniates can be found in *RHC, Grecs*, I, as well as in Migne, and the *Corpus Scriptorum Historiae Byzantinae.* Gregory the Presbyter continued the Armenian chronicle of Matthew of Edessa to 1163 (*RHC, Arm.*, I). Michael the Syrian's chronicle is edited and translated by J. B. Chabot (4 vols., Paris, 1899–1900) and (in part) in *RHC, Arm.*, I.

By the middle of the twelfth century the Latin states had reached a point in their development where each could manage its own affairs. There was, as a consequence, a tendency to disregard such feudal ties as had earlier bound the three states together. Rare, for example, were the instances when the counts of Tripoli recognized the suzerainty of Jerusalem. At most, the king of Jerusalem possessed a superior dignity as *primus inter pares*. His intervention in Tripoli or Antioch — as also the intervention of northern princes in Jerusalem — usually resulted from ties of blood relationship or followed a formal request for aid from the local *curia*. Common danger was the most important element in uniting the forces of the three states. But even in times of crisis coöperation was disappointingly difficult to secure. Without a common policy the Latin states were at best a loose federation.

The greatest problem confronting the Syrian Latins was military security. They were a minority in an alien land and the number of troops which the various baronies and military orders could provide was limited. Native auxiliaries were occasionally useful but not consistently reliable. Numerical inferiority was in part offset by certain other factors. To natural barriers of mountain, river, and desert, the crusaders added formidable fortresses at critical points along the frontier. In the later years of the twelfth century most of these were garrisoned by Templars and Hospitallers. Command of the sea was maintained by the Italians,

These sources can be supplemented by a number of other chronicles, letters, and documents which are cited in the standard secondary reference works. For the details of narrative history the most important of these are: R. Grousset, *Histoire des croisades et du royaume franc de Jérusalem*, vol. II, *Monarchie franque et monarchie musulmane: l'équilibre* (Paris, 1935); R. Röhricht, *Geschichte des Königreichs Jerusalem, 1100–1291* (Innsbruck, 1898); S. Runciman, *A History of the Crusades*, vol. II: *The Kingdom of Jerusalem* (Cambridge, 1952); and W. B. Stevenson, *The Crusaders in the East* (Cambridge, 1907). Institutional history is covered by J. L. LaMonte, *Feudal Monarchy in the Latin Kingdom of Jerusalem, 1100–1291* (Cambridge, Mass.: Mediaeval Academy, 1932).

Additional material can be found in C. Cahen, *La Syrie du nord à l'époque des croisades et la principauté franque d'Antioche* (Paris, 1940); F. Chalandon, *Les Comnène: Jean II Comnène (1118–1143) et Manuel I Comnène (1143–1180)* (Paris, 1912), and "The Later Comneni," *Cambridge Medieval History*, IV; Annie Herzog, *Die Frau auf den Fürstenthronen der Kreuzfahrerstaaten* (Berlin, 1919); J. L. LaMonte, "The Lords of Sidon in the Twelfth and Thirteenth Centuries," *Byzantion*, XVII (1944–1945), 183–211; "The Lords of Caesarea in the Period of the Crusades," *Speculum*, XXII (1947), 145–161; [with Norton Downs] "The Lords of Bethsan in the Kingdom of Jerusalem and Cyprus," *Medievalia et Humanistica*, fasc. VI; S. Lane-Poole, *Saladin and the Fall of the Kingdom of Jerusalem* (New York, 1898, new ed., 1926); Jean Richard, *Le Comté de Tripoli sous la dynastie toulousaine (1102–1187)* (Paris, 1945), *Le Royaume latin de Jérusalem*, Paris, 1953; Leopoldo Usseglio, *I Marchesi di Monferrato in Italia ed in Oriente*, 2 vols., Casale Monferrato, 1926; G. Schlumberger, *Campagnes du roi Amaury Ier en Égypte* (Paris, 1906), and *Renaud de Châtillon* (Paris, 1898); H. F. Tournebize, *Histoire politique et religieuse de l'Arménie* (Paris, 1910); and A. A. Vasiliev, *History of the Byzantine Empire*, Madison, 1952.

and although reinforcements from Europe were never adequate, supplies were assured.

From years of experience the Syrian Latins had learned their own capacities and limitations. Especially had they become familiar with the weaknesses of their opponents. The divisions in Levantine Islam which had facilitated the original conquest were an important element in their continuing security. Judicious alliances with friendly Moslem powers — a procedure never understood by crusaders fresh from Europe — helped to maintain a Levantine balance of power. This advantage was destined to be lost during the second half of the twelfth century as Near Eastern Islam was progressively unified under able leadership.

Partly as a consequence of the military and political successes of Islam, the role of Constantinople in the grand strategy of the Levant became more significant. John Comnenus, it will be recalled, had revived Byzantine power in Cilicia and northern Syria. At his death in 1143 Franco-Byzantine relations were severely strained. Manuel Comnenus (1143–1180) added to his predecessors' claims over Antioch an ambition to extend Byzantine influence southward and westward in the Mediterranean. In the face of a resurgent Islam the Latins were forced to solicit his aid and make concessions which earlier crusaders had refused. For a number of years Manuel was a kind of arbiter of Near Eastern politics.

Frequent mention will also be made in the following pages of Cilician Armenia. Although there were occasional border conflicts with Antioch, Armenia was generally friendly to the Latins, as the number of prominent intermarriages testifies. The kingdom was formally a vassal state of Byzantium. To maintain some sort of independence against Constantinople and against its Moslem neighbors was its hope. Its efforts to do so form part of the complex pattern of contemporary Near Eastern diplomacy.

When king Fulk died, his son Baldwin was only thirteen years old, and the high court (the Haute Cour of the Assises de Jérusalem) devised a somewhat unusual arrangement for the succession. On Christmas day, 1143, queen Melisend and her son were both crowned. Melisend's government, therefore, was less a regency than a joint rule. Like most divisions of power, it was not an unqualified success once Baldwin reached an age where he could fend for himself. It was especially unfortunate in the period of crisis following the fall of Edessa. The loss of Edessa, which was described in two previous chapters, was a grievous blow to the

Latin orient. Not only was the capital of a Christian principality captured — and the remaining towns east of the Euphrates could not survive long — but the possibility of menacing communications between Aleppo and Mesopotamia was removed. Christian loss was Moslem gain and the union of Moslem Syria was a step nearer.

Fortunately for the Franks, Zengi was not able to follow up his initial successes and within two years (September 1146) he was assassinated. His lands were partitioned between two of his sons, Saif-ad-Dīn Ghāzī, who took Mosul and the east, and Nūr-ad-Dīn, to whom fell the western territories and Aleppo.[1] It was Nūr-ad-Dīn, therefore, with whom the Latins had to reckon. Although he was deprived of the strength Zengi had derived from Mesopotamia, Nūr-ad-Dīn was also free of many political complications which had plagued his father. Thus he could concentrate on creating a power in Moslem Syria capable of challenging the Latins without help from Mosul. Nūr-ad-Dīn was admired as well as feared by his enemies. William of Tyre generously described him as "a wise and prudent man and according to the superstitious traditions of his people, one who feared God." The Franks were soon to test his strength in a second and final siege of Edessa.

Encouraged by the news of Zengi's death the Armenian residents of Edessa communicated with its former count, Joscelin II, and plotted the recovery of the city. Sometime in October 1146 Joscelin and Baldwin of Marash appeared before the city, but they were not adequately equipped. Before they could reduce the inner citadel, Nūr-ad-Dīn had surrounded the town with ten thousand men. In a desperate sortie some Christians escaped, among them Joscelin, but Baldwin of Marash fell, and thousands of luckless native Christians were massacred. Thus the second siege of Edessa proved far worse than the first and the city never recovered its former prominence.

An immediate consequence of the fall of Edessa was the added danger to Antioch. Although Raymond of Poitiers, the prince of Antioch, had not assisted his fellow Christians of Edessa, he now realized his predicament and sought a rapprochement with Manuel Comnenus. No Byzantine troops came to his assistance, however, and in the course of the years 1147 and 1148 Nūr-ad-Dīn captured Artāḥ, Māmūlah, Basarfūt, and Kafarlāthā. Most of the principality's possessions beyond the Orontes, therefore, were lost.

[1] For the development of Nūr-ad-Dīn's power see above, chapter XVI.

With losses sustained in the north, the security of the Latin Levant depended more than ever on the relations between Jerusalem and those Moslem states, notably Damascus, which still resisted the southward advance of the Aleppans. Earlier chapters have described Frankish relations with Damascus; and it will be recalled that Muʿīn-ad-Dīn Unur (or Önör), the governor, had allied with king Fulk. On Zengi's death, Unur had quickly occupied Baalbek and entered into negotiations with the governors of Homs and Hamah. At the same time his astute sense of diplomacy had prompted him to appease Zengi's successor. In March 1147 Unur's daughter married Nūr-ad-Dīn. But he had ample reason to continue his friendly dispositions toward Jerusalem, which a characteristic loyalty to treaty obligations dictated. It seems obvious too that the most elementary diplomatic and strategic considerations should have led the Latins to avoid any actions which might endanger this Levantine balance of power. Yet this was precisely the error committed by the leaders of the Second Crusade.[2]

Our fifteenth chapter has described in detail the Second Crusade of 1147–1149. To Christian Europe the failure represented a tragic shattering of high hopes. To the Latin east it was more than a military defeat. Christian prestige in the orient had been dangerously weakened. The one thing the Moslems feared most, a powerful expedition from Europe, had arrived and been repulsed. Further, the breach with Damascus, so long well disposed toward Jerusalem, upset the Levantine equilibrium and paved the way for the eventual union of Aleppo and Damascus.

After the Second Crusade, the Moslems, emboldened by success and assisted by continued quarrels in Christian ranks, pressed their advantage and made new gains in northern Syria. Count Raymond II of Tripoli actually sought Moslem assistance in dislodging Bertram, grandson of Raymond of St. Gilles, from al-ʿArīmah, the citadel of which was destroyed, and Bertram, along with others, was captured.[3] When Raymond of Antioch advanced to thwart Nūr-ad-Dīn's moves east of the Orontes, a bold attack with a small force won him an initial advantage. But on the night of

[2] Even before the Second Crusade, the bellicose elements in the king's council forced a similar error. In the spring of 1147 the authorities in Jerusalem accepted the tempting offer of a rebellious emir in the Hauran. The campaign proved to be a dismal failure redeemed only by the courageous conduct of Baldwin III and a well disciplined retreat. Cf. Runciman, *History of the Crusades*, II, 241–243.

[3] Bertram with Languedocian troops from the Second Crusade had besieged the castle. Raymond had then asked the assistance of Unur, who came with Nūr-ad-Dīn. Apparently Unur signed a truce with the kingdom in May 1149. Cf. Runciman, *Crusades*, II, 287–288.

June 29, 1149, his troops were surrounded, and Raymond with Reginald of Marash perished in the battle.[4] The atabeg then advanced toward Antioch ravaging the countryside as far as the coast where he exultantly bathed in the Mediterranean. The defenders of Antioch, directed by the patriarch Aimery, were accorded a short truce. Moslem troops were kept on guard, however, and Nūr-ad-Dīn returned to complete the capture of Ḥārim.

These Moslem successes and Raymond of Poitiers' death produced a situation which required intervention from Jerusalem. In Antioch the government had fallen to Raymond's young widow, Constance, who had been left with four children. Although the patriarch Aimery had rallied the discouraged defenders and messages had been sent to Europe, immediate reinforcement was vital. In fact, when Baldwin III arrived to assist Antioch, all the possessions of the principality east of the Orontes had been lost. An attempt to recapture Ḥārim failed, but Nūr-ad-Dīn was for the moment satisfied with his conquests, and a truce provided a much needed respite. It was possible, therefore, to put Antioch's defenses in order.

The king was also able to salvage, at least temporarily, the vestiges of the county of Edessa. The final liquidation of Edessa could not, however, be long delayed. On May 4, 1150, Joscelin was ambushed on the way to Antioch. His Turkoman captors were willing to set him free on payment of ransom, but the atabeg quickly sent a corps of soldiers who brought the count to Aleppo where he died nine years later. Despite threats of injury he refused to abjure his faith and, since he was unable to obtain a Latin priest, received the last rites at the hands of a Jacobite bishop.

On the news of Joscelin's capture, Mas'ūd, Selchükid sultan of Iconium (Konya), advanced into Latin territory and in May 1150 took Kesoun, Behesni, Raban, and other outlying possessions of Edessa. Considerable numbers of the inhabitants made their way to Tell Bashir where Joscelin's wife, Beatrice, was valiantly holdnig out. Meanwhile, Nūr-ad-Dīn took 'Azāz, which with Ḥārim made him master of the hinterland of Antioch.

These events brought Baldwin once again to Syria accompanied by Humphrey of Toron and Guy of Beirut. He was joined by Raymond II of Tripoli and his troops. When the royal party reached Antioch, the king found that although Mas'ūd had been

[4] Apparently Raymond of Antioch had the assistance of a Kurdish Assassin leader who also was killed. Cf. above, chapter IV, p. 120, and XVI, p. 515. See also chapter XVI, pp. 515–516, for an analysis of Nūr-ad-Dīn's own conception of his "mission" at this time.

called away, Nūr-ad-Dīn had invested the entire region of Tell Bashir. Some hope, however, was afforded by the intervention of Manuel Comnenus. He had offered financial support to Beatrice and her children in return for the surrender of the fortresses still in her possession. The matter was referred to king Baldwin, and when Byzantine envoys further explained the emperor's purpose to Baldwin, the latter decided to agree to the transfer. The magnates of both Antioch and Jerusalem who were present were divided in their opinion, but the king sided with those who argued that further delay would be fatal. Moreover, it was evident that with both northern states deprived of their rulers, there was not adequate strength in the Latin east to maintain authority beyond the now shrunken confines of Antioch. And if the territory were eventually lost, the failure would be attributed to the emperor and not to Jerusalem. Therefore, with the consent of the countess and her children, Tell Bashir and the other remaining possessions of the county — Ravendan, Aintab, Duluk, Bira, and Samosata — were surrendered to the Greeks. As many had predicted, the Byzantines were able to maintain their new acquisitions only a few months. The lands of the former county of Edessa were eventually divided among the Selchükids of Iconium, the Artukids, and Nūr-ad-Dīn.[5]

Busy though he was in the north, Baldwin did not neglect the defenses of Jerusalem. Probably during the winter of 1149–1150, Gaza, an important defense position against Ascalon, was rebuilt and assigned to the Templars. Twice, early in 1150 and again in the spring of 1151, Nūr-ad-Dīn's moves on Damascus were checked by Latin troop movements. Thus the king and barons of Jerusalem maintained and even improved the position of the kingdom to counteract the disasters in the north.

Throughout the years following the Second Crusade it was becoming evident to many that Baldwin had attained a political maturity which justified a full assumption of royal authority. Although Melisend had governed well and had firmly upheld the rights of the crown, her interests were too narrowly local, whereas the activities of her son bespoke a wider view of the needs of the Latin orient. For some time Baldwin had coöperated successfully with his mother, but the joint rule had been prolonged well past the customary age of majority, for in 1150 the king was twenty years old. A most unfortunate rift which had grown between the

[5] For a more detailed discussion of Moslem movements see above, chapter XVI, pp. 516–517.

mother and son was widened when Melisend appointed her cousin, Manasses of Hierges, as constable. Manasses was haughty, intolerant, and generally unpopular, but connected by marriage with the important Ibelin family, and so the queen was not without considerable support among the nobility. A number of barons, however, urged Baldwin to take the crown. Some, it is true, and among these was the patriarch Fulcher, counseled the young man to include his mother in the ceremony of coronation. But he preferred the advice of others and, after postponing the ceremony, was crowned alone two days after Easter 1151 (or 1152).[6] Partly as a consequence of his precipitate action, the rift between the supporters of the queen and those of Baldwin degenerated into civil war.

Following the coronation, the king summoned the high court. He then asked his mother to divide the kingdom and concede at least part of his rightful inheritance. This was done. The king received the coastal cities of Tyre and Acre with their dependencies, while Jerusalem and Nablus were left to the queen. Manasses, the queen's favorite, was deposed, and Humphrey II of Toron appointed constable. The division of authority satisfied no one and was soon followed by hostilities. Manasses was successfully besieged in his castle of Mirabel and forced to renounce his lands. Nablus was likewise taken, and Melisend sought refuge in Jerusalem. As Baldwin advanced in force, the queen with a few of her adherents, notably Philip of Nablus, Amalric, count of Jaffa and the king's brother, and Rohard the elder, retired to the citadel. Several days of furious assault followed before either side would accept mediation. Then Melisend agreed to relinquish Jerusalem, and Baldwin took a solemn oath to respect his mother's tenure of Nablus. Thus peace was restored, and the king could proceed with the important affairs of government.

During the years following king Baldwin III's assumption of full royal responsibility two developments stand out. First, the king frequently found it necessary to intervene in the concerns of Tripoli and Antioch. Sometime in 1152 Raymond II of Tripoli was attacked and killed at the city gates by a band of Assassins. The king was in Tripoli at the time, having come with his mother in an attempt to reconcile the count with his wife, the countess

[6] The date is not certain. According to the order of events as related by William of Tyre, XVII, 13, 14 (*RHC, Occ.*, I, 779–781), the coronation preceded the trip north for the final liquidation of Edessa (1150). There is reason to believe, however, that the rupture with Melisend occurred in 1151 or even in 1152. See Stevenson, *Crusaders*, p. 152; Röhricht, *Königreich*, pp. 265ff.; LaMonte, *Feudal Monarchy*, pp. 16–18; Krey, *William of Tyre*, II, 205, note 9; Runciman, *Crusades*, II, 333–334.

Hodierna. It was under the king's direction that the Tripolitan barons now swore allegiance to the countess and her children, Raymond III, then only twelve, and his younger sister Melisend. In Antioch, Byzantine pressure was still very evident, and Manuel Comnenus sought in various ways to extend his power southward. Both the emperor and king Baldwin had tried to induce the princess Constance of Antioch to remarry. Manuel urged her to accept a Byzantine prince. Baldwin suggested various noblemen whom he thought capable of shouldering the heavy responsibility of defending the exposed frontiers. At a council of notables held at Tripoli, everyone earnestly besought the young woman to take a husband if only for the sake of the principality. But Constance persistently refused. A more romantic solution was soon to present itself, and was perhaps already in her mind. Jerusalem and Constantinople were not, however, always in conflict. There were to be important periods of coöperation. And both were worried about the gradual encirclement of Christian Syria by Nūr-ad-Dīn. The second great concern of Baldwin's reign was the grand strategy of frontier expansion and defense against the menacing advance of Aleppo. Although these two major concerns, the northern states and the frontiers of Jerusalem, were clearly related, it will be convenient to consider first the frontier policy as it affected the kingdom of Jerusalem.

In previous years the intermittent skirmishes along the southern frontier, far less serious than in the north and east, had not greatly worried the Franks. But after the retreats in northern Syria, Baldwin wisely sought to counteract Moslem advances there by pushing southward. Moreover, in so doing, he was formulating a strategy which was to continue under his successor. The key to the situation was Ascalon, whose capture, long considered desirable, now seemed a necessity. Ascalon, the "bride of Syria", was highly prized by the Egyptians and provided a bulwark against the Latins. Hence it had been their policy to send supplies and reinforcements to its already large population four times a year. Situated on a semicircular area sloping toward the sea, it was surrounded by artificial mounds additionally fortified by heavy walls upon which many towers were mounted. Its four gates were also defended by massive towers. An outer line of solidly constructed fortifications added to the city's strength. Indeed, Ascalon was generally regarded as impregnable.

But although Ascalon itself was strong, the government at Cairo which stood behind it was weakening. The Fāṭimid caliphs had been largely supplanted by their vizirs. Assassinations were not infrequent. In fact, such was the decadence of the Fāṭimid dynasty that outside intervention seemed inevitable, if not from Christian Jerusalem, then from Moslem Syria. The Christian army which assembled before Ascalon in January 1153, augmented when a full siege was finally decided upon, contained the flower of Latin Syrian knighthood. William of Tyre mentions by name: Hugh of Ibelin, Philip of Nablus, Humphrey of Toron, Simon of Tiberias, Gerard of Sidon, Guy of Beirut, Maurice of Montréal (ash-Shaubak), and Walter of St. Omer, the last-named serving for pay. Bernard of Tremelay, master of the Temple, and Raymond of Le Puy, master of the Hospital, were also present. Five bishops in addition to the patriarch Fulcher of Jerusalem accompanied the troops and escorted the sacred relic of the True Cross. The city was speedily blockaded, and Gerard of Sidon, in command of some fifteen ships, was ordered to prevent exit and all attempts at reinforcement by sea. But such was the vigilance and strength of the defenders that two months passed without progress.

During the spring the Christian army was reinforced by a number of knights and foot-soldiers who had recently arrived on pilgrimage, but this advantage was counterbalanced, toward the end of the fifth month of siege, by the arrival of a powerful Egyptian fleet of seventy large vessels and a number of smaller craft. Gerard of Sidon's squadron was easily routed and substantial reinforcements in both men and supplies were safely delivered. Notwithstanding this change in fortune, the attackers pressed on and succeeded in causing serious losses. They fought from a huge movable tower which they had managed to bring up against the wall in the face of heavy arrow fire. Attempts to burn the tower failed, and with a shift in wind a large fire set between the tower and the wall was blown back against the defenders. As a consequence, a section of the wall collapsed, permitting the master of the Templars, Bernard of Tremelay, and about forty men to enter the breach. They were soon cut off, however, and the breach mended. The corpses of the fallen were suspended over the walls and their heads severed and sent as trophies to the caliph.

Thoroughly discouraged by this new reverse, Baldwin summoned his men to council in the presence of the True Cross. The king and almost all the lay barons were ready to end the siege. But the patriarch, the archbishop of Tyre, the master of the Hospital, and the bulk of the clergy strongly contended that what had been commenced and carried forward so long should not be abandoned. This view prevailed and was ultimately accepted unanimously.

Accordingly, with the fury of desperation — for all must have realized that this was the last chance — the attack was resumed. The defenders suffered such heavy losses that after three days a truce was requested in order that the dead might be exchanged and properly buried. Shortly afterward, a huge stone hurled by a Frankish siege machine killed forty citizens carrying a heavy beam. This seemed to crown the misfortunes of the defenders, for they agreed that envoys be sent to negotiate terms of surrender. Three days were granted the inhabitants to leave, and military escort was promised as far as al-ʿArīsh.

The city fell on August 22, 1153, and a considerable booty in the form of money, supplies, and war material was collected. King Baldwin and his retinue entered the city amidst great jubilation. The Cross was born in solemn procession to the principal mosque, a beautiful structure later dedicated to St. Paul, where services of thanksgiving were offered. The government of Ascalon was entrusted to Amalric, count of Jaffa, the king's brother.

Thus it was that a half century after the First Crusade the conquest of the Palestinian sea coast was finally completed. Defeat in the north had apparently been counterbalanced by a great victory and a new southward orientation of policy inaugurated. This was to become especially evident after the new count of Jaffa and Ascalon succeeded his brother as king.

Important as was the strategic advantage won by the Christians at Ascalon it was offset within a few months by Nūr-ad-Dīn's success at Damascus. In April 1154 he appeared in force, blockaded the city, and began to advance through the outskirts. Once again Damascus appealed to Jerusalem, and in desperation Mujīr-ad-Dīn offered Baalbek and part of the Biqāʿ in return for assistance. But Nūr-ad-Dīn moved first, and took Damascus on April 25 before a Frankish army could swing into action. As a consequence Moslem and Christian Syria now consisted of two long narrow bands of territory lying adjacent to each other. From Cilicia to Ascalon the coast was Christian. The hinterland was for the first time under a single Moslem government.

For a number of years after 1154 Nūr-ad-Dīn was inclined to maintain peaceful relations with the Christian states. He needed time to assimilate his conquests and consolidate an authority still far from perfect. Apparently he was even willing to continue the tribute paid to Jerusalem by the previous regime. Baldwin was also disposed to avoid hostilities. Not only was he then unable to take the initiative, but aggressive moves from Egypt, principally coastal raids by the Egyptian fleet, occupied his attention for a few years. Accordingly in 1156 a truce which had been negotiated in June 1155 by mutual agreement was extended for another year, and Nūr-ad-Dīn bound himself to pay eight thousand Tyrian dinars.[7]

However, the truce was broken in the following year by depredations from Jerusalem in the region around Banyas, where it had been the custom for nomadic Arabs and Turkomans to drive their cattle. Nūr-ad-Dīn replied by attacking Banyas. The outer city was destroyed, and the defenders under Humphrey of Toron forced to take refuge in the citadel. The king arrived in time to force Nūr-ad-Dīn's withdrawal, and the city was restored. But a part of the king's army was ambushed at Jacob's Ford (June 19, 1157). With great difficulty the king escaped to Safad and thence to Acre with a handful of companions. Almost all his knights were captured, among them Hugh of Ibelin, Odo of St. Amand, king's marshal, Rohard of Jaffa and his brother Balian, and Bertrand of Blancfort, now master of the Temple.

A second attempt on Banyas was repulsed by king Baldwin with the assistance of Reginald of Châtillon, recently installed, as we shall see, as prince of Antioch, and the young Raymond III of Tripoli. These men joined the king at Noire Garde near Chastel-Neuf (Ḥūnīn) whence they could see the besieged city. Nūr-ad-Dīn was unwilling to risk an engagement and withdrew. About a year later (July 15, 1158) a series of movements by the king's army and by Nūr-ad-Dīn in the Sawād east of Lake Tiberias culminated in a brilliant victory for the Christian forces on the plain of al-Baṭīḥah.

In 1158, therefore, the situation between Damascus and Jerusalem remained much as before. None of the actions described amounted to a serious campaign any more than did the raids of the Egyptian fleet at the same period. The really significant developments were in the north where Byzantine intervention profoundly altered an already difficult situation. To these events we must now turn, considering first the king's activities in Syria after the fall of Ascalon.

During the early weeks of the siege of Ascalon, a time when the king was too preoccupied to give proper attention to the affairs of northern Syria, Constance of Antioch finally decided to marry.

[7] Cf. above, chapter XVI, pp. 520–521.

Having spurned all the princes who had been suggested and who might have advanced the development of the principality, she chose Reginald of Châtillon, a knight who had recently arrived in the east and entered the king's service. The choice was unfortunate. Reginald's lack of standing caused considerable gossip and subsequently complicated his dealings with those whose superior rank was well established. It soon became evident, too, that Reginald was of a turbulent and unruly disposition. An adventurer to the end, he was destined to waste his good qualities and to bring disaster to the Latin east, but he was a brave and dashing warrior and a handsome man. It is not difficult to understand why the young widow preferred him to less attractive men of higher estate.

Although the romantic pair were secretly betrothed, Constance was unwilling to celebrate the marriage publicly without the permission of king Baldwin. Reginald presented his case to the king when he was engaged before Ascalon (January 1153). No doubt Baldwin was too occupied to give the matter much consideration and Antioch would now have a protector. At any rate he consented and the marriage took place in the spring of 1153.

Among those who resented Constance's marriage was the patriarch of Antioch, Aimery. Not without ambition himself, he may have hoped Constance would prolong a regency which gave him considerable authority. Aimery's criticism eventually reached Reginald's ears. Aimery also refused Reginald's demands for money. Unable to control his wrath, the prince had the patriarch seized, brutally humiliated, and thrown into prison. King Baldwin was astounded as well as angered and sent the chancellor, Ralph, bishop of Bethlehem, and bishop Frederick of Acre to reprove and warn Reginald. Reluctantly the prince released Aimery and restored his property. But the patriarch decided to quit Antioch for Jerusalem, where he remained for some years.

Reginald displayed the same truculence in his early dealings with Manuel Comnenus, who was also far from pleased at Reginald's marriage. In return for campaign expenses, the prince had agreed to suppress a revolt in Cilician Armenia. Ṭoros II, a son of Leon I, who had once been a prisoner at Constantinople, had defeated Andronicus Comnenus and by 1152 had brought under his control the important Cilician cities. In 1155 the region of Alexandretta (İskenderun) was the scene of hostilities. Although there seems to be some doubt concerning the outcome, Ṭoros ceded areas along the gulf to the Templars in Antioch. Since the campaign benefited Antioch and not Byzantium, Manuel found reasons for postponing the promised payment. Whereupon Reginald turned in anger against the emperor and, apparently accompanied by Ṭoros, raided the island of Cyprus. The Greek governor, John Comnenus, Manuel's nephew, and his lieutenant, Michael Branas, vainly attempted to oppose the landing. Both were captured and the island so effectively pillaged that it never entirely recovered. An indefensible act, the raid was so much energy wasted in an enterprise of no military significance whatever.

Since Reginald had thus far accomplished nothing toward improving the position of his principality, the initiative fell to the king of Jerusalem. Toward the end of the summer of 1157 count Thierry of Alsace had arrived in Jerusalem with a considerable retinue. Moreover, in July and August several Moslem cities had been badly damaged by earthquakes. It was with great expectations, therefore, that Baldwin and the count moved northward and, together with Reginald and Raymond III of Tripoli, assembled a formidable army in the Buqai'ah valley in the vicinity of Krak des Chevaliers (Ḥiṣn al-Akrād). Thence an advance was made into the Orontes valley. Chastel-Rouge resisted successfully, and on the advice of Reginald the armies moved toward Antioch.

Meanwhile Nūr-ad-Dīn advanced to Inab, probably with the intention of crossing the Orontes and marching against Antioch. At Inab, however, he was taken so ill that his life was despaired of. This was probably in October of 1157. Having arranged for the disposition of his territories if he should die, he was carried on a litter to Aleppo while Shīrkūh went to defend Damascus. Sensing a perfect opportunity to strike, Baldwin and the other Christian leaders dispatched a message to Ṭoros urgently requesting his assistance. The Armenian responded promptly and led a considerable force to Antioch. The combined armies then marched on Shaizar. Shaizar was a city which, somewhat after the manner of Damascus, had escaped the full power of the Zengid dynasty. After the death of a pro-Frankish ruler in August 1157 and the destruction of part of the city in the earthquake of the same month, Shaizar had fallen into a sort of anarchy. Thus the situation was highly favorable to the Christians.

Capture of the lower city proved comparatively easy. Tight blockade forced the citizens within the walls, and well placed siege machines battered down the defenses. Not, apparently, warlike folk, the inhabitants abandoned the walls after several days and retreated to the citadel. This presented no great problem, but a most inopportune controversy over the disposition of the newly conquered territory stalled the Latin attack. The king intended to concede Shaizar to count Thierry, knowing that his strength, backed by the resources of a prominent European family, would be more than sufficient to maintain the city. Perhaps he envisaged a new Latin state beyond the Orontes, a buffer state to replace the lost Edessa. At any rate the plan was applauded by everyone except Reginald, who argued that since Shaizar was a former tributary of the principality, anyone who held it must swear fealty to him. But a count of Flanders could hardly be expected to do homage to a minor French baron. Thierry, therefore, refused such a condition. Unfortunately for the Franks this quarrel became so serious that the siege had to be abandoned.[8]

Nūr-ad-Dīn sent an emir to take over the city. Later, when his health was fully restored, he visited Shaizar in person, saw that the damage caused by earthquake and siege was repaired, and had the defenses put in order. Thus Shaizar, the last of the towns of middle Syria to maintain some degree of autonomy, and one which might have become a Christian principality, fell to the all-embracing power of Aleppo. Although Shaizar was lost, it was agreed that the opportunity presented by the atabeg's illness should not be entirely wasted. Accordingly Ḥārim was besieged and taken after a siege of two months (February 1158). The city was returned, this time without dispute, to the jurisdiction of Antioch. The king and the count of Flanders returned to Jerusalem, count Raymond accompanying them as far as Tripoli. Later in the same year Thierry and Baldwin raided the Damascus region, forced Nūr-ad-Dīn to raise the siege of Ḥabīs Jaldak, southeast of Lake Tiberias, and soundly defeated his troops. A truce followed.

Not long before the northern campaign an embassy had been sent to Constantinople for the purpose of seeking a consort for king Baldwin. It had been felt for some time that the royal dynasty should be carried on, but the decision to approach Byzantium at this juncture was especially significant. European aid was manifestly inadequate and not to be relied upon. It was, therefore, imperative to seek assistance elsewhere. It was probably shortly after the arrival of count Thierry in the autumn of 1157 that the envoys set out for the Byzantine capital. After some time was consumed in discussion it was agreed that Theodora, Manuel's niece, should

[8] Apparently Assassins of Maṣyāf defended the citadel. On this and on Nūr-ad-Dīn's illness see above, chapter XVI, pp. 521–522.

be sent as a bride for the king. Though only thirteen she was exceptionally beautiful. A large dowry was provided, a magnificent trousseau, and high-ranking attendants to accompany the bridal party to Jerusalem. On his part Baldwin had sent a written guarantee accepting whatever his envoys arranged and further promising Acre as a marriage portion in the event of his own death. The bridal party landed at Tyre in September 1158 and journeyed directly to Jerusalem where Theodora was married to Baldwin and solemnly crowned. Aimery, patriarch of Antioch, who had sought refuge from Reginald in the holy city, performed the ceremonies. The king was much taken with his young bride and remained a devoted husband.

If Baldwin's purpose in seeking a Byzantine alliance is clear, it seems equally evident that Manuel was ready to resume pressure on Antioch. In the fall of 1158 he entered Cilicia with a sizeable army. His first objective, the recovery of Cilicia, he achieved without great difficulty, for Ṭoros was so completely taken by surprise that he had barely time to escape to the mountains. When Reginald learned of the emperor's approach, he consulted his barons as to how he might justify his recent conduct. He may also have appealed to Baldwin. But Manuel arrived too quickly for the king to intervene. Reginald, therefore, set out for the emperor's camp at Mamistra (Misis). Bishop Gerard of Latakia and a few barons accompanied him.

In the presence of the emperor's court, where there were to be found not only a number of Byzantine dignitaries, but envoys from various Moslem rulers and from the king of Georgia, Reginald publicly repented his misdeeds. Barefooted and clad in a short-sleeved woolen tunic, he presented his sword to the emperor, holding it by the point. He then prostrated himself on the ground. Restored to favor by this abject submission, Reginald swore allegiance and promised to surrender the citadel of Antioch on demand. He also agreed to admit a Greek patriarch whom the emperor should designate. Thus Manuel amply avenged the pillage of Cyprus and obtained a clear recognition of his suzerainty over Antioch. Further, the installation of a Greek patriarch would symbolize a victory for the Byzantine church.

It was not long before Baldwin arrived at Antioch accompanied by Amalric, his brother, and by several distinguished nobles. An embassy was sent to Manuel, who responded through his chancellor by inviting the king to his presence and by directing that he be met by his nephews, John, the *protosebastos*, and Alexius, the chamberlain, and a suitable retinue of nobles. Thus Baldwin was received with considerable ceremony. He was saluted with the kiss of peace and seated by the emperor's side in a place only slightly lower than that of the emperor himself.[9] For ten days the two rulers held important conversations, and Baldwin won the respect and esteem of the imperial court. Precisely what was decided at these conferences has not been recorded. Presumably some sort of pact was arranged whereby Manuel agreed to participate in a crusade against Islam. Apparently Baldwin was also able to effect a reconciliation between the emperor and Ṭoros. The Armenian agreed to surrender one fortress, was fully restored to favor, and took an oath of fealty. This diplomacy reflected great credit on the king of Jerusalem and won him the gratitude of both Greeks and Armenians.

The imperial entry into Antioch which took place shortly after Easter (April 12, 1159) was a veritable "triumph". Wearing the diadem of the empire, Manuel was welcomed by the king, Reginald, their respective followers, and the city notables. He was escorted first to the cathedral and then to the palace. For eight days the imperial standard floated over the citadel, and gifts were distributed liberally among the population. There were tournaments and hunting expeditions and Manuel distinguished himself in both. When Baldwin was thrown from his horse and broke his arm, the emperor amazed everyone by ministering to the king with his own hands. Manuel prided himself on his medical knowledge and skill. Although these events heralded a period of almost twenty years during which Byzantium was to dominate Syrian politics, the emperor's actual power in Antioch must not be exaggerated. There is no trace during these years of any direct administration in Antioch comparable, for example, to that in Cilician Armenia. Nor did Manuel insist at this time on the installation of a Greek patriarch. Moreover, Baldwin's part in the negotiations should not be underestimated. As a consequence of his marriage and through the use of considerable diplomatic finesse he had secured the Byzantine alliance.

[9] Although there is a clear recognition of the emperor's suzerainty over Antioch, the ceremonies implied no claim to or recognition of suzerainty over Jerusalem in the western feudal sense. See especially LaMonte, "To what Extent was the Byzantine Empire the Suzerain of the Latin Crusading States?" *Byzantion*, VII (1932) 258–260, where the arguments of Chalandon, *Les Comnène*, II, 447–449, are discussed. See also Cahen, *La Syrie du nord*, pp. 400–402, who contends that the king's position as Reginald's suzerain "à titre personnel" mitigated the humiliating character of his vassalage to the emperor. On the possible conspiracy of the emperor, Baldwin, and the patriarch Aimery to remove Reginald see Krey, *William of Tyre*, II, 277, note 71; LaMonte, *Feudal Monarchy*, p. 195, note 3; Grousset, *Croisades*, II, 405.

All these celebrations were merely preliminaries to the serious business of planning a joint expedition against Nūr-ad-Dīn. Meanwhile the Moslems began preparations to resist the expected attack. The atabeg ordered all his emirs and governors of fortified places to make their defenses ready. He then moved with the bulk of his forces toward the middle Orontes. If he really expected an attack in the region of Shaizar, Homs, or Hamah, he was deceived. It was the intention of Manuel and the Frankish leaders to strike at Aleppo, the heart of Nūr-ad-Dīn's empire. Machines and engines of war were assembled and the entire army proceeded to the ford of Balana some forty miles northwest of Aleppo.

At this juncture, Nūr-ad-Dīn, evidently concerned at the size of the forces arrayed against him, entered into negotiation with Manuel. The result was the liberation of a number of Christian prisoners, including Bertram of Toulouse and the master of the Temple. Since the mere appearance of the Christian armies opened the prison gates, the consequent and expected military operations might have achieved decisive results. But to the disgust of the Franks and for reasons not adequately explained, Manuel returned to Constantinople. There was nothing left for the king to do, except to withdraw likewise and to return to Jerusalem. The great combined Graeco-Latin crusade, from which so much had been expected, thus failed to materialize.

To understand this defection on the part of Manuel it is necessary to emphasize that the emperor's journey into Syria had as its purpose the recovery of Cilicia and the reassertion of suzerainty over Antioch. Success in these matters, and particularly in the latter, was in part owing to Nūr-ad-Dīn's pressure against the Franks. Without the atabeg's recent conquests, Baldwin and Reginald would probably have been unwilling to admit Manuel's claims. The atabeg must, therefore, be restrained but not crushed. Further, peace with Nūr-ad-Dīn fitted in with the emperor's plans for a reckoning with Iconium. Under the command of John Contostephanus troops from Antioch, Jerusalem, and Cilicia — evidently the alliance was still in force — routed a part of Kilij (or Kilich) Arslan's army in the autumn of 1161. As Manuel moved south the sultan was encircled and sought peace. After restoring certain captured towns and engaging to attack the empire's enemies Kilij Arslan went in person to Constantinople and was received as a vassal and ally. Byzantine diplomacy was grounded on an oriental balance of power in which

Moslem states were to be played against each other and against the Franks.[10]

It should, however, be added that the basileus evidently had no intention of breaking completely with the Latins. Sometime in 1160 (or 1161) an imperial embassy approached king Baldwin requesting as a future consort for the emperor one of the king's kinswomen, either the sister of the count of Tripoli or Constance of Antioch's daughter. Perhaps in order to avoid strengthening the emperor's claims over Antioch the king and his advisers suggested Melisend, Raymond of Tripoli's sister. The bride-elect was provided with a suitable retinue and expensive adornments. The king and a number of barons assembled at Tripoli to wish her Godspeed. But the Byzantine envoys, constantly in communication with Manuel, delayed a year. At length a messenger was sent to Constantinople who returned with the information that the emperor had decided against Melisend. Count Raymond was so enraged that he ordered a pillaging expedition along the Greek coast. The king was equally disgusted, but important developments at Antioch required the utmost in diplomatic finesse.

In November 1160 (or 1161), perhaps somewhat after the Byzantine embassy had left Constantinople, Reginald was ambushed and captured. Sixteen years' imprisonment was to be the consequence of a futile marauding foray, sixteen years during which the Latins were at once deprived of a valiant warrior and relieved of the embarrassment of an intemperate adventurer.

Reginald's capture again created a vacancy at Antioch. The barons, apparently fearing Constance's leanings toward Byzantium, appealed to Baldwin, who was then at Tripoli. The king came directly, assumed charge of the principality as *bailli*, and before he returned to Jerusalem rebuilt a fort at the "iron bridge" over the Orontes. The patriarch, Aimery, who had evidently returned, was temporarily placed in charge of the administration.

While he was at Antioch the king was surprised to discover the same imperial envoys with whom he had been negotiating at Tripoli. It had been supposed that they had gone back to Constantinople. Instead, they had commenced discussions with Constance regarding her daughter, Maria. It is also possible that Constance had appealed to the emperor when her husband had been captured. Although the king feared Manuel's designs over Antioch, he gave his consent, being unwilling to break completely with

[10] Cf. also above, chapter XVI, p. 523.

Byzantium. Manuel and Maria were married at Constantinople on December 25, 1161.

Actually the situation in Antioch was not stabilized until 1163, probably shortly after Baldwin's death. At that time the barons of the principality, still suspecting Constance of complicity with Constantinople, solicited the aid of Ṭoros, expelled the princess, and installed her son, Bohemond III, who had come of age.

King Baldwin's days were numbered. He had been saddened by the death of his mother, queen Melisend, on September 11, 1161. While at Antioch he was taken seriously ill and was first removed to Tripoli, where he remained several months. Then, realizing that recovery was not likely, he asked to be transported to Beirut where he summoned the nobles and clergy of the realm. Having confessed his sins he died on February 10, 1163.[11] His body was borne to Jerusalem and buried in the church of the Holy Sepulcher. As the funeral cortège passed from Beirut to Jerusalem, people came from the towns and countryside to pay their last respects. Moslems joined the faithful in grief. Nūr-ad-Dīn, it was reported, indignantly rejected a suggestion that the kingdom be invaded and spoke words of high praise of the departed king.

Baldwin III deserved well of his subjects. Faced in the early years with the consequences of two disasters, the loss of Edessa and the failure of the Second Crusade, he had preserved Antioch and pushed the boundaries of Jerusalem southward. At the time of his death there was still reason to hope that the Byzantine alliance, a product of his skillful diplomacy, might bear fruit. He was respected by his contemporaries, Moslem as well as Christian, Greek and Syrian as well as Latin.

To the historian William of Tyre, who probably knew him well, Baldwin was the ideal king. Directly following his account of Fulk's death, William inserted into his history a detailed description which, though it pictures Baldwin as a youth, was composed later and contains many references to the king's more mature years.[12] Apparently he was unusually gifted. Tall and well formed, albeit somewhat heavy, he carried himself with dignity. His features were comely. His manners were perfect, and he was at once affable and vivacious. He was eloquent of speech and possessed of a keen intellect and an accurate memory which were no

[11] On the date of Baldwin III's death, see Krey, *William of Tyre*, II, 293, note 91, where reasons for rejecting 1162 are marshalled.

[12] William of Tyre, XVI, 2, (*RHC*, *Occ.*, I, 705–706). William's reference to Nūr-ad-Dīn's forbearance is in XVIII, 34 (p. 881). See Grousset, *Croisades*, II, 310–313.

doubt sharpened by his devotion to reading and to converse with men of learning. His conversation could be witty and he mingled easily with people of varied backgrounds and gave audience whenever requested. Criticism he bestowed freely and publicly, but never with rancor. Moreover, he could listen quietly to sharp words directed at himself. His courage, steadfastness, endurance, his foresight and presence of mind in war have been amply emphasized in the preceding pages. He was well versed in the laws of the kingdom and older men often consulted him. A Godfearing man, he respected the institutions and possessions of the church. Though unusually abstemious in food and drink, he indulged, during his early years, the desires of the flesh and was addicted to gambling. But these failings diminished as he grew older and ceased altogether after his marriage. Baldwin III was one of the great kings of Jerusalem and his reign was a distinguished period in its history.

Since Baldwin III left no children, he was succeeded by his younger brother, Amalric I (1163–1174).[13] Totally unlike his brother in temperament and character, Amalric, nevertheless, possessed qualities which made him an admirable king. He was a man of medium height and, despite his habitual moderation in food and drink, excessively fat. He was more fond of active amusements like the chase, than the performances of minstrels. But he was singularly gifted intellectually and enjoyed reading and discussion with such men as William of Tyre. In fact, it was at his request that William, then archdeacon, commenced that record of the king's doings which he later expanded into a fullfledged history. Brave, even daring, in battle, cool and decisive in command, well informed on the strategic problems of the orient, Amalric was well suited to that military leadership so necessary to a Levantine ruler.

With all his accomplishments, Amalric did not inspire the affection or popularity which his brother had enjoyed. He lacked Baldwin's affability and was inclined to be taciturn and sometimes arbitrary. Married women were not safe from his advances. Clergy complained that he illegally violated their rights and properties. Excessive taxes, never popular, he justified on the grounds

[13] The standard work on king Amalric, R. Röhricht, "Amalrich I., König von Jerusalem," *Mittheilungen des Instituts für Österreichische Geschichtsforschung*, XII (1891), 432–481, has been reprinted as chapters XVII and XVIII of the same author's *Königreich Jerusalem*. The description of the king, from William of Tyre, XIX, 2–3 (pp. 884–888), is paraphrased in Grousset, *Croisades*, II, 438–442.

of military necessity. Amalric's succession to the throne was not unopposed. The clergy and people together with a few magnates approved, but a number of barons expressed objection, presumably because of the king's wife, Agnes of Courtenay, whom they declared to be unworthy. Although no specific complaints were mentioned, it is true that in later years Agnes was to prove herself an accomplished intriguer and to exert a sinister influence on the affairs of the realm. Widow of Reginald of Marash, and sister of Joscelin III, she was related to Amalric; and a former patriarch, Fulcher, had opposed the marriage in the first place. Evidently Amalric regarded the barons' opposition as serious, for he promptly obtained an annulment from the patriarch, Amalric of Nesle, and the papal legate, the cardinal John. Their two children, Baldwin and Sibyl, were recognized as legitimate and their succession rights guaranteed. The appointment of Miles of Plancy as seneschal also aroused antagonism. Miles was to marry Stephanie, widow of Humphrey of Toron, and thus control the fief of Montréal (1173–1174). Although the king may have felt it necessary to appease the magnates in order to assure his succession to the throne, legislation enacted in the first year of his reign strengthened his position measurably. By his *Assise sur la ligece* he required all rear vassals to render liege homage to the king directly. Thus the power of the tenants-in-chief was lessened since rear vassals could now seek redress in the king's court. So long as a strong king stood at the center of this system, in fact so long as Amalric lived, this legislation fortified royal power in a manner more reminiscent of the Norman rulers of England than of their Capetian confrères. Amalric also appears to have established two new courts for maritime litigation, the *Cour de la Fonde* and the *Cour de la Chaîne*. Indeed, Amalric's role in the legal development of Jerusalem is evidenced by a number of significant references to his name in the *Assises* of the kingdom. These matters will receive more extended treatment in a later volume.

The foreign policy of Amalric, largely a series of attempts to conquer Egypt, had been foreshadowed by Baldwin III when he captured Ascalon. And it was logical that Amalric, who had been entrusted with the government of Ascalon, should be interested in the south.[14] The combination of circumstances which had motivated Baldwin still existed. The union of Aleppo and Damas-

[14] On the Egyptian campaigns of Amalric, see G. Schlumberger, *Campagnes du roi Amaury Ier en Égypte*. For the career of Saladin, see Lane-Poole, *Saladin*, pp. 77–128; and below, chapter XVIII.

cus under Nūr-ad-Dīn made the whole matter more urgent. For if Egypt fell into the power of the Syrian Sunnite Moslems, the Latin states would be encircled. Add to these strategic considerations the immense commercial value of Egypt with its great port of Alexandria, and it is not difficult to understand why Amalric persistently pushed southward.

Unfortunately for the success of Amalric's ventures, Nūr-ad-Dīn, as we have seen in an earlier chapter, was equally concerned over developments in Egypt.[15] Moreover, the atabeg was able not only to intervene directly in Egypt, but also to hamper Latin action by creating diversions along the frontiers of the kingdom and the northern states. Indeed, these border attacks were often costly to the Franks. The heavy losses thus sustained must be considered in any estimate of Amalric's Egyptian policy.

The king's first venture was in September 1163. Taking as a pretext the non-payment of tribute promised in the time of Baldwin III, Amalric crossed the isthmus of Suez and besieged Bilbais. Only by cutting dikes were the Egyptians able to force a withdrawal. Meanwhile, Shavar, a former vizir recently ejected from Cairo by his enemies, had persuaded Nūr-ad-Dīn to support his cause. Accordingly, in April 1164 an expeditionary force under the Kurdish emir Asad-ad-Dīn Shīrkūh set out with Shavar for Egypt. At the same time the atabeg provided an important diversion by continuing operations on the frontiers of northern Syria. As a consequence, Shīrkūh reached Cairo safely and Shavar was restored to power (May 1164).

Once he was reinstated, Shavar proved recalcitrant and refused to pay a tribute which had been promised Shīrkūh. The latter thereupon seized Bilbais and the entire province of Sharqiya to the east of the delta. Accordingly, Shavar, following a precedent set by his former enemies, appealed to the Franks, promising military support and financial aid. Since a number of crusaders arrived from Europe about this time, Amalric felt able to equip an invasion army without seriously depleting the kingdom's defenses. He therefore took counsel with his barons, put Bohemond III of Antioch in charge of the realm, and set out a second time for Egypt. Junction with Shavar was made and Shīrkūh was besieged in Bilbais. After three months (August–October, 1164) the city's fall seemed near. But Amalric had learned of formidable attacks in northern Syria by Nūr-ad-Dīn and proposed to Shīrkūh that both abandon their projects. Nearly at the end of his resour-

[15] Cf. above, chapter XVI, p. 523.

ces, Shīrkūh agreed and returned to Syria. Thus an otherwise promising campaign ended in a stalemate owing partly to the king's overly optimistic judgment regarding the strength of the northern frontiers. Notwithstanding, prompt action had preserved the independence of Egypt.

Nūr-ad-Dīn's activities which had so alarmed Amalric had commenced with a siege of Ḥārim and an invasion of the plain of Buqai'ah southwest of Krak des Chevaliers. Forces composed of Greeks and Armenians from Cilicia and a number of Latin knights from the northern states at first routed the invaders. But not long after, Nūr-ad-Dīn was able to divide the Christian troops and captured Bohemond III of Antioch, Raymond III of Tripoli, Constantine Coloman, Greek governor of Cilicia, Hugh of Lusignan, and Joscelin III, titular count of Edessa.[16] Ḥārim fell to the atabeg on August 12, 1164. Captured flags and the heads of fallen Christians were sent to Shīrkūh with instructions to exhibit them on the walls of Bilbais to frighten the besiegers. Ḥārim had been a bastion potentially menacing to Aleppo. Its capture opened the way for a Moslem invasion of Antioch.

Whether or not Nūr-ad-Dīn could have taken Antioch is a question. Certainly its defenses were weakened and its ruler was a captive. But the atabeg countered the urgings of his own officers by pointing out that in an emergency the Franks would summon Byzantine aid. No such misgivings prevented him from attacking farther south. Moreover, since the king and the bulk of the Latin troops were still in Egypt, and Bohemond and other leaders were in captivity, the kingdom was vulnerable. After circulating a rumor that he would attack Tiberias, Nūr-ad-Dīn besieged Banyas, the important stronghold some miles north of the city. Probably because of incompetence, although treason was suggested, the defenses failed and Banyas fell to the atabeg.

As soon as the king reached Jerusalem from Egypt and learned further details of the situation, he hastened northward accompanied by Thierry of Alsace, who had returned to the orient. Defenses were set in order, and arrangements were made for the liberation of Bohemond III in the summer of 1165. In Tripoli Raymond III had been able to designate Amalric as regent. Indeed, the king held the *bailliage* of Tripoli for the ten years of the count's captivity. Thus Amalric's forthright action and Nūr-ad-

[16] William of Tyre XIX, 9. According to other sources Joscelin was taken in 1160. Cf. Röhricht, *Königreich*, p. 318, note 3; Runciman, *Crusades*, II, 358.

Dīn's fear of Byzantine intervention restored the balance of power in northern Syria.[17]

In January 1167 the persistent Shīrkūh set out once again to recoup his fortunes in Egypt. Amalric heard of his preparations and summoned an important assembly at Nablus where he publicly outlined the danger which threatened the kingdom. Indeed, his words so moved his hearers that they voted a ten per cent tax. Since a preliminary expedition into the southern desert failed to intercept Shīrkūh, the king reassembled his forces at Ascalon. On January 30 a Christian army marched a third time toward Egypt and reached Bilbais without incident. Thence they moved south past Cairo and camped near Fustat (Babylon). At first Shavar, apparently unaware of Shīrkūh's movements, doubted Amalric's intentions. Indeed, he received from Shīrkūh an invitation to unite against the foes of Islam. But on learning more of the Turkish advance, he elected to renew his engagements with Amalric in a formal treaty. In addition to the annual tribute, the sum of four hundred thousand gold pieces, half to be paid at once, was agreed upon as adequate compensation to the Franks. The king, on his part, pledged himself not to leave Egypt until Shīrkūh and his army had been destroyed or driven from the country. Hugh of Caesarea was chosen to head a delegation to ratify the treaty with the caliph.

In a remarkable passage, William of Tyre describes the amazement and wonder of the Frankish delegation as they saw for the first time the caliph's magnificent palace, lavishly but exquisitely decorated.[18] They were led past fish pools, cages of strange birds and animals, through even more beautifully appointed buildings to the caliph's presence. There, to the consternation of all present and to the embarrassment of the caliph, Hugh insisted that the contract be sealed in the Frankish manner by each party holding the bare hand of the other. After considerable hesitation, the caliph offered his gloved hand. Still Hugh refused. At length the caliph, whom Hugh later described as "of an extremely generous disposition", consented and repeated after him the words "in good faith, without fraud or deceit".

[17] On Raymond III and the regency in Tripoli, see Baldwin, *Raymond III of Tripolis*, p. 11; Richard, *Le Comté de Tripoli*, pp. 33–34. About this time (1164 or 1167) if we may believe Ernoul, *Chronique* (ed. Mas Latrie), pp. 27–30, Ṭoros visited Jerusalem and suggested the colonization of a large number of Armenians. Amalric and the barons agreed, but owing to the opposition of the Latin clergy the project never materialized. Grousset, *Croisades*, II, 602–604, discusses this development in detail.

[18] William of Tyre, XIX, 18–19 (pp. 910–911). It is possible that the Templar Geoffrey Fulcher had more part in making the treaty than would appear from William's narrative. See Krey, *William of Tyre*, II, 351, note 11.

The following days were spent in various attempts to make contact with Shīrkūh's army which had, meanwhile, successfully crossed the Nile, and camped at Giza across the river from Fustat and Cairo. After a month of stalemate broken only by minor engagements, Shīrkūh moved rapidly southward at night. Amalric crossed the river, pursued his enemy, and made contact at al-Bābain (March 18, 1167). Apparently the Christians were outnumbered. Nevertheless, Shīrkūh hesitated to give battle and was only persuaded to do so by his more warlike officers, among whom was his nephew Saladin (Ṣalāḥ-ad-Dīn). In the ensuing engagement many Christian knights were killed or captured and a great deal of equipment taken, but the survivors retreated in good order. Moreover, when Amalric counted his forces he discovered only one hundred men lost as against an estimated fifteen hundred for the Moslems.

After the battle Shīrkūh marched to Alexandria, where the citizens welcomed him, but where he was soon besieged by the Christian army. All means of entrance or exit were carefully guarded and a fleet blocked all river traffic. After about one month had elapsed and conditions within the city had deteriorated, Shīrkūh managed to lead a small force secretly past the king into upper Egypt. Amalric at first pressed south in pursuit, but was dissuaded by the advice of an Egyptian nobleman who pointed out that Alexandria was in desperate straits and close to surrender.

Accordingly, reinforced by another contingent from the kingdom, the Christians began bombarding the city and making repeated assaults. Saladin, whom Shīrkūh had left in command, desperately tried to stem the growing tide of defeatism and secretly informed his superior of the critical conditions within the city. At length Shīrkūh, after one or two unsuccessful raids, decided to sue for peace. Arnulf of Tell Bashir, one of the Latin captives, was sent to negotiate with Amalric. The king was not unwilling to end hostilities. His own losses had been serious, and he was again concerned about Nūr-ad-Dīn's movements in the north. It was agreed, therefore, that both armies would return prisoners, evacuate Egypt, and leave Shavar in possession of power. Shīrkūh, disconsolate over his failures, reached Damascus in September 1167. The Christian army was permitted to "tour" Alexandria before departing for Palestine. The men marveled at the city's magnificence and wondered that so small an army could shut up a city with so many able to bear arms. Amalric reached Ascalon in August 1167.

Before leaving Alexandria, Amalric had accorded the courtesies of war to Saladin, for whom he provided an escort, and, according to his original agreement with Shavar, raised his flag on Pharos island. Shavar also agreed again to an annual tribute and to the installation of a Frankish commissioner and guard in Cairo. Shīrkūh had not been destroyed, but for the moment the Latins were in the ascendant in Egypt.

If the events of the early years of Amalric's reign demonstrated the weakness of Egypt, they also brought into clear focus the precarious nature of Frankish defenses in northern Syria. As a consequence, the position of the Byzantine emperor Manuel Comnenus took on added significance. Indeed, he held the balance of power in the Levant, and the Latins, though fearful of the emperor's designs on Antioch, were coming to realize their dependence on his support. An ambitious ruler, whose far-reaching plans envisaged a reconciliation with Rome and an extension of Byzantine power westward as well as to the east and south, Manuel on his part showed a marked willingness during this period to coöperate with westerners. It was not long before these developments that Manuel had married Maria, sister of Bohemond of Antioch, and somewhat later that Bohemond married the emperor's niece, Theodora.

It is not surprising, therefore, that Bohemond should have hastened to Constantinople shortly after his release from captivity. When he returned with gifts which perhaps enabled him to pay off his ransom, he was accompanied by a Greek patriarch, Athanasius, whom he installed in Antioch. Aimery, the Latin patriarch, placed the city under an interdict and took refuge in the castle of Quṣair some miles to the south. And although the Latin clergy continued their protests which were supported by pope Alexander III, and echoed by the Jacobite Christians, Athanasius remained in Antioch until 1170 when he lost his life in an earthquake. Evidently Bohemond was sufficiently appreciative of Byzantine assistance to risk the opposition of his subjects.

There were also important relations between the emperor and Jerusalem. Following his separation from Agnes, Amalric had sent a delegation to Constantinople. And shortly before the close of the recent Egyptian campaign, Hernesius, archbishop of Caesarea, and Odo of St. Amand, the king's marshal, returned bringing with them Maria Comnena, daughter of John, Manuel's nephew and *protosebastos*. Amalric met the party at Tyre, and he and Maria were married there on August 29, 1167, just after his return from Egypt.

In the following months a plan for a joint Franco-Byzantine military expedition to conquer and partition Egypt was elaborated. It is possible that the project was first proposed by Amalric. But Manuel's interest in the Egyptian situation is evident and the first discussions of which we have certain knowledge resulted from the visit of two imperial envoys in the summer of 1168. A formal treaty of alliance was drawn up and William, who had recently been named archdeacon of Tyre, accompanied the envoys on the return journey. He was empowered to ratify the agreement in the emperor's presence. Since the negotiations were deemed urgent, William was taken to the emperor's military headquarters in Serbia. His mission was successfully accomplished and he set out for Palestine on October 1, 1168. Before William reached home, however, Amalric had already started again for Egypt.

What prompted the king to proceed without Byzantine aid and to break his agreements with Shavar is not clear. Although in retrospect it is easy to understand William of Tyre's disappointment, and to agree that the venture was a mistake, it is difficult to believe that Amalric would have jeopardized the Latin predominance in Egypt without adequate reason. Moreover, there are certain possible explanations. It appears that the tribute which Shavar had agreed to pay seemed even less palatable to the Egyptians after the immediate danger had past. More irritating was the presence of the Frankish commissioner and guard who, apparently, behaved with inexcusable insolence. As a consequence, certain negotiations were commenced between Cairo and Damascus, and disquieting rumors reached Jerusalem. An immediate invasion, opposed by the Templars under Philip of Milly, was vigorously urged by their Hospitaller rivals under Gilbert of Assailly. A warlike and greedy element among the barons, perhaps unwilling to contemplate a division of Egypt with the Greeks, added its pressure. It appears that the king withstood this pressure for a while, but the decision was ultimately made and the army set out for Egypt in October 1168.

Undeterred by the pleadings of Shavar's emissaries the Christian army entered Egypt and took Bilbais on November 4. A shocking slaughter followed, and captives were taken indiscriminately. Many of the victims were native Christians. The siege of Cairo was commenced on November 13, but, according to William of Tyre, not pressed energetically because the king only wanted to force a money payment. It is, however, possible that Amalric realized that the city would resist to the end rather than suffer the fate of Bilbais. Further, on November 12, Shavar had inaugurated a scorched earth policy by ordering that Fustat be burned. The conflagration lasted fifty-four days, a horrible example of what might happen in Cairo. Thus a kind of haggling between the king and Shavar continued. The latter paid one hundred thousand dinars as ransom for his son and nephew, who had been captured, and gave hostages for the payment of another one hundred thousand. Accordingly Amalric withdrew to al-Maṭarīyah and then proceeded to Siryāqūs about sixteen miles northeast of Cairo. Meanwhile, a Christian fleet appeared at the entrance to the Nile and occupied Tinnis. Further progress was blocked by Egyptian ships and before Humphrey of Toron and a detachment of the king's army could seize the opposite shore, rumors of Shīrkūh's approach reached the king and he ordered the fleet home.

Amalric then hastily returned to Bilbais, left a guard, and on December 25 marched out to intercept Shīrkūh. But Shīrkūh successfully crossed the Nile. Since Amalric knew that his enemies could now easily be reinforced, he elected to abandon the project entirely. By January 2, 1169, the army was on its return journey. Shīrkūh, who was generously supported by Nūr-ad-Dīn, was able, therefore, to reach Cairo unhindered. There he was welcomed by the caliph and the citizens. Shavar was assassinated (January 18, 1169), and Shīrkūh became vizir. Within two months, however, he had died and was succeeded by his nephew, Saladin. By August of the same year the young Kurd had replaced a number of the caliph's officials, dispossessed Egyptian landowners and substituted Syrians, massacred the caliph's negro guard, and, in short, made himself master of Egypt.

These events produced a revolution in the balance of power in the Levant. The Frankish protectorate over Egypt with all its advantages, economic as well as political, was ended. To all intents and purposes Moslem Egypt and Syria were united, and there began that encirclement of the Christian states which in future years was to prove so disastrous.[19]

The gravity of the situation was well understood in Jerusalem, and early in 1169 ambassadors and letters were sent to Europe. Western princes were too occupied with their own concerns, and the ambassadors returned without accomplishing anything. Fortunately for the Latins, Manuel Comnenus was still anxious to

[19] For further details see above, chapter XVI. For the career of Saladin, see below, chapter XVIII.

fulfil his part of the agreement arranged by William of Tyre in September 1168. Indeed, the fleet and equipment which arrived at Acre in September 1169 were more imposing than had been stipulated, and restored Christian command of the sea.[20]

The Latins were overjoyed and obviously impressed by the Byzantine preparations. But since Amalric had to reorganize his forces after the previous Egyptian expedition and post sufficient troops to guard against any action by Nūr-ad-Dīn, prompt attack with the element of surprise was impossible. Byzantine food supplies, for some unexplained reason not sufficiently provided for, began to run short, and it was found necessary for the Greek troops to disembark at Acre and march overland with the Latins. On October 15, 1169, the combined armies left Ascalon and after nine days reached Pelusium (al-Faramā') near the sea on the eastern branch of the Nile where the fleet had preceded them. They were ferried across the Nile and by following the shore of Lake Manzala reached Damietta two or three days later.

Since Saladin had evidently not expected attack at this point, the city was inadequately defended. William of Tyre insists that a quick attack could have succeeded, and it appears that Saladin was worried. But there was a delay of three days. Moreover, although the river was blocked by an iron chain, it was open above the city. Thus Damietta was speedily reinforced by boats from the south. A full siege was, as a consequence, necessary, and the Christians had to construct war machines with considerable labor. At length a huge engine of seven storeys was built. But the defenders, now constantly reinforced, fought back with skill and bravery. Meanwhile, taking advantage of a strong onshore wind, the Moslems launched a fire boat which was blown into the Byzantine fleet riding at anchor in close array. Six ships were burned, and a disaster was averted only by the prompt action of Amalric, who roused the crews.

As the siege was prolonged, food ran short in the Christian camp. Torrential rains added to the discomfort. Finally, Andronicus, commanding the Byzantine forces, proposed a desperate all-out assault. Amalric was opposed, holding that the city's defenses were too strong and needed further battering by the machines. Although he had been directed to obey Amalric, Andronicus made preparations to attack alone. But before he had started, the king's

[20] William of Tyre, XX, 13 (p. 961). Among the Byzantine vessels were ships with stern openings for unloading, and bridges for embarking and landing men and horses. The description strikingly resembles modern invasion ships.

messengers informed him that negotiations for withdrawal had begun. After a few days of fraternizing, during which the Christians were permitted to enter Damietta and trade as they pleased, war machines were burned and the withdrawal commenced. The Latin and Greek troops reached Ascalon on December 21, 1169. Less fortunate was the fleet. A violent storm wrecked many ships, and others were deserted by sailors who feared the emperor's wrath. Disappointment accentuated the mutual recriminations of Latins and Greeks as each blamed the other for the expedition's failure.

Although it was not apparent at the time, the failure of the combined Franco-Byzantine expedition of 1169 marks a turning point in Levantine history. Had Amalric not acted on his own in 1168, the alliance might have prevented the union of Egypt and Syria. With more careful preparation — and in the matter of food, the Byzantines were possibly to blame — the combined forces could perhaps have defeated Saladin before he consolidated his hold over Egypt. As it turned out, no other joint expedition was undertaken and the final victory lay with Saladin.

Although the Christian failure strengthened Saladin's position in Egypt, communication between Syria and Egypt was still endangered by Frankish possessions in the south, especially the fortresses of Kerak or Krak des Moabites, sometimes mistakenly termed by the crusaders Petra Deserti, and Krak de Montréal (ash-Shaubak). Moreover, a temporary lull in hostilities resulted from the terrible earthquakes of June 1170. A large part of northern Syria, both Christian and Moslem, was devastated; thousands were killed; and many churches and castles destroyed. But in December 1170 Saladin attacked Darum and Gaza. The outer defenses of Darum were breached. A number of persons, including women and children, refugees from the surrounding country, were killed at Gaza. Saladin, evidently unwilling to risk an engagement with the royal army, withdrew to Egypt on its approach.

Early in 1171 Amalric summoned the high court to discuss the critical problems which now faced the kingdom. Although Frederick, archbishop of Tyre, had not yet returned from the embassy of 1169, it was agreed that another appeal to western rulers should be made. Europe remained uninterested in the plight of the Holy Land. Frederick finally returned having accomplished nothing, and his companion, Stephen of Sancerre, on whose assistance the king had counted and who had been chosen as a prospective son-in-law, left after six months of disgraceful conduct. Indeed, there is no further mention of the European legation, and the members of the high court realized that their only salvation lay in again securing Byzantine aid. The king insisted on leading an embassy to Constantinople himself. He set sail from Acre on March 10 with an impressive retinue and ten galleys.

Manuel, overjoyed though at first surprised, went out of his way to receive and entertain the royal party in a suitable manner. Daily conferences alternated with visits to churches and other places of interest. There were games and musical and dramatic performances at the circus. The visitors were shown the most precious relics and presented with costly gifts. Although Greek sources describe Amalric as performing a kind of homage, William of Tyre mentions only that at the initial reception, the king occupied a throne slightly lower than that of the basileus. Presumably, as in 1159, such gestures carried no implication of vassalage in the western feudal sense.[21] At any rate Amalric succeeded, at whatever cost, in persuading the emperor of the necessity and feasibility of subjugating Egypt. As a consequence, the Franco-Byzantine alliance was renewed and put in writing over the seals of both parties. The king returned in July 1171, his mission accomplished, but with no productive results.

Manuel Comnenus, like his father John and his grandfather Alexius, had proved himself an able emperor, pursuing the best interests of his realm with single-minded determination, but his conception of the best method of accomplishing this was both less prudent and less favorable to the Franks than his predecessors' had been. The unfounded accusations against Alexius and John, the bitter hostility common to Normans of Antioch and Latin Christians of western Europe, the failure to unite Christians of either high or low degree against the Moslems — all these were intensified during Manuel's reign, with more basis in his own actions than had previously been the case.[22] His obstructionism and other hostile relations with the Second Crusade have been examined in a previous chapter, while we have covered in some detail his ineffective alliance with Amalric against Egypt, as well as his fruitless purchase in 1150 of the remnants of the county of

[21] William of Tyre, XX, 23 (p. 984). Grousset, *Croisades*, II, 577, following Chalandon, *Les Comnène*, II, 549–550, accepts this tentatively as vassalage. But in "The Later Comneni," *Cambridge Medieval History*, IV, 377, Chalandon notes that since the Greek chronicler Cinnamus's statement cannot be verified, "it is impossible to speak decidedly." The best discussion of this whole matter is LaMonte, "To What Extent was the Byzantine Empire the Suzerain of the Latin Crusading States?" *Byzantion*, VII (1932), 262–263.

[22] The reign of Manuel, as well as those of his great predecessors and his miserable successors, is examined in a chapter of volume II.

Edessa and the devastation of Cyprus by Reginald and Ṭoros II in 1156.

The recovery before 1150 of the Taurus fortresses by the Ṛoupenid prince Ṭoros had not seriously affected Greek power, but his conquest of Mamistra in 1151 and the rest of Cilicia in 1152 had necessitated the great expedition of 1158, which like John's two decades earlier won great renown but little of permanent value: control of Cilicia for a few years, suzerainty over Antioch effective only during the presence of a Byzantine army, a truce with Nūr-ad-Dīn which postponed the full onslaught of Moslem Syria against the Frankish littoral. His peace in 1161 with the Selchükids of Iconium was more fruitful, but its effects were to be dissipated in 1176 at Myriokephalon, the absolute end of Byzantine control over any part of Anatolia except the coastal cities, since Mleh the Ṛoupenid ex-Templar had reconquered Cilicia in 1173.

To return to Amalric's visit to Constantinople, however, we may note that it marks the climax of his reign. The situation in the Moslem world was serious, but so long as the rift between Nūr-ad-Dīn and Saladin continued, not yet hopeless. The Byzantine alliance should have insured power adequate to break Saladin's hold over Egypt. This project, however, so full of promise was destined never to be carried out. Events beyond the frontiers of Jerusalem and Byzantium delayed the expedition.[23] On Amalric's death in 1174 the alliance lapsed.

Furthermore, in 1171, Saladin, at first reluctantly following Nūr-ad-Dīn's directives, had ordered that at Friday prayers in Egyptian mosques the name of the caliph of Baghdad be substituted for the Shī'ite, al-'Āḍid. Then, on September 13, al-'Āḍid had died, and no successor was named. The politico-religious revolution which had been thus quietly consummated in Cairo was of tremendous importance. A schism of centuries' duration which had contributed materially to the security of the Latin states had ended. Only the strained relations between Saladin and Nūr-ad-Dīn prevented the encirclement from being fully effective.

[23] In 1171–1173 there were disturbances in Cilician Armenia and in Iconium, the latter prompting the intervention of Nūr-ad-Dīn (Stevenson, *Crusaders*, pp. 200–201). In 1172 Henry the Lion of Saxony completed a pilgrimage, but remained in the east only a short time. See E. Joranson, "The Palestine Pilgrimage of Henry the Lion," *Medieval and Historiographical Essays in Honor of James Westfall Thompson*, ed. J. L. Cate and E. N. Anderson (Chicago, 1938), pp. 190–202. It was also during this period that the murder by a Templar of an envoy from the Assassins who had the king's safe conduct prompted Amalric to severe measures against the order. Since the king soon died, nothing was done except to

King Amalric's reign was drawing to a close. In the summer of 1173, despite the Byzantine alliance, the king once again sought assistance from the west. Sometime in the fall of 1173 or early in 1174 Raymond III of Tripoli was released from captivity. The king, who had helped procure the ransom money, welcomed him and restored the county over which he had acted as *bailli*. On May 15, 1174, Nūr-ad-Dīn died and Amalric immediately tried to take advantage of the discord which followed by attacking Banyas.[24] After a short campaign he agreed to a truce. On his return he complained of illness. Neither oriental nor Latin physicians were able to give more than temporary relief and the king died on July 11, 1174, at the age of thirty-eight.

The death of Amalric came at a most unfortunate time for the Latins. It is impossible to say whether, had he lived, he could have averted the eventual union of Damascus and Cairo. In any event the Latins derived no advantage from the death of Nūr-ad-Dīn. Amalric's own death caused the Franco-Byzantine alliance to lapse, and the field was left free for Saladin. Although the historian may thus reproach Amalric for the inopportuneness of his death, he was one of the best kings of Jerusalem, the last man of genuine capacity to hold the reins of government. In the years to come men were to see the resources of the kingdom — and they were still great — wasted through want of adequate leadership.

discipline the guilty member. B. Lewis (above, chapter IV, p. 123) suggests that this episode may reflect an actual rapprochement between the Assassins and Jerusalem.

[24] For the immediate consequences of Nūr-ad-Dīn's death, see below, chapter XVIII, pp. 566–567.

Aleppo: The Main Gateway to the Citadel

XVIII
THE RISE OF SALADIN
1169–1189

The reign of Saladin is more than an episode in the history of the crusades. It is one of those rare and dramatic moments in human history when cynicism and disillusion, born of long experience of the selfish ambitions of princes, are for a brief period dislodged by moral determination and unity of purpose. Without this foundation the Moslem armies could never have sustained the exhausting struggle of the Third Crusade. If that achievement is to be seen and understood in its historical setting, an attempt must be made to show how, using — as he had to use — the materials to his hand within the political circumstances of his age, Saladin triumphed over all obstacles to create a moral unity which, though never perfectly achieved, proved just strong enough to meet the challenge from the west.

The childhood of Ṣalāḥ-ad-Dīn Yūsuf ibn-Aiyūb (Righteousness of the Faith, Joseph son of Job) was spent in Baalbek, where his father Aiyūb was governor, first for Zengi and subsequently for the princes of Damascus. In 1152, at the age of fourteen, he joined his uncle Shīrkūh at Aleppo in the service of Nūr-ad-Dīn, and was allotted a fief; in 1156 he succeeded his elder brother Turan-Shāh as his uncle's deputy in the military governorship of Damascus, but relinquished the post after a short time in protest against the fraudulence of the chief accountant. He rejoined Nūr-ad-Dīn at

The fundamental source for this chapter is *Al-barq ash-Sha'mi* of Saladin's secretary 'Imād-ad-Dīn al-Iṣfahānī (only vols. III and V extant in MS.; the others summarized with other contemporary materials in *Ar-rauḍatain* ["The Two Gardens"] of abū-Shāmah, partially translated in *RHC, Or.*, IV, V). Bahā'-ad-Dīn's biography of Saladin (*RHC, Or.*, III) becomes a direct source only from 1186; for 1187 onwards 'Imād-ad-Dīn's earlier and shorter work *Al-fatḥ al-qussī* (ed. Leyden, 1888) is equally authoritative. Ibn-al-Athīr's narratives in his general history (*Al-kāmil*, vols. XI and XII, ed. Leyden, 1851–1853; extracts in *RHC, Or.*, I, II) are mostly derived from 'Imād-ad-Dīn. A desideratum is a corpus of the extant documents of al-Qāḍī al-Fāḍil; there is an incomplete list in A. H. Helbig, *Al-Qāḍī al-Fāḍil* (Leipzig, 1908). S. Lane-Poole's *Saladin and the Fall of the Kingdom of Jerusalem* (London and New York, 1898; new ed. by H. W. C. Davis, 1926) rests mainly on Ibn-al-Athīr and Bahā'-ad-Dīn.

Aleppo and became one of his close associates, "never leaving him whether on the march or at court."[1] Later on he again held the office of deputy commandant of Damascus for an unspecified period. Apart from his skill at polo, inherited from his father, and an interest in religious studies, probably inspired by his admiring emulation of Nūr-ad-Dīn, almost nothing else is known of his early years.

During the first campaigns in Egypt Saladin had played a subordinate but not inglorious part under the command of Shīrkūh. When, for the third time, Shīrkūh was ordered into Egypt at the end of 1168, at the urgent entreaty of the Fāṭimid caliph al-ʻĀḍid, Saladin, on his own statement, submitted unwillingly to Nūr-ad-Dīn's command to accompany him. It seems evident that the occupation was intended to be a permanent one this time; according to Ibn-al-Athīr, the Fāṭimid caliph had even made provision for the allocation of fiefs to the Syrian officers. Saladin's first exploit on this occasion was the seizure of the intriguing vizir, Shavar, who had been responsible for calling in the Franks, and his execution on the caliph's orders. Shīrkūh was invested with the vizirate, and the administration was directed on his behalf by Saladin.

When Shīrkūh died suddenly nine weeks later, Saladin was thus his natural successor, although some of Nūr-ad-Dīn's Turkish officers resented his appointment and returned to Syria. The voluminous diploma of his investiture on March 26, 1169, with the official title of *al-malik an-nāṣir*, is still extant. It was composed by his devoted friend and counsellor the *qāḍī* al-Fāḍil, and among its grandiloquent periods there is one strikingly prophetic phrase: "As for the holy war [Arabic, *jihād*], thou art the nursling of its milk and the child of its bosom. Gird up therefore the shanks of spears to meet it and plunge on its service into a sea of sword-points.... until God give the victory which the Commander of the Faithful hopeth to be laid up for thy days and to be the witness for thee when thou shalt stand in his presence."

His first task was to meet the problems raised by his position in Egypt. In effect, though Saladin was officially designated vizir, he was "the sultan", and was generally called by that title, with al-Qāḍī al-Fāḍil as his vizir. The apparent anomaly of a Sunnite vizir of a Fāṭimid caliph was no novelty; for nearly a century there had been Sunnite vizirs at intervals in Egypt. But until recently the ʻAbbāsid caliphs had been the more or less passive instruments

[1] Ibn-abi-Ṭaiyī, quoted by abū-Shāmah, I, 100.

of the Selchükid sultans, the sworn enemies of the Fāṭimids, and adherence to the Sunnite sect did not necessarily imply political recognition of the ʿAbbāsids. Now, however, the ʿAbbāsids were reasserting their sovereignty against the Selchükids; and the jihad movement in Syria, born of a revival of Sunnite orthodoxy, had placed itself under their banner. There could be no effective union with Egypt except on these terms. Saladin was consequently bound by his own principles to restore Egypt to the ʿAbbāsid allegiance, but it was necessary to prepare the ground for the change.

The main danger lay in the Egyptian army, composed of several regiments of white cavalry and some 30,000 Sudanese infantry. Saladin immediately began to build up his own army at the expense of the Egyptian officers, and when a revolt of the blacks broke out he already had enough regular troops of his own to decimate them and to drive them out of Cairo into upper Egypt, where his brothers, in the course of the next five years, gradually crushed their resistance. The white troops made no move and seem to have coöperated with Saladin in repelling Amalric's attack on Damietta (1169), and in the raid on Gaza and the subsequent capture of Ailah in December 1170.[2] But Nūr-ad-Dīn was pressing him to take the decisive step of proclaiming the ʿAbbāsid caliphate in Egypt, and at length in June 1171 sent him a formal order to do so, at the same time notifying the ʿAbbāsid caliph himself of his action. The order was obeyed, with no immediate outward disturbances. On al-ʿĀḍid's death shortly afterwards the members of the Fāṭimid house were placed in honorable captivity and the sexes separated, so that it should die out in the natural course of time, and the immense treasures of their palaces were shared between Saladin's officers and Nūr-ad-Dīn.

The good relations which had subsisted up to this point between Nūr-ad-Dīn and Saladin, however, gradually grew strained. Some suspicion may have been aroused by Saladin's failure to assist his suzerain during the expedition to Krak de Montréal (ash-Shaubak) in October 1171, whatever good reasons he may have put forward for his withdrawal. In the following year his gift to Nūr-ad-Dīn from the Fāṭimid treasures was found insufficient. At bottom, the causes of the strain lay more probably in a divergence of political views. Nūr-ad-Dīn regarded Syria as the main battlefield against the crusaders, and looked to Egypt firstly as a source of revenue to meet the expenses of the jihad, and secondly as a source of

[2] On the Egyptian campaign of Amalric see above, chapter XVII, pp. 557–558.

additional manpower. Saladin, on the other hand, judging from the former competition for Egypt and the attempt on Damietta in 1169, and probably informed of the tenor of Amalric's negotiations with the Byzantine emperor in 1171, seems to have been convinced that for the time being, at least, the main point of danger lay in Egypt. He was more conscious also than Nūr-ad-Dīn could be of the dangers arising from the hostility of the former Fāṭimid troops and their readiness to join with the Franks. In his view, therefore, it was his first duty to build up a new army strong enough to hold Egypt in all contingencies, and to spend what resources he could command on this object.

It was also largely for reasons of internal security that he sent troops to occupy the hotbeds of Fāṭimid activity on the upper Nile and in the Yemen, although the ambition of his elder brother Turan-Shāh had some share in the second of these expeditions. How real the danger was to Saladin is shown by the fact that to the end of his life the defense of Egypt against sudden attack remained one of his constant preoccupations. Nevertheless, the continuous expansion of his influence and military power, which by 1171 already equalled, if it did not even exceed, the forces at Nūr-ad-Dīn's disposal, might well have made Nūr-ad-Dīn uneasy, and there was some talk of his intention to go down to Egypt himself. Saladin's good faith was, however, evidenced by an expedition against the bedouins of Kerak in 1173, in order to safeguard communications with Syria, and for the moment Nūr-ad-Dīn was content to send a controller to audit and report on Saladin's finances and military expenditure. Whatever further plans he may have had in view were cut short by his death on May 15, 1174.

The chief officers of Nūr-ad-Dīn's army at once entered into competition for the guardianship of his young son al-Malik aṣ-Ṣāliḥ. Saladin could not remain indifferent to this outbreak of rivalries, but for the time being took no action beyond acknowledging aṣ-Ṣāliḥ as his suzerain. In June Amalric laid siege to Banyas, but Saladin, having received warning from Constantinople to expect an attack by the Sicilian fleet, was unable to move. It was not until the end of July that the naval assault on Alexandria was made and beaten off, and in the meantime affairs in Syria had taken a grave turn. The emirs of Damascus had made a separate peace with Jerusalem on payment of tribute; Nūr-ad-Dīn's nephew at Mosul had invaded and annexed all his provinces beyond the Euphrates; and in August the eunuch Gümüshtigin, having secured the person of aṣ-Ṣāliḥ, established himself at

Aleppo and threw Nūr-ad-Dīn's lieutenants into his dungeons. The unity of Islam in face of the crusaders was disrupted. In reply to Saladin's remonstrances and hints of intervention, the emirs appealed to him to be loyal to the house that had raised him up. His answer was categorical: "In the interests of Islam and its people we put first and foremost whatever will combine their forces and unite them in one purpose; in the interests of the house of the atabeg we put first and foremost whatever will safeguard its root and its branch. Loyalty can only be the consequence of loyalty. We are in one valley and those who think ill of us are in another."

It was therefore with full consciousness of his mission as the true heir of Nūr-ad-Dīn that he set himself to rebuild the shattered edifice of his empire, and on an urgent appeal from the commandant at Damascus occupied it, almost without opposition, on October 28, 1174. Fully justified as Saladin's action was to himself and in the light of history, his contemporaries and rivals could not be expected to see it in the same light. In their eyes, naturally enough, he was only one of themselves and presumably inspired by the same motives of self-interest and lust for power, cloak them as he might by high-sounding appeals to the principles and interests of Islam. His occupation of Damascus seemed only a clever move to forestall them. When he appointed his brother Tughtigin as its governor, and himself pressed northwards in December with a small force to occupy Homs and Hamah and to demand that Aleppo should open its gates to him as the rightful guardian of aṣ-Ṣāliḥ, they concluded that he was bent upon nothing but the aggrandizement of his own house at the expense of the house of Zengi.

This is the view of Saladin which is presented by the Mosul chronicler, and it was the view of aṣ-Ṣāliḥ himself, who appealed to the population of Aleppo to protect him from his self-appointed deliverer. The emirs had recourse to the familiar expedients: the hiring of assassins (Arabic singular, *fidā'ī*) from Sinān, the "Old Man of the Mountain," to assassinate Saladin, an agreement with Raymond of Tripoli, the *bailli* of the kingdom of Jerusalem, that in return for favors past and to come he should execute a diversion by attacking Homs, and an appeal to Mosul in the name of family solidarity. The attempted assassination failed, but Saladin withdrew to defend Homs.[3] Two months later, in face of the combined forces of Mosul and Aleppo, he consented to retrocede northern Syria and content himself with holding Damascus as the lieutenant

[3] Cf. above, chapter IV, p. 123.

of aṣ-Ṣāliḥ. The allies tried to press their advantage, and on his refusal to yield further they attacked, only to be routed at the Horns of Hamah (Qurūn Ḥamāh), thanks to the timely arrival of the Egyptian regiments. When Saladin posted his forces round Aleppo for the second time, Gümüshtigin had no alternative but to accept his terms, which left Aleppo in the hands of aṣ-Ṣāliḥ on condition that the two armies should combine in operations against the Franks.

This was at the end of April 1175. A few days later, at Hamah, the envoys from the caliph brought his formal investiture with the governments of Egypt and Syria.[4] For most princes of his time this was a mere formality, but for Saladin it was much more. If the war to which he had vowed himself against the crusaders was to be a real jihad, a true "holy war", it was imperative to conduct it with scrupulous observance of the revealed law of Islam. A government which sought to serve the cause of God in battle must not only be a lawful government, duly authorized by the supreme representative of the divine law, but must serve God with equal zeal in its administration and in its treatment of its subjects. Already, during his first years in Egypt, and following the example set by Nūr-ad-Dīn, he had abolished all forms of taxation which were contrary to Islamic law, and his first action in Damascus was to abolish them there. This was his invariable practice on each addition to his territories, and was formally stipulated in the diplomas issued to his vassals. It is true that they did not always observe the condition, but an offender was likely to find himself summarily dispossessed of his government in consequence. The sources vividly portray the repeated amazement of his officers and subjects that the personal acquisitions and exercise of power which were the first objects of most princes and governors, including those of his own house, were of no interest to him, and that wealth was a thing to be used in prosecution of the holy war or to be given to others. The fact was patent even to the crusaders. As early as 1175, when Raymond agreed to terms with Aleppo in order to draw off Saladin, William of Tyre observed that "any increase of Saladin's power was cause for suspicion in our eyes.... For he was a man wise in counsel, valiant in war, and generous beyond measure. It seemed wiser to us to lend aid to the boy king... not for his own sake, but to encourage him as an adversary against Saladin."[5]

[4] There is no evidence that he was at any time formally invested by the caliph with the title of sultan (Arabic, *sulṭān*).

[5] William of Tyre, XXI, 6.

No greater justification than this could well be found for the policy which Saladin had adopted. Eight years later he used the same argument in an outspoken despatch to the caliphate: "Your servant believes that there is no stratagem more fraught with mischief for the enemy and the infidel, no effort more effective against the misguided, no favor more profitable in stirring up to anger the leaders of heresy, than to enlarge your servant's power to increase his opportunity of service. For let it be considered, is there among all the rulers of Islam another one whose extension of power is a source of grief and affliction to the infidels?"

The facts were not so patent at Mosul, where the terms of the agreement with Aleppo, and probably also the diploma from the caliph, were received with incredulous anger. It was not only that a prince of the Zengid house was reduced virtually to being a vassal of one of his father's creatures. What was still more disagreeable was that the creature was a Kurd, who challenged the monopoly of sovereignty enjoyed by the Turks for a century and a half, and bestowed his conquests upon his own kinsmen. To what extent, indeed, personal motives were mingled with Saladin's genuine devotion to the cause and the ideals of Islam is a question which it may never be possible to resolve. But in the circumstances of his time, however unselfregarding his motives were, the only way in which his object could be realized was by concentrating power in his own hands, and delegating it to persons on whose loyalty he could count with absolute assurance. The attitude of the Zengids drove him in the same direction, when events showed him the futility of relying upon alliances and confederations.

Before leaving northern Syria, Saladin retaliated against the Assassins by raiding the Ismā'īlite territories in Jabal as-Summāq, then withdrew to Damascus and made a truce with Jerusalem. An envoy had been sent to Mosul to ensure Saif-ad-Dīn's acceptance of the agreement, and had obtained satisfactory assurances. When, however, the envoy of Mosul in turn came to Damascus to swear Saladin to its terms, he presented in error a document which provided for an offensive alliance against him between Mosul and Aleppo. He was prepared, therefore, when in April 1176 the allies mustered their forces again. Marching northwards, he met them on the 22nd at Tall as-Sulṭān, fifteen miles from Aleppo, and drove them headlong from the field. Restraining his army from pursuit, he distributed among them the immense booty, released the captives, and sent back to Saif-ad-Dīn the cages of doves, nightingales, and parrots found in his canteen with an ironical message to amuse himself with them and keep out of military adventures in the future. The disgusted sultan, says the contemporary Aleppo chronicler, "found the Mosul camp more like a tavern, with all its wines, guitars, lutes, bands, singers, and singing girls, and showing it to his troops prayed that they might be preserved from such an affliction."

In spite of Saladin's magnanimity Aleppo still held out. But when, after storming its protecting fortresses to east and north, Buzā'ah, Manbij, and 'Azāz, he again invested it on June 25, its defenders consented to a renewal of the arrangement made the year before. A general peace was signed a month later between Saladin, his brother Turan-Shāh (now "sultan" at Damascus), the princes of Aleppo and Mosul, and the Artukid vassals of Mosul (the princes of Ḥiṣn Kaifā and Mardin), all parties swearing to join together against any one of them who should break the agreement. Aṣ-Ṣāliḥ was given back 'Azāz on the intercession of his little sister, and undertook to furnish Saladin with the assistance of the army of Aleppo should he require it.

During the siege of 'Azāz, a second and more determined attempt had been made on Saladin's life by Assassin emissaries.[6] On his return from Aleppo, therefore, he marched on Maṣyāf, the Syrian headquarters of the sect, and laid siege to it, while his troops ravaged the neighborhood. What followed is largely enveloped in legend; but Saladin withdrew to Damascus and dismissed his forces to their homes. All that is certain is that for the rest of his life he had nothing to fear from the Assassins.

After marrying at Damascus the widow of Nūr-ad-Dīn, Saladin returned to Egypt, which had been governed in his absence by his brother al-'Ādil Saif-ad-Dīn, and occupied himself for a year with internal affairs. His chief attention was directed to the construction of the citadel and the great walls of Cairo which he had begun in 1171 as a precaution against future Frankish invasions, together with the reorganization of the fleet. At the same time he was earnestly concerned to foster in Egypt the orthodox reform movement which Nūr-ad-Dīn had encouraged in Syria, and both he and al-'Ādil set the example of founding the new colleges from which it was diffused. Meanwhile, his nephew Taqī-ad-Dīn 'Umar, the most warlike and impetuous member of the family, who had watched with a jealous eye the distribution of kingdoms and governments to his relatives, was engaged in attempting to carve

[6] Cf. above, chapter IV, pp. 123–124.

out a kingdom for himself in the west, an attempt which was ultimately to lead to a clash with the Muwaḥḥid (Almohad) sultan of Morocco. Saladin, so far as the evidence goes, took no hand in organizing these expeditions, but certainly connived at them, and even took credit for them in his despatches to Baghdad.

In August 1177 the news of the arrival in Palestine of Philip of Flanders gave the signal for fresh preparations for war. Whether or not he was informed of the proposals made to Philip to invade Egypt, it was a condition of the truce with the Franks that "if any king or great noble arrived they were free to give him assistance, and the armistice should be renewed on his withdrawal."[7] As the crusaders, after attacking Hamah, moved up to besiege Ḥārim, Saladin planned a large-scale raid on Ascalon and Gaza. ʿImād-ad-Dīn gives a vivid picture of the light-hearted confidence of the Egyptian troops as they assembled at the advance base and dispersed on plundering raids over the countryside. Baldwin IV's well-timed surprise attack on the regiment of guards at Mont Gisard on November 25 threw the whole force into confusion, and the remnants straggled back to Egypt as best they could, harassed by the Franks and the bedouins, and by lack of both food and water. To Saladin himself, who owed his escape to the loyalty and foresight of al-Qāḍī al-Fāḍil, it was a lesson that he never forgot.

So far from decisive was this defeat, however, that only four months later he was able to set out again with a refitted army, and yet leave sufficient forces behind to guard the security of Egypt. The expedition this time had the definite object of attacking the besiegers of Ḥārim, and although Saladin was forestalled in this by the raising of the siege on payment of an indemnity by the government of Aleppo, he pushed on to Homs and encamped there in readiness to take the field at the first opportunity. The withdrawal of the count of Flanders automatically brought the armistice into effect again; in addition, a bad year had brought severe scarcity in Syria. Yet Saladin was eager to resume the jihad, and although all the eloquence of al-Qāḍī al-Fāḍil was exerted to persuade him to hold his hand until conditions were more favorable, he was already assuring the caliph's ministers that, if all went well and if the troops duly mustered, he would attack Jerusalem in the following year.

[7] ʿImād-ad-Dīn, *Barq*, iii, f. 25v (quoted by abū-Shāmah, I, 275). See also below, chapter XIX, p. 595.

In August the Franks broke the armistice by an attack on Hamah. It was driven off without much difficulty and the prisoners were brought to Saladin, who ordered their execution for breach of faith. A more serious breach occurred when Baldwin began to construct a fortress at Jacob's Ford, at the instance of the Templars, in October. Saladin was unable to intervene at once owing to a delicate situation which had arisen at Damascus. His brother Turan-Shāh had completely neglected his duties as governor, besides being on suspiciously good terms with aṣ-Ṣāliḥ at Aleppo. Saladin had accordingly appointed his nephew Farrukh-Shāh as military commandant at Damascus. Turan-Shāh now demanded that he should be given the fief of Baalbek, which was held by the former governor of Damascus, Ibn-al-Muqaddam. Very unwillingly, Saladin consented to the investment of Baalbek, and when Ibn-al-Muqaddam eventually surrendered he was given extensive fiefs in the north; the loyal relationship between him and Saladin remained unbroken, and on the death of Farrukh-Shāh in 1183 he was reappointed to the governorship of Damascus. The episode temporarily weakened Saladin's diplomatic position as against his rivals; but in the long run it was largely due to his firm, yet conciliatory, attitude towards Ibn-al-Muqaddam in this conflict that he had never again to take military measures against an insubordinate officer.

With this problem out of the way, Saladin was free to resume the offensive in the spring of 1179. He began by reorganizing the commands in the north, appointing Taqī-ad-Dīn to Hamah and Naṣīr-ad-Dīn ibn-Shīrkūh to Homs, to hold Raymond of Tripoli in check. A second winter without rains had created famine conditions in Syria; his troops were suffering severely and remonstrated with him, but he answered only "God will provide", and sent the most incapacitated back to Egypt with Turan-Shāh, asking al-'Ādil to send him 1500 picked men in return, along with supplies. Early in April, on receiving reports of a projected raid by Baldwin, he sent out Farrukh-Shāh with the Damascus regiment, numbering about 1000 slave troops (Arabic singular, *mamlūk*), with orders to shadow the Franks and send back information on their movements. Farrukh-Shāh, however, found himself engaged almost by accident near Belfort (Shaqīf Arnūn), and gained a brilliant success, the more welcome to the Moslems because the constable Humphrey of Toron was among the killed.

Shortly afterwards Saladin moved out to Banyas and, trusting to receive warning from his spies of any concentration of Frankish troops, posted a guard at Tall al-Qāḍī and dispersed his forces to loot for forage and supplies. Bands of starving Arab tribesmen who had followed him up were dispatched into the districts of Sidon and Beirut to reap all the grain that they could find. In the plain of Marj ʿUyūn, he was surprised by the appearance of a large force under Baldwin, but hastily mounted all the available troops and turned an initial reverse into a notable victory. The date was June 10, 1179, and ʿImād-ad-Dīn, who drew up the register of the prisoners, relates that over two hundred and seventy knights were among them, exclusive of lower ranks.

Adequately supplied now for a major operation, Saladin enlisted large auxiliary forces of Turkomans and siege troops to supplement the Syrian regiments and the fresh Egyptian contingent, and on August 25 invested the newly-constructed castle at Jacob's Ford. The siege was prosecuted with unremitting vigor and resolution; on the sixth day, the castle was stormed, the seven hundred defenders were taken prisoner, and the Moslem captives were released. In spite of the heat and the stench of dead bodies, Saladin would not leave until the last stone had been razed, and made a series of forays into the territories of Jerusalem before returning to Damascus.

In all these operations, the Zengids of Aleppo and Mosul had shown no readiness to assist him in the reconquest of Palestine. The modest successes that he had been able to gain made it clear to him that the struggle with the crusaders could not be pressed to a conclusion with only the forces of Damascus and those which could be spared from the defense of Egypt. It was not merely that the 6000 troopers whom he could now maintain in the field at one time were insufficient for a decisive campaign. So long as the Nūrīyah at Aleppo were under the command of others, they constituted a potentially hostile force on his flank. But even if they were securely brought over to his side, that very operation would only deepen the hostility of the Zengids of Mosul, who with their 6000 troops could still effectually neutralize him. The conclusion was inescapable: since he could not concentrate the forces of Syria and Egypt against the crusaders so long as he was endangered by flank or rear attacks from Mosul, the forces of Mosul too must be brought under his control and turned into auxiliaries in the jihad.

That this could not be accomplished without armed conflict must have been clear to him; but he was reluctant to take up arms against those who were to be his future allies. Persuasion and diplomacy would yield better returns than conquest, and he knew himself to possess one powerful advantage. In the eyes of all Islam he had established his claim to the spiritual succession of Nūr-ad-Dīn, and those moral forces which had been fanned into life by Nūr-ad-Dīn were ranging themselves on his side. However much the interests of the Zengids might be supported by the narrower loyalties of local patriotism and military tradition, he enjoyed the sympathies of an increasingly powerful faction, not only at Aleppo, but also at Mosul. The rivalries and secret or overt communications of the Zengids with the Franks undermined their own cause, and it seems that even the doctrine of legal rights, so industriously pursued by Saladin, helped to turn the scale. He had only to repeat the tactics employed by Nūr-ad-Dīn himself against Damascus: to weaken the opposing party by encouraging defections and by organizing military demonstrations at appropriate moments, and at the same time to observe to the letter his treaty obligations and the sovereign rights of the caliph.

Saladin's history during the next six years, 1179 to 1185, is the record of his successive advances toward this aim. The complex tale of campaigns and negotiations with the minor princes of Mesopotamia, the Zengids of Mosul, and the envoys of the caliphate, though not difficult to unravel, is difficult to present without entering into a mass of detail. With this main thread in the narrative two others are interwoven: the continued warfare with Jerusalem, and the problems of internal administration and relations between his relatives and vassals. For the sake of clarity, we shall deal with these aspects separately.

During the campaigns of 1179 the Selchükid sultan of Rūm, Kilij (or Kilich) Arslan II, who had in the previous year sent an envoy to assure Saladin of his friendship, suddenly demanded the cession of Raban, taken by Saladin in 1176 from aṣ-Ṣāliḥ. Taqī-ad-Dīn, in whose command it lay, was dispatched to defend it, and by a stratagem routed the Selchükid army with his small force of 1000 horsemen. Early in 1180 a quarrel broke out on a domestic issue between the Selchükid sultan and the Artukid prince of Ḥiṣn Kaifā, Nūr-ad-Dīn. Although the latter was a vassal of Mosul he appealed to Saladin, presumably in virtue of the Aleppo treaty of 1176. This was just the kind of occasion for which Saladin was waiting. In order to establish his control over Mosul, the first step was to detach the great vassals of Mesopotamia and Diyār-Bakr, who furnished more than half of the effective forces of the Mosul army. The most powerful of these were the Artukid princes of Ḥiṣn Kaifā and Mardin, who had never reconciled themselves to Zengid domination. Already in 1178 they had approached Saladin, to obtain his support against the aggressive designs of the Selchükid sultan, and, dubious as the present *casus belli* was, he was impelled to seize the opportunity, in order to gain their interest and display a *de facto* suzerainty over Diyār-Bakr. A truce signed with Baldwin in the spring left him free to lead his army to the borders of the Selchükid dominions, less for the purpose of military operations than to force Kïlïj Arslan to cease these provocations and accept his mediation. The plan achieved even greater success than he could have anticipated. The two sultans met on the river Sanja (Gök-Su) in June and there, apparently, concluded the alliance which was to mean so much to Saladin in later years. Its first fruits were a short and successful campaign against Reuben (West Armenian, Ṛoupen) of Little Armenia, on the pretext of harsh treatment of the Turkoman tribes in his territories.

Bahā'-ad-Dīn relates that after this campaign a general peace was concluded, on the initiative of Kïlïj Arslan, between Saladin, the Selchükid sultan, Mosul, and the princes of Diyār-Bakr, at a meeting on the Sanja, near Samosata, on October 2, 1180. There is no confirmation of this statement in any other contemporary source, and indeed the evidence is all against it. For on June 29 Saif-ad-Dīn of Mosul had died, and his brother ʿIzz-ad-Dīn, setting aside Saif-ad-Dīn's nomination of his son Sanjar-Shāh, had succeeded him. On his accession ʿIzz-ad-Dīn sent an envoy to Saladin to ask his agreement to the continuance of the suzerainty of Mosul over the Mesopotamian cities seized by Saif-ad-Dīn after Nūr-ad-Dīn's death in 1174. Saladin refused point-blank. These provinces, he said, were included in the general grant made to him by the caliph, and he had left them in Saif-ad-Dīn's possession only in return for his promise to assist Saladin with his troops. At the same time he sent a despatch to Baghdad, pointing out that he could not draw indefinitely on the Egyptian forces for his Syrian campaigns but needed the armies of those provinces, and asking for a confirmation of the grant, which was sent to him accordingly.

The breach with Mosul was consummated by the death of aṣ-Ṣāliḥ at Aleppo on December 4, 1181. Saladin was in Egypt at the time, and on learning of aṣ-Ṣāliḥ's illness had sent urgent orders to Farrukh-Shāh at Damascus and Taqī-ad-Dīn at Hamah to occupy the western Jazira (Arabic, *jazīrah*: upper Mesopotamia), and prevent the army of Mosul from crossing the Euphrates. But Farrukh-Shāh was engaged in countering Reginald's schemes of invading Arabia from Kerak (Krak des Moabites), and Taqī-ad-Dīn was unable to prevent ‘Izz-ad-Dīn from entering Aleppo. There he appointed his brother ‘Imād-ad-Dīn as governor of the city, in exchange for Sinjar, and after emptying the contents of its treasury and arsenal returned to Mosul. Saladin's intense anxiety over the situation is shown by the succession of letters addressed to the caliph's council (Arabic, *dīwān*), criticizing the conduct of the prince of Mosul in seizing a province which had been assigned to him while his own troops were in the very act of protecting the city of the prophet from the "infidel", complaining that the disputes between the Moslem princes were hindering the jihad, reasserting his claim to Aleppo on the basis of his diploma, and declaring that "if the Exalted Commands should ordain that the prince of Mosul be invested with the government of Aleppo, then it were better to invest him with all Syria and Egypt as well." The urgent tone of these letters is no doubt explained partly by the need to counteract the similar pressure of the partisans of Mosul at Baghdad, but though propaganda points may be difficult to disentangle from religious zeal there can be no doubt that Saladin was genuinely in earnest over the stalemate that would follow from a reunion of Aleppo with Mosul.

In May 1182 he left Cairo, accompanied by half of the newly reorganized army of Egypt, some 5000 troopers in all, and rejoined his lieutenants in Syria. After an unsuccessful *coup de main* against Beirut by sea and land, he marched on Aleppo, fortified in his purpose by the caliph's diploma. But before investing it, he was visited by Muẓaffar-ad-Dīn Gökböri, the governor of Harran, with an urgent invitation to cross the Euphrates and assurances that he would be welcomed on all sides. Accordingly, since he was, in fact, by virtue of the caliph's diploma, lawful ruler of the Euphrates and Khabur provinces, Saladin crossed the Euphrates at the end of September, and with only scattered opposition occupied the former possessions of Nūr-ad-Dīn in the Jazira. ‘Izz-ad-Dīn attempted to take the field against him, but was foiled by the opposition of his own officers and the open adhesion to Saladin of his chief vassal, the Artukid prince of Ḥiṣn Kaifā, Nūr-ad-Dīn ibn-Kara-Arslan. The sole result of his action was to supply Saladin with a valid pretext for advancing on Mosul itself, an action justified by him in a lengthy despatch to Baghdad, accusing the rulers of Mosul of paying the Franks to attack him, of oppression of their subjects, and finally of appealing to the sworn enemy of the caliphate, the Selchükid atabeg in Persia. The last accusation is confirmed by the Mosul sources; in desperation 'Izz-ad-Dīn was seeking allies in every direction, and sent Bahā'-ad-Dīn himself to ask for the caliph's support against Saladin. In response to this appeal, the caliph sent a delegate, the *shaikh ash-shuyūkh*, to mediate between the parties, and for a month protracted negotiations went on while the siege continued.

It must be emphasized that the point at issue in these negotiations was not at any time Saladin's claim to the physical possession of Mosul, but the terms on which its prince would adhere to Saladin and send his armies to coöperate in the war against the Franks. On this first occasion the main object of the Zengid prince was to retain his suzerainty over Aleppo, and although Saladin, anxious to reach an agreement, yielded to all his demands short of this, he refused to ratify the terms. At the urgent intercession of the shaikh, Saladin agreed to withdraw from Mosul, but refused to continue the negotiations. The fact that they had been set on foot had severely strained the confidence of his new vassals in the Jazira, and in order to reassure them he announced to the diwan his firm determination not to leave the province until he had completed the conquest of it.

He began by besieging 'Izz-ad-Dīn's brother in Sinjar, with the assistance of the Artukid Nūr-ad-Dīn. It was surrendered on terms after fifteen days (December 30), and the garrison was evacuated to Mosul. After Dara also had been surrendered by its Artukid prince Bahrām, Saladin went into winter quarters at Harran. But that he had no intention of relaxing the pressure upon 'Izz-ad-Dīn is shown by the stream of correspondence addressed to the chief ministers at Baghdad and reiterated requests for his recognition as suzerain of Mosul. Though this was still withheld, his application to receive the caliph's diploma for Amida (modern Diyarbakīr) was granted. In April 'Izz-ad-Dīn made an attempt to rally his remaining allies, but Saladin called up Taqī-ad-Dīn from Hamah, and on his approach the coalition dissolved. Without waiting for the remainder of his forces he at once laid siege to the all-but-impregnable fortress of Amida in Diyār-Bakr, in pursuance of a promise made to Nūr-ad-Dīn. Its surrender within three weeks set the seal on his reputation; and his quixotic generosity, both to the defeated governor and in handing it over with its immense military stores intact to Nūr-ad-Dīn, disproved once and for all his enemies' imputations of selfish ambition.

In his despatches to the caliphate after the capture of Amida Saladin pointed the moral. The caliph's authority to take and govern Amida had unlocked its gates to him; why was the patent for Mosul still denied? This alone stood in the way of the union of Islam and the recovery of Jerusalem. Let the commander of the faithful compare the conduct of his clients and judge which of them had most faithfully served the cause of Islam. If Saladin insists on the inclusion of Mesopotamia and Mosul in his dominions, it is because "this little Jazira [*i.e.* Mesopotamia] is the lever which will set in motion the great Jazira [*i.e.* the whole Arab east]; it is the point of division and center of resistance, and once it is set in its place in the chain of alliances, the whole armed might of Islam will be coördinated to engage the forces of unbelief."

The submission of Amida brought the remaining Artukids at Maiyafariqin and Mardin over to Saladin, and he now turned to settle his account with Aleppo, receiving on the way the surrender of the last of its outer fortresses, Tall Khālid and Aintab (Gaziantep). By May 21, 1183, he was already encamped before Aleppo, with a reasonable expectation of its early surrender. Saladin's secretary vividly portrays the complexity of the conflict; neither 'Imād-ad-Dīn Zengi nor Saladin was eager to fight, the former because he had set his heart on returning to Sinjar, the latter because the Nūrīyah, Nūr-ad-Dīn's old guard, were "the soldiers of the jihad, who had in the past done great service for Islam, and whose gallantry and courage had gained his admiration," whereas they for their part "stirred up the flames of war," and the younger and more ardent of Saladin's own troops plunged eagerly into the fray. After a few days he withdrew to the hill of Jaushan, overlooking the city, set his builders to construct a fortress there, and started to distribute the territories of Aleppo in fiefs to his own officers. 'Imād-ad-Dīn Zengi saw that the critical moment had come, and secretly arranged the exchange of Aleppo for Sinjar and the eastern Jazira, on condition of coöperating in the war with the Franks. On June 11 Saladin's yellow banner was hoisted on the citadel; the Nūrīyah in turn made their submission with what, from the external events, would seem surprising readiness, were received by Saladin as old comrades in arms, and were overwhelmed by his generosity. The governor of Ḥārim alone held out and attempted to gain support from Antioch, but was arrested by his own men, who surrendered the castle to Saladin in person on June 22.

A truce with Bohemond of Antioch having been arranged on condition of the liberation of Moslem prisoners, Saladin was now in a position to retaliate against the Franks of Jerusalem for their raiding expeditions during his absence in Mesopotamia, and more especially on Reginald of Kerak for his forays in Arabia and on the Red Sea. Announcing to the diwan at Baghdad his decision to prosecute the jihad, now that the main obstacles had been removed, he set out with the regular troops of Aleppo and the Jazira, together with the Turkoman cavalry and a large force of volunteers and auxiliaries. After a brief halt at Damascus he crossed the Jordan to Baisan on September 29, but failed to bring the main forces of the kingdom to battle.[8] Returning to Damascus, he summoned al-ʻĀdil to join him before Kerak with a body of the Egyptian troops, and laid siege to the castle in November. The Moslems were so confident of success that the failure of their mangonels to effect a breach produced a corresponding discouragement, and when news was received of the arrival of a relieving force at Wālā, they found excuses for putting off the attack, and Saladin withdrew to rest and refit his armies.

During this interval another attempt was made to solve the problem of Mosul by negotiation. The initiative came from ʻIzz-ad-Dīn, whose nephew Sanjar-Shāh at Jazīrat-Ibn-ʻUmar, with Gökböri's brother at Irbil and the governors of Takrīt and Ḥadīthah, had thrown themselves on the protection of Saladin and obtained from him a guarantee of support. ʻIzz-ad-Dīn appealed to the caliph to send the *shaikh ash-shuyūkh* once more to mediate with Saladin, "knowing," as Saladin's secretary wrote, "that our policy was one of strict obedience to the caliph's commands." An agreement was reached with the shaikh on the basis that ʻIzz-ad-Dīn's rights in Mosul should be respected and that his former vassals should be left free to choose between Saladin and him, but it was rejected by the envoy from Mosul, and so matters remained as they were, or rather worse than they had been.

For his fresh assault on Kerak (August–September 1184) Saladin assembled the most powerful army that had yet operated in Syria, comprising the forces of Damascus, Aleppo, the Jazira and Sinjar, Ḥiṣn Kaifā and Mardin, and a contingent from Egypt. Again it failed, and the armies were dismissed after a raiding expedition through Samaria. Back at Damascus, he found the shaikh awaiting him with the caliph's patents for his new provinces. This was followed by graver news. ʻIzz-ad-Dīn of Mosul

[8] Cf. below, chapter XIX, pp. 599–600.

had accepted the offers of the atabeg of Persia, and had received a reinforcement of 3000 horsemen from the atabeg Kizil Arslan of Azerbaijan for an attack on Irbil. Although the attack was unsuccessful, the governor called on Saladin to honor his promise, and thus provided the occasion for Saladin's renewed assault on Mosul.

Before setting out in the following year, however, he had the good fortune to be invited by Raymond of Tripoli to agree to a truce for four years. With his rear thus protected, he assembled his forces at Aleppo in May 1185 and marched on Mosul, although he had been warned by the sultan Kilij Arslan that he would be opposed by a coalition of the "eastern princes". But Mosul was in fact left to its fate, and even the caliph refused to intervene further, presumably because — as Saladin lost no opportunity of reminding him — 'Izz-ad-Dīn had been forced to acknowledge the Selchükid Tughrul as his suzerain. During the summer heat Saladin slackened the siege and, leaving part of his forces in front of Mosul, led the rest northwards to deal with a confused situation which had arisen there after the deaths of Nūr-ad-Dīn and the princes of Akhlat (or Khilat) and Mardin. Returning to Mosul in November, he prepared to continue the siege through the winter. In a last attempt to stave off the inevitable end, 'Izz-ad-Dīn appealed to Saladin's chivalry by sending out a delegation of the Zengid princesses to intercede. But the issue at stake was too serious, and Saladin could promise no more than to accept the mediation of 'Imād-ad-Dīn Zengi of Sinjar. What followed is not quite clear. Saladin suddenly fell ill, and "repenting of his rebuff to the envoys, sent to 'Imād-ad-Dīn to dispatch a mission to Mosul." Without waiting for the conclusion of the negotiations he left Mosul on December 25 for Harran and withdrew his troops to Nisibin. In the following February 'Izz-ad-Dīn sent the *qāḍī* Bahā'-ad-Dīn as his envoy to Harran with instructions to get a sworn agreement on the best terms that he could. Saladin restored to him the small district of Baina-n-Nahrain, between Nisibin and the Tigris, and on swearing to these conditions was recognized as suzerain of Mosul; 'Izz-ad-Dīn in return undertook to send his troops to assist in the reconquest of Palestine. The grand coalition was formed at last.

Throughout all these years, in which Saladin was devoting his chief attention to organizing the forces for the coming struggle, it was clearly to his advantage to avoid any major operations against the Franks. In 1180 he had willingly agreed to a truce with

Baldwin on both land and sea.[9] Raymond of Tripoli had, it seems, refused to become a consenting party and was brought to reason only by a series of devastating raids as well as the seizure of the island of Ruad by the Egyptian fleet. One of the most important stipulations for Saladin was the freedom of trade, since the route between Egypt and Damascus was precariously exposed, and in times of warfare caravans had to be convoyed by bodies of troops. It was the violation of this condition by Reginald of Kerak which gave the signal for the reopening of hostilities. In the summer of 1181 he had made a raid on Taimā' in the northern Hejaz, from which he was recalled by an energetic counterattack on the Transjordan by Farrukh-Shāh from Damascus. This was bad enough, but Saladin made no move until Reginald seized a caravan on its way from Damascus to Mecca. After all efforts to right the wrong had failed, he took the field in the spring of 1182. Though his forces were not yet strong enough for a decisive blow, he no doubt hoped to inflict some further losses on the Franks. Baldwin's defensive tactics, however, prevented a major engagement but left the countryside open to the raids of Farrukh-Shāh's cavalry, with the booty from which the Moslem forces retired well-content to Damascus.

Saladin's next operation was of a more audacious kind. As early as 1177 he had begun to reorganize the Egyptian fleet, making it a separate and independent department under its own head, with power to take all the materials and impress all the men that it needed. By the middle of the same year, the fleets of Alexandria and Damietta were already engaged in raiding, and in 1179 they carried out a daring attack on Acre and the Syrian coast. The seizure of Ruad in 1180 has already been mentioned. In the general reorganization of the Egyptian forces which Saladin made in 1181 the fleet was still further strengthened. He now planned a combined land and sea operation against Beirut, in the hope of taking it by surprise. The plan was skillfully carried out (August 1182), but the garrison held off his assaults until Baldwin was ready to relieve them, when Saladin, who had come out with only light raiding equipment, reassembled his forces at Baalbek and marched northwards.

During the campaigns in Mesopotamia and the struggle for Aleppo, Farrukh-Shāh was left in Damascus with instructions to meet, as best he could with the troops at his disposal, the raids made by the Franks into Moslem territory. "While they knock

[9] Cf. below, chapter XIX, p. 595.

down villages," Saladin is reported as saying on the news of Baldwin's raids into the Hauran, "we are taking cities." Much more serious was the news of Reginald's commerce-raiding in the Red Sea and penetration into the Hejaz in February 1183. Saladin's admiral, Ḥusām-ad-Dīn Lu'lu', taught the raiders a drastic lesson, but not before the report of the exploit sent a thrill of consternation and horror round the Moslem world. This episode probably did as much as any other single event to enhance Saladin's reputation and strengthen his position.

The expeditions in the latter half of 1183, already mentioned, though inconclusive, served to throw the Franks back on the defensive. The equally unsuccessful siege of Kerak in August 1184 and subsequent raid on Palestine served nevertheless one useful purpose, in that they brought together for the first time most of the diverse contingents of Saladin's army and gave them some practice in joint operations. The Egyptian fleet also continued its activities in both of these years, although in less spectacular ways. Raymond of Tripoli and the barons were therefore ready enough to ask for the armistice which, in the spring of 1185, freed Saladin for his final campaign against Mosul.[10]

Saladin's military forces, though organized on the same lines as those of Nūr-ad-Dīn, differed in one important respect. The proportion of Kurds in his regiments was much greater, and the mamluk element less prominent. A common loyalty to him kept in check the rivalries that might otherwise have issued in conflicts between them, and in his selection of fiefholders and the lesser governors he seems to have held the balance fairly evenly. In the disposal of provinces, however, his own family had first claim. His viceroys and governors enjoyed uncontrolled authority, on condition of equitable treatment of their subjects, a contribution to the war-chest of the jihad, and maintenance of their regiments in good order and discipline, in readiness to take the field when they were called for. To all of them he gave his complete confidence, and expected of them equal loyalty in return. Himself indifferent to the material rewards of power, he seems to have been unaware of the corrupting influence of power and wealth on others, and only in flagrant cases of disregard of these conditions did he intervene. He had little patience with the perpetual and petty but necessary details of daily administration, and the lack of his personal supervision made itself felt in the provinces. With this weakness in the field of administration went also an imprudent gener-

[10] Cf. below, chapter XIX, p. 604.

osity in the disposal of his revenues. Everything was given away without a thought to all who asked; "I used to blush," wrote Bahā'-ad-Dīn, "at the size of the demands made upon him." His campaigns were as much occasions of princely largesse as of military operations. His intendants saw to it that all present military needs were adequately met, but no reserves were accumulated, and this deficiency was to prove a serious embarrassment during the Third Crusade.

On the occupation of Aleppo in 1183 Saladin at first invested his ten-year-old son aẓ-Ẓāhir Ghāzī "as sultan", with a number of trusted officers to support him, but this arrangement was challenged by al-'Ādil, who asked that he might exchange the government of Egypt for that of Aleppo. Whatever Saladin's regrets at deposing his favorite son may have been, he agreed without demur, and the diploma of appointment, which was drawn up in terms of brotherly affection unusual for such formal documents, conferred on al-'Ādil unrestricted authority, subject to the usual stipulations. On the advice of al-Qāḍī al-Fāḍil he replaced al-'Ādil in Egypt by Taqī-ad-Dīn 'Umar, but with a justified fear of his impetuosity reluctantly sent the qadi with him to exercise a moderating influence. During his grave illness several of his relatives, anticipating his death, began to make dispositions in their own interests. Partly because of this, partly because he was anxious to establish his sons, he redistributed the provinces in 1186. Al-'Ādil, on his own suggestion, was reappointed to Egypt, not, however, in full possession but as guardian of Saladin's son al-'Azīz 'Uthmān. Taqī-ad-Din took his deposition in bad part, and for a moment threatened to go out west, taking a large part of the Egyptian army with him. At length, however, he obeyed Saladin's order to present himself in Damascus, and was reappointed to his fiefs in the north, together with Maiyafariqin in Diyār-Bakr. Aleppo was restored to aẓ-Ẓāhir Ghāzī.

In any estimate of Saladin's career the chief place must be given to the efforts by which he built up the material power now about to be discharged upon the Franks with accumulated force. But there was another, less obvious, group of activities which were being prosecuted at the same time and to the same end. The extent to which Saladin's diplomacy was employed to isolate the Franks in Syria and to ensure that he should be, as far as possible, on terms of peace, if not of friendship, with every potential external antagonist before opening his decisive campaign, has not been sufficiently appreciated. His diplomacy was directed on two fronts. The Moslems in Syria and Egypt were well aware of the large place that the trading interests of the Italian republics represented in the maintenance of the Latin states, and of the rivalries among Pisa, Genoa, and Venice. From the beginning of his government Saladin made efforts to attract their trade to Egypt, which would have the double advantage of increasing his own resources and diminishing the value of the Syrian trade, especially in view of his control of the Red Sea. The earliest treaty which has so far been attested was one with Pisa in 1173, and its utility was demonstrated in the following year, when the Pisans and other European merchants assisted the Egyptian forces against the Sicilians at Alexandria. Saladin's own letter to Baghdad on this occasion affirms the existence of treaties with Genoa and Venice as well: "There is not one of them but supplies our land with its materials of war..., and treaties of peaceful intercourse have been negotiated with them all." Three years later, a letter from al-Qāḍī al-Fāḍil to Saladin refers in passing to "the envoys of the different peoples" in Cairo, and there can be no doubt that this trade greatly assisted the reconstruction of the Egyptian fleet.

Still more effective for Saladin's purpose were the diplomatic negotiations with Constantinople. The efforts of the Greeks to persuade the Latins in Syria to coöperate in attacks on Egypt constituted a standing threat to its security. At the same time, it was difficult to reach agreement with them without turning the Selchükids of Anatolia against him. The disaster inflicted on Manuel's army by Kïlïj Arslan at Myriokephalon in 1176, however, ended for a time direct hostilities between them, and on Manuel's death in 1180 his successors took the initiative in opening relations with Saladin, which were affirmed by treaty in 1181. The growing hostility between Greeks and Latins increased the utility and frequency of these relations, which were maintained between Saladin and both Isaac Angelus at Constantinople and Isaac Comnenus in Cyprus. Such terms of friendship with the traditional foes of Islam were no doubt sufficiently justified in Saladin's eyes by their immediate advantage, but they gave him the further satisfaction of restoring, if only temporarily, the old institution of Moslem worship at Constantinople in the name of the ʿAbbāsid caliph.

By the end of 1186 everything was organized and ready for the signal. But Saladin was still bound by the terms of the treaty of 1185 and had to wait until he was furnished with a *casus belli.* A promising opening had been offered by the conflict between Raymond of Tripoli and Guy, and the ensuing alliance between Raymond and the sultan.[11] Some of his troops were actually sent to reinforce the garrison of Tiberias; consequently, Guy's first intention, under Templar instigation, to attack Tiberias would have had the effect of setting the war in motion. Early in 1187 Reginald of Kerak made his fatal blunder of attacking a caravan from Cairo to Damascus, violating the truce, and refused to yield up his booty in response either to the threats of Saladin or the appeals of the king. The summonses went out to all Saladin's viceroys and vassals, while he himself set out with his guard on March 14 to protect a homeward-bound pilgrim-caravan. The Egyptian contingent, arriving after some delay, joined in ravaging the lands of Kerak and Montréal, and returned with him to Damascus two months later; meanwhile the contingents from Damascus, Aleppo, Mesopotamia, Mosul, and Diyār-Bakr assembled at Ra'ṣ al-Mā', and raided the county of Tiberias. At Ṣaffūrīyah a body of Templars and Hospitallers, disregarding Raymond's instructions, engaged a powerful force making a demonstration raid on May 1, and were killed or captured almost to a man.

At the end of May Saladin reviewed the combined armies at al-'Ashtarā in the Hauran. The regular cavalry contingents mustered 12,000, with possibly as many again of auxiliary troops and irregulars. "To each emir he assigned his place on the left or right wing, from which he might not depart; no contingent must absent itself, nor a single man leave. From each company he picked out the advance guard of archers..., and said, 'When we enter the enemy's territory, this is the order of our forces and these the positions of our companies'."[12] On Friday, June 26, he set out for Palestine and after a halt of five days at al-Uqḥuwānah, at the south end of the lake, advanced into the hills above Tiberias. While the two armies lay opposite one another Saladin, whether by accident or design, led his guards and siege personnel to Tiberias on Thursday, July 2. Raymond's countess held the castle against his assault, but her appeal to Guy for help secured the opportunity that had been denied to him all these years, a set encounter in the field with the forces of the kingdom.

The overwhelming character of the victory at Hattin (July 4, 1187) was proved immediately by the tale of cities and fortresses that fell either to Saladin personally (Acre, Toron, Sidon, Beirut) or to separate contingents under their generals (Nazareth, Caesa-

[11] Cf. below, chapter XIX, p. 605.
[12] 'Imād-ad-Dīn, *Fatḥ*, 19. On the battle of Hattin, see below, chapter XIX, pp. 608 ff.

rea, Nablus, etc.). Then, passing Tyre by for the time being, he joined forces with al-ʻĀdil, who had already stormed Jaffa, and besieged Ascalon, which was surrendered on September 5 on his promise to release Guy and the master of the Temple, a promise eventually fulfilled. The remaining castles in this region were captured either on the march to Ascalon or just after. Finally, reuniting his armies, Saladin marched to the goal of his ambitions, the capture of Jerusalem. After a siege of less than a fortnight the city surrendered on October 2 on terms which confirmed, if confirmation were needed, his reputation for limitless courtesy and generosity.[13]

The collapse of the kingdom encouraged Saladin to hope that Tyre too might be captured before the winter began, and he laid siege to it on November 13. The tenacious defense of Conrad of Montferrat disheartened the eastern contingents, who, now that winter was at hand, were eager to return home with their booty. The disastrous defeat of the Egyptian blockading fleet at the end of December strengthened their impatience, and in spite of Saladin's arguments for perseverance, supported by the commanders of the Aleppo contingent, the emirs took their men off and dispersed. On January 1 Saladin was compelled to relinquish the siege and retired to winter at Acre, where a succession of embassies brought him the congratulations of all the Moslem princes, including his former rivals in Azerbaijan and Persia.

Leaving Acre to be refortified under the charge of his trusted mamluk Bahā'-ad-Dīn Karakush, Saladin returned to Damascus in the spring, halting for a short time before the still unsubdued castle of Belvoir (Kaukab). On May 10 he marched north with his guard to join the Mesopotamian contingents under Gökböri and ʻImād-ad-Dīn of Sinjar, while al-ʻĀdil remained with the Egyptian regiments to guard the south and to deal with Kerak and Krak de Montréal. The Aleppo and Hamah troops were ordered to stand on guard at Tīzīn against any movement on Bohemond's part. The remaining forces at his disposal were too light to undertake prolonged siege operations, but adequate for the capture of the isolated towns and castles of the principality, as far as its northern frontiers at Baghrās and Darbsāk. Although Antioch itself was not in any real danger, Bohemond in September asked for and was unwillingly granted an armistice of eight months, after the negotiation of which the Mesopotamian contingents returned to their homes and Saladin to Damascus. There he was rejoined by

[13] Cf. below, chapter XIX, pp. 616–618.

al-'Ādil with his troops and at once besieged and captured the two remaining castles in Palestine, Safad and Belvoir. After the surrender of the latter on January 5 the rest of his forces dispersed, and Saladin made a tour of inspection of his coastal fortresses from Ascalon to Acre.[14]

The spectacular success of Saladin in reducing the holdings of the crusaders in Syria to three cities, Tyre, Tripoli, and Antioch, with a few outlying fortresses, within the short space of eighteen months, has led both Moslem and western historians to regard him primarily as a great and successful general, whose victories were due to the same military qualities as those of other successful commanders of armies. This is a complete misapprehension. Saladin possessed, indeed, personal military virtues of a high order; but his victories were due to his possession of moral qualities which have little in common with strategic gifts. He was a man inspired by an intense and unwavering ideal, the achievement of which involved him necessarily in a long series of military activities. Down to 1186 these activities were directed to imposing his will upon the prevailing feudal military system and shaping it into the instrument which his purpose required; and the preceding pages have shown that their military aspect was subordinate, in his own mind and to a large extent in practice, to uniting the political forces of western Asia "in one purpose" and imbuing them with something of his own tenacity and singleness of outlook. It was by these means, and not by superior strategic ability, that he succeeded in assembling the army that was to destroy the kingdom of Jerusalem. Even the striking campaigns of 1187 and 1188 cannot be held to prove that Saladin possessed outstanding generalship. The victory at Hattin owed as much to the mistakes of the Franks as to his strategy, even when every credit is given to the skill with which the opportunity was seized. The subsequent crumbling of the inner defenses of Jerusalem and Antioch demonstrate rather the fundamental weaknesses of the crusading states than the military genius of the conquerors, a point emphasized by the fact that many of them fell to small detached forces.

Furthermore, these very successes were due largely to the exercise of the qualities which most sharply distinguished him from his military contemporaries. Nothing is more remarkable in the sources than his reiterated appeal from the criticisms of his officers to the principles of honor, of good faith, and of a firm religious conviction. When the turn of the Christian cities and castles came,

[14] For the campaigns of 1187–1189, see also below, chapter XIX, pp. 615–619.

it was chiefly because of his reputation for scrupulous observance of his plighted word and for uncalculating generosity that they surrendered so easily. Those critics who have found fault with him for allowing such numbers of knights and merchants to find a refuge in Tyre and so to build up a bridgehead there for the counterattack have generally failed to consider what the course of the Third Crusade might have been if on its arrival it had found Saladin still engaged in the task of reducing one by one the castles of the interior, without complete freedom of movement and complete security in his rear. That he did not in fact capture Tyre as well was the result partly of the accident of Conrad's arrival, and partly of the impatience and insubordination of the eastern regiments.

The second of these causes illustrates sharply the persisting defects of the forces with which he had to meet the later struggle with the crusaders. But this was still in the future, and it is unhistorical to imagine Saladin as preparing plans and disposing his forces to meet the forthcoming invasion from the west. His thought had from the beginning been concentrated upon offensive, not defensive, warfare; it was for this purpose that he had built up his armies, and it had now been largely, and brilliantly, fulfilled. Though he grieved over the lack of staying-power of his vassals before Tyre and again in 1188 before Antioch, he saw in these no more than temporary checks, and confidently expected to make up for them in later campaigns. The first hint of the coming invasion reached him from the Sicilian admiral Margarit at Latakia in the autumn of 1188, and so little disturbed was he by the report that he granted Bohemond a truce only until May 1189, and busied himself during the winter with preparations to attack Antioch and Tripoli.

In all probability, therefore, he was taken by surprise when the first convoys arrived and Guy's troops succeeded in marching to Acre and investing the city, on August 27, 1189. From that moment his role was transformed, and he was faced with a new and grimmer task which no Moslem commander, for centuries before him, had ever attempted: the task of holding an army in the field for three years, and that with every circumstance of discouragement. Had he been no more than a leader of armies, he could not have achieved it; his feudal troops would have melted away and left the field to the Franks. But it was in this wholly unexpected conjunction that the true greatness of Saladin and the inner strength of the instrument which he had created were put to the test. He had a double conflict to wage: the external struggle with the crusaders, and the internal struggle with the fissiparous tendencies and the instability of the feudal armies. Military genius had but a small part in the combination of qualities by which he fought the crusade to a standstill. The long campaign was an almost unbroken succession of military reverses and disasters; his generals were openly critical, his troops often mutinous. It was by the sheer force of personality, by the undying flame of faith within him, and by his example of steadfast endurance, that he inspired the dogged resistance which finally wore down the invaders.

XIX
THE DECLINE AND FALL OF JERUSALEM, 1174–1189

The history of the Latin orient following king Amalric's death is overshadowed by the disaster of 1187, the loss of Jerusalem. And yet, if this tragic conclusion may be for a moment forgotten, these same years brought continued prosperity to the three Latin colonies remaining in the Levant. Despite losses and the costly failures in Egypt, the combined resources of Antioch, Tripoli, and Jerusalem were still formidable. Even in 1187 when Saladin controlled the Moslem world from the Nile to Mesopotamia, the crusaders sent out an army the equal of his. Those who maintain that Saladin's conquest was "inevitable" too often forget this. Indeed, to attribute the crusaders' failure in 1187 solely to Saladin's power is to oversimplify a complex problem. The defeat of that year stunned Europe. The problem of the "fall of Jerusalem" has fascinated historians ever since. The modern historian cannot be content merely to relate the story. He must attempt an explanation.

Most of the works cited in the bibliographical note to chapter XVII are pertinent to the period from 1174 to 1189. William of Tyre's *Historia* remains the principal Latin source up to the year 1183. He was appointed chancellor of the kingdom in 1174 and made archbishop of Tyre in the following year. Except for an absence of two years (1178–1180), he was always in a position to obtain first-hand information. The section of his work which deals with the period after 1174 was written after 1180. The so-called *Continuation of William of Tyre* or *L'Estoire de Eracles empereur*, carries the narrative forward. This is cited below as *Eracles* (referring to the edition in *RHC, Occ.*, II) or as *Ernoul* (referring to the edition by L. de Mas Latrie, *Chronique d'Ernoul et de Bernard le trésorier*, Société de l'histoire de France, XXXV, Paris, 1871). There is also a Latin continuation edited by M. Salloch, *Die lateinische Fortsetzung Wilhelms von Tyrus* (Greifswald, 1934), which was written by an unknown but well informed author. It is apparently independent of the Old French version.

Bahā'-ad-Dīn, *An-nawādir as-sulṭānīyah* ... (extracts ed. and tr. as "Anecdotes et beaux traits de la vie du sultan Youssof," *RHC, Or.*, III, 1–370), is important for the career of Saladin. See also H. A. R. Gibb, "The Arabic Sources for the Life of Saladin," *Speculum*, XXV (1950), 58–72; S. Lane-Poole, *Saladin and the Fall of the Kingdom of Jerusalem* (New York, 1898; new ed. 1926); and especially chapter XVIII above.

For the internal politics of the kingdom of Jerusalem before 1187 and for the battle of Hattin, see M. W. Baldwin, *Raymond III of Tripolis and the Fall of Jerusalem (1140–1187)* (Princeton, 1936), and S. Runciman, *History of the Crusades*, vol. II, *The Kingdom of Jerusalem* (Cambridge, 1952). On the period after 1187 see F. Groh, *Der Zusammenbruch des Reiches Jerusalem* (Jena, 1909). For Reginald of Kerak, see G. Schlumberger, *Renaud de Châtillon* (Paris, 1898).

Contemporary chroniclers generally agree that the men of Jerusalem had brought disaster on themselves through their own mistakes. It is true that the short reigns of Baldwin IV and Baldwin V witnessed quarrels over the regency, dissension, wasted effort, and, above all, ill-conceived diplomacy and blundering strategy. But the contemporary historian, lacking the perspective of later years, was too much concerned with apportioning the blame. Since the kingdom of Jerusalem was split into two factions during its last years, partisan historians handed down to posterity two sets of villains and heroes. As a consequence, although the accounts of William of Tyre and his continuators have gradually for sound reasons found favor, modern interpretations have long echoed the ancient controversies. Hence an understanding of the opposing factions is essential.

In the kingdom of Jerusalem, as in the Latin east generally, baronial participation in government was exceptionally well developed. It is also a fact of capital importance that Amalric's capable administration was followed by the troubled reigns of Baldwin IV (1174–1185) and Baldwin V (1185–1186). Since each, for reasons of health or youth, was unable consistently to assume full executive responsibility, baronial rule — or, as it sometimes happened, misrule — triumphed over royal power. The normal functioning of administration was upset because the proper balance between the two organs of government, the king and the high court, was destroyed.

History records few more tragic careers than that of Baldwin IV, the "leper king". Only thirteen at the time of his father's death, afflicted with a terrible disease which sapped his strength and caused an untimely death, he nevertheless in the short years of his life displayed heroic fortitude and remarkable intelligence. He had been tutored by William of Tyre and during most of his reign owed much to that exceptional man's wisdom and experience. Baldwin possessed an admirable understanding of the needs of the monarchy of Jerusalem. Unfortunately, his health frequently forced him to relinquish the responsibilities of government to various regents, who were called *baillis* or procurators. The very choice of a *bailli*, whether by royal appointment or baronial selection, often raised opposition and ultimately contributed largely toward dividing the kingdom into two factions. Each faction endeavored to control policy. Each attempted to promote the interests of its adherents through influencing the helpless king or securing the *bailliage*.

There is no simple explanation for the development of these two parties. To a great extent their existence is attributable to the divergence in viewpoint between the well established so-called "native barons" and the "newcomers" from the west. Broadly speaking, the native barons, already in possession of their fiefs, were devoted to a prudent defensive military policy and anxious to preserve as far as was still possible the balance of power among Moslem and Christian states. The newcomers, on the other hand, were likely to be warlike adventurers, immigrants, anxious to win renown and fortune. But these labels are not entirely satisfactory. Associated with the newcomers, for example, were the Templars and the Hospitallers whose dedication to the military life perhaps accentuated the desire for aggressive action. Finally, purely personal loyalties and animosities often dictated adherence to one faction or the other. But whatever their origin, the existence of the two factions proved disastrous. In the last days of the kingdom, as the parties became more distinct and their mutual opposition more bitter, there developed a serious cleavage in the matter of diplomatic and military policy which prevented unified action and in 1187 directly caused military disaster. In a short time, therefore, the unified kingdom of Amalric became a realm divided. In the following pages attention will be centered on the affairs of the kingdom of Jerusalem, for it was there that the events which determined the fate of all three states took place. Developments in Tripoli and Antioch will, therefore, be mentioned only as they bear on the common situation.

The early years of Baldwin IV's reign passed without any serious crisis. They were significant as illustrating, first, the administrative difficulties created by the young king's precarious health and, second, the beginnings of Saladin's efforts to control Moslem Syria. The first important regency after Amalric's death was that of count Raymond III of Tripoli, who took office late in the autumn of 1174.[1] Supported by the higher clergy and the principal native barons, Humphrey of Toron, the constable, Baldwin of Ramla (sometimes found as Rama) and his brother Balian of Ibelin, and Reginald of Sidon, Raymond held office until Baldwin IV came of age, presumably in the fall of 1176. Not only did Raymond possess the proper legal title to the *bailliage* as the king's closest male relative, but he was highly esteemed by

[1] The administration was temporarily carried on by Miles of Plancy, the seneschal. He lost support and shortly after Raymond's elevation was murdered. His wife, Stephanie of Kerak and Montréal, apparently regarded Raymond as the murderer.

the native barons, now evidently in the ascendant, as one of themselves. His ancestral inheritance, it is true, was the county of Tripoli, but through marriage to Eschiva, widow of Walter of Tiberias, he secured control over Tiberias, one of the important lordships of the kingdom. Except for a relatively unimportant expedition into northern Syria, Raymond's administration was uneventful. It is worth mentioning, however, that William, the historian, was appointed chancellor and archbishop of Tyre.

At best, *bailliage* was a temporary expedient. Since the king's condition precluded the possibility of direct succession, the hope of the dynasty rested with his elder sister, Sibyl. Hence, sometime during 1175 or early in 1176 it was decided by Baldwin IV and the high court that some provision for the future of the dynasty must be made. Accordingly, William Longsword, son of William of Montferrat, was invited to the Holy Land. On his arrival in October 1176, he was married to Sibyl with the county of Jaffa and Ascalon as dowry and given what apparently amounted to the procuratorship or regency. Unfortunately, William Longsword died in June 1177, a scant few months after his marriage. Moreover, the birth of a son, the future Baldwin V, shortly afterward foreshadowed another regency problem unless Sibyl should marry again. Even this last possibility was not without its dangers as subsequent events were to prove.

The hopes so abruptly dashed by Montferrat's death were raised again later in the same year (1177) by the arrival of count Philip of Flanders, a relative of king Baldwin, who was accompanied by a considerable retinue of knights. Here at least was the prospect of real assistance against Saladin, and so he was offered the regency. To the consternation and disappointment of all he declined with a display of modesty which, to judge from his subsequent behavior, was insincere. Eventually it was decided that Reginald of Châtillon, who on his release from captivity had married Stephanie of Kerak (Krak des Moabites) and Montréal (ash-Shaubak), should act as *bailli* with Philip's assistance.[2] Having thus embarrassed the high court in its attempt to provide for the administration, Philip proceeded in various other ways to make himself thoroughly a nuisance. Later in 1177, the king himself was again active and apparently continued to exercise power until

[2] Reginald of Kerak (originally, of Châtillon) had been released from captivity in 1176. He married Stephanie, widow of Humphrey of Toron and Miles of Plancy, and as lord of Kerak and Montréal was one of the kingdom's most important barons. For Reginald's career see Schlumberger, *Renaud de Châtillon*.

1183. At least there is no record until then of the appointment of any *bailli*.

During these same years (1174–1180), the diplomatic and military situation grew steadily worse. It will be recalled that the center of interest during Amalric's reign had been Egypt where the collapse of the Fāṭimid caliphate invited outside intervention. Amalric's failure permanently to profit by that opportunity had left the field to Saladin. As the preceding chapter has indicated, Saladin's success in supplanting the caliphate of Cairo had ended, at least in that area, the old Sunnite-Shī'ite feud which had been an important element in Christian security.[3] So long as Nūr-ad-Dīn had lived, however, his jealousy and suspicion of the young conqueror of Egypt had prevented the political unity of Egypt and Syria. Nūr-ad-Dīn's death (May 1174), just two months before that of Amalric, therefore removed one obstacle to Syrian-Egyptian coöperation. Saladin was quick to take advantage of the situation. His capture of Damascus on October 28, 1174, with the resulting political union of Egypt and Syria, was his first step toward encircling the crusaders' states. The old Latin policy of balancing a friendly Damascus against its rivals in Egypt and northern Syria was now largely thwarted. What was worse, Saladin then proceeded from Damascus north against Aleppo, the key to northern Syria.

This objective, however, Saladin did not then attain, partly because of Aleppan resistance, partly because of the presence of a Frankish army under Raymond of Tripoli, then *bailli*. Yet his campaign was otherwise a great success. Before he returned to Egypt in September 1176, he had taken Homs and Hamah and defeated a contingent from Mosul. Somewhat later Baalbek was invested. Further, the caliph of Baghdad now recognized him as ruler of Egypt and Syria. Thus, the crusaders' policy of balancing dissident Moslem states against each other was gradually losing its efficacy in the face of Saladin's Syrian successes.

The Near Eastern equilibrium was also seriously upset by the Byzantine defeat at Myriokephalon in September 1176. It had been the emperor Manuel Comnenus's intention to break the Turkish hold in Asia Minor. Instead, his army was routed. The basileus accepted Kilij (or Kilich) Arslan's terms and retreated with the remnants of his troops. Myriokephalon has been compared with Manzikert a century earlier; and, indeed, for the Latin east the defeat was crucial. Militarily, Byzantium never recovered.

[3] For further details regarding Saladin's career see above, chapter XVIII.

Rivalry over Antioch, it is true, was now ended, but the strong Byzantine power in Asia Minor, so long a deterrent against Moslem expansion, was also removed.

In the following year (1177), at the time of Philip of Flanders' visit to the Holy Land, a splendid opportunity for separating Egypt from Syria was lost. Emperor Manuel, whose fleet was still formidable, offered to fulfil arrangements made previously with Amalric to renew the project of a joint Latin-Byzantine expedition against Egypt. Unfortunately for the Christian cause, Philip, after offering all sorts of excuses and causing interminable delays, flatly refused to participate, and the project was abandoned. Since Manuel died in 1180 and since, after the death of young Alexius II (1180–1183), the empire was ruled by the violent Andronicus Comnenus (1183–1185) and the incompetent Isaac Angelus (1185–1195), both unfriendly to the crusaders, this was in fact the last opportunity to renew the Byzantine alliance. A remarkable victory of the royal army under king Baldwin IV at Mont Gisard temporarily restored Latin morale. Saladin was badly worsted (November 25, 1177). But the crusaders were not able permanently to follow up their victory; and Saladin, who had lost a battle, had by no means exhausted his resources as the succeeding months were to show. Therefore, despite the victory of Mont Gisard, the Christians were far from secure.

The campaigns of these years have been described in the preceding chapter.[4] But it may be well to recall here that they cost the Latins heavily. The eminent constable, Humphrey of Toron, was mortally wounded, and many distinguished knights, including Odo of St. Amand, master of the Temple, Hugh of Tiberias, Raymond of Tripoli's stepson, and Baldwin of Ramla, were captured. Saladin also captured and destroyed a newly built castle at Jacob's Ford in August 1179. Further, he had, with a reorganized Egyptian fleet, menaced the Frankish coastal possessions. Ruad, an island off Tortosa in the county of Tripoli, was seized, and in May 1180 king Baldwin proposed a truce which, because of the threat of a famine in the Damascus region, Saladin was willing to accept. Somewhat later in the summer, after sea and land raids, Saladin also concluded a truce with count Raymond of Tripoli and returned once again to Egypt where he remained until 1182. The breathing spell was welcome, but it only postponed the issue. Indeed, it is important to remember that Frankish security still depended on Moslem disunion. So long as the Aleppans and

[4] Cf. above, chapter XVIII, pp. 567–572.

Mosulites continued to resist his northward advance, Saladin could not press his advantage or follow up fully his minor victories. How energetically and successfully he strove to eliminate these obstacles, the preceding chapter has related.[5]

During these critical years the Christians never ceased trying to secure assistance from outside. The eastern bishops, among whom was William of Tyre, who attended the Third Lateran Council of 1179 were commissioned to broadcast word of the danger facing Jerusalem. But although the council attempted to discourage trade with the Moslems, especially in war materials, no real aid was organized. Therefore, although a few new crusaders arrived from the west in 1179, no substantial betterment in the crusaders' position can be noted.

It is evident from what has already been described of the first six years of Baldwin IV's reign that the instability of the executive power had seriously handicapped policy. So long as it was uncertain whether the young king's health would permit him personally to govern or would force him to shift the burden of responsibility to another, there was bound to be a certain feeling of tension within the high court. During the years 1180–1182, when the foreign danger was temporarily removed, this tension increased markedly. In fact those years brought the first open division into two hostile factions of barons. While not all the circumstances attending these fatal quarrels can be determined, the main outlines are clear.

The occasion for the first outburst seems to have been the marriage of Sibyl to Guy of Lusignan in the spring of 1180.[6] Guy of Lusignan, a young Poitevin noble with an indifferent record, had recently arrived in the Holy Land. With the help of some advance publicity on the part of his brother Aimery, a favorite of Agnes of Courtenay, Sibyl's mother, he had won the young lady's favor. In fact, this fickle widow, who seems already to have tenta-

[5] Cf. above, chapter XVIII, pp. 572–580.

[6] William of Tyre who is the principal authority for these developments left the Holy Land for Europe in September 1178, attended the Lateran Council of 1179, and made an extended visit to Constantinople. He did not return to the east until May 1180 and did not reach Jerusalem until July 1180 (Röhricht, *Königreich*, pp. 381, 390). As a consequence, his narrative at this point (XXII, 1, pp. 1062–1063), lacks details which can be tentatively supplied from the first part of the chronicle of Ernoul. The first part of this version of the *Continuation of William of Tyre* does not appear in most MSS. Unlike those versions which follow William verbatim until 1183–1184, it is a brief summary of the events of the period up to about 1180. From that point it is independent and contains information not found in William of Tyre. In particular it gives here the details concerning Aimery of Lusignan, Agnes, and Baldwin of Ramla. The author, a servant of the Ibelins, was presumably well informed. Cf. A. C. Krey, "The Making of an Historian in the Middle Ages," *Speculum*, XVI (1941), p. 160, note 1. For further details see Baldwin, *Raymond III of Tripolis*, pp. 31ff.

tively offered her hand to Baldwin of Ramla, was completely captivated by the handsome Poitevin. Apparently Agnes and Baldwin IV were also persuaded by the Lusignans to agree to the match. Guy's suit for Sibyl's hand, carrying with it the presumption of regency, possibly even of succession to the throne, was apparently not favored by most of the barons. It was particularly abhorrent to Raymond of Tripoli who, presumably on hearing of the projected match, entered the kingdom in force along with his friend, Bohemond III of Antioch. Thereupon the king took alarm at their appearance and ordered the marriage performed at once even though it was still Lent (March 5–April 30, 1180). Raymond and Bohemond then left the kingdom, the former remaining away for two years.[7] In this affair, as in its sequel two years later, there is ample evidence of personal intrigue on the part of the Lusignans and Agnes, which was directed toward the stakes of power as well as of love. Agnes seems to have been an especially sinister influence. Indeed, her accomplishments as an intriguer were considerable.

Agnes had been married four times. Two husbands had died; and two of her marriages had been annulled. Exercising a powerful influence over her son, Baldwin IV, especially during his periods of illness, she promoted the cause of her relatives and favorites. Among the former were Sibyl, her daughter, and Joscelin III, her brother. To compensate for the loss of his Edessan inheritance, the latter had built up a considerable fief in the neighborhood of Acre and was seneschal of the kingdom (1176–1190). As was mentioned above, Aimery of Lusignan, and now presumably his brother Guy also, were numbered among her favorites. In addition, Heraclius, a handsome though incompetent and immoral cleric, apparently owed to her his appointment as archdeacon of Jerusalem and then archbishop of Caesarea. Late in 1180, when Amalric of Nesle died and Baldwin IV had to choose between William of Tyre and Heraclius for the patriarchate, Agnes influenced her son to pick the utterly worthless Heraclius. William of Tyre's defeat undoubtedly strengthened his already existing antipathy toward this "odious and grasping woman" and all her associates.[8]

[7] Bohemond III caused considerable trouble at this time. On the death of Manuel in 1180, he repudiated his Greek wife and married a lady of dubious reputation named Sibyl. The opposition of the patriarch and barons of the principality nearly caused a civil war which was averted only by a deputation from Jerusalem. Between 1182 and 1185 Bohemond was also involved with Reuben (Roupen) of Armenia, Isaac Comnenus, a rebellious governor of Cilicia, and the Templars. Temporary gains made by Bohemond in Cilicia were ultimately lost. For further details see Runciman, *Crusades*, II, 429–430.

[8] William of Tyre, XXII, 9. See also Krey, *William of Tyre*, I, 22. The building of

The baneful influence of Agnes is again evident in 1182. In the spring of that year, Raymond of Tripoli set out for his barony of Tiberias after an absence of almost two years. Before he had crossed the frontier of his county he was ordered by the king not to enter the kingdom. In this instance, William of Tyre clearly explains how certain people, jealous of the count, were able to persuade the king of Raymond's intent to seize the throne. Among them were Agnes, Joscelin, and a few others. Evidently the associates of Agnes and Joscelin enjoyed in 1182 an ascendancy over Baldwin IV which they probably had established earlier. At this point, however, their designs were frustrated by a group of the "most experienced" among the barons who finally prevailed upon the king to reconsider. Thus peace was made, and although William of Tyre mentions no names, it seems clear that among the supporters of Raymond were those native barons, Baldwin of Ramla, Balian of Ibelin, Reginald of Sidon, and others, who had helped him secure the procuratorship in 1174.

Therefore, by 1182 two mutually antagonistic parties had appeared within the kingdom of Jerusalem. One, which might well be called the "court party," was composed of the relatives and favorites of Agnes and the Lusignans. Bound together by blood relationship, marriage, and the pursuit of power, they sought to establish their ascendancy over the helpless Baldwin IV. The other party consisted of the native barons who increasingly looked to Raymond of Tripoli for leadership. Each group attempted to control policy, either through the high court, presumably the normal constitutional procedure, or, as the court party seems to have done, by gaining power over the king and acting quickly. The latter method worked in 1180; and the remaining barons were faced with a *fait accompli*. It failed in 1182 as the native barons reorganized their ranks.

The year 1183 is important in the annals of Jerusalem for two reasons. First, Saladin was able by the conquest of Aleppo to complete the encirclement of the crusaders' states along the coast. Second, an additional crisis in the internal affairs of Jerusalem weakened the resistance of the kingdom. These two developments are so closely related as to warrant a somewhat detailed chronological treatment.

As the preceding chapter has described, Reginald of Kerak broke the truce in the summer of 1181 by attacking a caravan

Joscelin's fief is described by J. L. La Monte, "The Rise and Decline of a Frankish Seigneury in Syria in the Time of the Crusades," *Revue du Sud-Est Européen*, 1938, nos. 10–12. On Agnes, see Rey-Ducange, *Les Familles d'outre-mer*, pp. 300–301.

bound for Mecca; and Saladin left Egypt for the north in May 1182.[9] Pushing through Syria and Mesopotamia, he was able to capture Sinjar and Amida (Diyarbakir). As he turned south again, Aleppo and Ḥārim fell to his arms in June 1183. With Egypt, Damascus, and Aleppo in his possession, the encirclement was complete. Mosul still resisted, but Iconium (Konya) was friendly and, as we have seen, the fear of a diversion from Byzantium had been removed by Manuel's death.

This triumphal campaign had been carried forward without serious hindrance on the part of the Latins. That they understood the gravity of the situation is clear, for in February 1183 an extraordinary tax for defense was decided upon in Jerusalem. Meanwhile an exceptionally large concentration of troops assembled at Ṣaffūrīyah, a village near Tiberias. In this vulnerable area on the border an attack by Saladin was expected. While the army remained in readiness at Ṣaffūrīyah, king Baldwin's illness took a sharp turn for the worse. He summoned all the barons and, in the presence of his mother and the patriarch, made Guy of Lusignan *bailli*. For himself he reserved only the royal dignity, the city of Jerusalem, and an annual revenue of one thousand gold pieces. Guy was further required to promise neither to seek the crown while the king lived nor to alienate any of the king's castles or cities of the public domain.

Although the barons were then commanded to swear fealty to Guy, many made no attempt to conceal their resentment. William of Tyre, as might be expected, echoes the view that Guy was utterly unfit for the task thrust upon him. Moreover, his explicit mention of the presence of Agnes and Heraclius, together with his intimation that Guy had obligated himself to a number of knights by unwise promises, lends support to the conclusion that the court party, or at least its principal members, had regained their ascendancy over the king. At any rate, the renewal of dissension came at a most inopportune time.

Toward the end of September Saladin, who had left Aleppo and returned to Damascus, crossed the Jordan and plundered Baisan. The main body of his army then encamped at 'Ain Jālūt, leaving bands of skirmishers to reconnoiter elsewhere. The Christian army, numbering according to William of Tyre thirteen hundred knights and fifteen thousand foot, probably the largest ever assembled up to that time, moved from Ṣaffūrīyah to al-Fūlah closer to Saladin.

[9] Chapter XVIII, pp. 576, 581. It was in August 1182 that a combined land and sea operation against Beirut was thwarted by the appearance of Baldwin's relief army.

No attack was made, however, and after a week of unimportant maneuvers, Saladin, finding it impossible to obtain adequate provisions, withdrew. He regained Damascus on October 13. Two great armies had faced each other and had not risked a decisive engagement.

There are two possible explanations of the campaign of 1183. One, which has been developed at some length, approves the crusaders' strategy and further insists that they did precisely what they should have done four years later at Hattin. The campaign was, in this view, a success. The limited Christian forces had not been depleted; yet Saladin had been forced to withdraw. No such interpretation was accepted by the contemporary historian, William of Tyre. Although he cautiously disclaims more than hearsay information and admits that a difficult military situation existed, he strongly intimates that personal quarrels immobilized this great Christian army. A number of barons, he suggests, were unwilling to have Guy, whose *bailliage* they opposed, receive the credit for a victory. Hence a glorious opportunity was wasted.[10]

Probably there is truth in both explanations. The waiting strategy had succeeded in frustrating a possible attack. Moreover, it must be remembered that Saladin's control over the disparate elements of the Moslem Levant was recently won and depended on constant vigilance and continued success. Armies could not be kept in the field indefinitely. Soldiers were also farmers and merchants and had to return to their fields and shops. On the other hand, it is possible that Saladin could better afford to be patient than the crusaders. Certainly his strength remained undiminished during the subsequent critical years.

At any rate, there is no denying the poisonous nature of the dissension in Jerusalem. Shortly after the campaign of 1183, the king came to the conclusion that Guy's incapacity had been amply demonstrated. In November he removed Guy from the procuratorship, specifically denied his rights of succession to the throne and, in the presence of the clergy and the barons, had his five-year-old nephew crowned and anointed. Among those present were Bohemond of Antioch, Raymond of Tripoli, Reginald of Sidon, Baldwin of Ramla, and Balian of Ibelin. Balian held the child, the future Baldwin V, on his shoulder.

There followed in the next few weeks an unedifying quarrel between Baldwin IV and Guy, the details of which need not con-

[10] William of Tyre, XXII, 27, and cf. Grousset, *Croisades*, II, 723 ff.

cern us here. The latter, understandably enough, was not prepared to submit quietly. Nor was he without friends; for the patriarch and the masters of the Templars and Hospitallers pleaded before the high court in his behalf. Neither the king nor his barons were moved, however. Finally in December 1183 or early in 1184 the king strengthened his nephew's position and concluded his action against Guy by bestowing the *bailliage* on Raymond of Tripoli. The move seems to have been popular. Certainly the count's elevation to the regency a second time marked a personal triumph for himself. Further, it seems a clear indication that the native barons, of whom he was the most prominent, had recovered their influence in the kingdom. To provide against all possible contingencies and especially to forestall the expected resistance of the court party, elaborate arrangements were made concerning the *bailliage* and the guardianship of the boy-king.

The *bailliage* was to last until the majority of Baldwin V, that is, ten years. To defray expenses Raymond was given Beirut and its revenues. All other castles were to be kept by the military orders. The guardianship of the boy-king was entrusted to Joscelin, the next nearest male relative, lest Raymond be held responsible in the event of the boy's death. If Baldwin V died before the ten years had elapsed, a committee consisting of the pope, the emperor, and the kings of France and England, was to choose between Sibyl and Isabel, the two daughters of king Amalric by different marriages. Until the choice was made Raymond was to continue as procurator. All were required to give their oath to him and to the boy-king.

The barons' hesitation to admit Sibyl's rights without the action of the committee is understandable. They feared her husband, not herself, and presumably hoped to invalidate her claims (and Guy's) with the help of outside arbitration. Isabel had married Humphrey, the son of Stephanie of Kerak and Montréal, and therefore now the stepson of Reginald. No doubt the barons hoped he would prove more amenable to their wishes than Guy, although in this they were to be disappointed. In the main the provisions adequately guaranteed an orderly solution of all foreseeable contingencies as far as law was concerned. As will be seen, they failed because a conspiracy successfully defied the law.

We have seen that after 1180 the existence of two parties contesting the control of the kingdom of Jerusalem was increasingly evident. The events of 1183–1184 so aggravated the dissension between these two groups as to make their composition more clear.

On the one hand were the native barons, including such men as Baldwin of Ramla, Balian of Ibelin, and Reginald of Sidon. Their acknowledged leader in 1175 and more prominently after 1183 was Raymond of Tripoli. A man of proved capacity, an excellent strategist, he had even won the respect of his Moslem enemies. These native barons were united in opposition to Guy and his associates for personal reasons and on grounds of public policy. To them, the blooded nobility of the land secure in their ancient fiefs, Guy was an upstart and adventurer whose rise to power aroused a natural jealousy and a fear that continued success might eventually jeopardize their own vested interests. In addition there is reason to believe that these men favored a purely defensive military policy. Certainly this was true of Raymond of Tripoli in 1187. At any rate they were opposed to rash adventures which the "newcomers" with everything to gain and nothing to lose might advocate.

It is also evident that the principal historian of these events, William of Tyre, must be counted among the adherents of Raymond of Tripoli. Like the Ibelins he was a native of the Levant and shared their suspicions of Guy and his fellows. Thus his excellent account, though faithful to the facts as he learned them, is colored by his personal attitude. Unfortunately his service as chancellor and his support of Raymond's cause came to an end with his death, perhaps early in 1185. His history closes with the events we have just described.[11]

The court party which continued to support Guy of Lusignan was grouped around Sibyl, Agnes, Joscelin of Edessa, Aimery of Lusignan, and Heraclius. The masters of the two military orders, Arnold of Toroge and Roger of Les Moulins, it will be recalled, had also pleaded on Guy's behalf in 1183. Perhaps they were among those to whom Guy had made rash promises. Possibly, as was frequently the case with the Templars and Hospitallers, they opposed the conservative military policy of the native barons. Together with the patriarch they toured Europe in 1184 seeking aid for the Holy Land. Arnold died on the journey and was succeeded as master of the Templars in 1186 by Gerard of Ridefort.

Gerard was already a personal enemy of Raymond of Tripoli. Some years previously, when Gerard had first arrived in the east, he obtained from Raymond a promise of the first good marriage in his county. Somewhat later the lord of al-Batrūn died leaving only

[11] Cf. Krey, *William of Tyre*, I, 24ff. The details of the *bailliage* arrangements are found in the *Continuation* (Ernoul, pp. 115–19; *Eracles*, pp. 4–10). For a discussion of the conflicting testimony as to dates and other matters, see Baldwin, *Raymond III*, pp. 57–59, and La Monte, *Feudal Monarchy*, pp. 31–33, 51–54.

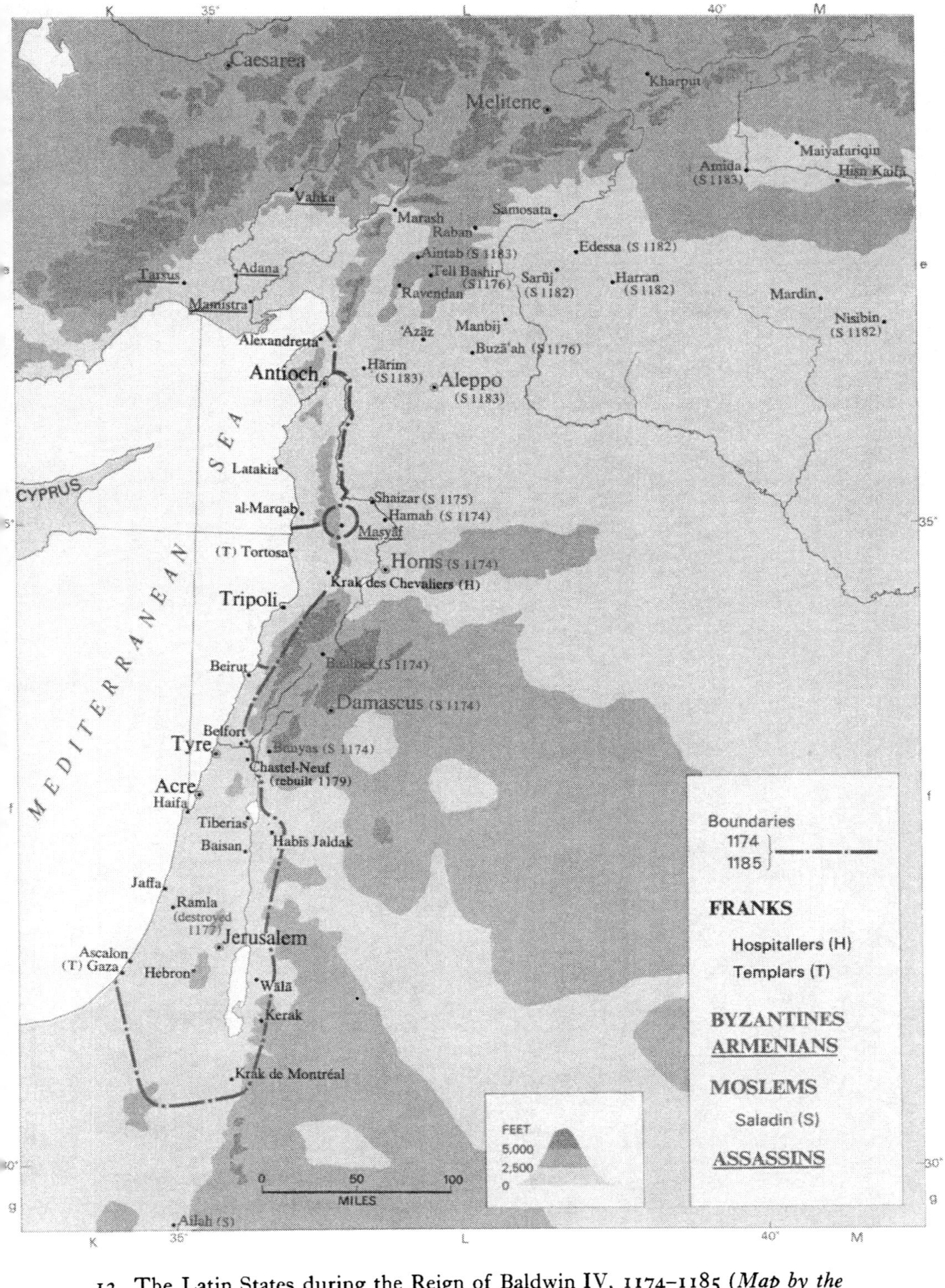

13. The Latin States during the Reign of Baldwin IV, 1174–1185 (*Map by the University of Wisconsin Cartographic Laboratory*)

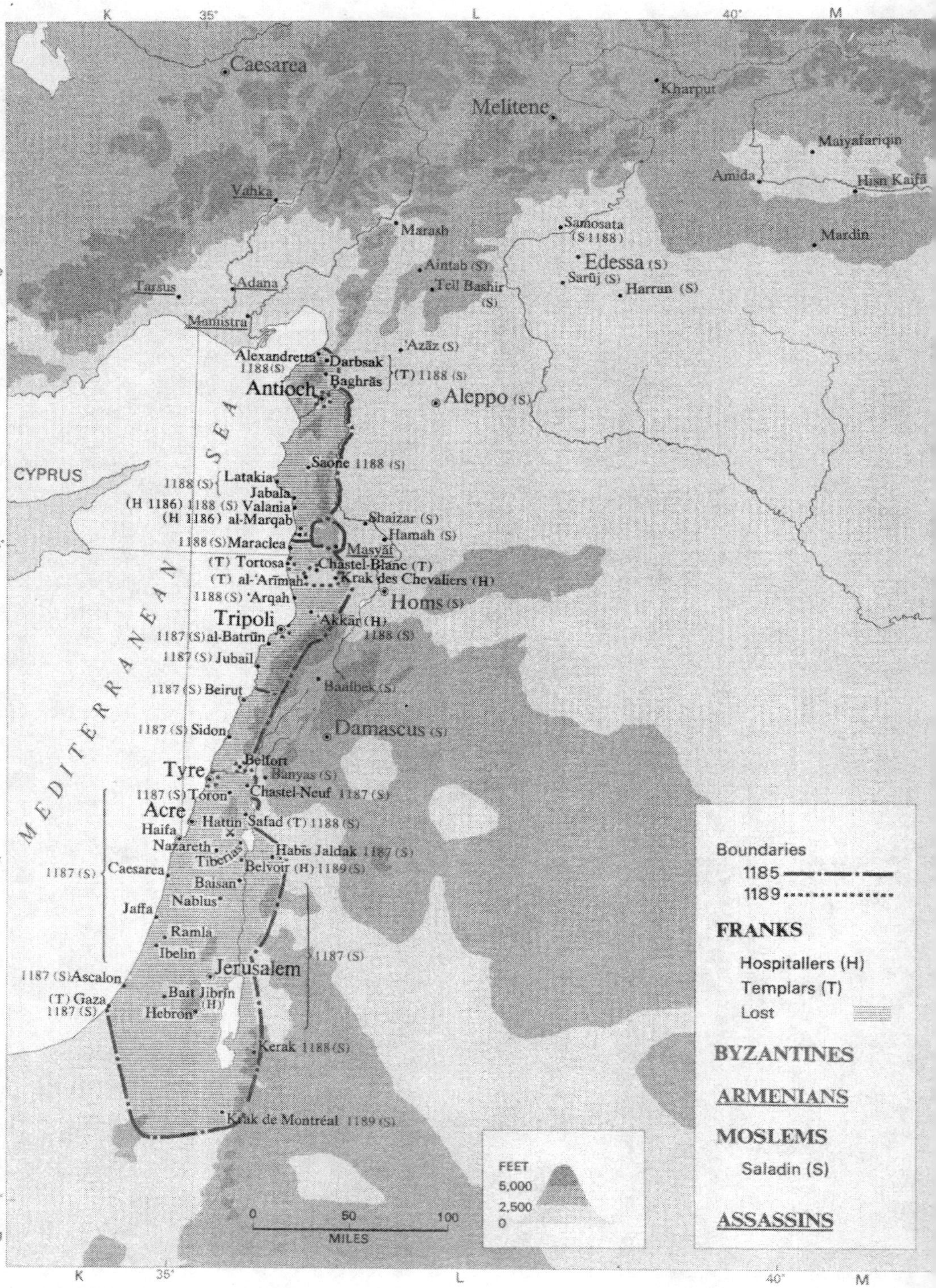

14. The Conquest by Saladin, 1185–1189 (*Map by the University of Wisconsin Cartographic Laboratory*)

a daughter. Raymond allowed himself to be dissuaded from fulfilling his promise to Gerard by a handsome financial offer from Plebanus, a wealthy Pisan. As a consequence Plebanus got the fief, and Gerard remained thereafter an irreconcilable adversary of Raymond. Therefore, although up to this point Gerard had not been prominent in the affairs of the kingdom, he must be numbered among the confederates of Guy.

Another baron soon to be found among Guy's followers was Reginald of Châtillon, ruler of Kerak. An uncontrollably adventurous knight, Reginald had already had a remarkable career both in Antioch, where through his marriage to Constance he was for a time prince, and in the kingdom. His marriage to Stephanie, heiress of Kerak and Montréal, gave him control over that important southern barony and provided him with a constant temptation to attack the caravans passing between Egypt and Syria. On more than one occasion he broke the truce with the Saracens, and in 1182–1183 he audaciously, though unsuccessfully, launched a fleet on the Red Sea to pillage the coast.[12] Hardly to be classified as a newcomer, since he had been in the east for more than a quarter of a century and possessed a handsome fief, he was none the less a restless spirit who found the company of men like Guy and Gerard more congenial than that of the conservative native barons.

Guy's character, like that of all controversial figures, is difficult to estimate. That he was not without soldierly and statesmanlike qualities his later career in Cyprus seems to indicate. But, being largely responsible for the loss of the kingdom in 1187, he became the target of bitter criticism in a whole class of contemporary chronicles. Yet, even if the partisan character of much of this criticism be admitted, it seems abundantly clear that in 1186–1187 Guy was the one led, not the leader. He did not further any consistent policy. Rather he was the rallying point for a collection of ambitious, jealous, or discontented individuals. The events of those fateful years point to the conclusion that, with the exception of Sibyl, men and women followed Guy either for reasons of personal advantage or because they opposed the other party. In himself he was not important.

Far more important than the motives of individuals was the fact of schism. At the most critical moment in its history, Jerusalem was a state divided, indeed, a kingdom verging on civil war.

[12] Cf. above, chapter XVIII, p. 582.

The arrangements made for the administration of the kingdom by Raymond of Tripoli and the provisions for the future of the dynasty brought temporary internal peace. Except for one or two minor engagements the military situation remained approximately the same. The patriarch and the master of the Hospital returned from Europe with a sum of money, contributed by the king of England, which was to be placed in the care of the military orders. But they brought no substantial promise of armed assistance. A passive defensive strategy was, therefore, still the only hope particularly as Saladin, despite his tremendous successes, continued to meet resistance in Mesopotamia. In fact it was the coincidence of renewed difficulties in that region with a severe drought in Jerusalem that led to the arrangement, probably early in 1185, of a four-year truce between Saladin and the kingdom.

Meanwhile Raymond's administration proceeded smoothly even after the death of the afflicted Baldwin IV in March 1185. A severer test came with the death of the young Baldwin V in the late summer of 1186, for this event provided the opportunity evidently awaited by the court party. In spite of their oath to follow the procedure laid down in 1183–1184, the associates of Guy conspired to overthrow Raymond's regency by methods which amounted to a palace revolution. The conspiracy was launched by count Joscelin immediately following the death of Baldwin V at Acre. First, Raymond of Tripoli and the barons were somehow persuaded to avoid Jerusalem, and permit the Templars to bury the late boy-king. Therefore, while the count of Tripoli went to Tiberias, Joscelin was able to secure Acre, and then to seize Beirut, the city supposedly held by Raymond. Having thus strengthened his own position, he sent word to Sibyl to go to Jerusalem, where she was joined by the patriarch, the masters of the two military orders, and William III of Montferrat, Baldwin V's grandfather, who had just arrived in the east.[13]

When Raymond discovered how he had been betrayed, he summoned all the barons to Nablus. Actually those who assembled there with him were the native barons. Joscelin remained at Acre. Reginald of Kerak absented himself and was soon persuaded to join those in Jerusalem. Thus the division followed party lines, and the court party was strongly entrenched in the capital. It was obviously the intention of the conspirators in Jerusalem to defy the regency of Raymond and to proceed with the coronation of

[13] William III of Montferrat was the father of William Longsword who married Sibyl in 1176 and of Conrad who arrived at Tyre in 1187.

Sibyl and Guy before the complicated machinery of arbitration by the pope, the emperor, and the kings of France and England could be set in motion. Only Roger of Les Moulins, master of the Hospital, demurred. For several hours he refused to surrender his key to the treasury — he and the master of the Temple each had one — where the crowns were kept. Finally, he thrust the key from him, thus disclaiming responsibility for an action which he was powerless to prevent. Gerard and Reginald then took two crowns from the treasury. First, the patriarch crowned Sibyl. Afterwards, Sibyl herself crowned her husband, assisted according to the chronicler by Gerard, who uttered the famous words: "This crown is well worth the marriage of Botron." The coronation took place late in the summer of 1186.

Betrayed, out-maneuvered, now faced with a *fait accompli*, Raymond and the barons with him at Nablus were at their wits' end. Baldwin of Ramla, who not only shared his associates' estimate of Guy, but, it will be remembered, had once himself aspired to Sibyl's hand, threatened to leave the country. Raymond suggested that they crown Isabel and Humphrey, the alternate pair mentioned in 1183–1184, and force their way into Jerusalem. The plan was accepted. Unfortunately for the kingdom, Humphrey fled that same night to Jerusalem and made his peace with Sibyl and Guy. Since no other course remained, the barons with Raymond's consent went to Jerusalem to accept what they had failed to prevent. Probably it was the wisest course, in view of the military crisis facing the kingdom. Only Raymond and Baldwin of Ramla held aloof. The former went to his barony of Tiberias to await developments.[14] Baldwin finally appeared before Guy, after the king had threatened to disinherit his son. Even then he refused to kiss the king's hand. Afterwards he left the kingdom.

Since Raymond remained in Tiberias, and since, as every one knew, his services in the coming trial of strength with Saladin were indispensable, Guy turned to Gerard for advice. The master of the Temple, still harboring thoughts of revenge, urged the king to assemble troops and force the count's surrender. Raymond refused to be intimidated. Instead, he took a step which loosed a train of fateful consequences. He sent messengers to Saladin, with whom he presumably had been in communication as *bailli*, and requested assistance against Guy's threatened attack. Saladin replied by sending him a number of troops and a promise of more. Obviously he hoped to profit by civil war in Jerusalem.

[14] In the opinion of Runciman, *Crusades*, II, 449, note 2, Raymond wanted the throne.

Certain things must be remembered in estimating the significance of the count's action. First, the truce was still in force. Raymond, therefore, clearly intended no formal alliance with Islam against his fellow Christians. He was acting in self-defense, and doing what many far more truculent Christian knights had done before with less justification in Spain and in the Levant. Viewed by itself, soliciting Saladin's help was neither an act of treason nor particularly unusual. Raymond's decision to resist, however justifiable under normal conditions, aggravated the crisis already facing the kingdom and led to developments which he could hardly have foreseen.[15] At first the count's action seemed to produce the result desired. On the advice of Balian of Ibelin and some other barons, the king agreed to disband his troops and sent an embassy to Tiberias. But, having won this initial success, Raymond declined to submit until the city of Beirut was returned. For the moment the king opposed any further concessions, and, therefore, the mission returned without having achieved its objective. Thus matters rested until after Easter 1187.

At this point a new crisis was precipitated by the impulsive Reginald of Kerak. Probably early in 1187, although the exact date is uncertain, Reginald attacked a caravan passing between Cairo and Damascus. Not only did he carry off considerable booty, but he broke the truce between the kingdom and Saladin. This was a serious matter, as even Reginald's friends realized. Indeed, Guy tried to force the lord of Kerak to make restitution. When Reginald flatly refused on the interesting grounds that he was absolute sovereign in his lands and had no truce with Saladin, the latter swore to kill him with his own hands if he should capture him, and proclaimed the holy war (*jihād*) against Jerusalem. The final reckoning was at hand.

The expectation of renewed hostilities made a reconciliation with Raymond of Tripoli more necessary than ever. Moreover, the count was now in an equivocal position. With the truce broken, Saladin was no longer merely a friend helping him out of difficulties. Notwithstanding, he remained reluctant to come to terms with Guy until properly compensated. From this time on, his actions are less easily justified. Shortly after Easter (March 29,

[15] The various charges against Raymond and the conflicting testimony of the sources are discussed in Baldwin, *Raymond III*, p. 84, note 35, and Appendix C. To the sources cited there should be added *Die Lateinische Fortsetzung Wilhelms von Tyrus*, ed. M. Salloch, which reports a number of accusations against Raymond as contemporary hostile rumors. See especially pp. 13 ff., 66–67, 70. Cf. also Groh, *Der Zusammenbruch des Reiches Jerusalem*, pp. 70–73, and above, chapter XVIII, p. 585.

1187) the king, on the advice of his barons, sent another mission to Tiberias. Gerard, Roger of Les Moulins, Joscius, archbishop of Tyre, Balian of Ibelin, Reginald of Sidon, and others set out, stopping at Nablus and the Templar castle of al-Fūlah, which they reached on April 30. Balian, however, remained an extra day at Nablus; and Reginald of Sidon took another route altogether. But before they had left the castle of al-Fūlah an extraordinary thing happened.

One of Saladin's sons, who was then in camp across the Jordan near Jacob's Ford, was ordered by his father to raid Christian territory in retaliation for Reginald's attack on the caravan. Since he would have to pass through Raymond's lordship of Tiberias, he asked the count's permission to traverse his territory. Raymond, sorely embarrassed by this strange request, but still unwilling to risk losing Saladin's help against his rivals, granted the permission on certain conditions. The Moslem leader must enter the kingdom after sunrise and leave before sunset. Meanwhile, in order to warn his fellow Christians of what he had done, he sent word to Nazareth and all the surrounding country and to the embassy at al-Fūlah. On April 30 he closed Tiberias.

Some historians have doubted the authenticity of this admittedly romantic tale.[16] Yet there is good reason to accept its essential features. Certainly a raid took place with the count's permission and without any effort on his part to prevent it. Further, although he may have expected his warning to have been better heeded than was the case, he must in a large part be held responsible for what subsequently happened.

On May 1 the raid took place. The Templars and the others at al-Fūlah, probably at the instigation of Gerard and certainly contrary to the intention of Raymond, decided to resist. The result was a battle at "the spring of Cresson" near Nazareth, in which the hastily assembled Christian troops were badly defeated by a superior Saracen force. Gerard and one or two of his knights escaped, but some sixty Templars were killed, and forty men from Nazareth were captured. The kingdom could ill afford the loss in manpower and morale, and the animosity between Raymond and Gerard was further aggravated. Gerard, in fact, did not continue

[16] Stevenson, *Crusaders*, p. 242, note 2, questions the story. Röhricht, *Königreich*, pp. 423–424; Grousset, *Croisades*, II, 782–783; Baldwin, *Raymond III*, pp. 88–90; and Runciman, *Crusades*, II, p. 452, accept it. It is given in the *Continuation* (*Eracles*, pp. 37–38; Ernoul, pp. 144–145). The Moslem authorities do not contradict the story and in certain matters substantiate it. H. A. R. Gibb, above, chapter XVIII, p. 585, calls it a "demonstration raid", and locates the battle at Ṣaffūrīyah.

with the mission to Tiberias. Balian of Ibelin, who escaped the disaster at Nazareth because he had spent the previous night at Nablus instead of al-Fūlah, and Reginald of Sidon, who had taken a different route, joined the archbishop of Tyre in the remainder of the journey to Tiberias.

Shocked by the news of the disaster, Raymond was now willing to become reconciled to Guy and to do what he could to save the kingdom. Accordingly he dismissed the Saracens Saladin had sent him, and accompanied the envoys to one of the Hospitallers' castles where Guy awaited them. Together they all went to Jerusalem where Raymond did homage to Guy and Sibyl. Thus, at long last, the quarrel between Guy and Raymond was ended after bringing great misfortune to the kingdom. Unfortunately, ill-feeling between the two parties still smoldered under the surface of apparent harmony. Gerard and Reginald, for example, still hated the count of Tripoli, still suspected him of treason, and in the weeks to come refused the advice and counsel he was so eminently able to give. Since these men had the ear of the king, the continuance of this animosity was serious. Truly spoken were the words of the chronicler: "... Ceste haine et cest despit firent perdre le roiaume de Jerusalem."[17]

The situation facing the kingdom of Jerusalem in the early summer of 1187 was the most serious in its history. While internal dissension brought the country to the verge of suicidal civil war, Saladin had taken the last steps in preparation for his great offensive. In March 1186 a treaty with Mosul which permitted 'Izz-ad-Dīn to retain control of the Mesopotamian region in return for an acknowledgment of Saladin's suzerainty removed the last obstacle to his power in the Moslem world. In addition, Saladin directed the emir of Aleppo to arrange a truce with Antioch in order that he might be free to give assistance. As we have seen, the jihad was proclaimed early in 1187, after Reginald's attack on the caravan. About twenty thousand troops, some lightly, others heavily armed, with the usual predominance of mounted archers customary in Moslem armies, assembled at Tall al-'Ashtarā in the third week of June. On Saturday the twenty-sixth the army crossed the Jordan south of Lake Tiberias and encamped near the river bank.[18]

[17] *Eracles*, p. 63.

[18] On the literature of the battle of Hattin, see Baldwin, *Raymond III*, Appendix B, and Runciman, *Crusades*, II, Appendix II. A detailed description of the battle is given in Baldwin, *op. cit.*, chapter VI. J. Richard has discovered a new source in a manuscript in the Vatican Library (Reg. lat. 598) which he has published, with significant comments regarding certain

Meanwhile the troops of Jerusalem were gathering in force at Ṣaffūrīyah, the rendezvous previously agreed upon. The *arrière-ban* was published. This was an emergency summons, beyond the regular feudal levy, to all able-bodied men. The patriarch, although he did not go himself, sent the relic of the True Cross. Knights and foot-soldiers were hired with the money sent by the king of England. A few additional troops arrived from Tripoli and Antioch. Obviously neither northern state could afford to denude itself of defenders. Both, therefore, remained technically neutral while sending such assistance as they could in a moment of common danger. The size of the Latin army is difficult to determine accurately, but it probably numbered about twenty thousand. Roughly speaking it equalled the Moslem force. It was composed of some twelve hundred heavily armed knights, three or four thousand lightly armed mounted sergeants, several thousand foot-soldiers, and a large number of native auxiliaries equipped as mounted bowmen. Capable, therefore, of meeting Saladin on equal terms, this great Christian army gathered at Ṣaffūrīyah and awaited the sultan's next move.

It has often been assumed that Saladin's progressive unification of a large and important section of the Moslem world rendered an ultimate victory over the Christian states inevitable. It is true that his brilliant chain of successes in Egypt and Syria seemed to point inexorably to that greatest success, the recovery of the coast lands. Nevertheless, Saladin's position in 1187, far from making his victory inevitable, still left the crusaders two possible courses of action. First, they could delay, as they had done in 1183, avoiding an open battle in the hope that Saladin would not be able to maintain his army intact for long. The intense summer heat in the arid Galilaean hill country would be an added factor in their favor. The success of such a policy depended on the sultan's decision not to risk a battle under unfavorable circumstances, and the expected disintegration of his army and consequently of his political power if he failed to win a decisive victory. In many respects Saladin's control of the Moslem hinterland from the Euphrates to the Nile was more apparent than real. It is significant, for example, that when he discussed the plan of campaign with his subordinates on the eve of the invasion of Jerusalem, he rejected the suggestion that the Christians be opposed only by small raids, sieges, and devastation of the countryside and insisted

aspects of the battle, in "An Account of the Battle of Hattin Referring to the Frankish Mercenaries in Oriental Moslem States," *Speculum*, XXVII (1952), 168–177.

strongly on a major engagement. Apparently he realized that he was not popular at the caliph's court and that he was thought by many to be more eager to fight Moslems than Christians.

A second course open to the crusaders, which assumed the desirability or inevitability of a decisive engagement, was perhaps more likely to succeed and was in fact advocated by the best strategists in the Christian army. After all, they had staked everything on this campaign and had mobilized their entire resources. Since the two forces were roughly equal, victory might well lie with that army which could induce the other to attack in unfavorable terrain. Being on the defensive in a well chosen position, the crusaders were admirably situated to try this and in fact so decided. The plan was not carried out partly because of a clever ruse by Saladin, but more because of a renewed outburst of wrangling within the Christian ranks. This is the tragic significance of Hattin. It was a battle which perhaps need not have been fought and certainly should not have been lost.

The Christian army was encamped near the Fountains of Ṣaffūrīyah, a spring with plenty of water even in summer, about a mile south of the village. Ample provisions could be obtained in the neighborhood. Between Ṣaffūrīyah and Lake Tiberias, some fifteen miles to the east, the terrain was high and plateaulike with rock swells and small depressions and with almost no water during the summer. This barren area was bounded on the east and north by a curving range of hills whose northern and eastern slopes descended sharply, well below the level of the plateau to the lake shore. Thus, the hills which would appear steep and high to a person standing to the north and east would seem only a low ridge from the viewpoint of the rugged plateau to the west and south. Only a few passes traversed these hills. Five miles west of Tiberias, which was situated on the lake shore, was one pass through the northern ridge. Close to the point where it penetrated was a curious double hill known as the Horns of Hattin, famous ever since as the site of the battle.

Saladin, it will be recalled, had crossed the Jordan south of the lake where he too had access to water and provisions. Well aware of the nature of the terrain east of Ṣaffūrīyah, he evidently hoped to take advantage of it by drawing the Christians out. When the crusaders wisely refused to budge, he moved some of his troops north to Kafr Sabt on the southern edge of the plateau and attempted to provoke an attack by small raids. Since the Christian army still did not move, he decided on a daring ruse, a sudden attack on Tiberias itself. This was to prove the turning point of the campaign.

On Thursday, July 2, he moved the main body of his army to the high ground under the ridge west of Tiberias. At this point he could block the direct route to Tiberias, yet at the same time command the passes through the eastern ridge down to Tiberias and water. Then with a small detachment he entered Tiberias easily and began to attack the citadel where Raymond's wife had retired with a small garrison of troops. This maneuver meant that Saladin had risked everything on a gamble. Defeat would have meant disaster since orderly retirement through the narrow passes would have been impossible. To advance would have meant crossing the arid plateau to meet a Christian army well based. But he calculated that the news of his attack on Tiberias and the consequent danger to the lady of Tiberias would arouse the chivalrous ardor of the more impulsive crusaders, and possibly in this instance of the more conservative count of Tripoli. Then, he hoped, they would move out across the arid and difficult ground now lying directly between the two armies and fight under conditions dictated by himself.

As soon as the news of the attack on Tiberias reached the crusaders, the king summoned a council of war and turned first to the count of Tripoli for advice. In spite of the fact that Tiberias was his barony and that it was his wife who was in danger, Raymond strongly urged the king not to venture forth. Rather let him retire to the fortified cities of the coast. If anyone was to cross the plateau, let it be Saladin. Considered in retrospect the soundness of the advice is evident; and despite the ominous grumblings of Gerard and Reginald it was immediately accepted. But the suspicion of Raymond still harbored by Gerard, his old enemy, was to prove a factor more decisive than cool consideration of military tactics. Late that evening Gerard had an interview with the king alone. Calling Raymond a traitor and implying that the king would be a coward to relinquish a city without a blow, he prevailed upon the weak-willed Guy to reverse the decision. Thus, the fate of a kingdom hinged on the will of two conspirators, one acting from personal spite, the other a victim of his own ambition and the associations into which it had led him.

Therefore, when in the early hours of the morning the other knights received Guy's command to march, they were amazed and terribly disturbed. They begged him to reconsider, but this time the king was stubborn. Nor did he offer any explanation. Like good soldiers they obeyed their commander-in-chief. Sad at heart they prepared for the worst. The army set out toward Tiberias early in the morning, on Friday, July 3, with Raymond in the van since the march was through his barony. As they proceeded slowly eastward, bands of Saracen skirmishers harassed them from all sides. The heat increased and with it their thirst. Meanwhile, Saladin, overjoyed that his plan had succeeded, withdrew from Tiberias leaving only a small force and arranged his main army on the hills west of the city.

Toward the middle of the day, when the army had reached Marescallia, about half the distance to Tiberias, progress became so difficult, especially for the Templars, who were in the rear, that the king ordered a halt and encampment. Just who was responsible for this decision and when it was made, it is not easy to determine. Contemporary accounts of the battle, some presumably written by men in different sections of the army, differ markedly. Probably Raymond, who was in the advance guard, realized that the direct way to Tiberias was blocked and urged the king to turn north from Marescallia toward the Horns of Hattin and the pass through the northern ridge. It may be that he had nearly reached that place himself and felt that the only remaining course was to escape the desperate situation on the plateau as soon as possible. Then, either because the Templars in the rear were so hard pressed or because the Saracens intercepted the van before it reached the northern pass, or possibly owing to a combination of such circumstances, the king decided to halt.

Although the chroniclers differ in allocating the blame for the decision, they all agree that it was a fatal mistake. And yet the modern historian may be permitted tentatively to suggest what the participants may in retrospect have forgotten or hesitated to add. Perhaps the crusaders were in fact exhausted. Unable to carry through a real advance, unwilling to retrace their steps across the waste, they were caught in the trap Saladin had laid. The decisive mistake was in starting at all.

The night of July 3 was a frightful ordeal. No water was available for man or beast. The enemy now surrounded them so closely "that not even a cat could have escaped". The Moslems, on the other hand, had access to water and provisions and were exultant at the promise of victory. Their cries of triumph taunted the thirst-racked crusaders during the entire night. Early the next morning (Saturday, July 4) Raymond again led the advance guard in another attempt to reach the pass by the Horns through the northern ridge; but again the Moslems, although giving way slightly, intercepted them. Toward nine o'clock the main forces of the two armies joined in battle on the plain south of the Horns of Hattin.

Since each army employed the tactics which experience had proved successful, the battle is a classic illustration of medieval warfare in the Levant. The crusaders formed their foot and cavalry into a compact body in order that the former, armed with cross-bows and pikes, and protected by heavy leather cloaks (gambesons) sometimes covered with mail, might help shield the horses from arrows and provide a rallying-point for each successive charge of the heavily armed knights. They had learned from experience that when infantry and cavalry coöperated in some such manner they were usually successful. When, on the other hand, the Saracens could separate the two arms, they often broke the Christian heavy cavalry by killing their horses. In this battle, therefore, Saladin's troops, while constantly harassing the crusaders from all sides with quick charges of light-armed horsemen, let loose a devastating storm of arrows.

The Christian infantry, being exhausted before the battle started, failed to keep in formation after the first few charges of the knights. Crying out that they were perishing with thirst, they broke ranks and rushed up a hill, presumably one of the Horns, where they were later cut to pieces. As a consequence the heavily armed knights were thrown back in confusion and finally herded themselves together near the king and the Holy Cross. The collapse of the infantry was the turning point in the battle. Without the support of the foot, the desperate courage of the Christian knights — and it was everywhere in evidence — could postpone but not change the final outcome. Some knights, led by Raymond of Tripoli, who had become separated from the rest, escaped. Those who fought on were subjected to further agony when Saladin took advantage of a favorable breeze to set the dry prairie grass afire. Moreover, the Holy Cross, their source of spiritual inspiration, was captured. Finally, late in the day, after the last desperate charges of the crusaders had been repulsed, Saladin ordered a final advance which ended the battle.

The loss of Christian manpower was terrific as thousands were killed or captured. Actual figures given by different chroniclers are hopelessly confusing. But apparently few besides those in the rear guard with Balian of Ibelin and Reginald of Sidon, or in the van with Raymond of Tripoli, had much chance to escape. In other words, the bulk of the main body of the army with the king was lost either by death or capture. Knights fared better than the foot, not only in escaping injury, but in receiving better treatment as captives. No code of chivalry or hope of ransom money protected the lowly-born. With the exception of Reginald of Kerak, whom Saladin executed with his own hand as he had promised, and the two hundred Templars and Hospitallers whom he ordered to be executed, the captive knights were honorably treated. Many were later released, usually in return for the cession of a castle or town. The foot-soldiers, on the other hand, and presumably also the mounted sergeants, who escaped the slaughter, were taken away and sold into slavery by individual Moslem soldiers. Sometimes thirty or forty were seen tied together by rope. Reports of a glut in the slave markets of Syria further illustrate the extent of the debacle. A significant observation made by one Moslem chronicler gives further evidence that the separation of the infantry from the cavalry had been decisive. He noticed that although scarcely a horse was left alive, few of the heavily armed knights were injured.[19] These well protected warriors were made helpless by the loss of their mounts and were easily captured.

Since the failure of the infantry seems to have been due as much to their thirst and exhaustion as to the Moslem attacks, it should again be emphasized that this great and decisive battle should have been either avoided or fought under circumstances unfavorable to Saladin. A formidable Christian army, skilled in Levantine tactics and hardened by campaigns, had permitted itself to be maneuvered into a trap largely because of personal and political animosities. The irreparable blunder of the march across the arid plateau toward Tiberias was the direct consequence of Gerard's hatred and suspicion of Raymond and his baneful influence over king Guy. It is perhaps idle to speculate on what might have been; yet it seems clear that if there had been no party dissension in Jerusalem there might well have been no Hattin. But now the disasters which followed were the unavoidable consequences of a major defeat.

The far-reaching consequences of Hattin must be considered from two points of view. First, Saladin's victory led directly to the conquest of the greater part of the three Latin states, although not all this was permanent. Second, the replacement of Christian by Moslem rule wrought profound changes in the religious, social, and economic life of the former Christian territories. It has seemed

[19] Cf. abū-Shāmah (*RHC, Or.*, IV), pp. 271–273, 288–289.

advisable to treat these two subjects separately and to turn first to a brief survey of the Moslem reconquest.

The military situation facing the kingdom of Jerusalem, and now also Tripoli and Antioch, was certainly desperate. Saladin's resounding victory had all but denuded the kingdom of defenders. Everything had been staked on the Hattin campaign. It is true that a number of castles and towns still had, or managed to muster, garrisons capable of stiff resistance. But since these had no supporting army to relieve them, Saladin's troops were in the end able to starve out those forts which they could not readily or quickly storm. The only hope left for the Christians was speedy reinforcement from Europe. But it was evident that since Europe did not awake to the danger before 1187, it would be some time before help came in any quantity, if indeed it came at all. Closely linked with the problem of reinforcements was the control of the coast; for without adequate facilities for landing troops and supplies, recovery would have been more difficult. Thus the gathering of the refugees from the Christian army at Tyre, where the first reinforcements arrived, was highly significant.

Saladin's first efforts after Hattin were directed toward obtaining a maximum number of important strongholds in a minimum amount of time. Thus, he struck immediately at the essential ports and paused only long enough to take those inland castles and towns which offered little resistance. Then after capturing Jerusalem itself, he moved northward along the coast of Tripoli and Antioch.

The campaign in the kingdom of Jerusalem proceeded immediately after Hattin. Indeed, Saladin delayed only a day to secure the capitulation of Tiberias (July 5) before marching toward Acre. This vital port surrendered on July 9 after a two-day siege. Meanwhile some of his lieutenants moved southward into Galilee and Samaria and the southern parts of the kingdom. So successful were these operations that before the siege of Jerusalem, which commenced in September 1187, all the major ports south of Tripoli, with the exception of Tyre, were in Moslem hands. These included Beirut, Jaffa, Ascalon, and Sidon, together with Jubail and al-Batrūn in the county of Tripoli. In addition, virtually all the inland towns and castles south of Tiberias, except Krak de Montréal (ash-Shaubak) and Kerak (Krak des Moabites), capitulated. These two southern strongholds and other formidable castles such as Belvoir (Kaukab), Safad, and Belfort (Shaqīf Arnūn) in the north held out. In order to hasten his conquest Saladin usually permitted defending garrisons to go free and often released important prisoners in return for the surrender of towns. Gaza, for example, was surrendered at the request of Gerard of Ridefort, who at Guy's request had been spared in the general execution of Templars. In Galilee and Samaria Saladin's lieutenants were not always as merciful as their master, and it is probable that large numbers of Latin Christians at least were sold into slavery. Most of the refugees went to Tyre where, with those who had escaped from Hattin, they were joined in mid-July by Conrad of Montferrat and several knights from Europe. Although Saladin tried to bargain for the surrender of Tyre in return for the liberation of William of Montferrat, Conrad's father, this offer was refused.[20] Having at that time no fleet he gave up the siege after a week. Thus, the first preparations for Christian recovery were permitted to continue. Saladin's success in the summer of 1187 was, therefore, striking but not complete. He has been criticized for permitting so many refugees to assemble at Tyre. Notwithstanding, it seems likely that failure there was more than offset by the greater speed of his conquest of the other sections of the kingdom.

Saladin arrived before Jerusalem, a city which had sacred associations for Moslems as well as for Christians, in September 1187. Balian of Ibelin was in charge.[21] But since most of the refugees had gone to Tyre, the holy city was extremely short of defenders and incapable of resisting the full force of Saladin's army. Nevertheless, when the attack began on the twentieth, the defenders resisted successfully for six days before it became clear that they could hold out no longer. Although Saladin may have originally hoped to spare Jerusalem a siege, it seems that he later intended to avenge the destruction wrought by the crusaders a hundred years earlier. But after Balian had threatened to destroy the city and massacre all the Moslem inhabitants, Saladin agreed to a capitulation on just and statesmanlike terms.

All those who could pay at the rate of ten gold pieces for a man, five for a woman, and one for a child might have forty days' time to depart. Horses and weapons were to be left behind. Saladin

[20] On the problem of the capture of William of Montferrat, see the collection of sources and discussion of Leopoldo Usseglio, *I Marchesi di Monferrato in Italia ed in Oriente*, II (1926), 100–101 ff.

[21] Balian had asked Saladin's permission to enter Jerusalem for the purpose of removing his wife and children. Saladin had granted the request on the condition that Balian stay only one night and promise never again to take up arms against him. On the advice of Heraclius, who absolved him from the oath to an "infidel", Balian remained. Nevertheless, Saladin gave safe conduct to Balian's wife and children and nephews and to one or two other people of rank (*Eracles*, pp. 81 ff.).

next offered to release all the poor, of whom there were more than twenty thousand who could pay nothing, for the sum of one hundred thousand gold pieces. Although the remainder of the king of England's gift was then in the hands of the military orders, Balian, fearful that the Templars and Hospitallers would not pay such an amount, was forced to accept freedom for seven thousand of the poorest (two women or ten children regarded as the equivalent of one man) for thirty thousand gold pieces. As a result there were several thousand unredeemed whose probable fate was slavery. The fault was presumably the Templars' and Hospitallers', but Balian was blamed.

The Moslem occupation, which commenced on October 2 (a Friday, and therefore considered a good omen by the Moslems), was carried out with a minimum of confusion. To keep order Saladin placed two knights and ten sergeants at every street. Moslem officers were also stationed at the gates to receive the ransom money of those leaving immediately. Moreover, it seems that the accounting was not overexact, and some less generous emirs complained. A great many apparently escaped over the walls or in disguise or successfully used bribery. Further, Saladin not only proved himself unusually liberal to prominent individuals like Stephanie of Kerak, but he and his emirs personally set free three or four thousand poor. In fulfilling his promise of safe conduct for the refugees Saladin was equally conscientious, although they were not permitted to join the Christian garrison at Tyre. They were protected and fed on the journey north. Indeed, such mistreatment as they received was at the hands of their fellow Christians. Outside Nephin they were robbed and the Tripolitans permitted only the wealthy to enter the city. The others reached Antioch or Cilicia after great hardships.

Some thousands remained in Jerusalem and in the environs, either to enter the sultan's service or to pay the usual tribute. Presumably, as in the other cities which changed hands, most of those who stayed were native Syrian or Greek Christians, although ten Hospitallers were allowed to remain for one year to care for the sick who could not leave. Four Syrian priests were permitted to remain at the Holy Sepulcher.

Moslem banners were unfurled and the mosques reopened amid great celebration. Vengeful tendencies which so far had been notably absent began to appear among the jubilant victors as they pillaged Christian churches and cloisters. Since the city had been occupied late in the day, the formal religious celebration was postponed until the following Friday (October 9). It was held in the Aqṣâ mosque, and Saladin attended. After the surrender of Jerusalem, Saladin pushed northward along the coast into Syria. Without delaying to storm the fortresses capable of withstanding a long siege which he felt could be isolated by the conquest of the coast, he proceeded to attack the major ports. Except in one or two instances he had remarkable success.

The most important exception was Tyre where Conrad of Montferrat had organized the refugees into a defense capable of withstanding a second siege. An important factor was the command of the sea, for while Saladin's troops encircled the city from the land side, his ships which had arrived from Acre blockaded the town from the sea. Finally, a sudden bold attack by a squadron of small vessels in the harbor dispersed or captured the Moslem fleet. This, combined with a skillful defense, forced Saladin to raise the siege (January 1, 1188). Most of his now weary troops he sent home. It was his first major reverse. Further, command of the sea and possession of this vital port eventually guaranteed reinforcements from Europe and made possible an extensive Christian reconquest. Failure at Tyre signified more than an unsuccessful siege.

In May 1188 Saladin had reassembled his army for the campaign in northern Syria while his lieutenants continued operations in the kingdom. Al-Batrūn and Jubail, it will be recalled, had already been taken. His plan of action contemplated immediate attack on the ports. Fortresses capable of standing a long siege would then be isolated and more easily subdued later. Adequate leadership for such an emergency was lacking in both Tripoli and Antioch. Raymond III of Tripoli had probably died by this time, and the designated successor, Bohemond, the second son of Bohemond III of Antioch, was presumably in charge, although he is nowhere mentioned by name. Throughout Saladin's campaign in Antioch, Bohemond III showed a lamentable inability to offer any substantial assistance to his beleaguered garrisons. Some of the stronger castles and towns offered resistance, a few of them successfully. A Sicilian fleet under admiral Margarit prevented a siege of the city of Tripoli, and seriously menaced Saladin's passage along the narrow coast road near al-Marqab. Notwithstanding, Saladin's northern campaign was speedily completed. By September (1188) he had surrounded Antioch. Only negotiations for a truce prevented the city's fall. On September 26, Bohemond sent his wife and brother to arrange for an armistice in return for an exchange of prisoners. Saladin's troops were tired from long campaigning, and the month of Ramaḍān was approaching when according to Moslem tradition no fighting should occur. It was agreed that if in seven months no help came from his fellow Christians, Bohemond would surrender Antioch.

Meanwhile, in the southern part of the kingdom of Jerusalem, hunger finally forced the heroic garrison of Kerak to capitulate. Al-Malik al-ʿĀdil received the message from the nearly starved garrison and gave them free egress (November 1188). Shortly afterward (April–May 1189), Krak de Montréal and a few other smaller places surrendered, and Humphrey was given his liberty. Saladin himself had left Damascus (November 7) where he had rested a month, and joined al-Malik al-ʿĀdil at Safad, where they besieged the fort. On December 6 the garrison capitulated and was permitted to go to Tyre. Belvoir gave in on January 5, 1189. Of the great castles in the kingdom only Belfort remained. Held by Reginald of Sidon, it commanded the route from Tyre to Damascus and was considered impregnable. Saladin arrived on May 5, 1189, but the siege was interrupted by the first Latin counterattack at Acre. (The castle was not to surrender until April 22, 1190.) The fall of Belvoir completed two years of triumphant campaigning. The kingdom of Jerusalem was entirely conquered with the exception of Belfort and Tyre. In the county of Tripoli, the city of Tripoli, one tower in Tortosa, two small Templar castles, and the great Hospitaller fortress of Krak des Chevaliers held out. Only Antioch and al-Marqab remained of the principality of Antioch.

In disposing of the conquered territories Saladin was both merciful and statesmanlike. He was anxious to lay the foundations for the future and to disrupt normal economic and social life as little as possible. Above all he hoped to avoid giving occasion for another crusade. Moreover, he well understood the importance of preserving as far as possible the economic prosperity of the ports. In laying down conditions for the surrender of Acre, for example, he offered attractive terms to the merchants, evidently hoping to induce them to remain. Most of them, however, departed and the rich stocks they abandoned were left to the mercies of the conquerors. In Latakia, also, a port in the principality of Antioch, Saladin's chancellor, ʿImād-ad-Dīn, describes with sorrow the deliberate destruction by "our emirs" of a once beautiful city.[22] It is permissible to suppose that Saladin shared his feelings.

[22] Abū-Shāmah (*RHC, Or.*, IV), pp. 361–363, quoted in Grousset, *Croisades*, II, 827. At Acre Saladin apparently offered to allow merchants to remain on payment of the usual

In most cases, as has been pointed out, Saladin was content to allow the inhabitants of captured cities free egress with their movable property, and loyally kept his word. Often a payment of ransom was demanded. But his emirs were usually less farsighted as well as less merciful, and Saladin either would not or could not curb them. Therefore, some thousands of the former inhabitants were either killed or enslaved. We can only suggest Saladin's attitude toward such occurrences by recalling that it was not his own usual procedure.

In the agricultural districts there seems to have been less disruption of normal life. Probably most of the peasants were Moslems or native Christians living in *casalia* as tributaries to the western military aristocracy. The former certainly welcomed their new masters and, as in Nablus, hastened to loot the abandoned dwellings of the Franks. The native Christians were as a rule permitted to stay. Significant religious changes also resulted from the reconquest. Everywhere, of course, Islam was officially restored; and many churches were converted (or reconverted) into mosques. Latin Christianity lost its predominant position. On the other hand, the native Greek and Syrian Christians whose establishments antedated the crusades were apparently unmolested, although the usual Moslem tribute was exacted.

The attitude of the Greek Orthodox and other native Christian sects presents an interesting problem upon which evidence is disappointingly scanty. In the main they seem rather to have welcomed the Moslem reconquest than otherwise. This was particularly true of the Greeks, whose dislike of Rome was of long standing. Moreover, as we have seen, the attitude of the Byzantine emperors after Manuel's death had become increasingly hostile toward the crusaders and had apparently led Andronicus Comnenus toward a sort of alliance with the Moslems. Isaac Angelus sent his official congratulations to Saladin after the capture of Jerusalem, asked for a renewal of the alliance against the Latins, and requested that the holy places be returned to Orthodox priests. Certainly Greek and Syrian Christians remained in the city.

One or two isolated references indicate a similar situation elsewhere. When Nablus was taken over by one of Saladin's nephews, the native Greek and Syrian Christians were apparently allowed to stay. Similarly, in Latakia, the native Christians preferred to remain in the captured city and pay the customary Moslem tax.

Moslem tribute. This privilege seems to have been offered elsewhere only to non-Latin Christians.

Toward the Jews Saladin's attitude was less consistent. In Jerusalem he apparently encouraged Jewish immigration, perhaps hoping that they would prove valuable allies in the event of a new crusade. In the region of Darbsāk and Baghrās in Antioch, on the other hand, he converted the synagogues into mosques.

The picture we have briefly presented of the end of a colony is far from complete and is admittedly drawn from scattered sources. Nevertheless, it indicates the main outlines of the transformation from Latin to Moslem administration. Saladin's policy, although not always consistent, nor properly followed by his subordinates, was at once merciful and statesmanlike. It probably preserved some of the normal economic life of the captured area, although much must have been lost. Presumably, it left unmolested the majority of the population, that is, the Moslems, the Jews, and the native Greek and Syrian Christians. For the former ruling class, the western Christians, the Moslem reconquest was a major catastrophe. Bereavement, loss of home and property, even slavery must have been the lot of thousands of the less fortunate. The aristocracy, although they had lost their lands and castles, could always hope for recovery. A few outposts still remained. The success at Tyre was also encouraging, but, most of all, Europe now understood well enough the grim prospects of the Latin Christians who were left in Palestine and Syria. News soon reached the Holy Land that a new crusade was on its way, with the German emperor and the kings of France and England, and Latin hopes rose again in the Levant. Our next volume will begin with the spectacular history of the Third Crusade.

IMPORTANT DATES AND EVENTS

1054 July	Schism precipitated by patriarch Cerularius and cardinal Humbert
1055 December	The Selchükid Tughrul-Beg enters Baghdad
1064–1065	Great German pilgrimage to Jerusalem
1071 April 16	The Normans take Bari
1071 August 26	The Selchükid Turks under Alp Arslan defeat the Byzantines at Manzikert
1071	The Turkoman Atsïz occupies Jerusalem
1074–1077	Badr al-Jamālī pacifies Egypt for the Fāṭimid caliph al-Mustanṣir; shift of power to the military
1078	The Selchükid Tutush, brother of Malik-Shāh, granted Syria and Palestine
1079 October	Atsïz surrenders Damascus to Tutush; Artuk his lieutenant at Jerusalem
1081 April	Accession of emperor Alexius I Comnenus
1081 May	Robert Guiscard invades Byzantine Albania
1085 May 25	Alfonso VI of Castile and Leon conquers Toledo
1085 July 17	Death of Robert Guiscard; the Normans abandon invasion of Albania
1086 October 23	The Murābiṭs defeat the Spanish at Zallaca
1087 August 6	The Italians sack Mahdia in Tunisia
1087–1090 or 1091	Pilgrimage of count Robert I of Flanders
1088 March 12	Odo of Lagery elected pope Urban II
1089	The Fāṭimids acquire Acre, Tyre, and other ports
1090	The Assassins established at Alamut
1091	The Normans complete the conquest of Sicily
1091 April 29	The Pechenegs annihilated by the Byzantines and Kumans
1092 November	Death of Malik-Shāh; Kïlïj Arslan I dominates west central Anatolia
1095 February 26	Tutush killed; succeeded by his sons: Rïdvan at Aleppo, Dukak at Damascus
1095 March	The Council of Piacenza opens
1095 November 27	Urban II preaches the crusade at the Council of Clermont
1096 July–August	Peter the Hermit, Walter Sans-Avoir, and the people's crusade arrive at Constantinople
1096 October 21	The people's crusade annihilated near Nicaea by the Turks
1096 November–December	The First Crusade: Hugh of Vermandois, Godfrey of Bouillon, and the first armies arrive at Constantinople
1097 May	Robert of Normandy, Stephen of Blois, and the last armies of the First Crusade leave Constantinople
1097 June 19	Nicaea surrendered by the Turks to the Byzantines
1097 July 1	The crusaders defeat Kïlïj Arslan I at Dorylaeum
1097 September	Tarsus taken by Tancred, surrendered to Baldwin of Boulogne
1097 October 21	Crusaders commence siege of Antioch
1098 March 10	Baldwin of Boulogne assumes rule of Edessa, with the title of count
1098 June 3	The crusaders capture Antioch; Bohemond of Taranto claims the city, assumes the title of prince
1098 June 28	Kerbogha of Mosul defeated by the crusaders at Antioch
1098 August 26	The vizir al-Afḍal takes Jerusalem from the Artukids for the Fāṭimids
1099 July 15	The crusaders conquer Jerusalem from the Fāṭimid governor Iftikhār-ad-Daulah
1099 July 22	Godfrey of Bouillon elected Advocate of the Holy Sepulcher

1099 July 29	Death of Urban II; Rainerius of Blera elected pope Paschal II August 14
1099 August 12	The crusaders defeat the Fāṭimid army near Ascalon
1100 July 18	Death of Godfrey of Bouillon
1100 August	Bohemond captured by Dānishmendid Turkomans
1100 October 2	Baldwin of Boulogne departs for Jerusalem, leaving Baldwin of Le Bourg as count of Edessa
1100 December 25	Baldwin I crowned king at Bethlehem
1101 March	Tancred regent of Antioch for Bohemond
1101 March	Crusade of 1101: the first armies arrive at Constantinople, cross to Nicomedia April 21
1101 August	Lombard crusaders defeated by Turks near Mersivan
1101 August	Nivernais crusaders defeated near Heraclea
1101 September	Crusaders from Aquitaine and Germany defeated near Heraclea
1103 May	Bohemond freed, resumes rule of Antioch
1104 May 7	Baldwin of Edessa and Joscelin of Courtenay captured at Harran
1104	The Byzantines regain Cilicia
1104 June 14	Tughtigin independent ruler at Damascus
1104 autumn	Bohemond leaves for Europe; Tancred regent of Antioch; Richard of Salerno governor at Edessa
1105 February 28	Raymond of St. Gilles dies while besieging Tripoli; William Jordan takes his place
1105–1107	Bohemond, with papal authorization, organizes a "crusade" against Byzantium
1107 June 3	Kilij Arslan I killed at the Khabur by the Selchükids of Iraq
1107 autumn	Bohemond's army captures Avlona, besieges Dyrrachium (Durazzo)
1107–1110	Crusade of Norwegians under king Sigurd
1108	Baldwin of Le Bourg and Joscelin released; Baldwin recovers Edessa from Tancred and Richard September 18
1108 September	Collapse of Bohemond's expedition; treaty affirms Byzantine suzerainty over Antioch
1109 March	Bertram, son of Raymond of St. Gilles, arrives to claim the area around Tripoli
1109 July 12	Tripoli falls to the crusaders; Bertram assumes the title of count
1112 January or February	Bertram dies; his son Pons count of Tripoli
1112 December	Tancred dies; succeeded by Roger of Salerno
1113 October 2	Maudūd of Mosul killed by Assassins at Damascus
1113 November	Ridvan dies; Aleppo under his son and the regent Lu'lu' (dies 1117)
1115 September 14	Roger of Antioch defeats Bursuk at Dānith
1115	Baldwin I builds the castle of Krak de Montréal (ash-Shaubak) south of the Dead Sea
1118 April 2	Death of Baldwin I; Baldwin of Le Bourg, count of Edessa, consecrated king April 14
1118 August 15	Death of Alexius I Comnenus; his son John emperor
1119 June 28	Roger of Antioch defeated and killed by Īl-Ghāzī near Darb Sarmadā (the *ager sanguinis*); Baldwin II later becomes regent of Antioch for Bohemond II
1119 August or September	Baldwin II installs Joscelin of Courtenay as count of Edessa
1122 September 13	Joscelin captured by Belek at Sarūj
1123 April 18	Baldwin II captured by Belek at Shenchrig
1123	Joscelin escapes, fails to rescue king Baldwin
1124 July 7	Tyre falls to Franks and Venetian fleet
1124 August 29	Baldwin II freed by Timurtash
1126 October or November	Bohemond II arrives to be prince at Antioch
1126 November 26	Aksungur al-Bursukī killed by Assassins at Mosul
1127 September	Zengi appointed governor at Mosul
1128 June 18	Zengi enters Aleppo
1130 February	Bohemond II of Antioch killed in Cilicia
1131 August 21	Death of Baldwin II; his son-in-law, Fulk of Anjou, king September 14

1131 autumn	Joscelin I dies; his son Joscelin II count of Edessa
1132 or 1133	The Assassins purchase al-Qadmūs, begin settlement in the Nuṣairī mountains (Jabal Anṣārīyah)
1136	Raymond of Poitiers marries Constance, becomes prince of Antioch
1137 March 25	Pons killed; his son Raymond II count of Tripoli
1137	Emperor John Comnenus invades Cilicia, besieges Antioch August 20
1138 April–May	Franco-Byzantine alliance fails at Shaizar, John Comnenus enters Antioch, but withdraws
1140 winter	Unur (Önör) of Damascus and king Fulk ally to thwart Zengi
1142	Fortress of Kerak (Krak des Moabites) built in the Transjordan
1142 autumn	John Comnenus again appears before Antioch, withdraws, to Cilicia
1143 April 8	John dies; succeeded by son Manuel Comnenus
1143 November 10	Death of king Fulk; Melisend and son Baldwin III crowned together December 25
1144 December 24–26	First capture of Edessa by Zengi
1145 December 1	Second Crusade: pope Eugenius III issues the bull for a new crusade
1146 March 31	St. Bernard preaches the crusade at Vézelay
1146 September 14	Zengi killed; succeeded by his sons: Saif-ad-Dīn Ghāzī at Mosul, Nūr-ad-Dīn at Aleppo
1146 November 3	Final capture and sack of Edessa by Nūr-ad-Dīn
1147 July–September	The German expeditions against the Wends
1147 September	Second Crusade: Conrad III and the German crusaders arrive at Constantinople
1147 October 4	Louis VII and the French crusaders arrive at Constantinople
1147 October 17	Almeria taken by the Spanish
1147 October 24	Lisbon falls to the Portuguese and English
1147 October	Conrad III and the Germans defeated near Dorylaeum
1148 January	Louis VII and the French defeated near Cadmus
1148 July 24–28	Failure of the Second Crusade before Damascus
1149 June 29	Army of Antioch defeated by Nūr-ad-Dīn near Inab; Raymond killed
1149 September 6	Saif-ad-Dīn Ghāzī of Mosul dies; succeeded by brother Quṭb-ad-Dīn Maudūd
1150 May 4	Joscelin II captured (dies in captivity 1159)
1150 summer	Tell Bashir and other Edessan fortresses sold to Manuel Comnenus
1151 July 12	Nūr-ad-Dīn takes Tell Bashir, last remnant of the county of Edessa, from the Byzantines
1151 (or 1152) spring	Baldwin III breaks with queen Melisend, assumes full royal authority
1152	Raymond II of Tripoli is killed by Assassins; his son Raymond III becomes count under the regency of his mother Hodierna
1153 spring	Reginald of Châtillon marries Constance of Antioch and becomes prince
1153 August 22	Ascalon surrenders to king Baldwin III
1154 April 25	Damascus submits to Nūr-ad-Dīn
1158 September	Marriage of Baldwin III to Theodora, niece of emperor Manuel
1158 autumn	The Byzantine army enters Cilicia
1159 April 12	Emperor Manuel enters Antioch as suzerain; Franco-Byzantine expedition ended by truce between Manuel and Nūr-ad-Dīn
1160 (or 1161) November	Reginald of Antioch captured; Baldwin III regent
1163 February 10	Death of Baldwin III; his brother Amalric I crowned February 18
1163	Bohemond III becomes prince of Antioch
1163 September	Amalric's first Egyptian expedition
1164 May	Shīrkūh, for Nūr-ad-Dīn, restores the vizir Shavar in Cairo
1164 August–October	Amalric's second Egyptian expedition
1164 August 10	Nūr-ad-Dīn captures Bohemond III and Raymond III, takes Ḥārim August 12; Amalric later assumes regency of Tripoli
1165 summer	Bohemond III released, visits Constantinople, returns to Antioch with Greek patriarch (to 1170)
1167 January-August	Amalric fails to intercept Shīrkūh on the way to Egypt, leads third Egyptian expedition
1167 August 29	Amalric marries Maria Comnena
1168 October	Amalric's fourth Egyptian expedition (to January 1169)
1169 January 18	Shīrkūh, assisted by his nephew Saladin, replaces Shavar as vizir of Egypt

1169 March 23	Shīrkūh dies; Saladin succeeds, granted diploma of investiture by Nūr-ad-Dīn March 26, soon masters Egypt
1169 October–December	Amalric's fifth Egyptian expedition, with Byzantine alliance
1171 January 22	Mosul recognizes suzerainty of Nūr-ad-Dīn
1171 March–July	Amalric visits Constantinople; temporary renewal of Franco-Byzantine alliance
1171 September 10	At order of Nūr-ad-Dīn, Saladin proclaims the 'Abbāsid caliphate in Egypt
1171 September 13	The last Fāṭimid caliph, al-'Āḍid, dies
1173 or 1174	Raymond III of Tripoli released
1174 May 15	Death of Nūr-ad-Dīn
1174 July 11	Death of Amalric; his leper son Baldwin IV crowned July 15
1174 autumn	First regency of Raymond III at Jerusalem (to 1176)
1174 October 28	Saladin occupies Damascus
1174 December or 1175 January	First Assassin attempt on the life of Saladin
1175 May	The caliph formally invests Saladin with the governments of Egypt and Syria
1176 May 22	Second Assassin attempt on the life of Saladin
1176 September 17	The Selchükids defeat the Byzantines at Myriokephalon
1177 November 25	Baldwin IV routs Saladin's army at Mont Gisard
1179 August 25–30	Saladin captures and destroys the fortress at Jacob's Ford
1179	A reorganized Egyptian fleet raids Frankish ports, takes Ruad in 1180
1180 March or April	Marriage of Sibyl and Guy of Lusignan
1180 May	Truce between Saladin and Baldwin IV
1180 September 24	Death of Manuel Comnenus; succeeded by son Alexius II
1181 summer	Reginald of Kerak breaks the truce by attacking a caravan to Mecca
1182 spring	Raymond III of Tripoli denied entrance to the kingdom
1182 August	Saladin's land-sea attack on Beirut fails
1182–1183 February	Reginald of Kerak raids Red Sea ports
1183 early	Illness of Baldwin IV; regency of Guy of Lusignan
1183 June 11	Aleppo submits to Saladin
1183 October	Large Frankish army faces Saladin near Ṣaffūrīyah; Saladin withdraws
1183 November 20	Guy deposed from regency; the king's child nephew, Baldwin V, crowned
1183 December or 1184 January	Second regency of Raymond III begins; provisions regarding the succession to the throne
1185 March	Death of Baldwin IV
1185 early	Truce between Saladin and kingdom of Jerusalem
1186 March 3	Saladin recognized as suzerain of Mosul
1186 late summer	Death of Baldwin V; coronation of his mother Sibyl and Guy of Lusignan
1187 early	Reginald of Kerak breaks the truce by attacking a caravan from Cairo to Damascus
1187 May 1	Templars under Gerard of Ridefort routed near Nazareth
1187 July 4	Saladin defeats the army of Jerusalem decisively at Hattin, captures Guy, executes Reginald
1187 July 14	Arrival of Conrad of Montferrat at Tyre
1187 October 2	Jerusalem surrenders to Saladin
1187 November–December	Saladin's unsuccessful siege of Tyre
1187–1189	Saladin conquers almost all the Latin states
1189 August 27	Guy of Lusignan besieges Acre; preliminary to the Third Crusade

GAZETTEER AND NOTE ON MAPS

This gazetteer has been prepared to fulfill a variety of functions. Every place name found in the text or on the maps is here alphabetized and identified, variant spellings and equivalent names in other languages are supplied, and the map location is indicated by key letters. Thus it not only serves as an index to the maps, and a supplement to them, but is in itself a source for reference on matters of historical geography and changing nomenclature. Names originating in Arabic, Turkish, Persian, or Armenian have been carefully transliterated according to the systems described in the prefatory note on transliteration and nomenclature.

In the gazetteer, alphabetization is by the first capital letter of the form used in maps and text, disregarding such lower-case prefixes as *al-* and such geographical words as Cape, Gulf, Lake, Mount, and the like. The designation classical may mean Greek, Latin, biblical, or other ancient usage, and the designation medieval generally means that the name in question was in common use among speakers of various languages during the crusades, or appears in contemporary sources.

The maps themselves fall into two groups: six locational and eight historical. On the locational maps may be found every place name occurring in the text, with these exceptions: a few whose exact location is unknown (like Xerigordon, Saint John, and ʿAqr as-Sudan), a few outside the regions mapped (like Iceland, Aden, and Delhi), a few too ancient (like Lusitania) or too modern (like Israel or Turkey), several in areas overcrowded with names (like Sorrento, the Golden Horn, and Marescallia), several of minimal importance (like Lorto or Narni) or common knowledge (like France or Africa), and a large number which occur only in names or titles of crusaders and other persons (like Bouillon, Vermandois, and Aguilers). Four of these maps cover the area from Ireland and Morocco to Transoxiana and Sind in a series of overlapping vertical panels; two are detailed maps of the crusading area. All maps are vertical for convenient reference, with north at the top.

The historical series comprises maps showing the changing fortunes of the crusaders and their Christian rivals and Moslem opponents between 1097 and 1189. All place names on this series also occur on the locational maps. The political power controlling each locality, at the beginning of the eight periods mapped, is indicated by a color code, the name appearing in black for the Franks, green for the Byzantines, green with an underline for the Armenians, brown for the Moslems, and brown with an underline for the Assassins. Dates of conquest are similarly coded, so that, for example, on the 1100-1118 map Ma'arrat-an-Nu'mān in black, followed by 1104 in brown and 1109 in black, indicates that this town was Frankish in 1100, lost to the Moslems in 1104, and regained in 1109. A fuller list of such dates follows this gazetteer.

All maps for the second edition have been newly designed and prepared in the University of Wisconsin Cartographic Laboratory under the direction of Randall D. Sale, assisted by Michael P. Conzen. Base information was compiled from U.S.A.F. Jet Navigation Charts, at a scale of 1:2,000,000. Historical data have been supplied by Dr. Harry W. Hazard from such standard works as Sprüner-Mencke, Stieler, Andree, and Baedeker for Europe and Ramsey, Honigmann, Dussaud, Deschamps, Cahen, and LeStrange for the Near East. Additional information was found in the text of this volume, in *The Encyclopaedia of Islam* and *İslâm Ansiklopedisi*, in Yāqūt and other Arabic sources, and in *The Columbia Lippincott Gazetteer of the World*.

Aachen (German), Aix-la-Chapelle (French): city — F2b5, 1, 2.
Aalst: town — see Alost.
Abana: river — see Barada.
Ablasṭa: town — see Albistan.
Abū-Qubais (Arabic): village — L2e5, 5.
Achrida: town — see Ochrida.
Acre; Ptolemaïs (classical), Saint John or Saint Jean (medieval), 'Akkā (Arabic): city, port — L1f3, 3, 6, 7, 8, 9, 10, 11, 12, 13, 14.
Adalia (medieval), Attalia (classical), Antalya (Turkish): port — K1e4, 2, 3, 8, 11.
Adana (classical, West Armenian, Turkish): city — L1e3, 3, 5, 7, 8, 9, 10, 11, 12, 13, 14.
Aden; 'Adan (Arabic): port in sw Arabia — not in area mapped.
Ādharbādhagān: region of NW Persia — see Azerbaijan.
Admont (German): town 65 miles east of Salzburg.
Adria (Italian): port, now town — G3c5, 2.

Adrianople; Hadrianopolis (classical), Edirne (Turkish): city — J2d4, 2, 3, 7, 8.
Adriatic Sea — 2.
Aegean Sea — 2, 3.
Afāmiyah: town — see Apamea.
Aflis (medieval), Afīs (Arabic): village 3 miles east of Sarmīn.
'Afrīn (Arabic): valley — L2e4, 5.
Afula: village — see al-Fūlah.
Aghmat; Aghmāt (Arabic): town, now abandoned — C4f3, 1.
Agrigento or Girgenti (Italian): town — G4e3, 2.
Aguilers (medieval), Aighuile or Aiguilhe (French): village just north of Le Puy.
al-Aḥaṣṣ (Arabic: the bald): district of Syria — L3e5, 5.
Ahlat: town — see Akhlat.
'Aidhāb (Arabic): port, now abandoned — L2h3, 3.
Aighuile or Aiguilhe: village — see Aguilers.
Ailah (medieval Arabic), al-'Aqabah (modern Arabic): port — L1g1, 3, 8, 9, 10, 11, 12, 13.
'Ain Jālūt (Arabic: well of Goliath), Well of Harod (medieval): village — L1f3, 6.
'Ain Zarbâ or 'Ain Zarbah: town — see Anazarba.
'Ainjar or 'Ain al-Jarr (Arabic: spring at the mountain's foot): village — L1f2, 6.
Aintab; 'Ainṭāb (Arabic: spring of good taste), Anṭap̓ (Armenian), Gaziantep (modern Turkish: warrior Aintab): city — L3e3, 3, 5, 7, 8, 9, 10, 11, 12, 13, 14.
Aix; Aix-en-Provence (French): town — F1d2, 1; Albert of "Aix" came from Aachen.
Aix-la-Chapelle: city — see Aachen.
Akhlat or Ahlat (Turkish), Akhlāṭ or Khilāṭ (Arabic), Khlaṭ (Armenian): town — M3e2, 3, 7, 8, 11.
'Akkā: city, port — see Acre.
'Akkār (Arabic), Gibelcar (medieval): fortress — L2f1, 5, 10, 14.
al-Akmah: village — see Lakmah.
Aksaray: town — see Aqserai.
Akshehir: town — see Philomelium.
Alamannia — see Allemania.
Alamut; Alamūt (Persian, Arabic): fortress — O1e4, 3, 4, 7, 8, 11.
Alashehir: town — see Philadelphia.
Albania; Shqipni or Shqipri (Albanian): region NW of Epirus.
Albara (medieval), al-Bārah (Arabic): town — L2e5, 5, 7.
Albistan; Arabissus (classical), Ablasṭa (West Armenian), Albistān (Arabic), Elbistan (Turkish): town — L3e2, 3.
Alburz: mountain range — see Elburz.
Alcalá de Henares (Spanish), al-Qal'ah (Arabic: the fort): town — D2d5, 1.
Aleppo; Beroea or Chalybon (classical), Ḥalab (Arabic), Haleb (Turkish): city — L3e4, 3, 5, 7, 8, 9, 10, 11, 12, 13, 14.
Alexandretta; İskenderun (Turkish): port — L2e4, 5, 7, 9, 10, 11, 12, 13, 14.
Alexandretta, Gulf of; Sinus Issicus (classical), İskenderun Körfezi (Turkish) — L1e4, 5.
Alexandria (classical), al-Iskandarīyah (Arabic): city, port — J5f4, 2, 3, 7, 8, 11.
Allemania or Alamannia: medieval name for Germany.
Almeria; Almería (Spanish), al-Marīyah (Arabic): city, port — D3e4, 1.
Alost (French), Aalst (Flemish): town 18 miles SE of Ghent.
Alps: mountain range — FGc, 1, 2.
Alsace (French), Elsass (German): region west of the upper Rhine — Fc, 1, 2.
Altai: mountain range in Turkestan — not in area mapped.
Altenahr (German): town — F2b5, 2.
Amalfi (Italian): port — G5d5, 2.

Amanus (classical), Gavur Daghi or Elma Daghi (Turkish): mountain range — L2e4, 5.
Amanus Gates; Maṛi (Armenian): pass south of Marash — L2e3, 5.
Amasya (Turkish), Amasia (classical): town — L1d5, 3, 8.
Ameria (classical), Amelia (Italian): village 45 miles north of Rome.
Amida (classical), Āmid or Diyār-Bakr (Arabic), Diyarbekir or Diyarbakir (Turkish): town — M1e3, 3, 7, 8, 9, 10, 11, 12, 13.
Amorium or Amorion (classical), 'Ammurīyah (Arabic): town, now abandoned — K2e1, 3.
Amu Darya: river — see Oxus.
al-'Amuq or al-'Amq (Arabic), Amik (Turkish): district NW of Artāḥ — L2e4, 5.
'Amwās: village — see Emmaus.
Anafah: town — see Nephin.
'Ānah (Arabic): town — M3f1, 3.
Anatolia; Romania (medieval), Anadolu (Turkish): region south of the Black Sea, now Asiatic Turkey.
Anazarba; Anazarbus (classical), Anavarza (Armenian), 'Ain Zarbâ or 'Ain Zarbah (Arabic): fortress 16 miles south of Sis, now abandoned.
Ancona (Italian): port — G4d2, 2.
Ancyra: town — see Ankara.
Andalusia; al-Andalus (Arabic): region of southern Spain.
Andechs (German): priory 85 miles SW of Regensburg.
Angers (French): town — D5c3, 1.
Angora: town — see Ankara.
Angoulême (French): town 55 miles west of Limoges.
Anhalt (German): district of Saxony on Elbe river.
Ani (Armenian), Ānī (Arabic): town, now unimportant — M4d5, 3.
Anjou (French): region of NW France — D4c3, 1.
Ankara (Turkish), Ancyra (classical), Angora (medieval): town — K3e1, 2, 3, 7, 8.
Anse (French): town — E5c5, 1.
Antakya or Anṭākiyah: city — see Antioch.
Antalya: port — see Adalia.
Anṭap: city — see Aintab.
Antaradus or Anṭarṭūs: port — see Tortosa.
Anti-Lebanon; al-Jabal ash-Sharqī (Arabic: the eastern mountain) — L2f1, 5, 6.
Anti-Taurus: mountains between the Sarus and Pyramus rivers.
Antioch; Antiochia (classical), Anṭākiyah (Arabic), Antakya (Turkish): city — L2e4, 3, 5, 7, 8, 9, 10, 11, 12, 13, 14.
Antioch, Carian: town, now abandoned — J4e3, 3, 11.
Antioch, Pisidian: town, now abandoned in favor of Yalvach — K2e2, 3, 7.
Antwerp; Antwerpen (Flemish), Anvers (French): city, port — E5b4, 1, 2.
Apamea (classical), Afāmiyah or Qal'at al-Muḍīq (Arabic): town, now unimportant — L2e5, 5, 11, 12.
Apollonia-Sozusa: town — see Arsuf.
Apulia (classical), Puglie (Italian): region of SE Italy — Hd, 2.
al-'Aqabah: port — see Ailah.
'Aqr as-Sudan or 'Aqr as-Sadan (Arabic): village near Basra on road to Wāsiṭ.
Aqserai; Archelais (classical), Aksaray (Turkish: white market): town in Cappadocia, 50 miles south of Nyssa.
Aquitaine (French): region of western France — DEc, 1.
Arabia: peninsula — LMNgh, 3, 4, 6.
Arabissus: town — see Albistan.
Aradus: island — see Ruad.

Aragon; Aragón (Spanish): region of NE Spain — Dd, 1.
Aral Sea — PQcd, 4.
Araxes (classical), Aras (Turkish): river — N5e1, 3, 4.
Arbela: town — see Irbil.
Arbrissel (French): village 50 miles NW of Angers.
Arca: town — see 'Arqah.
Archelais: town — see Aqserai.
Arcy (French): village 8 miles north of Vézelay.
Arḍ ar-Rūm: city — see Erzerum.
Ardagger or Ardacker (German): town, now unimportant — G5c2, 1, 2.
Ardahan: town — see Artan.
Ardèche (French): district of NE Languedoc.
Arevîntan: fortress — see Ravendan.
Arīḥā: town — see Jericho.
al-'Arīmah (Arabic), Aryma (medieval): village — L2f1, 5, 14.
al-'Arīsh (Arabic), Rhinocolura (classical): town — K4f4, 3, 6, 8, 9.
Arjish (West Armenian), Arsissa (classical), Arjīsh (Arabic), Erjish (Turkish): town — M4e2, 3.
Arles (French): town 18 miles SE of Nîmes.
Arm of Saint George (medieval): the Sea of Marmara and Bosporus.
Armenia; Hayastan (Armenian), Ermenistan (Turkish): region north of Lake Van — Mde, 3.
'Arqah or 'Irqah (Arabic), Arca or Irqata (classical): town — L2f1, 5, 7.
Arras (French): town — E3b5, 1.
Arsinga: town — see Erzinjan.
Arsissa: town — see Arjish.
Arsuf; Apollonia-Sozusa (classical), Arsur (medieval), Arsūf (Arabic): town, now unimportant — K5f3, 6, 8.
Artāḥ (Arabic): town, now abandoned in favor of Reyhanlî — L2e4, 5, 9, 11, 12.
Artan (medieval), Artahan (East Armenian), Ardahan (Turkish): town — M3d4, 3.
Artlenburg (German): town, now unimportant — G1b2, 2.
Arwād: island — see Ruad.
Aryma: village — see al-'Arīmah.
Arzghān or Arzighān (Arabic), Ercican (classical): town, now unimportant — L2e5, 5.
Ascalon; Ashkelon (classical), 'Asqalān (Arabic): port, now unimportant — K5f4, 3, 6, 7, 8, 9, 10, 11, 12, 13, 14.
Ascanius or Ascania, Lake (classical), İznik Gölü (Turkish): lake west of Nicaea.
Ashdod; Azotus (classical), Isdūd (Arabic): town — K5f4, 6.
al-'Ashtarā (Arabic), Ashtaroth (classical): village — L1f3, 6.
Ashturqah: town — see Astorga.
al-'Āṣī: river — see Orontes.
Asia Minor (classical): region equivalent to western Anatolia.
'Asqalān: port—see Ascalon.
Assailly (French): suburb of Lorette, 17 miles SSW of Lyons.
Asti (Italian): town — F4d1, 1.
Astorga (Spanish), Ashturqah (Arabic): town — C4d3, 1.
Asturias (Spanish): region of NW Spain — Cd, 1.
al-Athārib (Arabic), Cerep (medieval): fortress — L2e4, 5, 10.
Athens; Athēnai (ancient Greek), Athínai (modern Greek): city — I4e3, 2.
Atlantic Ocean — 1.
Atlas Mountains — Cf, 1.
Attalia: port — see Adalia.

Augustopolis (medieval): town, now abandoned in favor of Nighde, 50 miles NE of Heraclea.
Aulon: port — see Avlona.
Aulps or Aups (French): village 50 miles NE of Marseilles.
Aura (German): village 85 miles NW of Nuremberg.
Aurillac (French): town 70 miles SSW of Clermont.
Austria; Ostmark (German): region east of Bavaria, smaller than modern nation — GHc, 2.
Autun (French): town — E5c4, 1.
Auvergne (French): region of southern France — Ecd, 1.
Auxerre (French): town 26 miles NNW of Vézelay.
Avesnes-sur-Helpe (French): town 45 miles NNE of Laon.
Avignon (French): city — E5d2, 1.
Avlona (medieval), Aulon (classical), Valona (Italian), Vlonë (Albanian): port — H5d5, 2.
Axius: river — see Vardar.
'Azāz (Arabic), Hazart (medieval): town — L3e4, 5, 9, 10, 12, 13, 14.
Azerbaijan; Ādharbādhagān or Āzerbaijān (Persian): region of NW Persia — Ne, 3, 4.
Azotus: town — see Ashdod.

Baalbek; Heliopolis (classical), Ba'labakk (Arabic): town — L2f1, 5, 6, 8, 9, 10, 11, 12, 13, 14.
al-Bāb or Bāb Buzā'ah (Arabic: the gate, or gate of Buzā'ah): town — L3e4, 5.
Bāb al-Abwāb: town — see Derbent.
al-Bābain (Arabic: the two gates): village — K1g3, 3.
Bābalū: fortress — see Bibol.
Babylon: town — see Fustat.
Bactra: city — see Balkh.
Badajoz (Spanish), Baṭalyaus (Arabic): town — C4e2, 1.
Badulia (classical): ancient name for Castile.
Bafra (Turkish): port — L1d4, 3, 8.
Baghdad; Baghdād (Arabic): city — M5f2, 3, 7, 8, 11.
Baghrās (Arabic), Pagrae (classical), Gaston (medieval), Baghra (Turkish): town — L2e4, 5, 14.
Bahasnā or Bahasnī: fortress, now town — see Behesni.
Baḥr an-Nīl: river — see Nile.
Baḥr Lūṭ — see Dead Sea.
Bahrain; al-Baḥrain (medieval Arabic: the two seas), al-Ḥasā (modern Arabic): coastal region of NE Arabia — Lg, 4.
Bailleul (French): town 33 miles north of Arras.
Baina-n-Nahrain (Arabic: between the rivers): district of Mesopotamia between Mosul and the Khabur river.
Bairūt: port — see Beirut.
Baisan; Scythopolis or Bethshan (classical), Bethsan or Bessan (medieval), Baisān (Arabic): town — L1f3, 6, 7, 8, 9, 11, 12, 13, 14.
Bait al-Mā': town — see Daphne.
Bait Jibrīn or Bait Jibrīl (Arabic), Eleutheropolis (classical), Beth Gibelin (medieval): town — K5f4, 6, 10, 14.
Bait Laḥm: town — see Bethlehem.
Bait Nūbā (Arabic), Betenoble (medieval): village — L1f4, 6, 10.
Ba'labakk: town — see Baalbek.
Balad (Arabic): town — M3e4, 3.
Balana (medieval): ford — L2e4, 5.
Balansiyah: city, port — see Valencia.

Balarm: city, port — see Palermo.
al-Balāṭ (Arabic: the level ground): village — L2e4, 5.
Baleares (Spanish): island group — Ee, 1.
Balikh; Balīkh (Arabic), Belikh or Belih (-Nehri) (Turkish): river — L5e4, 3.
Bālis (Arabic), Barbalissus (classical): town — L4e5, 5, 9.
Balkans: mountain range and peninsula — Id, 2, 3.
Balkh (Persian, Arabic), Bactra (classical): city, now unimportant — R2e4, 4.
Balona or Bālū: fortress — see Palu.
Baltic Sea — 1, 2.
Baluchistan: region north of the Indian Ocean — Qg, 4.
Banbalūnah: town — see Pamplona.
Bāniyās: port — see Valania.
Banyas; Paneas or Caesarea-Philippi (classical), Belinas (medieval), Bāniyās (Arabic): town — L1f2, 6, 9, 10, 11, 12, 13, 14.
Bar (French): district between Champagne and Lorraine east of Châlons.
Barada; Abana (classical), Baradâ (Arabic): L2f2, 6.
al-Bārah: town — see Albara.
Barbalissus: town — see Bālis.
Barbastro (Spanish), Barbashtrū (Arabic): town — E1d3, 1.
Barcelona (Spanish), Barshilūnah (Arabic): city, port — E3d4, 1.
Bari (Italian): port — H2d4, 2.
Ba'rīn or Bārīn (Arabic), Montferrand (medieval): fortress — L2f1, 5.
Barres or Barr (French): village 19 miles sw of Strassburg.
Barzenona (medieval): unidentified Italian bishopric, not Barcelona in Spain.
Bas-Poitou (French): district of western Poitou.
Basarfūt (Arabic): fortress — L2e5, 5.
Basra; al-Baṣrah (Arabic): city, port — N3f5, 3, 4, 7, 8, 11.
Baṭalyaus: town — see Badajoz.
Bathnae: town — see Sarūj.
Bathys (classical), Sarî (-Su) (Turkish): river — K1e1, 3.
al-Baṭīḥah or al-Buṭaiḥah (Arabic: the stream-bed): plain north of Lake Tiberias — L1f3, 6.
al-Batrūn (Arabic), Botrys (classical), Botron (medieval): town — L1f1, 6, 9, 14.
Bavaria; Bayern (German): region of southern Germany — Gc, 1.
Bayeux (French): town 25 miles east of Carentan.
Béarn (French): district of sw France — Dd, 1.
Beaufort: crusader castle — see Belfort.
Beauvoir: crusader castle — see Belvoir.
Bebou: fortress — see Bibol.
Bec (French): abbey 23 miles sw of Rouen.
Behesni; Behesnou (West Armenian), Bahasnī or Bahasnā (Arabic), Besni (modern Turkish): fortress, now town — L3e3, 5, 9.
Beirut; Berytus (classical), Bairūt (Arabic): port — L1f2, 3, 5, 6, 7, 8, 9, 10, 11, 12, 13, 14.
Belen Boghazî: pass — see Syrian Gates.
Belfort or Beaufort (medieval), Shaqīf Arnūn or Qal'at ash-Shaqīf (Arabic: fort of the rock): crusader castle — L1f2, 6, 10, 13, 14.
Belgrade; Beograd (Serbian): town — I1d1, 2.
Belikh or Belih (-Nehri): river — see Balikh.
Belinas: town — see Banyas.
Belvoir or Beauvoir (medieval), Kaukab al-Hawā' (Arabic: star of the sky): crusader castle — L1f3, 6, 10, 14.
Benevento (Italian): city — G5d4, 2.
Beograd: town — see Belgrade.

Bergen: city — see Mons.
Beroea: city — see Aleppo.
Berry (French): region of central France — Ec, 1.
Berytus: port — see Beirut.
Besançon (French): town 45 miles east of Dijon.
Besni: fortress, now town — see Behesni.
Bessan: town — see Baisan.
Betenoble: village — see Bait Nūbā.
Beth Gibelin: town — see Bait Jibrīn.
Bethlehem; Bait Laḥm (Arabic: house of flesh): town — L1f4, 6, 7, 9.
Bethsan or Bethshan: town — see Baisan.
Beyoghlu: port — see Pera.
Biandrate (Italian): village 10 miles north of Vercelli.
Bibol (Turkish), Bebou (West Armenian), Bābalū (Arabic): fortress — L5e2, 10.
Bieda: village — see Blera.
Bijāyah: port — see Bougie.
Bilbais or Bilbīs (Arabic): town — K2f5, 3.
Binkath: city — see Tashkent.
al-Biqā' (Arabic: the hollow), Coele-Syria (classical): district of central Lebanon — L1f2, 5, 6.
Bīr (Arabic: colloquial for Bi'r: well): village — L3e4, 5.
Bira; al-Bīrah (Arabic), Birtha (classical), Bir (West Armenian), Birejik (Turkish): town — L3e3, 3, 5, 9, 10, 12.
Bisanthe: port — see Rodosto.
Biscay, Bay of — Dcd, 1.
Bithynia (classical): region of NW Anatolia — JKd, 2.
Bitolj: town — see Monastir.
Bivar: town — see Vivar.
Black Sea — KLd, 2, 3.
Blancfort or Blanquefort (French): town 6 miles NW of Bordeaux.
Blanche Garde (medieval), at-Tall aṣ-Ṣāfiyah (Arabic: the glittering hill): crusader castle — K5f4, 6, 10.
Blera (classical), Bieda (Italian): village 5 miles SSW of Vetralla.
Blois (French): town 34 miles ENE of Tours.
Bogen (German): village 28 miles east of Regensburg.
Bohemia; Čechy (Czech): region between upper Elbe and Austria — Gb, 1, 2.
Bokhārā: city — see Bukhara.
Bologna (Italian): town — G2d1, 1, 2.
Bolvadin: town — see Polybotus.
Bona (medieval), Hippo Regius (classical), Būnah (Arabic): port — F3e4, 1, 2.
Bordeaux (French): city, port — D5d1, 1.
Borysthenes: river — see Dnieper.
Bosporus (classical), Karadeniz Boghazî (Turkish): strait — J5d4, 3.
Botron or Botrys: town — see al-Batrūn.
Boudantē: town — see Podandus.
Bougie (French), Saldae (classical), Bijāyah (Arabic): port — F1e4, 1.
Bouillon (French): town 60 miles NE of Rheims.
Boulogne-sur-Mer (French): port 60 miles NW of Arras.
Bourbon (French): town 50 miles SE of Bourges.
Bourges (French): town — E3c3, 1.
Bourgogne: region — see Burgundy.
Brač: island — see Brazza.
Braga (Portuguese), Brāqarah (Arabic): town — C2d4, 1.

Branits; Viminacium (classical), Brandiz or Branichevo (medieval), Brnjica (Serbian): town, now unimportant — I3d1, 2.
Braunschweig: city — see Brunswick.
Bray (French): village 50 miles SSE of Ghent.
Brazza (Italian), Brač (Croatian): island — H2d2, 2.
Breiz: region — see Brittany.
Bremen (German): city, port — F4b2, 1, 2.
Brescia (Italian): city 30 miles NNE of Cremona.
Breslau (German), Wrocław (Polish): city — H3b4, 2.
Brest (French): port — D1c2, 2.
Bretagne: region — see Brittany.
Breteuil (French): village 35 miles NW of Chartres.
Brindisi (Italian): port — H3d5, 2.
Britain or Great Britain: island comprising England, Scotland, and Wales.
Brittany; Bretagne (French), Breiz (Breton): region of NW France — Dc, 1.
Brnjica: town — see Branits.
Broyes (French): village 25 miles NE of Provins.
Brucheville: village — see Brus.
Bruck an der Leitha (German): town at confluence of the Leitha and the Danube, possibly medieval Tollenburg.
Bruges (French), Brugge (Flemish): port, now city — E4b4, 1.
Brunswick; Braunschweig (German): city — G1b3, 2.
Brus (medieval), Brucheville (French): village 6 miles NNE of Carentan.
Buda (Hungarian): city — H5c3, 2.
Buḥairat al-Manzalah — see Manzala, Lake.
Buḥairat Ṭabarīyah — see Tiberias, Lake.
Buis (French): village 50 miles SSE of Valence.
Bukhara; Bokhārā (Persian), Bukhārā (Arabic): city — Q5e1, 4.
Bulgaria: region south of the lower Danube, larger than modern nation — Id, 2, 3.
Bulunyās: port — see Valania.
Būnah: port — see Bona.
al-Buqai'ah (Arabic: the little hollow): valley — L1f1, 5.
Bures (French): village 14 miles SW of Paris.
Burgos (Spanish), Burghush (Arabic): city — D2d3, 1.
Burgundy; Bourgogne (French): region of eastern France, extending farther south than now — Ec, 1.
Burj Ṣāfīthā: crusader castle — see Chastel-Blanc.
Burj Sibnā (Arabic): fortress — L3e5, 5.
Burṭuqāl: port — see Oporto.
Bury (French): village 30 miles north of Paris.
al-Buṭaiḥah: plain — see al-Baṭīḥah.
Büyük Menderes: river — see Maeander.
Buzā'ah (Arabic): town — L3e4, 5, 10, 13.
Byblos: town — see Jubail.
Byzantium: city — see Constantinople.

Cadmus (classical), Khonaz or Honaz (Daghî) (Turkish): mountain south of Chonae.
Caen (French): city 40 miles east of Carentan.
Caesarea (classical), Qaisārīyah (Arabic): port, now unimportant — K5f3, 6, 7, 9, 14.
Caesarea ad Argaeum or Caesarea-Mazaca (classical), Kayseri (Turkish): city — L1e2, 3, 7, 8, 9, 10, 11, 12, 13.

Caesarea-Philippi: town — see Banyas.
Caiffa or Caiphas: port — see Haifa.
Cairo; al-Qāhirah (Arabic): city — K2f5, 2, 3, 7, 8.
Calabria (Italian): region of sw Italy — He, 2.
Cambrai (French): town 22 miles ESE of Arras.
Campania (Latin, Italian): region around Naples.
Candia: medieval name for Crete.
Cangas de Onís (Spanish): village — C5d2, 1.
Cannae (classical): village — H2d4, 2.
Canosa (Italian): town — H2d4, 2.
Canossa (Italian): town, now unimportant — G1d1, 1, 2.
Cantabria: region of northern Spain.
Cantabrian Mountains; Cordillera Cantábrica (Spanish) — Cd, 1.
Canterbury: town 55 miles ESE of London.
Capharda: village — see Kafarṭāb.
Cappadocia (classical): region of central Anatolia — KLe, 3.
Capua (Italian): town — G5d4, 2.
Carcassonne (French): town — E3d2, 1.
Carentan (French): town — D4c1, 1.
Caria (classical): region of sw Anatolia — Je, 2, 3.
Carinthia; Kärnten (German): region of the upper Drava — Gc, 1, 2.
Carmel, Mount; Jabal Mār Ilyās (Arabic: Mount St. Elias) — K5f3, 6.
Carpathians: mountain range — Ic, 2, 3.
Carrhae: town — see Harran.
Carthage; Carthago (Latin): town — G1e4, 2.
Caspian Sea — NOde, 3, 4.
Cassandria; Cassandrea, Pallene, or Potidaea (classical), Kassándra or Potídhaia (modern Greek): peninsula south of Thessalonica.
Castello: district on lagoon of Venice — see Olivola.
Castile; Badulia (classical), Castilla (Spanish): region of north central Spain — D2d4, 1.
Castillon (French): town 55 miles ssw of Toulouse.
Castoria (medieval), Celetrum (classical), Kastoría (modern Greek): town — I2d5, 2.
Castra Comnenon: town — see Kastamonu.
Castrum Cepha: town — see Ḥiṣn Kaifā.
Catalonia; Cataluña (Spanish), Catalunya (Catalan): region of NE Spain — Ed, 1.
Catania (Italian): town — H1e3, 2.
Caucasus; Kavkaz (Russian): mountain range — MNd, 3, 4.
Čechy: region — see Bohemia.
Celetrum: town — see Castoria.
Central Asia: region stretching north and east from Turkestan.
Cephalonia; Kephallēnia (ancient Greek), Kephallōnia (medieval Greek), Kefallinía (modern Greek): island — I1e2, 2.
Cerami (Italian): town — G5e3, 2.
Cerdagne (French): district north of the Pyrenees — Ed, 1.
Cerep: fortress — see al-Athārib.
Ceuta (Spanish), Septa (classical), Sabtah (Arabic): port — C5e5, 1.
Cevennes (French): mountains — Ed, 1.
Chabannes (French): village near Limoges.
Chahan: river — see Pyramus.
Chaise-Dieu (French): village 20 miles NNW of Le Puy.
Chalcedon (classical), Kalkhēdōn (ancient Greek), Khalkēdōn (medieval Greek), Kadiköy (Turkish): town — J5d5, 3.
Chalcis ad Belum: town — see Qinnasrīn.

Châlons-sur-Marne (French): town — E5c2, 1.
Chalybon: city — see Aleppo.
Champagne (French): region of NE France — Ec, 1.
Chanakkale Boghazî: strait — see Dardanelles.
Chankirî: town — see Gangra.
Chardak Boghazî: pass — see Myriokephalon.
Chariopolis (medieval), Hayrabolu (Turkish): village 25 miles NW of Rodosto.
Chartres (French): town — E2c2, 1.
Chartreuse (French: charterhouse): monastery 50 miles ESE of Lyons.
Chastel-Arnoul (French): fortress near Bait Nūbā.
Chastel-Blanc (medieval), Burj Ṣāfīthā (Arabic): crusader castle — L2f1, 5, 14.
Chastel-Neuf (medieval), Ḥūnīn (Arabic): crusader castle — L1f2, 6, 12, 13, 14.
Chastel-Rouge or Rugia (medieval): crusader castle — L2e5, 5.
Chastel-Rouge: fortress — see Yaḥmur.
Châtillon-sur-Loing (French): town 23 miles east of Sully.
Cherso (Italian), Cres (Croatian): island — G5d1, 2.
Chersonesus Heracleotica: port, now ruined — see Kherson.
China: region of eastern Asia — not in area mapped.
Chocques (French): village 19 miles NNW of Arras.
Chonae (classical), Khonaz or Honaz (Turkish): village — J5e3, 3.
Chorasmia: region — see Khorezm.
Chorsa: town — see Kars.
Chrysoceras: bay — see Golden Horn.
Cibotus: port — see Civetot.
Ciciliano (Italian): town — G3d4, 2.
Cilicia (classical): region of southern Anatolia — KLe, 5.
Cilician Gates; Pylae Ciliciae (classical), Külek (or Gülek) Boghazî (Turkish): pass through the Taurus range north of Lampron.
Cintra: Sintra (Portuguese): town 14 miles NNW of Lisbon.
Cîteaux (French): abbey 12 miles south of Dijon.
Civetot (medieval), Cibotus (classical): port, now abandoned — J5d5, 3.
Civita Vecchia (Italian: old city): port — G2d3, 2.
Clairvaux (French): abbey — E5c2, 1.
Clermont (French): town — E4c5, 1.
Cluny (French): abbey — E5c4, 1.
Cocussus: town — see Coxon.
Coele-Syria: district of central Lebanon — see al-Biqā'.
Coible: fortress — see al-Khawābī.
Coimbra (Portuguese), Qulumrīyah (Arabic): town — C2d5, 1.
Coliat: fortress — see al-Qulai'ah.
Cologne (French), Köln (German): city — F2b5, 1, 2.
Comacchio (Italian): port — G3d1, 2.
Comana or Placentia (medieval): town, now abandoned — L2e2, 3, 7.
Como (Italian): town — F5c5, 1.
Compostela or Santiago de Compostela (Spanish): town — C2d3, 1.
Constance (French), Konstanz (German): town 90 miles SE of Strassburg.
Constantinople; Byzantium or Constantinopolis (classical), İstanbul (Turkish): city, port — J4d4, 2, 3, 7, 8, 11.
Cordillera Cantábrica — see Cantabrian Mountains.
Cordova; Córdoba (Spanish), Qurṭubah (Arabic): city — D1e3, 1.
Corfu (Italian); Corcyra (Latin), Kerkyra (ancient Greek), Kérkira (modern Greek): island — H5e1, 2.
Coria (Spanish), Qūriyah (Arabic): town — C4e1, 1.
Corice: town — see Cyrrhus.

Corinth; Korinthos (Greek; now Palaiá Kórinthos: Old Corinth): town — I3e3, 2.

Corsica; Corse (French): island — Fd, 1, 2.

Corvey (French), Korvey (German): abbey at Höxter 45 miles west of Goslar.

Corycus (classical), Goṛigos (West Armenian), Korgos (Turkish): port, now unimportant — K5e4, 3.

Coucy-le-Château (French): village 15 miles west of Laon.

Courtenay (French): village 40 miles ssw of Provins.

Covadonga (Spanish): battlefield — D1d2, 1.

Coxon (medieval), Cocussus (classical), Gogîson (West Armenian), Göksun (Turkish): town — L2e2, 3, 7.

Crac — see Krak.

Cracow; Kraków (Polish): town — H5b5, 2.

Craon (French): town 33 miles NW of Angers.

Cremona (Italian): town — G1c5, 1.

Cres: island — see Cherso.

Crete; Candia (medieval), Krētē (medieval Greek), Kríti (modern Greek): island — IJe, 2, 3, 7, 8, 11.

Croatia; Meran (medieval), Hrvatska (Croatian): region north of Dalmatia — Hcd, 2.

Cursat: town — see Quṣair.

Cydnus (classical), Tarsus (-Chayï) (Turkish): river flowing past Tarsus.

Cyprus; Kypros or Kipros (Greek), Kîbrîs (Turkish): island — Kef, 3, 7, 8, 9, 10, 11.

Cyrrhus (classical), Gouris (West Armenian), Qūriṣ (Arabic), Corice (medieval): town, now unimportant — L2e4, 5, 9.

Cyrus (classical), Kura (modern): river — N5e1, 3, 4.

Dailam (Persian): district of northern Persia — N4e3, 3, 4.

Dalmatia; Dalmacija (Croatian): coastal region east of the Adriatic — Hd, 2.

Damascus; Dimashq or ash-Sha'm (Arabic: the left): city — L2f2, 3, 6, 7, 8, 9, 10, 11, 12, 13, 14.

Damietta; Dimyāṭ (Arabic): port — K2f4, 3.

Dan: village — see Tall al-Qāḍī.

Dandānqān or Dandāngān (Persian): village — Q2e3, 4.

Danelaw: region of NE England.

Dānīth (Arabic): village — L2e5, 5, 8.

Dāniyah: port — see Denia.

Danmark: region — see Denmark.

Danube: river — J5c5, 1, 2, 3.

Daphne (classical), Bait al-Mā' (Arabic: house of the water): town — L2e4, 5.

Dara (classical), Dārā (Arabic): town — M1e3, 3.

Dāraiyā (Arabic): village — L2f2, 6.

Darb Sarmadā (Arabic): pass north of Sarmadā.

Darband: town — see Derbent.

Darbsāk (Arabic), Trapesac (medieval): town, now unimportant — L2e4, 5, 14.

Dardanelles; Hellespontus (classical), Chanakkale Boghazî (Turkish): strait — J2d5, 3.

Darsous: city — see Tarsus.

Dartmouth: port — D2b5, 1.

Darum or Daron (classical), ad-Dārum (Arabic): town, now unimportant — K5f4, 6.

Deabolis or Diabolis (medieval): town, now abandoned, on Devol river 30 miles south of Ochrida.

Dead Sea; Baḥr Lūṭ (Arabic: sea of Lot) — L1f4, 3.
Delhi: city in NW India — not in area mapped.
Delta (classical): region at mouth of the Nile.
Demmin (Slavic, German): town — G4b2, 2.
Demotika; Dēmotika (medieval Greek), Dhidhimótikhon (modern Greek): town — J2d4, 2, 7.
Denia (Spanish), Dāniyah (Arabic): port — E1e2, 1.
Denmark; Danmark (Danish): region, then including the southern part of Sweden — Ga, 1, 2.
Derbent; Darband (Persian), Bāb al-Abwāb (Arabic: gate of the gates): town — N4d3, 3, 4.
Deuil (French): town 8 miles north of Paris.
Deutschland: region — see Germany.
Dhidhimótikhon: town — see Demotika.
Diabolis: town — see Deabolis.
Die (French): village 27 miles ESE of Valence.
Dijlah or Dijle: river — see Tigris.
Dijon (French): city — F1c3, 1.
Dillingen (German): town 65 miles SSW of Nuremberg.
Dimashq: city — see Damascus.
Dimyāṭ: port — see Damietta.
Diyār-Bakr, Diyarbakír, Diyarbekir: town — see Amida.
Diyār-Bakr (Arabic): region of the upper Tigris — L5e2, 3.
Djerba: island — see Jerba.
Dlouḳ: town — see Duluk.
Dnieper; Borysthenes (classical), Dnepr (Russian): river — K3c4, 2, 3.
Dniester; Tyras (classical), Dnestr (Russian), Nistru (Rumanian): river — K1c4, 2, 3.
Dobin (Slavic): town, now unimportant — G2b2, 2.
Dog; Kalb (Arabic: dog): river — L1f2, 6.
Dol (French): town 60 miles SSW of Carentan.
Doliche: town — see Duluk.
Domfront (French): town 60 miles NW of Le Mans.
Don; Tanaïs (classical): river — L5c3, 3.
Doornijk: town — see Tournai.
Dorylaeum (classical): town, now abandoned in favor of Eskishehir — K1e1, 2, 3, 7, 8, 11.
Douro (Portuguese), Duero (Spanish): river — C2d4, 1.
Dracon (medieval): village on Dracon river, 10 miles south of Civetot.
Dracon (medieval), Yalak (-Deresi) (Turkish): river flowing past Civetot.
Dramelay: village — see Tremelay.
Drava or Drave (Croatian), Drau (German), Dráva (Hungarian): river — H4c5, 1, 2.
Dreux (French): town 23 miles NNW of Chartres.
Dristra (medieval), Durostorum (classical), Silistra (Romanian), Silistria (Bulgarian): town — J3d1, 2, 3, 7.
Dropuli: unidentified town near Viyosa river, probably classical Hadrianopolis, medieval Drinopolis, east of modern Argyrokastron and 60 miles SE of Avlona.
Dubrovnik: port — see Ragusa.
Dueñas (Spanish): town — D1d4, 1.
Duero: river — see Douro.
Duluk; Doliche (classical), Dlouḳ (West Armenian), Dulūk (Arabic), Dülük (Turkish): town — L3e3, 5.
Durostorum: town — see Dristra.

Dyrrachium or Epidamnus (classical), Durazzo (Italian), Durrës (Albanian): port — H5d4, 2.

East Anglia: region of eastern England.
Ebrach (German): village 40 miles NW of Nuremberg.
Ebro (Spanish): river — E1d5, 1.
Ecbatana: city — see Hamadan.
Edessa (medieval), Ourha (Armenian), ar-Ruhā' (Arabic), Urfa (Turkish): city — L4e3, 3, 5, 7, 9, 10, 12, 13.
Édhessa: town — see Vodena.
Edirne: city — see Adrianople.
Egypt; Miṣr (Arabic): region — 2, 3.
Eichstädt or Eichstätt (German): town 40 miles south of Nuremberg.
Eire: island — see Ireland.
Elbe (German), Labe (Czech): river — F5b2, 1, 2.
Elbistan: town — see Albistan.
Elburz; Alburz (Persian): mountain range — Oe, 3, 4.
Eleutheropolis: town — see Bait Jibrīn.
Elma Daghî: mountain range — see Amanus.
Elsass: region west of the upper Rhine — see Alsace.
Emesa: city — see Homs.
Emmaus; 'Amwās (Arabic): village — K5f4, 6.
England: region — Db, 1.
Enna (Italian): town — G5e3, 2.
Ephesus (classical): town, now abandoned — J3e3, 3, 7, 8, 11.
Epidamnus: port — see Dyrrachium.
Epiphania: city — see Hamah.
Epirus; Épeiros (ancient Greek), Ípiros (modern Greek): region — I1e1, 2.
Eppenstein (German): town 90 miles ESE of Salzburg.
Ercican: town — see Arzghān.
Ereghli: port — see Heraclea.
Erjish: town — see Arjish.
Ermenek (Turkish), Germanicopolis (classical): town — K3e4, 3, 8.
Ermenistan: region — see Armenia.
Erzerum; Theodosiopolis (classical), Garin (West) or Karin (East Armenian), Qālīqalā or Arḍ ar-Rūm (Arabic: land of Rome), Erzurum (Turkish): city — M2e1, 3, 7, 8, 11.
Erzinjan (Turkish), Arsinga (classical): town — L5e1, 3, 7, 8, 11.
Esch (German): town 30 miles NNW of Metz.
Eskihisar: town — see Laodicea.
España: region — see Spain.
Esseron (medieval): village — J3e1, 3, 11.
Estanor: port — see Pera.
Esztergom: town — see Gran.
Étampes (French): town — E3c2, 1.
Euboea (classical), Evripos (medieval Greek), Negroponte (Italian), Évvoia (modern Greek): island — I5e2, 2.
Euphrates (classical), al-Furāt (Arabic), Firat (Nehri) (Turkish): river — N4f5, 3, 4, 5.
Évreux (French): town 30 miles south of Rouen.

Falkenberg; Fauquembergue (French): town 38 miles NW of Arras.
al-Faramā': town — see Pelusium.
Farfa (Italian): abbey 24 miles NE of Rome.

Faroes: island group north of the Shetlands — not in area mapped.
Fars; Fārs (Persian), Fāris (Arabic): region of sw Persia — Og, 4.
Fauquembergue: town — see Falkenberg.
Feke: fortress — see Vahka.
Fez; Fās (Arabic): city — D1f1, 1.
Filistīn: region — see Palestine.
Fırat (Nehri): river — see Euphrates.
Flanders; Vlaanderen (Flemish): region of northern France and Belgium — EFb, 1.
Flavigny (French): abbey 28 miles NW of Dijon.
Florence; Firenze (Italian): city — G2d2, 1, 2.
Fontevrault (French): town 35 miles WSW of Tours.
Forez (French): district east of Clermont.
Fortore (Italian): river in SE Italy, flowing into the Adriatic west of Monte Gargano.
Fraga (Spanish), Ifrāghah (Arabic): town — E1d4, 1.
France: region, smaller than modern nation.
Franconia; Franken (German): region of western Germany — FGbc, 1, 2.
Frankfurt am Main (German): city — F4b5, 1, 2.
Fraxinet or Fraxinetum: fortress — see La Garde-Freinet.
Freising (German): city 45 miles SSW of Regensburg.
Frisia; Friesland (Dutch, German): region of northern Netherlands and NW Germany — Fb, 1, 2.
al-Fū'ah (Arabic): village — L2e5, 5.
al-Fūlah (Arabic: the bean), La Fève (medieval), Afula (modern): village — L1f3, 6.
al-Furāt: river — see Euphrates.
Fustat; al-Fusṭāṭ (Arabic), Babylon (medieval): town — K2f5, 3.

Gabala: port — see Jabala.
Gadres: town — see Gaza.
Gaeta (Italian): port — G4d4, 2.
Galatia (classical): region of central Anatolia — Ke, 2, 3.
Galicia; Halicz (Polish): region of SE Poland.
Galicia (Spanish): region of NW Spain — Cd, 1.
Galilee: region of northern Palestine — L1f3, 6.
Galilee, Sea of — see Tiberias, Lake.
Gand: city, port — see Ghent.
Gangra or Germanicopolis (classical), Chankiri (Turkish): town — K4d5, 3, 8.
Gargar; Gargaṛ (West Armenian), Karkar or Qarqar (Arabic), Gerger (Turkish): town — L4e3, 3, 7, 8, 9, 10, 12.
Garigliano (Italian): river flowing into the Tyrrhenian Sea east of Gaeta.
Garin: city — see Erzerum.
Garonne (French): river — D5c5, 1.
Gascony; Gascogne (French): region of SW France — Dd, 1.
Gaston: town — see Baghrās.
Gâtinais (French): district between Courtenay and Châtillon.
Gaul: ancient name for France.
Gavur Daghı: mountain range — see Amanus.
Gaza; Gadres (medieval), Ghazzah (Arabic): town — K5f4, 6, 12, 13, 14.
Gazara: hill — see Mont Gisard.
Gaziantep: city — see Aintab.
Genoa; Genova (Italian): city, port — F4d1, 1, 2.
Gent: city, port — see Ghent.

Georgia; Sakartvelo (Georgian): region east of the Black Sea and south of the Caucasus range — Md, 3.
Gerasa: town — see Jarash.
Gerger: town — see Gargar.
Germanicia: town — see Marash.
Germanicopolis: town — see Ermenek.
Germanicopolis: town — see Gangra.
Germany; Allemania or Alamannia (medieval), Deutschland (German): region of north central Europe.
Gerona (Spanish), Jarundah (Arabic): town — E3d3, 1.
Gezer: hill — see Mont Gisard.
al-Ghāb (Arabic): swampy region of the middle Orontes — L2c5, 5.
Gharnāṭah: city — see Granada.
Ghaznah (Arabic), Ghaznī (Persian): town — R4f2, 4.
Ghazzah: town — see Gaza.
Ghent; Gent (Flemish), Gand (French): city, port — E4b4, 1.
Ghor; al-Ghaur (Arabic: the bottom): valley of the lower Jordan — L1f4, 3.
al-Ghūṭah (Arabic): district SE of Damascus — L2f2, 6.
Gibelcar: fortress — see 'Akkār.
Gibelet: town — see Jubail.
Gibraltar; Jabal Ṭāriq (Arabic): rock — C5e4, 1.
Gibraltar, Strait of: strait between Spain and Morocco.
Girgenti: town — see Agrigento.
Giza; al-Jīzah (Arabic): town — K2f5, 3.
Gnesen (German), Gniezno (Polish): town — H3b3, 2.
Gogison or Göksun: town — see Coxon.
Gök(-Su): river — see Sanja.
Golden Horn; Chrysoceras (classical), Halich (Turkish): bay between Constantinople and Pera.
Göle: town — see Kola.
Gorigos: port — see Corycus.
Gorizia (Italian): town 22 miles NE of Grado.
Goslar (German): town — G1b4, 1, 2.
Gothia: district of southern France, between Narbonne and Nîmes — E4d2, 1.
Gouris: town — see Cyrrhus.
Grado (Italian): port — G4c5, 2.
Gran (German), Esztergom (Hungarian): town — H4c3, 2.
Granada (Spanish), Ighranāṭah or Gharnāṭah (Arabic): city — D2e3, 1.
Grandpré (French): village 40 miles east of Rheims.
Grant-Mesnil or Grandmenil (French): village 24 miles south of Liége.
Gray (French): town 27 miles ENE of Dijon.
Great Britain: island — see Britain.
Great Saint Bernard Pass: Alpine pass 120 miles east of Lyons.
Greece; Hellas (Greek): region west of the Aegean Sea, smaller than modern nation — Ie, 2.
Greenland: large island west of Iceland — not in area mapped.
Guadalajara (Spanish), Wādī-l-Ḥijārah (Arabic: river of the stones): town — D2d5, 1.
Guadarrama Mountains; Sierra de Guadarrama (Spanish), ash-Shārrāt (Arabic) — Dd, 1.
Guarenne: castle — see Warenne.
Guienne; Guyenne (French): region around Bordeaux.
Gujerat: coastal district of western India — not in area mapped.

Gurgānj (Persian), al-Jurjānīyah (Arabic): city, now abandoned for Novo Urgench — Q1d4, 4.

Hāb (Arabic), Hapa (medieval): town — L2e5, 5.
Ḥabīs Jaldak (Arabic): cave fortress — L1f3, 6, 9, 12, 13, 14.
Habor: river — see Khabur.
Ḥabrūn: town — see Hebron.
Ḥadīthah (Arabic): town — M3f1, 3.
Hadrianopolis: city — see Adrianople.
Hadrumetum: port — see Susa.
Haifa; Caiphas or Caiffa (medieval), Ḥaifā (Arabic): port — L1f3, 3, 6, 7, 8, 9, 10, 11, 12, 13, 14.
Hainault; Hainaut (French), Henegouwen (Flemish): district around Mons.
al-Hajīrah (Arabic): village — L2f2, 6.
Ḥalab, Haleb: city — see Aleppo.
Halich: bay — see Golden Horn.
Halicz: region of SE Poland — see Galicia.
Halys (classical), Kizil (Irmak) (Turkish: red): river — K1d4, 3.
Hamadan; Ecbatana (classical), Hamadān (Persian): city — N4f1, 3, 4, 7, 8, 11.
Hamah; Epiphania or Hamath (classical), Ḥamāh (Arabic): city — L2e5, 3, 5, 7, 8, 9, 10, 11, 12, 13, 14.
Hamburg (German): city, port — G1b2, 1, 2.
Hapa: town — see Hāb.
Ḥārim (Arabic), Harenc (medieval): town — L2e4, 5, 13.
Harput: fortress — see Kharput.
Harran or Haran (Turkish), Carrhae (classical), Ḥarrān (Arabic): town — L5e4, 3, 7, 8, 9, 10, 11, 12, 13.
al-Ḥasā: coastal region of NE Arabia — see Bahrain.
Hasankeyf: town — see Ḥiṣn Kaifā.
Ḥāṣbaiyā (Arabic): town — L1f2, 6.
Hastings: port 55 miles SE of London.
Hattin; Madon (classical), Ḥaṭṭīn or Ḥiṭṭīn (Arabic): village — L1f3, 6, 14.
Hauran; Ḥaurān (Arabic): district of southern Syria — L2f3, 6.
Hauteville (French): village 13 miles SSW of Carentan.
Havelberg (German): town — G3b3, 2.
Hayastan: region — see Armenia.
Hayrabolu: village — see Chariopolis.
Hazart: town — see 'Azāz.
Hebron; Ḥabrūn or Khalīl (Arabic), Saint Abraham (medieval): town — L1f4, 6, 7, 8, 9, 11, 13, 14.
Hejaz; al-Ḥijāz (Arabic): region of western Arabia — Lgh, 3.
Helenopolis (medieval): village 5 miles SW of Civetot.
Heliopolis: town — see Baalbek.
Hellas: region — see Greece.
Hellespontus: strait — see Dardanelles.
Henegouwen: district — see Hainault.
Heraclea or Heraclea-Cybistra (classical), Ereghli (Turkish): town — K5e3, 3, 7, 8.
Herat; Herāt (Persian): city — Q3f1, 4.
Hermon, Mount; al-Jabal ash-Shaikh or Jabal ath-Thalj (Arabic: the hoary, or snow-covered, mountain) — L1f2, 6.
Hierapolis: town — see Manbij.
Hierges (French): castle 55 miles SW of Liége.
Hierosolyma: city — see Jerusalem.

al-Ḥijāz: region — see Hejaz.
Hilla; al-Ḥillah (Arabic): town — M5f3, 3, 7, 8.
Ḥimṣ: city — see Homs.
Hippo Regius: port — see Bona.
Ḥiṣn ad-Dair (Arabic: stronghold of the monastery): fortress — L2e4, 5.
Ḥiṣn al-Akrād: fortress — see Krak des Chevaliers.
al-Ḥiṣn ash-Sharqī (Arabic: the eastern stronghold): fortress — L2f1, 5.
Ḥiṣn Kaifā (Arabic), Castrum Cepha (classical), Hasankeyf (Turkish): town — M2e3, 3, 8, 9, 10, 11.
Hispania: medieval name for the Iberian peninsula.
Ḥiṭṭīn: village — see Hattin.
Holstein (German): region south of Denmark — FGb, 1.
Homs; Emesa (classical), Ḥimṣ (Arabic): city — L2f1, 3, 5, 7, 8, 9, 10, 11, 12, 13, 14.
Honaz: village — see Chonae.
Honaz (Daghi̊): mountain — see Cadmus.
Horeb, Mount — see Sinai, Mount.
Horns of Hamah: hills near Hamah.
Hṛomgla: fortress — see Qal'at ar-Rūm.
Hrvatska: region north of Dalmatia — see Croatia.
Huesca (Spanish), Washqah (Arabic): town — D5d3, 1.
Ḥulwān (Arabic) : town, now unimportant — N1f1, 3, 4.
Hungary; Magyarország (Hungarian): region of central Europe — HIc, 2.
Ḥūnīn: crusader castle — see Chastel-Neuf.

Ibelin (medieval), Jabneel or Jamnia (classical), Yabnâ (Arabic): town — K5f4, 6, 10, 14.
Iberia (classical): region south of the central Caucasus range — MNd, 3.
Iceland; Island (Icelandic): island in North Atlantic — not in area mapped.
Iconium (medieval), Qūniyah (Arabic), Konya (Turkish): city — K3e3, 2, 3, 7, 8, 11.
Ifrāghah: town — see Fraga.
Ifrīqiyah: region of North Africa — see Tunisia.
Ighranāṭah: city — see Granada.
Île de France (French): region around Paris.
'Imm (Arabic), Imma (classical), Yenishehir (Turkish: new town): town — L2e4, 5.
Inab (Arabic), Napa (medieval): village — L2e5, 5, 12.
India: region east of Sind — not in area mapped.
Indian Ocean — 4.
Indus: river — Rgh, 4.
Ípiros: region — see Epirus.
Iran: modern nation holding most of medieval Persia.
Īrān: region of sw Asia — see Persia.
Iraq: modern nation, approximately equivalent to Mesopotamia.
al-'Irāq: region — see Mesopotamia.
Irbil (Arabic), Arbela (classical): town — M5e4, 3.
Ireland; Eire (Irish): island — Cb, 1.
'Irqah or Irqata: town — see 'Arqah.
Ischia (Italian): island — G4d5, 2.
Isdūd: town — see Ashdod.
Isfahan; Iṣfahān or Ispahān (Persian), Iṣbahān (Arabic): city — O2f3, 4.
Ishbīliyah: city — see Seville.
al-Iskandarīyah: city, port — see Alexandria.

İskenderun: port — see Alexandretta.
Island: island — see Iceland.
İsmil: town — see Salamia.
Ispahān: city — see Isfahan.
İstanbul: city, port — see Constantinople.
Istria (classical): peninsula — G5c5, 1, 2.
Italy; Italia (Italian): peninsula, now a nation.
Itil: river — see Volga.
Ivrea (Italian): town 30 miles WNW of Vercelli.
İzmir: city, port — see Smyrna.
İzmit: town — see Nicomedia.
İznik: town — see Nicaea.
İznik Gölü: lake west of Nicaea — see Ascanius.

Jabal Anṣārīyah (Arabic: mountain of the Nuṣairīs) or Jabal Bahrā' (Arabic): mountain — L2e5, 5.
Jabal as-Summāq (Arabic: mountain of the sumac) — L2e5, 5.
al-Jabal ash-Shaikh or Jabal ath-Thalj — see Hermon, Mount.
al-Jabal ash-Sharqī — see Anti-Lebanon.
Jabal aṭ-Ṭūr — see Olives, Mount of.
Jabal Bahrā': mountain — see Jabal Anṣārīyah.
Jabal Lubnān — see Lebanon, Mount.
Jabal Mār Ilyās — see Carmel, Mount.
Jabal Mūsâ — see Sinai, Mount.
Jabal Ṭāriq: rock — see Gibraltar.
Jabala; Gabala (classical), Jabalah (Arabic): port — L1e5, 5, 9, 14.
Jabneel: town — see Ibelin.
Jacob's Ford; now Jisr Banāt Ya'qūb (Arabic: bridge of the daughters of Jacob): ford across the upper Jordan — L1f2, 6.
Jaffa or Joppa; Yāfā (Arabic): port — K5f3, 3, 6, 7, 9, 10, 11, 12, 13, 14.
Jaiḥān: river — see Pyramus.
Jaiḥūn: river — see Oxus.
Jamnia: town — see Ibelin.
Jarash (Arabic), Gerasa (classical): town — L1f3, 6, 9.
Jarbah: island — see Jerba.
Jarundah: town — see Gerona.
Jaulan; al-Jaulān (Arabic): district NE of Lake Tiberias — L1f3, 6.
Jaushan (Arabic): hill near Antioch.
Jaxartes (classical), Saiḥūn (Persian, Arabic), Syr Darya (modern): river — Q2c4, 4.
Jazira; al-Jazīrah (Arabic: the island, or peninsula): the upper Mesopotamian region.
Jazīrat-Ibn-'Umar (Arabic: island of the son of Omar), Jezire or Jizre (Turkish): town — M3e3, 3.
al-Jazr (Arabic): district SW of Aleppo — L2e4, 5.
Jerba; Meninx (classical), Jarbah (Arabic), Djerba (French): island — G1f2, 1, 2.
Jericho; Arīḥā or ar-Rīḥā (Arabic): town — L1f4, 6.
Jerusalem; Hierosolyma (classical), al-Quds (Arabic: the holy): city — L1f4, 3, 6, 7, 8, 9, 10, 11, 12, 13, 14.
Jeyhan: river — see Pyramus.
Jezire or Jizre: town — see Jazīrat-Ibn-'Umar.
al-Jibāl (Arabic: the mountains): district of western Persia — N2e5, 3, 4.
Jisr Banāt Ya'qūb: bridge — see Jacob's Ford.
al-Jīzah: town — see Giza.

Joppa: port — see Jaffa.
Jordan; al-Urdunn (Arabic): river — L1f4, 3, 6.
Jubail (Arabic: small mountain), Byblos (classical), Gibelet (medieval): town — L1f1, 5, 6, 9, 10, 14.
al-Jurjānīyah: city — see Gurgānj.

Kabul; Kābul (Persian, Arabic): city — R5f1, 4.
Kadiköy: town — see Chalcedon.
Kafar Rūm (Arabic: village of Rome): town — L2e5, 5.
Kafarlāthā (Arabic): village — L2e5, 5, 10, 11.
Kafarṭāb (Arabic), Capharda (classical): village — L2e5, 5, 9, 10.
Kaffa: port — see Theodosia.
Kafr Nāṣiḥ (Arabic): village — L2e4, 5.
Kafr Sabt (Arabic: village of Saturday): village — L1f3, 6.
al-Kahf (Arabic: the cavern): cave fortress — L2e5, 5.
Kairawan; al-Qairawān (Arabic): city — G1e5, 1, 2.
Kaisūn: fortress — see Kesoun.
Kalb: river — see Dog.
Kalkhēdōn: town — see Chalcedon.
Kandahar; Qandahār (Persian, Arabic): city — R1f4, 4.
Kara-Su: river — see an-Nahr al-Aswad.
Karadeniz Boghazi: strait — see Bosporus.
al-Karak: fortress — see Kerak.
Karbalā': town — see Kerbela.
Karin: city — see Erzerum.
Karkar: town — see Gargar.
Kärnten: region — see Carinthia.
Kars (East Armenian, Turkish), Chorsa (classical): town — M4d5, 3.
Kassándra: peninsula — see Cassandria.
Kastamonu (Turkish), Castra Comnenon or Kastamuni (medieval): town — K4d4, 3, 8.
Kastoría: town — see Castoria.
Kaukab al-Hawā': castle — see Belvoir.
Kavkaz: mountain range — see Caucasus.
Kayseri: city — see Caesarea.
Kazvin; Qazvīn (Persian), Qazwīn (Arabic): city — N5e4, 4.
Kephallēnia, Kephallōnia, or Kefallinía: island — see Cephalonia.
Kerak; Kir-hareseth (classical), Krak des Moabites or Krak of Moab (medieval), al-Karak (Arabic): fortress, now town — L1f4, 3, 6, 10, 11, 12, 13, 14.
Kerbela; Karbalā' (Arabic): town — M5f3, 3.
Kerkyra or Kérkira: island — see Corfu.
Kerman; Kirmān (Persian): region of southern Persia — Pg, 4.
Kerman; Kirmān (Persian): town — P3f5, 4.
Keshan: town — see Roussa.
Kesoun; Ḳesoun (West Armenian), Kaisūn (Arabic), Keysun (Turkish): fortress, now town — L3e3, 5, 9, 10.
Khabur; Habor (classical), Khābūr (Arabic): river — M1e5, 3.
Khalīl: town — see Hebron.
Khalkēdōn: town — see Chalcedon.
Khanāṣir: town — see Khunāṣirah.
Kharībah (Arabic): fortress — L2e5, 5.
Khwārizm: region at mouth of Oxus River — see Khorezm.
Kharput or Harput (Turkish), Kharpert (West Armenian), Kharpūt or Khartabirt (Arabic): fortress, now town — L5e2, 3, 8, 9, 10, 11, 12, 13.

al-Khawābī (Arabic), Coible (medieval): fortress — L2f1, 5.
Kherson (medieval Russian), Chersonesus Heracleotica (classical), Korsun (Slavic): port, now ruined (not modern Kherson on the Dnieper) — K4d1, 2, 3.
Khilāṭ or Khlaṭ: town — see Akhlat.
Khonaz: village — see Chonae.
Khonaz (Daghî): mountain south of Chonae — see Cadmus.
Khorezm; Chorasmia (classical), Khʷārizm (Persian): region at mouth of the Oxus River — Q1d3, 4.
Khunāṣirah or Khanāṣir (Arabic): town — L3e5, 5.
Khurasan; Khorāsān (Persian): region of NE Persia — PQe, 4; misapplied to Pontus in the medieval period.
Khuzistan; Susiana (classical), Khūzistān (Persian, Arabic): region of SW Persia — Nf, 4.
Kîbrîs or Kipros: island — see Cyprus.
Kiev (Russian): city — K1b5, 2.
Kir-hareseth: fortress, now town — see Kerak.
Kirmān: region and town of southern Persia — see Kerman.
Kîzîl (Irmak): river — see Halys.
Kola (medieval), Kogh (East Armenian), Göle (Turkish): town — M3d5, 3.
Köln: city — see Cologne.
Konstanz: town — see Constance.
Konya: city — see Iconium.
Korgos: port — see Corycus.
Korinthos: town — see Corinth.
Korsun: port, now ruined — see Kherson.
Korvey: abbey — see Corvey.
Kozan: town — see Sis.
Krak de Montréal (medieval), ash-Shaubak (Arabic): fortress — L1f5, 3, 8, 9, 10, 11, 12, 13, 14.
Krak des Chevaliers (medieval), Ḥiṣn al-Akrād (Arabic: stronghold of the Kurds): fortress — L2f1, 5, 11, 12, 13, 14.
Krak des Moabites or Krak of Moab: fortress — see Kerak.
Kraków: town — see Cracow.
Krētē or Kríti: island — see Crete.
Kufa; al-Kūfah (Arabic): town — M5f3, 3.
Külek (or Gülek) Boghazî: pass — see Cilician Gates.
Kura: river — see Cyrus.
Kurdistan; Kurdistān (Persian, Arabic): region between Armenia and Persia — MNe, 3.
Kyburg (German): village 45 miles south of Strassburg.
Kypros: island — see Cyprus.

La Châtre (French): town 45 miles SSW of Bourges.
La Fère (French): village 14 miles NW of Laon.
La Ferté (French): village 32 miles NW of Chartres.
La Fève: village — see al-Fūlah.
La Garde-Freinet (French), Fraxinetum (classical), Fraxinet (medieval): fortress — F2d2, 1, 2.
La Garnache (French): village 75 miles SW of Angers.
La Portelle: pass — see Syrian Gates.
Labe: river — see Elbe.
Ladder of Tyre: ascent south of Tyre.
al-Lādhiqīyah: port — see Latakia.
Lagery (French): village 14 miles west of Rheims.

Laicas: fortress — see al-ʿUllaiqah.
Lailūn (Arabic): hill NW of Aleppo — L2e4, 5.
Laish: village — see Tall al-Qāḍī.
Lakmah or al-Akmah (Arabic): village — L2f1, 5.
Lamego (Portuguese): town — C3d4, 1.
Lampedusa (Italian): island — G3e5, 2.
Lampron (West Armenian), Namrun (Turkish): fortress — K5e3, 3, 7, 9, 10.
Langres (French): town 40 miles NNE of Dijon.
Languedoc (French): region of southern France — Ed, 1.
Laodicea: port — see Latakia.
Laodicea ad Lycum (classical), Eskihisar (Turkish): town, now abandoned in favor of Denizli — J5e3, 3, 7, 8, 11.
Laon (French): town — E4c1, 1.
Lāridah: town — see Lerida.
Larissa: fortress — see Shaizar.
Latakia; Laodicea (classical), al-Lādhiqīyah (Arabic): port — L1e5, 3, 5, 7, 8, 9, 12, 13, 14.
Laṭmīn (Arabic): village — L2e5, 5.
Lauria: town — see Loria.
Le Bourg (French): castle just north of Rethel, 25 miles NE of Rheims.
Le Mans (French): town — E1c3, 1.
Le Monestre or Le Moinestre: fortress — see al-Munaiṭirah.
Le Puiset (French): castle 25 miles SE of Chartres.
Le Puy (French): town — E4c5, 1.
Lebanon; Lubnān (Arabic): region north of Palestine.
Lebanon, Mount; Jabal Lubnān (Arabic) — L2f1, 5, 6.
Lefke: town — see Leucae.
Leiningen (German): village 15 miles SW of Worms.
Leipzig (German), Lipsk (Slavic): town — G3b4, 1, 2.
Leitha (German): river — H3c2, 2.
Lentini (Italian): town — H1e3, 2.
Leon; León (Spanish): region of northern Spain — Cd, 1.
Leon; León (Spanish), Liyūn (Arabic): town — C5d3, 1.
Leontes (classical), al-Līṭānī (Arabic): river — L1f2, 6.
Leopoli (Italian): village near Civita Vecchia.
Lerida; Lérida (Spanish), Lāridah (Arabic): town — E1d4, 1.
Les Moulins or Moulines (French): village 45 miles NNE of Le Mans.
Leucae (medieval), Lefke (Turkish): village — K1d5, 3, 7.
Levkōsia: town — see Nicosia.
Libya: region of NE Africa — If4, 2.
Licosa, Point — G5d5, 2.
Liége or Liège (French), Luik (Flemish): city — F1b5, 1, 2.
Limoges (French): town — E2c5, 1.
Limousin (French): region of central France — E2c5, 1.
Lipsk: town — see Leipzig.
Lisbon; Lisboa (Portuguese), al-Ushbūnah (Arabic): city, port — C1e2, 1.
Lisieux (French): town 45 miles WSW of Rouen.
al-Līṭānī: river — see Leontes.
Liyūn: town — see Leon.
Loire (French): river — D3c3, 1.
Lombardy; Lombardia (Italian): region of NW Italy — Fc, 2.
London: city, port — D5b4, 1.
Longiniada or Longinias (medieval): port, now abandoned for Mersin, 15 miles SW of Tarsus.

Lopadium (classical), Ulubad (Turkish): town — J4d5, 3, 11.
Lorraine (French), Lothringen (German): region of eastern France — EFc, 1, 2.
Lorto (Italian): village near Civita Vecchia.
Low Countries: region of the lower Rhine, modern Belgium and Netherlands.
Lower Lorraine: district of southern Belgium.
Lübeck (German): city, port — G1b2, 1, 2.
Lubnān: region north of Palestine — see Lebanon.
Lucca (Italian): town — G1d2, 1.
al-Ludd: town — see Lydda.
Luik: city — see Liége.
Lund (Swedish): city — G4a5, 1, 2.
Luni (Italian): town — G1d1, 2.
Lusignan (French): town 17 miles SW of Poitiers.
Lusitania (classical): ancient name for Portugal.
Lychnidus: town — see Ochrida.
Lydda; Saint George (medieval), al-Ludd (Arabic): town — K5f4, 6.
Lyons; Lyon (French): city — E5c5, 1.

Ma'arrat-an-Nu'mān (Arabic): town — L2e5, 5, 7, 8, 10.
Ma'arrat-Miṣrīn (Arabic): town — L2e4, 5.
Maas: river — see Meuse.
Macedonia: region around Vardar river — Id, 2.
Mâcon (French): town 13 miles SE of Cluny.
al-Madīnah: city — see Medina.
Madon: village — see Hattin.
Maeander (classical), Büyük Menderes (Turkish): river — J3e3, 2, 3.
Magdeburg (German): town — G2b3, 1, 2.
al-Maghrib al-Aqṣâ: region of NW Africa — see Morocco.
Maguelonne (French): port, now unimportant, 10 miles south of Montpellier.
Magyarország: region of central Europe — see Hungary.
Mahdia; al-Mahdīyah (Arabic): city, port — G2e5, 1, 2.
Main (German): river — F4b5, 1, 2.
Maine (French): region of NW France — Dc, 1.
Mainz (German), Mayence (French): city — F4b5, 1, 2.
Maiyafariqin; Martyropolis (classical), Maiyāfāriqīn (Arabic), Miyafarkin or Silvan (Turkish): town — M2e2, 3, 8, 9, 10, 11, 12, 13.
al-Majdal (Arabic: the place of contention): plain north of Ascalon.
Makkah: city — see Mecca.
Malaga; Málaga (Spanish), Mālaqah (Arabic): city, port — D1e4, 1.
Malatya or Malaṭiyah: city — see Melitene.
Malazgirt or Malāzjird: town — see Manzikert.
al-Mallāhah (Arabic: the salt-mine): village — L1f2, 6.
Malmesbury: town 90 miles west of London.
Malta; Māliṭah (Arabic): island — G5e5, 2.
Mamistra (medieval), Mopsuestia (classical), Msis (Armenian), Misis (Turkish): town — L1e4, 3, 5, 7, 8, 9, 10, 11, 12, 13, 14.
Māmūlah (Arabic): village — L2e4, 5.
Man, Isle of — D1b1, 1.
Manbij (Arabic), Hierapolis (classical): town — L3e4, 5, 9, 13.
al-Manīqah (Arabic): fortress — L2e5, 5.
Manzala, Lake; Buḥairat al-Manzalah (Arabic): lake between Tinnis and Pelusium.
Manzikert; Mandzgerd (West) or Mantskert (East Armenian), Malazgirt (Turkish), Malāzjird (Arabic): town — M3e1, 3.

Maraclea (medieval), Maraqīyah (Arabic): port — L1e5, 5, 7, 14.
Maragha; Marāgheh (Persian): town — N2e3, 3, 4, 7, 8, 11.
Marash (Armenian, Turkish), Germanicia (classical), Mar'ash (Arabic): city — L2e3, 3, 5, 8, 9, 10, 11, 12, 13, 14.
Ma'ratah (Arabic): village — L2e4, 5.
Mardin (Turkish), Māridīn (Arabic): town — M1e3, 3, 8, 9, 10, 11, 12, 13.
Marescallia or Marescalcia (medieval): village, now abandoned, just south of Hattin.
Margat: fortress — see al-Marqab.
Margiana: city — see Merv.
Marį: pass south of Marash — see Amanus Gates.
Māridīn: town — see Mardin.
al-Marīyah: city, port — see Almeria.
Marj Aksās (Arabic): plain opposite Bālis — L4e4, 5.
Marj aṣ-Ṣuffar (Arabic): plain south of Damascus — L2f2, 6.
Marj Dābiq (Arabic): plain east of 'Azāz — L3e4, 5.
Marj 'Uyūn (Arabic: meadow of springs): plain between the Leontes and the upper Jordan — L1f2, 6.
Marmara, Sea of; Propontis (classical), Marmara Denizi (Turkish) — J4d5, 2.
al-Marqab (Arabic: the watch-tower), Margat (medieval): fortress — L1e5, 5, 9, 10, 12, 13, 14.
Marrakesh; Marrākush (Arabic): city — C2f4, 1.
Marseilles; Marseille (French): city, port — F1d2, 1.
Marturana (medieval), Martirano (Italian): town in Calabria 80 miles NE of Messina.
Martyropolis: town — see Maiyafariqin.
Marv: city — see Merv.
Marzban or Parzman (West Armenian), Marzubān (Arabic), Merzban (Turkish): fortress — L3e3, 5.
Mashḥalā (Arabic): village — L2e4, 5.
Maṣyāf or Maṣyāth or Maṣyād or Miṣyāf (Arabic): fortress — L2e5, 5, 10, 11, 12, 13, 14.
al-Maṭarīyah (Arabic): village 8 miles NE of Cairo.
Matera (Italian): town — H2d5, 2.
Maurienne (French): district of southern Savoy.
al-Mauṣil: city — see Mosul.
Mayence: city — see Mainz.
Mazara (Italian): port — G3e3, 2.
Mecca; Makkah (Arabic): city — L5h4, 3, 7, 8, 11.
Medina; al-Madīnah (Arabic: the city): city — L5h1, 3, 7, 8, 11.
Mediterranean Sea — 1, 2, 3.
Melas (classical): river east of Roussa.
Melfi (Italian): town — H1d4, 2.
Melitene (classical), Malaṭiyah (Arabic), Melden (West Armenian), Malatya (Turkish): city — L4e2, 7, 9, 10, 11, 12, 13.
Melk (German): town — H1c2, 2.
Melun (French): town 26 miles SE of Paris.
Meninx: island — see Jerba.
Meram (Turkish): valley west of Iconium.
Meran: medieval name for Croatia.
Mersivan (medieval), Merzifon (Turkish): town — L1d5, 3, 8.
Merv or Marv (Persian), Margiana (classical): city, now abandoned for nearby Mary — Q2e3, 4.
Merzban: fortress — see Marzban.

Mesopotamia; al-'Irāq (Arabic): region between the Euphrates and Tigris rivers — Mf, 3.
Messina (Italian): port — H1e2, 2.
Messina, Strait of: strait between Sicily and Italy.
Messines (French): village 33 miles north of Arras.
Metz (French): city — F2c1, 1.
Meuse (French), Maas (Flemish, Dutch): river — E5b4, 1.
Milan; Milano (Italian): city — F5c5, 1, 2.
Milly (French): village 50 miles NE of Châlons.
Mineo (Italian): town — G5e3, 2.
Minho (Portuguese), Miño (Spanish): river — C2d3, 1.
Mirabel (medieval): crusader castle 9 miles NNE of Lydda.
Miseno, Cape: point west of Naples.
Misilmeri (Italian): town — G4e2, 2.
Misis: town — see Mamistra.
Miṣr: region of NE Africa — see Egypt.
Miṣyāf: fortress — see Maṣyāf.
Miyafarkin: town — see Maiyafariqin.
Modena (Italian): town 24 miles WNW of Bologna.
Modica (Italian): town — G5e4, 2.
Moissac (French): town — E2d1, 1.
Molesme (French): village 65 miles NW of Dijon.
Monastir; Bitolj (Serbian): town — I2d4, 2.
Mondego (Portuguese): river — C2d5, 1.
Monferrato: district — see Montferrat.
Mons (French), Bergen (Flemish): city 45 miles south of Ghent.
Mons Pelegrinus: hill — see Pilgrim Mountain.
Mont Gisard (medieval), Gezer or Gazara (classical), Tall al-Jazar (Arabic): hill between Ramla and Ibelin.
Montaigu (French): town 50 miles SW of Angers.
Monte Cassino (Italian): abbey — G4d4, 2.
Monte Gargano (Italian): mountain shrine — H1d4, 2.
Montebello (Italian): village 13 miles south of Pavia.
Monteil (French): village 50 miles ENE of Moissac.
Montferrand: fortress — see Ba'rīn.
Montferrat (French), Monferrato (Italian): district south of upper Po river.
Montfort (French): village 25 miles WSW of Paris.
Montier-en-Der (French): village 40 miles SSE of Châlons.
Montlhéry (French): village 17 miles south of Paris.
Montmorency (French): village 10 miles north of Paris.
Montpellier (French): town — E4d2, 1.
Mopsuestia: town — see Mamistra.
Morava (Serbian): river — I2d, 2.
Moravia; Morava (Czech): region SE of Bohemia — Hc, 2.
Morocco; al-Maghrib al-Aqṣâ (Arabic: the farthest west): region of NW Africa — Cf, 1.
Mörs (German): town between Xanten and Neuss.
Moselle (French), Mosel (German): river — F3b5, 1, 2.
Moson: town — see Wieselburg.
Mosul; al-Mauṣil (Arabic), Musul (Turkish): city — M4e4, 3, 7, 8, 11.
Mozac (French): town, now unimportant — E4c5, 1.
Msis: town — see Mamistra.
al-Munaiṭirah (Arabic: the little lookout), Le Monestre or Le Moinestre (medieval): fortress — L1f1, 6.

Murcia (Spanish), Mursiyah (Arabic): city — D4e3, 1.
Musul: city — see Mosul.
Myriokephalon (classical), Chardak Boghazî (Turkish): pass — K4e1, 3.

Nablus; Neapolis (classical), Nābulus (Arabic): town — L1f3, 6, 7, 8, 14.
an-Nahr al-Aswad (Arabic: the black river), Kara-Su (Turkish: same) — L2e4, 5.
an-Nahr al-'Aujā' (Arabic: the crooked river) — K5f3, 6.
an-Nahr al-Auwalī (Arabic: the nearer river) — L1f2, 6.
Naisābūr: city — see Nishapur.
Naissus: town — see Nish.
Namrun: fortress — see Lampron.
Namur (French): town 36 miles wsw of Liége.
Napa: village — see Inab.
Naples; Napoli (Italian): city, port — G5d5, 2.
an-Naqīrah (Arabic): district south of Manbij — L3e4, 5.
an-Naqūrah (Arabic): hills along coast south of Tyre — L1f2, 6.
Narbonne (French): town — E4d2, 1.
Narni (Italian): town 40 miles north of Rome.
Naṣībīn: town — see Nisibin.
Natura: unidentified town near Constantinople.
Navarre; Navarra (Spanish): region of northern Spain — Dd, 1.
Nazareth; an-Nāṣirah (Arabic): town — L1f3, 6, 14.
Neapolis: town — see Nablus.
Near East: region from Egypt to Persia and Turkey to Aden.
Nederland: nation — see Netherlands.
Negroponte: island — see Euboea.
Neocaesarea, Pontic; Niksar (Turkish): town — L2d5, 3, 8.
Nephin (medieval), Anafah (Arabic): town — L1f1, 6.
Nesle (French): village 40 miles south of Arras.
Netherlands; Nederland (Dutch) : modern nation, larger than medieval Holland.
Neumünster (German): town — F5b1, 2.
Neuss (German): town — F2b4, 1, 2.
Nevers (French): town 35 miles east of Bourges.
Nicaea (classical), İznik (Turkish): town — J5d5, 2, 3, 7, 8, 11.
Nice (French): port — F3d2, 1, 2.
Nicomedia (classical), İzmit (Turkish): town — J5d5, 3, 7, 8, 11.
Nicomedia, Gulf of; İzmit Körfezi (Turkish): gulf west of Nicomedia.
Nicosia; Levkōsia (medieval Greek): town — K4e5, 3.
Niksar: town — see Neocaesarea.
Nile; Baḥr an-Nīl (Arabic): river — K3f4, 2, 3.
Nîmes (French): city — E5d2, 1.
Nish (Turkish, Serbian), Naissus or Nissa (classical): town — I2d2, 2.
Nishapur; Nīshāpūr (Persian), Naisābūr (Arabic): city — P4e4, 4.
Nisibin or Nusaybin (Turkish), Nisibis (classical), Naṣībīn or Nuṣaibīn (Arabic): town — M2e3, 3, 13.
Nistru: river — see Dniester.
Nitra (Czech): town — H4c2, 2.
Nogent (French): town 7 miles east of Paris.
Noire Garde (medieval): crusader castle — L1f2, 6.
Normandy; Normandie (French): region of northern France — DEc, 1.
North Africa: region from Morocco to Libya, north of the Sahara.
North Sea — 1, 2.

Norway; Norge (Norwegian): region of western Scandinavia — not in area mapped.
Noto (Italian): town — H1e4, 2.
Novalesa (Italian): village 70 miles west of Vercelli.
Novgorod (Russian): city and district in northern Russia — not in area mapped.
Noyon (French): town 29 miles west of Laon.
Nuremberg; Nürnberg (German): city — G2c1, 1, 2.
Nuṣaibīn or Nusaybin: town — see Nisibin.
Nyssa (classical): town, now abandoned — K5e1, 3.

Ochrida (medieval), Lychnidus or Achrida (classical), Ohrid (Serbian): town — I1d4, 2.
Ödenburg (German), Sopron (Hungarian): town — H2c3, 2.
Oder (German), Odra (Polish): river — G5b2, 1, 2.
Oea: city, port — see Tripoli.
Ofanto: river in SE Italy, flowing past Canosa into the Adriatic.
Ohrid: town — see Ochrida.
Olives, Mount of; Jabal aṭ-Ṭūr (Arabic): hill east of Jerusalem.
Olivola (medieval), Olivolo or Castello (Italian): district on lagoon of Venice.
Olmütz (German), Olomouc (Czech): town — H3c1, 2.
Oman; 'Umān (Arabic): region of eastern Arabia — Ph, 4.
Oporto; Pôrto (Portuguese), Burṭuqāl (Arabic): port — C2d4, 1.
Orange (French): town 13 miles north of Avignon.
Orense (Spanish), Ūriyah (Arabic): town — C3d3, 1.
Orkhon: river in Mongolia — not in area mapped.
Orkneys: island group north of Scotland — not in area mapped.
Orléans (French): city 75 miles SSW of Paris.
Orontes (classical), al-'Āṣī (Arabic: the rebellious): river — L1e4, 3, 5, 6.
Orte (Italian): village 35 miles north of Rome.
Ossero (Italian), Osor (Croatian): village on west coast of Cherso.
Ostia (Italian): village — G3d4, 2.
Ostmark: region east of Bavaria — see Austria.
Oultrejourdain: region east of the Jordan — see Transjordan.
Ourha: city — see Edessa.
Oviedo (Spanish): town — C5d2, 1.
Oxus (classical), Jaiḥūn (Persian, Arabic), Amu Darya (modern): river — P5d2, 4.

Pagrae: town — see Baghrās.
Palaiá Kórinthos: town — see Corinth.
Palanka (Croatian): town — H5c5, 2.
Palermo (Italian), Balarm (Arabic): city, port — G4e2, 2.
Palestine; Palaestina (classical), Filistīn (Arabic): region — KLf, 3.
Pali, Cape: headland near Dyrrachium — H5d4, 2.
Pallene: peninsula — see Cassandria.
Palmela (Portuguese): town 17 miles SE of Lisbon.
Palu (Turkish), Balona (medieval), Palou (West Armenian), Bālū (Arabic): fortress — L5e2, 3.
Pamplona (Spanish), Pampeluna (medieval), Banbalūnah (Arabic): town — D4d3, 1.
Paneas: town — see Banyas.
Panidos (medieval): port, now abandoned, 5 miles SSW of Rodosto.
Pannonhalma: monastery — see Saint Martin.
Pantelleria: island — G3e4, 1, 2.

Paphlagonia (classical): region of northern Anatolia — Kd, 3.
Paphos (medieval Greek): island, port — K3f1, 3.
Paris (French): city — E3c2, 1.
Parma (Italian): town 55 miles WNW of Bologna.
Partzapert (medieval), Partsrpert (West Armenian): fortress — L1e3, 9, 10.
Parzman: fortress — see Marzban.
Passau (German): town — G4c2, 1, 2.
Pavia (Italian): town — F5c5, 1.
Payens or Payns (French): village NW of Troyes, 35 miles ESE of Provins.
Peiting (German): village 100 miles west of Salzburg.
Pelagonia (classical): district NW of Macedonia.
Pelecanum or Pelecanon (medieval): fortress — J5d5, 3, 7.
Pelusium (classical), al-Faramā' (Arabic): town — K3f4, 3, 8.
Pera or Estanor (medieval), Beyoghlu (Turkish): port east of the Golden Horn opposite Constantinople.
Perche (French): district west of Chartres.
Périgueux (French): town 50 miles SW of Limoges.
Persia; Īrān (Persian): region — NOf, 3, 4.
Persian Gulf — NOg, 4.
Philadelphia (classical), Alashehir (Turkish): town — J4e2, 2, 7, 11.
Philippopolis (classical), Plovdiv (Bulgarian): town — I5d3, 2, 3.
Philomelium (Latin), Philomēlion (medieval Greek), Akshehir (Turkish: white city): town — K2e2, 3, 7, 8.
Phrygia (classical): region of central Anatolia — Ke, 2.
Piacenza (Italian): town — F5c5, 1.
Picardy; Picardie (French): region of northern France — Eb, 1.
Picos de Europa (Spanish): peak in Cantabrian mountains.
Picquigny (French): town 40 miles SW of Arras.
Pilgrim Mountain; Mons Pelegrinus (medieval): hill overlooking Tripoli.
Pisa (Italian): port, now city — G1d2, 1, 2.
Pisidia (classical): region of southern Anatolia — Ke, 2, 3.
Pistoia (Italian): town — G1d2, 1.
Placentia: town — see Comana.
Plancy (French): village 35 miles SW of Châlons.
Plötzkau (German): village 28 miles south of Magdeburg.
Plovdiv: town — see Philippopolis.
Po (Italian): river — G3d1, 1, 2.
Podandus (classical), Boudantē (West Armenian), Pozantî (Turkish): town 40 miles east of Heraclea.
Poissy (French): town — E3c2, 1.
Poitiers (French): town — E1c4, 1.
Poitou (French): region of western France — Dc, 1.
Poland; Polska (Polish): region — HIb, 2.
Polotsk (Russian): town — J4a5, 2.
Polybotus (classical), Bolvadin (Turkish): town — K2e2, 3, 7.
Pomerania; Pommern (German): region south of the Baltic — Hb2, 1, 2.
Pontarlier (French): town — F2c4, 1.
Ponthieu (French): district of western Picardy.
Pontus (classical): region of northern Anatolia — Ld, 3.
Ponza (Italian): island — G3d5, 2.
Porsuk (-Su): river — see Tembris.
Port Said: modern port at northern end of Suez Canal.
Porto (Italian): village — G3d4, 2.
Pôrto: port — see Oporto.

Portugal; Lusitania (classical): region north of the Douro river, now a nation extending farther south — Cd, 1.
Posen (German), Poznań (Polish): town — H2b3, 2.
Potidaea or Potídhaia: peninsula — see Cassandria.
Pozanti?: town — see Podandus.
Prague; Praha (Czech): city — G5b5, 1, 2.
Preslav (Bulgarian): town — J2d2, 2, 3, 7.
Propontis — see Marmara, Sea of.
Provence (French): region of SE France — EFd, 1.
Provins (French): town — E4c2, 1.
Ptolemaïs: city, port — see Acre.
Puglie: region of SE Italy — see Apulia.
Pylae Ciliciae: pass — see Cilician Gates.
Pyramus (classical), Chahan (West Armenian), Jaiḥān (Arabic), Jeyhan (Turkish): river — L1e4, 3, 5.
Pyrenees: mountain range — DEd, 1.

al-Qadmūs (Arabic): fortress — L2e5, 5.
al-Qāhirah: city — see Cairo.
al-Qairawān: city — see Kairawan.
Qaisārīyah: port — see Caesarea.
al-Qal'ah: town — see Alcalá de Henares.
Qal'at al-Muḍīq: town — see Apamea.
Qal'at ar-Rūm (Arabic: fort of Rome), Ranculat (medieval), Hṛomgla (West Armenian), Rum Kalesi (Turkish): fortress — L3e3, 5.
Qal'at ash-Shaqīf: crusader castle — see Belfort.
Qal'at Ja'bar or Qal'at Dausar (Arabic): fortress — L4e5, 5, 9, 12.
Qal'at Najm (Arabic: fort of a star): fortress — L4e4, 5.
Qālīqalā: city — see Erzerum.
Qandahār: city — see Kandahar.
Qarqar: town — see Gargar.
Qazvīn or Qazwīn: city — see Kazvin.
Qinnasrīn (Arabic), Chalcis ad Belum (classical): town, now unimportant — L2e4, 5.
al-Quds: city — see Jerusalem.
al-Qulai'ah (Arabic: the small fort), Coliat (medieval): fortress — L2f1, 5, 10.
Qulumrīyah: town — see Coimbra.
Qūniyah: city — see Iconium.
Qūriṣ: town — see Cyrrhus.
Qūriyah: town — see Coria.
Qurṭubah: city — see Cordova.
Quṣair (Arabic: little castle), Cursat (medieval): town, now unimportant — L2e4, 5, 10.

Raban (Turkish), Ṛaban (West Armenian), Ra'bān (Arabic): fortress — L3e3, 5, 9, 10, 13.
Rafanīyah (Arabic): town — L2f1, 5, 9, 10.
Ragusa (Italian): town — G5e4, 2.
Ragusa (medieval), Rhausium (classical), Dubrovnik (Serbian): port — H4d3, 2.
Rahba; ar-Raḥbah (Arabic): town — M1e5, 3, 12.
Raiy: town — see Rayy.
Rametta or Rometta (Italian): town 5 miles SW of Messina.
Ramla; Rama or Rames (medieval), ar-Ramlah (Arabic: the sandy): town — K5f4, 6, 7, 8, 9, 11, 12, 13, 14.

Rancon (French): village 22 miles north of Limoges.
Ranculat: fortress — see Qal'at ar-Rūm.
Raqqa; ar-Raqqah (Arabic: subject to flooding): town — L5e5, 3.
Ra's al-'Ain (Arabic: headland of the spring): town — M1e4, 3.
Ra's al-Mā' (Arabic: headland of the water): village — L2f3, 6.
Ra's ash-Shaq'ah or (colloquial) Ra's Shakkā (Arabic): cape SW of Tripoli — L1f1, 6.
Ratisbon: town — see Regensburg.
Ravendan; Rāwandān (Arabic), Arevîntan (West Armenian), Ravendel (medieval), Ravanda (Turkish): fortress — L3e4, 5, 7, 13.
Ravenna (Italian): port, now town — G3d1, 1, 2.
Rayy; Rhages or Rhagae (classical), Raiy (Persian): town, now abandoned in favor of Teheran — O2e5, 4.
Red Sea — Lgh, 3.
Regensburg (German), Ratisbon (medieval): town — G3c1, 1, 2.
Reggio di Calabria (Italian): port — H1e2, 2.
Rhausium: port — see Ragusa.
Rheims; Reims (French): city — E5c1, 1.
Rhine; Rhin (French), Rhein (German), Rijn (Dutch): river — E5b4, 1, 2.
Rhineland: region of the middle Rhine.
Rhinocolura: town — see al-'Arīsh.
Rhodes; Rhodus (classical), Ródhos (modern Greek): island — Je, 2, 3, 7, 8, 11.
Rhoedestus: port — see Rodosto.
Rhone; Rhône (French): river — E5d2, 1.
Ribagorza (Spanish): district south of central Pyrenees, east of Sobrarbe.
Ribemont (French): village 19 miles NNW of Laon.
Ridefort (French): unidentified place, perhaps Rochefort or Bedford.
ar-Rīḥā: town — see Jericho.
Rijn: river — see Rhine.
Roaix or Rouaix (French): village 23 miles NNE of Avignon.
Robecque or Robecq (French): village 23 miles NNW of Arras.
Rochefort (French): town 35 miles SSW of Liége.
Rodez (French): town 80 miles NE of Toulouse.
Ródhos: island — see Rhodes.
Rodosto (medieval), Bisanthe or Rhoedestus (classical), Tekirdagh (modern Turkish): port — J3d5, 2, 3.
Romania: medieval name for Anatolia.
Rome; Roma (Italian): city — G3d4, 1, 2.
Rometta: town — see Rametta.
Rouaix: village — see Roaix.
Roucy (French): village 14 miles NW of Rheims.
Rouen (French): city — E2c1, 1.
Roussa or Rusköy or Ruskeshan (medieval), Keshan (Turkish): town — J2d5, 2.
Ruad; Aradus (classical), Arwād or Ruwād (Arabic): island — L1f1, 5.
Rue (French): village 55 miles west of Arras.
Rufinel: unidentified fortress near Pelecanum.
Rugia (medieval), ar-Rūj (Arabic): valley — L2e5, 5.
Rugia: crusader castle — see Chastel-Rouge.
ar-Ruhā': city — see Edessa.
Rum Kalesi: fortress — see Qal'at ar-Rūm.
ar-Ruṣāfah (Arabic): fortress 4 miles SW of Maṣyāf.
Ruskeshan or Rusköy: town — see Roussa.
Russia: region of eastern Europe — JKb, 2.
Ruwād: island — see Ruad.

Sabtah: port — see Ceuta.
Sachsen: region — see Saxony.
Sacralias or Sagrajas: battlefield — see Zallaca.
Safad; Saphet (medieval), Ṣafad (Arabic): town — L1f3, 6, 10, 14.
Ṣaffūrīyah (Arabic), Sepphoris (classical): village 5 miles NNW of Nazareth.
Ṣāfīthā or Ṣāfītā (Arabic): town just west of Chastel-Blanc.
Sagitta: port — see Sidon.
Sahan or Saiḥān: river — see Sarus.
Sahara; aṣ-Ṣahrā' (Arabic): desert — EFGf, 1, 2.
Ṣahyūn: crusader castle — see Saone.
Ṣaidā': port — see Sidon.
Saiḥūn: river — see Jaxartes.
Saijar: fortress — see Shaizar.
Saint Abraham: town — see Hebron.
Saint Amand (French): town 25 miles south of Bourges.
Saint Aubin (French): abbey at Angers.
Saint Bénigne (French): abbey at Dijon.
Saint Bertin (French): abbey 45 miles NW of Arras.
Saint Cybar (French): abbey at Angoulême, 55 miles west of Limoges.
Saint Denis (French): town 7 miles north of Paris.
Saint George: town — see Lydda.
Saint Gilles (French): village 13 miles SSE of Nîmes.
Saint John or Saint Jean: city, port — see Acre.
Saint John: village near Gargar.
Saint Martin; Pannonhalma (Hungarian): monastery 50 miles west of Buda.
Saint Médard (French): town 8 miles WNW of Bordeaux.
Saint Omer (French): town 40 miles NW of Arras.
Saint Simeon (medieval), as-Suwaidīyah (Arabic), Süveydiye (Turkish): port — L1e4, 5, 9.
Saintonge (French): district of SW Aquitaine.
Sakartvelo: region east of the Black Sea — see Georgia.
Sakarya: river — see Sangarius.
Salamanca (Spanish), Salmantiqah (Arabic): city — C5d5, 1.
Salamia (medieval), İsmil (Turkish): town — K4e3, 3, 8.
Salamyah or (colloquial) Salamīyah (Arabic): town — L3e5, 5.
Saldae: port — see Bougie.
Salerno (Italian): port — G5d5, 2.
Salisbury: city 80 miles WSW of London.
Salmantiqah: city — see Salamanca.
Salonika: port — see Thessalonica.
Salzburg (German): city — G4c3, 1, 2.
Sam (Turkish), Sām (Arabic): town — L3e3, 5.
Samaria: district of northern Palestine — L1f3, 6.
Samarkand; Samarqand (Persian, Arabic): city — R2e1, 4.
Samarra; Sāmarrā' (Arabic): town — M4f1, 3.
Sammūrah: town — see Zamora.
Samosata (medieval), Samousad (West Armenian), Sumaisāṭ (Arabic), Samsat (Turkish): town — L4e3, 5, 7, 8, 9, 10, 11, 12, 13, 14.
San Chrysogono (medieval), San Crisogono (Italian): church at Rome with titular cardinal-priest.
San Vincenzo (Italian: Saint Vincent): abbey 17 miles NE of Monte Cassino.
Sangarius (classical), Sakarya (Turkish): river — K1d4, 2, 3.
Sanja; Singa (classical), Shnchē (West Armenian), Sanjah (Arabic), Gök (-Su) (Turkish): river — L4e3, 5.

Sansego (Italian), Sušak (Croatian): island SW of Cherso.
Santarem; Santarém (Portuguese), Shantarīn (Arabic): town — C2e1, 1.
Santiago de Compostela: town — see Compostela.
Saone (medieval), Ṣahyūn or Ṣihyaun (Arabic): crusader castle — L2e5, 5, 10, 14.
Saphet: town — see Safad.
Saracinesco (Italian): town — G3d3, 2.
Saragossa; Zaragoza (Spanish), Saraqusṭah (Arabic): city — D5d4, 1.
Sardica: city — see Sofia.
Sardinia; Sardegna (Italian): island — Fde, 1, 2.
Sardone: village — see Zardanā.
Sarì (-Su): river — see Bathys.
Sarmadā (Arabic): village — L2e4, 5.
Sarmīn (Arabic), Sermin (medieval): town — L2e5, 5.
Sarūj (Arabic), Bathnae (classical), Sororgia (medieval), Suruch or Sürüch (Turkish): town — L4e4, 5, 7, 9, 10, 11, 12, 13, 14.
Sarus (classical), Sahan (Armenian), Saiḥān (Arabic), Seyhan (Turkish): river — K5e4, 3.
Sava or Save (Croatian), Sau (German), Száva (Hungarian): river — Ic5, 1, 2.
Savoy; Savoie (French): region west of Lombardy — F2c5, 1, 2.
as-Sawād (Arabic: the black lands): district east of Lake Tiberias — L1f3, 6.
Saxony; Sachsen (German): region then of NW Germany — F5b3, 1, 2.
Scandinavia: region of northern Europe.
Scheyern (German): village 45 miles SW of Regensburg.
Schwaben: region of SW Germany — see Swabia.
Sclavonia: medieval name for Dalmatia, and other Slavic regions.
Scotland: region north of England — Da, 1.
Scutari (Italian), Scodra (classical), Shkodër (Albanian): town — H5d3, 2.
Scythopolis: town — see Baisan.
Sebastia (classical), Sīwās (Arabic), Sìvas (Turkish): city — L3e1, 3, 7, 8, 11.
Segni (Italian): town 30 miles ESE of Rome.
Seine (French): river — E1c1, 1.
Seleucia (medieval), Selevgia (West Armenian), Silifke (Turkish): port, now town — K4e4, 3, 7, 8.
Selymbria (classical), Silivri (Turkish): port — J4d4, 2.
Semlin (medieval), Zemun (Croatian): town — I1d1, 2.
Sennabris: village — see aṣ-Ṣinnabrah.
Sens (French): town 27 miles south of Provins.
Sepphoris: village — see Ṣaffūrīyah.
Septa: port — see Ceuta.
Serbia; Srbija (Serbian): region east of Croatia and Dalmatia — HId, 2.
Sermin: town — see Sarmīn.
Sestus (Latin), Sēstos (medieval Greek): town, now abandoned — J2d5, 2, 11.
Seville; Sevilla (Spanish), Ishbīliyah (Arabic): city — C5e3, 1.
Seyhan: river — see Sarus.
Shabakhtan; Shabakhtān (Arabic): district east of Harran.
Shahrazūr (Persian): district east of the Tigris — MNe, 3.
Shaizar (medieval Arabic), Larissa (classical), Saijar (modern Arabic): fortress — L2e5, 5, 7, 8, 9, 10, 11, 12, 13, 14.
ash-Sha'm: city — see Damascus.
ash-Sha'm: region — see Syria.
Shantarīn: town — see Santarem.
Shaqīf Arnūn: crusader castle — see Belfort.
Shaqīf Tīrūn: cave fortress — see Tyron.
Sharqiya; ash-Sharqīyah (Arabic: the eastern): district between the Nile and Sinai.

ash-Shārrāt — see Guadarrama Mountains.
ash-Shaubak: fortress — see Krak de Montréal.
Shenchrig; Singae Pons (classical), Shnchrig (West Armenian): fortress — L4e3, 5, 9.
Shetlands: island group north of the Orkneys — not in area mapped.
Shiraz; Shīrāz (Persian, Arabic): city — O3g1, 4.
Shirvan; Shirvān (Persian): coastal region east of the Caucasus — N4d4, 2, 4.
Shkodër: town — see Scutari.
Shnchē: river — see Sanja.
Shnchrig: fortress — see Shenchrig.
Shqipni or Shqipri: region NW of Epirus — see Albania.
Sibilla: town — see Zawīlah.
Sicily; Sicilia (Italian), Ṣiqillīyah (Arabic): island — Ge, 1, 2.
Sidon; Ṣaidā' (Arabic), Sagitta (medieval): port — L1f2, 3, 6, 7, 8, 9, 11, 12, 14.
Ṣiffīn (Arabic): village — L4e5, 5, 9.
Ṣihyaun: crusader castle — see Saone.
Sijilmasa; Sijilmāsah (Arabic): city, now abandoned — D1f4, 1.
Sijistān: region of Afghanistan — see Sistan.
Silifke: port, now town — see Seleucia.
Silistra or Silistria: town — see Dristra.
Silivri: port — see Selymbria.
Siloam, Pool of: pool SE of Jerusalem.
Silpius, Mount (classical), Ziyaret Daghî (Turkish) — L2e4, 5.
Silvan: town — see Maiyafariqin.
Simancas (Spanish): town — D1d4, 1.
Sinai; Sīnā' (Arabic): peninsula — Kg, 3.
Sinai, Mount, or Mount Horeb; Jabal Mūsâ (Arabic: mountain of Moses): mountain monastery — K4g2, 3.
Sind: region west of the Indus — Rg, 4.
Singa: river — see Sanja.
Singae Pons: fortress — see Shenchrig.
Sinjar; Sinjār (Arabic): town — M2e4, 7, 8, 11.
aṣ-Ṣinnabrah or Sinn an-Nabrah (Arabic), Sennabris (classical): village west of the Jordan and south of Lake Tiberias.
Sinope; Sinōpē (medieval Greek), Sinop (Turkish): port — L1d3, 3, 8.
Sintra: town — see Cintra.
Sinus Issicus — see Alexandretta, Gulf of.
Sion or Zion, Mount: hill NE of Jerusalem.
Ṣiqillīyah: island — see Sicily.
Siracusa: town — see Syracuse.
Siryāqūs (Arabic): town 12 miles NNE of Cairo.
Sis (Armenian, medieval), Kozan (Turkish): town — L1e3, 5.
Sistan; Sijistān or Sīstān (Persian): region of Afghanistan — Qf, 4.
Sîvas or Sīwās: city — see Sebastia.
Smolensk (Russian): city — K3b1, 2.
Smyrna (medieval), İzmir (Turkish): city, port — J3e2, 2, 3, 7, 8, 11.
Sobrarbe (Spanish): district south of central Pyrenees.
Sofia; Sardica (classical), Sofiya (Bulgarian): city — I4d3, 2.
Soghdia: ancient name for Transoxiana and adjacent regions.
Soissons (French): town 20 miles SW of Laon.
Sopron: town — see Ödenburg.
Sororgia: town — see Sarūj.
Sorrento (Italian): port 12 miles west of Amalfi.
Spain; España (Spanish): region south of the Pyrenees.

Spalato (medieval), Split (Serbian): port — H2d2, 2.
Speyer (German), Spires (French): town — F4c1, 1, 2.
Spoleto (Italian): town 55 miles north of Rome.
Srbija: region — see Serbia.
Stavelot (French): town 25 miles SE of Liège.
Steiermark: region — see Styria.
Stenay (French): town 55 miles NW of Metz.
Stettin (German), Szczecin (Polish): port — G5b2, 1, 2.
Strassburg (German), Strasbourg (French): city — F3c2, 1, 2.
Studium: monastery in Constantinople.
Styria; Steiermark (German): region east of Carinthia — Hc, 2.
Subiaco (Italian): town — G4d4, 2.
Sudan; as-Sūdān (Arabic: the Negro-lands): region south of Egypt — Kh, 3.
Suez; as-Suwais (Arabic): isthmus and port — K3g1, 3.
Sully (French): town — E3c3, 1.
Sultan Daghî (Turkish): mountain between Philomelium and Pisidian Antioch.
Sulzbach (German): town 30 miles east of Nuremberg.
Sumaisāṭ: town — see Samosata.
Ṣūr: port — see Tyre.
Sūriyah: region — see Syria.
Surrey: region of England south of London.
Suruch or Sürüch: town — see Sarūj.
Susa; Hadrumetum (classical), Sūsah (Arabic): port — G1e5, 1, 2.
Sušak: island — see Sansego.
Susiana: region of SW Persia — see Khuzistan.
Süveydiye or as-Suwaidīyah: port — see Saint Simeon.
as-Suwais: isthmus and port — see Suez.
Swabia; Schwaben (German): region of SW Germany — Fc, 1, 2.
Sweden; Sverige (Swedish): region of eastern Scandinavia, smaller than modern nation — not in area mapped.
Switzerland: region in Alps.
Syr Darya: river — see Jaxartes.
Syracuse; Siracusa (Italian): town — H1e3, 2.
Syria (classical), ash-Sha'm or Sūriyah (Arabic): region — Lf, 3.
Syrian Gates; La Portelle (medieval), Touṛn (Armenian), Belen Boghazî (Turkish): pass over Amanus range — L2e4, 5.
Száva: river — see Sava.
Szczecin: port — see Stettin.

Tabaristan; Ṭabaristān (Persian, Arabic): region between Caspian Sea and the Elburz range — Oe, 3, 4.
Ṭabarīyah: town — see Tiberias.
Tabriz; Tabrīz (Persian), Tibrīz (Arabic): city — N2e2, 3, 4.
Tagus (classical), Tajo (Spanish), Tejo (Portuguese): river — C1e2, 1.
Taik; Tayḳ (East Armenian): region of western Armenia — Md, 3.
Taimā' (Arabic): town — L4g3, 3.
Takrīt (Arabic): village — L2f1, 5.
Talavera or Talavera de la Reina (Spanish), Ṭalabīrah (Arabic): town — D1e1, 1.
Tall Aghdī or A'dī (Arabic): village — L2e4, 5.
Tall al-'Ashtarā (Arabic): hill overlooking al-'Ashtarā.
Tall al-Jazar: hill — see Mont Gisard.
Tall al-Qāḍī (Arabic: hill of the judge), Dan or Laish (classical): village just west of Banyas.
at-Tall aṣ-Ṣāfiyah: crusader castle — see Blanche Garde.

Tall as-Sulṭān (Arabic: hill of the sultan): village — L2e5, 5.
Tall ash-Shaikh (Arabic: hill of the chieftain): village — L2f1, 5.
Tall Bāshir: fortress — see Tell Bashir.
Tall Dānīth (Arabic): hill east of Dānīth.
Tall Khālid (Arabic): village — L3e4, 5.
Tall Qabbāsīn (Arabic): village — L3e4, 5.
Tanaïs: river — see Don.
Tangier; Tingis (classical), Ṭanjah (Arabic): port — C5e5, 1.
Taormina (Italian): port — H1e3, 2.
Ṭarābulus: city, port — see Tripoli.
Ṭarābulus al-Gharb: city, port — see Tripoli.
Taranto (Italian): port — H3d5, 2.
Tarragona (Spanish), Ṭarrakūnah (Arabic): port — E2d4, 1.
Tarsus (classical, Turkish), Darsous (West Armenian): city — K5e4, 3, 7, 8, 9, 10, 11, 12, 13, 14.
Tarsus-Chayi̊: river — see Cydnus.
Ṭarṭūs: port — see Tortosa.
Tashkent; Binkath or Tāshkand (Arabic), Tāshkend (Persian): city — R5d4, 4.
Ṭaudhah: town — see Tuy.
Taurus (classical), Toros Daghlari̊ (Turkish): mountain range — KLe, 2.
Tayḳ: region — see Taik.
Tbilisi: city — see Tiflis.
Tejo: river — see Tagus.
Tekirdagh: port — see Rodosto.
Tell Bashir; Tall Bāshir (Arabic), Ṭlbashar (West Armenian), Turbessel (medieval), Tilbeshar (Turkish): fortress — L3e4, 5, 7, 8, 9, 10, 11, 12, 13, 14.
Tembris (classical), Porsuk (-Su) (Turkish): river — K2e1, 3.
Tevere: river — see Tiber.
Thabaria: town — see Tiberias.
Thebes; Thēvai (ancient Greek), Thívai (modern Greek): city — I4e2, 2.
Theodosia or Kaffa (medieval): port, now unimportant — L1c5, 3.
Theodosiopolis: city — see Erzerum.
Thessalonica (medieval), Salonika (Italian), Thessaloníki (modern Greek): port — I3d5, 2.
Thēvai or Thívai: town — see Thebes.
Thouars (French): town 40 miles NW of Poitiers.
Thrace; Thracia (Latin), Thrakē (ancient Greek), Thráki (modern Greek), Trakya (Turkish): region south of Bulgaria — Jd, 3.
Thuringia; Thüringen (German): region of central Germany — Gb, 1, 2.
Tiber; Tevere (Italian): river — G3d4, 2.
Tiberias; Ṭabarīyah (Arabic), Thabaria (medieval): town — L1f3, 3, 6, 7, 8, 9, 11, 12, 13, 14.
Tiberias, Lake, or Sea of Galilee; Buḥairat Ṭabarīyah (Arabic) — L1f3, 6.
Tibnīn (Arabic): village just west of Toron.
Tibrīz: city — see Tabriz.
Tiflis; Tiflīs (Persian, Arabic), Tbilisi (Georgian): city — M5d4, 3, 4.
Tigris (classical), Dijlah (Arabic), Dijle (Turkish): river — N4f5, 3, 4.
Tilbeshar: fortress — see Tell Bashir.
Tilimsān: city — see Tlemcen.
Tingis: port — see Tangier.
Tinnis; Tinnīs (Arabic): town, now unimportant — K3f4, 3, 8.
Tīzīn (Arabic): village — L2e4, 5.
Ṭlbashar: fortress — see Tell Bashir.

Tlemcen; Tilimsān (Arabic): city — D4f1, 1.
Toëni: castle — see Tosni.
Toledo (Spanish), Ṭulaiṭulah (Arabic): city — D1e1, 1.
Tollenburg — see Tulln and Bruck an der Leitha.
Tonnerre (French): town 45 miles WSW of Clairvaux.
Torino: town — see Turin.
Toro (Spanish): town — C5d4, 1.
Toroge (medieval), Tour Rouge (French): unidentified place, probably in Spain.
Toron (medieval): fortress — L1f2, 6, 14.
Toros (Daghlarï): mountain range — see Taurus.
Tortona (Italian): town 24 miles SW of Pavia.
Tortosa (Spanish), Ṭurṭūshah (Arabic): town — E1d5, 1.
Tortosa; Antaradus (classical: opposite Aradus), Anṭarṭūs or Ṭarṭūs (Arabic): port — L1f1, 5, 7, 8, 9, 12, 13, 14.
Toscana: region of central Italy — see Tuscany.
Tosni (medieval), Toëni (French): castle just west of Conches, 35 miles south of Rouen.
Toul (French): town — F1c2, 1.
Toulouse (French): city — E2d2, 1.
Tour Rouge — see Toroge.
Touraine (French): region of central France — E1c3, 1.
Tourn: pass — see Syrian Gates.
Tournai (French), Doornijk (Flemish): town 35 miles NE of Arras.
Tours (French): town — E1c3, 1.
Trabzon: city, port — see Trebizond.
Trajetto (Italian): village on the Garigliano river, 10 miles ENE of Gaeta.
Trakya: region — see Thrace.
Trani (Italian): port — H2d4, 2.
Transjordan; Oultrejourdain (medieval): region east of the Jordan — L1f3, 6.
Transoxiana: region NE of the Oxus — QRde, 4.
Trapesac: town — see Darbsāk.
Trebizond; Trapezus (classical), Trapezunt (medieval), Trabzon (Turkish): city, port — L5d5, 3, 7, 8, 11.
Tremelay or Dramelay (French): village 45 miles east of Cluny.
Trier (German), Trèves (French): city — F2c1, 1, 2.
Tripoli; Tripolis (classical), Ṭarābulus (Arabic): city, port — L1f1, 3, 5, 6, 7, 8, 9, 10, 11, 12, 13, 14.
Tripoli; Oea (classical), Ṭarābulus al-Gharb (Arabic): city, port — G4f3, 2.
Troia (Italian): town — H1d4, 2.
Troina (Italian): town — G5e3, 2.
Troyes (French): town 35 miles WNW of Clairvaux.
Tudela (Spanish), Tuṭilāh (Arabic): town 50 miles NW of Saragossa.
Ṭulaiṭulah: city — see Toledo.
Tulln (German): town 18 miles NW of Vienna, possibly medieval Tollenburg.
Tunis; Tūnis (Arabic): city — G1e4, 1, 2.
Tunisia; Ifrīqiyah (Arabic): region of North Africa — Fe, 1, 2.
Turbessel: fortress — see Tell Bashir.
Turenne (French): village 60 miles SSE of Limoges.
Turin; Torino (Italian): town 28 miles WNW of Asti.
Turkestan: region NE of the Jaxartes — QRc, 4.
Turkey; Turkiye (Turkish): modern nation, holding Anatolia, Armenia, and parts of Thrace and Kurdistan.
Ṭurṭūshah: town — see Tortosa.
Tuscany; Toscana (Italian): region of central Italy — Gd, 1, 2.

Tuṭīlah: town — see Tudela.
Tuy (Spanish), Ṭaudhah (Arabic): town — C2d3, 1.
Tyana (medieval): town, now abandoned in favor of Bor, 38 miles NE of Heraclea.
Tyras: river — see Dniester.
Tyre; Tyrus (classical), Ṣūr (Arabic): city, port — L1f2, 3, 6, 7, 8, 9, 10, 11, 12, 13, 14.
Tyron (medieval), Shaqīf Tīrūn (Arabic): cave fortress — L1f2, 6, 10, 12.
Tyrrhenian Sea — Gd, 1, 2.

al-'Ullaiqah (Arabic), Laicas (medieval): fortress — L2e5, 5.
Ulubad: town — see Lopadium.
'Umān: region of eastern Arabia — see Oman.
al-Uqḥuwānah (Arabic): battlefield — L1f3, 6.
al-Urdunn: river — see Jordan.
Urfa: city — see Edessa.
Ūriyah: town — see Orense.
al-Ushbūnah: city, port — see Lisbon.
Utica (classical): port, now abandoned — G1e3, 2.
Utrecht (Dutch): city — F1b3, 1, 2.

Vahka; Vahga (West Armenian), Feke (Turkish): fortress — L1e3, 3, 9, 10, 12, 13, 14.
Val Demone (Italian): eastern district of northern coast of Sicily.
Valania (medieval), Bulunyās (medieval Arabic), Bāniyās (modern Arabic): port — L1e5, 5, 14.
Valence (French): town — E5d1, 1.
Valencia (Spanish), Balansiyah (Arabic): city, port — D5e1, 1.
Valentinois (French): district around Valence.
Vallombrosa (Italian): monastery 15 miles east of Florence.
Valois (French): district NE of Paris.
Valona: port — see Avlona.
Van, Lake; Van Gölü (Turkish) — M3e2, 3.
Vardar (medieval, modern), Axius (classical): river — I3d5, 2.
Varenne: castle — see Warenne.
Vaspurkan; Vaspourakan (East Armenian): region east of Lake Van — Me, 3.
Vaudémont (French): village 21 miles SE of Toul.
Vendeuil (French): village 16 miles NW of Laon.
Vendôme (French): town 35 miles NE of Tours.
Venice; Venezia (Italian): city, port — G3c5, 1, 2.
Venosa (Italian): town 9 miles ESE of Melfi.
Vercelli (Italian): town — F4c5, 1.
Verdun (French): town 35 miles west of Metz.
Vermandois (French): district of eastern Picardy.
Verona (Italian): city 65 miles west of Venice.
Vetralla (Italian): town — G3d3, 1, 2.
Vézelay (French): town — E4c3, 1.
Vienna; Wien (German): city — H2c2, 2.
Vienne (French): town 16 miles south of Lyons.
Vijosë: river — see Viyosa.
Viminacium: town — see Branits.
Viseu or Vizeu (Portuguese): town — C2d5, 1.
Vistula; Wisla (Polish), Weichsel (German): river — HIb, 2.
Vitry (French): town 19 miles SE of Châlons.
Vivar or Bivar or Viver (Spanish): town — D5e1, 1.

Viyosa; Vijosë (Albanian): river — H5d5, 2.
Vizeu: town — see Viseu.
Vlaanderen: region of northern France and Belgium — see Flanders.
Vlachia: region north of Bulgaria — see Wallachia.
Vlonë: port — see Avlona.
Vodena (medieval), Édhessa (modern Greek): town — I3d5, 2.
Volga (Russian), Itil (Tartar): river — N3c4, 3, 4.
Volturno (Italian): river flowing past Capua.

Wādī Buṭnān (Arabic): valley east of Aleppo — L3e4, 5.
Wādi-l-ʿArabah (Arabic): valley — L1f5, 3.
Wādī-l-Ḥijārah: town — see Guadalajara.
Wādī-t-Taim (Arabic): valley west of Mount Hermon — L1f2, 6.
Wālā (Arabic): village — L1f4, 6, 13.
Wales: region west of England — Db, 1.
Wallachia; Vlachia (medieval): region north of Bulgaria — Jd, 2, 3.
Warenne; Varenne or Guarenne (French): castle just south of Arques, 32 miles north of Rouen.
Washqah: town — see Huesca.
Wāsiṭ (Arabic: middle): town, now abandoned — N2f4, 3, 4.
Weichsel: river — see Vistula.
Weser (German): river — F5b2, 1.
Wevelinghofen (German): town 7 miles ssw of Neuss.
Wien: city — see Vienna.
Wieselburg (German), Moson (Hungarian): town — H3c3, 2.
Wisla: river — see Vistula.
Worms (German): town — F4c1, 1, 2.
Wrocław: city — see Breslau.

Xanten (German): town — F2b4, 2.
Xerigordon (medieval): fortress near Nicaea.

Yabnâ: town — see Ibelin.
Yāfā: port — see Jaffa.
Yaghra; al-Yaghrā (Arabic): village — L2e4, 5.
Yaḥmur (Arabic), Chastel-Rouge (medieval): fortress — L1f1, 5.
Yalak (-Deresi): river — see Dracon.
Yarmuk; Yarmūk (Arabic): river — L1f3, 6.
Yemen; al-Yaman (Arabic: the right hand): region of sw Arabia — not in area mapped.
Yenishehir: town — see ʿImm.

az-Zabadanī (Arabic): town — L2f2, 6.
Zagreb (Croatian): town — H1c5, 2.
Zähringen (German): village 39 miles south of Strassburg.
Zallaca; Sacralias or Sagrajas (Spanish), az-Zallāqah (Arabic): battlefield — C4e2, 1.
Zamora (Spanish), Sammūrah (Arabic): town — C5d4, 1.
Zaragoza: city — see Saragossa.
Zardanā (Arabic), Sardone (medieval): village — L2e4, 5.
Zawīlah (Arabic), Sibilla (medieval): town — G2e5, 2.
Zemun: town — see Semlin.
Zion, Mount — see Sion, Mount.
Ziyaret Daghî — see Silpius, Mount.
Zūrʿ (Arabic): fortress — L2e5, 5.

Important Towns and Fortresses

Supplementing the dates appearing on the historical maps for changes in control of towns and fortresses, the following list provides as complete an outline as possible of this information for 100 of the most important places in or near the crusaders' states for the period 1097–1189. The initials of Armenians, Byzantines, Franks, and Moslems, and X for the Assassins, indicate their possession of a place in 1097 or its subsequent acquisition or construction by them in the year given. Within the Frankish period Hospitallers and Templars are similarly designated by initials; within the Moslem period Z indicates the rule of Zengi (until his death in 1146 unless otherwise specified), N the rule of Nūr-ad-Dīn (until his death in 1174), and S the rule of Saladin (until the volume closes in 1189).

The only possessions remaining to the crusaders after the fall of Belvoir and Krak de Montréal in that year were, in the principality of Antioch, the city of Antioch itself and the Hospitaller fortress of al-Marqab; in the county of Tripoli, the city of Tripoli, the Templar citadel in Tortosa and castles of al-ʿArīmah and Chastel-Blanc, and the Hospitaller stronghold of Krak des Chevaliers; in the kingdom of Jerusalem, Belfort (which was to fall to Saladin in 1190).

Acre M - F 1104 - M(S) 1187
Adana A - F 1097 - B 1099 - F 1101 - B 1104 - F 1108 - A 1130 - F 1131 - A 1131 - F 1136 - A 1136 - B 1137 - F 1143 - B 1144 - A 1152 - B 1158 - A 1173 - F 1185? - A 1185?
Ailah M - F 1116 - M(S) 1170
Aintab A - F 1097 - B 1150 - M 1151 (N 1155; S 1183)
ʿAkkār M - F 1109 - M(N) 1167? - F(H) 1170 - M(S) 1188
Aleppo M (Z 1128; N 1146; S 1183)
Alexandretta M - F 1097 - B 1099 - F 1101 - B 1137 - F 1143 - A 1152 - F 1155 - M(S) 1188
Anazarba A - F 1098 - B 1099 - F 1101 - B 1104 - A 1105? - F 1130 - A 1130 - F 1131 - A 1131 - B 1137 - F 1143 - B 1144 - A 1152 - B 1158 - A 1162 - B 1163? - A 1173
Antioch M - F 1098
Apamea M - F 1106 - M 1149 (N; S 1175)
ʿArqah M - F 1109 - M(Z) 1138 - F 1138 - M(N) 1171 - F 1171 - M(S) 1188
Arsuf M - F 1101 - M(S) 1187
Artāḥ M - F 1097 - M 1104 - F 1105 - M 1147/8 (N; S 1183)

Arzghān M - F 1098 - M(N) 1149 - F 1159 - M 1160 (N; S 1183)
Ascalon M - F 1153 - M(S) 1187
al-Athārib M - F 1110 - M 1119 - F 1123 - M(Z) 1135 - B 1138 - M 1138 (Z; N 1146; S 1184)
ʿAzāz M - F 1111 ? - M 1113 ? - F 1118 - M 1150 (N; S 1176 - 1176, 1183)

Baalbek M (Z 1139; N 1155; S 1174)
Baisan M - F 1099 - M(S) 1187
Bait Jibrīn - F built 1136 (H 1137) - M(S) 1187
Bait Nūbā - F built 1133 - M(S) 1187
Banyas M - X 1126 - F 1129 - M 1132 (Z 1137) - F 1140 - M 1164 (N; S 1174)
Baʿrīn M - F 1115 - M 1115 - F 1126 - M 1137 (Z 1137 - 1138; N 1146; S 1174)
Basarfūt M - F 1104 - M 1119 - F 1119 - M 1147/8 (N; S 1184)
al-Batrūn M - F 1104 ? - M(S) 1187
Beirut M - F 1110 - M(S) 1187
Belfort - F built 1139
Belvoir - F built 1140 (H 1168) - M(S) 1189
Bethlehem M - F 1099 - M(S) 1187
Bira A - F 1099 - A 1104 - F 1117 - B 1150 - M 1150 (S 1182)
Blanche Garde - F built 1142 - M(S) 1187
Buzāʿah M - F 1119 - M 1119 (Z 1129) - B 1138 - M 1138 (Z; N 1146 - 1170) - X 1170 - M(S) 1176

Caesarea M - F 1101 - M(S) 1187
Chastel-Neuf - F rebuilt 1179 - M(S) 1187
Cyrrhus A - F 1117 - M 1150 (N; S 1176)

Damascus M (N 1154; S 1174)

Edessa A - F 1098 - M 1144 (Z; N 1146; S 1182)

Gargar A - F 1117 - M 1123 - A 1136 - M 1149
Gaza - F rebuilt 1150 (T) - M(S) 1187

Ḥabīs Jaldak M - F 1118 - M(S) 1182 - F 1182 - M(S) 1187
Haifa M - F 1100 - M(S) 1187
Hamah M (Z 1129 - 1133, 1135 - 1146; N 1147; S 1174)
Ḥārim M - F 1097 - M 1097 - F 1098 - M(N) 1149 - F 1158 - M 1164 (N; S 1183)
Harran M (Z 1127; N 1146; S 1182)
Hebron M - F 1099 - M(S) 1187
Homs M (Z 1138; N 1149; S 1174)

Ibelin - F built 1141 - M(S) 1187

Jabala M - B 1104 - M 1104 - F 1109 - M(S) 1188
Jacob's Ford - F built 1178 - M(S) destroyed 1179
Jaffa M - F 1099 - M(S) 1187
Jarash - M built 1120 - F destroyed 1121
Jerusalem M - F 1099 - M(S) 1187
Jubail M - F 1104 - M(S) 1187

Kafarlāthā M - X 110x - F 1109 - M 1119 - F 1119 - M 1147/8 (N; S 1183)
Kafarṭāb M - F 1100 - M 1104 - F 1106 - M 1115 - F 1119 - M 1125 - F 1128 - M(Z) 1135 - B 1138 - M 1138 (Z; N 1146; S 1175)
al-Kahf M - X 1135
Kerak - F built 1142 - M(S) 1188

Kesoun A - F 1116 - M 1150 (N 1160 - 1166/7, 1173 - 1174)
Kharībah M - F 1105 - X 1136/7
al-Khawābī M - F 1117/8 - X 114x
Krak de Montréal - F built 1115 - M(S) 1189
Krak des Chevaliers M - F 1099 - M 1099 - F 1110 (H 1142)

Lampron A - B 1137 - A 1145 ?
Latakia M - F 1097 - B 1098 - F 1103 - B 1104 - F 1108 - M(S) 1188
Lydda M - F 1099 - M(S) 1187

Ma'arrat-an-Nu'mān M - F 1098 - M 1104 - F 1109 - M 1119 - F 1119 - M(Z) 1135 - B 1138 - M 1138 (Z; N 1146; S 1175)
Mamistra M - F 1097 - B 1099 - F 1101 - B 1104 - F 1108 - A 1130 - F 1131 - A 1131 - F 1136 - A 1136 - B 1137 - F 1143 - B 1144 - A 1151 - B 1158 - A 1162 - B 1163 ? - A 1173 - F 1185 ? - A 1185 ?
Manbij M (Z 1129; N 1146; S 1176)
al-Manīqah M - F 1118 ? - X 1151 ?
Maraclea M - F 1099 - B 1099 - F 1102 - M(S) 1188
Marash A - B 1097 - F 1104 - M 1149 (N 1160 - 1166/7, 1173 - 1174)
al-Marqab M - F 1118 (- H 1186)
Maṣyāf M (Z 1129) - X 1140 ?
Melitene A - F 1100 - M 1103

Nablus M - F 1099 - M(S) 1187
Nazareth M - F 1099 - M(S) 1187

Partzapert A - B 1138 - A 1145 ?

al-Qadmūs M - F 1129 - M 1131 - X 1132
al-Qulai'ah M - F 1118 - X 114x

Raban A - F 1116 - M 1150 (N 1160 - 1166/7; S 1176)
Rafanīyah M - F 1099 - M 1099 - F 1104 ? - M 1105 - F 1115 - M 1115 - F 1126 - M 1137 (Z 1137 - 1138; N 1146; S 1174)
Ramla M - F 1099 - M 1102 - F 1103 (M destroyed 1177) - M(S) 1187
Ravendan M - F 1097 - B 1150 - M 1150 (N; S 1176)

Safad - F built 1102, rebuilt 1140 ? (T 1167 ?) - M(S) 1188
Saint Simeon M - F 1097 - M(S) 1188
Samosata M - F 1098 - B 1150 - M 1150 (S 1188)
Saone M - F 1098 - M(S) 1188
Sarūj M - F 1097 - M 1145 (Z; N 1146; S 1182)
Shaizar M (Z 1135) - X 1157 - M 1157 (N; S 1175)
Sidon M - F 1110 - M(S) 1187

Tarsus M - F 1097 - B 1099 - F 1101 - B 1104 - F 1108 - A 1130 - F 1131 - A 1131 - B 1137 - M 1138 - B 1138 - F 1143 - B 1144 - A 1152 - B 1158 - A 1173 - F 1182 ? - A 1183 ?
Tell Bashir M - F 1097 - B 1150 - M 1151 (N; S 1176)
Tiberias M - F 1099 - M(S) 1187
Toron - F built 1105 - M(S) 1187
Tortosa M - F 1099 - M 1100 - F 1102 - M(N) 1152 - F(T) 1152
Tripoli M - F 1109
Tyre M - F 1124
Tyron M - F after 1133 - M 1167 (N; S 1174)

Vahka A - B 1138 - M 1138 - A 1144 ? - B 1158 - A 1162
Valania M - F 1099 - B 1099 - F 1103 - B 1104 - M 1104 - F 1109 (H 1186) - M(S)1188

INDEX

Abak, Mujīr-ad-Dīn, son of Jamāl-ad-Dīn Muḥammad, Börid ruler of Damascus 1140–1154: 442, 459, 516, 518, 519, 538
'Abbādids, Arab dynasty at Seville 1023–1091: 38; *see also* al-Mu'tamid 1068–1091
al-'Abbās, uncle of Mohammed, 82
'Abbāsids, Arab caliphal dynasty at Baghdad 749–1258; 749–842: 42, 82–85, 93, 101, 142, 154–156, *and see* Hārūn ar-Rashīd 786–809, al-'Amīn 809–813, al-Ma'mūn 813–833, al-Mu'taṣim 833–842; 842–1094: 73, 83–87, 89, 92, 93, 97, 104–106, 144–147, 179; 1094–1180: 370, 560, 564, 565, 571, 574, 594, *and see* al-Mustaẓhir 1094–1118, al-Mustarshid 1118–1135, ar-Rāshid 1135–1136, al-Muqtafī 1136–1160; 1180–1258: 569, 575, *and see* an-Nāṣir 1180–1225
Abbots, in western Europe, 18, 23–24
'Abd-al-Massīḥ, Fakhr-ad-Dīn, Zengids' governor at Mosul in 1168: 525, 527
'Abd-Allāh ibn-Qais, Arab general in Sicily about 652: 41
'Abd-ar-Raḥmān III, Umaiyad emir 912–929 and caliph 929–961 at Cordova, 35–36
Ablgharib, *see* abū-l-Gharīb
Abū-Bakr, aṣ-Ṣiddīq, orthodox caliph at Medina 632–634: 99
Abū-Qubais, emir of, 123
Acre, 129, 363, 369, 396; under Moslems to 1104: 93, 95, 98, 331, 375, 376, 385, 386; under Franks 1104–1187: 432, 435, 505, 506, 535, 539, 543, 557, 559, 581, 585, 597, 604, 615; under Saladin after 1187: 585–588, 615, 618, 619; archdeacon of, 443; bishops of, 506, 540
Adalbero, archbishop of Bremen, 493
Adalbert, bishop of Stettin, 494
Adalia, 319, 445, 499–503
Adam, abbot of Ebrach, 478
Adam, archdeacon of Acre, elected bishop of Banyas, 443
Adana, 299–301, 387, 390
Adelaide of Sicily, wife of Baldwin I, 1113–1116: 385; marriage annulled, 406; death in 1118: 407
Adelchis, duke of Benevento, 48
Adèle, daughter of William the Conqueror, wife of Stephen of Blois, 21, 247, 276, 277, 320, 349
Aden, 96
Adhémar of Chabannes, chronicler, 39
Adhémar of Monteil, bishop of Le Puy, 234, 267, 330, 335, 338, 352, 373, 374 note, 491; appointed legate, 239, 249, 250, 257; with first crusade to Constantinople, 272, 274, 287; at Dorylaeum, 293; at Antioch, 247, 309, 311–313, 316, 319–325
al-'Āḍid, Fāṭimid caliph 1160–1171: 525, 552, 556, 560, 564, 565
al-'Ādil Saif-ad-Dīn, son of Aiyūb, Aiyūbid ruler of Egypt and Syria 1199–1218: 128, 570, 572, 579, 583, 586, 587, 619
Admont, abbot of, 350
Adolf, count of Holstein, 493, 494
Adria, 47
Adrian, brother of Alexius I, 216
Adrianople, 184–187, 190, 257; people's crusade at, 262, 281; crusade of 1101 at, 353, 360; second crusade at, 485, 489
Adriatic Sea, 46–49, 64, 180, 252; crossing of, 75, 257, 275, 276, 278, 281, 358; eastern side of, 270; northern end of, 257, 273
Aegean Sea, islands of, 213; shores of, 150, 157, 163, 280
Aetheria, pilgrim, 69
al-Afḍal Shāhānshāh, son of Badr al-Jamālī, vizir of Egypt 1094–1121: 94–98, 409; 1094–1099: 95, 97, 106, 166, 316; 1099–1105: 98, 340, 341, 370, 376, 385, 386; 1105–1121: 118, 386, 387, 411, 422 note, 454
Aflis, 518
'Afrīn valley, 514
Aftigin, Turkish commander at Damascus to 978: 88
Aga Khan, Ismā'īlite leader in India in 1955: 132
Ager sanguinis, *see* Darb Sarmadā
Aghlabids, Arab dynasty in Tunisia 800–909: 42–44, 59; *see also* Ibrāhīm I 800–812, Ziyādat-Allāh I 817–838
Agnes, German empress, mother of Henry IV, 224
Agnes of Courtenay, daughter of Joscelin II, mother of Baldwin IV and Sybil, 596–599, 602; marriage to king Amalric annulled, 549
Agriculture, European, 3–9; Moslem, in Sicily, 55–56
Agrigento, 44, 58, 63
Aguilers, *see* Raymond

296, 390–391, 407, 408, 488, 490–492, 496, 502, 511
Anti-semitism, *see* Jews
Anti-Taurus mountains, 292, 296–299
Antioch, 308; before 1098: 84, 88–91, 97, 150, 152, 159, 160, 164, 191, 193, 309; first crusade to, 287 note, 291, 292, 296–298, 302–304, 309, at, 310–329, 345, 349, 365, 401, letters from, 221, 247, 248, 250; 1098–1104: 172, 359, 362–364, 366, 369–373, 378, 381–385, 388, 395, 396; 1104–1112: 391, 393, 397, 400; 1112–1119: 413; 1119–1126: 413, 415, 417, 418, 420, 425, 428, 452; 1126–1130: 428; 1130–1136: 431, 433, 434, 437; 1136–1149: 437, 439, 440, 444–445, 458, 459, 490; second crusade to, 497, 501–504, at, 503–506; 1149–1153: 516, 517, 533; 1153–1160: 521–523, 540, 541, 543, 544; 1160–1189: 523, 524, 526, 547, 551, 554, 586–588, 618, 619; patriarchs of, 159, 217, 325, 413, 423, 428, 429, 441 note, 543, 544, *and see* John the Oxite (Greek) to 1100, Bernard of Valence 1100–1135, Ralph of Domfront 1135–1139, Aimery of Limoges 1139–1196 ?, Athanasius (Greek) to 1170
Antioch, principality, under Bohemond I 1099–1100: 372–374, 378, 380; regency of Tancred 1101–1103: 382, 387–388, 395–396; under Bohemond I 1103–1104: 388–390; regency of Tancred 1104–1112: 390, 392, 397–401; regency of Roger 1112–1119: 401–406, 412–413; regency of Baldwin II 1119–1126: 413–419, 428; under Bohemond II 1126–1130: 428, 431; regency of Joscelin I 1130–1131: 431–432; regency of Fulk 1132–1136: 433–437; under Raymond 1136–1149: 437–440, 444–445, 458–459, 470, 503–504, 514–515, 530–533; regency of Constance 1149–1153: 516, 533–534, 536, 540; regency of Reginald 1153–1160: 540–546; regency of Constance 1160–1163: 546–547; under Bohemond III after 1163: 524, 547, 551, 554, 560, 608, 615, 618, 619; princes of, *see* Bohemond I, Bohemond II, Raymond of Poitiers, Bohemond III; princesses of, *see* Cecilia, Alice, Constance, Theodora, Sibyl; regents of, *see* Tancred, Roger of Salerno, Baldwin II, Joscelin I, Fulk, Constance, Reginald of Châtillon
Antioch in Caria, 499
Antioch in Pisidia, 294–295
Antoninus Martyr, pilgrim, 71
Antwerp, margraviate of, 267
Anushtigin ad-Dizbirī, Turkish general in Syria in 1029: 91
Apamea: under Moslems to 1106: 112, 165, 173, 392; under Franks 1106–1149: 112, 113, 392, 404, 441, 515, 516; under Moslems after 1149: 516, 521
Apokapes, *see* Basil Apokapes
Apulia, 19, 47, 64, 75, 180, 208, 226, 279, 281, 391, 411, 428, 487; bishops of, 189, 213, 224; duke of, 19, 59, *and see* Robert Guiscard; people of, 66; seamen from, 64; *see also* Robert, William
'Aqr as-Sudan, 120
al-Aqṣâ (Arabic: farthest), mosque at Jerusalem, 337, 527 note, 618
Aqserai, 520
Aqsonqor, Aqsunqur, *see* Aksungur
Aquitaine, 236, 251; crusaders from, in 1101: 346, 349, 351, 354 note, 359–361; crusaders from, in 1147: 487; dukes of, 11, 12, 17; fleet from, 43; *see also* Eleanor
abū-l-'Arab, Arabic poet, about 1060: 64, 65 note
Arabia, 81–86, 103, 137; Frankish invasions of, 576, 579
Arabic language, transliteration and nomenclature, xxii–xxiv
Arabs, Semitic people, in Arabia, 81–84, 86, 103, 137; in Italy, the Mediterranean, Sicily, and Spain, *see* Moslems; in North Africa, 40–44, 48, 50–53, 56, 470; in Syria before 1098, 71, 81–84, 86–94, 103, 107, 164; in Syria after 1098, 165, 175, 327, 333, 371, 375, 381, 402, 409, 456, 462, 520, 521, 525, 539, 573; elsewhere, 81–84, 86–88, 100, 103, 107, 137, 143, 145, 146, 157, 423, 452
Aragon, 18, 31, 33, 34, 37, 38; kings of, *see* Ramiro I 1035–1063, Peter I 1094–1104
Arbrissel, *see* Robert
Archers, crusaders', 500, 613; Turkish, 293, 323, 355, 500, 585, 608, 613
Architecture, in western Europe, 28–29
Arculf, Frankish bishop, 71
Arcy, count of, 73
Arda, daughter of Ṭaṭoul, wife of Baldwin I until 1113: 372, 406
Ardagger, 483
Ardèche, count of, 73
Ardent, *see* Raoul Ardent
Ardoin of Turin, 51
Ardouin of St. Médard, 360
Argyrus, Byzantine governor in Italy, 208, 209
al-'Arīmah, 515, 532
al-'Arīsh, 407, 538
Aristocracy, Byzantine landed, 195–199, 202
Arjish, 144, 625
Arles, *see* Gibelin
Arm of St. George, 242, 353, 358
Armenia, or Greater Armenia, 84, 143, 144, 147–149, 157, 159, 163, 179, 180, 192, 196, 299, 371
Armenian language, transliteration and nomenclature, xxii, xxv
Armenians, Indo-European people, in Armenia, 179, 189, 190; around Edessa, 165, 302–304, 399, 419, 462, 513, 517, 531; in Cappadocia, 179, 189, 295, 297–299; in Cilicia, 299–302, 371, 390, 552 note; in Syria, 97, 297, 309, 318; princes,

Stephanie; lord of, 537, *and see* Reginald of Châtillon; *see also* Krak de Montréal
Moors, *see* Moslems
Morava river, 484
Moravia, 481; dukes of, 21
Morfia, daughter of Gabriel, wife of Baldwin II, 392, 423
Morocco, 39, 42, 638; ruler of, 571
Mörs, 265 note
Moselle river, valley of, 264
Moslems (Arabic, al-Muslimūn), members of Islamic community, xxiii, 68, 100, 362 note, 512, 582; in Italy, 3, 40–53, 63–64, 72; in the Mediterranean, 9, 40–53, 58, 181; in Sicily, 19, 41–45, 49–51, 54–67, 181, 385; in Spain, 20–21, 31–39, 41–44, 51–53, 63, 81, 232, 233, 249, 346, 349, 386, 465, 475, 476, 481–483
Mosul, 86, 115, 121, 152, 166, 169, 175, 316, 323, 393, 394, 425, 427, 434, 436, 449, 453–456, 458–462, 520, 522, 524, 525, 531, 567, 569, 574, 576–580, 582, 585, 594, 596; governors of, 113, 120, 169, 170, 173, 303, 309, 315, 389, 393, 399, 403, 420, 424, 429, 451, 452, 461, 527; rulers of, 122, 146, 151, 508, 513, 516, 526, 566, 569, 573, 575, 599, 608
Mount Carmel, 331
Mount Hermon, 371
Mount Lebanon, 110, 330, 371, 437, 438, 508
Mount of Olives, 334, 336
Mount Silpius, 308, 309, 311, 315
Mount Sinai, 69, 406
Mount Sion, 333, 334, 336
Mozac, 235
Mu'āwiyah, Umaiyad caliph at Damascus 661–680: 41
Muḍar, Qaisī Arab tribe, 81–82
abū-Muḥammad, Assassin master in Syria, died about 1169: 120, 121
Muḥammad, Jamāl-ad-Dīn, son of Böri, Börid ruler of Damascus 1139–1140: 441–442, 459
Muḥammad, son of Malik-Shāh, Selchükid sultan 1105–1118: 114, 167–171, 175, 371, 372, 388, 389, 393, 394, 405, 450; *jihād* against Franks, 169, 170, 175, 399, 403
Muḥammad, *see* Nūr-ad-Dīn
Muḥammad ibn-al-Ḥanafīyah, son of 'Alī, died about 701: 101
Muḥammad ibn-Tughj, al-Ikhshīd, Ikhshīdid ruler of Egypt 935–946: 86–87
Mu'īn-ad-Dīn Unur, *see* Unur
al-Mu'izz, Fāṭimid caliph 953–975: 88, 104–105, 107
al-Mu'izz, Zīrid emir in Tunisia 1016–1062: 62
Mu'izz-ad-Daulah, Buwaihid ruler at Baghdad 946–967: 86
al-Mujāhid, Arab emir of Denia 1017–1044: 52
Mujāhid-ad-Dīn Qaimāz, *see* Qaimāz
Mujīr-ad-Dīn Abak, *see* Abak
Mukhtār, Persian 'Alid leader at Kufa in 685: 100
Mulūk aṭ-ṭawā'if (Arabic, petty kings, of Andalusia), 38
al-Munaiṭirah, 525
Munqidhites, *see* Banū-Munqidh
al-Muqtafī, son of al-Mustaẓhir, 'Abbāsid caliph 1136–1160: 169, 170, 461, 519
al-Muqtanâ, Druze missionary in 1036: 112
Murābiṭs, Berber sect and dynasty in Morocco and Spain 1056–1147: xxv, 39, 63, 232; *see also* Yūsuf 1061–1106
Mūsâ, son of Ja'far, Shī'ite imam, died 799: 102
Mūsâ, son of Saif-al-Mulk, Arab chief of al-Kahf about 1135: 119
Mūsâ ibn-Nuṣair, Arab governor of Tunisia in 700: 41
al-Musta'lī, son of al-Mustanṣir, Fāṭimid caliph 1094–1101: 95–96, 106, 107, 370
al-Mustanṣir, Fāṭimid caliph 1036–1094: 93, 95, 105, 106
al-Mustarshid, son of al-Mustaẓhir, 'Abbāsid caliph 1118–1135: 168–169, 435, 436, 452, 454, 456–458
al-Mustaẓhir, 'Abbāsid caliph 1094–1118: 329, 372, 400
al-Mu'tamid, 'Abbādid king of Seville 1068–1091: 39, 65 note
al-Mu'taṣim, son of Hārūn, 'Abbāsid caliph 833–842: 84
Muwaḥḥids, Berber sect and dynasty in North Africa and Spain 1130–1269: xxv, 571
Myriokephalon pass, 560, 584, 594

Nablus, 340, 377, 402, 438, 535, 552, 586, 604, 605, 607, 608, 620; lords of, 506, 535, 537, 555
an-Nahr al-Aswad, 515
an-Nahr al-'Aujā', 382
an-Nahr al-Auwalī, 331
Najm-ad-Dīn, Assassin master in Syria, died 1274: 130–131
Najm-ad-Dīn Aiyūb, *see* Aiyūb
Namur, count of, 473
Nangis, *see* Bartolf
Naples, 43–51; dukes of, 45–48; ships from, 46
an-Naqīrah, 415–417, 426
an-Naqūrah, heights, 331
Narbonne, 9; count of, 234; crusaders from, 483; *see also* Peter
Narni, 77
an-Nāṣir, 'Abbāsid caliph 1180–1225: 122, 127–128, 576–580, 584, 610
Nāṣir-ad-Daulah, Ḥamdānid general in Egypt, died 1073: 93, 94
Naṣīr-ad-Dīn, son of Shīrkūh, Aiyūbids' governor at Homs in 1179: 572
Naṣr, Persian Assassin master in Syria in 1194: 127